Finite Element Simulations with

ANSYS Workbench 12

Huei-Huang Lee
Department of Engineering Science
National Cheng Kung University, Taiwan

ISBN: 978-1-58503-604-2

SDC PUBLICATIONS
Schroff Development Corporation
www.schroff.com

Schroff Development Corporation
P.O. Box 1334
Mission KS 66222
(913) 262-2664
www.schroff.com

Publisher: Stephen Schroff

Contents

Preface

Usage of the Book

Learning finite element simulations needs much background knowledge, not just a textbook like this. The book is a guidance in learning finite element simulations. This textbook is designed mainly for graduate students and senior undergraduate students. It is designed for use in three kinds of courses: (a) as a first course of finite element simulation before you take any theory-intensive courses, such as Finite Element Methods, (b) as an auxiliary parallel tutorial in a course such as Finite Element Methods, or (c) as an advanced (in an application-oriented sense) course after you took a theoretical course such as Finite Element Methods.

Why ANSYS?

ANSYS has been a synonym of finite element simulations. I've been using ANSYS both as a learning platform in a course of finite element simulations and as a research tool in the university for over 20 years. The reasons I love ANSYS are due to its multiple physics capabilities, completeness of on-line documentations, and popularity among both academia and industry. Equipping engineering students with interdisciplinary capabilities is becoming a necessity. A complete documentation allows the students finding solutions themselves independently, especially for those problems not taught in the classroom. Popularity, implying a high percentage of market share, means that after the students graduate and work as CAE engineers, they will be able to work with the software without any further training.

Recent years, I have another reason to advocate this software, the user-friendliness.

ANSYS Workbench

The Workbench has evolved for years but matured more in recent years, and the version 12 has been an important bench mark, worth a "wow" or 4.5 stars.

Before the Workbench gets mature enough, I have been using the Classic (now it is dubbed ANSYS APDL). The Classic is essentially driven by text commands (its GUI provides no essential advantages over text commands). The user-unfriendly language imposes unnecessary constraints that make the use of the software extremely difficult and painful. The difficulty comes from many aspects, for examples, modeling geometries, setting up contacts or joints, setting up nonlinear material properties, transferring data between two analysis systems. As a result, the students or engineers often restrict themselves within limited types of problems, for example, working on mechanical component simulations rather than mechanical system simulations.

Comparing with the Classic, the real power of the Workbench is its user-friendliness. It releases many unnecessary constraints. In a cliche, the only limitation is engineers' imagination.

Why a New Tutorial?

Preparing a tutorial for the Workbench needs much more effort than that for the Classic, due to the graphic nature of the interface. I think that is why the number of books for the Workbench is still so limited. So far, the most complete tutorial, to my knowledge, is the training tutorials prepared by ANSYS Inc. However, they may not be suitable for direct use as a university textbook for the following reasons. First, the cases used in these tutorials are either too trivial or too complicated. Some cases are too complicated for students to create from scratch. The students need to rely on the geometry files accompanied with the tutorials. Students usually obtain a better comprehension by working from scratch. Second, the tutorial covers too little on theory aspect while too much on the software operations aspect. Many of nonessential software operations should not be included for a semester course. On the other hand, it contains limited theoretical background about solid mechanics and the finite element methods. Besides, the tutorials are not available in any bookstores. To access the tutorials, the students need to attend the training courses offered by ANSYS, Inc. or authorized firms. Other reasons include that they are in a form of PowerPoint presentation files; much of effort is needed to furnish it to a university textbook, for example, adding homework problems.

Structure of the Book

The structure of the book will be detailed in Section 1.1. Here is an overall picture.

With the help of a case study, Section 1.1 overviews the Workbench simulation procedure. During the overview, as more concepts or tools are needed, specific chapters or sections will be pointed out to the students. In-depth discussion will be provided in these chapters or sections. The rest of Chapter 1 provides necessary background of structural mechanics, which will be used in the later chapters. These backgrounds include equations that govern the behavior of a mechanical or structural system, the finite element methods that solve these governing equations, and the failure criteria of materials. Chapter 1 is the only chapter that doesn't have any hands-on exercises. It is so designed because, in the very beginning of a semester, students may not be able to access the software facilities yet.

Chapters 2 and 3 introduce 2D geometric modeling and simulations. Chapters 4-7 introduce 3D geometric modeling and simulations. Up to Chapter 7, we almost restrict our discussion on linear static structural simulations. Chapter 8 is dedicated to optimization and Chapter 9 to Meshing. Chapter 10 deals with buckling and its related topic: stress stiffening. Chapters 11 and 12 discuss dynamic simulations. Chapters 13 and 14 dedicate to a more in-depth discussion of nonlinear simulations, although several nonlinear simulations have been performed in the previous chapters. Chapter 15 devotes to an exciting topic: explicit dynamics, which is becoming a necessary discipline for a simulation engineer.

Features of the Book

Comprehensiveness and comprehensibility are the ultimate goals of every textbook. There is no exception for this book. To achieve these goals, following features are incorporated into the design of the book.

Real-World Cases. There are 45 step-by-step hands-on exercises in this book; each exercise is conducted in a single section. These exercises center on 27 cases. These cases are neither too trivial nor too complicated. Many of them are industrial or research projects; prototype pictures are presented in many cases. The size of the problems are not too large so that they can be simulated in an academic version of ANSYS Workbench 12, which has a limitation on the number of nodes or elements. They are not too complicate so that the students can build each project step by step by themselves. Throughout the book, the students don't need any supplement files to work on these exercises. The files in the DVD that comes with the book are provided for the students only in cases they need (see Usage of the Accompanying DVD).

Review of Background Knowledge. Relevant background knowledge is reviewed whenever necessary, such as solid mechanics, finite element methods, structural dynamics, nonlinear solution methods (Newton-Raphson methods), nonlinear materials, explicit integration methods, etc. To be efficient, the review is conceptual rather than mathematical, short, yet comprehensive.

Learning by Hands-on Experiencing. A learning approach emphasizing hands-on experience spreads through the entire book. In my own experience, this is the best way to learn a complicated software such as ANSYS Workbench. A typical chapter, such as Chapter 3, consists of 6 sections. The first two sections provide two step-by-step examples. The third section tries to complement the exercises by providing a more systematic view of the chapter subject. The following two sections provide more exercises. Most of these additional exercises in the book are also presented in a step-by-step fashion. The final section provides review problems.

Learning by Building Motivation and Curiosity. After complete an exercise in a section, the students often raise more questions than what they have learned. For example, we will introduce problems involving nonlinearities as early as in Chapter 3, without further in-depth discussion. Nonlinearities will be formally discussed in Chapters 13 and 14. Learning is more efficient after building enough motivation and curiosity.

Key Concepts. Key concepts are inserted in places whenever appropriate. Must-know concepts, such as structural error, finite element convergence, stress singularity, are taught by using designed hands-on exercises, rather than by abstract lecturing. For example, how finite element solutions converge to their analytical solutions, as the meshes get finer and finer, is illustrated by guiding the students to plot convergence curves. That way, the students should have strong knowledge of the finite elements convergence behaviors (and, after hours of working, they will not forget it for the rest of their life). Step-by-step guiding the students to polt curves to illustrate important concepts is one of the featuring teaching methods in this book.

Inside Blackbox. How the Workbench internally solves a model is conceptually illustrated throughout the book. Understanding these procedures, at least conceptually, is crucial for a simulation engineer.

On-line Reference. One of the objectives of this book is to serve as a guiding book toward the huge repository of ANSYS on-line documentation. As mentioned, the ANSYS on-line documentation is so complete that it even includes a theory manual; it should be a well of knowledge for many students and engineers. The discussions in the textbook often point to the on-line documentation as a further study aid whenever helpful.

Homework Exercises. Additional exercises or extension research problems are provided as homework exercises at the ending section of each chapter.

Summary of Key Concepts. Key concepts are summarized at the ending section of each chapter. One goal of this textbook is to train the engineering student to comprehend the terminologies and use them properly. That is not so easy for some students. For example, whenever asked "What is shape functions?" most of the students cannot satisfyingly define the terminology. Yes, many books of finite element methods spend pages teaching students what the shape functions are, but the challenge is how to define or describe a term in less than two lines of words. This part of the textbook demonstrates how to define or describe a term in an efficient way, for example, "Shape functions serve as interpolating functions, to calculate continuous displacement fields from discrete nodal displacements."

Ordered Speech Bubbles. Screenshots with ordered speech bubbles are used throughout the book. Although not an orthodox way for a university textbook, it has been proven to be very efficient in my classroom. My students love it. I personally feel proud of creating this way of presentation for a textbook.

Classroom Tryout. The entire book has been tried out on my classroom for a semester. The purpose is to minimize mistakes. How the tryout proceeds is described as follows.

To Instructor: How I Use the Textbook

I use this textbook in a course offered each fall semester. There are 3 classroom hours a week; and the semester lasts 18 weeks. The progress is one chapter per week, except Chapter 1, which takes 2 weeks to complete.

The textbook is designed much like a workbook. The students must complete all the hands-on exercises and read the text of a chapter before they go to my classroom. Every student has to prepare an **one-page report** and turns it in at the end of the class. The one-page report should include questions and comments. The students must propose their questions in the classroom. In my classroom, there are only **discussions** of students' questions: NO traditional lecturing. The instructor's main responsibility in the classroom is to answer the students' questions. I mark and grade the one-page reports as part of performance evaluations. The main purpose of the one-page report is to ensure that the students compete the exercises and thoroughly read the text of the chapter each week. The idea is that a student who completes the exercises and reads the text must be full of questions in his/her mind, and a teacher should be able to grade the students' comprehension from the level of the questions. The emphasis here is that we grade students' performance according to their questions, not their answers.

The course load is not light as all; some chapters are as lengthy as 50 pages. Nevertheless, most of students were willing to spend hours working on these step-by-step exercises, because these exercises are tangible, rather than abstract. Students of this generation are usually better in picking up knowledge through tangible software exercises rather than abstract lecturing.

At the end of the semester, each student has to turn in a project. Students are free to choose topics for their projects as long as they use ANSYS Workbench to complete the project. Students who are working as engineers may choose topics related to their job. Other students who are working on their theses may choose topics related to their studies. They are also allowed to repeat a project from journal papers, as long as they go through all details by themselves. The purpose of the final project is to ensure that the students are capable of carrying out a project independently, which is an ultimate goal of the course, not just following the step-by-step procedure in the textbook.

To Students: How My Students Use the Book

Many students in my classroom reported to me that, when following the steps in the textbook, they often made mistakes and ended up with completely different results from that in the textbook. In many cases they cannot figure out which steps the mistakes were made. In these case, they have to redo the exercise from the beginning. It is not uncommon that they redid the exercise twice and finally saw the beautiful results.

What I want to say is that you may come across the same situation, but you are not wasting your time when you redo the exercises. You are learning from the mistakes. Each time you fix a mistake, you gain more insight. After you obtain the same results as the textbook, redo it and try to figure out if there are other ways to accomplish the same results. That's how I learn finite element simulations when I was a young engineer.

Finite element methods and solid mechanics are the foundation of mechanical simulations. If you haven't taken these courses, plan to take them after you complete this course of simulation. If you've already taken them and feel not "solid" enough, review them.

Why Different Numerical Results?

Many students often puzzled because they obtained slightly difference numerical results, but they insist that they followed exactly the same steps in the textbook. One of the reasons is that different way of creating a geometry may end up with slightly different mesh, and this in turn ends up with slightly different numerical results. For example, when you draw a straight line, the order of the end points may affect mesh slightly. Limited differences in numerical values are normal, particularly when the mesh are coarse. As the mesh becomes finer, the solution will converge to a theoretical value, which will be independent of mesh variations, and this kind of puzzle should be resolved.

Usage of the Accompanying DVD

The files in the DVD that accompanies with the book is organized according to the chapters and sections of the book. Each folder of a section stored finished project files for that section. If everything works smoothly, you may not need the DVD at all. Every project can be built from scratch according to the steps described in the book. We provide this DVD just in some cases you need it. For examples, when you want to skip the creation of geometry, or when you run into troubles following the steps and you don't want to redo from the beginning, you may find that these files are useful. Another situation may happen when you have troubles following the geometry details in the textbook, you may need to look up the geometry details in the DVD files.

However, It is suggested that, in the beginning of a step-by-step exercise when previously saved project files are needed, you use the project files stored in the DVD rather than your own files, in order to obtain results that have exact the same numerical values as shown in the textbook.

Numbering and Self-Reference System

To efficiently present the material, the writing of this textbook is not always done in a traditional format. Chapters and sections are numbered in a traditional way. Each section is further divided into subsections, for example, the 8th subsection of the 3rd section of Chapter 4 is denoted as "4.3-8." Each speech bubble in a subsection is assigned a number. The number is enclosed by a pair of square brackets (e.g., [9]). When needed, we may refer to that speech bubble such as "4.3-8[9]." When referring to a speech bubble in the same subsection, we drop the subsection identifier, for the foregoing example, we simply write "[9]." Equations are numbered in a similar way, except that the equation number is enclosed by a pair of round brackets (parentheses) rather than square brackets. For example, "1.2-3(2)" refers to the 2nd equation in the Subsection 1.2-3. Numbering notations are summarized as follows:

1.2-3	The number after a hyphen is a subsection number.
[1], [2], ...	Square brackets are used to number speech bubbles.
(1), (2), ...	These notations are used to number equations
(a), (b), ...	These notations are used to number items in the text.
Reference^{1,2}	Superscripts are used to number references.
<DesignModeler>	Angle brackets are used to highlight Workbench keywords.

Workbench Keywords

There are literally thousands of keywords used in the Workbench. For example: DesignModeler, Project Schematic, etc. To maintain readability and efficiency of the text, Workbench keywords are normally enclosed by a pair of angle brackets, for examples, <DesignModeler>, <Project Schematic>. Sometimes, however, the angle brackets may be dropped, whenever it doesn't cause any readability or efficiency problems.

Acknowledgement

I feel thankful to the students who had ever sat in my classroom, listening to my lectures. They are spreading out across the world, working as engineers or dedicated researchers. Some of them still discuss problems with me through e-mail. I hope that, as they become aware of this textbook by their old-time professor, they will go get one and refresh their knowledge right away. It is my students, past and present, that motivated me to give birth to this textbook. Thanks.

Many of the cases discussed in this textbook are selected from turned-in final projects of my students. Some are industry cases while others are thesis-related research topics. Without these real-world cases, the textbook would never be useful. The following is a list of the names who contributed to the cases in this book.

"Pneumatic Finger" (Sections 1.1 and 9.1) is contributed by Mr. C. S. Fun, ME, NCKU.
"Microgripper" (Sections 2.6 and 13.3) is contributed by Mr. C. I. Cheng, ES, NCKU.
"Cover of Pressure Cylinder" (Sections 4.2 and 9.2) is contributed by Mr. M. H. Tsai, ME, NCKU.
"Lifting Fork" (Sections 4.3 and 12.2) is contributed by Mr. K. Y. Lee, ES, NCKU.
"LCD Display Support" (Sections 4.5 and 5.4) is contributed by Mr. Y. W. Lee, ES, NCKU.
"Bellows Tube" (Section 6.1) is contributed by W. Z. Liu, ME, NCKU.
"Flexible Gripper" (Sections 7.1 and 8.1) is contributed by S. Y. Shu, ME, NCKU.
"3D Truss" (Section 7.2) is contributed by T. C. Hung, ME, NCKU.
"Translational Joint" (Section 13.2) is contributed by J. H. Lieu, ME, NCKU.
"Snap Lock" (Section 13.4) is contributed by C. N. Chen, ME, NCKU.

The textbook had been tried out in my classroom. Many students volunteered to proofread the text and pointed out many errors. They wrote down those errors in their one-page reports that I collected at the end of the class. Thanks to these students.

Much of information about the ANSYS Workbench are obtained from training tutorials prepared by ANSYS Inc. I didn't specifically cite them in the text, but I appreciate these training tutorials very much. As I mentioned, these training tutorials are the most complete tutorials about the ANSYS Workbench, as far as I've known.

I'm thankful for the environment provided by National Cheng Kung University and the Department of Engineering Science. The campus is cozy, the library facility is excellent, and the working atmosphere is so free of pressure that I was able to accomplish this textbook within a short time.

I want to thank Mrs. Lilly Lin, the CEO, and Mr. Nerow Yang, the general manager, of Taiwan Auto Design, Co., the partner of ANSYS, Inc. in Taiwan. The couple, my long-term friends, provided much of substantial support during the writing of this book.

Special gratitude is due to Professor S. J. Huang, of the Department of Mechanical Engineering, NCKU, and Professor D. Y. Huang, of Chung Hwa University of Medical Technology. They are my long-term research partners. Together, we have accomplished many projects, and, in carrying out these projects, I've learned much from them.

Lastly, thanks to my family, including my wife, my son, and the dogs (Penny, Beagle, and Shiba), for their patience and sharing the excitement with me.

Huei-Huang Lee

Associate Professor
Department of Engineering Science
National Cheng Kung University
Tainan, Taiwan
hhlee@mail.ncku.edu.tw

Chapter 1
Introduction

Purpose of the Chapter

The ANSYS Workbench is a software implementation of finite element simulations. Its functionalities includes structural, mechanical, fluid dynamics, electromagnetic, etc. This book scopes on structural and mechanical simulations only. Objectives of this chapter are to (a) show how we perform a structural/mechanical simulation with the Workbench, (b) show how this textbook is organized, and (c) equip the students with the necessary basics about solid mechanics.

About Each Section

The first two objectives are accomplished in Section 1 by using a case study. The section also brings up the topics provided in Sections 2, 3, and 4.

Section 2 gives a quick derivation of the equations governing the behavior of a solid mechanical system, such as the one in Section 1. Another purpose of this section is to refresh the concepts, such as displacements, stresses, and strains, that will be used throughout the book.

Finite element methods are used to solve these governing equations. Section 3 introduces the basic ideas and the procedure of the finite element methods. The introduction is conceptual rather than theoretical or mathematical. These concepts are important to understand the topics in the later chapters.

One goal of mechanical simulations is to know whether the system will fail or not under the design loads. We usually compare the calculated stresses with certain criteria. If the calculated stresses are too large then the system is said to fail, otherwise okay. What is the theory behind these failure criteria? This is the subject of Section 4.

A Chapter without Hands-Ons

All chapters of the book include step-by-step hands-on exercises, except this chapter. There are no hands-on exercises in this chapter. The chapter is so designed because, in the first week of the semester, students may not be able to access the software facility yet.

Section 1.1

Case Study: Pneumatically Actuated PDMS Fingers

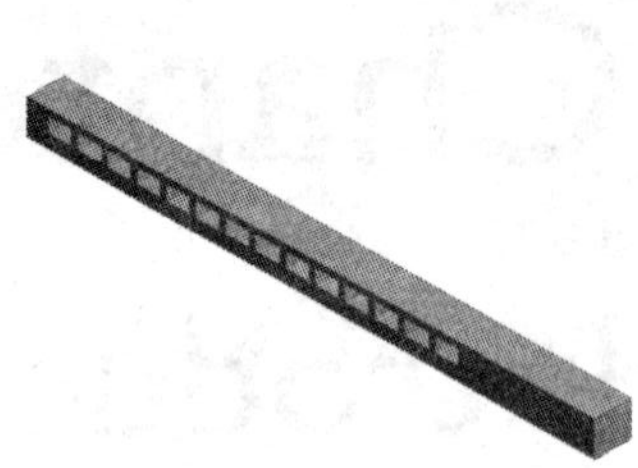

The purposes of this section are to (a) overview the functionality of the ANSYS Workbench through a case study, (b) present an overall structure of the textbook by bringing up topics of the chapters through a case study, and (c) build motivation for learning the topics in Sections 2, 3, 4 of this chapter: structural mechanics, finite element methods, and the failure criteria.

Although this case study is presented in a step-by-step fashion, it does not intend to guide the students working in front of a computer. In fact, only the relevant steps are presented, and some steps are purposely omitted to make the presentation more instructional. There will be many hands-on exercises in the later chapters. So, be patient.

1.1-1 Problem Description

About the Pneumatic Fingers

The pneumatic fingers [1] are designed as part of a surgical parallel robot system which is remotely controlled by a surgeon through the Internet[1].

The robot fingers are made of a PDMS-based (polydimethylsiloxane) elastomer material. The geometry of a finger is shown in the figure [2]. Note that 14 air chambers are built in the finger.

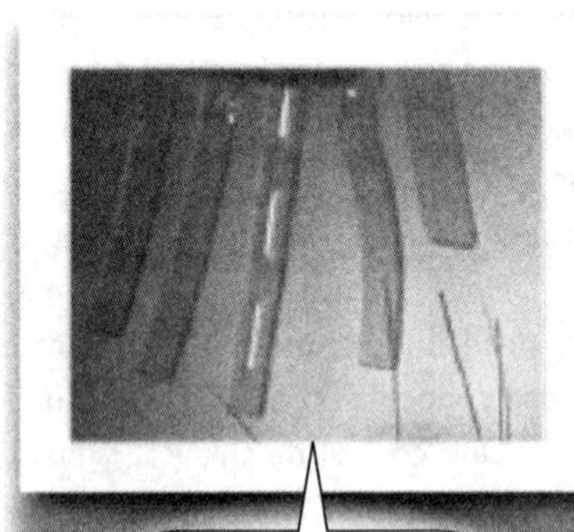

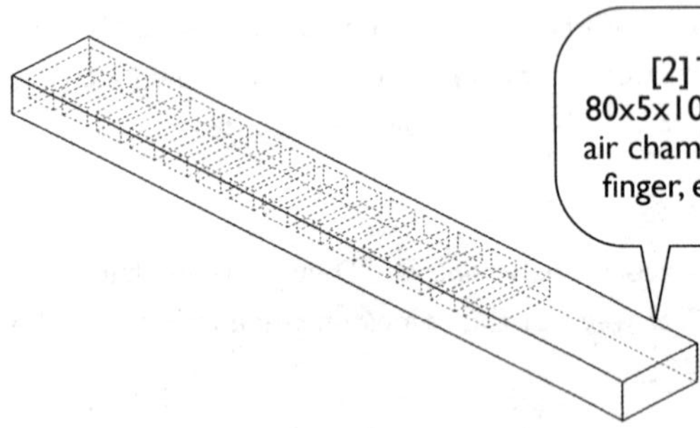

The chambers are located closer to the upper face than the bottom face so that when the air pressure applies, the finger bends downward [3]. Note that only half of the model is rendered, so you can see the chambers. The undeformed model is also shown in the figure [4].

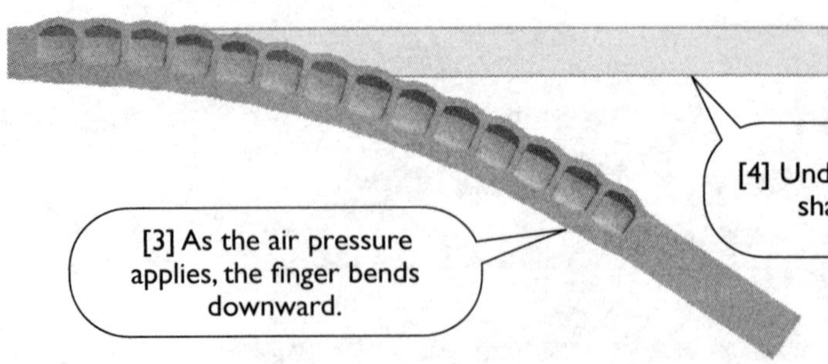

Note: In this book, each speech bubble has a unique number in a subsection. The number is enclosed with a pair of square brackets. When you read figures, please follow the order of numbers; the order is important. These numbers also serve as reference numbers when referred.

About the PDMS Elastomer

The mechanical properties of PDMS elastomers depend on the ingredients, especially the curing agent. The chart on the right shows the strain-stress curve of the PDMS elastomer used in this case[2] [5].

The experimental data show that the material exhibits linear strain-stress relationship in quite a large strain range. In this range, the Young's modulus is calculated to be 2.0 MPa. The Poisson's ratio is 0.48 from other experimental data.

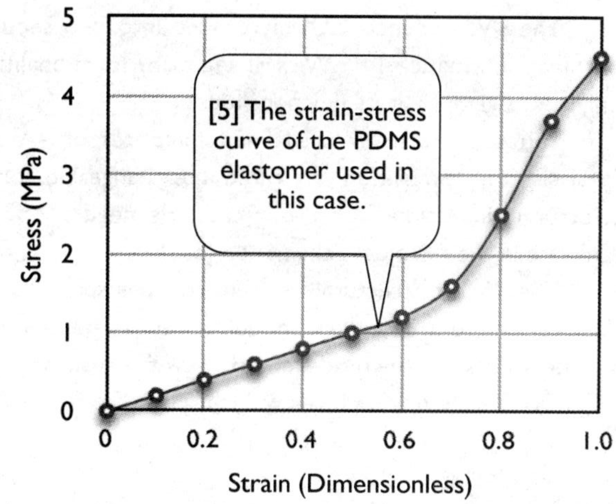

Goal of the Simulation

The purpose of the simulation is to evaluate the efficiency of the design. The efficiency of the pneumatic finger is defined as the magnitude of the actuation, the vertical deflection, under a working air pressure up to 200 KPa. Specifically we want to plot a pressure-versus-deflection chart.

1.1-2 Workbench GUI

After launching the Workbench [1], you will see the <Workbench GUI> (graphic user interface) [2]. The Workbench GUI is the gateway to all of ANSYS applications. It can be thought of as the "main program" of the Workbench. It supports two types of applications: *native applications* and *data integrated applications*.

Native applications are those directly supported in the Workbench GUI, i.e., their program codes and database bind together with the Workbench GUI. The native applications currently supported are <Project Schematic>, <Engineering Data>, and <Design Exploration>.

Data integrated applications are independent programs; they have their own GUI's and databases. They communicate with the Workbench GUI or other applications through out-of-core database files. Data integrated applications currently supported include <DesignModeler>, <Mechanical>, <Mechanical APDL>, <Fluent>, <CFX>, etc.

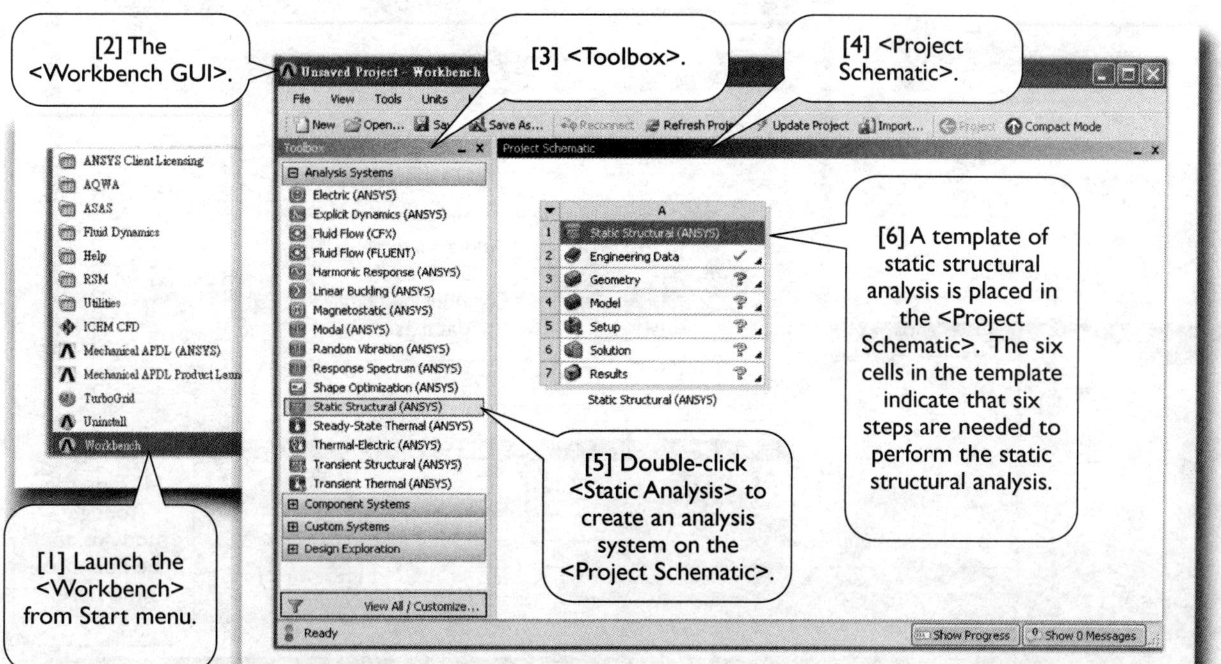

The <Workbench GUI> is divided into two sections: on the left is a <Toolbox> [3], and on the right is the <Project Schematic> [4]. We will see many functionalities of the <Workbench GUI> in later chapters. For now, we only take a glimpse at its functionalities.

You can see many predefined templates of <Analysis Systems> in the <Toolbox> [5]. In Workbench, the "analysis" and "simulation" are often interchangeable, for example, "static structural analysis" is synonymous to "static structural simulation." For our case, we need a <Static Structural> analysis system. A double-click places that template in the <Project Schematic> [5, 6].

The <Static Structural> system contains six "cells," implying that it consists of six steps: (a) prepare engineering data, (b) create a geometric model, (c) divide the geometric model into a finite element mesh, (d) setup loads and supports, (e) solve the model, and (f) view the results.

Double-clicking each cell will bring up a fresh application to process that step.

Note: In this book, a pair of angle brackets "< >" is used to highlight a Workbench keyword. Sometimes, if they do not add any clarity, the angle brackets may be dropped.

1.1-3 Prepare Engineering Data

By double-clicking the <Engineering Data> cell in the <Static Structural> analysis system [1], you will see the <Engineering Data> application [2] show up on the top of the <Workbench GUI>. For this case, we need to prepare the material properties of the PDMS elastomer. We will model the material as an <Isotropic Elasticity> material, in which we need to input the Young's modulus (2.0 MPa) and the Poisson's ratio (0.48) as material parameters [3, 4].

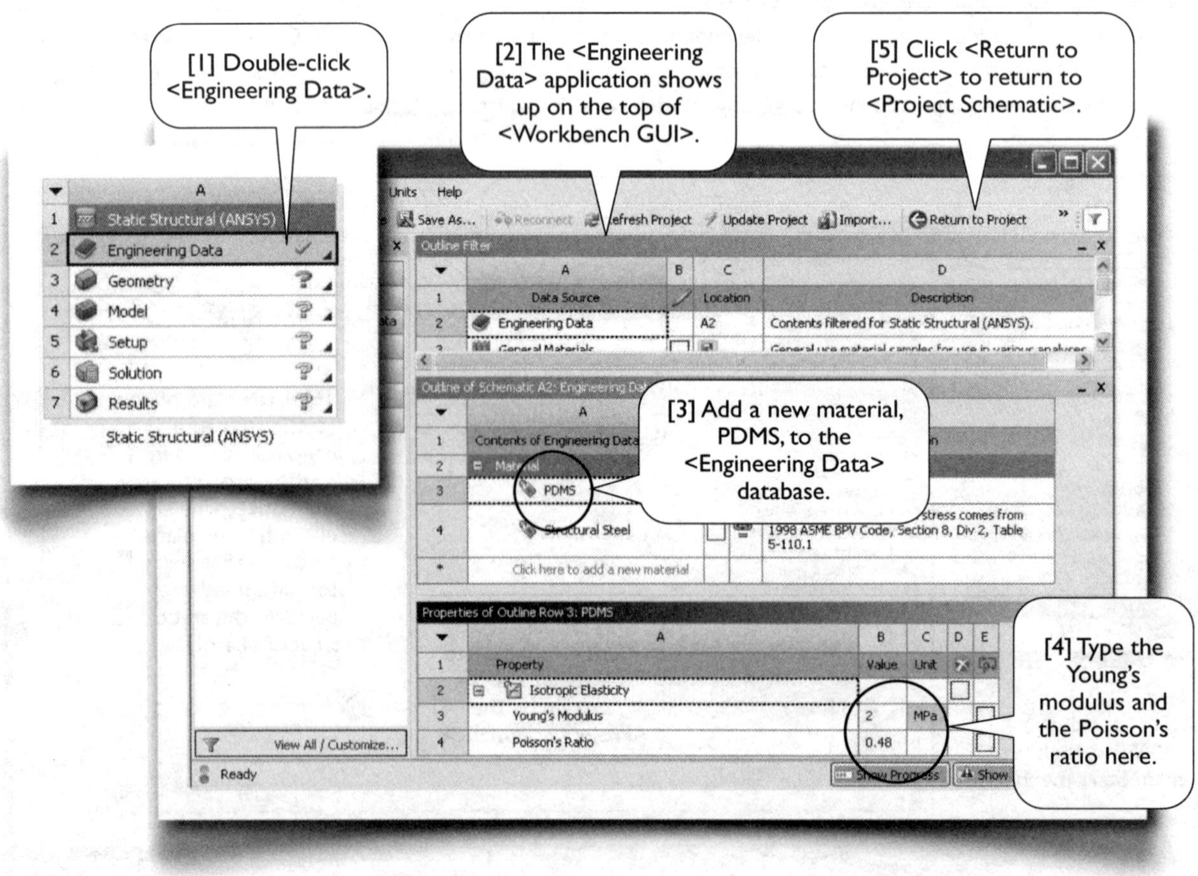

1.1-4 Create Geometric Model

Double-click <Geometry> cell in the analysis template [1], the <DesignModeler> application shows up [2]. Functions of <DesignModeler> are similar to any other CAD software such as Pro/Engineer, SolidWork, etc., except that <DesignModeler> is specifically designed to create geometric models for use in ANSYS Workbench simulations. In our case, we want to construct a geometric model for the pneumatic finger [3]. Note that, due to the symmetry, we model only half of the pneumatic finger.

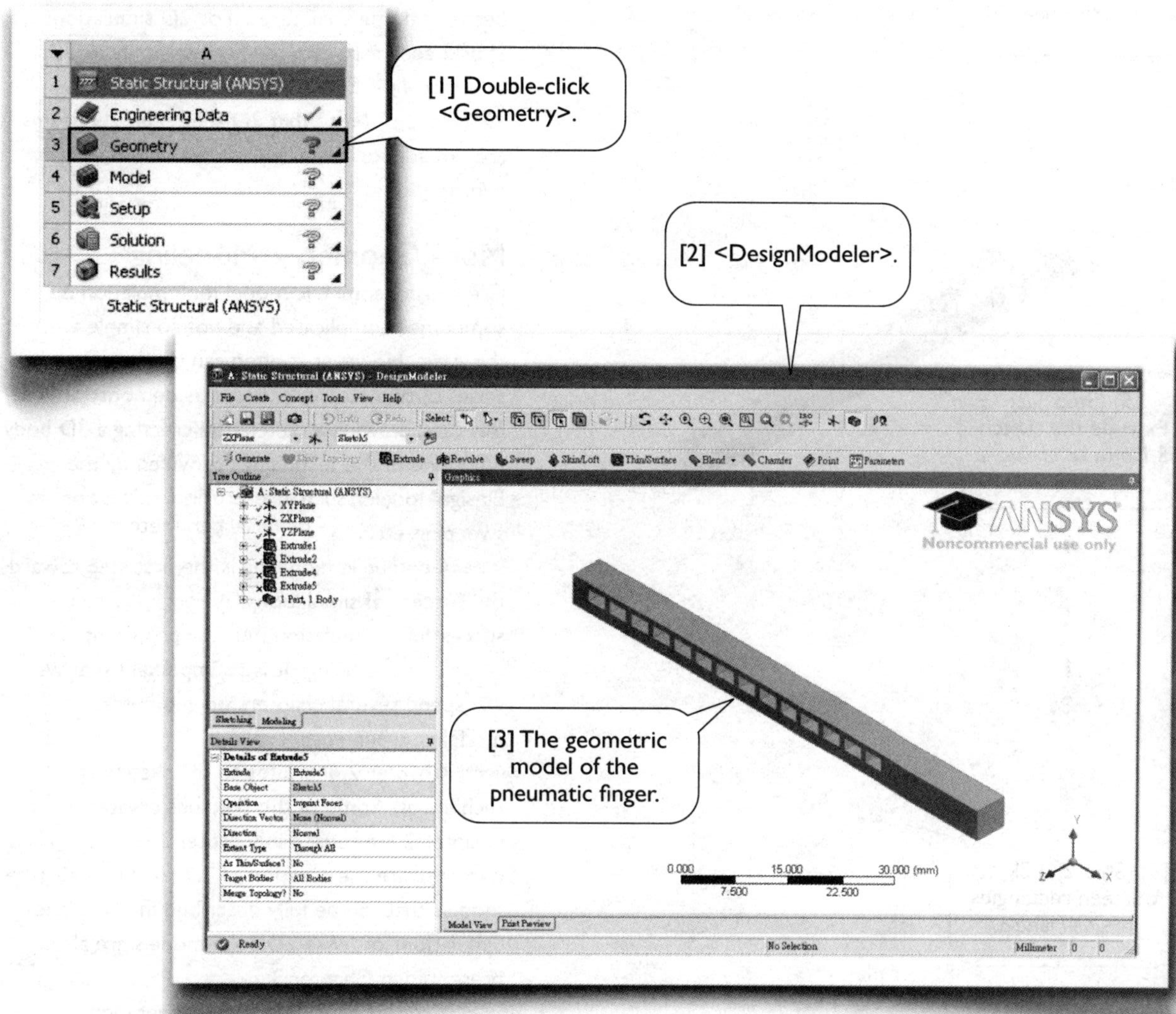

The creation of the 3D geometric model in our case [3] is relatively simple. It involves two steps, each step consists of a 2D sketching and a 3D extrusion, summarized as follows.

Step 1. Create an 80x5x5.1 mm solid.
- Step 1.1. Sketch an 80x5 mm rectangle [4].
- Step 1.2. Extrude the sketch 5.1 mm to create the solid [5].

Step 2. Create fourteen 3.2x2x4 mm air chambers.
- Step 2.1. Sketch fourteen 3.2x2 mm rectangles [6].
- Step 2.2. Extrude the sketch 4 mm to cut material from the solid [7].

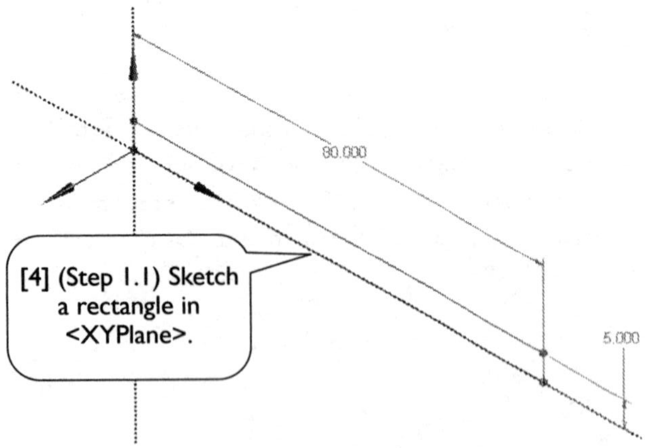

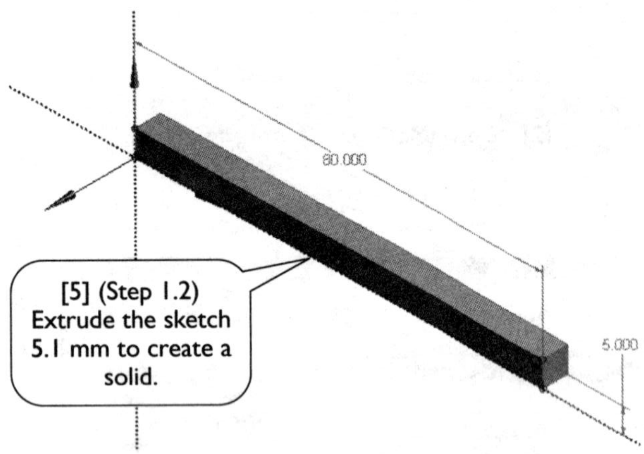

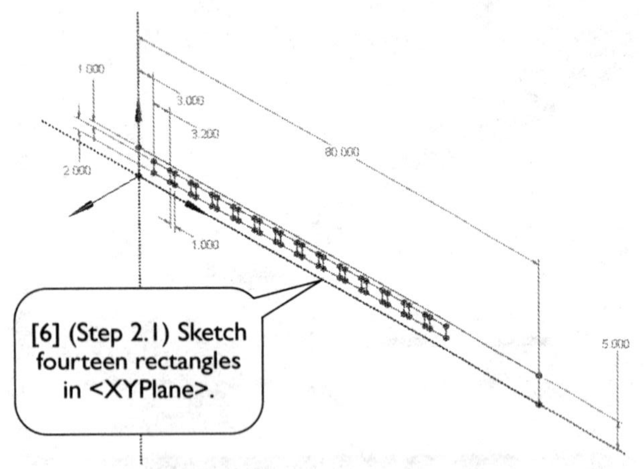

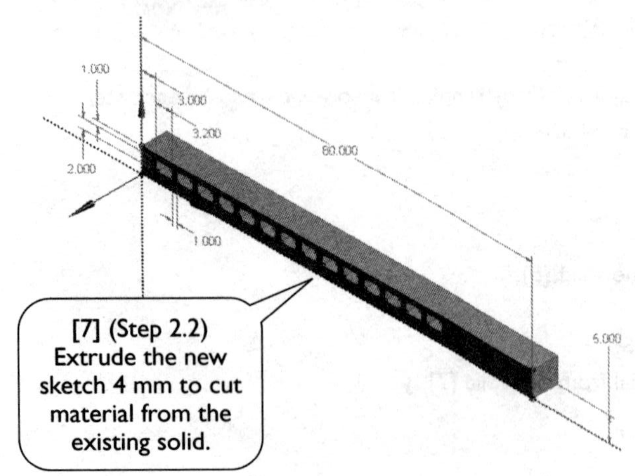

2D and 3D Simulations

ANSYS Workbench supports 2D and 3D simulations. For 3D simulations, Workbench supports three types of geometric models: *solid models* (models that have volumes), *surface models* (models that do not have volume but have surface area), and *line models* (models that do not have surface area). Examples of surface models include shell structures; examples of line models include beam or frame structures. For 2D simulations, Workbench supports solid models only. A *2D solid model* must be created entirely on the <XYPlane>. Note that 2D shells and 2D beams are not supported in the current version of Workbench.

More Geometric Modeling

Creating a geometric model for simulation is sometimes complicated and not so simple as in this case. However, it often can be viewed as a series of two-step operations as demonstrated in this case: drawing a sketch, and creating a 3D body using one of the techniques provided by the DesignModeler, such as extrusion, revolution, sweeping, etc.

Geometric modeling is the first step toward the success of simulations. An engineer to be successful in simulation must be proficient in geometric modeling. It is so important that we will spend several chapters on geometric modeling techniques.

Chapter 2 dedicates to the sketching techniques. Some of the sketches created in Chapter 2 are reused in Chapter 3 to demonstrate the creation of 2D solid models (the models that can be fully described in <XYPlane>). Simulations of these 2D solid models are also presented in Chapter 3.

Chapters 4-7 devote to 3D geometric modeling and linear static simulations. Chapter 4 discusses the creation of 3D solid models and Chapter 5 demonstrated 3D simulations using the models created in Chapter 4. Chapter 6 dedicates to 3D surface modeling and simulations, and Chapter 7 to 3D line modeling and simulations. In real-world, there are no such things as surface/line geometries, so surface/line models (as well as the 2D solid models) are aptly called *conceptual models*.

1.1-5 Divide the Geometry into Finite Elements

The procedure that Workbench solves an engineering problem can be viewed as two main steps: establishing the equations governing the behavior of the problem and solving the equations. The problem domain, i.e., the geometric model, is usually so complicated that it is almost impossible to establish the governing equations directly, without any further processing. A core idea in the *finite element methods* is to divide the entire problem domain into many smaller and simpler domains called the *finite elements*, so that the governing equations can be established for each element, and all the equations are solved simultaneously. We will dig into more details in Section 3 of this chapter.

The dividing of a geometric model into elements is called *meshing*, and the collection of the elements is called the *finite element mesh*, or sometimes called the *finite element model*. Strictly speaking, a finite element model should mean a finite element mesh PLUS its *environment conditions*, which we will introduce in the next subsection.

Double-click <Model> cell in the analysis template [1], the <Mechanical> application will show up [2]. The rest of the simulation is done in the <Mechanical>, i.e., the functions of the <Mechanical> include meshing, setup of loads and supports, solution, and viewing results [3].

The Workbench performs meshing task as your request. In our case, most of elements are hexahedral [4]. In the <Details of Mesh>, a <Statistics> displays the number of nodes and elements [5].

More Meshing

Quality of meshing cannot be overemphasized. Although it is possible to let the ANSYS Workbench perform the meshing automatically, its quality is not guaranteed. Achieving a high quality mesh is not trivial. It needs much background knowledge and experience. Chapter 9 demonstrates many meshing techniques.

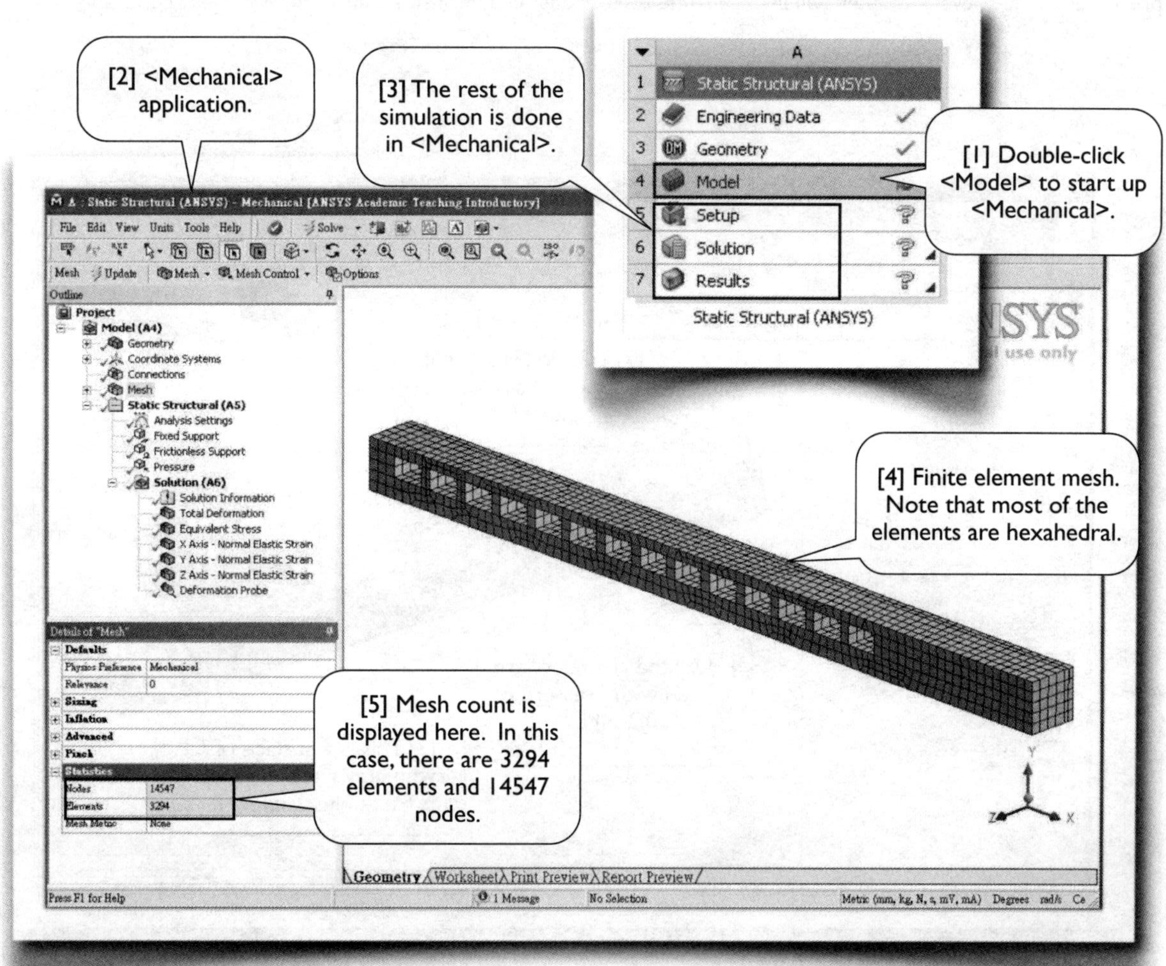

1.1-6 Setup Loads and Supports

In the real-world, all things are part of the world, they interact with each other. When we take an object apart for simulation, we are cutting it away from the rest of the world. The cutting surfaces of the model are called the *boundary* of the model. Where we cut the boundary is arbitrary--AS LONG AS we can specify the *boundary conditions* for ALL of the boundary surfaces. In Workbench, all conditions affecting the response of an object are called the *environment conditions* of the object. Most of time, environment conditions are synonymous to boundary conditions. Strictly speaking, environment conditions are more than boundary conditions.

In our case, things surrounding the pneumatic finger are: pressurized air in the chambers [1], the material connecting the root of the finger [2], the material on the other half side of the model [3], and the atmosphere air around all the other boundary surfaces.

Modeling the pressurized air in the chambers is straightforward: specify pressure of 0.2 MPa for all the surfaces of the chambers [1]. The root of the finger is modeled as fixed support [2]. The surface of symmetry is modeled as frictionless support [3]. Finally, assuming the atmosphere air has very little interaction with the model, we simply neglect it. We model all other boundary surfaces as *free boundaries*, boundaries without any boundary conditions on them.

More Environment Conditions

Modeling environment conditions is sometimes not so simple as in this case, and is often challenging for a simulation engineer. The challenge mostly comes from the need of domain knowledge. For example, it is not possible to perform a structural analysis if an engineer doesn't have enough domain knowledge of structural mechanics.

We will start to introduce environment conditions in Chapters 3 and 5-7, where linear static simulations are presented. In fact, every chapter will involve some discussions or demonstrations of environment conditions.

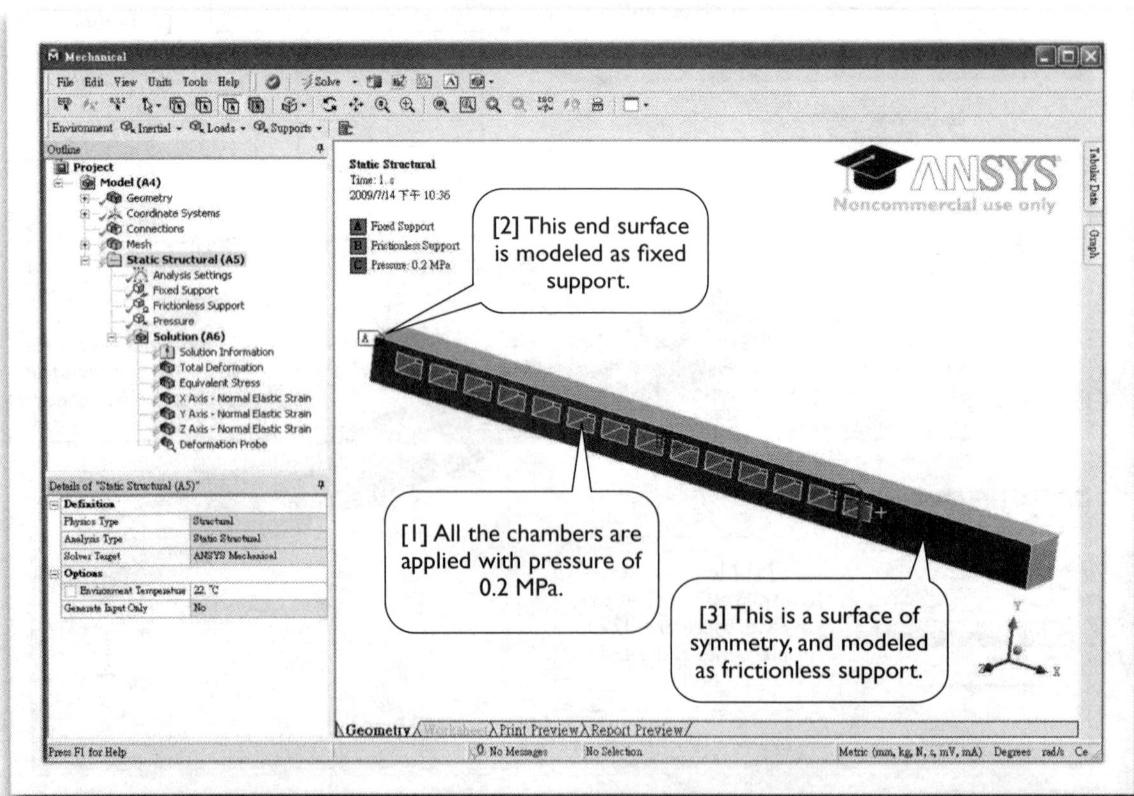

1.1-7 Solve the Finite Element Model

As mentioned, in a strict sense, a finite element model consists of a finite element mesh and its environment conditions. We will use this strict definition throughout the book. Make sure you can distinguish the following three terms: *geometric model*, *finite element mesh*, and *finite element model*.

Now, we want to solve the finite element model. In Workbench, simply click <Solve> in the <Mechanical> GUI [1]. The solution procedure is entirely automatic. The time to complete a simulation depending on the problem size and complexity. After the solution, the numerical results are stored in databases.

Inside Workbench

As we mentioned, the solution procedure can be viewed as two main steps: establishing governing equations and solving the governing equations. Section 2 of this chapter is an overview of structural mechanics. The goal is to summarize a list of equations that govern the structural behaviors. How does ANSYS Workbench solve the governing equations? The answer is: the *finite element methods*. Section 3 of this chapter is a summary of the finite element methods. The goal is to equip the readers with enough concepts of finite element methods to expedite the learning for the rest of the book.

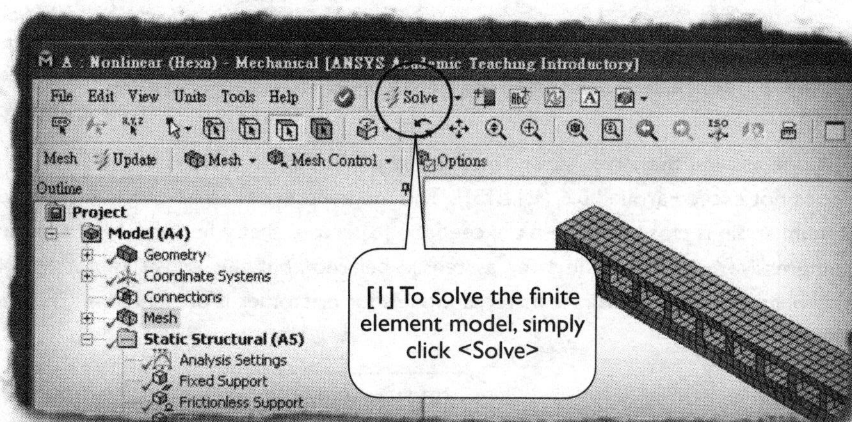

1.1-8 View the Results

After the solution, the numerical results are stored in databases, they can be viewed upon your request. In our case, we are most concerned about the vertical deflection [1, 2, 3]. Another useful information is to plot a pressure-versus-deflection chart [4, 5]. Note that the deflection is measured at the tip of the finger [6]. The deformation also can be animated in the GUI [7].

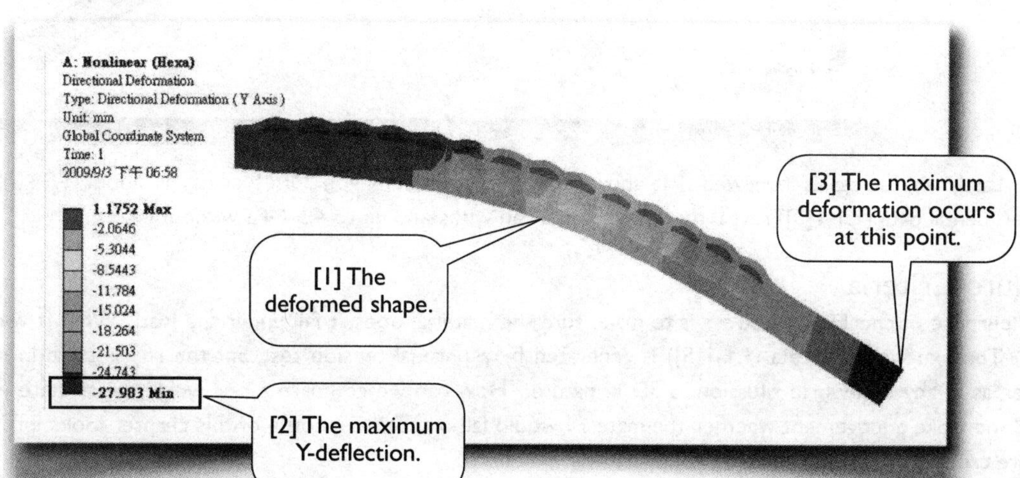

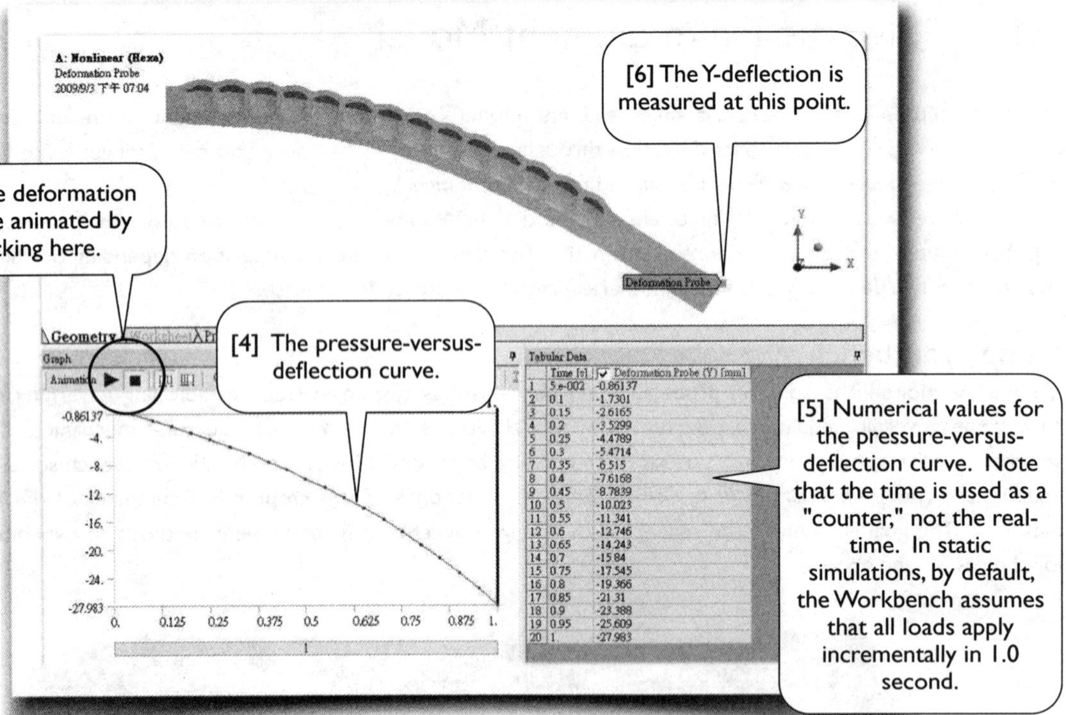

In Section 1.1-1, we assume the stress-strain relationship of the PDMS material is linear. This is equivalently to say that the strain does not exceed around 0.6 (1.1-1[5]). This assumption has to be checked at this point. The results show that the maximum strain is close but doesn't exceed 0.6 [8]. Note that when assuming a linear material, we are also assume the compressive behavior is the same as tensile behavior, but this is usually not true for an elastomer under such a large deformation. More accurate material models for elastomer is presented in Chapter 14.

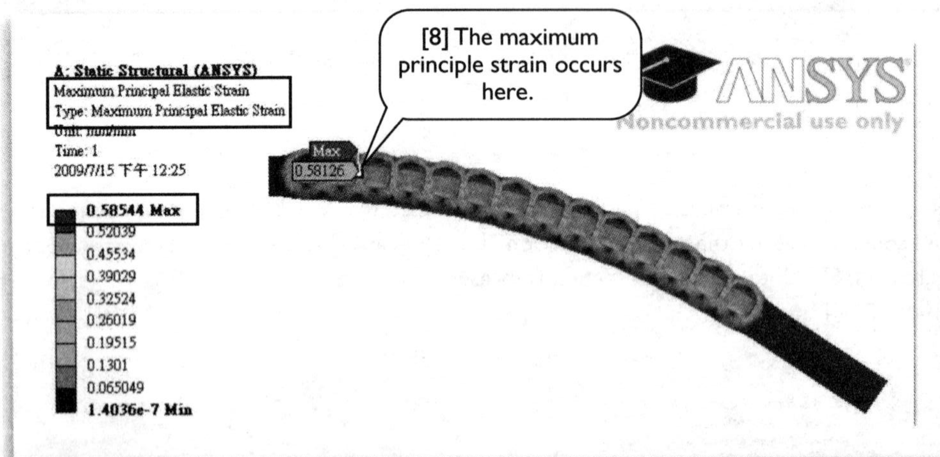

Lastly, the stress is reviewed. It shows that the maximum von Mises stress is about 1.34 MPa [9]. The experimental data (1.1-1[5]) reveal that the material can withstand up to 4.5 MPa without failure.

Failure Criteria

The purpose of checking the stress is to make sure the material doesn't fail under the load. What is von Mises stress [9]? The experimental data (1.1-1[5]) is generated by a uniaxial tension test, but the stress state in the pneumatic finger, as in any real-world situation, is 3D in nature. How can we compare a real-world stress state with a uniaxial one, and make a judgement whether the material would fail or not? Section 4 of this chapter looks into the details of failure criteria.

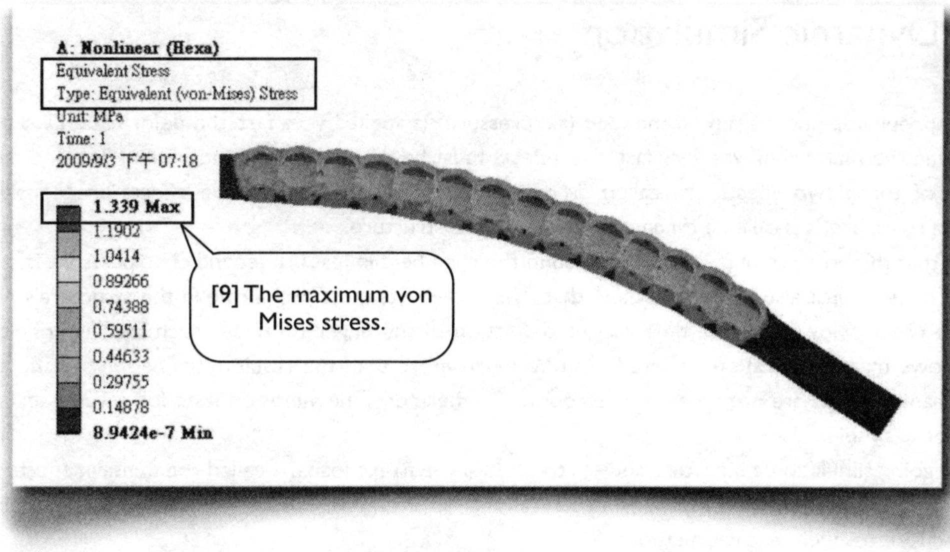

1.1-9 Buckling and Stress-Stiffening

Everyone knows that as he/she stretches a guitar string more, he/she needs more force to pluck it. In technical words, the string's lateral stiffness increases with the increase of its tensile stress. By lateral direction, we mean the direction orthogonal to the direction of tensile stress. This effect can also be justified by the fact that the string's vibrating frequency (pitch) increases with the increase of its tensile stress. This effect is called the *stress-stiffening effect*: a structure's lateral stiffness increases with the increase of its longitudinal tensile stress.

Does the opposite also hold? That is, the lateral stiffness of a structure (for example, a column subject to an axial compressive force) decreases with the increase of its axial compressive stress. The answer is YES. A more dramatic phenomenon is that, as the compression is increasing and the lateral stiffness is decreasing, the lateral stiffness would eventually vanish. Physically, that means a tiny lateral force would deflect the structure infinitely. This phenomenon is called *buckling*. When the buckling occurs, the structure is said to be in an unstable state.

In real-world, the buckling usually occurs in a compressive structural component where its lateral dimension is much smaller than the longitudinal dimension, for examples, slender columns subject to axial loads, thin-walled pipes subject to a circumferential twist.

Return to the pneumatic finger. Instead of air pressure applied in the chambers, we now apply an upward lifting at the finger tip [1]. The upper surface, which is essentially a layer of thin PDMS film, would undergo compressive stress [2]. Our concern then is to know the magnitude of the lifting force that will cause the thin film buckle.

Simulations of buckling and stress-stiffening will be covered in Chapter 10.

1.1-10 Dynamic Simulation

Consider the pneumatic finger again. If the load (air pressure) is applied very fast, the deformation would also occur very fast. When the material moves very fast, two effects must be taken into account: *inertia effect* and *damping effect*. Combination of these two effects are called *dynamic effects*. When the dynamic effects are considered in the simulation of a structure, it is called a *dynamic simulation* of the structure.

Imagine that the pressure of 0.2 MPa is applied in the chambers in just 0.1 second. The pressure is applied so fast that the deformation must also be very fast and that dynamic effects must play a role in the structure's behavior. The figure and the chart below show the time-varying deflection of the finger tip under such loading condition [1, 2, 3]. The curve shows that the vibration amplitude can be much more than the results obtained in a static simulation, in which the dynamic effects are not taken into account. Furthermore, the vibration lasts for several seconds. This, in this case, is not desirable.

The foregoing simulation, a structure subject to arbitrary dynamic loads, is called the *transient structural simulation*. Chapters 12 and 15 will introduce transient structural analysis in depth; Chapter 12 discusses the implicit methods while Chapter 15 introduces explicit methods.

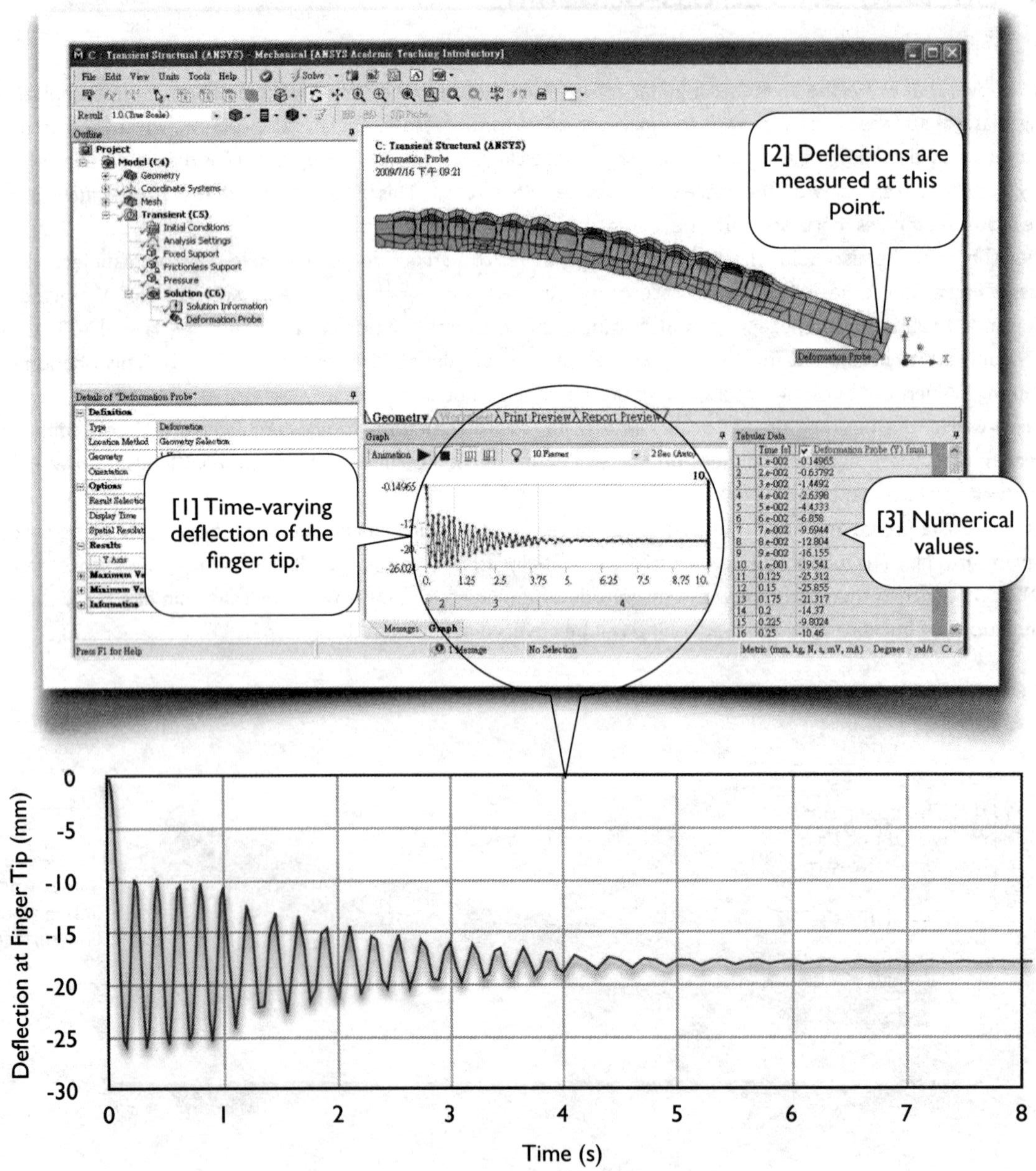

1.1-11 Modal Analysis

A special case of dynamic simulation is the *free vibration* simulation, the vibration of a structure without any loading (prestress is allowed). Consider that you suddenly apply a force during a short period on a structure. After the short period, the force has been removed but the structure is still vibrating, and the vibration will last for a while. We want to know the nature of this "free" vibration of the structure. It is called the *modal analysis*. The results of modal analysis include the *natural frequencies* and the *vibration modes* of the structure [1-4]. The figure below shows the first four natural frequencies and the corresponding vibration modes of the pneumatic finger.

A modal analysis is usually needed before a transient analysis, to obtain preliminary dynamic characteristics of the structure. A modal analysis is also much less expensive, in terms of engineer's work hours and computer resource, than a transient analysis. Chapter 11 will discuss modal analysis in depth.

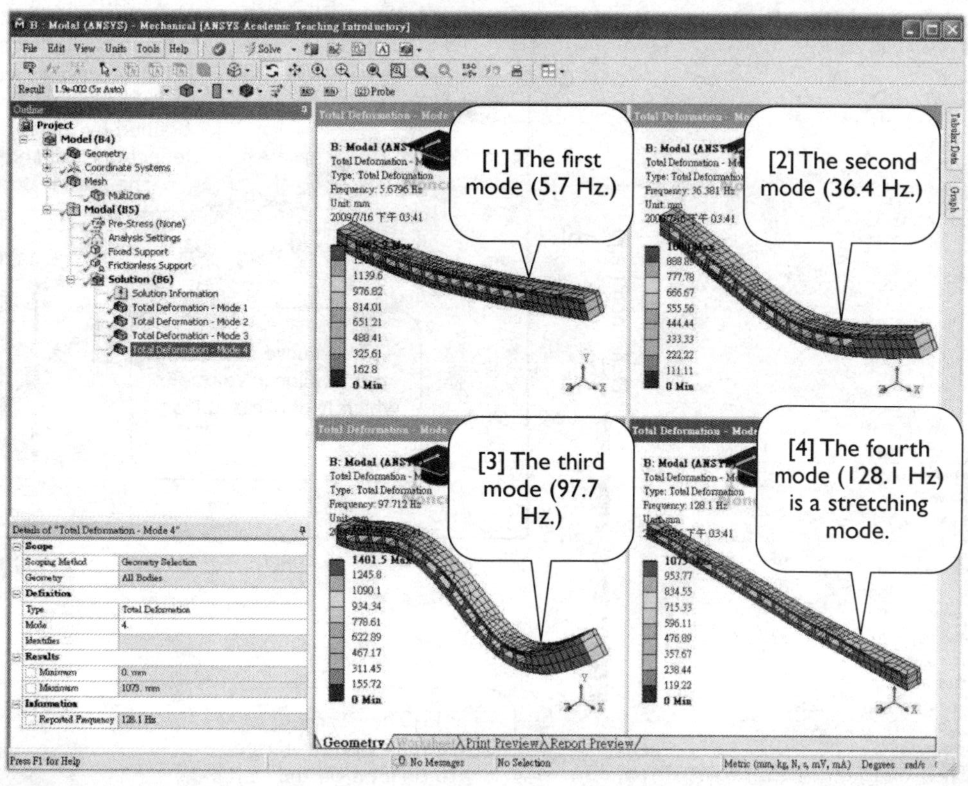

1.1-12 Structural Nonlinearities

When the responses (deflection, stress, strain) of a structure is linearly proportional to the loads, the structure is called a *linear structure* and the simulation is called a *linear simulation*. Otherwise the structure is called a *nonlinear structure* and the simulation is called a *nonlinear simulation*.

The structural nonlinearity commonly comes from three sources. (a) Due to large deformation. This is called *geometry nonlinearity*. (b) Due to topological change of the structure. This is called *topology nonlinearity*. A common case of topology nonlinearity is the change of contact status, and this is called *contact nonlinearity*. (c) Due to nonlinear stress-strain relationship of the material. This is called *material nonlinearity*.

In our case, the stress-strain relationship of the PDMS is modeled as linear and there is no contact between any parts; there is no material nonlinearity or contact nonlinearity. This case, however, has a deflection so large that it exhibits certain degree of geometry nonlinearity.

The curve [1] in the figure shown below is a duplicate from the curve in 1.1-8[4]. It shows a nonlinear relationship between the response (deflection) and the load (pressure). For comparison, we also include a linear solution [2] in the figure. The linear solution is obtained by turning <Large Deflection> off [3] and solving the model again.

A comparison between the nonlinear solution and the linear solution concludes that, in our case, the error would be huge if geometry nonlinearity were not taken into account.

Solving a nonlinear problem is always challenging (and sometimes frustrating). Real-world problems often involve more-or-less nonlinearities. We will experience nonlinear simulation as early as in Chapter 3, without detail explanation of many nonlinear solution controls. But, near the end of the book, we will spend two chapters dedicated to the discussion of nonlinear simulations. Chapter 13 discusses general nonlinear solution methods. It also discusses geometry nonlinearity and contact nonlinearity. Chapter 14 dedicates to the discussion of material nonlinearity.

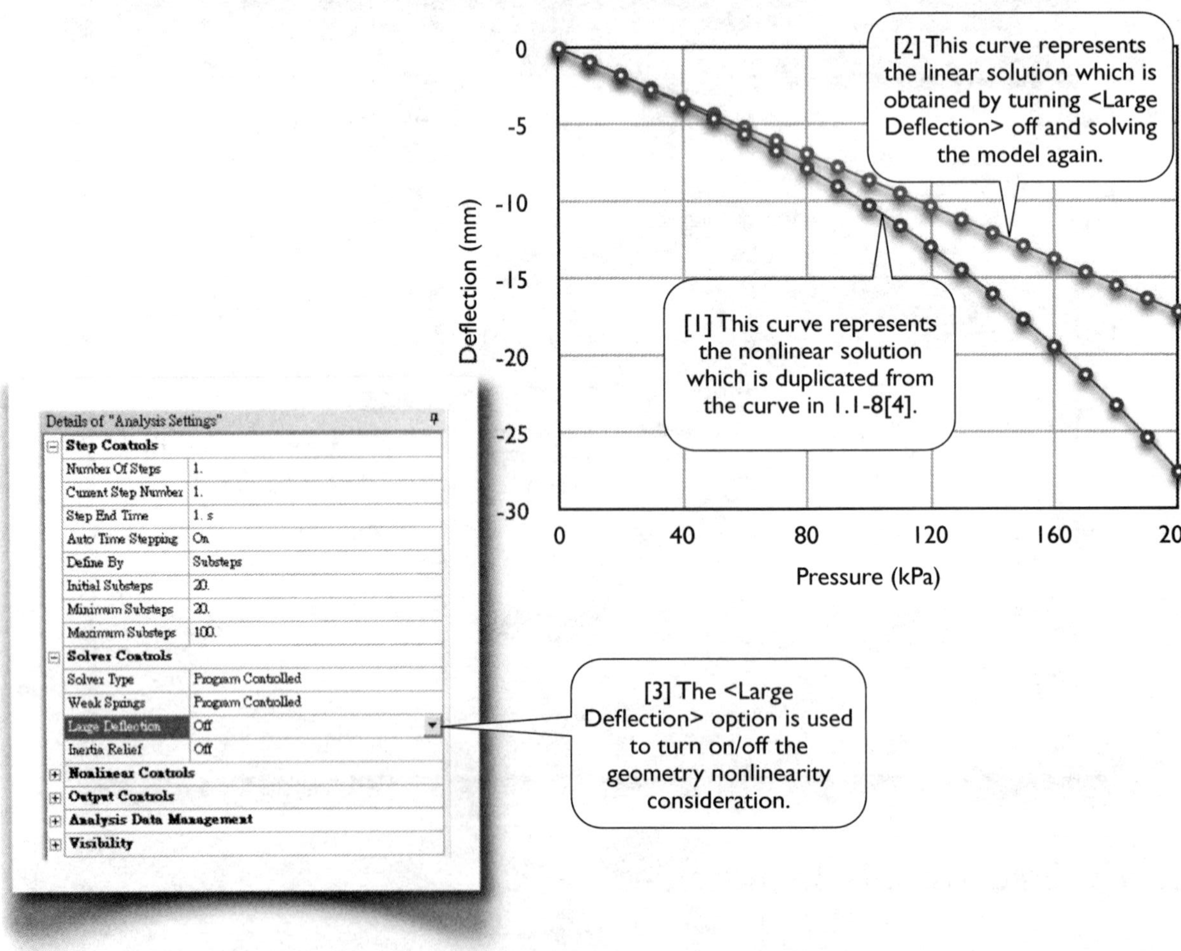

References

1. Jeong, O. K and Konishi, S., "All PDMS Pneumatic Microfinger With Bidirectional Motion and Its Application," Journal of Microelectomechanical Systems, Vol. 15, No. 4, August 2006, pp. 896-903.
2. Draheim, J, Kamberger, R., and Wallrabe, U, "Process and material properties of polydimethylsiloxane (PDMS) for Optical MEMS," *Sensors and Actuators A: Physical*, Vol. 151, Issue 2, April 2009, pp. 95-99.

Section 1.2

Structural Mechanics: A Quick Review

The purposes of this quick review are to (a) define a structural simulation problem so that the students have a clear picture of the input and the output of a structural simulation system; (b) bring up terminologies relevant to structural mechanics, such as displacement, stress, and strain, that will be used throughout the book; (c) and summarize equations that govern the behavior of structures so that the students know what the Workbench is solving.

We will restrict our review on homogeneous, isotropic, linear static structural analysis. More specifically, (a) the material is assumed to be homogeneous, isotropic, and linearly elastic; the last item implies that Hooke's law is applicable; (b) the deformation is small enough so that we assume a linear relationship between the displacements and the strain; (c) there is no status changes, for example, contacts, during the deformation; (d) the deformation is slow enough so that the dynamic effects are not taken into account.

The concepts we will draw can be generalized to include non-homogeneous, anisotropic, nonlinear, dynamic problems.

1.2-1 Structural Simulation Problems

Many engineering simulation problems (e.g., structural, mechanical, flow, electromagnetic) can be defined as the process of finding the *responses* of a *problem domain* subject to some *environmental conditions*.

In structural simulation, the problem domain consists of *solid bodies*; the environmental conditions include loads and supports; the responses can be described by the displacements, stresses, or strains.

For the pneumatic fingers case (Section 1.1), the problem domain is a body of the PDMS elastomer. There are two support conditions: fixed support at one end surface and frictionless support at the surface of symmetry. There is only one loading condition: the air pressure applied on the surfaces of the air chambers.

Note that these environmental conditions apply on boundary surfaces, so these conditions are also called *boundary conditions*. In general, environmental conditions do not necessarily apply on boundary surfaces. Common environmental conditions that do not apply on boundary surfaces include temperature changes and inertia forces; these loads distribute over the volumes (rather than boundary surfaces) of the problem domain.

1.2-2 Displacement

Deformation of a body can be described by a *displacement field* $\{u\}$ [1-5]. Note that the quantity $\{u\}$ is a function of position and, since it is a vector, we can expressed the displacement in terms of three components

$$\{u\} = \{\ u_X \quad u_Y \quad u_Z\ \} \qquad (1)$$

All three components are, of course, functions of position. The SI unit for displacements is meter (m).

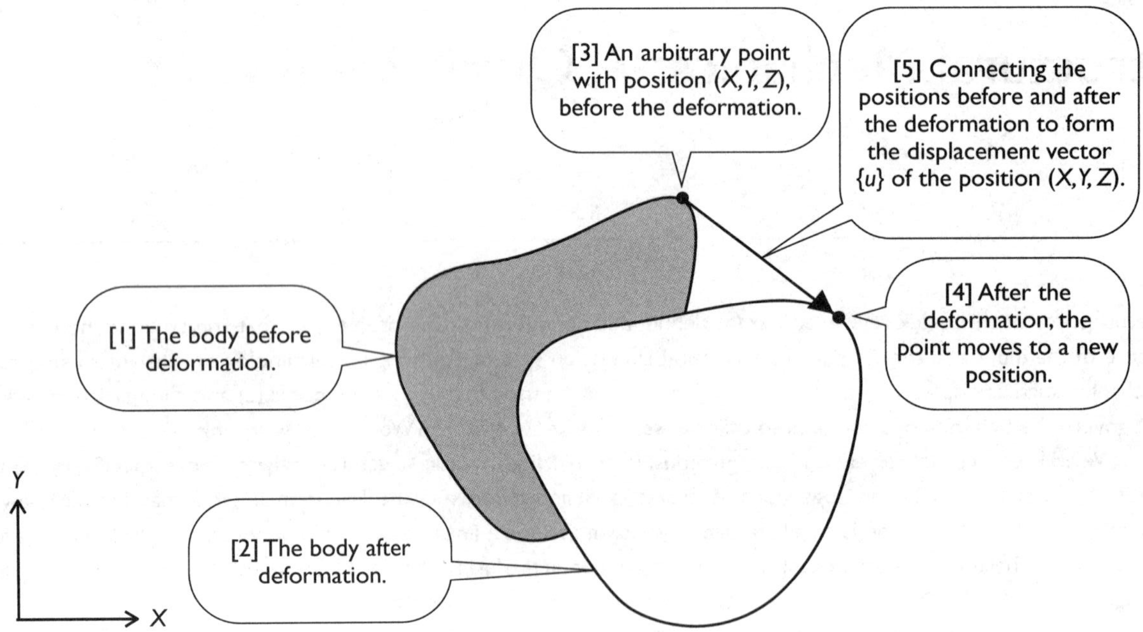

1.2-3 Stress

Concepts of displacement are relatively easy to understand, since the displacement can be represented by a vector, and most of college students are familiar with the mathematics of vector. On contrast, the concepts of stress is not so obvious.

The stress is similar to pressure. A pressure, which can be represented by a vector, is a quantity to describe the intensity of a force acting on a surface (note that the surface defines a direction). The SI unit for the pressure is pascal (Pa). Unlike the pressure in still water, in which the magnitudes of the pressure are the same on any surfaces and the directions of the pressure are alway normal to the surfaces, the magnitudes and the directions of the stress of a solid body may not be the same on any two surfaces.

Imagine that you are buried underground. You should feel different pressures in different surfaces of your body. For example, the pressure on your top surface is usually larger than that on your cheek surface. In addition, the pressure is not necessarily normal to the surface. This is quite different from as if you were under still water, where you should feel the same pressure magnitudes on any surfaces (neglecting the length of your body), and the pressure directions are always normal to your surfaces.

Therefore, to describe the stress state at your position, you should tell the outside people two sets of information: (a) which face you are describing and (b) the magnitude and direction of the pressure. You might repeat this description for ALL the faces in order to FULLY describe the stress state at your position. Of course, that is not really necessary. In 3D space, you only need to describe the pressures in three independent faces, or directions. Pressures in other directions can be derived from those in these three directions.

It is practical to set up a reference coordinate system, *XYZ* [1] and describe the pressures along these three directions, *X*, *Y*, and *Z*. In the figure below, the box represents a small cube at the point of our concern in the structure body. There are six faces in the cube. We can denote them as X-face, negative X-face [2, 3], etc.

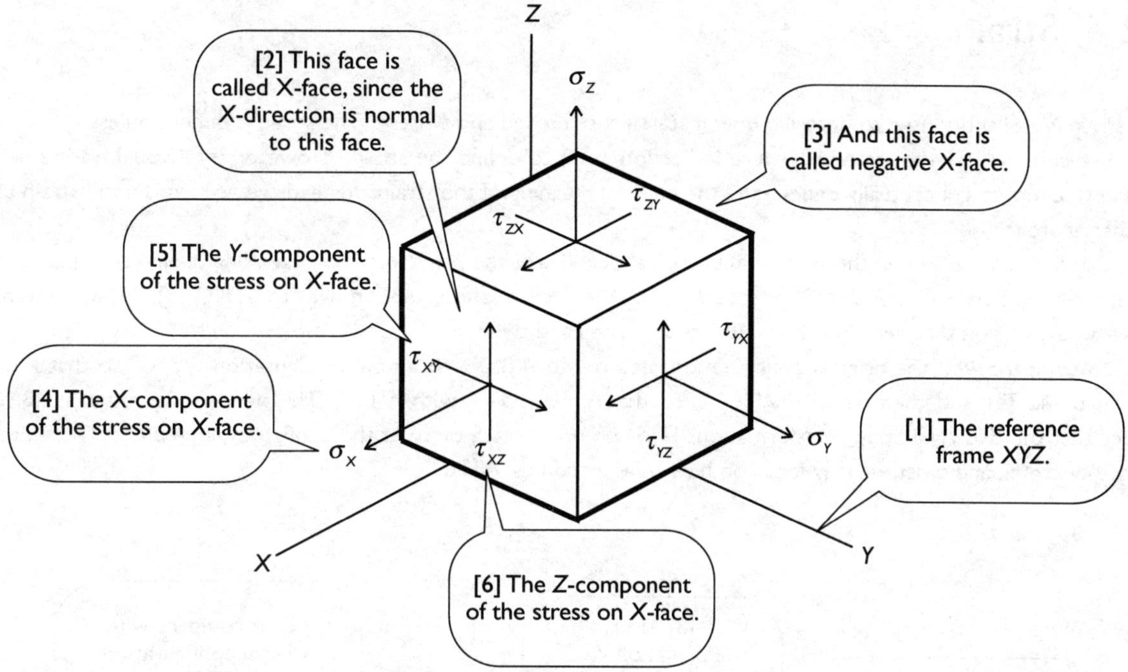

Consider the pressure on X-face. The pressure in general is not normal to the face, we however can decompose it into X-, Y-, and Z-components, and denote them as σ_X, τ_{XY}, and τ_{XZ} respectively [4, 5, 6]. The component σ_X is called the *normal stress* on the X-face; τ_{XY} is called the Y-component of *shear stress* on the X-face; τ_{XZ} is called the Z-component of shear stress on the X-face. Other stress components are defined in a similar way. In this way, to fully describe the stress state at a certain point, we need 9 components; they can be conveniently arranged in a matrix form

$$\{\sigma\} = \left\{ \begin{matrix} \sigma_X & \tau_{XY} & \tau_{XZ} \\ \tau_{YX} & \sigma_Y & \tau_{YZ} \\ \tau_{ZX} & \tau_{ZY} & \sigma_Z \end{matrix} \right\} \tag{1}$$

Note that in the negative faces, the stresses are exactly the same as those in the positive faces except the directions are reversed. This can be proved by simply applying the force equilibrium along X-, Y-, and Z-directions respectively.

By applying moment equilibrium along X-, Y-, and Z-direction respectively, i.e.,

$$\sum M_X = 0, \quad \sum M_Y = 0, \quad \sum M_Z = 0, \tag{2}$$

we can prove that the stress state matrix is symmetric, i.e.,

$$\tau_{XY} = \tau_{YX}, \quad \tau_{YZ} = \tau_{ZY}, \quad \tau_{XZ} = \tau_{ZX} \tag{3}$$

Therefore, only 6 independent components are needed to describe the stress state at a certain point. We now rewrite the stress state in a more concise form:

$$\{\sigma\} = \{ \sigma_X \quad \sigma_Y \quad \sigma_Z \quad \tau_{XY} \quad \tau_{YZ} \quad \tau_{ZX} \} \tag{4}$$

These 6 components are, of course, functions of position.

1.2-4 Strain

The strain is a quantity used to describe how material is stretched and twisted. The strain is dimensionless.

We could follow the same procedure in Section 1.2-3 to define the strain. However, that would not be helpful for the students to conceptually understand the physical meaning of the strain. Instead, we will explain the strain using another approach.

Consider a particle A in the structural body. Particle B is at the neighborhood of A along X-direction and particle C is at the neighborhood of A along Y-direction [1, 2]. After deformation, ABC moves to $A'B'C'$ [3]. Now, we want to derive an expression that describes how ABC is stretched and twisted.

To compare with the original configuration, let's rotate $A'B'C'$ to a new configuration $A'B''C''$ so that $A'C''$ is parallel to AC [4], and then translate $A'B''C''$ so that A' coincident with A [5]. The new configuration is $AB'''C'''$. Notice that the two rigid body transformations [4, 5] do not stretch or twist the configuration $A'B'C'$. Therefore, to study the stretch and twist, we may focus on how ABC becomes $AB'''C'''$.

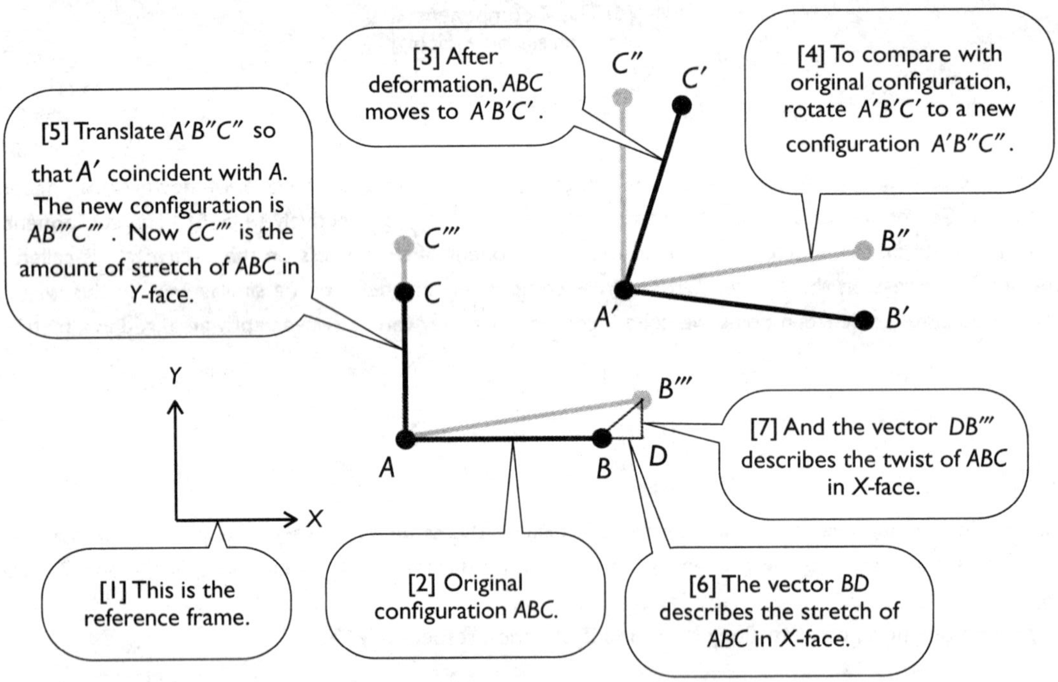

It is now easier to see how ABC is stretched and twisted to become $AB'''C'''$. The vector BB''' represents the displacement of B in X-direction (or X-face). We can define the strain on X-face as the vector BB''' divided by the original length AB, i.e.,

$$\text{Strain on X-face} = \frac{BB'''}{AB}$$

The strain can be decomposed into two components: X-component and Y-component [6, 7]. The former is called the *normal strain* ε_X (since it is normal to the X-face) the latter is called the *shear strain* (since it is parallel to the X-face) in Y-direction, γ_{XY}, i.e.,

$$\varepsilon_X = \frac{BD}{AB}, \quad \gamma_{XY} = \frac{DB'''}{AB} \qquad (1)$$

Now the physical meaning of the strain becomes obvious: the normal strain ε_X is the percentage of stretch of a fiber which lies along X-direction; the shear strain γ_{XY} is the angle change (in radian) of two fibers lying on XY-plane and originally forming a right angle.

We can define the strains in Y-face and Z-face in a similar way and conclude that, to fully describe the strain state at a point, we need 9 components; they can be conveniently arranged in a matrix form:

$$\{\varepsilon\} = \begin{Bmatrix} \varepsilon_X & \gamma_{XY} & \gamma_{XZ} \\ \gamma_{YX} & \varepsilon_Y & \gamma_{YZ} \\ \gamma_{ZX} & \gamma_{ZY} & \varepsilon_Z \end{Bmatrix} \tag{2}$$

From the geometry (by swapping X-axis and Y-axis [1]), we can prove that the strain matrix is symmetric, i.e.,

$$\gamma_{XY} = \gamma_{YX}, \quad \gamma_{YZ} = \gamma_{ZY}, \quad \gamma_{XZ} = \gamma_{ZX} \tag{3}$$

Therefore, only 6 independent components are needed to describe the strain state at a certain point. We can rewrite the strain state in a more concise form:

$$\{\varepsilon\} = \{\ \varepsilon_X \quad \varepsilon_Y \quad \varepsilon_Z \quad \gamma_{XY} \quad \gamma_{YZ} \quad \gamma_{ZX}\ \} \tag{4}$$

These 6 components are, of course, functions of position.

1.2-5 Governing Equations

Let's summarize what we've come up with so far. In structural analysis, we can use following quantities (all or part of them) to describe the response of a structure subject to environmental conditions:

$$\{u\} = \{\ u_X \quad u_Y \quad u_Z\ \} \qquad \text{Copy of 1.2-2(1)}$$

$$\{\sigma\} = \{\ \sigma_X \quad \sigma_Y \quad \sigma_Z \quad \tau_{XY} \quad \tau_{YZ} \quad \tau_{ZX}\ \} \qquad \text{Copy of 1.2-3(4)}$$

$$\{\varepsilon\} = \{\ \varepsilon_X \quad \varepsilon_Y \quad \varepsilon_Z \quad \gamma_{XY} \quad \gamma_{YZ} \quad \gamma_{ZX}\ \} \qquad \text{Copy of 1.2-4(4)}$$

These 15 quantities are not independent each other. Physical principles and mathematical relationships exist among these quantities. We must establish 15 equations to solve these 15 quantities. These equations are called governing equations, since they govern the structure's behaviors. These equations are: 3 equilibrium equations, 6 strain-displacement relations, and 6 stress-strain relations.

1.2-6 Equilibrium Equations

The stress components in 1.2-3(4) must satisfy equilibrium principle:

$$\sum F_X = 0, \ \sum F_Y = 0, \ \sum F_Z = 0 \tag{1}$$

If we apply Equations (1) on a point INSIDE the structural body, we can obtain three equilibrium equations involving the stress components:

$$\begin{aligned}
&\frac{\partial \sigma_X}{\partial X} + \frac{\partial \tau_{XY}}{\partial Y} + \frac{\partial \tau_{XZ}}{\partial Z} + b_X = 0 \\
&\frac{\partial \tau_{YX}}{\partial X} + \frac{\partial \sigma_Y}{\partial Y} + \frac{\partial \tau_{YZ}}{\partial Z} + b_Y = 0 \\
&\frac{\partial \tau_{ZX}}{\partial X} + \frac{\partial \tau_{ZY}}{\partial Y} + \frac{\partial \sigma_Z}{\partial Z} + b_Z = 0
\end{aligned} \tag{2}$$

where b_X, b_Y, b_Z are components of body forces (forces distributed in the body, with SI unit N/m^3). If we apply Equations (1) on a point ON the boundary surface of the structural body, the three equilibrium equations will have the form:

$$\begin{aligned}
\sigma_X n_X + \tau_{XY} n_Y + \tau_{XZ} n_Z + S_X &= 0 \\
\tau_{YX} n_X + \sigma_Y n_Y + \tau_{YZ} n_Z + S_Y &= 0 \\
\tau_{ZX} n_X + \tau_{ZY} n_Y + \sigma_Z n_Z + S_Z &= 0
\end{aligned} \tag{3}$$

where S_X, S_Y, S_Z are components of surface forces (forces distributed on the boundary, with SI unit N/m^2), and n_X, n_Y, n_Z are components of the unit normal vector on the boundary surface.

We will not discuss the derivations of Equations (2) and (3) further; they can be found in any textbook of solid mechanics. Here, we want to emphasize again that the equilibrium equations originate from Eq. (1). Note that the moment equilibrium has been used to prove the symmetry of the shear stresses (Eqs. 1.2-3(2, 3)). Furthermore, the three equilibrium equations, in either form of Eqs. (2) or (3), involve 6 quantities to be solved; of course that is not possible. We need to establish more equations to solve the response of the structure.

1.2-7 Strain-Displacement Relation

There exist geometric relations between displacement and strain. Under the assumption of small deformation, the relations are linear:

$$\begin{aligned}
&\varepsilon_X = \frac{\partial u_X}{\partial X}, \quad \varepsilon_Y = \frac{\partial u_Y}{\partial Y}, \quad \varepsilon_Z = \frac{\partial u_Z}{\partial Z} \\
&\gamma_{XY} = \frac{\partial u_X}{\partial Y} + \frac{\partial u_Y}{\partial X}, \quad \gamma_{YZ} = \frac{\partial u_Y}{\partial Z} + \frac{\partial u_Z}{\partial Y}, \quad \gamma_{ZX} = \frac{\partial u_Z}{\partial X} + \frac{\partial u_X}{\partial Z}
\end{aligned} \tag{1}$$

Again, we will not discuss the derivations of Eq. (1) further; they can be found in any textbook of solid mechanics. Here, we want to emphasize that Eq. (1) is derived from mathematics (geometry) without applying any physical principles. You also see that the strain-displacement relation in Eq. (1) is consistent with what we have illustrated in Eq. 1.2-4(1). Second, if the assumption of small deformation is removed, a strain-displacement relation still exists but is no longer linear; there will be some high-order derivative terms in the equations. Third, combining Eq. (1) with either Eq. 1.2-6(2) or 1.2-6(3), we now have 9 equations involving 15 quantities to be solved. We need to establish 6 more equations, to solve the response of a structure.

1.2-8 Stress-Strain Relation

To solve the response of a structure, it is practical to assume a relation between stress and strain. Experiments show that a linear relation between stress and strain often can be adopted; it is called the Hooke's law:

$$\begin{aligned}
\varepsilon_X &= \frac{\sigma_X}{E} - \nu\frac{\sigma_Y}{E} - \nu\frac{\sigma_Z}{E} \\
\varepsilon_Y &= \frac{\sigma_Y}{E} - \nu\frac{\sigma_Z}{E} - \nu\frac{\sigma_X}{E} \\
\varepsilon_Z &= \frac{\sigma_Z}{E} - \nu\frac{\sigma_X}{E} - \nu\frac{\sigma_Y}{E} \\
\gamma_{XY} &= \frac{\tau_{XY}}{G}, \quad \gamma_{YZ} = \frac{\tau_{YZ}}{G}, \quad \gamma_{ZX} = \frac{\tau_{ZX}}{G}
\end{aligned} \tag{1}$$

Although Eq. (1) is purely an assumption (no physical or mathematical principles applied), it is proved to be very useful and often accurate enough, depending on the material and the application. Eq. (1) is called a *material model*; it characterizes the behavior of a material, independent of the geometry and environmental conditions.

There are three *material parameters* in Eq. (1): the Young's modulus E, the Poisson's ratio ν, and the shear modulus G. In SI units, the Young's modulus and the shear modulus are pascal (Pa) and the Poisson's ratio is dimensionless. Elementary mechanics of material shows that these three quantities are not independent to each other. They satisfy the relation

$$G = \frac{E}{2(1+\nu)} \tag{2}$$

We conclude that, for an isotropic, linearly elastic material, two independent material parameters are needed to describe the stress-strain relation; you can choose any two of E, ν, and G. In Workbench, it requires the input of Young's modulus and Poisson's ratio to define the <Isotropic Elasticity> (1.1-3[4]).

Consider that the temperature changes over the structural body. Since a temperature change of ΔT causes a strain of $\alpha\Delta T$, in which α is the *coefficient of thermal expansion*, this *thermal strain* should be added to Eq. (1), i.e.,

$$\begin{aligned}
\varepsilon_X &= \frac{\sigma_X}{E} - \nu\frac{\sigma_Y}{E} - \nu\frac{\sigma_Z}{E} + \alpha\Delta T \\
\varepsilon_Y &= \frac{\sigma_Y}{E} - \nu\frac{\sigma_Z}{E} - \nu\frac{\sigma_X}{E} + \alpha\Delta T \\
\varepsilon_Z &= \frac{\sigma_Z}{E} - \nu\frac{\sigma_X}{E} - \nu\frac{\sigma_Y}{E} + \alpha\Delta T \\
\gamma_{XY} &= \frac{\tau_{XY}}{G}, \quad \gamma_{YZ} = \frac{\tau_{YZ}}{G}, \quad \gamma_{ZX} = \frac{\tau_{ZX}}{G}
\end{aligned} \tag{3}$$

1.2-9 Summary

We now have 15 equations, including three equilibrium equations, either (INSIDE the structural body)

$$\begin{aligned}
\frac{\partial \sigma_X}{\partial X} + \frac{\partial \tau_{XY}}{\partial Y} + \frac{\partial \tau_{XZ}}{\partial Z} + b_X &= 0 \\
\frac{\partial \tau_{YX}}{\partial X} + \frac{\partial \sigma_Y}{\partial Y} + \frac{\partial \tau_{YZ}}{\partial Z} + b_Y &= 0 \\
\frac{\partial \tau_{ZX}}{\partial X} + \frac{\partial \tau_{ZY}}{\partial Y} + \frac{\partial \sigma_Z}{\partial Z} + b_Z &= 0
\end{aligned} \qquad \text{Copy of 1.2-6(2)}$$

or (ON the boundary surface)

$$\begin{aligned} \sigma_X n_X + \tau_{XY} n_Y + \tau_{XZ} n_Z + S_X &= 0 \\ \tau_{YX} n_X + \sigma_Y n_Y + \tau_{YZ} n_Z + S_Y &= 0 \\ \tau_{ZX} n_X + \tau_{ZY} n_Y + \sigma_Z n_Z + S_Z &= 0 \end{aligned}$$ Copy of 1.2-6(3)

and six equations describe the strain-displacement relation

$$\varepsilon_X = \frac{\partial u_X}{\partial X},\quad \varepsilon_Y = \frac{\partial u_Y}{\partial Y},\quad \varepsilon_Z = \frac{\partial u_Z}{\partial Z}$$
$$\gamma_{XY} = \frac{\partial u_X}{\partial Y} + \frac{\partial u_Y}{\partial X},\quad \gamma_{YZ} = \frac{\partial u_Y}{\partial Z} + \frac{\partial u_Z}{\partial Y},\quad \gamma_{ZX} = \frac{\partial u_Z}{\partial X} + \frac{\partial u_X}{\partial Z}$$ Copy of 1.2-7(1)

and six equations describe the stress-strain relation

$$\begin{aligned} \varepsilon_X &= \frac{\sigma_X}{E} - \nu\frac{\sigma_Y}{E} - \nu\frac{\sigma_Z}{E} \\ \varepsilon_Y &= \frac{\sigma_Y}{E} - \nu\frac{\sigma_Z}{E} - \nu\frac{\sigma_X}{E} \\ \varepsilon_Z &= \frac{\sigma_Z}{E} - \nu\frac{\sigma_X}{E} - \nu\frac{\sigma_Y}{E} \end{aligned}$$
$$\gamma_{XY} = \frac{\tau_{XY}}{G},\quad \gamma_{YZ} = \frac{\tau_{YZ}}{G},\quad \gamma_{ZX} = \frac{\tau_{ZX}}{G}$$ Copy of 1.2-8(1)

In theory, these 15 equations can be solved for 15 unknown quantities:

$$\{u\} = \{\ u_X\ \ u_Y\ \ u_Z\ \}$$ Copy of 1.2-2(1)

$$\{\sigma\} = \{\ \sigma_X\ \ \sigma_Y\ \ \sigma_Z\ \ \tau_{XY}\ \ \tau_{YZ}\ \ \tau_{ZX}\ \}$$ Copy of 1.2-3(4)

$$\{\varepsilon\} = \{\ \varepsilon_X\ \ \varepsilon_Y\ \ \varepsilon_Z\ \ \gamma_{XY}\ \ \gamma_{YZ}\ \ \gamma_{ZX}\ \}$$ Copy of 1.2-4(4)

In practice, only a few of extremely simple "textbook problems" can be solved analytically. Most of real-world problems are too complicated to be solved analytically. The complexity comes from either the geometry or the environmental conditions. Numerical methods become the only feasible methods. The finite element methods, which is one of the most successful numerical methods for the boundary-value problems such as the problems summarized in this section, are implemented in the ANSYS Workbench to solve the governing equations.

Remark

By "governing equations" of a structural simulation problem, we usually mean the equilibrium equations: Eq. 1.2-6(2) governs the behavior in the body and Eq. 1.2-6(3) governs the behavior on the boundary. The two sets of equations constitute a boundary value problems.

It is possible to replace the stress components in the equilibrium equations by strain components using Eq. 1.2-8(1), and in turn replace the strain components by displacement components using Eq. 1.2-7(1). That will end up with a set of three equilibrium equations involving three displacement components, and we can solve the three differential equations for three displacement components.

Actually, this is how the ANSYS Workbench solves the structural problems.

Section 1.3

Finite Element Methods: A Conceptual Introduction

The purposes of this introduction are to (a) bring up terminologies relevant to the finite element methods, such as degrees of freedom, shape functions, stiffness matrix, etc., that will be used throughout the book; (b) to present the procedure of the finite element methods, so that the students have better understanding of how the Workbench performs a simulation.

1.3-1 Basic Procedure

As mentioned, most of real-world problems are too complicated to be solved analytically, because of the geometry or the environmental conditions. If we add the complexity of nonlinearity and dynamic effects into the problems, then analytical solutions are practically unreachable.

A basic idea of the finite element methods is to divide the entire structural body into many smaller and geometrically simpler bodies, called *elements*, so that equilibrium equations of each element can be written down, and all the equilibrium equations are then solved simultaneously.

The elements are assumed to be connected by *nodes* located on the elements' edges and vertices. Another idea is to solve unknown discrete values (e.g., displacements at the nodes) rather than to solve unknown functions (e.g., displacement fields). In 3D cases, since the displacement on each node is a vector and has three components, the number of total unknown quantities to be solved is three times the number of nodes [1].

The available element shapes in the ANSYS Workbench and their specific configuration of nodes will be discussed in Section 1.3-3.

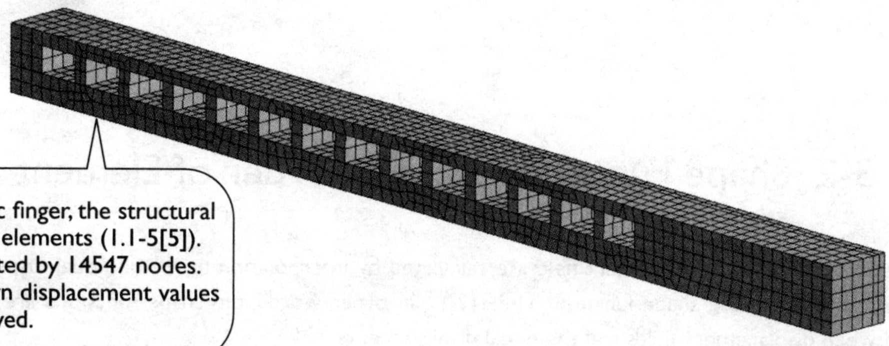

[1] In case of the pneumatic finger, the structural body is divided into 3294 elements (1.1-5[5]). The elements are connected by 14547 nodes. There are 3x14547 unknown displacement values to be solved.

The nodal displacement components, collectively denoted by the vector {*D*}, are called the *degrees of freedom* (DOF's) of the structure. They are so called because these values fully define the response of the structure. Assuming a static case, the system of equilibrium equations in terms of degrees of freedom has the following form (also see the remark in the end of Section 1.2):

$$[K]\{D\} = \{F\} \qquad (1)$$

The size of Eq. (1) is determined by the degrees of freedom, which is, in 3D cases, three times the number of nodes. The vector {*F*} is the external forces acting on the nodes, which is calculated from the environmental conditions. Physical meaning of the matrix [*K*] can be understood by thinking of the structure as a spring, {*F*} as external force, and {*D*} as the displacement of the spring, then [*K*] would be the spring constant, or the stiffness of the spring. In finite element methods, [*K*] is called the *stiffness matrix* of the structure. More precisely, physical meaning of the values on its ith column is the forces required on all the DOFs to make the ith DOF a unit displacement while restrain other DOFs from displacement.

Note that, for linear structure, [*K*] is a constant matrix; this is contrast to nonlinear cases (Section 1.1-12) where [*K*] is a function of {*D*}; we will extend the equilibrium equations to include nonlinearity in Chapters 13 and 14. For dynamic cases (Sections 1.1-10 and 1.1-11), dynamic effects have to be included in the Eq. (1); we will extend the equilibrium equations to include dynamic effects in Chapters 11 and 12.

After the discrete nodal displacements in Eq. (1) are solved, the displacement fields, Eq. 1.2-2(1), which are continuous functions, are calculated by interpolation using these nodal displacements, either linearly or quadratically [2]. These interpolating functions are called *shape functions*. Concepts of shape functions are crucial in the finite element methods; they will be discussed further in Section 1.3-2.

As soon as the displacement fields become known, the strain fields can be calculated by using Eq. 1.2-7(1), the strain-displacement relation. The stress fields in turn can be calculated by using Eq. 1.2-8(1), the stress-strain relation.

[2] After the discrete nodal displacements become known, the displacement field are calculated by interpolation using these nodal displacements. The interpolating functions are called shape functions. Note the displacement fields are continuous over the structural body.

1.3-2 Shape Functions and the Order of Element

As mentioned, the displacement field are calculated by interpolation using the nodal displacements. The interpolating functions are called shape functions (1.3-1[2]). In other words, the shape functions are used to establish a relation between displacement fields and the nodal displacements.

As an example, consider a 2D 4-node quadrilateral element [1]. The nodal displacements, collectively denoted by a vector {*d*}, has 8 components

$$\{d\} = \{\, d_1 \;\; d_2 \;\; d_3 \;\; d_4 \;\; d_5 \;\; d_6 \;\; d_7 \;\; d_8 \,\} \tag{1}$$

The displacement field {*u*} in the element is related to the nodal displacements by

$$\{u\} = [N]\{d\} \tag{2}$$

Where $[N]$ is the matrix of shape functions. The role of shape functions is to interpolate displacement field $\{u\}$ using the nodal displacements $\{d\}$. Let's summarize again: the components of nodal displacements $\{d\}$ are discrete values and the components of displacement field $\{u\}$ are continuous functions of (X,Y, Z). The shape functions in $[N]$ are to bridge the continuous functions and the discrete values. Other features of shape functions are addressed as follows.

First, let's examine the dimension of the $[N]$ matrix using the same example. Since $\{d\}$ has 8 components and $\{u\}$ has 3 components (Eq. 1.2-2(1)), the matrix $[N]$ must be of dimension 3x8.

Second, since $\{u\}$ contains functions of (X, Y, Z) and $\{d\}$ contains discrete values, therefore $[N]$ must contains functions of (X, Y, Z). Besides, for the element shown [1], since the interpolating points are on the vertices of the element, the shape functions must be a linear form. When the shape functions are linear polynomials, the element is called a *linear element, first-order element*, or *lower-order element* [2].

Often, using quadratic polynomials as shape functions can be more efficient. In such case, a node is added on the middle of each edge of the element; the added nodes are called the *midside nodes*; the element is called a *quadratic element, second-order element*, or *higher-order element*. In this book, we will not use the term linear element, to avoid confusing with the terms such as linearly elastic material.

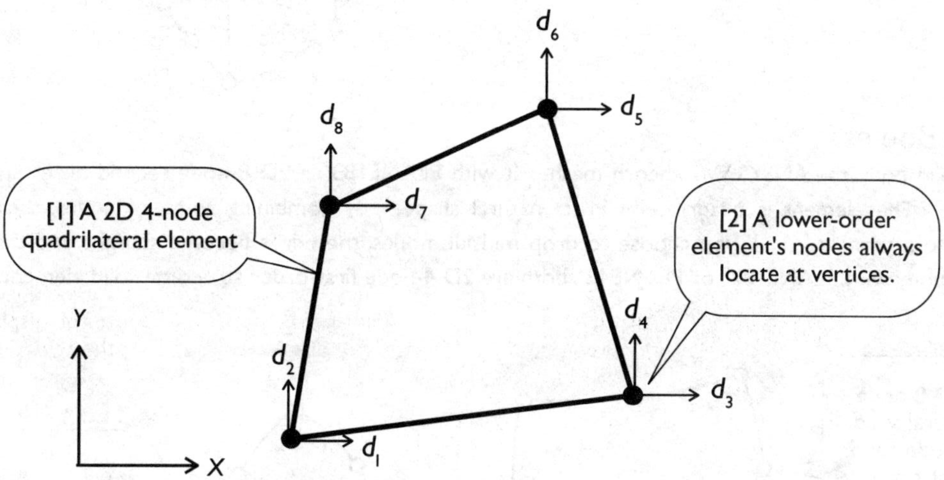

1.3-3 Element Shapes

ANSYS literally provides hundreds of element types[1]. The ANSYS Workbench, however, directly supports only a portion of them[2], other element types can be accessed with APDL (ANSYS Classic). To identify these elements, each element type is assigned a code name (e.g., SOLID186, PLANE183, etc.).

In 2D cases, the element shapes available are quadrilateral (4-sided) or triangular (3-sided). In 3D cases, the popular shapes include hexahedral (6-faced), triangle-based prism (5-faced), quadrilateral-based pyramid (5-faced), and tetrahedral (4-faced). By default, the ANSYS Workbench automatically chooses appropriate element type from its element library[2] according to the type of the structural body: 3D solid body, 2D solid body, 3D surface body, or 3D line body. Current version of ANSYS Workbench supports only these 4 body types. Note that 3D surface bodies are geometrically 2D but spatially 3D, while 3D line bodies are geometrically 1D but spatially 3D.

3D Solid Bodies

For a 3D solid body, the ANSYS Workbench meshes it with SOLID186[3] or SOLID95[4]; both are 3D 20-node second-order structural solid elements [1]. The element is hexahedral in its natural shape. By combining some of nodes, the element can degenerate to a triangle-based prism [2], quadrilateral-based pyramid [3], or tetrahedron [4]. Capability of degeneration is useful since it allows different shapes of elements mixed up in a body. If a body is to be meshed with tetrahedral elements exclusively, ANSYS Workbench meshes the body with SOLID187[5] or SOLID92[6]; both are 3D 10-node tetrahedral second-order structural solid elements, which have shapes exactly the same as the one degenerated from SOLID92 or SOLID186 [4]. Note that the Workbench allows an option to drop off elements' midside nodes; in that case the edges become straight.

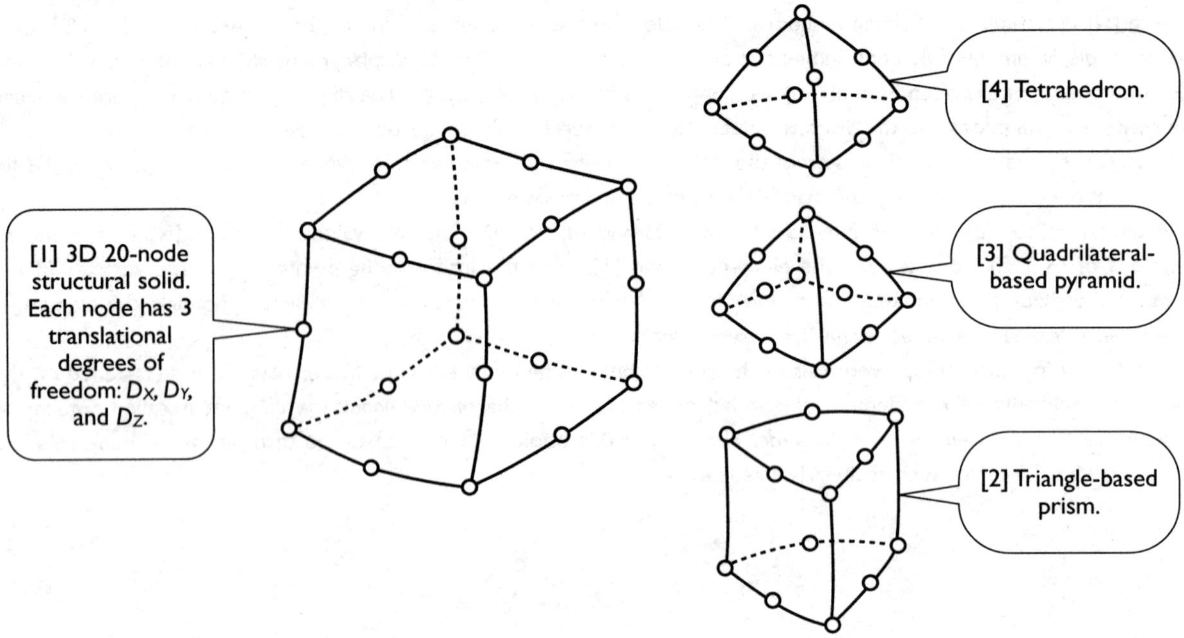

2D Solid Bodies

For a 2D solid body, the ANSYS Workbench meshes it with PLANE183[7], a 2D 8-node second-order structural solid element [5]. The element is quadrilateral in its natural shape. By combining some of nodes, the element can degenerate to a triangle [6]. If you choose to drop midside nodes, the edges become straight, and the Workbench meshes the body with PLANE182[8] or PLANE42[9]; both are 2D 4-node first-order structural solid elements.

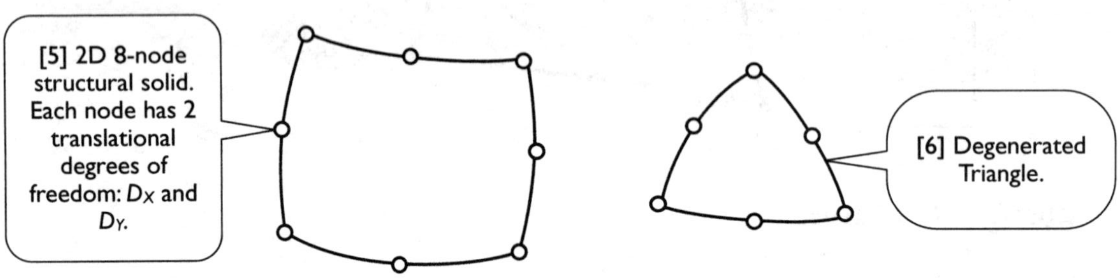

3D Surface Bodies

For a 3D surface body, the ANSYS Workbench meshes it with SHELL181[10], a 3D 4-node first-order structural shell element [7]. The element is quadrilateral in its natural shape, but can degenerate to form a triangle [8]. Note that shell elements, although planar by themselves, are not necessarily arranged on a plane.

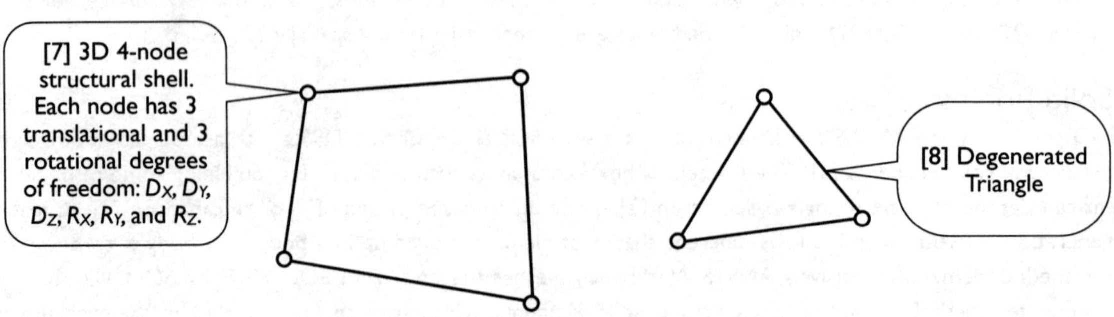

3D Line Bodies

For a 3D line body, ANSYS Workbench meshes it using BEAM188[11], a 3D 2-node first-order beam element [9]. Note that the beam element can be arranged in 3D space. Note that beam elements are not necessarily arranged in a straight line or on a plane.

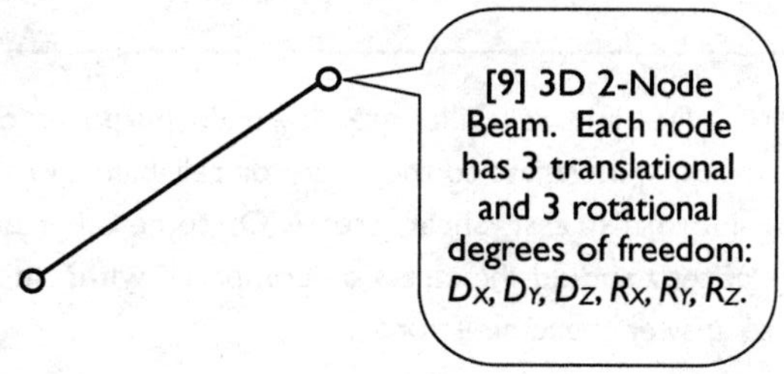

References

1. ANSYS Help System>Mechanical APDL>Element Reference>Element Library
2. ANSYS Help System>Mechanical APDL>Theory Reference>1.4.1. Elements Used by the ANSYS Workbench Product.
3. ANSYS Help System>Mechanical APDL>Element Reference>SOLID186.
4. ANSYS Help System>Mechanical APDL>Element Reference>SOLID95.
5. ANSYS Help System>Mechanical APDL>Element Reference>SOLID187.
6. ANSYS Help System>Mechanical APDL>Element Reference>SOLID92.
7. ANSYS Help System>Mechanical APDL>Element Reference>PLANE183.
8. ANSYS Help System>Mechanical APDL>Element Reference>PLANE182.
9. ANSYS Help System>Mechanical APDL>Element Reference>PLANE42.
10. ANSYS Help System>Mechanical APDL>Element Reference>SHELL181.
11. ANSYS Help System>Mechanical APDL>Element Reference>BEAM188.
12. ANSYS Help System>Mechanical APDL>Element Reference>2.17. Legacy vs. Current Element Technologies

Section 1.4

Failure Criteria of Materials

Achieving functionality, safety, and reliability are the main purposes of structural simulations. Deformation usually relates to the functionality, while stress to the safety or reliability. Which stress should we look into to ensure that a structure doesn't fail? Normal stress? Shear stress? Or some other quantities? How can we say a stress value is too large, or okay? What criteria should the stress be compared with? In short, what are the failure criteria of materials? This section intends to answer these questions.

1.4-1 Ductile versus Brittle Materials

From structural engineering point of view, stress-strain relation is the most important characteristics of a material. We often draw a stress-strain relation from standardized uniaxial tensile test data.

Two examples of stress-strain relation are shown in the figure below [1, 2]. On the left, the material displays large amount of strain before it fractures [3]; it is termed *ductile material*. On the right, the material's fracture strain is relatively small [4]; it is called a *brittle material*. Fracture strain is a measure of ductility. There are essential differences between these two types of materials.

Yield or Fracture?

Mild steel is a typical ductile material. For ductile materials, there often exists an obvious yield point [5], beyond which the deformation would be too large so that the material is no longer reliable or functional; the failure is due to excess deformation. Therefore, for ductile material, we are most concerned about whether the material reaches the yield point. In a uniaxial tensile test, the yield point is characterized by a yield stress σ_Y [5]. This is the stress we want to compare with. But, by which stress we want to compare with? σ_X? σ_Y? σ_Z? τ_{XY}? τ_{YZ}? τ_{ZX}? Sections 1.4-4 and 1.4-5 will answer this question.

Cast iron and ceramics are two examples of brittle materials. For brittle materials, there usually doesn't exist obvious yield point, and the failure is in a form of fracture. In a uniaxial tensile test, the fracture point is characterized by a fracture stress σ_f [4]. This is the stress we want to compare with. But, again, by which stress we want to compare with? σ_X? σ_Y? σ_Z? τ_{XY}? τ_{YZ}? τ_{ZX}? Section 1.4-2 and 1.4-3 will answer this question.

Tensile Failure or Shear Failure?

The fracture of brittle materials is mostly due to *tensile failure*; the yielding of ductile materials is mostly due to *shear failure*. The tensile failure of brittle material is easier to understand, because the failure always occurs after cracking, that is in turn due to the tensile stress. The shear failure of ductile materials can be justified in a standard uniaxial tensile test, in which the failure is accompanied by a necking process and a cone-shape breaking surface. It is important to note that a material may fail due to a mix-up of both mechanisms.

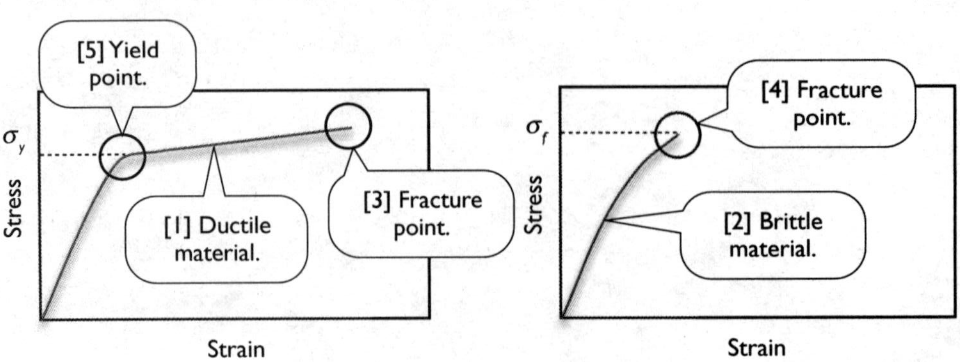

1.4-2 Principal Stresses

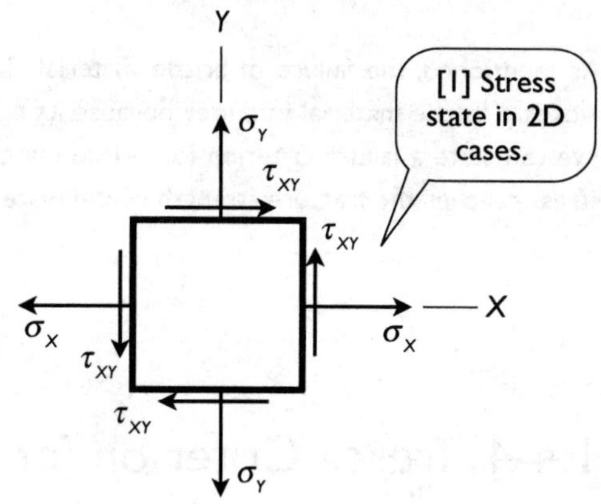

In Section 1.2-3, we reviewed the concepts of stress. We've learned that, at a certain point, the stresses are different in different directions. It then naturally raises questions such as these: In which direction does the normal stress reach its maximum? And, in which direction does the shear stress reach its maximum?

To present the concepts efficiently, consider a 2D case as shown in the figure [1], in which let's called the X-direction the base direction. In the base direction, the stress can be expressed with a stress pair (σ_X, τ_{XY}). In any direction, stress can be expressed with a stress pair (σ, τ). Our objective now is to find a relationship between normal stress σ and shear stress τ: how does σ vary with τ?

First we lay out a σ-τ space, and then mark the stress (σ_X, τ_{XY}) in the σ-τ space [2]. Second, noting that the stress (σ_Y, τ_{XY}) is also a stress pair, whose direction forms 90° with the base direction, we mark the stress (σ_Y, τ_{XY}) in the σ-τ space [3]. Similarly, we could draw other stress pairs in the σ-τ space [4].

What we want to point out is that the collection of these points form a circle in the σ-τ space [5], called the *Mohr's circle*. The proof can be found in any textbook of solid mechanics. Here, we only emphasize the concepts: a Mohr's circle represents a stress state. If you can seize this concept, then finding the maximum normal stress and maximum shear stress becomes straightforward.

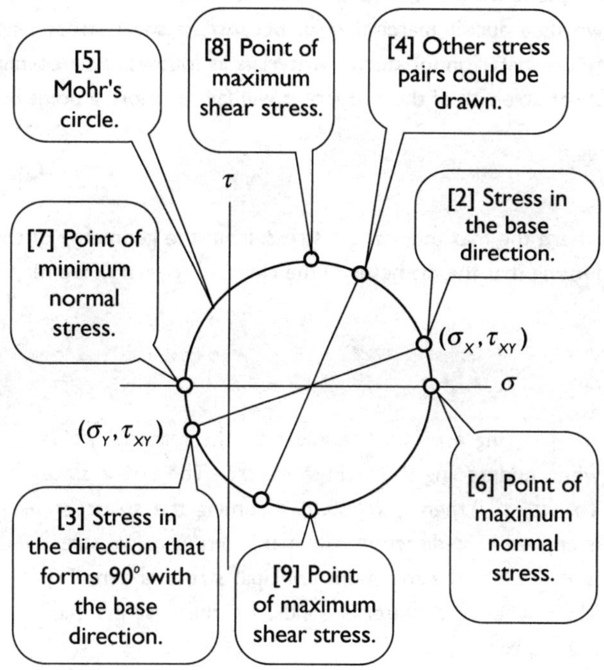

A stress state defines a Mohr's circle, and vice versa. Here, the stress state $(\sigma_X, \sigma_Y, \tau_{XY})$ fully defines the Mohr's circle as shown. Once we have a Mohr's circle, the points of maximum normal stress, minimum normal stress, and maximum shear stress can be located. The point of maximum normal stress is located at the right-most of the Mohr's circle [6]. The point of minimum normal stress is located at the left-most of the Mohr's circle [7]. The points of *maximum shear stress* are located at the upper-most and the lower-most of the Mohr's circle [8, 9]. Note that at points of maximum and minimum normal stresses, the shear stress vanishes.

The maximum normal stress is called the *maximum principal stress* and denoted by σ_1; The minimum normal stress is called the *minimum principal stress* and denoted by σ_3. Their corresponding directions are called *principal directions*. In 3D solid, there are three principal directions and three principal stresses. The *medium principal stress* is denoted by σ_2. The maximum principal stress is usually a positive value, a tension. The minimum principal stress is often a negative value, a compression.

Given $(\sigma_X, \sigma_Y, \tau_{XY})$, from the geometry of the Mohr's circle, we can easily calculate the values and their corresponding directions of the principal stresses and the maximum shear stress. We will not derive these formula in this book; the Workbench can report for you on your request. More importantly, make sure you understand the concepts and can generalize them to the 3D cases on your own.

1.4-3 Failure Criterion for Brittle Materials

As mentioned, the failure of brittle materials is due to fracture, and the fracture is due to tensile failure. In other words, a brittle material fractures because its tensile stress reaches the fracture strength of the material σ_f (1.4-1[4]). We can state a failure criterion for brittle materials as follows. At a certain point of a body, if the maximum principal stress reaches the fracture strength of the material, it will fail. In short, a point of material fails if

$$\sigma_1 \geq \sigma_f \tag{1}$$

1.4-4 Tresca Criterion for Ductile Materials

As mentioned, the failure of ductile materials is due to yielding, and the yielding is due to shear failure. In other words, a ductile material yields because its shear stress reaches the shear strength of the material τ_y. We can state a failure criterion for ductile materials as follows. At a certain point of a body, if the maximum shear stress reaches the shear strength of the material, it will fail. In short, a point of material fails if

$$\tau_{max} \geq \tau_y \tag{1}$$

where the maximum shear stress, from the geometry of the Mohr's circle, is simply the radius of the circle (1.4-2[5]). Noting that the diameter of the circle is $(\sigma_1 - \sigma_3)$, we may write down

$$\tau_{max} = \frac{\sigma_1 - \sigma_3}{2} \tag{2}$$

During a uniaxial tensile test, the material yields when undergoing the yield stress σ_y. The stress state $(\sigma_X, \sigma_Y, \tau_{XY})$ then is $(\sigma_y, 0, 0)$, assuming the stress σ_y is applied in X-direction. Its maximum principal stress is σ_y while the minimum principal stress is zero [1]. Thus, when the material yields, its shear stress (i.e., shear strength) is

$$\tau_y = \frac{\sigma_y}{2} \tag{3}$$

Substituting Eqs. (2) and (3) into (1), we have

$$\frac{\sigma_1 - \sigma_3}{2} \geq \frac{\sigma_y}{2} \tag{4}$$

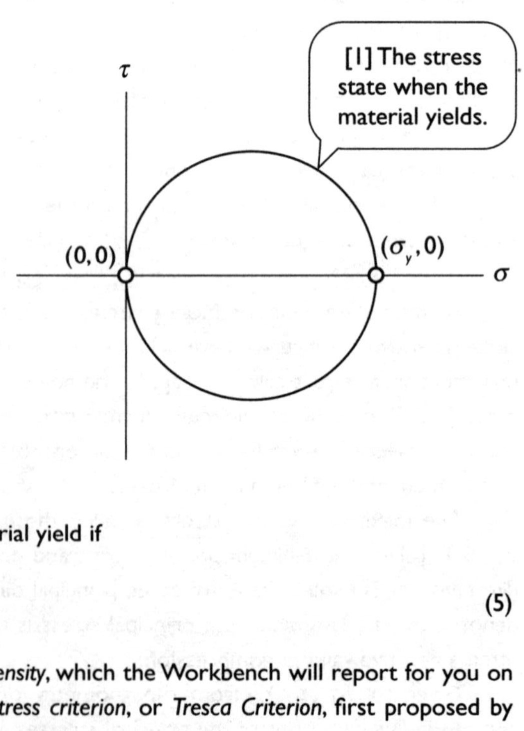

Simplifying the above equation, we reach a conclusion that the material yield if

$$\sigma_1 - \sigma_3 \geq \sigma_y \tag{5}$$

The quantity on the left-hand side, $(\sigma_1 - \sigma_3)$, is called the *stress intensity*, which the Workbench will report for you on your request. This failure criterion is called the *maximum shear stress criterion*, or *Tresca Criterion*, first proposed by Henri Tresca, a French mechanical engineer, in 1864.

1.4-5 Von Mises Criterion for Ductile Materials

The Tresca criterion is easy to understand but not accurate enough for predicting the yielding of many ductile materials. The theory discussed in 1.4-4 is too simplified and deviate from real-world situations. For example, the medium principal stress σ_2 plays no role in Eq. 1.4-4(5), but generally that is not true. A more sophisticated theory, called von Mises criterion, often predicts yielding more accurately than Tresca criterion.

Hydrostatic Stress and Deviatoric Stress

Without loss of generality, any stress state

$$\{\sigma\} = \begin{Bmatrix} \sigma_X & \tau_{XY} & \tau_{XZ} \\ \tau_{YX} & \sigma_Y & \tau_{YZ} \\ \tau_{ZX} & \tau_{ZY} & \sigma_Z \end{Bmatrix} \qquad \text{Copy of Eq. 1.2-3(1)}$$

can be rewritten in a form of principal stresses

$$\{\sigma\} = \begin{Bmatrix} \sigma_1 & 0 & 0 \\ 0 & \sigma_2 & 0 \\ 0 & 0 & \sigma_3 \end{Bmatrix} \qquad (1)$$

Note that, as mentioned in Section 1.4-2, from the Mohr's circle, in the directions where principal stresses occur, the shear stresses vanish.

The *hydrostatic stress* is defined as the average of the normal stresses

$$p = \frac{\sigma_1 + \sigma_2 + \sigma_3}{3} \qquad (2)$$

A stress state (1) can be thought of a superposition of two parts

$$\{\sigma\} = \begin{Bmatrix} \sigma_1 & 0 & 0 \\ 0 & \sigma_2 & 0 \\ 0 & 0 & \sigma_3 \end{Bmatrix} = \begin{Bmatrix} p & 0 & 0 \\ 0 & p & 0 \\ 0 & 0 & p \end{Bmatrix} + \begin{Bmatrix} \sigma_1 - p & 0 & 0 \\ 0 & \sigma_2 - p & 0 \\ 0 & 0 & \sigma_3 - p \end{Bmatrix} \qquad (3)$$

or, written in a more compact form,

$$\{\sigma\} = \{\sigma^p\} + \{\sigma^d\} \qquad (4)$$

The first part is the hydrostatic stress, and the second part is called the *deviatoric stress*, the stress deviate from the hydrostatic stress.

The material deformation also can be thought of a superposition of a dilation (volumetric change) and a distortion. The hydrostatic stress contributes exclusively to the dilation, while the deviatoric stress contributes exclusively to the distortion. The dilation plays no role in shear failure; it is the distortion that causes shear failure. In sort, the deviatoric stress

$$\{\sigma^d\} = \begin{Bmatrix} \sigma_1 - p & 0 & 0 \\ 0 & \sigma_2 - p & 0 \\ 0 & 0 & \sigma_3 - p \end{Bmatrix} \qquad (5)$$

can be used to establish a shear failure criterion. But, it is not a scalar value; how can we use it to compare with the uniaxial yield stress σ_y? We need more elaborate theory to derive a useful criterion.

Von Mises Yielding Criterion

In 1913, Richard von Mises, an Austria-Hungary born scientist, proposed a theory for predicting the yielding of ductile materials. The theory states that the yielding occurs when the deviatoric strain energy density (or deviatoric energy for short) reaches a critical value.

For linearly elastic material, the *total strain energy density* is half of the inner product of the stress state and the strain state,

$$w = \frac{1}{2}\{\sigma\}\cdot\{\varepsilon\} \tag{6}$$

The total strain energy can be decomposed into two part: energy caused by the hydrostatic stress and energy caused by the deviatoric stress,

$$w = w^p + w^d \tag{7}$$

It is equivalent to say that the *deviatoric energy* may be calculated by subtracting the energy caused by the hydrostatic stress, w^p, from the total energy w,

$$w^d = w - w^p \tag{8}$$

The von Mises criterion can be stated as follows: the yielding occurs when

$$w^d \geq w^{dy} \tag{9}$$

where w^{dy} is the deviatoric energy when the material yields in the uniaxial tension test.

Deviatoric Energy in Uniaxial Test

The stress state, when yielding occur in the uniaxial tension test, is

$$\begin{Bmatrix} \sigma_y & 0 & 0 \\ 0 & 0 & 0 \\ 0 & 0 & 0 \end{Bmatrix} = \begin{Bmatrix} \sigma_y/3 & 0 & 0 \\ 0 & \sigma_y/3 & 0 \\ 0 & 0 & \sigma_y/3 \end{Bmatrix} + \begin{Bmatrix} 2\sigma_y/3 & 0 & 0 \\ 0 & -\sigma_y/3 & 0 \\ 0 & 0 & -\sigma_y/3 \end{Bmatrix}$$

The first part of the right-hand-side is the hydrostatic stress and the second part is the deviatoric stress. The Hooke's law, Eq. 1.2-8(1) is used to obtain the strains. The strains correspond to the total stress and the hydrostatic stress are respectively

$$\frac{\sigma_y}{E}\begin{Bmatrix} 1 & 0 & 0 \\ 0 & -\nu & 0 \\ 0 & 0 & -\nu \end{Bmatrix} \text{ and } \frac{(1-2\nu)\sigma_y}{3E}\begin{Bmatrix} 1 & 0 & 0 \\ 0 & 1 & 0 \\ 0 & 0 & 1 \end{Bmatrix}$$

Calculated using Eq. (6), the energies correspond to the total stress and the hydrostatic stress are respectively

$$w^y = \frac{\sigma_y^2}{2E} \text{ and } w^{yp} = \frac{(1-2\nu)\sigma_y^2}{6E}$$

From Eq. (8), the deviatoric energy is

$$w^{yd} = w^y - w^{yp} = \frac{(1+\nu)\sigma_y^2}{3E} \tag{10}$$

Deviatoric Energy in General 3D Cases

Let's return to the general 3D stress state, Eq. (3). The strains corresponds the total stress and the hydrostatic stress are, using Eq. 1.2-8(1), respectively

$$\frac{1}{E}\begin{Bmatrix} \sigma_1 - \nu(\sigma_2+\sigma_3) & 0 & 0 \\ 0 & \sigma_2 - \nu(\sigma_3+\sigma_1) & 0 \\ 0 & 0 & \sigma_3 - \nu(\sigma_1+\sigma_2) \end{Bmatrix} \text{ and } \frac{(1-2\nu)p}{E}\begin{Bmatrix} 1 & 0 & 0 \\ 0 & 1 & 0 \\ 0 & 0 & 1 \end{Bmatrix}$$

Calculated using Eq. (6), the energies correspond to the total stress and the hydrostatic stress are respectively

$$w = \frac{1}{2E}\left[\sigma_1(\sigma_1 - \nu\sigma_2 - \nu\sigma_3) + \sigma_2(\sigma_2 - \nu\sigma_3 - \nu\sigma_1) + \sigma_3(\sigma_3 - \nu\sigma_1 - \nu\sigma_2)\right] \text{ and } w^p = \frac{3(1-2\nu)p^2}{2E}$$

From Eqs. (8) and (2), the deviatoric energy is

$$w^d = \frac{1}{2E}\left[\sigma_1(\sigma_1 - \nu\sigma_2 - \nu\sigma_3) + \sigma_2(\sigma_2 - \nu\sigma_3 - \nu\sigma_1) + \sigma_3(\sigma_3 - \nu\sigma_1 - \nu\sigma_2)\right] - \frac{3(1-2\nu)}{2E}\left(\frac{\sigma_1+\sigma_2+\sigma_3}{3}\right)^2 \quad (11)$$

After moderate manipulations (see the exercise in Section 1.5-2), it can be simplified as

$$w^d = \frac{1+\nu}{6E}\left[(\sigma_1-\sigma_2)^2 + (\sigma_2-\sigma_3)^2 + (\sigma_3-\sigma_1)^2\right] \quad (12)$$

Von Mises Stress

Substituting Eqs. (10) and (12) into the von Mises Yield criterion, (9), we conclude that the material yields when

$$\frac{1+\nu}{6E}\left[(\sigma_1-\sigma_2)^2 + (\sigma_2-\sigma_3)^2 + (\sigma_3-\sigma_1)^2\right] \ge \frac{1+\nu}{3E}\sigma_y^2 \quad (13)$$

or, in a more concise form

$$\sqrt{\frac{1}{2}\left[(\sigma_1-\sigma_2)^2 + (\sigma_2-\sigma_3)^2 + (\sigma_3-\sigma_1)^2\right]} \ge \sigma_y \quad (14)$$

The quantity on the left-hand-side is termed *von Mises stress* or *effective stress*, and denoted by σ_e; in ANSYS, it is also referred to as *equivalent stress*.

$$\sigma_e = \sqrt{\frac{1}{2}\left[(\sigma_1-\sigma_2)^2 + (\sigma_2-\sigma_3)^2 + (\sigma_3-\sigma_1)^2\right]} \quad (15)$$

To get more insight of Eq. (14), let's plot Eq. (14) in $\sigma_1 - \sigma_2 - \sigma_3$ space and consider only equal sign. It will be a cylinderical surface aligned with the axis $\sigma_1 = \sigma_2 = \sigma_3$ and with a radius of $\sqrt{2}\sigma_y$ (see 14.1-4[1]). It is called the *von Mises yield surface*. Condition of Eq. (14) is equivalent to say that the material fails when the stress state is outside the von Mises yield surface. When $\sigma_1 = \sigma_2 = \sigma_3$, the material is under hydrostatic pressure. It is the portion of stress that deviates from the axis contributes to the failure of the material.

Equivalent Strain

The *equivalent strain*, or *effective strain* ε_e is defined by

$$\varepsilon_e = \frac{\sigma_e}{E} \quad (16)$$

Section 1.5

Problems

1.5-1 Key Concepts

Define or describe following terms as concise as possible.

Workbench GUI

The gateway to all ANSYS applications. It supports two types of applications: native applications and data integrated applications.

Engineering Data

A native application of the Workbench GUI. Material properties are the most important type of engineering data. Loads and boundary conditions can also be stored as engineering data.

DesignModeler

An application of the Workbench GUI. Its function is similar to any other CAD software, except that it is specifically used to create geometric models for use in the ANSYS Workbench simulations.

Mechanical

An application of the Workbench GUI. It performs structural and mechanical simulations, including meshing, setting up environment conditions, solving finite element models, and viewing results.

Isotropic Elasticity

In <Engineering Data>, this term is used for materials whose stress-strain relation is described by Hooke's law and can be characterized by two material parameters: Young's modulus and Poisson's ratio.

Finite Element Mesh

A collection of elements and nodes.

Finite Element Model

A finite element mesh plus its environment conditions.

Boundary Conditions

Conditions that applied on the boundaries of a finite element mesh.

Environment Conditions

Conditions that applied on the boundaries or interior of a finite element mesh.

Free Boundary

A boundary that is free of boundary conditions.

Stiffness
The stiffness of a structure is the forces required to deform the structure.

Stress Stiffening
The phenomenon that in a structure member subjecting to tensile stress, its lateral stiffness increases with the increasing tensile stress.

Buckling
In a structure member subjecting to compression, when the compression large enough to zero out the lateral stiffness, the structure is said to be unstable, or buckling.

Dynamic Simulation
A simulation in which the dynamic effects are included.

Modal Analysis
Also called free vibration analysis. It is a special case of dynamic analysis, in which no loads apply on the structure. Results of modal analysis include natural frequencies and their corresponding vibration modes.

Linear Simulation
When the responses of a system are linearly proportional to the loading, it is called a linear system. The simulation is called a linear simulation.

Nonlinear Simulation
When the responses of a system are not linearly proportional to the loading, it is called a nonlinear system. The simulation is called a nonlinear simulation.

Displacement
Displacement of a particle in a body is the vector connecting from its initial position to its final position after deformation.

Stress
Stress, of a particle in a body, in a certain direction, or face, is a vector describing the force intensity on that face. The vector can be decomposed into two components: one that is normal to the face and the other that is parallel to the face.

Stress State
Stress state, of a point in a body, is a group of values describing the force intensity on the point in all directions. In 3D, three independent directions are needed to complete the description.

Strain
Strain, of a point in a body, in a certain direction, or face, is a vector describing the stretch and twist in the direction. The vector can be decomposed into two components: one that is normal to the face and the other that is parallel to the face.

Strain State
Strain state, of a point in a body, is a group of values describing the stretch and twist in all directions. In 3D, three independent directions are needed to complete the description.

Governing Equations
Governing equations of a structural system is a mathematical model of the structural system, usually in a form of differential equations.

Finite Elements
A finite element is a small portion of the problem domain. Its geometry is so simple that the governing equations can be pre-formulated in terms of discrete nodal degrees of freedom.

Node
Nodes are portion of an element that overlaps other elements. The overlapping implies that the elements share the same degree of freedom values on the nodes.

Degrees of Freedom
In the finite element methods, the discrete nodal values to be solved are called degrees of freedom. In Workbench structural simulations, they are nodal displacements. In 3D, the number of degrees of freedom is 3 times the number of nodes.

Stiffness Matrix
The matrix that describes the linear relation between displacement vector and the force vector. Physical meaning of the values on i^{th} column is the forces required on all the DOFs to make the ith DOF a unit displacement while restrain other DOFs from displacement.

Shape Functions
In finite element methods, shape functions are used as interpolating functions to calculate continuous displacement fields from discrete nodal displacements. Linear and quadratic polynomials are commonly used as shape functions.

First-Order Element
If linear polynomials are used as shape functions, the element is called a first-order element, or a lower-order element, in which the nodes are attached on each vertex.

Second-Order Element
If quadratic polynomials are used as shape functions, the element is called a second-order element, or a higher-order element, in which the nodes are attached on each vertex as well the middle of each edge.

Degenerated Element
A 3D solid element, hexahedral in its natural shape, may combine some of nodes to form a triangle-based prism, quadrilateral-based pyramid, or tetrahedron; they are called degenerated elements. A 2D solid element, quadrilateral in its natural shape, may degenerate to a triangle.

Ductile Material
If the strain is large before it is stretched up to fracture, the material is said to be ductile. The fracture is mostly due to a shear failure. There is usually an obvious yield point in its stress-strain curve.

Brittle Material
If the strain is small before it is stretched up to fracture, the material is said to be brittle. The fracture is mostly due to a tensile failure. There is usually no obvious yield point in its stress-strain curve.

Principle Stress
At a point in a body, different directions have different stress. There exist directions in which the normal components are in extremity and the shear components vanish; the directions and the corresponding normal stresses are called principle directions and the principle stresses respectively. In 3D, there are 3 principle stresses, they are denoted as, in order starting from the largest, σ_1, σ_2, and σ_3 respectively.

Stress Intensity
Stress intensity is defined as the difference between the maximum principle stress and the minimum principle stress. It equals to twice the maximum shear stress.

1.5-2 Questions

Describe procedure of finite element methods.

(a) Calculate stiffness matrix for each element. (b) Add up the element matrices to form a global stiffness matrix. The force vector is calculated according to the loading conditions. (c) Eq. 1.3-1(1) is solved for the nodal displacements. (d) For each element, the displacement field is calculated according to Eq. 1.3-2(2), the strain field is calculated according to Eq. 1.2-7(1), and the stress field is calculated according to Eq. 1.2-8(1).

Describe Failure Criteria of Materials.

For a brittle material, it fails if the maximum principle stress reaches the fracture stress. For a ductile materials, Tresca criterion or von Mises criterion may be used. The Tresca criterion states that the material fails if the stress intensity reaches the yield stress. The von Mises criterion states that the material fails if the von Mises stress reaches the yield stress.

Derive Eq. 1.4-5(12) from Eq. 1.4-5(11).

$$
\begin{aligned}
w^d &= \frac{1}{2E}\left[\sigma_1(\sigma_1 - \nu\sigma_2 - \nu\sigma_3) + \sigma_2(\sigma_2 - \nu\sigma_3 - \nu\sigma_1) + \sigma_3(\sigma_3 - \nu\sigma_1 - \nu\sigma_2)\right] - \frac{3(1-2\nu)}{2E}\left(\frac{\sigma_1+\sigma_2+\sigma_3}{3}\right)^2 \\
&= \frac{1}{2E}\left[\sigma_1^2+\sigma_2^2+\sigma_3^2 - 2\nu(\sigma_1\sigma_2+\sigma_2\sigma_3+\sigma_3\sigma_1)\right] - \frac{1-2\nu}{6E}\left[\sigma_1^2+\sigma_2^2+\sigma_3^2+2(\sigma_1\sigma_2+\sigma_2\sigma_3+\sigma_3\sigma_1)\right] \\
&= \frac{1}{6E}\left[3(\sigma_1^2+\sigma_2^2+\sigma_3^2) - 6\nu(\sigma_1\sigma_2+\sigma_2\sigma_3+\sigma_3\sigma_1) - (1-2\nu)(\sigma_1^2+\sigma_2^2+\sigma_3^2) - (2-4\nu)(\sigma_1\sigma_2+\sigma_2\sigma_3+\sigma_3\sigma_1)\right] \\
&= \frac{1}{6E}\left[(2+2\nu)(\sigma_1^2+\sigma_2^2+\sigma_3^2) - (2+2\nu)(\sigma_1\sigma_2+\sigma_2\sigma_3+\sigma_3\sigma_1)\right] \\
&= \frac{1+\nu}{3E}\left[\sigma_1^2+\sigma_2^2+\sigma_3^2 - \sigma_1\sigma_2 - \sigma_2\sigma_3 - \sigma_3\sigma_1\right] \\
&= \frac{1+\nu}{6E}\left[(\sigma_1-\sigma_2)^2+(\sigma_2-\sigma_3)^2+(\sigma_3-\sigma_1)^2\right]
\end{aligned}
$$

Chapter 2
Sketching

A simulation project starts with the creation of a geometric model. To be proficient at simulations, an engineer has to be proficient at geometric modeling first. In a simulation project, it is not uncommon to take the majority of human-hours to create a geometric model, that is particularly true in a 3D simulation.

A complex 3D geometry can be viewed as a collection of simpler 3D solid bodies. Each solid body is often created by first drawing a sketch on a plane, and then the sketch is used to generate the 3D solid body using tools such as extrude, revolve, sweep, etc. In turn, to be proficient at 3D bodies creation, an engineer has to be proficient at sketching first.

Purpose of the Chapter

The purpose of this chapter is to provide exercises for the students so that they can be proficient at sketching using DesignModeler. Five mechanical parts are sketched in this chapters. Although each sketch is used to generate a 3D models, the generation of 3D models is so trivial that we should be able to focus on the 2D sketches without being distracted. More exercises of sketching will be provided in later chapters.

About Each Section

Each sketch of a mechanical part will be completed in a section. Sketches in the first two sections are guided in a step-by-step fashion. Section 1 sketches a cross section of W16x50; the cross section is then extruded to generate a solid model in 3D space. Section 2 sketches a triangular plate; the sketch is then extruded to generate a solid model in 3D space.

Section 3 does not mean to provide a hands-on case. It overviews the sketching tools in a systematic way, attempting to complement what were missed in the first two sections.

Sections 4, 5, and 6 provide three cases for more exercises. Sketches in these sections are in a not-so-step-by-step fashion; we purposely leave some room for the students to figure out the details.

Section 2.1

Step-by-Step: W16x50 Beam

2.1-1 About the W16x50 Beam

Consider a structural steel beam with a W16x50 cross-section [1-4] and a length of 10 ft. In this section, we will create a 3D solid body for the steel beam.

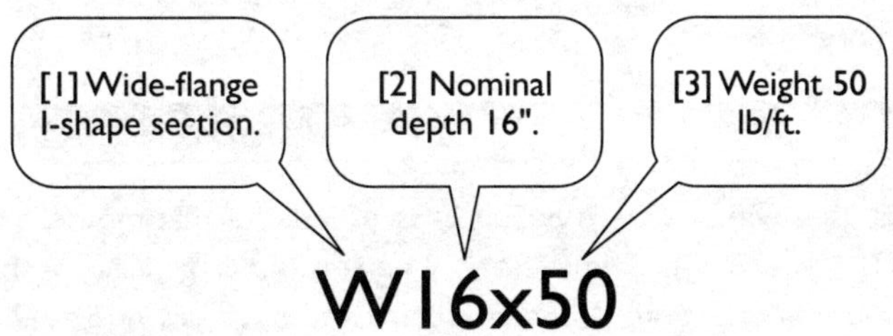

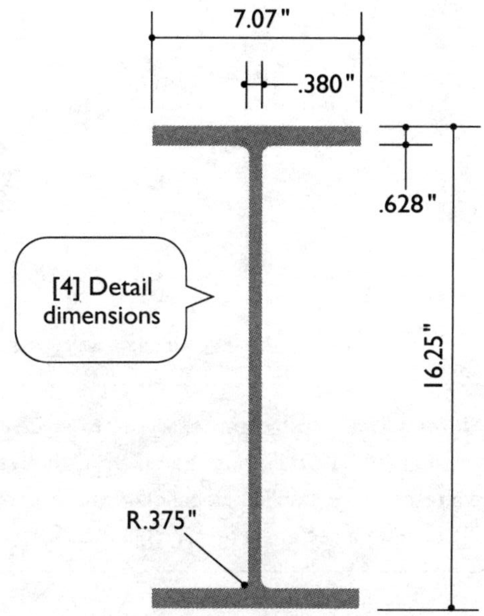

2.1-2 Start Up <DesignModeler>

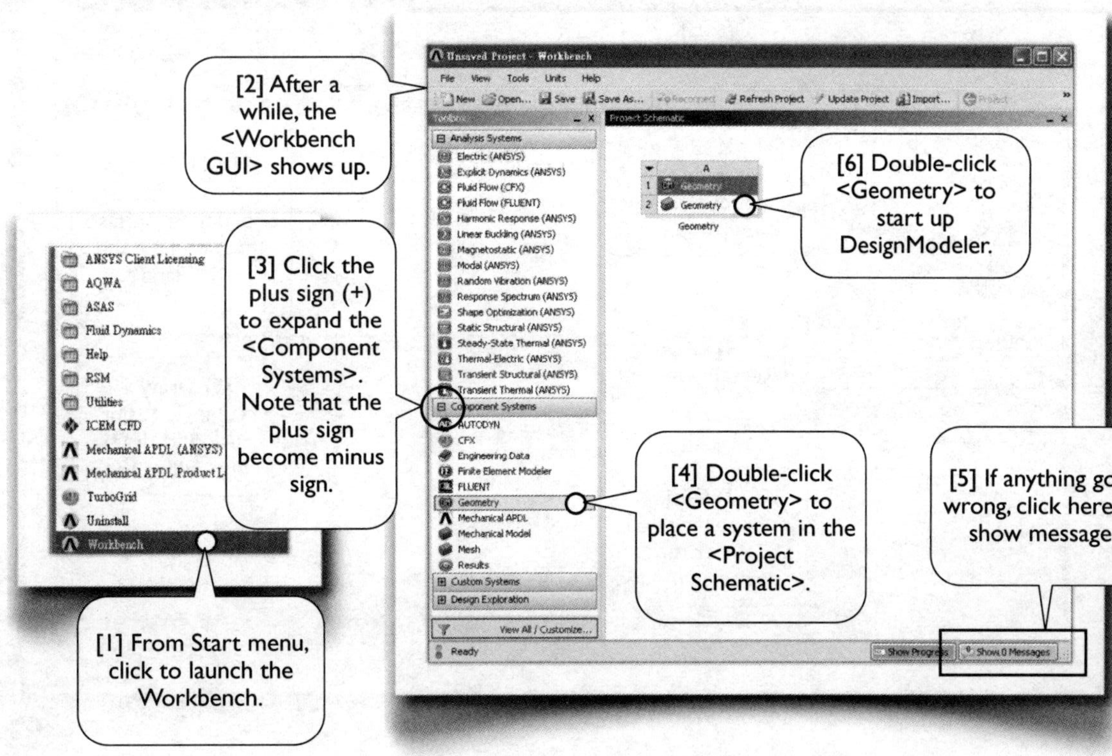

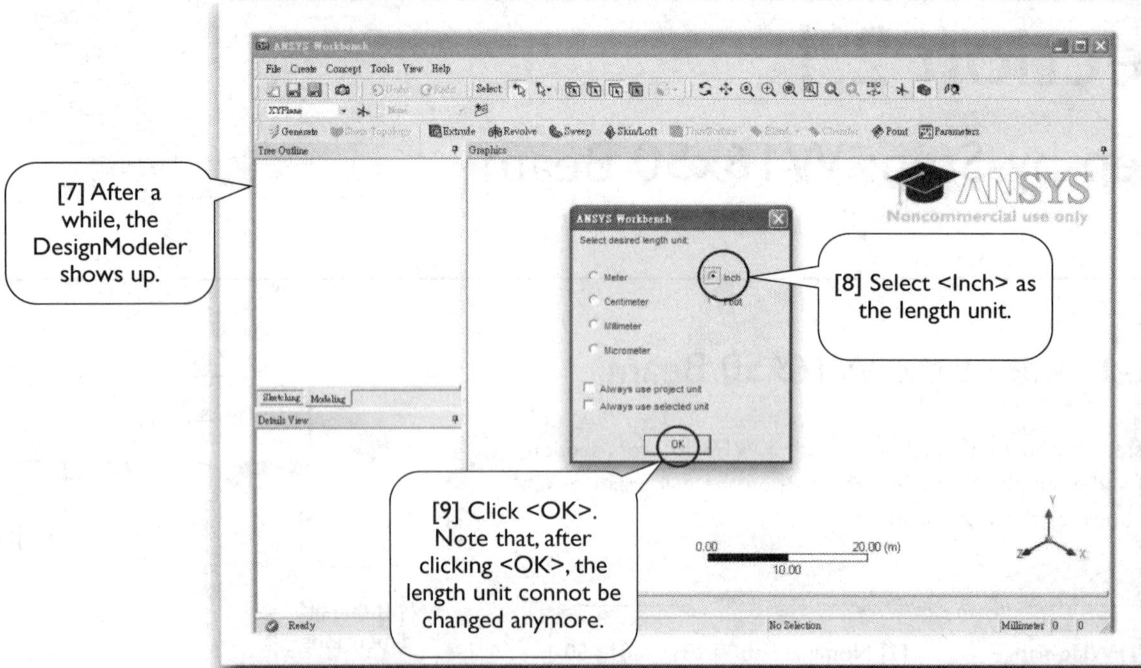

Notes: In a step-by-step exercise, whenever a circle is used with a speech bubble, it is to indicate that mouse or keynoard ACTIONS must be taken in that step (e.g., [1, 3, 4, 6, 8, 9]). The circle may be small or large, filled with white color or unfilled, depending on whichever gives more information. A speech bubble without a circle (e.g., [2, 7]) or with a rectangle (e.g., [5]) is used for commentary only, no mouse or keyboard actions are needed.

2.1-3 Draw a Rectangle on <XYPlane>

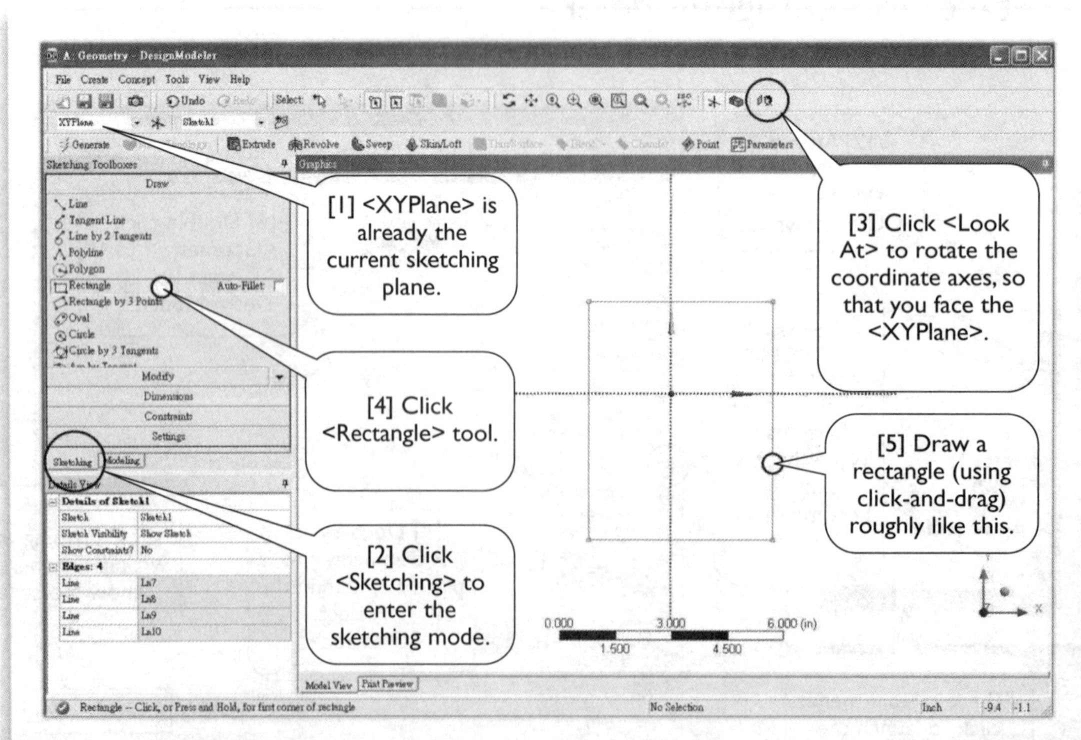

Impose symmetry constraints...

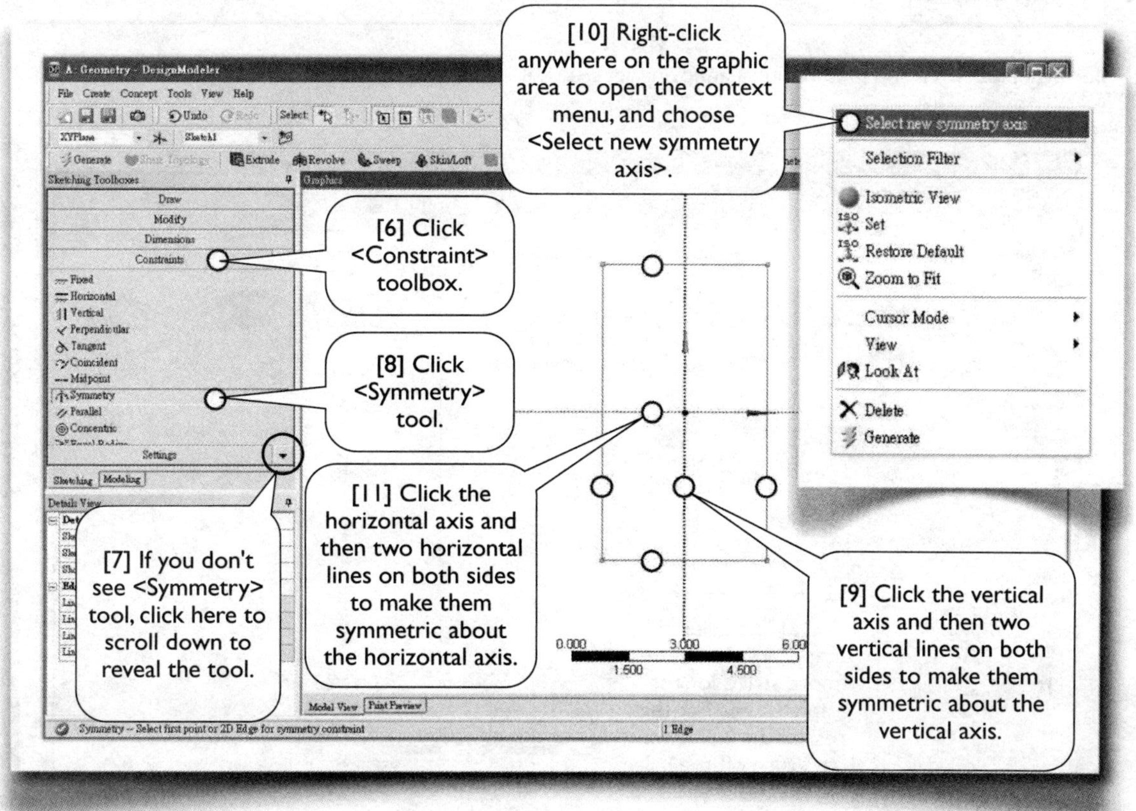

Specify dimensions...

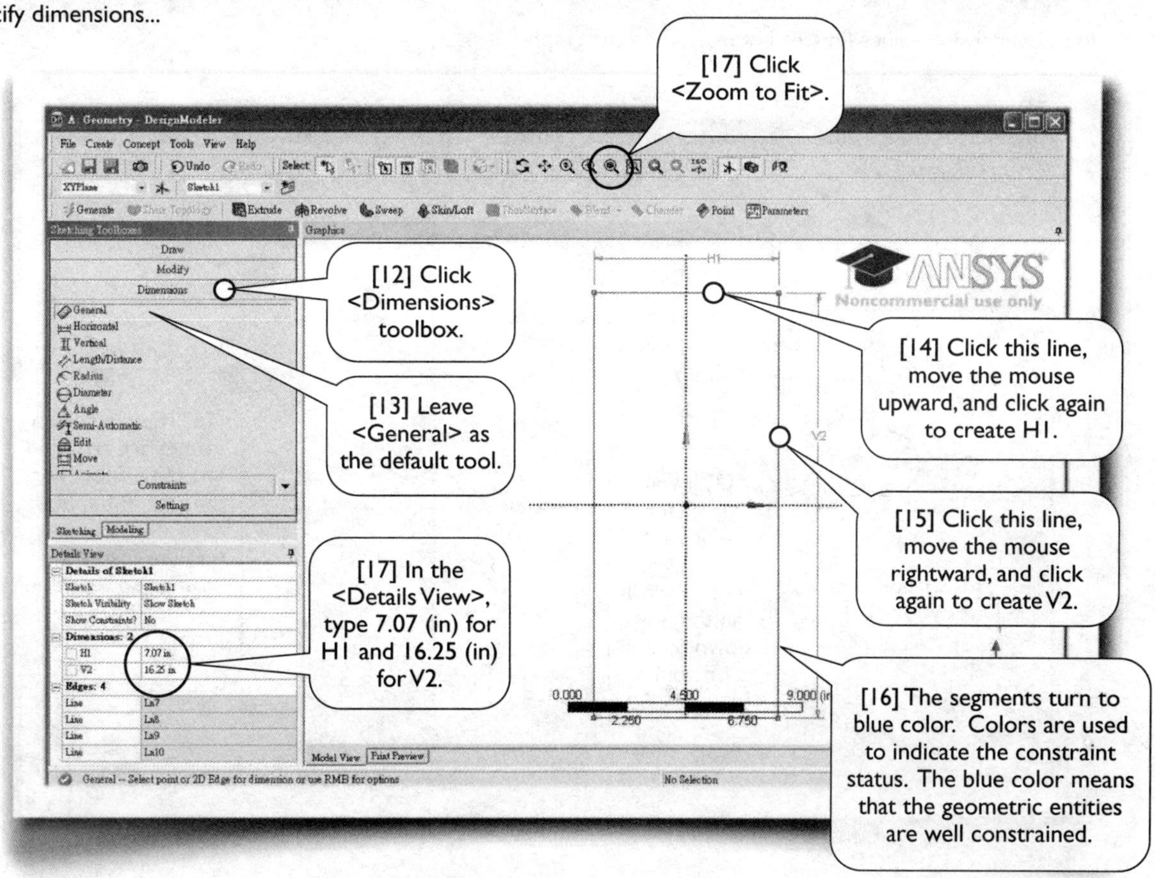

2.1-4 Clean up the Graphic Area

The ruler occupies space and is sometimes annoying; let's turn it off...

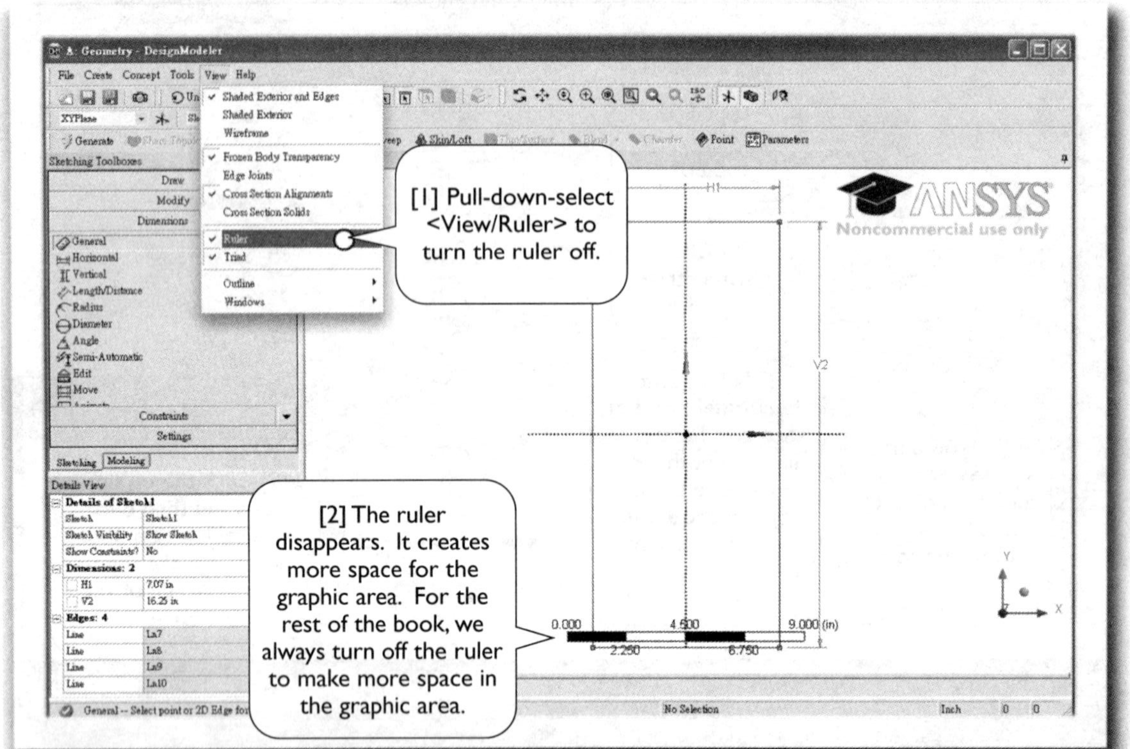

Let's display dimension values (in stead of names) on the graphic area...

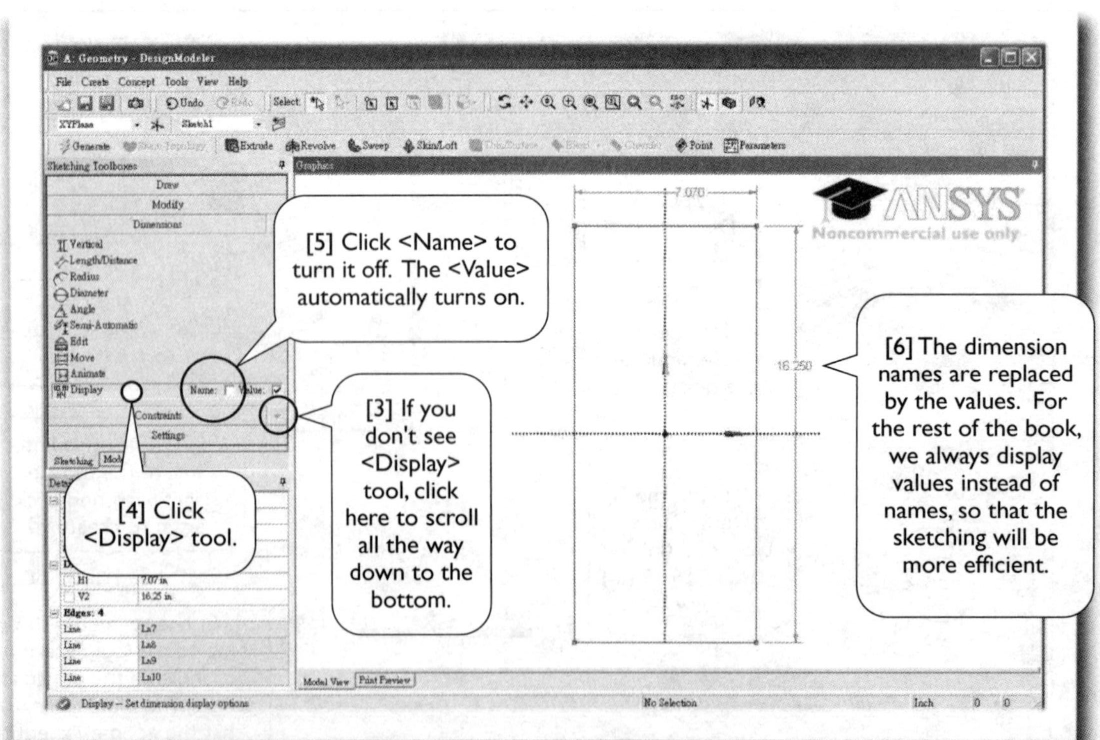

2.1-5 Draw a Polyline

Draw a polyline; the dimensions are not important for now...

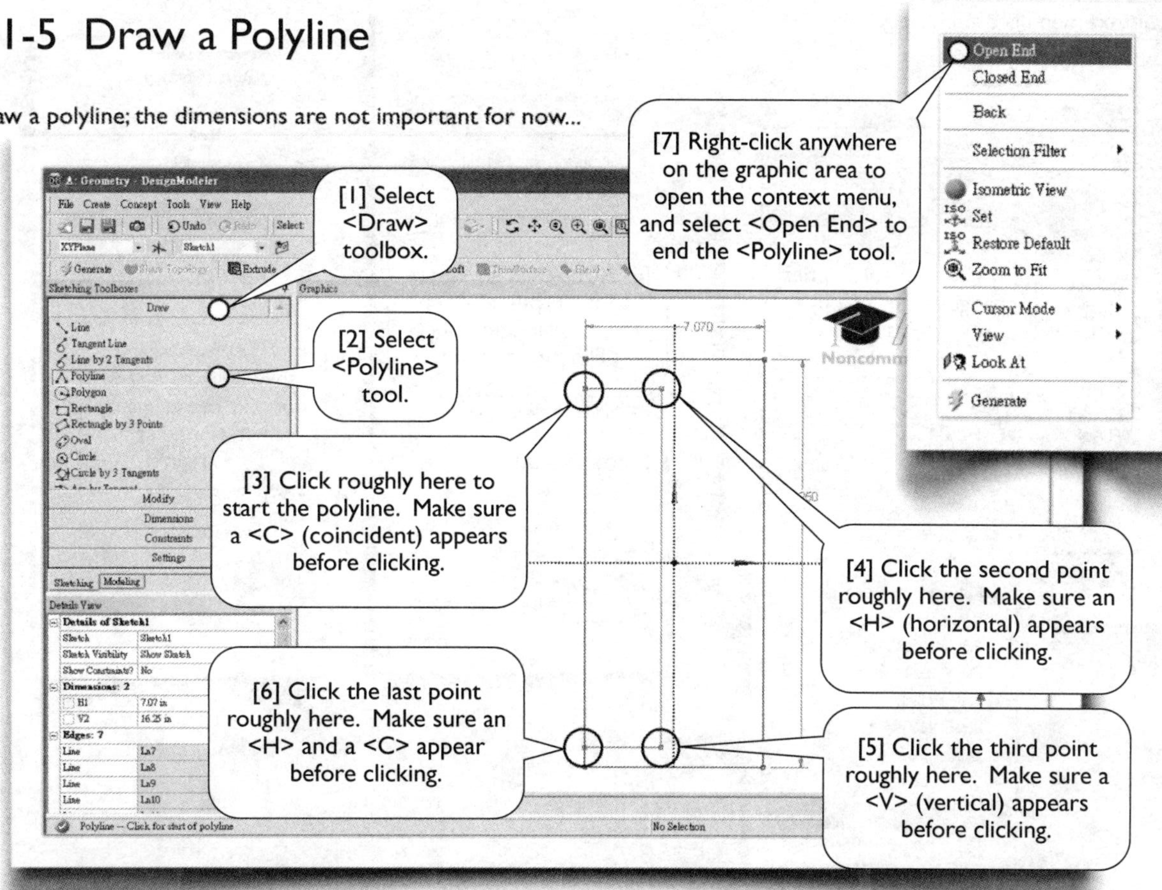

2.1-6 Copy the Polyline

Copy the newly created polyline to the right side, flip horizontally...

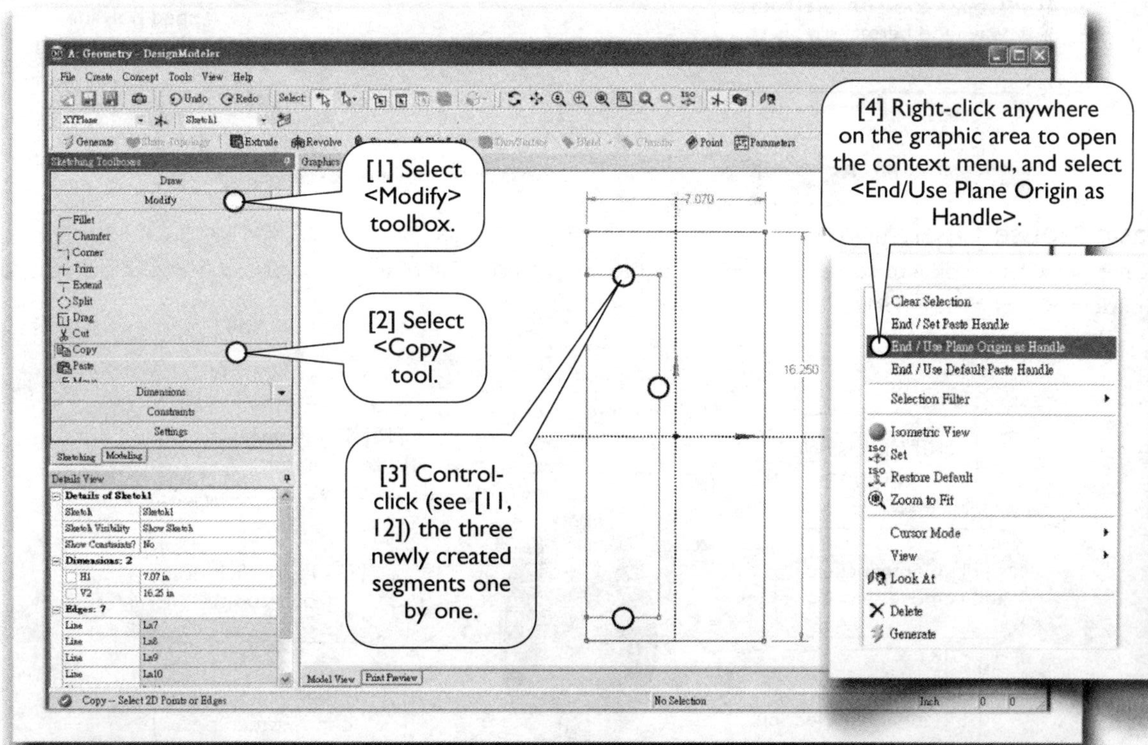

Context menu is used heavily...

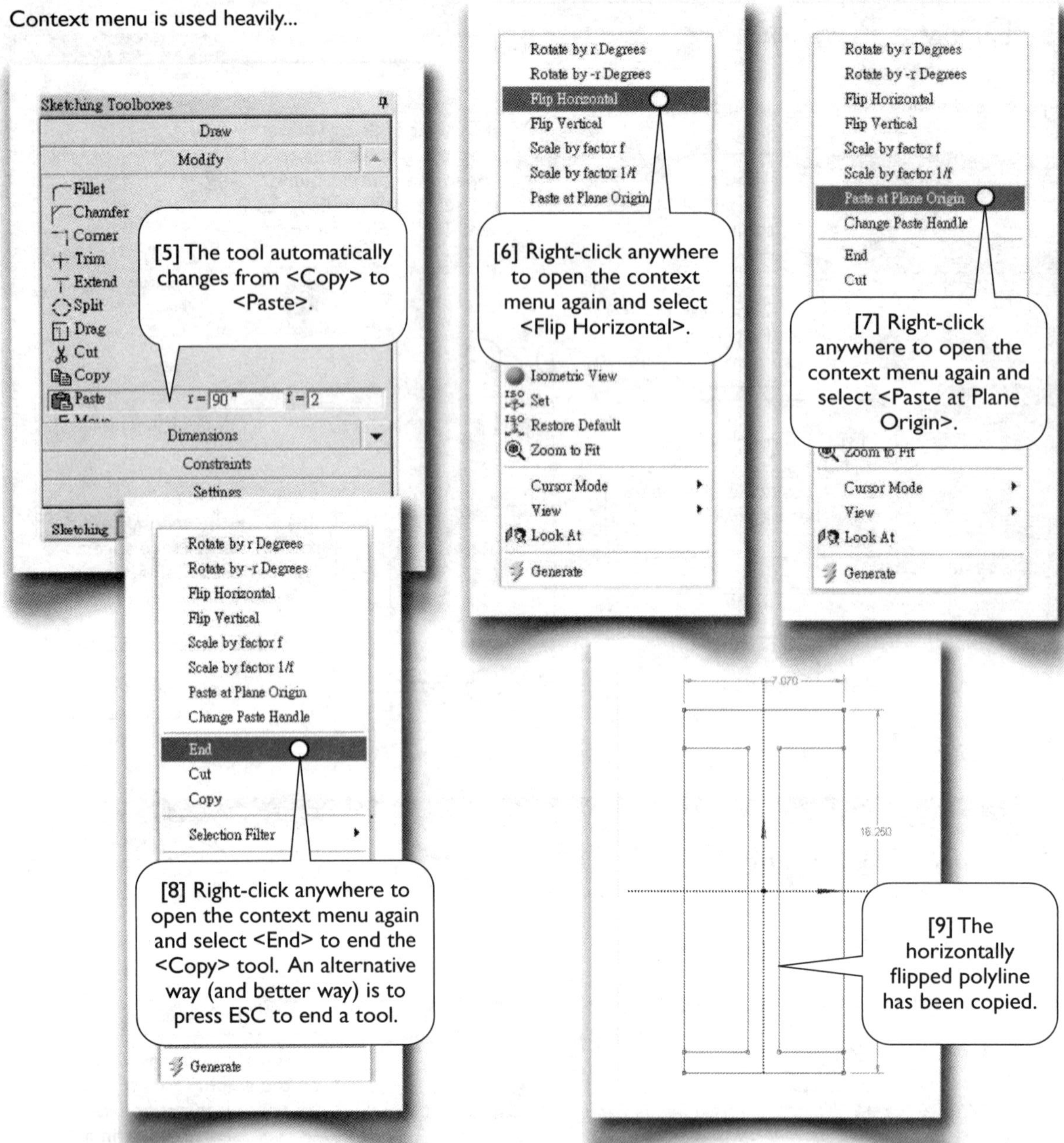

Basic Mouse Operations

At this point, let's look into some basic mouse operations [10-16]. Skill of these operations is one of the keys to be proficient at geometric modeling.

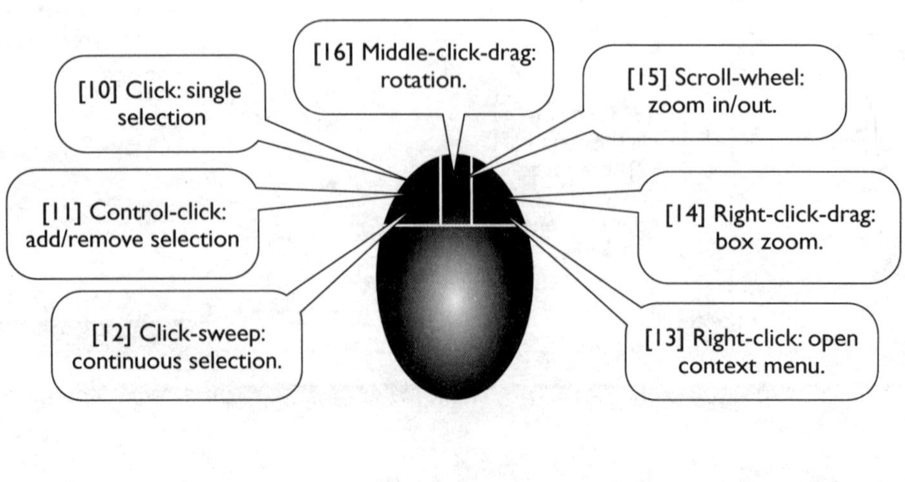

2.1-7 Trim Away Unwanted Segments

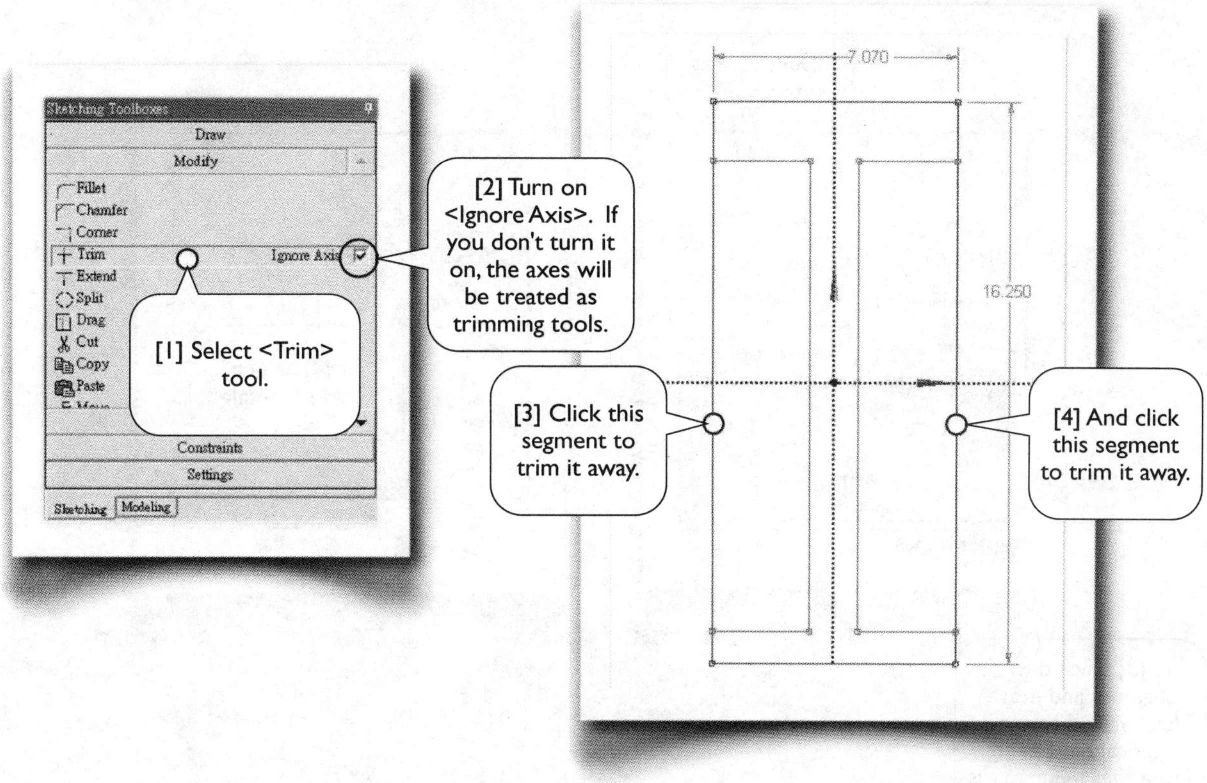

2.1-8 Impose Symmetry Constraints

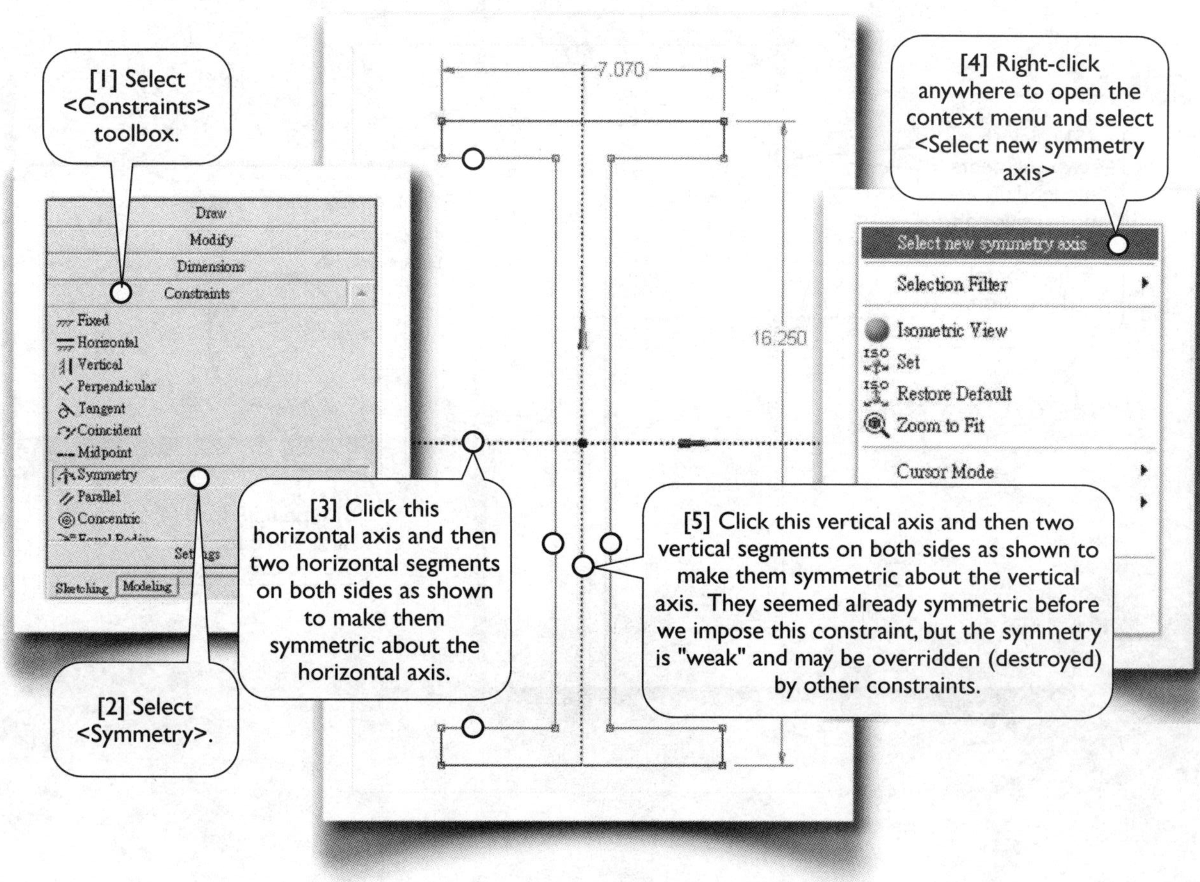

2.1-9 Specify Dimensions

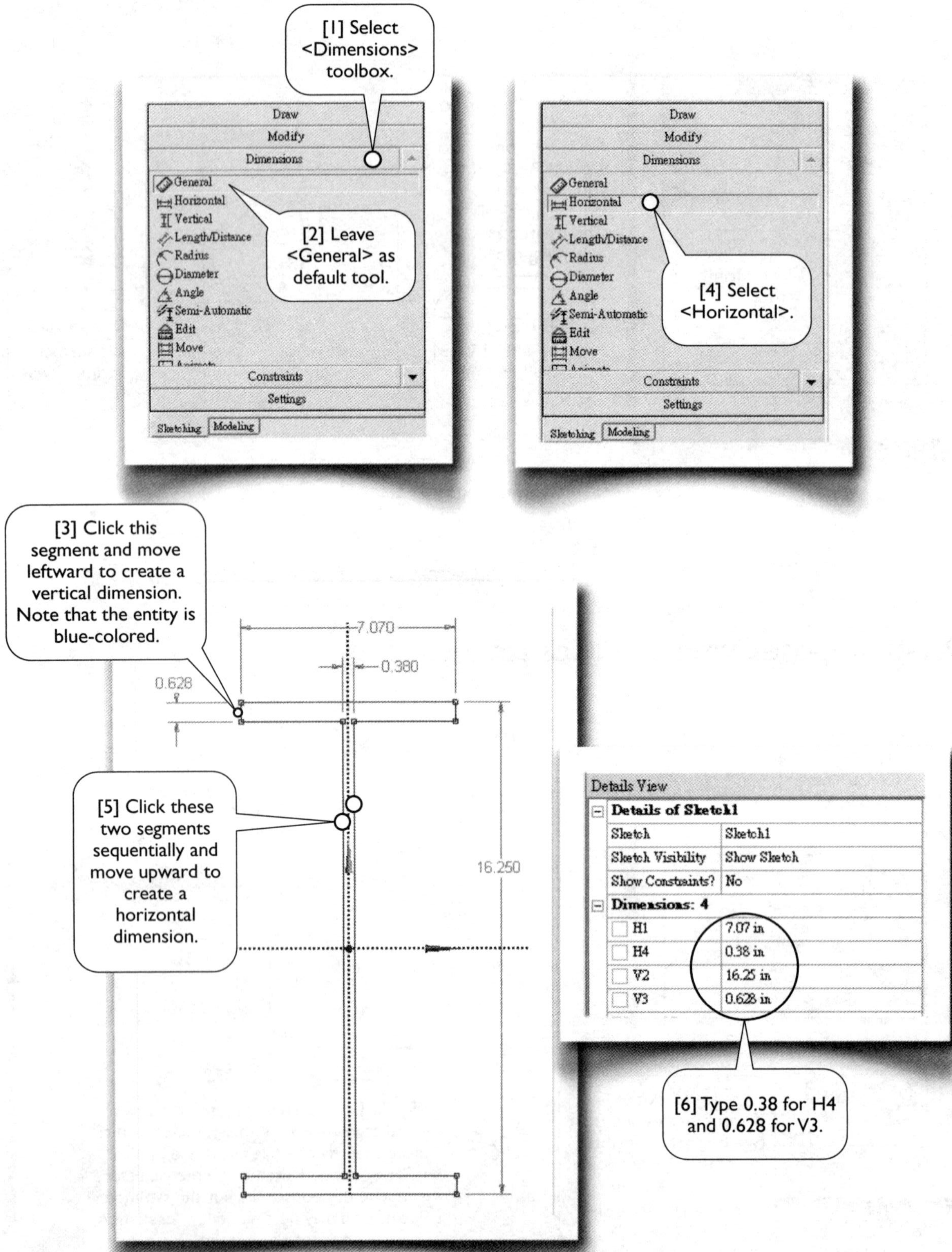

2.1-10 Add Fillets

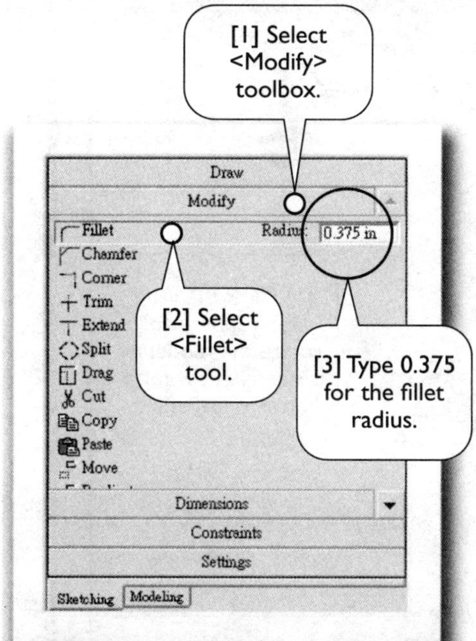

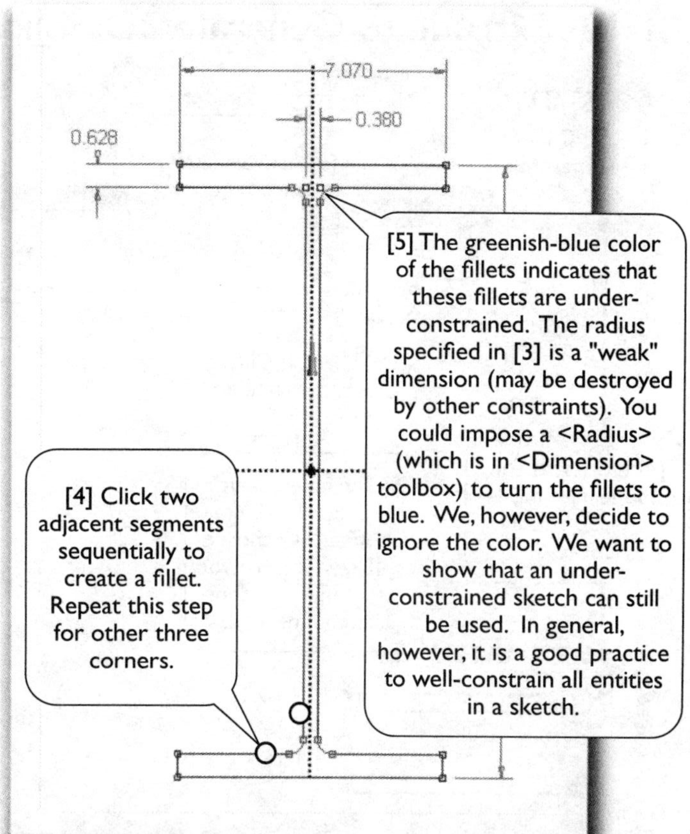

2.1-11 Move Dimensions

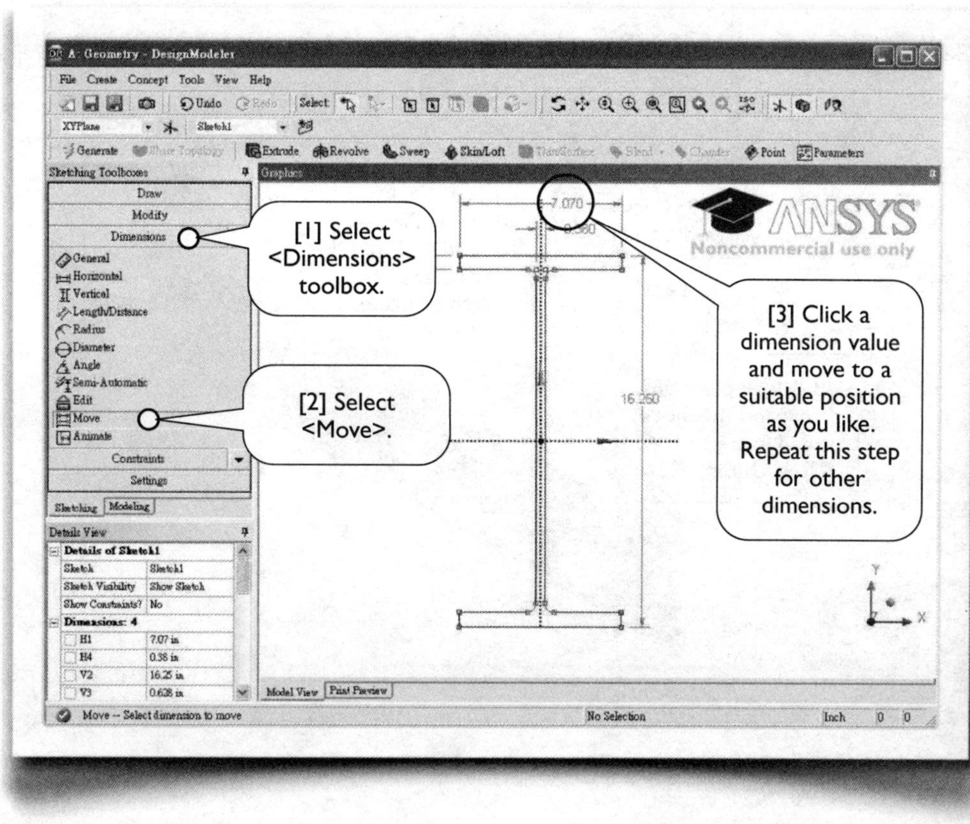

2.1-12 Extrude to Generate 3D Solid

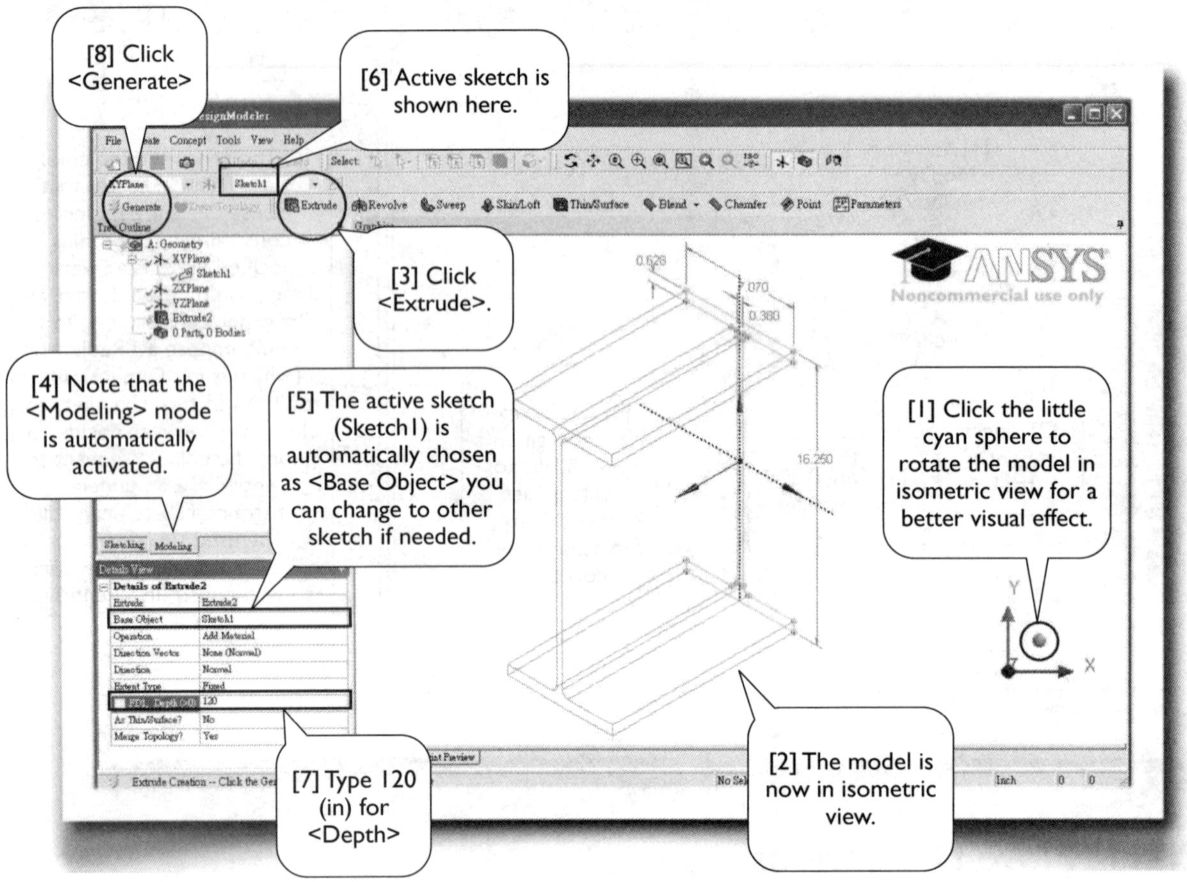

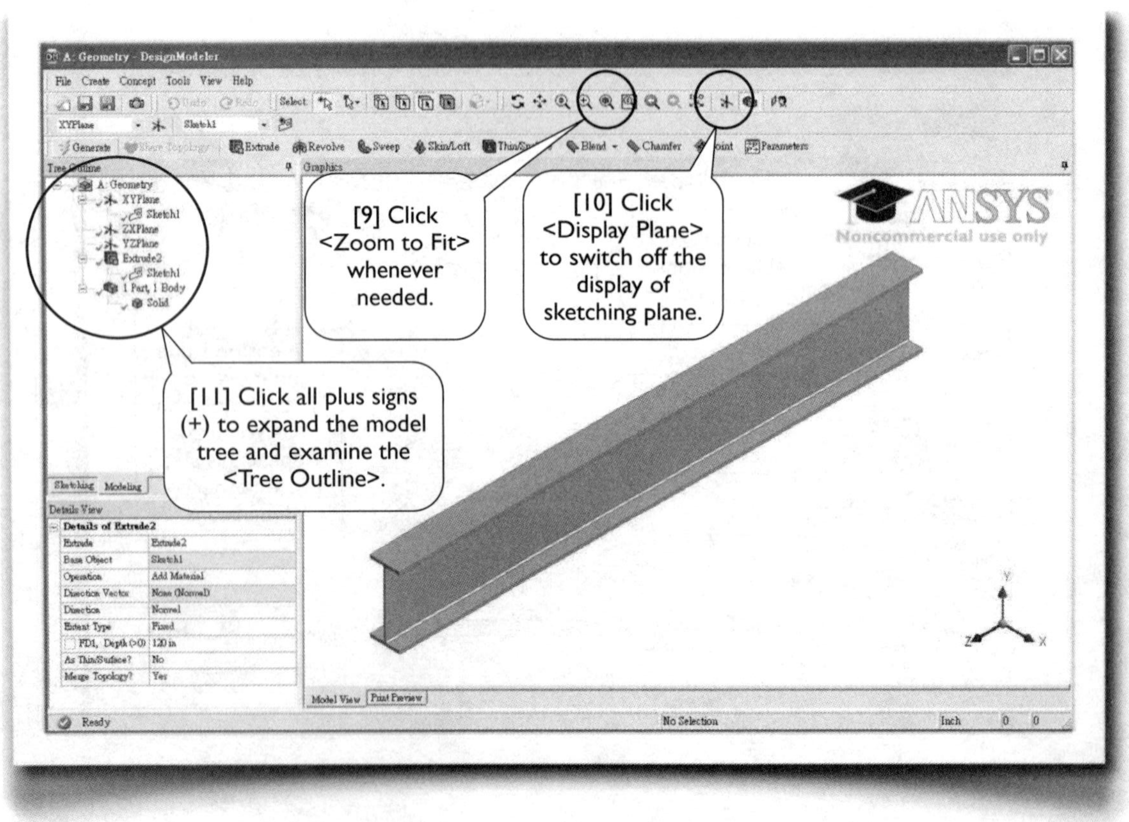

2.1-13 Save the Project and Exit Workbench

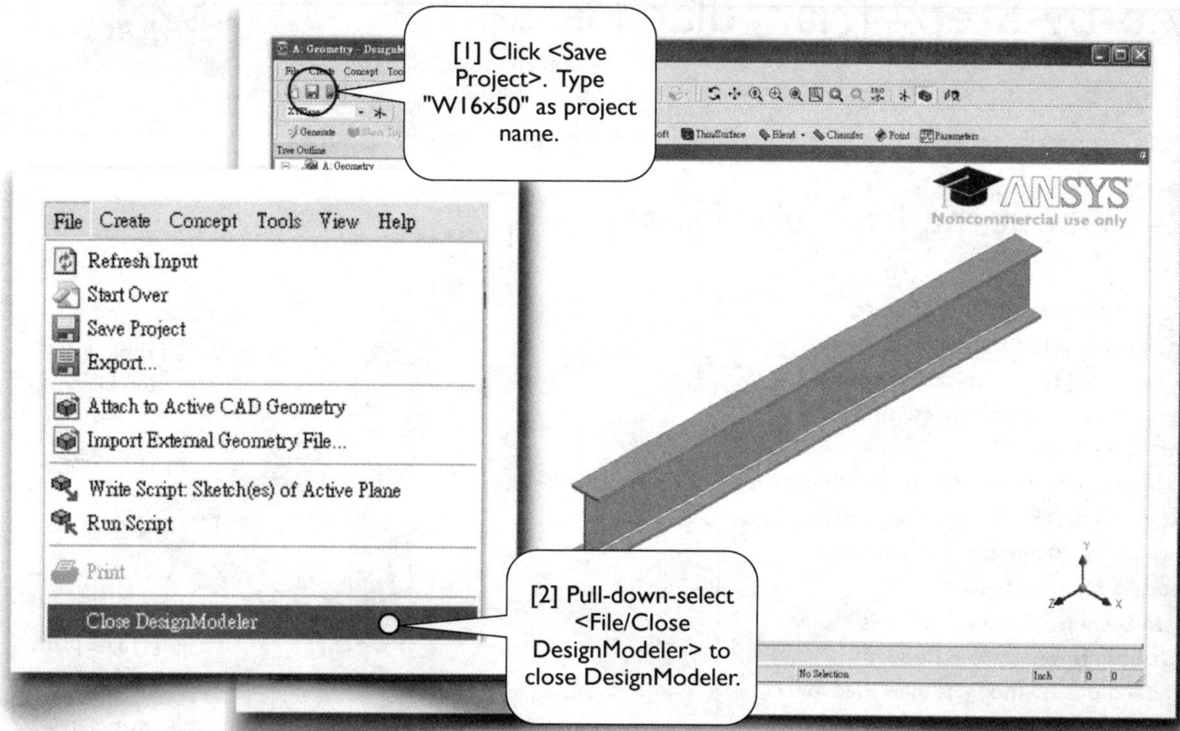

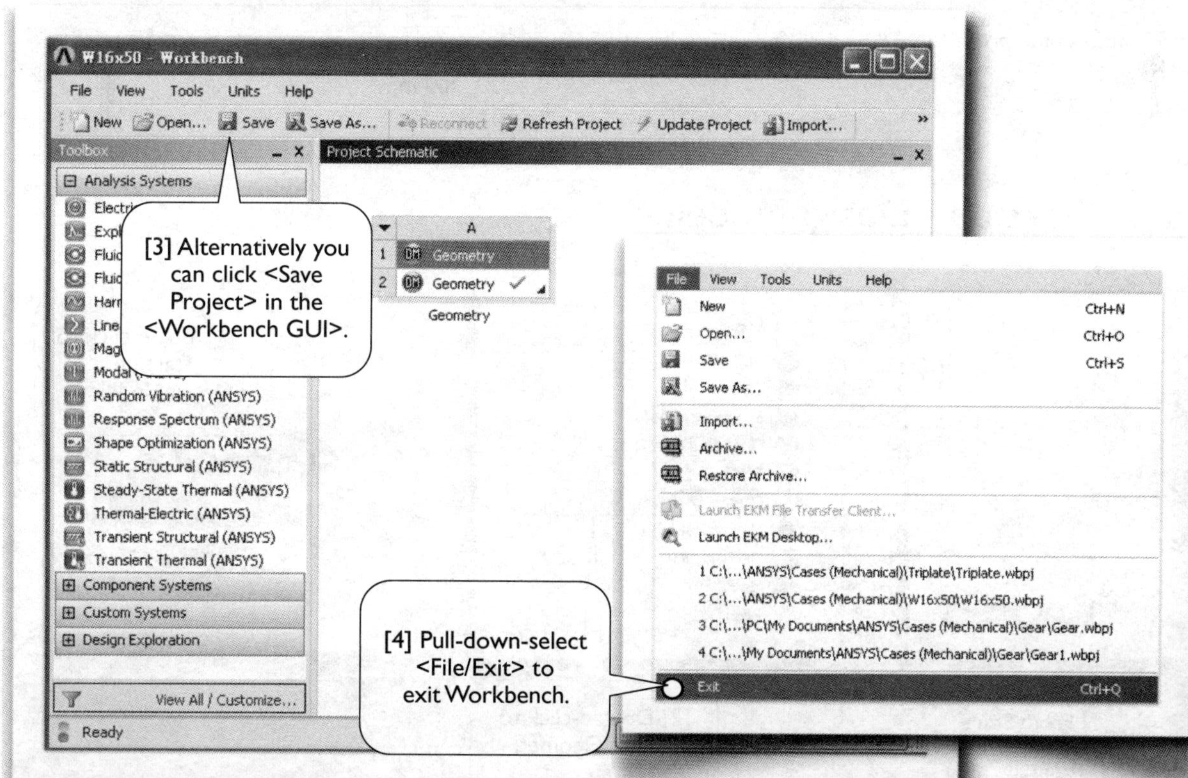

Section 2.2

Step-by-Step: Triangular Plate

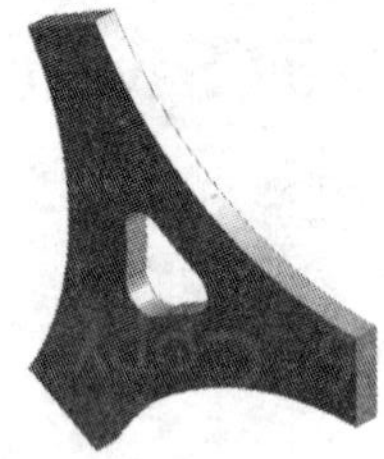

2.2-1 About the Triangular Plate

The triangular plate [1, 2] is made to withstand a tensile stress of 50 MPa on each side face [3]. The thickness of the plate is 10 mm. Other dimensions are shown in the figure.

In this section, we want to sketch the plate on <XYPlane> and then extrude a thickness of 10 mm along Z-axis to generate a 3D solid body.

In Section 3.1, we will use this sketch again to generate a 2D solid model, and the 2D model is then used for a static structural simulation to assess the stress under the loads.

The 2D solid model will be used again in Section 8.2 to demonstrate a design optimization procedure.

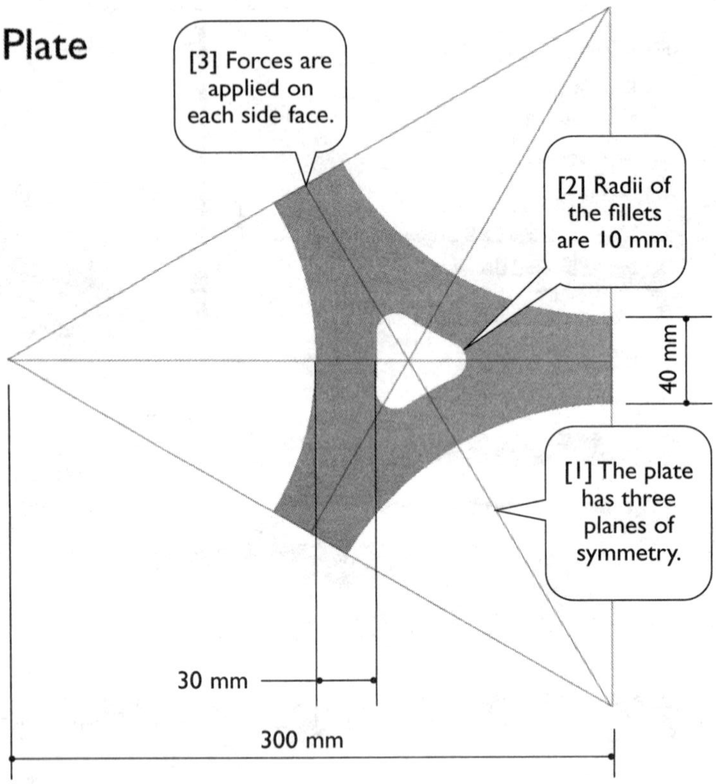

2.2-2 Start up <DesignModeler>

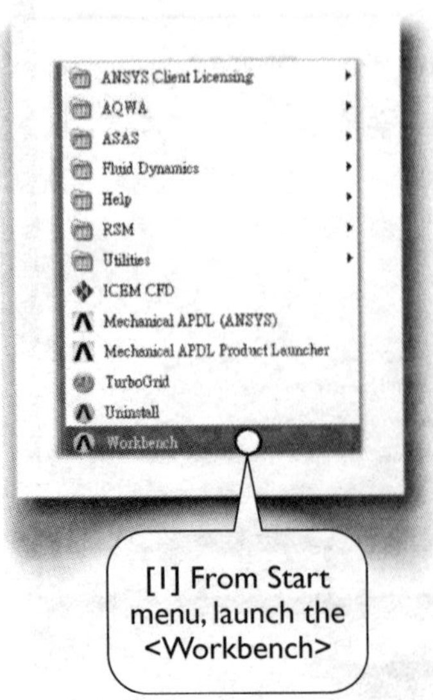

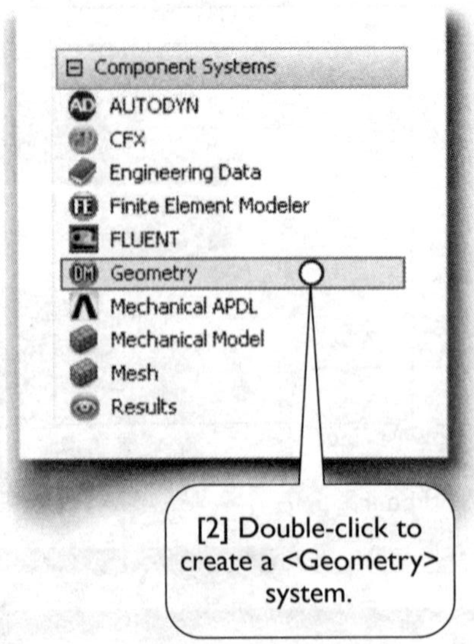

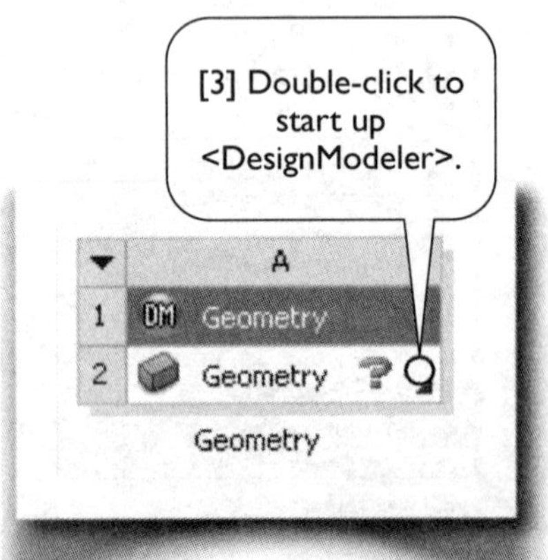

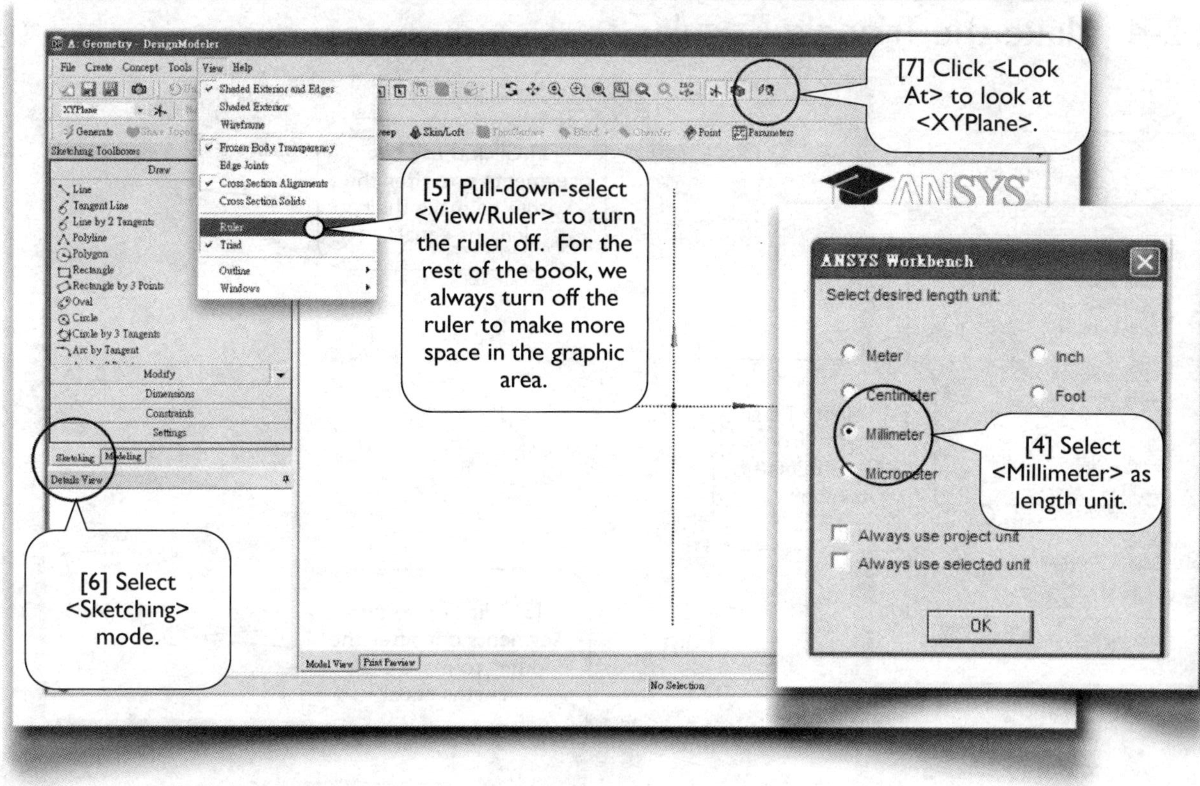

2.2-3 Draw a Triangle on <XYPlane>

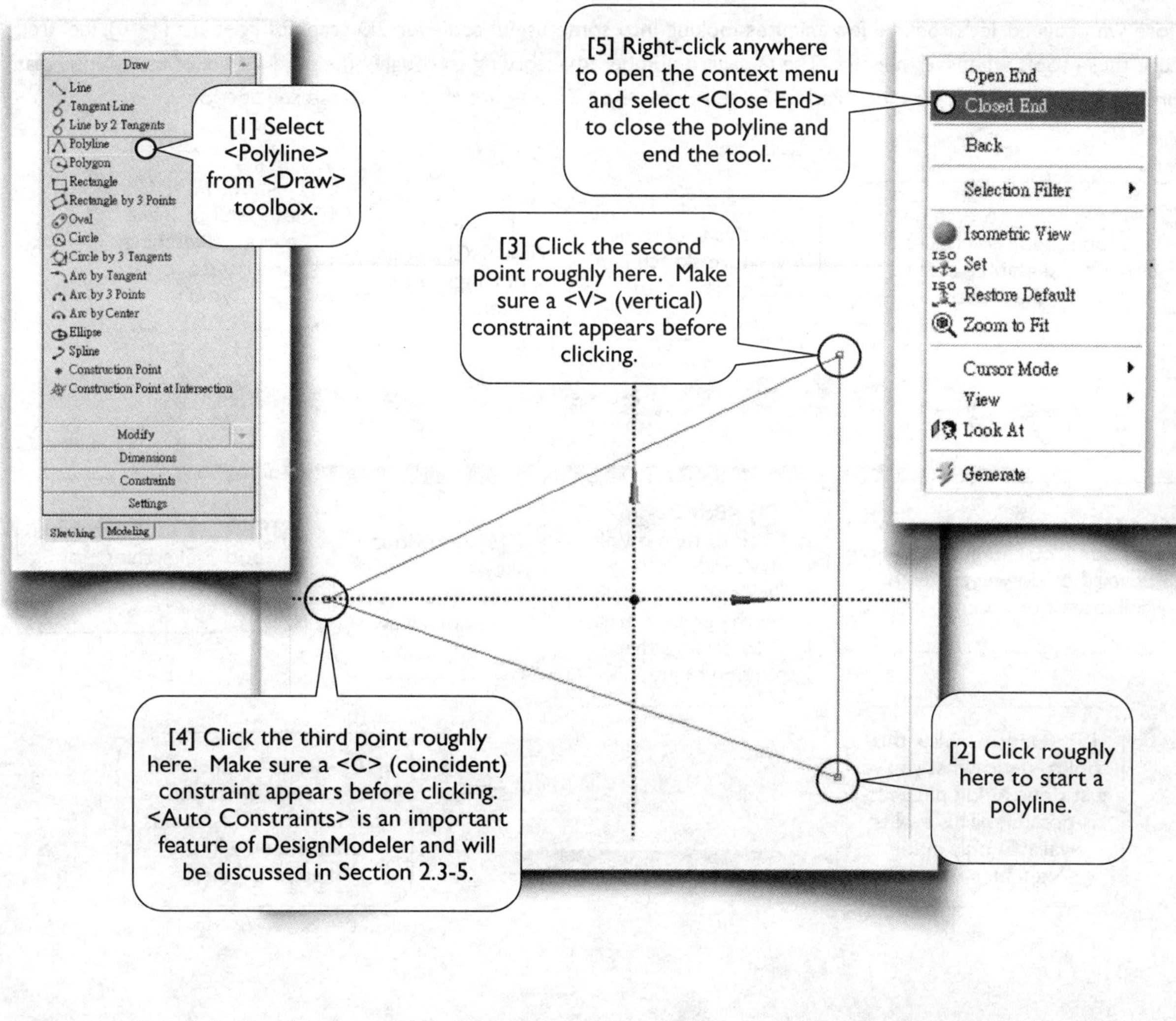

2.2-4 Make the Triangle Regular

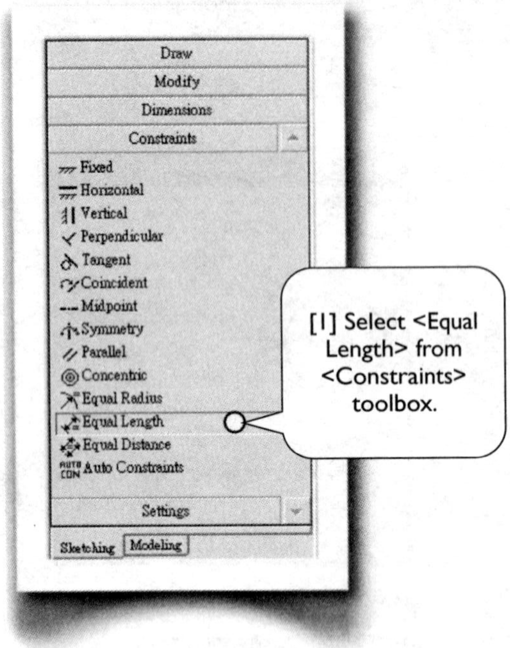

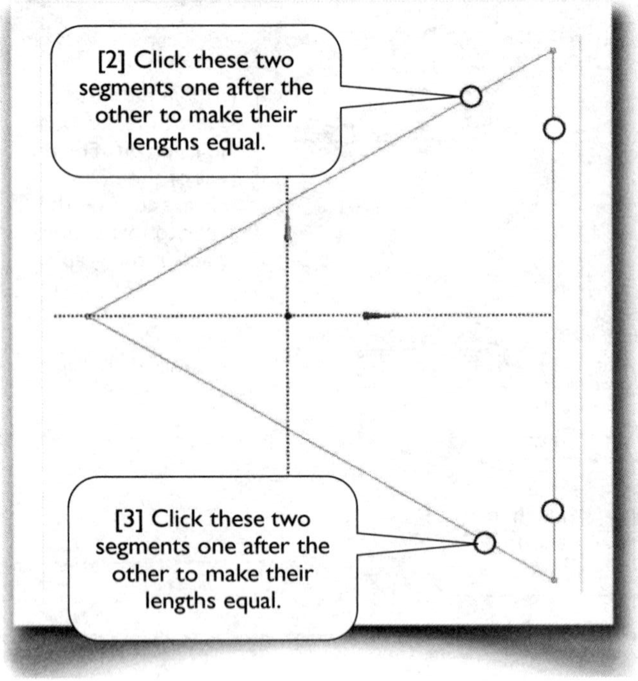

2.2-5 2D Graphics Controls

Before we proceed, let's spend a few minutes looking into some useful tools for 2D graphics controls [1-10]; feel free to use these tools whenever needed. The tools are numbered according to roughly their frequency of use. Note that more useful mouse short-cuts for <Pan>, <Zoom>, and <Box Zoom> are available; please see Section 2.3-4.

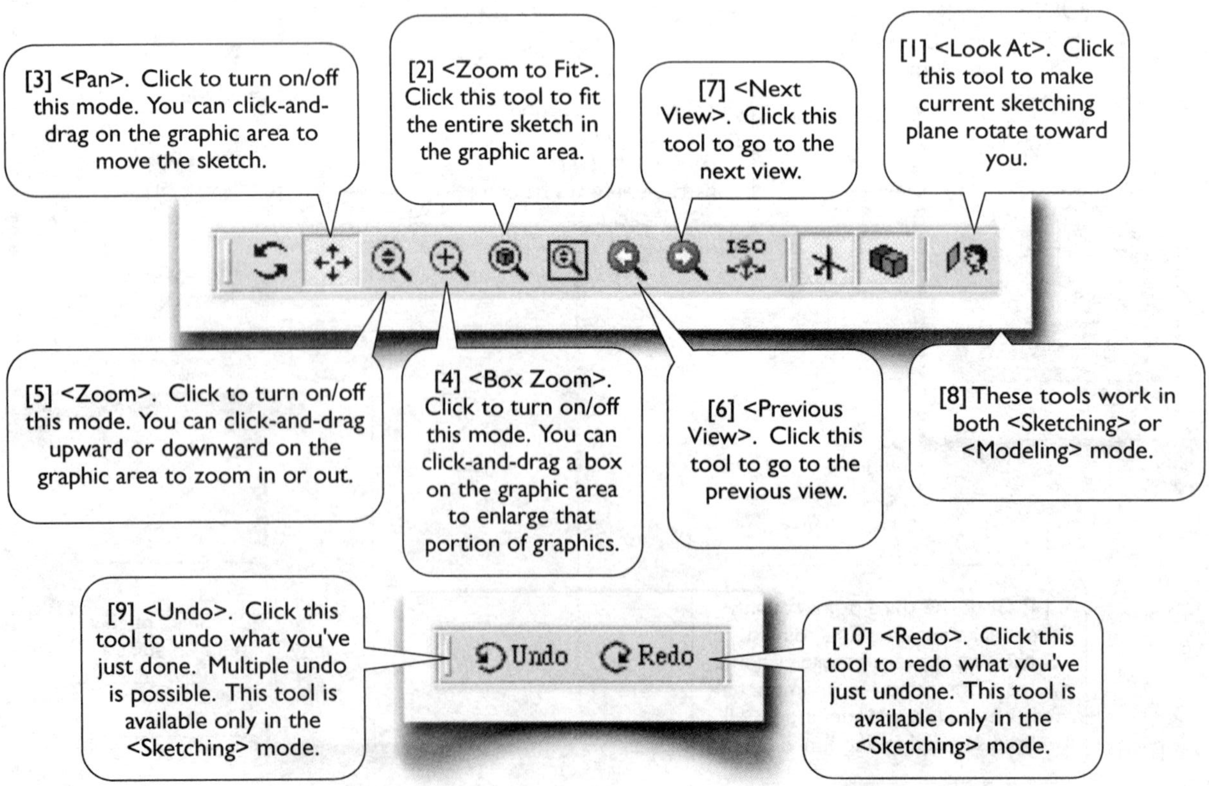

2.2-6 Specify Dimensions

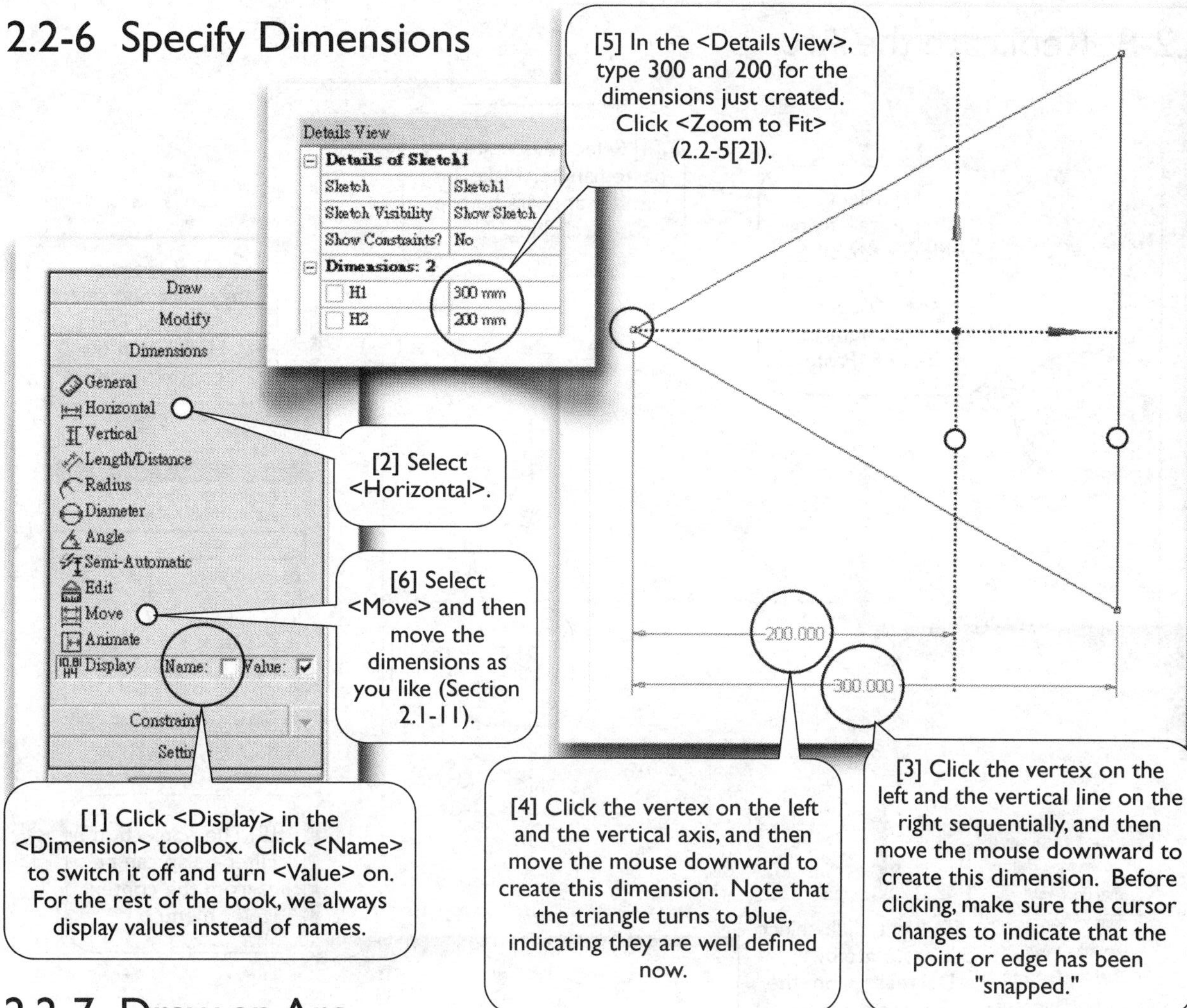

2.2-7 Draw an Arc

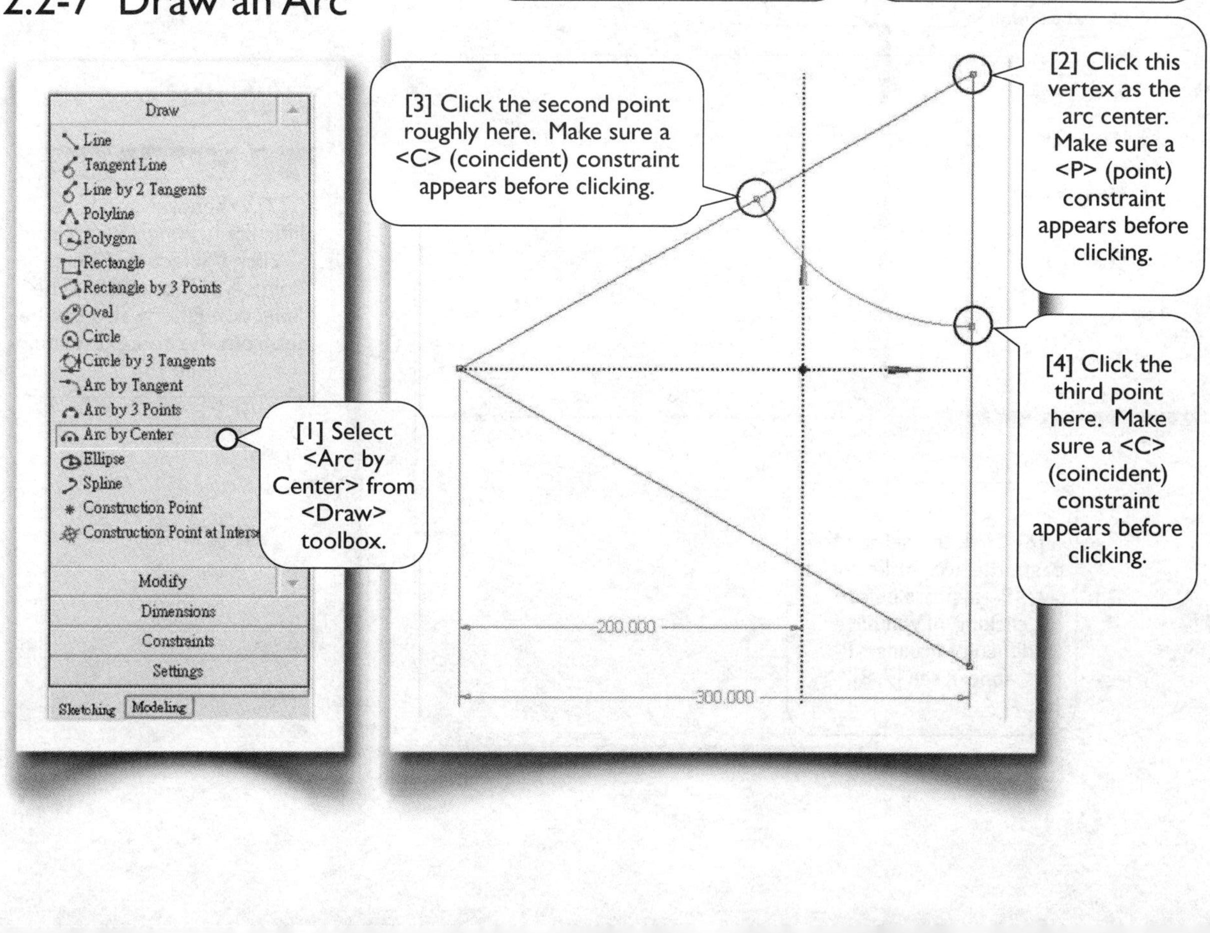

2.2-8 Replicate the Arc

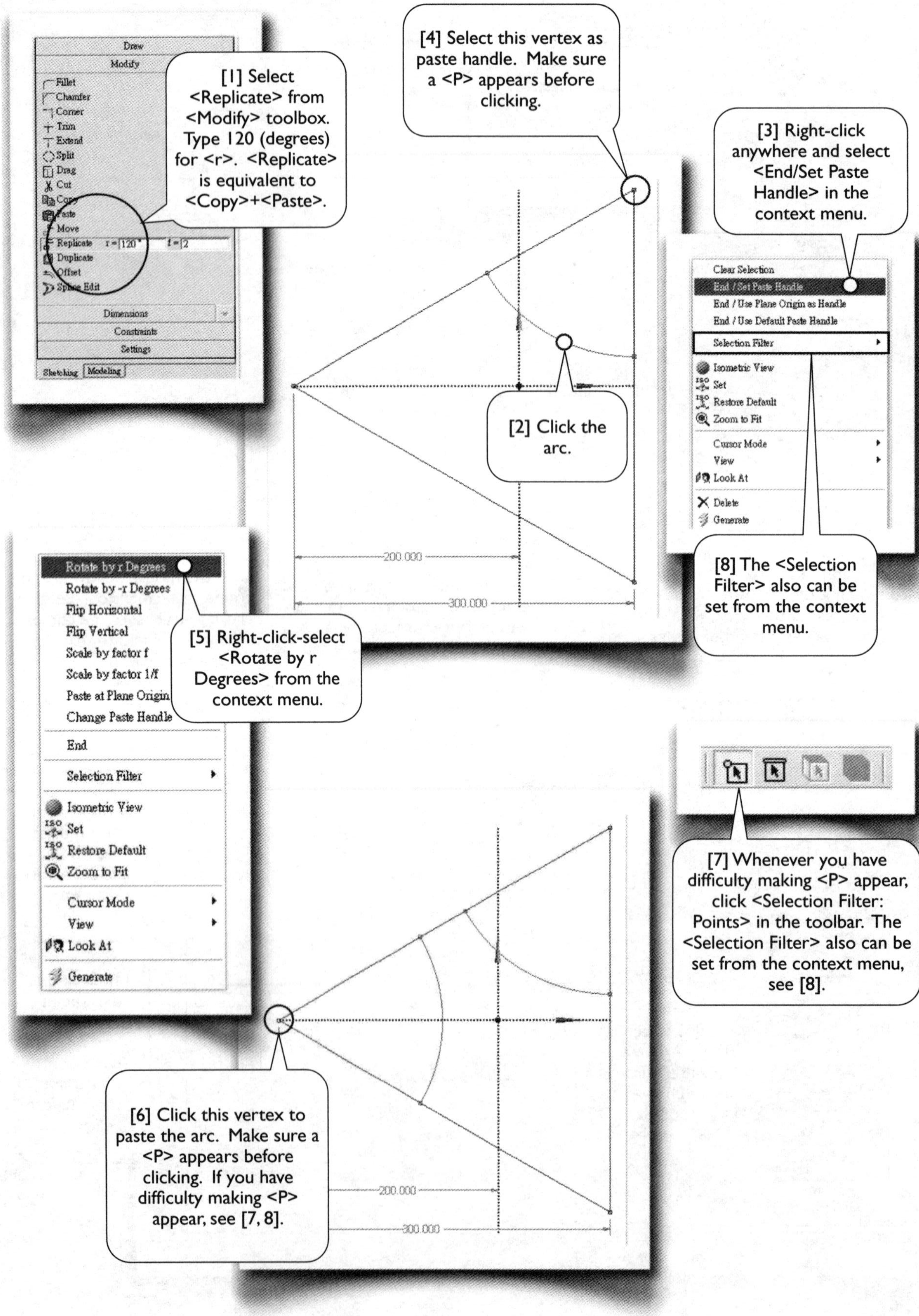

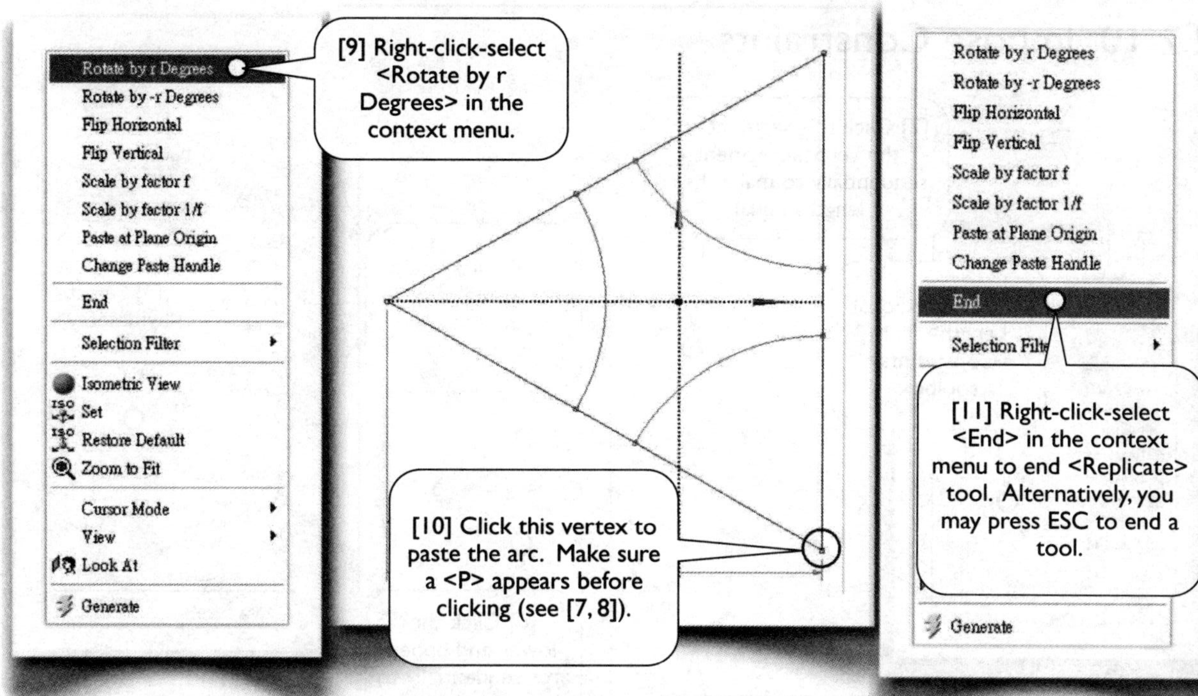

For instructional purpose, we chose to manually set the paste handle [3] on the vertex [4]. We could have used plane origin as handle. In fact, that would have been easier since we wouldn't have to struggle to make sure whether a <P> appears or not. Whenever you have difficulty to "snap" a particular point, you should take advantage of <Selection Filter> [7, 8].

2.2-9 Trim Away Unwanted Segments

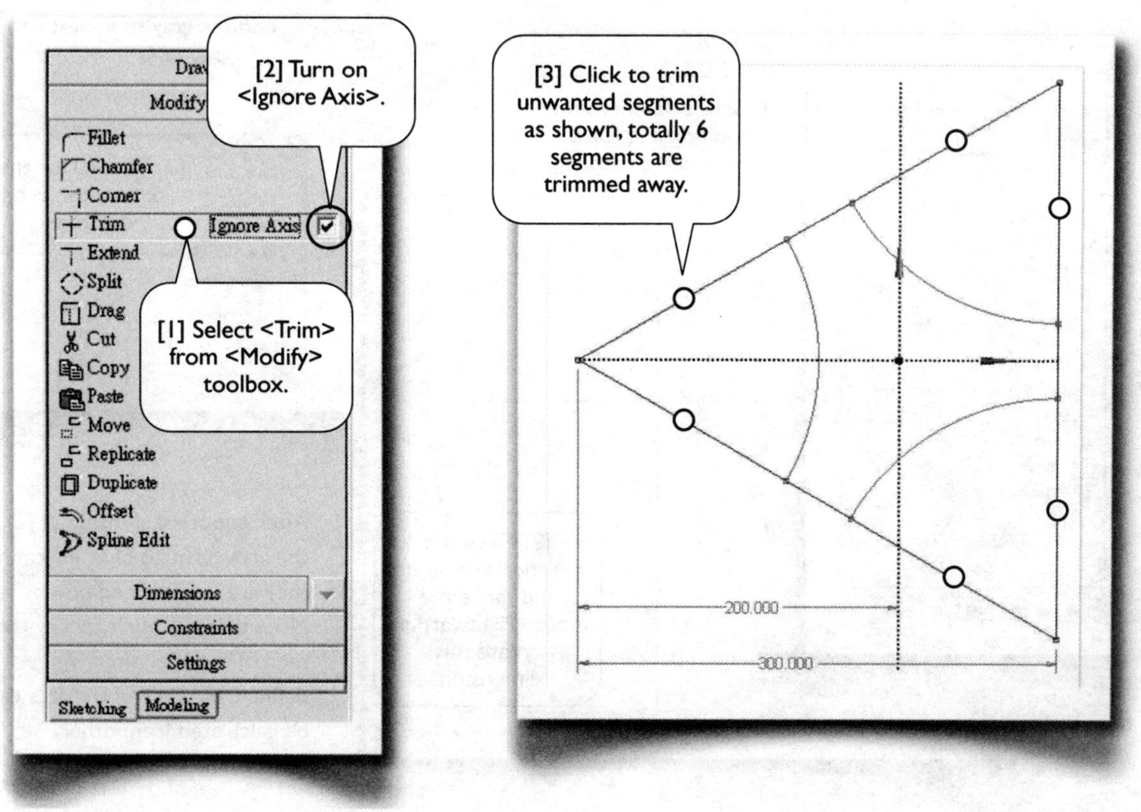

2.2-10 Impose Constraints

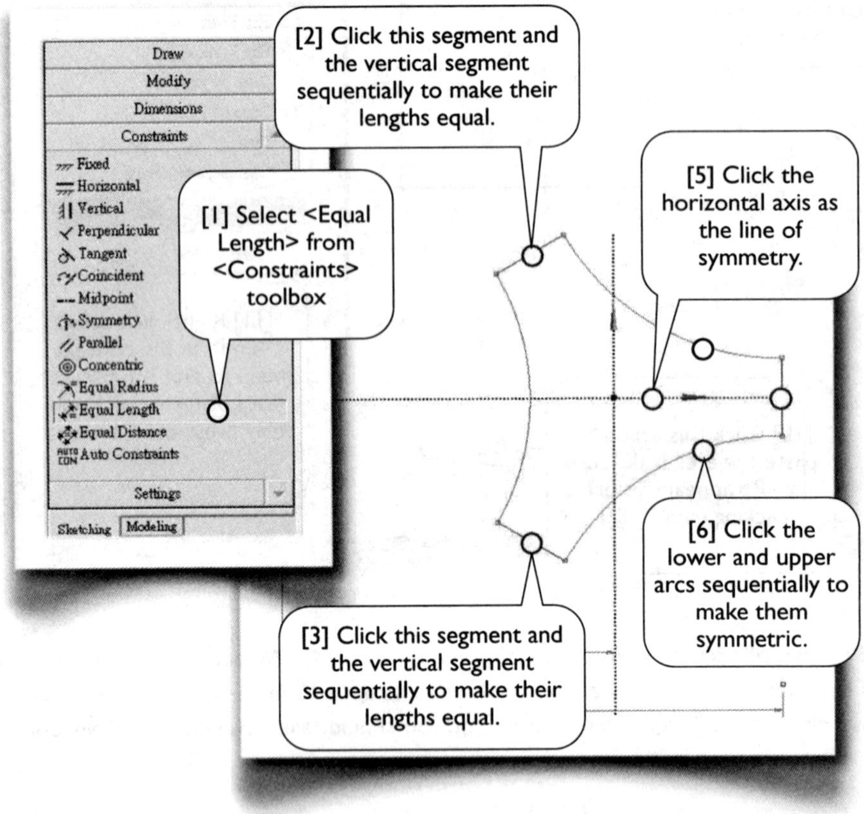

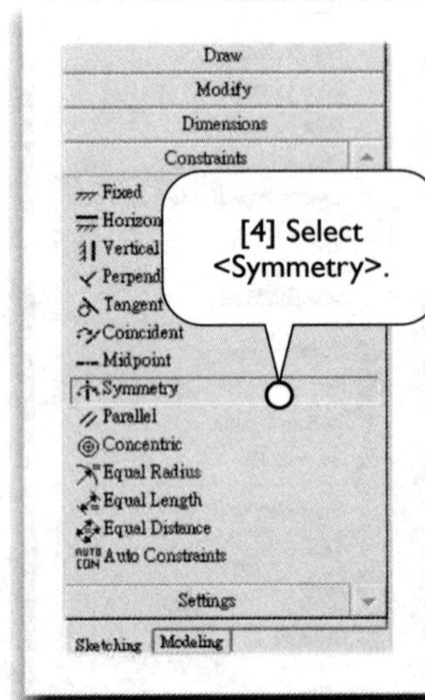

Constraint Status

Note the arcs have a greenish-blue color, indicating they are not well defined yet (i.e., under-constrained). Other color codes are: blue and black colors for well defined entities (i.e., fixed in the space); red color for over-constrained entities; gray to indicate an inconsistency.

2.2-11 Specify Dimension of Side Faces

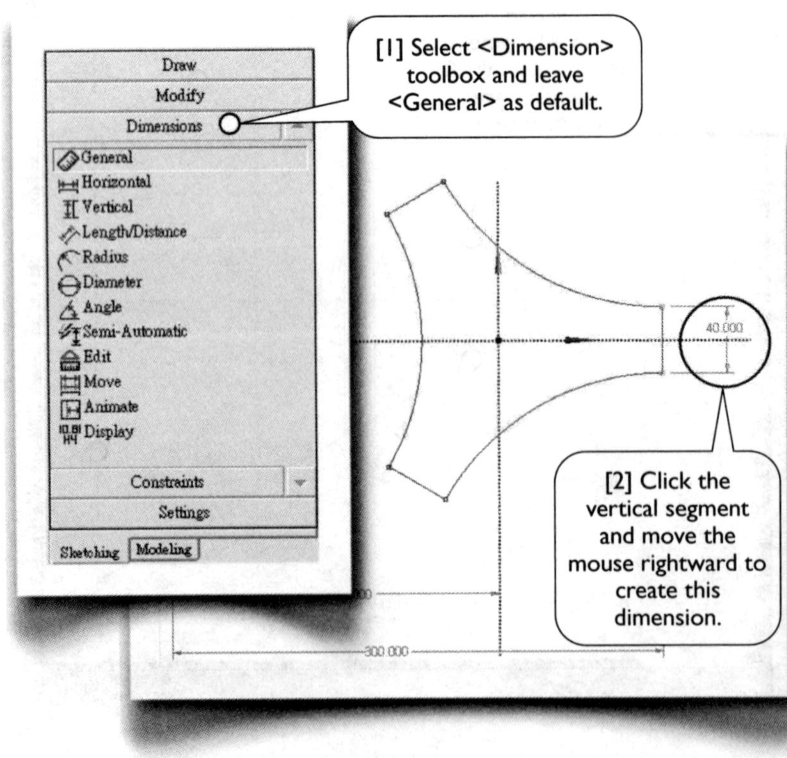

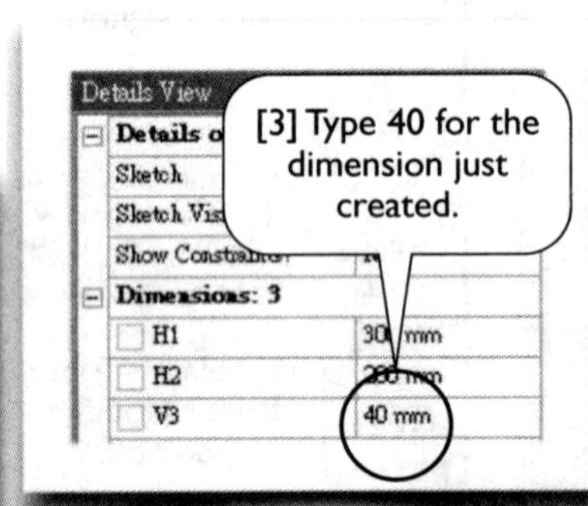

After impose dimension in [2], the arcs turns to blue, indicating they are well defined now. Note that we didn't specify the radii of the arcs; after well defined, the radii of the arcs can be calculated from other dimensions.

2.2-12 Create Offset

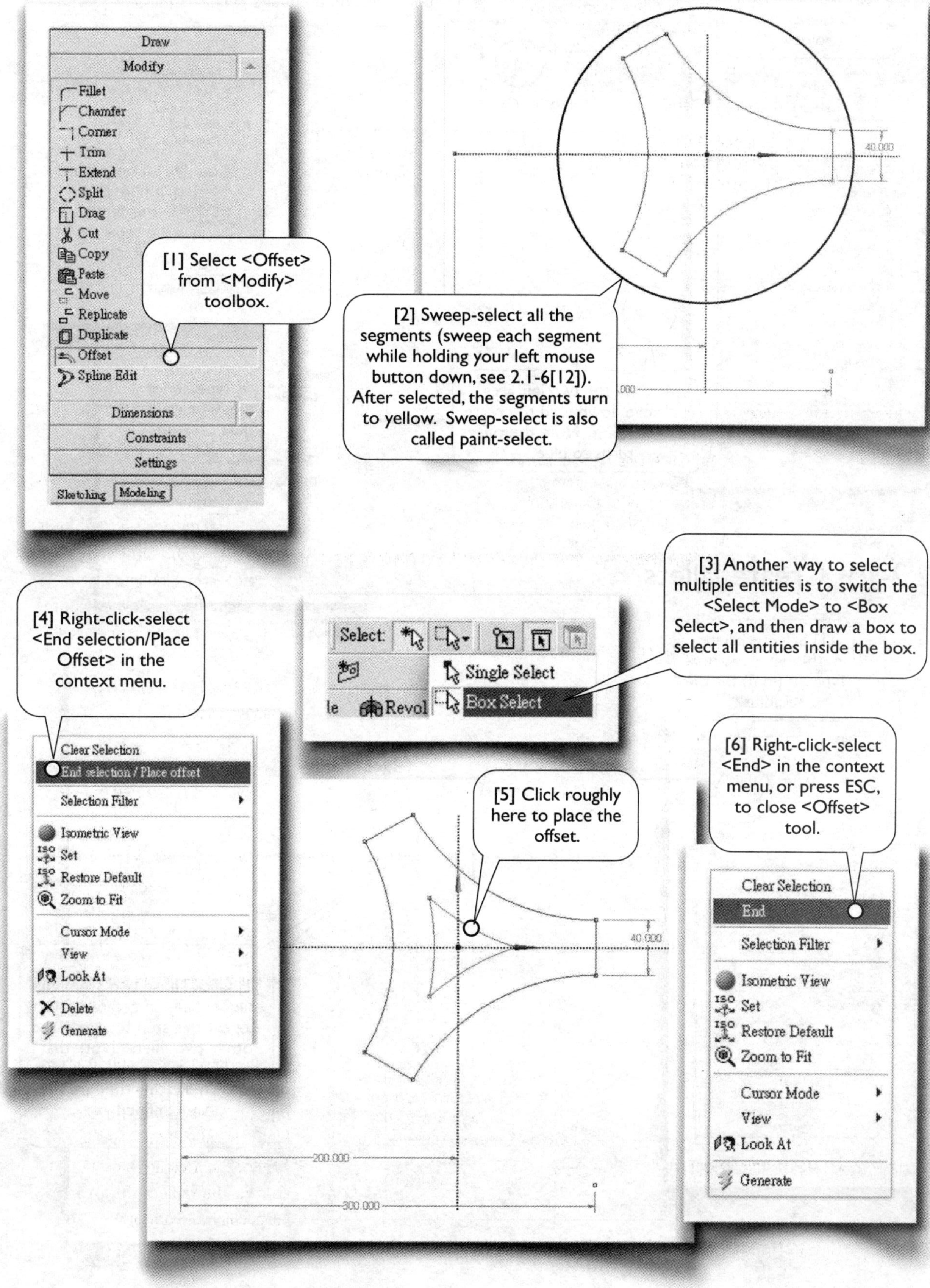

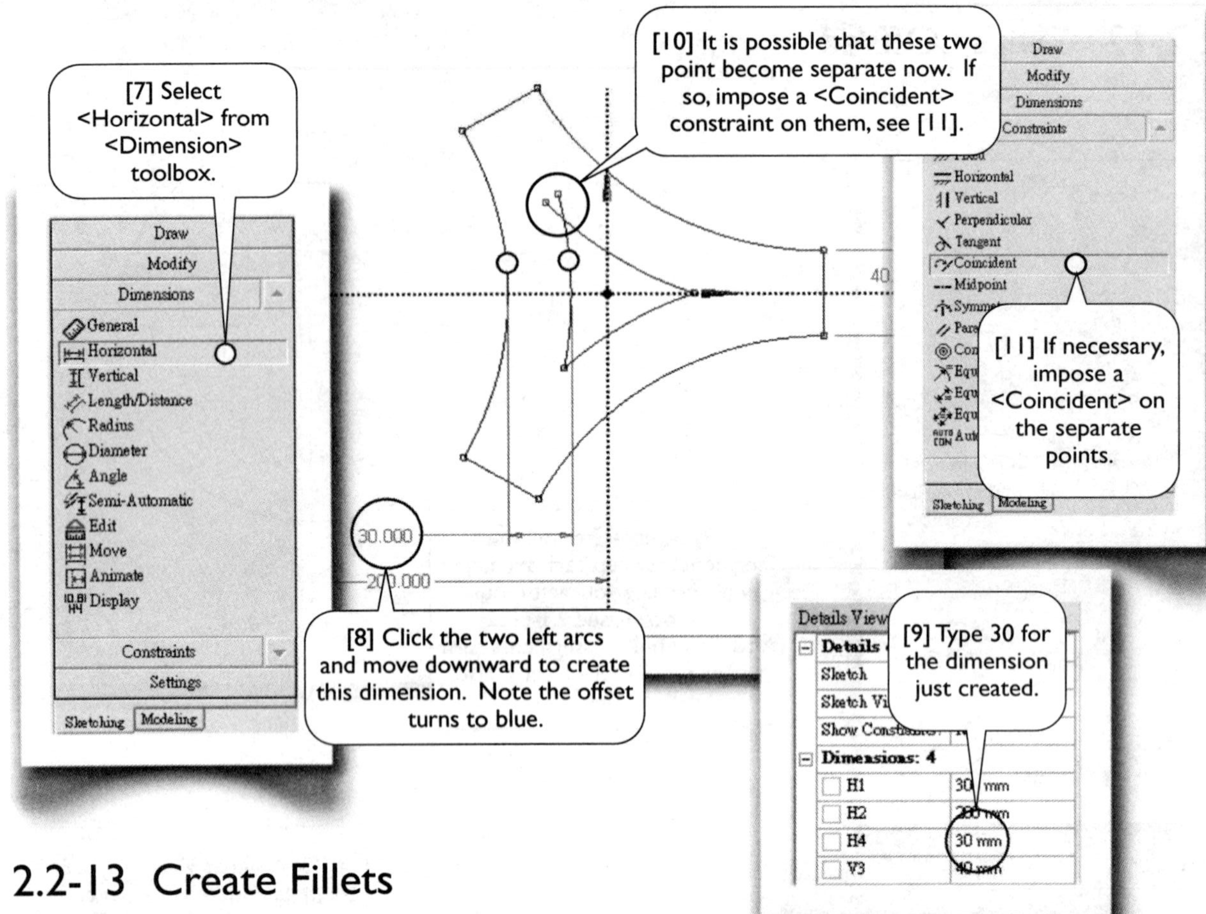

2.2-13 Create Fillets

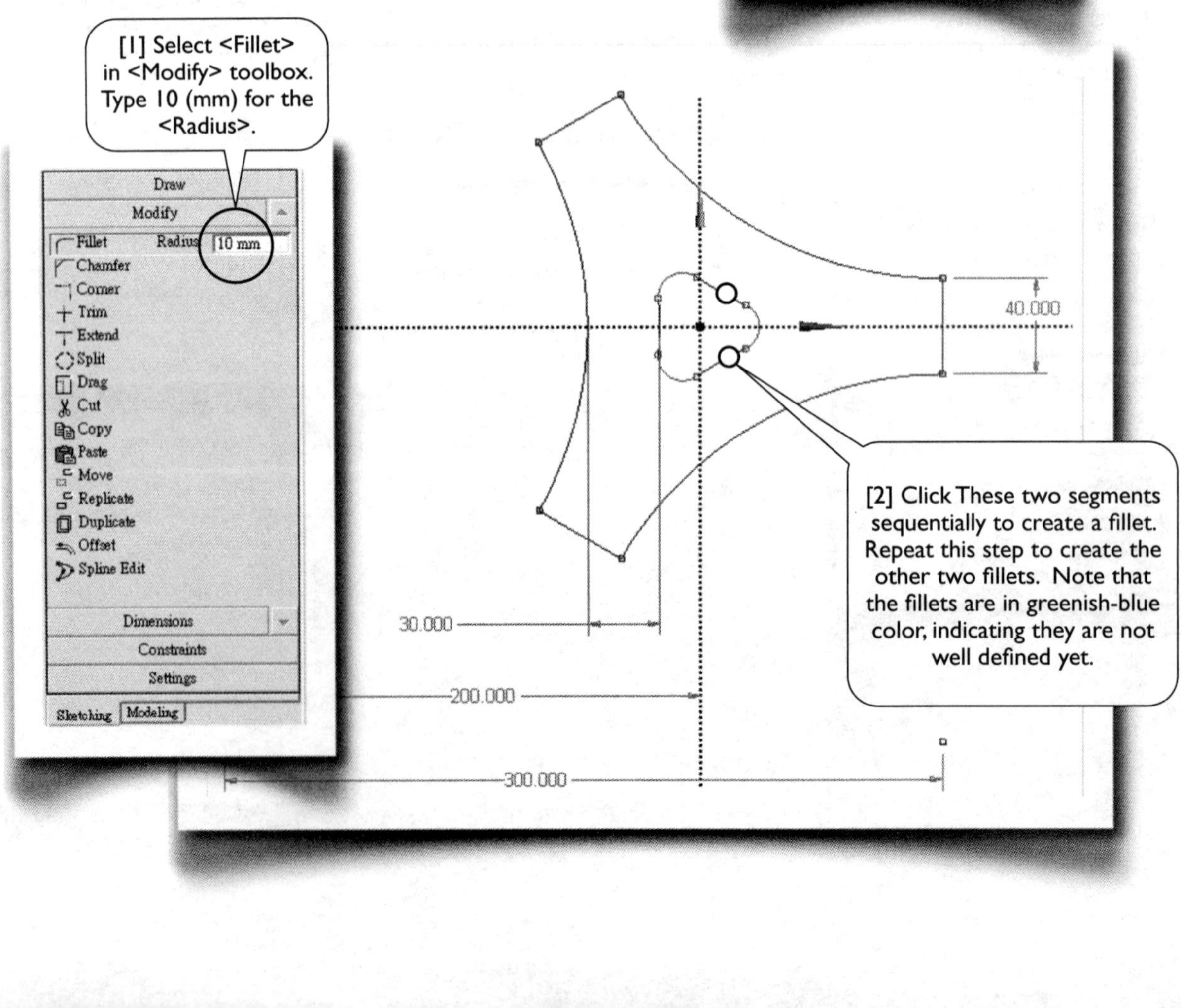

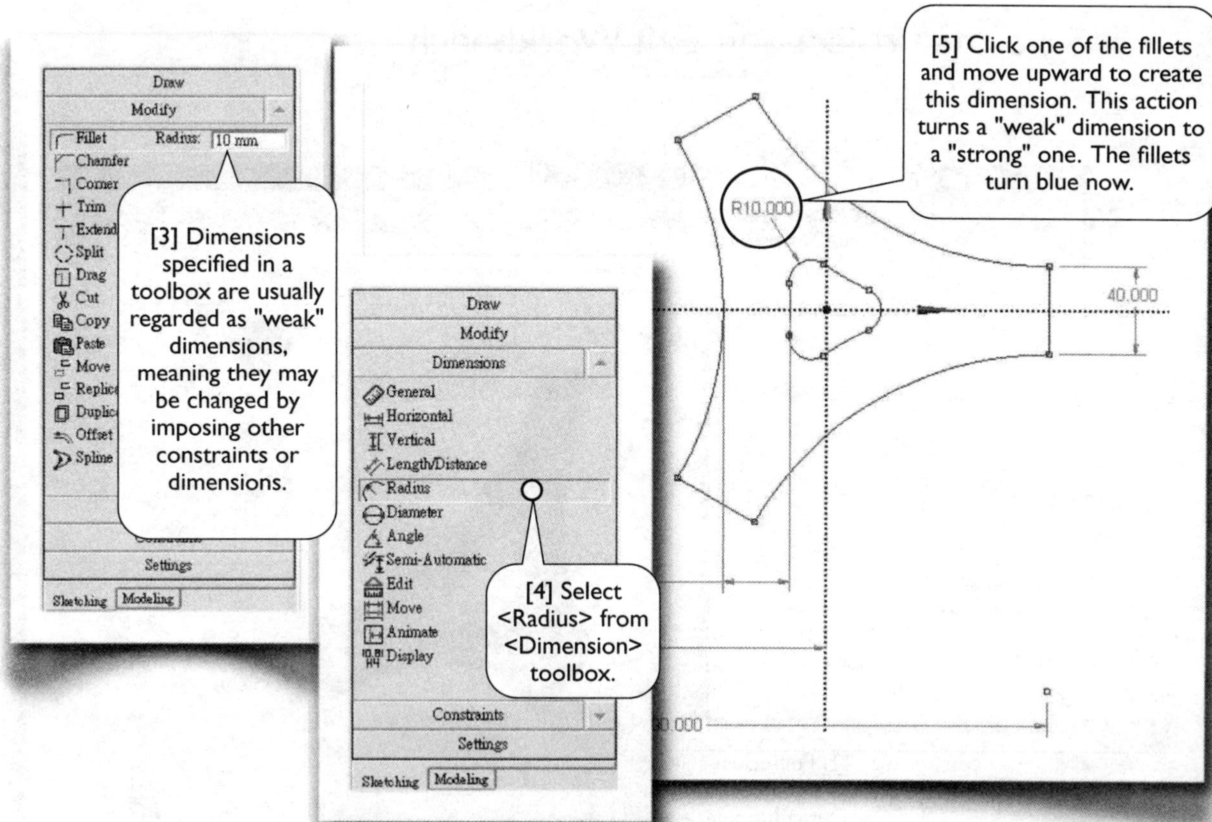

2.2-14 Extrude to Create 3D Solid

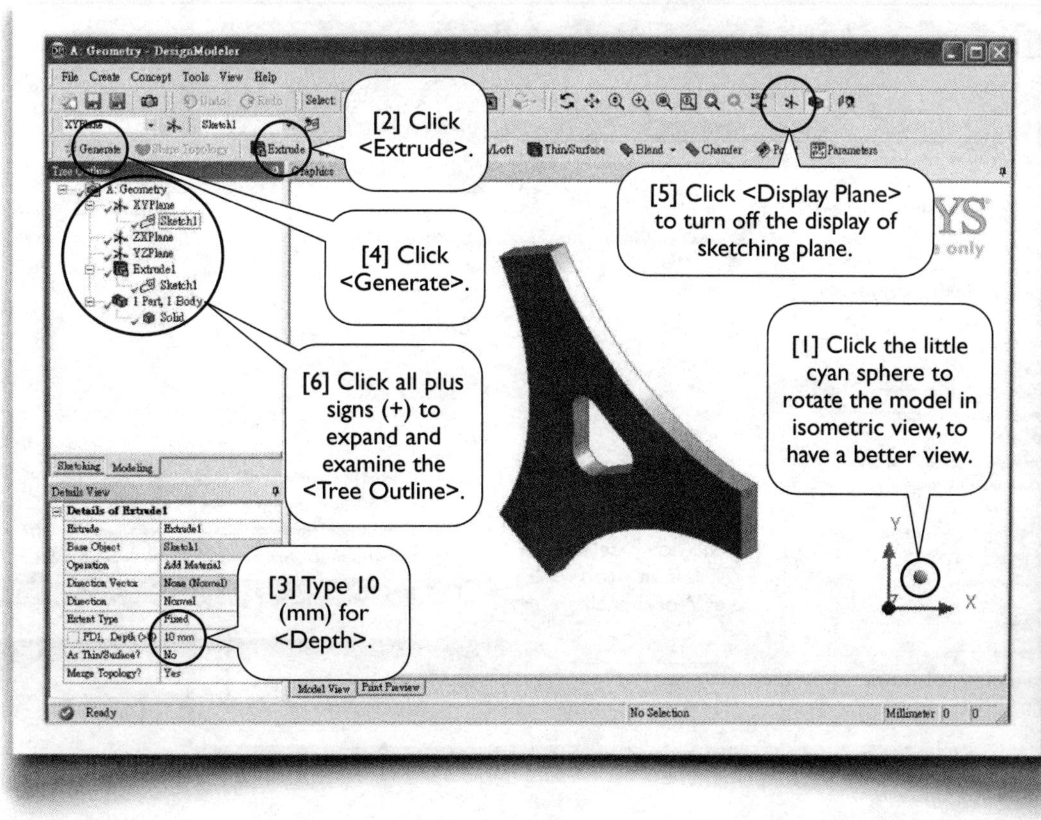

2.2-15 Save the Project and Exit Workbench

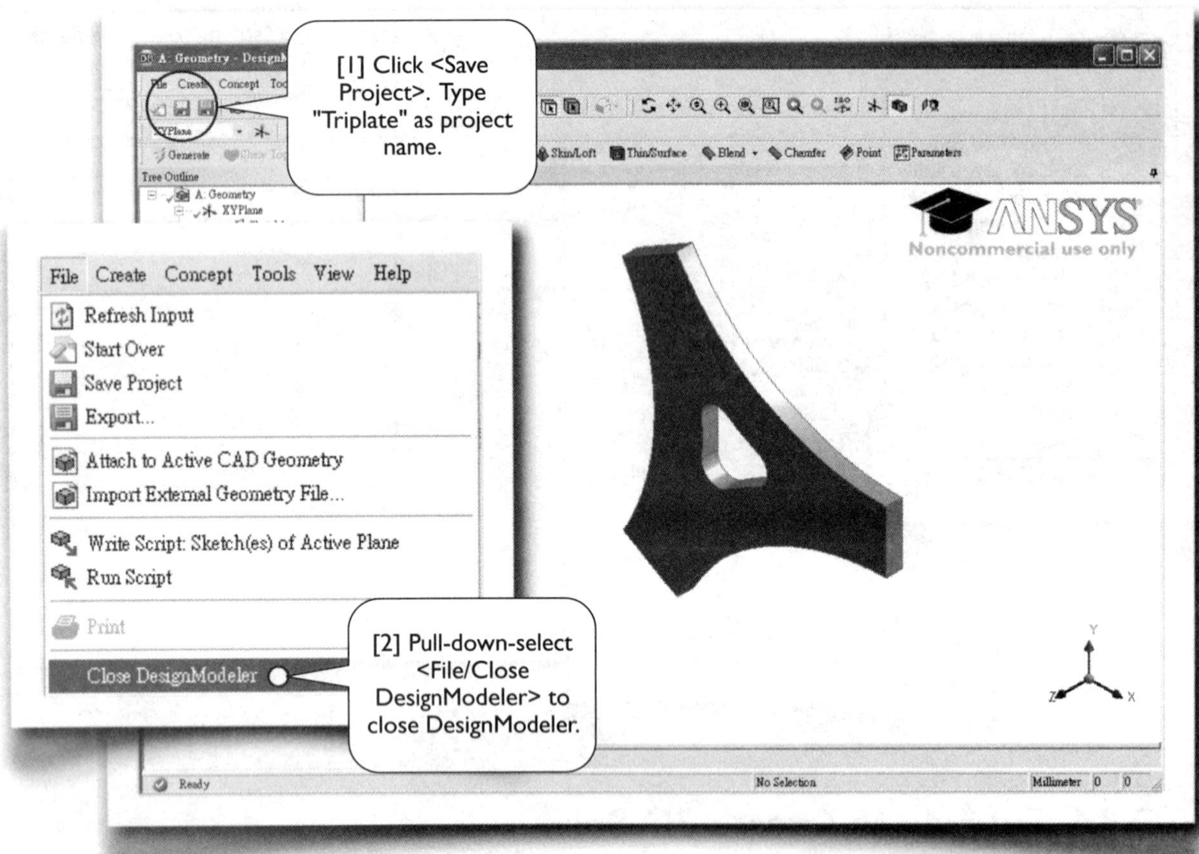

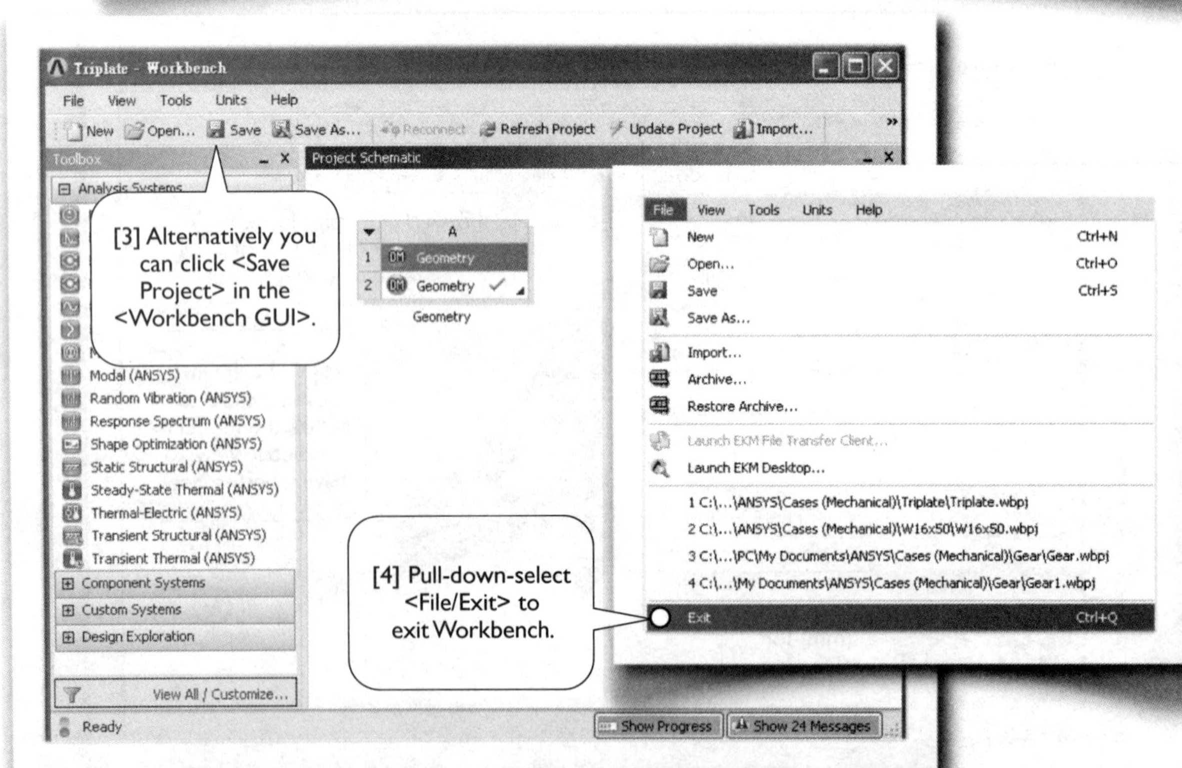

Section 2.3

More Details

2.3-1 DesignModeler GUI

The DesignModeler GUI is composed of several areas [1-7]. On the top are pull-down menus and toolbars [1]; on the bottom is a status bar [7]. In-between are several "window panes". A separator [8] between two window panes can be dragged to resize the window panes. You even can move or dock a pane by dragging its title bar. Whenever you mess up the workspace, simply pull-down-select <View/Windows/Reset Layout> to reset the default layout.

The <Tree Outline> [3] shares the same area with the <Sketching Toolboxes> [4]; you switch between these two "modes" by clicking the "mode tab" [2]. The <Details View> [6] shows the detail information of the geometry you currently work with. The graphics area [5] displays the model when in <Model View> mode; you can click a tab to switch to <Print Preview>. We will cover more details of DesignModeler GUI in Chapter 4.

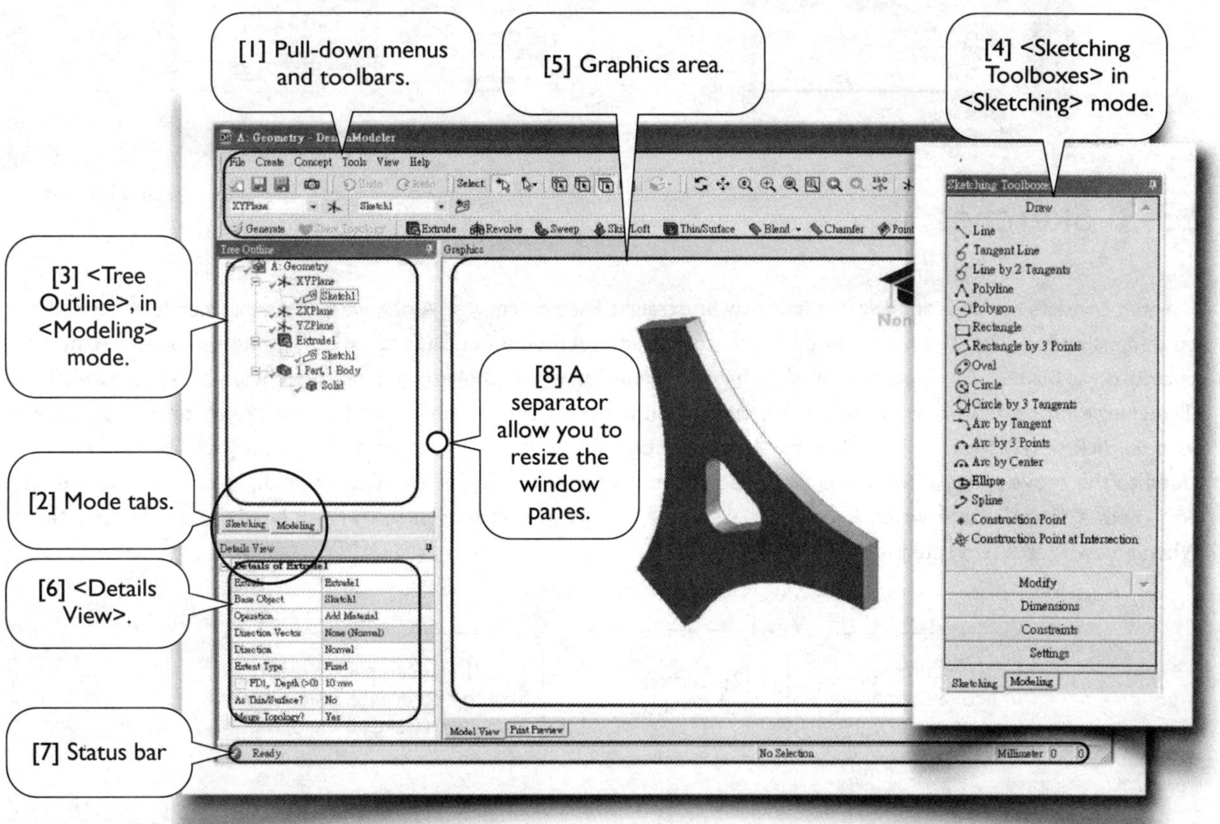

Model Tree

The <Tree Outline> contains an outline of the *model tree*, the tree representation of the geometric model. Each *leaf* and *branch* of the tree is called an *object*. A branch is an object containing one or more objects under itself. A model tree consists of *planes*, *features*, and a *part* branch. The parts are the only objects that are exported to <Mechanical>. Right-clicking an object and select a tool from the context menu, you can operate on the object, such as delete, rename, duplicate, etc.

The order of the objects is often relevant. DesignModeler renders the geometry according to the order. New objects are normally added one-by-one before the parts branch. If you want to insert a new object BEFORE an existing object, right-click the existing object and select <Insert/...> from the context menu. After insertion, DesignModeler will re-render the geometry again.

2.3-2 Sketching Planes

Sketches are created on *sketching planes*, or simply *planes*. Each sketch must be associated with a plane; each plane may have multiple sketches on it. In the beginning of a DesignModeler session, three planes are created automatically: <XYPlane>, <YZPlane>, and <ZXPlane>. Currently active plane is shown on the toolbar [1]. You can create new planes as needed [2]. There are many ways of creating a new plane [3]. In this chapter, since we assume sketches are created on the <XYPlane>, we will not discuss how to create sketching planes further, which will be discussed in Chapter 4. Usage of planes is not limited for storing sketches. Section 4.3-8 demonstrates another usage of planes.

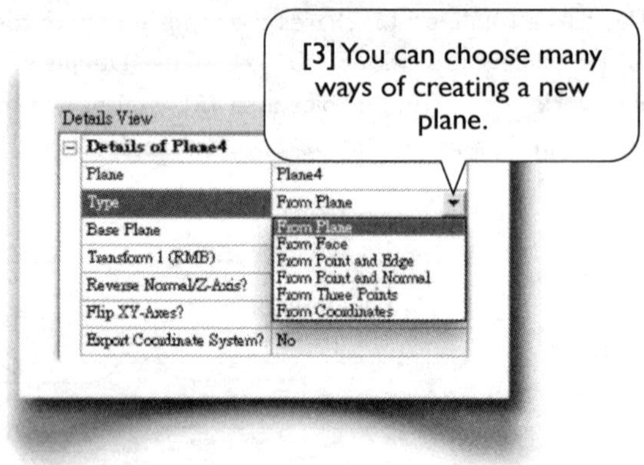

2.3-3 Sketches

A sketch consists of *points* and *edges*; edges may be straight lines or curves. Along with these geometric entities, there are dimensions and constraints imposed on these entities. As mentioned (Section 2.3-2), multiple sketches may be created on a plane. To create a new sketch on a plane on which there is yet no sketches, you simply switch to <Sketching> mode and draw any geometric entities on it. Later, if you want to add a new sketch on that plane, you need to click <New Sketch> [3]. Only one plane and one sketch is active at a time [1, 2]: newly created sketches are added to the active plane, and newly created geometric entities are added to the active sketch. In this chapter, we only work with a single sketch which is on the <XYPlane>. More on creating sketches will be discussed in Chapter 4. When a new sketch is created, it becomes the active sketch.

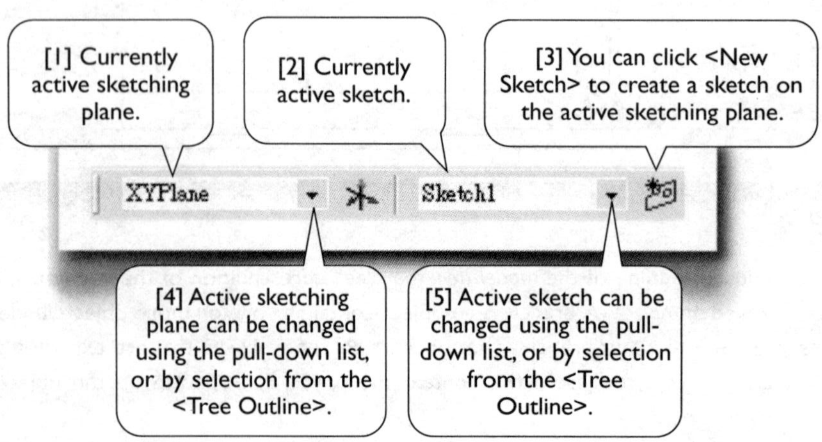

2.3-4 Sketching Toolboxes

When you switch to <Sketching> mode by clicking the mode tab (2.3-1[2]), you will see a <Sketching Toolboxes> (2.3-1[4]). The <Sketching Toolboxes> consists of five toolboxes: <Draw>, <Modify>, <Dimensions>, <Constraints>, and <Settings> [1-5]. Most of the tools in the toolboxes are self-explained. The most efficient way to learn the tools is to try them out. During the tryout, whenever you want to clean up the graphics area, pull-down-select <File/Start Over>, or select all entities and then delete them. Some tools need further explanation, as described in the rest of this section.

Before we jump to discuss each of the toolboxes, some tips relevant to sketching are worth emphasizing first.

Pan, Zoom, and Box Zoom

Besides the <Pan> tool (2.2-5[3]), the graphics can be panned by dragging your mouse while holding down both control key and the middle mouse button. Besides the <Zoom> tool (2.2-5[5]) the graphics can be zoomed in/out by simply rolling forward/backward your mouse wheel. The <Box Zoom> (2.2-5[4]) can be done by right-clicking and then dragging a rectangle in the graphics area. When you get use to these basic mouse actions, you probably don't need <Pan>, <Zoom>, and <Box Zoom> tools in the toolbar any more.

Context Menu

While most of operations can be done by issuing commands using pull-down menus or toolbars, many operations either require or are more efficient using the context menu. The context menu can be popped-up by right-clicking the graphics area or objects in the model tree. Try to explore whatever available in the context menu.

Status Bar

The status bar (2.3-1[7]) contains instructions on completing each operations. Look at the instruction whenever you wonder about what actions to do next. The coordinates of your mouse pointer are also shown in the status bar; they are sometimes useful.

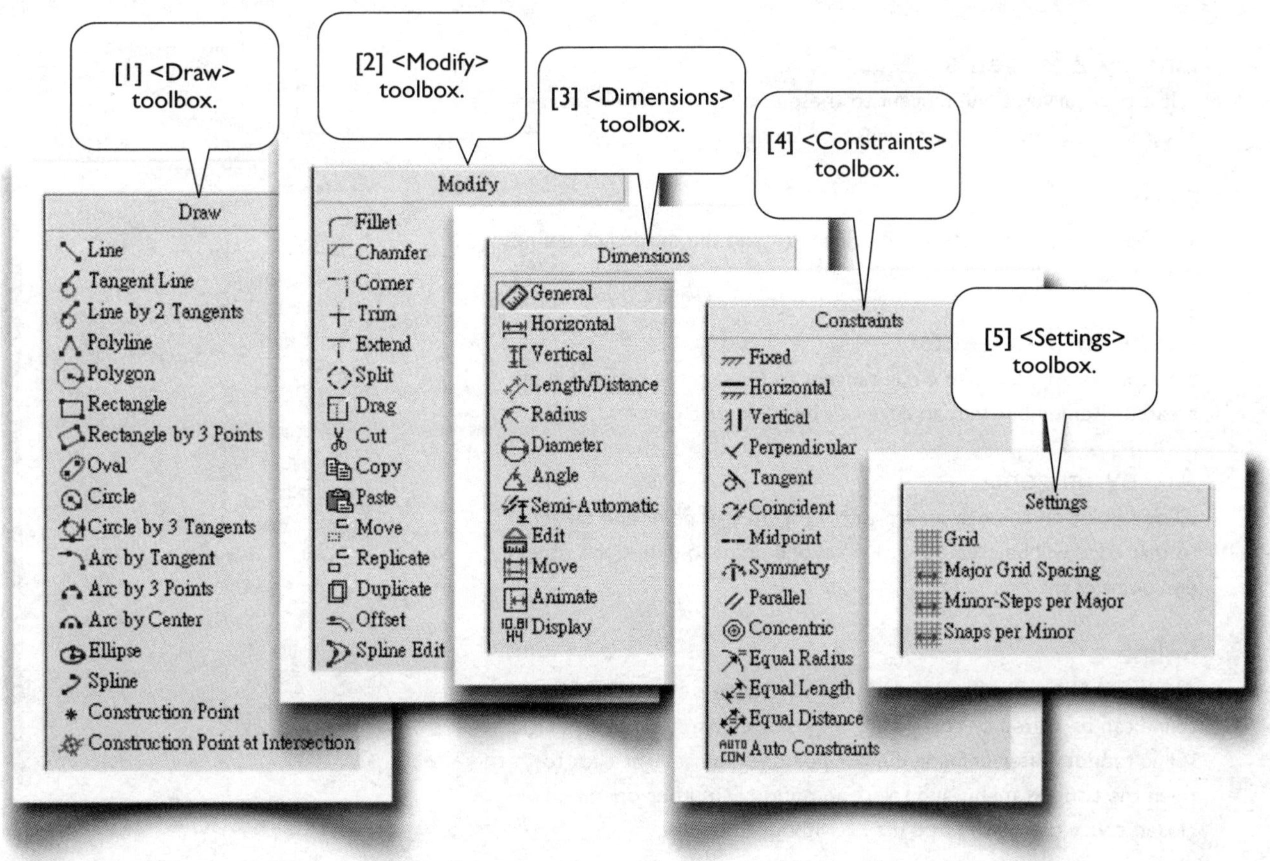

2.3-5 Auto Constraints[1, 2]

By default, DesignModeler is in <Auto Constraints> mode, both globally and locally. While drawing, DesignModeler attempts to detect the user's intentions and try to automatically impose constraints on the points or edges. The following cursor symbols indicate the kind of constraints that will be applied:

C - The point is coincident with a line.
P - The point is coincident with another point.
H - The line is horizontal.
V - The line is vertical.
// - The line is parallel to another line.
T - The point is a tangent point.
⊥ - The point is a perpendicular foot.
R - The circle's radius is equal to another circle's.

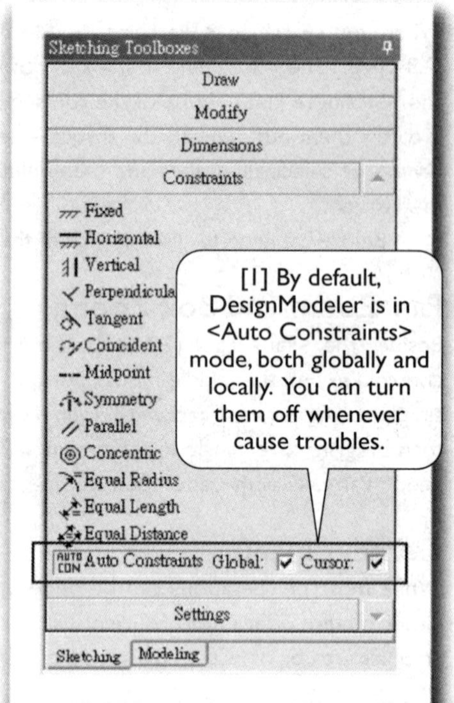

Both <Global> and <Cursor> modes are based on all entities of the active plane, not just the active sketch. The difference is that <Cursor> mode only examines the entities nearby the cursor, while <Global> mode examines all the entities in the active plane.

Note that while <Auto Constraints> can be useful, they sometimes can lead to problems and add noticeable time on complicated sketches. Turn off them if desired [1].

2.3-6 <Draw> Tools[3]

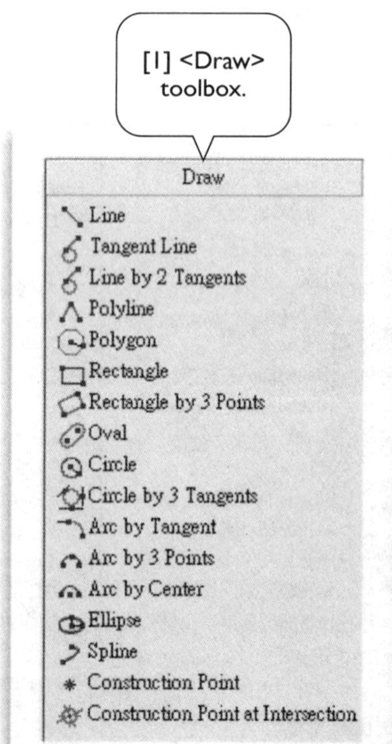

Line by 2 Tangents
Select two curves, a line tangent to these two curves will be created. The curves can be circle, arc, ellipse, or spline.

Oval
The first two clicks define the two centers, and the third click defines the radius.

Circle by 3 Tangents
Select three edges, then a circle tangent to these three edges will be created. Remember that an edge can be a line or a curve.

Arc by Tangent
Click a point on an edge, an arc starting from that point and tangent to that edge will be created; click a second point to define the other end point of the arc.

Spline
A spline is either rigid or flexible. The difference is that a flexible spline can be edited or changed by imposing constraints, while a rigid spline cannot. After defining the last point, you must right-click to open the context menu, and select an option [2]: either open end or closed end; either with fit points or without fit points.

Construction Point at Intersection

Select two edges, a construction point will be created at the intersection.

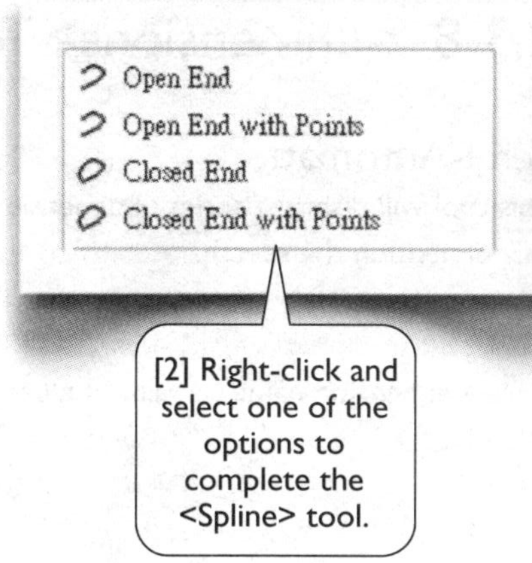

Delete Entities

There are no tools in the <Sketching Toolboxes> to delete entities. To delete entities, select them and right-click-select <Delete>. Multiple selection methods (e.g., control-selection and sweep-selection, see Section 2.1-6 and 2.2-12[2]), can be used to select entities.

Abort a Tool

To cancel a tool in any of toolbox, simply press <ESC>.

2.3-7 <Modify> Tools[4]

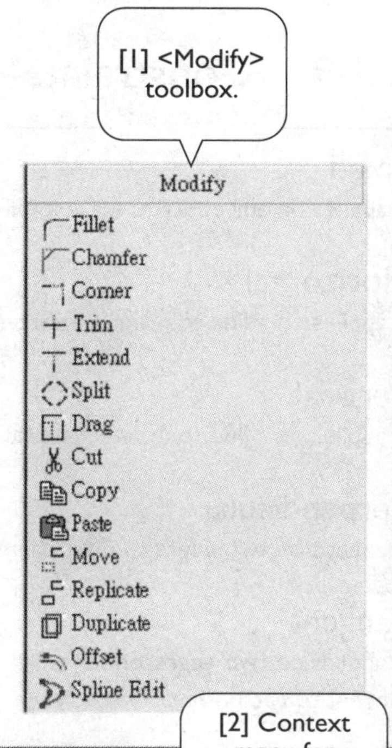

Corner

Click two entities, which can be lines or curves, the entities will be trimmed or extended up to the intersection point and form a sharp corner. The clicking points decide which sides to be trimmed.

Split

This tool split an edge into several segments depending on the options [2]. <Split Edge at Selection>: you click an edge, the edge will be split at the clicking point. <Split Edges at Point>: you click a point, all the edges passing through that point will be split at that point. <Split Edge at All Points>: you select an edge, the edge will be split at all points on the edge. <Split Edge into n Equal Segments>: You specify the value *n*, and select an edge, the edge will be split equally into *n* segments.

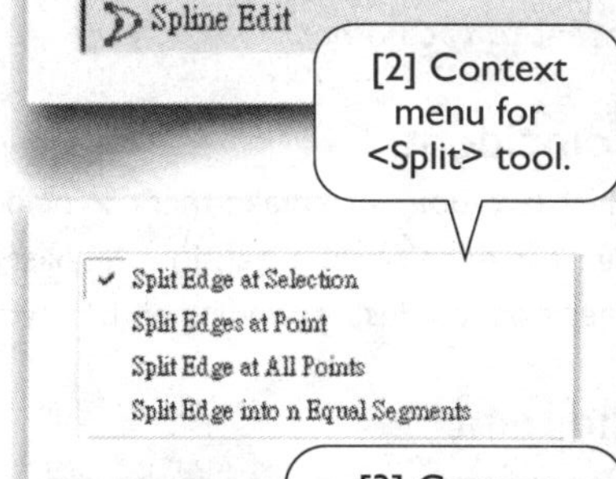

Drag

Drag a point or an edge to a new position. All the constraints and dimensions are preserved.

Cut

It is the same as <Copy>, except the originals are deleted.

Move

It is equivalent to a <Cut> followed by a <Paste>.

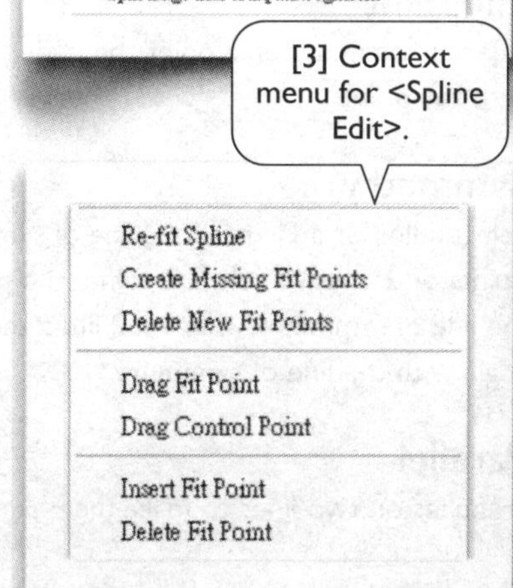

Replicate

It is equivalent to a <Copy> followed a <Paste>.

Duplicate

It is equivalent to <Replicate>, except the entities are pasted on the same place as the originals and become part of the current sketch. It is often used to duplicate plane boundaries.

Spline Edit

It is used to modify flexible splines. You can insert, delete, drag the fit points, etc. For details, see the reference[4].

2.3-8 <Dimensions> Tools[5]

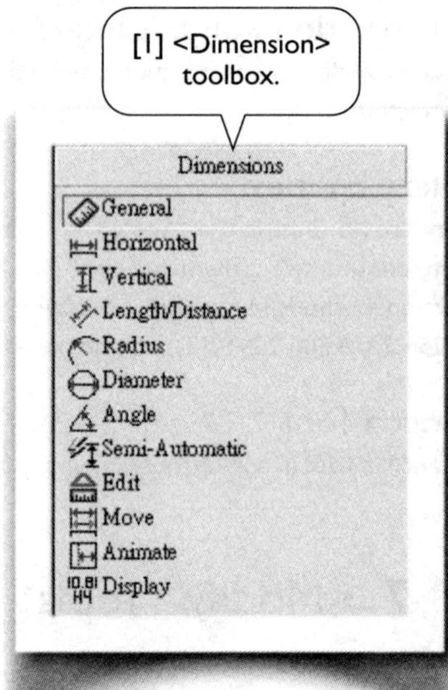

Semi-Automatic
This tool will display a series of dimensions automatically to help you fully dimension the sketch.

Edit
Click a dimension name or value, it allows you to change its name or value.

2.3-9 <Constraints> Tools[6]

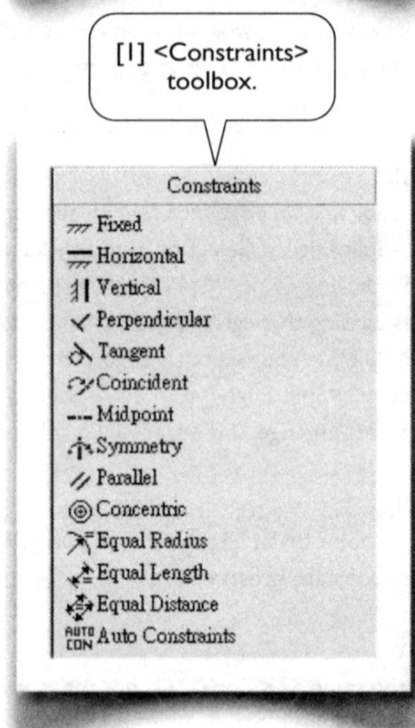

Fixed
It applies on any entity to make it fully constrained.

Horizontal
It applies on a line to make it horizontal.

Vertical
It applies on a line to make it vertical.

Perpendicular
It applies on two edges to make them perpendicular to each other.

Tangent
It applies on two edges, one of which must be a curve, to make them tangent to each other.

Coincident
Select two points to make them coincident. Select a point and an edge, the edge or its extension will pass through the point. There are other possibilities, depending on how you select the entities.

Midpoint
Select a line and then a point, the midpoint of the line will coincide with the point.

Symmetry
Select a line or an axis, as the line of symmetry, and either select 2 points or 2 lines. If select 2 points, the points will be symmetric about the line of symmetry. If select 2 lines, the lines will form the same angle with the line of symmetry.

Parallel
It applies on two lines to make them parallel to each other.

Concentric
It applies on two curves, which may be circle, arc, or ellipse, to make their centers coincident.

Equal Radius
It applies on two curves, which may be circle or arc, to make their radii equal.

Equal Length
It applies on two lines to make their lengths equal.

Equal Distance
It applies on two distances to make them equal. A distance can be defined by selecting two points, two parallel lines, or one point and one line.

2.3-10 <Settings> Tools[7]

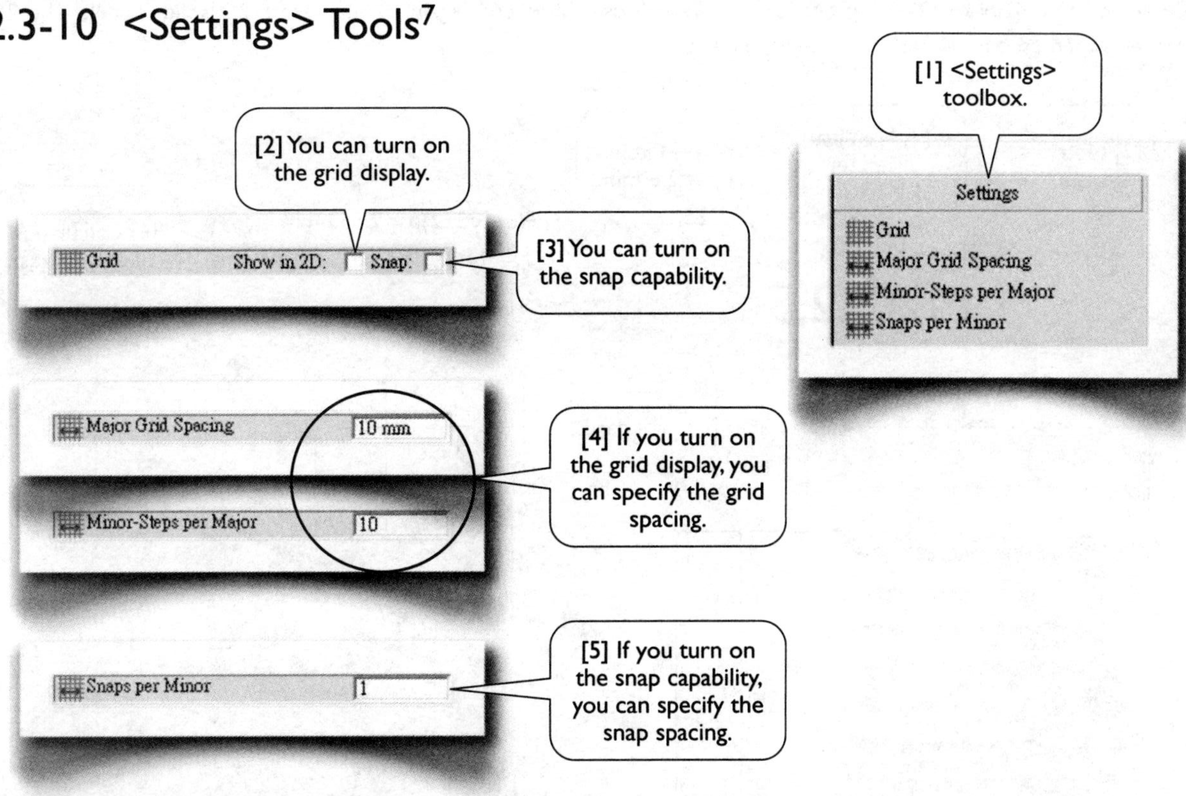

References

1. ANSYS Help System>DesignModeler>2D Sketching>Auto Constraints
2. ANSYS Help System>DesignModeler>2D Sketching>Constraints Toolbox>Auto Constraints
3. ANSYS Help System>DesignModeler>2D Sketching>Draw Toolbox
4. ANSYS Help System>DesignModeler>2D Sketching>Modify Toolbox
5. ANSYS Help System>DesignModeler>2D Sketching>Dimensions Toolbox
6. ANSYS Help System>DesignModeler>2D Sketching>Constraints Toolbox
7. ANSYS Help System>DesignModeler>2D Sketching>Settings Toolbox

Section 2.4

Exercise: M20x2.5 Threaded Bolt

2.4-1 About the M20x2.5 Threaded Bolt

Consider a pair of threaded bolt and nut. The bolt has external threads while the nut has internal threads. This exercise is to created a sketch and revolve the sketch 360° to generate a solid body for a portion of the bolt [1] threaded with M20x2.5 [2-6]. In Section 3.2, we will use this sketch again to generate a 2D solid model. The 2D model is then used for a static structural simulation.

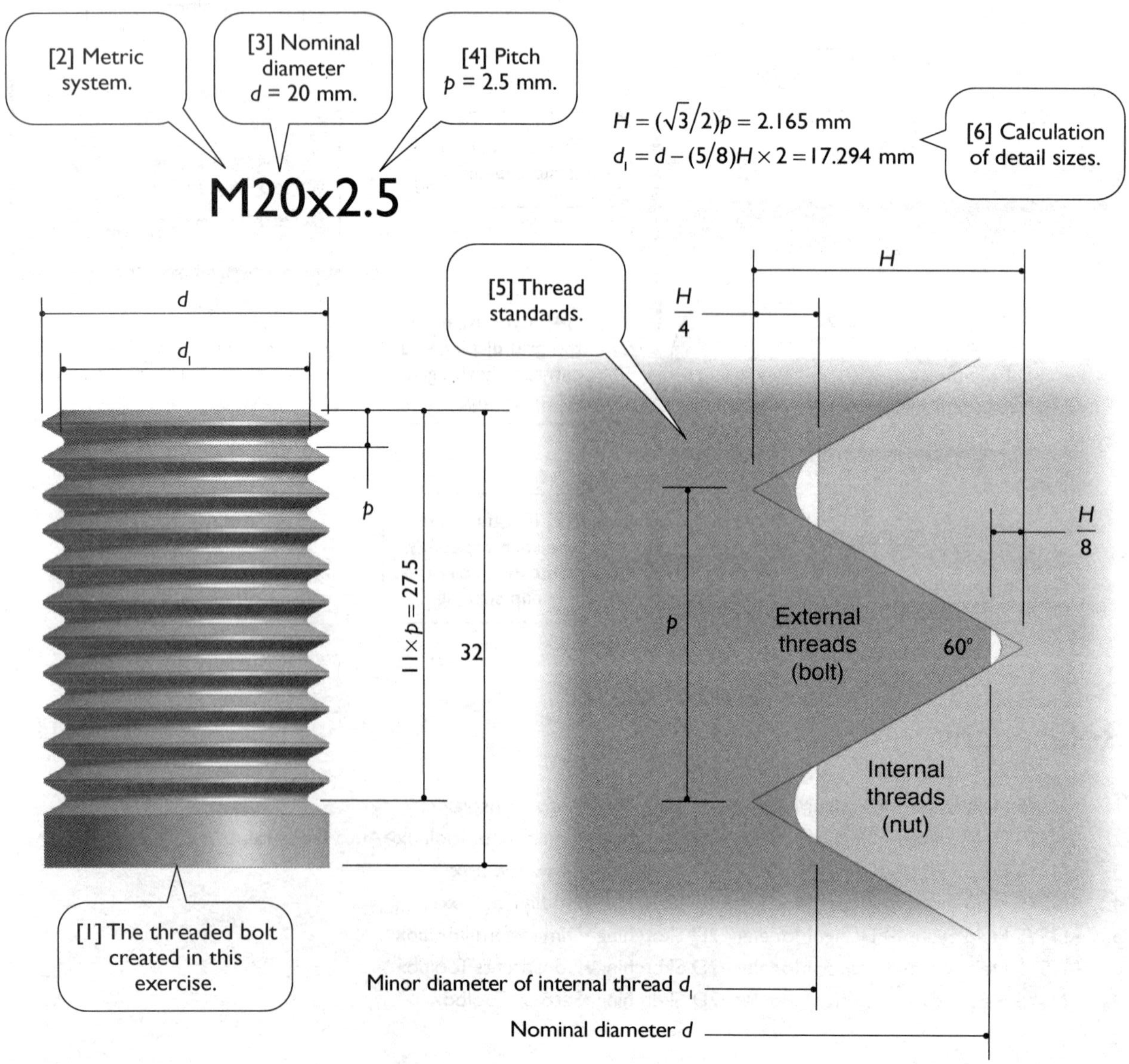

2.4-2 Draw a Horizontal Line

Launch <Workbench>. Create a <Geometry> System. Save the project as "Threads." Start up <DesignModeler>. Select <Millimeter> as length unit.

Draw a horizontal line on the <XYPlane>. Specify the dimensions as shown [1].

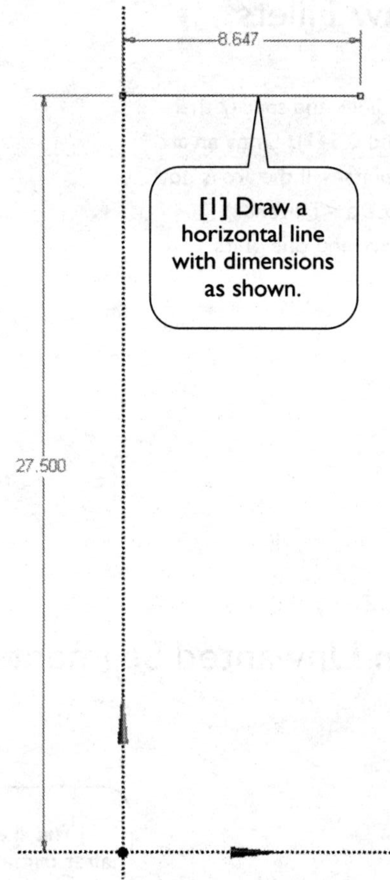

2.4-3 Draw a Polyline

Draw a polyline (totally 3 segments) and specify dimensions (30°, 60°, 60°, 0.541, and 2.165) as shown below. Note that, to avoid confusion, we explicitly specify all the dimensions. You may apply constraints instead. For example, using <Parallel> constraint in stead of specifying an angle dimension [1].

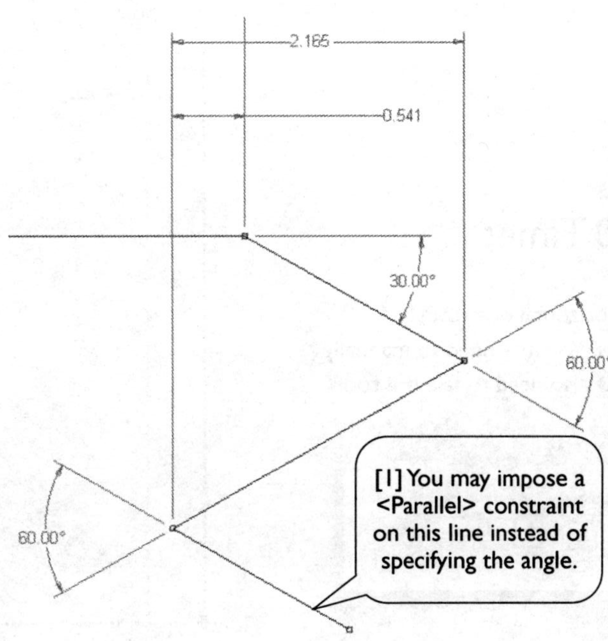

2.4-4 Draw Fillets

Draw two vertical lines and specify their positions (0.271 and 0.541). Draw an arc using <Arc by 3 Points>. If the arc is not in blue color, impose a <Tangent> constraint on the arc and one of its tangent line [1].

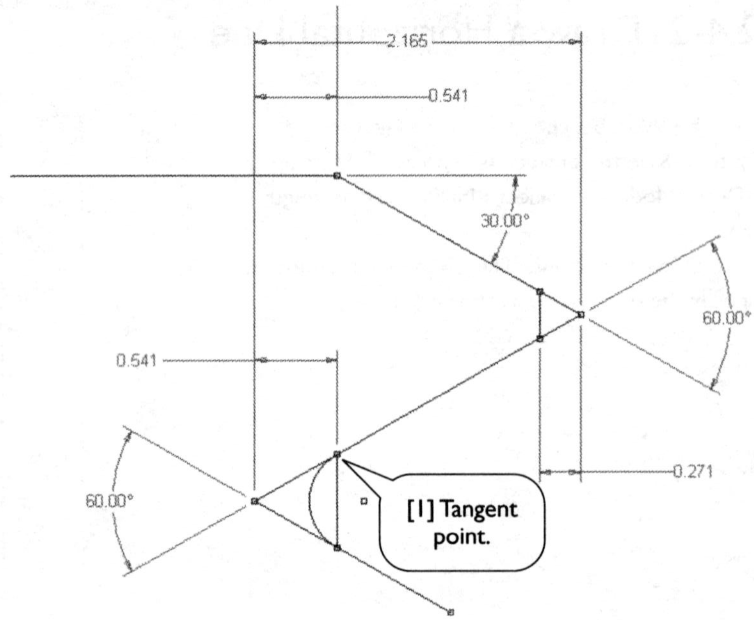

2.4-5 Trim Unwanted Segments

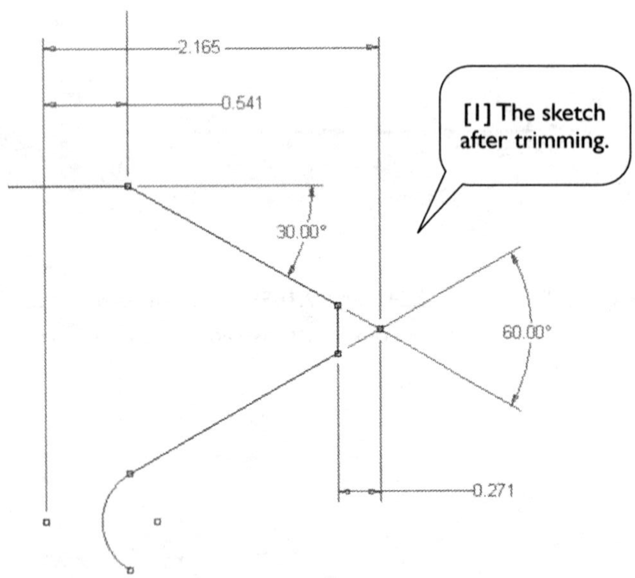

2.4-6 Replicate 10 Times

Select all segments except the horizontal one (totally 4 segments), and replicate 10 times. You may need to manually set the paste handle [1]. You may also need to use the tool <Selection Filter: Points> [2].

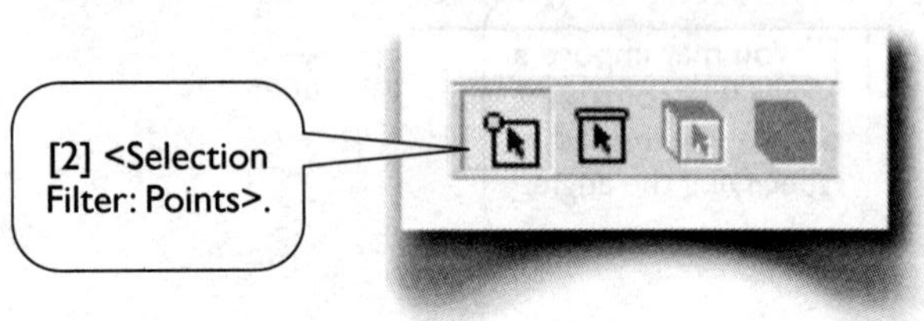

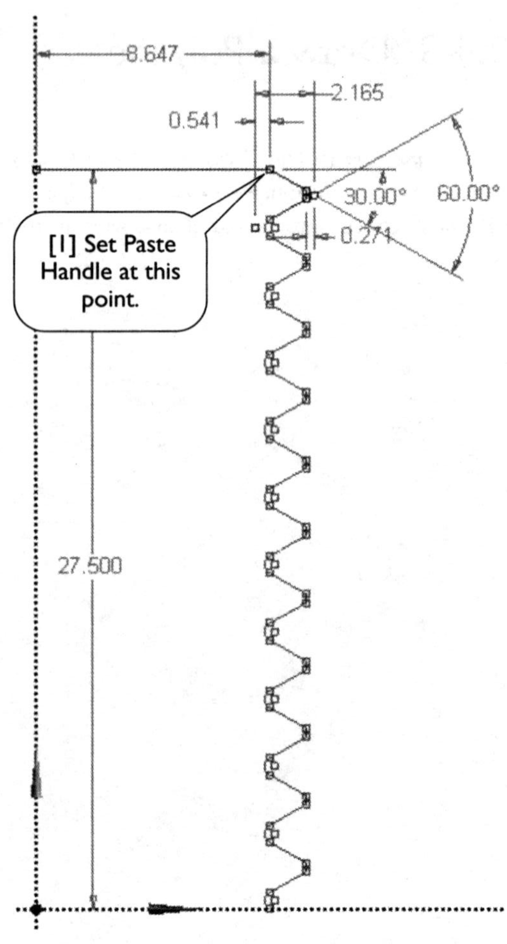

2.4-7 Complete the Sketch

Follow the steps [1-5] to complete the sketch. Note that, in step [4], you don't need to worry about the length. After step [5], you can trim the vertical segment created in step [4].

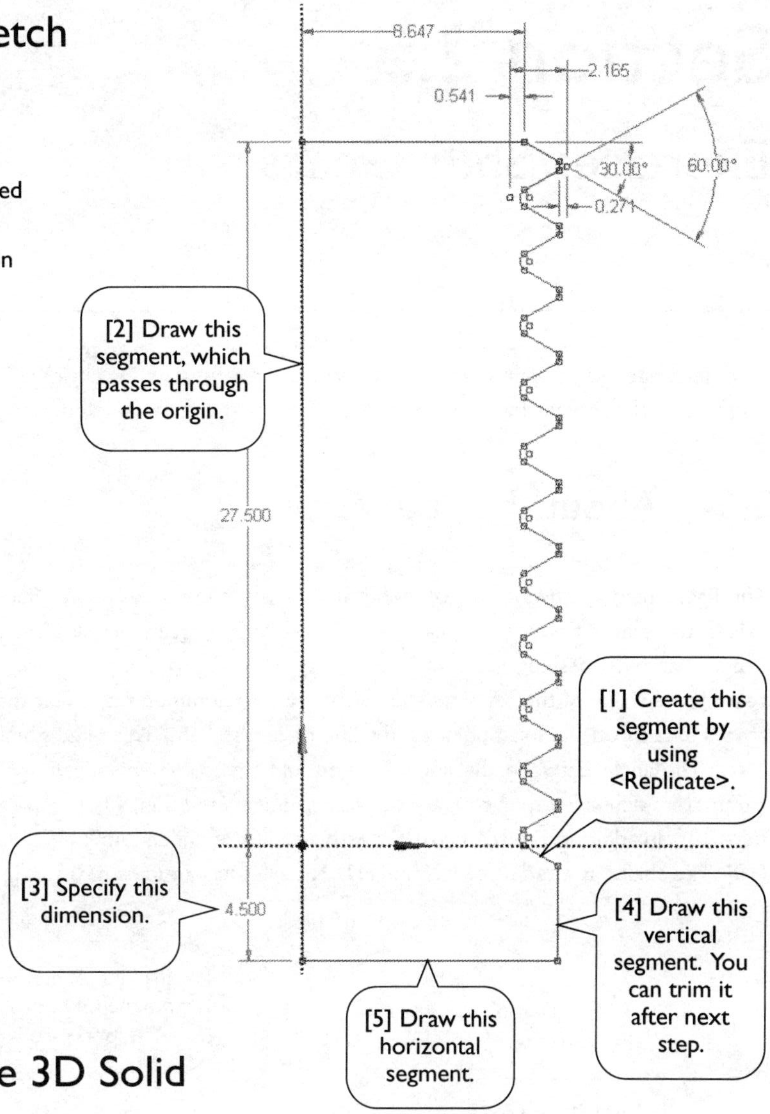

2.4-8 Revolve to Create 3D Solid

Revolve the sketch to generate a solid of revolution. Select the Y-axis as the axis of revolution.

Save the project and exit from the Workbench. We will resume this project again in Section 3.2.

References

1. Zahavi, E., *The Finite Element Method in Machine Design*, Prentice-Hall, 1992; Chapter 7. Threaded Fasteners.
2. Deutschman, A. D., Michels, W. J., and Wilson, C. E., *Machine Design: Theory and Practice*, Macmillan Publishing Co., Inc., 1975; Section 16-6. Standard Screw Threads.

Section 2.5

Exercise: Spur Gears

Geometric details of spur gears are important for a mechanical engineer. However, if you are not concerned about these geometric details for now, you may skip the first two subsections and jump directly to Subsection 2.5-3.

2.5-1 About the Spur Gears

The figure below shows a pair of identical spur gears in mesh [1-12]. Spur gears have their teeth cut parallel to the axis of the shaft on which the gears are mounted. Spur gears are used to transmit power between parallel shafts. In order that two meshing gears maintain a constant angular velocity ratio, they must satisfy the fundamental law of gearing: the shape of the teeth must be such that the common normal at the point of contact between two teeth must always pass through a fixed point on the line of centers[1] [5]. This fixed point is called the *pitch point* [6].

The angle between the line of action and the common tangent [7] is known as the *pressure angle* [8]. The parameters defining a spur gear are its pitch radius (r_p = 2.5 in) [3], pressure angle (α = 20°) [8], and number of teeth (N = 20). In addition, the teeth are cut with a radius of addendum r_a = 2.75 in [9] and a radius of dedendum r_d = 2.2 in [10]. The shaft has a radius of 1.25 in [11]. The fillet has a radius of 0.1 in [12]. The thickness of the gear is 1.0 in.

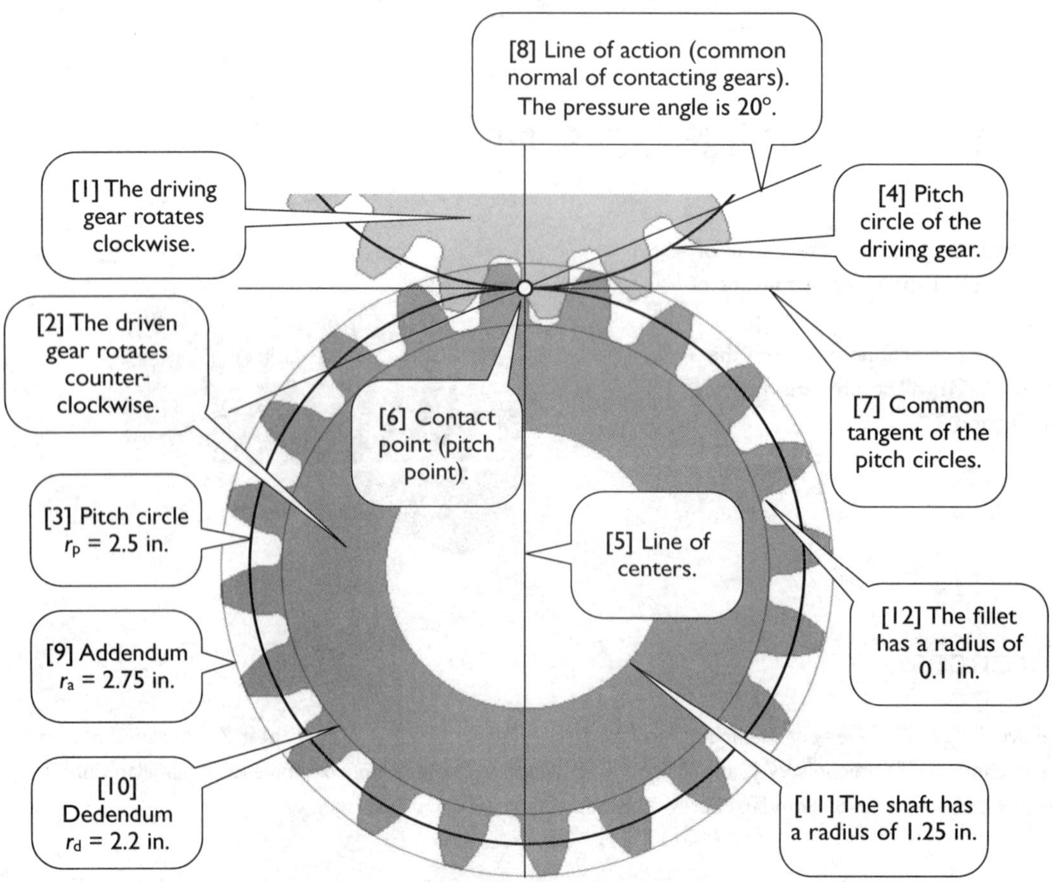

2.5-2 About Involute Curves

To satisfy the fundamental law of gearing, most of gear profiles are cut to an *involute curve* [1]. The involute curve may be constructed by wrapping a string around a cylinder, called the *base circle* [2], and then tracing the path of a point on the string.

Given the gear's pitch radius r_p and pressure angle α , we can calculated the coordinates of each point on the involute curve. For example, consider an arbitrary point *A* [3] on the involute curve; we want to calculate its polar coordinates (r,θ), as shown in the figure. Note that *BA* and *CP* are tangent lines of the base circle, and *F* is a foot of perpendicular.

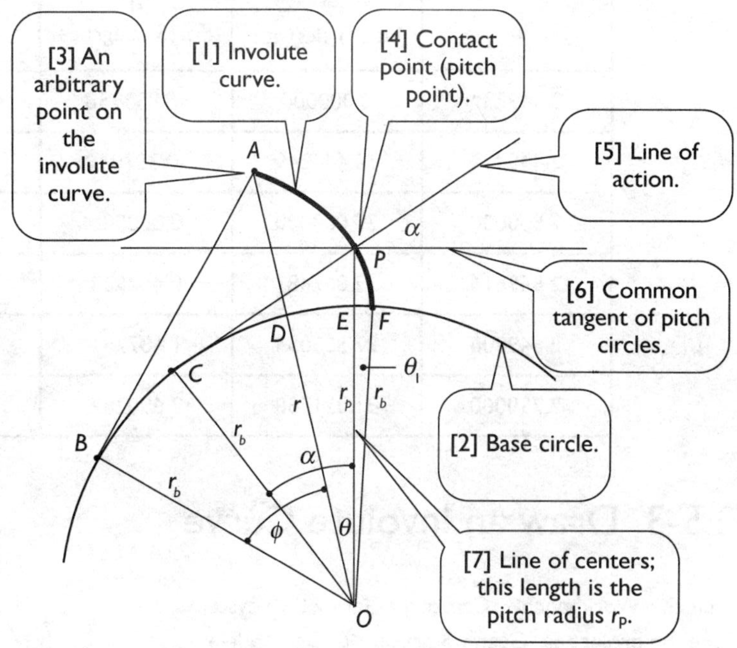

Since *APF* is an involute curve and $\overset{\frown}{BCDEF}$ is the base circle, by the definition of involute curve,

$$\overline{BA} = \overset{\frown}{BC} + \overline{CP} = \overset{\frown}{BCDEF} \qquad (1)$$

$$\overline{CP} = \overset{\frown}{CDEF} \qquad (2)$$

From ΔOCP,

$$r_b = r_p \cos\alpha \qquad (3)$$

From ΔOBA,

$$r = \frac{r_b}{\cos\phi} \qquad (4)$$

Or equivalently,

$$\phi = \cos^{-1}\frac{r_b}{r} \qquad (5)$$

To calculate θ, we notice that

$$\overset{\frown}{DE} = \overset{\frown}{BCDEF} - \overset{\frown}{BCD} - \overset{\frown}{EF}$$

Dividing the equation with r_b and using Eq. (1),

$$\frac{\overset{\frown}{DE}}{r_b} = \frac{\overline{BA}}{r_b} - \frac{\overset{\frown}{BCD}}{r_b} - \frac{\overset{\frown}{EF}}{r_b}$$

If radian is used, then the above equation can be written as

$$\theta = (\tan\phi) - \phi - \theta_1 \qquad (6)$$

The last term θ_1 is the angle $\angle EOF$, which can be calculated by dividing Eq. (2) with r_b,

$$\frac{\overline{CP}}{r_b} = \frac{\overset{\frown}{CDEF}}{r_b}, \text{ or } \tan\alpha = \alpha + \theta_1, \text{ or}$$

$$\theta_1 = (\tan\alpha) - \alpha \qquad (7)$$

Eqs. (3-7) are all we need to calculate polar coordinates (r,θ). The polar coordinates can be easily transformed to rectangular coordinates, using *O* as origin and *OP* as y-axis,

$$x = -r\sin\theta,\ \ y = r\cos\theta \qquad (8)$$

Numerical Calculations

In our case, the pitch radius $r_p = 2.5$ in, and pressure angle $\alpha = 20^\circ$; from Eqs. (2) and (7),

$$r_b = 2.5\cos 20^\circ = 2.349232 \text{ in}$$

$$\theta_1 = \tan 20^\circ - \frac{20^\circ}{180^\circ}\pi = 0.01490438$$

The calculated coordinates are listed in the table below. Notice that, in using Eqs. (6) and (7), radian is used as the unit of angles; in the table below, however, we translated the unit to degrees.

r in.	ϕ Eq. (4), degrees	θ Eq. (5), degrees	x	y
2.349232	0.000000	-0.853958	-0.03501	2.34897
2.449424	16.444249	-0.387049	-0.01655	2.44937
2.500000	20.000000	0.000000	0.00000	2.50000
2.549616	22.867481	0.442933	0.01971	2.54954
2.649808	27.555054	1.487291	0.06878	2.64892
2.750000	31.321258	2.690287	0.12908	2.74697

2.5-3 Draw an Involute Curve

Launch <Workbench>. Create a <Geometry> system. Save the project as "Gear." Start up <DesignModeler>. Select <Inch> as length unit. Start to draw sketch on the XYPlane.

Draw six <Construction Points> and specify dimensions as shown (the vertical dimensions are measured down to the X-axis). Note that the dimension values display three digits after decimal point, but we actually typed with five digits (refer to the above table). Impose a <Coincident> constraint on the Y-axis for the point which has a Y-coordinate of 2.500.

Connect these six points using <Spline> tool, keeping <Flexible> option on, and close the spline with <Open End>. Note that you could draw <Spline> directly without creating <Construction Points> first, but that would be not so easy.

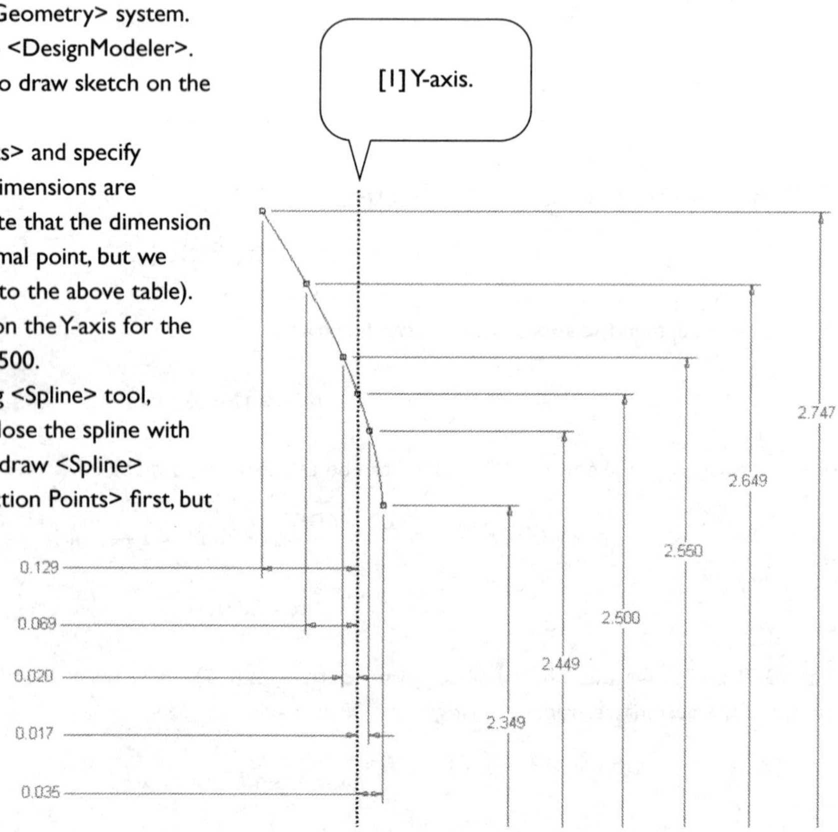

2.5-4 Draw Circles

Draw three circles [1-3]. Let the addendum circle "snap" to the outermost construction point [3]. Specify radii for the circle of shaft (1.25 in) and the dedendum circle (2.2 in).

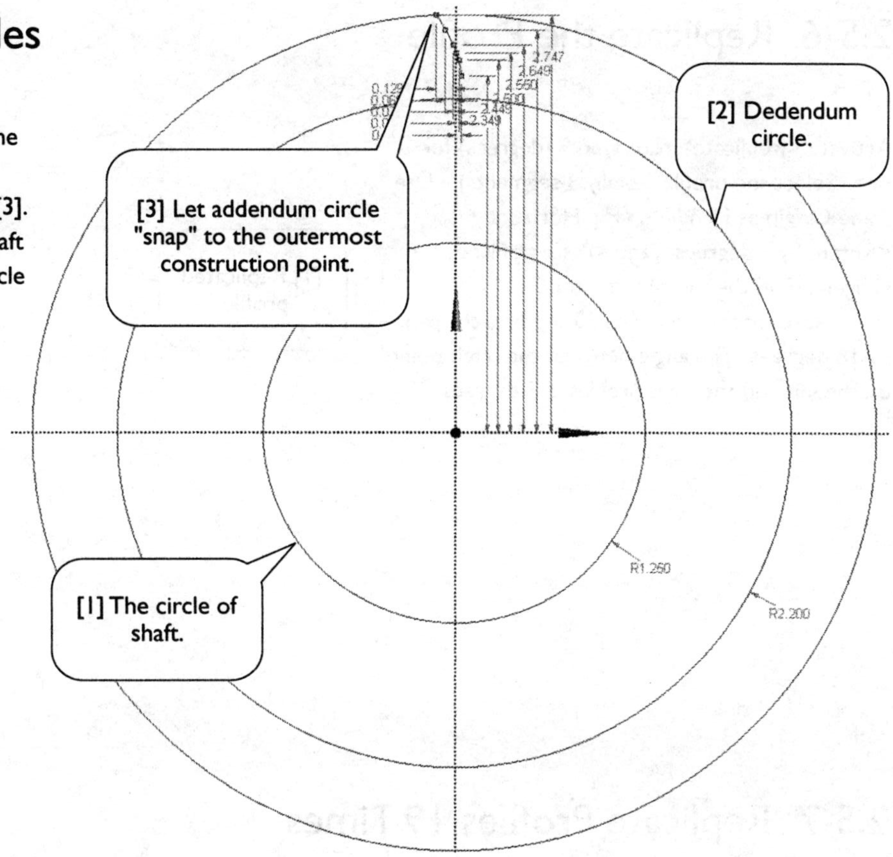

2.5-5 Complete the Profile

Draw a line starting from the lowest construction point, and make it perpendicular to the dedendum circle [1-2]. Note that, when drawing the line, avoid a <V> auto-constraint.

Draw a fillet [3] of radius 0.1 in to complete the profile of a tooth.

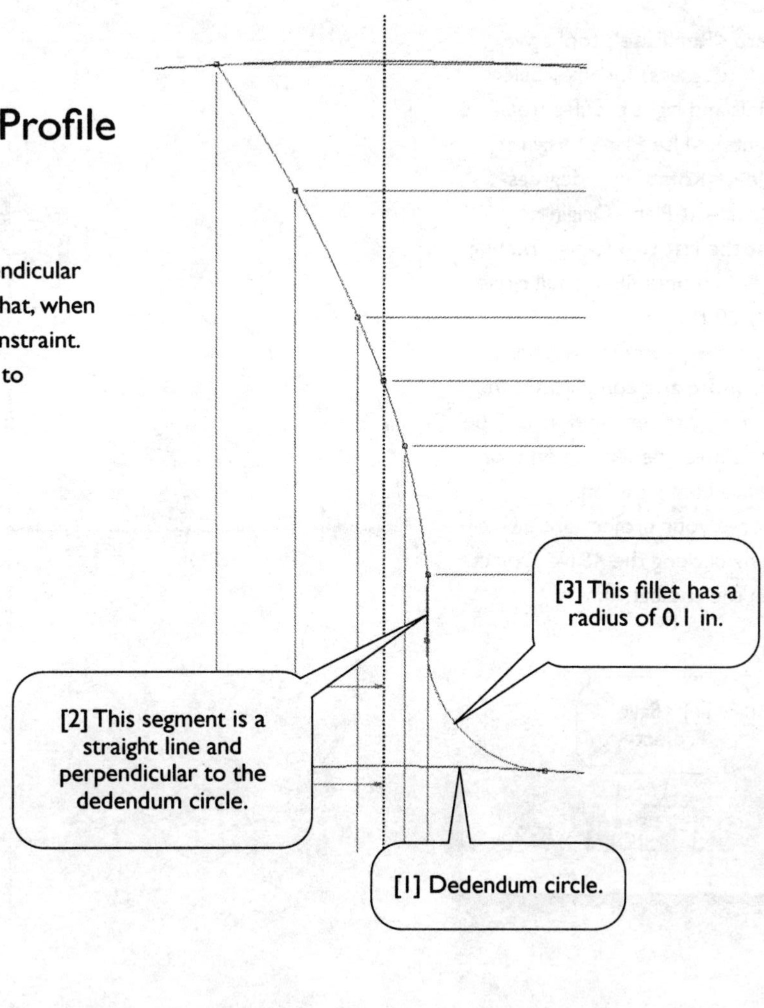

2.5-6 Replicate the Profile

Activate <Replicate> tool, type 9 (degrees) for <r>. Select the profile (totally 3 segments), <Use Plane Origin as Handle>, <Flip Horizontal>, <Rotate by r degrees>, and <Paste at Plane Origin>. End the <Replicate> tool.

Note that the gear has 20 teeth, each spans by 18 degrees. The angle between the pitch points on the left and the right profiles is 9 degrees.

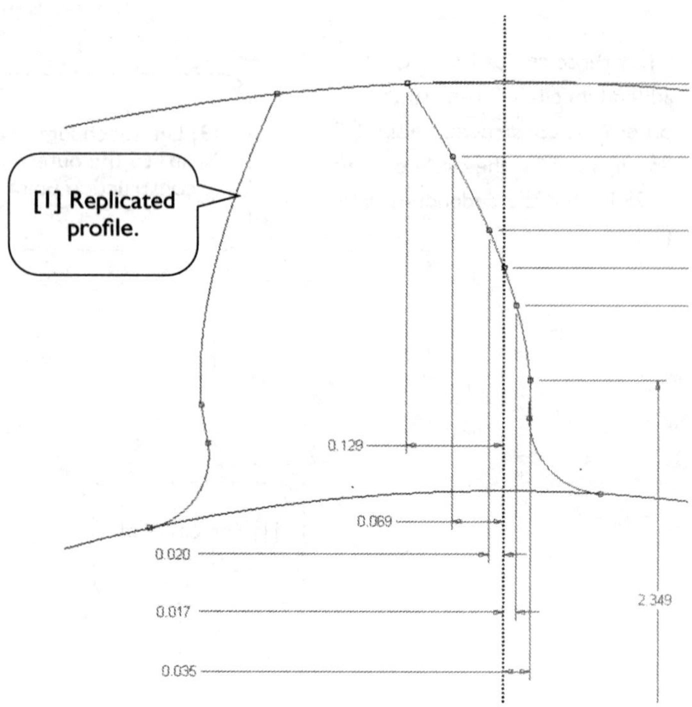

2.5-7 Replicate Profiles 19 Times

Activate <Replicate> tool again, type 18 (degrees) for <r>. Select both left and right profiles (totally 6 segments), <Use Plane Origin as Handle>, <Rotate by r degrees>, and <Paste at Plane Origin>. Repeat the last two steps (rotating and pasting) until fill-in a full circle (totally 20 teeth).

As the geometric entities is getting more and complicated, the computer's processing time may be getting slower, depending on your hardware configuration.

Save your project once a while by clicking the <Save Project> tool in the toolbar.

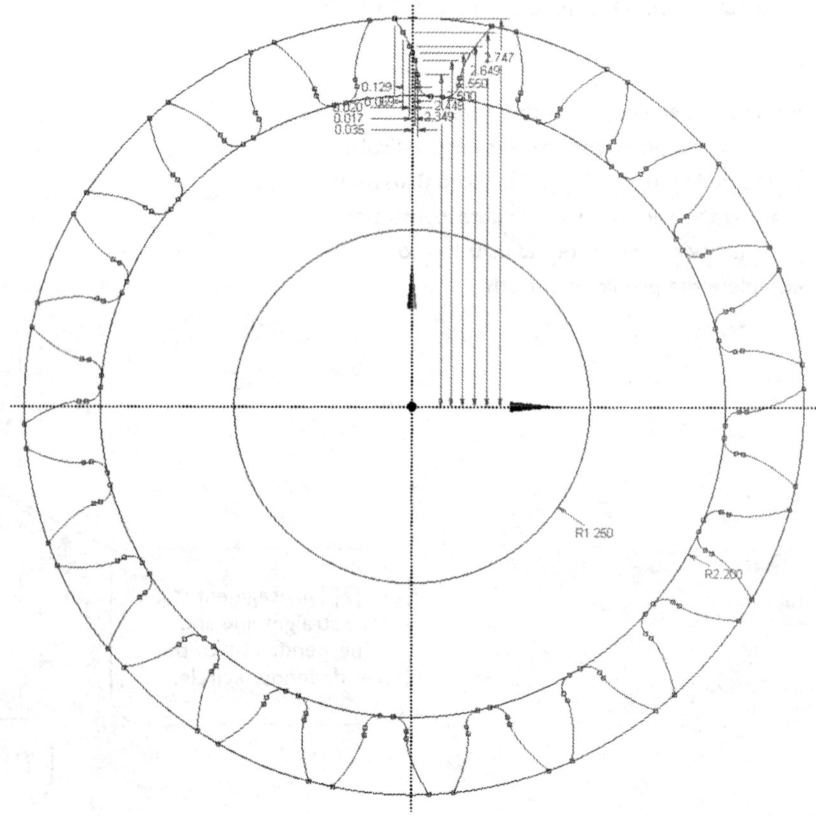

2.5-8 Trim Away Unwanted Segments

Trim away unwanted portion on the addendum circle and the dedendum circle.

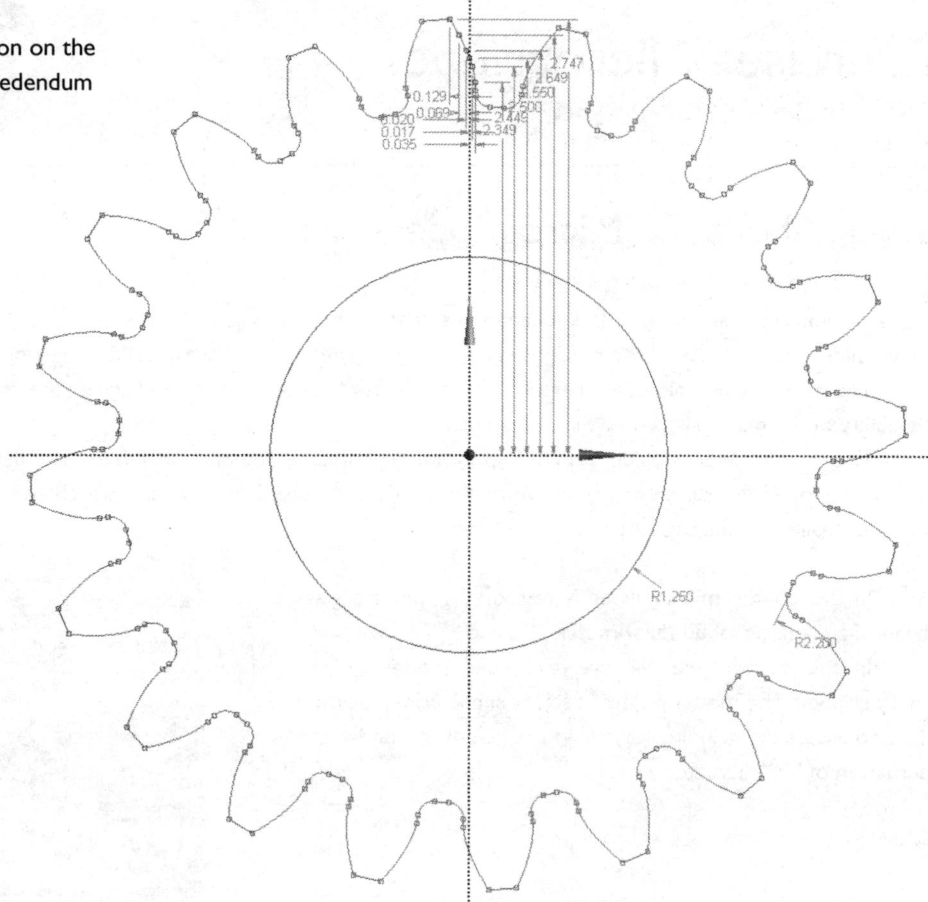

2.5-9 Extrude to Create 3D Solid

Extrude the sketch 1.0 inch to create a 3D solid as shown. Save the project and exit from <Workbench>. We will resume this project again in Section 3.4.

References

1. Deutschman, A. D., Michels, W. J., and Wilson, C. E., *Machine Design: Theory and Practice*, Macmillan Publishing Co., Inc., 1975; Chapter 10. Spur Gears.
2. Zahavi, E., *The Finite Element Method in Machine Design*, Prentice-Hall, 1992; Chapter 9. Spur Gears.

Section 2.6

Exercise: Microgripper

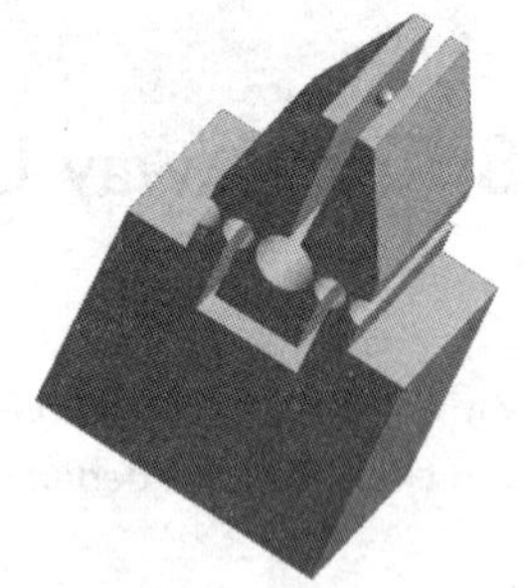

2.6-1 About the Microgripper

Many manipulators are designed as mechanisms, that is, they consist of bodies connected by joints, such as revolute joints, sliding joints, etc., and the motions are mostly governed by the laws of rigid body kinematics.

The microgripper discussed here [1-2] is a structure rather than a mechanism; the mobility are provided by the flexibility of the materials, rather than the joints.

The microgripper is made of PDMS (polydimethylsiloxane, see Section 1.1-1). The device is actuated by a shape memory alloy (SMA) actuator [3], of which the motion is caused by temperature change, and the temperature is in turn controlled by electric current.

In the lab, the microgripper is tested by gripping a glass bead of a diameter of 30 micrometer [4].

In this section, we will create a solid model for the microgripper. The model will be used for simulation in Section 13.3 to assess the gripping forces on the glass bead under the actuation of SMA actuator.

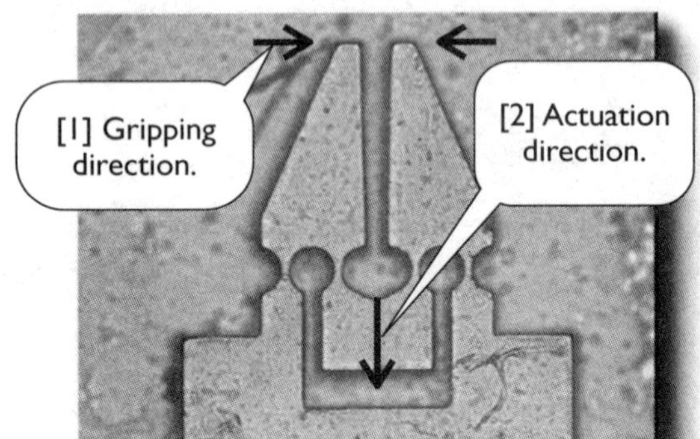

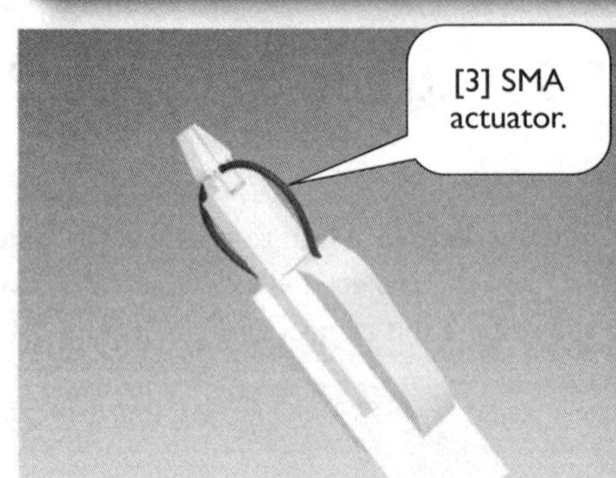

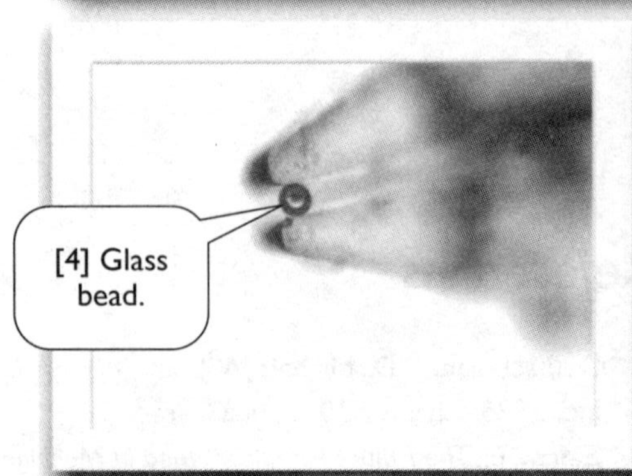

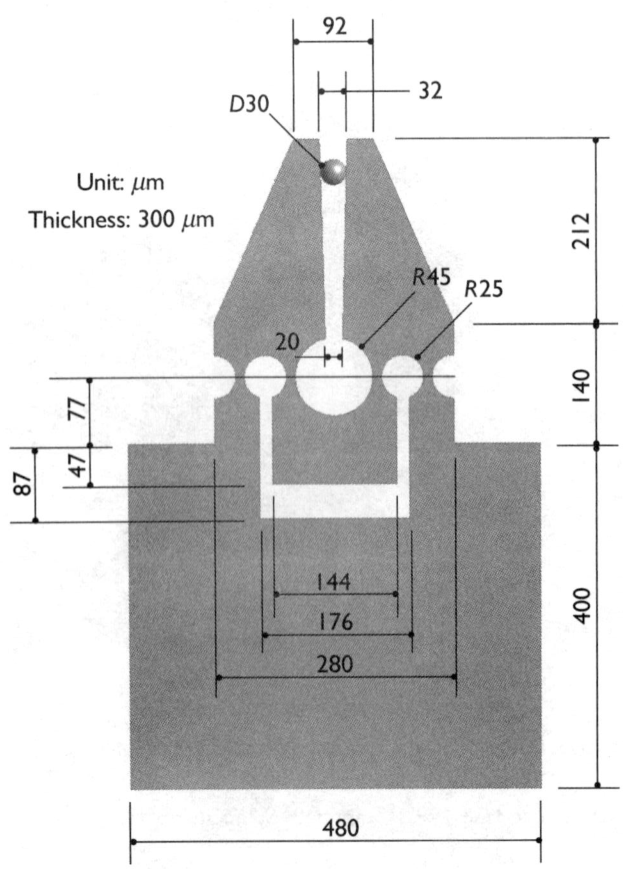

2.6-2 Create Half of the Model

Launch <Workbench>. Create a <Geometry> system. Save the project as "Microgripper." Start up <DesignModeler>. Select <Micrometer> as length unit. Start to draw sketch on the XYPlane.

Draw the sketch as shown on the right side [1]. Note that two of the three circles have equal radii. Trim away unwanted segments as shown below [2]. Note that we drew half of the model, due to the symmetry. Extrude the sketch 150 microns both sides of the plane symmetrically (total depth is 300 microns) [3]. Now we have half of the gripper [4].

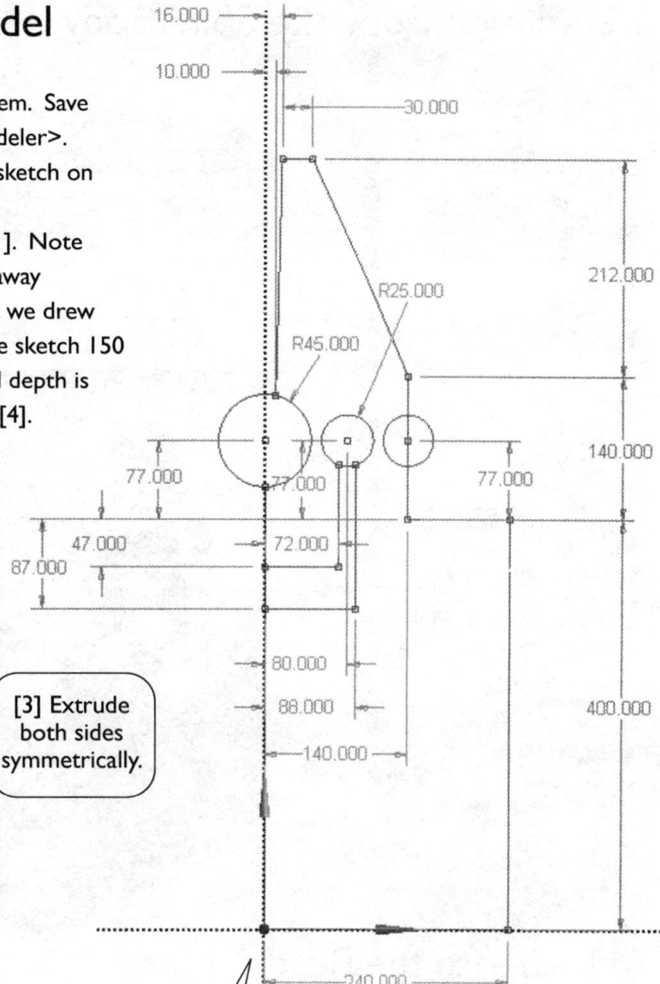

[1] Before trimming.

Details View

Details of Extrude1	
Extrude	Extrude1
Base Object	Sketch1
Operation	Add Material
Direction Vector	None (Normal)
Direction	Both - Symmetric
Extent Type	Fixed
FD1, Depth (>0)	150 μm
As Thin/Surface?	No
Merge Topology?	Yes

[3] Extrude both sides symmetrically.

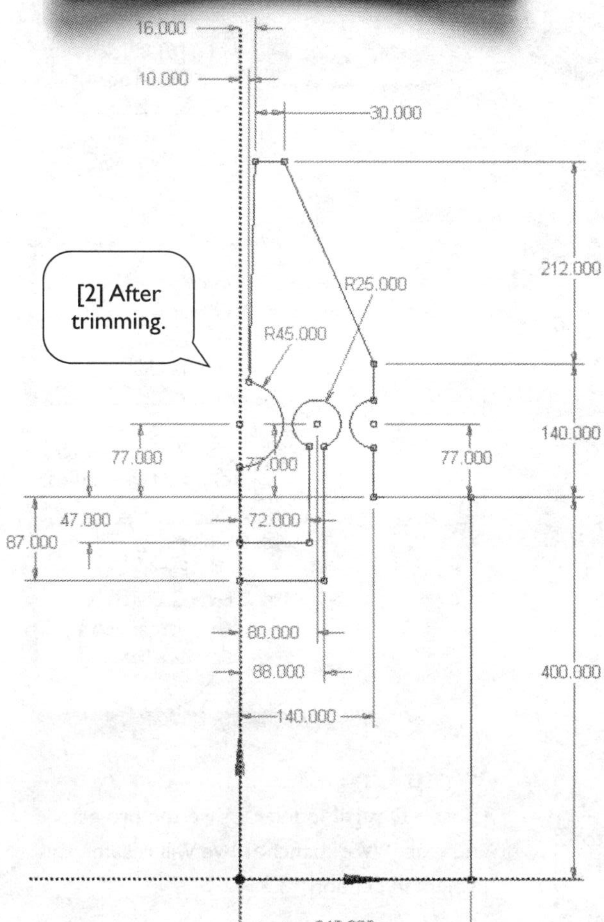

[2] After trimming.

[4] Half of the gripper.

2.6-2 Mirror Copy the Solid Body

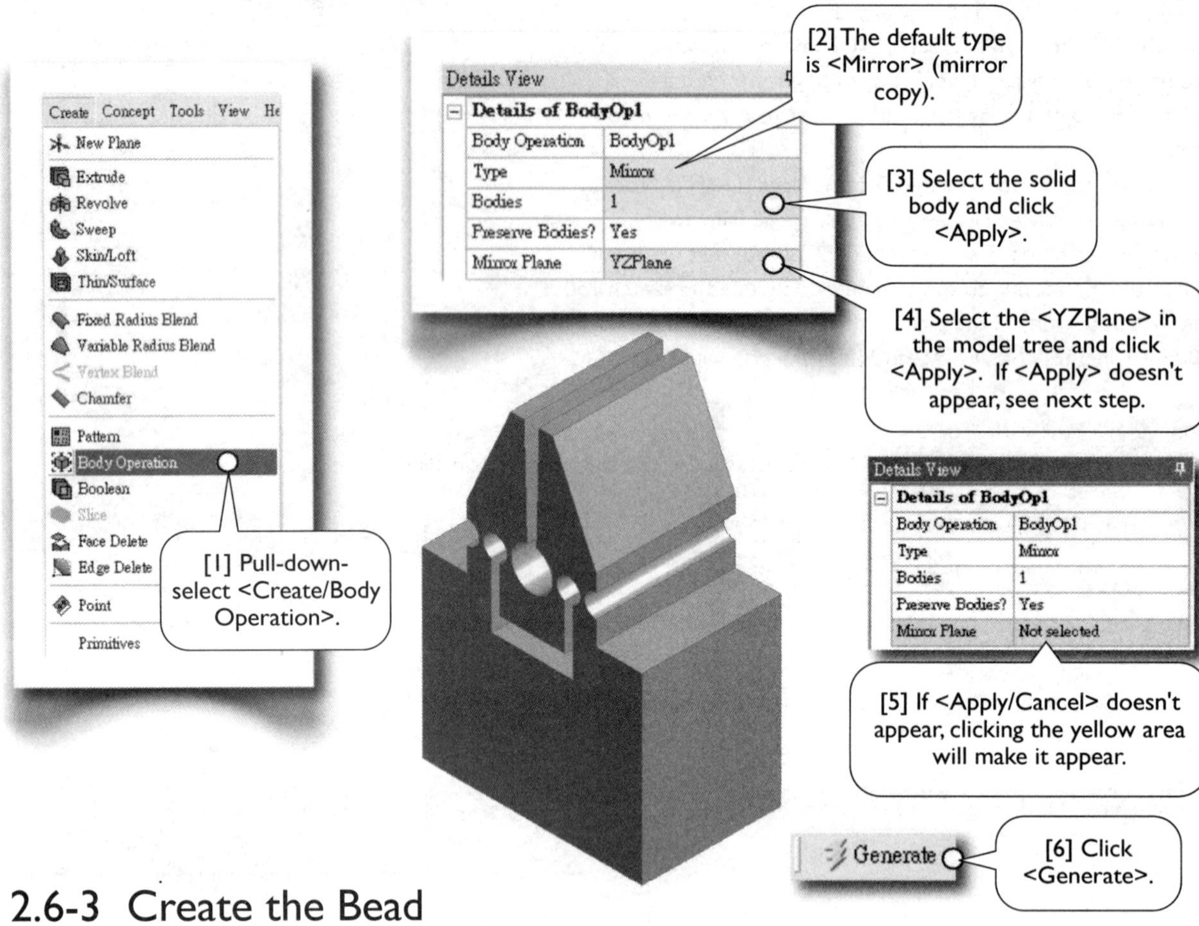

2.6-3 Create the Bead

Create a new sketch on XYPlane and draw a semicircle as shown [1-4]. Revolve the sketch 360 degrees to create the glass bead. Note that the two bodies are treated as two parts. Rename two bodies [5].

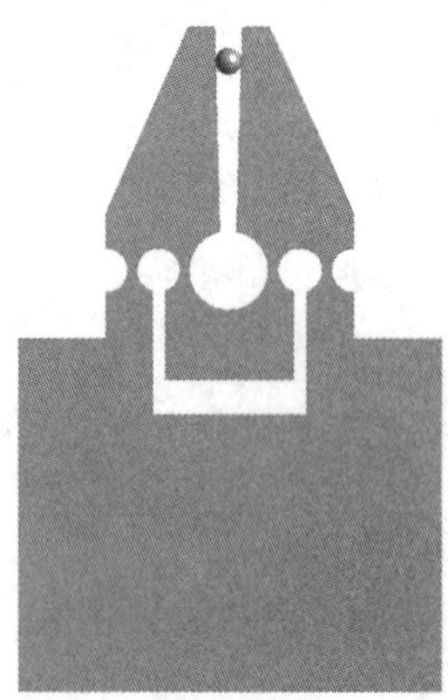

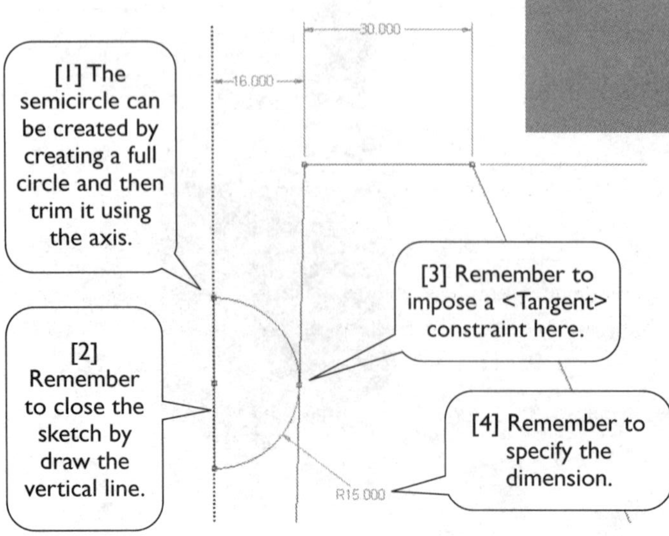

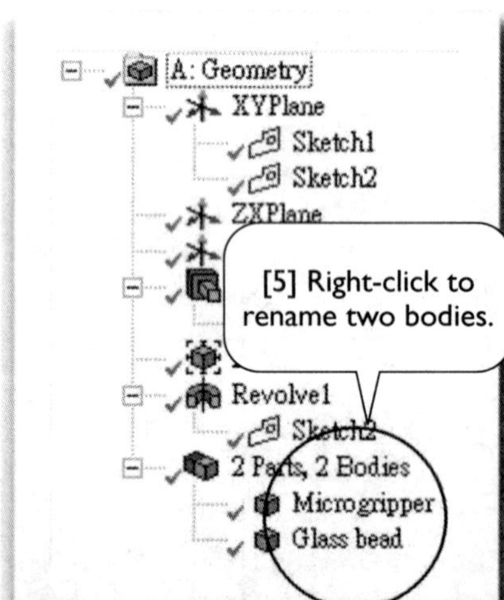

Wrap Up

Close <DesignModeler>, save the project and exit <Workbench>. We will resume this project in Section 13.3.

Section 2.7
Problems

2.7-1 Key Concepts

Sketching Mode
An environment under DesignModeler, configured for drawing sketches on planes.

Modeling Mode
An environment under DesignModeler, configured for creating 3D or 2D bodies.

Sketching Plane
The plane on which a sketch is created. Each sketch must be associated with a plane; each plane may have multiple sketches on it. Usage of planes is not limited for storing sketches.

Edge
In <Sketching Mode>, an edges may be a (straight) line or a curve. A curve may be a circle, ellipse, arc, or spline.

Sketch
A sketch consists of points and edges. Dimensions and constraints may be imposed on these entities.

Model Tree
A model tree is the structured representation of a geometry and displayed on the <Tree Outline> in DesignModeler. A model tree consists of planes, features, and a part branch, in which their order is important. The parts are the only objects exported to <Mechanical>.

Branch
A branch is an object of a model tree and consists one or more objects under itself.

Object
A leaf or branch of a model tree is called an object.

Context Menu
The menu that pops up when you right-click your mouse. The contents of the menu depend on what you click.

Auto Constraints
While drawing in <Sketching Mode>, by default, DesignModeler attempts to detect the user's intentions and try to automatically impose constraints on points or edges. Detection is performed over entities on the active plane, not just active sketch. <Auto Constraints> can be switched on/off in the <Constraints> toolbox.

Selection Filter

A selection filter filters one type of geometric entities. When a selection filter is turned on/off, the corresponding type of entities become selectable/unselectable. In <Sketching> Mode, there are two selection filters which corresponding to points and edges respectively. Along with these two filters, face and body selection filters are available in <Modeling Mode>.

Paste Handle

A reference point used in a copy/paste operation. The point is defined during copying and will be aligned at a specified location when pasting.

Constraint Status

In <Sketching> mode, entities are color coded to indicate their constrain status: greenish-blue for under-constrained; blue and black for well constrained (i.e., fixed in the space); red for over-constrained; gray for inconsistent.

2.7-2 Workbench Exercises

Create the Triangular Plate with Your Own Way

After so many exercises, you should be able to figure out an alternative way of creating the geometric model for the triangular plate (Section 2.2) on your own. Can you figure out a more efficient way?

Chapter 3
2D Simulations

In the real-world, everything is 3D. There are no such things as 2D bodies. Some problems, however, can be simplified and simulated in a 2D space. As an example, for an axisymmetric body subject to axisymmetric loads, all the particles with the same radial and axial coordinates (*R* and *Z*) share the same behaviors regardless of their tangential coordinate (θ). Thus, we can eliminate the tangential coordinate and reduce the problem to a 2D problem. Other 2D cases include plane stress problems and plane strain problems; we will define these terms in Section 3.3, after two sections of step-by-step exercises.

Reducing a problem to 2D has many advantages over the original problem, and you should always do it whenever possible. These advantages include (a) simpler to build geometry, (b) better mesh quality, (c) less computing time, (d) easier display and analysis of the results, (e) more accurate solution if no other assumptions introduced. In short, the simulation model becomes smaller and easier to handle.

Purpose of the Chapter

Since 2D simulations are usually easier to handle than 3D simulations, we will kick-off the simulations by conducting some 2D static structural simulations in this chapter, using the mechanical parts that we created in Chapter 2. Besides exercising 2D simulations, the chapter also serves as a stepping stone toward the 3D simulations. Most of the techniques and concepts in this chapter can be extended to 3D simulations, starting from Chapter 5.

About Each Section

Each of the first two sections guides the students to perform a 2D simulation in a step-by-step approach. Section 3 looks into more details and tries to complement what we are not able to cover in the first two sections. Sections 4 and 5 provide two additional exercises. Problems in Sections 2 and 4 involve contacts nonlinearities, which will not be discussed in-depth in the respective sections. One of the purposes is to raise your curiosity and build motivation of learning nonlinear simulations, which will be detailed in Chapters 13 and 14.

Section 3.1

Step-by-Step: Triangular Plate

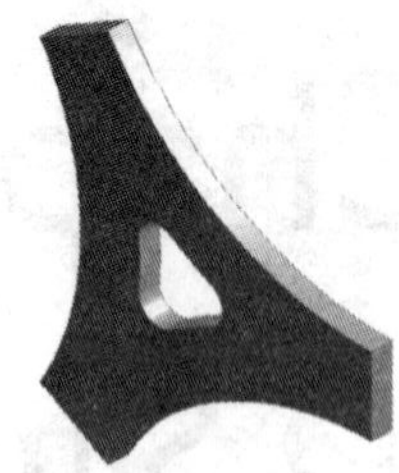

3.1-1 About the Triangular Plate

In this section, we want to use the triangular plate, introduced in Section 2.2, for a 2D static structural simulation. The plate is made of steel and designed to withstand tensile forces of 20,000 N on each of three side faces. The size of the side faces is 40x10 mm; so the applied tensile stress on the side faces is 50 MPa. We want to investigate the stresses in the plate.

We will model the problem as a 2D plane stress problem. The meaning of plane stress will be defined in Section 3.3-1. For now, all you need to know is that a thin plate subject to in-plane forces can be modeled as a plane stress problem.

There are two planes of symmetry in the model. In the first part of the section, we will analyze the full model and then, in the second part of the section, reanalyze the model by exploiting the symmetries.

3.1-2 Resume the Project "Triplate"

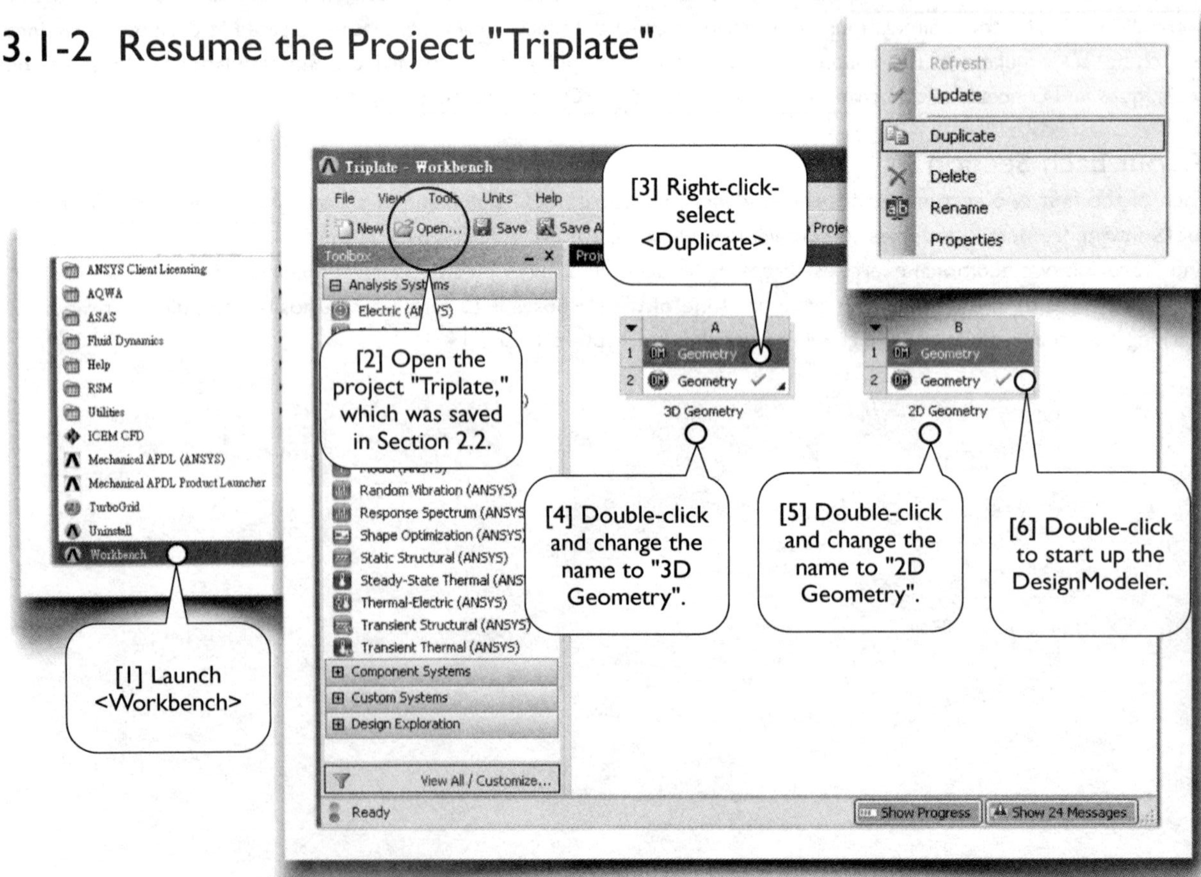

3.1-3 Delete the 3D Body and Create a 2D Body

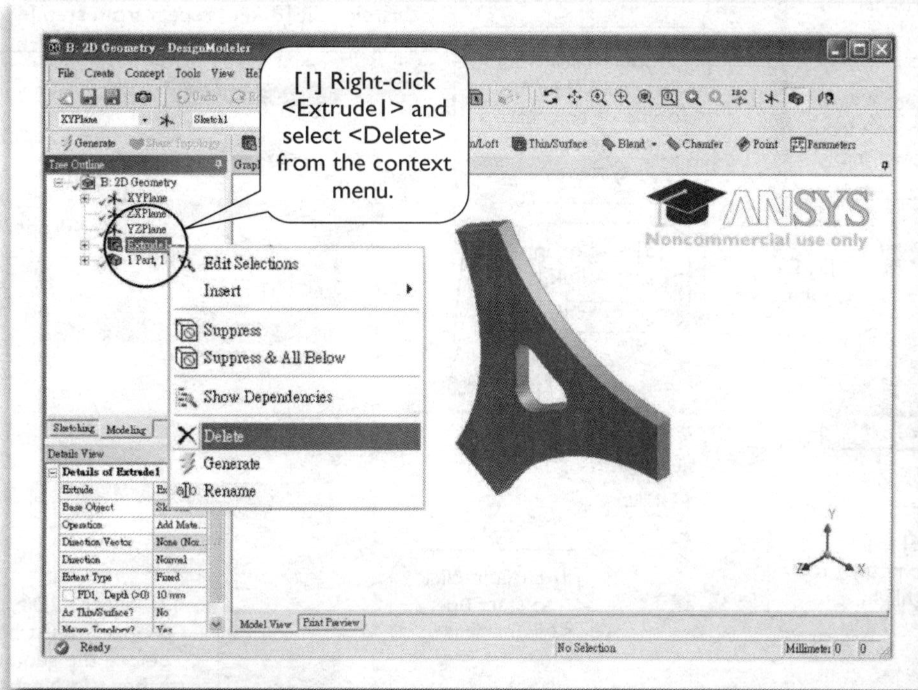

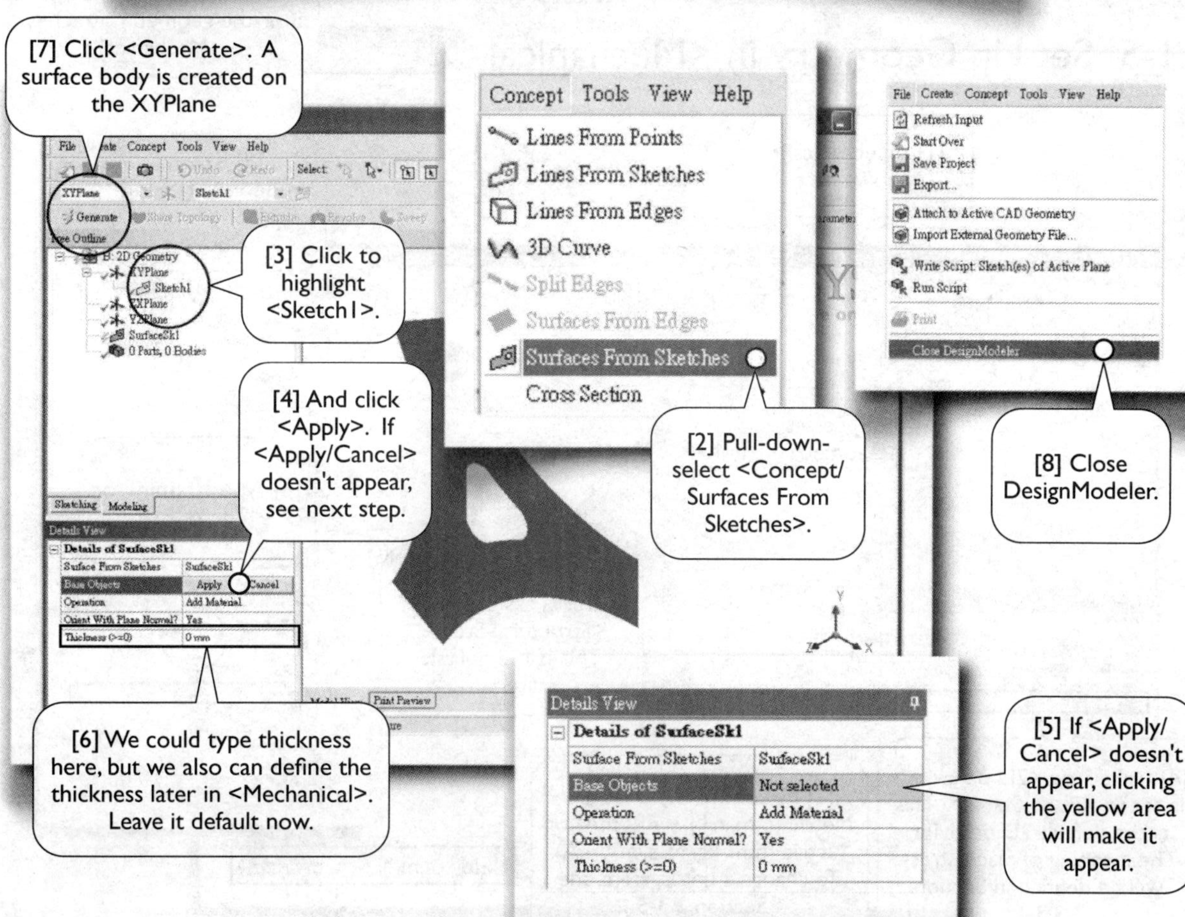

3.1-4 Create Analysis System and Specify <Analysis Type>

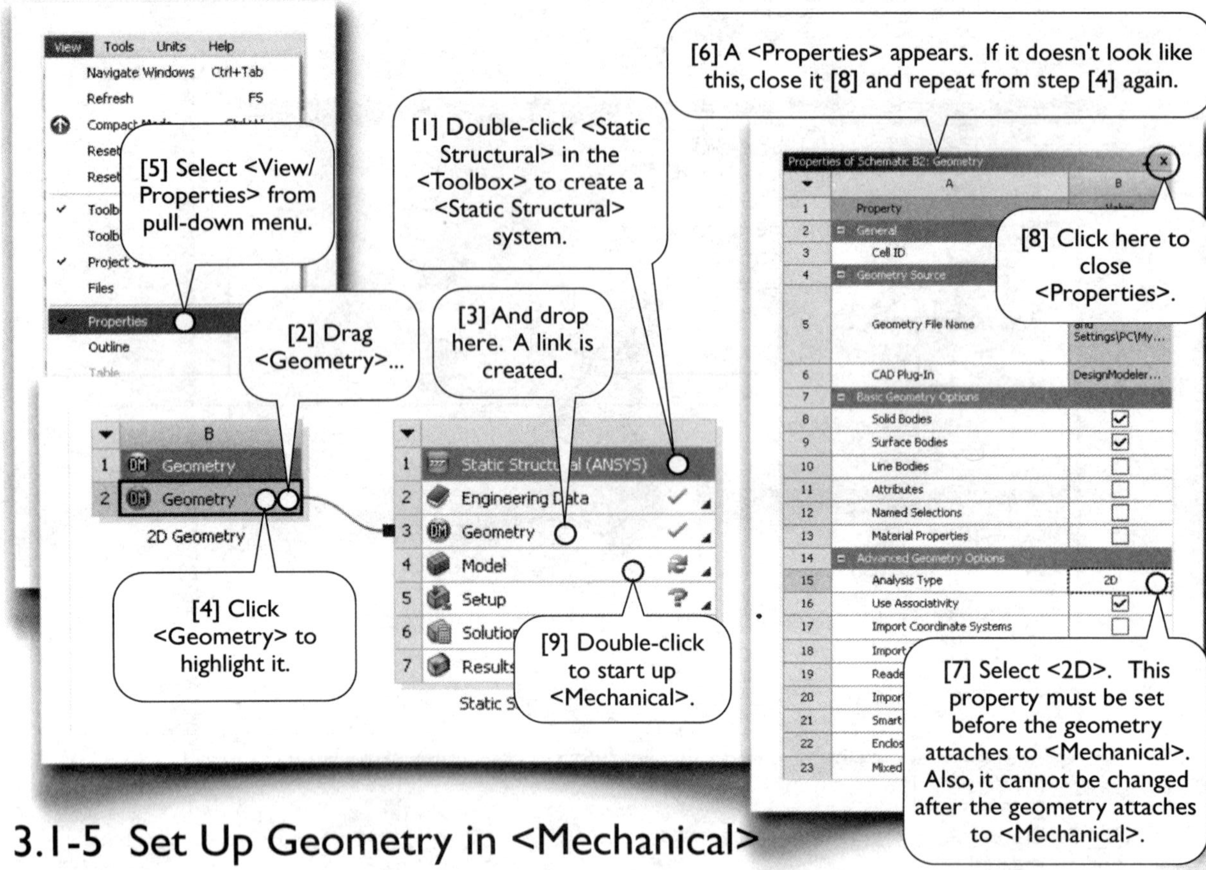

3.1-5 Set Up Geometry in <Mechanical>

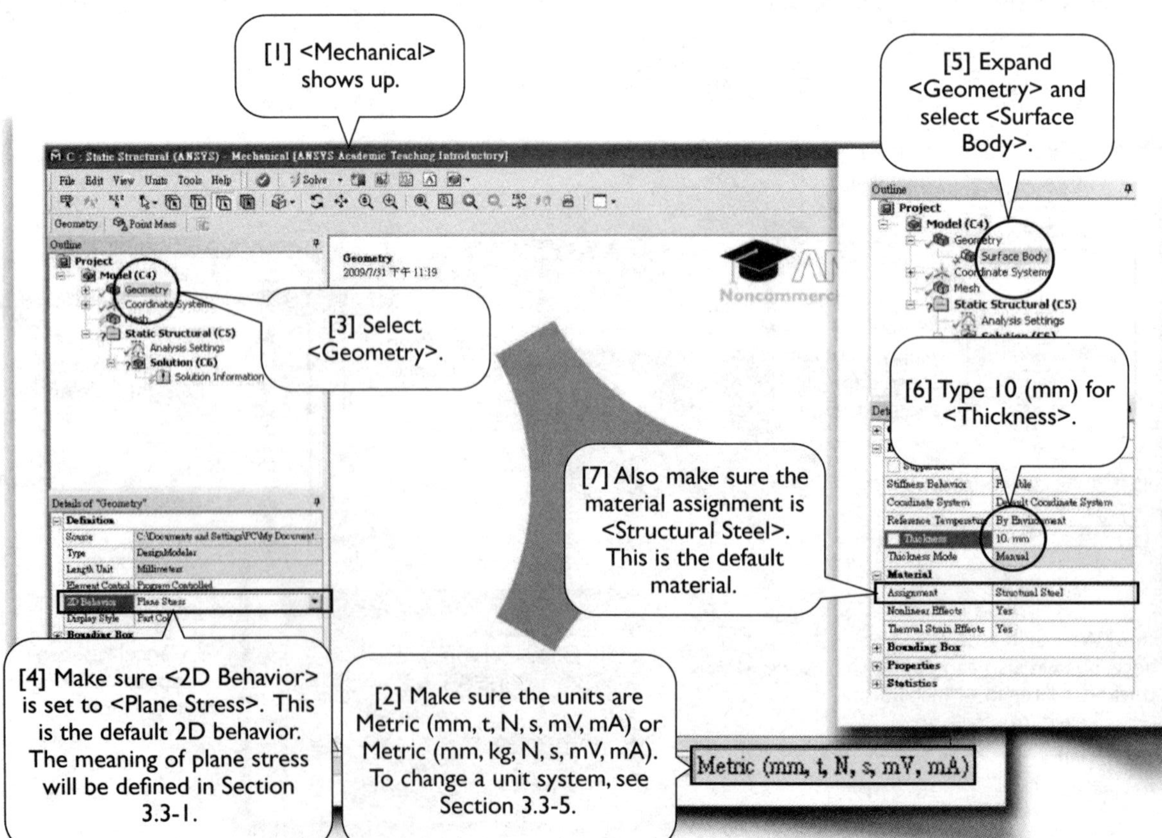

3.1-6 Generate Mesh

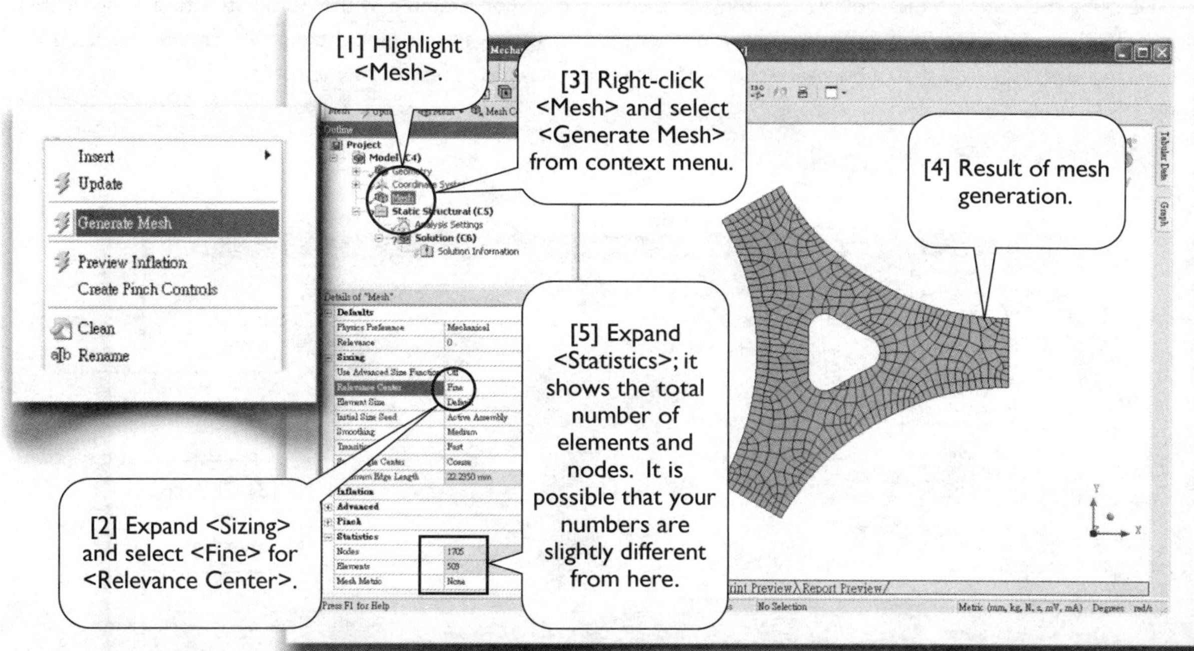

Generating a mesh before clicking <Solve> (3.1-8[1]) is not always necessary. When you issue a <Solve>, the Workbench automatically generates a mesh if it does not exist one. However it is a good practice to preview the mesh before clicking <Solve>. We usually generate mesh with default settings first, and then adjust mesh controls to improve the mesh, which will be discussed in Chapter 9.

3.1-7 Specify Loads

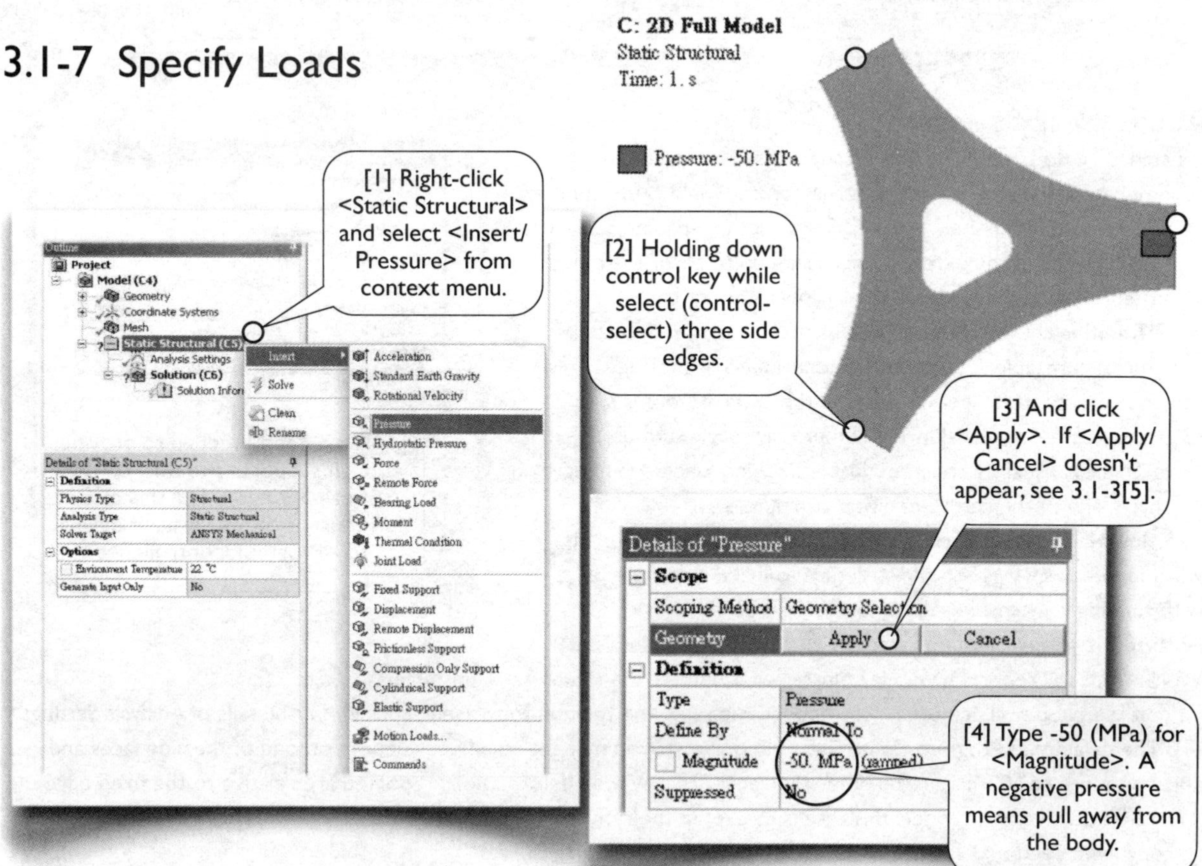

Use of context menus is instinctive: you select an object, right-click to open its context menu and choose a tool that operates on the object. Many frequently used tools can also be accessed from the toolbars. As you get familiar with the GUI, using the tools on the toolbars is often more convenient. For example, with <Static Structural> highlighted, pull-down-selecting <Loads/Pressure> also let you insert a <Pressure> in the model tree. When you work on the step-by-step exercises, you should be aware that there are many ways to access the same tool.

3.1-8 Solve the Model

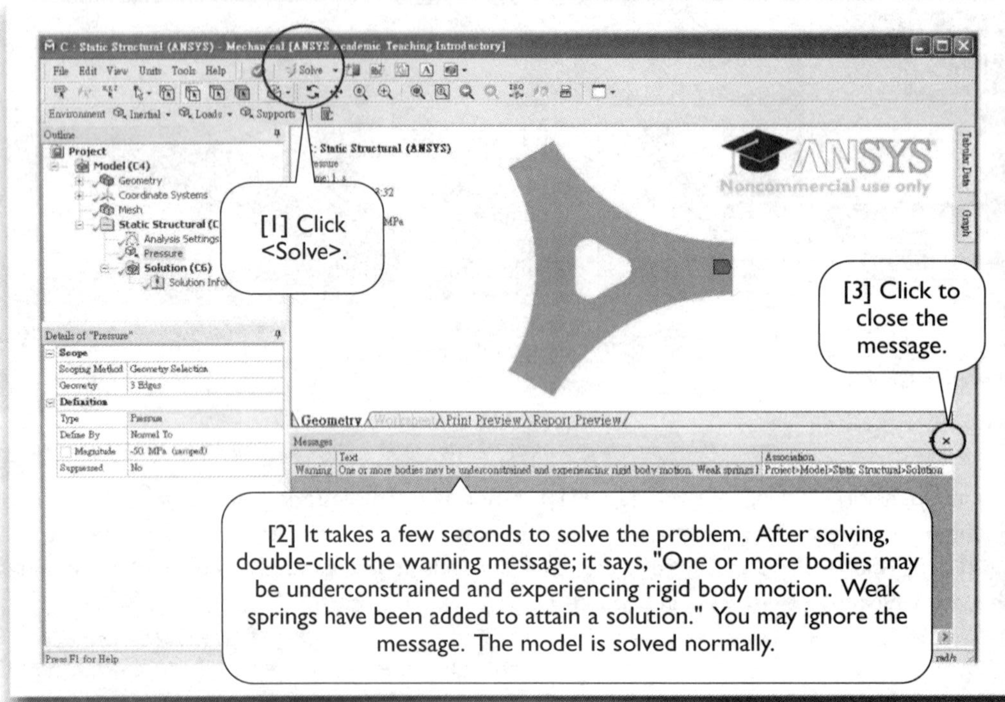

About Weak Springs

If a structure does not have enough supports, the structure become unstable: any non-zero external forces would cause the structure move indefinitely. An unstable structure still can achieve static equilibrium if the external forces sum up to zero; it is called an unstable equilibrium. This is what happens in our case.

Traditionally, whenever a finite element program detects a structure as unstable, it stops and reports an error message. This has been practiced for decades, even if the external forces sum up to zero, since the external forces numerically rarely sum up to zero. There is usually a small residual left behind when summing up; this is one of the nature of digital computers.

In ANSYS Workbench, if it detects an unstable structure, it will add "weak springs" on the structure to make it capable of withstanding very small external forces. It is called "weak" because the spring constants are very small and negligible. The Workbench still reports a warning message if it detects the structure as unstable.

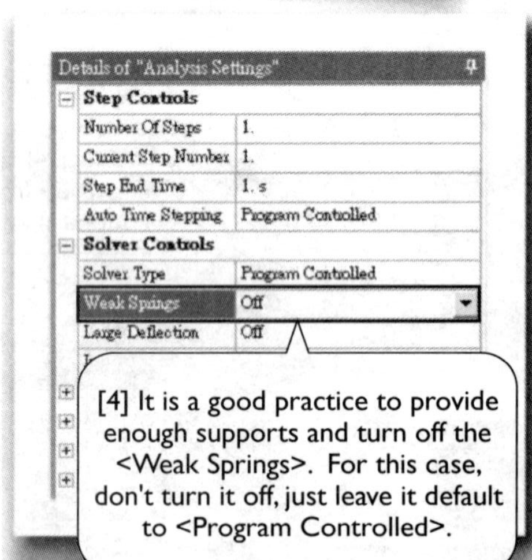

It is a good practice to provide enough supports and turn off the <Weak Spring> in <Details of Analysis Settings> [4]. The default is <Program Controlled>. In our case, you may set up a fixed support on one of the side faces and apply pressure of 50 MPa on the other two faces. That way, all deformations reported are relative to the fixed edge.

A better way is to model this case is to exploit the symmetries of the structure. We will present the procedure starting from Section 3.1-10.

3.1-9 View the Results

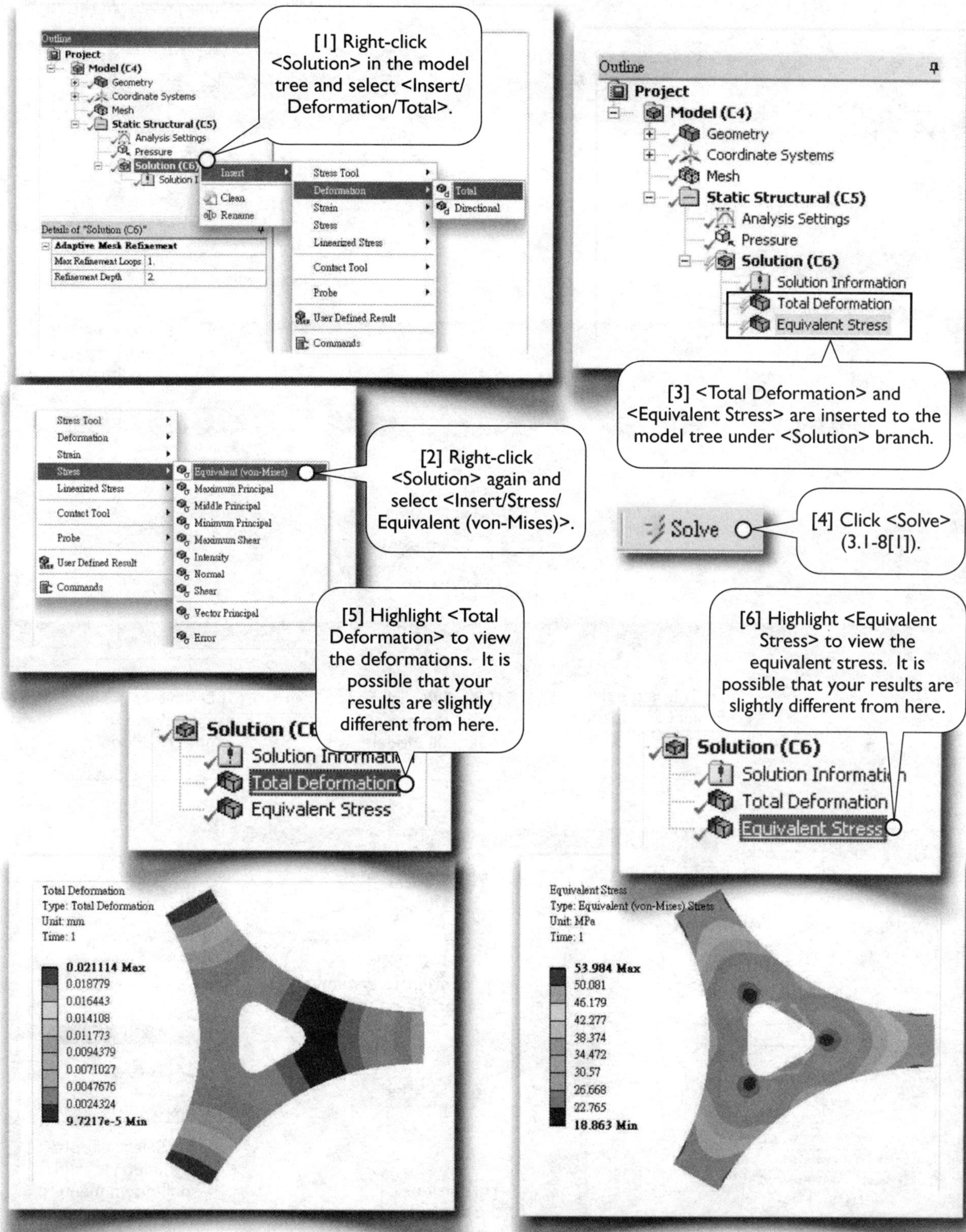

Symmetry of the Response

While the stress contour [6] is symmetric, you may wonder why the deformation contour [5] is not symmetric. The deformation should be symmetric. The numerical values are displacements relative to a certain point, which has been arbitrarily chosen to attach the weak springs. A way to avoid this kind of awkwardness is to exploit the symmetries.

3.1-10 Modify the Geometry

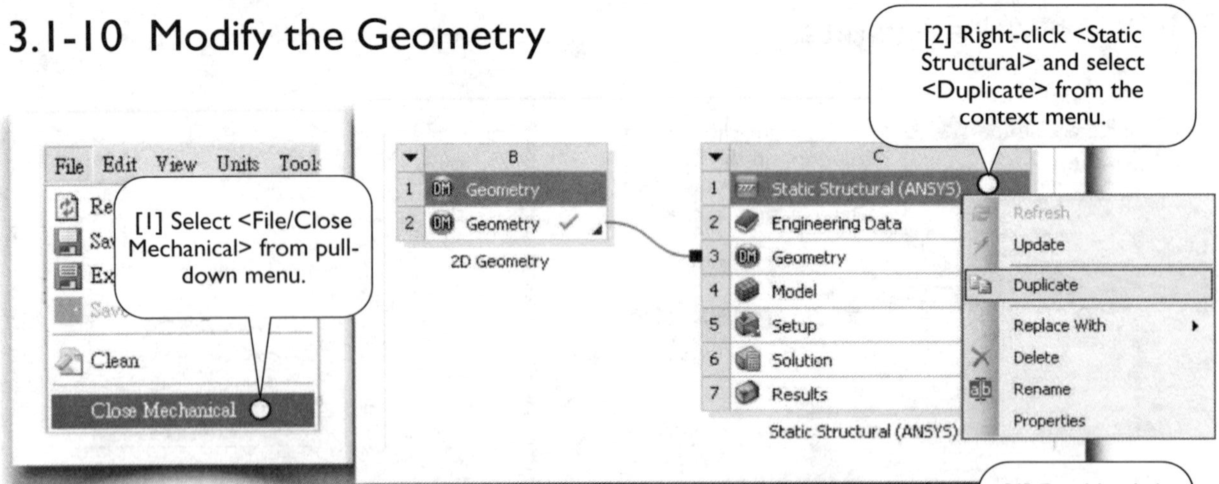

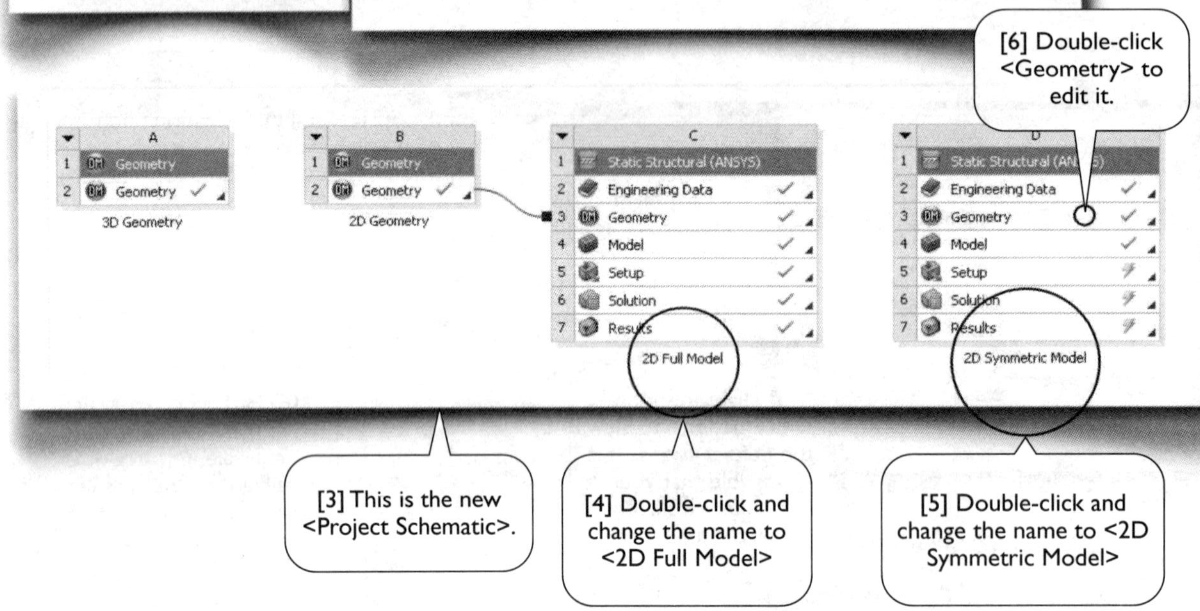

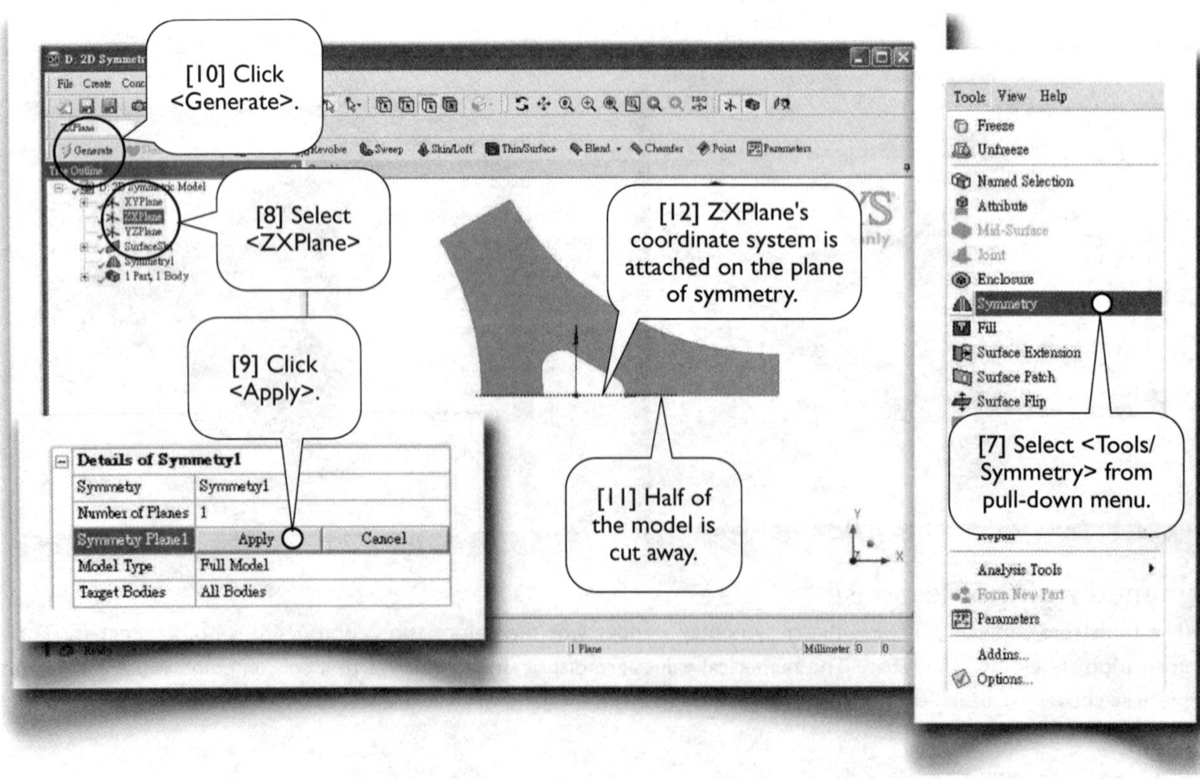

About Plane Coordinate System

There is a unique global coordinate system, the axes are shown in the bottom-right corner of the graphics area. Workbench uses R, G, B colors to represent X-, Y-, and Z-axis respectively: red arrow for X-axis, green arrow for Y-axis, and blue arrow for Z-axis. In this book, we use upper-case (X, Y, Z) for both global and local coordinate system, to be consistent with the notations used in the Workbench.

Each plane has its own local coordinate system, using the same color codes. Take ZXPlane as an example [12]. The local XY-plane coincides with global ZX-plane, and the local Z-axis points upward. When we specify a plane as the plane of symmetry, the plane's XY-plane is used by the Workbench to cut away the portion of the model which is on the plane's negative-Z side. The portion of the model on the plane's positive-Z side is reserved [12].

The triangular plate has another plane of symmetry. It is not any one of the default planes. We need to create one. The plane of symmetry can be derived from rotating ZXPlane by 60 degrees.

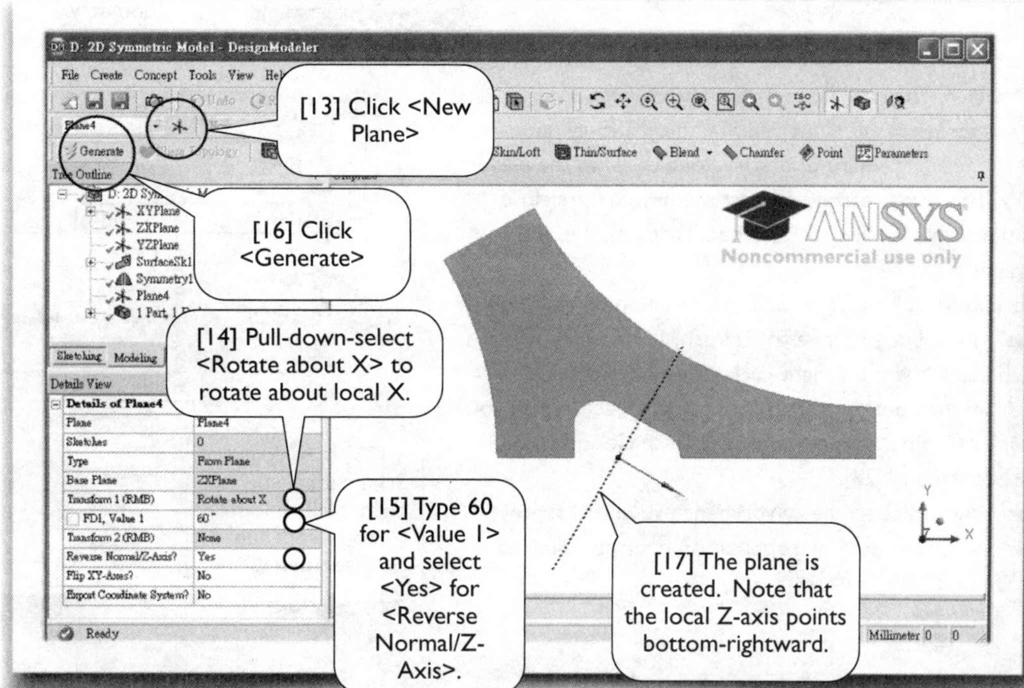

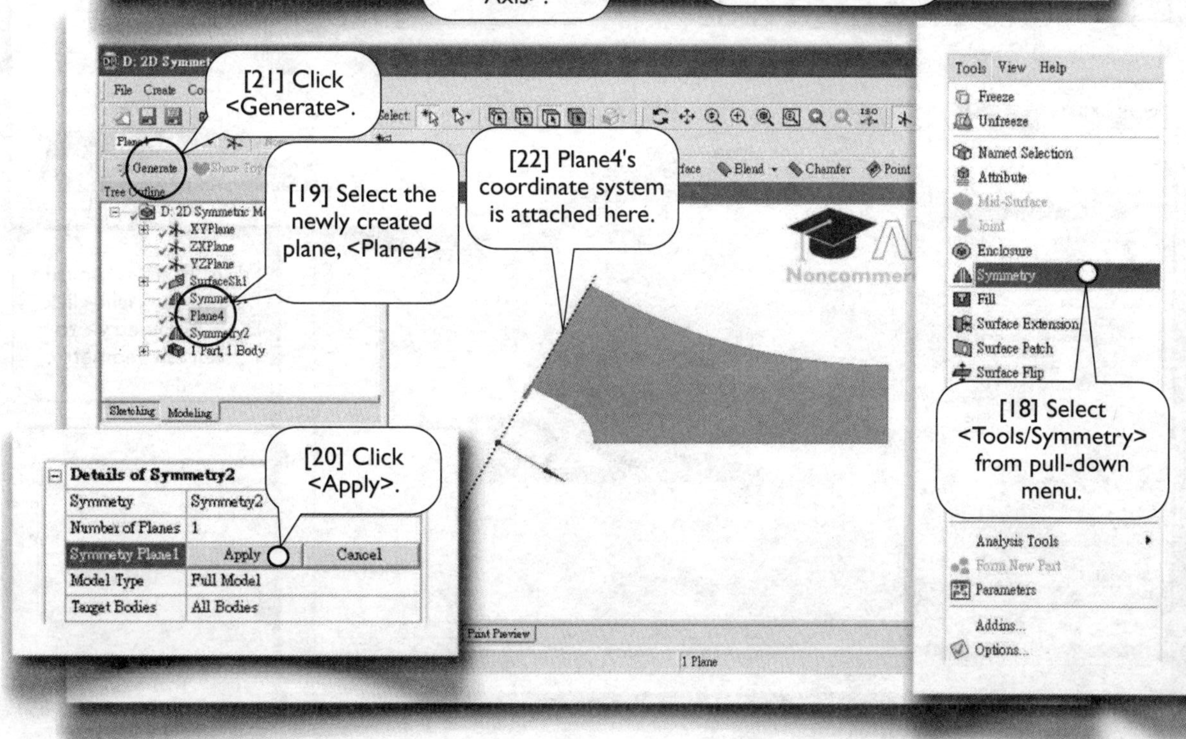

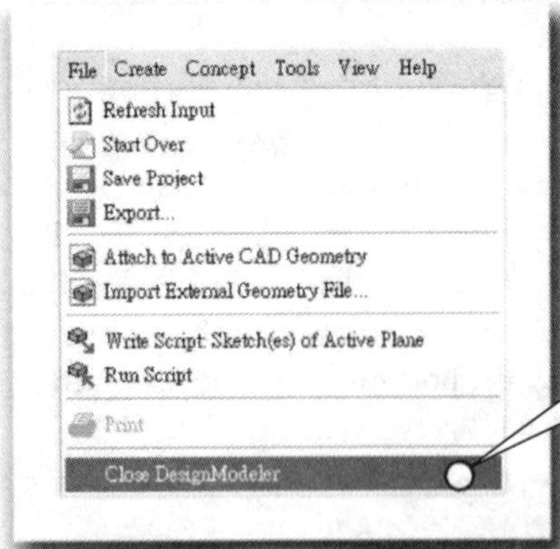

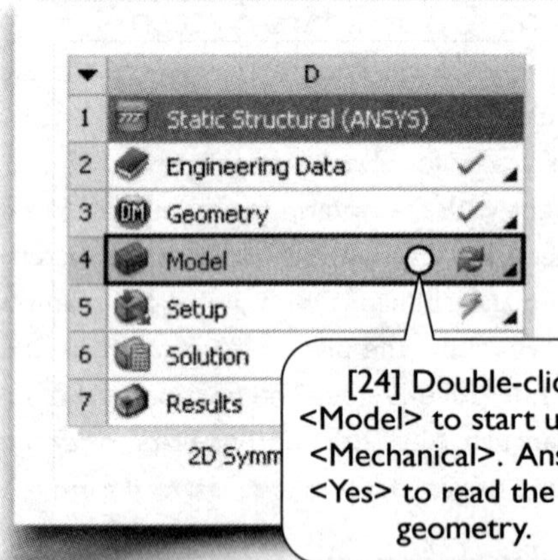

Do I need to close <DesignModeler> when working on <Mechanical>, or vice versa?

When starting up again, the <Mechanical> automatically updates the geometry, including adding boundary conditions on the planes of symmetry. That's the reason I suggest the newcomers close one application while working on another. That way, the update will be automatic.

Nope, you don't have to close any application when switch another application, but you have to "refresh" it manually. In <Project Schematic> you can right-click <Model> and select <Refresh> from the context menu [25]. Inside <Mechanical> you can right-click <Geometry> and select <Refresh Geometry> from the context menu [26].

Anyway, until you become a Workbench veteran, I suggest the newcomers to keep only one application open at a time to make your life simpler.

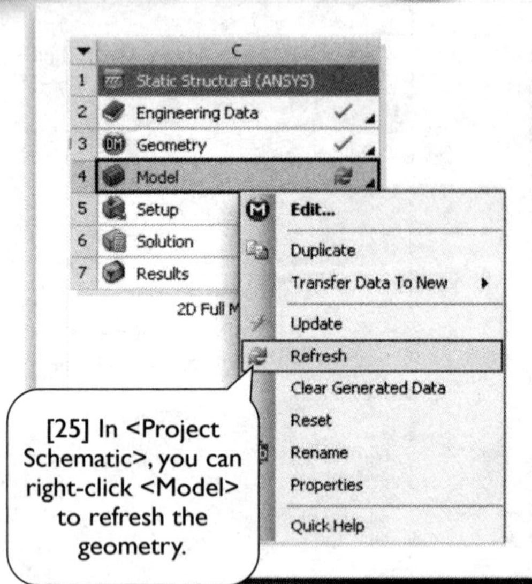

3.1-11 Solve the New Model

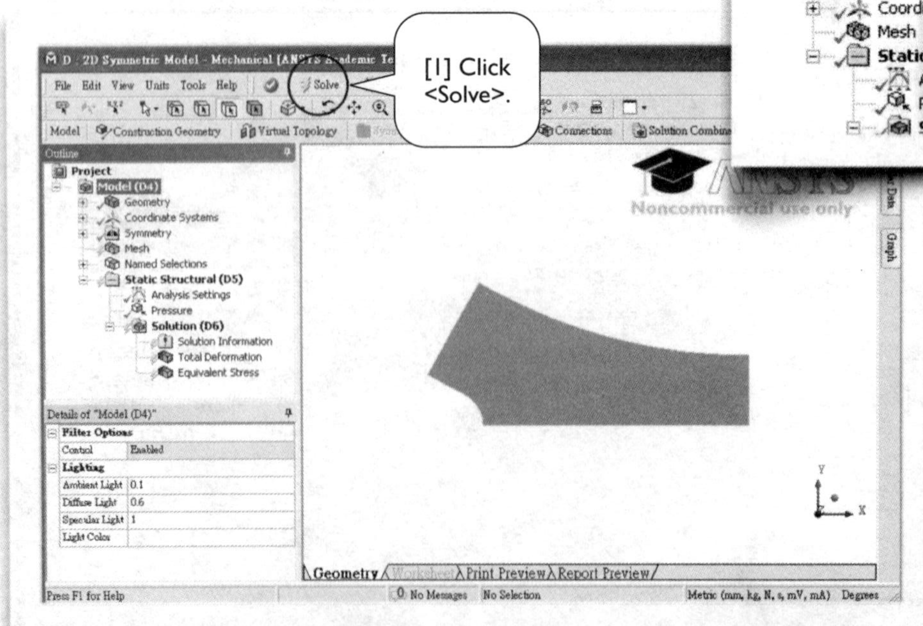

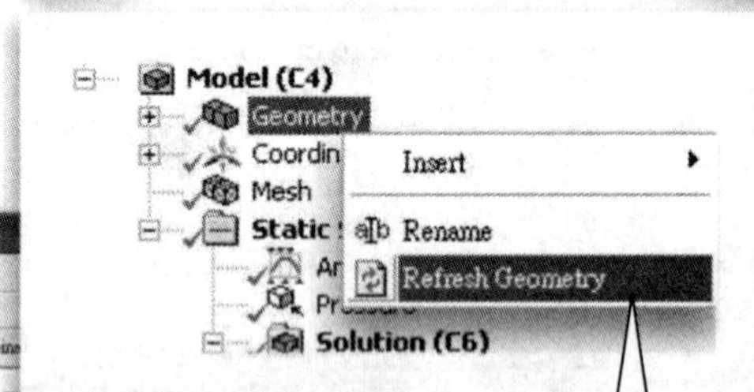

3.1-12 View the Results

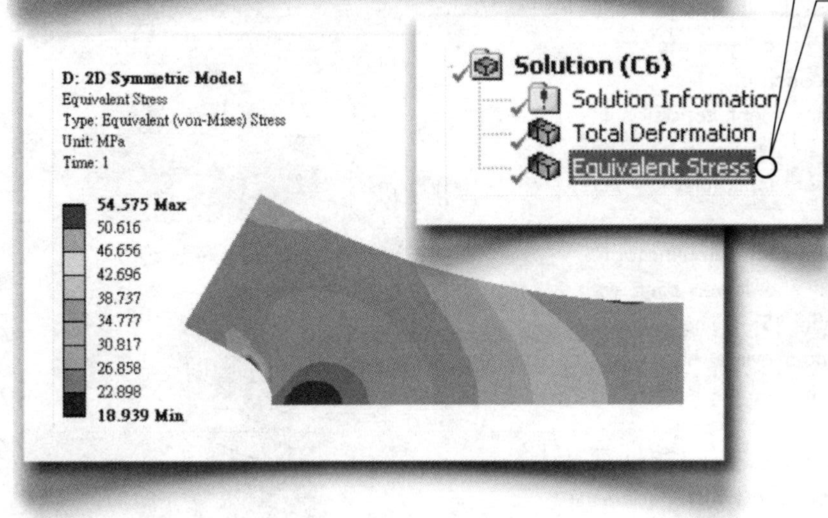

Check Environment Conditions After Modifying Geometry

In this case, you don't need to make any modification when solving the new model. In most of other cases, however, whenever you modify your geometry, you may need to redefine the environment conditions. As a good practice, always check your environment conditions each time you modify the geometry before solving it.

Wrap Up

Close <Mechanical>. Save the project and exit from the Workbench.

Why Different Numerical Results?

Your numerical results may be slightly different from here. This is one of the nature of the finite element methods: different meshes end up with different results. In general, the finer the mesh, the more accurate the results. The question is, how fine a mesh should be, to achieve enough accuracy. We will discuss this must-know behavior in Section 3.5. The discussion will be extended to 3D cases in Section 9.3.

Some students may be puzzled about why they obtained a mesh different from the one in the textbook if they follow EXACTLY the same steps in the textbook. The answer is that the students have no way to follow EXACTLY the same steps in the textbook. For example, a line in the textbook may be drawn from right to left while you drew it from left to right. It is possible that the direction of the line affects the meshing algorithm in the Workbench.

Limited differences in numerical values are normal, particularly when the mesh are coarse. As the mesh becomes finer, the solution will converge to a theoretical value, which will be independent of mesh variations. This kind of puzzle would disappear.

Section 3.2

Step-by-Step: Threaded Bolt-and-Nut

3.2-1 About the Threaded Bolt-and-Nut

The threaded bolt we created in Section 2.4 is part of a bolt-nut-plate assembly [1-4]. The bolt is preloaded with a tension. The pretension is applied by tightening the nut with torque. The pretension can be calculated by multiplying the maximum torque with a coefficient, which is empirically determined. The pretension in our case is 10 kN. We want to know the stress at the threads under such a pretension condition.

Pretension is a ready-to-use environment condition in 3D simulations, in which a pretension can apply on a body or cylindrical surface. It is, however, not applicable for 2D simulations.

In this 2D simulation, we will make some simplification. Assuming a symmetry between upper and lower part, we model only upper part of the assembly [5]. The plate is removed, to reduce the problem size and alleviate the contact nonlinearity, and its boundary surface with the nut is replaced by a frictionless support [6].

The pretension is replaced by a uniform force applied on the lower face of the bolt. The model somewhat deviates from the reality, which we will discuss at the end of this section, but for accessing the stress, it should be acceptable.

The coefficient of friction between the bolt and the nut is estimated to be 0.3.

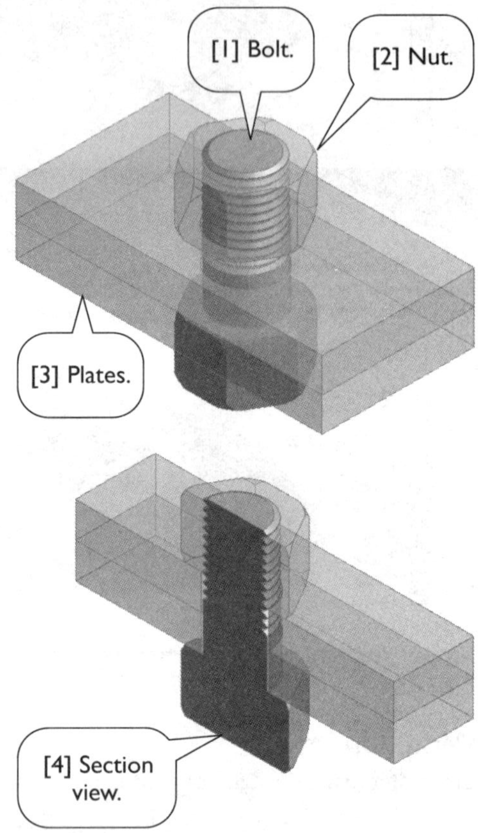

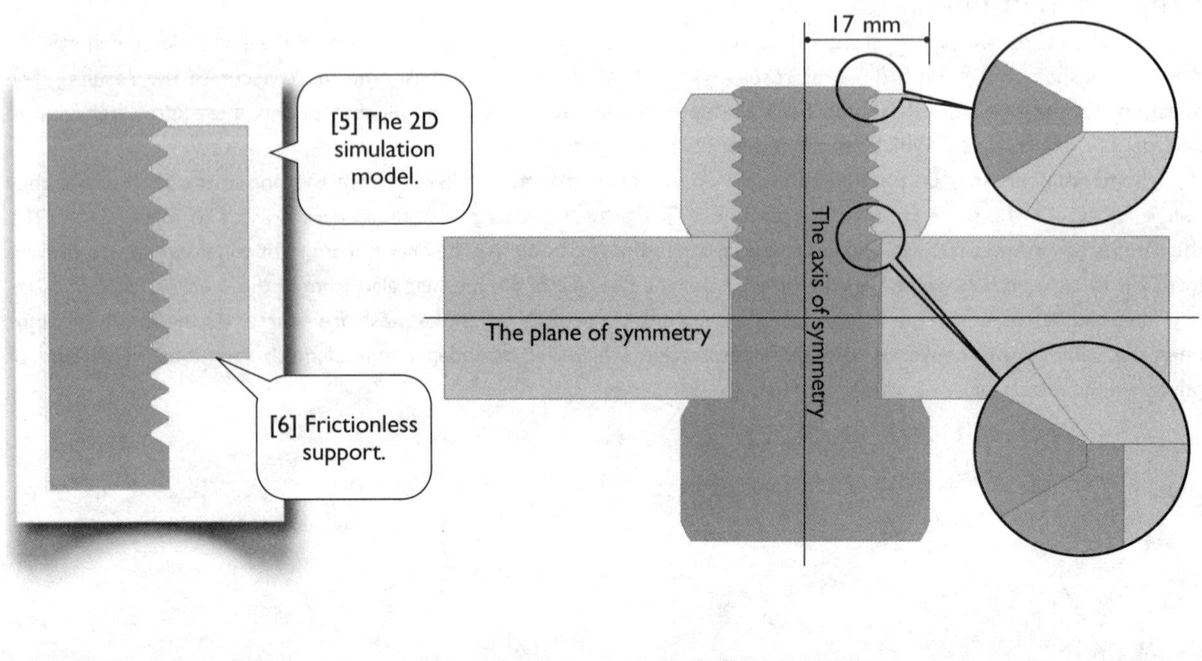

3.2-2 Open the Project "Threads"

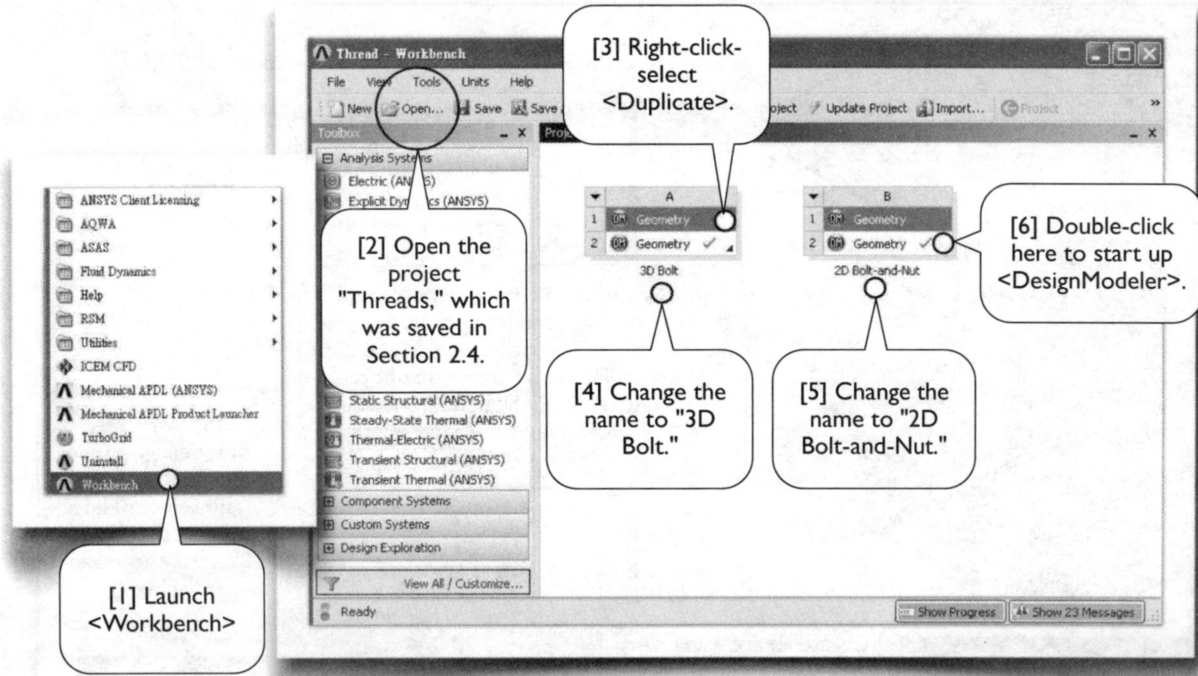

3.2-3 Delete the 3D Body and Create a 2D Body for the Bolt

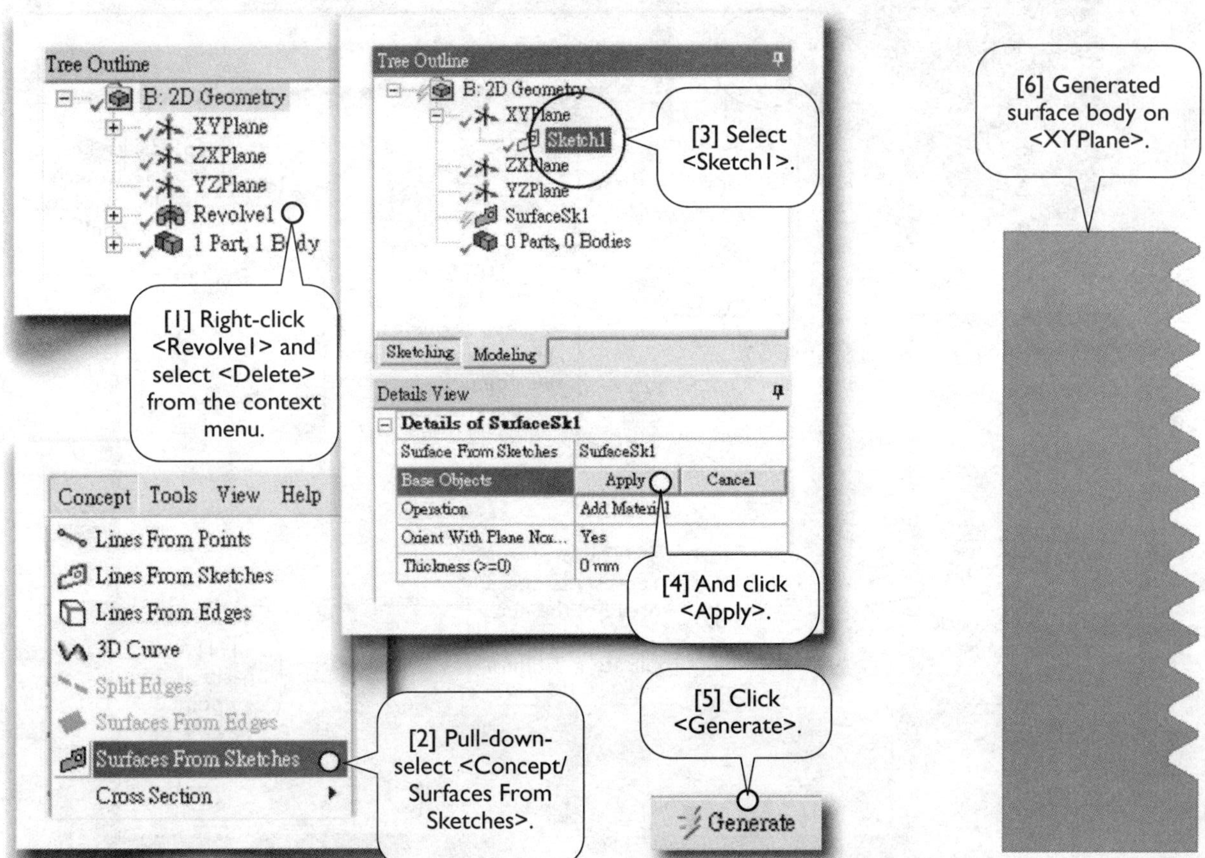

3.2-4 Create a 2D Body for the Nut

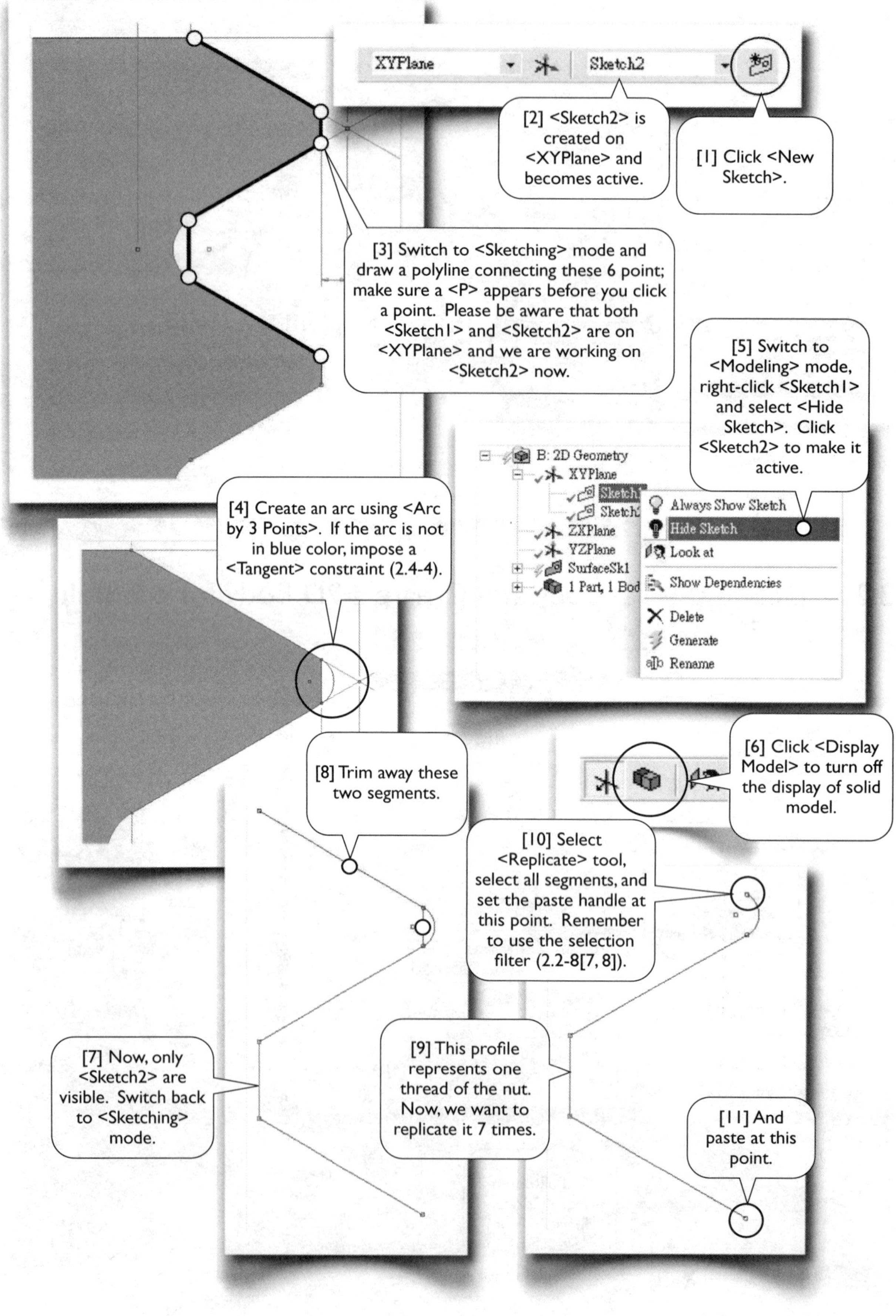

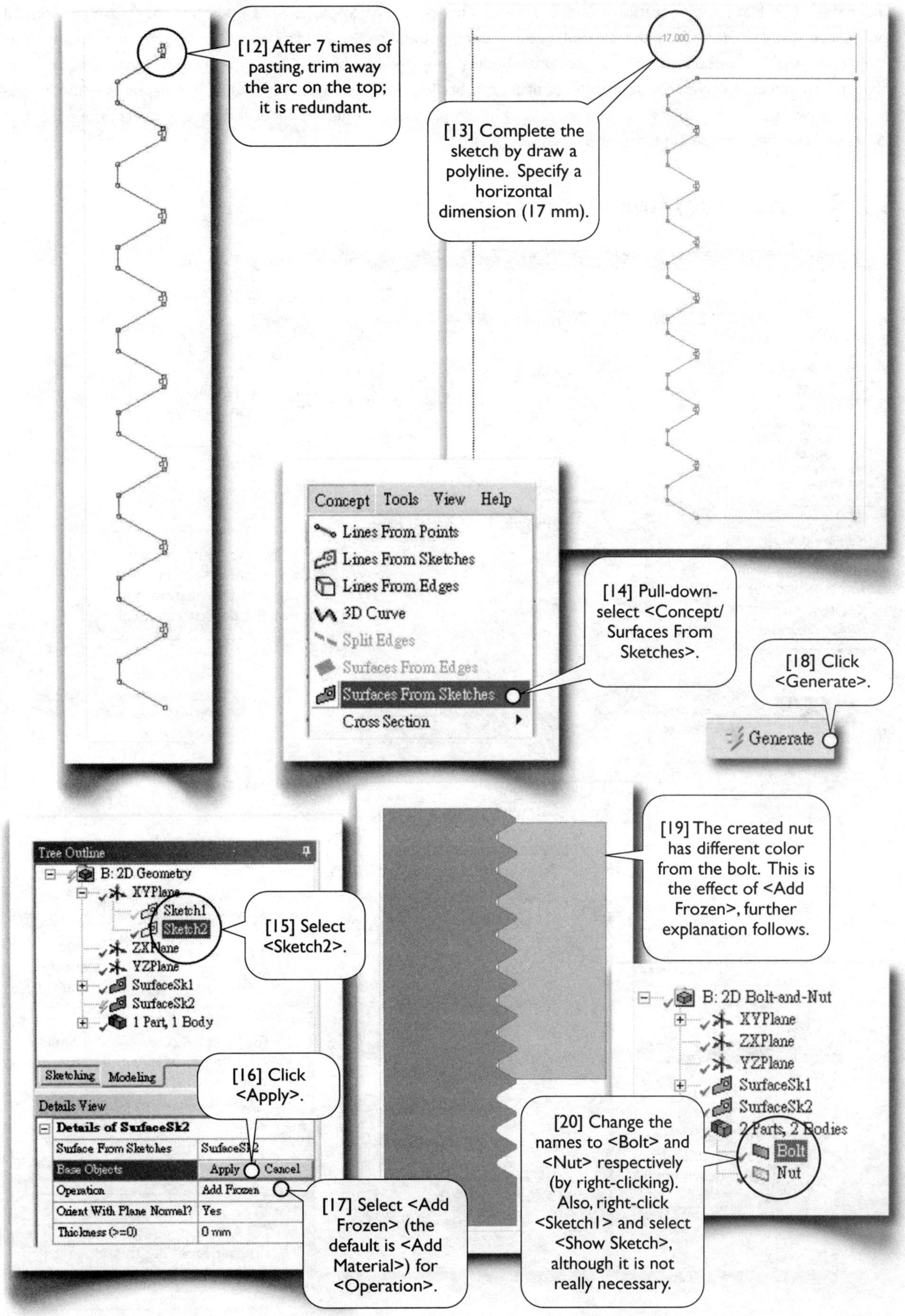
[12] After 7 times of pasting, trim away the arc on the top; it is redundant.
17.000
[13] Complete the sketch by draw a polyline. Specify a horizontal dimension (17 mm).
Concept Tools View Help
Lines From Points
Lines From Sketches
Lines From Edges
3D Curve
Split Edges
Surfaces From Edges
Surfaces From Sketches
Cross Section
[14] Pull-down-select <Concept/ Surfaces From Sketches>.
[18] Click <Generate>.
Generate
Tree Outline
B: 2D Geometry
XYPlane
Sketch1
Sketch2
ZXPlane
YZPlane
SurfaceSk1
SurfaceSk2
1 Part, 1 Body
[15] Select <Sketch2>.
Sketching Modeling
Details View
Details of SurfaceSk2
Surface From Sketches SurfaceSk2
Base Objects Apply Cancel
Operation Add Frozen
Orient With Plane Normal? Yes
Thickness (>=0) 0 mm
[16] Click <Apply>.
[17] Select <Add Frozen> (the default is <Add Material>) for <Operation>.
[19] The created nut has different color from the bolt. This is the effect of <Add Frozen>, further explanation follows.
B: 2D Bolt-and-Nut
XYPlane
ZXPlane
YZPlane
SurfaceSk1
SurfaceSk2
2 Parts, 2 Bodies
Bolt
Nut
[20] Change the names to <Bolt> and <Nut> respectively (by right-clicking). Also, right-click <Sketch1> and select <Show Sketch>, although it is not really necessary.

Add Material versus Add Frozen

Under the <Add Material> operation mode, the created material adds to the existing body (i.e., they form a union). If you choose <Add Frozen> [17], the created material does not add to the existing one; they become two bodies. This is what we want. The bolt and nut are separate bodies; they are not bonded each other; they interact each other through contacting. We will discuss more about frozen bodies in 3D geometric modeling in Chapter 4. Also notice that, here, two bodies are treated as two parts [20]. Each part will be meshed independently. Concepts of parts and bodies will also be discussed in Chapter 4.

3.2-5 Create an Analysis System

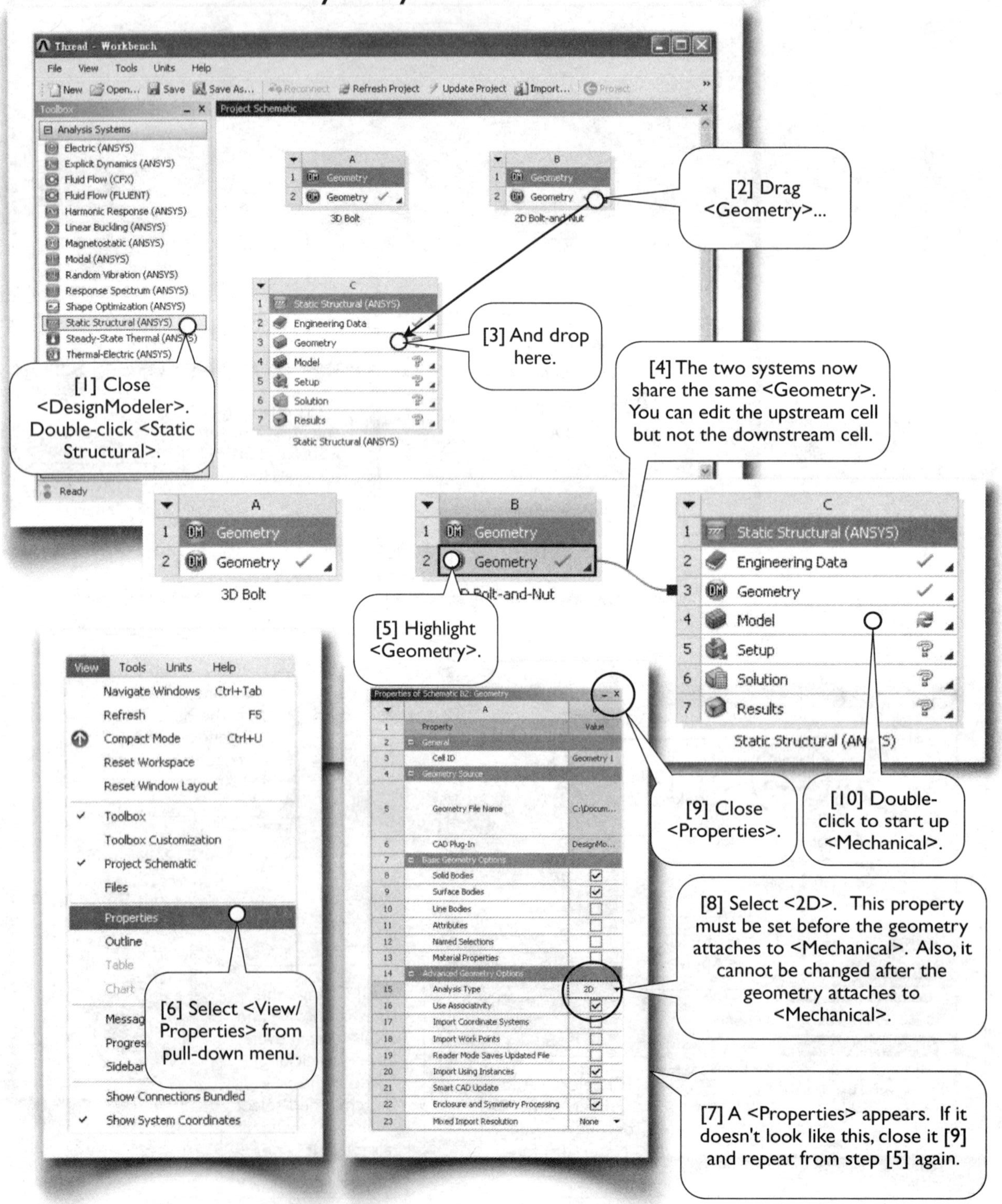

3.2-6 Set Up Geometry in <Mechanical>

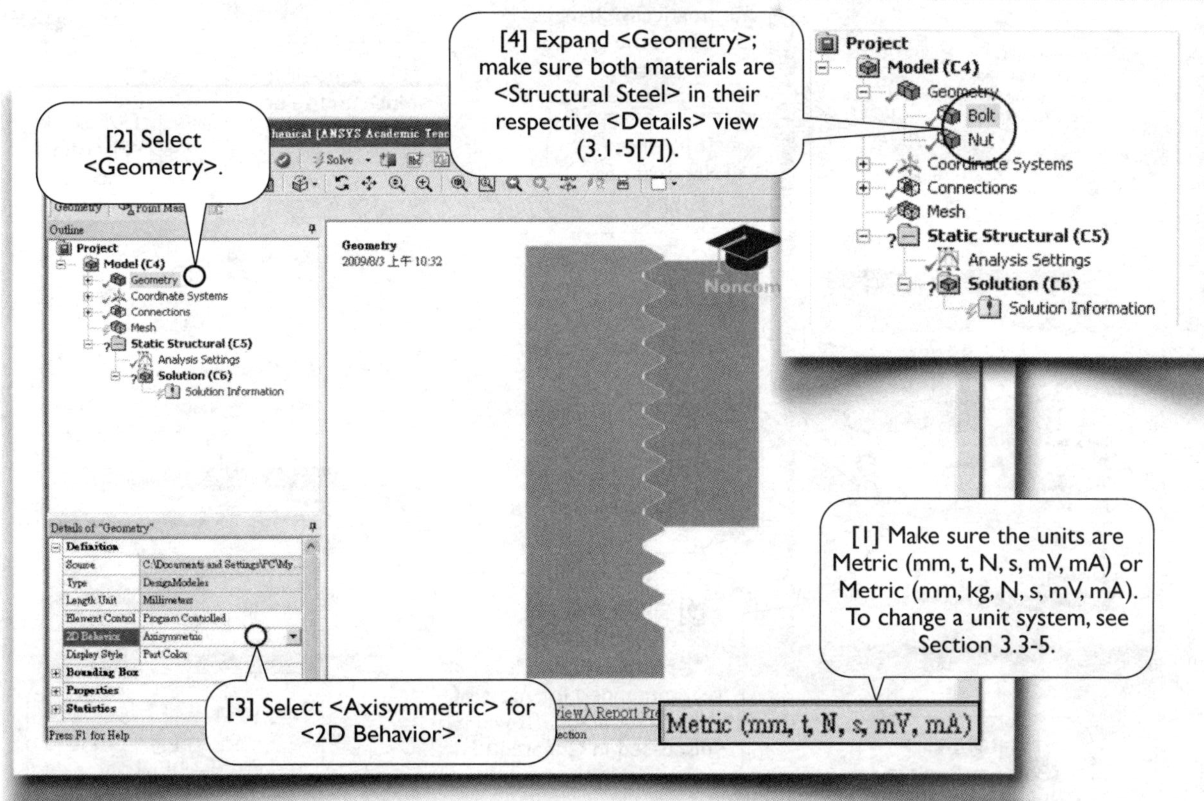

3.2-7 Set Up Contact Region

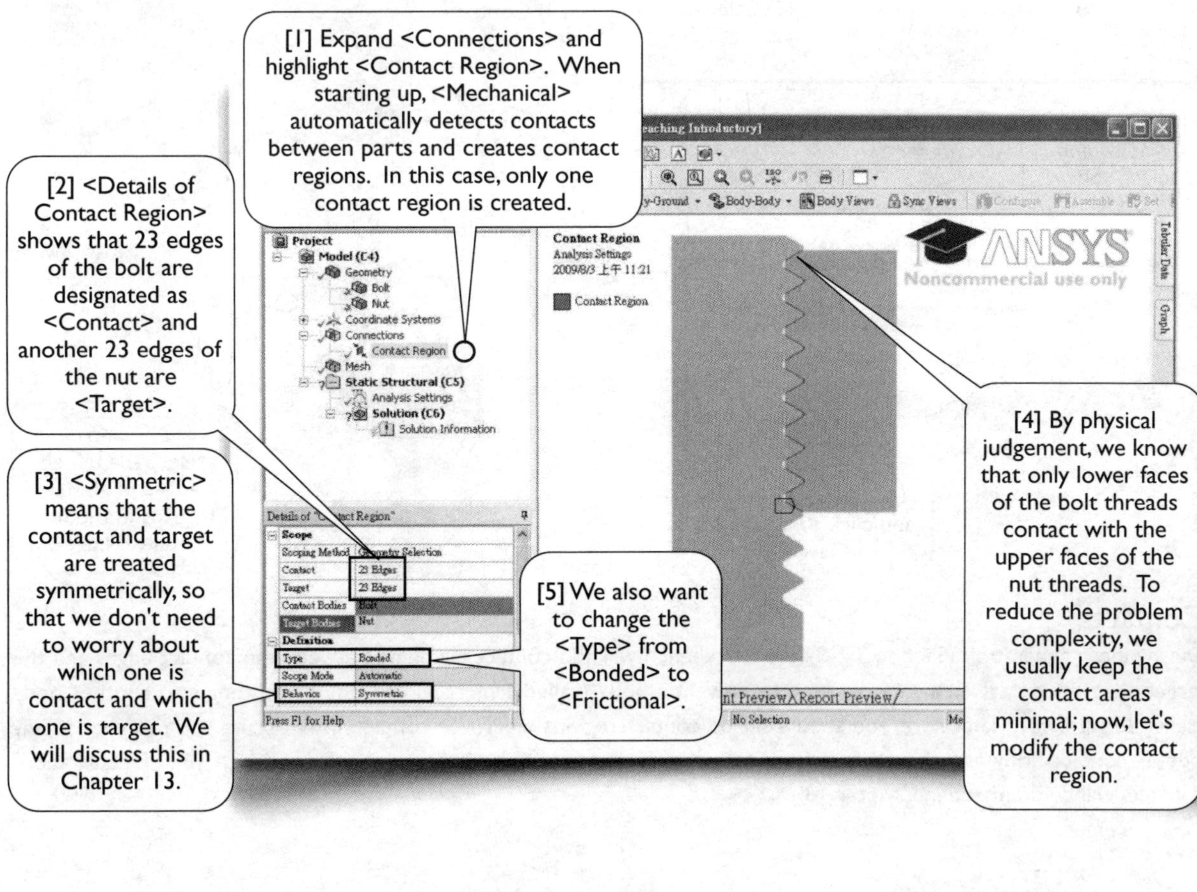

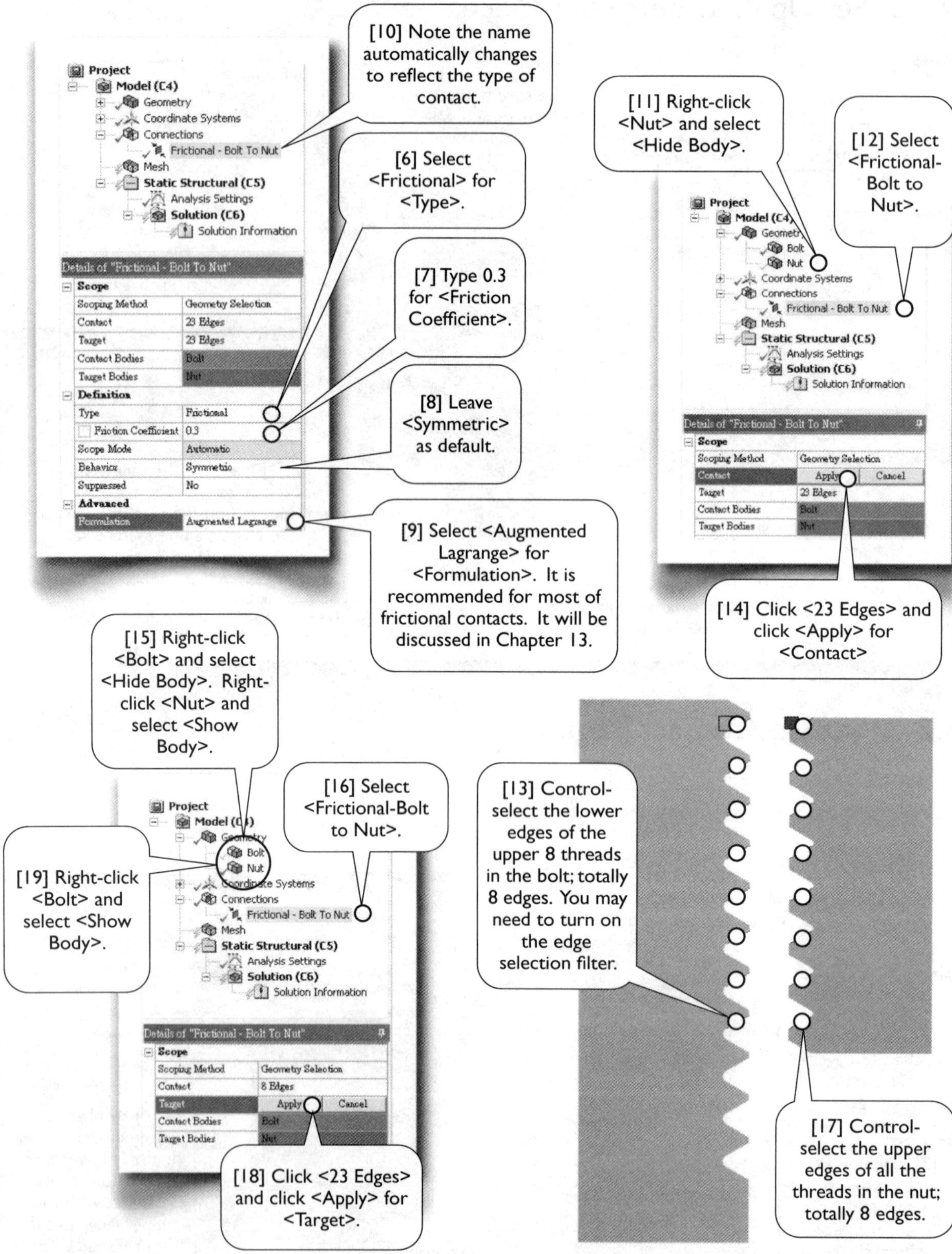

Contacts

During mesh generation (Section 3.2-8), the Workbench will add contact elements between the contact edges and the target edges. Contact elements are used to prevent a body (called *contact body*) from penetrating into another body (called *target body*). Therefore, you should set up contact regions wherever contacts may occur. You can choose any side as contact body and the other side as target body, as long as the behavior is <Symmetric> [8]. Details about contacts will be discussed in Chapter 13.

3.2-8 Generate Mesh

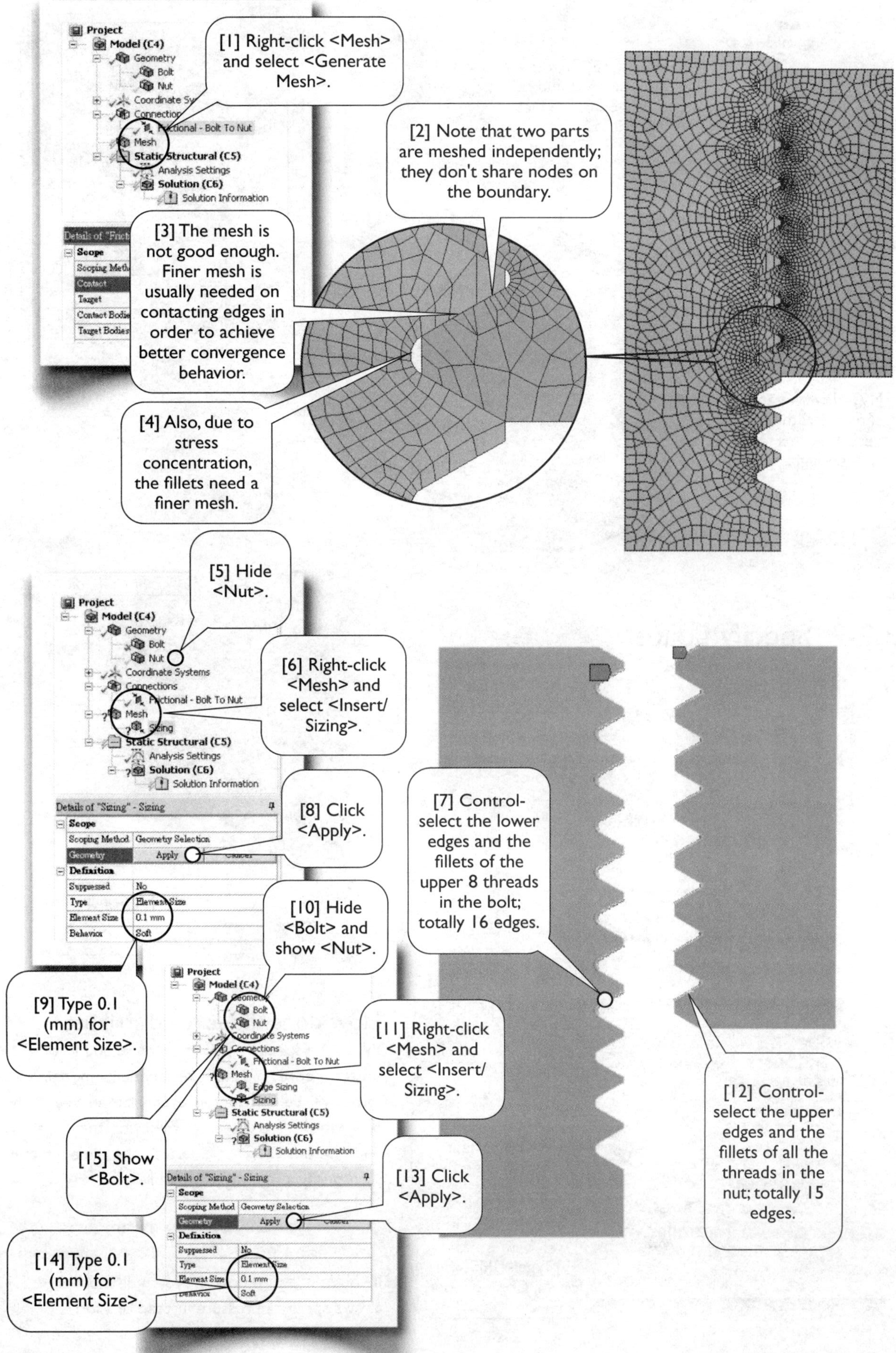

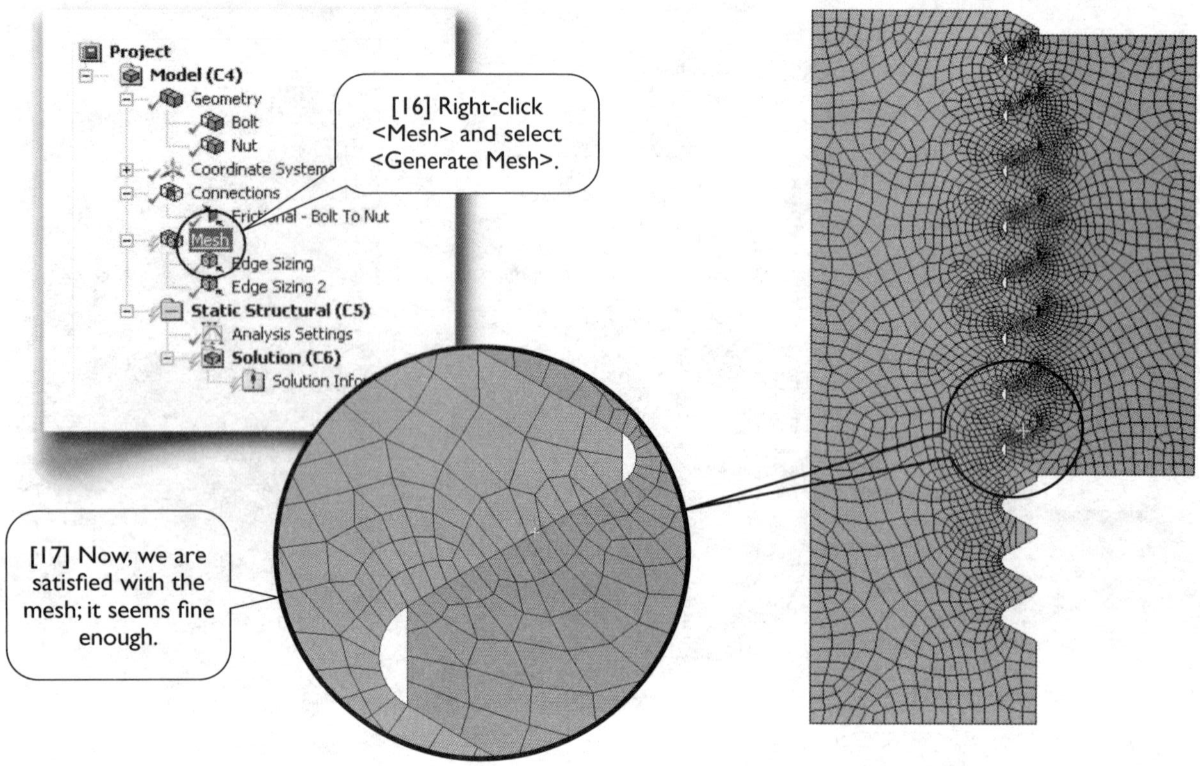

3.2-9 Specify Loads

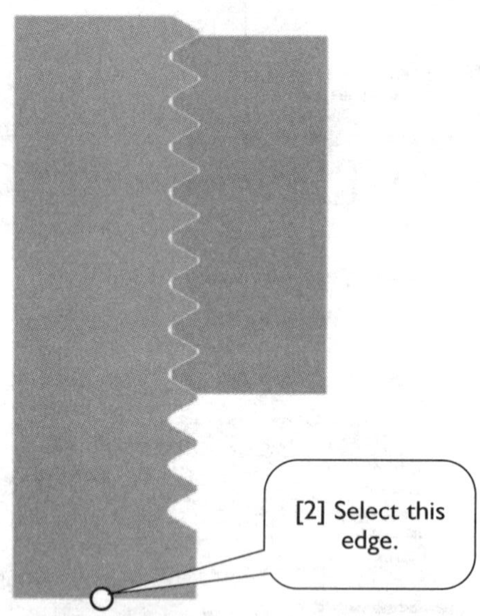

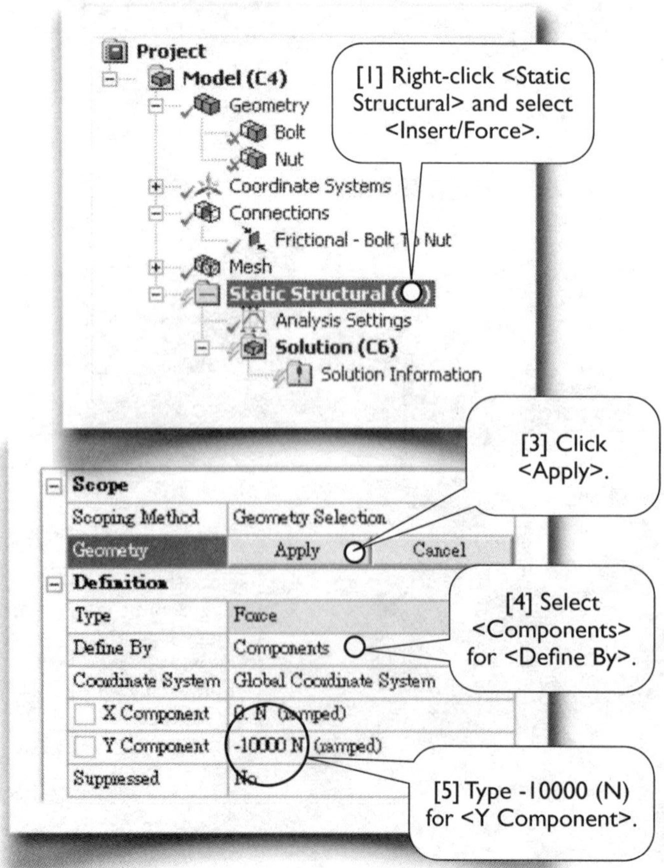

How does the force distribute?

When we specify a pull force of 10,000 N on the bottom edge of the axisymmetric model, the force will be distributed evenly on an imaginary face which is created by revolving the edge by 360°. In this case, it has exactly the same effect if you specify a (negative) pressure of

$$\frac{10000}{\left(\pi \times 20^2/4\right)} = 31.83 \text{ MPa}$$

If you're not sure how the force distributes, always specify a pressure instead of a force.

3.2-10 Specify Supports

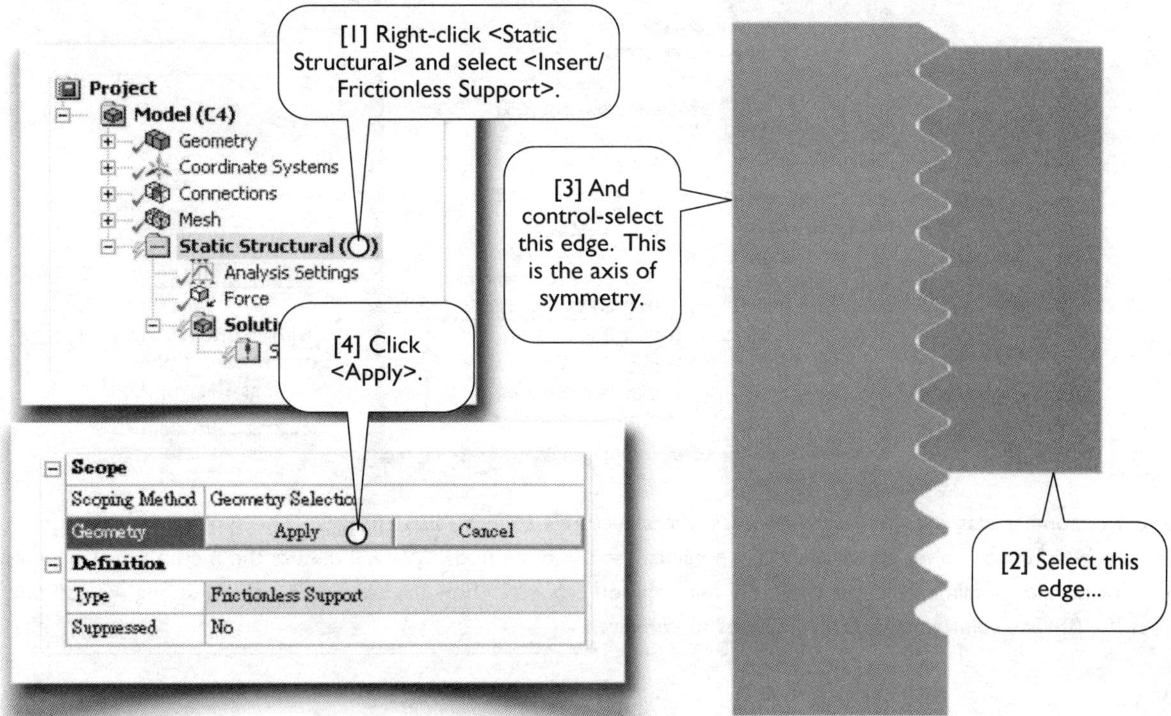

The Boundary Condition for the Axis of Symmetry

For an axisymmetric problem, the global Y-axis is always the axis of symmetry and the model MUST be placed on the +X side. Since all points on the axis of symmetry do not move in the X-direction, you must specify a zero X-displacement condition or, equivalently, a frictionless support on this edge. Some software can automatically take care of this boundary condition; however, as a good practice, always explicitly specify this boundary condition. If you leave it as a free boundary, the axis may become a small cylindrical "hole" after deformation.

3.2-11 Solve the Model

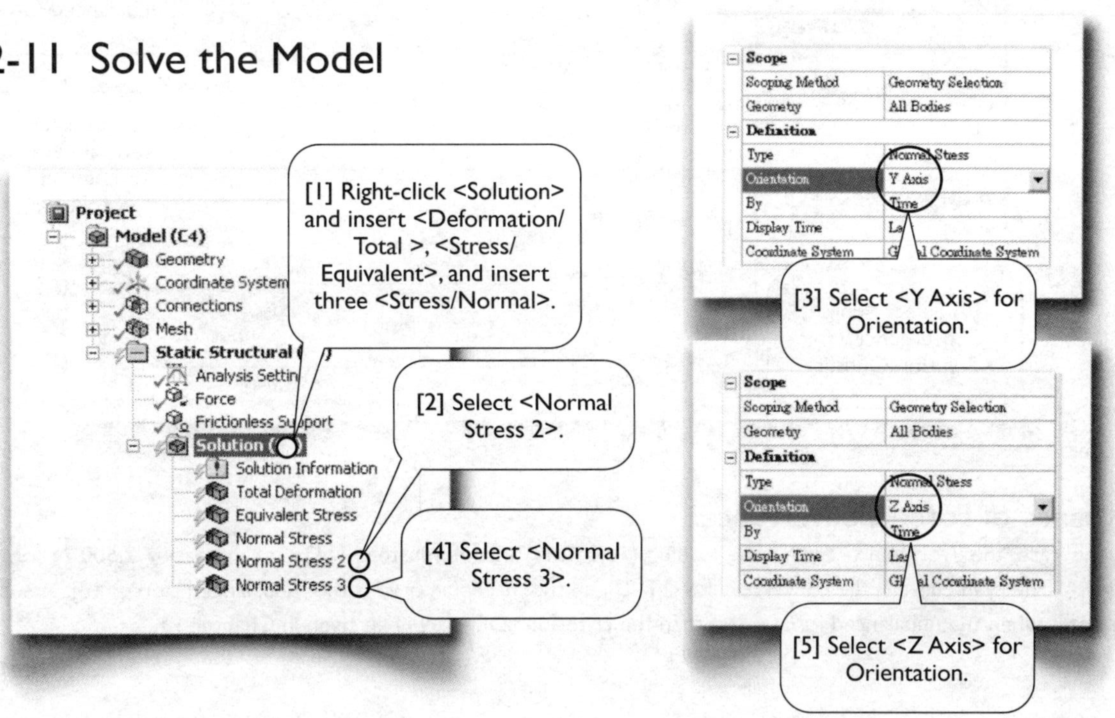

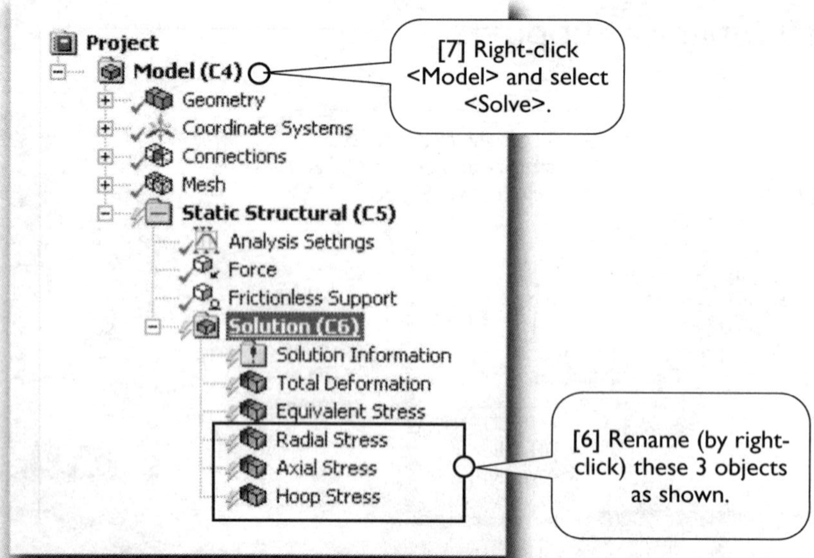

Due to the contact status, as the loads increase, the structure's stiffness also changes. The simulation is no longer linear. The Workbench solves the model using nonlinear solution methods. We will discuss the methods in Chapters 13-14. For now, to obtain a feeling of nonlinear solution, you can watch how the solution proceeds during the solution process [8-10]. The solution takes a few minutes to complete.

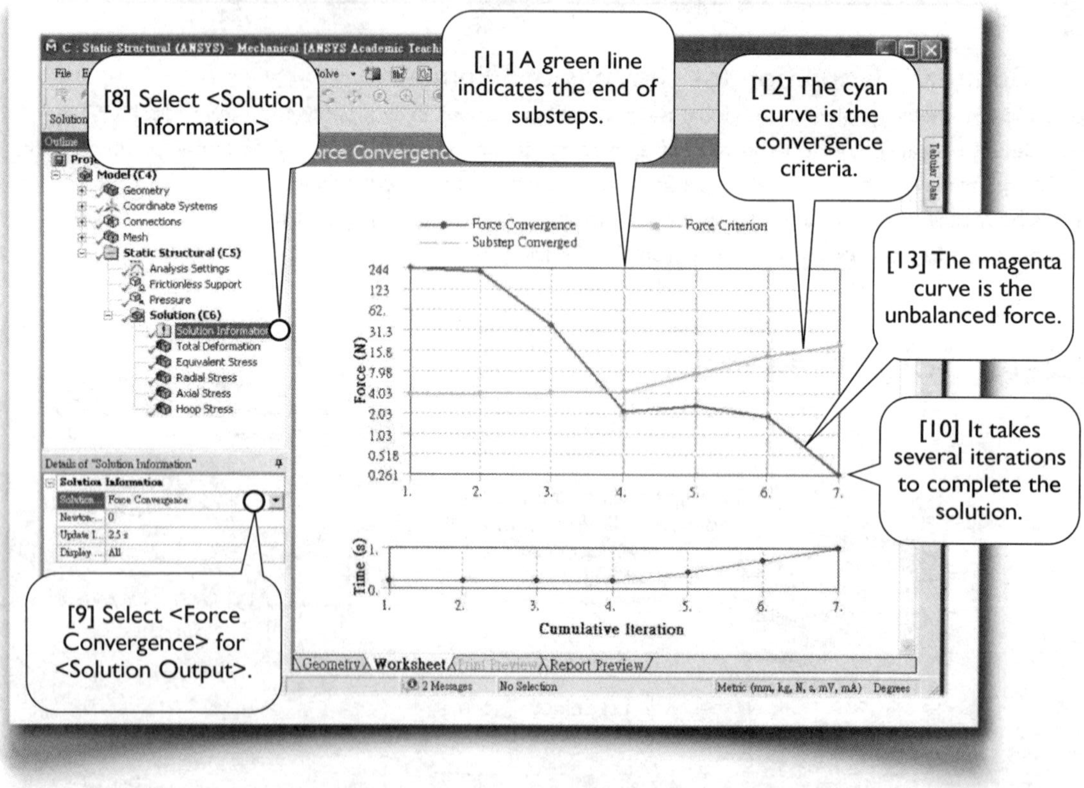

A Glance of Force Convergence

For this case, the Workbench divides the loading (10,000 N) into 4 substeps [11] (i.e., increasing 2,500 N for each substep). The cyan curve is the converge criteria [12] and the magenta curve is the "unbalanced" force [13]. A substep converges when the unbalanced force is less than the criterion. DEtails will be given in Chapter 13.

3.2-12 View the Results

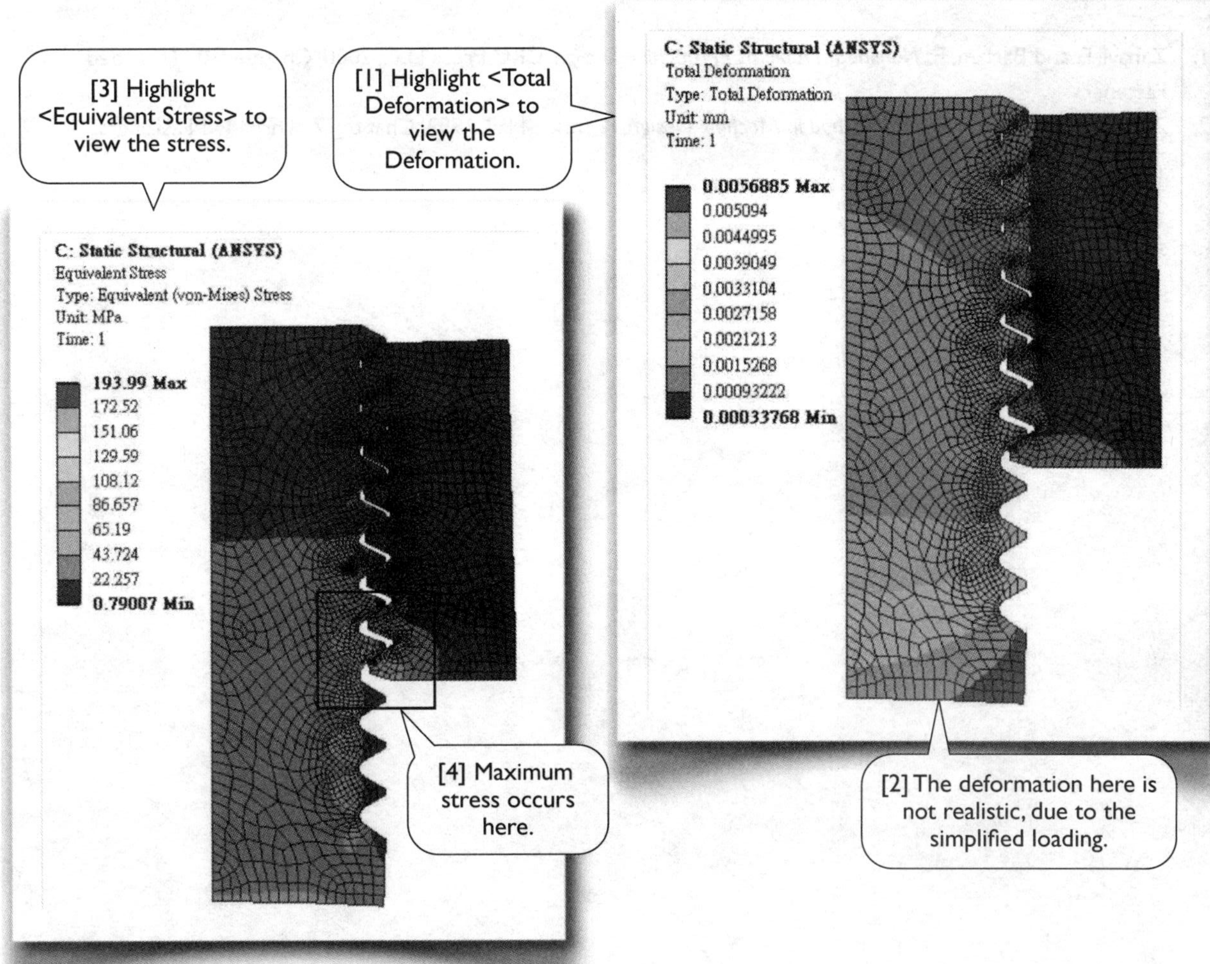

The bottom edge is actually a plane of symmetry; it should not have any vertically displacement. The plane of symmetry should be modeled as a frictionless support. However, a frictionless support cannot have an out-of-plane loading on it. In this dilemma, we choose to apply a force, and expect an unrealistic deformation near the plane of symmetry [2]. Because we concern about the stress on the threads only, and the region of influence of this faulty boundary condition seems not so large to reach the point that concern us [4], we decide to satisfy with this arrangement.

Wrap Up

View other results. Save the project. Close <Mechanical> and exit <Workbench>.

Remark

The quantities of bolt-and-nut used in daily industrial application is huge. Their behavior should be carefully investigated. In our preliminary study, it shows that the stresses are distributed unevenly that most of stresses are taken by a few lower contacting threads. To improve the efficiency of the bolt-and-nut, one way is to allot some of the stresses to the upper contacting threads. In his books[1, 2], Zahavi has provided several alternatives to reduce the maximum stress. This case is adapted based on an example in his books.

References

1. Zahavi, E. and Barlam, E., *Nonlinear Problems in Machine Design*, CRC Press LLC, 2000; Chapter 10. Threaded Fasteners.
2. Zahavi, E., *The Finite Element Method in Machine Design*, Prentice-Hall, 1992; Chapter 7. Threaded Fasteners.

Section 3.3

More Details

3.3-1 Plane-Stress Problems

Plane-Stress Condition

Consider a plate of zero thickness on *XY* plane subject to in-plane forces. The stress state at any point can be depicted as shown [1]. Notice that there are no stresses in *Z*-face,

$$\sigma_Z = 0, \quad \tau_{ZY} = 0, \quad \tau_{ZX} = 0 \qquad (1)$$

Eq. (1) is termed the *plane-stress condition.*

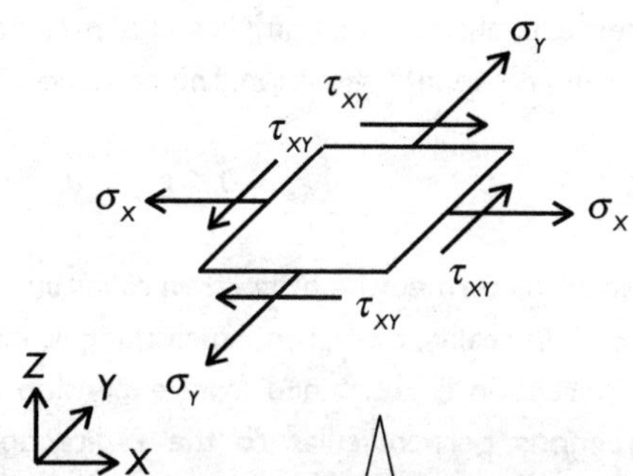

[1] Stress state at a point of a zero thickness plate, subject to in-plane forces.

In reality, there is no such thing as zero thickness. The triangular plate simulated in Section 3.1 is close to but not exactly what we described here, since the triangular plate has finite thickness of 10 mm. However, since its stresses in *Z*-direction are negligible, we usually assume the plane-stress condition (1) holds for such a finite thickness plate.

In practice, if its *Z*-direction is not restrained and thus free to expand or contract, the problem may assume the plane-stress condition (1). As an example, a simply supported beam as shown [2] is often solved by assuming the plane stress condition, even though its out-of-plane thickness is far from zero.

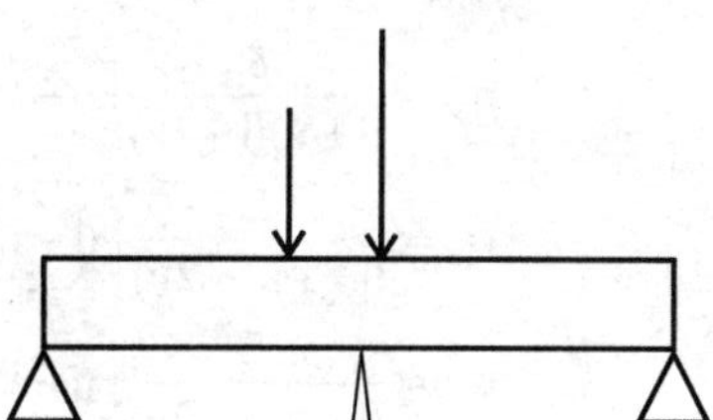

[2] A beam is often solved by assuming the plain-stress condition.

Reducing Plane-Stress Problems to 2D

Substituting the plane-stress condition (1) into Eq. 1.2-8(1), the Hooke's law becomes

$$\begin{aligned} \varepsilon_X &= \frac{\sigma_X}{E} - \nu \frac{\sigma_Y}{E} \\ \varepsilon_Y &= \frac{\sigma_Y}{E} - \nu \frac{\sigma_Z}{E} \\ \varepsilon_Z &= -\nu \frac{\sigma_X}{E} - \nu \frac{\sigma_Y}{E} \end{aligned} \qquad (2)$$

$$\gamma_{XY} = \frac{\tau_{XY}}{G}, \quad \gamma_{YZ} = 0, \quad \gamma_{ZX} = 0$$

Similar substitution of Eq. (1) into other equations (e.g., Eq. 1.2-6(2)) will conclude that all quantities are independent of *Z*. That is, the particles having the same *X* and *Y* coordinates share the same behaviors regardless of their *Z* coordinate. Thus, we can eliminate *Z* coordinate and reduce the problem to a 2D, on *X-Y* space.

Note, in Eq. (2), although ε_Z is not zero, it can be calculated independently from σ_X and σ_Y. The nonzero ε_Z is conceivable, since *Z*-direction is free to expand or contract.

3.3-2 Plane-Strain Problems

Plane-Strain Condition

Consider a structure of infinite length in Z-direction. The Z-direction is restrained such that no particles can move in Z-direction. If you take cross-sections perpendicular to the Z-direction, each cross-section has the same geometry, supports, and loading, which are all in the XY plane [1]. In such a case, the strain state at any point can be depicted as shown [2]. Notice that there are no strains in Z-face. That is, $\varepsilon_Z = 0$, otherwise the particle on the Z-face would move in Z-direction, and $\gamma_{ZX} = \gamma_{ZY} = 0$, otherwise the cube would twist in ZX and ZY planes respectively, and that implies the particles on the X-face and Y-face would move in Z-direction. The condition is summarized as follows

$$\varepsilon_Z = 0, \quad \gamma_{ZX} = 0, \quad \gamma_{ZY} = 0 \tag{1}$$

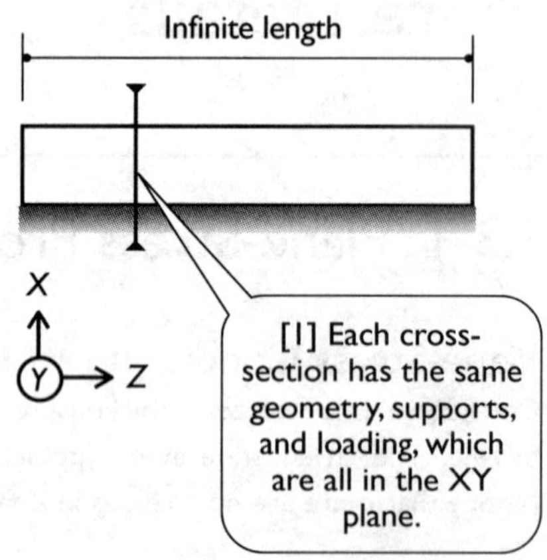

Eq. (1) is termed the *plane-strain condition.*

In reality, there is no such thing as infinite length. In practice, if its Z-direction is restrained from expansion or contraction, and all cross-sections perpendicular to the Z-direction have the same geometry, supports, and loadings, which are all in the XY plane, then the problem may assume the plane-strain condition (1). As an example, a pressurized pipe buried under the earth is often modeled as a plane-strain problem.

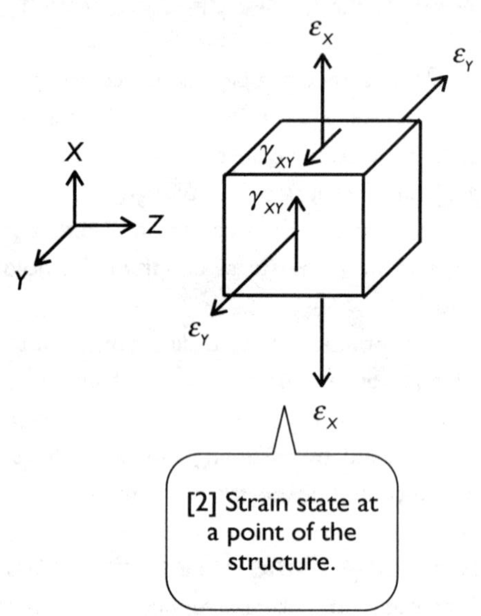

Reducing Plane-Strain Problems to 2D

Eq. 1.2-8(1), the Hooke's law, can be inverted and rewritten as

$$
\begin{aligned}
\sigma_X &= \frac{E}{(1+\nu)(1-2\nu)}\left[(1-\nu)\varepsilon_X + \nu\varepsilon_Y + \nu\varepsilon_Z\right] \\
\sigma_Y &= \frac{E}{(1+\nu)(1-2\nu)}\left[(1-\nu)\varepsilon_Y + \nu\varepsilon_Z + \nu\varepsilon_X\right] \\
\sigma_Z &= \frac{E}{(1+\nu)(1-2\nu)}\left[(1-\nu)\varepsilon_Z + \nu\varepsilon_X + \nu\varepsilon_Y\right] \\
\tau_{XY} &= G\gamma_{XY}, \quad \tau_{YZ} = G\gamma_{YZ}, \quad \tau_{ZX} = G\gamma_{ZX}
\end{aligned} \tag{2}
$$

The proof of Eq. (2), starting from Eq. 1.2-8(1), leaves as an exercise for you (Section 3.6-2).

Substitute the plane-strain condition (1) into Eq.(2), and the Hooke's law becomes

$$
\begin{aligned}
\sigma_X &= \frac{E}{(1+\nu)(1-2\nu)}\left[(1-\nu)\varepsilon_X + \nu\varepsilon_Y\right] \\
\sigma_Y &= \frac{E}{(1+\nu)(1-2\nu)}\left[(1-\nu)\varepsilon_Y + \nu\varepsilon_X\right] \\
\sigma_Z &= \frac{E}{(1+\nu)(1-2\nu)}\left[\nu\varepsilon_X + \nu\varepsilon_Y\right] \\
\tau_{XY} &= G\gamma_{XY}, \quad \tau_{YZ} = 0, \quad \tau_{ZX} = 0
\end{aligned} \tag{3}
$$

Similar substitution of Eq. (1) into other equations (e.g., Eq. 1.2-6(2)) will conclude that all quantities are independent of *Z*. That is, the particles having the same *X* and *Y* coordinates share the same behaviors regardless of their *Z* coordinate. Thus, we can eliminate *Z* coordinate and reduce the problem to a two dimensional, on *X-Y* space.

Note, in Eq. (3), although σ_Z is not zero, it can be calculated independently from ε_X and ε_Y. The nonzero σ_Z is conceivable, since *Z*-direction is restrained from expansion or contraction, it will develop stress to counteract the restriction.

3.3-3 Axisymmetric Problems

Consider a structure of which the geometry, supports, and loading are axisymmetric about a *Z*-axis. In such a case, all quantities are independent of θ coordinate. That is, the particles having the same *R* and *Z* coordinates share the same behaviors regardless of their θ coordinate. Thus, we can eliminate θ coordinate and reduce the problem to a two dimensional, on *R-Z* space.

The strain state at any point can be depicted as shown [1]. Notice that there are no shear strains in θ-face,

$$\gamma_{\theta R} = 0, \quad \gamma_{\theta Z} = 0 \tag{1}$$

otherwise the θR-face and the θZ-face would twist and the problem is no longer axisymmetric. Eq. (1) implies

$$\tau_{\theta R} = 0, \quad \tau_{\theta Z} = 0 \tag{2}$$

Eqs. (1) and (2) can be regarded as the *axisymmetric condition*. Stress state is also depicted as shown [2].

Axisymmetric problems are everywhere in engineering applications. Many problems are not strictly axisymmetric but can reasonably assume the axisymmetric condition, such as the bolt-and-nut problem simulated in Section 3.2, in which the threads are in fact spiral and the nut is hexagonal.

Note that both σ_θ and ε_θ are generally not zero. They are termed *hoop stress* and *hoop strain* respectively.

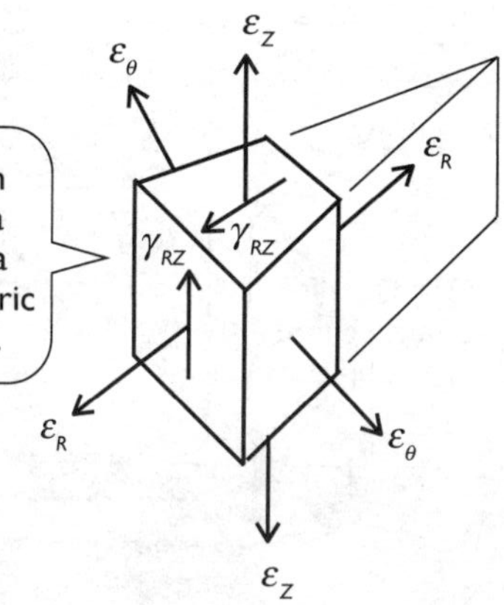

[1] Strain state at a point of a axisymmetric problem.

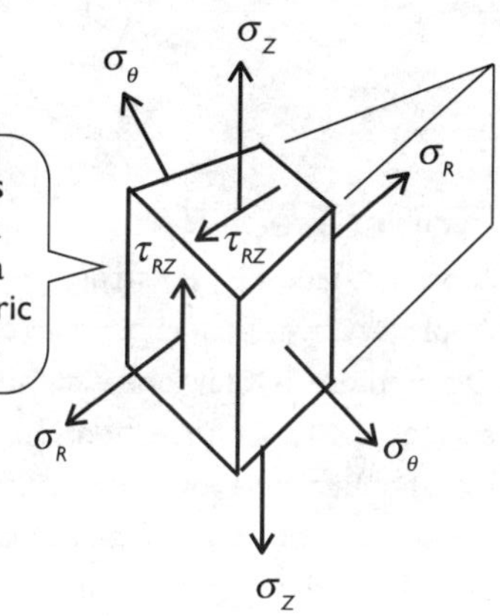

[2] Stress state at a point of a axisymmetric problem.

3.3-4 The <Mechanical> GUI

The <Mechanical> GUI is composed of several areas [1-7]; many of them are similar to those in DesignModeler GUI (Section 2.3-1). On the top are pull-down menus and toolbars [1]; on the bottom is a status bar [7]. In-between are several "window panes" [2-6]. A separator [8] between two window panes can be dragged to resize the window panes. You even can move or dock a pane by dragging its title bar. Whenever you mess up the workspace, simply pull-down-select <View/Windows/Reset Layout> to reset the default layout.

The <Outline> [2] display an outline of a *project tree*, which is a structured representation of the project. The <Details> [3] shows the detail information of the highlighted tree objects. The <Geometry> [4] area displays the model in various styles; you can click a tab to switch to <Print Preview> or <Report Preview>; Sometimes, a <Worksheet> is available to provide graphs or numerical data. The <Graph> shows quantities, which may be input or output quantities, varying with time. The <Tabular Data> is the numerical counterpart of the <Graph>. A set of animation tools are available along with the <Graph>, in which you can play, stop, or save the animation.

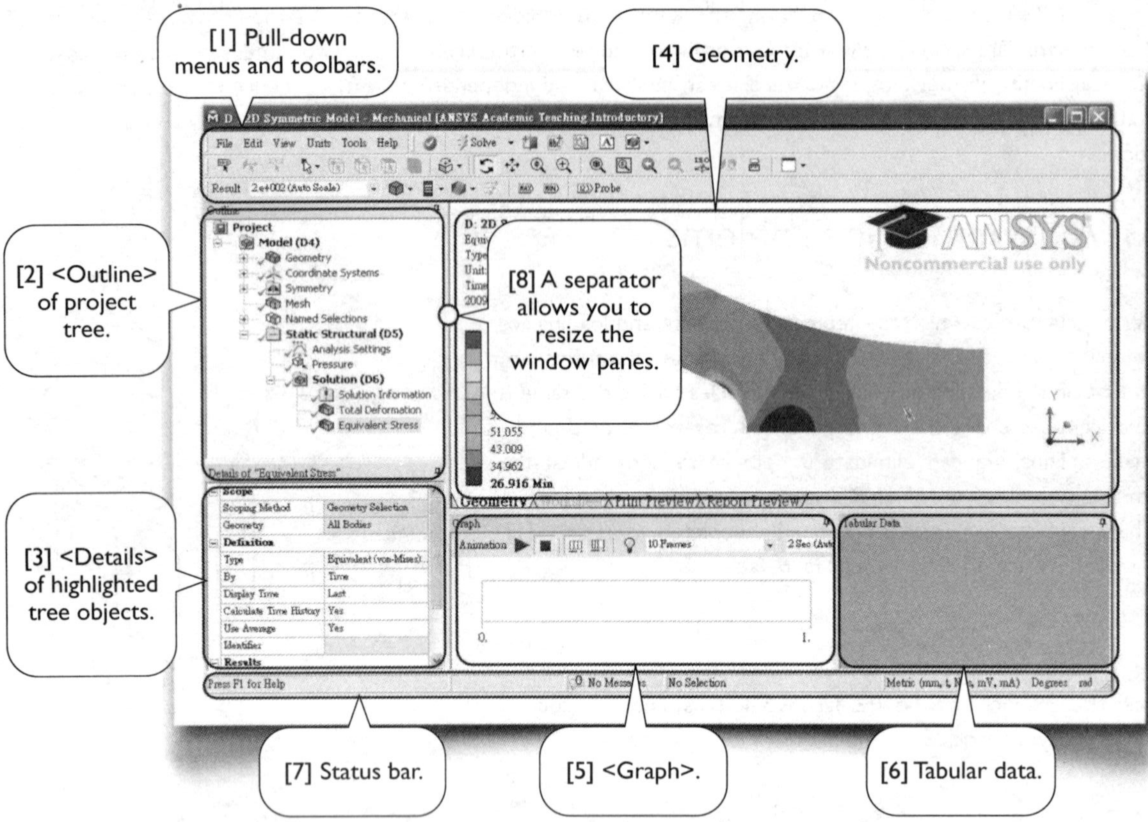

Project Tree[1, 11]

A project tree [9] is a structured representation of a project. A project tree contains one or more simulation models. Often, there is only one simulation model in a project tree, such as the cases in Sections 3.1 and 3.2. A simulation model may contain one or more <Environment> branches, along with other objects. Default name for the <Environment> branch is the name of the analysis system, for example: <Static Structural>. An <Environment> branch contains an <Analysis Settings>, several objects that define the environment conditions, and a <Solution> branch. The <Solution> branch contains a <Solution Information> and several results objects.

Right-clicking an object and select a tool from the context menu, you can operate on the object, such as delete, rename, duplicate, etc. Selecting multiple objects and operating on them at the same time are allowed.

Unlike the objects of a model tree in DesignModeler, in which their order is important, the order of the objects in a project tree is not relevant.

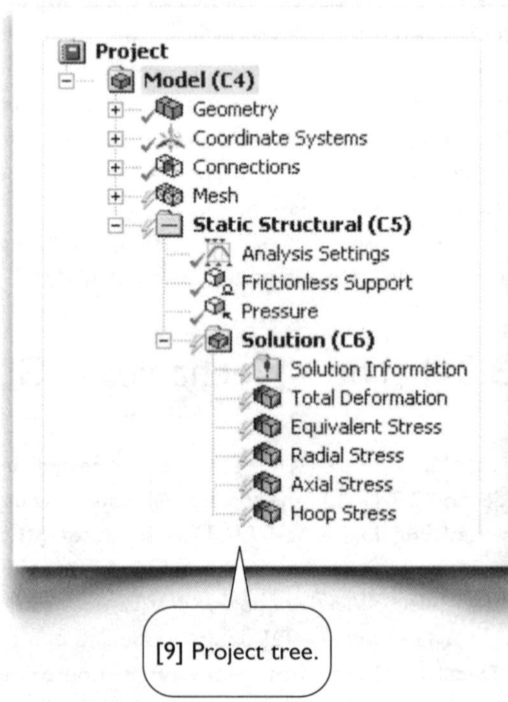

3.3-5 Unit Systems

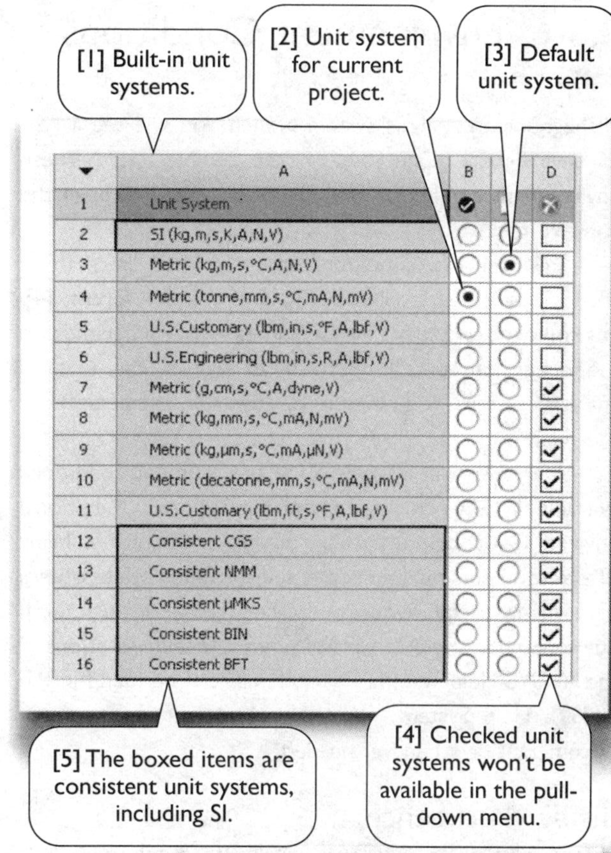

In geometric modeling, such as working with DesignModeler, the only unit used is for the length. In simulation, units are much more complicated. In the old days, you don't need to tell ANSYS Classic what unit system you are using. The users, however, have to carefully maintain the CONSISTENCY of a unit system. That was not trivial at all. In these days, it was not uncommon that a simulation fail just because of a mistake in unit system.

Fortunately, now, ANSYS Workbench takes care the consistency of the unit system. Your responsibility is to select a unit system suitable for your model. Selecting a suitable unit system for your model, in some cases, is crucial. In these cases the solution accuracy may deteriorate due to an accumulation of machine errors.

Choosing Unit Systems

As a guideline, select a unit system such that the values stored in the computer have about the same order. As an example, if you choose SI unit system for a micro-scale model, you would have the lengths of order 10^{-6} and a Young's modulus of order 10^{11}. That may raise the precision issue. On the other hand, if you choose the μMKS unit system, you would have the lengths of order 10^{0} and a Young's modulus of order 10^{5}. That is much better.

Unit Systems in Workbench

In <Workbench GUI>, pull-down-select <Units/Unit Systems...>, you will see a list of built-in unit systems [1-5]. Note that Workbench always uses a consistent unit system for internal computation. There are 6 *consistent unit systems* in the list: SI, CGS, NMM, μMKS, BIN, and BFT [5]. Highlight a unit system in the list, you will see the details of that unit system [6].

Other unit systems are *inconsistent* ones. They are, however, more convenient to use than consistent ones. When you select an inconsistent unit system for use in <Mechanical>, it internally uses a consistent unit system that is most close to the one you have chosen.

Unlike DesignModeler, in which you cannot change the unit, <Mechanical> allows you to change the unit system any time, using the pull-down menu <Units> [7]. The internal consistent unit system also changes accordingly.

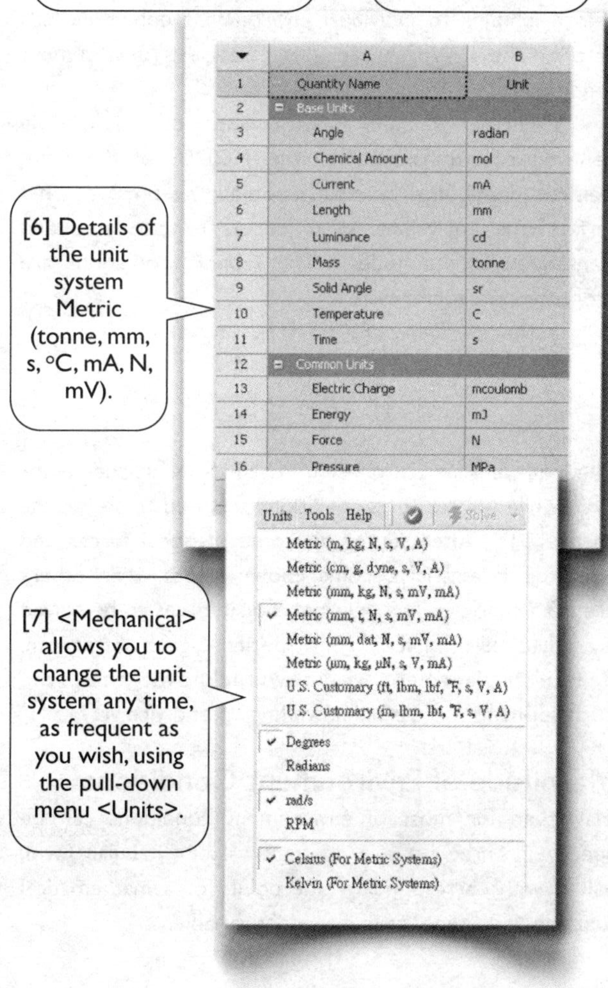

3.3-6 Environment Conditions

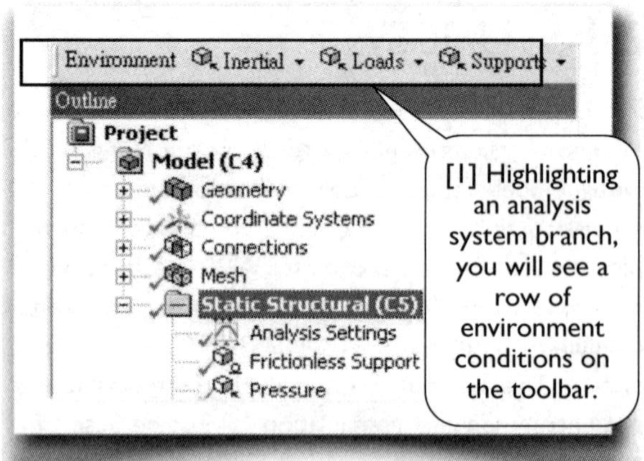

Highlighting an analysis system branch, you will see a row of environment conditions on the toolbar [1]. These environment conditions may also be accessed through the context menu.

Environment conditions are classified into three groups: loads [2], supports [3], and inertial forces [4]. Environment conditions available in each group depends on the dimensionality (2D or 3D) as well as the type of analysis system (e.g., static or dynamic, structural or thermal).

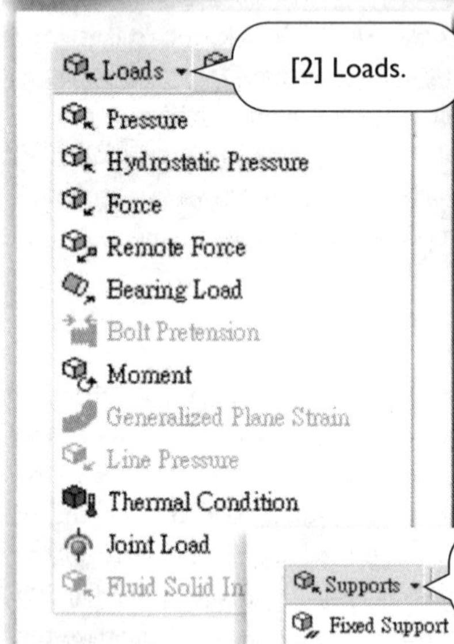

Here, we will introduce the environment conditions available in 2D static structural simulations. Additional environment conditions are introduced in Chapter 5. Many of environment conditions are self-explained while others have many useful features. When going through each environment condition, we will point out their locations in the ANSYS Help system. Many details can be found in the ANSYS Help System. You should consult these official documentation whenever needed.

Inside Workbench

Before jumping to individual environment condition, let's describe how Workbench processes the environment conditions.

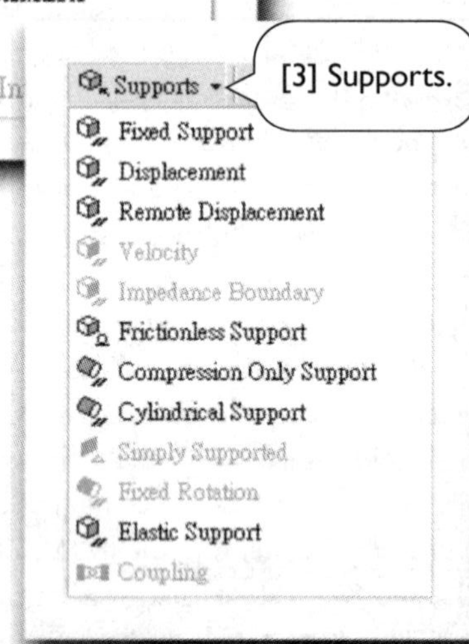

Wherever we apply an environment condition, it will be eventually transferred to the NODES of the finite element model. For example, if you apply a pressure on a surface, the equivalent nodal forces are calculated and transferred to the nodes. The support conditions are processed in a similar way.

In the paradigm of Eq. 1.3-1(1),

$$[K]\{D\}=\{F\}$$

The loads and inertia forces are used to set up the vector $\{F\}$, while the supports conditions are used to set up the vector $\{D\}$. After setting up, some of nodal forces and nodal displacements become known values while others are left unknown. The unknown nodal forces to be solved are called *reaction forces*. For a specific degree of freedom, if the displacement is known/unknown then the corresponding force is unknown/known, and vice versa.

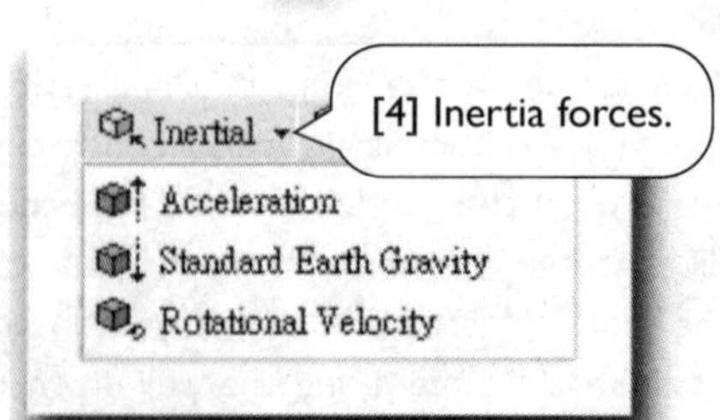

Magnitude of Environment Conditions[2]

Magnitude for most of environment conditions can be specify in three ways: a constant value; a tabular form, values with corresponding time points; or a mathematical function with "time" as independent variable.

3.3-7 Loads[3]

Pressure
Applies on 2D edges or 3D faces. It is possible to define a spatial varying pressure[4].

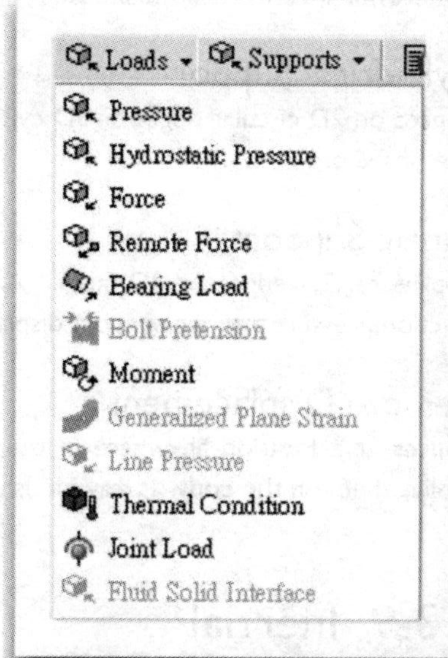

Force
Applies on vertices, edges, or faces. If applied on edges/faces, the force is evenly distributed on the edges/forces.

Thermal Condition
Applies on bodies. The temperature change ΔT (see Eq. 1.2-8(3)) is the difference between specified temperature and the reference temperature, which is part of information of the material properties, default to 22°C.

Bearing Load
Applies on 2D circular edges or 3D cylindrical faces. The total force is distributed on the compressive side of the circular edges or cylindrical faces.

Hydrostatic Pressure
Applies on 2D edges or 3D faces. It simulates pressure that occurs due to fluid weight. A free surface location may be specified, default to the surface at $X = 0$.

Moment
Applies on 2D edges or 3D faces. A statically equivalent pressure distributed on the edges/faces are calculated and applied on the edges/faces.

Remote Force
Applies at a location anywhere in the space. Workbench calculates the equivalent moment and force and applies them on the body. It may be used as an alternative to building a rigid part and applying a force to it.

Joint Load
Applies on a <Joint>[5]. You use a joint load to apply a kinematic driving condition in a multi-body dynamic simulation.

3.3-8 Supports[6]

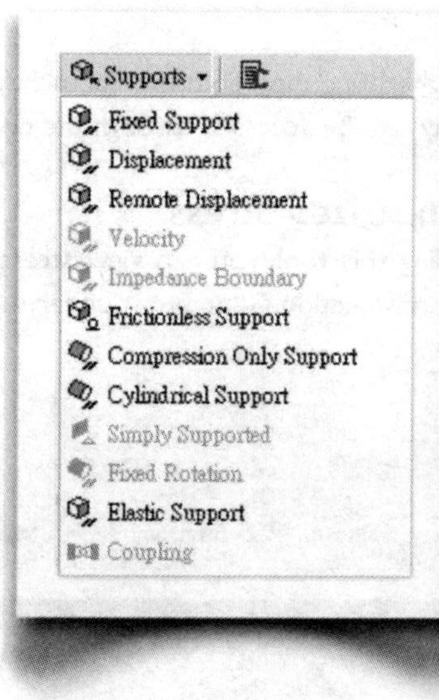

Fixed Support
Applies on vertices, edges, or faces. Prevents nodes from moving in X- Y- and Z-directions. Note that, it doesn't prevent nodes from rotations for beam/shell elements.

Displacement
Applies on vertices, edges, or faces. Displacements on X- Y- and Z-directions can be specified. A zero value prevents nodes from moving in that direction. An unspecified value set that direction free.

Frictionless Support
Applies on 2D edges or 3D faces. Prevents nodes from moving in the normal direction; allows nodes to freely move in the tangential direction.

Compression Only Support
Applies on 2D edges or 3D faces. The associated body is free to depart from the edges or faces, but cannot to penetrate them. It in effect sets up a frictionless contact region between the body and a rigid support; it introduces contact nonlinearity into the problem.

Cylindrical Support
Applies on 2D circular edges or 3D cylindrical faces. Each of radial, tangential, and axial (3D only) directions can be set free or fixed.

Elastic Support
Applies on 2D edges or 3D faces. A foundation stiffness must be specified to establish the relation between the reaction pressure and the support displacement.

Remote Displacement
Applies at a location anywhere in the space. Workbench calculates the equivalent displacement and rotation and applies them on the body. It may be used as an alternative to building a rigid part and applying a displacement to it.

3.3-9 Inertial[3]

Standard Earth Gravity
Applies on bodies. You must select a direction along which the gravitational force applies; it defaults to -Z direction.

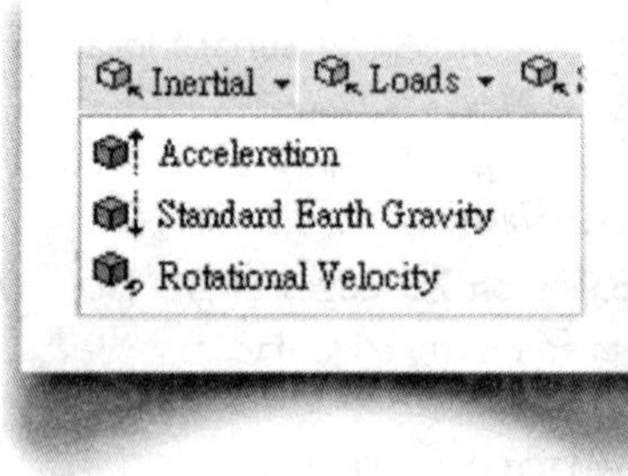

Acceleration
Applies on bodies. You must specify the magnitude and direction of acceleration. The direction is where the bodies moves. An "Inertia force" will apply in the opposite direction.

Rotational Velocity
Applies on bodies. You must specify the magnitude and direction of the angular velocity of the bodies. A distributed "inertia force" will apply in the opposite direction of rotation.

3.3-10 Solution[7]

Highlighting the <Solution> branch, you will see a row of results tools available on the toolbar [1]. These results tools may also be accessed through the context menu. Most of them are self-explained, some of them need to be explained.

Linearized Stress
Using this tool, you can view stresses along a straight line path. You need to first define a straight line path using <Construction Geometry> under <Model>.

[1] Results toolbar.

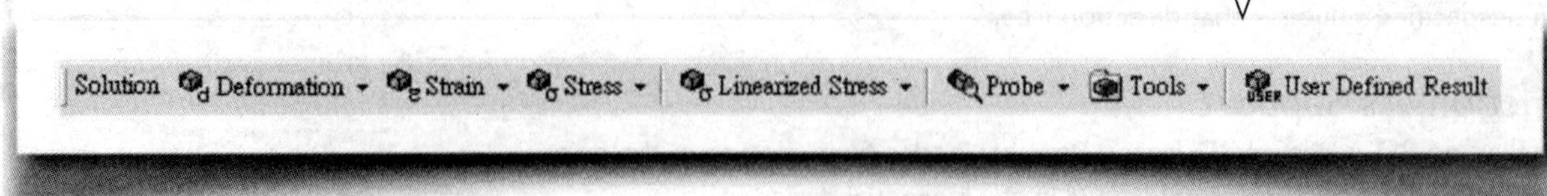

Probe[8]

It contains tools to explore the results of a point, or maximum/minimum values of the results of a scoped region, along the loading history. In other words, we concern about the results across the time domain instead of space domain.

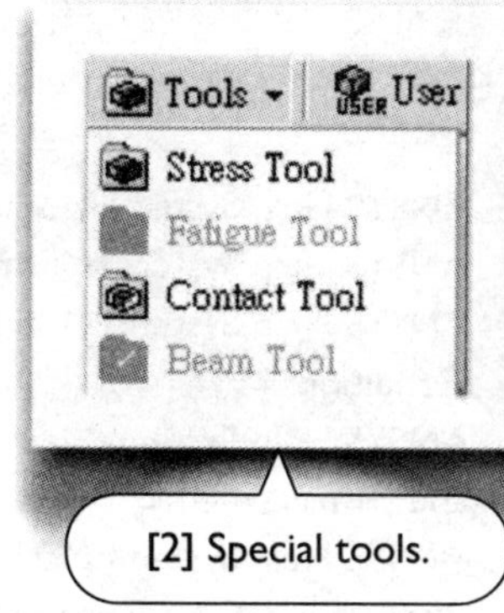

Tools[7]

It contains special tools: <Stress Tool>, <Fatigue Tool>, <Contact Tool>, and <Beam Tool> [2].

User Defined Results[9]

You may define a results expression using keywords. By highlighting <Solution> in the project tree and clicking <Worksheet> on the right side of the GUI, you will see a list of available keywords.

3.3-11 View Results[7]

To view results, simply highlight a results object. Tools to control the visual effects of the results are shown on the toolbar [1-6].

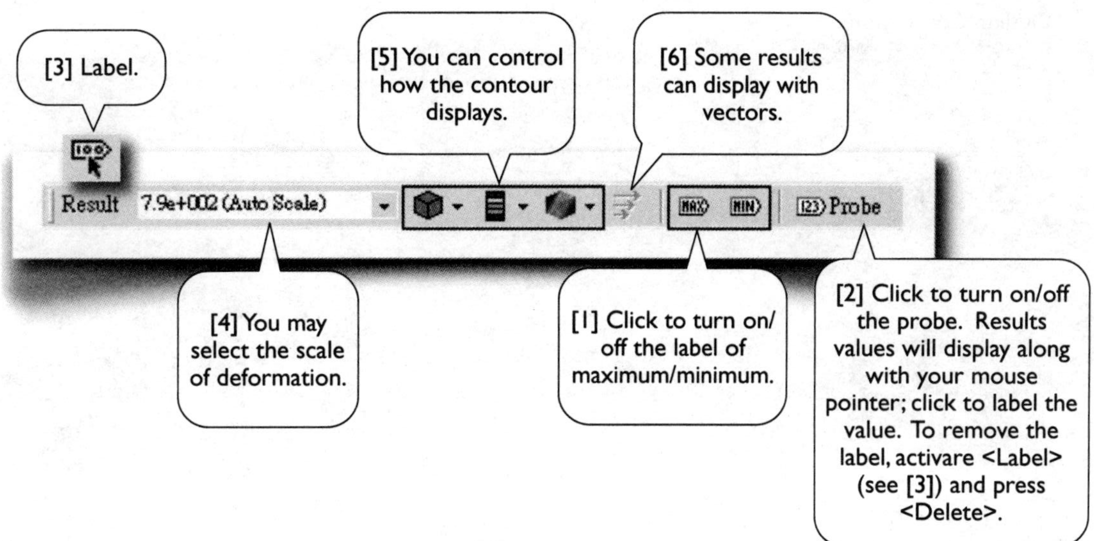

3.3-12 Insert APDL Commands[10]

An <Insert Commands> tool may appear on the toolbar [1], allowing you to insert APDL Commands. For those who are familiar with APDL, this may be useful, since the current version of Workbench doesn't include all the functionalities provided by APDL. For the newcomers, my suggestion is that you do not worry about APDL for now.

After click <Insert Commands> tool, a text editor is opened with several lines of comments telling you how the APDL commands will be executed. For example, an APDL commands object inserted under the <Environment> will be executed just before the <Solve> command.

References

1. ANSYS Help System>Mechanical>Mechanical Objects Reference
2. ANSYS Help System>Mechanical>Using the Mechanical Application Features>Applying Loads>How to Apply Loads
3. ANSYS Help System>Mechanical>Using the Mechanical Application Features>Applying Loads>Types of Loads and Conditions
4. ANSYS Help System>Mechanical>Using the Mechanical Application Features>Applying Loads>Spatial Varying Loads and Displacements
5. ANSYS Help System>Mechanical>Using the Mechanical Application Features>Geometry in the Mechanical Applicatin>Joints>Types of Joints
6. ANSYS Help System>Mechanical>Using the Mechanical Application Features>Applying Loads>Types of Supports
7. ANSYS Help System>Mechanical>Using the Mechanical Application Features>Results in the Mechanical application>Structural Results
8. ANSYS Help System>Mechanical>Using the Mechanical Application Features>Results in the Mechanical application>Results Related Topics>Probe
9. ANSYS Help System>Mechanical>Using the Mechanical Application Features>Results in the Mechanical Application>Results Related Topics>User Defined Results
10. ANSYS Help System>Mechanical>Using the Mechanical Application Features>Commands Objects
11. ANSYS Help System>Mechanical>The Mechanical Application Basics>The Mechanical Application Interface>Tree Outline Conventions

Section 3.4

Exercise: Spur Gears

3.4-1 About the Spur Gears

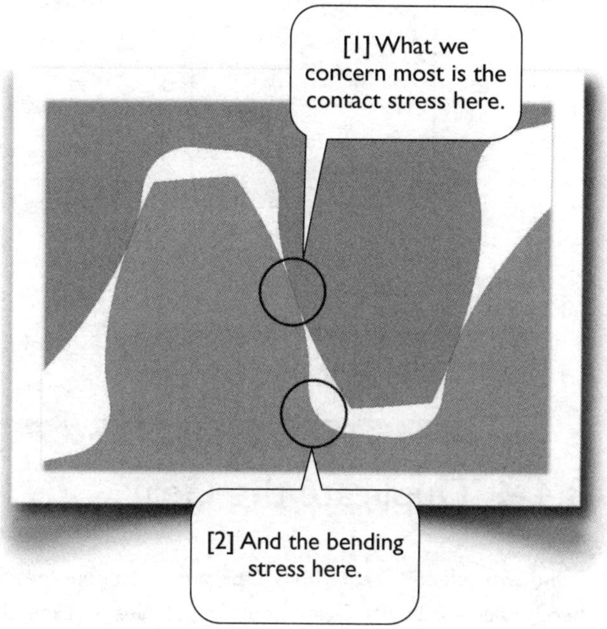

In this section, we want to conduct a simulation for the pair of spur gears introduced in Section 2.5. The goal is to assess the maximum stress during the transmission of a torque of 15,000 lb-in. According to engineering experience, the maximum stress occurs at either where the two teeth contact each other [1], or at the root of the contacting tooth due to the bending of the tooth [2].

The problem will be modeled as a plane stress problem, since the out-of-plane direction is without any restriction and thus free to expand or contract (Section 3.3-1).

The U.S. customary unit system is used in this exercise (to set up the unit system, see Section 3.3-5).

3.4-2 Set Up Project Schematic

Launch <Workbench>. Open the project "Gear" [1], which was saved in Section 2.5. Duplicate the <Geometry> system [2, 3]. Create a <Static Structural> system [4] by double-clicking in the <Toolbox>. Rename the three systems: <3D Gear>, <2D Gear Set>, and <2D Gear Set Simulation>. Share the geometry between the last two systems [5]. Double-click the <Geometry> cell in the <2D Gear Set> system to edit it [6].

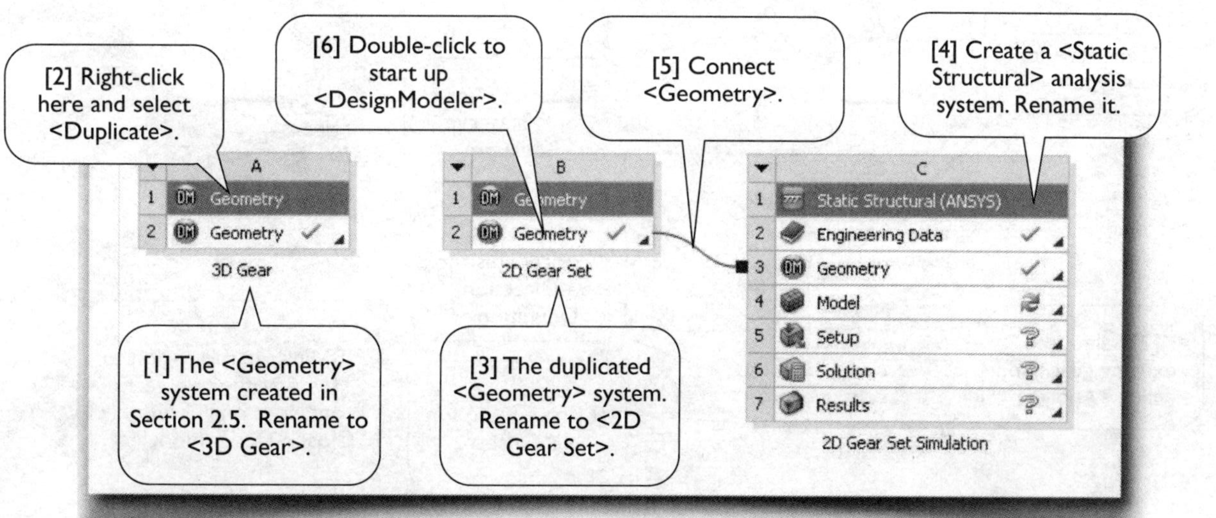

3.4-3 Delete the 3D Body and Creat a Surface Body

Delete <Extrude1> and create a surface body from <Sketch1> [1]. Remember to click <Generate>.

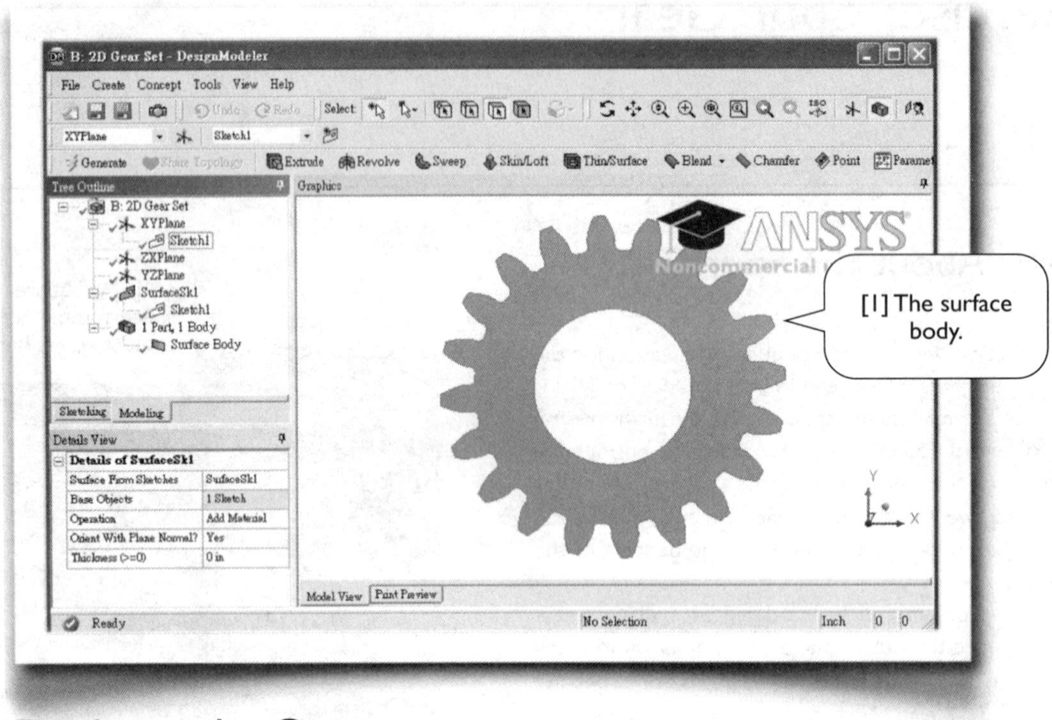

3.4-4 Duplicate the Gear

Pull-down-select <Create/Body Operation> to duplicate the gear [1-8]. Before closing <DesignModeler>, rename the two bodies as <Lower Gear> and <Upper Gear> respectively.

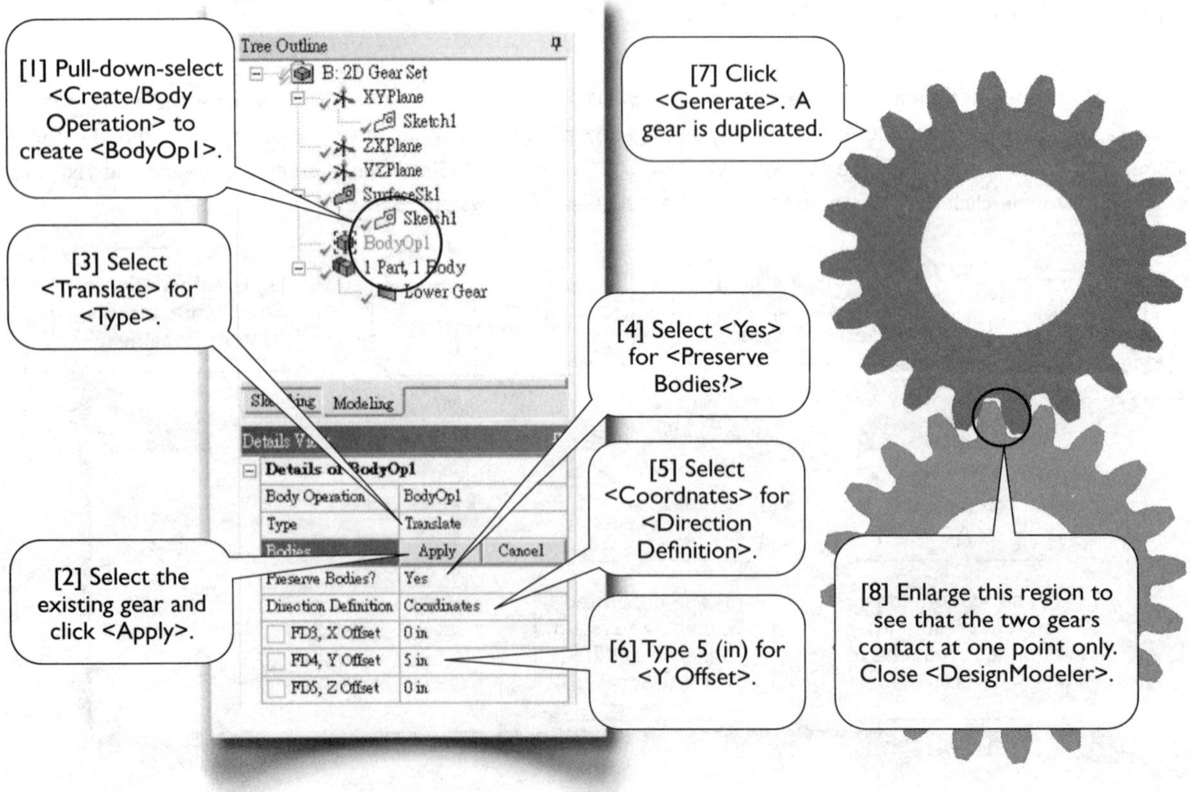

3.4-5 Set Up Geometry in <Mechanical>

Before entering <Mechanical>, remember to specify <2D> for <Analysis Type> in Workbench GUI (3.1-4[4-8]). This step is important since, after the geometry attaches to <Mechanical>, you cannot change it any more. Double-click <Model> in the <2D Gear Set Simulation> system to start up <Mechanical>.

In <Mechanical>, change the units to <U.S. Customary (in, lbm, lbf, s, V, A)> [1]. Make sure <2D Behavior> is set to <Plane Stress> [2]. Note that material defaults to <Structural Steel> and thickness defaults to 1.0 (in) [3].

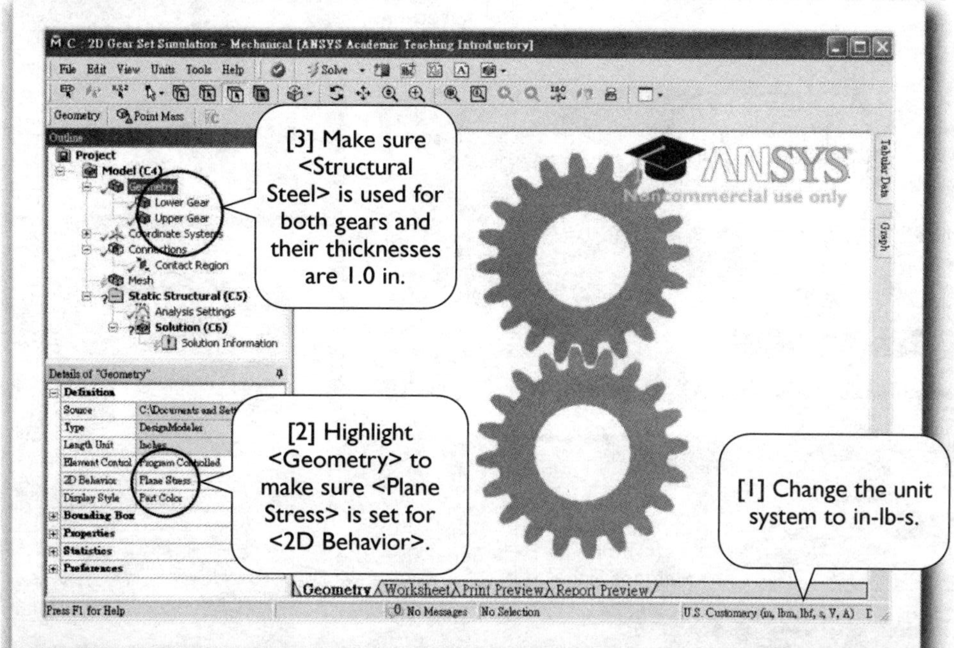

3.4-6 Set Up Contact Region

Redefine the contact region as follows. In the project tree, highlight <Connections/Contact Region> and define the <Contact> and <Target> as shown [1-4]. As we mentioned (3.2-7[3]), as long as the <Behavior> is <Symmetric>, the order of contact and target is irrelevant. Change the contact type to <Frictionless> [5]. Select <Argumented Lagrange> as <Formulation> [6]; this is generally recommended for frictionless contact (Section 13.1-10). Finally select <Adjust to Touch> for <Interface Treatment> [7] (Section 13.1-11).

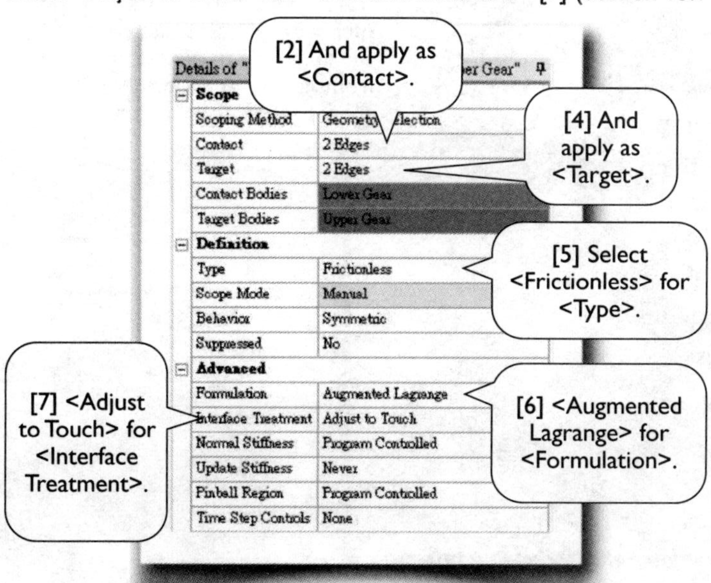

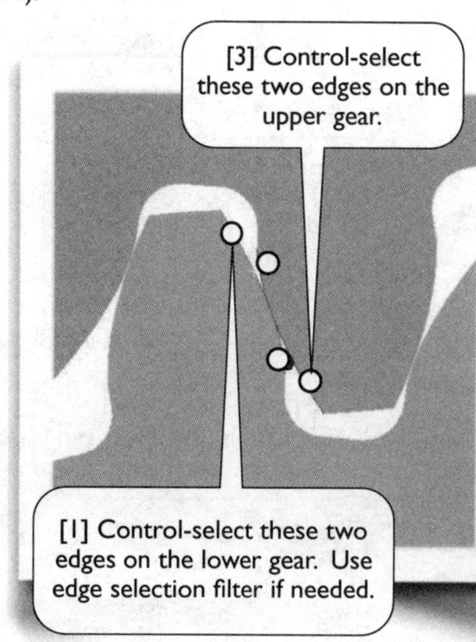

3.4-7 Generate Mesh

Generate mesh [1]. The mesh with default settings is not adequate. We need finer mesh on the contact areas and the fillets. Insert a <Sizing> for the mesh [2-4]. The new mesh should be adequate now.

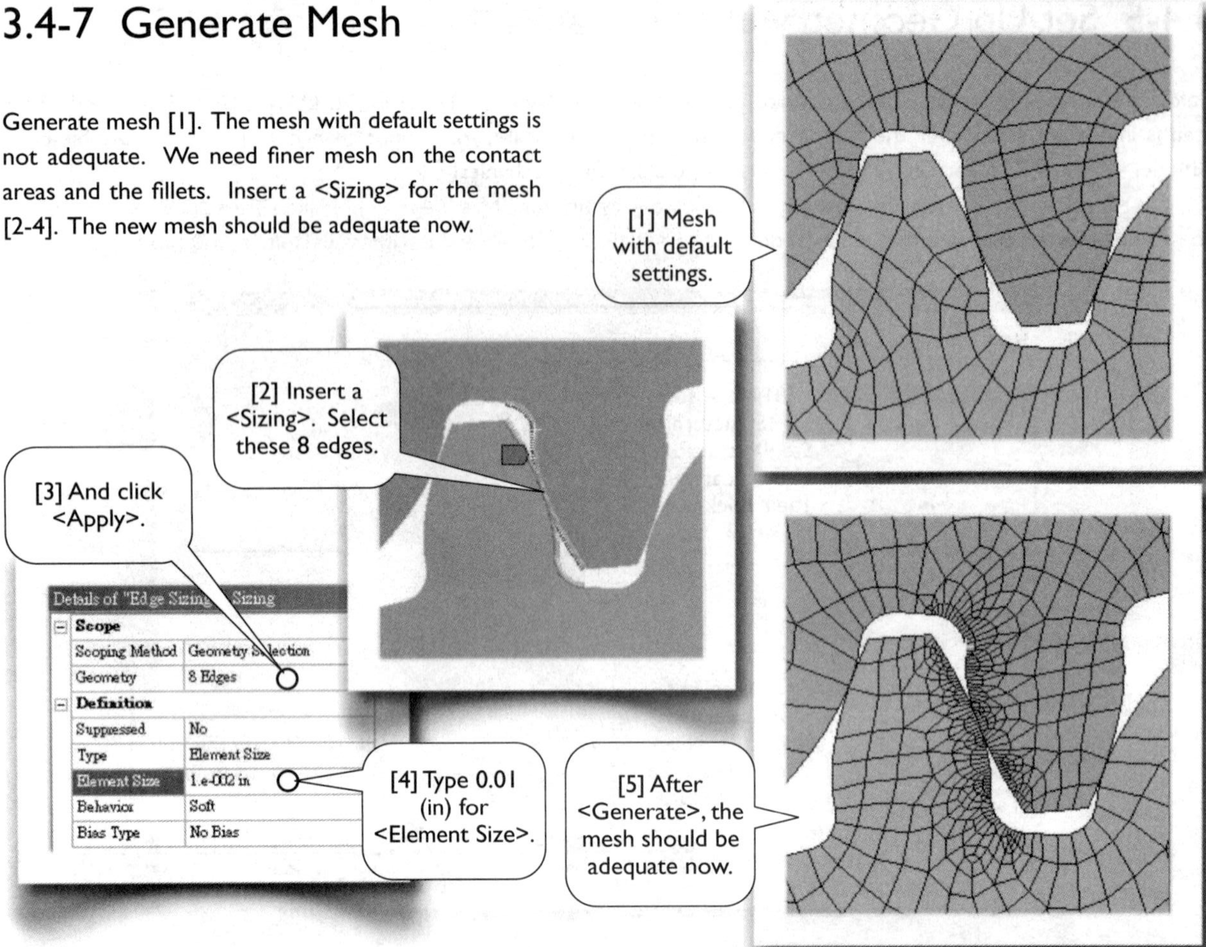

3.4-8 Specify Support and Load

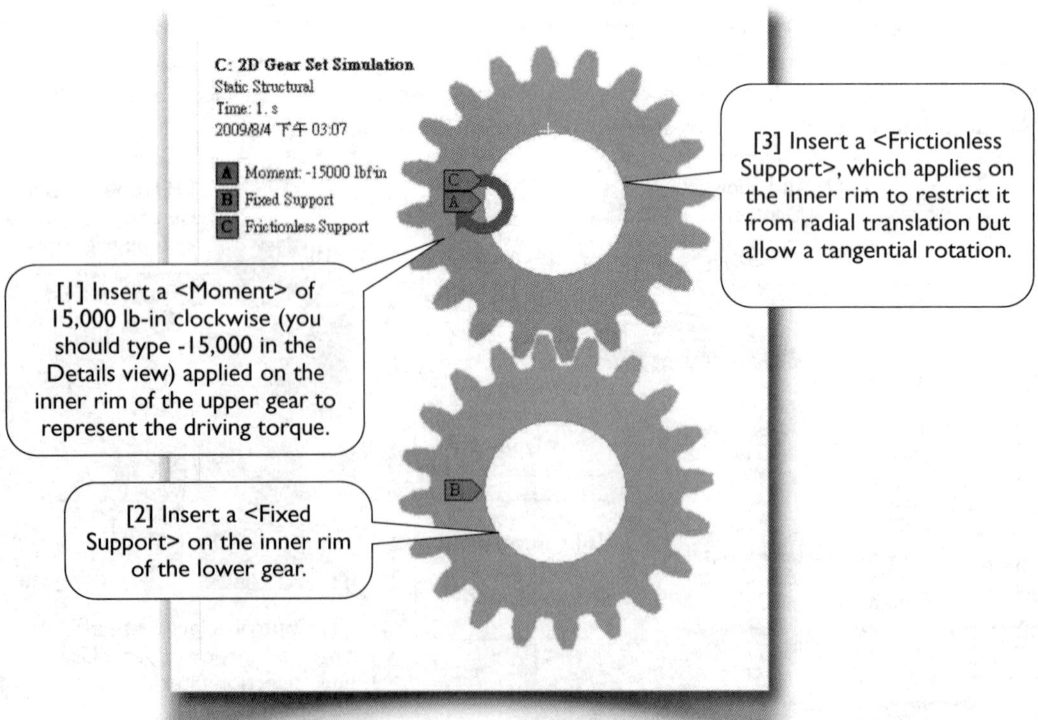

3.4-9 Solve the Model and View the Results

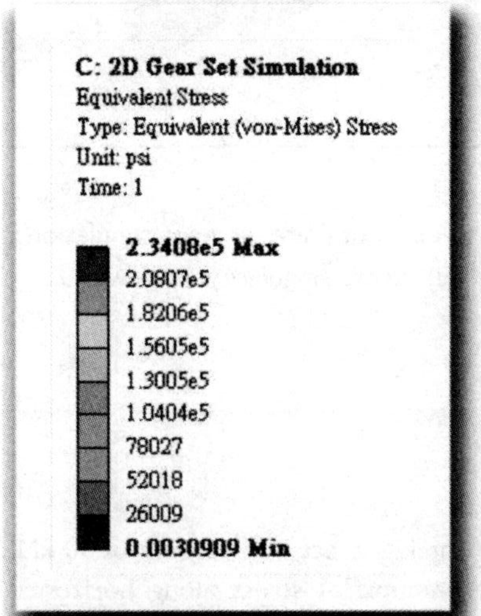

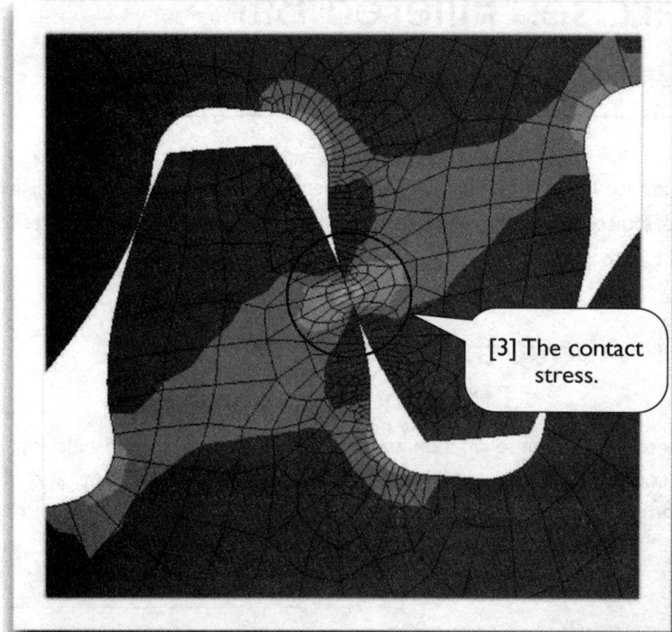

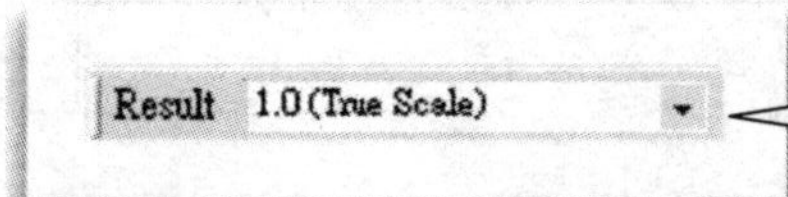

Wrap Up

Save the project. Close <Mechanical> and exit <Workbench>.

Section 3.5

Exercise: Filleted Bar

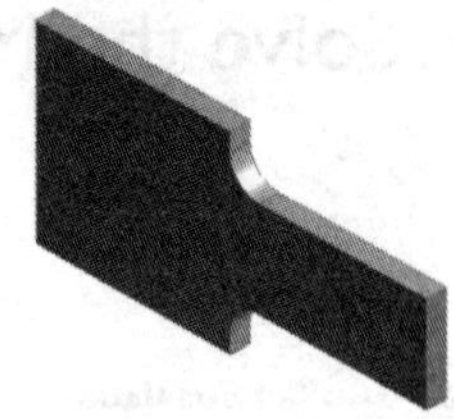

This exercise is designed to illustrate several must-know concepts regarding the solution of finite element simulations: (a) stress discontinuity, (b) structural error, (c) finite elements convergence, and (d) stress singularity. We will use a filleted bar to demonstrate these concepts.

3.5-1 About the Filleted Bar

The filleted bar is made of steel and has dimensions as shown below [1, 2]. The bar is subject to a tension of 50 kN. What concerns us are the maximum horizontal displacement, and the maximum normal stress along horizontal direction, which occurs near the fillets. The unit system used in this exercise is kg-mm-s-N (to set up this unit system, see Section 3.3-5).

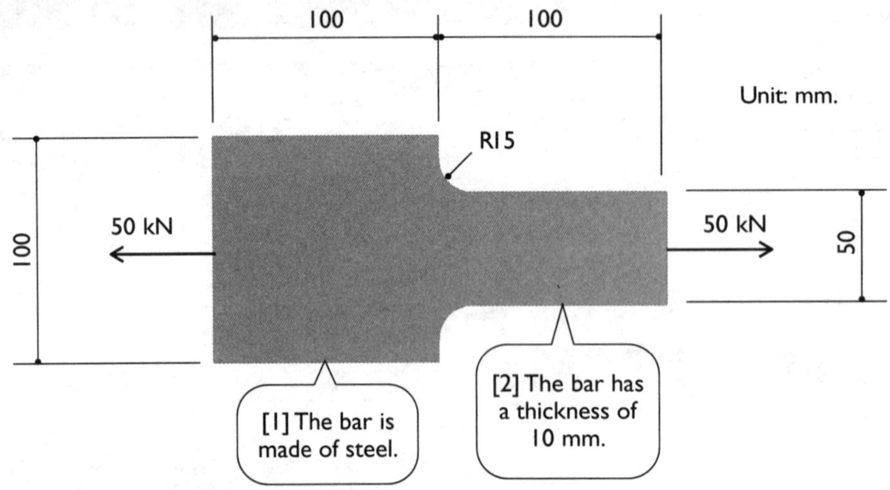

PART A. STRESS DISCONTINUITY

3.5-2 Start a New Project

Launch <Workbench>. Create a <Static Structural> system. Save the project as "Bar." Start up DesignModeler [1]. Select <Millimeter> as length unit.

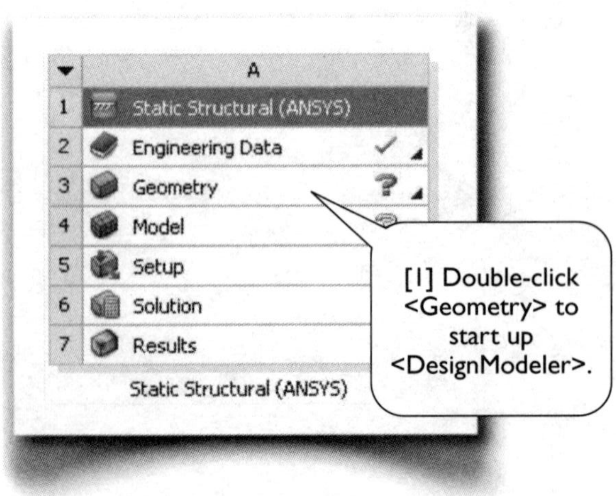

3.5-3 Create a 2D Model in DesignModeler

Create a sketch on XYPlane [1]. Create a surface body by pull-down-selecting <Concept/Surfaces from Sketches> [2, 3].

Close DesignModeler. In the Workbench GUI, specify <2D> (3.1-4[4-8]). In the <Project Schematic>, Double-click <Model> to start up <Mechanical>.

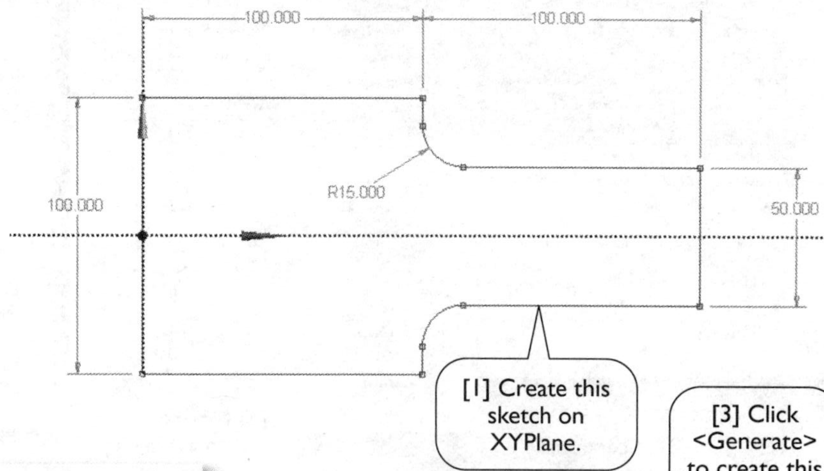

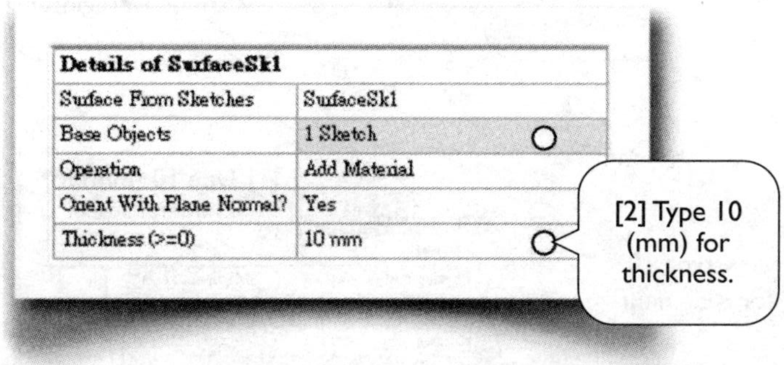

Details of SurfaceSk1	
Surface From Sketches	SurfaceSk1
Base Objects	1 Sketch
Operation	Add Material
Orient With Plane Normal?	Yes
Thickness (>=0)	10 mm

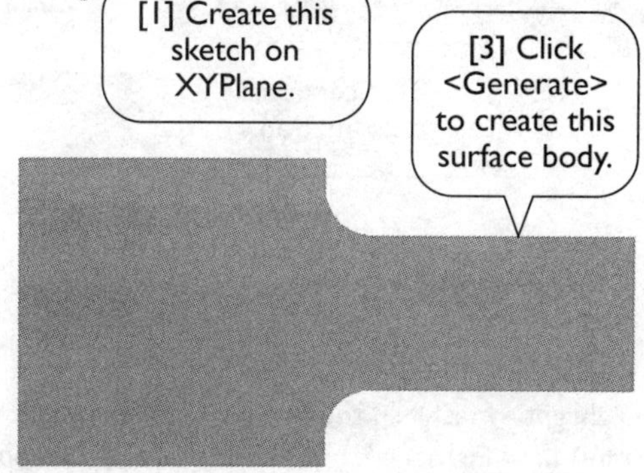

3.5-4 Set Up Support, Load, and Solution Objects

In <Mechanical>, select <mm, t, N, s> or <mm, kg, N, s> unit system.

Specify <Frictionless Support> on the left edge [1]; apply a force of 50,000 N on the right edge [2].

Insert a <Directional Deformation> and two <Normal Stress> under the solution branch as shown (next page) [3-5]. Rename the objects as shown (this page) [6].

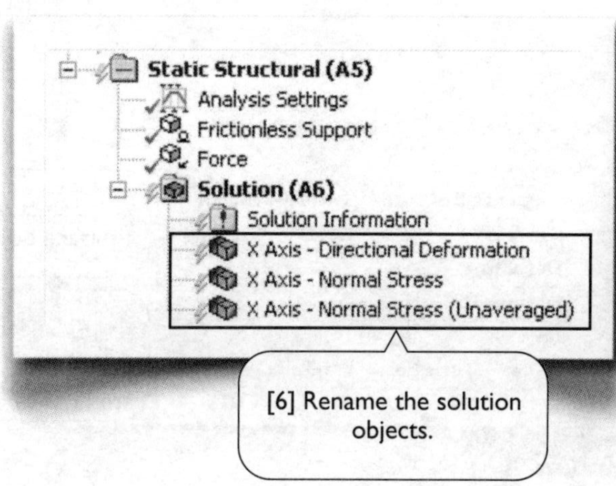

Averaged Stress

Note that, for the last solution object, we set <No> for <Use Average> [5]. The significance of this setting will be manifested after the stress results comes out.

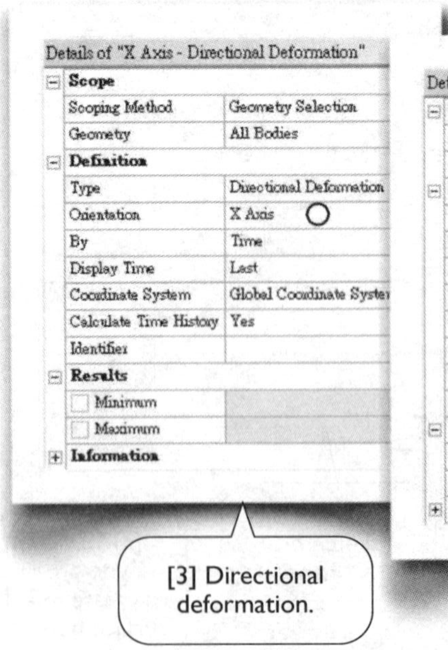

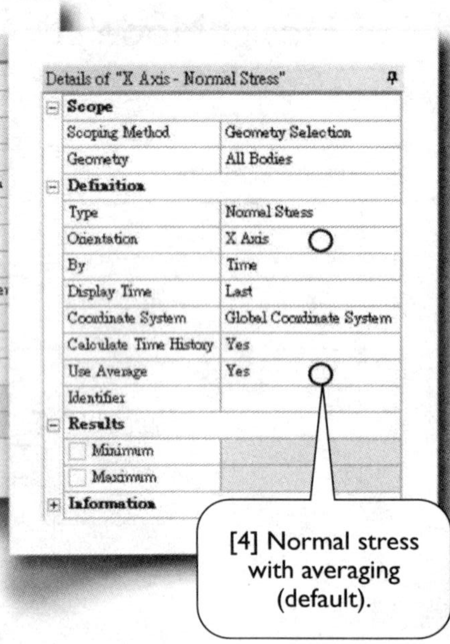

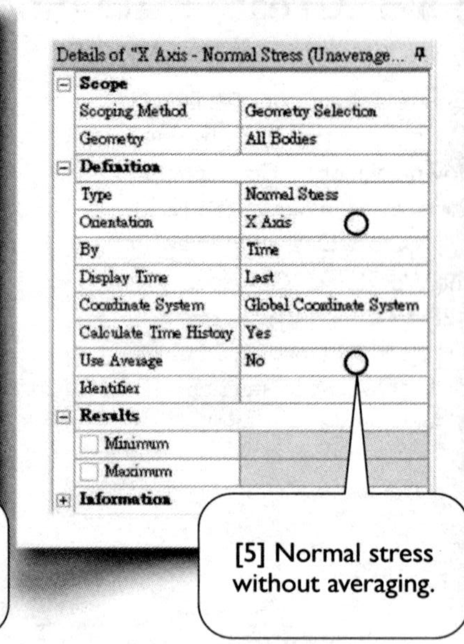

3.5-5 Set Up Mesh Controls

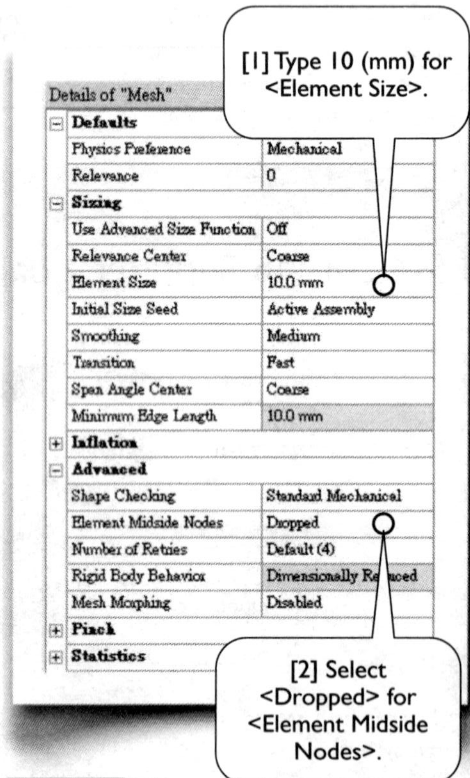

Highlight <Mesh> in the project tree. In the Details view, type 10 (mm) for <Element Size> [1] and select <Dropped> for <Element Midside Nodes>.

Select <Mesh Control/Method> to insert a method. In the Details view, select <Triangles> for <Method>. This sets up a <All-Triangles> method.

Generate the mesh [5]. Click <Solve> to solve the model.

Why Coarse Lower-Order Triangular Elements?

Remember that the purpose of this part of the simulation is to demonstrate the stress discontinuity, a must-know of finite element solution. Overall, we've set up a mesh that is coarse (about 10 mm of element size), and the element used are linear (midsize nodes dropped) triangular. The reason is to exaggerate the stress discontinuity behavior. Stress discontinuity is intrinsic in the finite element simulation, not limited to triangular or lower-order elements.

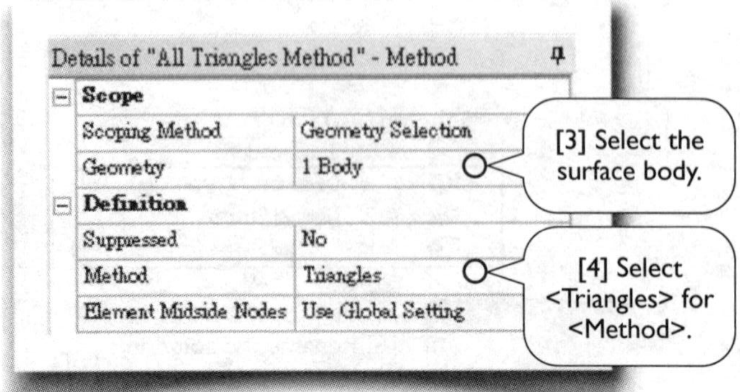

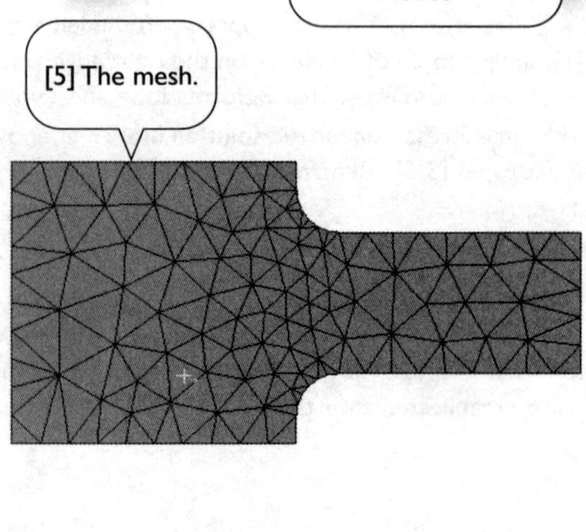

3.5-6 View the Results

Displacement Fields

Nodal displacements, calculated by solving Eq. 1.3-1(1), are single valued. Therefore the displacement fileds, calculated using Eq. 1.3-2(2), must be continuous over the entire body [1].

The displacement fields are continuous but not necessarily smooth. In fact, the use of continuous shape functions within the element guarantees the displacement field piecewise smooth only, but not smooth across the element boundaries.

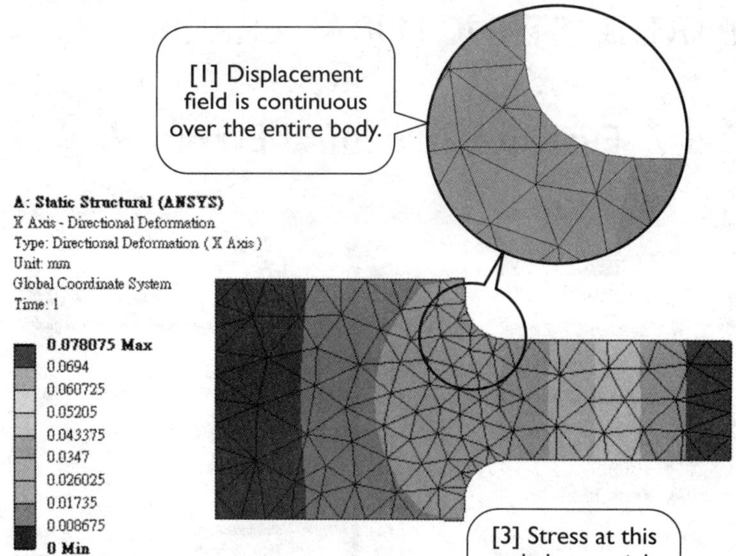

Stress Fields

After the displacement fields are calculated, the strain fields are calculated using Eq. 1.2-7(1), and stress field are in turn calculated using Eq. 1.2-8(1).

The calculations are element-by-element. The figure in the right is a typical results of stress calculation [2, 3]. Note that a node may have multiple stress values, since the node may connect to multiple elements, and each element calculation results a value.

This behavior is not difficult to understand. Since differentiations are involved in the Eq. 1.2-7(1), this makes the strain field and the stress fields become piecewise continuous only. They are not continuous across the element boundaries.

By default, stresses are averaged on the nodes, and the stress field is recalculated. After that, the stress field is continuous over the body.

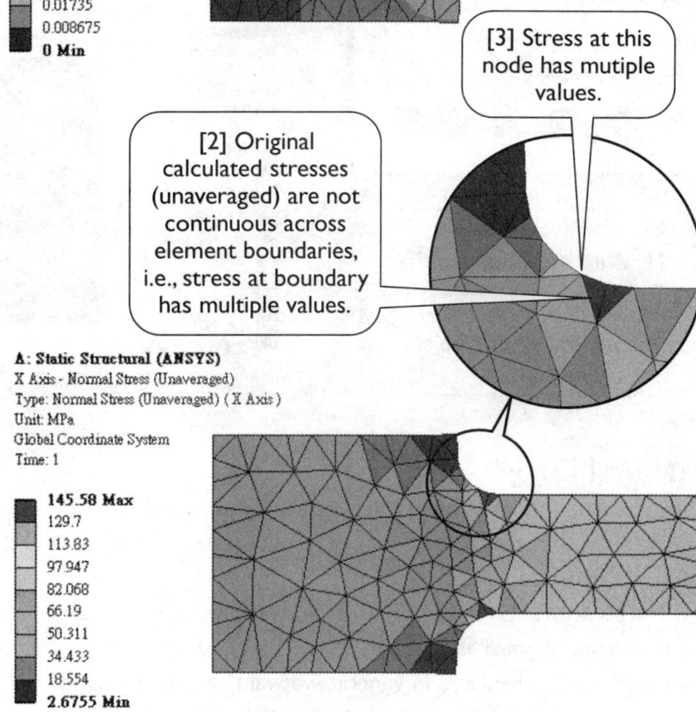

Useage of Unaveraged Stress Fields

The averaged stress fields are visually efficient for us to interpret the results, while unaveraged stress fields provide a way of assessing the solution accuracy.

In general, as the mesh is getting finer, the solution is more accurate, and the stress discontinuity is less obvious. Thus, stress discontinuity can be used as an index for solution accuracy: the less discontinuous of the stress field, the more accurate of the solution.

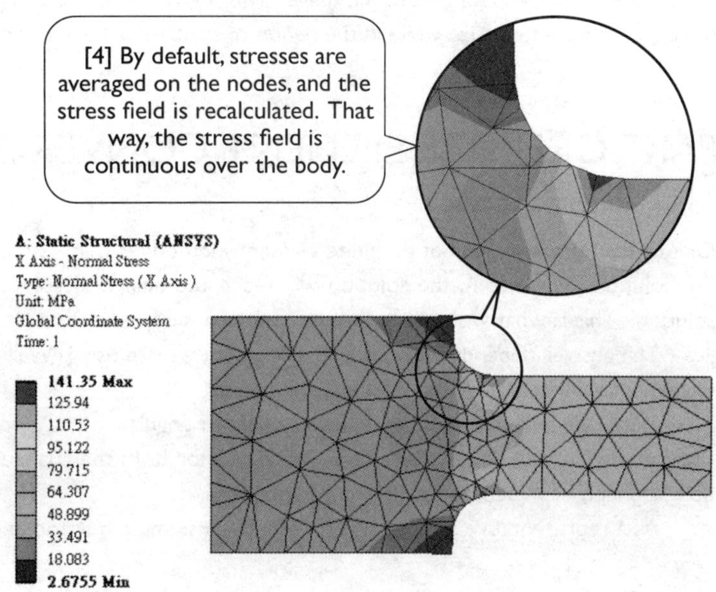

PART B. STRUCTURAL ERROR

3.5-7 Evaluate Structural Error

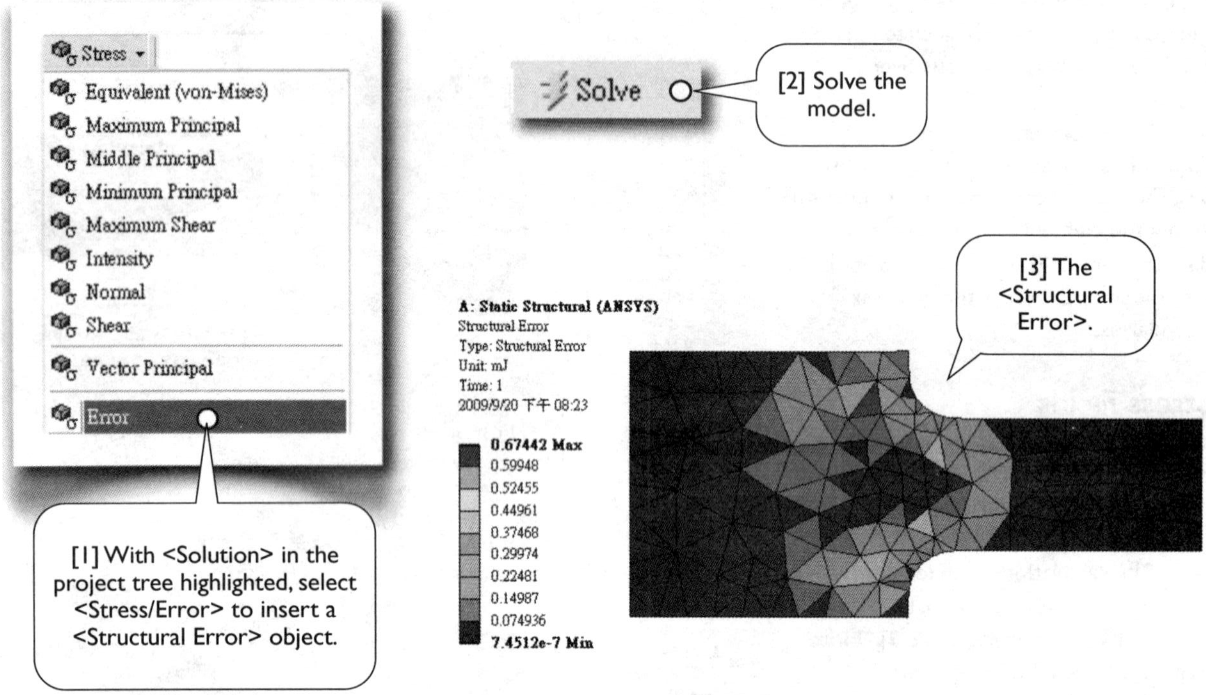

Structural Error[1]

For an element, strain energies calculated using averaged stresses and unaveraged stresses respectively are different. The difference between these two energy values is called <Structural Error> of the element. The finer the mesh, the smaller the structural error.

The structural error can be used for two purposes: (a) As an indicator of global mesh adequacy. In general, we want the values as small as possible. Refine the mesh globally is a way of reducing structural error. (b) As an indicator of the local mesh adequacy. In general, we want the structural error distribution as uniform as possible to maximize the efficiency of computing resource usage. This implies that in the region of large values of structural error we need to reduce the element size while in the region of small values we may enlarge the element size.

PART C. FINITE ELEMENT CONVERGENCE

One of the core concepts of the finite element methods is that, as mentioned, the finer the mesh, the more accurate the solution. Ultimately, the solution will reach the analytical solution. But, how fast it approaches the analytical solution? This is what we want to answer in this part of the section. It is called the *element convergence behavior*.

The answer depends on what kind of element we are using. We'll draw a conclusion that, in general, quadrilateral elements converges faster than triangular elements.

Here, we will only compare lower-order triangular with lower-order quadrilateral. To be meaningful, the comparison is made under the same problem size for both the triangular and the quadrilateral. The problem size can be reasonably represented by the number of nodes.

As a representative structural response, the maximum horizontal displacement is recorded for comparison.

3.5-8 Triangular Elements

Repeat the foregoing simulation. Change the element size each time [1], record the number of nodes [2], and the maximum displacement. Tabulate the your results somewhat like this:

Element Size (mm)	Number of Nodes	Max Displacement (mm)
10	132	0.078075
6	222	0.077965
4	407	0.078244
3	706	0.078428
2	1380	0.078536
1.5	2357	0.078585
1	5063	0.078625
0.7	10140	0.078636
0.6	13624	0.078640

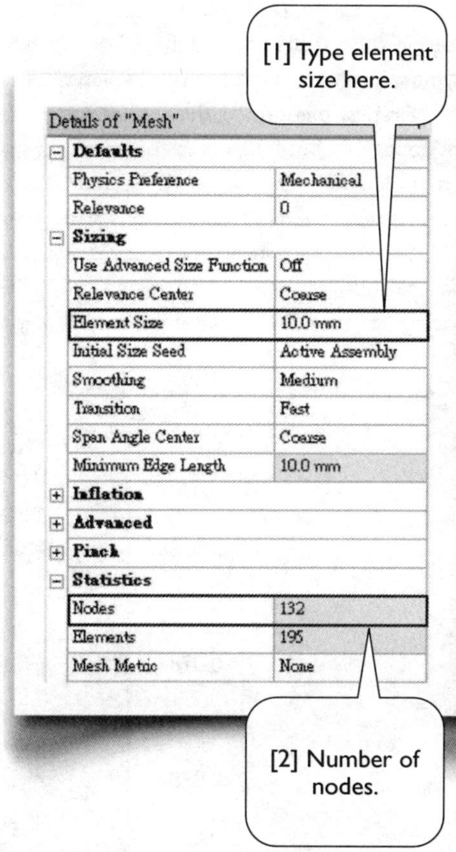

3.5-9 Quadrilateral Elements

Highlight <All Triangles Method> under the <Mesh> branch. In the Details view, change the method to <Quadrilateral Dominant> [3], and select <All Quad> for <Free Face Mesh Type> [4}. Repeat the simulation, and tabulate your results somewhat like this:

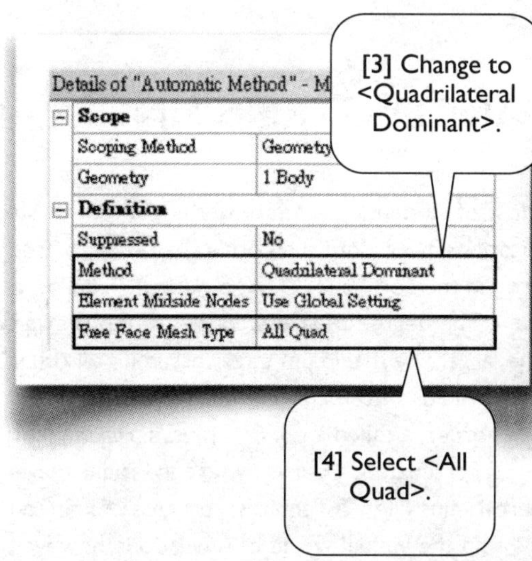

Element Size (mm)	Number of Nodes	Max Displacement (mm)
10	201	0.078420
6	501	0.078483
4	1048	0.078569
3	1835	0.078603
2	4022	0.078629
1.5	7104	0.078639
1	15924	0.078647
0.8	24814	0.078649

3.5-10 Comparison and Conclusions

Plotting the results in Sections 3.5-8 and 3.5-9, you have charts as shown [1-3]. Note two curves share the same asymptote, which is the analytical solution. Two important behaviors are also observed as follows.

First, as mentioned, the quadrilateral element converges faster than the triangular element. The difference does not appear to be dramatic in this case. In many other cases, however, the difference can be critical. We will discuss this topic more thoroughly in Section 9.3. In that section, we will generalize this concept to 3D, in which the convergence speeds of hexahedra is faster than prisms or tetrahedra (1.3-3[1-3]).

Second, the convergence curves approach the asymptote from below; the finite element solutions never exceed the analytical solution. That means the finite element solutions always underestimates the deformation, or in the language of Eq. 1.3-1(1), the stiffness matrix is always overestimated.

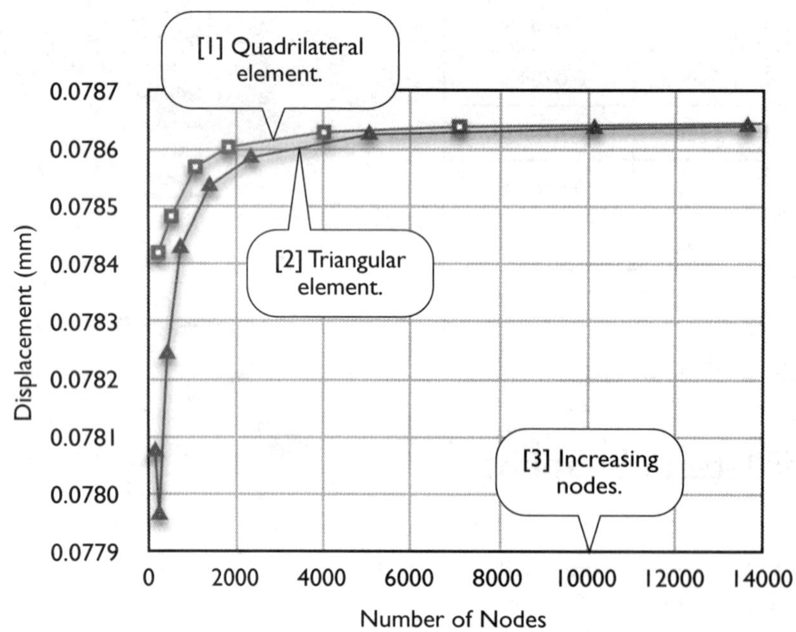

PART D. STRESS SINGULARITY

Most of students are aware of the concept of stress concentration: stress is larger at a concave corner than stress at locations away from the corner. In order to accurately evaluate the concentrated stress, finer mesh needs to be used around the corner [1, 2]. As a general guideline, around where the stress gradient is high, it requires finer mesh.

The degree of stress concentration is inversely proportional to the radius of the corner: the smaller the radius, the larger the maximum stress, assuming all other conditions remain the same. Naturally, a question raises: how about if the radius of the concave corner is zero? The answer is, in that case, the stress at that sharp corner is infinity, and the corner is called a point of *stress singularity*, or a *singular point*.

Fortunately, a corner with zero radius never happens in the real-world. You have no way to manufacture such a zero-radius fillet. It requires a process of infinite-high precision machining. That does not exist yet.

In the virtual-world of simulations, however, zero-radius fillets exist everywhere. Since many small features such as fillets do not contribute the global behavior of a structure too much, these small features are often not included in the simulation model. The result is that zero-radius fillets exist everywhere in the model.

It is important that the engineers be aware of the existence of stress singularity. For example, engineers may mistakenly use the maximum stress as the design stress, but, in fact, that is a singular stress—it doesn't exist in the real-world. Always check if the maximum stress comes from a singular point.

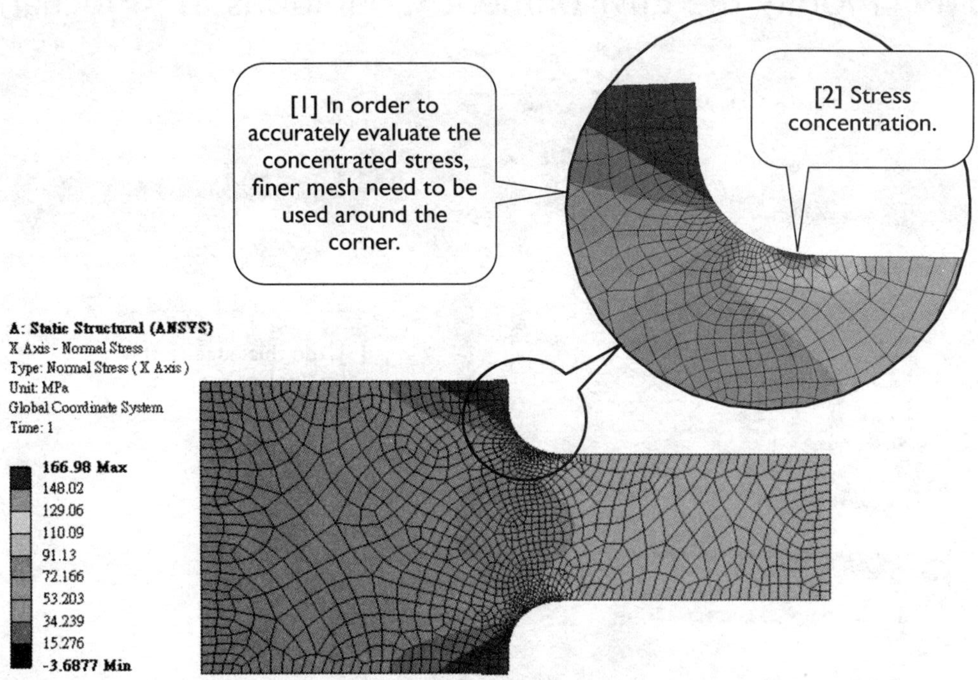

3.5-11 Modify the Model in DesignModeler

First, modify the sketch such that the fillet becomes sharp corners [1]. Second, since we need to use very fine mesh to study stress concentration, let's reduce the model to half by taking advantage of symmetry [2].

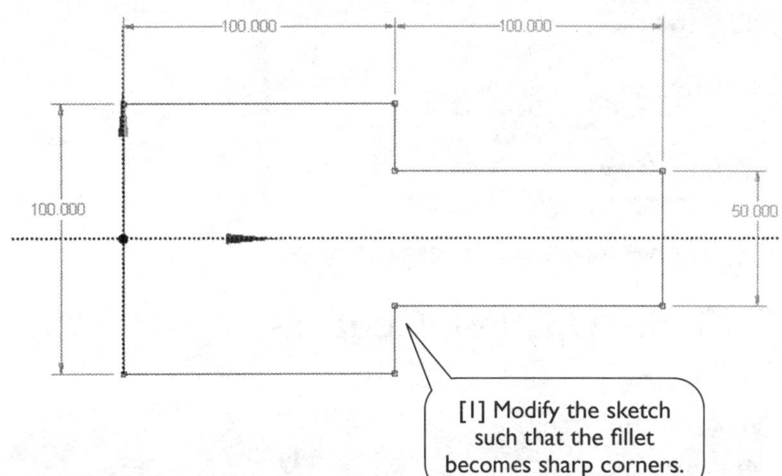

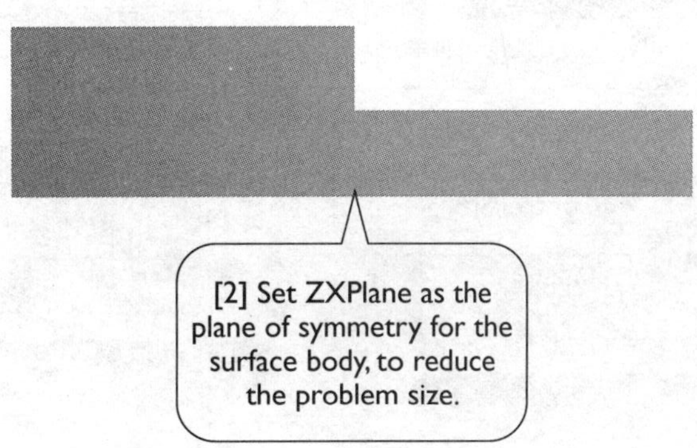

3.5-12 Modify the Environment Conditions in <Mechanical>

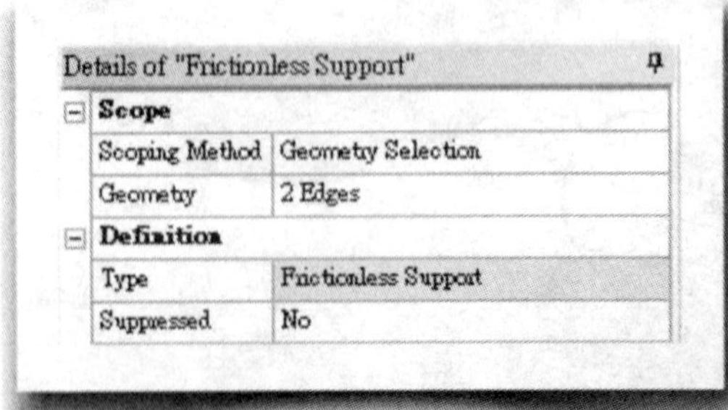

[1] Add this edge to the frictionless support.

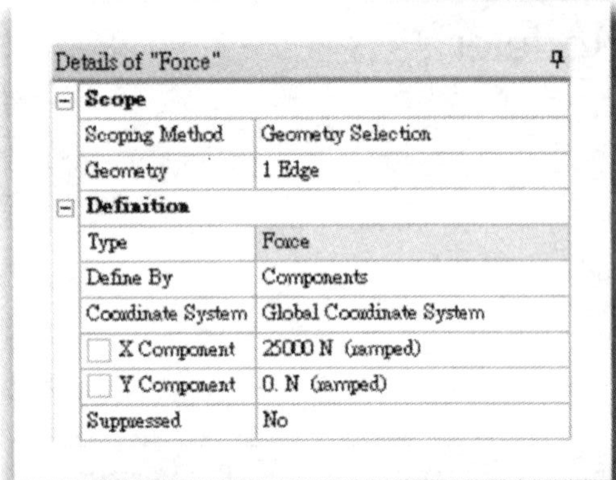

[2] Reduce the force to half (25,000 N), since the edge is half now.

3.5-13 Set Up Mesh Controls

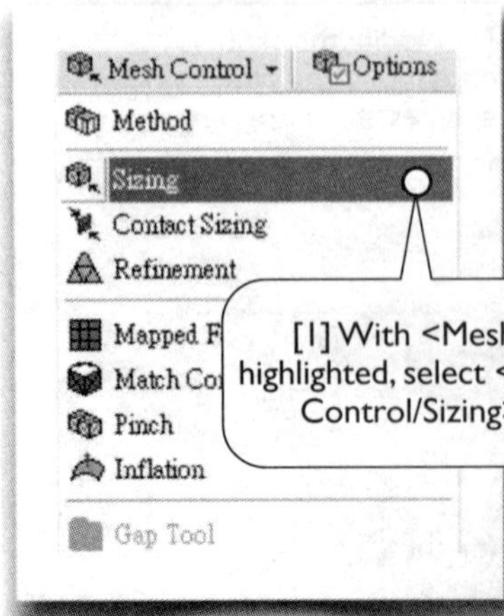

[1] With <Mesh> highlighted, select <Mesh Control/Sizing>.

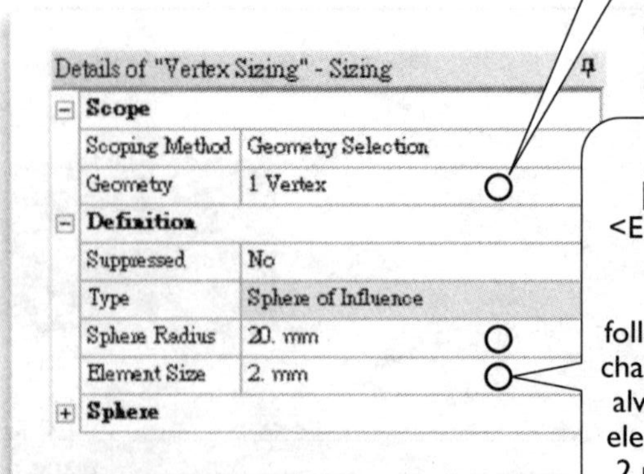

[2] In the Details view, select the vertex at the sharp corner and click <Apply>.

[3] Type 2 mm for <Element Size> and 20 mm for <Sphere Radius>. For the following study, we only change element size and always use 10 times of element size or at least 2 mm as the radius of sphere of influence.

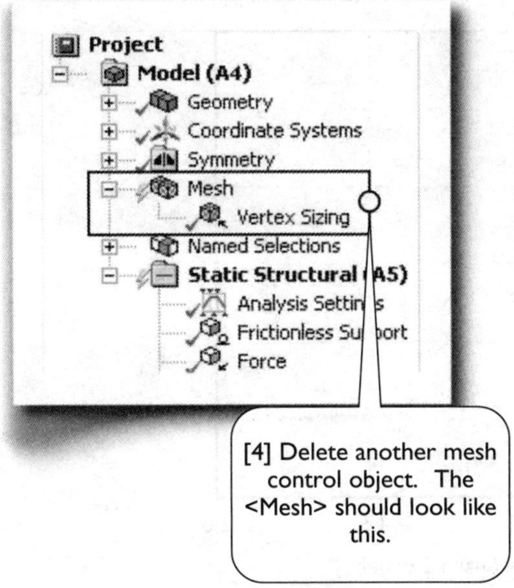

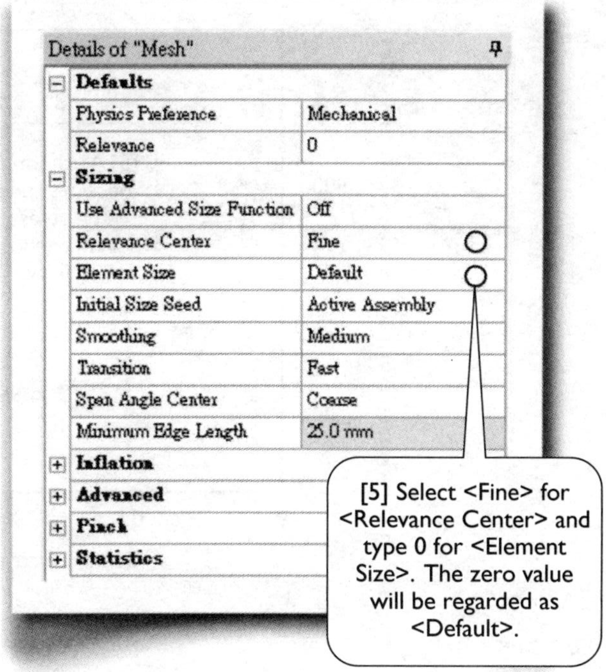

3.5-14 Perform Simulations and Conclusion

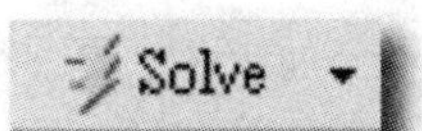

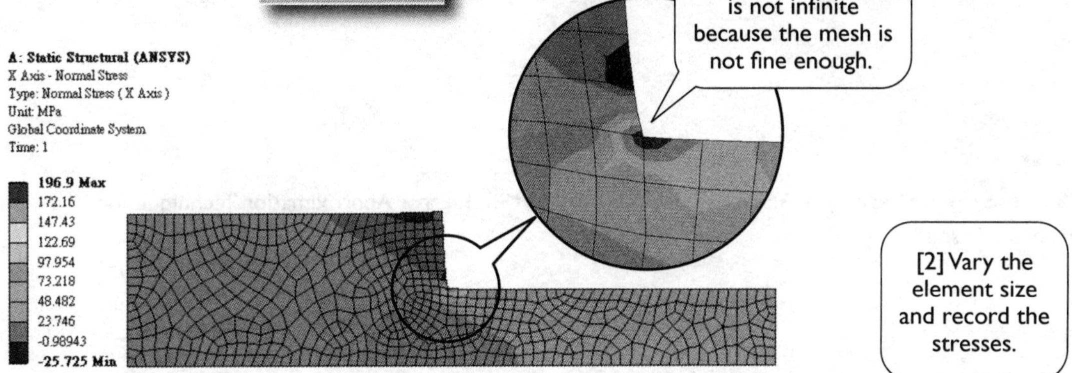

Element Size (mm)	Max Stress (MPa)
2	196.90
1	244.23
0.5	330.09
0.2	517.44
0.1	768.37
0.05	985.03

After solving the model, the stress at the zero-radius fillet is not infinite, the theoretical value. This is because our mesh is not fine enough. To achieve an infinite value of stress, you need a zero element size. That is, of course, not possible.

Reduce the element size, and record the maximum stress. Repeat this and you should obtain a table somewhat like the one on the right [2].

Interpretation of the data may be easier, if you put them in a graph [3]. It is obvious that, as the mesh gets finer (element size becomes closer to zero), the stress at the sharp corner will eventually reach an infinite value, consistent with the theory.

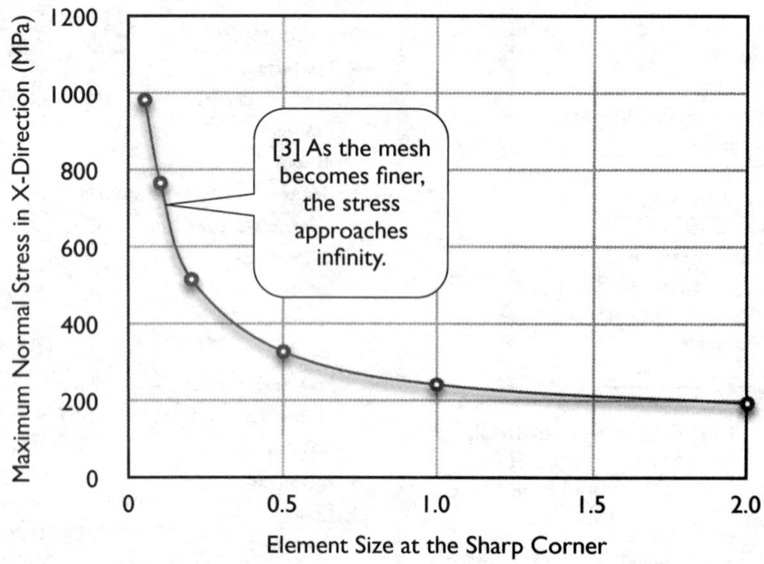

Remark

Stress Singularity is not limited to the sharp corner. Any locations that have stress of infinite large are called points of stress singularity. Besides a concave fillet of zero radius, a point of concentrated forces is also a point of singularity.

References

1. ANSYS Help System>Mechanical APDL>Theory Reference>19.7.1. Error Approximation Technique for Displacement-Based Problems.

Section 3.6
Problems

3.6-1 Key Concepts

Weak Spring
When Workbench detects a structure as unstable, it adds weak springs on the structure to make it capable of withstanding very small external forces.

Plane Stress Problem
In a structural simulation problem, if all the stresses in a direction, say Z-direction, vanish, the problem can be reduced to a 2D problem, and is called a plane stress problem.

Plane Strain Problem
In a structural simulation problem, if all the strains in a direction, say Z-direction, vanish, the problem can be reduced to a 2D problem, and is called a plane strain problem.

Project Tree
A project tree is a structured representation of an analysis system and displayed on the <Outline> in <Mechanical>. A project tree contains one or more simulation models. A simulation model contains one or more <Environment> branches.

Inconsistent Unit System
A unit system in which at least one unit is not consistent with other units. For example, the "Metric (mm, kg, N, s, mV, mA)" is inconsistent, since if mm and kg is used, the force must be mN (milli-newton) instead of N.

APDL
ANSYS Parametric Design Language. A set of text-based language that is used to drive ANSYS Classic program.

Environment Conditions
Consist of loads, supports, and inertial effects, which apply on the simulation model.

Stress Discontinuity
In the finite element methods, the shape functions are used to interpolate the displacement fields interior to the element. Across the element boundaries, the displacement fields are continuous but not smooth. The strains and stresses, which are calculated by differentiating the displacement fields, become discontinuous across the element boundaries.

Structural Error
For an element, strain energies calculated using averaged stresses and unaveraged stresses are different. The difference between these two energy values is called structural error of the element. The finer the mesh, the smaller the structural error. It is used as an indicator for mesh adequacy.

Element Convergence Study

Study of how the finite element solutions approaches to theoretical values as the mesh is getting finer. In 2D, quadrilateral elements converges faster than the triangular. In 3D, the order of convergence speeds are, from faster to slower, hexahedral, prism, pyramid, and tetrahedral.

Stress Singularity

Any locations that have infinitely large stress are called points of stress singularity. They are often found at concave fillets of zero radius, or at points subject to concentrated forces or displacement constraints.

3.6-2 Questions

Prove Eq. 3.3-2(2) from Eq. 1.2-8(1).

The first 3 and last 3 equations are decoupled, they can be proved independently. Proof of the last 3 equations from the last 3 equation in Eq. 1.2-8(1) is trivial. Now, we prove the first 3 equations. The first 3 equations in Eq. 1.2-8(1) can be written in matrix form

$$\begin{Bmatrix} \varepsilon_x \\ \varepsilon_y \\ \varepsilon_z \end{Bmatrix} = \frac{1}{E} \begin{bmatrix} 1 & -\nu & -\nu \\ -\nu & 1 & -\nu \\ -\nu & -\nu & 1 \end{bmatrix} \begin{Bmatrix} \sigma_x \\ \sigma_y \\ \sigma_z \end{Bmatrix} \quad \text{or} \quad \{\varepsilon\} = [D]\{\sigma\}$$

The first 3 equation in Eq. 3.3-2(2) can also be written in matrix form

$$\begin{Bmatrix} \sigma_x \\ \sigma_y \\ \sigma_z \end{Bmatrix} = \frac{E}{(1+\nu)(1-2\nu)} \begin{bmatrix} 1-\nu & \nu & \nu \\ \nu & 1-\nu & \nu \\ \nu & \nu & 1-\nu \end{bmatrix} \begin{Bmatrix} \varepsilon_x \\ \varepsilon_y \\ \varepsilon_z \end{Bmatrix} \quad \text{or} \quad \{\sigma\} = [F]\{\varepsilon\}$$

Then

$$[D][F] = \frac{1}{E} \cdot \frac{E}{(1+\nu)(1-2\nu)} \begin{bmatrix} 1 & -\nu & -\nu \\ -\nu & 1 & -\nu \\ -\nu & -\nu & 1 \end{bmatrix} \begin{bmatrix} 1-\nu & \nu & \nu \\ \nu & 1-\nu & \nu \\ \nu & \nu & 1-\nu \end{bmatrix} = \begin{bmatrix} 1 & 0 & 0 \\ 0 & 1 & 0 \\ 0 & 0 & 1 \end{bmatrix}$$

This completes the proof.

3.6-3 Workbench Exercises

Stress in a Long Cylinder

Consider the problem described in VM25 of the APDL verification manual[1]. Find the radial stress and the hoop stress at the inner and outer surfaces and at the middle wall thickness, for both loading cases. Model the problem as (a) axisymmetric problem and (b) plane strain problem.

Reference

1. ANSYS Help System>Mechanical APDL>Verification Manual for Mechanical APDL Application>Verification Test Case Description>VM25

Chapter 4
3D Solid Modeling

A 3D geometric model is usually much more complicated to construct than a 2D model. Fortunately, most of the techniques we learned in Chapters 2 and 3 for 2D solid modeling can also be used in 3D solid modeling. The types of 3D bodies that Workbench supports include *solid bodies*, *surface bodies*, and *line bodies*. Although different types of bodies can be mixed up in a model, in this chapter, we will mostly focus on models consisting of solid bodies only. The only exception is the model in Section 4.3, in which a surface body and several solid bodies constitute the model.

Purpose of the Chapter

The purpose of this chapter is to train the students' proficient at 3D solid modeling using DesignModeler. Four mechanical parts will be created in this chapters. These models are then used for static structural simulations in the next chapter.

About Each Section

We start with a beam bracket model in Section 4.1 to get familiar with 3D bodies creation basics. Section 4.2 jumps to a much more elaborated model, namely the cover of a pressure cylinder, to obtain some degree of proficiency at the 3D modeling techniques. In Section 4.3, we will create a model for a lifting fork, which is a combination of solid bodies and a surface body. Section 4.4 overviews all the 3D solid bodies creation and manipulation tools in a systematic way, intending to fill up what were missed in the first three sections. Section 4.5 provides an additional exercise.

Section 4.1

Step-by-Step: Beam Bracket

4.1-1 About the Beam Bracket

In constructing steel beam-column structures, such as high-rise buildings or manufacturing plants, columns are erected before beams can be elevated, positioned, and welded. The functions of the beam bracket [1] are to (a) precisely position the beam during the construction, and (b) safely transfer the loads from the beam to the column. The loads are determined by a thorough analysis of the entire structure subject to design loads, such as dead load, live load, earthquake, wind load, etc.

The beam bracket is made of a WT8x25 structural steel. It consists of a seat plate (the flange) and a web plate [2, 3]. The design considerations include (a) Would the maximum stress excess the allowable stress? (b) Would the web buckle under the load?

We will create a 3D solid model for the beam bracket in this section. The solid model will be used for a static structural simulation in Section 5.1 and then a buckling analysis in Section 10.3. In Section 6.2, the solid model will be transformed to a surface model, which is then simulated. The purpose is to demonstrate many capabilities of the Workbench.

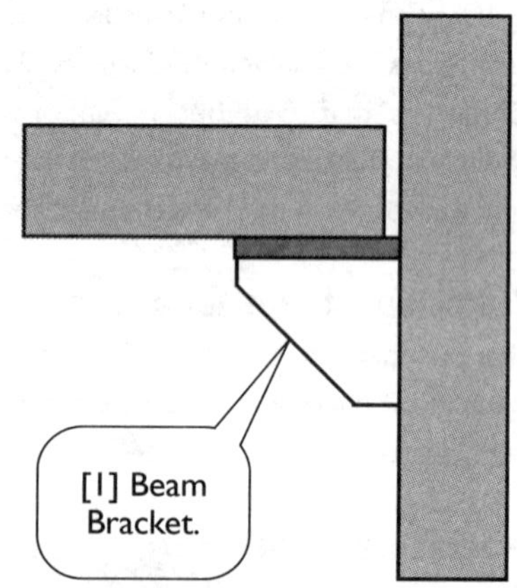

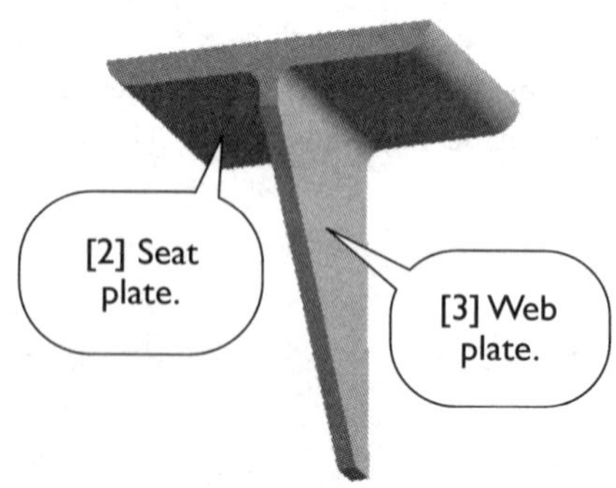

Global Coordinate System

Before creating a geometric model in DesignModeler, you need to set up a global coordinate system in mind. This is true both for 2D and 3D. For 2D, it is so trivial that we didn't mention it at all. For 3D, you'd better take it seriously. Many students are easily disoriented when working with 3D models on a 2D computer screen. In our case, the global coordinate system is set up as shown [4-7].

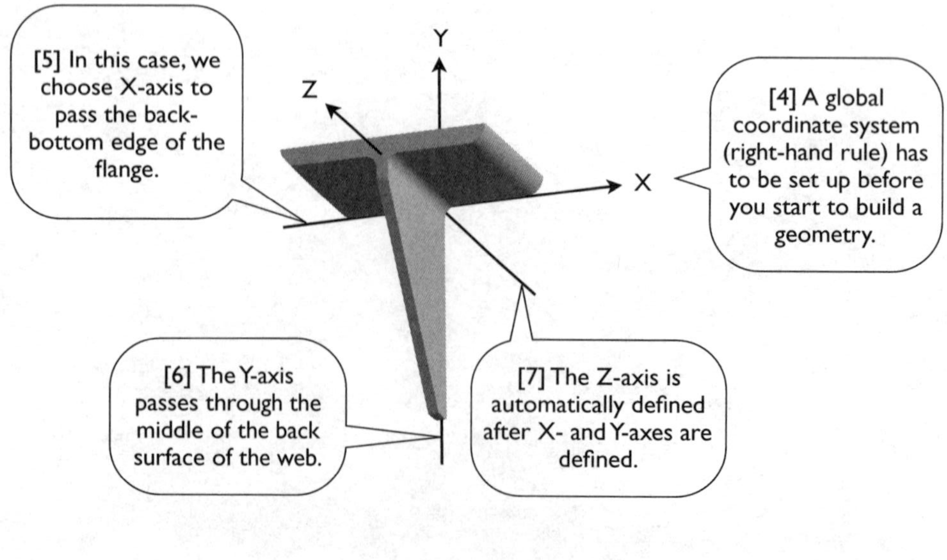

4.1-2 Start Up

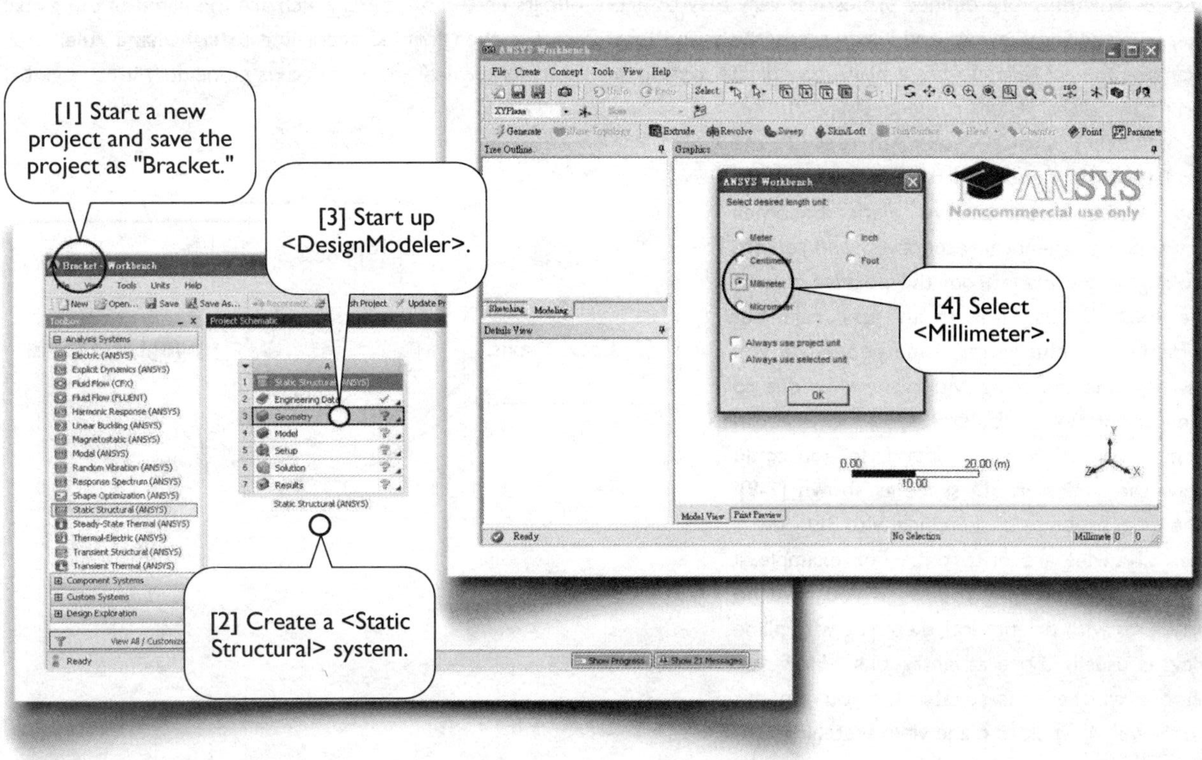

4.1-3 Sketch Seat Plate on <ZXPlane>

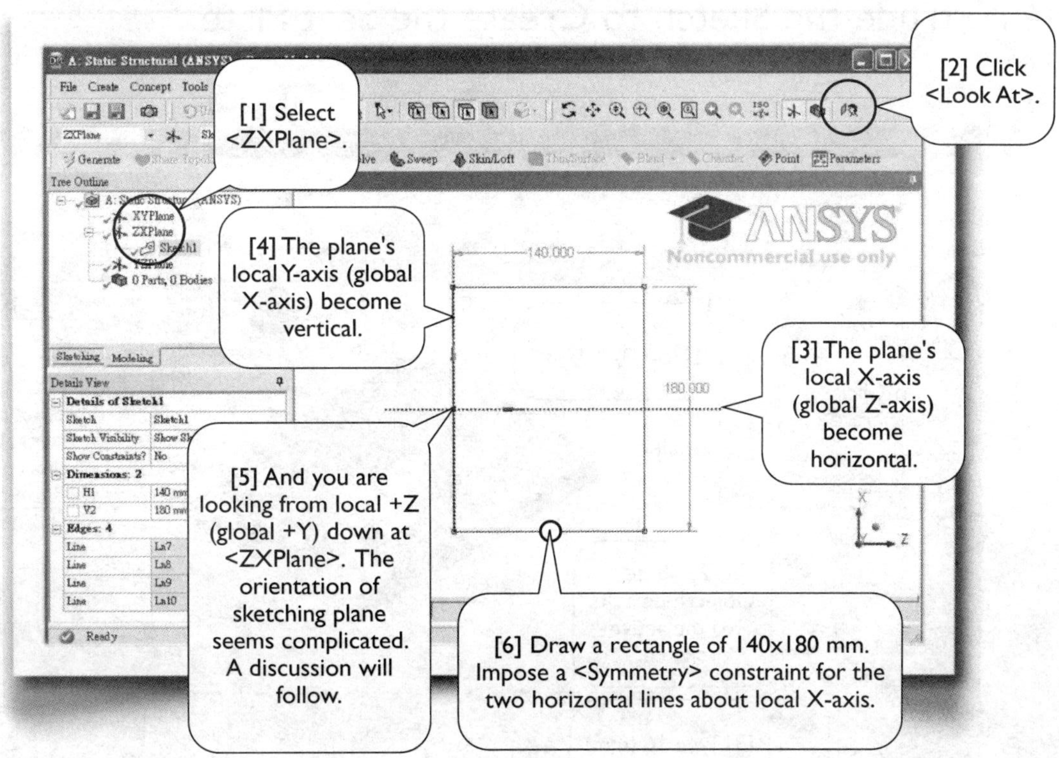

Local Coordinate Systems of Sketching Planes

We mentioned plane coordinate system in Section 3.1-10. Here is more. Each sketching plane has a local coordinate system. For three pre-defined planes, it is very easy to figure out: its first two letters, which are the name of the global axes, are the local X-axis and Y-axis respectively; the local Z-axis is then formed according to right-hand rule. For example, the <ZXPlane> has a plane coordinate system such that its local-X and local Y-axis coincide with the global Z-axis and global X-axis respectively [7-9].

When you click <Look At> tool [2], the model will reorient such that the local X-axis and Y-axis of the active plane becomes horizontal and vertical respectively, and you are looking at the plane from the positive side of the local Z-axis. It is an easy rule but sometimes confusing for some people. If you have trouble sketching with plane view due to the orientation problems, you always can sketch with 3D view. In our case, you could draw the sketch in 3D space as shown [7-9]. The main problem of sketching with 3D view is that all angles are distorted. For example, a right angle is no longer 90°. If you have no problems with orientation, sketching with plane view is usually more advantageous. However, choose whichever is suitable for you. In this book, we will stick to plane view sketching.

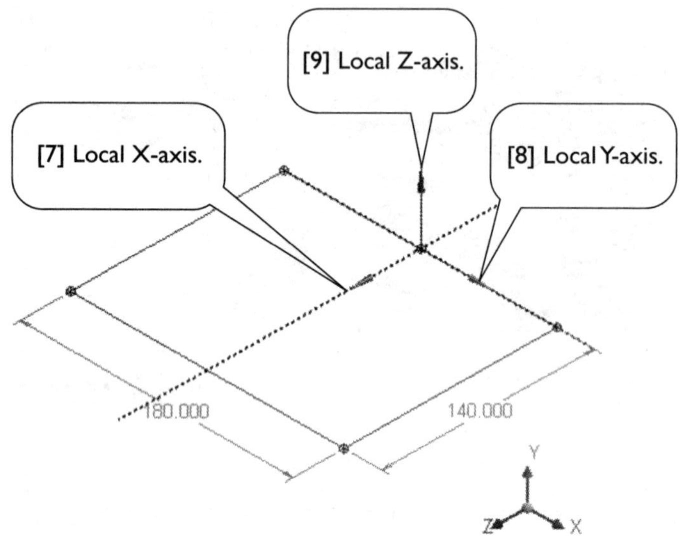

4.1-4 Extrude the Sketch to Create the Seat Plate

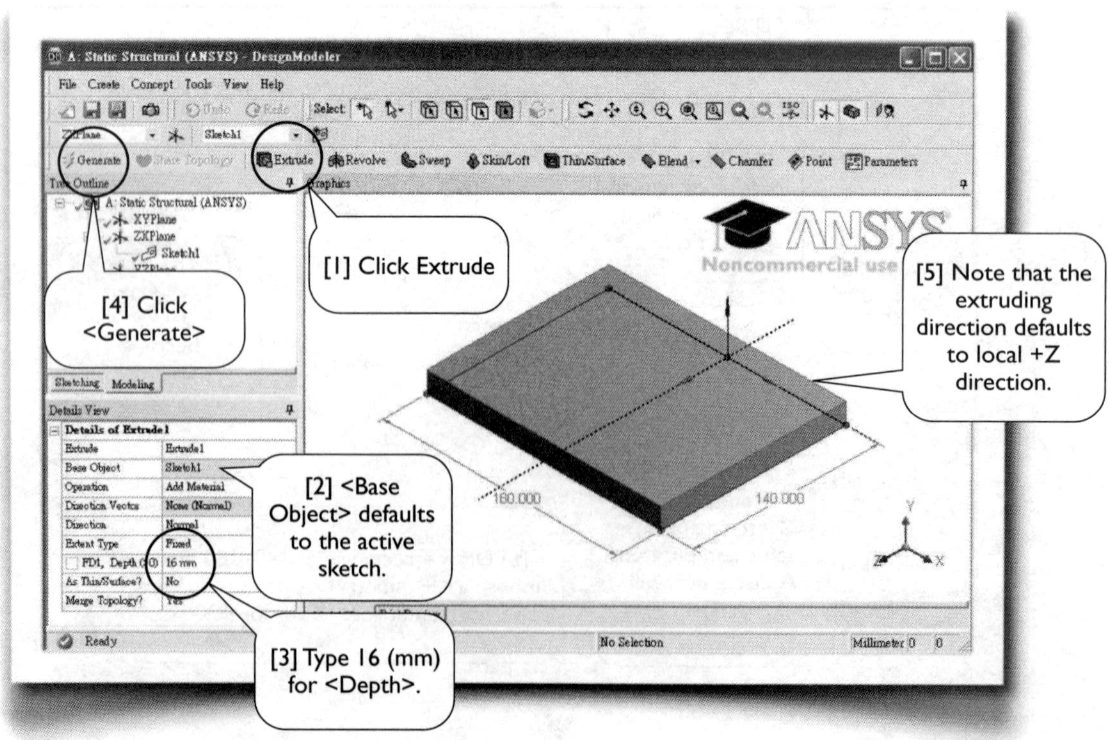

4.1-5 Sketch Web Plate on <YZPlane>

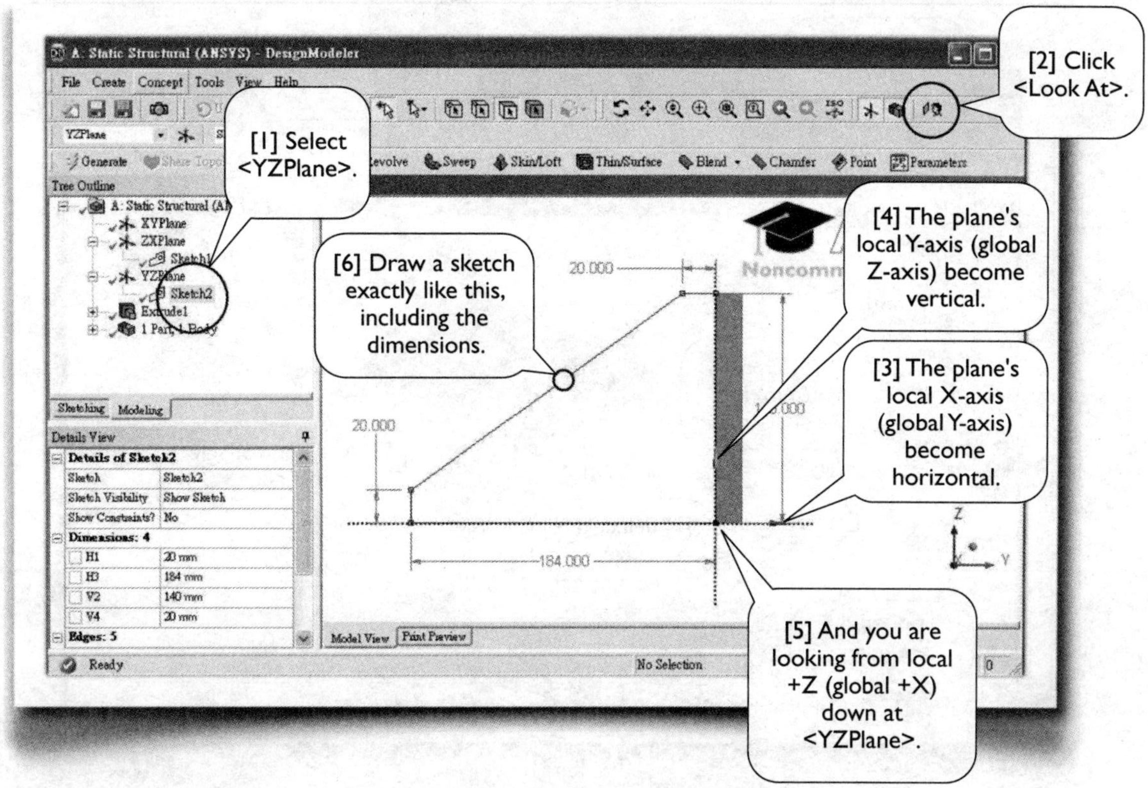

4.1-6 Extrude the Sketch to Create the Web Plate

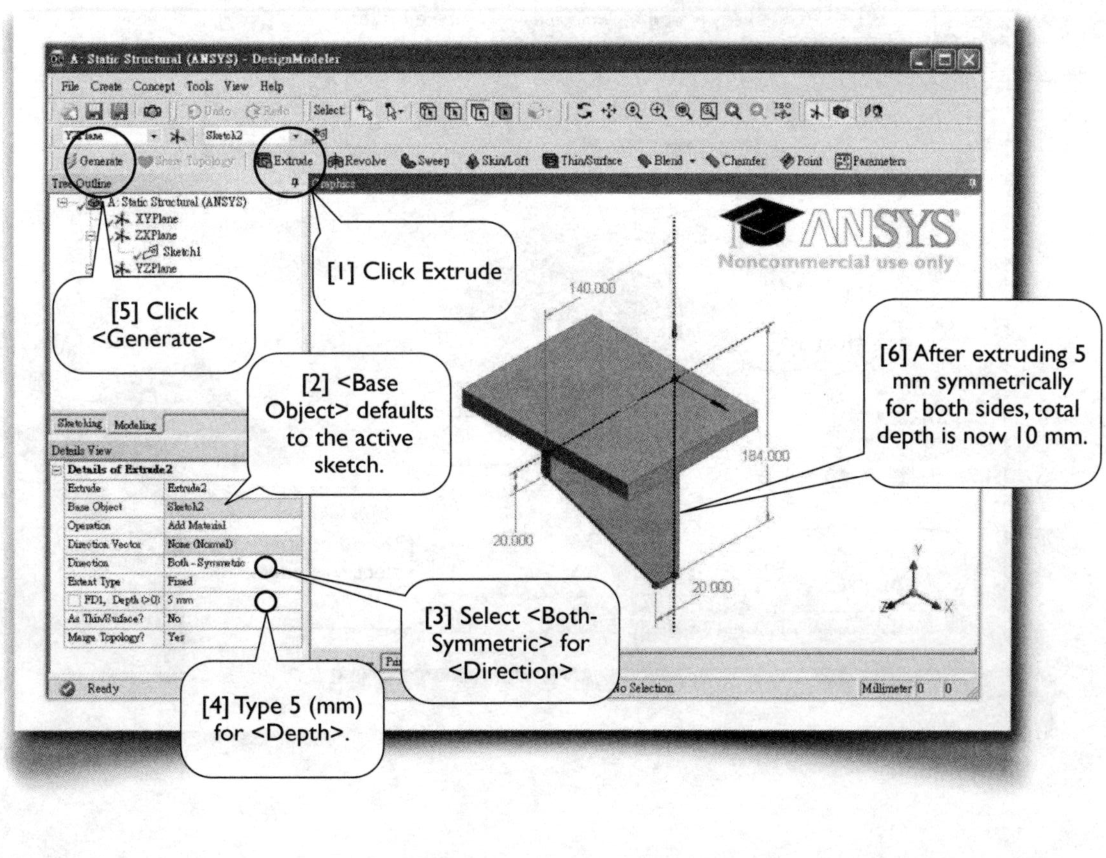

4.1-7 Create Rounds for the Flange

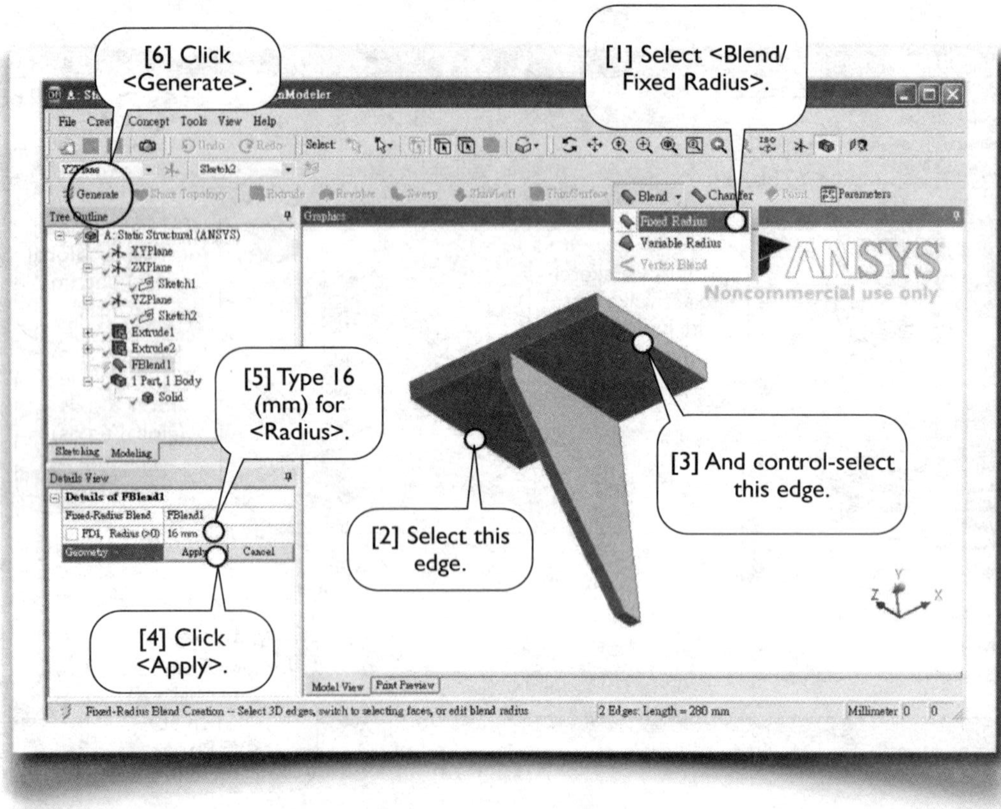

4.1-8 Create Fillets

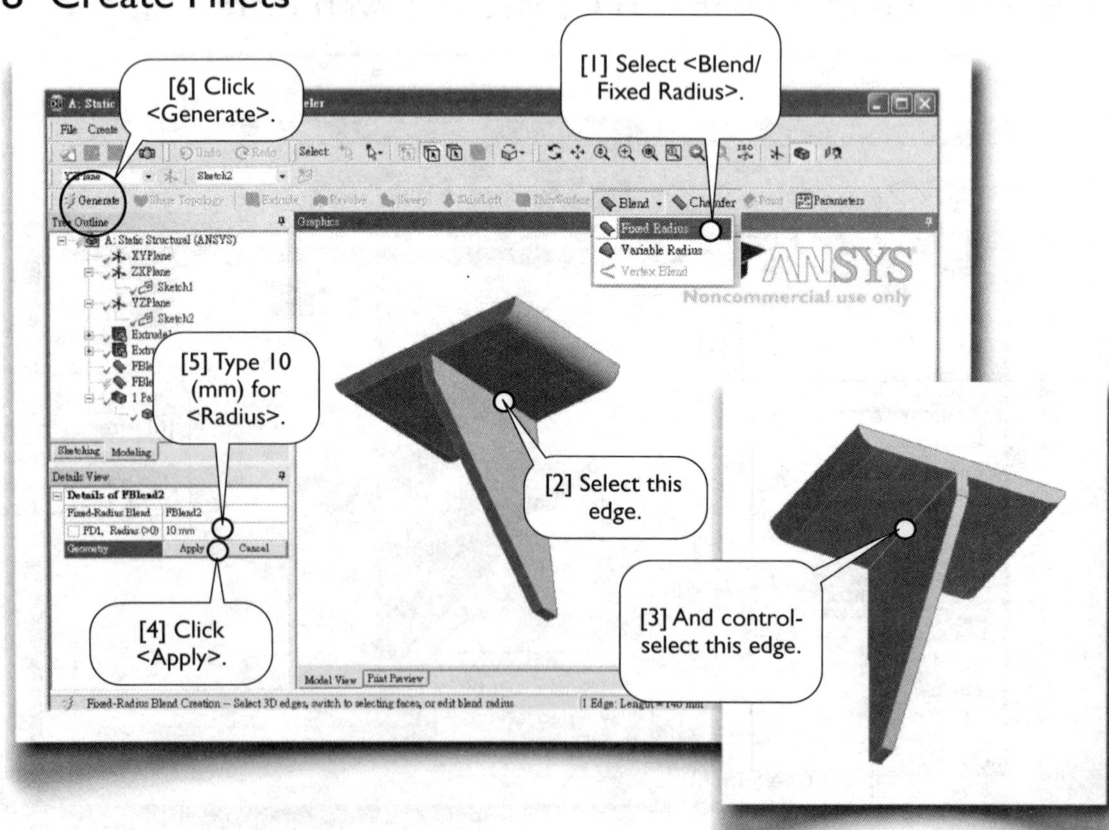

4.1-9 Wrap Up

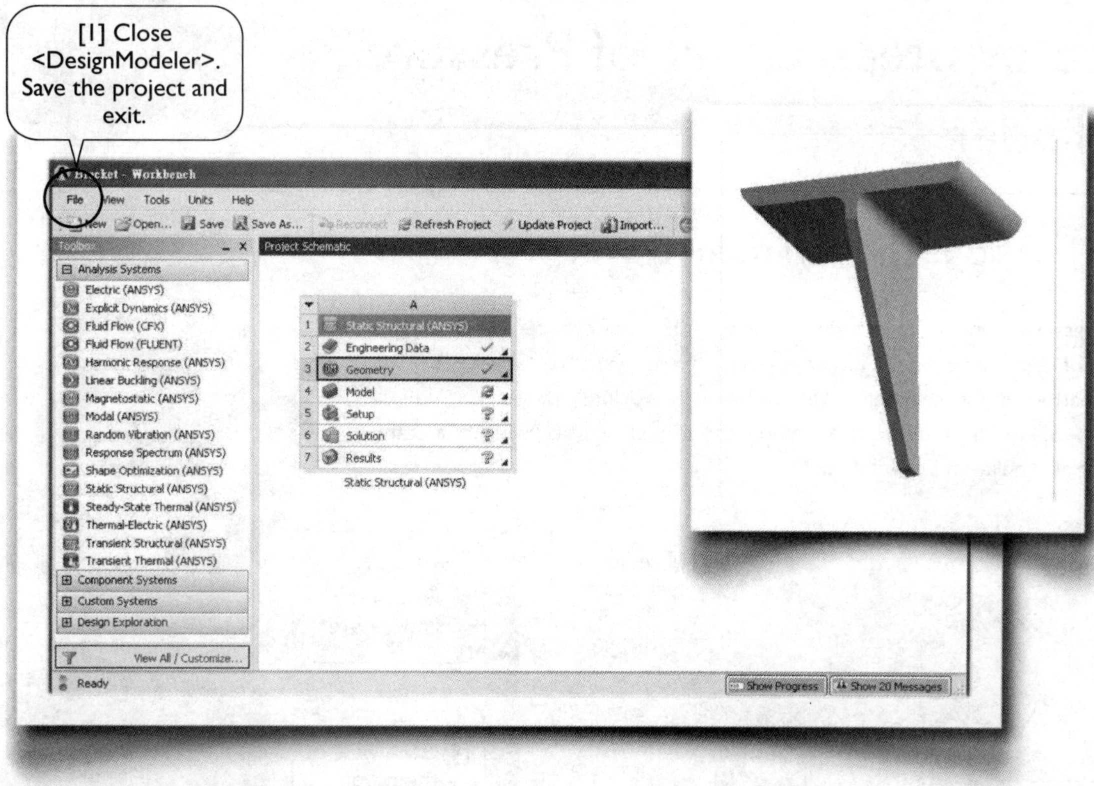
[1] Close <DesignModeler>. Save the project and exit.
Bracket - Workbench
File View Tools Units Help
New Open... Save Save As... Reconnect Refresh Project Update Project Import...
Toolbox
Analysis Systems
Electric (ANSYS)
Explicit Dynamics (ANSYS)
Fluid Flow (CFX)
Fluid Flow (FLUENT)
Harmonic Response (ANSYS)
Linear Buckling (ANSYS)
Magnetostatic (ANSYS)
Modal (ANSYS)
Random Vibration (ANSYS)
Response Spectrum (ANSYS)
Shape Optimization (ANSYS)
Static Structural (ANSYS)
Steady-State Thermal (ANSYS)
Thermal-Electric (ANSYS)
Transient Structural (ANSYS)
Transient Thermal (ANSYS)
Component Systems
Custom Systems
Design Exploration
View All / Customize...
Project Schematic
A
1 Static Structural (ANSYS)
2 Engineering Data
3 Geometry
4 Model
5 Setup
6 Solution
7 Results
Static Structural (ANSYS)
Ready
Show Progress
Show 20 Messages

Section 4.2

Step-by-Step: Cover of Pressure Cylinder

4.2-1 About the Cylinder Cover

The pressure cylinder [1] contains gas of 0.5 MPa. The cylinder cover [2-4] is made of carbon-fiber reinforced plastic. We want to investigate the deformation of the cylinder cover under such working pressure. We will create a 3D solid model in this section; the model will be used for a static structural simulation in Section 5.2.

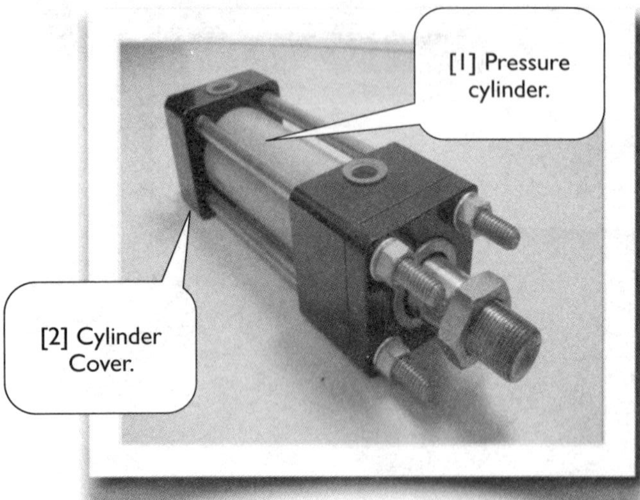

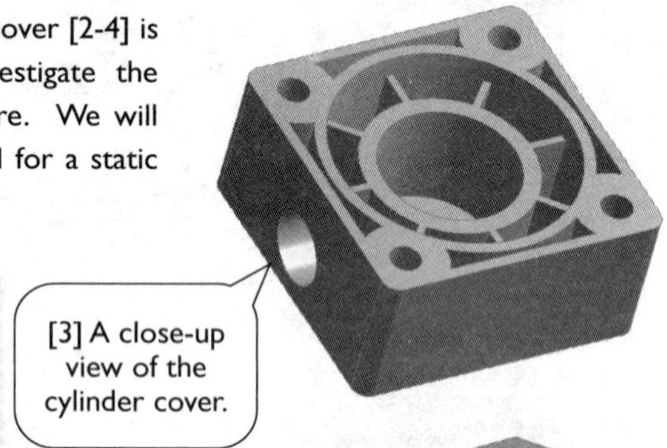

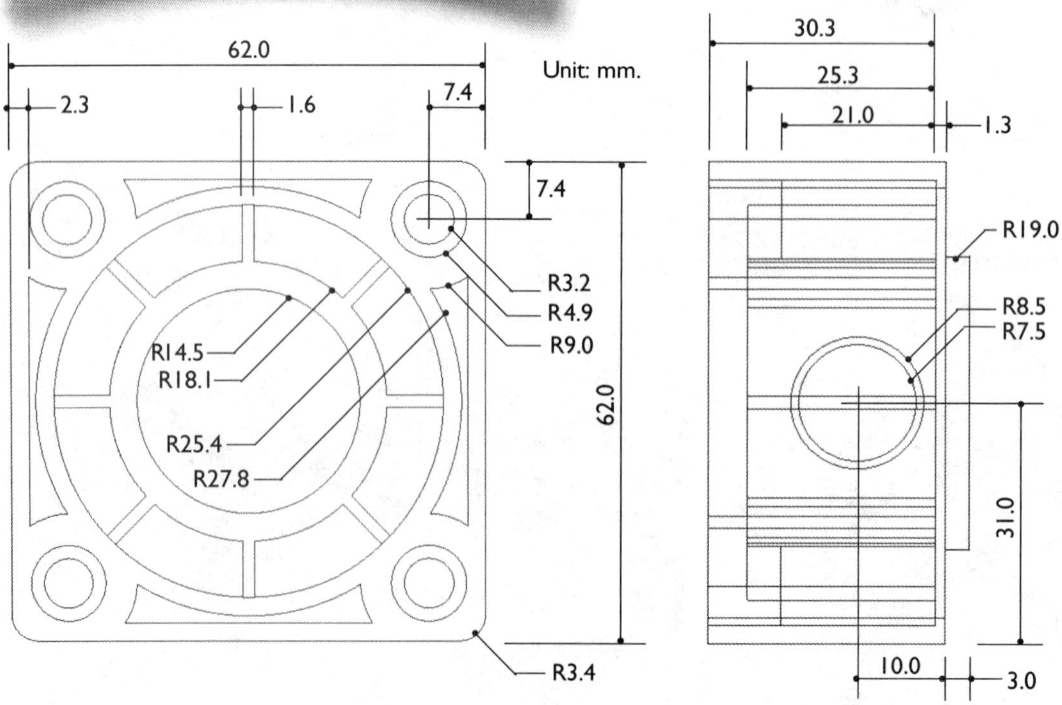

4.2-2 Start Up

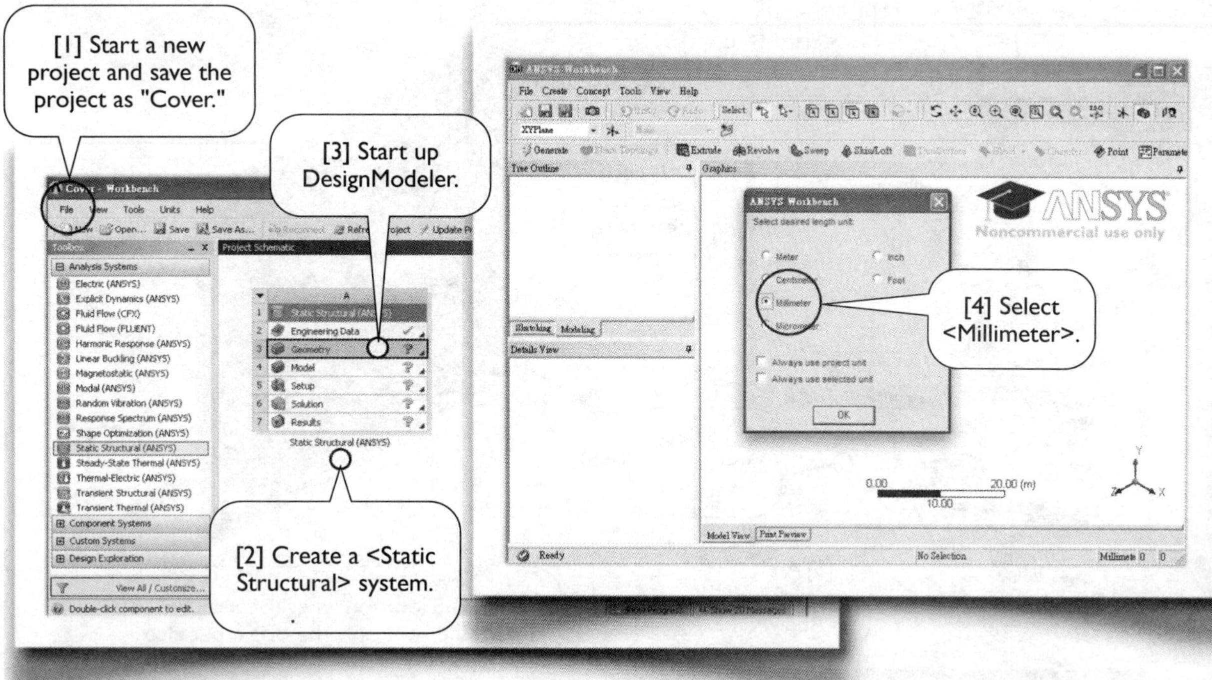

4.2-3 Create Base Plate

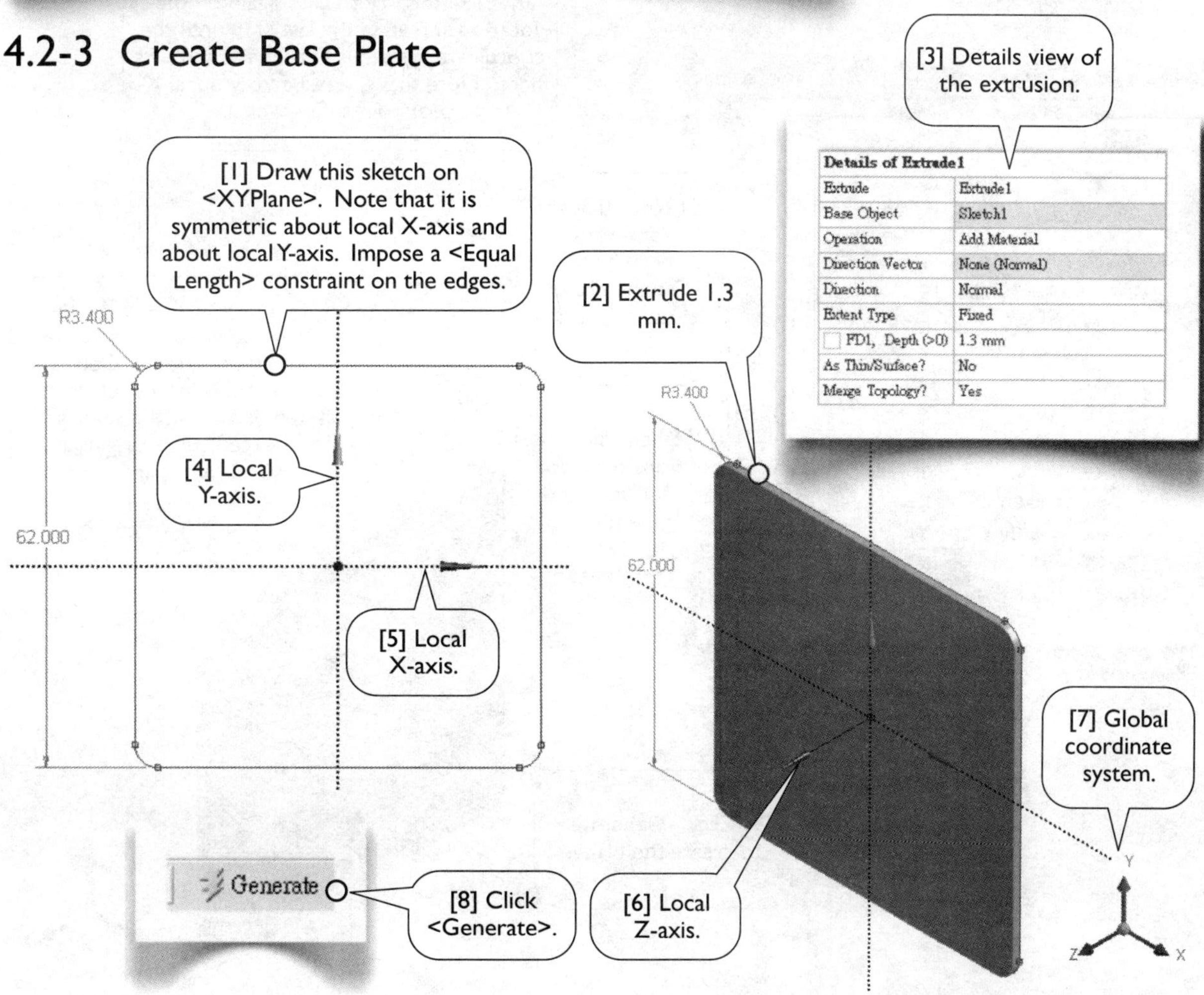

4.2-4 Create a New Sketching Plane

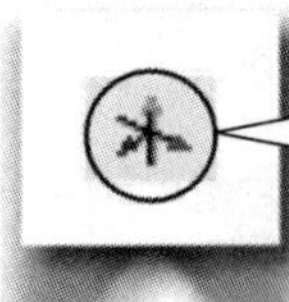

[1] Click <New Plane>. <Plane4> is created.

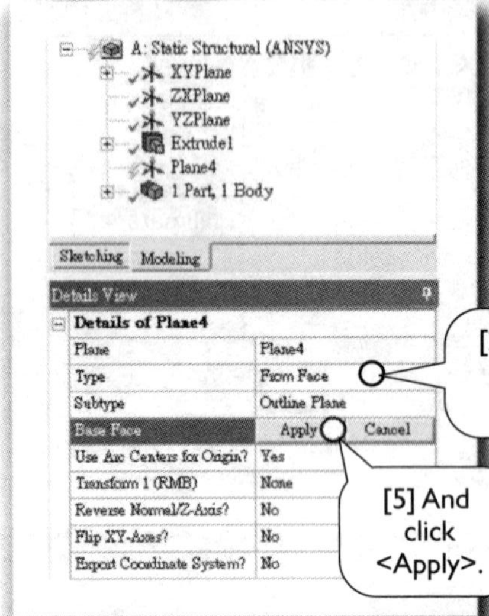

[2] Select <From Face>.

[5] And click <Apply>.

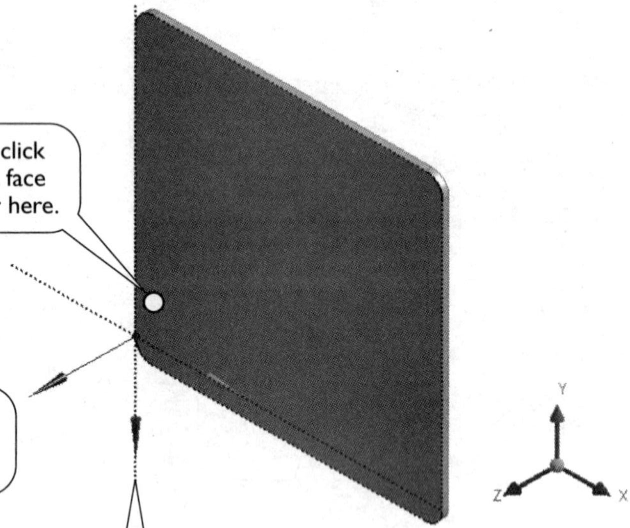

[3] click this face near here.

[4] The location where you click determines not only the origin but also the axes. If your coordinate system is not like this, try to click again on the location shown in the last step until the coordinate system is exactly the same as here. Note that the red-arrow (local X-axis) points downward.

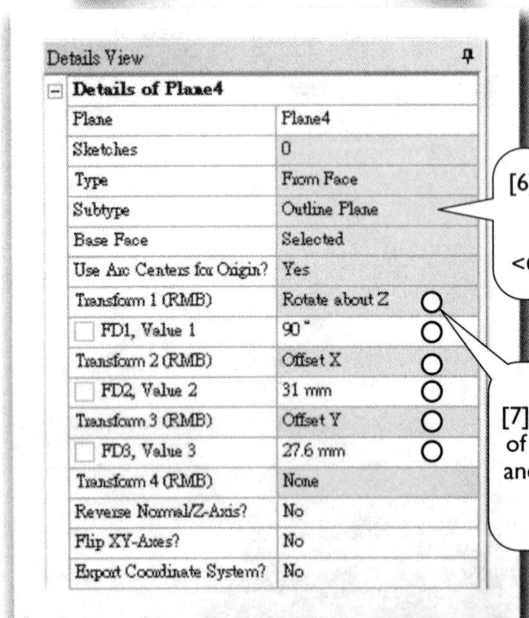

[6] Note that the <Subtype> defaults to <Outline Plane>.

[7] Select the type of transformation and set up exactly like this.

[8] You can visually see the local coordinate system transforms when you set up the Details. Note that this local coordinate system is almost the same as global except their origins are 1.3 mm apart.

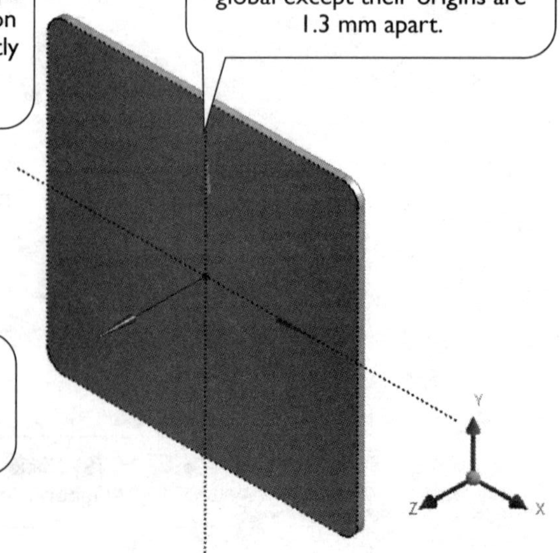

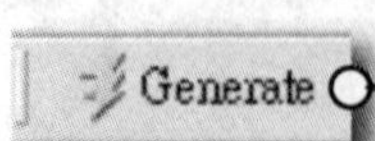

[9] Click <Generate> to create the plane.

4.2-5 Duplicate Plane Boundary on the New Plane

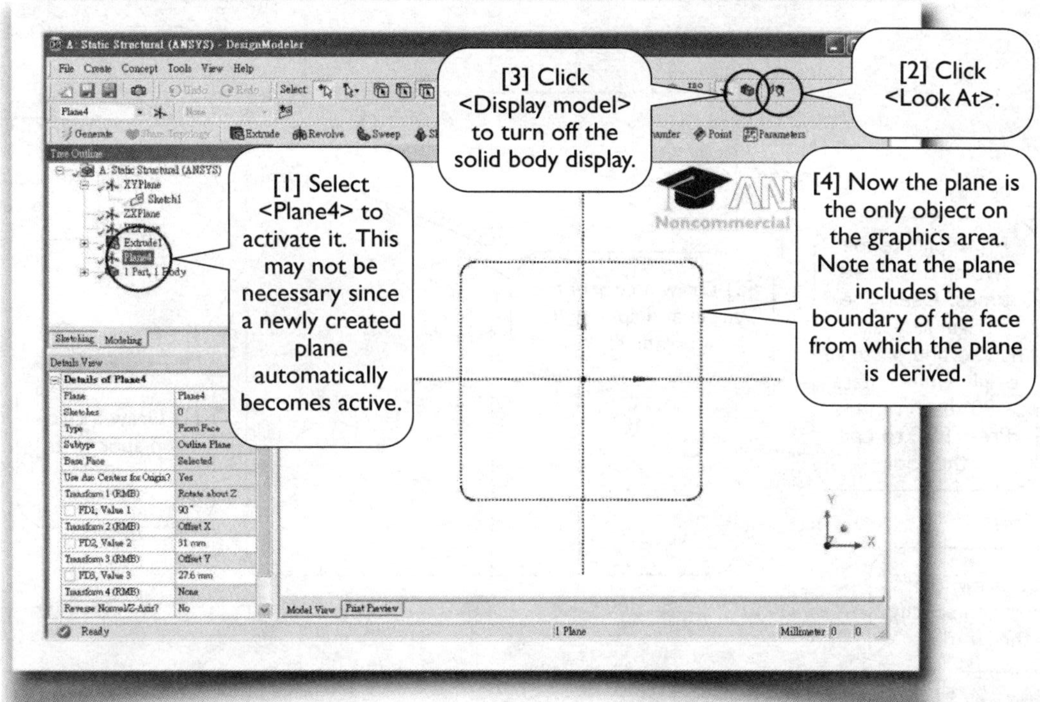

Plane with Boundary

When a plane is derived from a face and the <Subtype> is <Outline Plane>, the face boundary becomes part of the plane. You may call it "plane boundary." However, you can draw beyond that boundary. An important fact is that the boundary is not a geometric entity; you use it mainly as reference, or datum, just like you use local X-axis and Y-axis as datum. However, you may duplicate it to create geometric entities. Here we will demonstrate the duplication of the plane boundary.

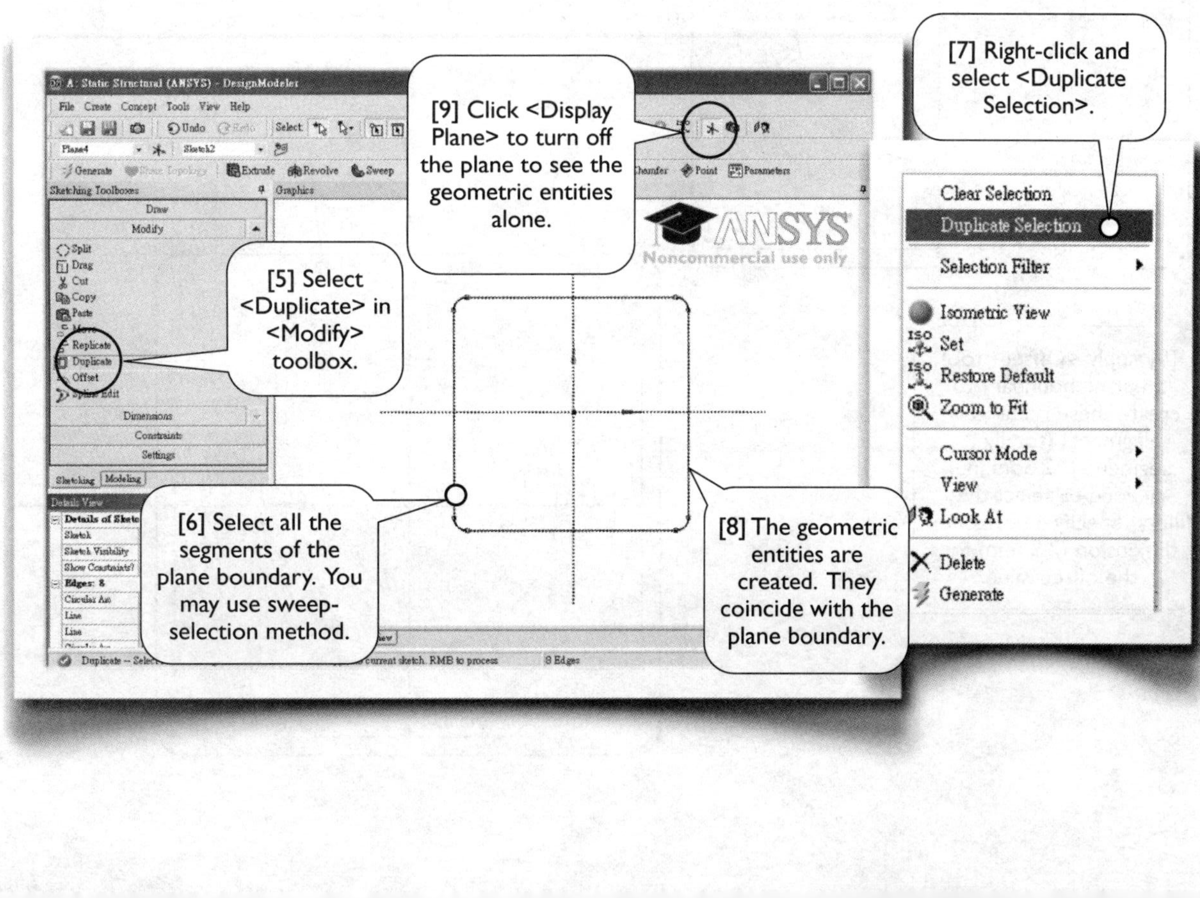

4.2-6 Sketch on the New Plane

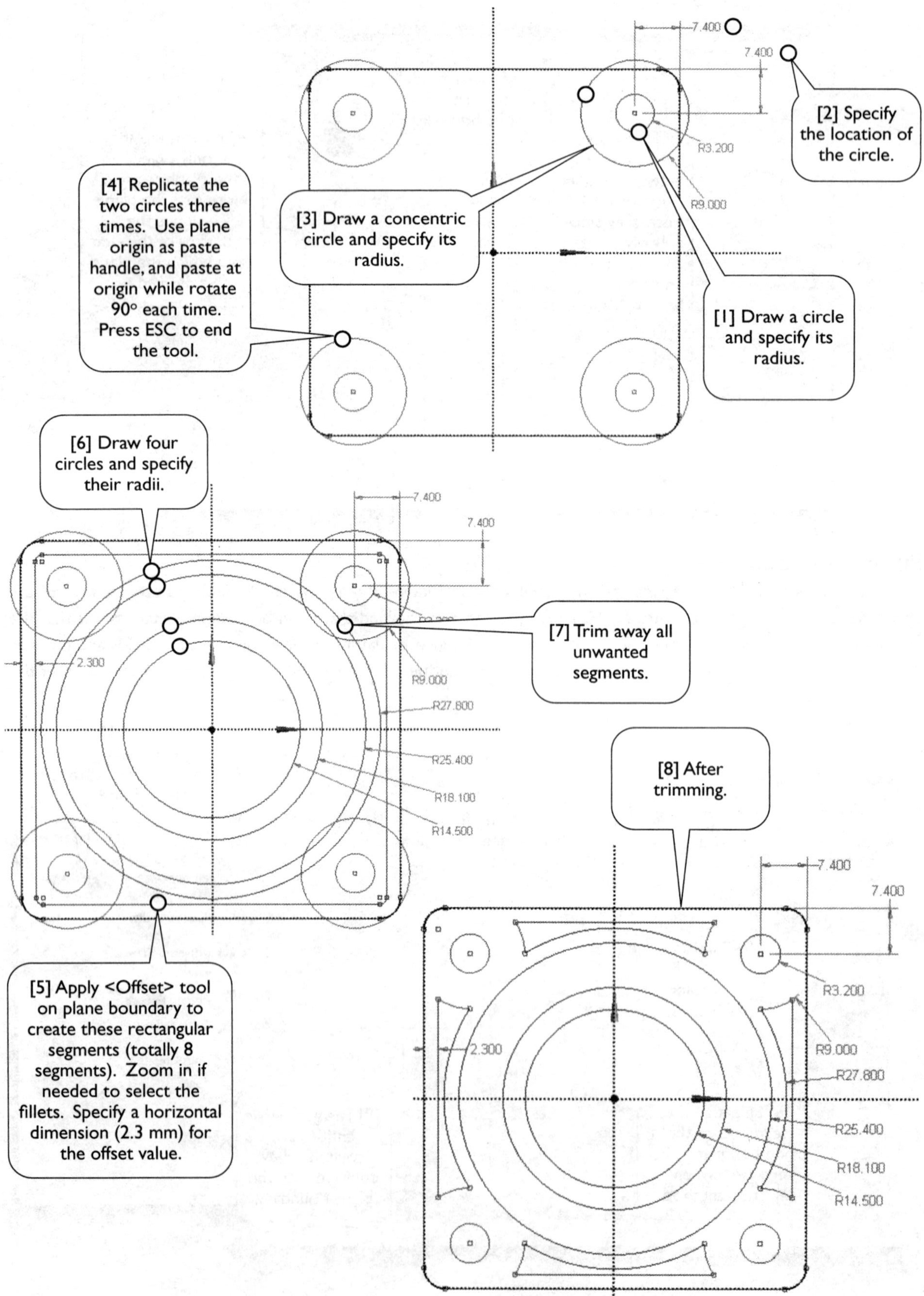

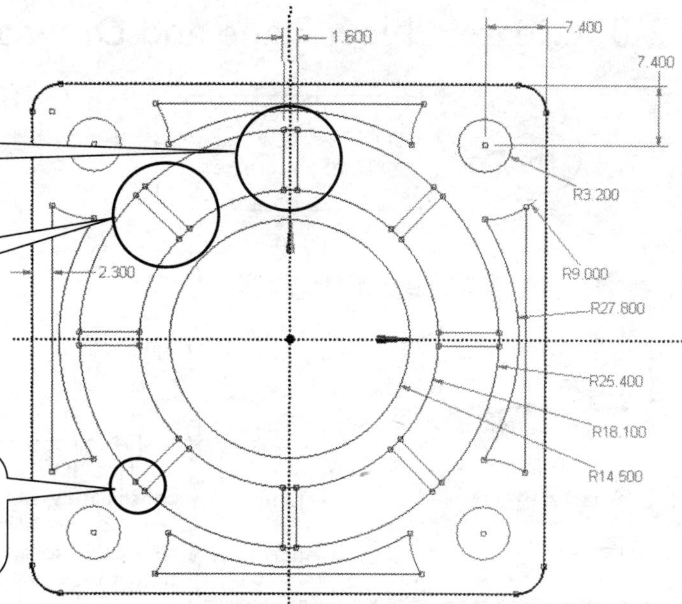

[9] Draw two vertical segments, impose <Symmetry> constraint, and specify horizontal dimension (1.6 mm).

[10] Replicate the two segments seven times. Use plane origin as paste handle, and paste at origin while rotate 45° each time. If you have trouble duplicating to horizontal positions, try other ways; you've run into the same problems as I did.

[11] Trim away all unwanted segments.

[12] After trimming.

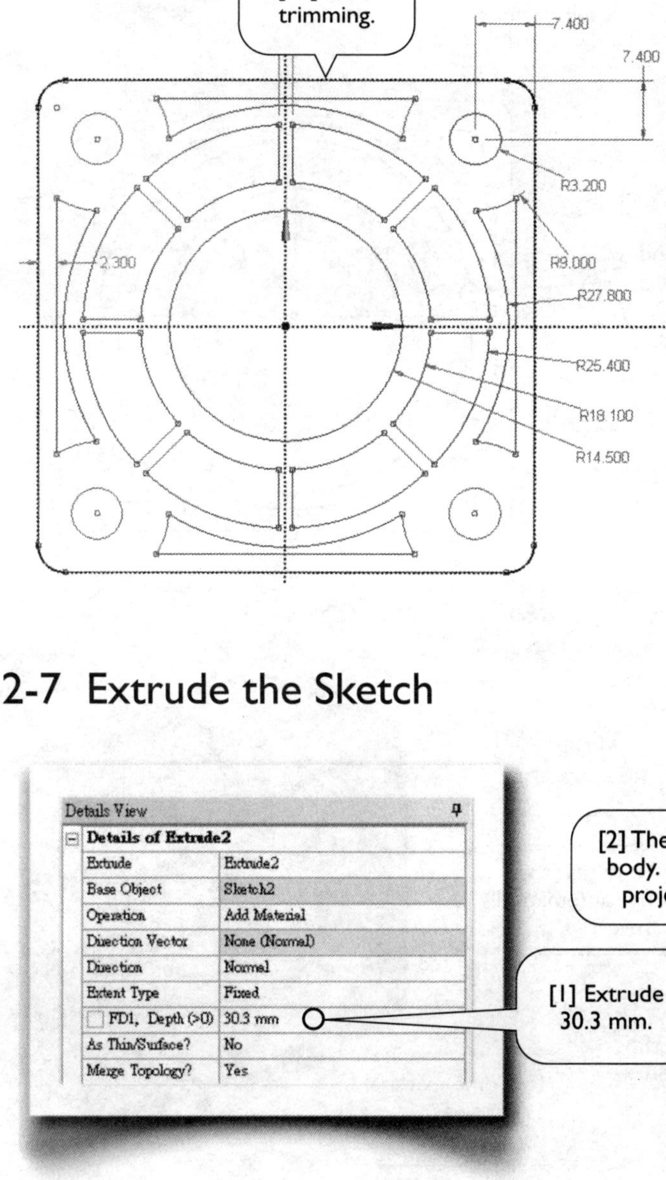

Working with Complicated Sketches

When you are working with a complicated sketch like this one, things may not be so smooth as you expected. You have to pan, zoom, turn on/off display modes frequently. Therefore, being familiar with the viewing control tools is critical. If your hardware configuration is not superb, the processing speed also slows down significantly, so please be patient. The worst thing is that some peculiar behaviors may happen. For example, the replication [10] is not smooth. These peculiar behavior is possibly due to some unnecessary constraints automatically imposed (2.3-5). Fortunately these small problems usually can be easily circumvented.

4.2-7 Extrude the Sketch

Details View

Details of Extrude2	
Extrude	Extrude2
Base Object	Sketch2
Operation	Add Material
Direction Vector	None (Normal)
Direction	Normal
Extent Type	Fixed
FD1, Depth (>0)	30.3 mm
As Thin/Surface?	No
Merge Topology?	Yes

[1] Extrude 30.3 mm.

[2] The solid body. Save project.

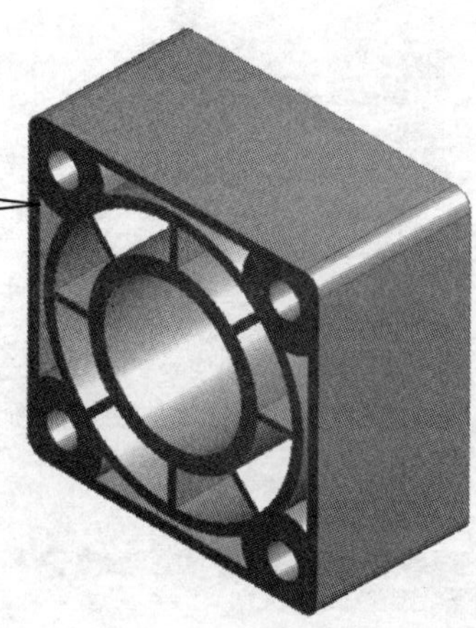

4.2-8 Create a New Plane and Draw a Circle on the Plane

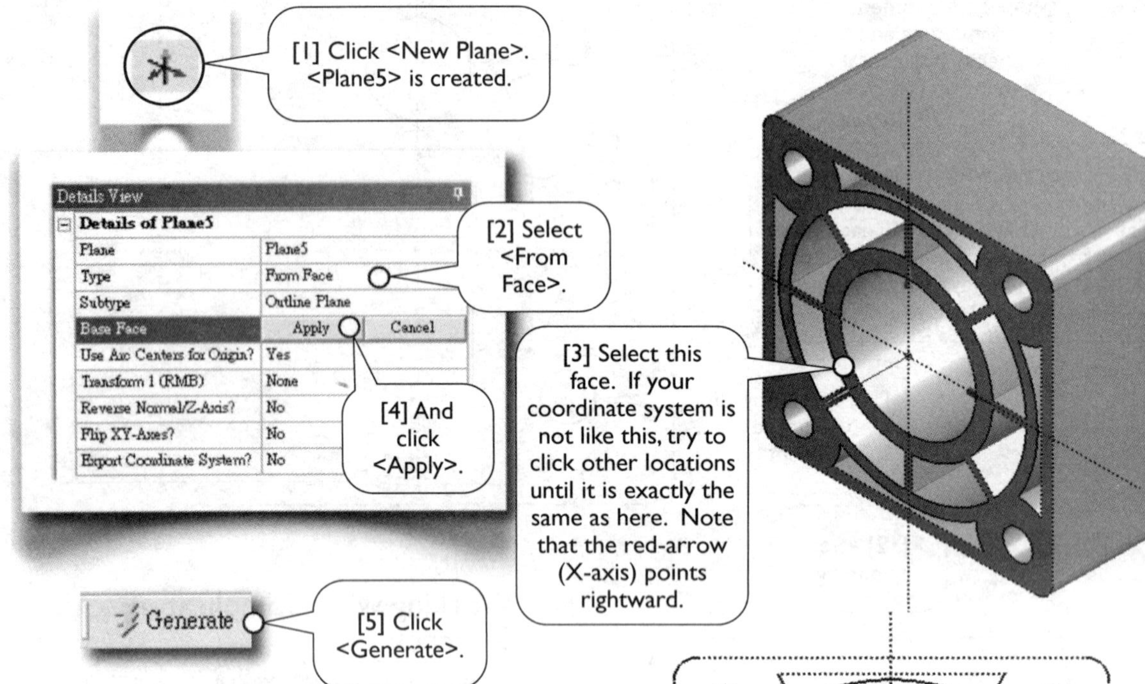

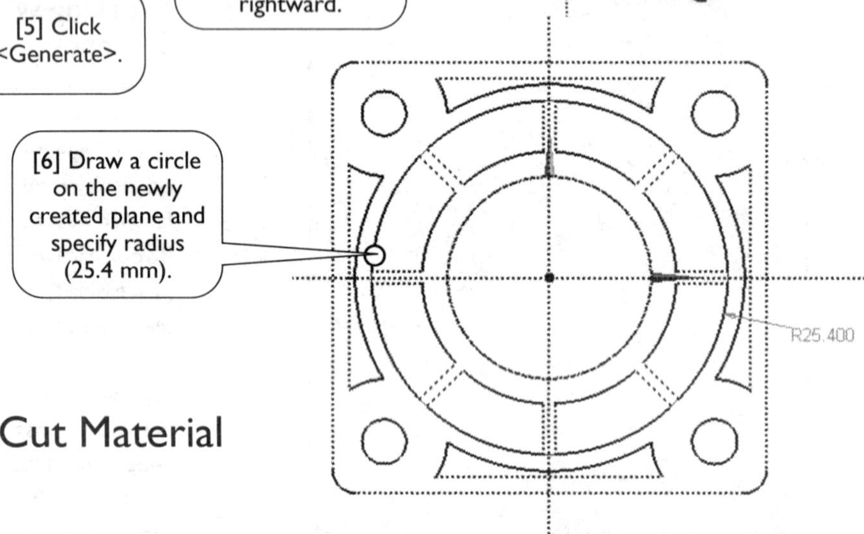

4.2-9 Extrude to Cut Material

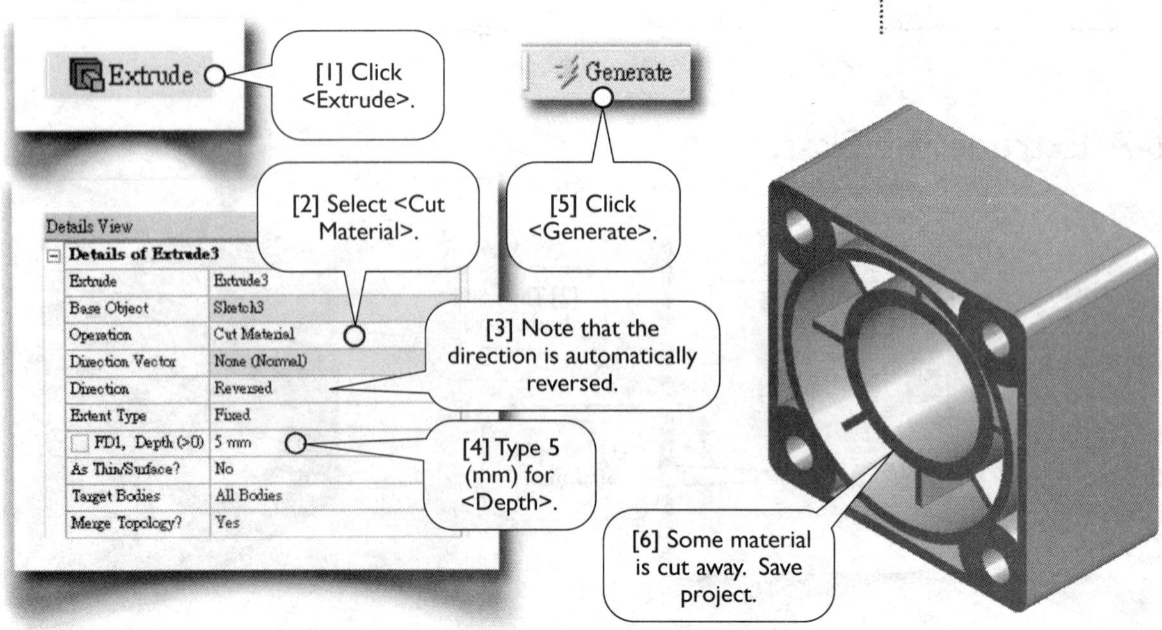

4.2-10 Create New Sketch on <XYPlane> and Draw Circles

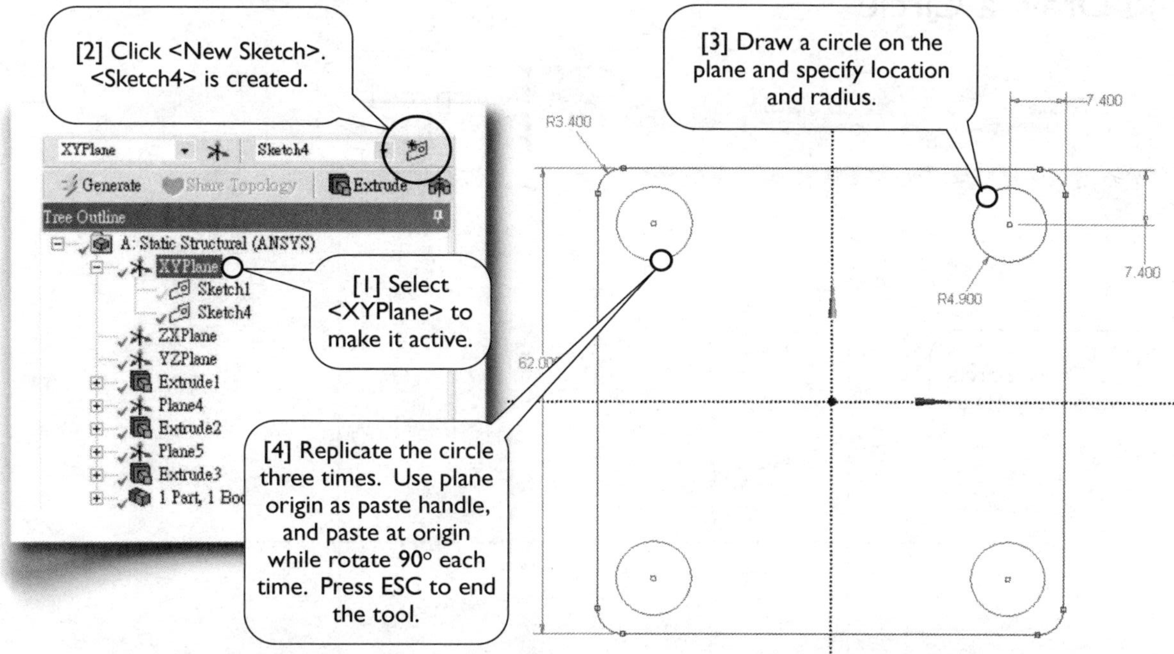

Create Second Sketch on a Plane

A plane may contain multiple sketches. When you begin to draw on a fresh plane, a sketch is automatically created; you don't have to explicitly click the <New Sketch> tool, although you may do that. When you want to add a second sketch on a plane, you MUST explicitly click the <New Sketch> tool, otherwise the entities you draw will become part of the first sketch.

4.2-11 Extrude to Cut Material

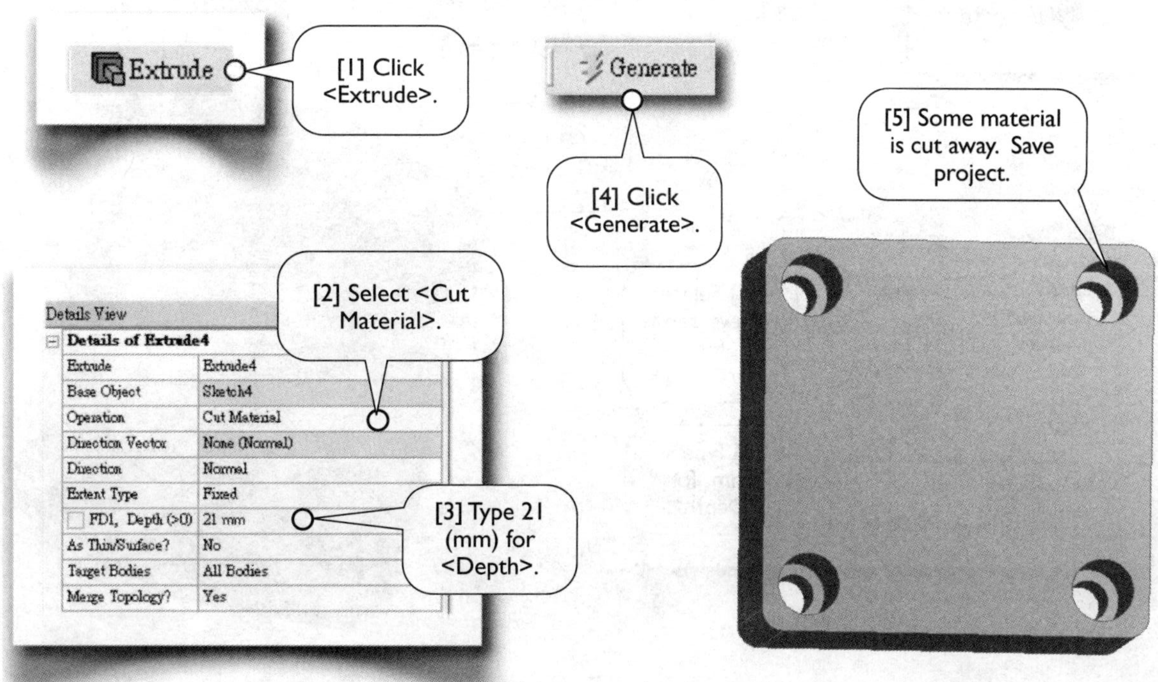

4.2-12 Create Another Sketch on <XYPlane> and Draw a Circle

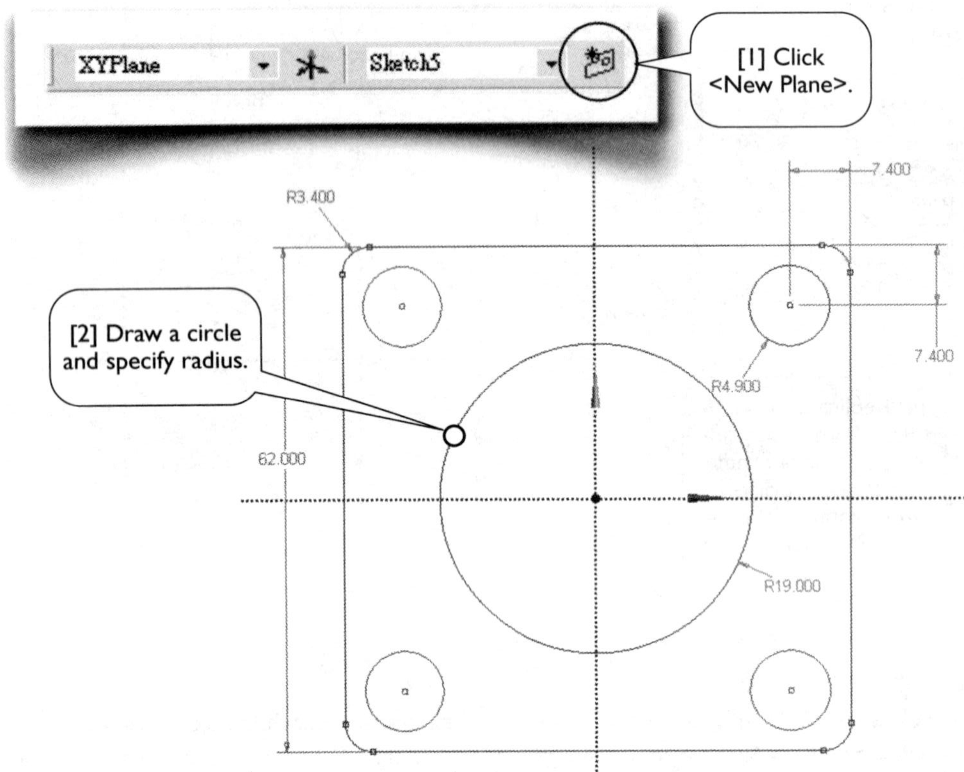

4.2-13 Extrude to Add Material

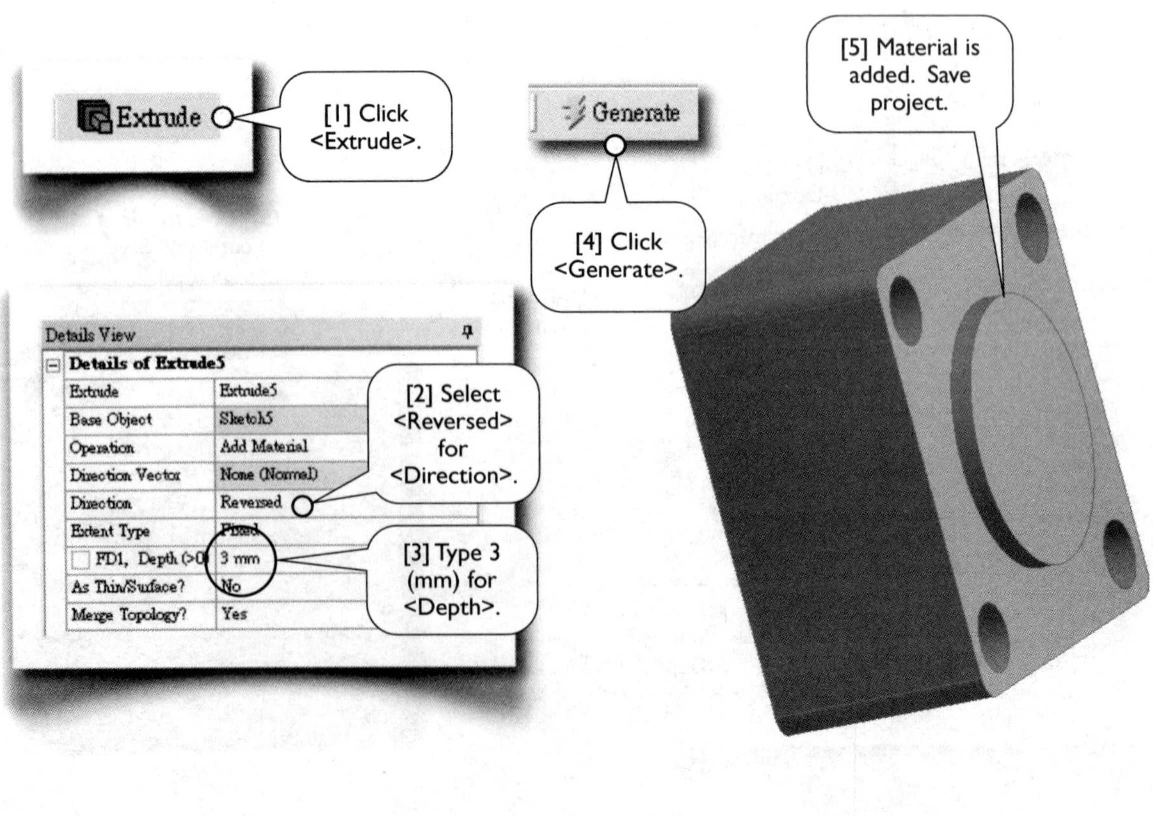

4.2-14 Create a New Plane on the Side Wall and Create two Sketches on the Plane

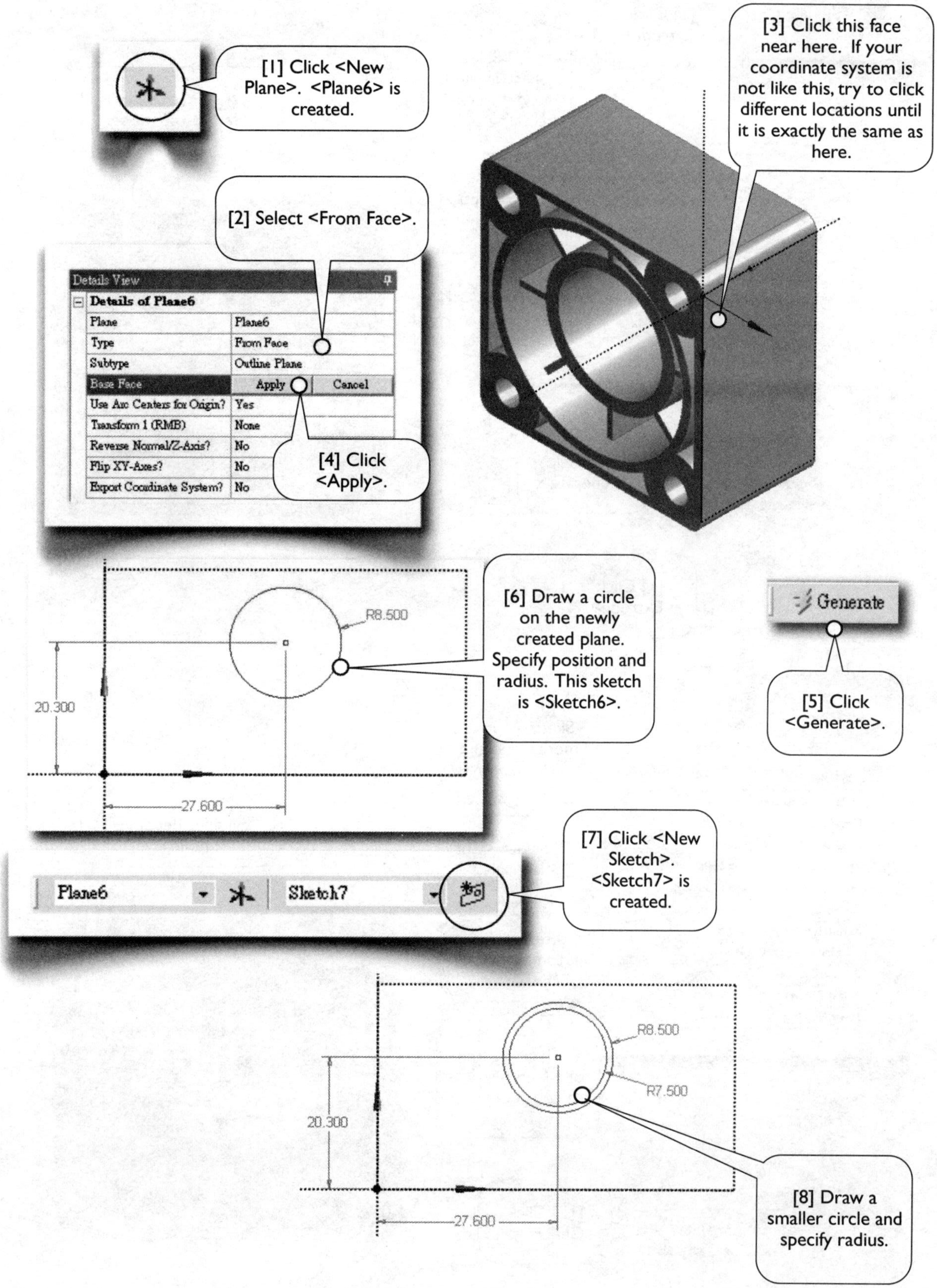

4.2-15 Complete the Model

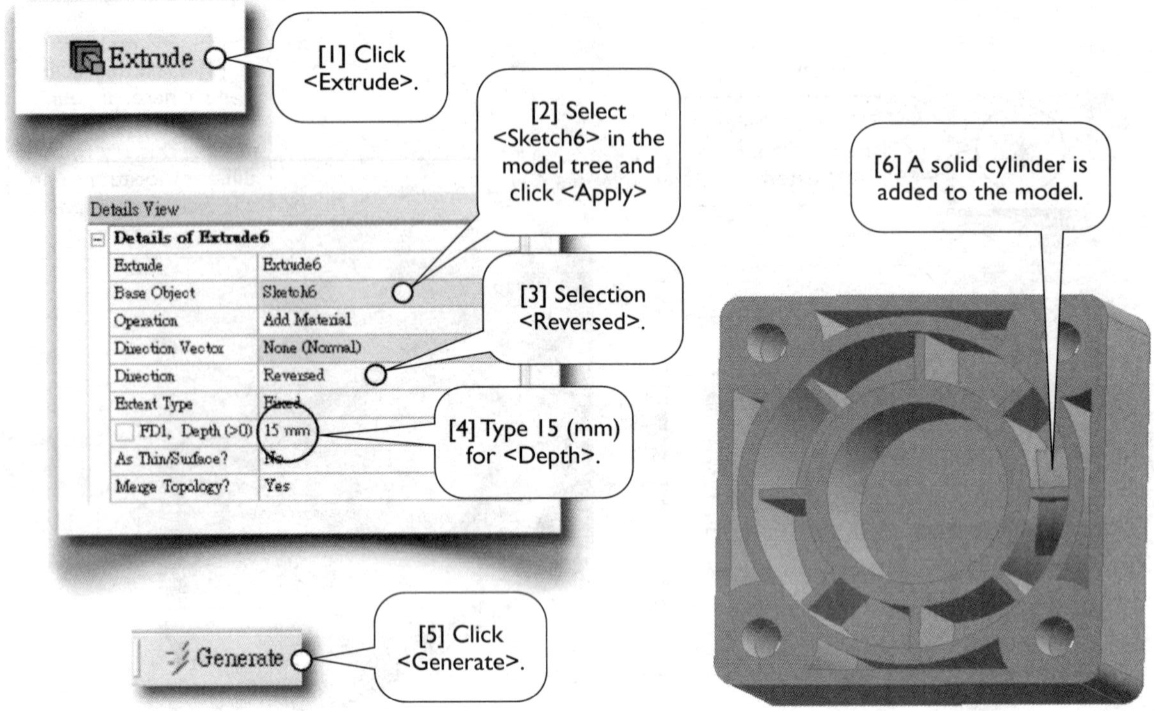

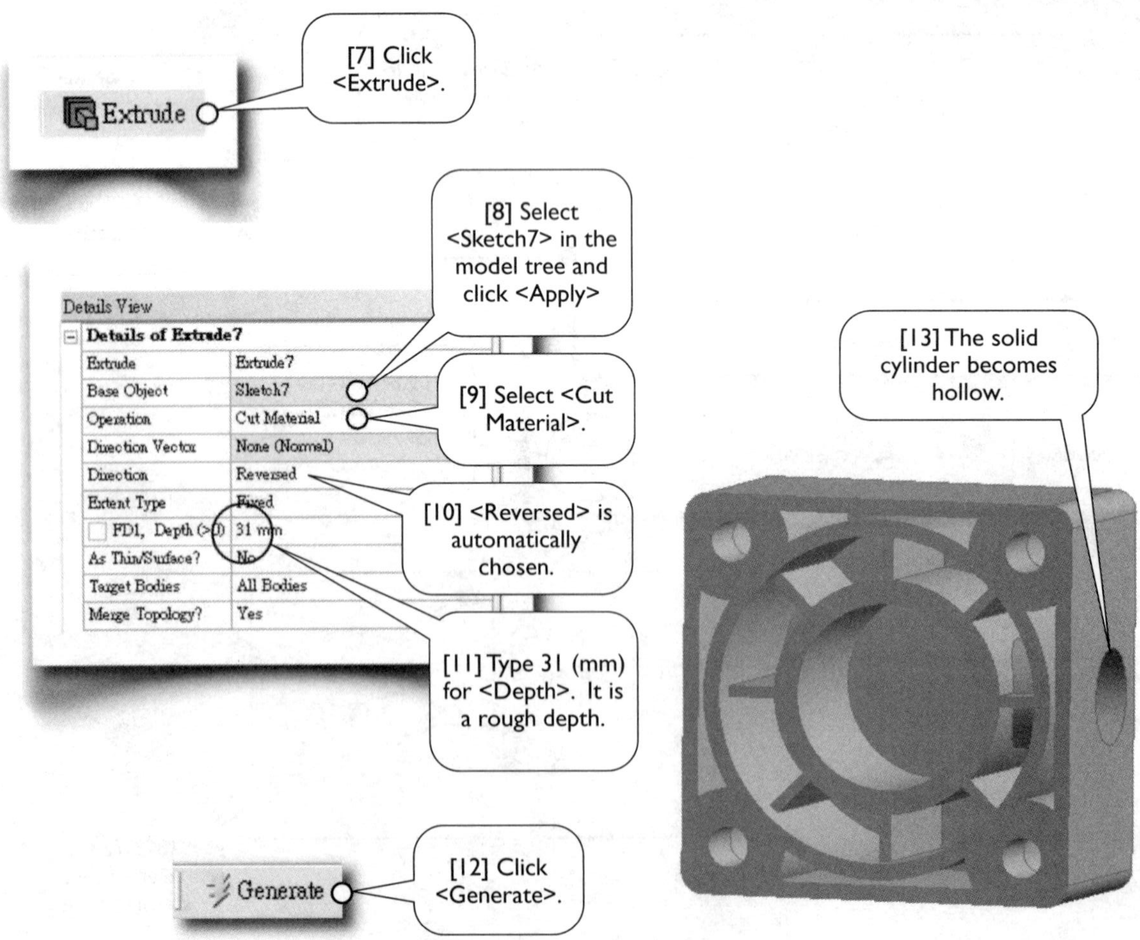

4.2-16 Wrap Up

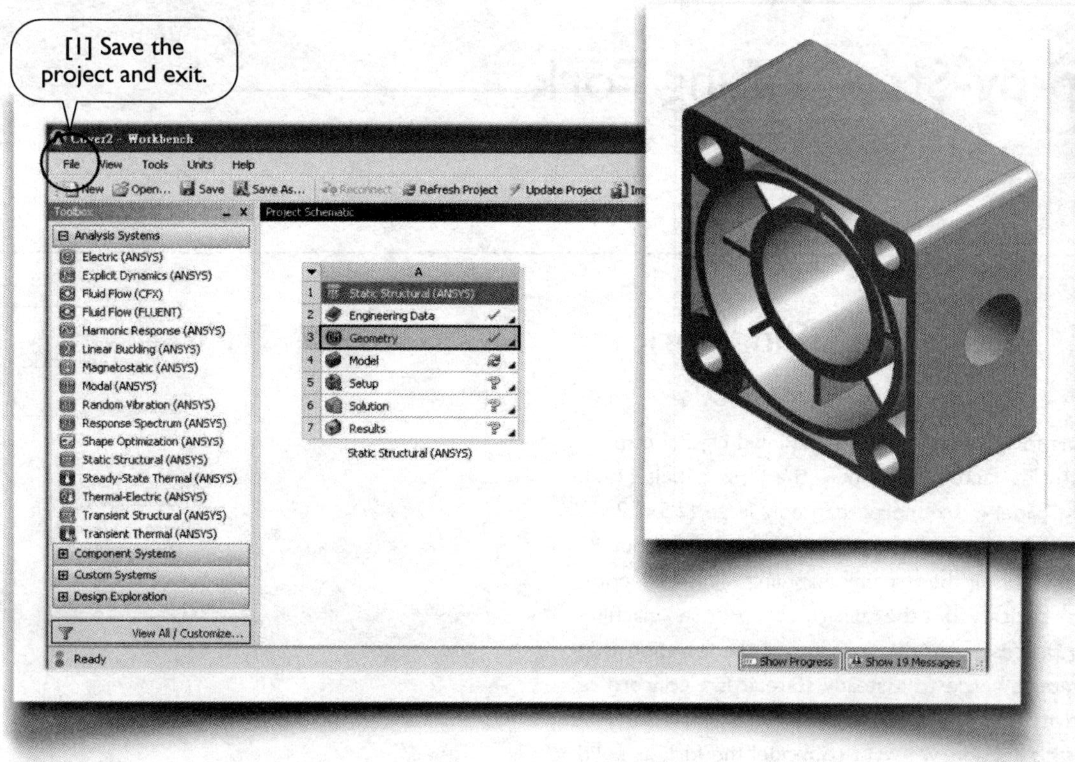
[1] Save the project and exit.
Cover2 - Workbench
File
View
Tools
Units
Help
New
Open...
Save
Save As...
Reconnect
Refresh Project
Update Project
Toolbox
Project Schematic
Analysis Systems
Electric (ANSYS)
Explicit Dynamics (ANSYS)
Fluid Flow (CFX)
Fluid Flow (FLUENT)
Harmonic Response (ANSYS)
Linear Buckling (ANSYS)
Magnetostatic (ANSYS)
Modal (ANSYS)
Random Vibration (ANSYS)
Response Spectrum (ANSYS)
Shape Optimization (ANSYS)
Static Structural (ANSYS)
Steady-State Thermal (ANSYS)
Thermal-Electric (ANSYS)
Transient Structural (ANSYS)
Transient Thermal (ANSYS)
Component Systems
Custom Systems
Design Exploration
View All / Customize...
Ready
A
1 Static Structural (ANSYS)
2 Engineering Data
3 Geometry
4 Model
5 Setup
6 Solution
7 Results
Static Structural (ANSYS)
Show Progress
Show 19 Messages

Section 4.3

Step-by-Step: Lifting Fork

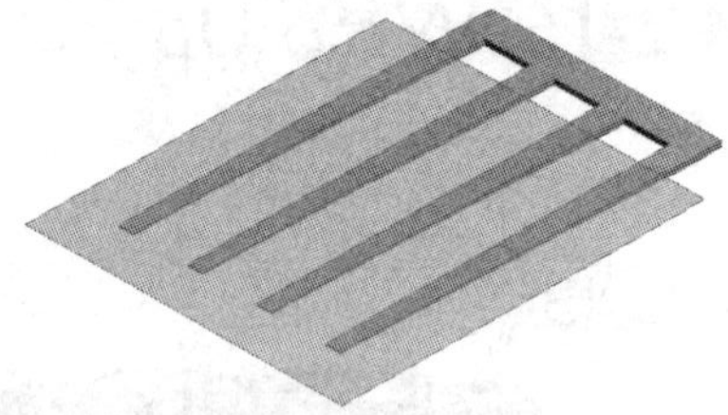

4.3-1 About the Lifting Fork

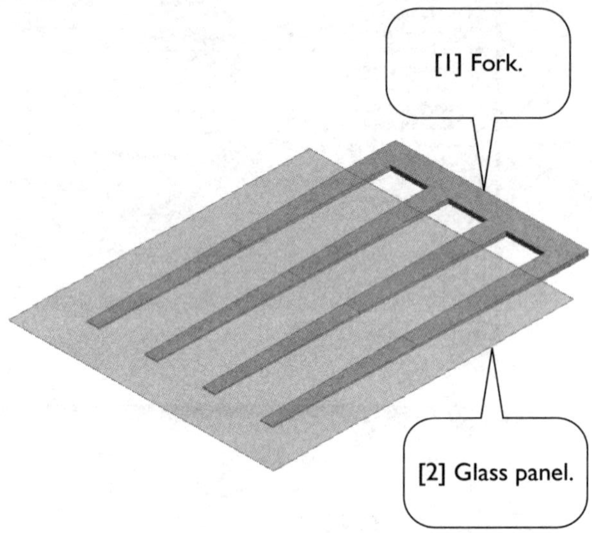

The lifting fork is used in an LCD (liquid crystal display) manufacturing factory to handle the glass panels [1-5]. The glass panel is so unprecedentedly large (2.5x2.2 m) and thin (1.0 mm) that the engineers concern about its deflections during the dynamic handling. This deflection value is critical for the design of precise machine handling process. Another concern is the duration that the vibrations settle to a steady state; it is a concern of productivity.

In this section, we want to model the fork as solid body and the glass panel as surface body. The model will be used for static, modal, and transient simulations in Section 12.2.

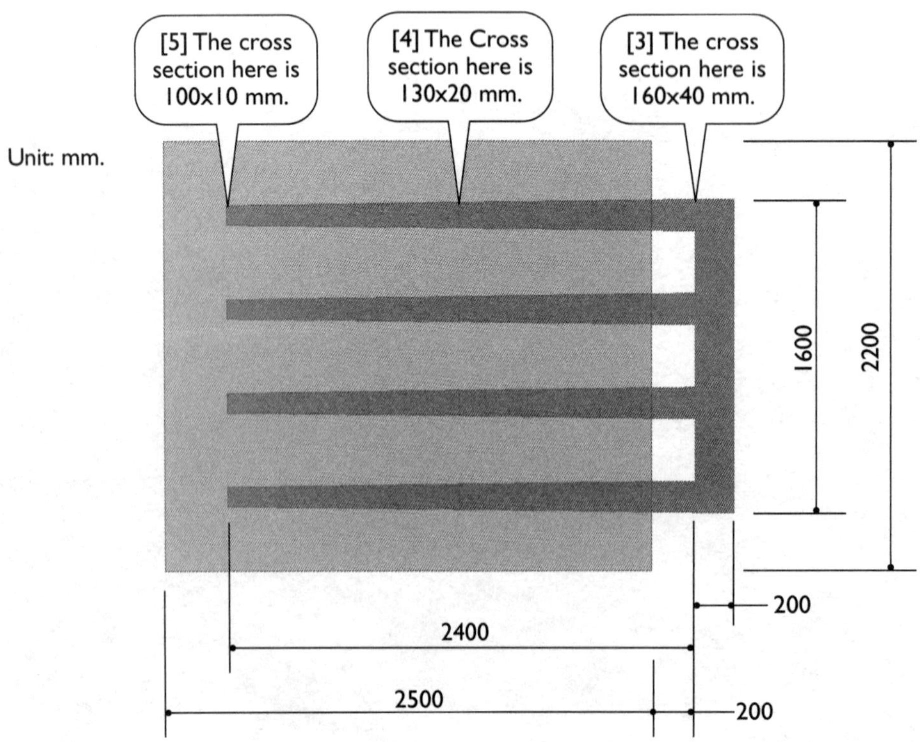

4.3-2 Start Up

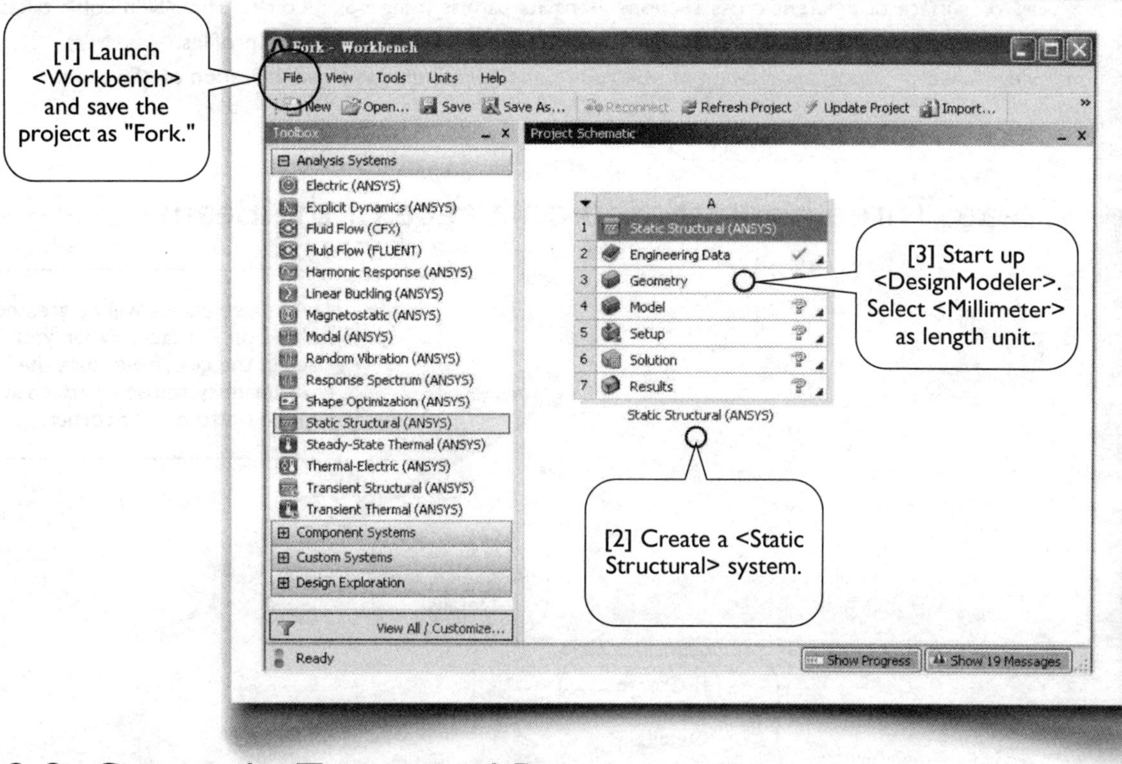

4.3-3 Create the Transversal Beam

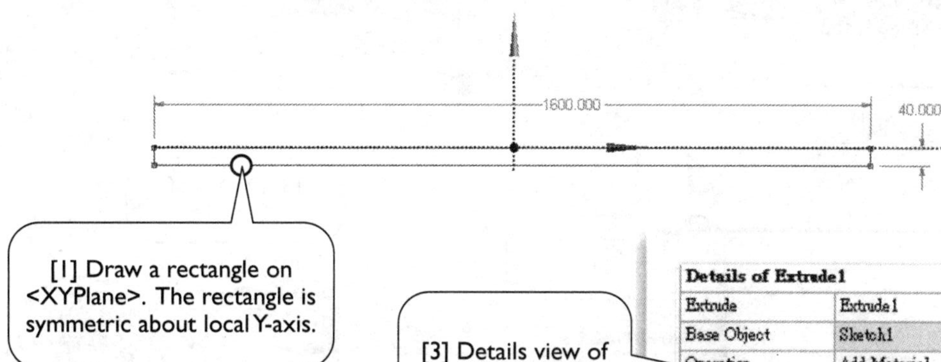

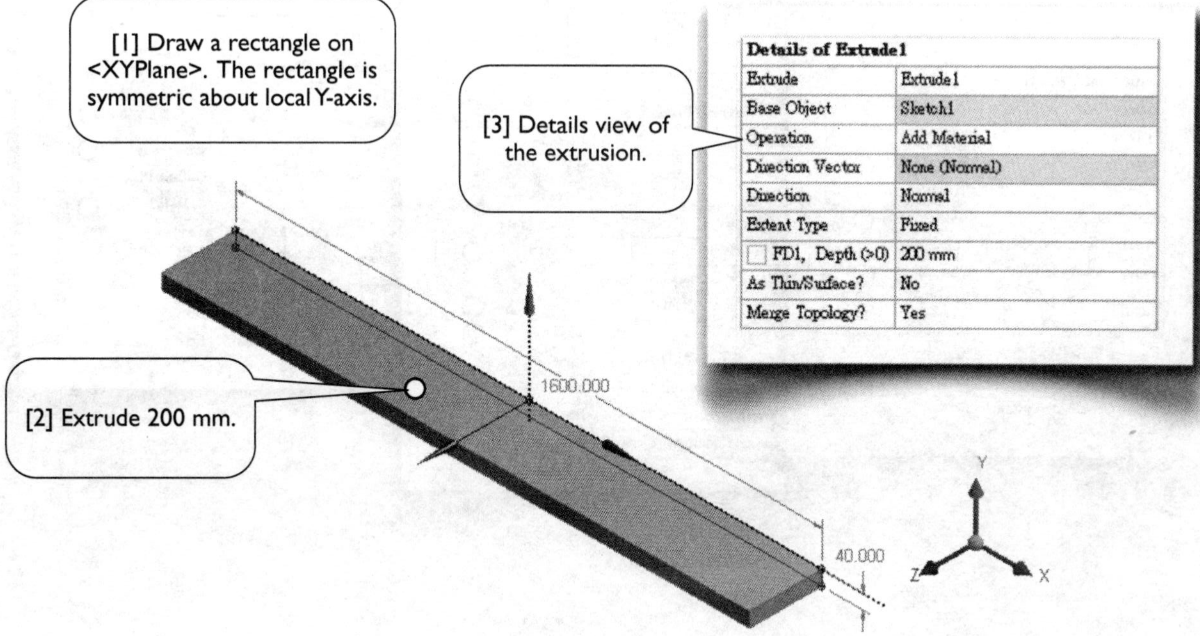

Skin/Loft

Now we want to create a prong, or finger. The prong is then duplicated three times to create other prongs. The prong's cross section is not uniform. You cannot create the prong using <Extrude> or <Sweep>. A more general way to create a solid or surface of different cross sections along its path is using <Skin/Loft>. The <Skin/Loft> takes a series of profiles from different planes and creates a solid or surface that fits through these profiles.

You may view <Sweep> as a generalization of <Extrude>, and <Skin/Loft> as a generalization of <Sweep>.

4.3-4 Create Three Planes Based on a Face of the Beam

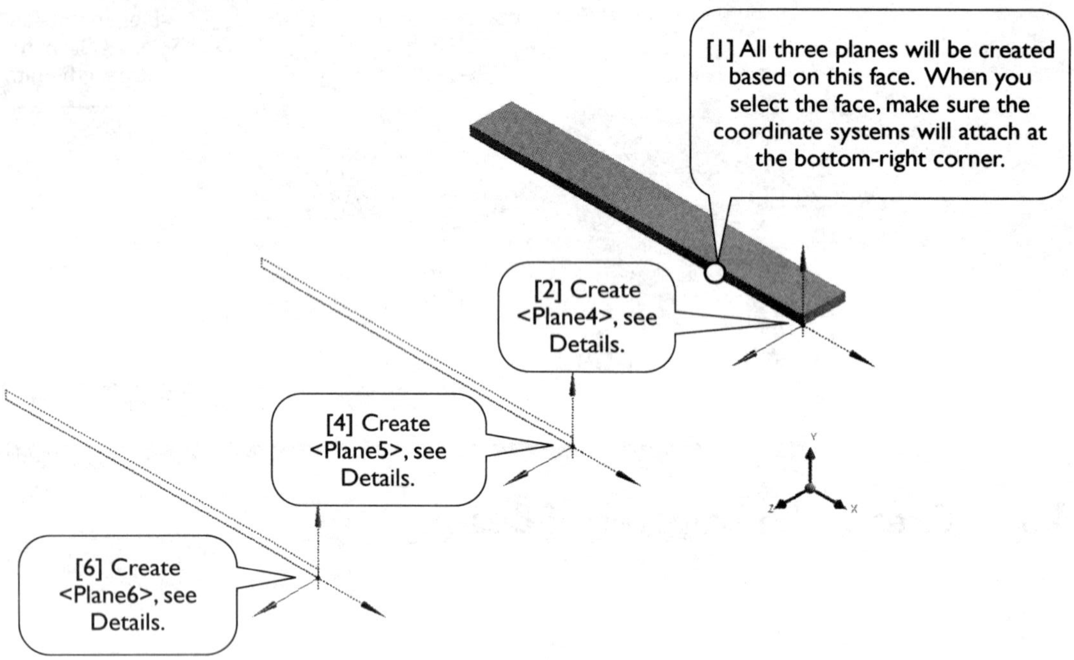

[3] Details of <Plane4>.

Details of Plane4	
Plane	Plane4
Sketches	0
Type	From Face
Subtype	Outline Plane
Base Face	Selected
Use Arc Centers for Origin?	Yes
Transform 1 (RMB)	None
Reverse Normal/Z-Axis?	No
Flip XY-Axes?	No
Export Coordinate System?	No

[5] Details of <Plane5>.

Details of Plane5	
Plane	Plane5
Sketches	0
Type	From Face
Subtype	Outline Plane
Base Face	Selected
Use Arc Centers for Origin?	Yes
Transform 1 (RMB)	Offset Z
FD1, Value 1	1200 mm
Transform 2 (RMB)	None
Reverse Normal/Z-Axis?	No
Flip XY-Axes?	No
Export Coordinate System?	No

[7] Details of <Plane6>.

Details of Plane6	
Plane	Plane6
Sketches	0
Type	From Face
Subtype	Outline Plane
Base Face	Selected
Use Arc Centers for Origin?	Yes
Transform 1 (RMB)	Offset Z
FD1, Value 1	2400 mm
Transform 2 (RMB)	None
Reverse Normal/Z-Axis?	No
Flip XY-Axes?	No
Export Coordinate System?	No

4.3-5 Create a Sketch on Each Plane

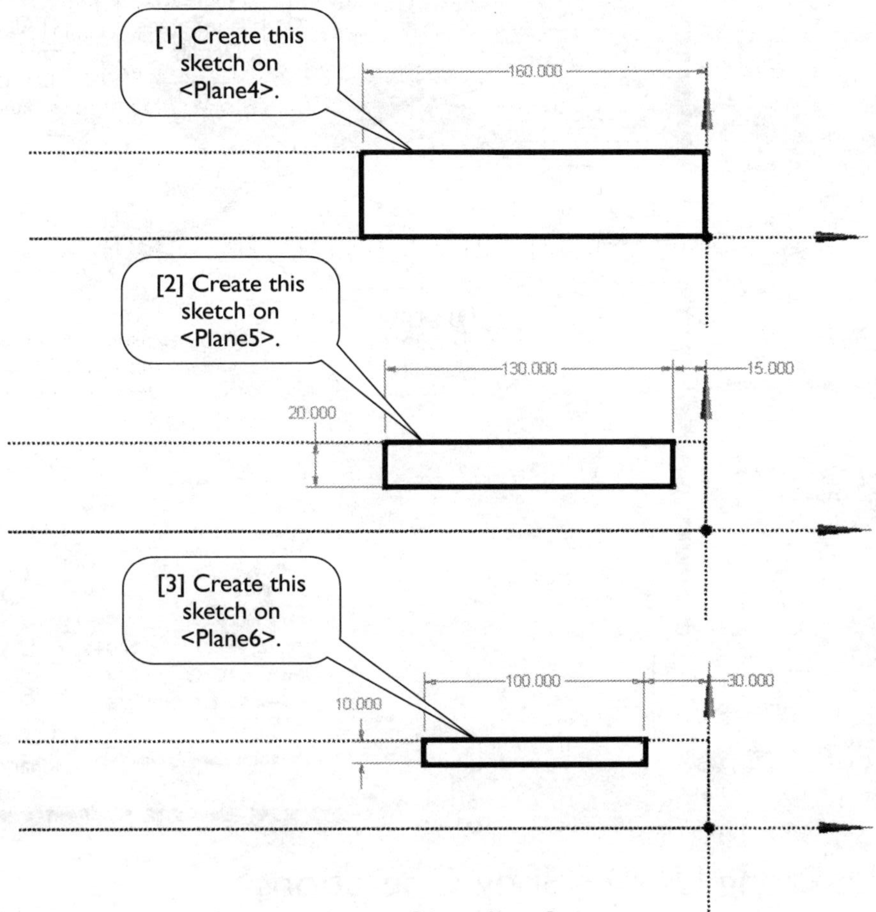

4.3-6 Create a Prong by <Skin/Loft>

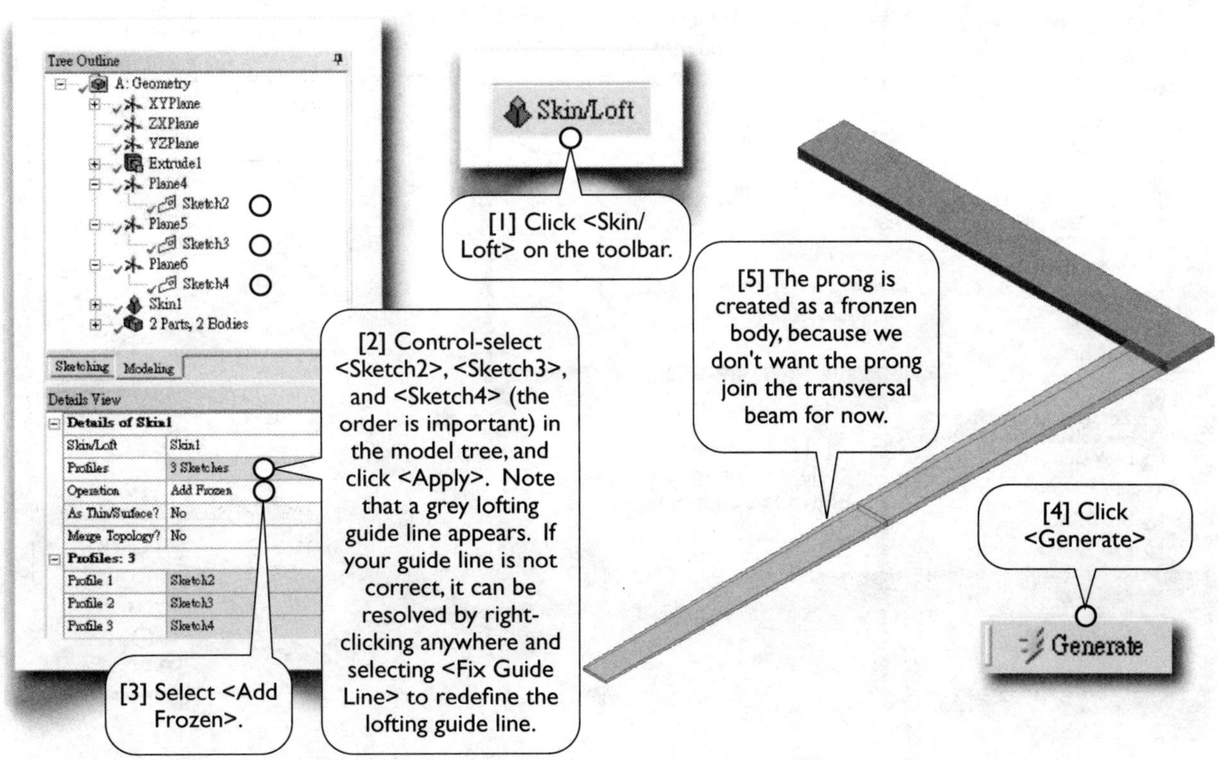

4.3-7 Create Three Planes Based on <Plane4>

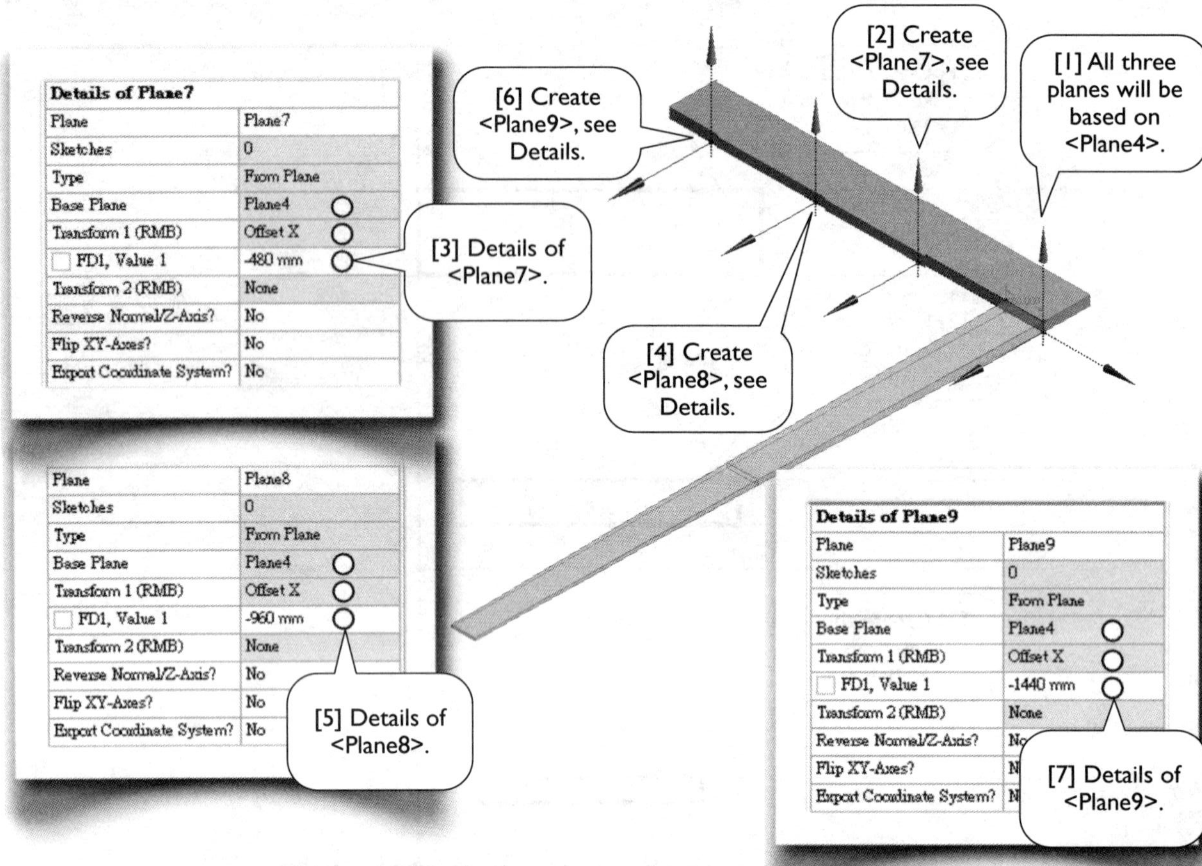

4.3-8 Copy the Prong Using <Body Operations>

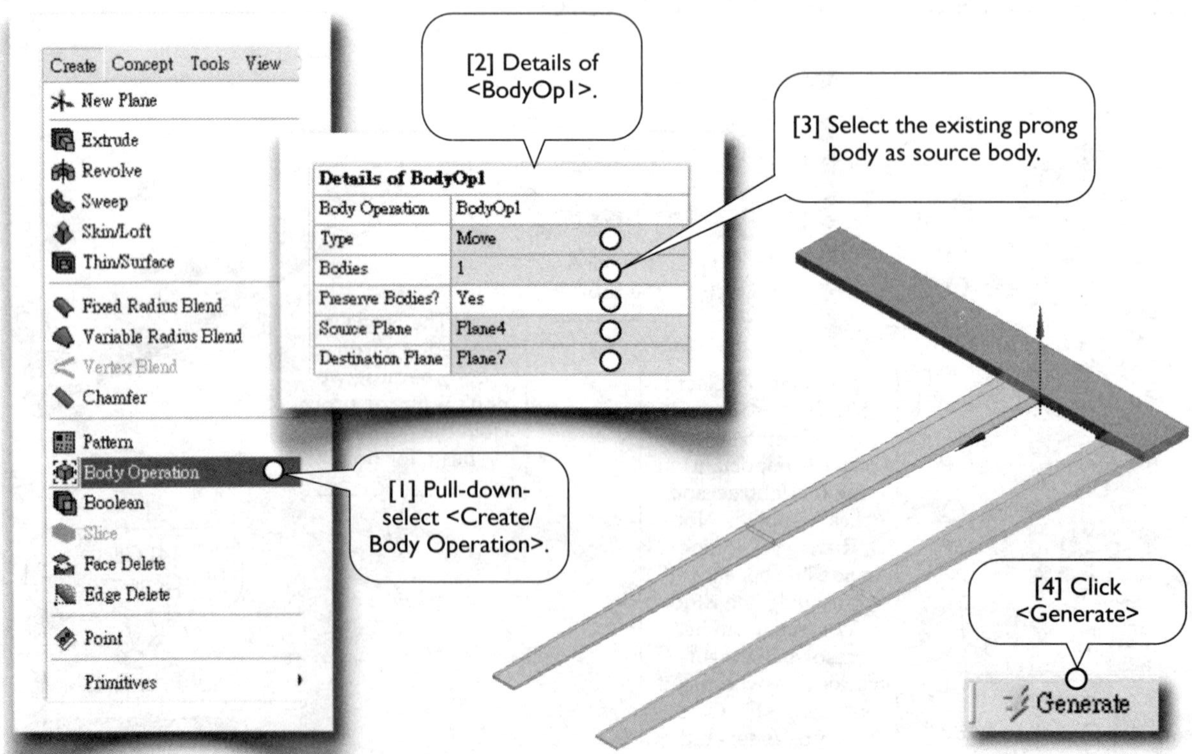

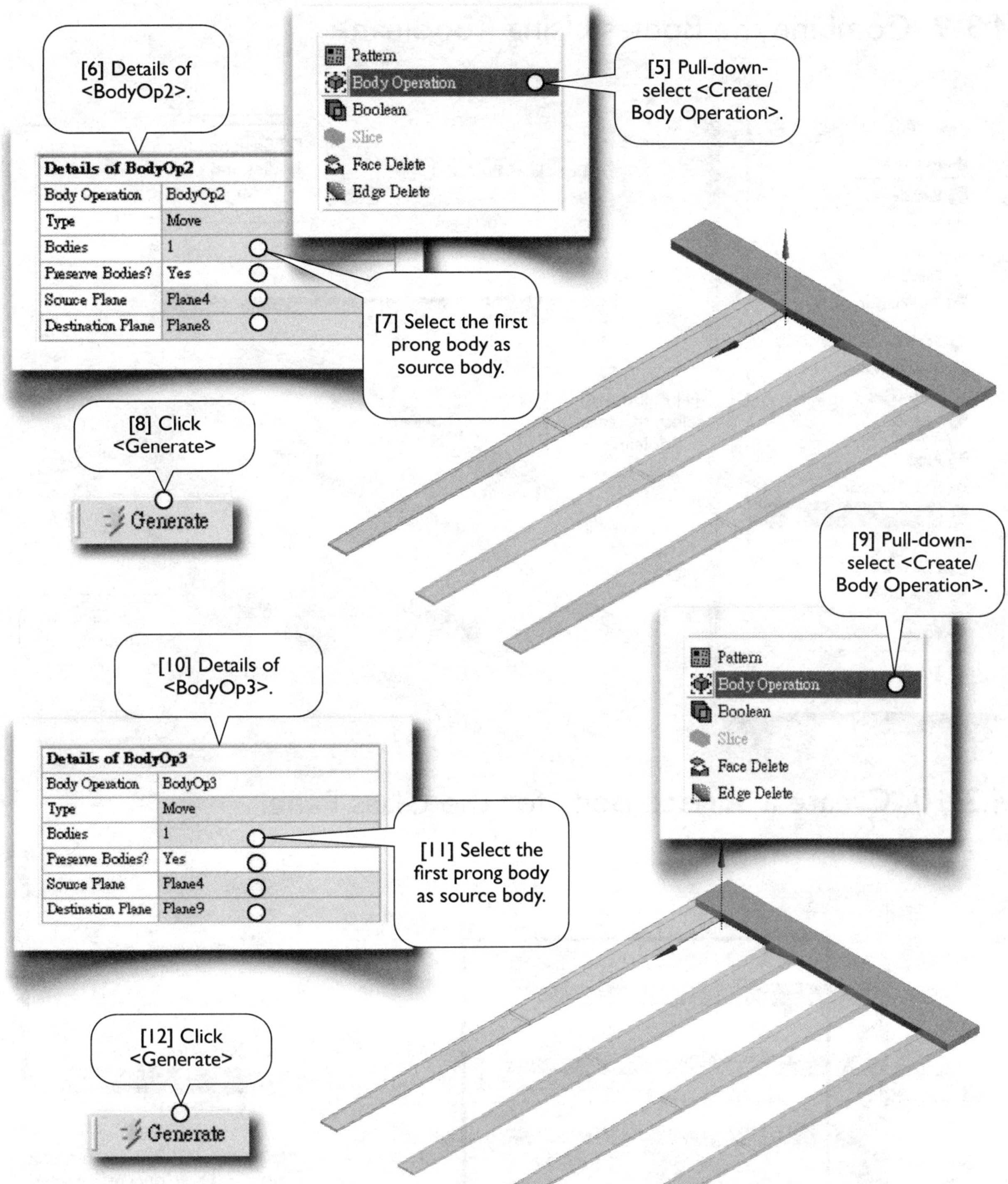

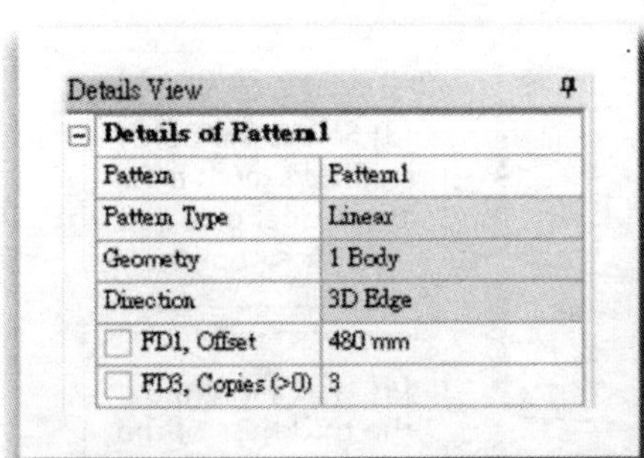

Copy the Prongs with <Pattern>

The above three times of copy can be replaced by using a <Pattern> operation. To do that, pull-down-selecting <Create/Pattern> and set up the Details as shown in the left. In this case, using <Pattern> to copy the prongs is much easier; try to redo the copying using <Pattern>. We used <Body Operations> to copy the prongs is just for instructional purpose.

The <Body Operation> includes a type <Translate>, which also can be used to copy bodies. Often, there are more than one way to accomplish the same job.

4.3-9 Combine the Bodies Using <Boolean>

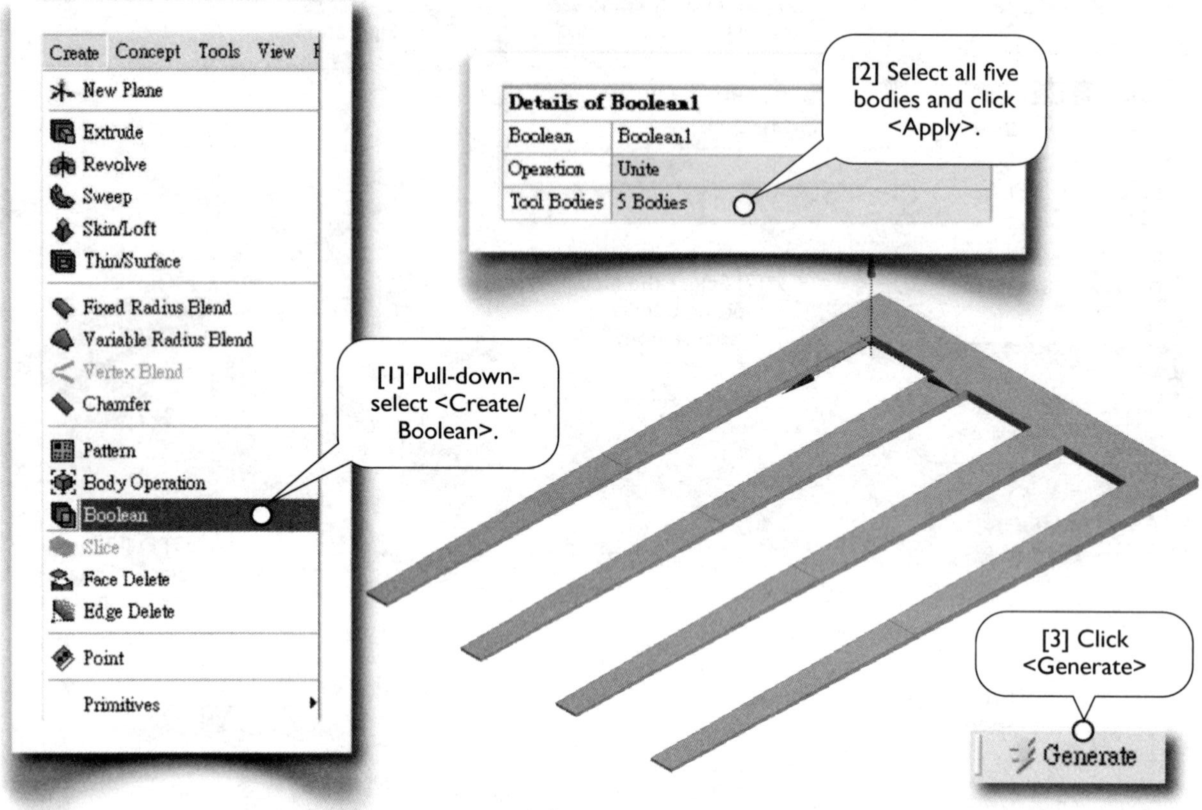

4.3-10 Create a Surface Body for the Glass Panel

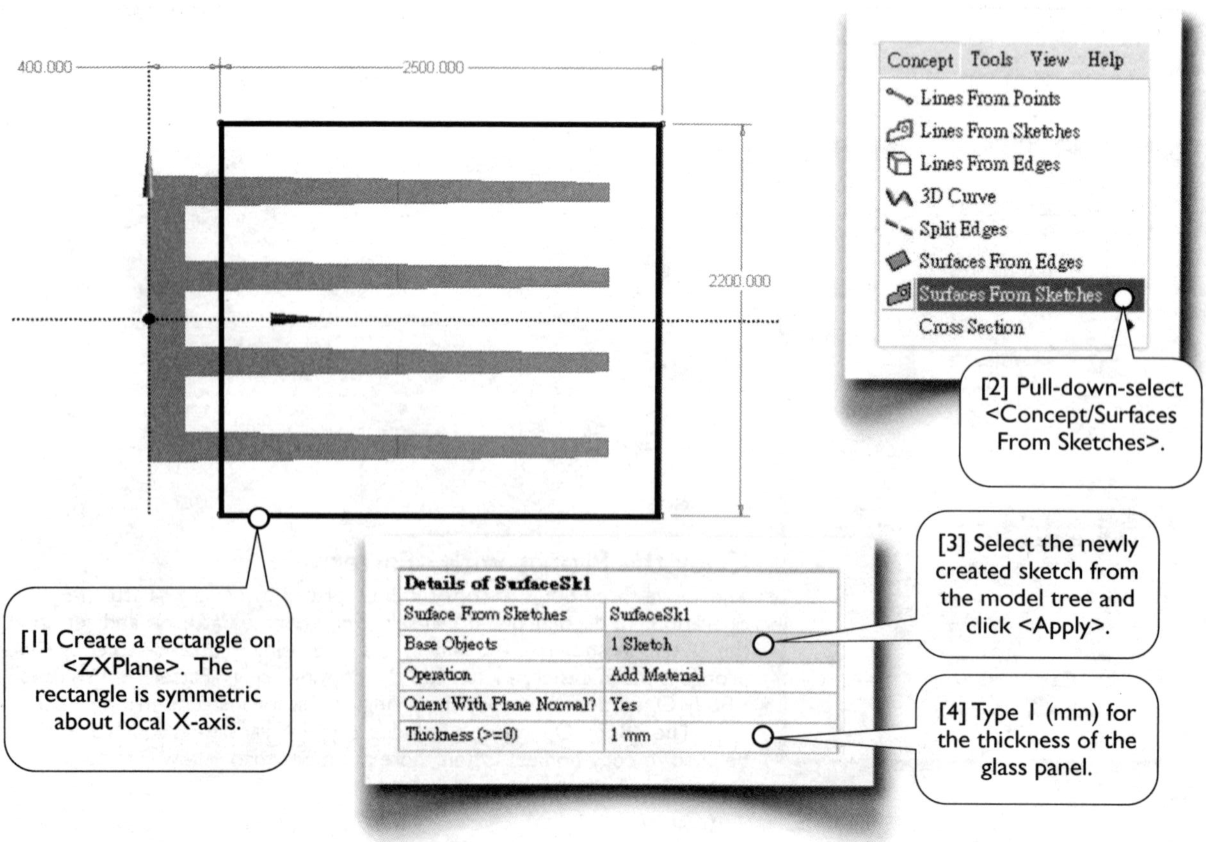

[5] Click <Generate>

[6] Although we specify <Add Material>, the surface body cannot add to the solid body. It is created as a separate body and as a separate part, because different body types cannot be combined to form a single body.

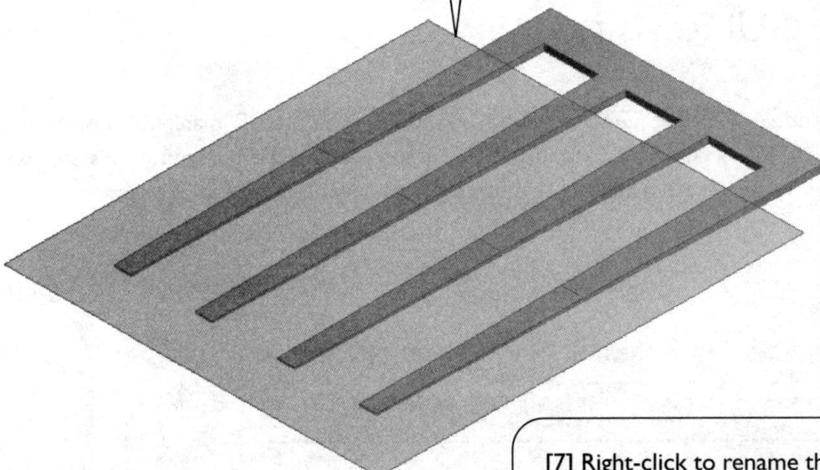

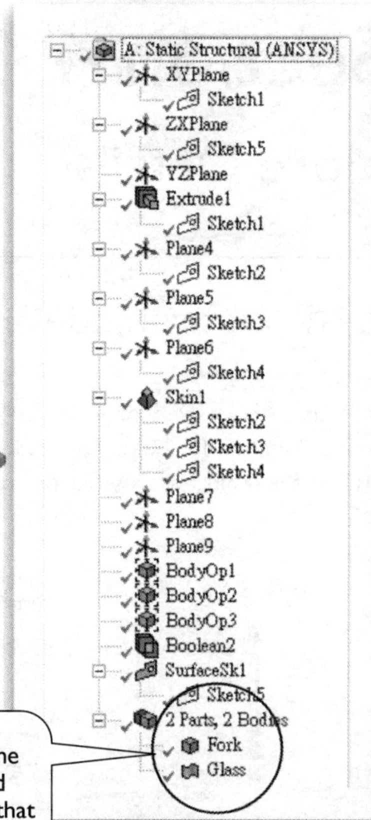

[7] Right-click to rename the two bodies as <Fork> and <Glass> respectively. Note that two bodies are treated as two parts. Each part will be meshed independently.

4.3-11 Wrap Up

[1] Save the project and exit.

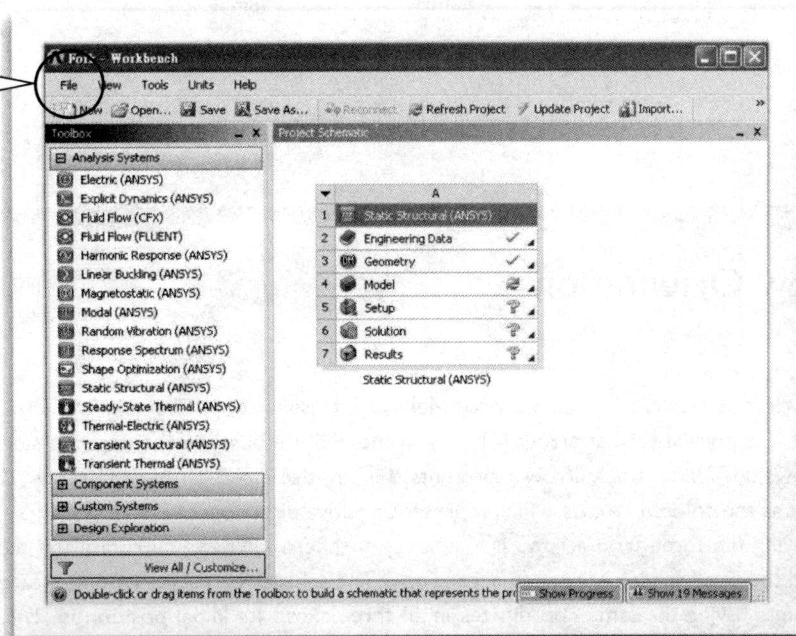

Section 4.4

More Details

4.4-1 DesignModeler GUI Revisit

In Section 2.3, we overviewed DesignModeler GUI, yet purposely skip some tools relating to 3D manipulations, such as view orientation [1, 2], model rotation [3], and entities selection [4-6]. These tools will be covered in this section. Also on the toolbar are a series of tools to create 3D features [7]; these tools are also discussed in this section.

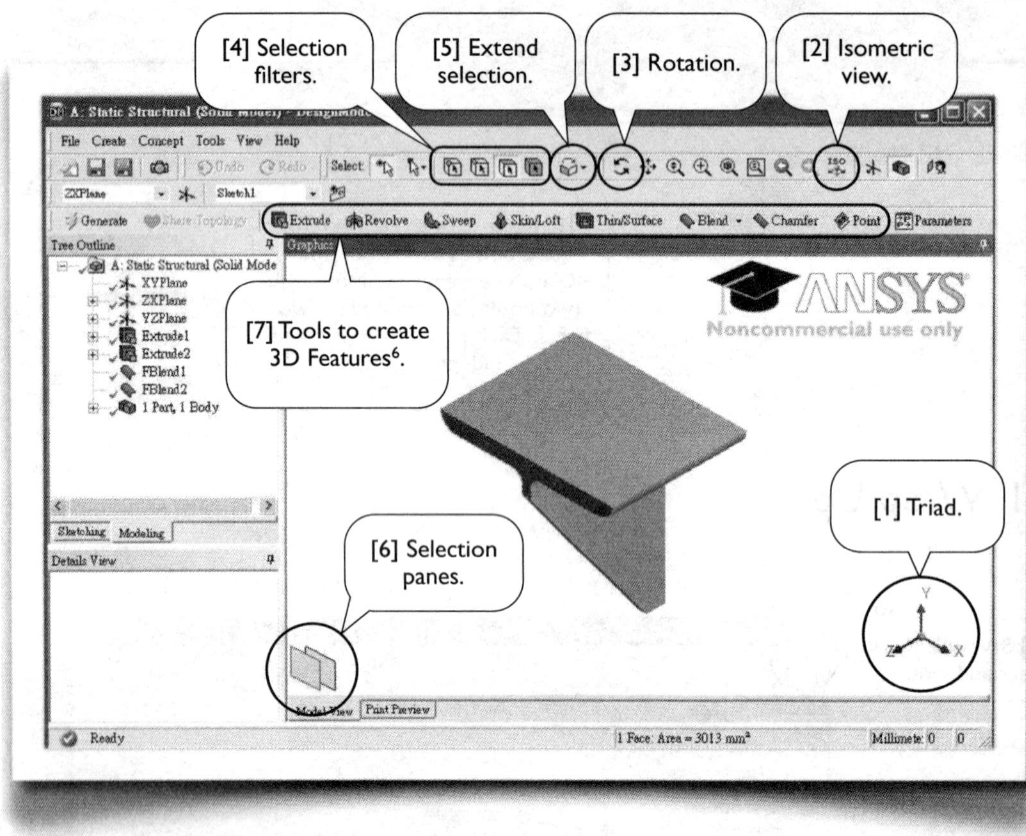

4.4-2 View Orientation

Triad[1]

On the bottom right corner of the GUI is a triad (4.4-1[1]), a useful tool. Click any of the triad arrows, the view will orient such that it is normal to that arrow [1]. If you move the mouse on the negative side of an arrow, you will a black arrow shows up [2]; this black arrow represents the negative direction of that arrow. Clicking black arrows has the similar effect as the colored arrows, which represent positive directions.

Accompanying the three triad arrows is a small cyan sphere. When you rotate the model (Section 4.4-3), the triad arrows and the small sphere will rotate accordingly. The sphere represents a point located at an "isometric axis," collection of points having the same coordinates in all three axes. Its initial position is (1, 1, 1). Thus, if the sphere coincides with the origin, that means your view is an isometric view [3]. When the sphere does not coincide with the origin, clicking the sphere will reorient the view to become isometric [4].

Isometric View[2]

As mentioned, the small cyan ball represents an isometric direction and initially it is (1, 1, 1). In 3D space, there are totally 8 such directions. For examples: (-1, 1, 1), (1, -1, 1), etc. These are all isometric views. When you click <Isometric View> tool (4.4-1[2]), the view will reorient to the isometric view closest to the current view, and the small cyan ball will move to new location accordingly. This tool let you override the initial isometric direction.

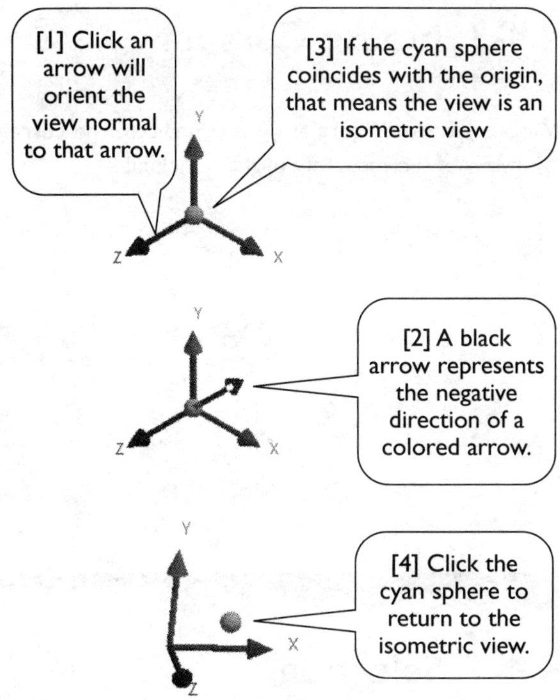

4.4-3 Rotation[3]

Rotate with Mouse Wheel

Hold the middle mouse button down while move around the graphic area, you can rotate the model [1]. It is convenient but sometimes not enough.

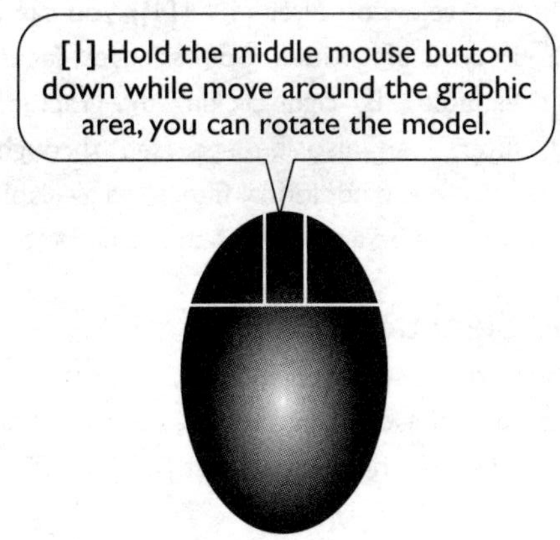

Rotate with <Rotate> tool

The <Rotate> tool (4.4-1[3]) gives you more controls for rotating the model. After activating the <Rotate> tool by clicking it, the mouse cursor becomes one of the four shapes [2-5], and the type of rotation depends on the location of your mouse cursor [6].

By default, the model center is the center of rotation. You can set the center of rotation (a red sphere) by clicking over the model. The red sphere will stay in the middle of the graphics window.

To restore the center of rotation to the model center, click anywhere in the graphics window away from the model. This will re-center the model in the middle of the graphics window.

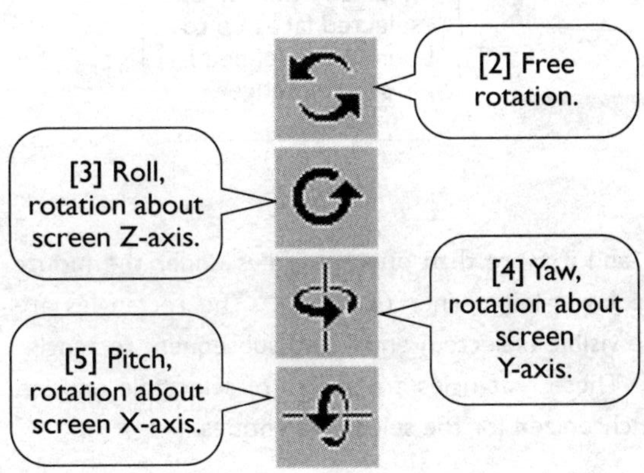

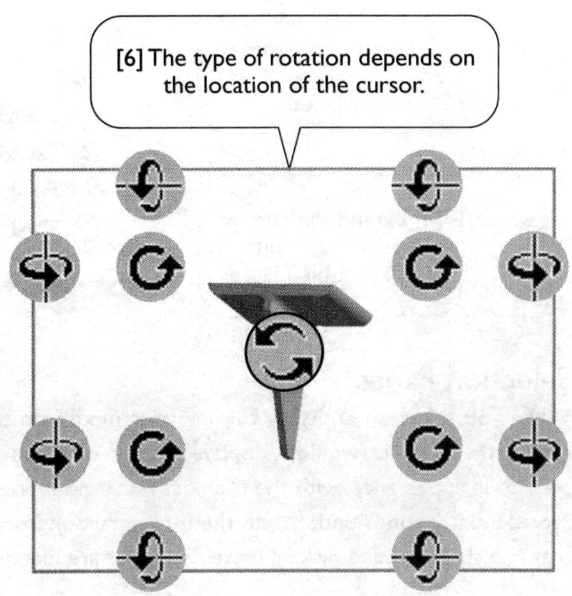

4.4-3 Mouse Cursor

Various mouse cursors are use to indicate the current operation [1]. An overview of these cursors might be helpful.

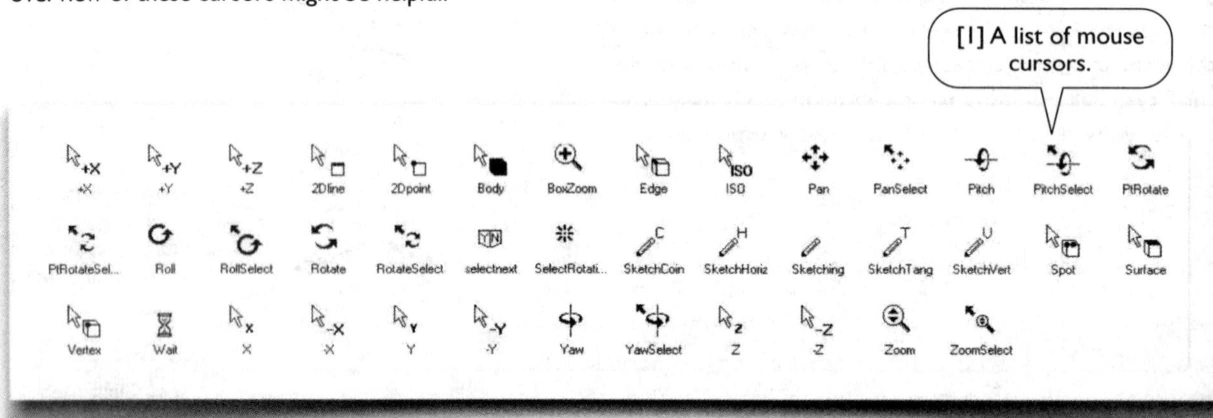

4.4-4 Selection

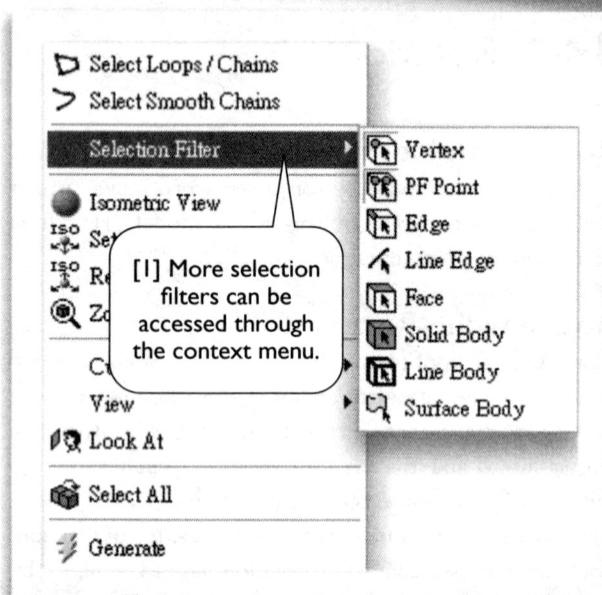

Selection Filters[4]

By activating a selection filter (4.4-1[4]), you can make one of four type of entities (points, edges, faces, and bodies) selectable. By right-clicking the graphic area, selection filters can also be accessed through the context menu, where additional filters are available [1]. Multiple filters can be activated at the same time.

Extend Selection[4]

Using the current selection as seed, these tools allow you to extend the seed to include various additional edges or faces into the selection set [2-5].

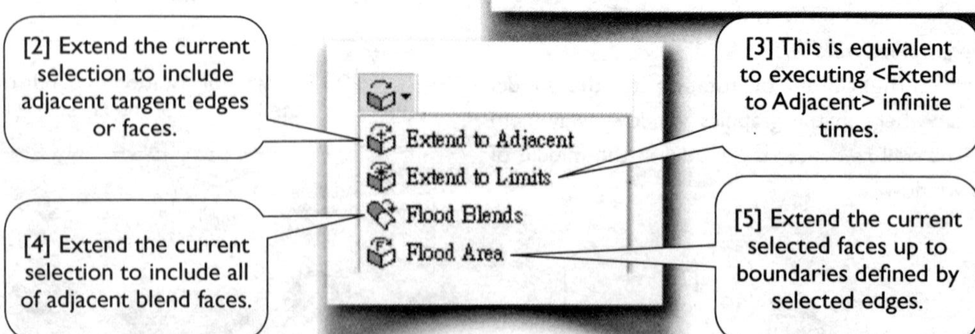

Selection Panes[5]

When you select an entity by clicking your mouse on the model, and if more than one entity lies under the mouse cursor, the graphics window displays a stack of rectangles in the lower-left corner (4.4-1[6]). The rectangles are stacked in appearance, with the topmost rectangle representing the visible (selected) entity and subsequent rectangles representing entities underneath the mouse cursor, front to back. These rectangles are aliases of selectable entities, that is, highlighting and picking these rectangles are identical and synchronized for the selectable entities.

4.4-5 Parts and Bodies

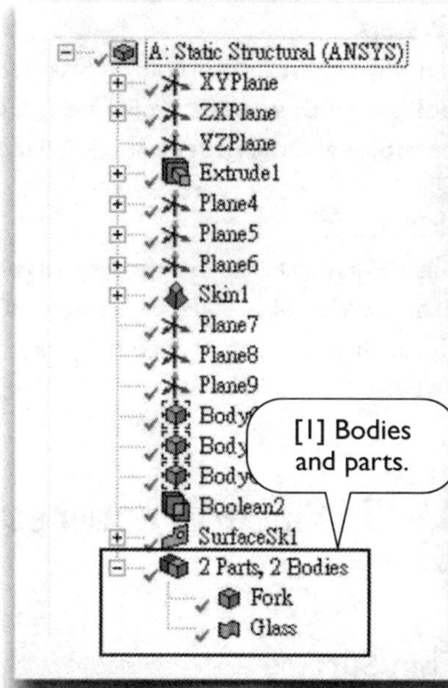

The last branch of the model tree contains the bodies and parts of the model [1]. This is the only geometric entities that will be attached to <Mechanical> for simulations.

A body is entirely made of one kind of material and is the basic building blocks of a model. A 3D body are either a solid body, a surface body, or a line body.

A part is a collection of same type of bodies. All bodies in a part are assumed to be bonded one another. In <Mechanical> parts are meshed independently—this is the most important concept about the part. Within a part, the boundary nodes are shared between contacting bodies.

A model may consist of one or more parts. Since parts are meshed independently, mesh at the boundaries between parts is not necessarily compatible. In <Mechanical>, connections[7] (e.g., contacts, joints) among parts must be established to complete a model.

4.4-6 Feature-Based 3D Bodies Modeling

A 3D body is created by combining various features. Features can be classified into two categories: base features and placed features.

Base Features

Base features are also called *sketched features* because they are created by first drawing one or more sketches, and then "growing" to 3D features by means of extrusion, revolution, sweeping, or lofting. A newly create base feature can add to or subtract material from the existing bodies.

Placed Features

Some features have predefined shapes and behaviors. To add these features to existing bodies, all we have to do is to specify where we want to place these features, along with a few other settings. Therefore, these features are called *placed features*, for examples: blends, chamfers.

4.4-6 Base Features[8]

Extrude

The tool is used to extrude a sketch along its normal direction to create a 3D body. The extrusion may be symmetric or asymmetric to the sketching plane. The extrusion depth may be a fixed value, through all bodies (used only for cutting the material), up to a face, or up to a surface. A *face* is a bounded region and has a finite area while a *surface* is an unbounded region and has infinite area. A surface is often the extension of a face.

Revolve

The tool is used to revolve a sketch about an axis to create a 3D body. An angle of revolution can be specified.

Sweep

The <Sweep> can be thought of a generalization of <Extrude>. The tool is used to sweep a profile along a path to create a 3D body. Both the profile and the path must be defined using sketches.

Skin/Loft

The <Skin/Loft> can be thought of a generalization of <Sweep>. It takes a series of profiles to create a 3D body by fitting through them. The profiles must be defined using sketches.

4.4-7 Placed Features[8]

Thin/Surface

The tool is used to convert a solid into a thin solid body or a surface body. Typically, you will select one or more faces to remove, and then specify a thickness. If the thickness is a positive value, then a thin solid body is created. If the thickness is zero, then a surface body is created.

Blend

The tool is used to create *rounds* or *fillets* on edges, or on vertices. The radius of the rounds or fillets may be fixed or variable.

Chamfer

The tool is used to create chamfer faces on edges.

References

1. ANSYS Help System>DesignModeler>Viewing>Model Appearance Controls>Triad
2. ANSYS Help System>DesignModeler>Viewing>Rotation Modes>Isometric View
3. ANSYS Help System>Mechanical>The Mechanical Application Basics>The Mechanical Application Interface>Triad and Rotation Cursors
4. ANSYS Help System>DesignModeler>Selection>Selection Toolbar
5. ANSYS Help System>DesignModeler>Selection>Graphical Selection>Depth Picking
6. ANSYS Help System>DesignModeler>3D Modeling>Bodies and Parts
7. ANSYS Help System>Mechanical>Mechanical Objects Reference>Connections
8. ANSYS Help System>DesignModeler>3D Modeling>3D Features

Section 4.5
Exercise: LCD Display Support

4.5-1 About the LCD Display Support

The LCD Display support is made of an ABS (acrylonitrile-butadiene-styrene) plastic. The thickness of the plastic is 3 mm [1]. Details of the hinge design is not shown in the figure [2] but will be detailed during the geometric modeling in this section.

The solid model will be used in Section 5.4 for a static structural simulation to assess the deformation and stress under a design load.

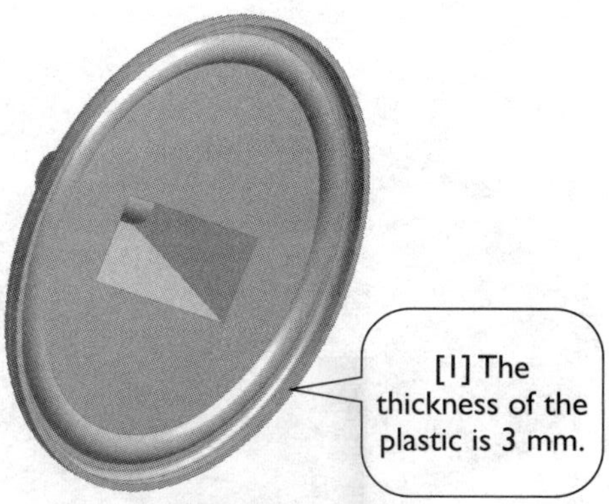

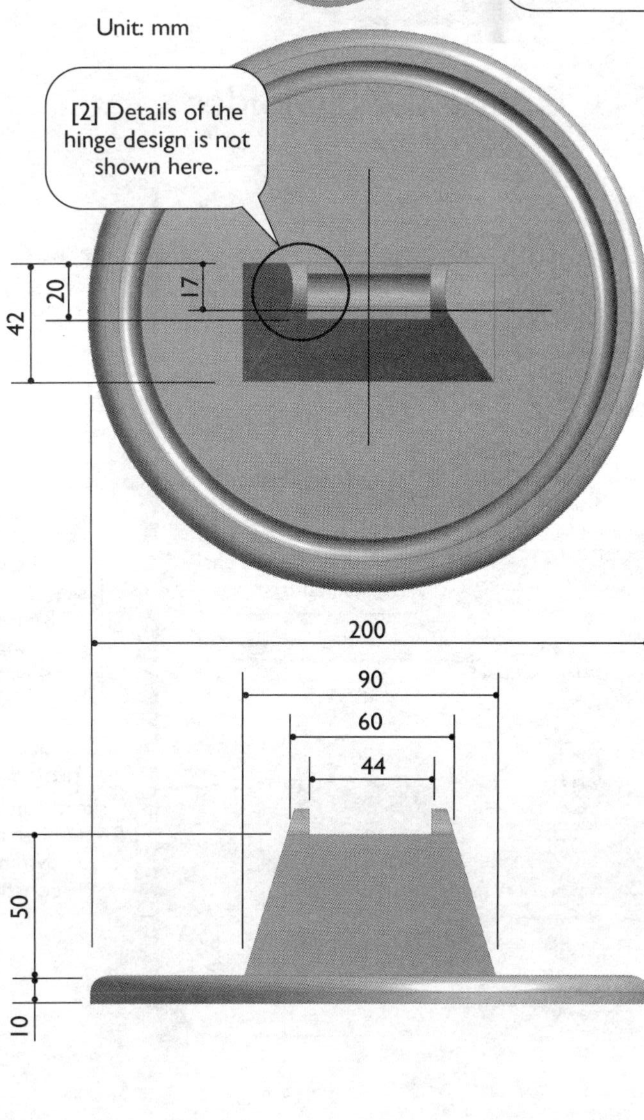

4.5-2 Create the Base

Launch <Workbench> as usual. Create a <Static Structural> system. Save the project as "Support." Start up <DesignModeler>; select <Millimeter> as length unit.

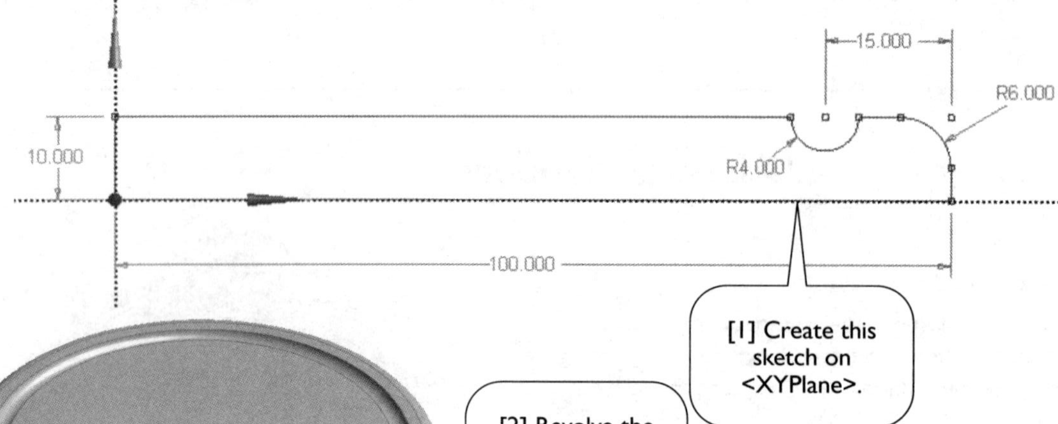

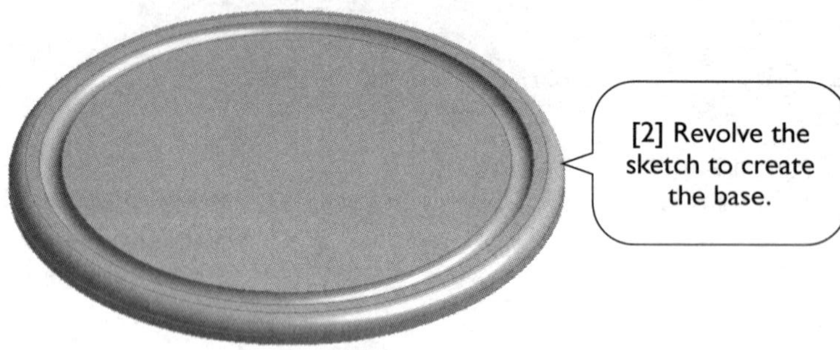

4.5-3 Create the Upholder

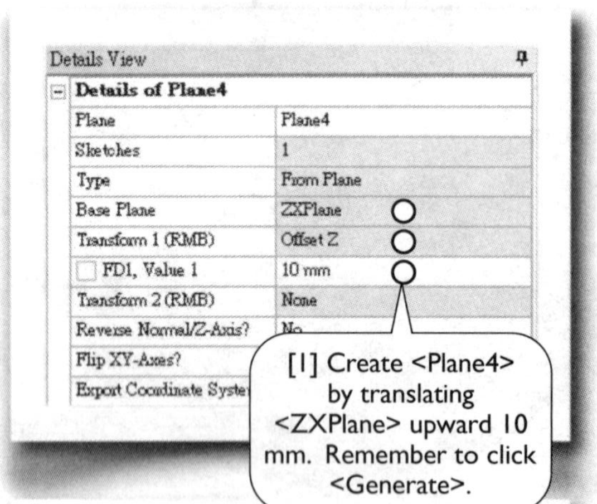

Details View

Details of Plane4	
Plane	Plane4
Sketches	1
Type	From Plane
Base Plane	ZXPlane
Transform 1 (RMB)	Offset Z
FD1, Value 1	10 mm
Transform 2 (RMB)	None
Reverse Normal/Z-Axis?	No
Flip XY-Axes?	
Export Coordinate Syste	

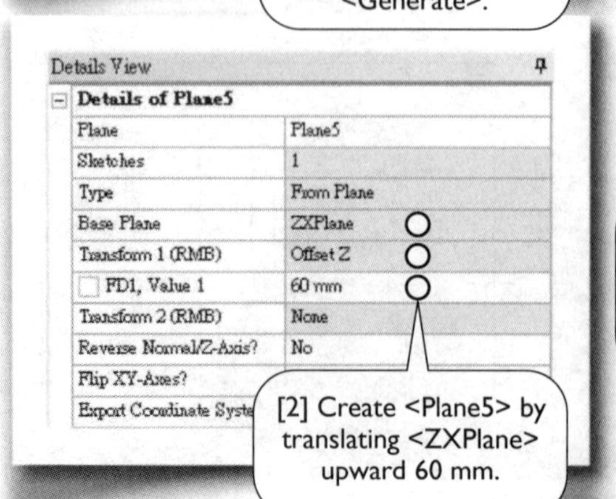

Details View

Details of Plane5	
Plane	Plane5
Sketches	1
Type	From Plane
Base Plane	ZXPlane
Transform 1 (RMB)	Offset Z
FD1, Value 1	60 mm
Transform 2 (RMB)	None
Reverse Normal/Z-Axis?	No
Flip XY-Axes?	
Export Coordinate Syste	

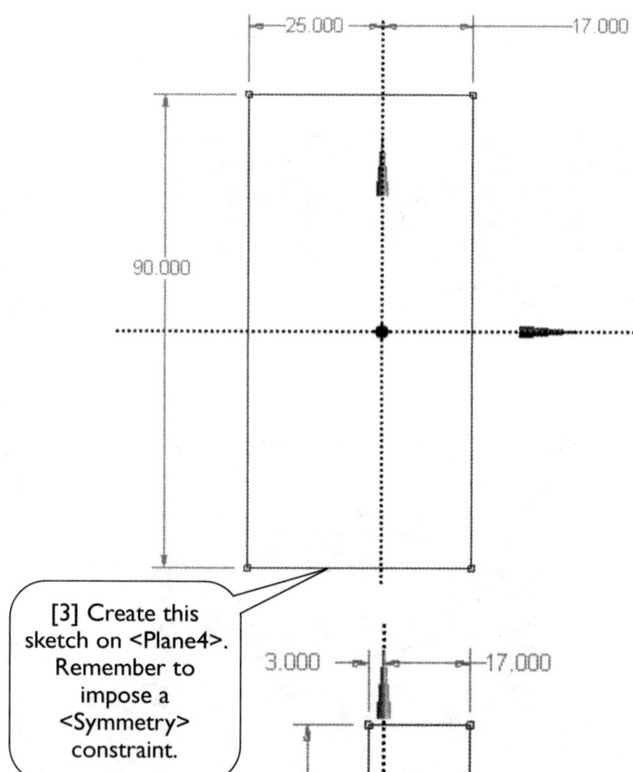

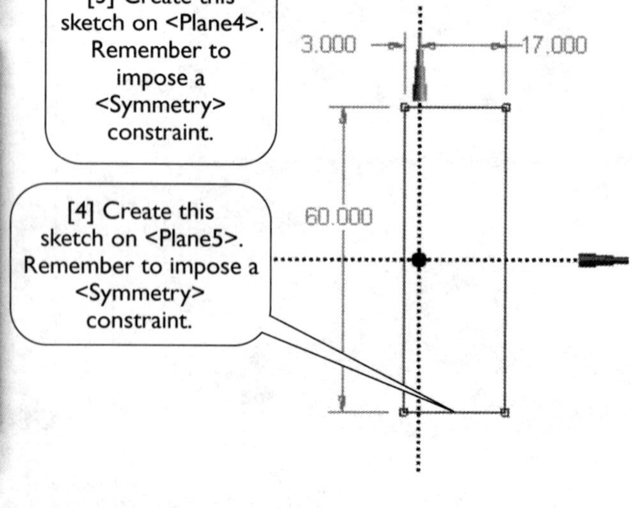

Details View

Details of Skin1	
Skin/Loft	Skin1
Profiles	2 Sketches
Operation	Add Material
As Thin/Surface?	No
Merge Topology?	No
Profiles: 2	
Profile 1	Sketch2
Profile 2	Sketch3

[5] Click <Skin/Loft> on the toolbar. Select the two sketches just created from the model tree and click <Apply>. Note that a grey lofting guide line appears. If your guide line is not correct, it can be resolved by right-clicking anywhere and selecting <Fix Guide Line> to redefine the lofting guide line.

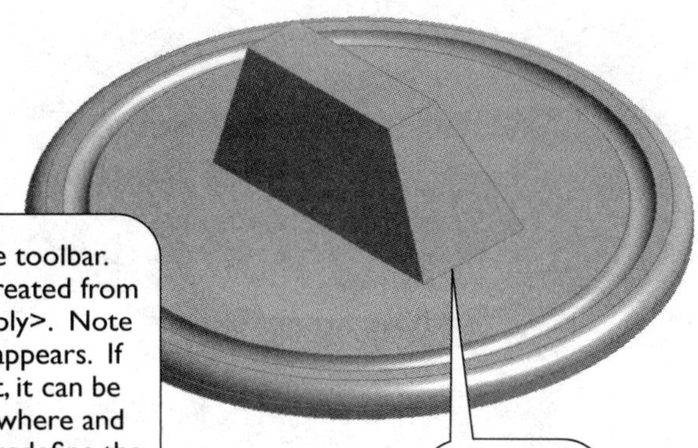

[6] <Skin1>.

4.5-4 Create the Hinge

[1] Create <Plane6> based on this face, and create <Plane7> based on the opposite face. The locations of coordinate systems are not important for upcoming operations; however, to be consistent with the textbook, set the coordinate systems as shown.

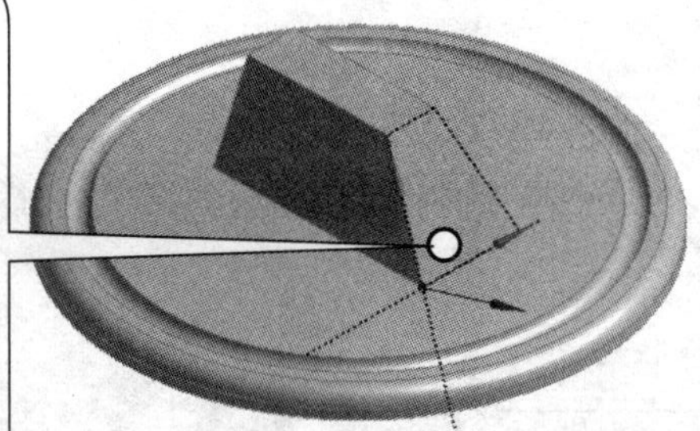

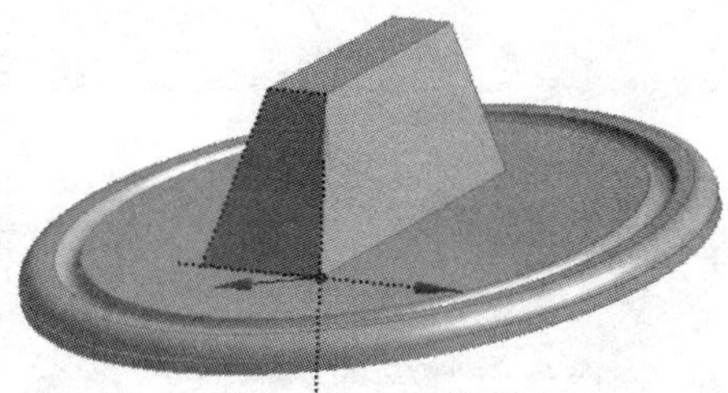

Details View

Details of Plane6	
Plane	Plane6
Sketches	1
Type	From Face
Subtype	Outline Plane
Base Face	Selected
Use Arc Centers for Origin?	Yes
Transform 1 (RMB)	None
Reverse Normal/Z-Axis?	No
Flip XY-Axes?	No
Export Coordinate System?	No

Details View

Details of Plane7	
Plane	Plane7
Sketches	1
Type	From Face
Subtype	Outline Plane
Base Face	Selected
Use Arc Centers for Origin?	Yes
Transform 1 (RMB)	None
Reverse Normal/Z-Axis?	No
Flip XY-Axes?	No
Export Coordinate System?	No

[2] Create this sketch on <Plane6>. The sketch consists of an arc and two straight lines. Don't forget the short line. For details, see next two steps.

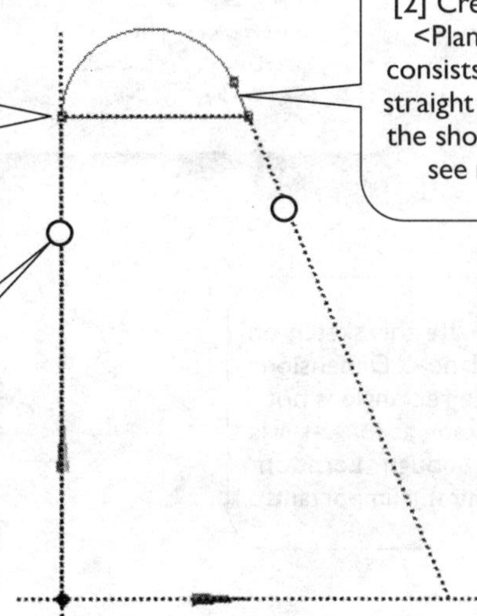

[4] Impose a <Perpendicular> constraint between the arc and the horizontal plane boundary line. Now the arc is fixed (the actual radius is 9.592 mm) and remains tangent to both plane boundary lines. Finally, draw the two straight lines by connecting the points.

[3] The arc can be created by using <Fillet> tool (temporarily set a radius of 10 mm) and selecting these two plane boundary lines. Note the arc is not fixed until next step.

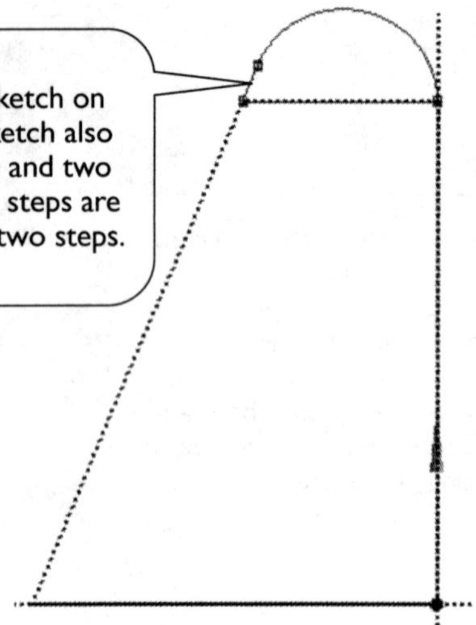

[5] Create this sketch on <Plane7>. The sketch also consists of an arc and two straight lines. The steps are similar to the last two steps.

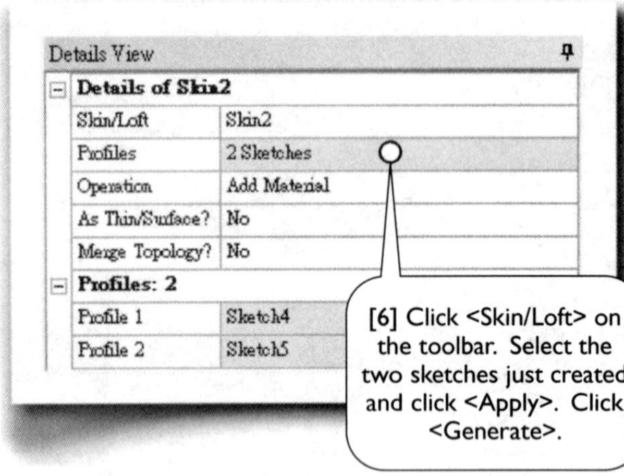

Details View

Details of Skin2	
Skin/Loft	Skin2
Profiles	2 Sketches
Operation	Add Material
As Thin/Surface?	No
Merge Topology?	No
Profiles: 2	
Profile 1	Sketch4
Profile 2	Sketch5

[6] Click <Skin/Loft> on the toolbar. Select the two sketches just created and click <Apply>. Click <Generate>.

[7] <Skin2>.

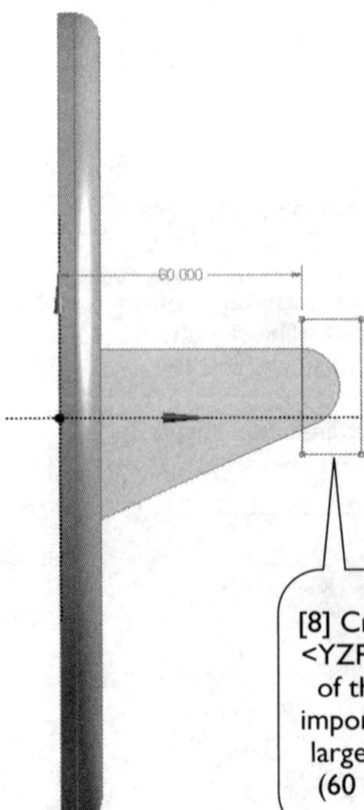

[8] Create this sketch on <YZPlane>. Dimensions of the rectangle is not important, as long as it is large enough. Location (60 mm) is important.

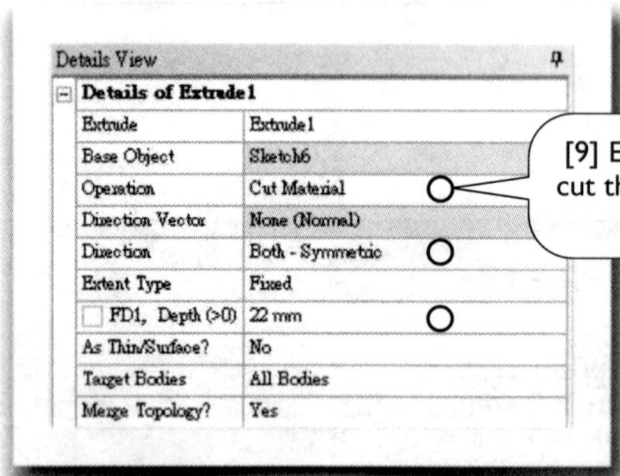

Details View

Details of Extrude1	
Extrude	Extrude1
Base Object	Sketch6
Operation	Cut Material
Direction Vector	None (Normal)
Direction	Both - Symmetric
Extent Type	Fixed
FD1, Depth (>0)	22 mm
As Thin/Surface?	No
Target Bodies	All Bodies
Merge Topology?	Yes

[9] Extrude to cut the material away.

[10] Some material is cut away.

Details View	
Details of Plane8	
Plane	Plane8
Sketches	1
Type	From Face
Subtype	Outline Plane
Base Face	Selected
Use Arc Centers for Origin?	Yes
Transform 1 (RMB)	None
Reverse Normal/Z-Axis?	No
Flip XY-Axes?	No
Export Coordinate System?	No

[11] Create <Plane8> based on this face. To be consistent with the textbook, please attach the coordinate system on the left corner as shown in the next step.

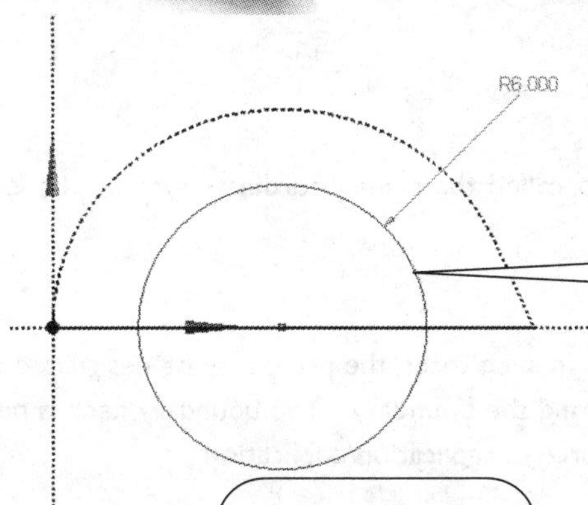

[12] Draw a circle on <Plane8>. Impose a <Concentric> constraint on the circle with the plane boundary circle. Note that, to avoid over-constrained, the center of the circle must not be on the horizontal axis before imposing the <Concentric> constraint.

Details View	
Details of Extrude2	
Extrude	Extrude2
Base Object	Sketch7
Operation	Cut Material
Direction Vector	None (Normal)
Direction	Both - Asymmetric
Extent Type	Fixed
FD1, Depth (>0)	47 mm
Extent Type 2	Fixed
FD4, Depth 2 (>0)	3 mm
As Thin/Surface?	No
Target Bodies	All Bodies
Merge Topology?	Yes

[13] Extrude the sketch asymmetrically to cut the material away.

[14] Some material is cut away.

4.5-5 Create the Thin Shell

Details View	
Details of Thin1	
Thin/Surface	Thin1
Selection Type	Faces to Remove
Geometry	1 Face
Direction	Inward
FD1, Thickness (>=0)	3 mm

[1] Click <Thin/Surface> on the toolbar. Select the bottom face to remove.

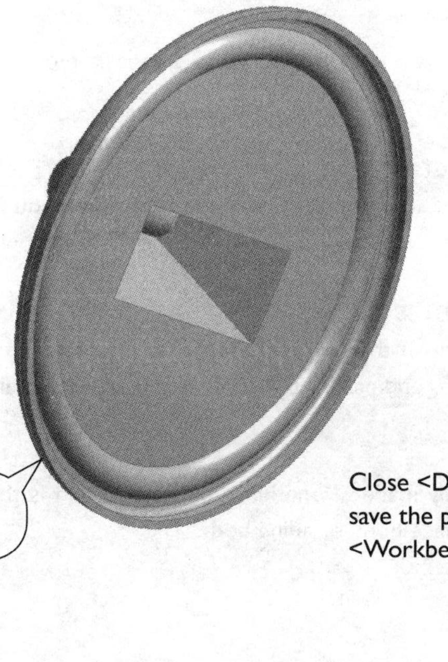

[2] The thin shell.

Close <DesignModeler>, save the project, and exit <Workbench>.

Section 4.6

Problems

4.6-1 Key Concepts

Plane Coordinate System
Each plane is attached a local coordinate system, called the plane coordinate system. Its Z-axis always points out of the plane.

Plane Boundary
A plane may be created by deriving from a face. In such cases, the plane may be designated as <Outline Plane> (i.e., a plane with boundary). You can draw entities beyond the boundary. The boundary itself is not a geometric entity. The plane boundary is used as datum edges, or as source of replication/duplication.

Isometric View
A model view in which the view direction follows an isometric axis, which forms the same angles with the three principle axes, is called an isometric view.

Roll
Rotate the model about the screen Z-axis.

Yaw
Rotate the model about the screen Y-axis.

Pitch
Rotate the model about the screen X-axis.

Selection Filters
A selection filter is a tool used to make a specific type of entities selectable. Multiple filters can be activated at the same time.

Extend Selection
Using the current selection as seed, these tools allow you to extend the seed to include additional edges or faces into the selection set.

Selection Panes
Rectangles appear in the lower-left corner of the graphics window. These rectangles are aliases of selectable entities, that is, highlighting and picking these rectangles are identical and synchronized for the selectable entities.

Body
A body is entirely made of one kinds of material and is the basic building blocs of a model. A 3D body are either a solid body, a surface body, or a line body.

Part
A part is a collection of same type of bodies. All bodies in a part are assumed to be bonded one another. In <Mechanical> parts are meshed independently. Within a part, the boundary nodes are shared between contacting bodies.

Connections
In <Mechanical>, connections are kinematic relations between parts. Typical connections are contacts, joints, etc.

Feature
A 3D body is created by combining various features. The features can be classified into two categories: base features and placed features.

Base Features
Base features are also called sketched features; they are created by first drawing one or more sketches, and then "growing" to 3D features by means of extrusion, revolution, sweeping, or lofting. A newly create base feature can add to or subtract material from the existing bodies.

Placed Features
Placed features have predefined shapes and behaviors. To add these features to existing bodies, all we have to do is to specify where we want to place these features, along with a few other settings.

4.6-2 Workbench Exercises

Create a 3D geometry for the Bolt-Nut-Plate Assembly
Create a model as shown in 3.2-1[1-3]. You can find the project file in the DVD that comes with the book.

Create a 3D model for a static mixer
Follow the steps described in the CFX-Mesh Tutorial 1, create a static mixer[1] [1]. The comprehensive description of each step in the tutorial might be helpful for those who need some more exercises. Sketching using grids (Section 2.3-10), for which we didn't give any examples, is detailed in this tutorial.

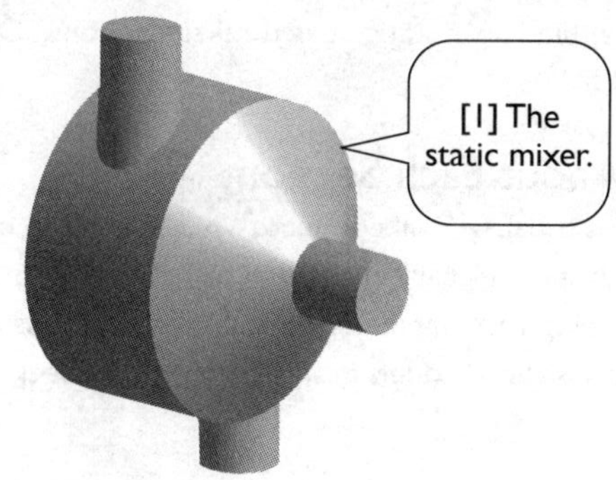

Create a 3D model for a catalytic converter
Follow the steps described in the CFX-Mesh Tutorial 7, create a catalytic converter[2] [2]. This provides additional exercise on creating 3D bodies using skin/lofting.

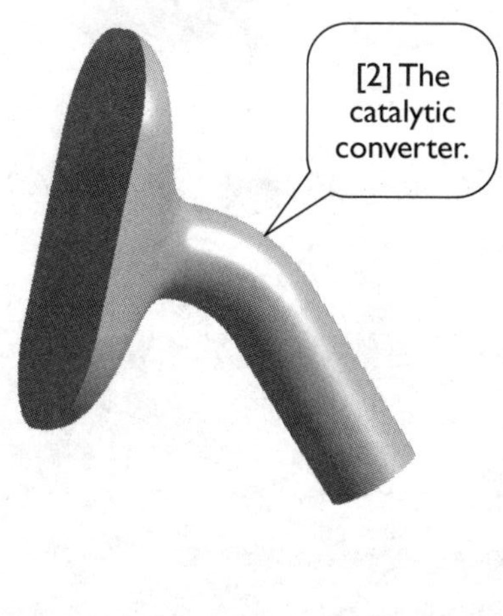

References

1. ANSYS Help System>CFX-Mesh>CFX-Mesh Tutorials>Tutorial 1: Static Mixer>Geometry Creation
2. ANSYS Help System>CFX-Mesh>CFX-Mesh Tutorials>Tutorial 7: Catalytic Converter>Geometry Creation

Chapter 5

3D Simulations

Many concepts and techniques in 2D simulations can be generalized to 3D simulations. Problem sizes in 3D cases are usually larger and the geometries are usually more complicated; that implies more computers and engineers time. On the other hand, we've been accustomed to the 3D world, and the 3D simulations seem more natural to us. As a result, newcomers often stick at 3D ways of thinking such that they forget that a problem may be modeled as 2D. Remember that, if a problem can be reduced to a 2D, you have no reasons to go for a 3D.

Purpose of the Chapter

This chapter deals with simulations using 3D solid models exclusively. 3D surface models and line models are introduced in Chapters 6 and 7 respectively. Like the 2D simulations in Chapter 3, this chapter limits the discussion within linear static structural simulations. Dynamic and nonlinear simulations will be presented starting from Chapter 11.

About Each Section

As usual, we will conduct two step-by-step examples in the first two sections. Section 1 is a simple example, serving as an introductory tutorial. Section 2 is a much more involved example. Section 3 provides a systematic discussion trying to complement what have been missed in the first two sections. Section 4 is an additional exercise. All the simulation models in this chapter have been created in Chapter 4.

Section 5.1

Step-by-Step: Beam Bracket

5.1-1 About the Beam Bracket

In Section 4.1, we created a 3D solid model for a beam bracket. The model will be used in this section for a static structural simulation. Besides a geometry, we need more information for a simulation. The additional information can be summarized into two categories: material properties and environmental conditions.

The bracket is made of structural steel [1], with a Young's modulus of 200 GPa and a Poisson's ratio of 0.3. Its yield strength is 250 MPa. The yield strength is needed for assessing safety factors.

As mentioned in Section 4.1-1, the design loads are determined by a thorough analysis of the entire structure. The design load for this bracket is 27 kN, which assumes a uniform distribution over the seat plate [2].

Besides the load, the environmental conditions include support conditions. In this case we assume the beam bracket's back face is rigidly welded on a steel column, that is, a fixed support [3].

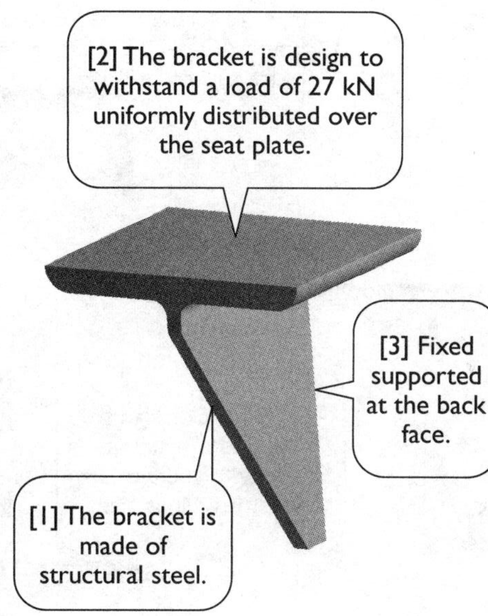

5.1-2 Open the Project "Bracket"

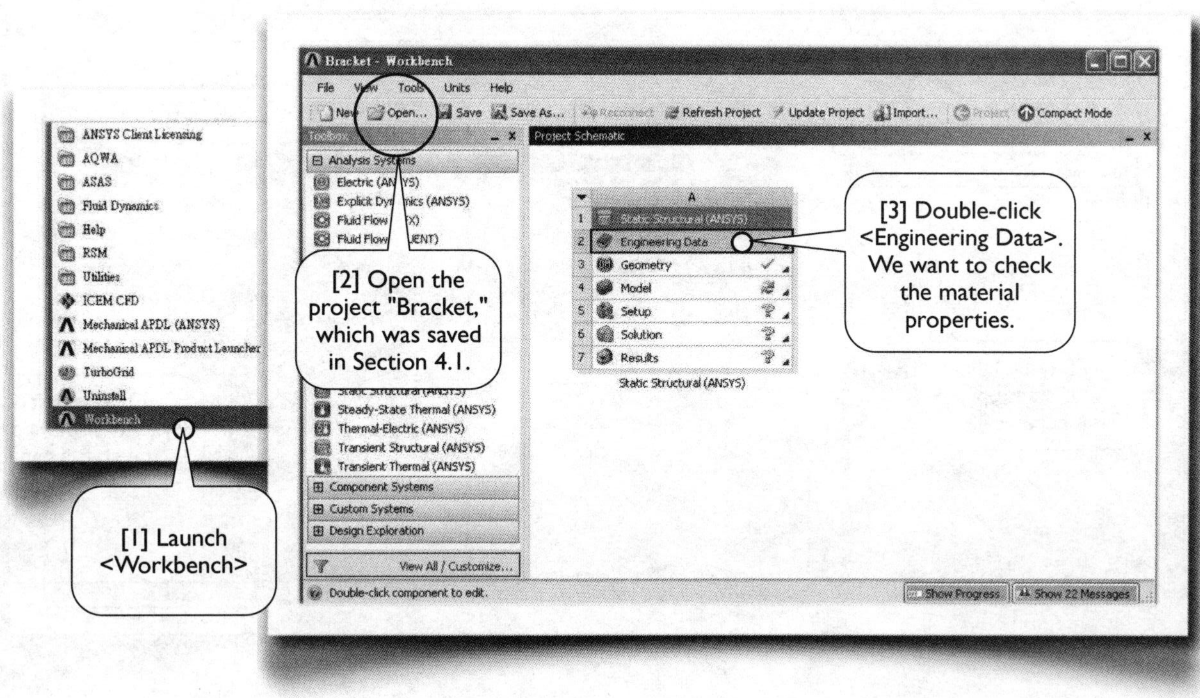

5.1-3 Check Material in <Engineering Data>

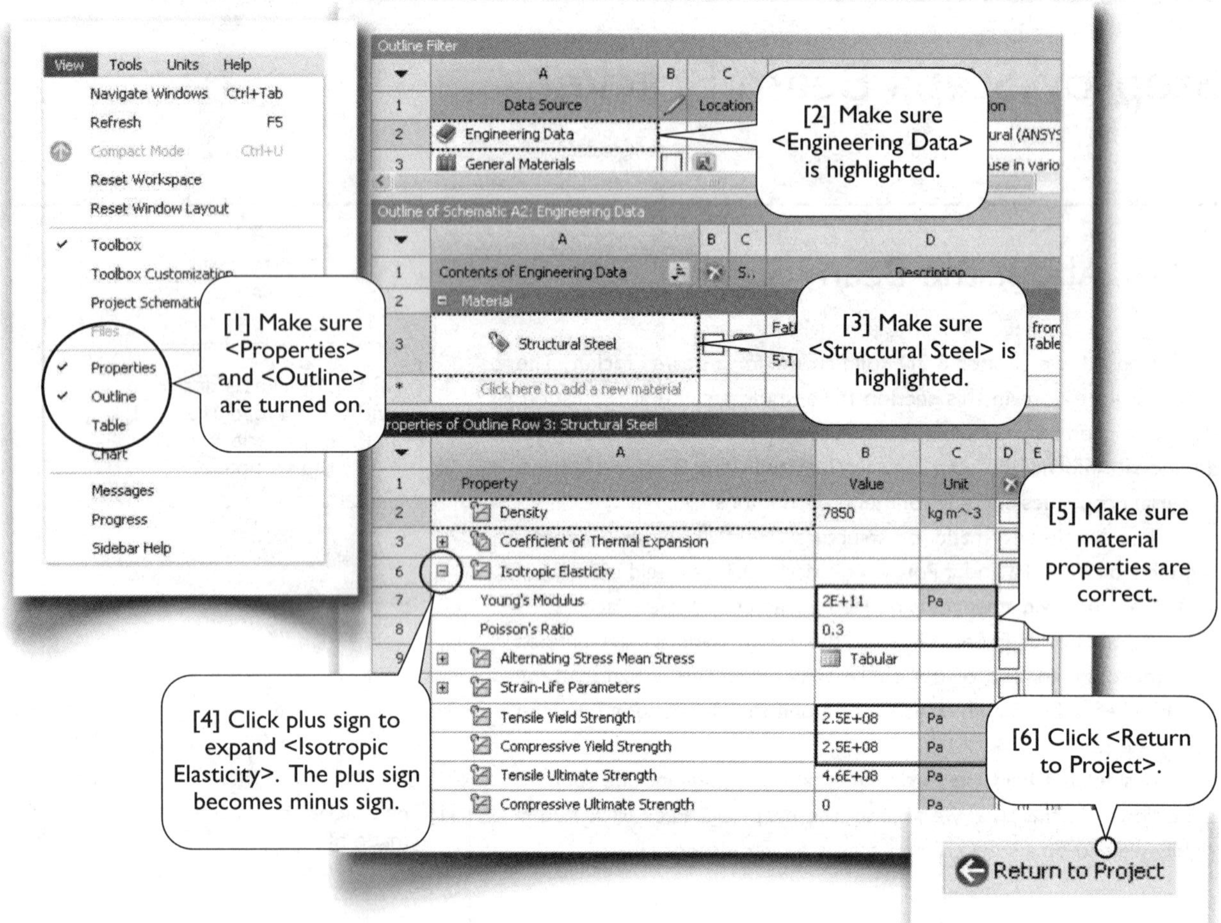

5.1-4 Start Up <Mechanical>

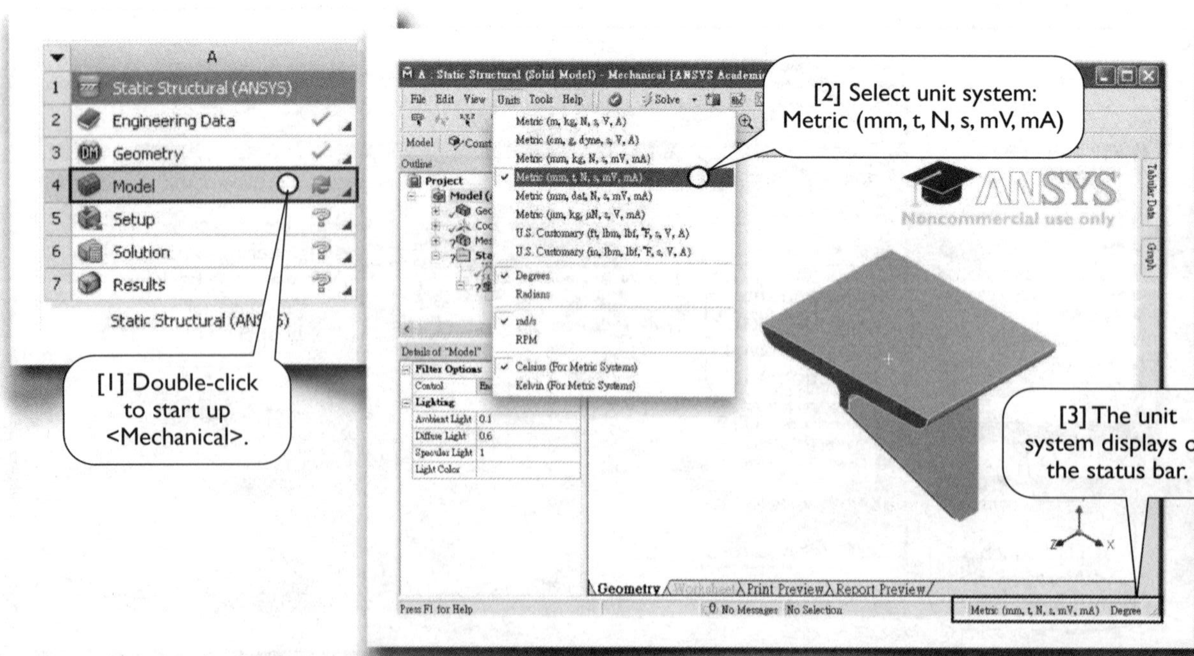

5.1-5 Check Material Assignment

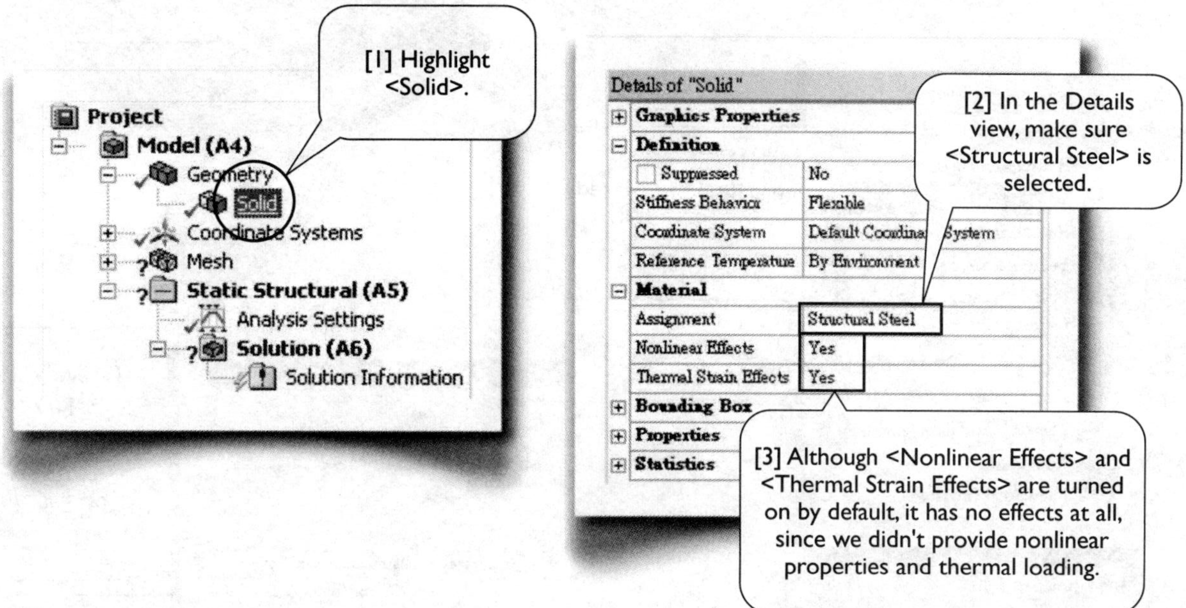

Material Assignment

By default, <Mechanical> assigns <Structural Steel> for each body. That is exactly what we want. Therefore we don't need to do anything for the material assignment in this case.

5.1-6 Specify Support

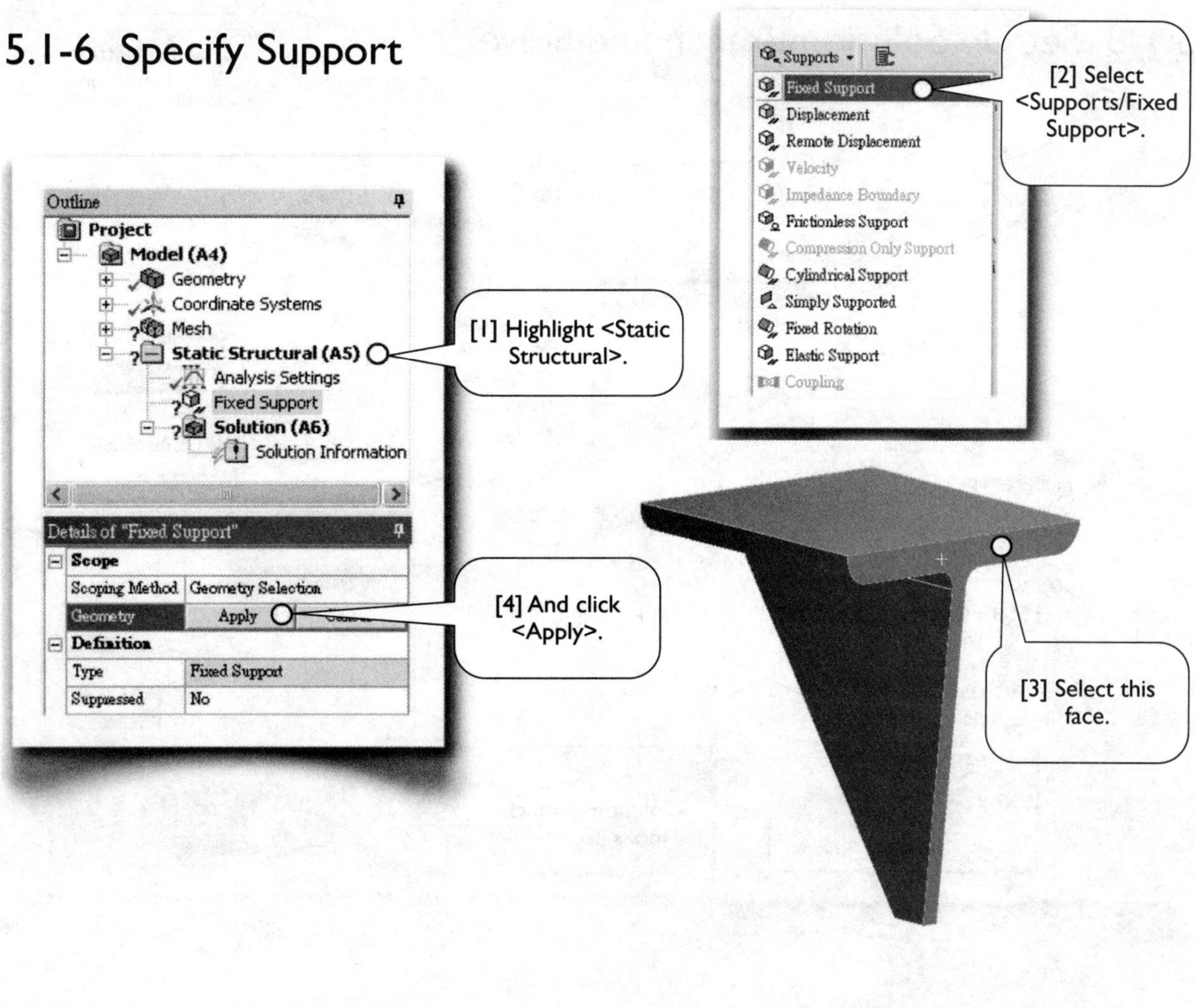

5.1-7 Apply Force

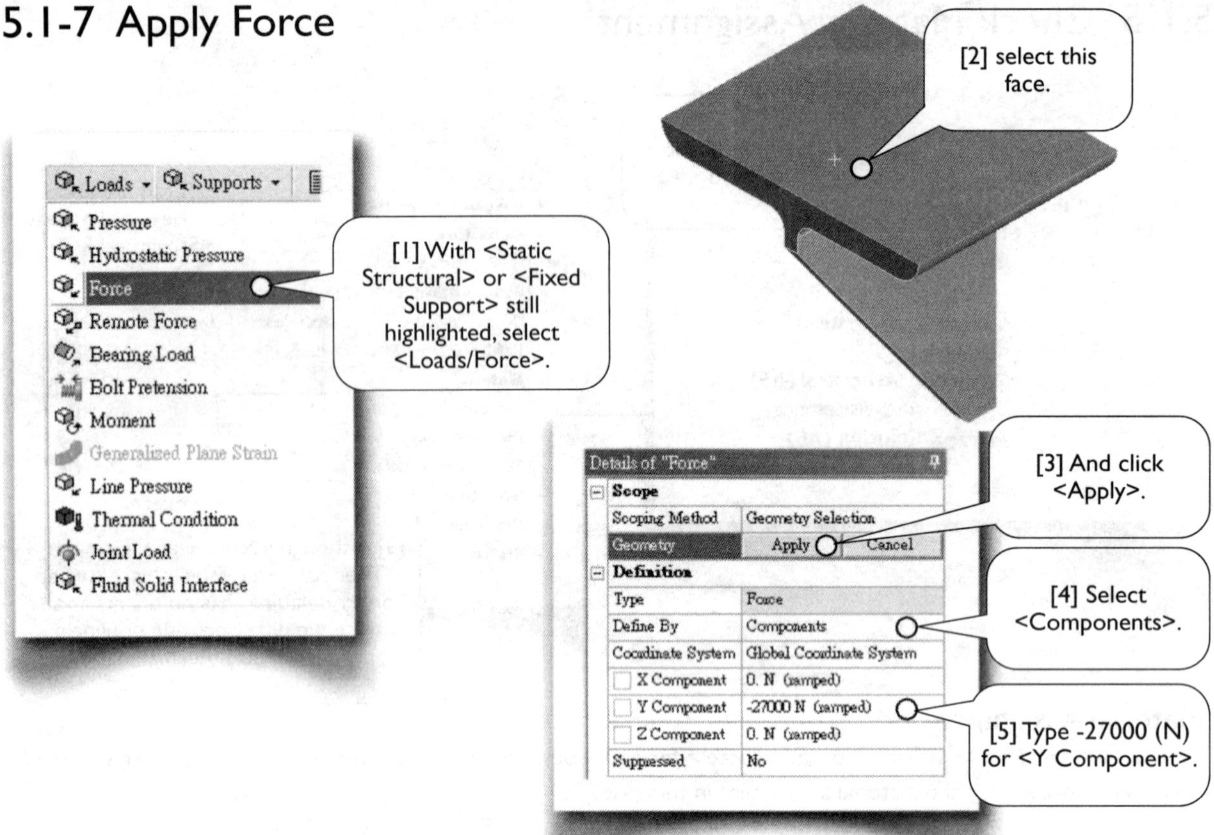

5.1-8 Set Up Solution Branch and Solve

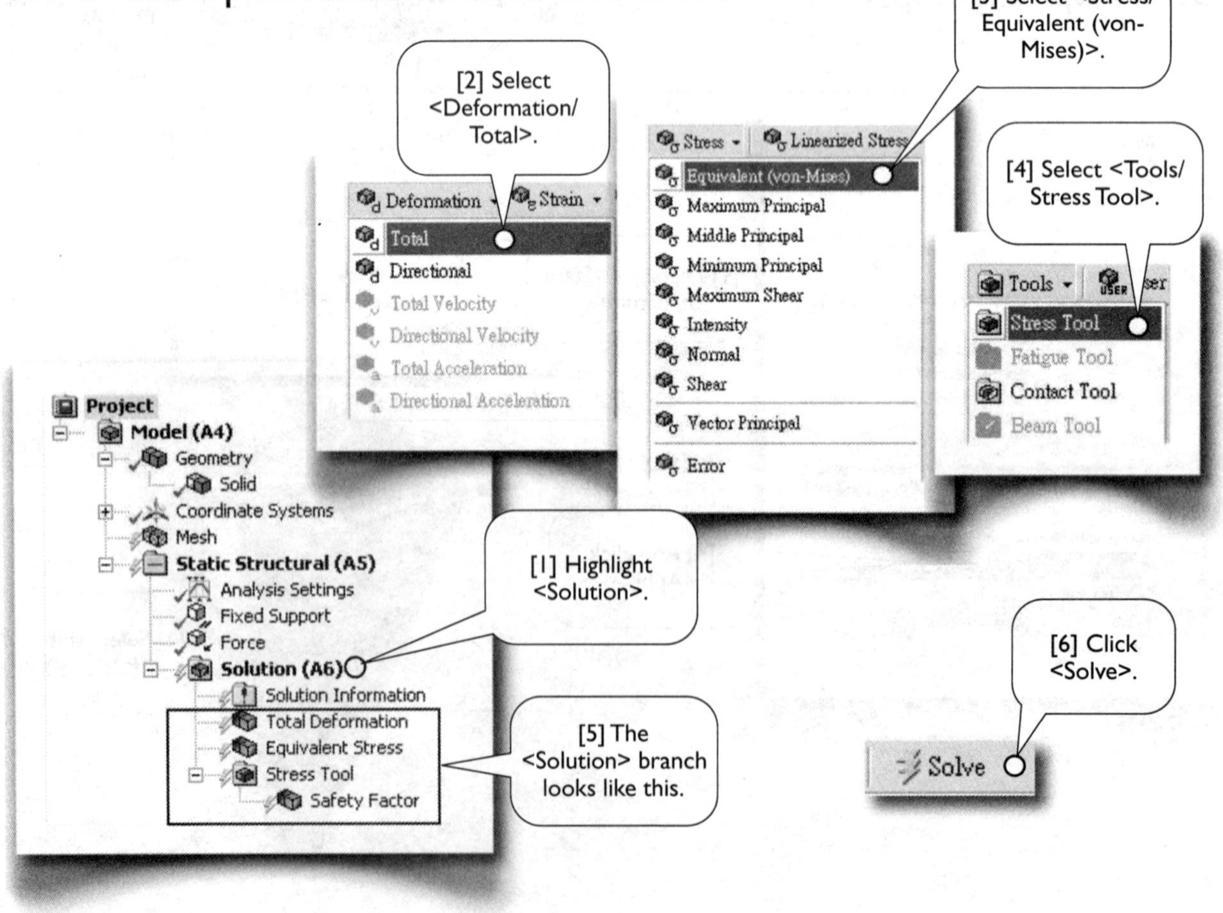

5.1-9 View the Results

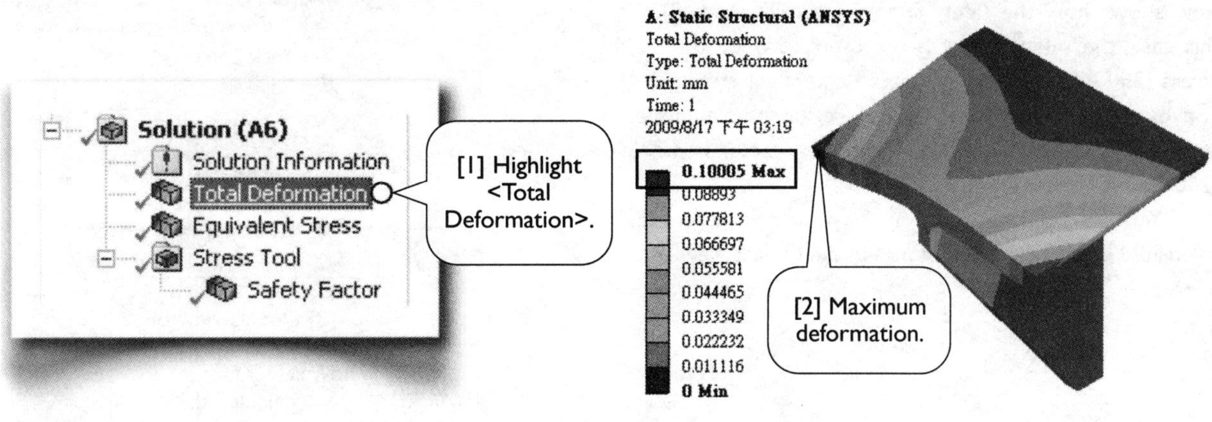

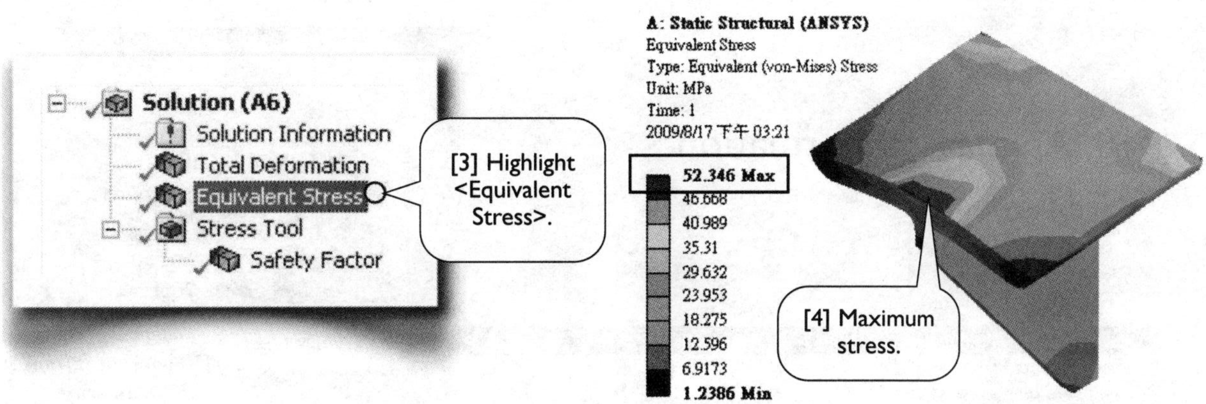

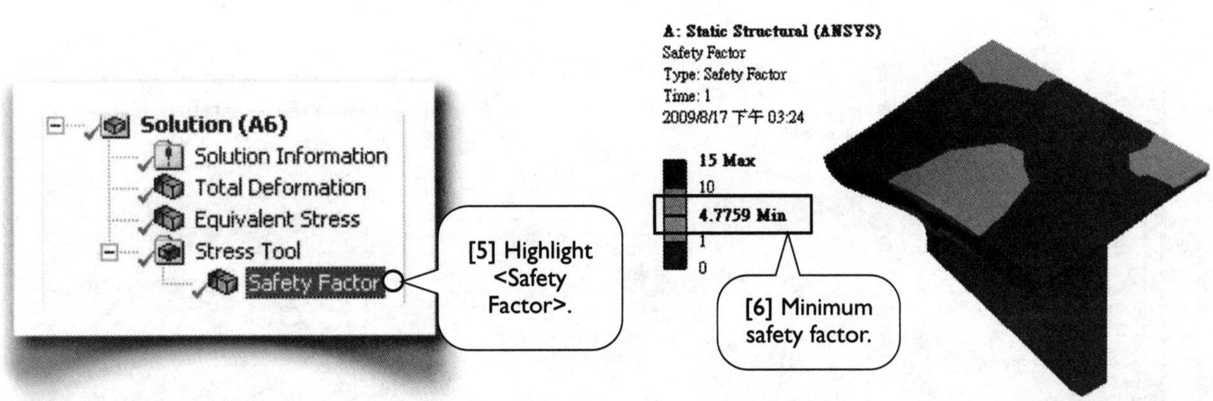

Safety Factors

Highlight <Stress Tool> in the model tree [7]. The Details view shows how the safety factors are calculated [8]. In this case, the safety factor is the ratio between the yield stress (250 MPa) and the calculated equivalent stress [3-4]. For example, at the most critical region, the equivalent stress is 52.346 MPa, therefore the safety factor is 4.7759 (250/52.346) [6].

You can change the way how safety factors are calculated by changing the settings in the Details view [8].

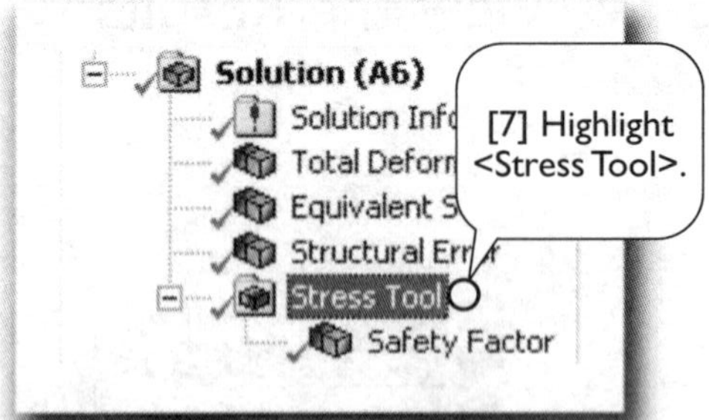

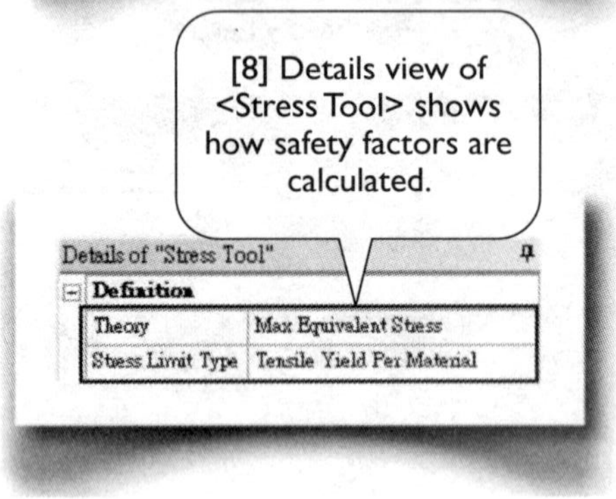

5.1-10 Animate Deformation

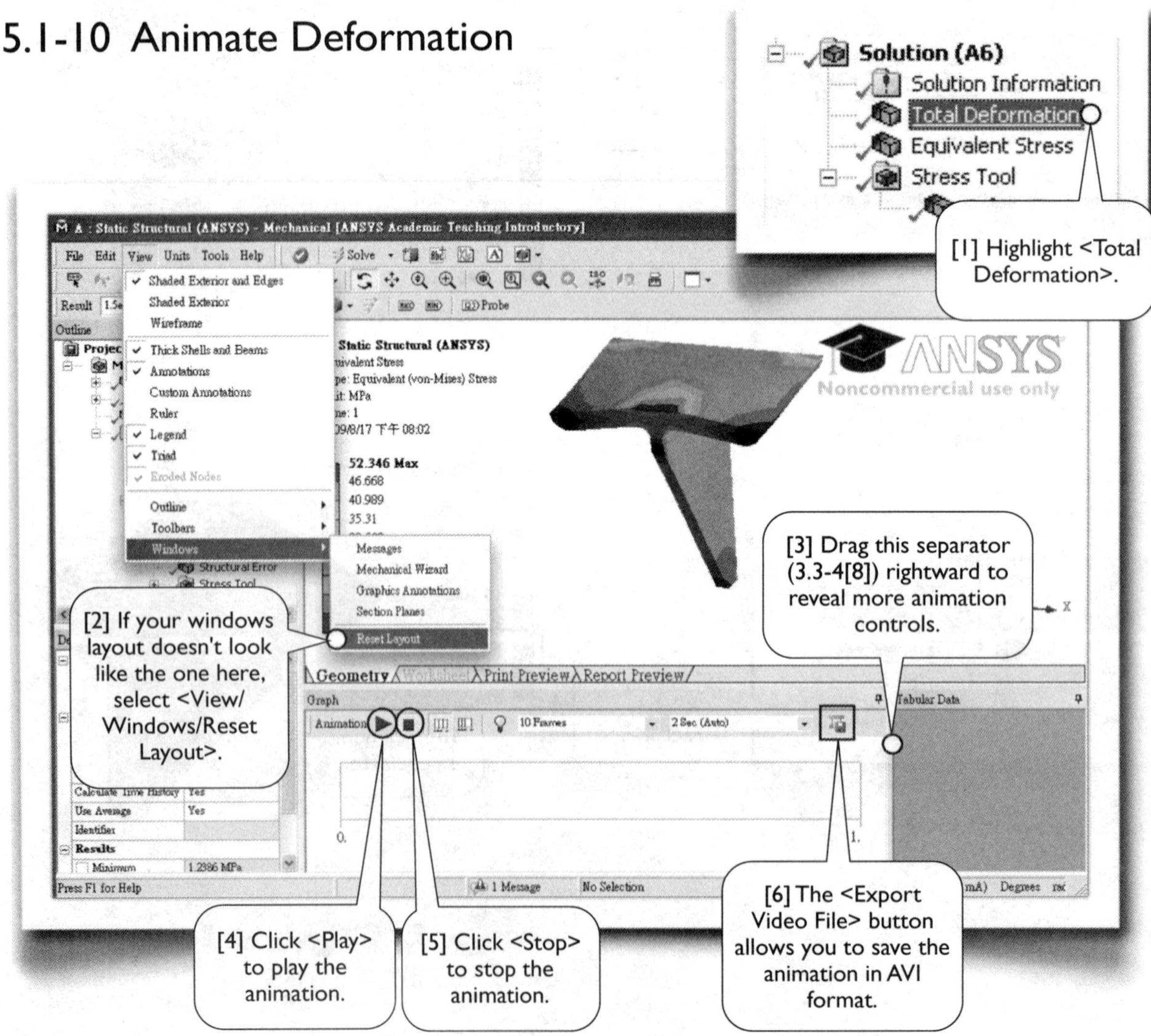

5.1-11 Evaluate Structural Error

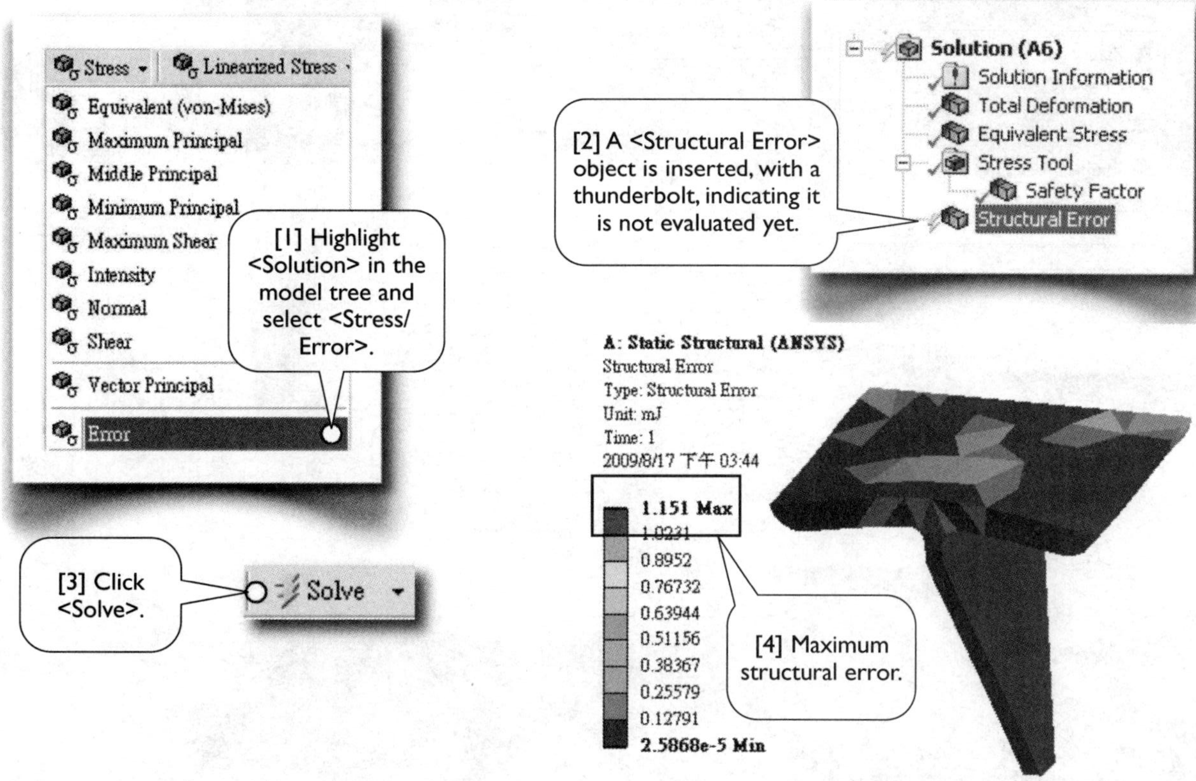

Structural Error

As mentioned in Section 3.5-7, the structural error can be used as an indicator of global mesh adequacy as well as local mesh adequacy. In general, we want the structural error as small as possible, and at the same time, we want the structural error distribution as uniform as possible.

5.1-12 Improve the Mesh Quality

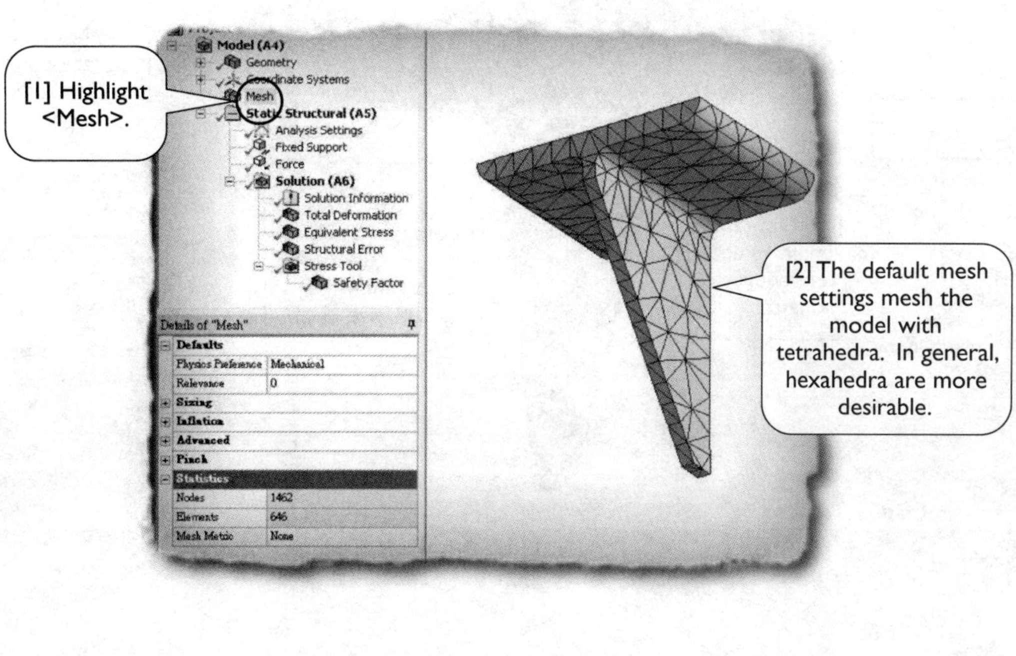

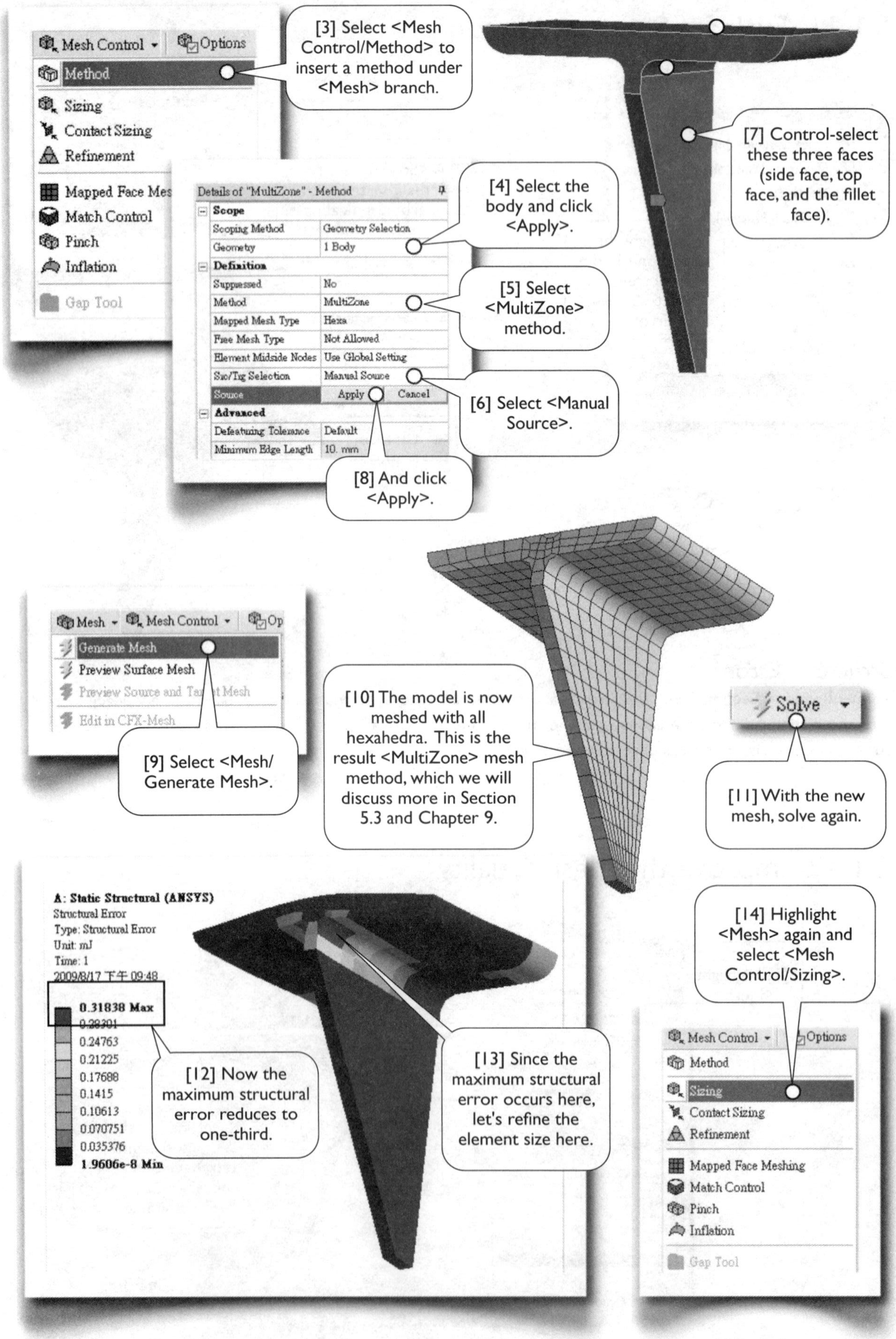
Mesh Control
Options
Method
Sizing
Contact Sizing
Refinement
Mapped Face Mes
Match Control
Pinch
Inflation
Gap Tool
[3] Select <Mesh Control/Method> to insert a method under <Mesh> branch.
Details of "MultiZone" - Method
Scope
Scoping Method Geometry Selection
Geometry 1 Body
Definition
Suppressed No
Method MultiZone
Mapped Mesh Type Hexa
Free Mesh Type Not Allowed
Element Midside Nodes Use Global Setting
Src/Trg Selection Manual Source
Source Apply Cancel
Advanced
Defeaturing Tolerance Default
Minimum Edge Length 10. mm
[4] Select the body and click <Apply>.
[5] Select <MultiZone> method.
[6] Select <Manual Source>.
[7] Control-select these three faces (side face, top face, and the fillet face).
[8] And click <Apply>.
Mesh
Mesh Control
Generate Mesh
Preview Surface Mesh
Edit in CFX-Mesh
[9] Select <Mesh/ Generate Mesh>.
[10] The model is now meshed with all hexahedra. This is the result <MultiZone> mesh method, which we will discuss more in Section 5.3 and Chapter 9.
Solve
[11] With the new mesh, solve again.
A: Static Structural (ANSYS)
Structural Error
Type: Structural Error
Unit: mJ
Time: 1
2009/8/17 下午 09:48
0.31838 Max
0.28301
0.24763
0.21225
0.17688
0.1415
0.10613
0.070751
0.035376
1.9606e-8 Min
[12] Now the maximum structural error reduces to one-third.
[13] Since the maximum structural error occurs here, let's refine the element size here.
[14] Highlight <Mesh> again and select <Mesh Control/Sizing>.
Mesh Control
Options
Method
Sizing
Contact Sizing
Refinement
Mapped Face Meshing
Match Control
Pinch
Inflation
Gap Tool

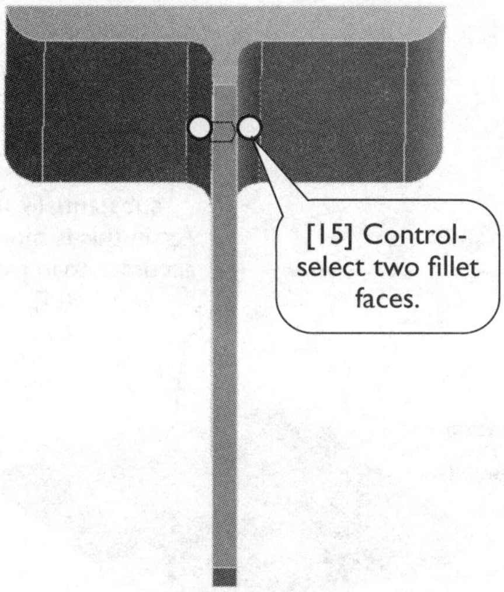

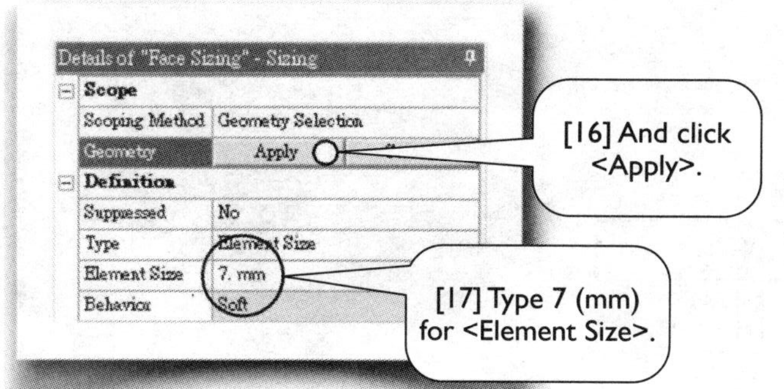

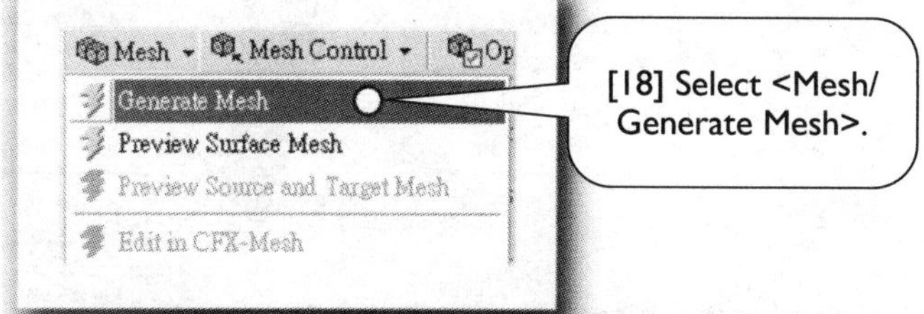

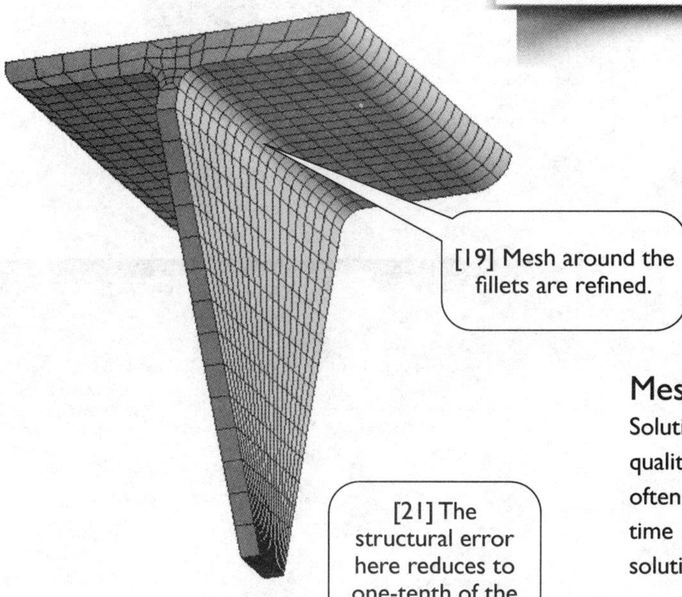

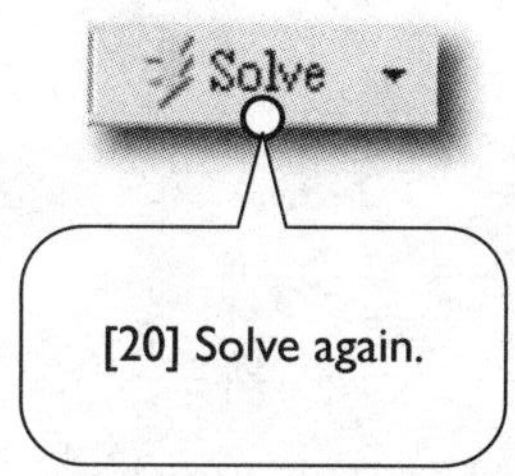

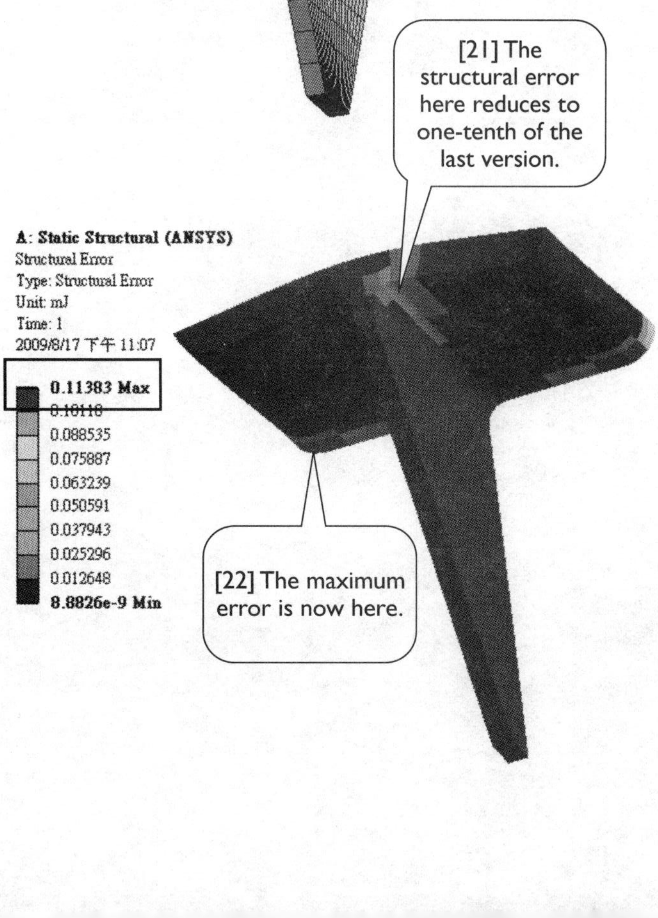

Meshing 3D Solid Bodies

Solution accuracy often depends on the mesh quality. In nonlinear problems, poor mesh quality often leads to huge consumption of computing time (several hours or even overnight) or even solution-finding failure.

Achieving a high mesh quality is, however, not trivial at all. In this section, we've exploited a new meshing technology, namely multi-zone method. It will be conceptually introduced in Section 5.3. Various meshing methods, including multi-zone method, will be detailed in Chapter 9.

For our case, we will not go further to improve the mesh. The reason is that the maximum structural error now occurs on a region of stress singularity. Improving mesh on a region of stress singularity makes little sense.

Stress singularity was demonstrated using an example in the sections from Sections 3.5-11 to 3.5-14. Phenomenon of stress singularity is extremely important. A well trained CAE engineer must be fully aware of the existence of stress singularity in the model.

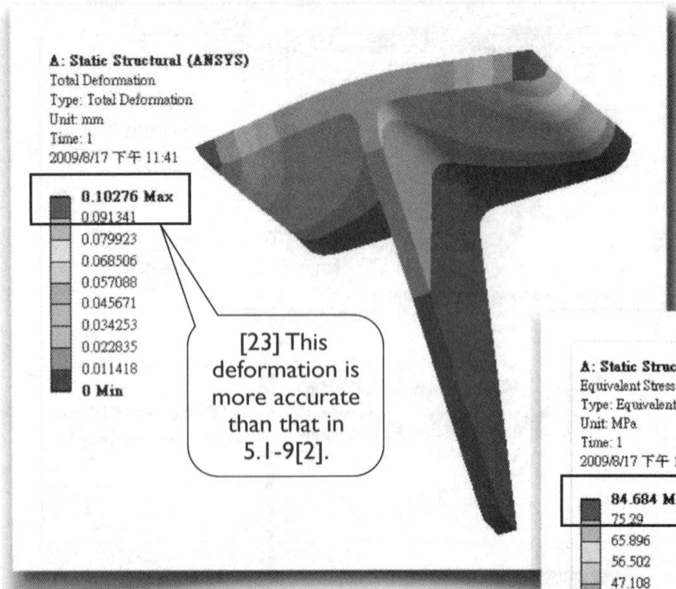

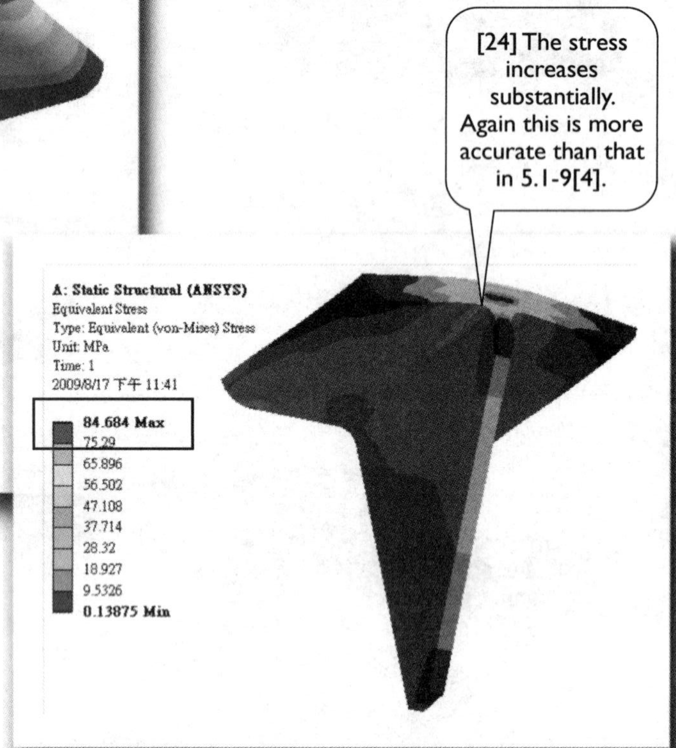

Wrap Up

Save the project and exit Workbench.

Section 5.2

Step-by-Step: Cover of Pressure Cylinder

5.2-1 About the Cylinder Cover

In Section 4.2, we created a 3D solid model for the cover of a pressure cylinder, which is designed to hold up a pressure of 0.5 MPa. The model will be used in this section for a static structural simulation.

The cover was originally made of aluminum alloy. The purpose of the simulation is to assess the possibility of replacing the aluminum alloy by a new type of engineering plastic. The engineering plastic has a Young's modulus of 22 GPa and a Poisson's ratio of 0.3.

The most concern is the deformation, specifically the circularity (more accurately, cylindricity) of the internal surface that encompasses the pressure cylinder [1]. The circularity of a profile can be defined as the difference between the radii of its circumscribed circle and inscribed circle.

The spec requires that the circularity should be less than 10 micrometers, excess of circularity beyond this value may impair the tightness and cause the gas leaking.

The unit system used in this exercise is mm-N-s (to set up a unit system, see Section 3.3-5)

5.2-2 Open the Project "Cover"

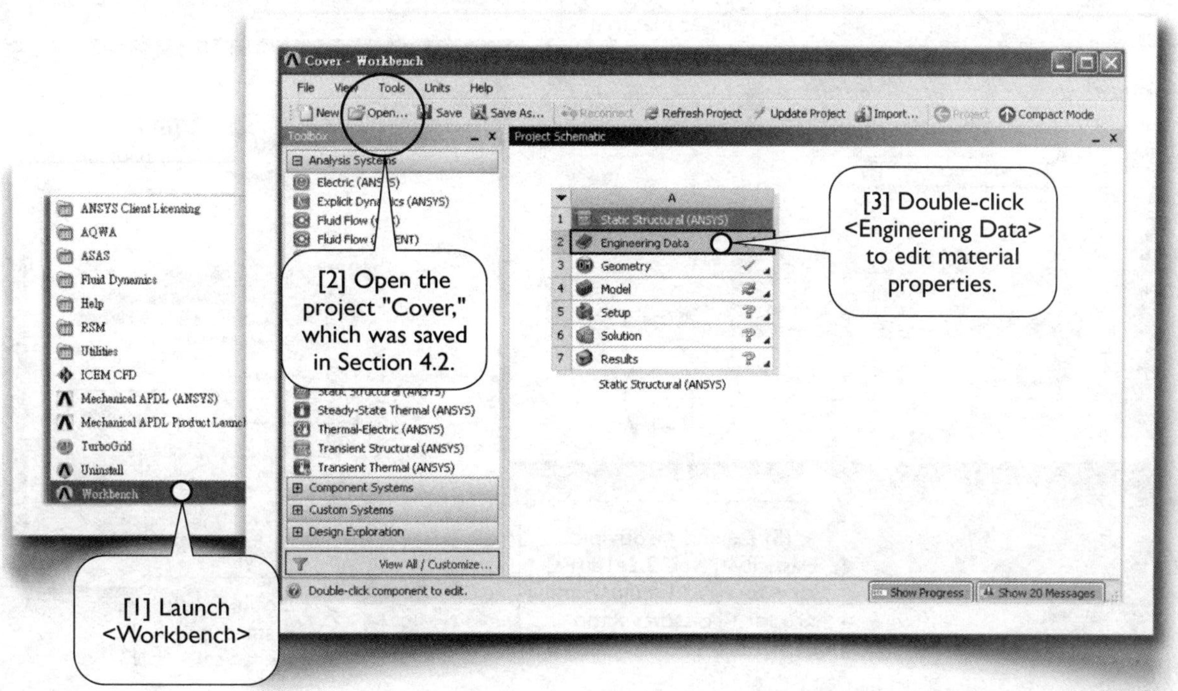

5.2-3 Prepare Material Properties

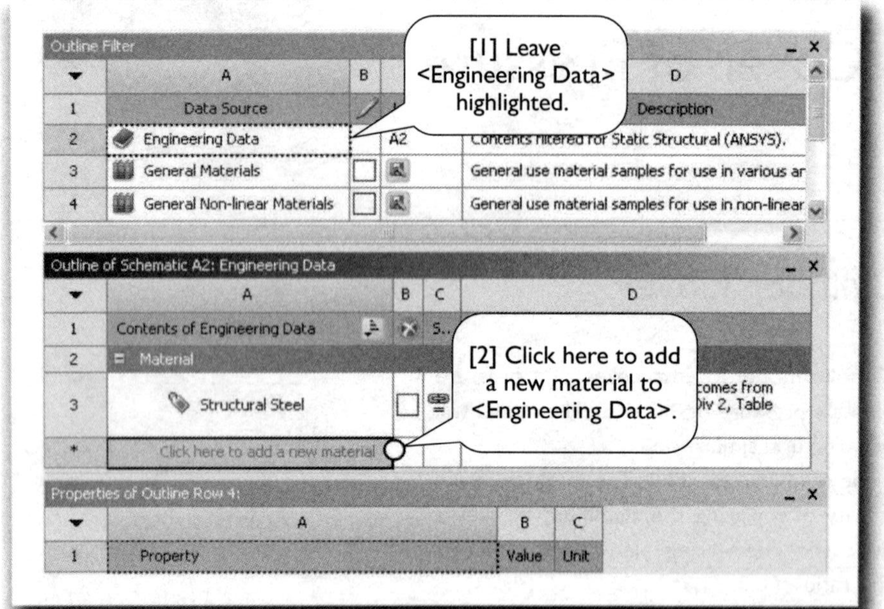

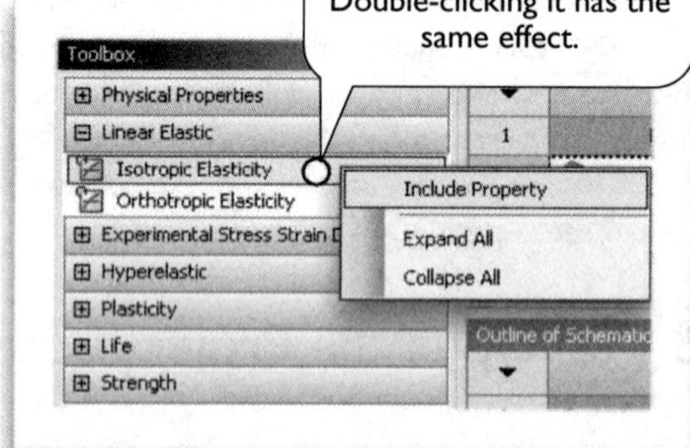

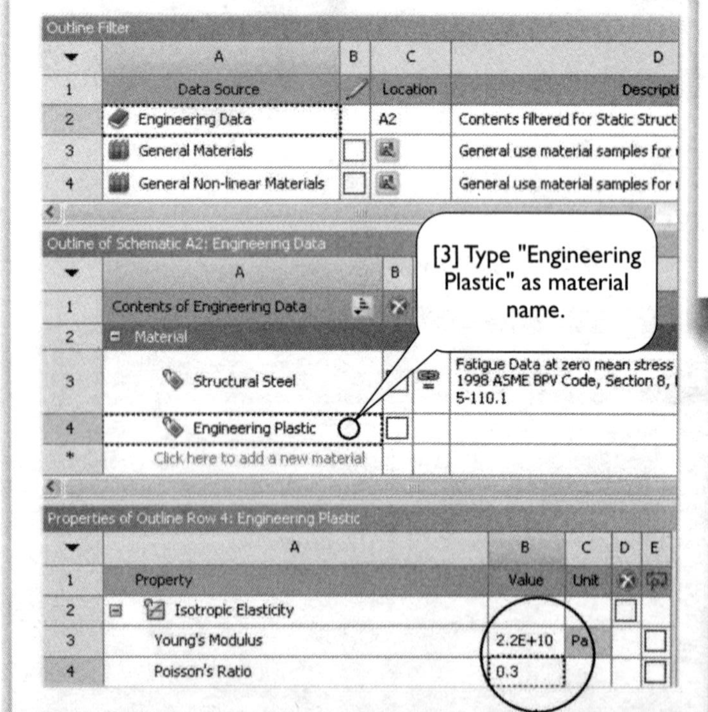

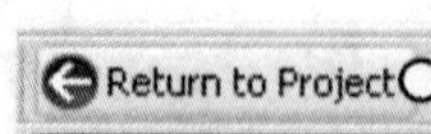

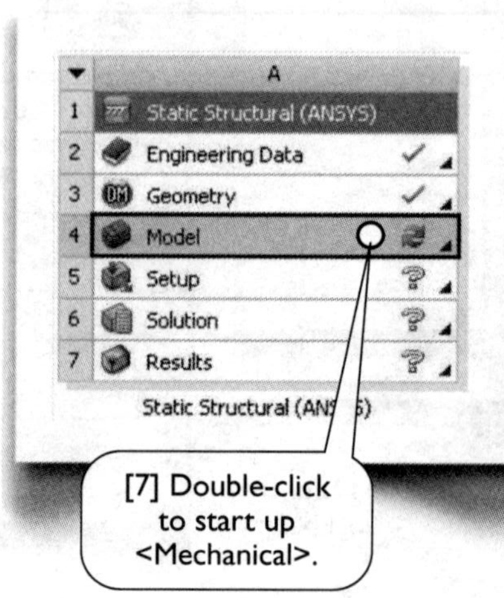

5.2-4 Assign Material to the Body

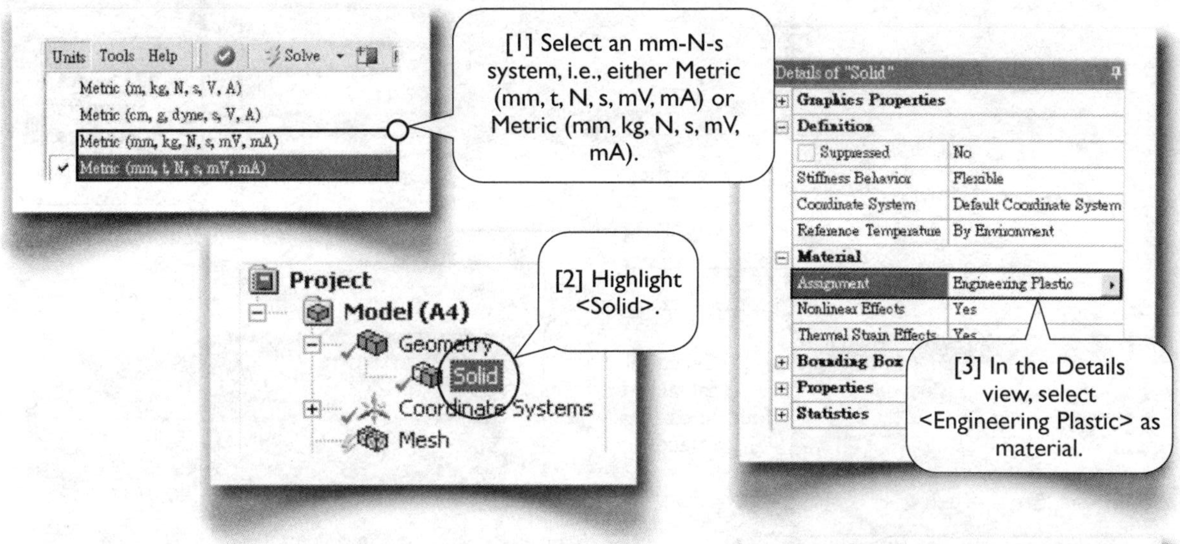

5.2-5 Generate Mesh

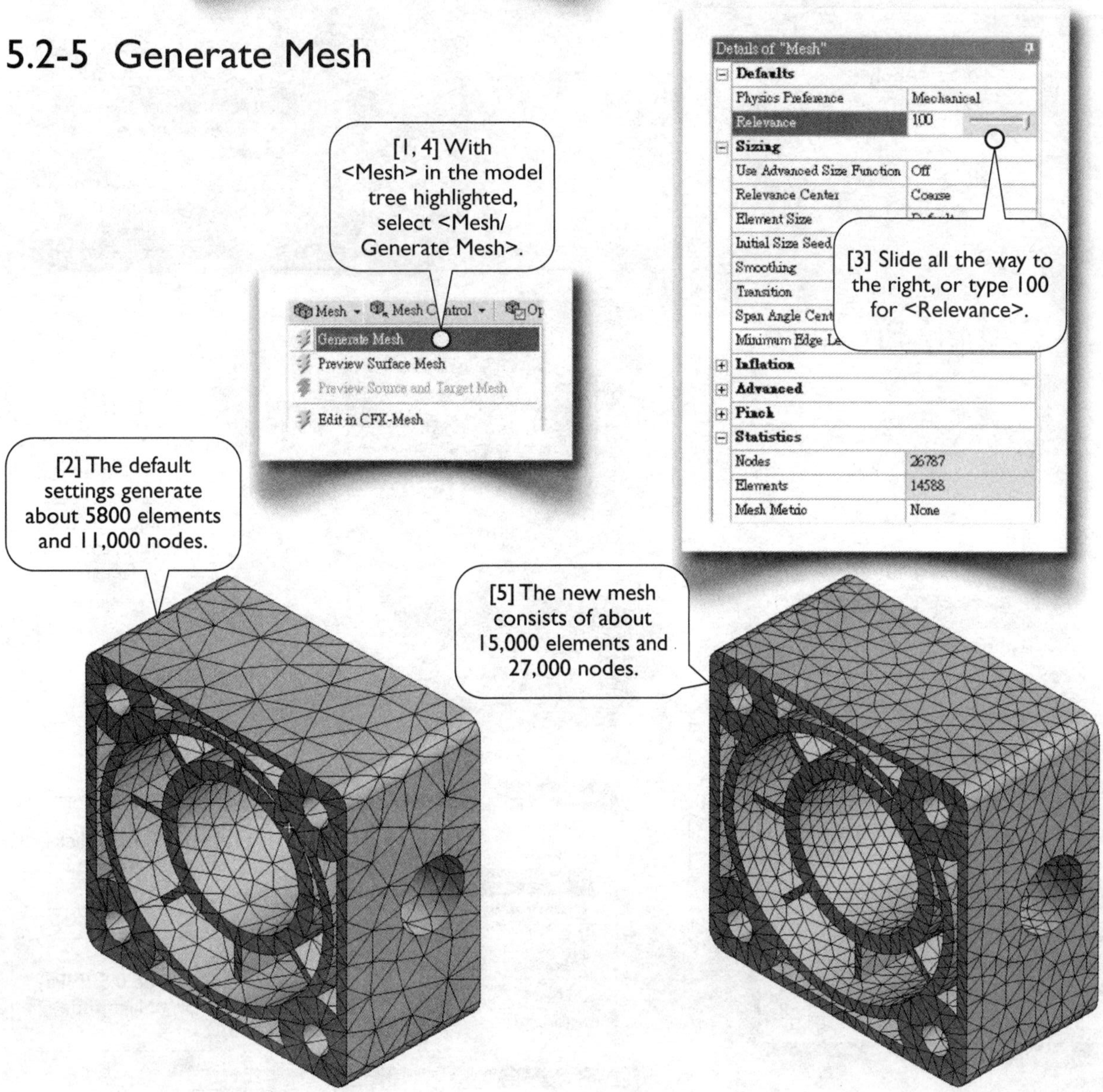

5.2-6 Specify Supports

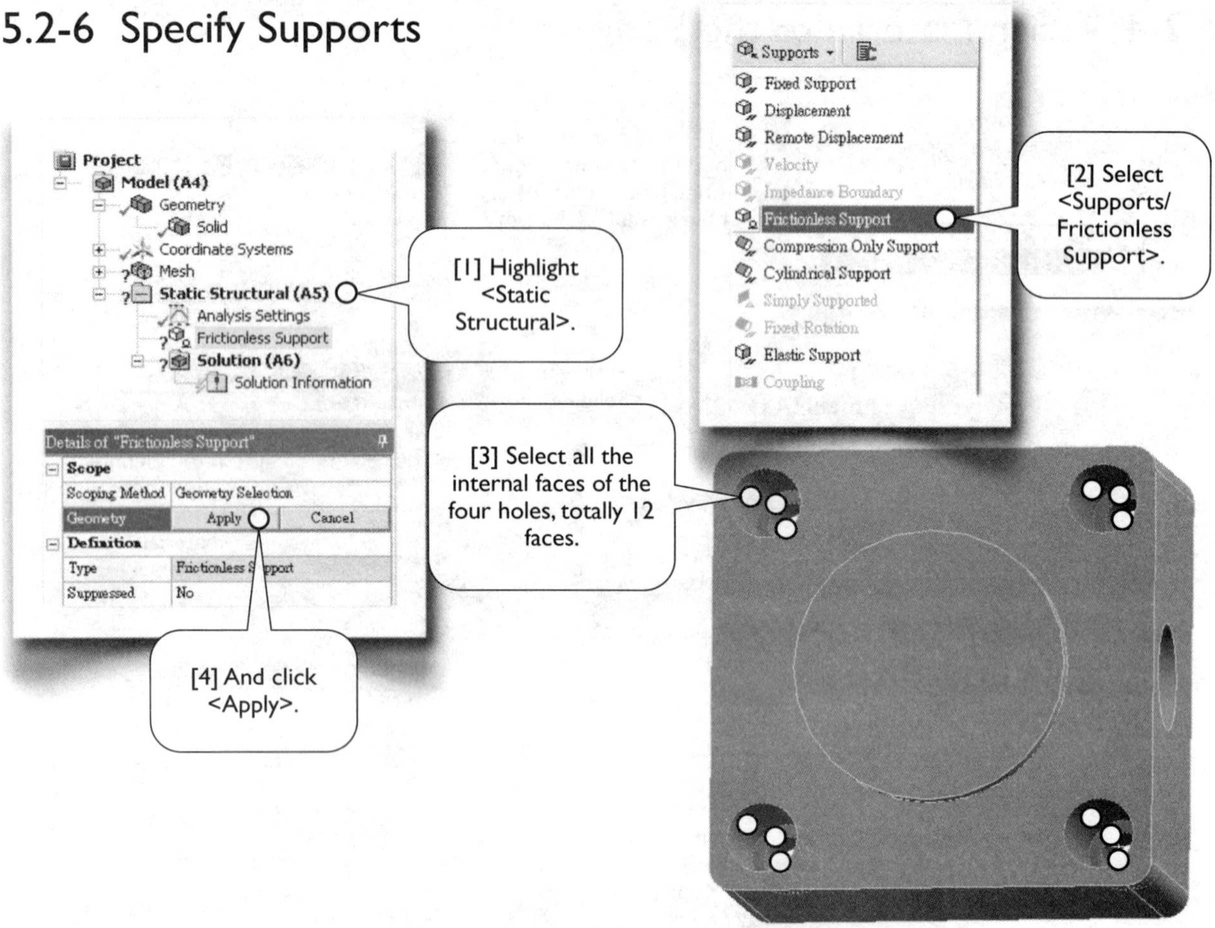

5.2-7 Apply Pressure

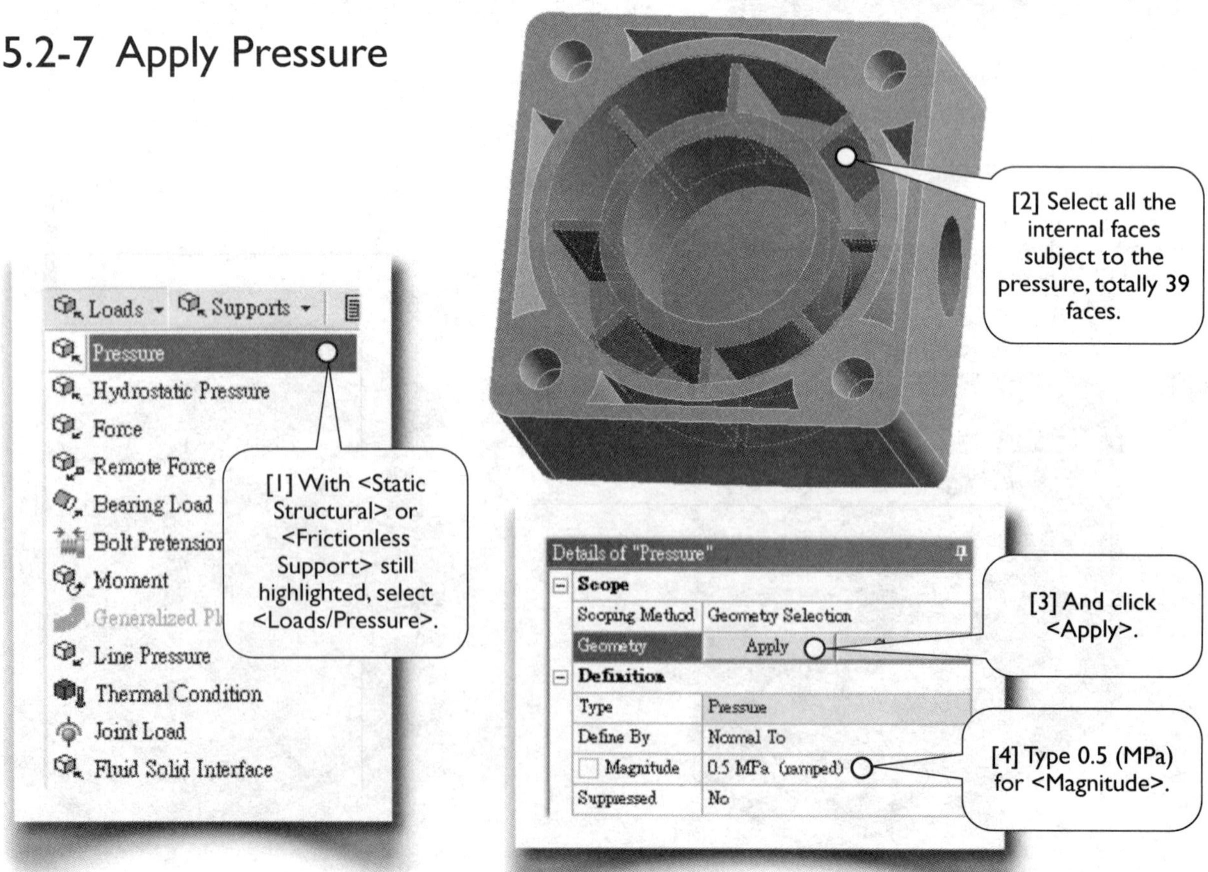

5.2-8 Set Up Solution Branch and Solve

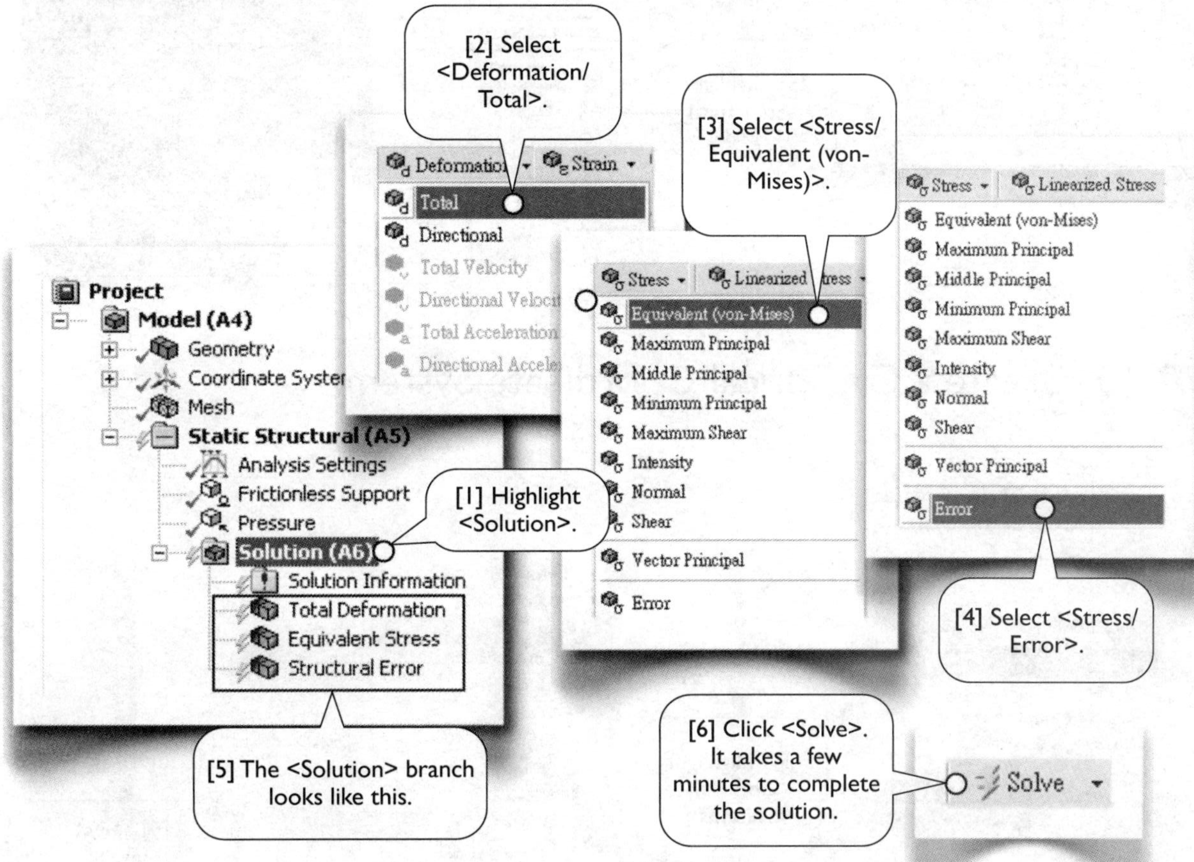

5.2-9 View the Results

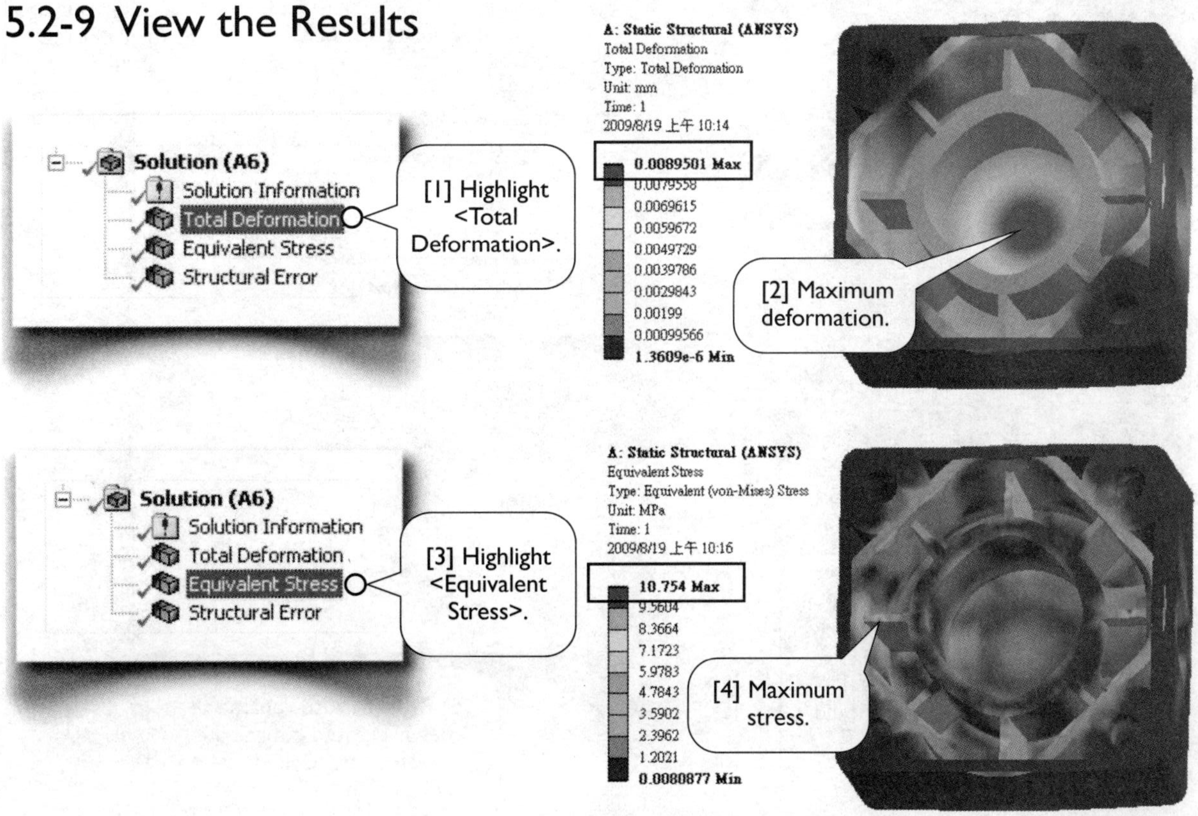

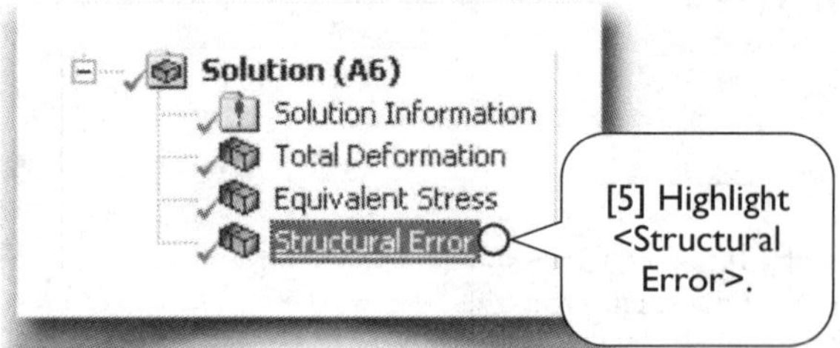

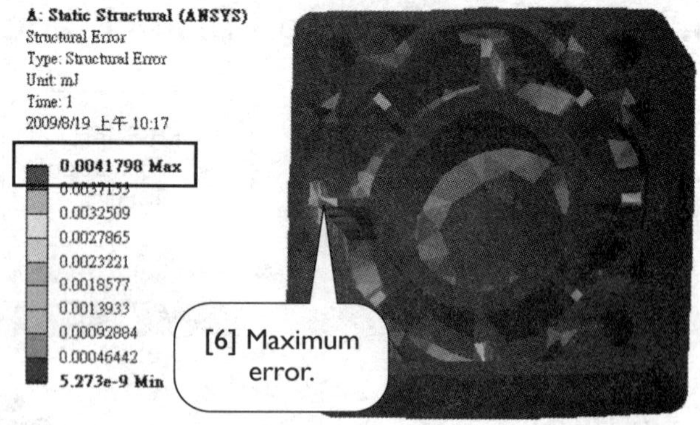

5.2-10 Create a Cylindrical Coordinate System

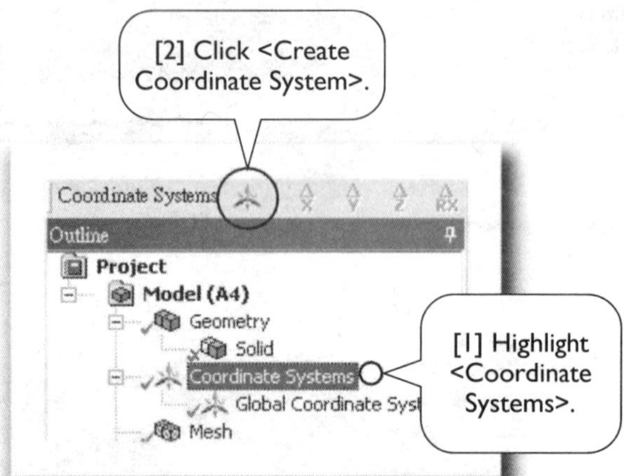

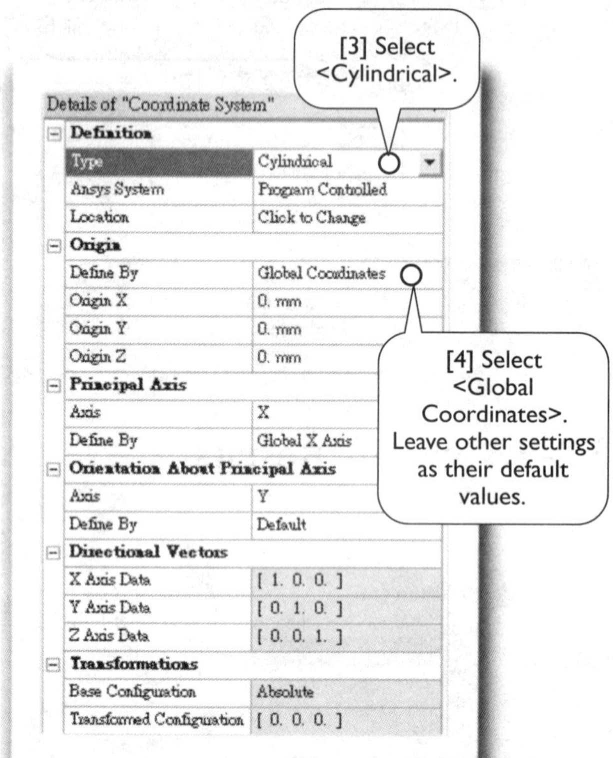

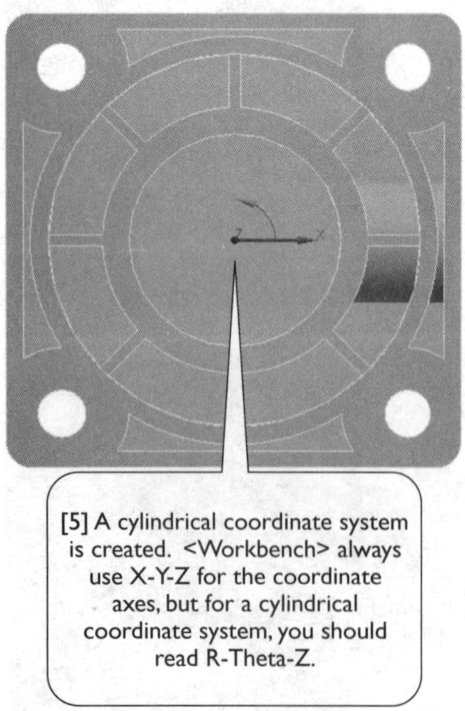

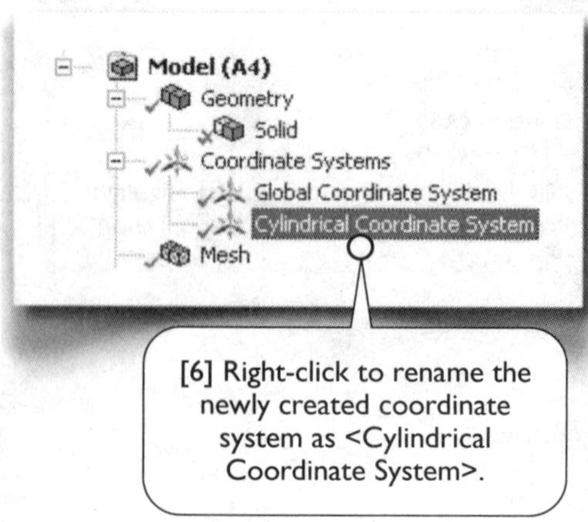

5.2-11 Assess the Circularity

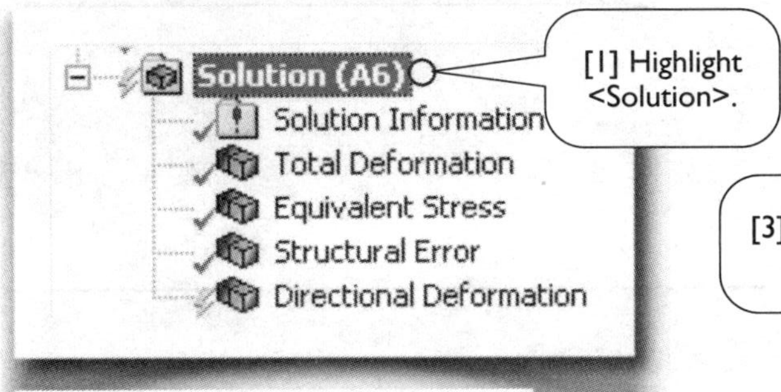

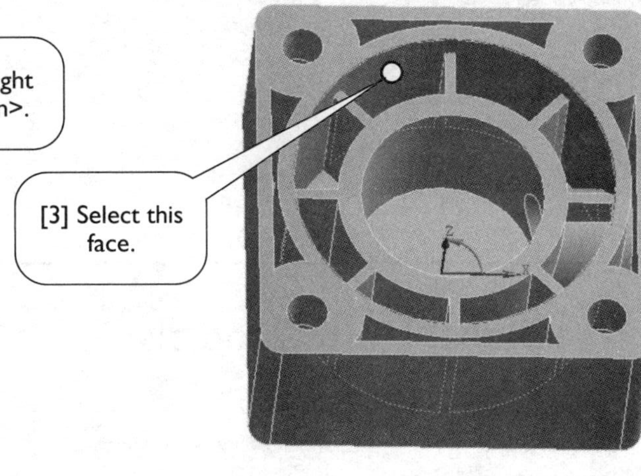

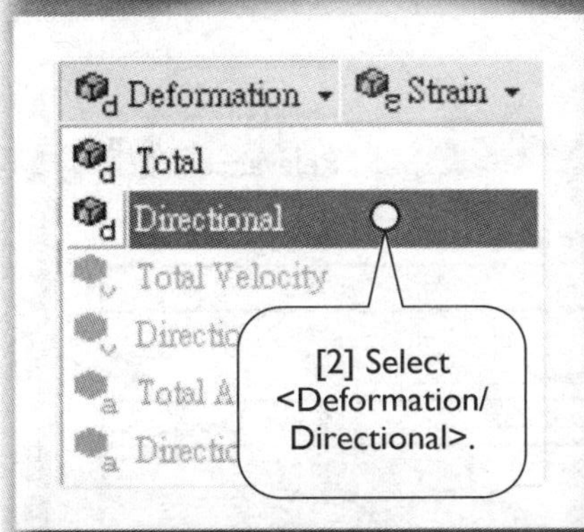

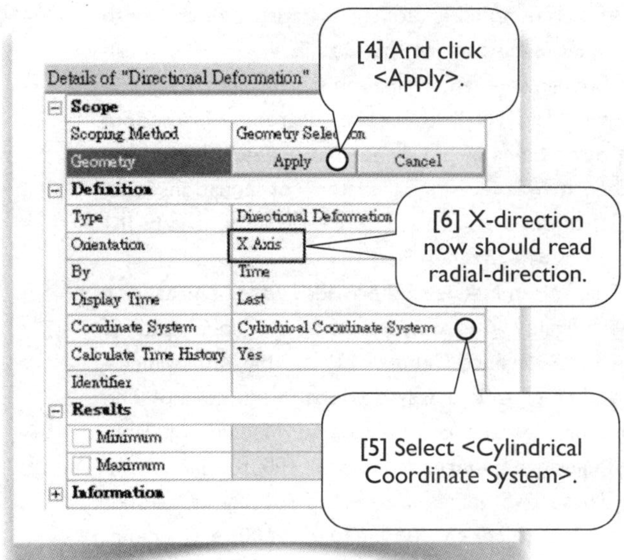

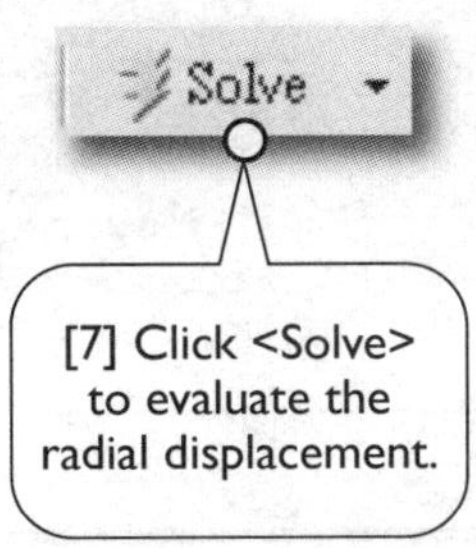

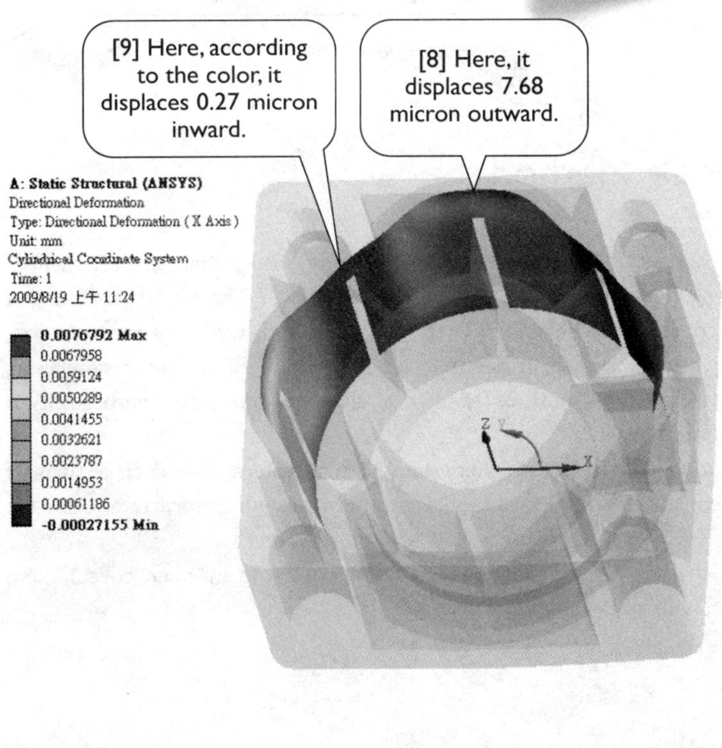

Conclusions

The circularity of the cover under the pressure, according to the definition, is 7.95 micrometer (7.68 + 0.27). It is within the spec requirement (10 micrometer).

We don't need to worry about he stress, since the stress (11 MPa, 5.2-9[4]) is much well below the fracture stress (50+ MPa).

Save the project, close <Mechanical> and exit <Workbench>.

Section 5.3

More Details

5.3-1 Global Mesh Controls[1]

By highlighting the <Mesh> in a model tree, you will see the Details view of the mesh.

After the model is meshed, a statistics of the mesh shows on the bottom of the Details view. The mesh count [1] provides an estimation of problem size. As mentioned (1.3-1[1]), the total degrees of freedom equals three times of the number of nodes. In this case, Workbench was solving a system of equations (Eq. 1.3-1(1)) of degrees of freedom 64,473. The matrix [K] has a size of 64,473x64,473!

The <Mesh Metric> [2] provides ways of measuring the mesh quality. This topic will be covered in Chapter 9.

The <Relevance Center> [3] and the <Relevance> [4] together provide a way of global mesh control. The <Relevance Center> can be Coarse, Medium, or Fine. The <Relevance> ranges from 0 to 100, the larger the finer. These two values are related roughly as follows: (Coarse, 0) = (Medium, -100), (Coarse, 100) = (Medium, 0) = (Fine, -100), and (Medium, 100) = (Fine, 0).

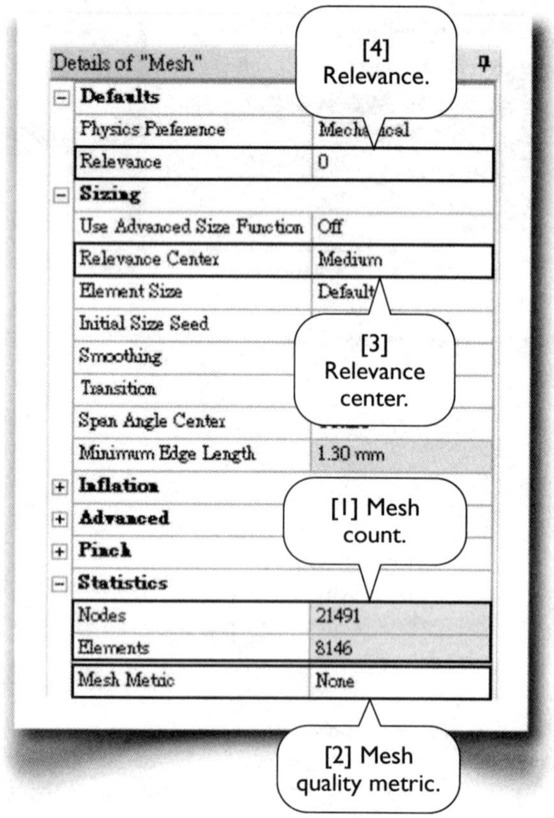

5.3-2 Mesh with <MultiZone> Method

We mentioned in 5.1-12[2] that hexahedral elements are generally more desirable than other shapes, such as tetrahedral. Similarly, in 2D cases, quadrilateral elements are more desirable than triangular. The main reason is that hexahedral (or quadrilateral in 2D) has better convergence behavior. That implies: (a) with the same problem size, hexahedral or quadrilateral gives more accurate results, and (b) it needs fewer iterations in a nonlinear simulation. Besides, mesh quality (5.3-1[2]) is also important though. A mesh of hexahedral elements with poor mesh quality is usually less desirable than tetrahedral with good mesh quality.

For 2D models, Workbench usually does good jobs and mesh them with all-quadrilateral elements, or at least quadrilateral-dominated. For examples, in Section 3.1, 3.2, and 3.4, all models are meshed with quadrilateral elements without further mesh controls.

For 3D models, meshing is much more challenging. In Section 5.2, the model (the cylinder cover) is so complicated that the Workbench choose to mesh with all-tetrahedral.

A simple idea of creating hexahedral elements is to mesh a face (or faces) of a body with quadrilaterals and then "sweep" along a path up to the other end faces of the body. The starting faces are called a *source* faces and the ending faces are *target* faces. The source or target faces can be either manually or automatically selected. Not all bodies are sweepable. In Section 5.1, the body (the bracket) is not sweepable without further decomposition.

The idea of <MultiZone> method is to decompose a non-sweepable body into several sweepable bodies, and then apply <Sweep> method on each of bodies. This is what we had done in Section 5.1-12, where we inserted a <MultiZone> method and manually selected the source faces. According to these information, Workbench decomposed the body into several sweepable bodies and easily "sweep" each body with hexahedral elements. The result is an all-hexa mesh.

5.3-3 Coordinate Systems[2]

Often, when you define an environment condition or a solution object by components, a coordinate system needed to be referred. By default, the <Global Coordinate System> is used, which is a Cartesian coordinate system. Sometimes this coordinate system is not convenient. In such cases, we may define additional coordinate systems for further use.

To define a coordinate system, you need to define the type of coordinate system [1], the origin [2], and the axes [3].

Currently, workbench supports only two types of coordinate system: Cartesian and Cylindrical [1].

Defining the origin is straightforward. You can click a location or type the coordinates [2].

There are many ways to define the axes. Basically, you need to define two of the three axes and the third axis is automatically defined using right-hand rule.

The first axis you define is called the <Principle Axis> and the second axis is the <Orientation About Principle Axis>.

For cylindrical coordinate system, you may be confused by such terminology. Fortunately, a triad appears on the graphics area and you are always visually aware when making a mistake.

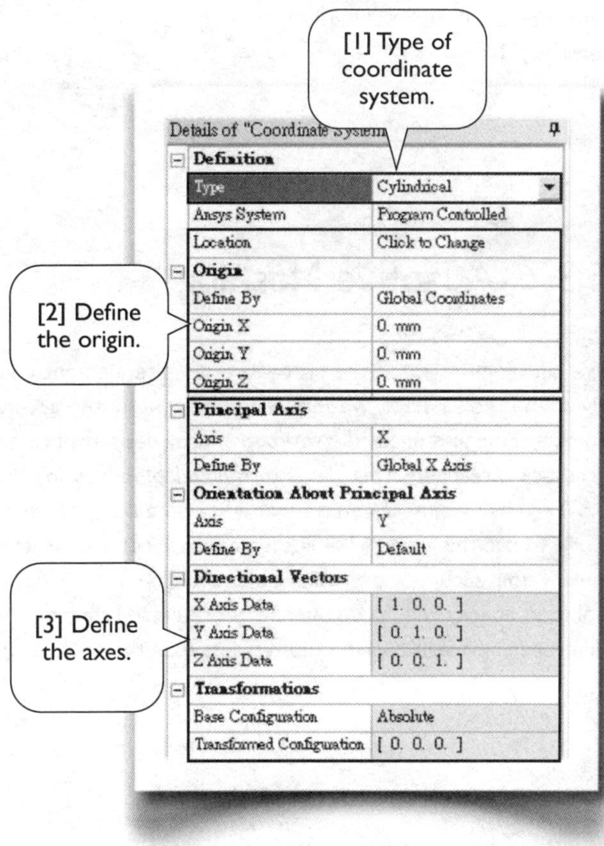

5.3-4 Results View Controls[3]

With a results object highlighted, the toolbar displays tools that can be used to control how the results are presented [1-6].

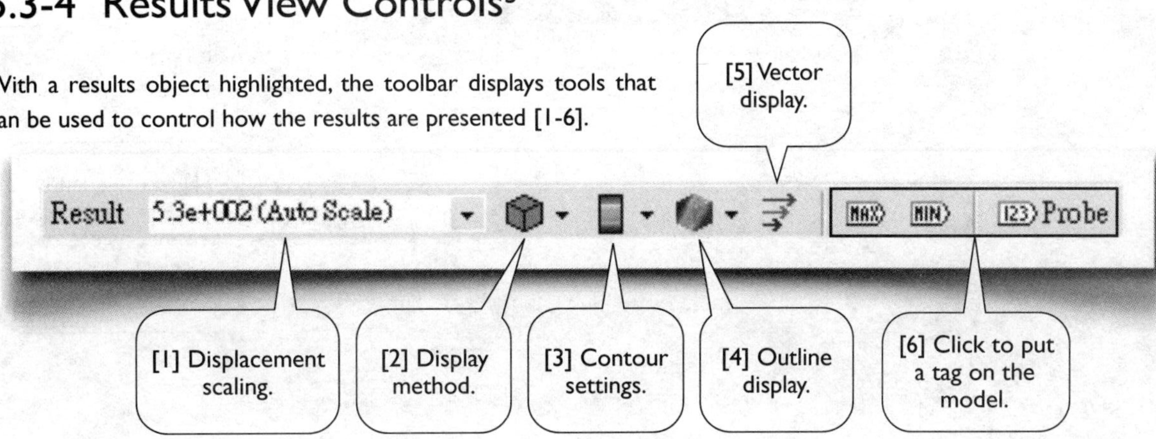

5.3-5 Legend Controls

Right-click on the legend in the graphics area allows the user to modify the legend [1-7].

Independent bands [6] allow neutral colors to represent regions of the model above or below the specified legend limits.

Whenever needed, Select <Reset All> to return to the default settings [7].

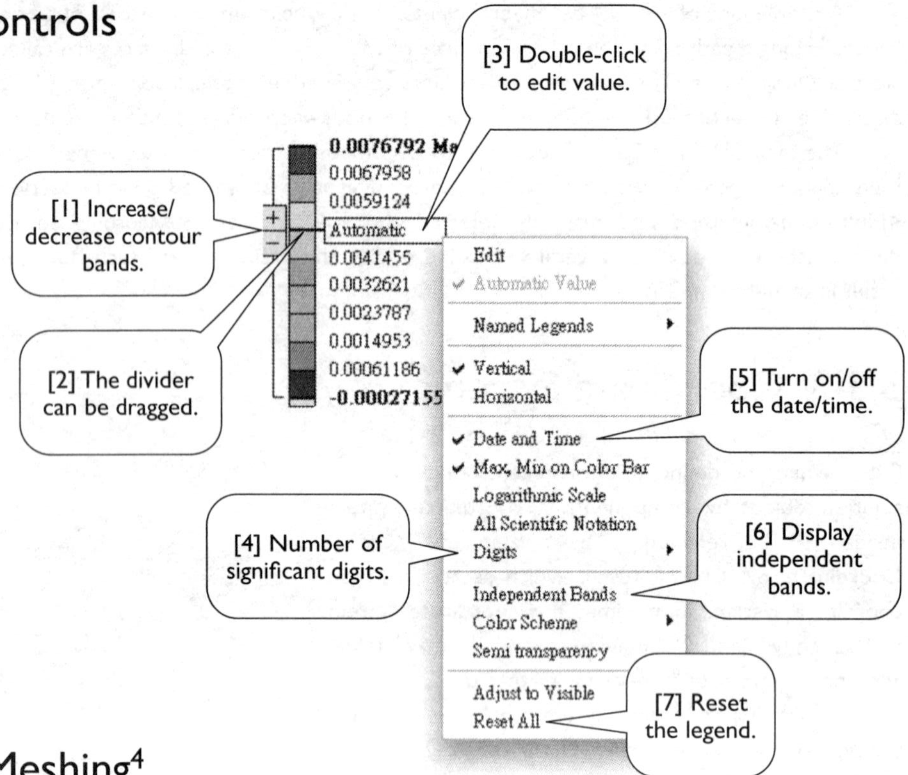

5.3-6 Adaptive Meshing[4]

We had demonstrated the procedure of finite element convergence study in Sections 3.5-8 to 3.5-10. Theoretically, given an error, say 5%, we may refine mesh until the accuracy reaches this level. Performing these tasks manually is cumbersome and inexact. Workbench provides a tool to automate the mesh refinement until a user-specified level of accuracy is reached. This idea is termed *adaptive meshing*. Internally, Workbench exploits the structural errors (Section 3.5-7) to help adjust the mesh, that is, it refine the mesh size in the area of large structural errors.

To use this tool, right-click a results object and select <Insert/Convergence> [1]. In the Details of Convergence, specify the accuracy, or <Allowable Change> [2]. Highlight <Solution> in the project tree and, in the Details of Solution, specify the maximum number of mesh refinement loops. Workbench will iterate to refine the mesh until the difference between two iterations is less than the <Allowable Change> or the <Max Refinement Loops> reaches.

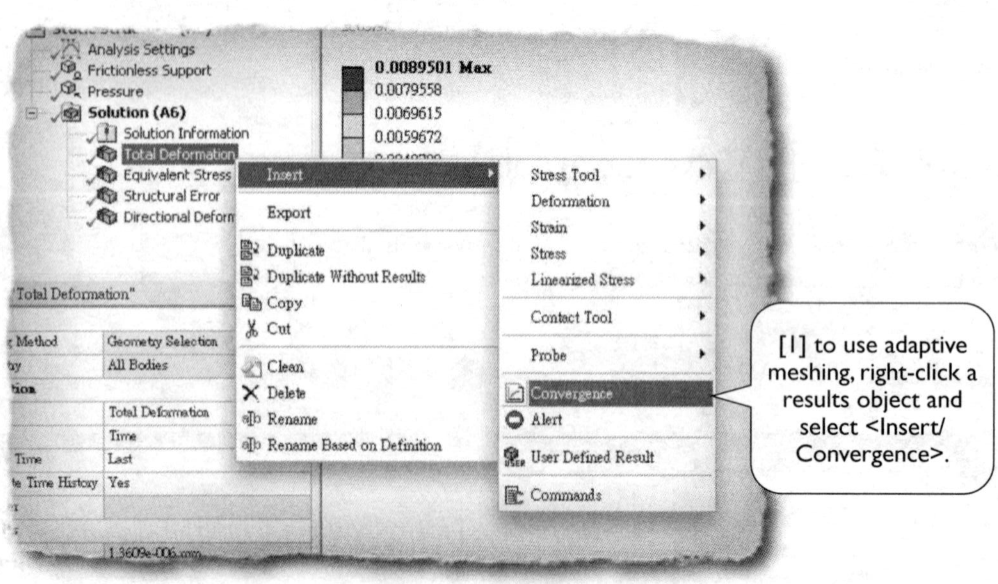

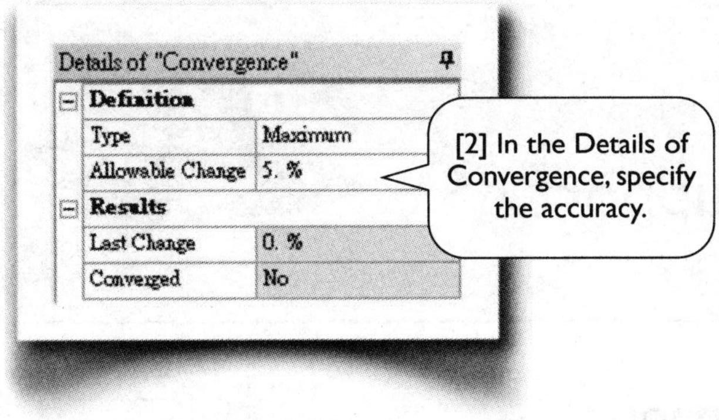

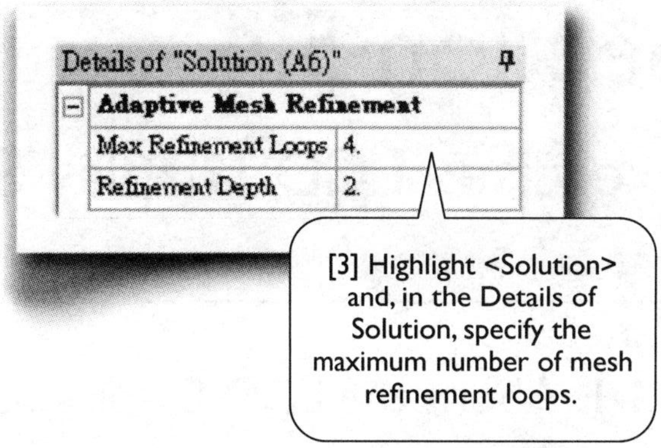

References

1. ANSYS Help System>Meshing>Global Mesh Controls
2. ANSYS Help System>Mechanical>Using the Mechanical Application Features>Coordinate Systems Overview>Creating Coordinate System
3. ANSYS Help System>Mechanical>The Mechanical Application Approach>Overall Steps to Using the Mechanical Application>Review Results.
4. ANSYS Help System>Mechanical>Mechanical Objects Reference>Convergence.

Section 5.4

Exercise: LCD Display Support

5.4-1 About the LCD Display Support

The geometry created in Section 4.5 will be used in this section for a static structural simulation to assess the deformation and stress under a design load.

The display support is made of an ABS (acrylonitrile-butadiene-styrene) plastic, of which the Young's modulus is 2.62 GPa and the Poisson's ratio is 0.34. In a tensile test, the material start to develop fine cracks at 37 MPa, and fracture at 54 MPa.

The support is designed for a 17" LCD display, which weighs 40 N. That will be the design load.

5.4-2 Prepare Material Properties

Open the project "Support," which was saved in Section 4.5. Double-click <Engineering Data> to edit material properties. Add a material to <Engineering Data> [1] and type the Young's modulus and Poisson's ratio [2].

Return to <Project Schematic> and double-click <Model> to start up <Mechanical>. In the <Mechanical>, the first thing is to assign the new material to the solid body [3].

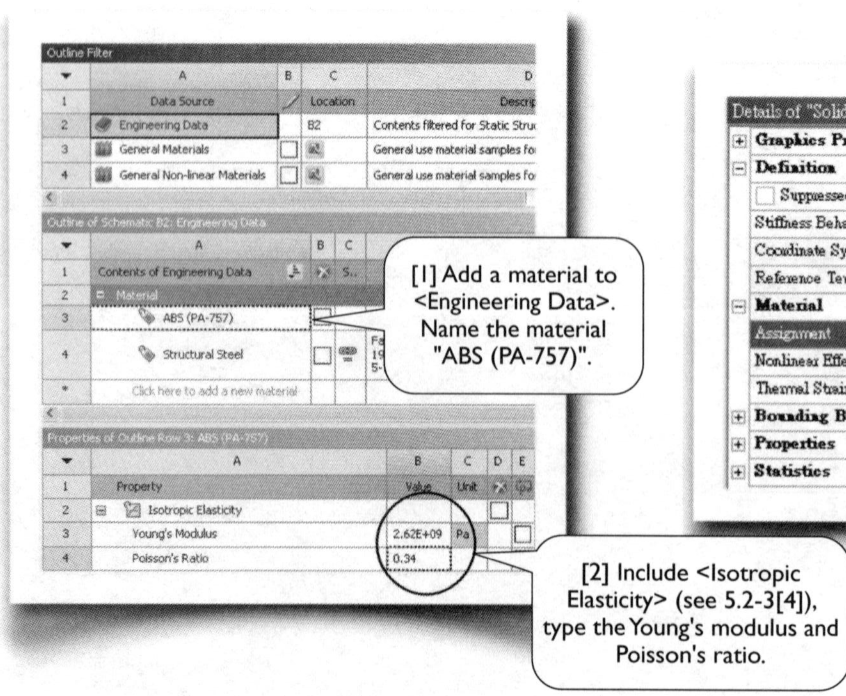

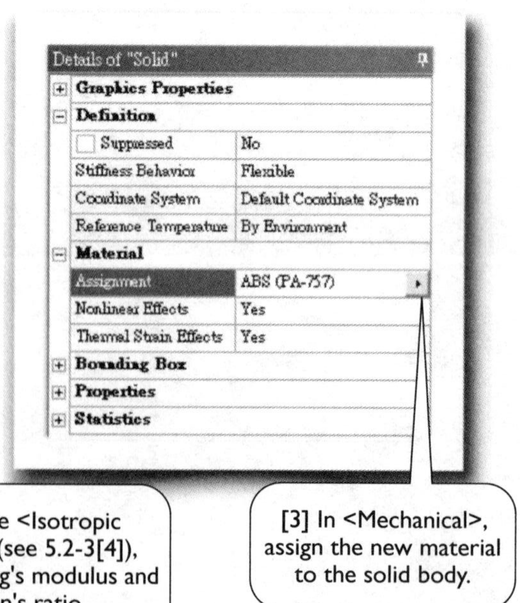

5.4-3 Specify Support

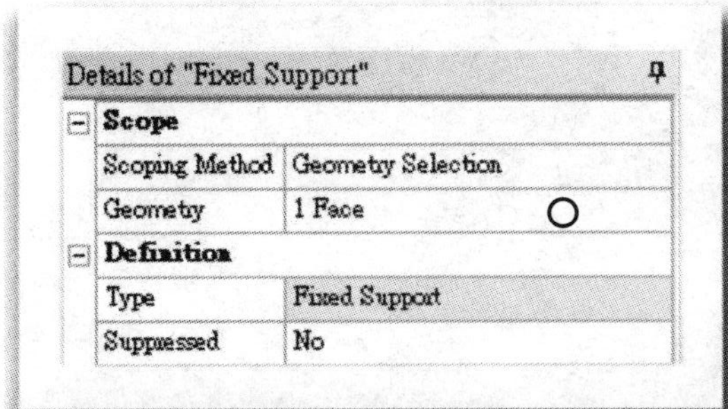

Details of "Fixed Support"	
Scope	
Scoping Method	Geometry Selection
Geometry	1 Face
Definition	
Type	Fixed Support
Suppressed	No

[1] The bottom rim face assumes a <Fixed Support>. That would be more realistic if it assume a <Compression Only Support>. For this case, however, there is no difference between them, since the rim face will not depart from the surface that support the model. A <Compression Only Support> would introduce contact nonlinearity into the problem.

5.4-4 Specify Load

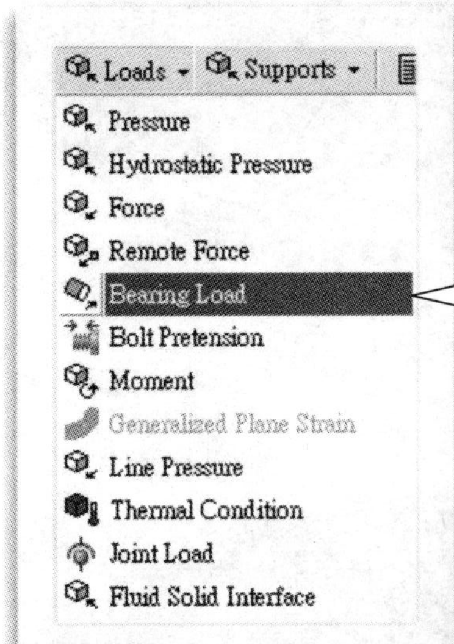

[1] The design load is applied as a <Bearing Load>.

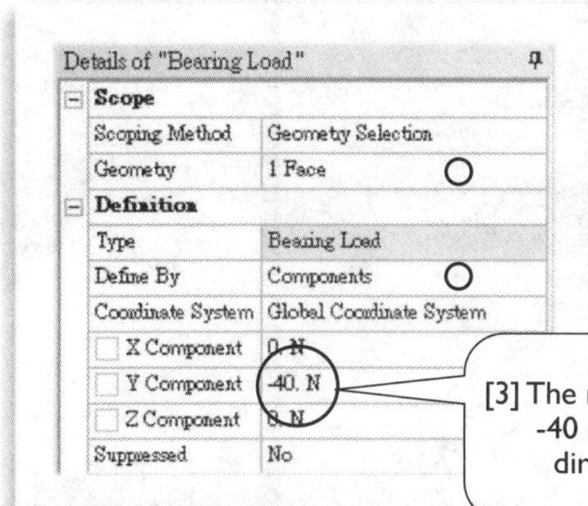

Details of "Bearing Load"	
Scope	
Scoping Method	Geometry Selection
Geometry	1 Face
Definition	
Type	Bearing Load
Define By	Components
Coordinate System	Global Coordinate System
X Component	0. N
Y Component	-40. N
Z Component	0. N
Suppressed	No

[3] The magnitude is -40 (N) in Y-direction.

[2] The bearing load is applied on this cylindrical surface.

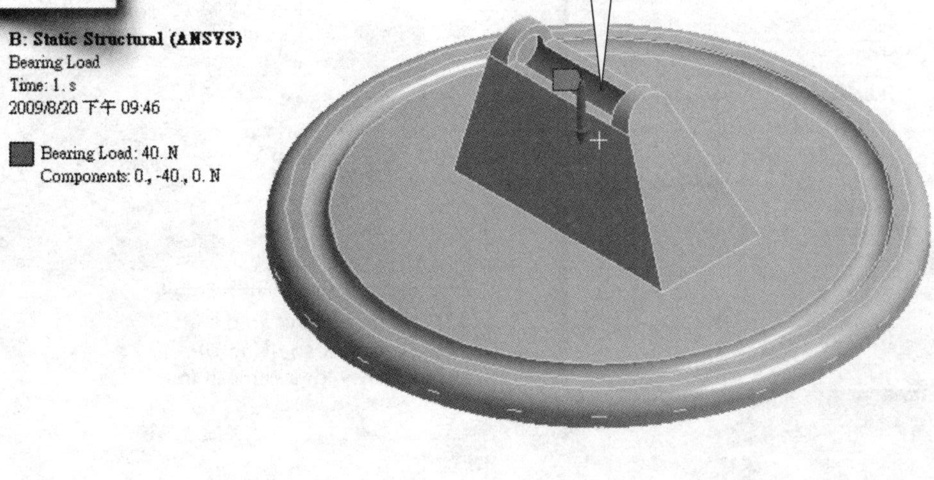

5.4-5 Generate Mesh

Details of "Mesh"	
Defaults	
Physics Preference	Mechanical
Relevance	0
Sizing	
Use Advanced Size Function	Off
Relevance Center	Coarse
Element Size	Default
Initial Size Seed	Active Assembly
Smoothing	Medium
Transition	Fast
Span Angle Center	Coarse
Minimum Edge Length	0.819530 mm
Inflation	
Advanced	
Pinch	
Statistics	
Nodes	8596
Elements	4282
Mesh Metric	None

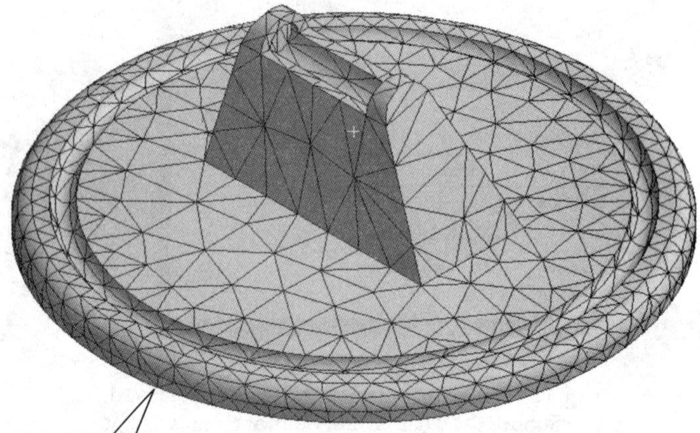

[1] The mesh generated with default settings, <Coarse, 0>.

Details of "Mesh"	
Defaults	
Physics Preference	Mechanical
Relevance	0
Sizing	
Use Advanced Size Function	Off
Relevance Center	Medium
Element Size	Default
Initial Size Seed	Active Assembly
Smoothing	Medium
Transition	Fast
Span Angle Center	Coarse
Minimum Edge Length	0.819530 mm
Inflation	
Advanced	
Pinch	
Statistics	
Nodes	10608
Elements	5263
Mesh Metric	None

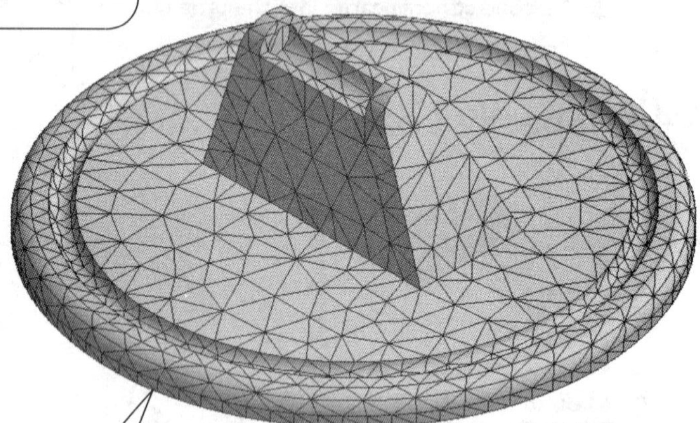

[2] The mesh generated with relevance set to <Medium, 0>

Details of "Mesh"	
Defaults	
Physics Preference	Mechanical
Relevance	0
Sizing	
Use Advanced Size Function	Off
Relevance Center	Fine
Element Size	Default
Initial Size Seed	Active Assembly
Smoothing	Medium
Transition	Fast
Span Angle Center	Coarse
Minimum Edge Length	0.819530 mm
Inflation	
Advanced	
Pinch	
Statistics	
Nodes	19853
Elements	9823
Mesh Metric	None

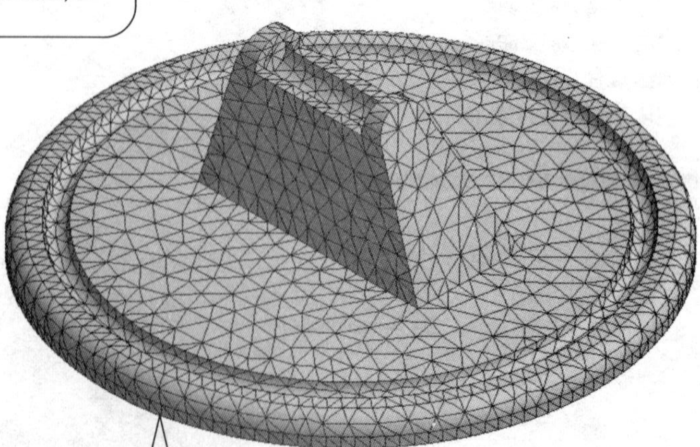

[3] The mesh generated with relevance set to <Fine, 0>. Let's satisfy with this mesh for now.

5.4-6 Set Up Solution Branch and Solve

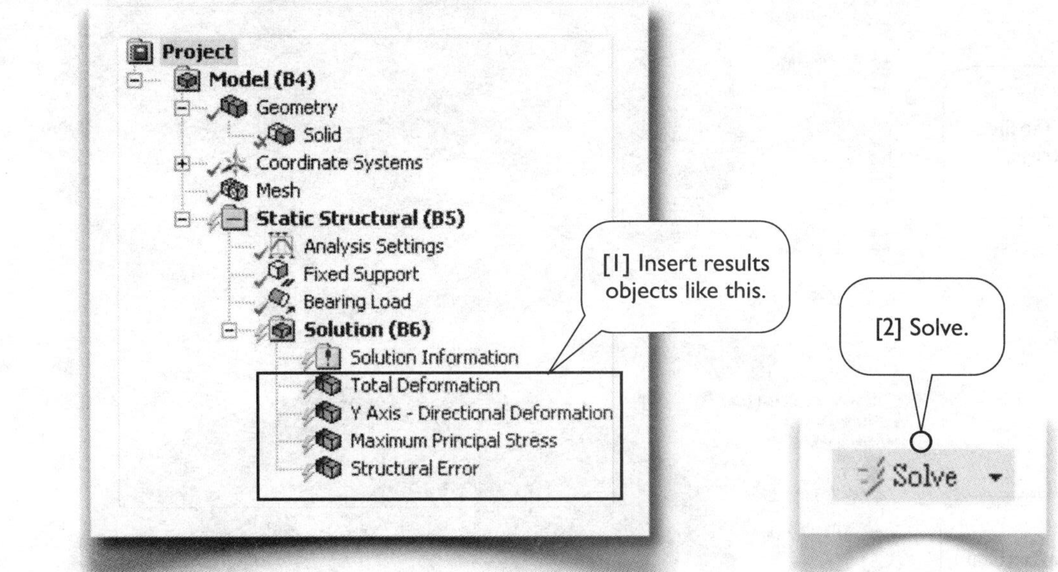

5.4-7 View the Results

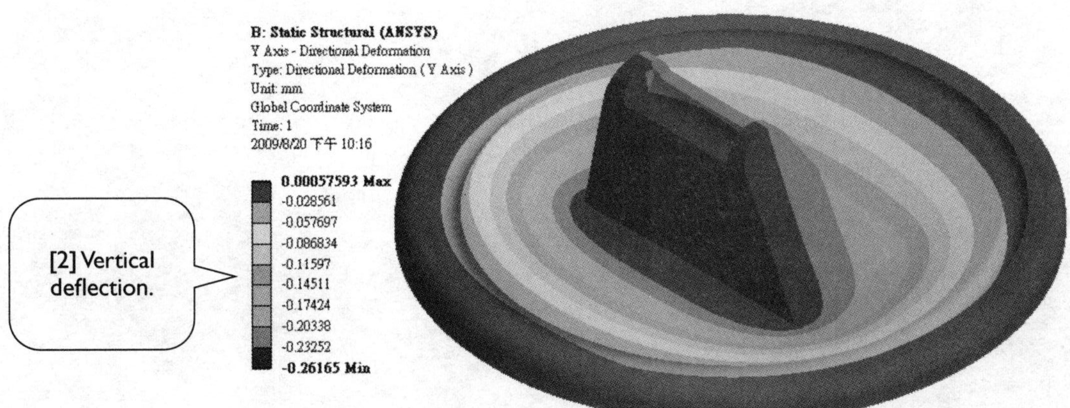

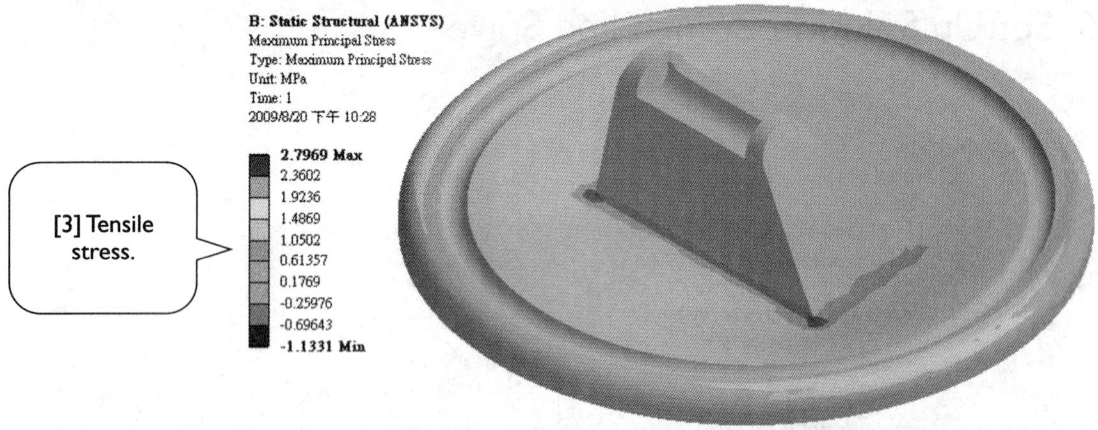

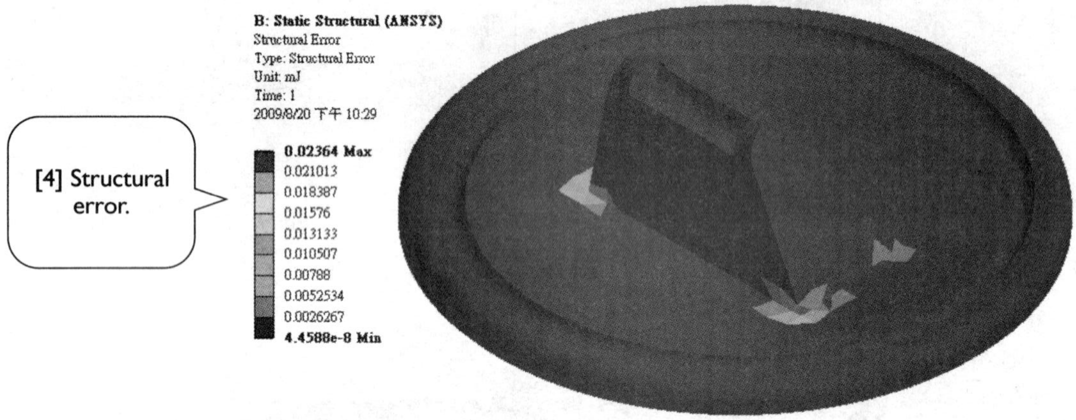

Wrap Up

Save the project, close <Mechanical> and exit <Workbench>.

Section 5.5
Problems

5.5-1 Key Concepts

Adaptive Meshing
An automatic and iterative solution process to meet a user-specified solution accuracy. Basic idea is to refine the mesh size in the area of large structural errors until the specified accuracy is satisfied.

Bearing Load
In 3D simulations, a bearing load applies on cylindrical faces. The total force is distributed on the compressive side of the cylindrical faces.

Coordinate System
To define a coordinate system, we need to specify the type of coordinate system, the location of origin, and the axes. The types of coordinate system may be Cartesian or Cylindrical in the current version of the Workbench.

Sweep Method
A meshing method, in which the source faces, selected manually or automatically, are meshed, and the 2D mesh grows to become 3D elements by sweeping along a path up to target faces. Not all 3D solid bodies are sweepable. A sweepable 3D solid body often can be meshed with hexahedral elements.

MultiZone Method
A meshing method. For a non-sweepable 3D solid body, the method tries to decompose the body into several sweepable bodies and then uses Sweep method to mesh each body.

5.5-2 Questions

Stress Singularity
In Section 5.1-12, we mentioned that the maximum structural error was at a region of stress singularity. How can you justify that this is a region of stress singularity? Are there any other regions of stress singularity in the bracket model? Also, point out all the regions of stress singularity in the LCD display support model.

Symmetries
We didn't take any advantages of symmetries in all three simulation cases of this chapters. Point out the planes of symmetry in each model.

5.5-3 Workbench Exercises

Simulation with Symmetric Models

It is a good exercise to redo the simulations in this chapter, taking advantages of the symmetries.

Additional Exercises

Additional Exercises of 3D simulations can be found in the Verification Manual for Workbench[1].

Reference

1. ANSYS Help System>Workbench>Verification Manual for Workbench>II. Mechanical Application Descriptions

Chapter 6
Surface Models

Many real-world objects can be modeled as surface bodies. In Section 4.3, we modeled a piece of glass as a surface body. The 2D bodies in Chapter 3, although created using <Surfaces From Sketches> in DesignModeler, are called 2D solid bodies in <Mechanical>. Remember that 2D solid bodies do not have out-of-plane bending.

When a real-world body is thin enough and subject to bending, it is usually a good candidate for a 3D surface body. The Workbench will mesh surface bodies with shell elements (1.3-3[7, 8]). There are many advantages of using surface models. First, creating surface models is usually easier than creating solid models. Second, the problem size is much smaller than using solid models. That implies a much less run-time for the problem. Third, it is possible to obtain a more accurate solution, even with less run-time, due to the efficiency of shell elements. Therefore, the engineers should consider using surface models over solid models whenever possible. In the old days, surface models are visually awkward since they have zero thickness and occupy zero volume in the space. Workbench eliminates this awkwardness by allowing the rendering of thickness, so that the surface bodies are visually the same as solid bodies.

Purpose of the Chapter

The main purpose of this chapter is to practice the use of shell elements (1.3-3[8]). This chapter guides the students to create surface models and perform simulations using these models. The chapter uses three examples, two of them are purely surface models while the other one is a model mixed up by solid bodies and surface bodies.

About Each Section

The first two sections present two step-by-step examples. Section 6.1 creates a bellows joint model and performs a simulation using the model. In Section 6.2, the bracket, which we introduced in Sections 4.1 and 5.1, is used as an example to demonstrate how an existing solid model can be transformed to a surface model using the tool <Mid-Surface>. The solution numerically is comparable with that obtained using the solid model in Section 5.1, while using much less computing time. Section 6.3 provides an additional exercise to demonstrate the mix-up of solid bodies and surface bodies.

Section 6.1

Step-by-Step: Bellows Joints

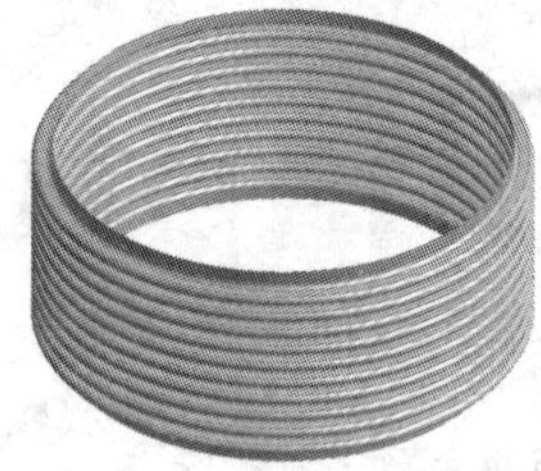

6.1-1 About Bellows Joints

The bellows joints [1-2] are used as expansion joints, which absorb thermal or vibrational movement in a piping system that transports high pressure gases. As part of the piping system, the bellows joints are designed to sustain internal pressure as well as external pressure. The external pressure must be considered when the piping system is used across the ocean. Under the internal pressure, the engineers mostly concern about its radial deformation (due to an engineering tolerance consideration) and hoop stress (due to the safety consideration). Under the external pressure, buckling is the main concern (see an exercise in Section 10.4-2).

In this section, we will create a full 3D surface model for the bellows joint and perform a static structural simulation under the internal pressure of 0.5 MPa. A buckling simulation under the external pressure will be left as an exercise in Section 10.4-2.

Note that the problem is axisymmetric both in geometry and loading. We could take advantage of this property and model the problem as 2D solid body or 2D line body (both as axisymmetric models). The latter, 2D line model, is not supported in the current version of <Mechanical> (it is supported through APDL). The former, 2D solid model, usually results a poorer solution than surface body, for this particular case, because the bending dominates its structural behavior.

[1] The bellows joints are made of SU316 steel, which has a Young's modulus of 180 GPa and Poisson's ratio of 0.28.

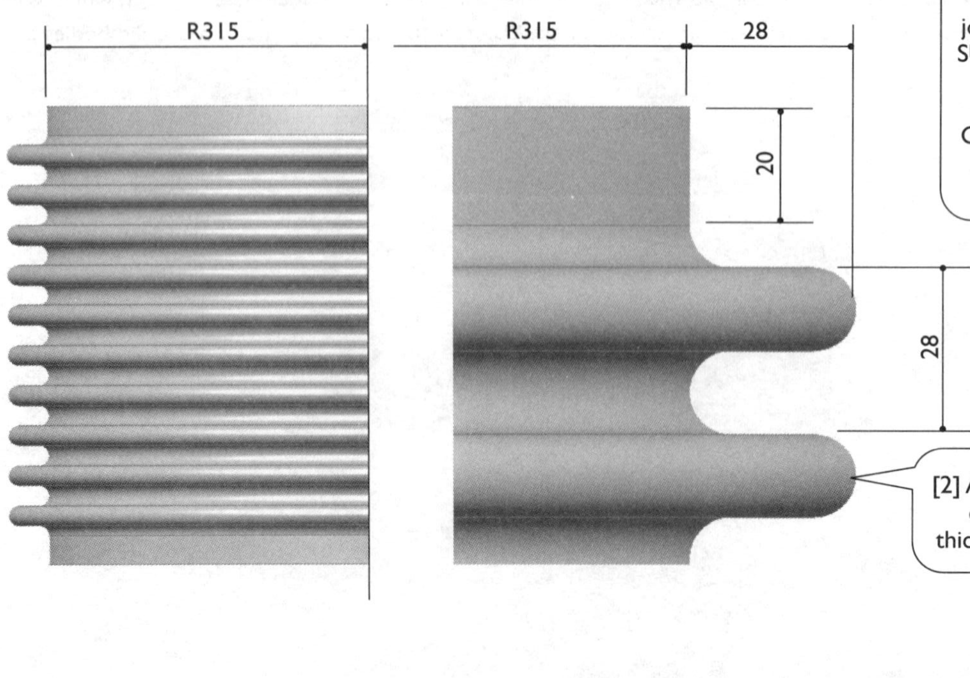

[2] All arcs have radii of 7 mm. The thickness is 0.8 mm.

PART A. GEOMETRIC MODELING

6.1-2 Start Up

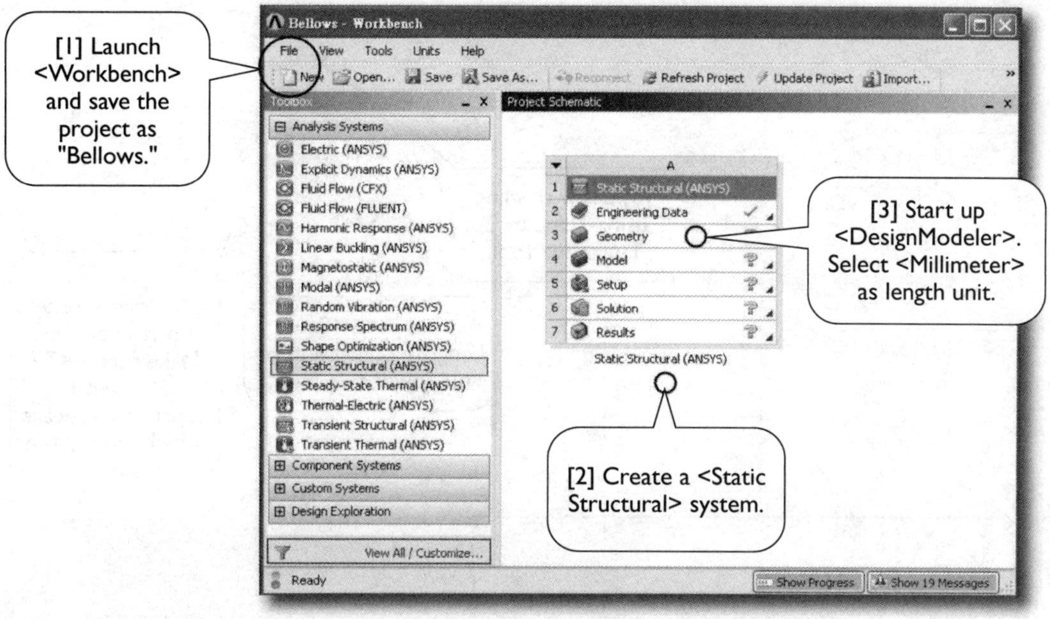

6.1-3 Draw a Pitch of the Bellows

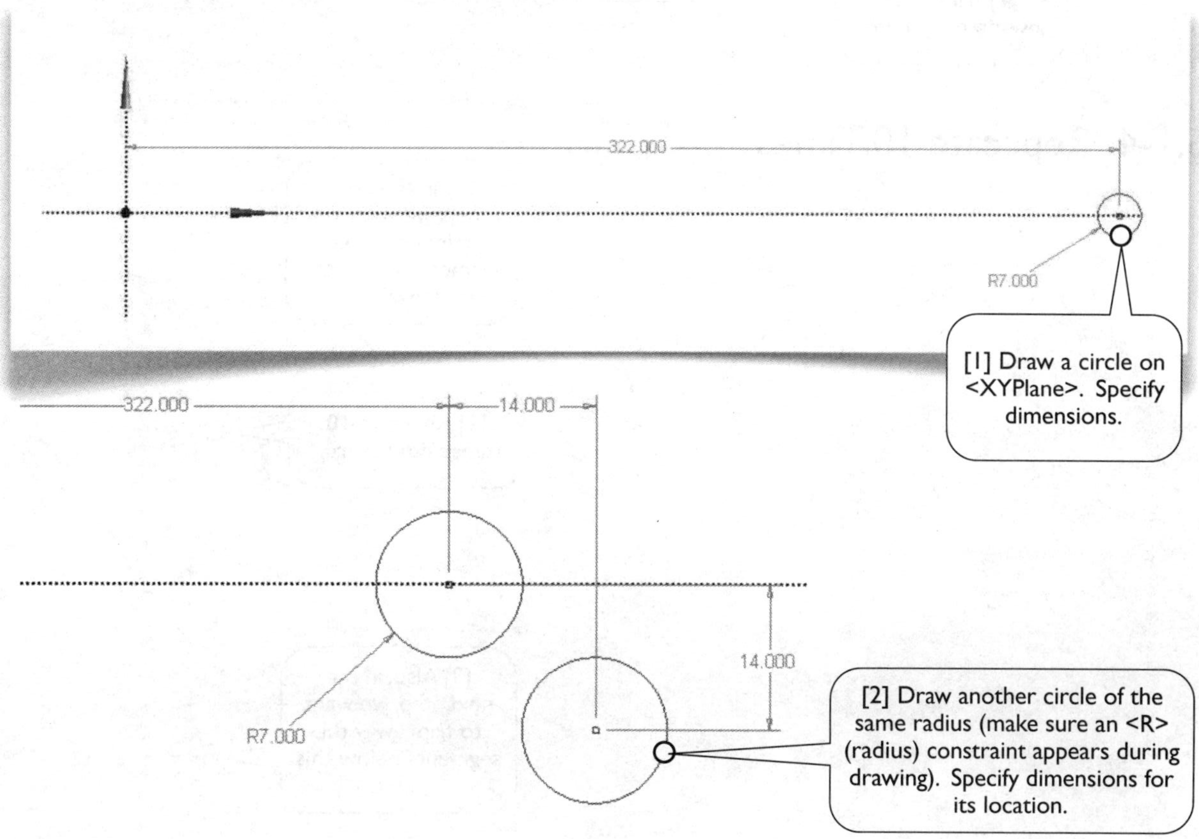

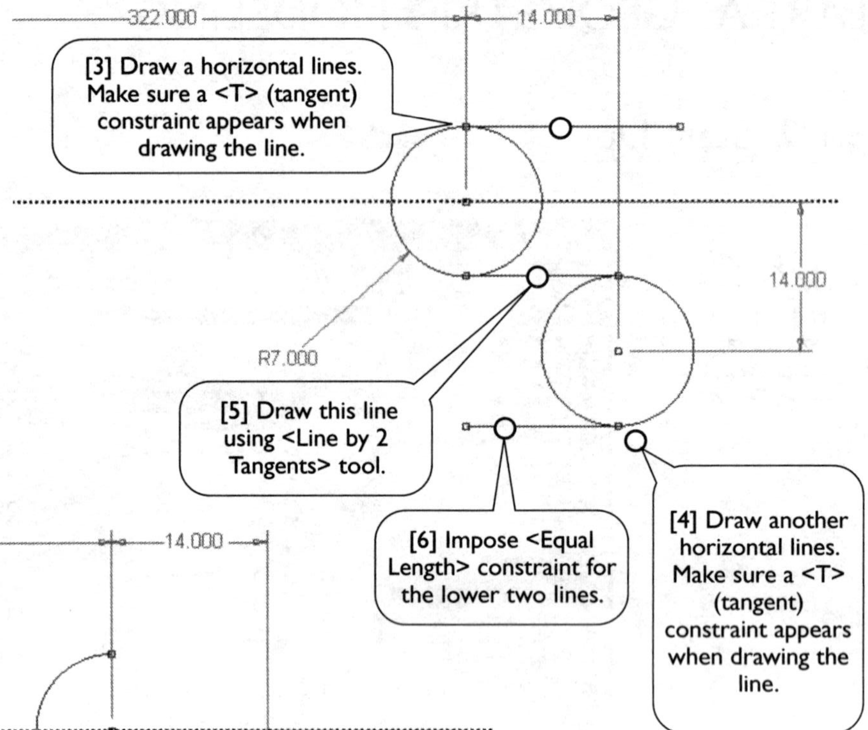

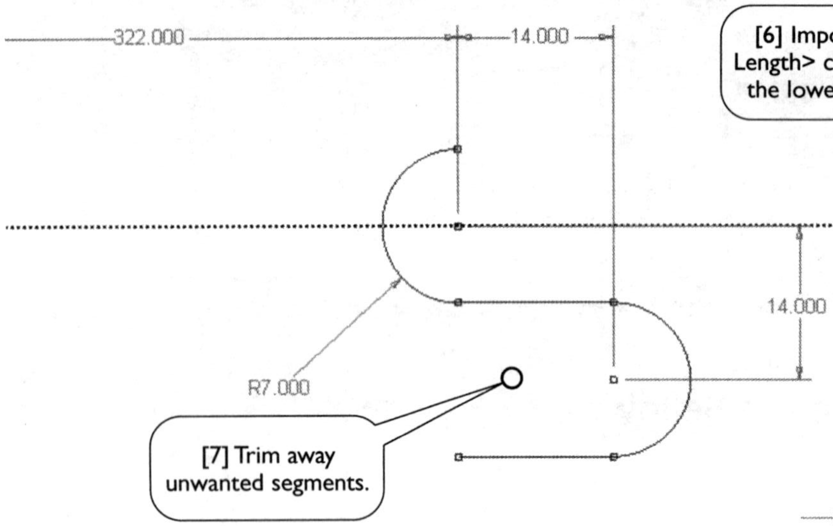

6.1-4 Replicate 10 Times

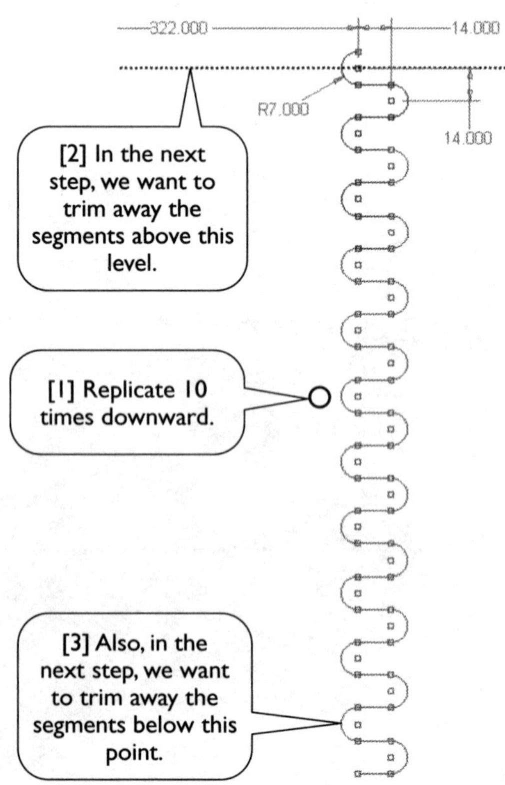

6.1-5 Finish Both Ends

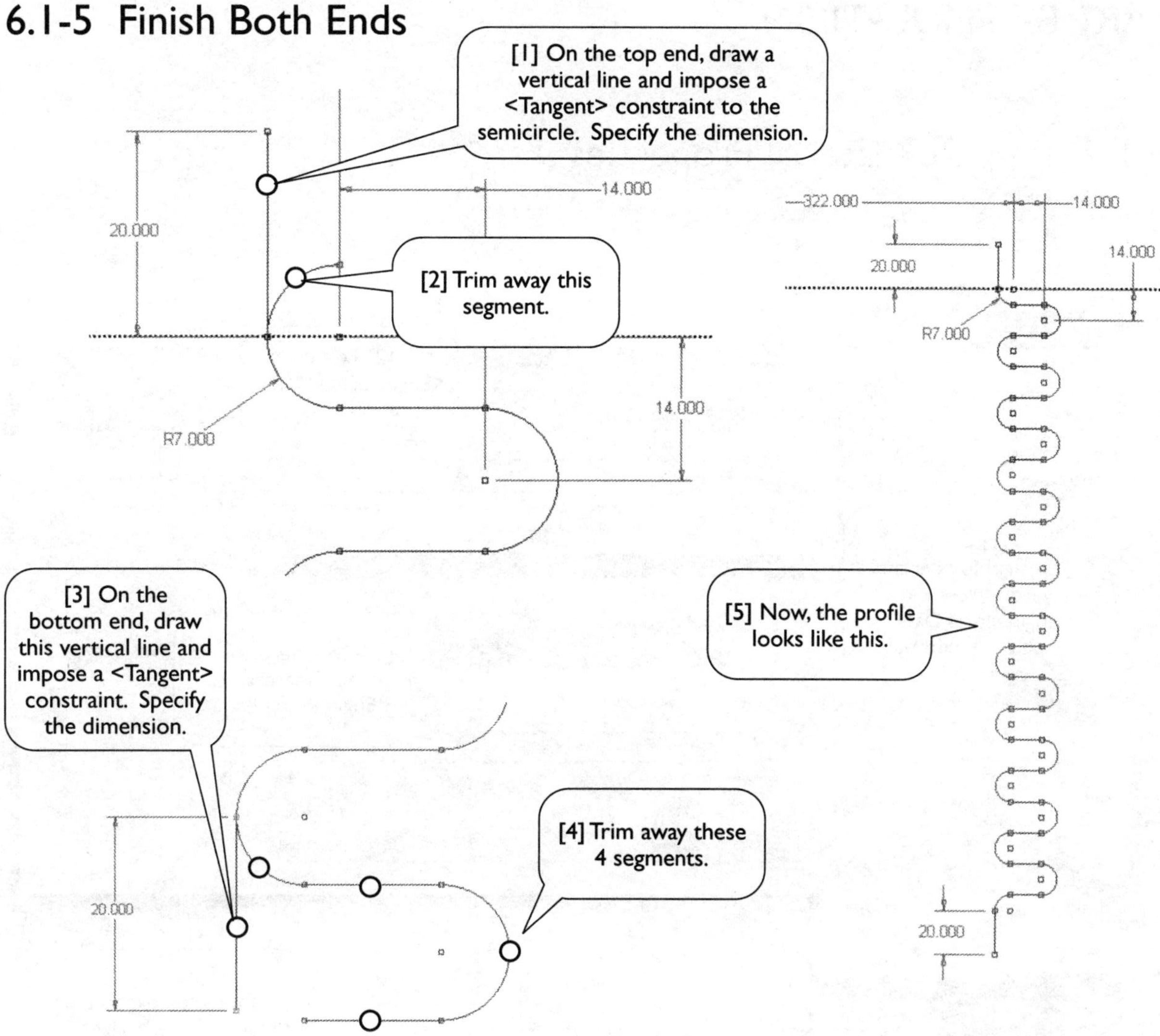

6.1-6 Revolve to Create Surface Body

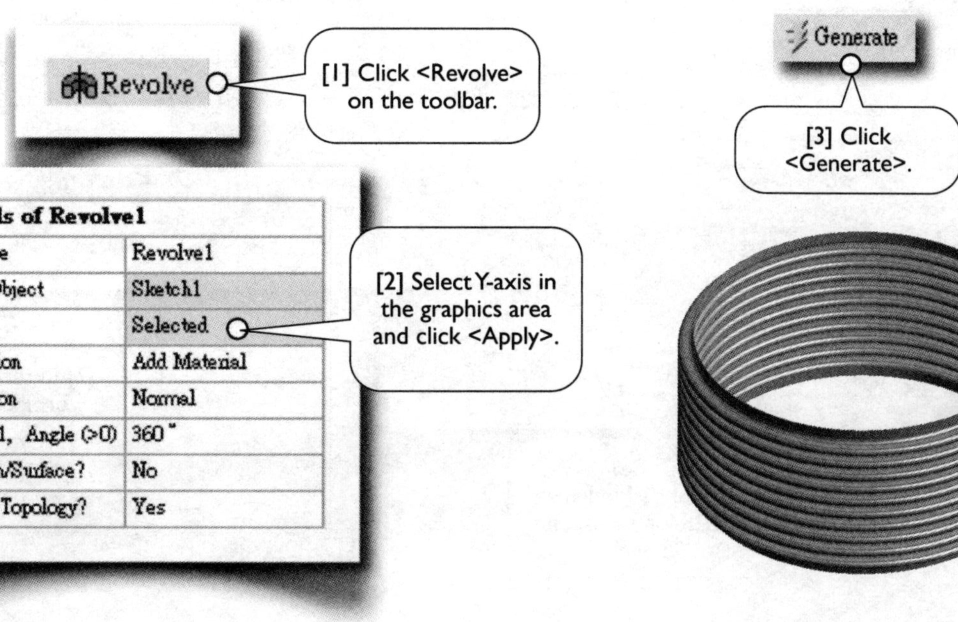

Details of Revolve1	
Revolve	Revolve1
Base Object	Sketch1
Axis	Selected
Operation	Add Material
Direction	Normal
FD1, Angle (>0)	360 °
As Thin/Surface?	No
Merge Topology?	Yes

PART B. SIMULATION

6.1-7 Prepare Material Properties

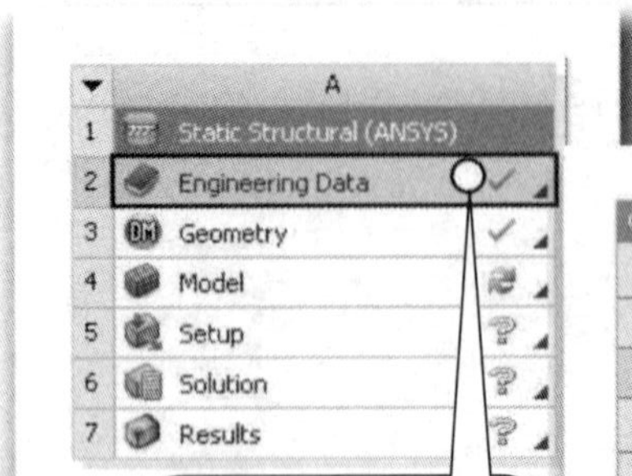

[1] Close DesignModeler and double-click <Engineering Data> to add the material.

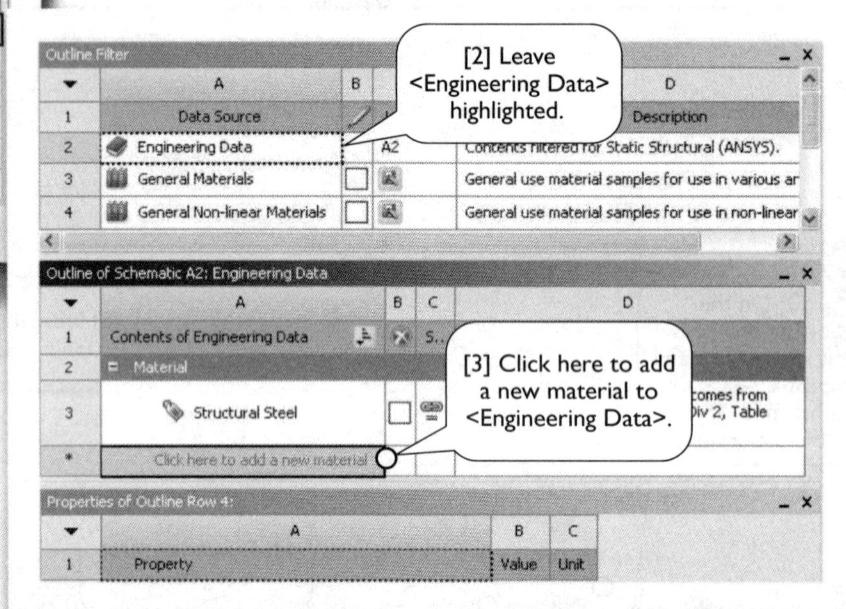

[2] Leave <Engineering Data> highlighted.

[3] Click here to add a new material to <Engineering Data>.

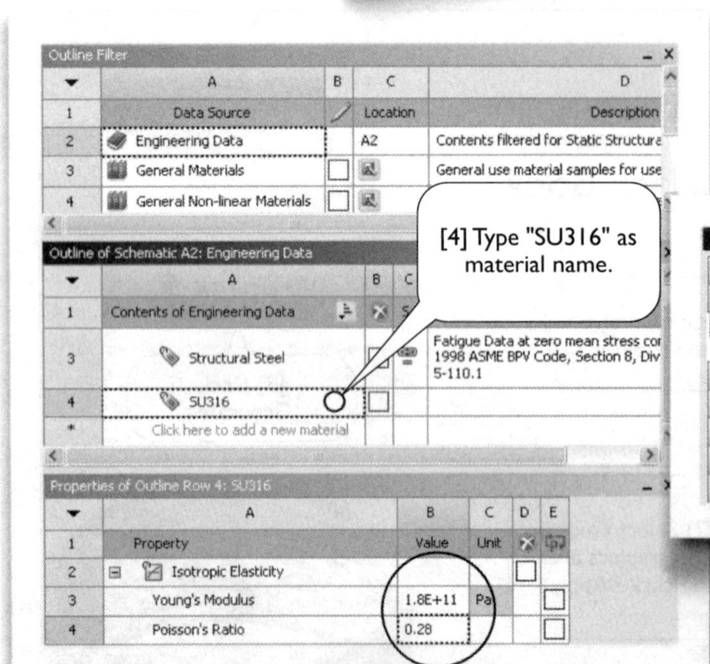

[4] Type "SU316" as material name.

[6] Type "1.8e11" (Pa) for <Young's Modulus> and 0.28 for <Poisson's Ratio>.

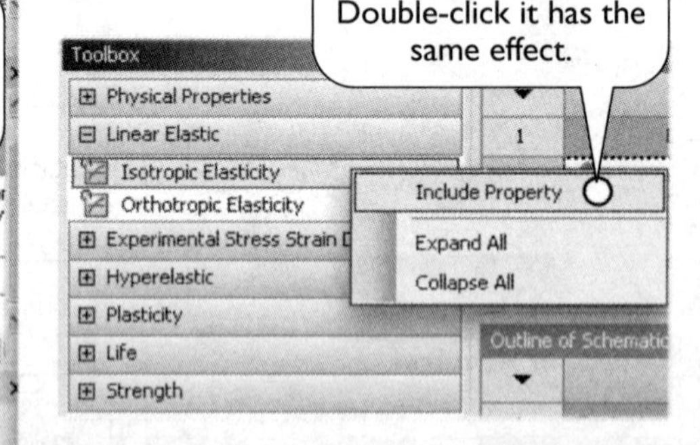

[5] In the <Toolbox>, expand <Linear Elastic>, right-click <Isotropic Elasticity>, and select <Include Property>. Double-click it has the same effect.

[7] Return to project.

6.1-8 Start Up <Mechanical>

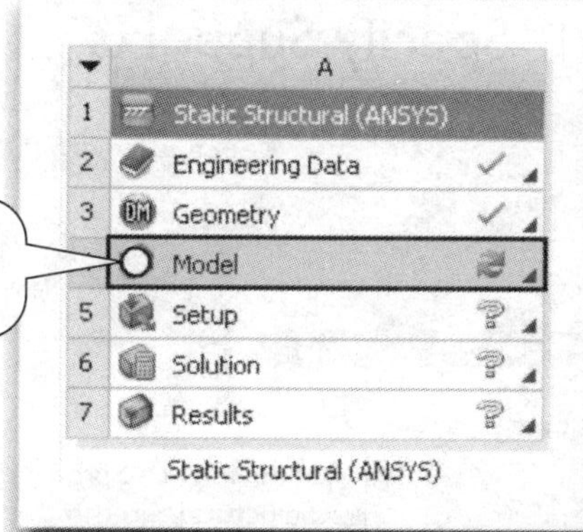

6.1-9 Assign Material and Thickness

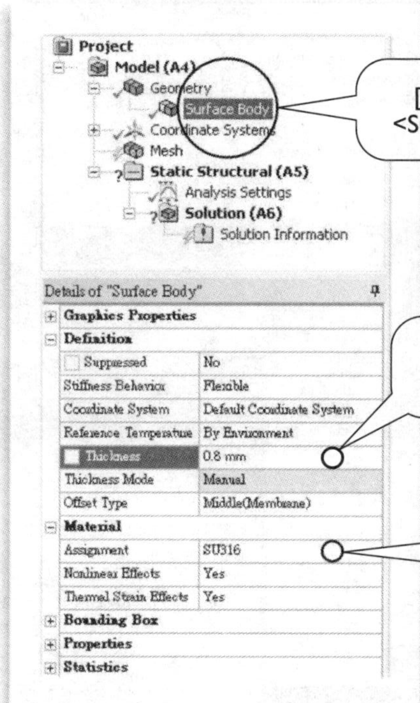

6.1-10 Generate Mesh

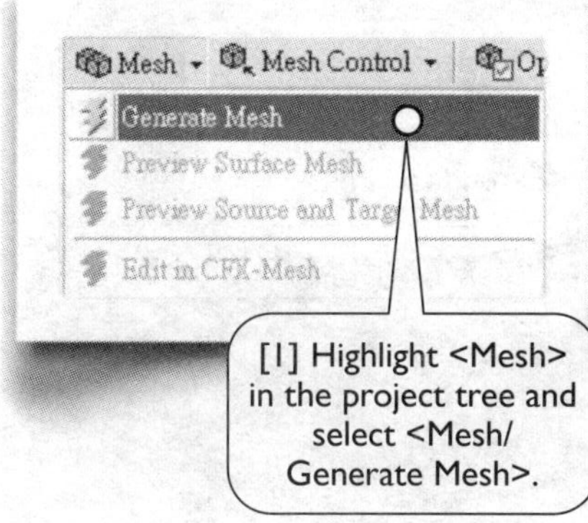

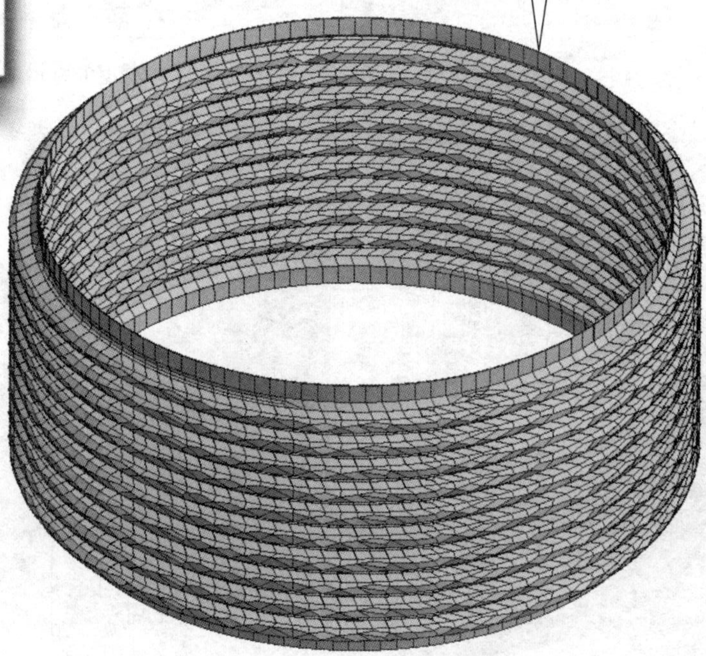

6.1-11 Specify Supports

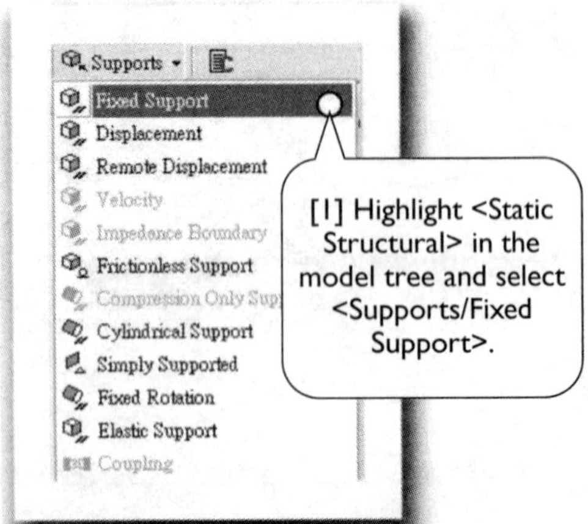

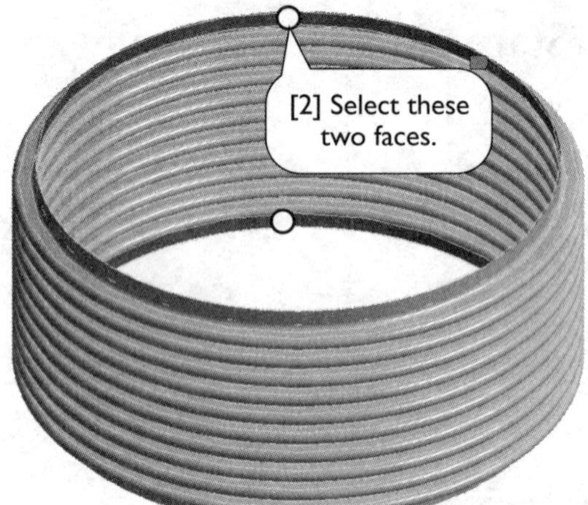

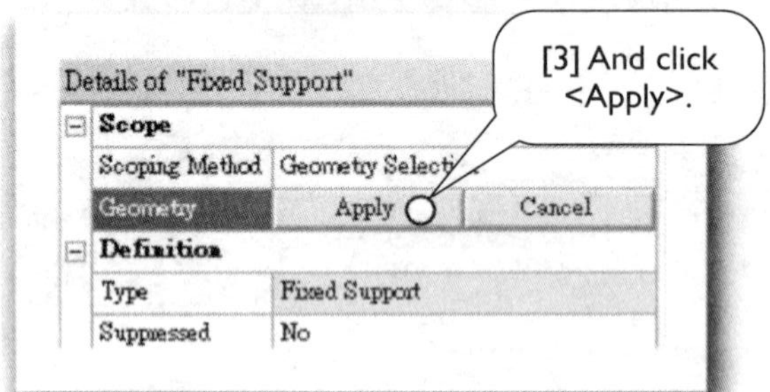

6.1-12 Apply Pressure

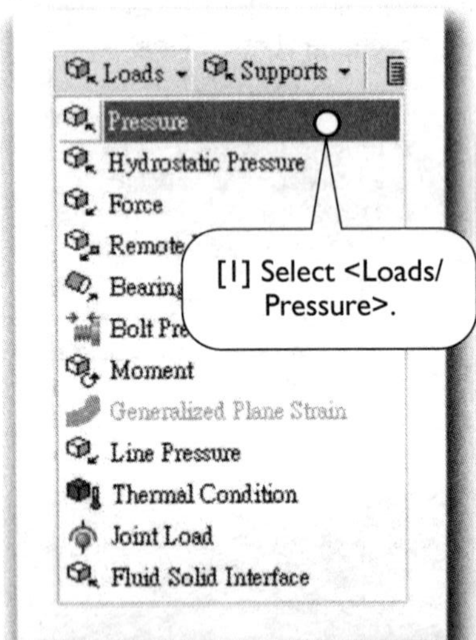

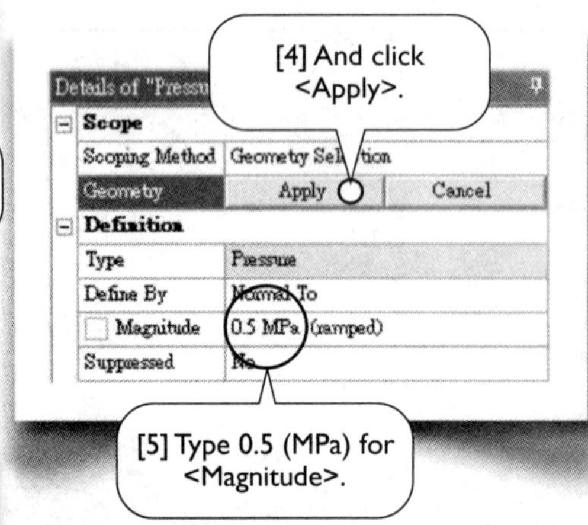

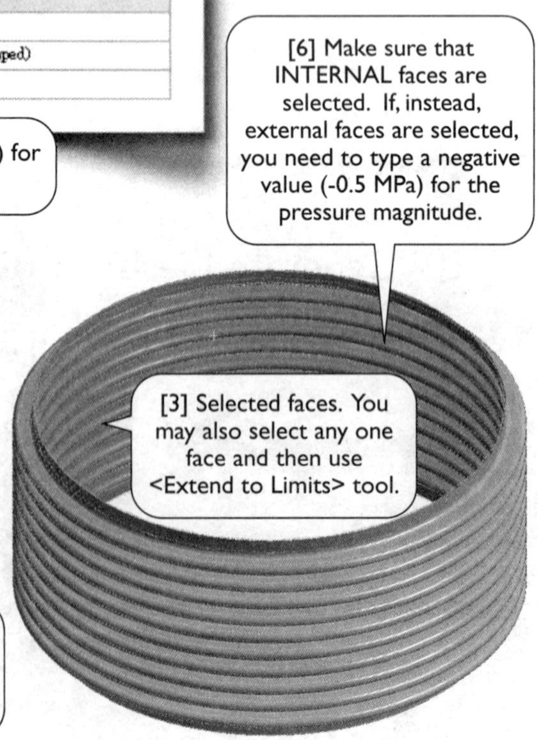

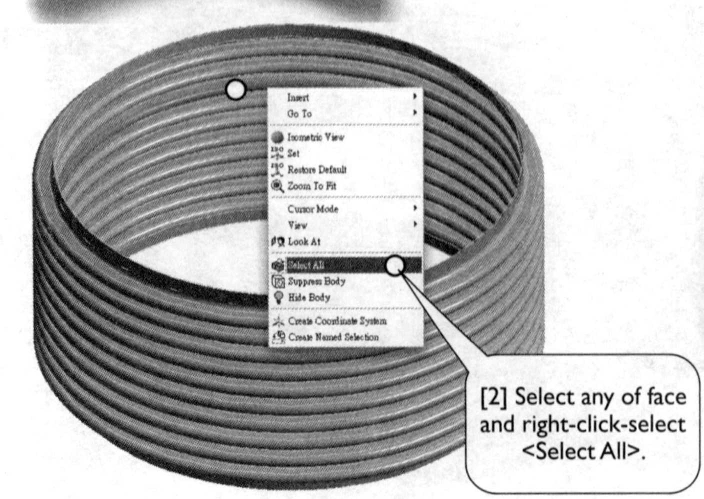

6.1-13 Create a Cylindrical Coordinate System

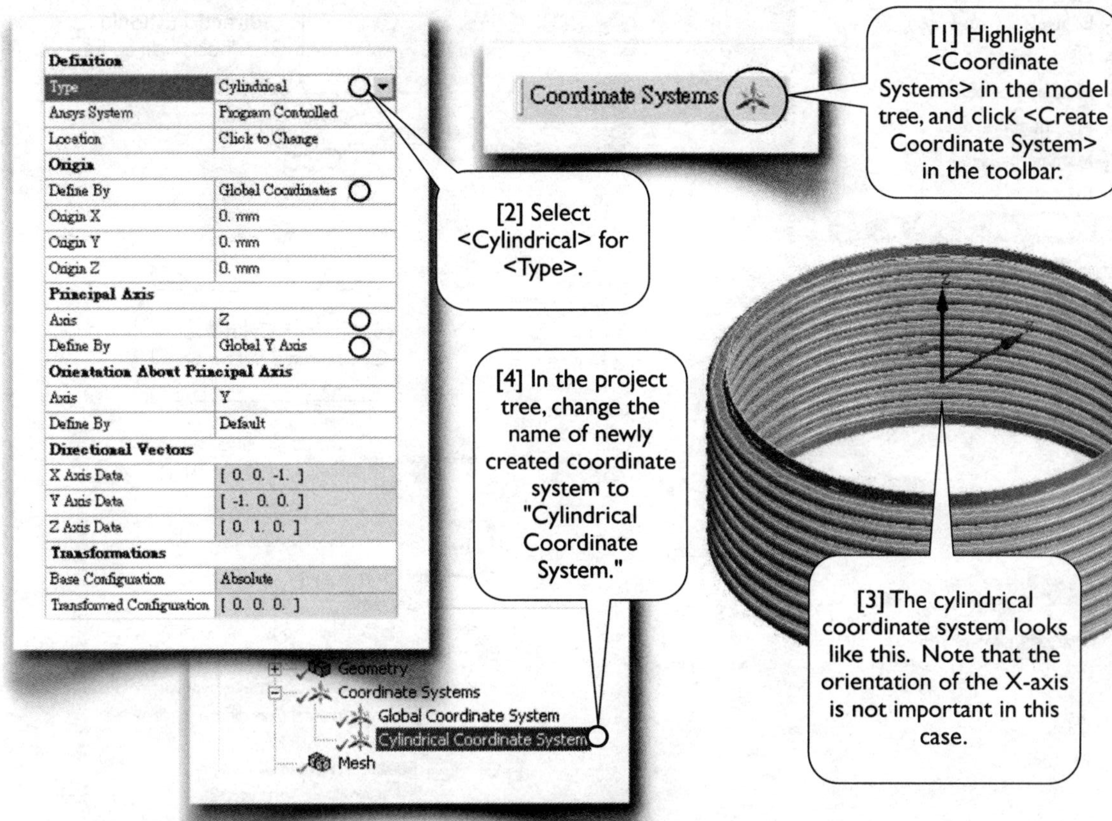

6.1-14 Set Up Solution Branch and Solve the Model

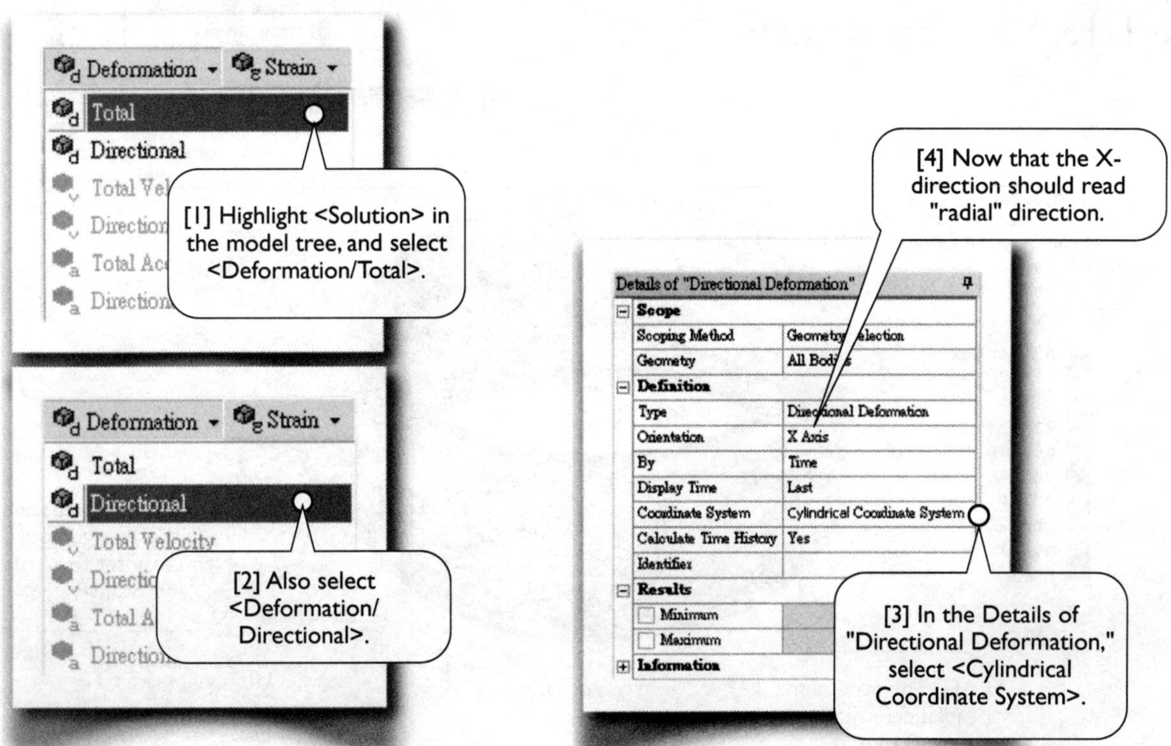

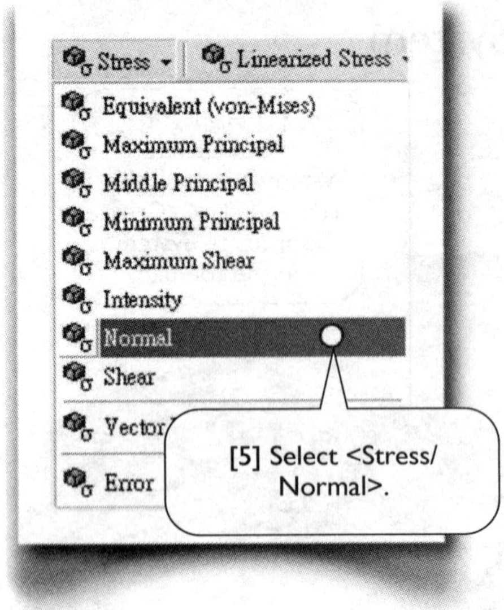

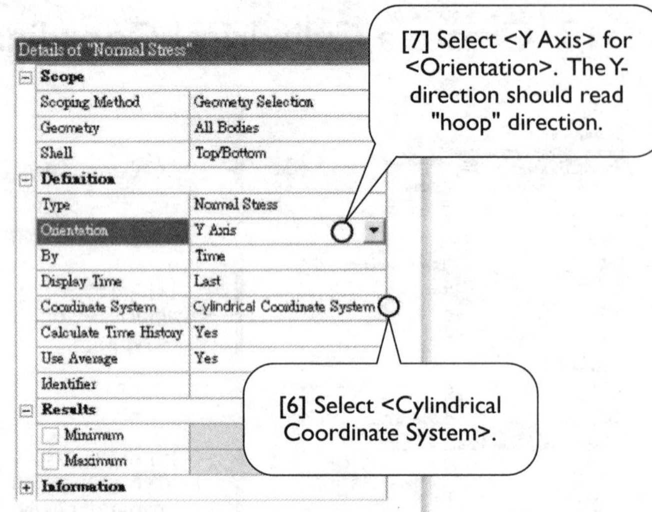

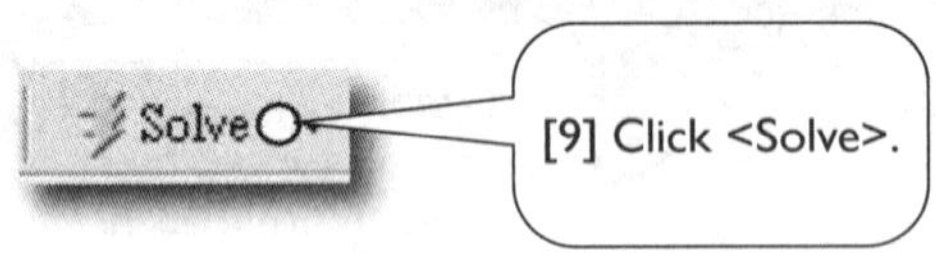

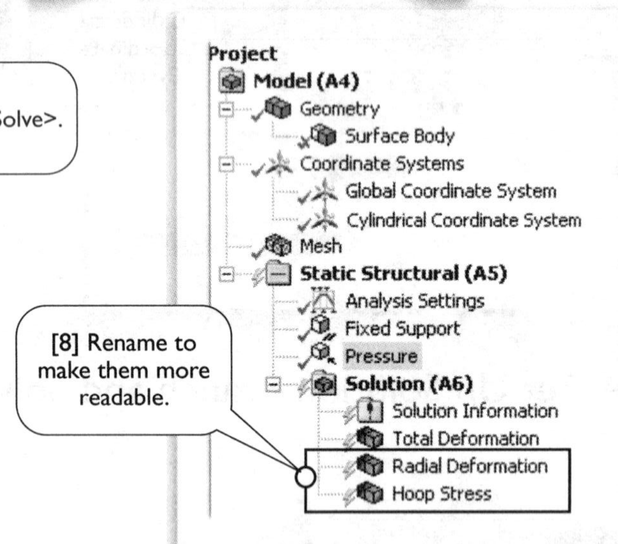

6.1-15 View the Results

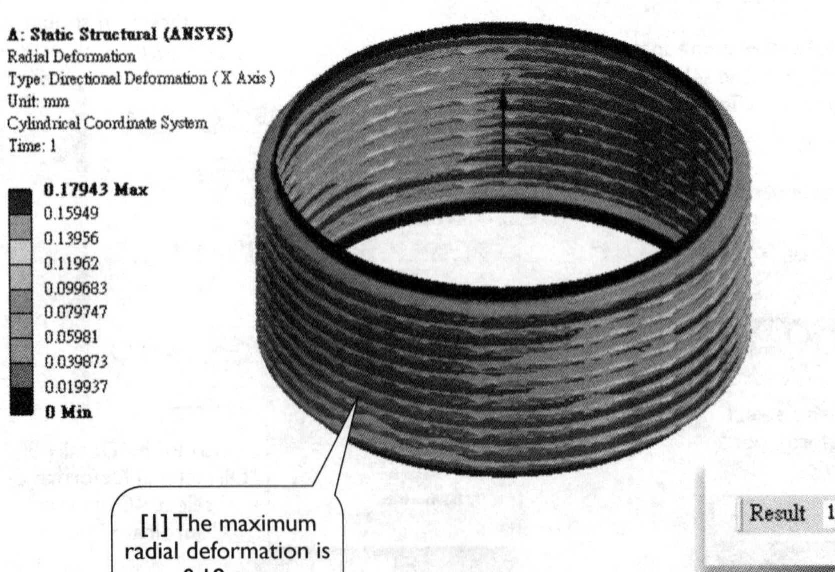

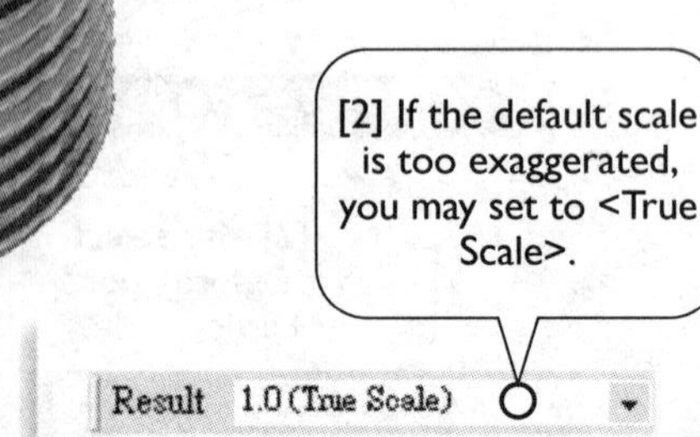

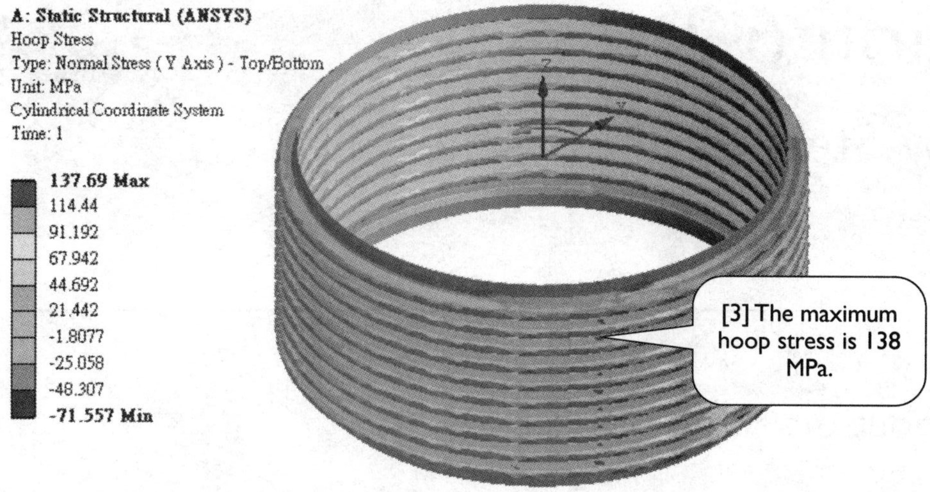

Wrap Up

Save the project and exit the Workbench.

Remark: Symmetry of the Model

As mentioned in Section 6.1-1, the model is axisymmetric. We could take advantage of this property and model the problem as 2D line body and mesh the body using axisymmetric shell elements (such as SHELL208[1]). For the current version of Workbench, that is possible only by inserting APDL commands.

In the foregoing simulation, we didn't take the advantage of axisymmetry. There are, however, at least three planes of symmetry we may exploit. This leaves for the students as an exercise (Section 6.4-3). The reason we model the bellows without taking the advantage of any symmetries is because we want to perform a buckling simulation in Section 10.4-2, as an exercise.

While the geometry and the loading are symmetric, the buckling mode may be not. If we model a problem as symmetric, then we would miss all asymmetric buckling modes. This is also true for a free vibration simulation (modal analysis), which if we model as symmetric, then we would miss all asymmetric vibration modes.

References

1. ANSYS Help System>Mechanical APDL>Element Reference>SHELL208.

Section 6.2

Step-by-Step: Beam Bracket

6.2-1 About the Beam Bracket

In Section 4.1, we created a 3D solid model for the beam bracket; the model was used for a simulation in Section 5.1. Since the seat plate (flange) and the web plate are relatively thin and have uniform thicknesses, it raises a curiosity that if it is possible to model the beam bracket as a surface body and obtain a comparable result.

To create a surface model for the beam bracket, we don't have to start from scratch; we can use a tool in the DesignModeler, called <Mid-Surface>. In fact, surface models are often created in this way. CAD models are usually created as 3D solids, since they are created for many purposes, and simulation is only one of them. When a surface model is needed for simulation, <Mid-Surface> is a powerful tool to extract a surface model from a solid model.

PART A. GEOMETRIC MODELING

6.2-2 Start Up

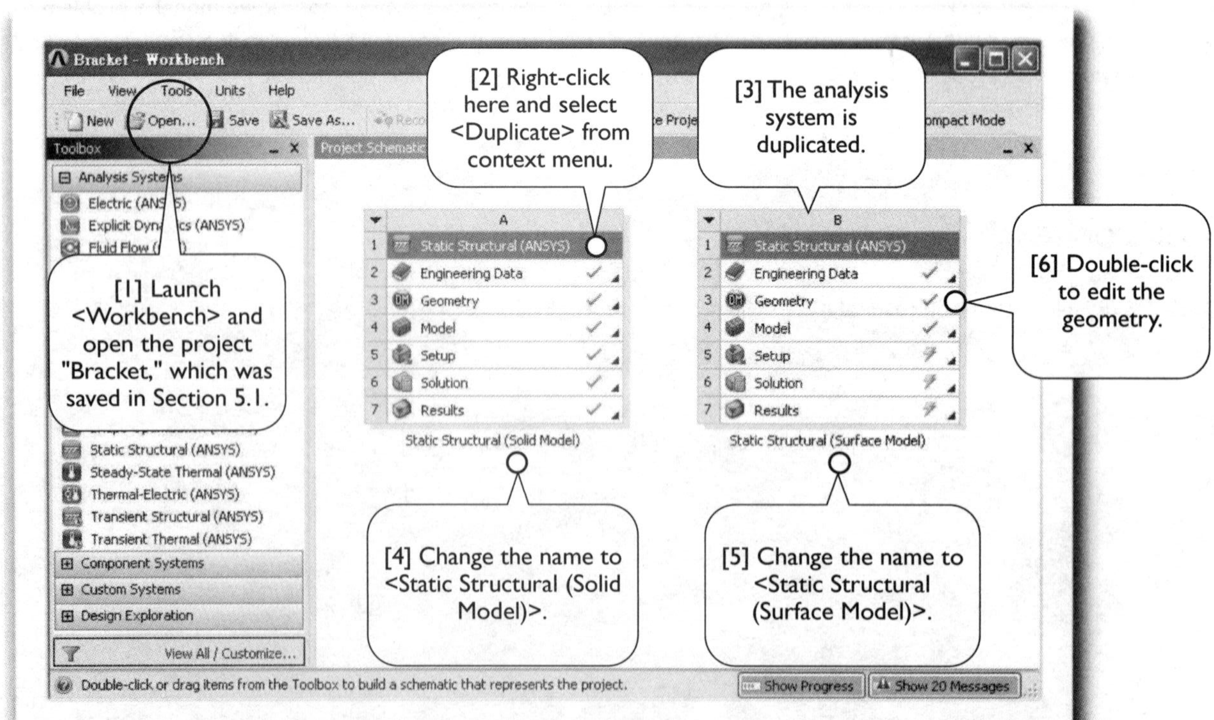

6.2-3 Automatically Find Face Pairs

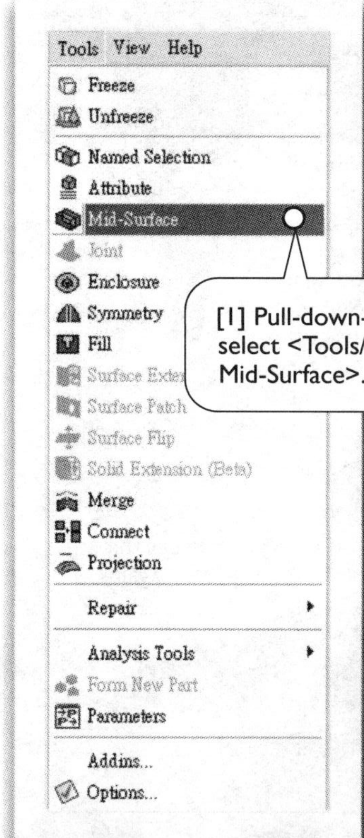

[1] Pull-down-select <Tools/Mid-Surface>.

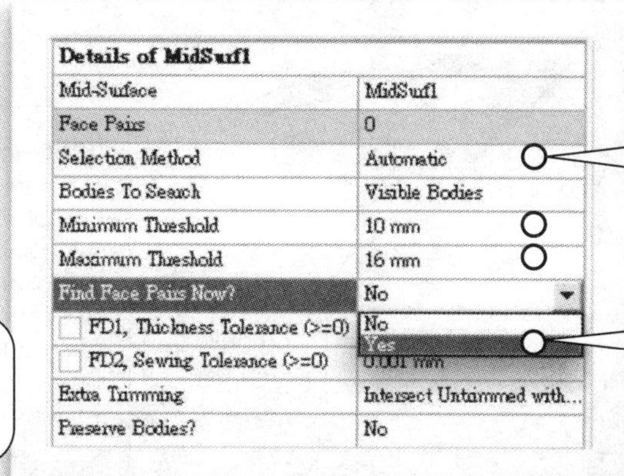

[2] Select <Automatic> to let the program search face pairs.

[3] As soon as you select <Yes>, face pairs are automatically found.

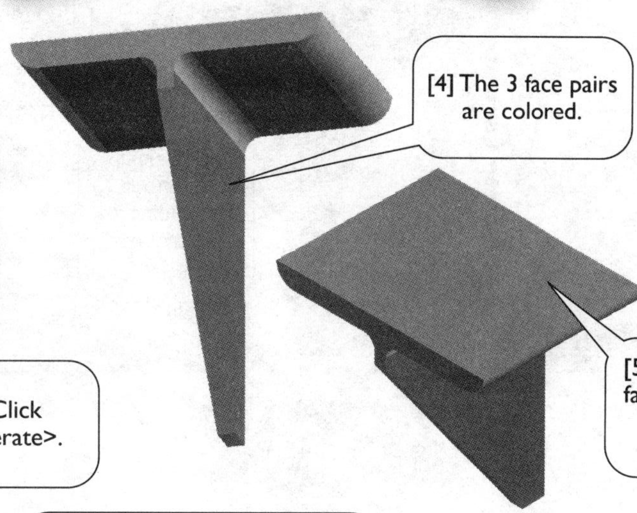

[4] The 3 face pairs are colored.

[5] Note that two faces of a face pair are in different colors.

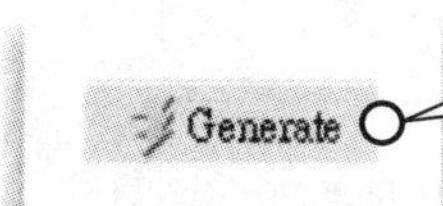

[6] Click <Generate>.

[7] Three surface bodies are generated. As you can see, they are not connected, because the face pairs do not cover all the model. The surface model needs to be further repaired.

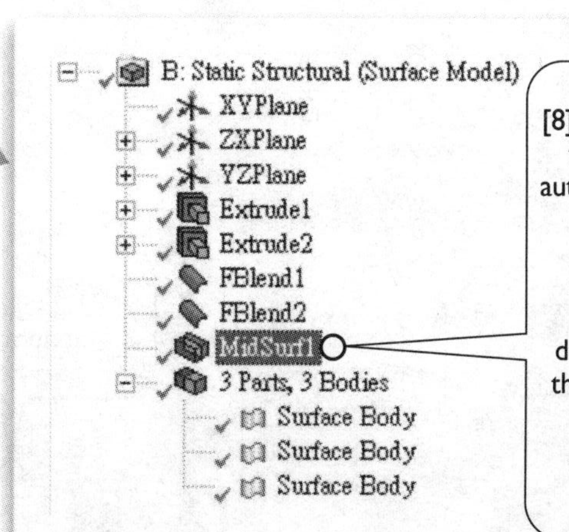

[8] This example is so simple that DesignModeler can automatically find all the face pairs. For complicated cases, you may need to manually select the face pairs. To illustrate, let's delete what we've done in this subsection, and redo it manually. Right-click <MidSurf1> and select <Delete>.

6.2-4 Manually Select Face Pairs

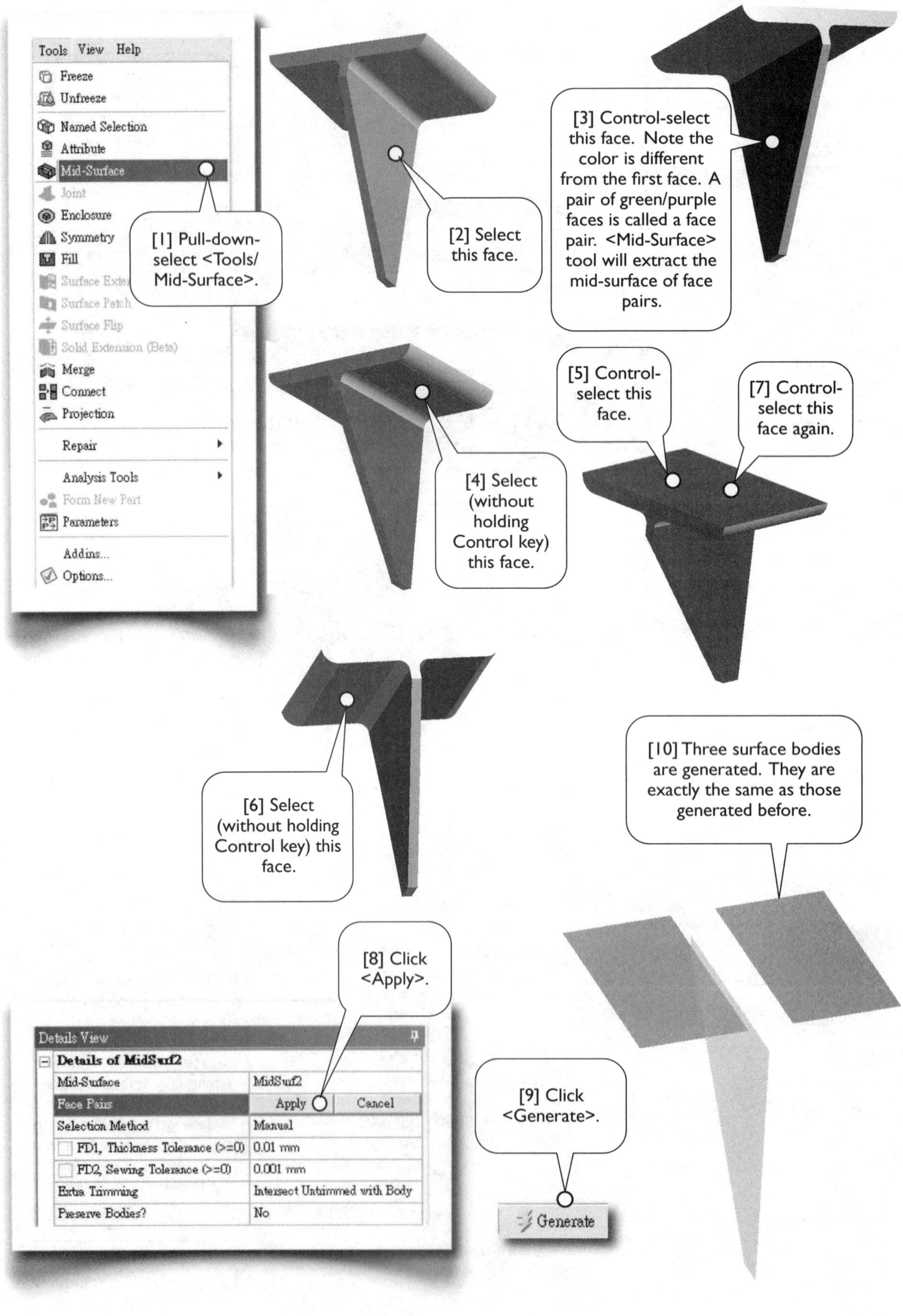

6.2-5 Extend the Web

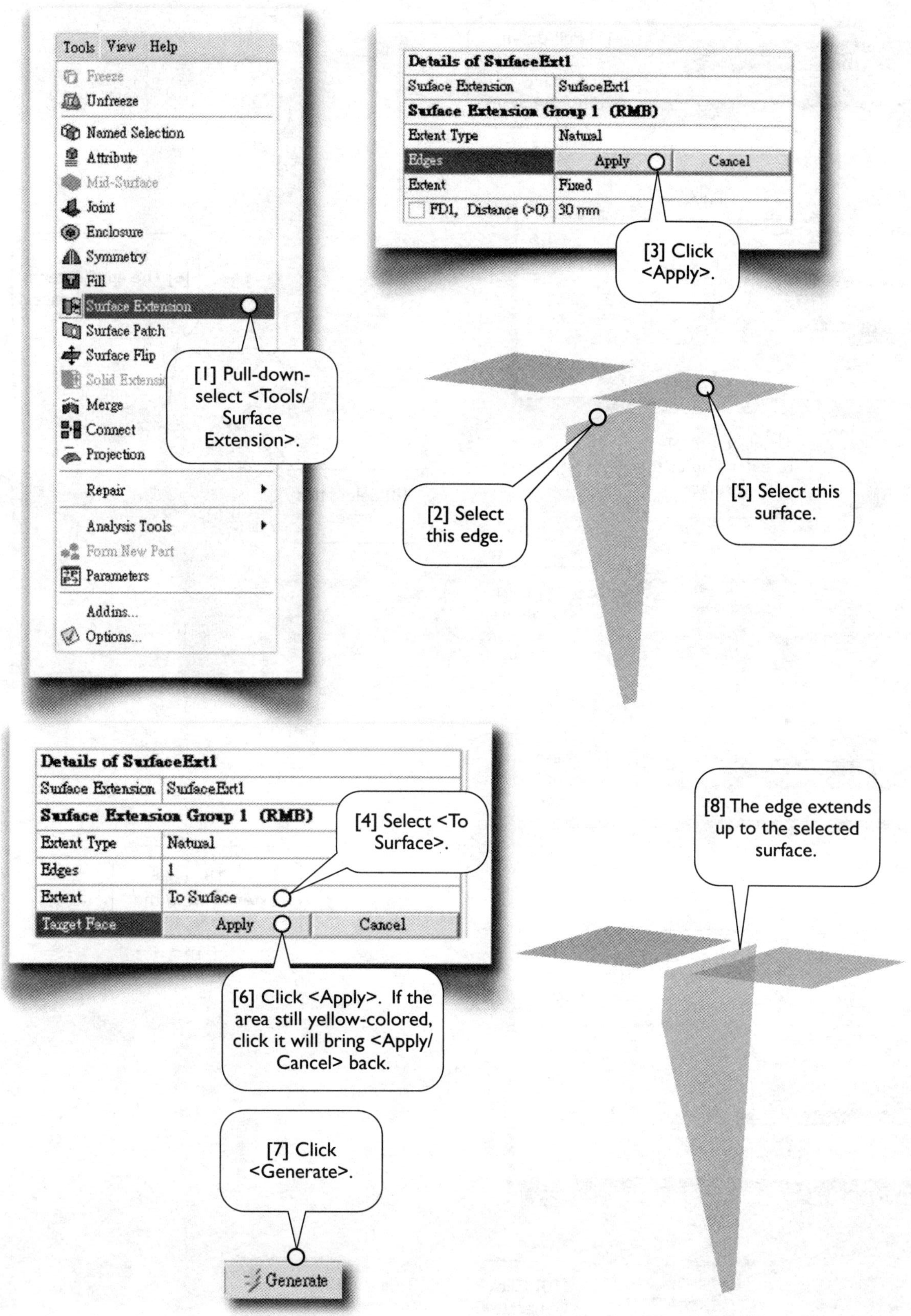

6.2-6 Extend the Flange

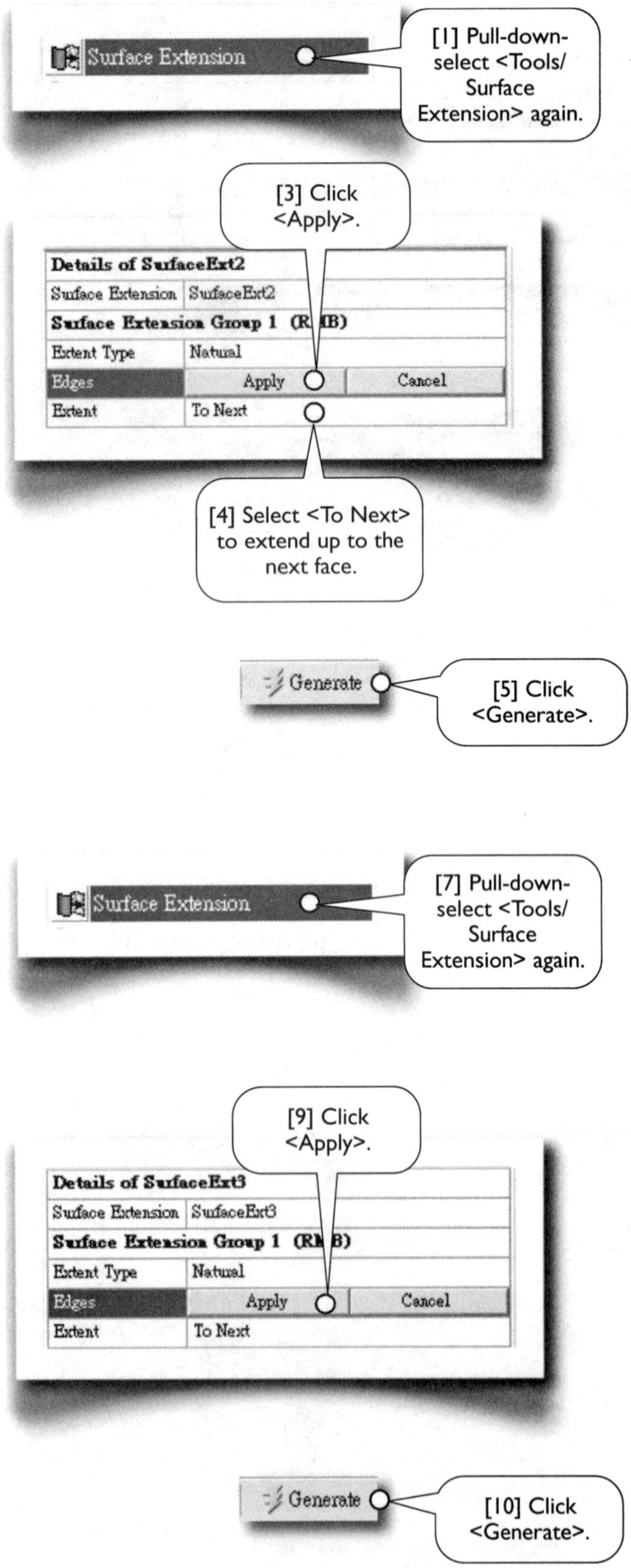

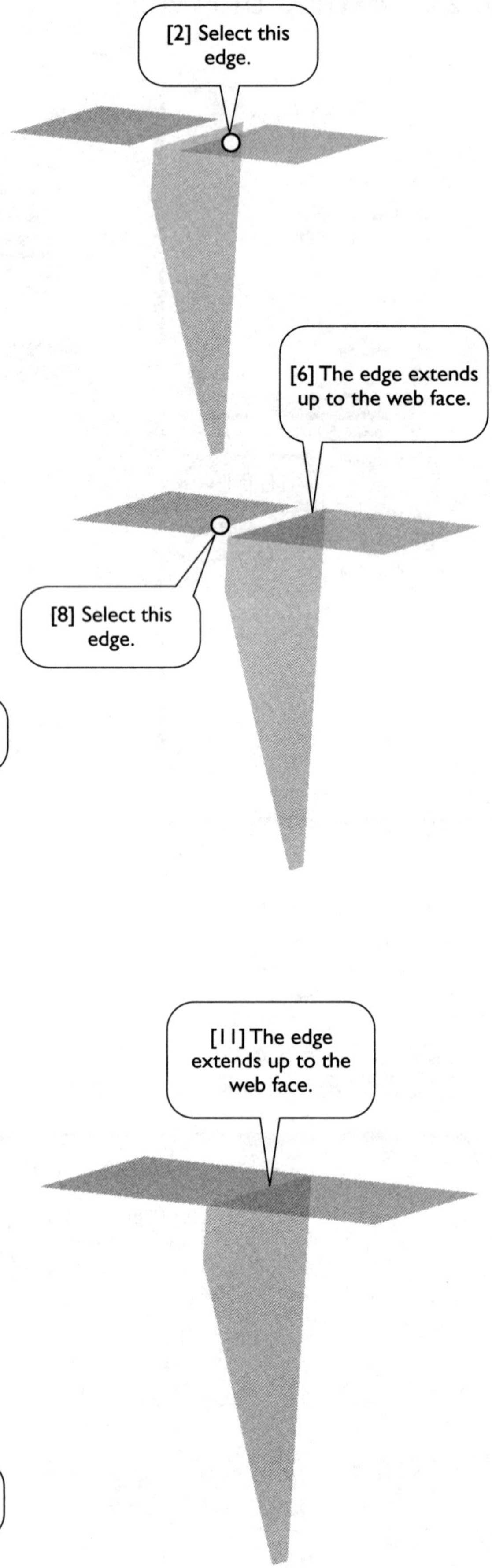

6.2-7 Form a Single Part

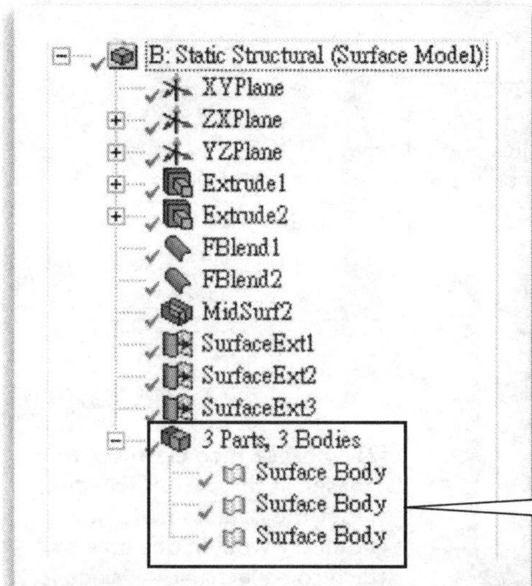

[1] Look at the model tree. There are three parts. Each part has one surface body. As we mentioned in Section 4.4-5, each part would be meshed independently. Let's join these three bodies together to form a single part (called a multi-body part). The reason we do this is to insure that, when meshed, each boundary recognizes its neighbor, and a continuous mesh is obtained. Also note <Boolean> (4.3-9[1]) does not work for surface bodies, so we cannot join them by using the tool <Create/Boolean>.

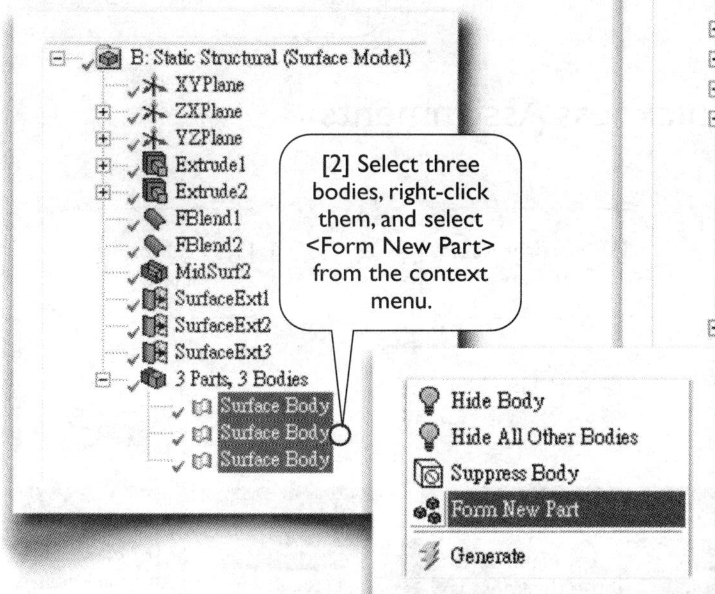

[2] Select three bodies, right-click them, and select <Form New Part> from the context menu.

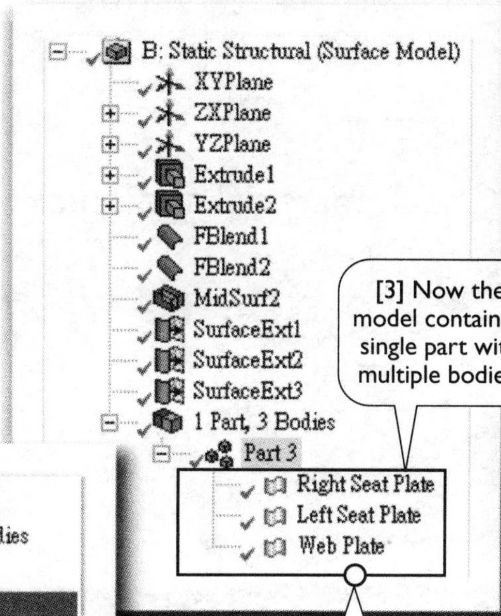

[3] Now the model contains a single part with multiple bodies.

[4] Right-click each body to rename it.

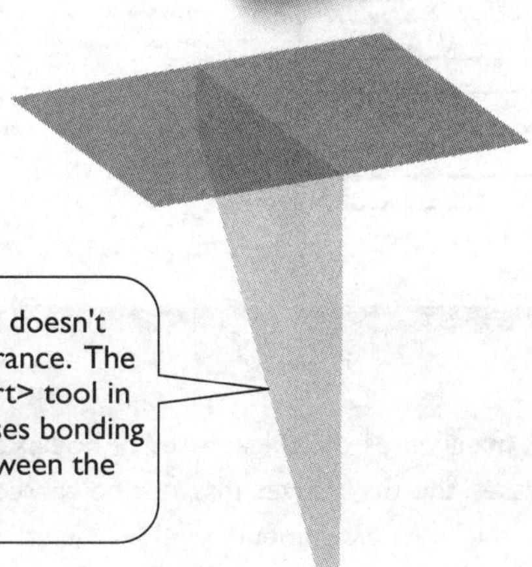

[5] The model doesn't change in appearance. The <Form New Part> tool in effect only imposes bonding conditions between the parts.

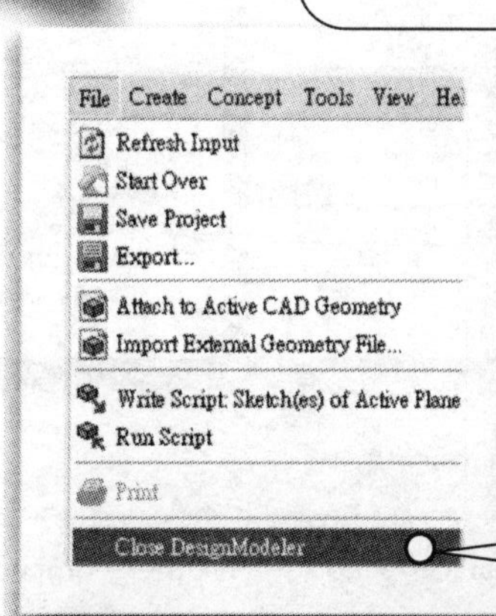

[6] Close DesignModeler.

PART B. SIMULATION

6.2-8 Start Up <Mechanical>

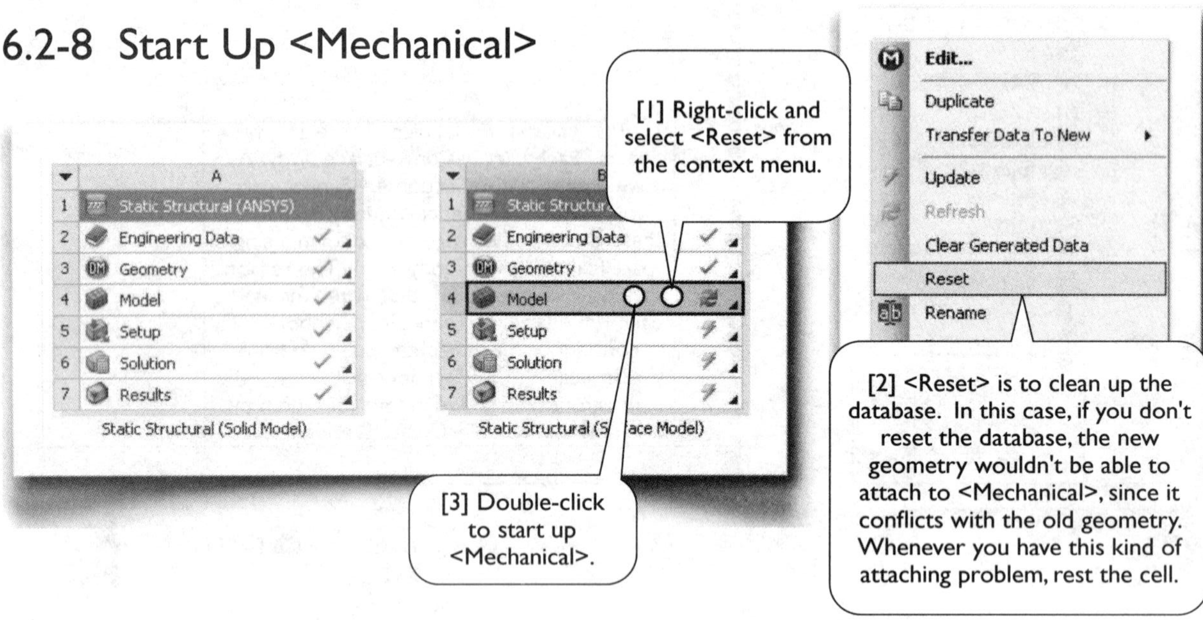

6.2-9 Check Material and Thickness Assignments

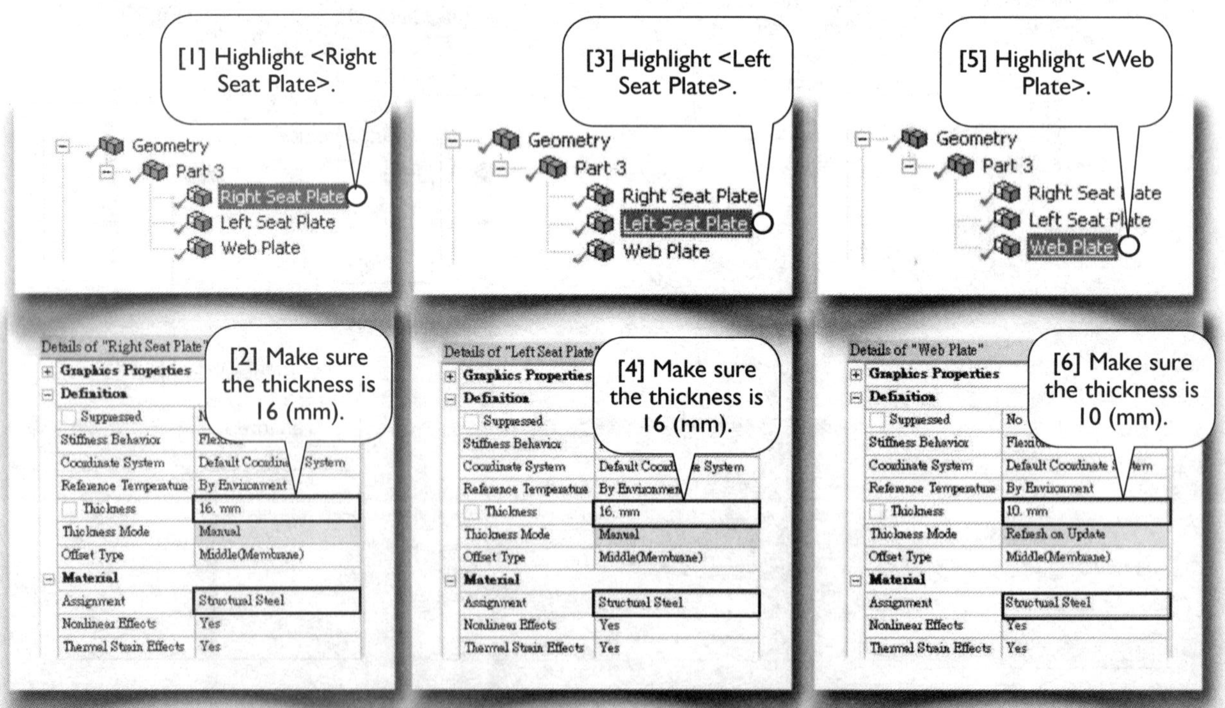

Thickness Assignment

The surface bodies are created using <Mid-Surface> tool. In many cases the thicknesses of bodies are calculated and transferred to <Mechanical>. For some other complicated cases, the thicknesses may not be correctly calculated and transferred. It is a good practice to always check material and thickness assignments in <Mechanical>.

6.2-10 Specify Support

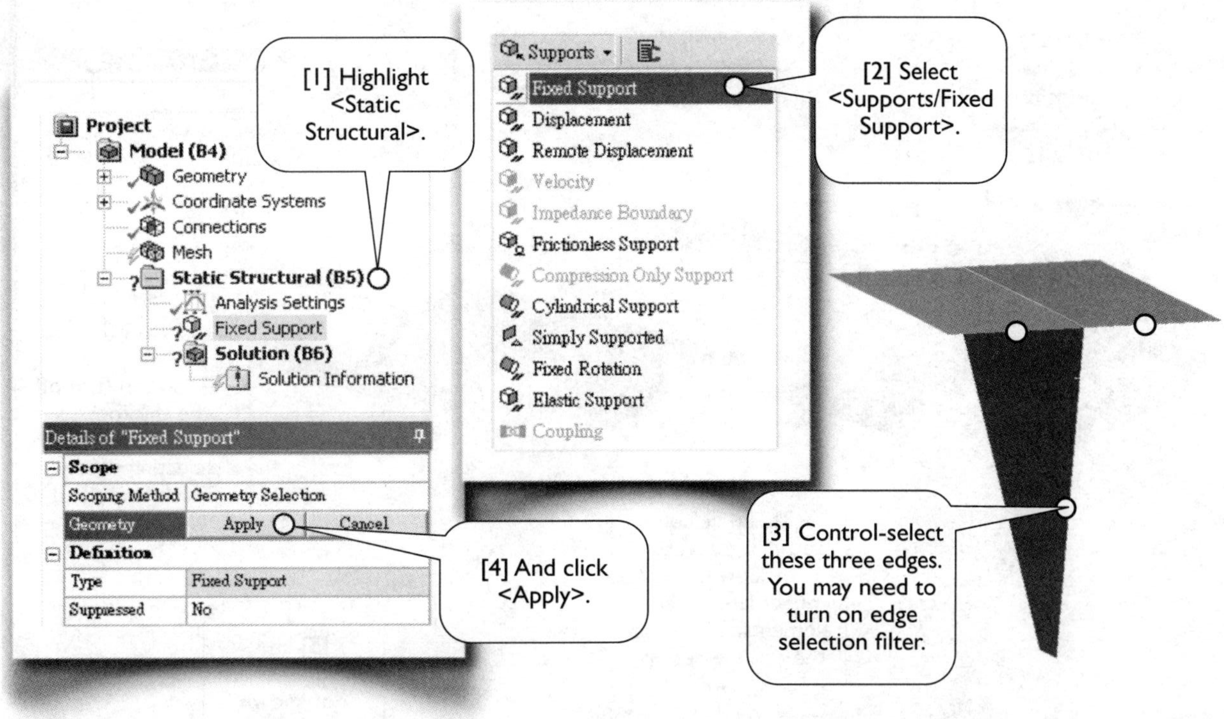

6.2-11 Apply Force

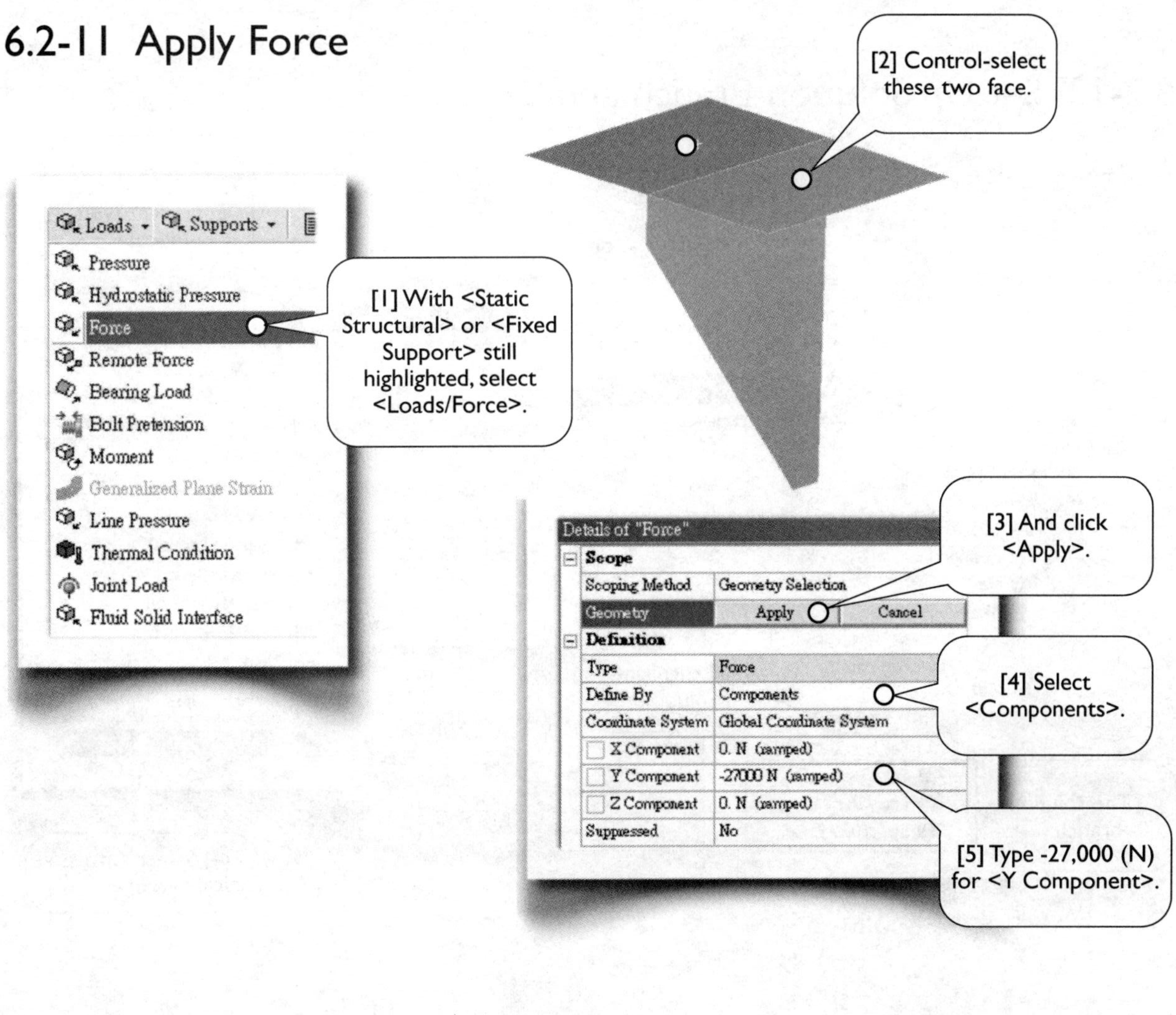

6.2-12 Generate Mesh

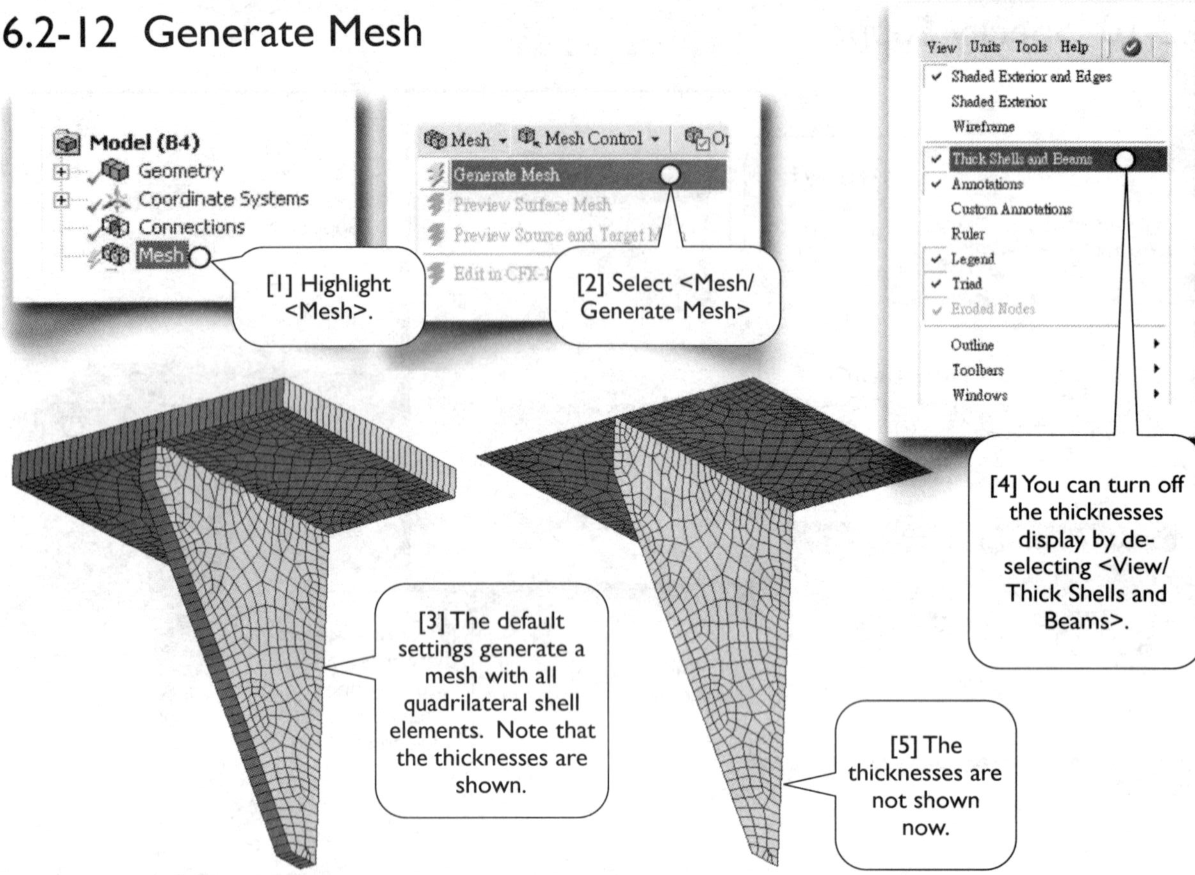

6.2-13 Set Up Solution Branch and Solve

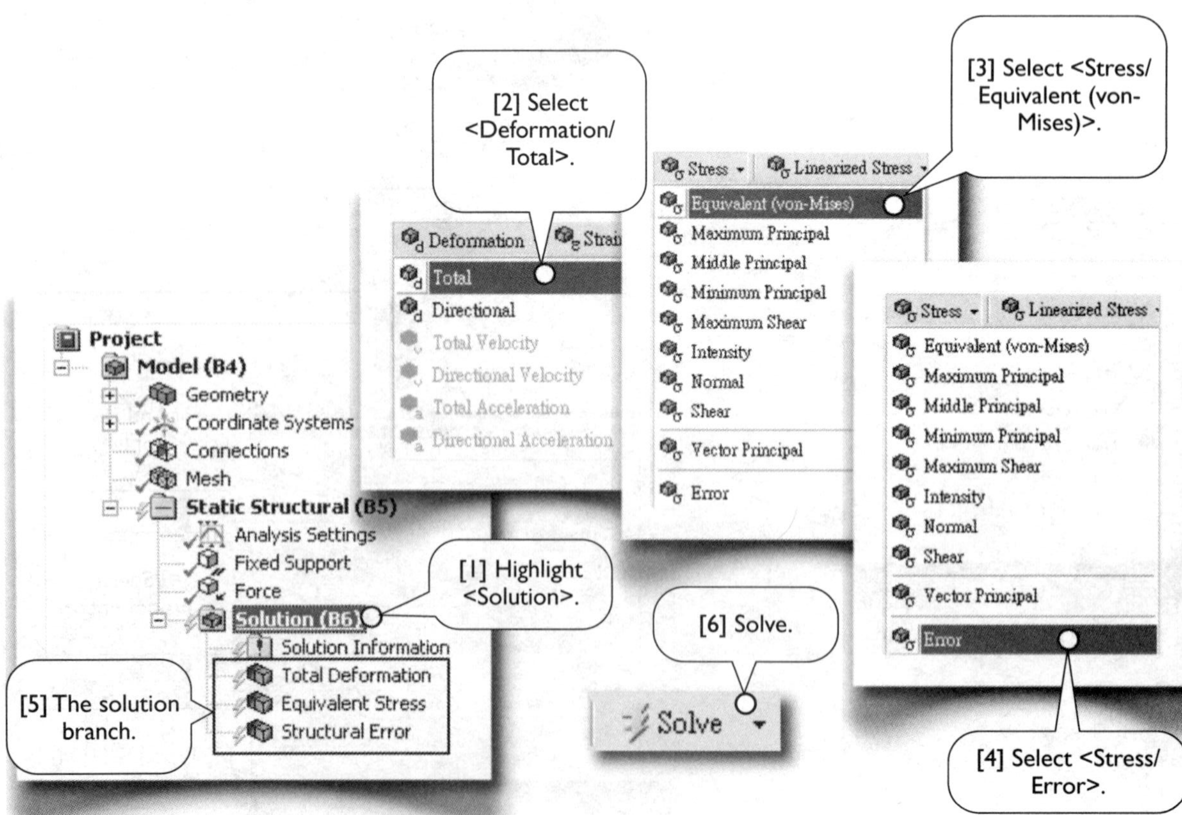

6.2-14 View the Results

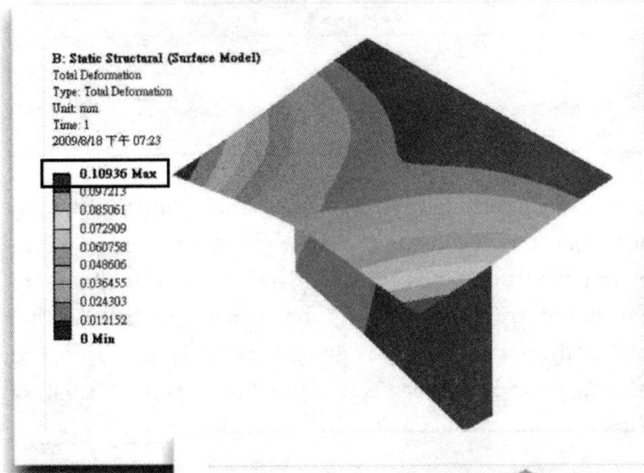

Surface Model versus Solid Model

The results are quite comparable to the results we obtained at the end of Section 5.1 (5.1-12[23, 24]). The surface model in this section consist of about 1,000 nodes while the solid model in Section 5.1-12 consists of 6,500 nodes! In general, before resorting to a solid modeling, consider a surface/line modeling first.

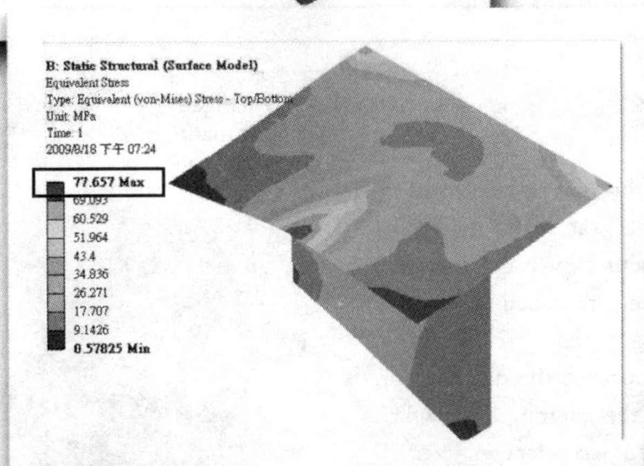

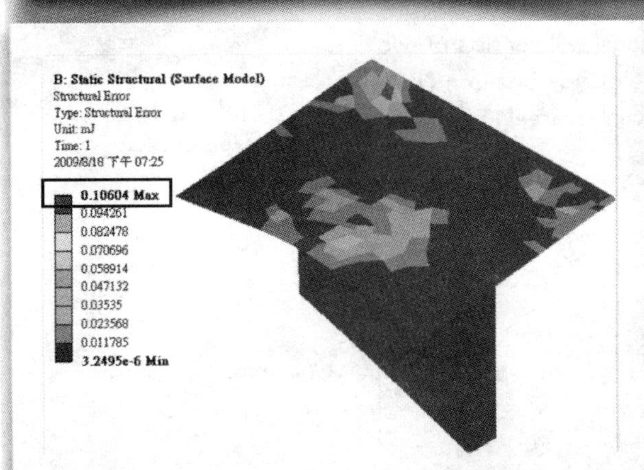

Wrap Up

Save the project and quit <Workbench>.

Section 6.3

Exercise: Gearbox

In DesignModeler, surface bodies are often created using four distinct techniques: (a) Create a 2D sketch and apply <Concept/Surface From Sketches> to create a planar surface body; this technique is demonstrated in Section 4.3 to create the planar glass. (b) Sketch lines or curves and then use <Extrude>, <Revolve>, <Sweep>, or <Skin/Loft> to create either planar or non-planar surfaces; this technique is demonstrated in Section 6.1 to create the bellows. (c) Apply <Tool/Mid-Surface> to extract mid-surface from a solid body; this technique is demonstrated in Section 6.2 to create a surface model for the beam bracket. (d) Use <Thin/Surface> tool; the idea is to extract the exterior "shell" of a solid body. We will demonstrate this technique in this Section.

6.3-1 About the Gearbox

Gears are used to transmit power. During the power transmission, gears exert forces on each other. Through the gear shafts, the forces eventually reach the bearing supports. A structure must exist to hold up the bearing forces. The gearbox in this case is designed to serve as a structural component to hold up the bearing forces.

Engineers' concern is the deformation, because the deformation of the gearbox may cause a displacement of the rotating axes, which may reach a point where the transmission becomes defective.

In this section, we will create a 3D model for the gearbox and conduct a simulation using the model. The model will consists of two solid bodies for the flange and the base, made of gray cast iron [1-2], and a surface body for the housing, made of stainless steel [3].

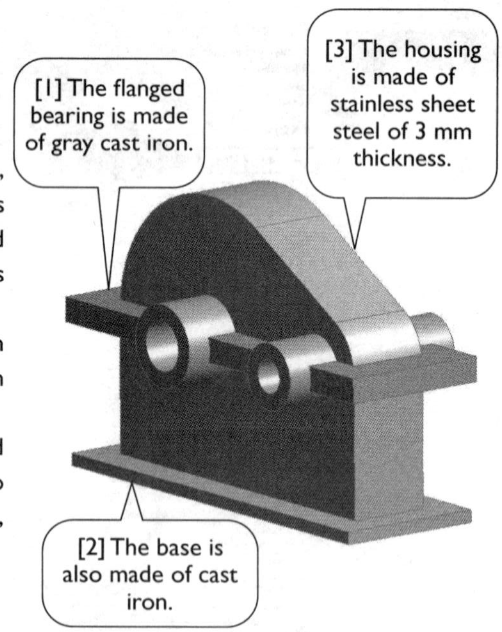

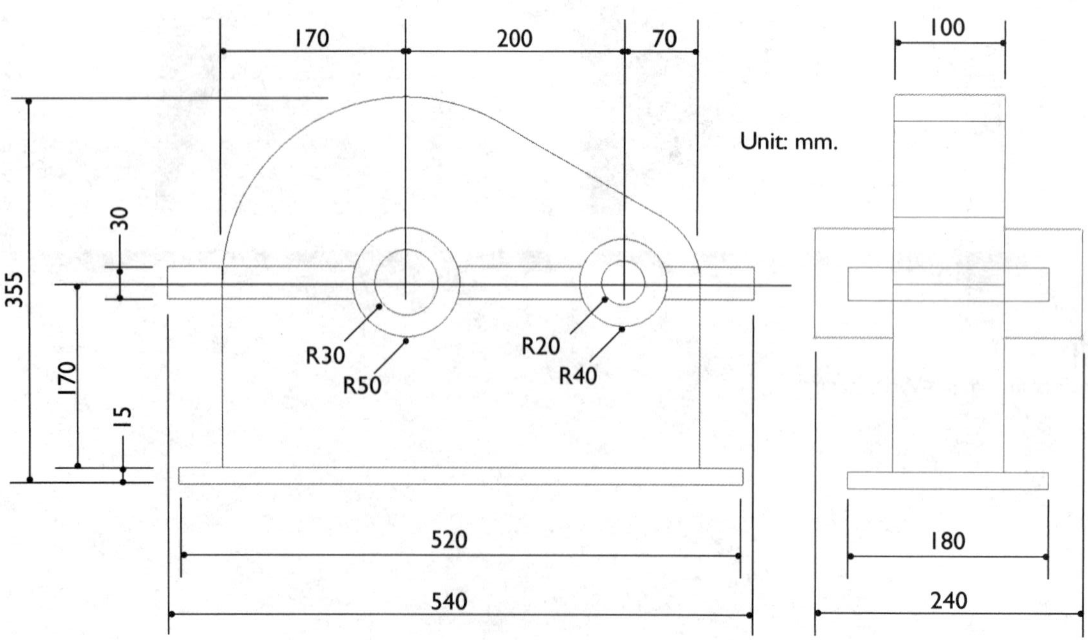

PART A. GEOMETRIC MODELING

6.3-2 Start Up

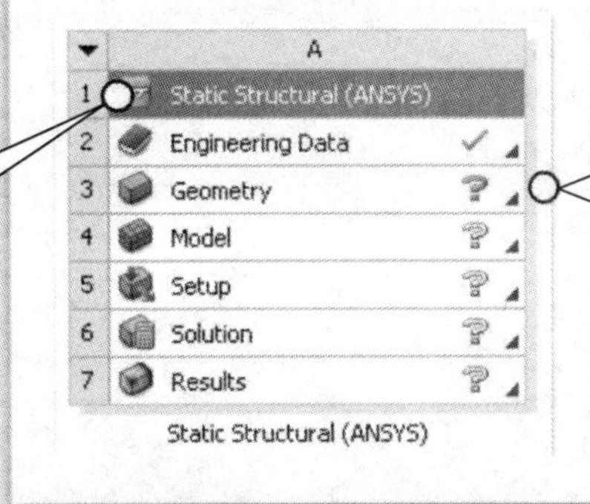

[1] Launch <Workbench>. Create a <Static Structural> system. Save the project as "Gearbox."

[2] Start up DesignModeler. Select <Millimeter> as length unit.

6.3-3 Create the Housing

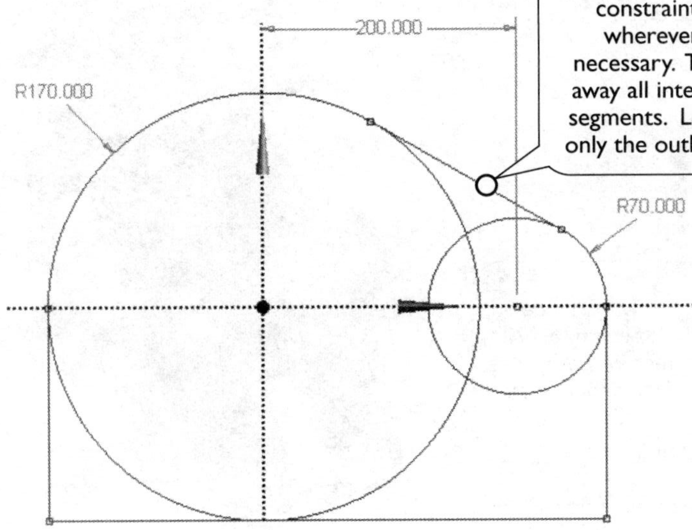

[1] Create a sketch on XYPlane. Impose <Tangent> constraints wherever necessary. Trim away all internal segments. Leave only the outlines.

Details of Extrude1	
Extrude	Extrude1
Base Object	Sketch1
Operation	Add Material
Direction Vector	None (Normal)
Direction	Both - Symmetric
Extent Type	Fixed
FD1, Depth (>0)	50 mm
As Thin/Surface?	No
Merge Topology?	Yes

[2] Extrude the sketch 50 mm for both directions.

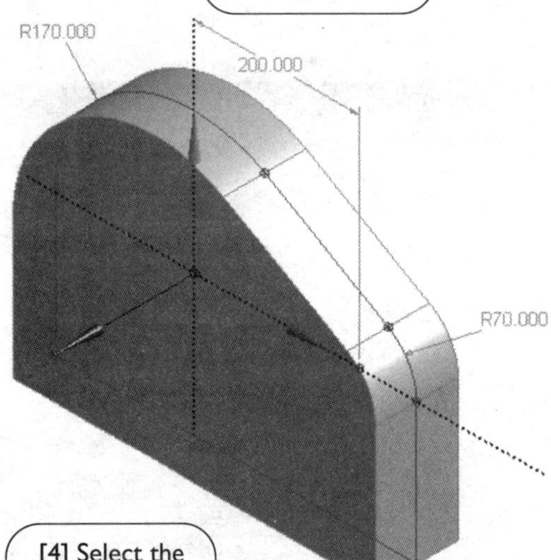

[3] Click <Thin/Surface> on the toolbar.

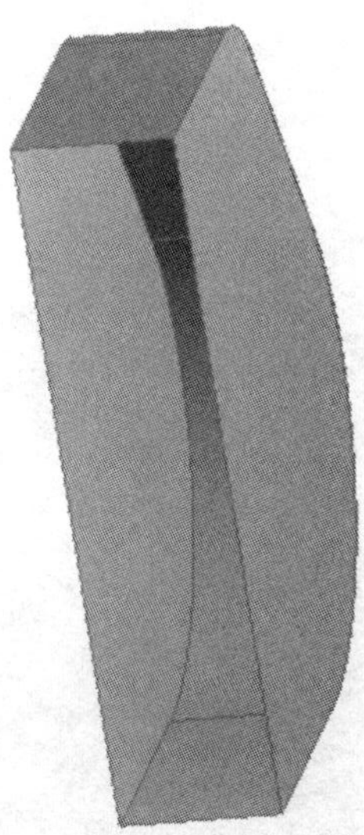

[4] Select the bottom face of the newly created solid body.

Details of Thin1	
Thin/Surface	Thin1
Selection Type	Faces to Remove
Geometry	1 Face
Direction	Inward
FD1, Thickness (>=0)	0 mm
FD2, Face Offset (>=0)	0 mm

[5] To create a surface body, you must type a zero value for the thickness. If you type a nonzero value, it would create a "thin solid body" instead of a surface body. Remember to click <Generate>.

6.3-4 Create the Bearings

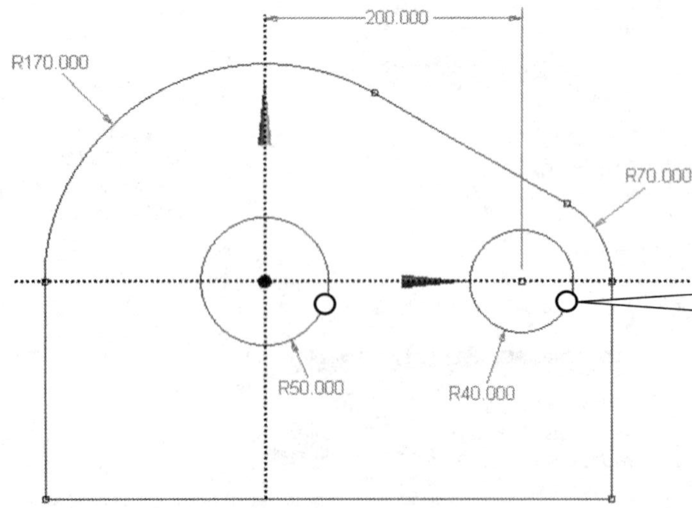

[1] Create a new sketch <Sketch2> on XYPlane. Draw two circles on <Sketch2>. Specify dimensions.

Details of Extrude2	
Extrude	Extrude2
Base Object	Sketch2
Operation	Add Material
Direction Vector	None (Normal)
Direction	Both - Symmetric
Extent Type	Fixed
FD1, Depth (>0)	120 mm
As Thin/Surface?	No
Merge Topology?	Yes

[2] Extrude <Sketch2> 120 mm for both sides. Remember to click <Generate>.

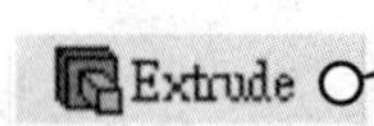

[3] Click <Extrude> again.

[4] <Sketch2> is automatically selected.

Details of Extrude3	
Extrude	Extrude3
Base Object	Sketch2
Operation	Cut Material
Direction Vector	None (Normal)
Direction	Both - Symmetric
Extent Type	Fixed
FD1, Depth (>0)	50 mm
As Thin/Surface?	No
Target Bodies	All Bodies
Merge Topology?	Yes

[5] Cut Material.

[6] Extrude 50 mm for both sides. Remember to click <Generate>.

6.3-5 Create the Flange

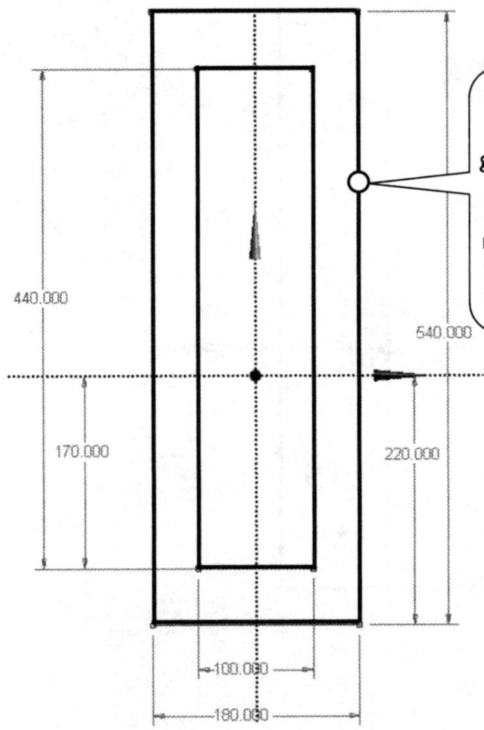

[1] Create a sketch on ZXPlane. Note the global Z- and X-axes are now horizontal and vertical axes respectively. Remember to impose <Symmetry> constraints.

Details View	
Details of Extrude4	
Extrude	Extrude4
Base Object	Sketch3
Operation	Add Material
Direction Vector	None (Normal)
Direction	Both - Symmetric
Extent Type	Fixed
FD1, Depth (>0)	15 mm
As Thin/Surface?	No
Merge Topology?	Yes

[2] Extrude 15 mm for both sides. Click <Generate>.

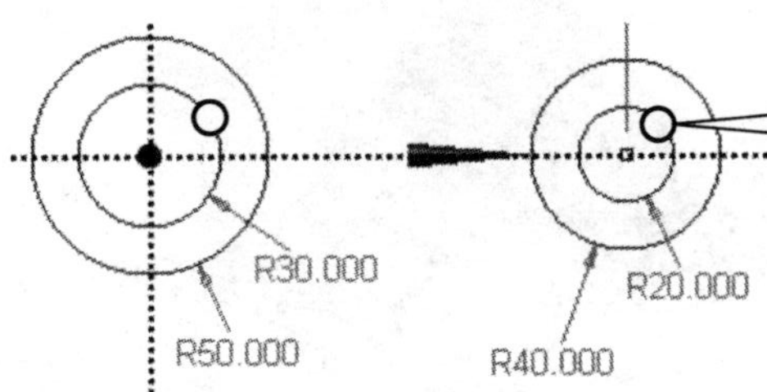

[3] Create a new sketch <Sketch4> on XYPlane. Draw two smaller circles on <Sketch>.

Details of Extrude5	
Extrude	Extrude5
Base Object	Sketch4
Operation	Cut Material
Direction Vector	None (Normal)
Direction	Both - Symmetric
Extent Type	Through All
As Thin/Surface?	No
Target Bodies	All Bodies
Merge Topology?	Yes

[4] Extrude to cut all material through. Click <Generate>.

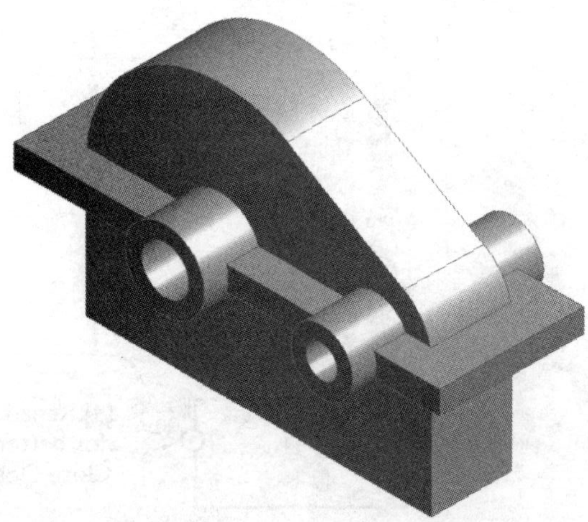

6.3-6 Create the Base

[1] Create a new plane by offsetting ZXPlane 170 mm downward. Click <Generate>.

Details of Plane4	
Plane	Plane4
Sketches	0
Type	From Plane
Base Plane	ZXPlane
Transform 1 (RMB)	Offset Z
FD1, Value 1	-170 mm
Transform 2 (RMB)	None
Reverse Normal/Z-Axis?	No
Flip XY-Axes?	No
Export Coordinate System?	No

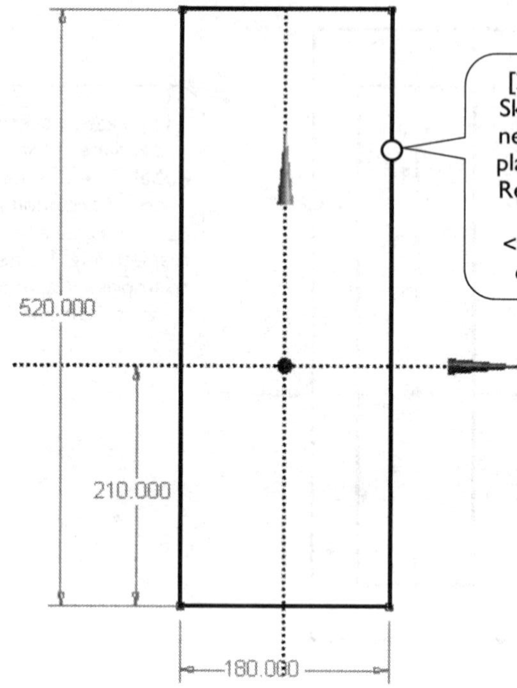

[2] Create a Sketch on the newly created plane (Plane4). Remember to impose <Symmetry> constraint.

Details of Extrude6	
Extrude	Extrude6
Base Object	Sketch5
Operation	Add Material
Direction Vector	None (Normal)
Direction	Reversed
Extent Type	Fixed
FD1, Depth (>0)	15 mm
As Thin/Surface?	No
Merge Topology?	Yes

[3] Extrude 15 mm downward to create the base. Click <Generate>.

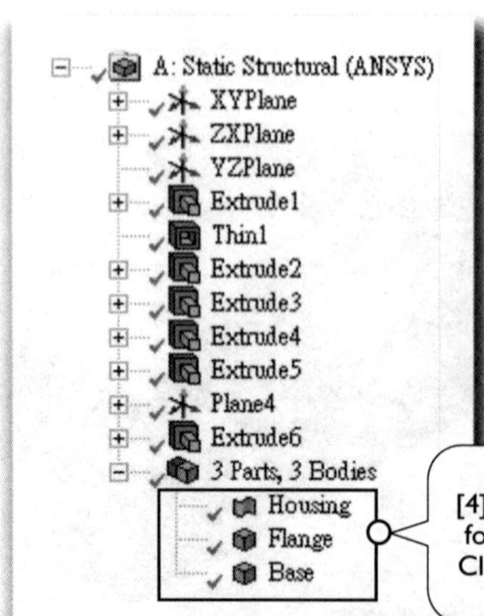

[4] Rename each body for better readability. Close DesignModeler.

PART B. SIMULATION

6.3-7 Bearing Loads

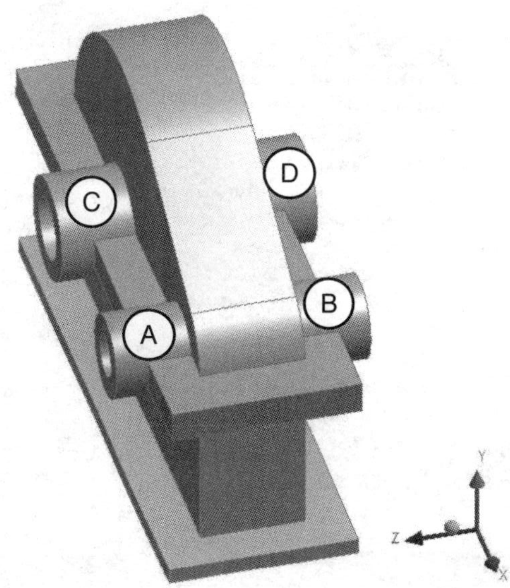

The bearing loads can be calculated according to the transmitted power, which is 175 hp in this case. Skipping the detail calculations (they are not the emphasis here; if you are interested in the detail calculation, please refer to the Zahavi's book[1]), we summarize the bearing loads as follows. Note that these forces sum up to zero.

Bearing	F_X (N)	F_Y (N)	F_Z (N)
A	16000	30000	16000
B	6000	30000	0
C	3000	-30000	0
D	-25000	-30000	-16000

Bearing Loads

In <Mechanical>, a bearing load of any direction can be specified on a cylindrical surface. However it is important to note that the load is distributed on compressive side using projected area. This implies that axial components (here, the Z-components) will disappear. In our case, the X- and Y-components of the bearing loads can be specified normally, but the Z-components cannot be specified as bearing load components. They are specified separately as surface forces.

6.3-8 Prepare Material Properties

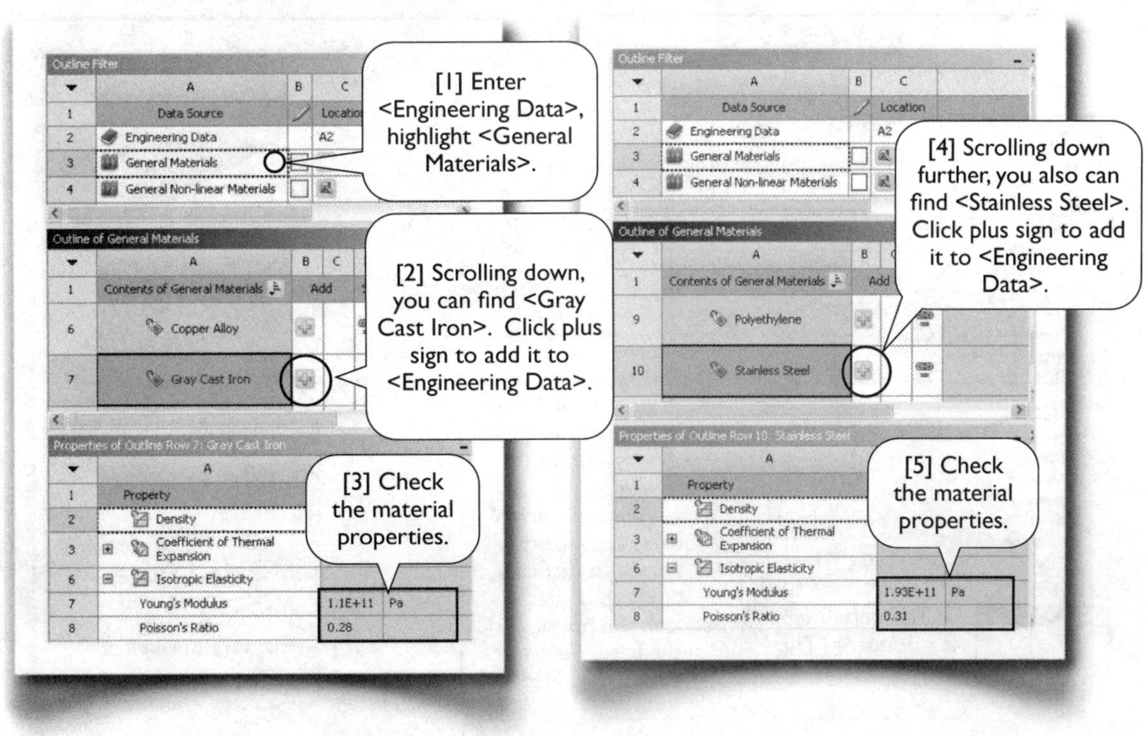

6.3-9 Assign Material and Thickness

Return to project. Start up <Mechanical>. Assign material and thickness for each body [1-4].

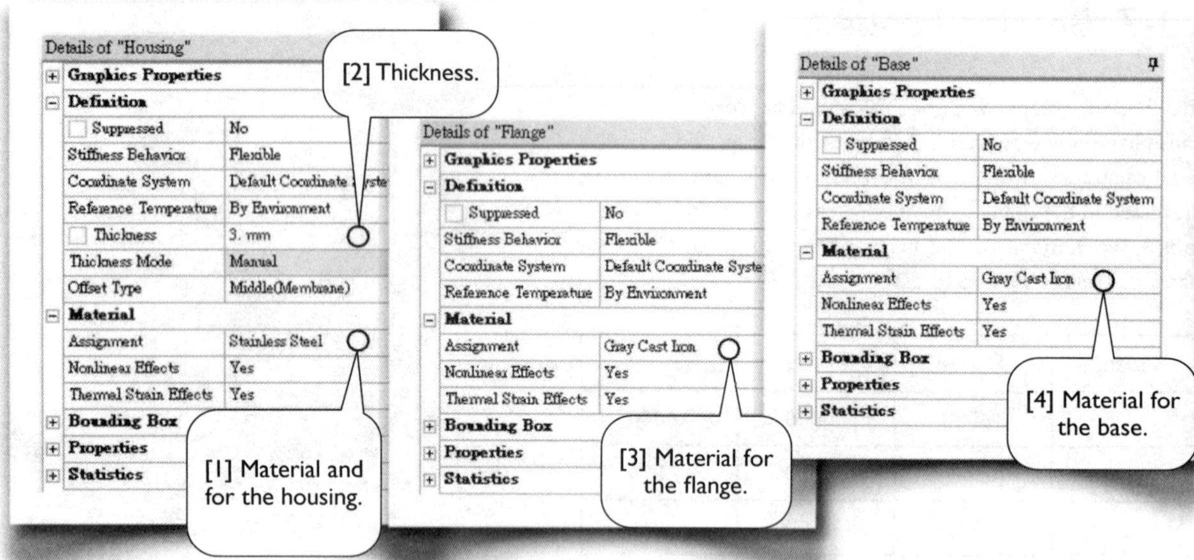

6.3-10 Set Up Connections between Parts

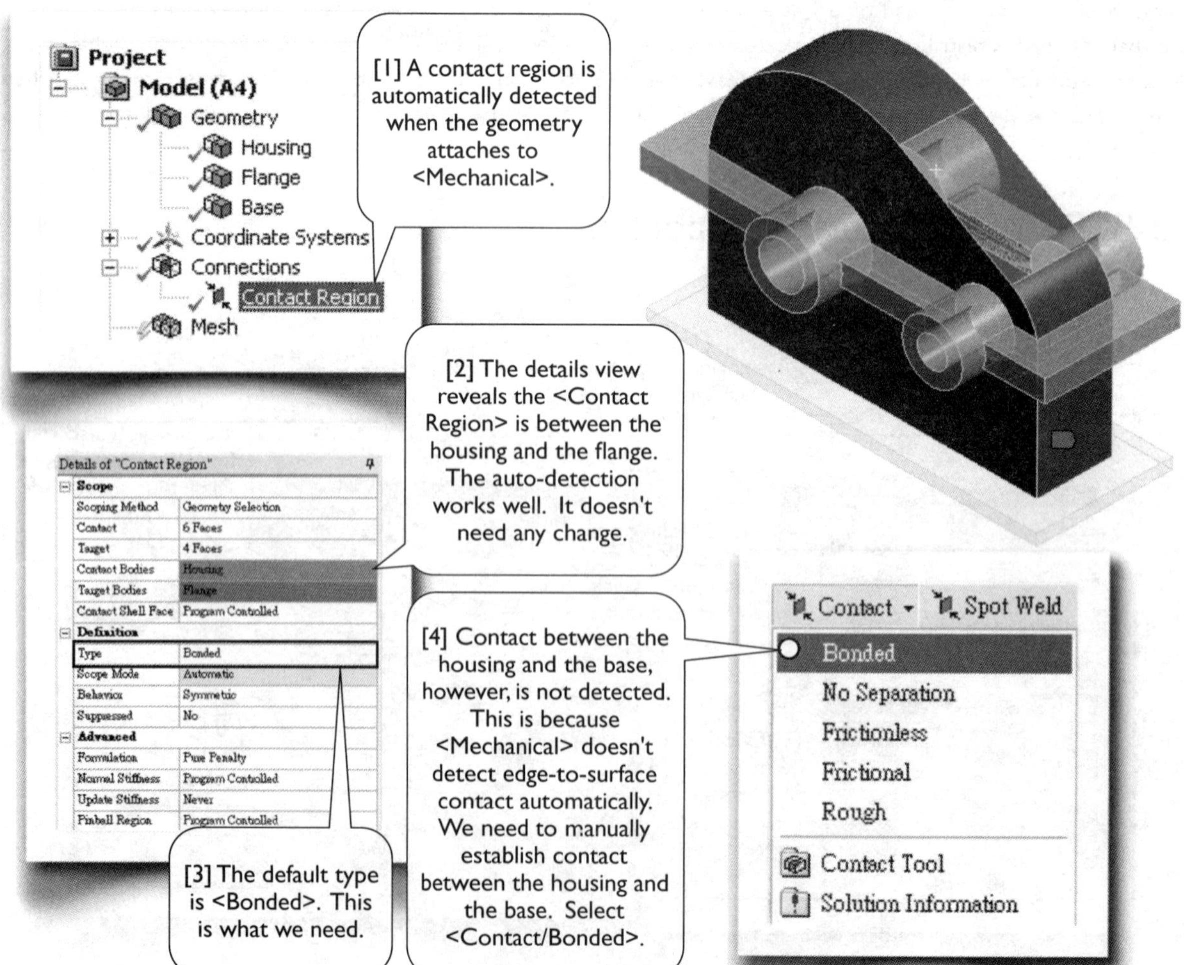

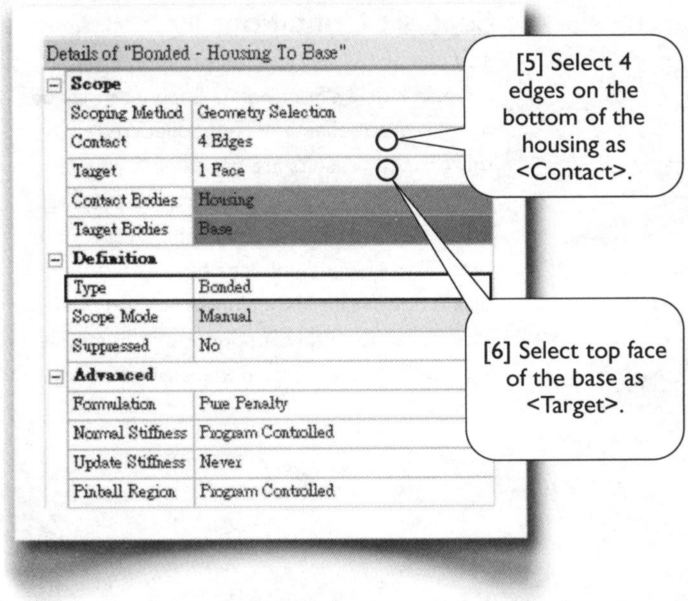

Details of "Bonded - Housing To Base"

Scope	
Scoping Method	Geometry Selection
Contact	4 Edges
Target	1 Face
Contact Bodies	Housing
Target Bodies	Base
Definition	
Type	Bonded
Scope Mode	Manual
Suppressed	No
Advanced	
Formulation	Pure Penalty
Normal Stiffness	Program Controlled
Update Stiffness	Never
Pinball Region	Program Controlled

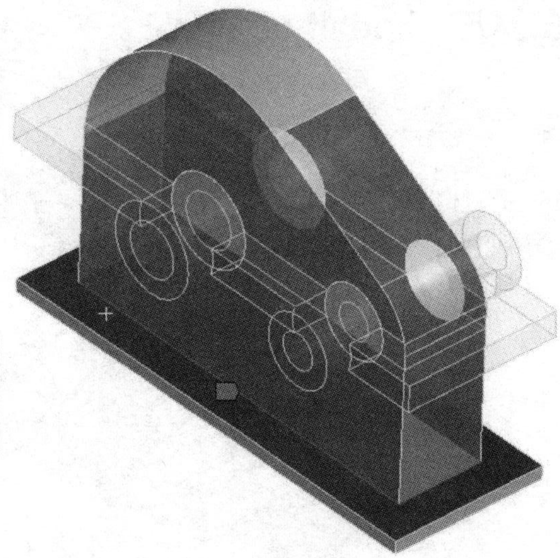

Do Contacts Imply Nonlinearity?

No. It depends on the type of contacts. In this case, the <Bonded> contacts do not introduce any nonlinearities. For details, see Section 13.1-8.

6.3-11 Set Up Mesh Controls

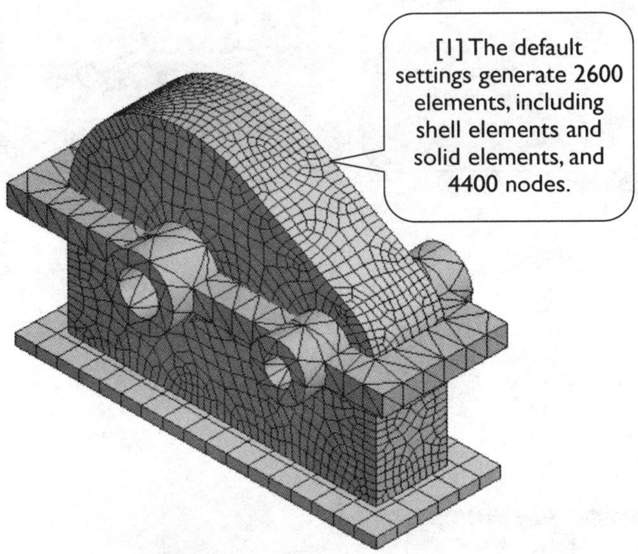

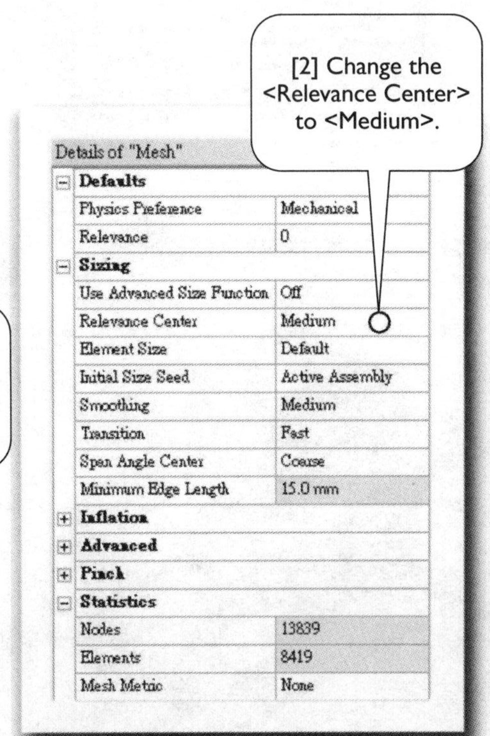

Details of "Mesh"

Defaults	
Physics Preference	Mechanical
Relevance	0
Sizing	
Use Advanced Size Function	Off
Relevance Center	Medium
Element Size	Default
Initial Size Seed	Active Assembly
Smoothing	Medium
Transition	Fast
Span Angle Center	Coarse
Minimum Edge Length	15.0 mm
Inflation	
Advanced	
Pinch	
Statistics	
Nodes	13839
Elements	8419
Mesh Metric	None

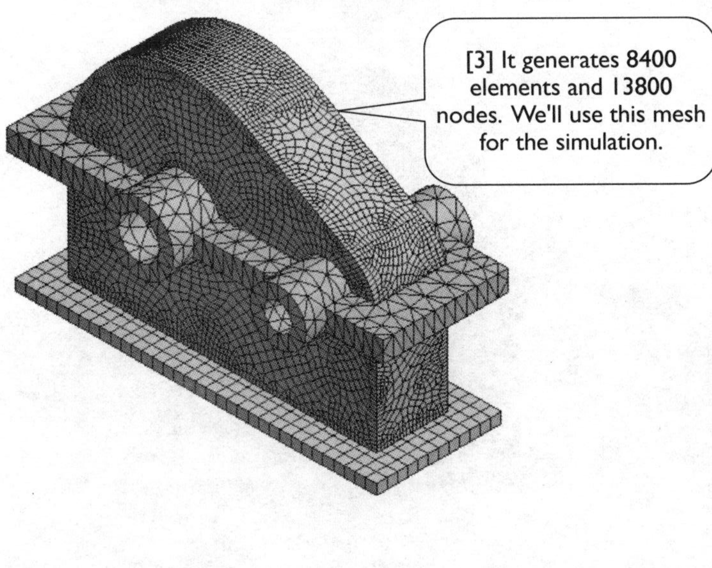

6.3-12 Specify Support

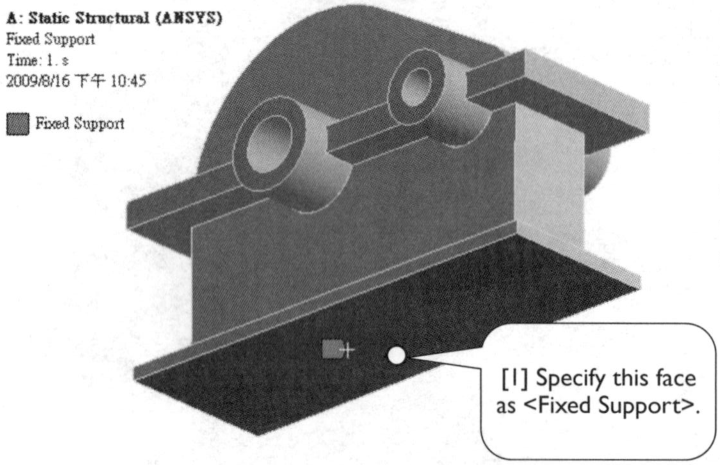

Support Conditions

You may think that a <Compression Only Support> or a <Frictionless Support> may be more realistic than a <Fixed Supported>. In this case, the results are the same for these three support conditions. Since the external forces sum up to zero, the support reaction is zero. The <Fixed Support> has an advantage that it doesn't introduce nonlinearities, while <Compression Only Support> or <Frictionless Support> do introduce nonlinearities.

6.3-13 Apply Bearing Loads

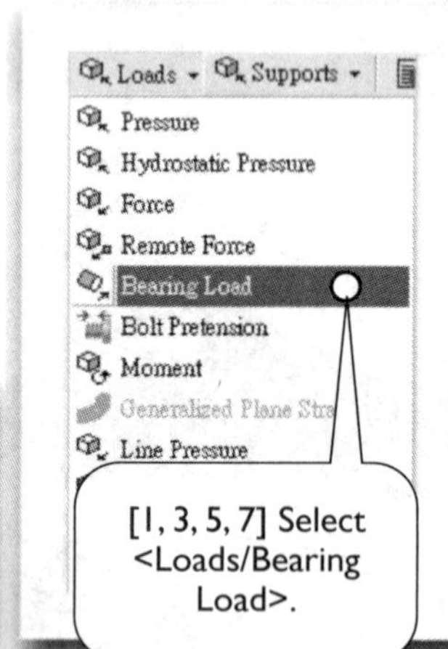

[2] Apply a bearing load on the internal cylindrical surface of bearing A.

Details of "Bearing Load A"

Scope	
Scoping Method	Geometry Selection
Geometry	1 Face
Definition	
Type	Bearing Load
Define By	Components
Coordinate System	Global Coordinate System
X Component	16000 N
Y Component	30000 N
Z Component	0. N
Suppressed	No

[4] Apply a bearing load on the internal cylindrical surface of bearing B.

Details of "Bearing Load B"

Scope	
Scoping Method	Geometry Selection
Geometry	1 Face
Definition	
Type	Bearing Load
Define By	Components
Coordinate System	Global Coordinate System
X Component	6000. N
Y Component	30000 N
Z Component	0. N
Suppressed	No

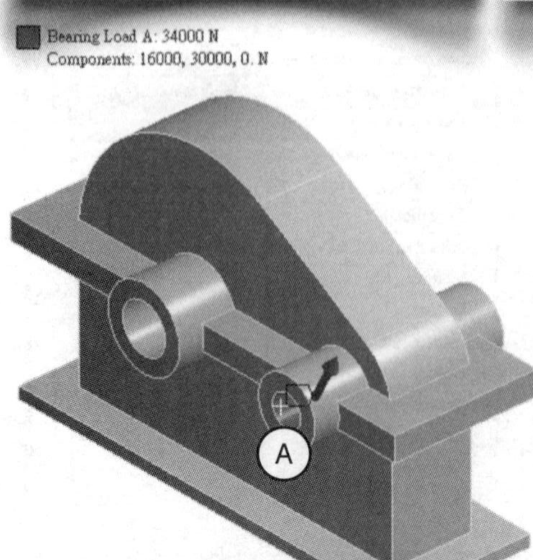

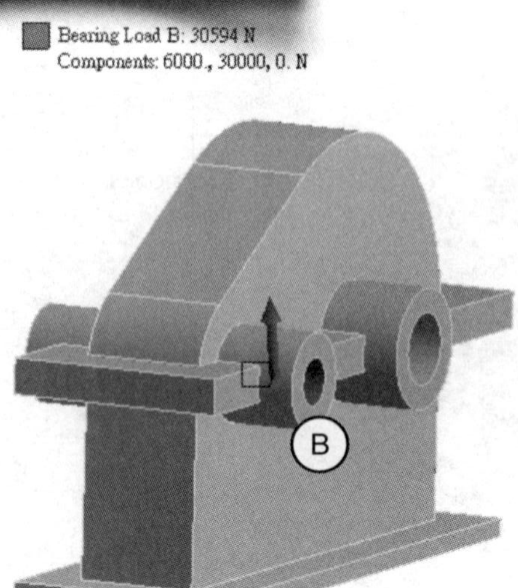

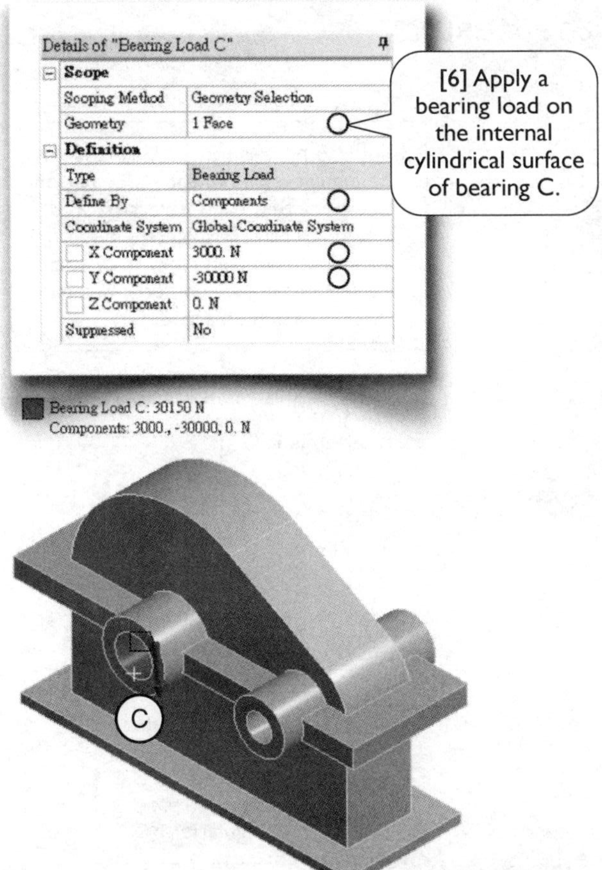

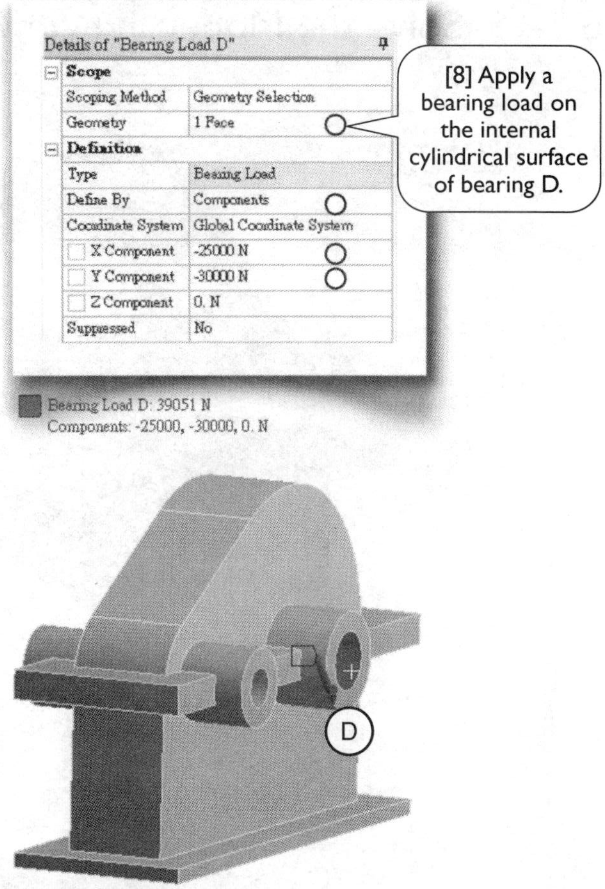

6.3-14 Apply Axial Loads

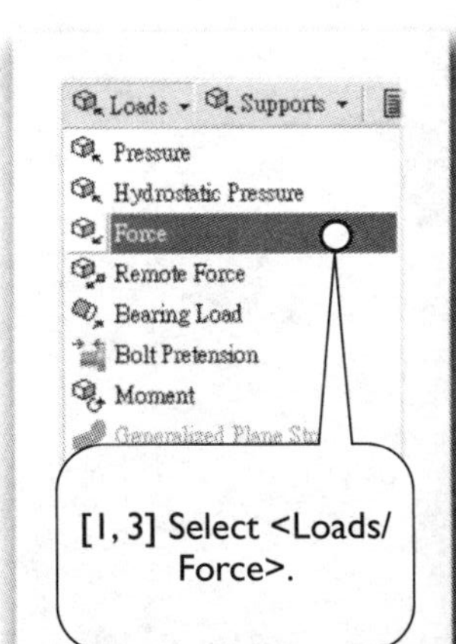

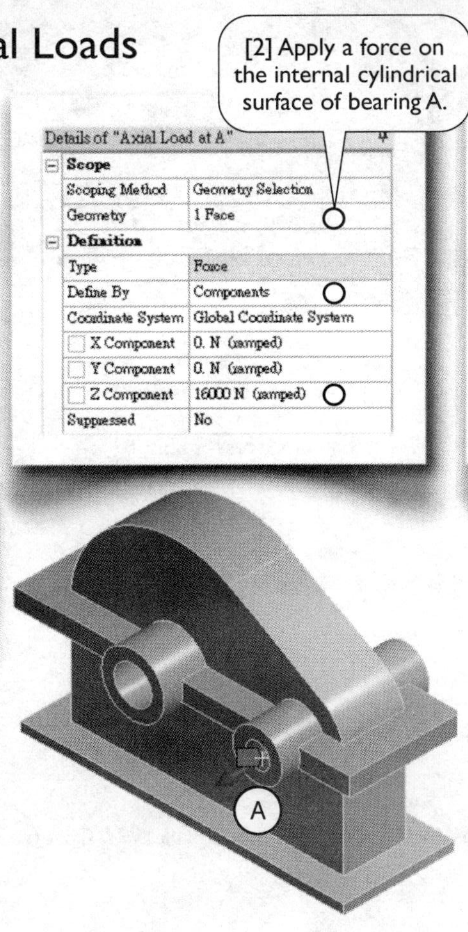

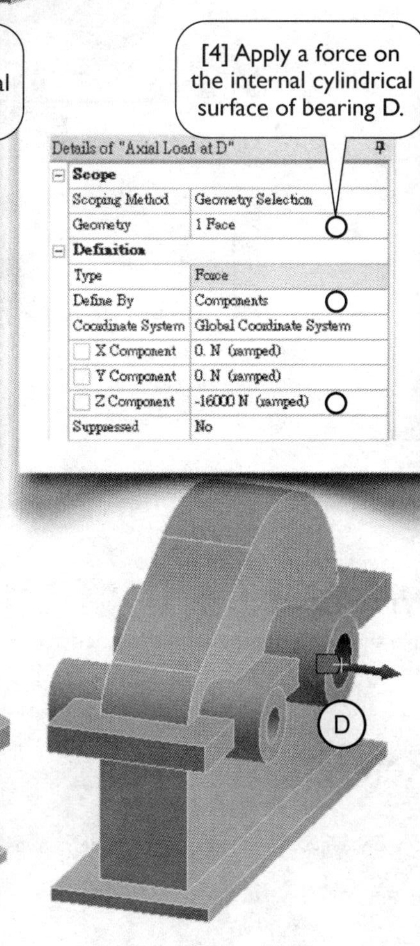

6.3-15 Solve the Model and View the Results

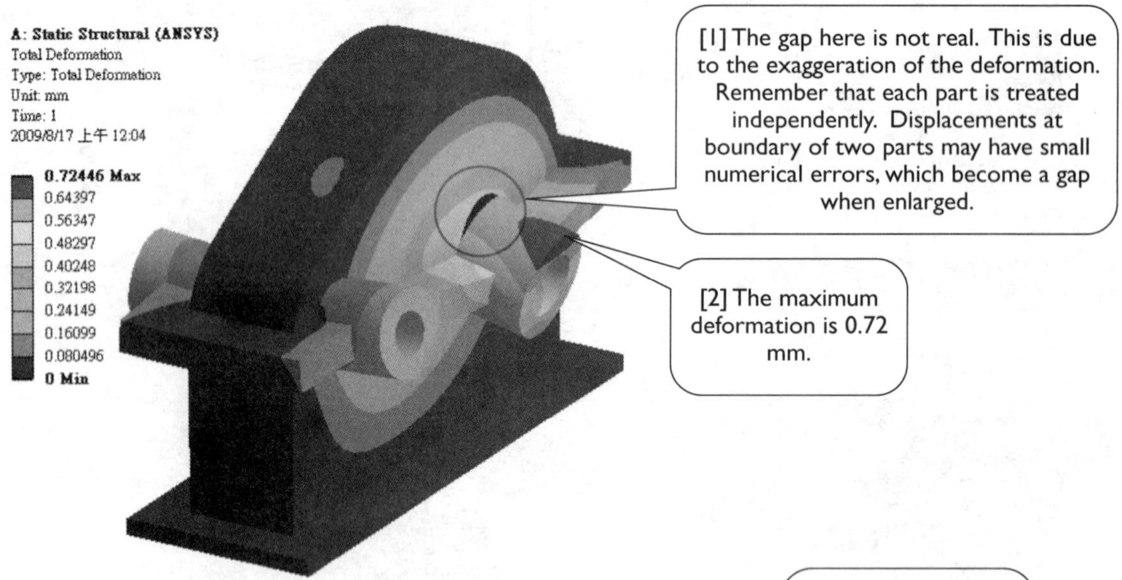

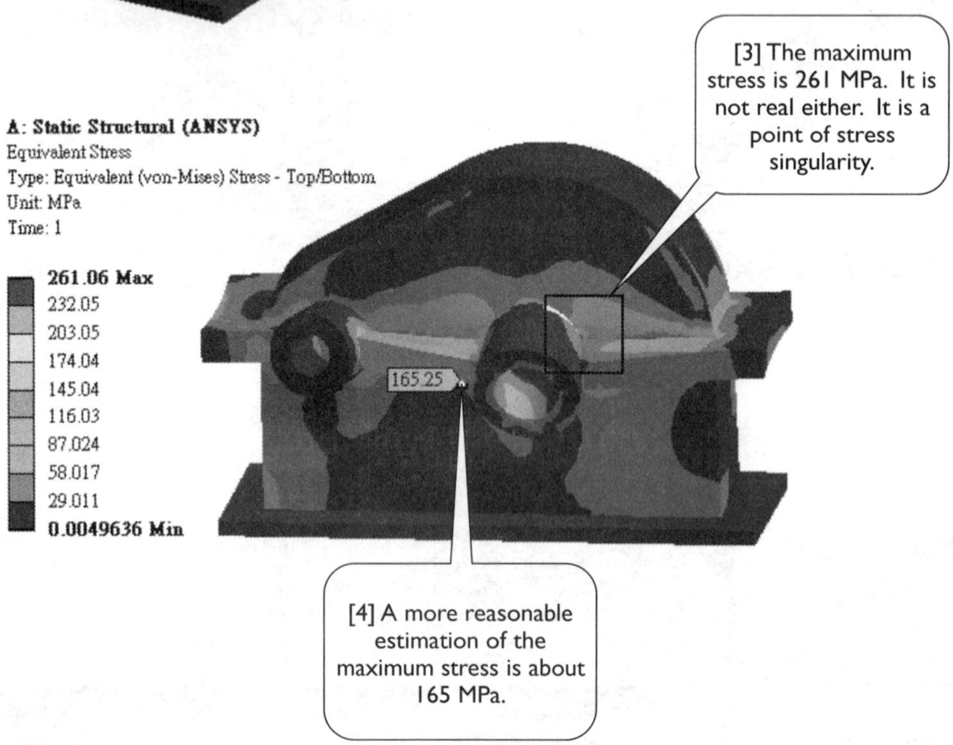

Wrap Up

Save the project and quit <Workbench>.

Reference

1. Zahavi, E., *The Finite Element Method in Machine Design*, Prentice-Hall, 1992; Chapter 10. Gear Box.

Section 6.4
Problems

6.4-1 Key Concepts

Shell Elements
A shell element is a planar (2D) element that can be arranged in the 3D space. It is used to mesh a body when one of its dimension are much smaller than the other two dimensions. Each node has 6 degrees of freedom: 3 translational and 3 rotational. Due to the present of rotational degrees of freedom, it is very efficient to model the problems dominated by the out-of-plane bending modes, contrasting to a solid element, which does not have rotational degrees of freedom.

Top/Bottom of Surface Body
Each surface body has a top side and a bottom side. When you select a surface body, only the top side is highlighted. Loads are applied on the top side. By default, results are reported on both sides.

Auto-Detection of Contacts
When a geometry attaches to <Mechanical>, it automatically detects and establishes possible contacts between parts, wherever the gaps between parts is less than a tolerance. The contact type is <Bonded> by default. The result of auto-detection may not be accurate and needs to be manually modified.

6.4-2 Questions

Surface Body versus Thin Solid Body
Q: In 6.3-3[5], you type a zero value for the thickness to create a surface body. If you type a nonzero value, it would create a "thin" solid body in stead of a surface body. What is the essential difference between a surface body and a thin solid body?

A: A surface body will be meshed with shell elements (1.3-3[7, 8]), while a thin solid body will be meshed with solid elements (1.3-3[1-4]).

Shell Elements versus Solid Elements
Q: What is the essential difference between shell elements and solid elements?

A: Besides the geometry, the shell elements have rotational degrees of freedom (1.3-3[7, 8]), while solid elements do not (1.3-3[1-4]).

Axisymmetric Bodies
In the beginning and the end of Section 6.1, we mentioned that we could model the bellows using axisymmetric 2D solid body or 2D line body. Show that you do understand the meaning of the statement.

Triangular Plate

Q: Can we perform a simulation with a 3D surface model for the triangular plate in Sections 3.1? If positive, is there any advantages of doing that over the 2D solid model?

A: Yes, we could, but there is no advantages of doing that. Remember that 3D surface bodies are meshed with shell elements. The essential difference between shell elements and 2D solid elements is that shell elements can have out-of-plane deformation (warpage) while 2D solid elements cannot. In the case of triangular plate, there is no out-of-plane deformation. There is no needs to use shell elements. The above discussions apply also on the spur gear of Section 3.4 and the filleted bar of Section 3.5.

6.4-3 Workbench Exercises

Exploring the Symmetries of the Bellows[1]

In the end of Section 6.1-15, we mentioned that there are at least three planes of symmetry we may exploit for a static structural simulation. In fact, there are infinite number of planes of symmetry: any planes passing through Z-axis are planes of symmetry. In 3D, however, we may use at most three planes of symmetry. In this exercise, you are asked to redo the static structural simulation, exploiting the symmetries to reduce the model. You can let Workbench automatically set up the boundary conditions on the symmetric planes (Section 3.1-10), or manually set them up yourself. How do you manually set up the rotational degrees of freedom on a plane of symmetry (see Section 7.1-12)? Also, after reducing the model by exploiting symmetries, refine the mesh and expect to obtain more accurate results.

Edge Joints[2]

In Section 6.2-7, we formed a single part by grouping three surface bodies to ensure the meshing continuity. Another way is using the <Edge Joints> feature. Edge joints are the glue that holds together bodies where a continuous mesh is desired. Edge joints can be created manually by pull-down-selecting <Tools/Joint>, and can be viewed by turning on <View/Edge Joints>. Explore this feature yourself.

Cover of Pressure Cylinder

Using <Mid-Surface> tool, transform the cover of pressure cylinder (Sections 4.2 and 5.2) to a surface model. Redo the simulation using the surface model.

References

1. ANSYS Help System>Mechanical>The Mechanical Application Approach>Special Analysis Topics>Using Symmetry
2. ANSYS Help System>DesignModeler>3D Modeling>Advanced Features and Tools>Joint

Chapter 7
Line Models

Many real-world objects can be modeled as line bodies. When a real-world body has small lateral dimension and has uniform cross-section, it is usually a good candidate for a line body. The most important applications of line models are frame, beam, and truss structures. The Workbench meshes a line body with beam elements (1.3-3[9]). Advantages of using line models against surface models or solid models are exactly analogous to the advantages of using surface models against solid models. These advantages include (a) creating line models is usually easier, (b) the problem size is much smaller, and (c) the solution accuracy is usually not compromised. Therefore, the engineers should consider using line models over surface or solid models whenever possible. Besides, the Workbench stores many built-in cross sections in the database to be chosen from by the users. Also, the Workbench allows the rendering of cross-sections when displaying the model, so that the line bodies visually look like the same as solid bodies.

Purpose of the Chapter

The main purpose of this chapter is to practice the use of beam elements (1.3-3[9]). This chapter guides the students to create line models and perform simulations using these models. The chapter provides three examples, two of them are entirely line models while the other one is a model mixed up by line bodies and surface bodies.

About Each Section

The first two sections present two step-by-step examples. Section 7.1 creates a flexible gripper model and performs a simulation using the model. Section 7.2 demonstrates the creation of a truss structure and the simulation. Section 7.3 uses a two-story building as an example to demonstrate the creation of a building structure and the simulation. Another purpose of Section 7.3 is to demonstrate how surface bodies and line bodies can be mixed-up to create a simulation model.

Section 7.1

Step-by-Step: Flexible Gripper

7.1-1 About the Flexible Gripper

Many manipulators are designed as mechanisms. That is, they consist of rigid bodies connected by joints, such as revolute joints, sliding joints, etc., and the motions are mostly governed by the laws of rigid body kinematics.

The gripper discussed here is a structure rather than a mechanism. The mobility are provided by the flexibility of the materials, rather than the joints. Therefore it is called a flexible gripper [1-4].

The gripper is made of POM (polyoxymethylene, a plastic polymer), which has a Young's modulus of 2 GPa and a Poisson's ratio of 0.35. It has a rectangular cross section of 1x5 mm.

One of the concern when designing this gripper is its geometric advantage, GA. The GA is defined as the ratio of the horizontal output displacement [4] to the input actuation [3]. The GA value can be used to assess the efficiency of the gripper, the larger the better. The main purpose of this simulation is to assess the GA value of the current design configuration as shown in the figure [5]. Note that only half of the gripper will be modeled due to the symmetry.

The profile consists of two smooth spline curves defined by 7 key points, whose numbering and coordinates are shown in the figure [5, 6]. The spline *P1-P2-P3-P4* has free ends on both ends. The spline *P4-P5-P6-P7* has free end at *P4* and a constraint on *P7*: it is perpendicular to the plane of symmetry. This constraint has to be imposed otherwise the smoothness of the curve across to the other half cannot be guaranteed.

We could model the problem as 2D. With 2D simulations, however, current version of <Mechanical> supports only solid models (doesn't support 2D surface or line model). Comparing with a 3D line model, 2D solid model is not efficient (in terms of accuracy and CPU time.) We decide to go for a 3D line model, although the geometry and the motion is entirely on a plane.

We will create a line model in the first part of this section. The model will be used in the second part of this section to simulate the motion of gripping and assess the GA value. The model will be used in Section 8.1 to demonstrate an optimization capability of the Workbench. That is, we want to re-configurate the positions of the key points to achieve an optimum GA value.

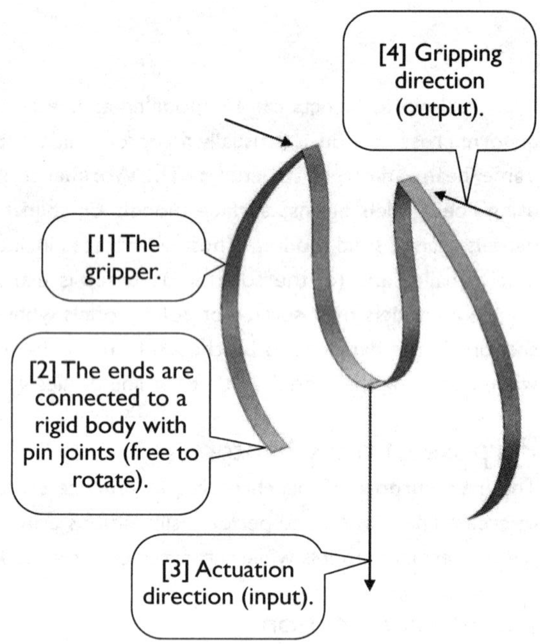

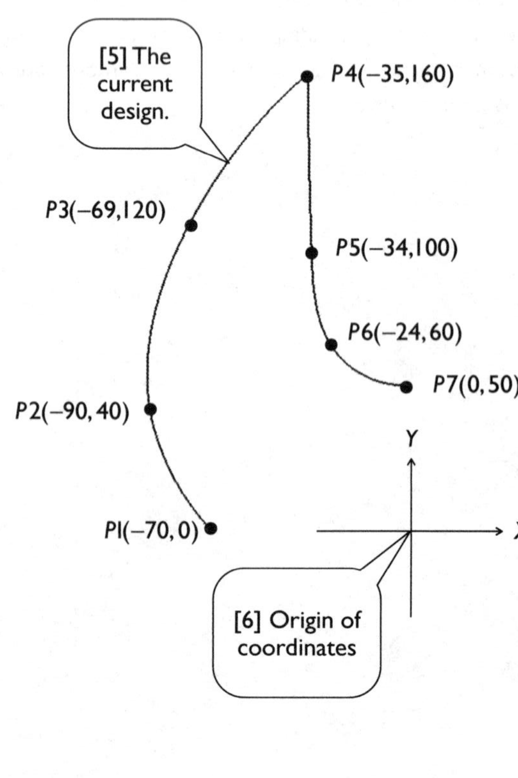

PART A. GEOMETRIC MODELING

7.1-2 Start Up

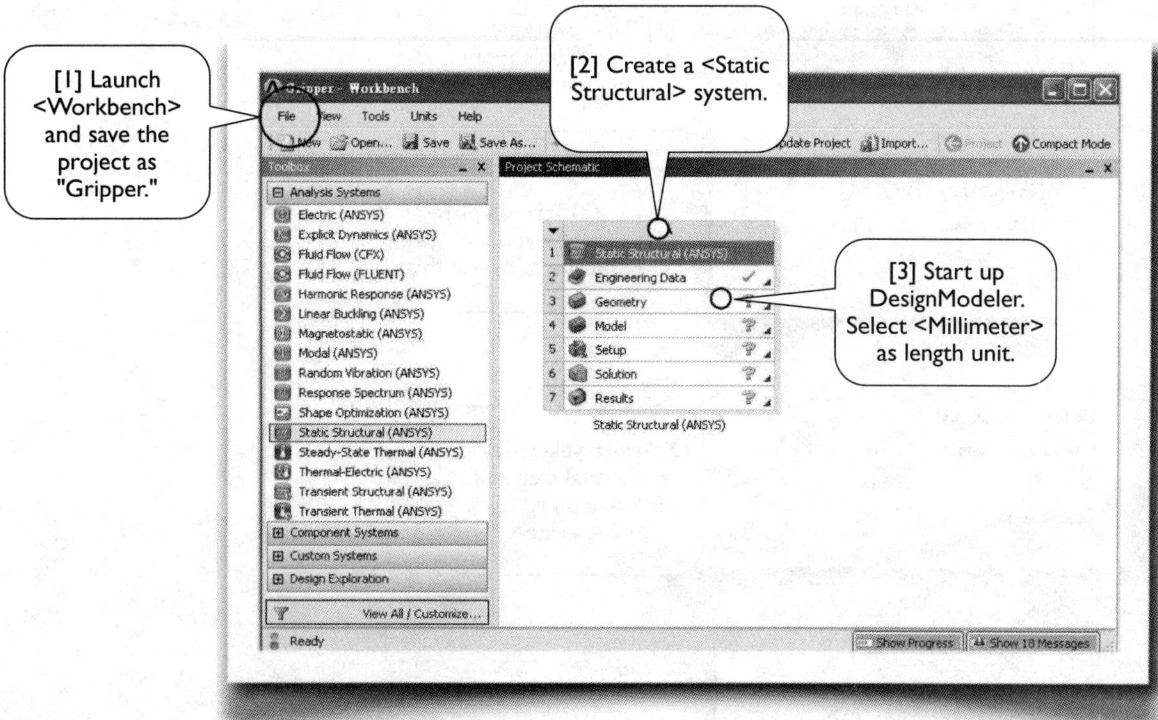

7.1-3 Create Sketch on XYPlane

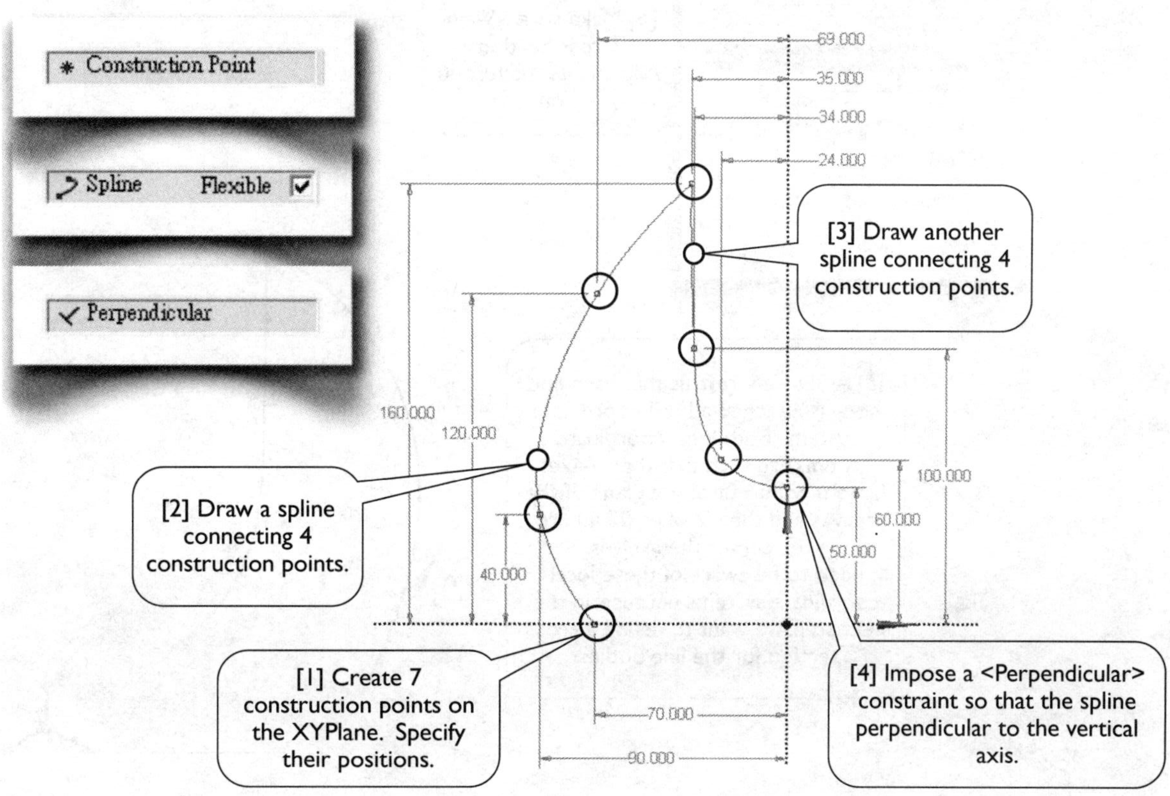

7.1-4 Create Line Body

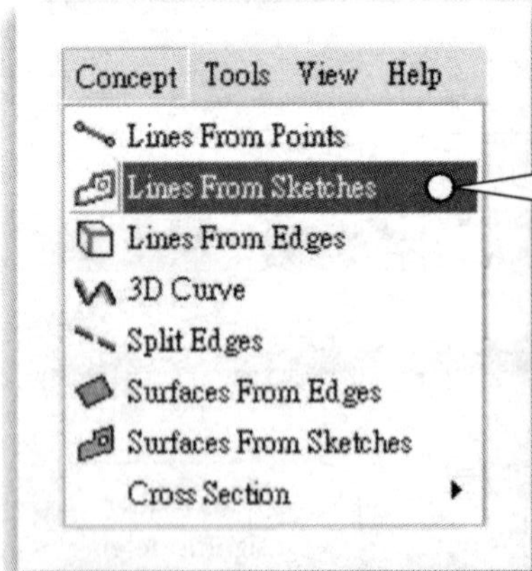

[1] Pull-down-select <Concept/Lines From Sketches>.

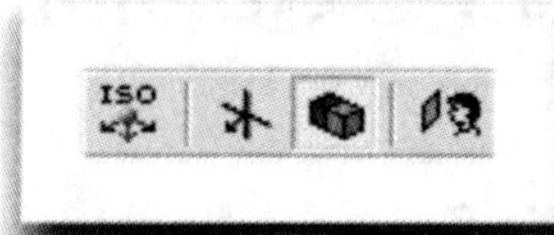

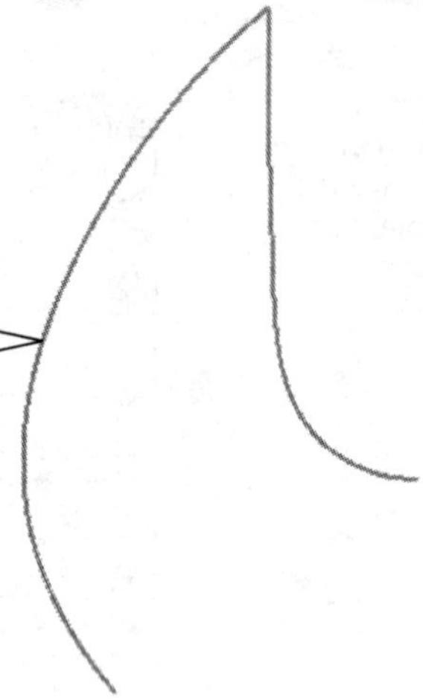

[3] Turn off plane display, you will see the line body like this.

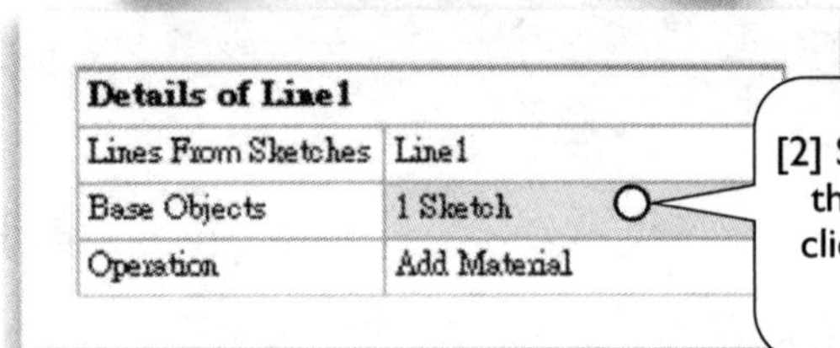

[2] Select <Sketch1> in the model tree and click <Apply>. Click <Generate>.

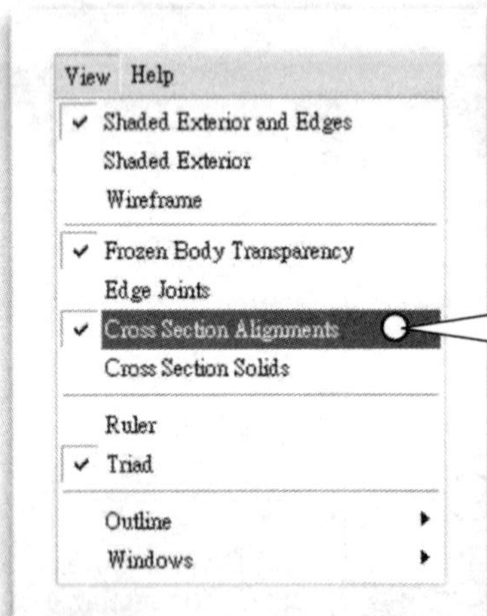

[4] Make sure <View/Cross Section Alignments> is turned on.

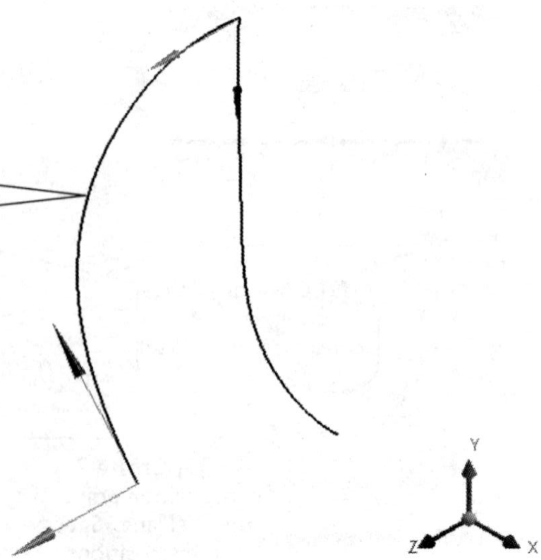

[5] A 3D view reveals that each line body is attached a local coordinate system. Both local coordinate systems are such that their Y-axes (green) point out of the plane of the curves and their Z-axes (blue) are along the curves themselves. We need to be aware of these local coordinate systems because, in the next step, we want to define a cross section for the line bodies.

7.1-5 Create a Rectangle Cross Section

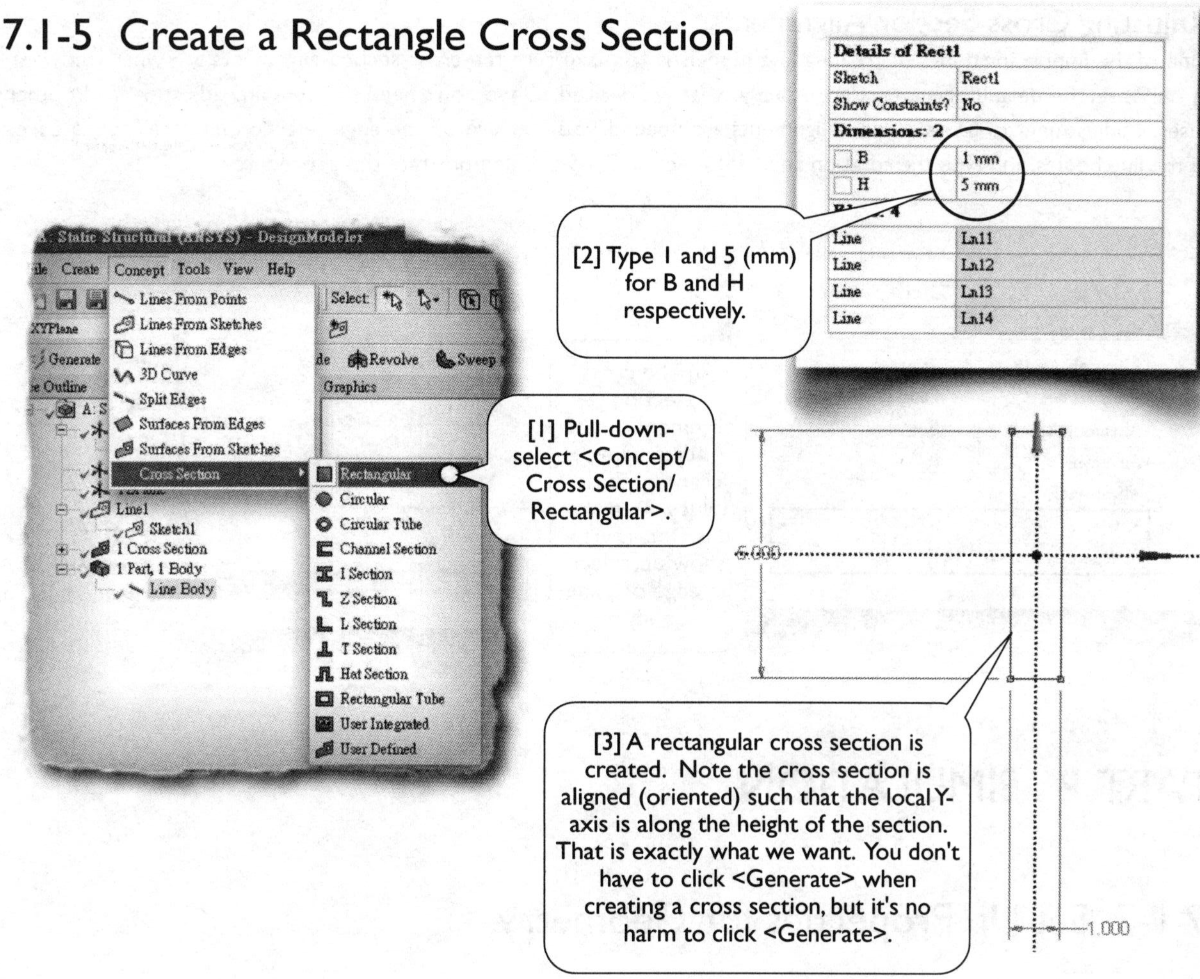

7.1-6 Assign the Cross Section to the Line Body

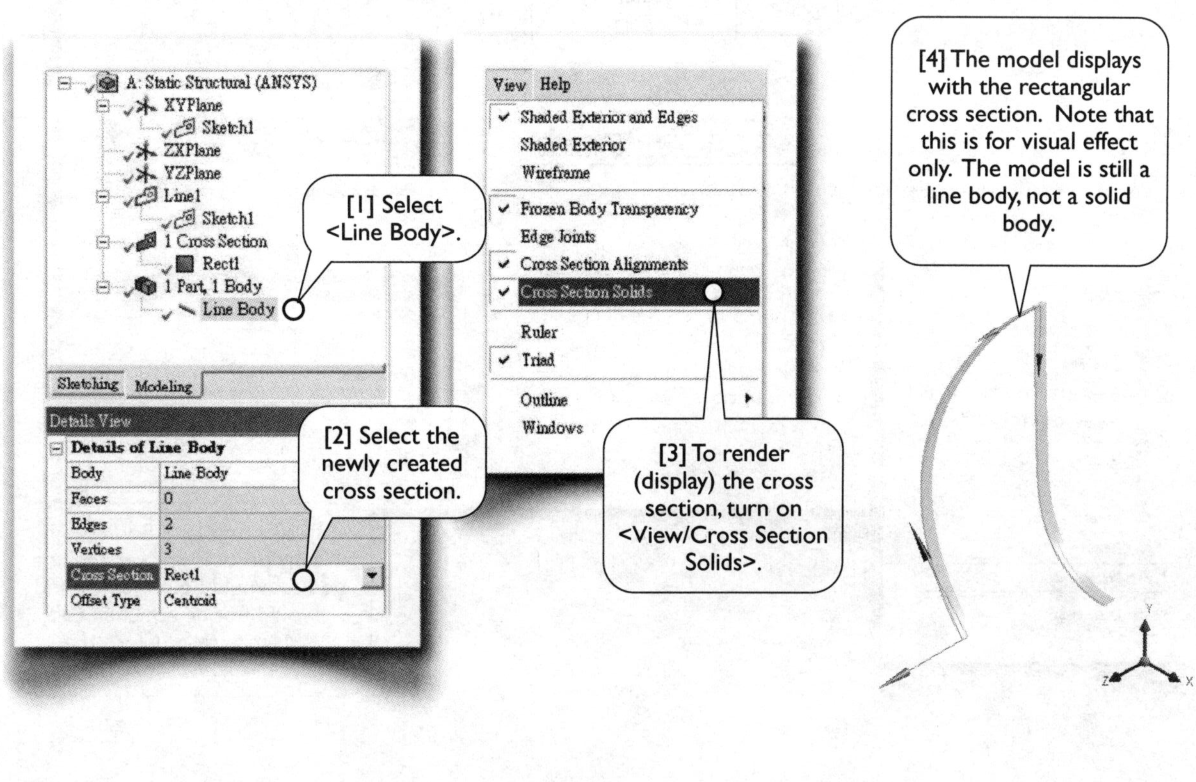

Adjusting Cross Section Alignments

One of the important things of creating line models is to make sure the cross section alignments are what you want. In our case, the default alignments are exactly what we desired, so we don't need to make any adjustment. In other cases, if adjustment of cross section alignments are needed, you can turn on the edge selection filter, select the edges of the line bodies, and type the rotation angle [5]. Section 7.3-9 will demonstrate this procedure.

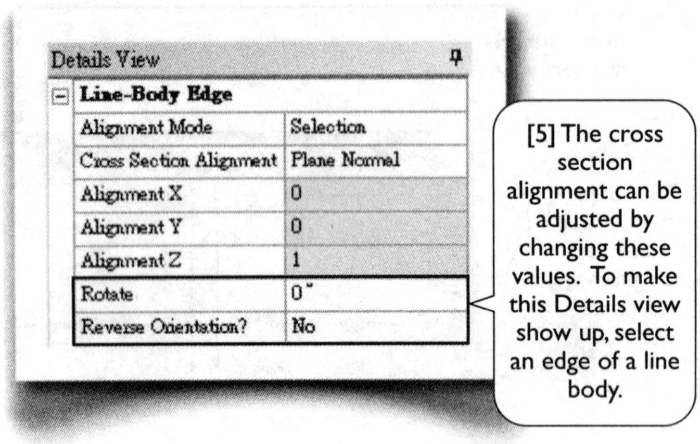

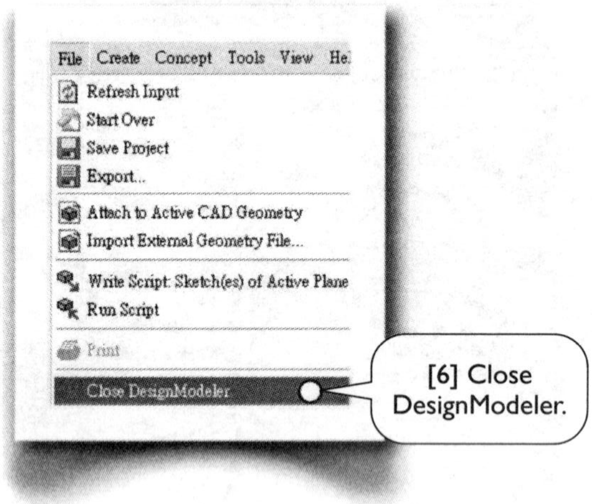

PART B. SIMULATION

7.1-7 Set Up Properties for Geometry

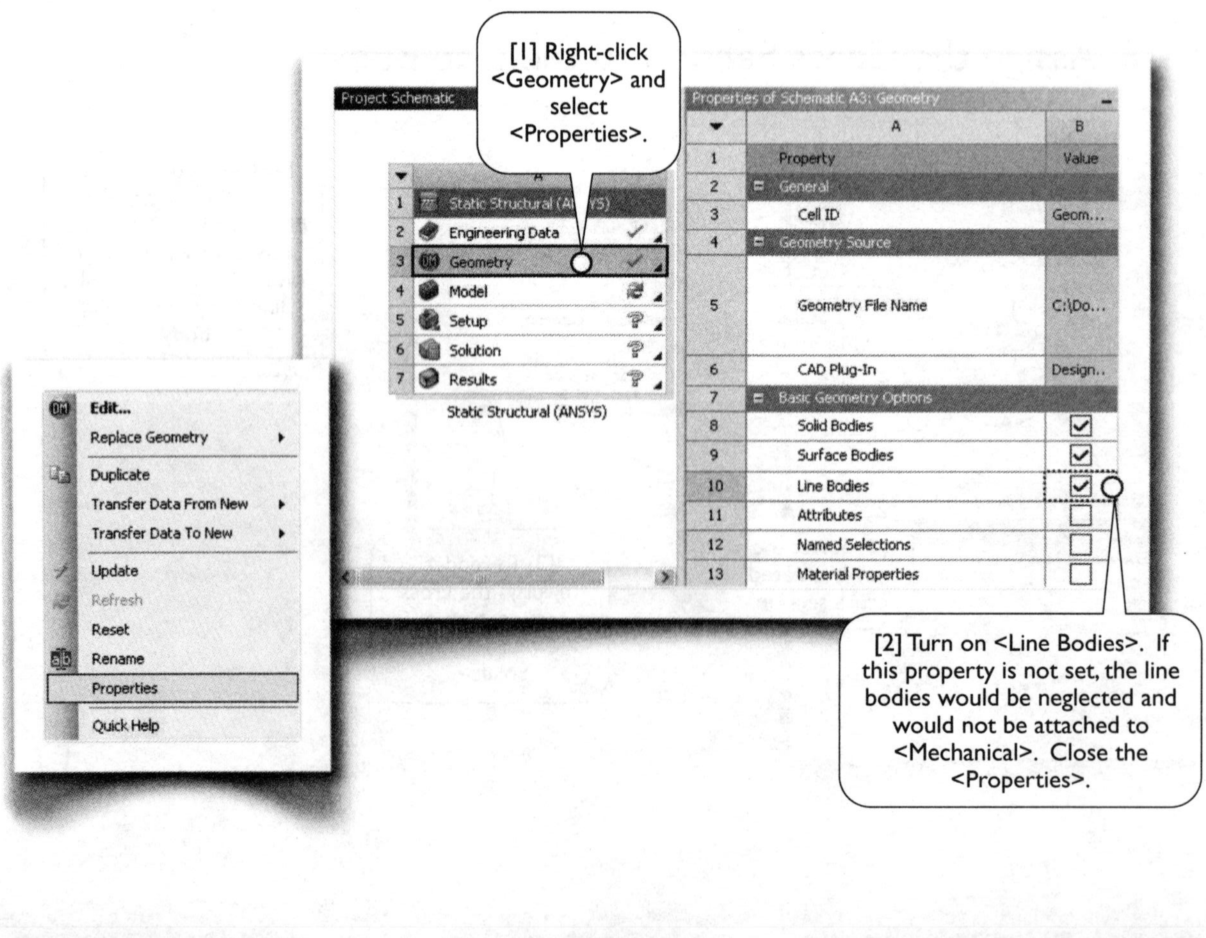

7.1-8 Prepare Material Properties

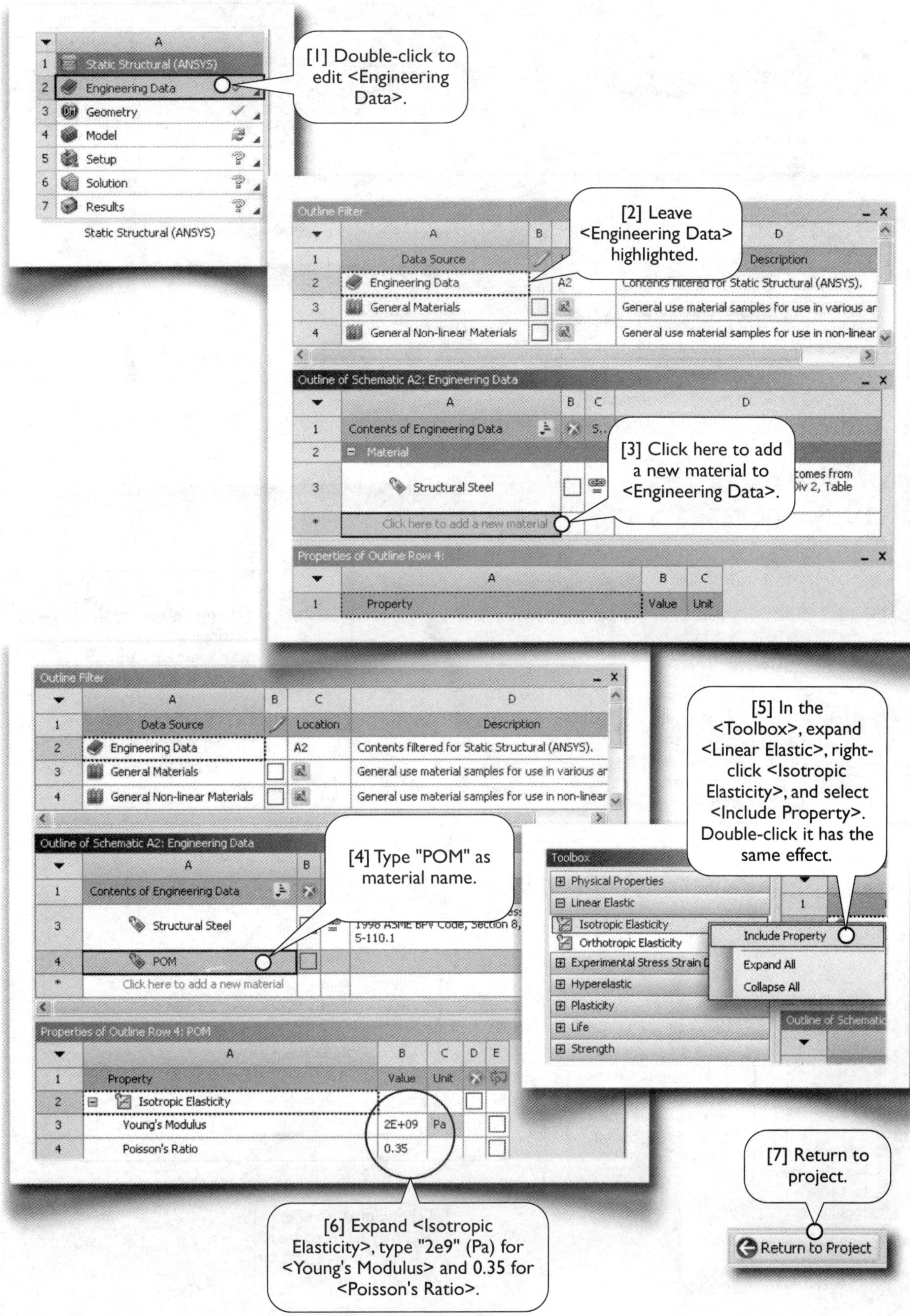

7.1-9 Start Up <Mechanical> and Assign Material

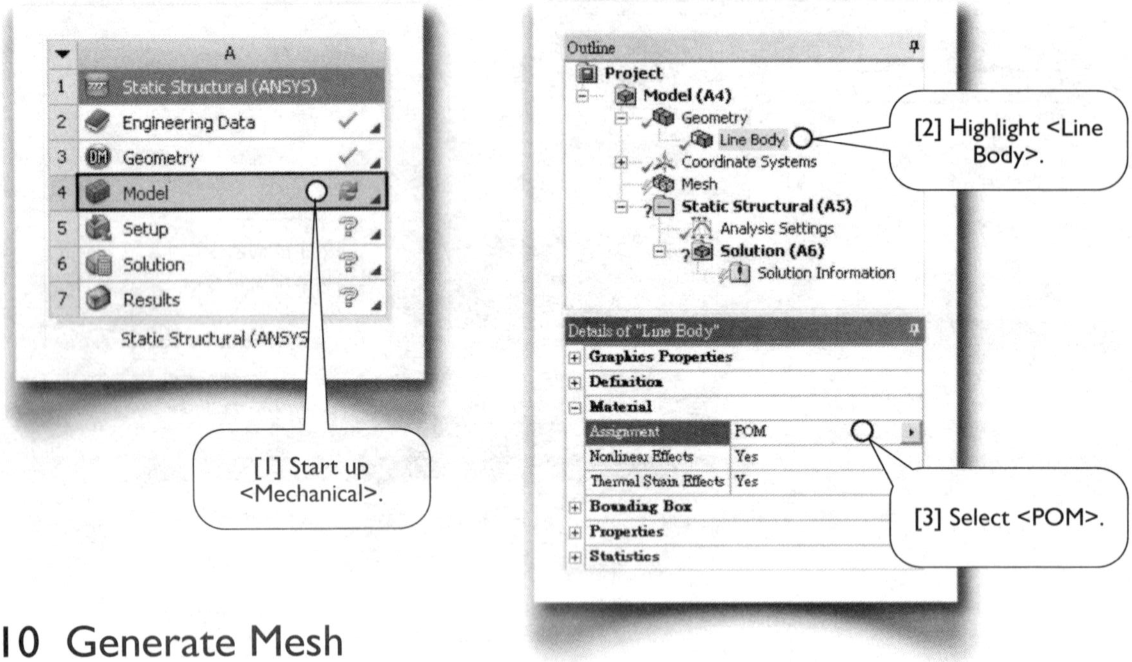

7.1-10 Generate Mesh

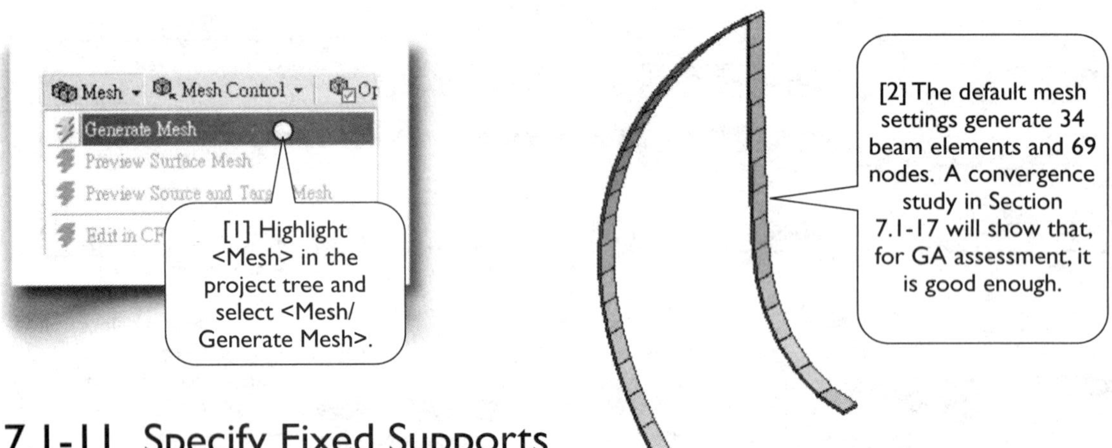

7.1-11 Specify Fixed Supports

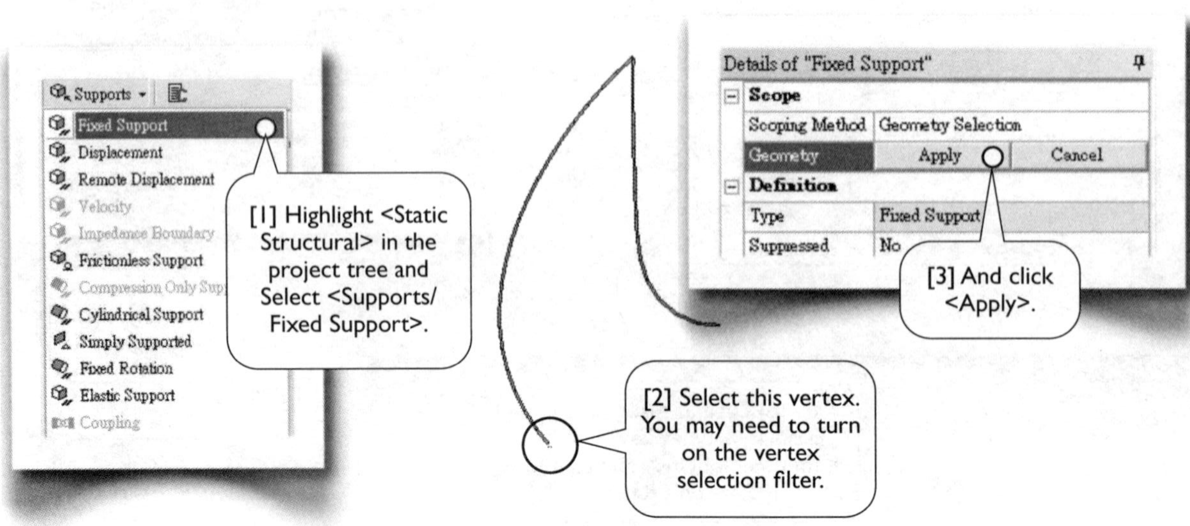

7.1-12 Specify Symmetry Condition and the Actuation

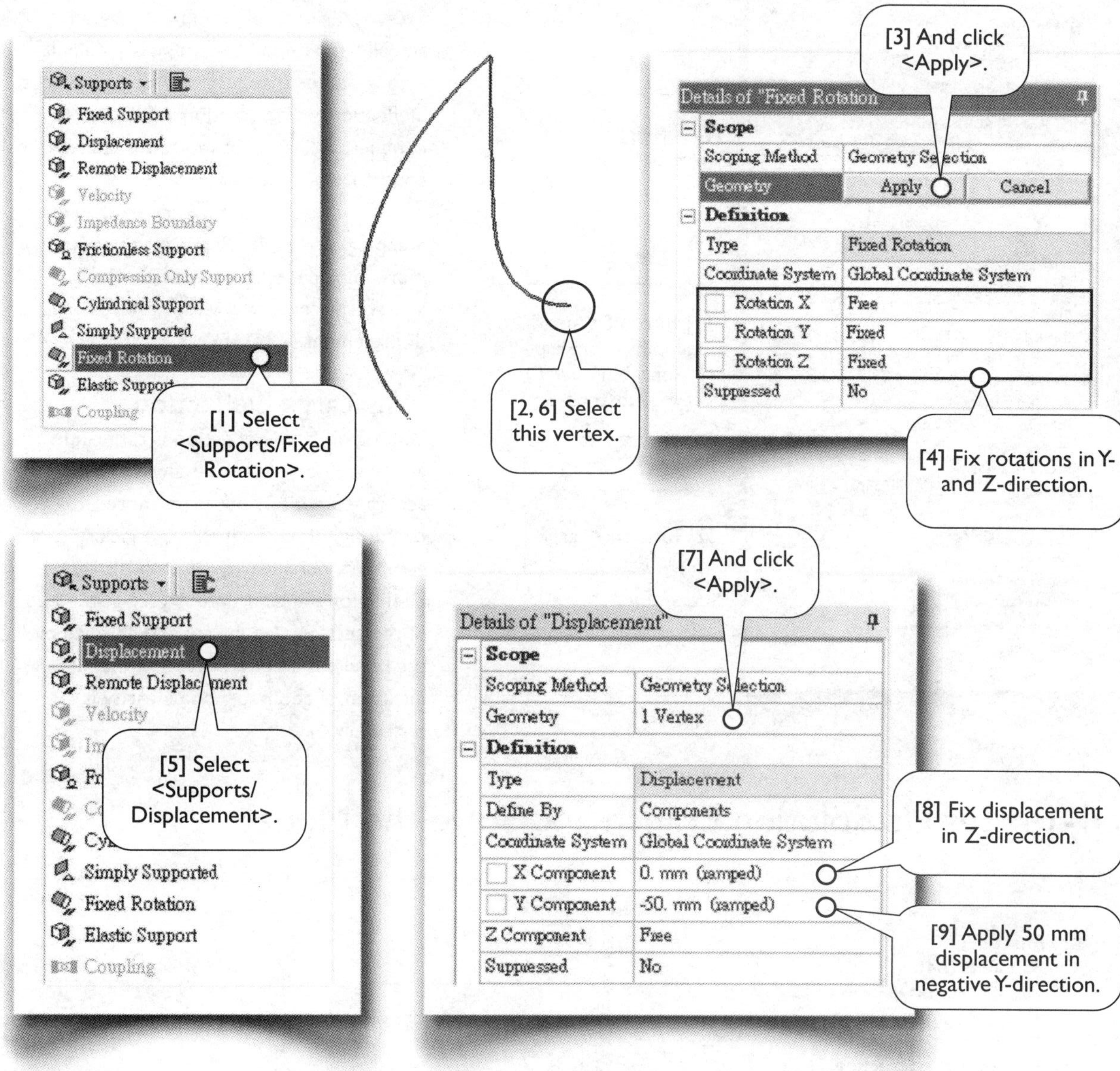

Symmetry Conditions for Shell and Beam Elements

Steps [1-8] are to set up condition of symmetry about YZPlane, while step [9] is to set up a downward actuation.

Recall that, in the first exercise of Section 6.4-3, you are asked how to set up the rotational degrees of freedom on a plane of symmetry. Beam elements, like shell elements, have rotational degrees of freedom (1.3-3[9]).

A general rule of symmetry conditions for shell and beam elements is to fix (set to zero value) the out-of-plane translations and in-plane rotations.

Consider the boundary conditions at the vertex [2, 6]. In this case, YZPlane is the plane of symmetry, X-displacement is the out-of-plane translations [8], Y-rotation and Z-rotation are the in-plane rotation [4]. Note that fixing Y-rotation may not needed in this case, since the loading automatically results with zero Y-rotation.

You could let Workbench automatically set up the symmetry boundary conditions (Section 3.1-10), but make sure you know how Workbench set up these symmetry boundary conditions. The Workbench will set up the symmetry boundary conditions as we described above: fix the out-of-plane translations and in-plane rotations. As a good engineer, use the software features only when you know how they work.

7.1-13 Set Up <Analysis Settings>

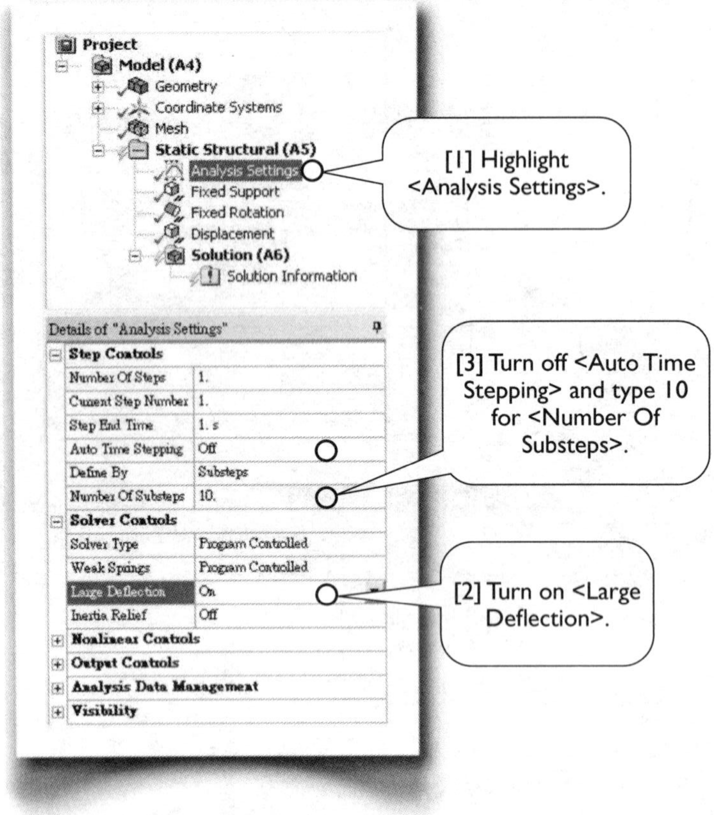

Auto Time Stepping

This model is simple enough that we actually don't need to change any default settings other than just turn on the <Large Deflection>. The solution would be complete in just 3 substeps, with a program controlled auto time stepping.

The reason we turn off <Auto Time Stepping> is because we want to gather more information for plotting a chart of input displacement versus output displacement (7.1-16[6]).

Why Large Deflection

Turning on large deflection is to include geometry nonlinearity. It always gives more accurate solutions but takes more computing time. To justify the inclusion of geometry nonlinearity, turn off <Large Deflection> and rerun this case at the end of the section. A substantial difference of the results is an indication that the inclusion of geometry nonlinearity is necessary.

7.1-14 Set Up Solution Branch and Solve the Model

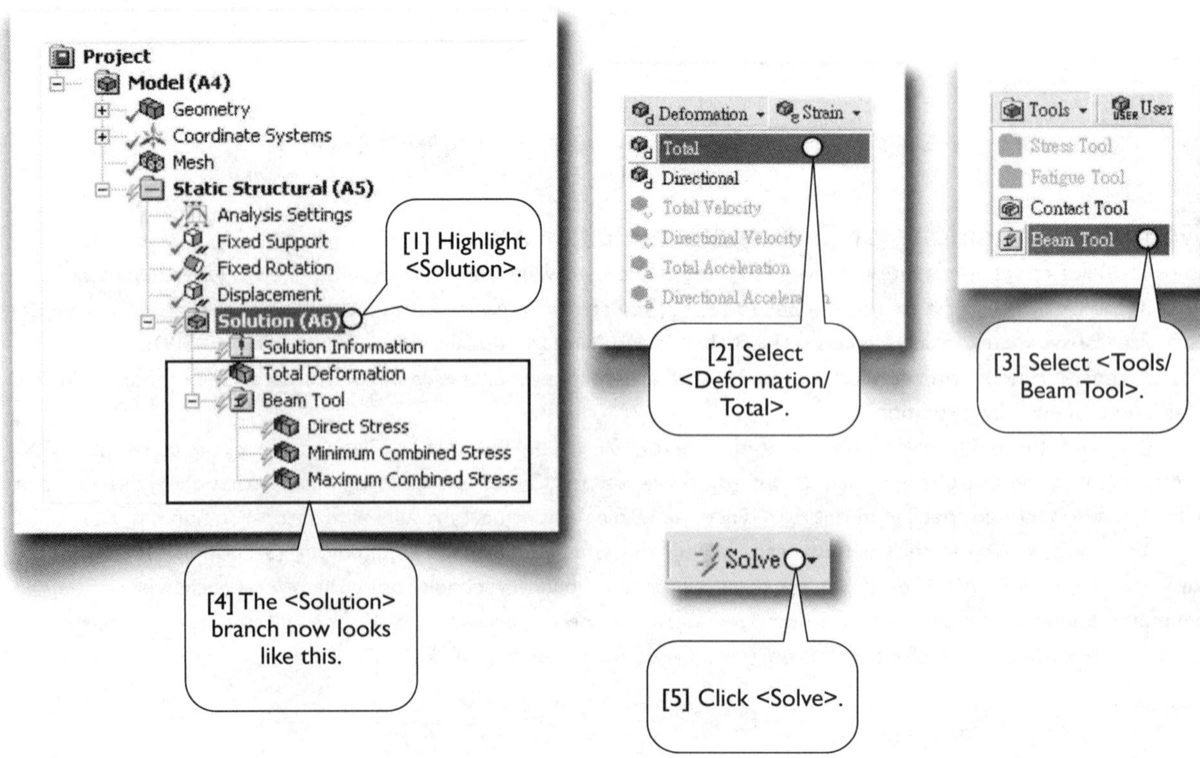

7.1-15 View Results

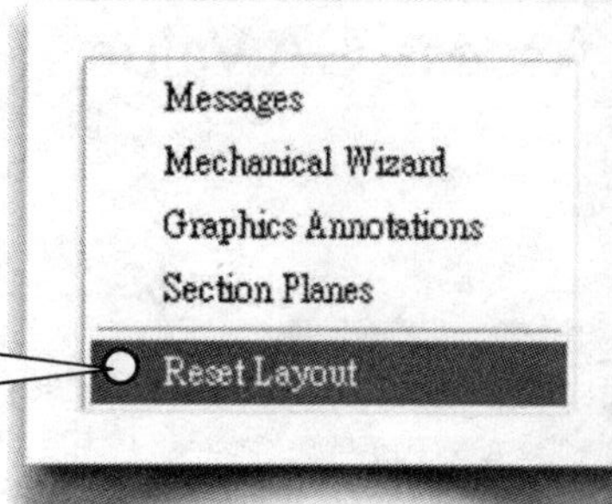

[3] If your window layout is different from what I have here, pull-down-select <View/Windows/Reset Layout>.

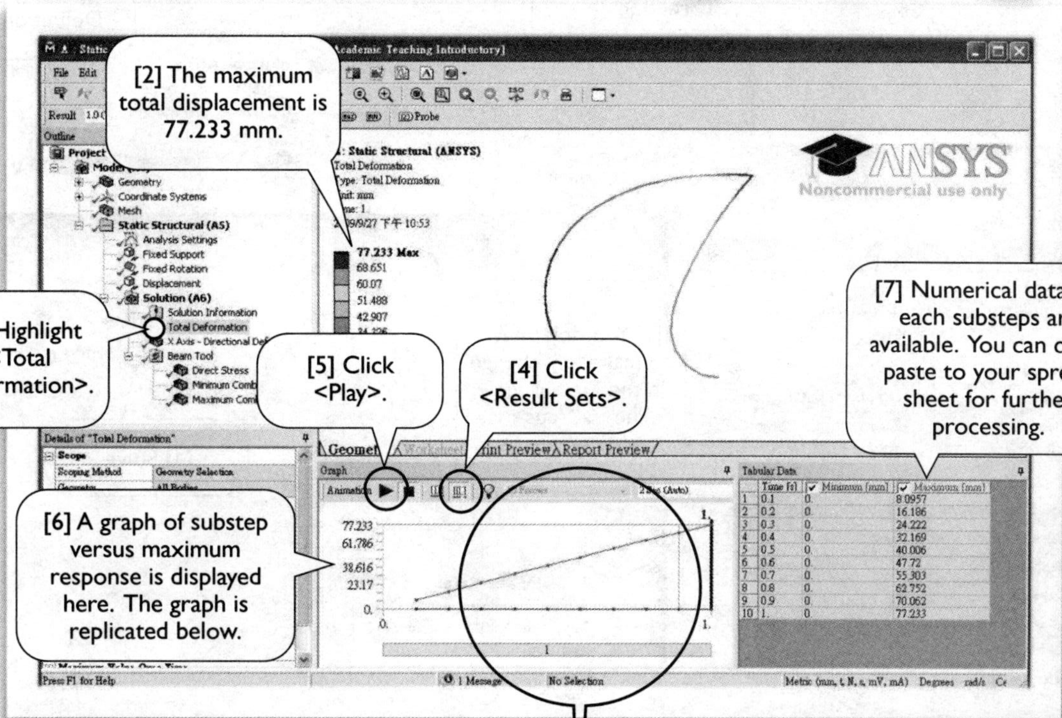

[1] Highlight <Total Deformation>.

[2] The maximum total displacement is 77.233 mm.

[4] Click <Result Sets>.

[5] Click <Play>.

[6] A graph of substep versus maximum response is displayed here. The graph is replicated below.

[7] Numerical data for each substeps are available. You can copy/paste to your spread sheet for further processing.

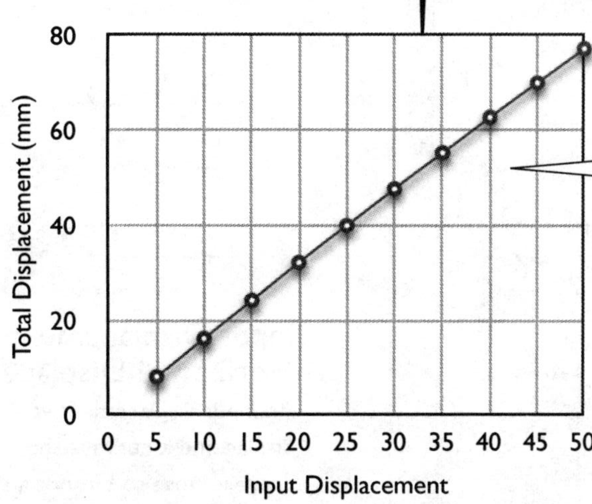

[8] The total input displacement (50 mm) is divided into 10 substeps, therefore each substep is 5 mm of input displacement.

[9] The input displacement versus total displacement curve is nearly a straight line.

7.1-16 Assess GA Value

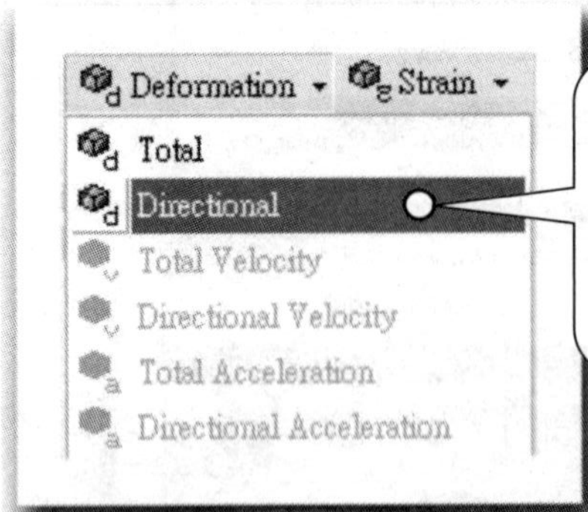

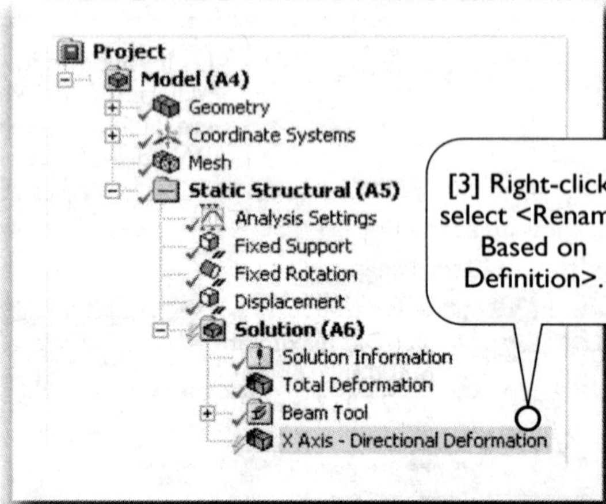

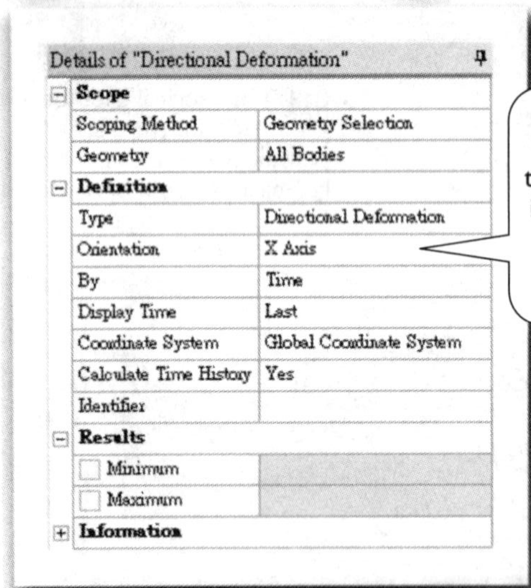

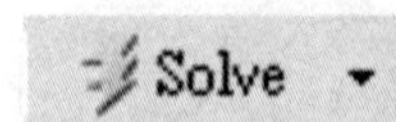

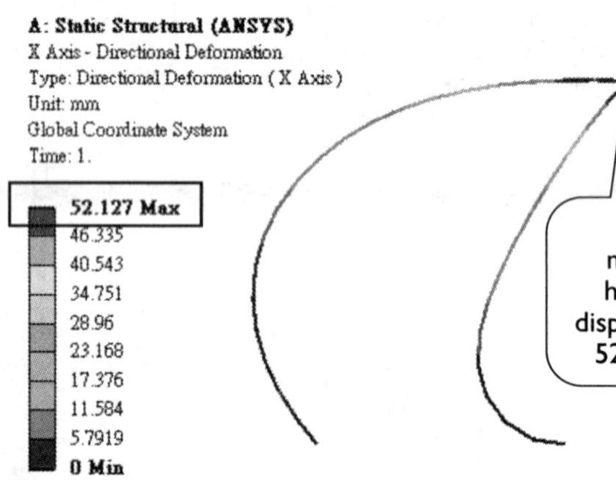

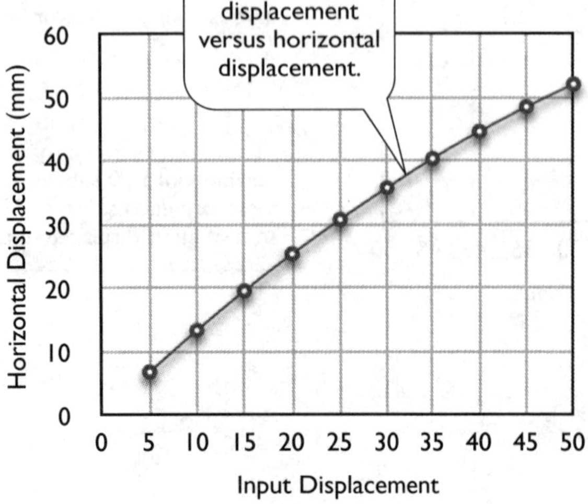

Input Displacement versus Horizontal Displacement

An input displacement versus horizontal displacement curve is shown on the left [6]. The curve is close to but not a straight line. A linear relationship usually more is desirable, because that would be easier for automatic control. The GA value in this case is about 1.04 (52/50).

Wrap Up

Save the project and quit <Workbench>.

7.1-17 Remark: Convergence of the Beam Element

A convergence study of the gripper model is summarized in the figure below [1-2]; this leaves an exercise for you. The figure shows that the displacement converges to 52.160 mm. In the foregoing simulation, we meshed with 34 elements under the default settings and obtain a displacement of 52.127 mm. That is good enough for the GA assessment, but may not be adequate for other purposes.

Generally, models meshed with beam elements or shell elements converge very fast. The meshing consideration is mostly geometric. In our case, since it is a curved structure, the major concern is to mesh the structure so that the meshed finite element model doesn't deviate the original geometry too much.

For a structure composed by straight beams, it is possible to obtain a solution equal to theoretical values by meshing each straight beam a single element! This will be demonstrated in Section 7.2.

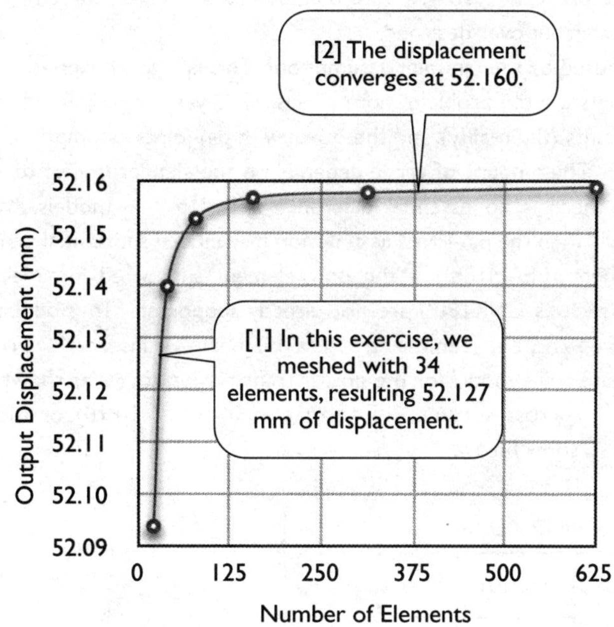

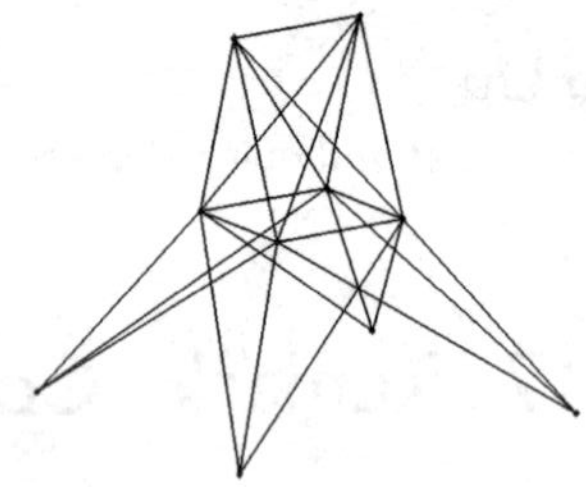

Section 7.2

Step-by-Step: 3D Truss

7.2-1 About the 3D Truss

Traditionally, a truss is defined as a structure consisting of two-force members. By two-force member, we mean that the members are pin-jointed at the ends and the loads apply on the joints so that the members are either stretched or compressed but not bent. Two members connected by a pin-joint can rotate about the joint independently. In reality, structural members are rarely connected each other by pin-joints. Modern structures are constructed using either welds or multiple bolt-and-nuts; the members are rigid jointed, not pin-jointed. Even in the old days, pin-jointed structures are not common. Main reason of pin-joint assumption is to ease the computational difficulty, in the days when computers were not widespread, if existing. Note that, due to the neglect of joint rigidity, pin-joint assumption leads to a conservative design: safer, but over-designed.

How much is the error caused by the pin-joint assumption? This is a good exercise problem for the engineering students (Section 7.4-2). Let me state the problem more precisely. Given a rigid-jointed structure, we perform twice of simulations: once with rigid joints (the reality), and the other with pin-joints assumption. What would the difference between these two models be? The amount of error depends on the slenderness of the structural member. If the members are slender enough, there is no essential difference between two models. On the other hand, if the members are not slender enough, then the pin-joints assumption may induce substantial errors.

Currently, the beam element (BEAM188[1]) is the only element supported in <Mechanical> to mesh the line bodies. The "truss elements" (such as LINK180[2]) are not directly supported. To model a pin-jointed structure, you need to explicitly specify revolute joints between the structural members, or insert APDL commands.

In this section, we will create a line model for the power transmission tower as shown. All members are made of structural steel angle of $1\frac{1}{2}\times 1\frac{1}{2}\times\frac{1}{4}$ cross section. Note that each joint (*P1*-*P10*) or member (1-25) is assigned a number. The design loads are also show below.

Design Loads for the Transmission Tower

Joint	F_X (lb)	F_Y (lb)	F_Z (lb)
P1	1,000	-10,000	-10,000
P2	0	-10,000	-10,000
P3	500	0	0
P6	600	0	0

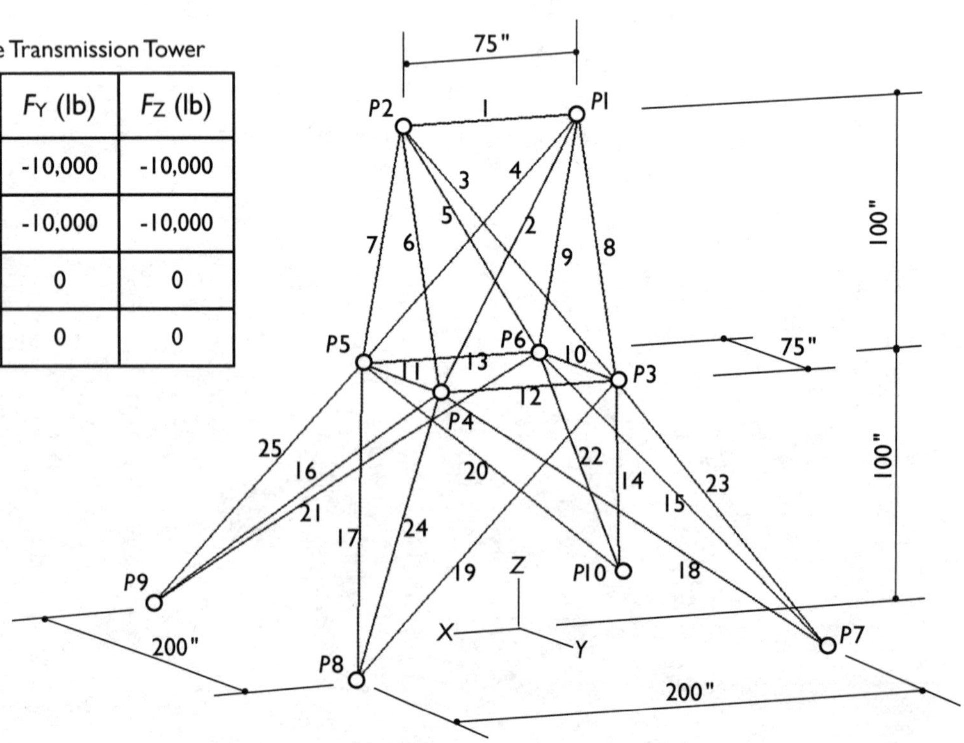

PART A. GEOMETRIC MODELING

7.2-2 Start Up

[1] Launch <Workbench> and save the project as "Truss."

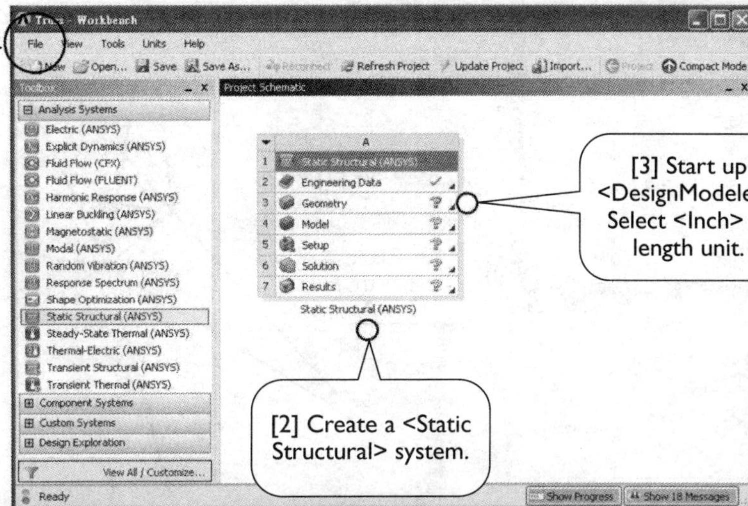

[2] Create a <Static Structural> system.

[3] Start up <DesignModeler>. Select <Inch> as length unit.

7.2-3 Create 10 Construction Points in the 3D Space

1	1	-37.5	0	200
1	2	37.5	0	200
1	3	-37.5	37.5	100
1	4	37.5	37.5	100
1	5	37.5	-37.5	100
1	6	-37.5	-37.5	100
1	7	-100	100	0
1	8	100	100	0
1	9	100	-100	0
1	10	-100	-100	0

[1] Prepare a TEXT FILE containing coordinates of 10 points, and save it in your disk. Note that the file has 5 columns (fields): (a) group number, (b) ID number, (c) X-coordinate, (d) Y-coordinate, and (e) Z-coordinate. The group number and the ID number are arbitrary, and they uniquely identify a point from others. Numbers can be separated by spaces or TABs.

[2] Click <Point> on the toolbar.

Details of Point1	
Point	Point1
Type	Construction Point
Definition	From Coordinates File
Coordinates File	C:\Documents and Settings\PC\My...\Points.txt
Tolerance	Normal
Refresh	No

[3] Select the TEXT FILE.

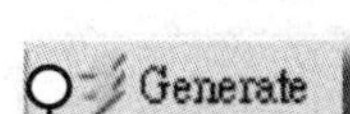

[4] Click <Generate>

[5] The points show up in the graphics space. Note that the model has been rotated such that XY plane lies horizontally.

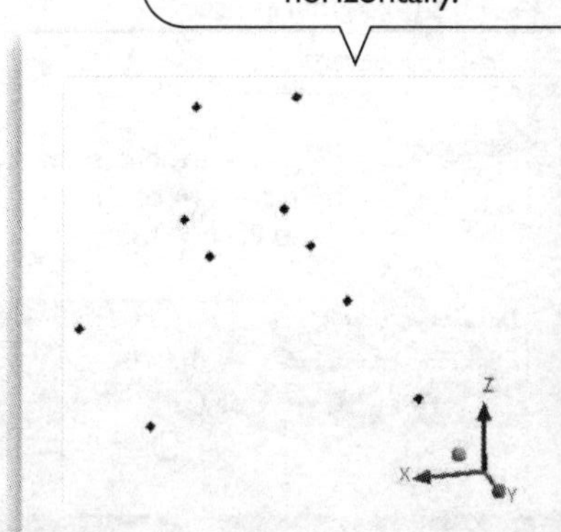

7.2-4 Create a Line Body for 19 Members

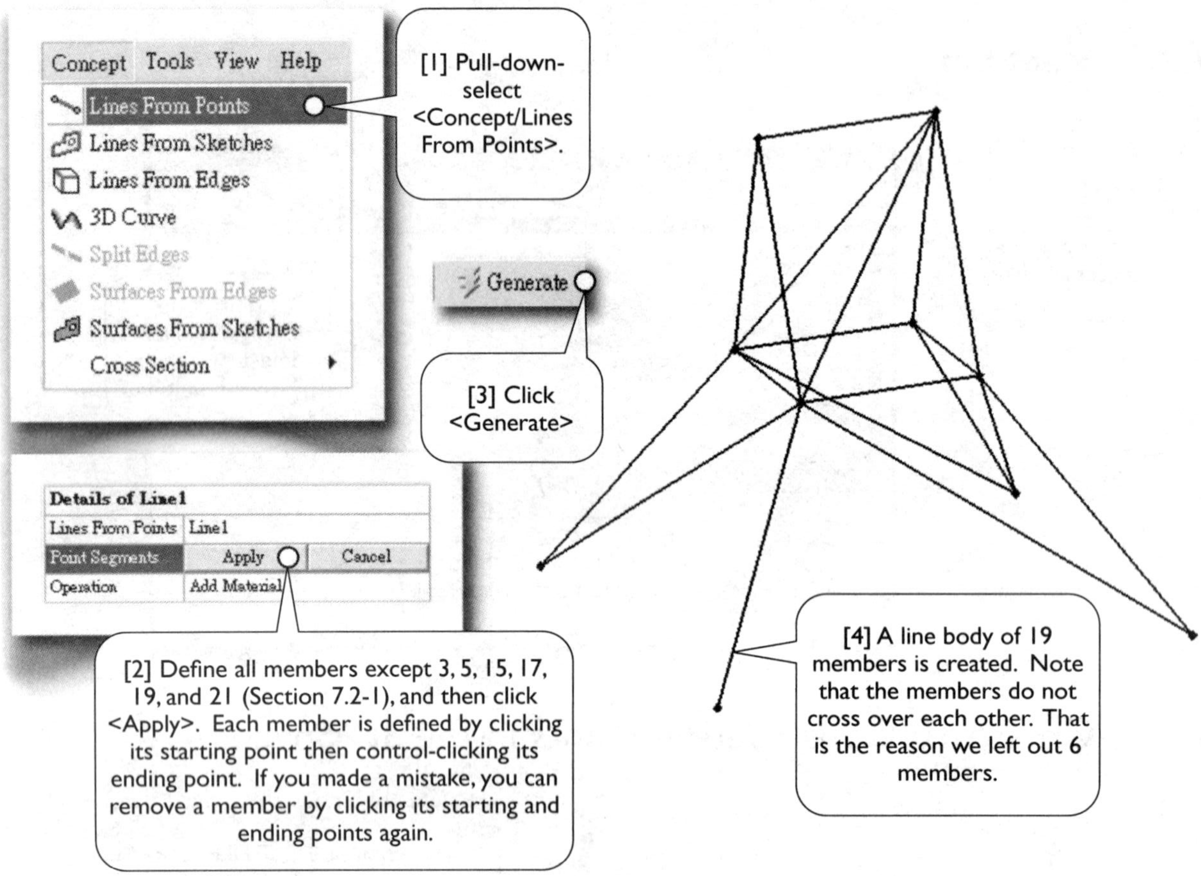

7.2-5 Create Another Line Body for the Rest of Members

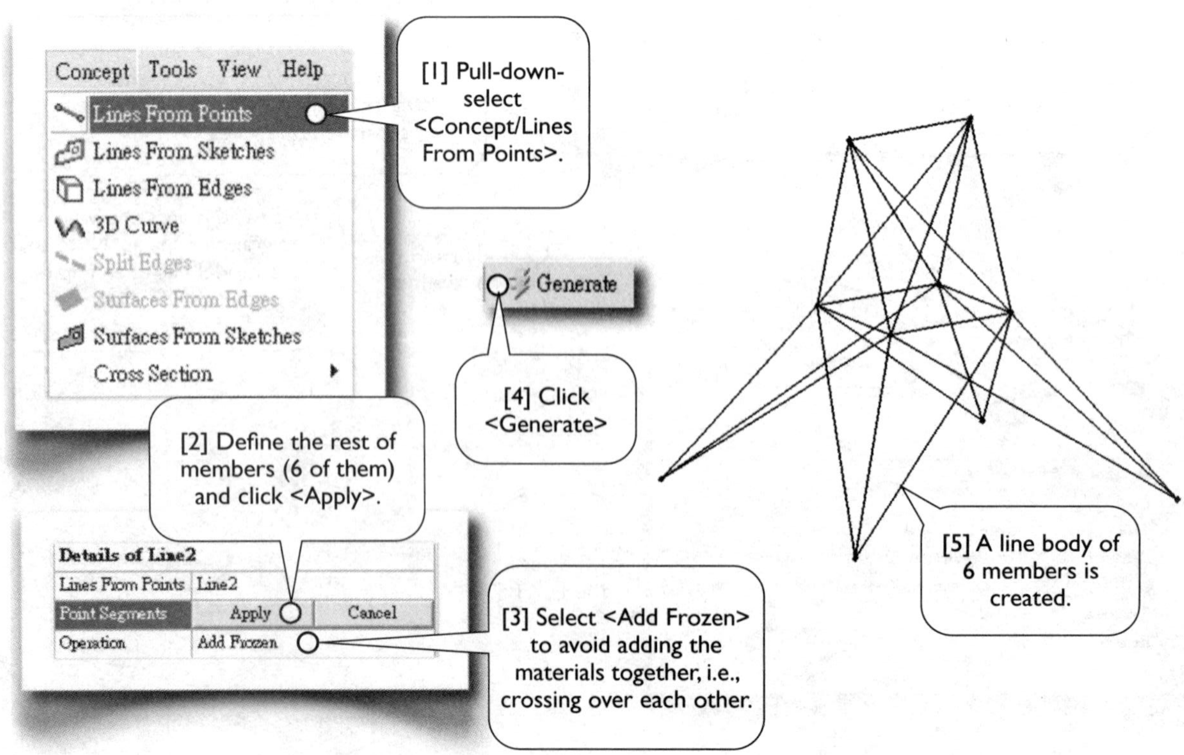

7.2-6 Form a Single Part

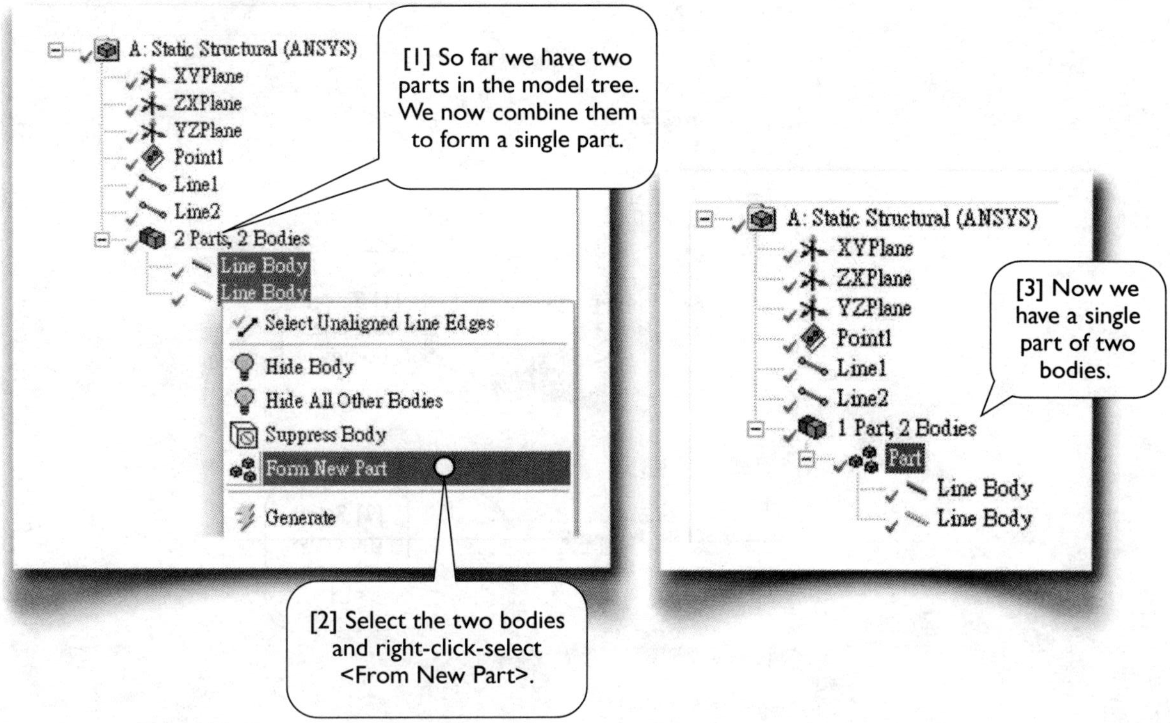

7.2-7 Create a Cross Section

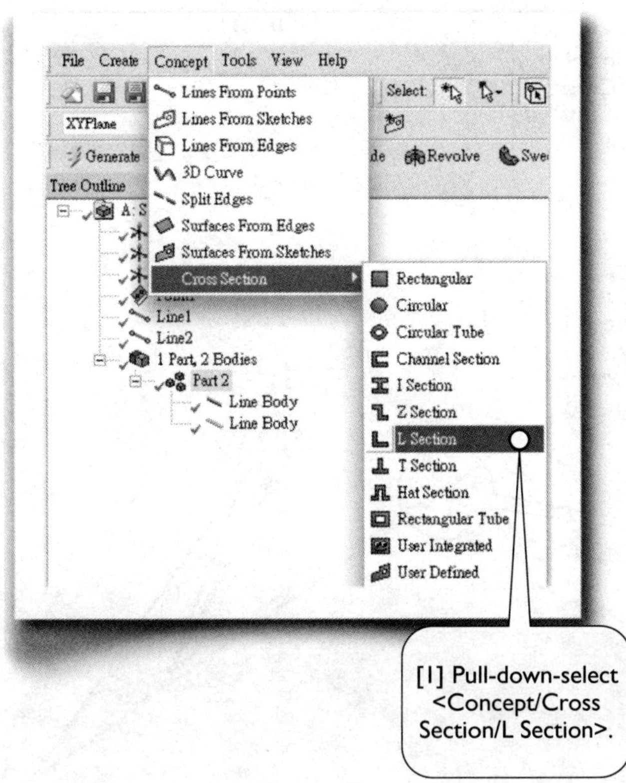

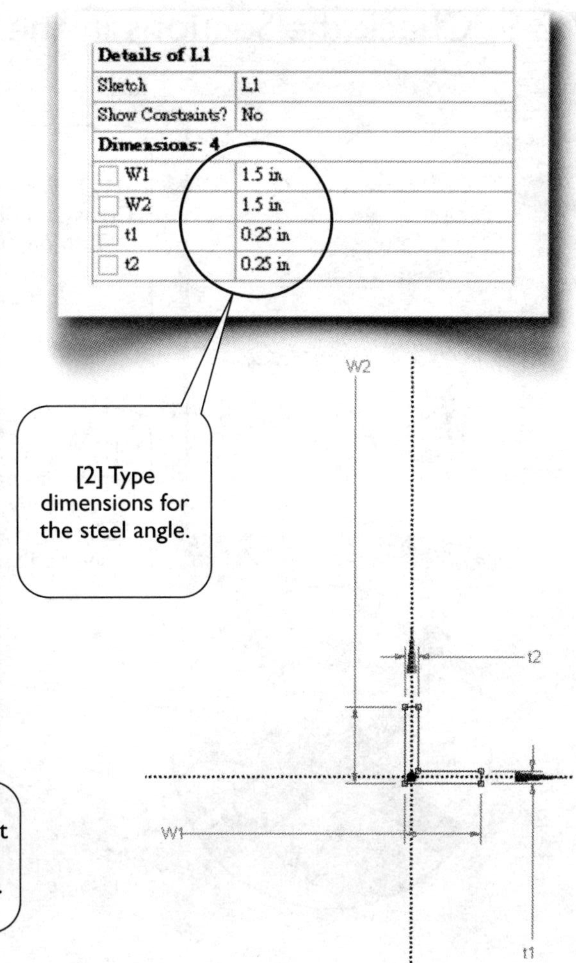

7.2-8 Assign the Cross Section to the Line Bodies

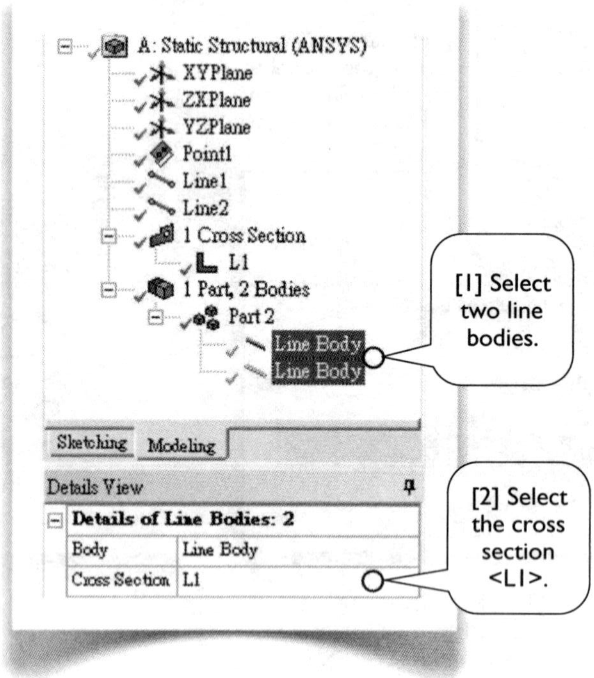

7.2-9 Check the Sections in the Model

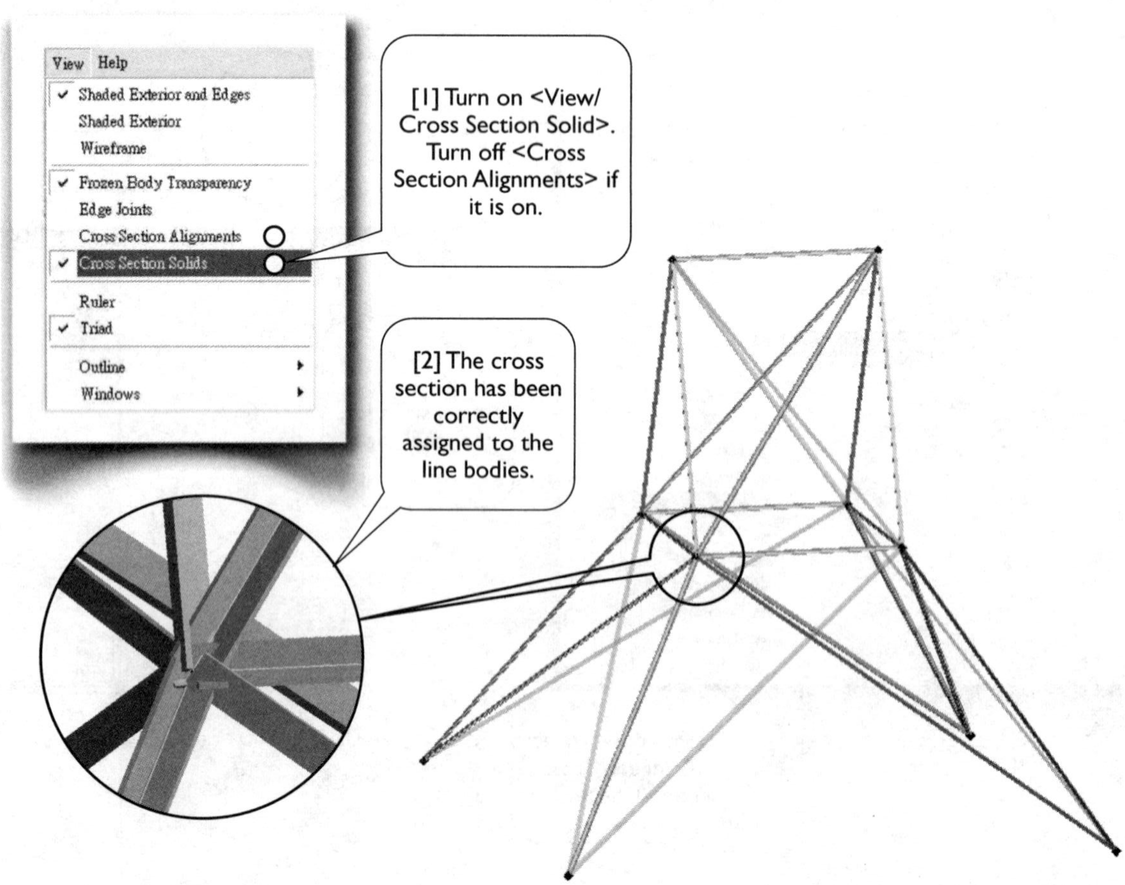

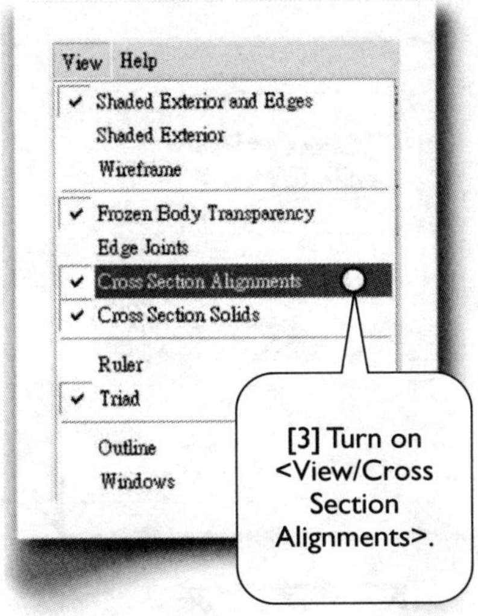

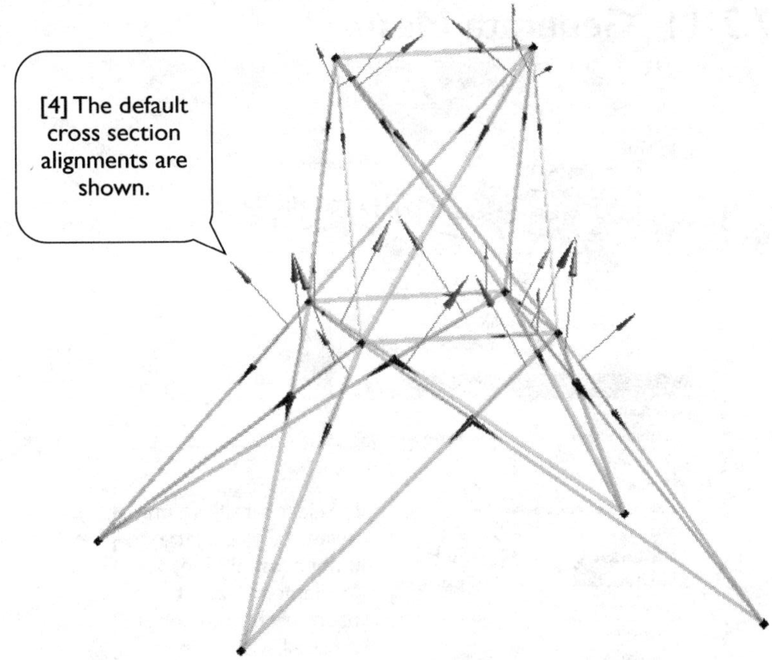

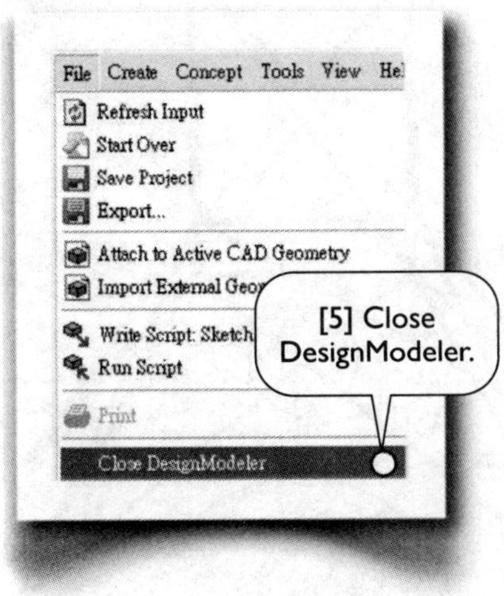

The default cross section alignments usually need to be adjusted to be consistent with the reality. In this case, we decided to leave them as default. Since the structural members are slender enough, the behaviors are close to two-force members, therefore alignments should not be critical. In other words, cross section alignments do not affect the structural response too much in this case. We will demonstrate the adjustment of cross section alignments in Section 7.3-9, in which the alignments must be adjusted, or it would deviate the reality too much.

PART B. SIMULATION

7.2-10 Set Up Properties for Geometry

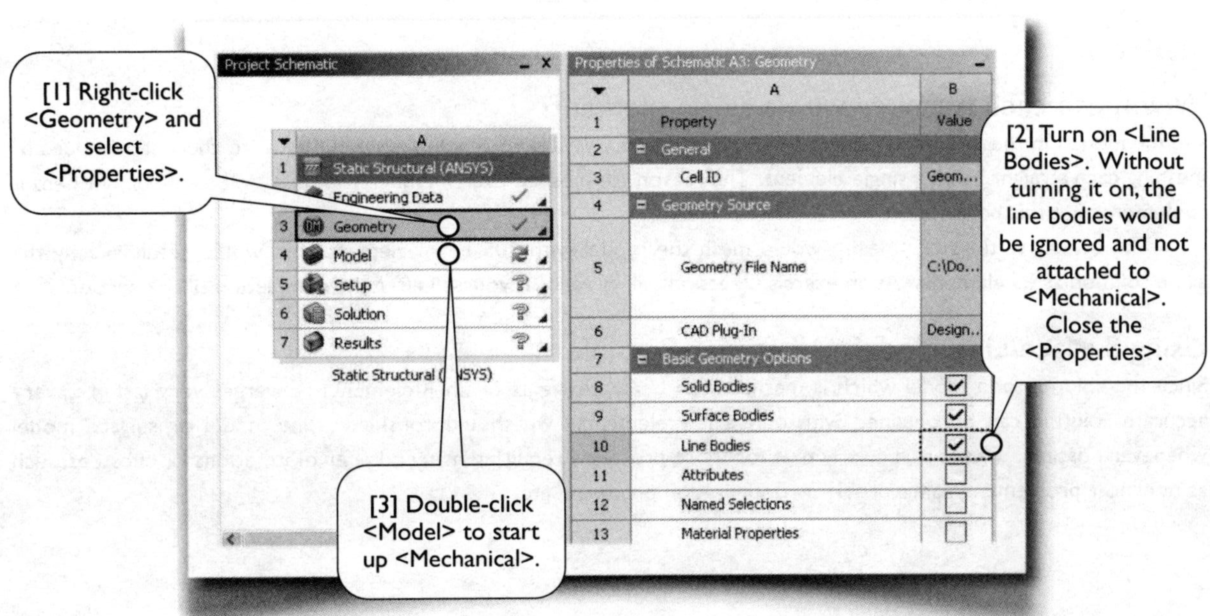

7.2-11 Generate Mesh

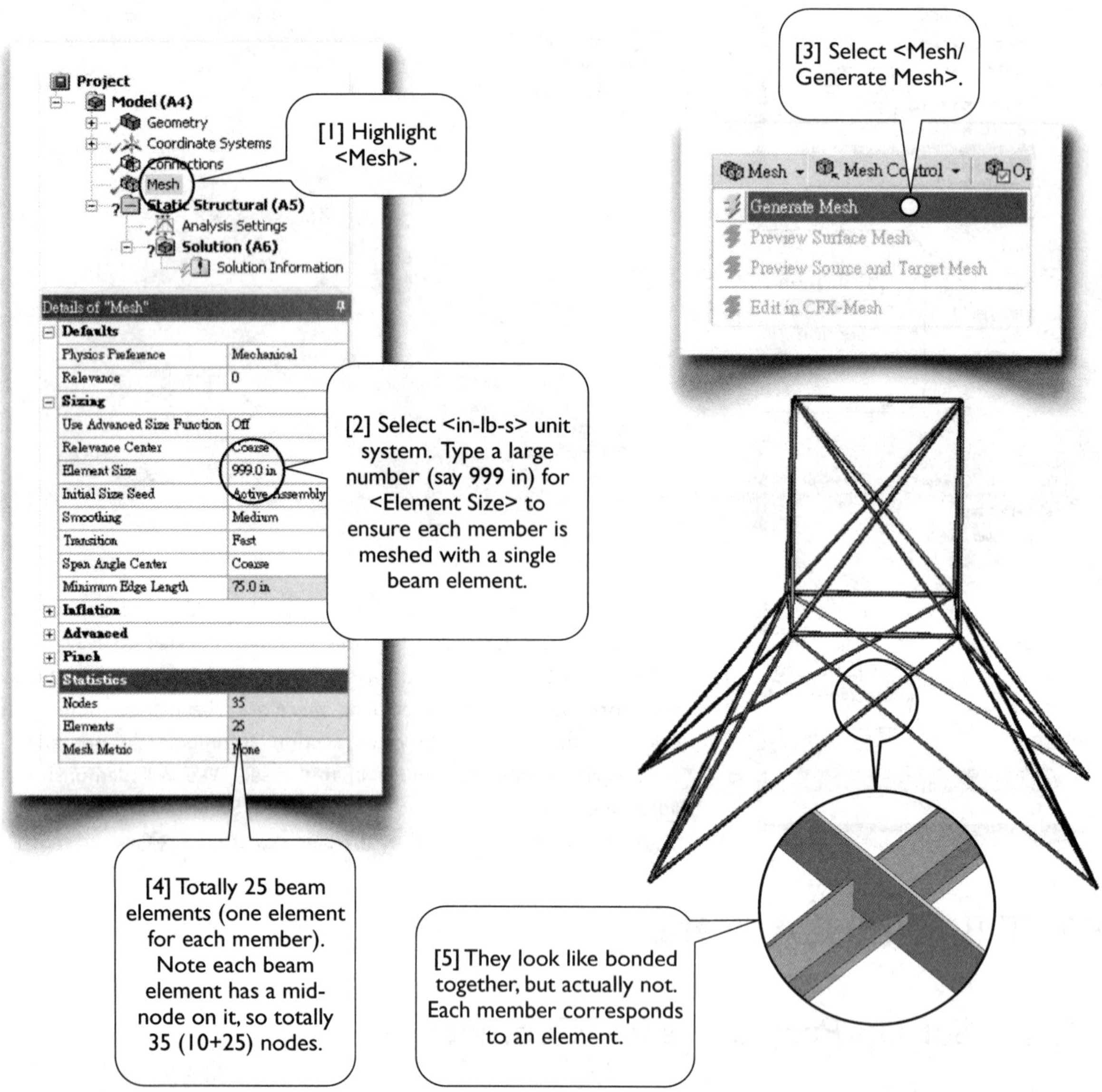

Why mesh each member with a single element?

We mentioned in the end of last section (7.1-17) that it is possible to obtain a solution equal to theoretical values by meshing each straight beam a single element. The reason we meshed each member with a single beam element here is to demonstrate this behavior.

The default settings of <Mesh> would mesh the model with 205 beam elements and would result exactly the same solution as 25 elements. As an exercise (Section 7.4-2), verify it yourself after the completion of this section.

Using Surface/Line Models Whenever Possible

Since the solution of a model which is meshed with beam elements or shell elements converges very fast (i.e., very accurate solution can be obtained with only a few elements), we should consider a line model or surface model whenever possible. This is particularly true for those problems requiring many number of iterations or substeps, such as nonlinear problems, dynamic problems, optimization problems, etc.

7.2-12 Specify Supports

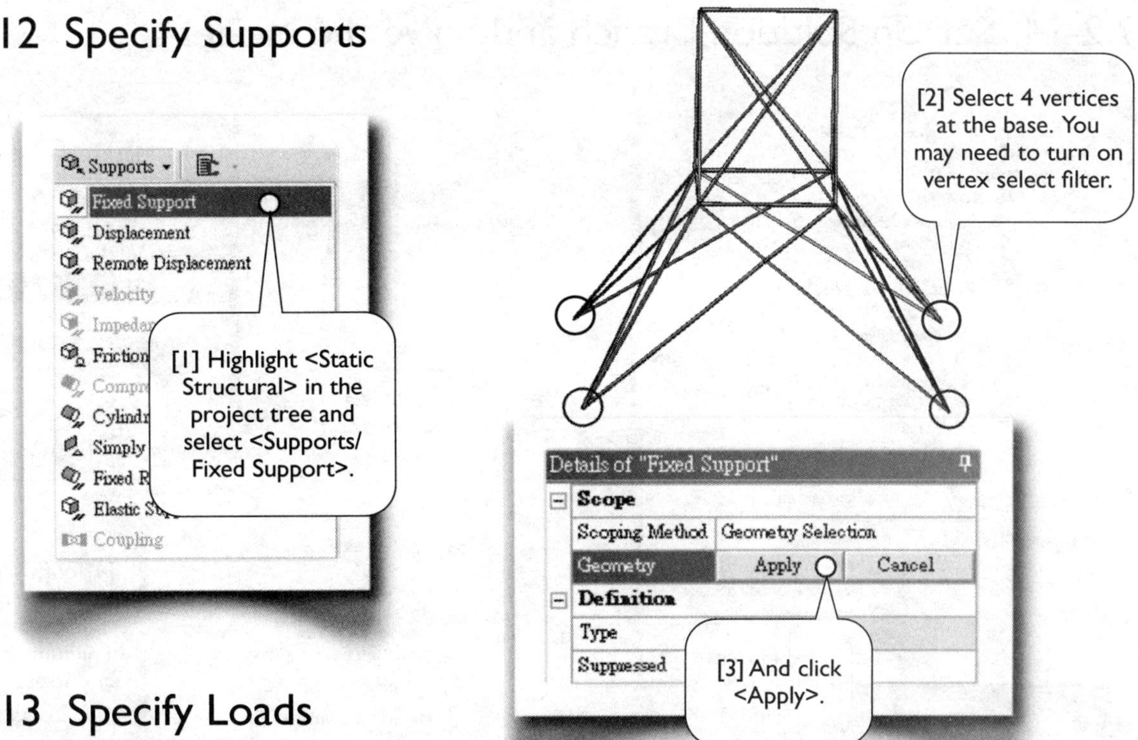

7.2-13 Specify Loads

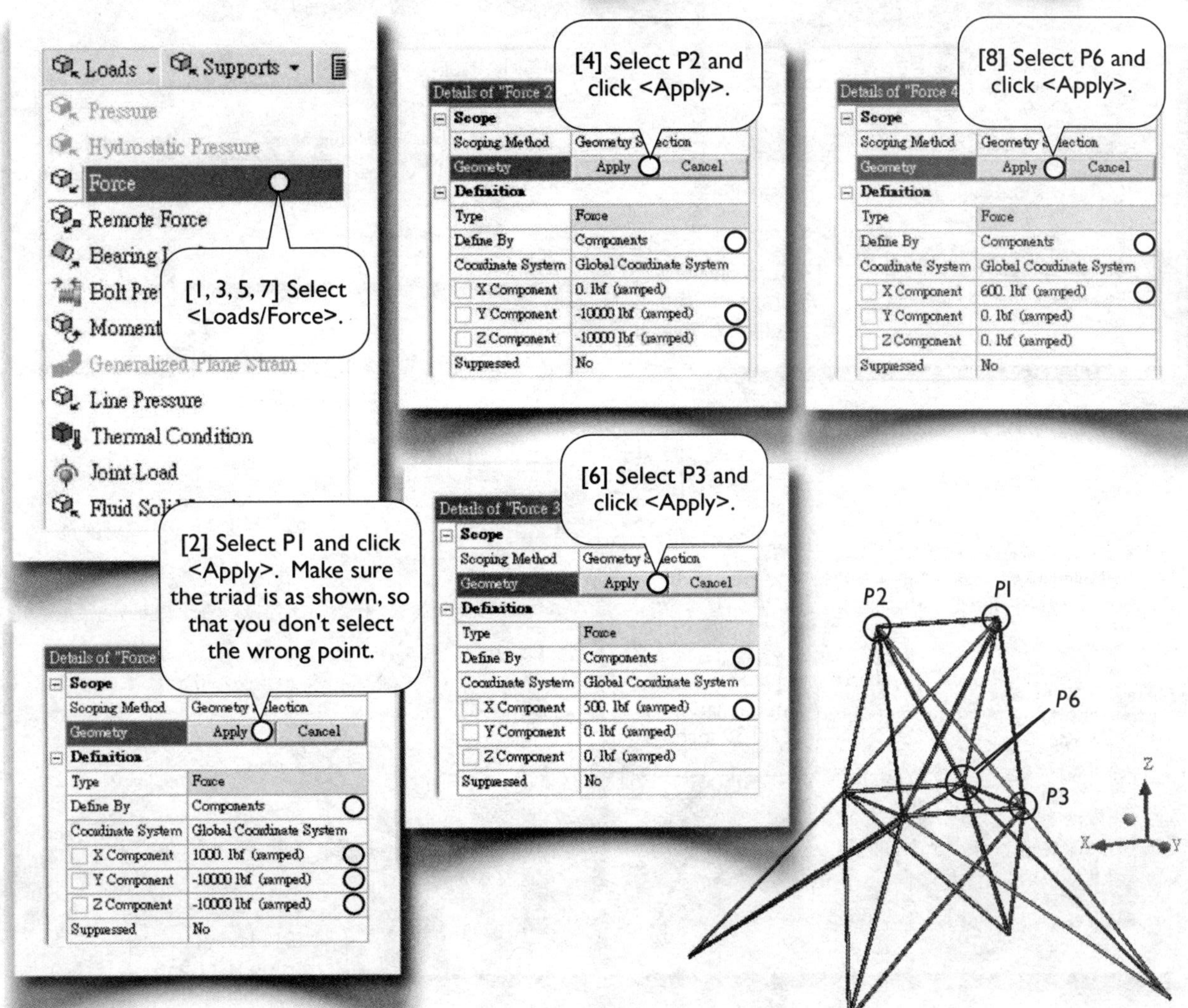

7.2-14 Set Up Solution Branch and Solve the Model

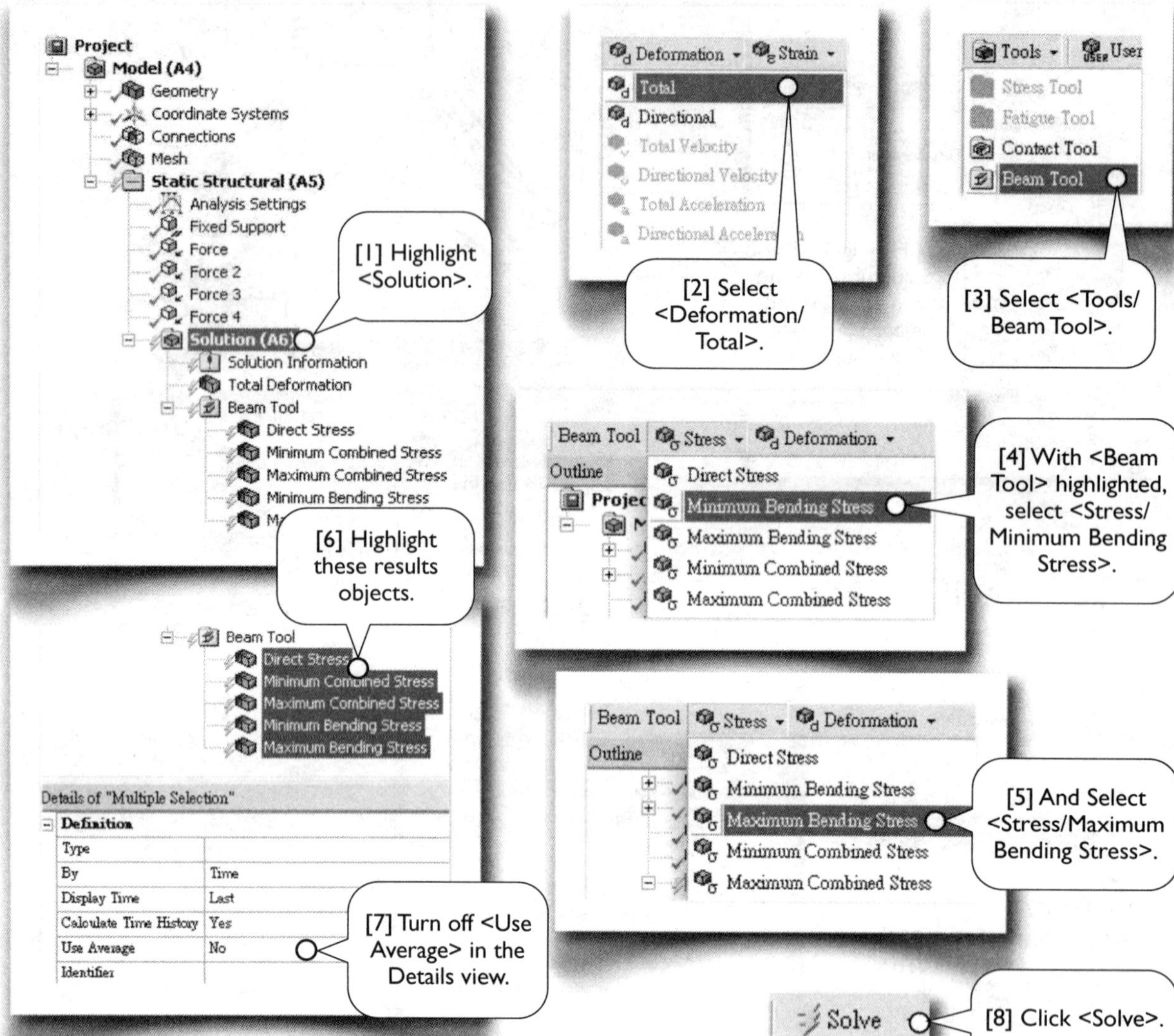

7.2-15 View the Results

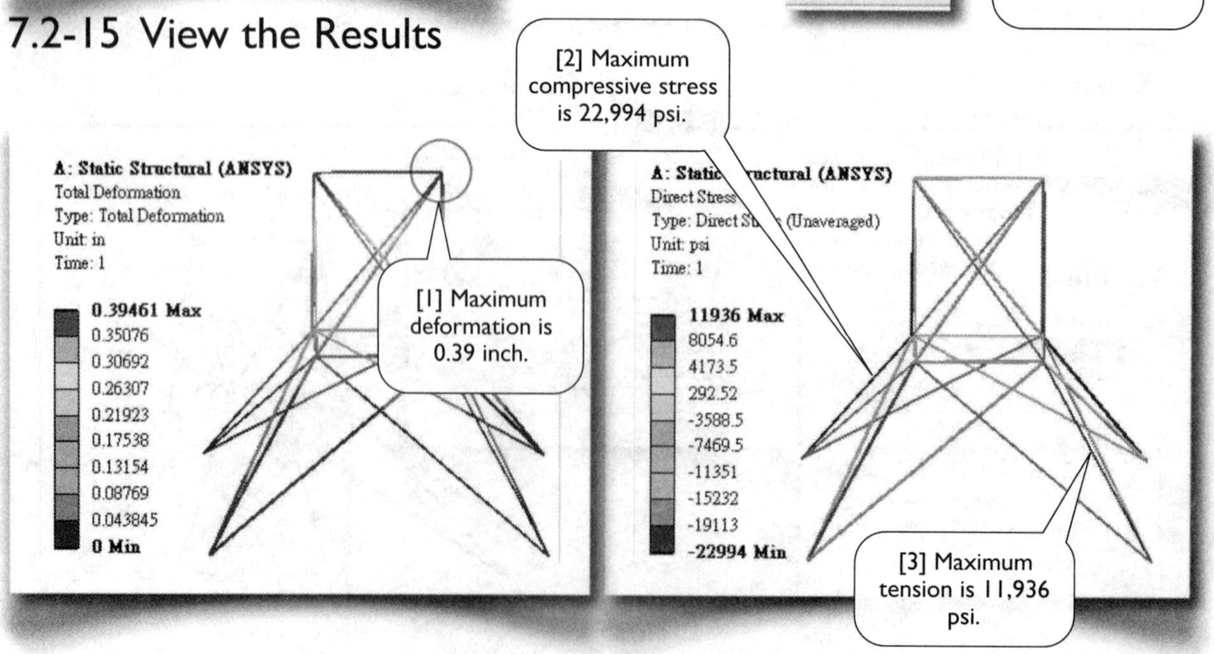

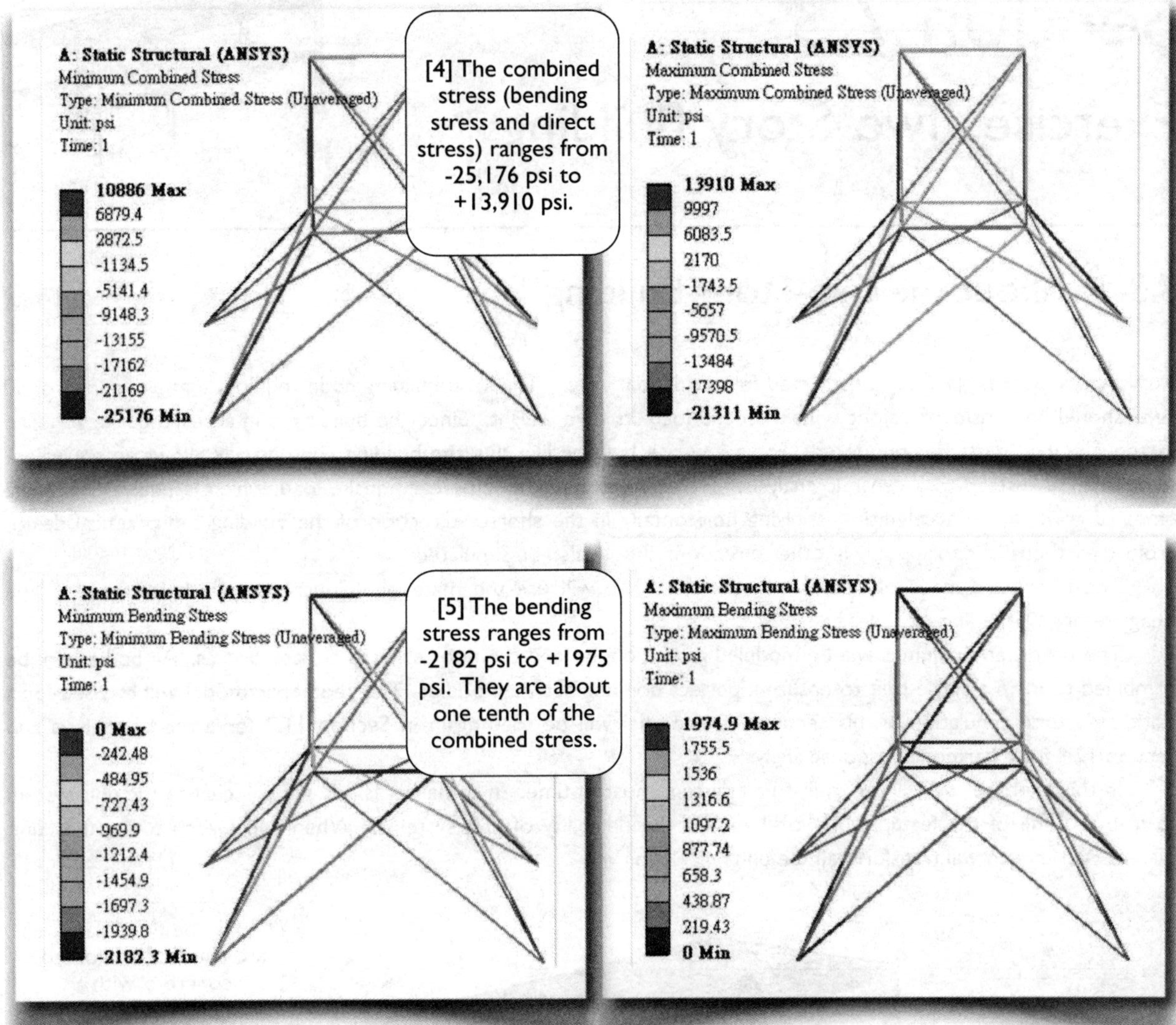

Why Turn Off <Use Average>?

We've introduced the notion of averaged and unaveraged stresses (Section 3.5-6). Unaveraged stresses are also called *element stresses*, since they are calculated at points (usually geometric center or integration points) inside elements. On the other hand, averaged stresses are also called *nodal stresses*, since they are calculated at nodes, which are located at element boundaries. Since we mesh each member with a single beam element, and if we didn't turn off <Use Average>, every two adjacent members' stresses would have been averaged and reported. The averaged stresses would not have any meaning.

Wrap Up

Save the project and quit <Workbench>.

References

1. ANSYS Help System>Mechanical APDL>Element Reference>BEAM188.
2. ANSYS Help System>Mechanical APDL>Element Reference>LINK180.

Section 7.3

Exercise: Two-Story Building

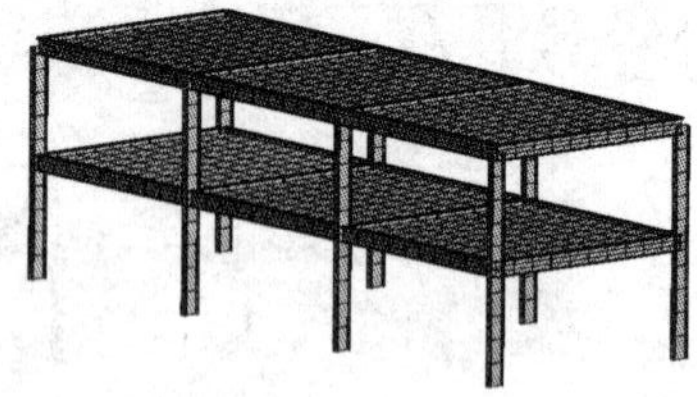

7.3-1 About the Two-Story Building

A two-story building [1-6] is constructed for residential usage. The local building code requires that a live load of 50 lb/ft^2 should be considered, along with the dead load, its own weight. Since the building is in an earthquake zone, an earthquake load must be considered. For a low-rise building like this, the building code usually allows an equivalent static analysis instead of a dynamic analysis. Here we consider a static earthquake load, which is equivalent to 0.2 times of gravitational acceleration, applying horizontally in the shorter direction of the building. In practical design project, earthquake load applying in other directions should also be simulated.

The floors are made of reinforced concrete. We will use the material <Concrete> which is stored in the <Engineering Data> library.

The beams and columns will be modeled as line bodies and the floor slabs as surface bodies. All bodies will be combined to form a single part to ensure a perfect bonding between bodies. The geometric model will be used for a static structural simulation in this section. The model will be used again in Section 11.2 for a modal analysis and Section 12.3 for a harmonic response analysis.

In this exercise, we will use in-lb-s unit system most of time. In some occasions, we will change the unit system to ft-lb-s. One of the features of Workbench is the flexibility of unit systems. When you switch to another unit system, Workbench will transform all the units nicely for you.

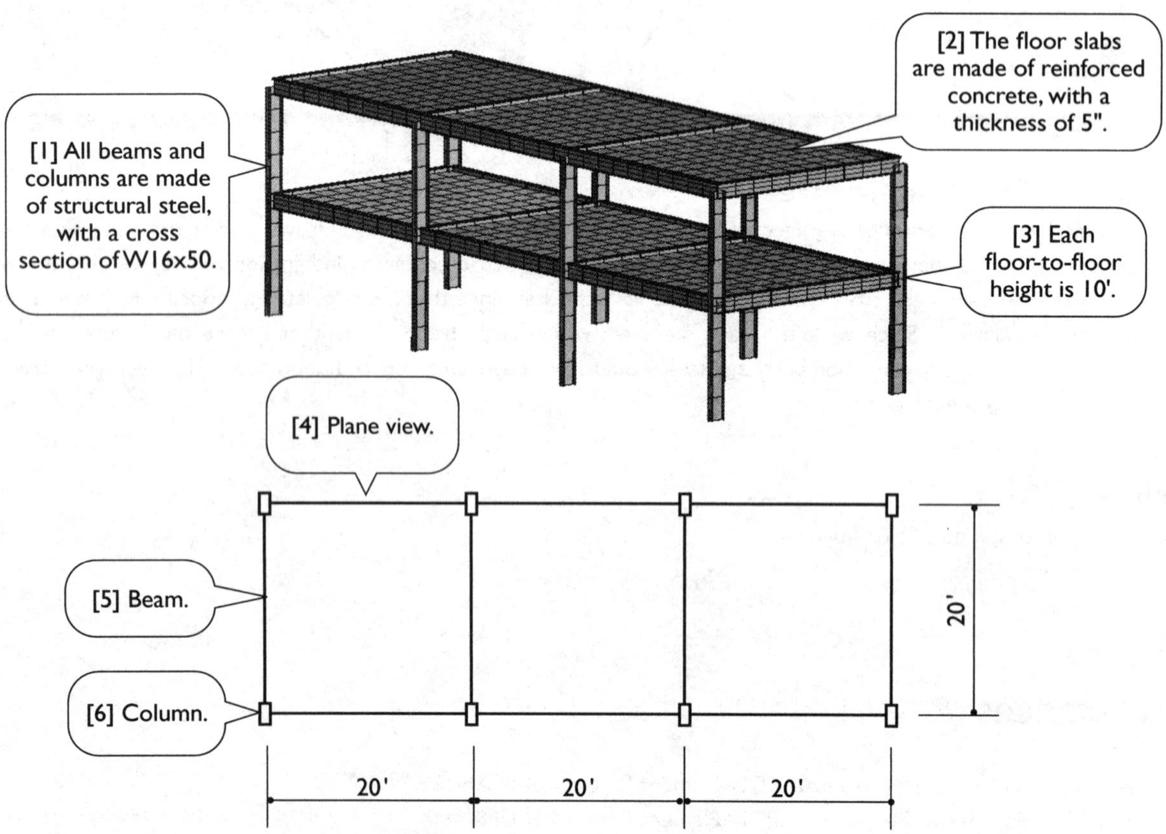

PART A. GEOMETRIC MODELING

7.3-2 Start Up

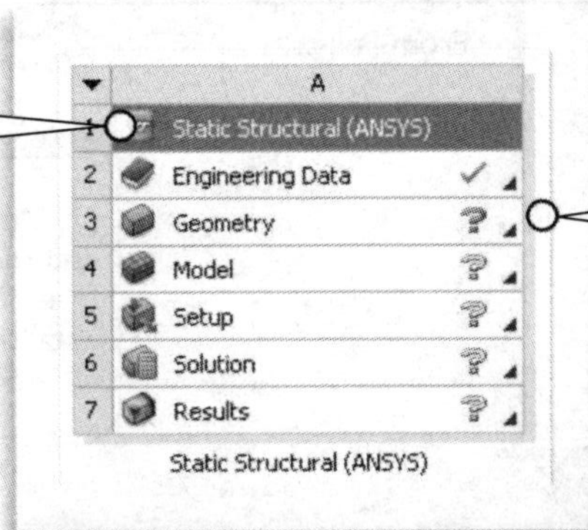

[1] Create a <Static Structural> system. Save the project as "Building."

[2] Start up DesignModeler. Select <Inch> as length unit.

7.3-3 Create 16 Construction Points in the 3D Space

1	1	0	0	0
1	2	240	0	0
1	3	480	0	0
1	4	720	0	0
1	5	0	0	240
1	6	240	0	240
1	7	480	0	240
1	8	720	0	240
2	1	0	120	0
2	2	240	120	0
2	3	480	120	0
2	4	720	120	0
2	5	0	120	240
2	6	240	120	240
2	7	480	120	240
2	8	720	120	240

[1] Prepare a text file containing coordinates of 16 points. Note the 5 columns (fields) in the text file are respectively group number, ID number, X-coordinate, Y-coordinate, and Z-coordinate. Numbers can be separated by spaces or TABs.

[2] Click <Point> on the toolbar.

Details of Point1	
Point	Point1
Type	Construction Point
Definition	From Coordinates File
Coordinates File	C:\Documents and Settin...\Columns.txt ...
Tolerance	Normal
Refresh	No

[3] Select the text file. Click <Generate>.

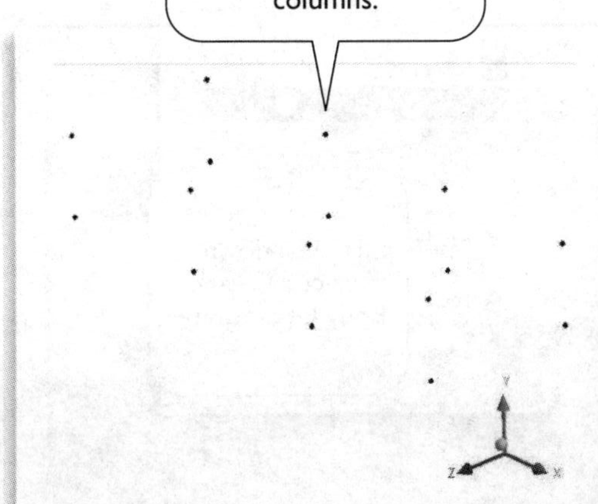

[4] These 16 points are starting and ending points of the first floor columns.

7.3-4 Create a Line Body of 10 Beams

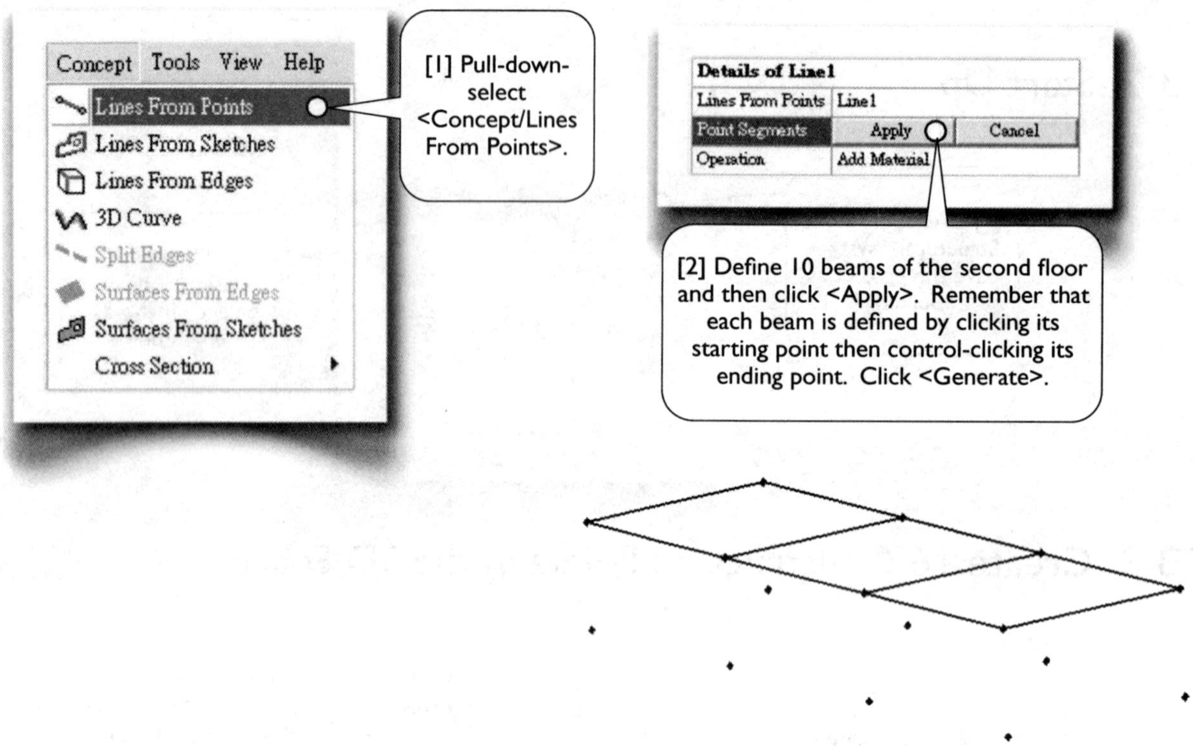

7.3-5 Copy the Line Body

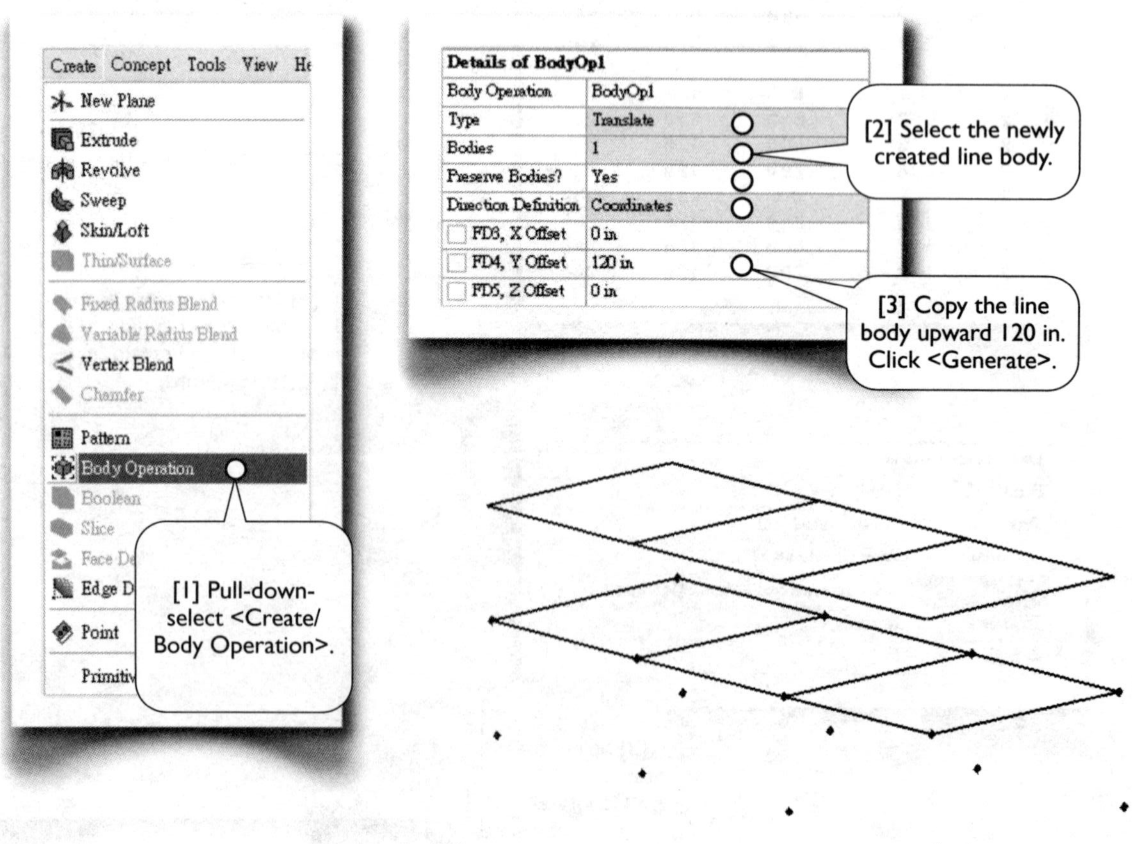

7.3-6 Create Line Body for Columns

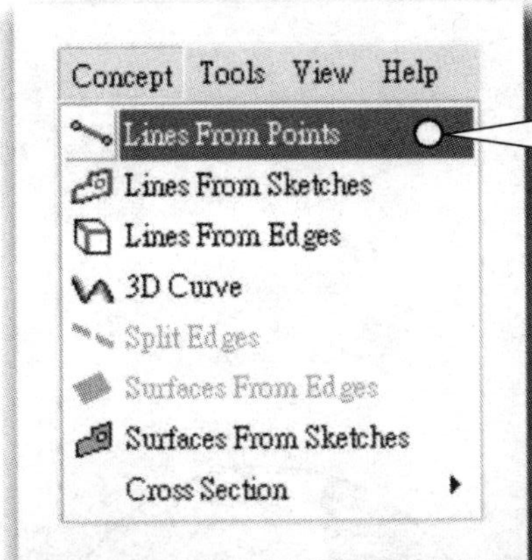

[1] Pull-down-select <Concept/Lines From Points>.

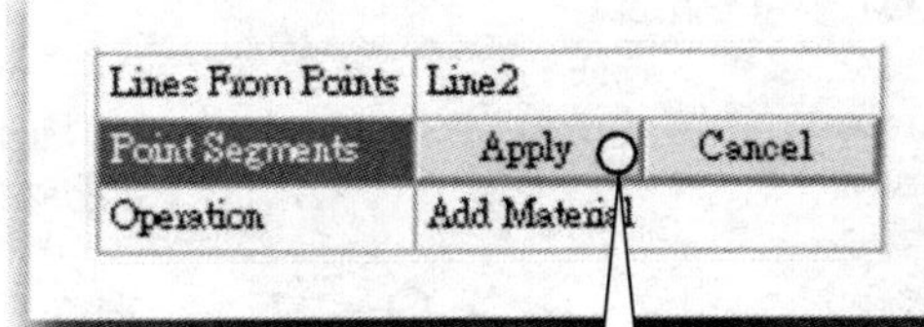

[2] Define 8 columns then click <Apply>. Each column is defined by clicking its starting point at the roof then control-clicking its ending at the ground. Click <Generate>. If you made a mistake, you can remove a member by clicking the starting and ending points again.

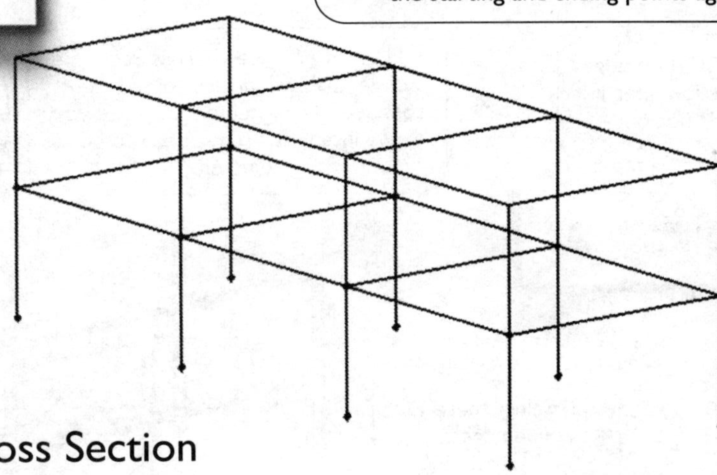

7.3-7 Create a Cross Section

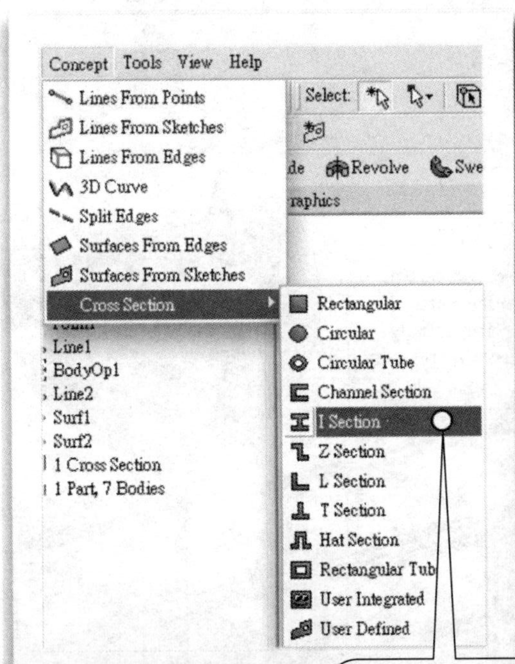

[1] Pull-down-select <Concept/Cross Section/I Section>.

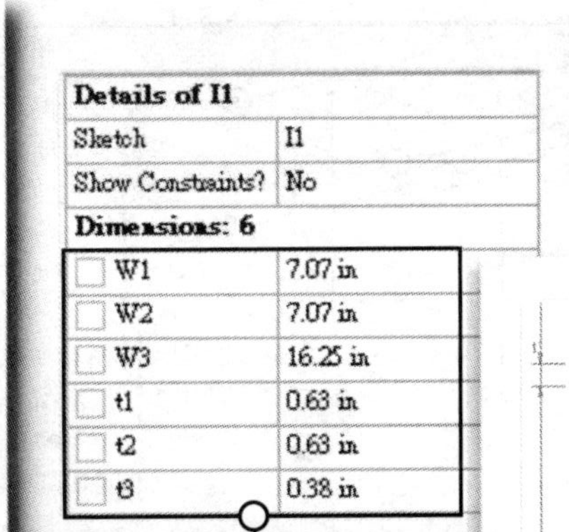

[2] Type dimensions for the W16x50 cross section.

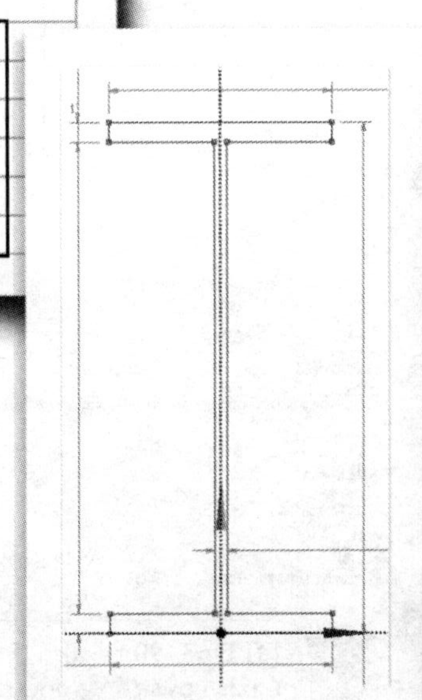

7.3-8 Assign the Cross Section to the Line Body

Details of Line Body	
Body	Line Body
Faces	0
Edges	36
Vertices	24
Cross Section	I1
Offset Type	Centroid

[1] Highlight the line body in the model tree and then, in the details view, select <I1> as cross section.

7.3-9 Adjust Cross Section Alignments

[2] Turn on edge selection filter if it is not on.

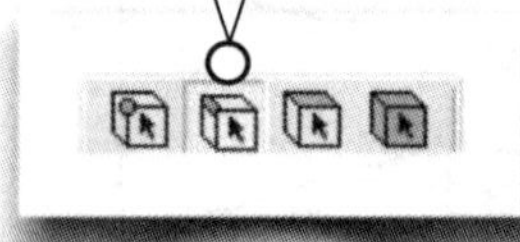

[1] Turn on <View/Cross Section Solid>. You will notice some beams' cross section alignements are not what we intend for. They need to be adjusted.

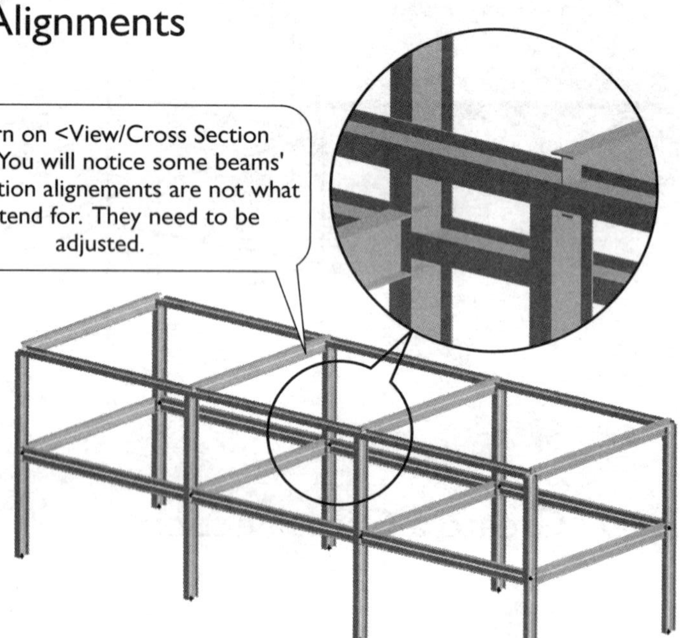

[3] Select these 12 line edges.

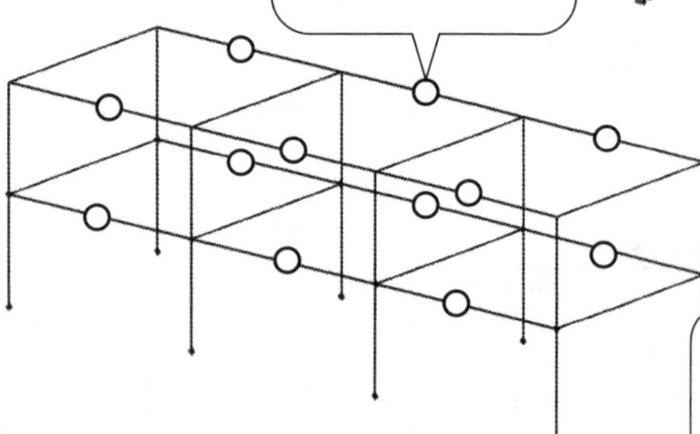

Line-Body Edge	
Alignment Mode	Selection
Cross Section Alignment	None (+Z by default)
Alignment X	0
Alignment Y	0
Alignment Z	1
Rotate	-90 °
Reverse Orientation?	No

[4] Type -90 to turn the sectional Y-axis upward. It doesn't matter if you type +90 to turn the Y-axis downward.

[5] Now the beams look more natural. Beams are usually constructed in this way.

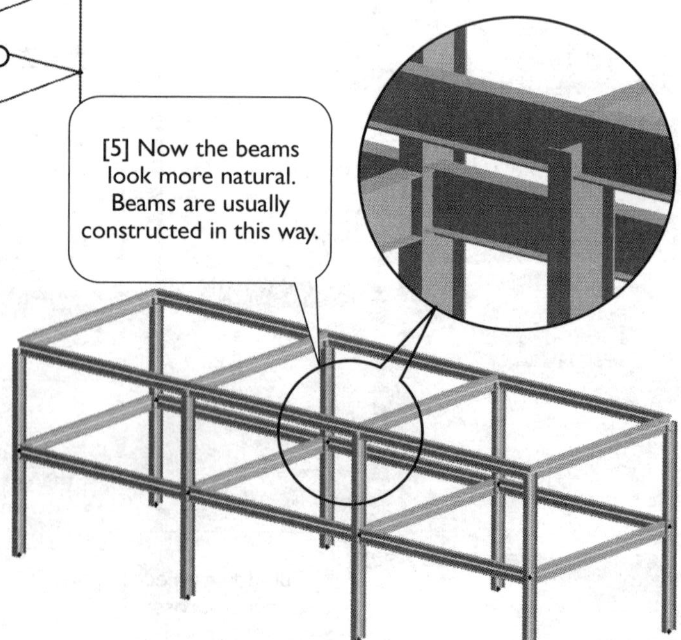

7.3-10 Create Surface Bodies

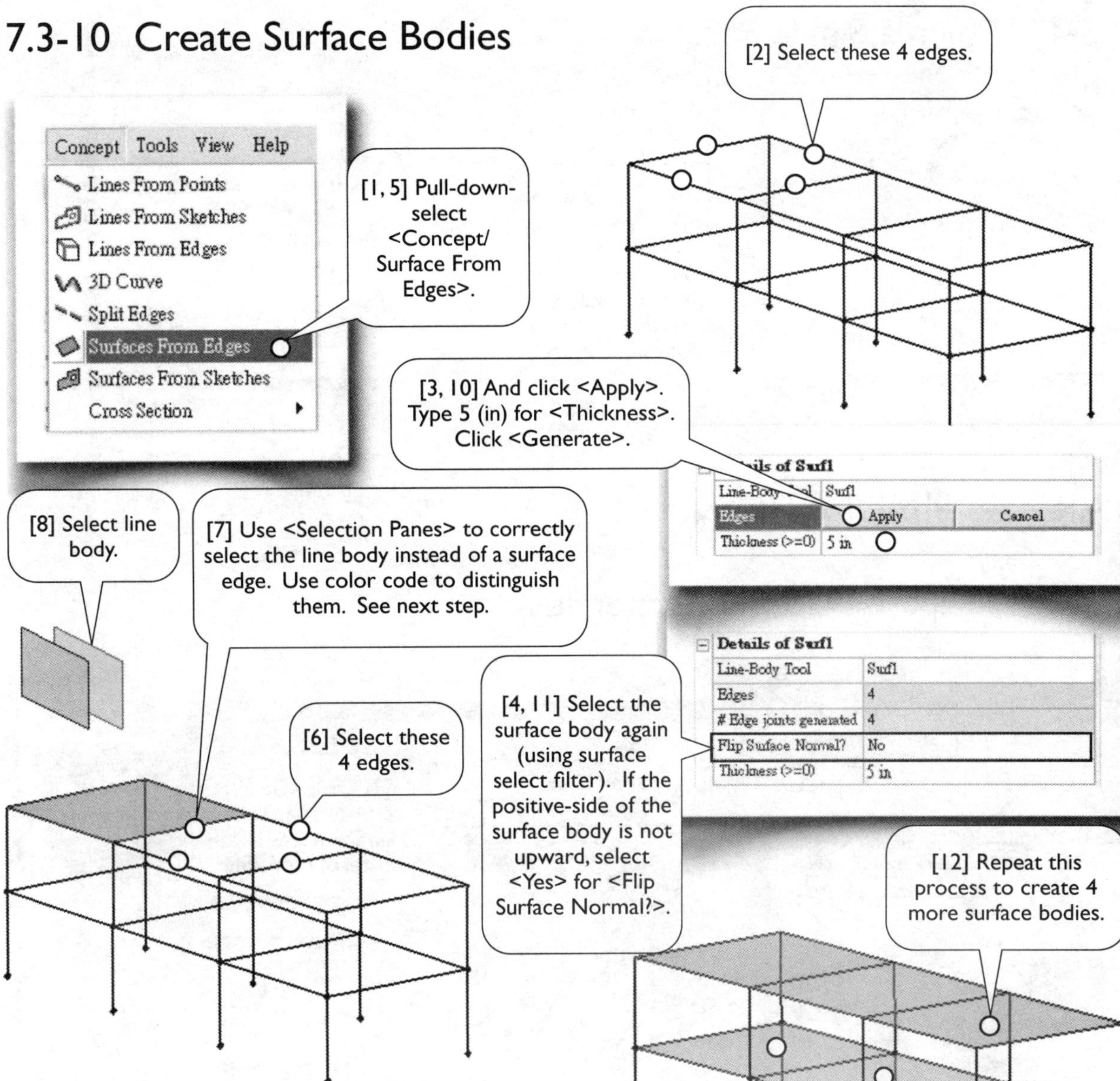

Edge Selection

When you select edges, you may need to use <Selection Panes> [7, 8] to correctly select the line body rather than a surface edge. If you select a surface edge instead of a line body, the slab would not connect to the line body, and would have a gap after deformation [9].

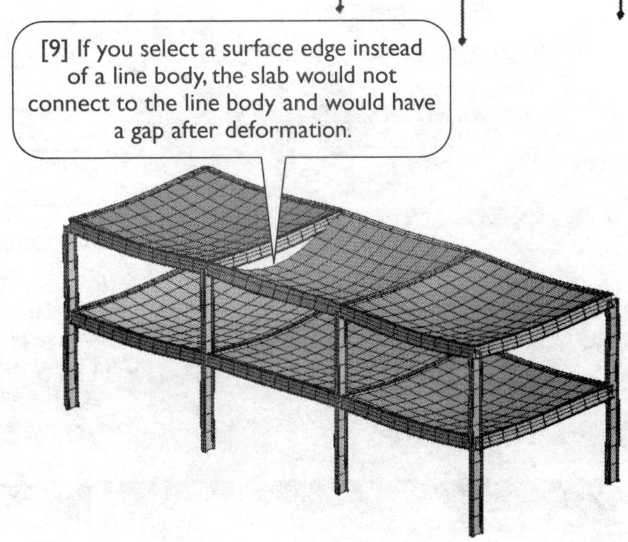

Direction of Surface Bodies

Each surface body has a positive-side and a negative-side. In <Mechanical>, the pressure always applies on the positive-side. Therefore it is important to know which side is the positive-side. Turn on the surface selection filter and click the surface body, the positive-side will highlighted with a deep green color. Make sure the positive-side of each surface body is upward in this case. If not, select <Yes> for <Flip Surface Normal> in the Details view [4, 11].

7.3-11 Form a Single Part

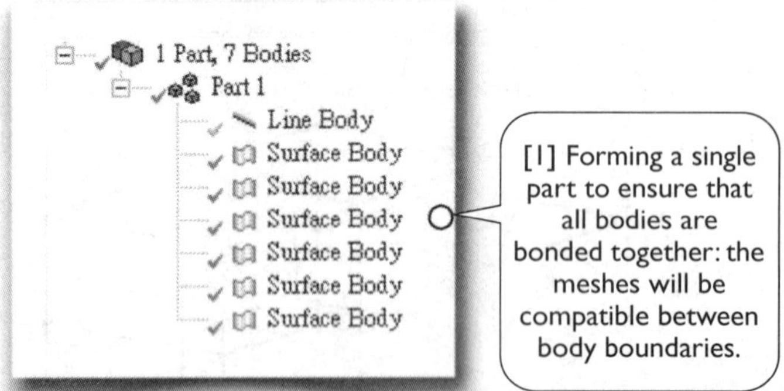

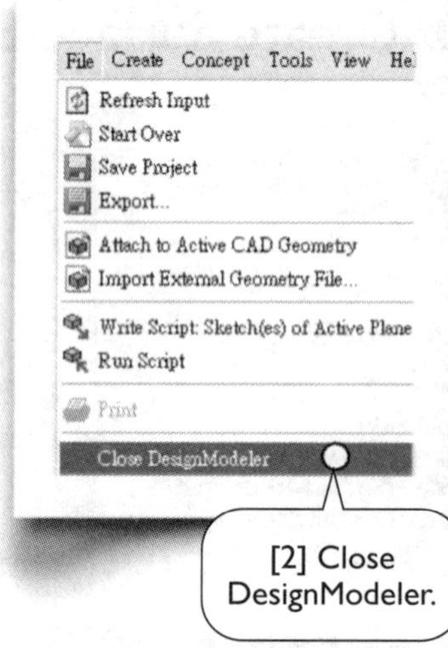

PART B. SIMULATION

7.3-12 Prepare Material Properties

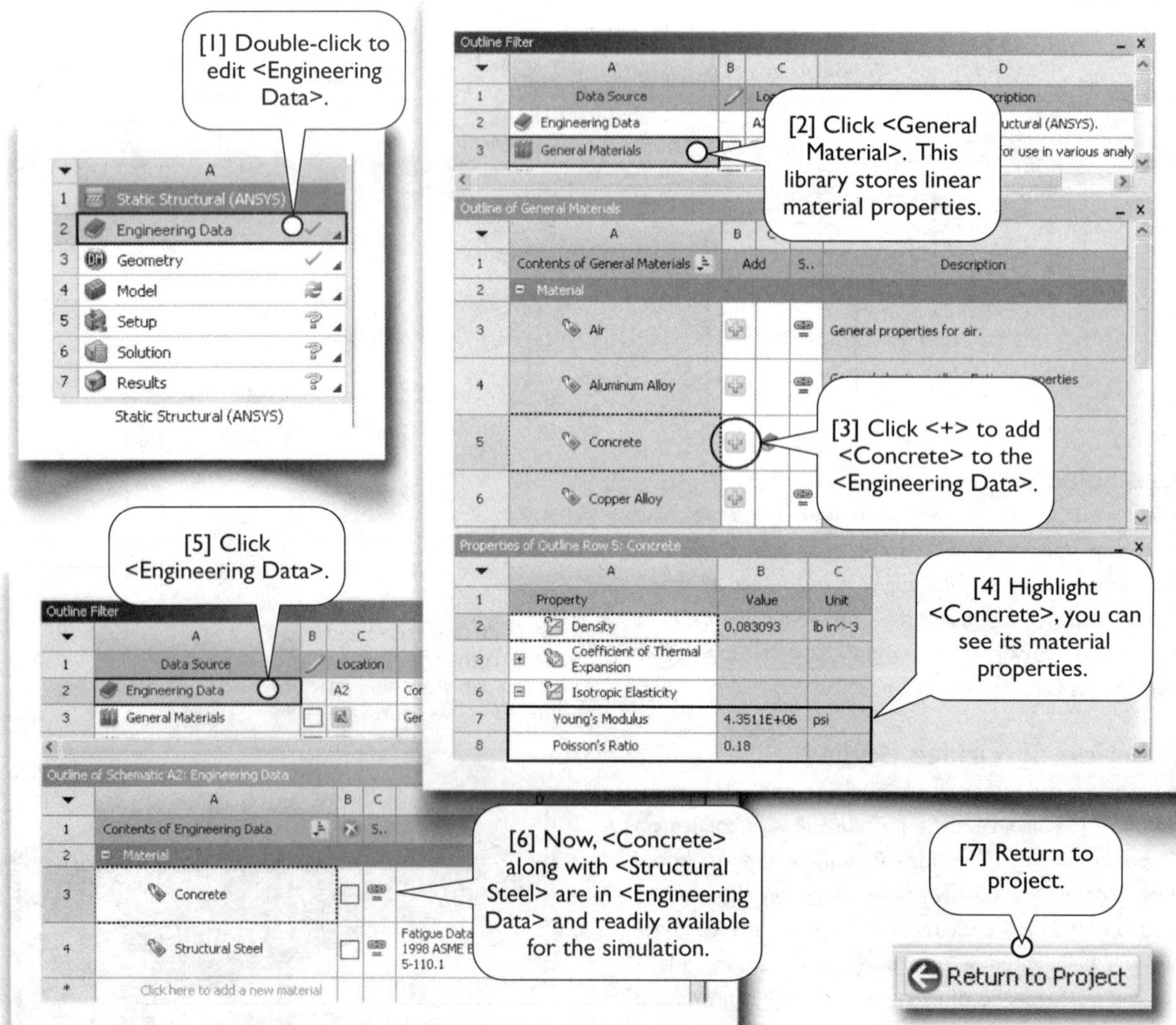

7.3-13 Start Up <Mechanical>

Before starting up <Mechanical>, remember to turn on <Line Bodies> property (see 7.1-7[2]).

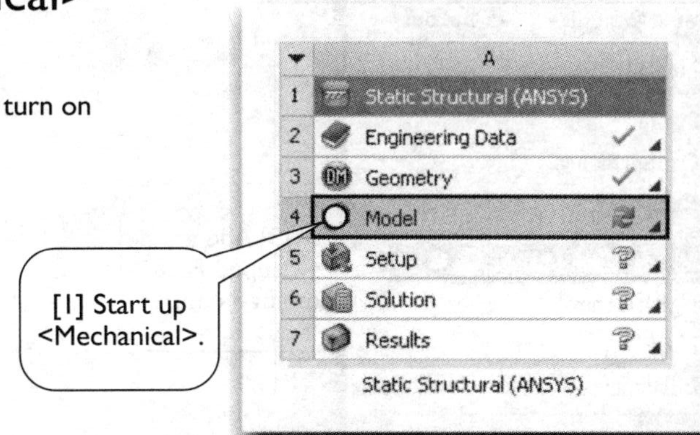

7.3-14 Assign Material

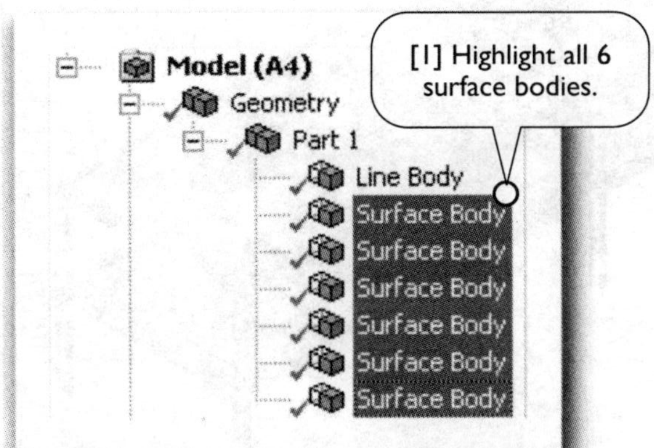

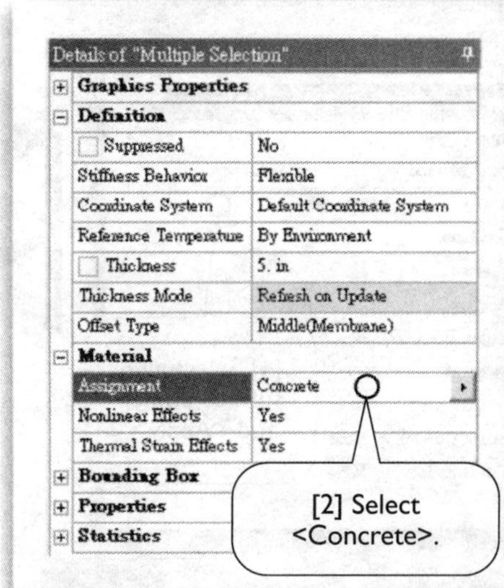

7.3-15 Set Up Mesh Controls

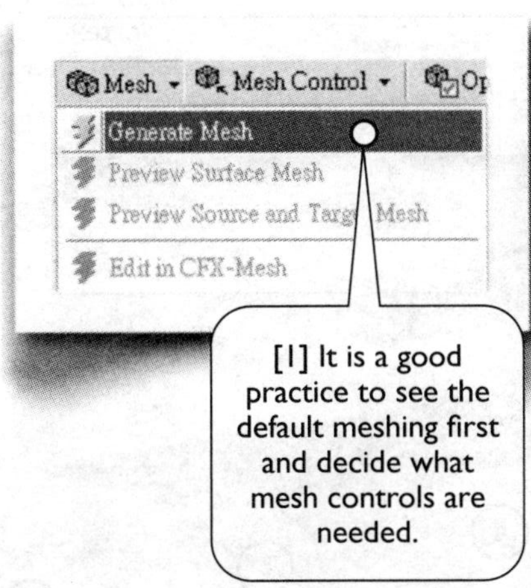

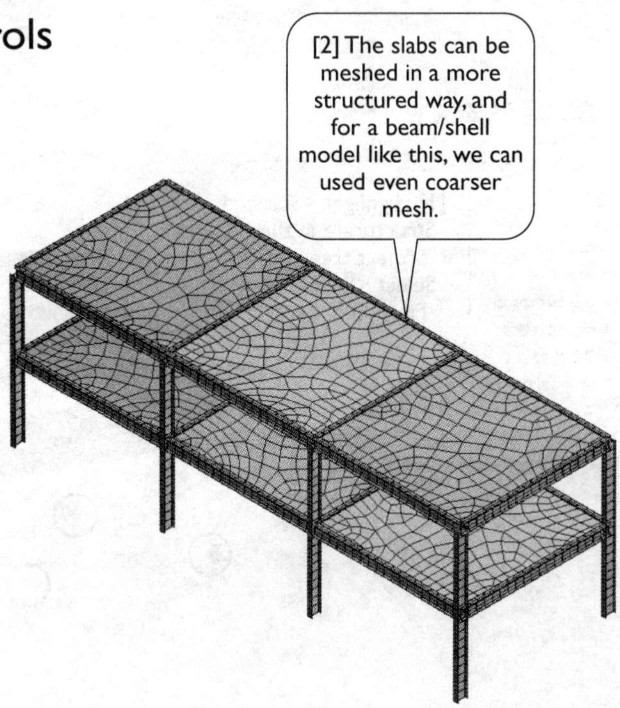

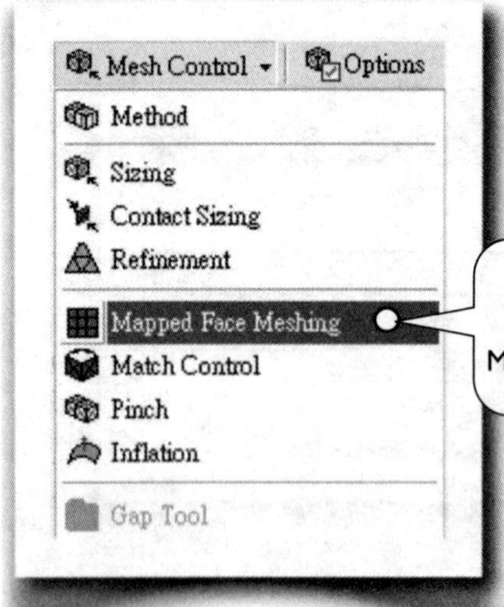

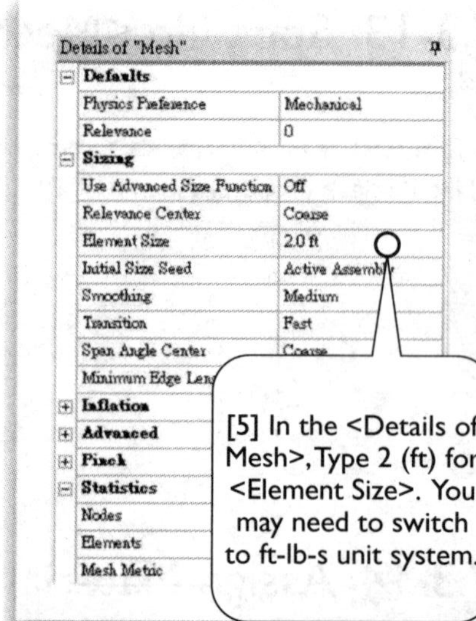

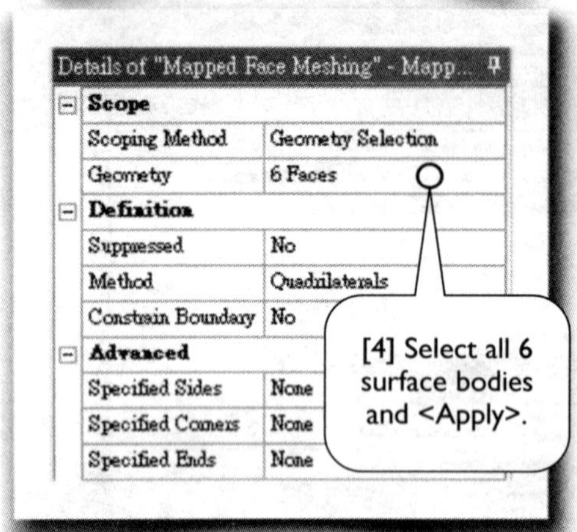

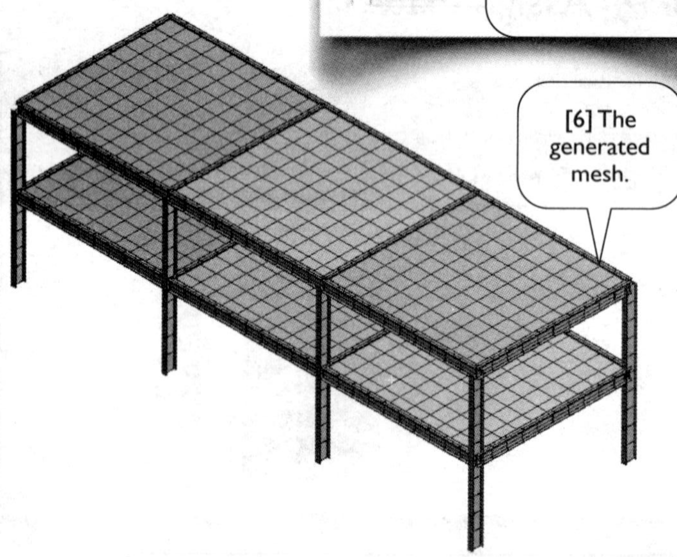

7.3-16 Specify Supports

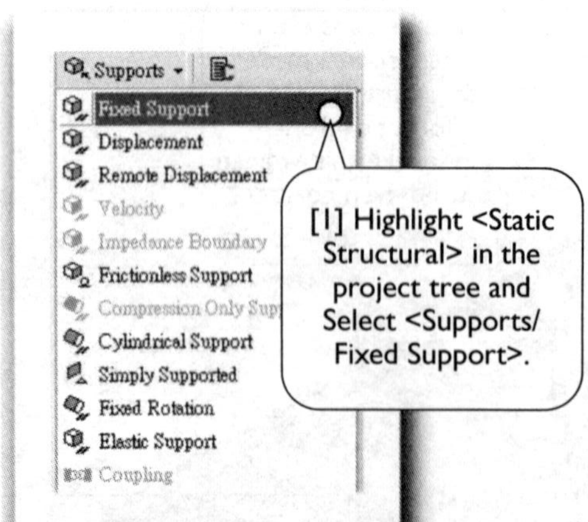

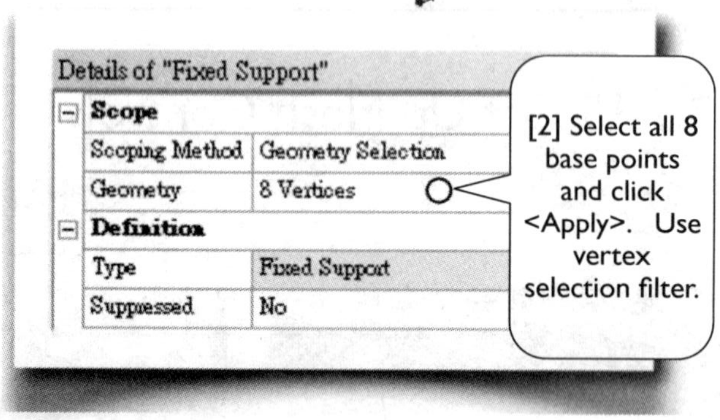

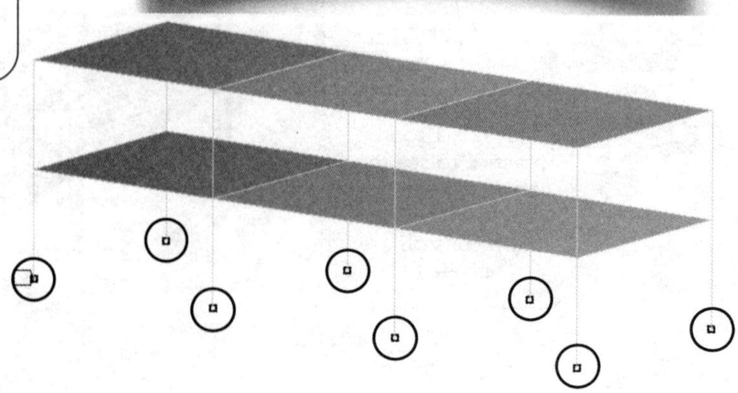

7.3-17 Apply the Live Load

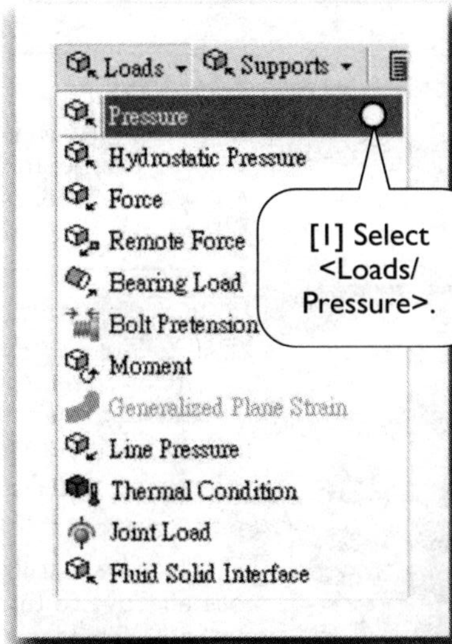

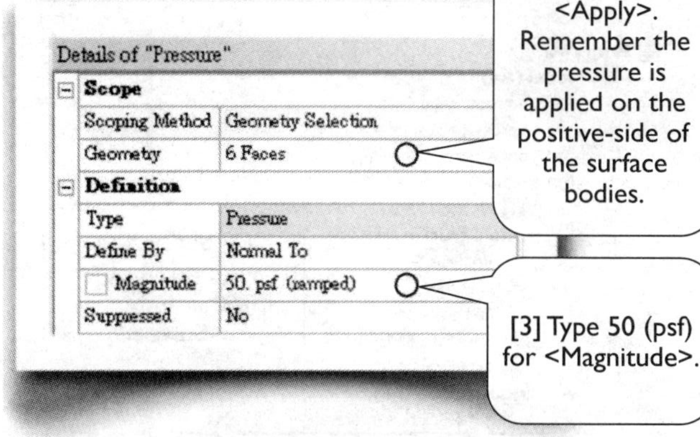

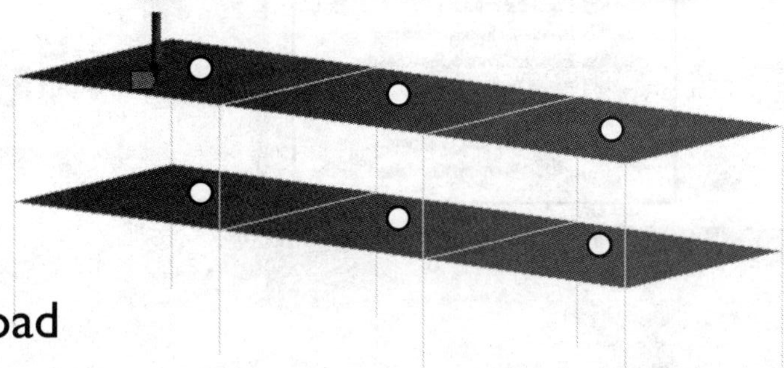

7.3-18 Apply the Dead Load

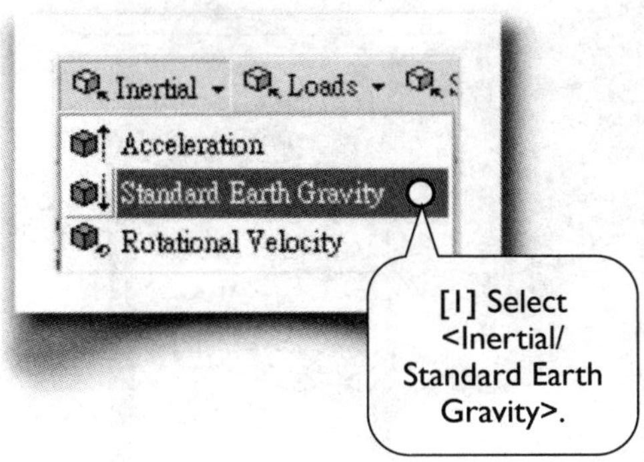

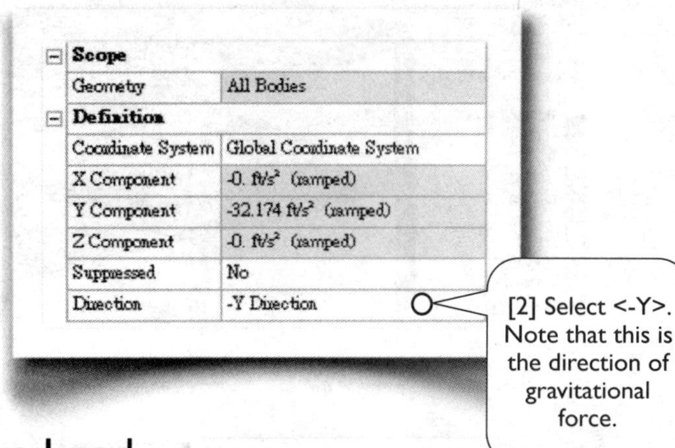

7.3-19 Apply the Earthquake Load

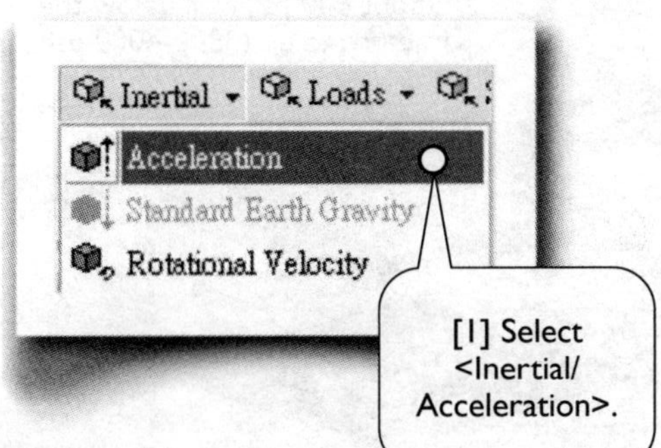

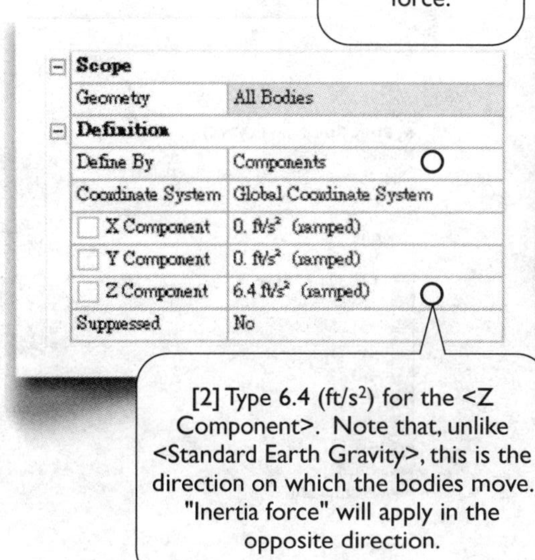

7.3-20 Solve the Model and View the Results

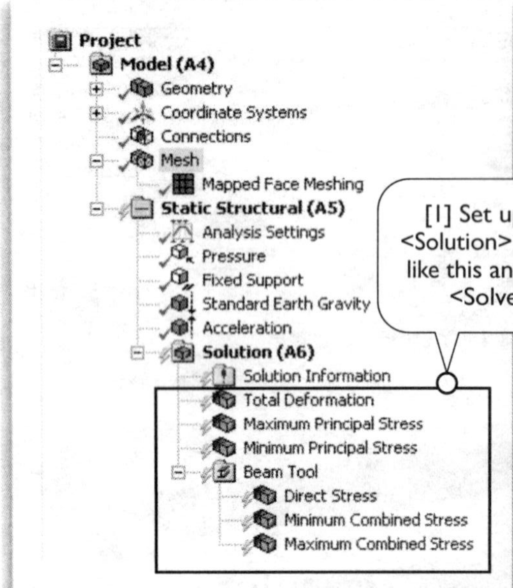

[1] Set up the <Solution> branch like this and issue <Solve>.

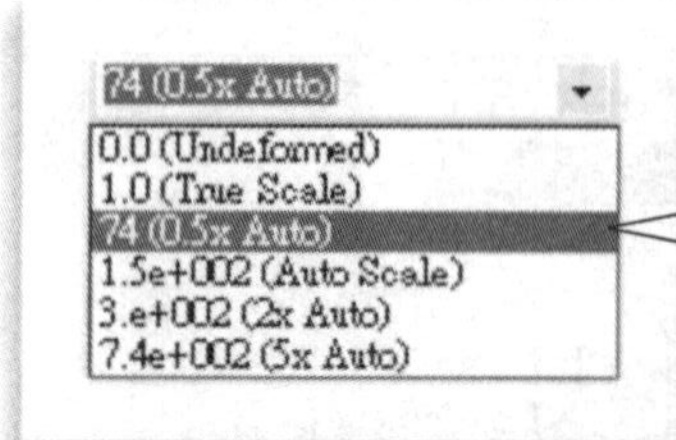

[2] If the deformation is too exaggerated, you can reduce the scale.

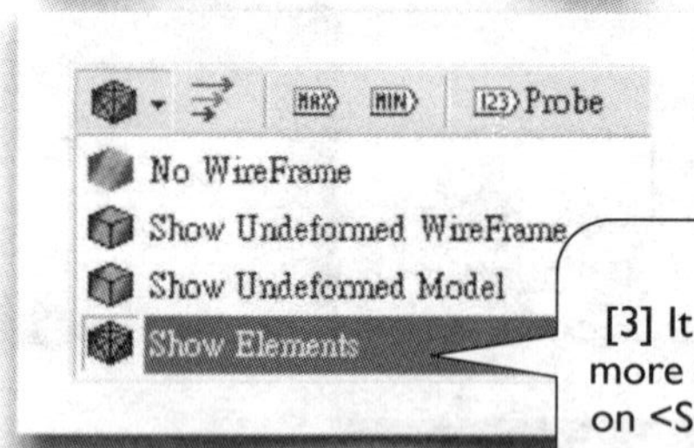

[3] It may be visually more effective to turn on <Show Elements>.

[4] The maximum deformation is 0.3 inch. (Please switch back to in-lb-s unit system.)

[5] Maximum compressive stress of the concrete slab is about 600 psi, well below the fracture value (3000-4000 psi).

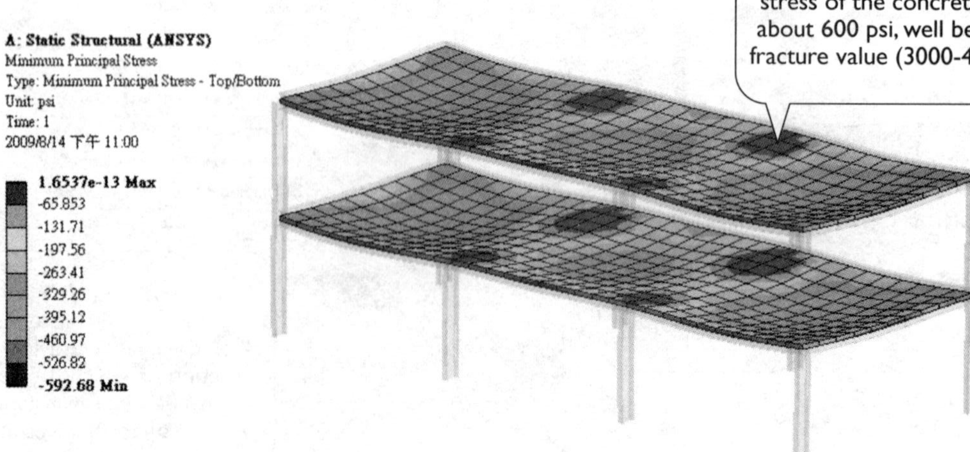

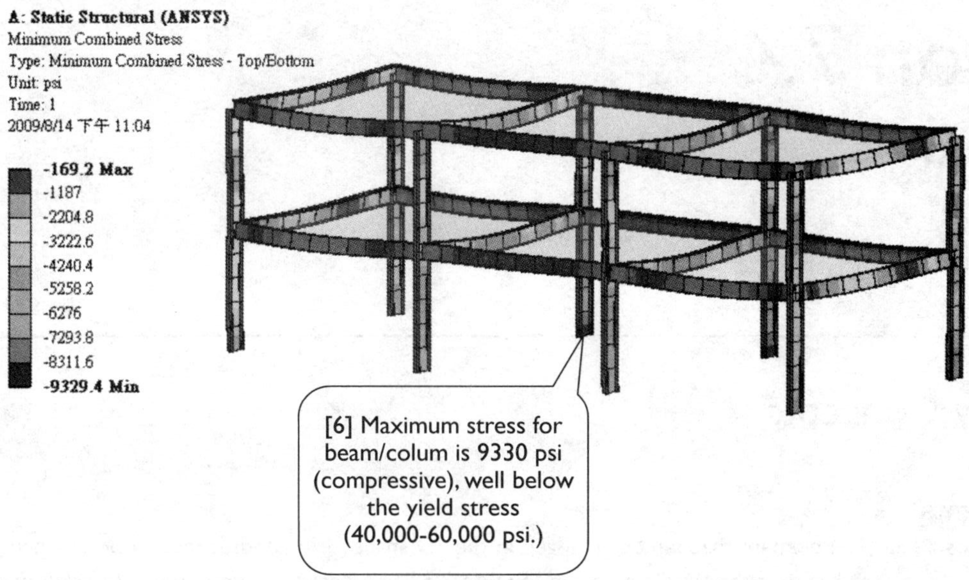

Wrap Up

Save the project and exit <Workbench>.

Section 7.4

Problems

7.4-1 Key Concepts

Beam Elements

A beam element is a line (1D) element that can be arranged in the 3D space. It is used to mesh a body when two of its dimensions are much smaller than the third dimension. Each node has 6 degrees of freedom: 3 translational and 3 rotational. Due to the presence of rotational degrees of freedom, it is very efficient to model the problems dominated by bending modes, contrasting to a solid element, which does not have rotational degrees of freedom.

Truss

A truss is defined as a structure consisting of two-force members. By two-force member, we mean that the members are pin-jointed at the ends, and the loads apply on the joints so that the members are either stretched or compressed but not bent.

Direct Stress and Bending Stress

The resultant forces acting on a beam cross section can be summarized into three components: direct force F, bending moment M, and shear force V. Only the direct force and the bending moment contribute to the axial stress. The axial stress caused by the direct force is called the direct stress $\sigma = F/A$, where A is the cross-sectional area. The direct stress can be tensile or compressive. The axial stress caused by the bending moment is called the bending stress $\sigma_b = My/I$, where y is the distance from the neutral axis to the point of concern, and I is the moment of inertia of the cross section.

Maximum/Minimum Bending Stress

The maximum or minimum bending stress occurs at the either top or bottom beam edge, depending on the direction of the bending moment. The maximum bending stress is always tensile while the minimum bending stress is always compressive.

Maximum/Minimum Combined Stress

The maximum combined stress is the superposition of the direct stress plus the maximum bending stress. The minimum combined stress is the superposition of the direct stress plus the minimum bending stress.

Coordinates File

A text file describing the coordinates of points. The file has 5 columns, or fields: (a) group number, (b) ID number, (c) X-coordinate, (d) Y-coordinate, and (e) Z-coordinate. The group number and the ID number are arbitrary and they uniquely identify a point from others.

7.4-2 Workbench Exercises

Convergence Study of Beam Elements

Generate a convergence curve like the one in Section 7.1-17 for the flexible gripper.

Mesh Each Member with More Elements

In Section 7.2-11, we mentioned that the default settings of <Mesh> would mesh the model into 205 beam elements and would result exactly the same solution as 25 elements. Verify this. Type 0 for <Element Size> to set the default element size.

Pin-Jointed or Rigid-Jointed?

In Section 7.2-1, we mentioned that if the members of a truss structure are slender enough, there is no essential difference between pin-jointed model and rigid-jointed model. Verify this. You may select a simple truss structure from any of your Engineering Mechanics textbook. With the pin-joint assumption, hand-calculate the solution. Solve the problem again in the Workbench using a rigid-jointed model. Compare the results and draw your conclusions.

Chapter 8
Optimization

Design Process

From engineering design point of view, simulation is a part of the design process. A typical design process involves several steps as shown in the right [1-6]. First, the engineer sets up an initial design [1], including the sizes, the materials, etc. The initial design is simulated [2] and the performance is evaluated [3]. If the performance is satisfied, then the design is accepted [6], otherwise the design must be improved somehow [5]. Note that it is an iterative process. After several iterations, the design ideally converges to an optimal design.

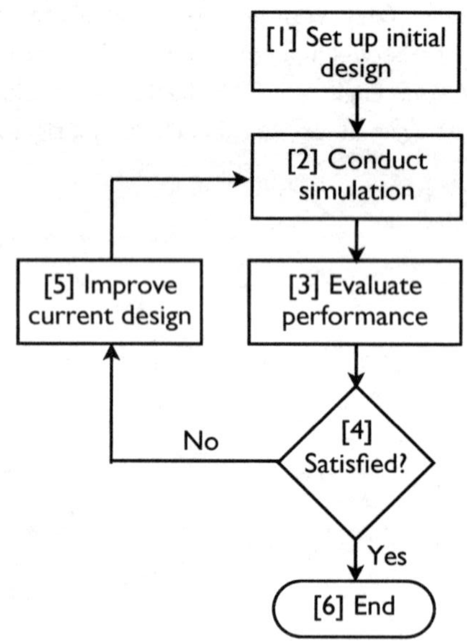

Now, let's examine the way of improving a design [5]. Conventionally, the way of improving a design pretty much relies on engineers' experience. For those engineers without much experience, it relies on their luck. Either way, the consequence is that the process is costly and often does not converge to an optimum.

This chapter focuses on a capability of the Workbench which automates the improvement of a design. Note that this capability does not mean to automate the entire design process [1-6]; rather, it automate the improvement of a design inside the loop of an iteration [5]. To complete the design process, the engineers themselves must decide how many iterations it should go through.

Purpose of the Chapter

This chapter is purposely arranged in the middle of the textbook because it is a suitable time to learn the optimization techniques before we look into more advanced topics. The idea is that the students should be aware as early as possible of the capabilities provided by the DesignXplorer, a native application of the Workbench, including optimization, so that they can exploit the features when doing their exercises.

This chapter provide two hands-on examples, which cover main ideas of optimization. After the exercises, the students should be able to use these capabilities on their own.

About Each Section

Section 1 revisits the flexible gripper, introduced in Section 7.1. This time, we want to improve the shape of the gripper to achieve a better geometric advantage. Section 2 provides an additional exercise, in which the triangular plate, introduced in Section 2.2 and simulated in Section 3.1, is to be improved to reduce the material used.

Section 8.1
Step-by-Step: Flexible Gripper

8.1-1 About the Flexible Gripper

[1] The gripper.

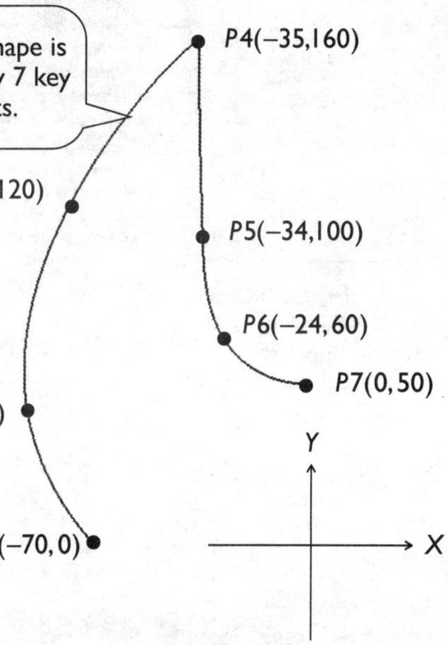

[2] The shape is defined by 7 key points.

In Section 7.1, we introduced a flexible gripper [1], created a line model for it, and performed a static structural simulation to assess the GA (geometric advantage, defined as the ratio of horizontal output displacement to input displacement) of the design. For that particular design, the GA value is 1.04 (7.1-16). In this section, we want to improve the GA value by adjusting the shape of the flexible gripper.

The shape of the gripper consists of two spline curves defined by 7 key points [2]. Positions of the *P1*, *P4*, *P5*, and *P7* are fixed (cannot be changed) due to constraints imposed by some functional requirements. The positions of the *P2*, *P3*, and *P6* are free to be changed.

The idea is to fix the X-coordinates of these three points and adjusting their Y-coordinates to achieve a better GA value. The allowable adjustment range on both sides of the Y-coordinates is 10 mm for *P2*, 20 mm for *P3*, and 5 mm for *P6*. Besides the GA value, we also have to watch out the maximum stress, which should not exceed 15 MPa for a reliability consideration.

We will use <DesignXplorer>, a native application of the Workbench, to complete the task.

The unit system used in this exercise is mm-s-N (to set up the unit system, see Section 3.3-5).

Keep the Number of Design Variables Minimum

The design parameters that can be changed to improve a design are called *design variables* (in this case, X-coordinates of *P2*, *P3*, and *P6*). The overall computing time of an optimization project will increase dramatically as the number of design variables increases. Therefore it is important to consider only minimum number of design variables.

In this case, we could have chosen both X-coordinates and Y-coordinates of *P2*, *P3*, *P6* as design variables. That would increase the number of design variables from 3 to 6, without earning any benefits at all, since the X-coordinate and the Y-coordinate of a point are not independent to each other.

8.1-2 Resume the Project "Gripper"

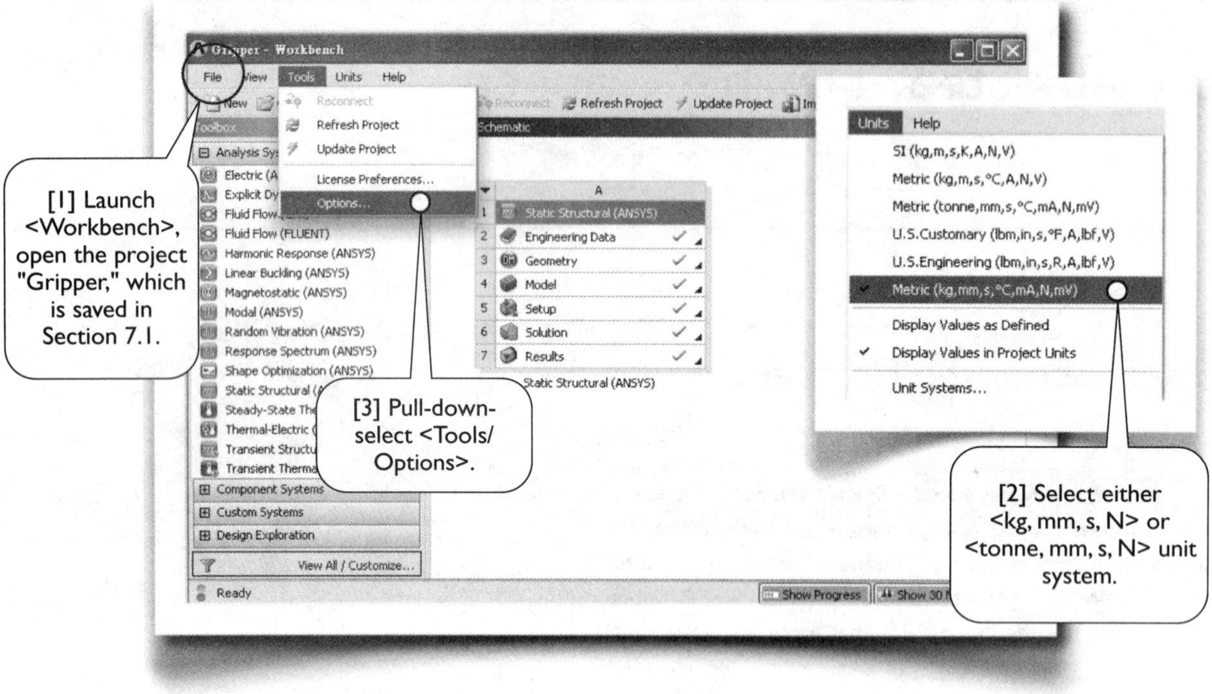

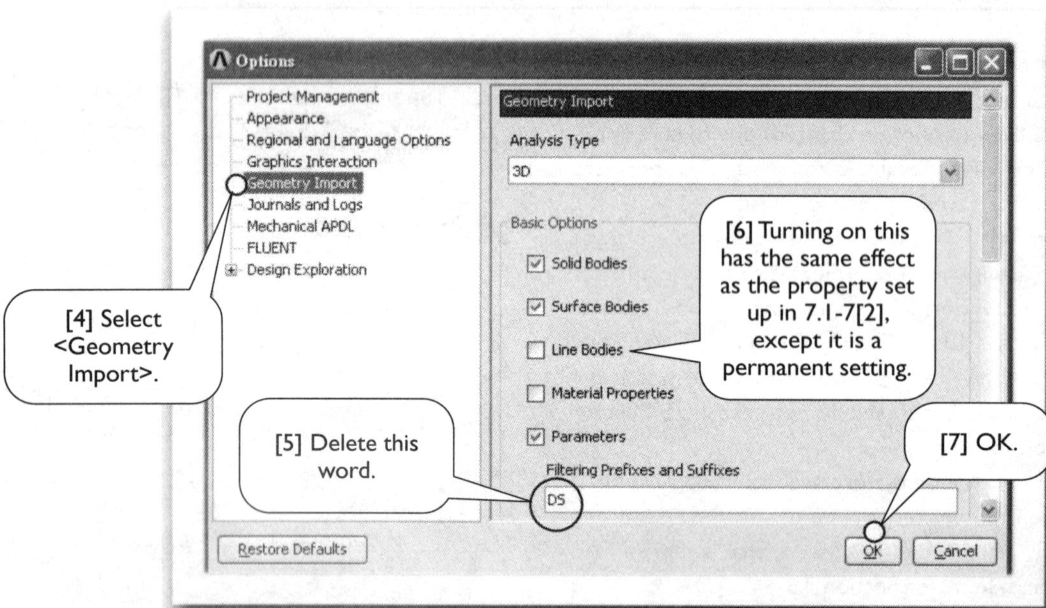

<Filtering Prefixes and Suffixes>

You can define as many parameters as you want in a CAD system, such as DesignModeler, or Pro/Engineer. However, only those parameters with names of prefix or suffix specified in the <Filtering Prefixes and Suffixes> are exposed (visible) to applications of the Workbench. The default prefix or suffix is "DS" (case insensitive, DS stands for Design Space, an obsolete name for the Workbench). For example, by default, following parameter names are exposed to the Workbench: DS_radius, ds_radius, Radius_DS, Radius_ds, where the underscore can be dropped.

In our case, we leave a blank for the <Filtering Prefixes and Suffixes>. That means any parameters defined in a CAD system are exposed to applications of the Workbench. Note that the changes of settings in the <Options> are permanent; they are effective even for other project. So, remember to change back if needed.

8.1-3 Define Parameters in DesignModeler

Start up <DesignModeler> by double-clicking <Geometry> in the <Static Structural> system. Highlight <Sketch1> in the tree outline and switch to <Sketching> mode.

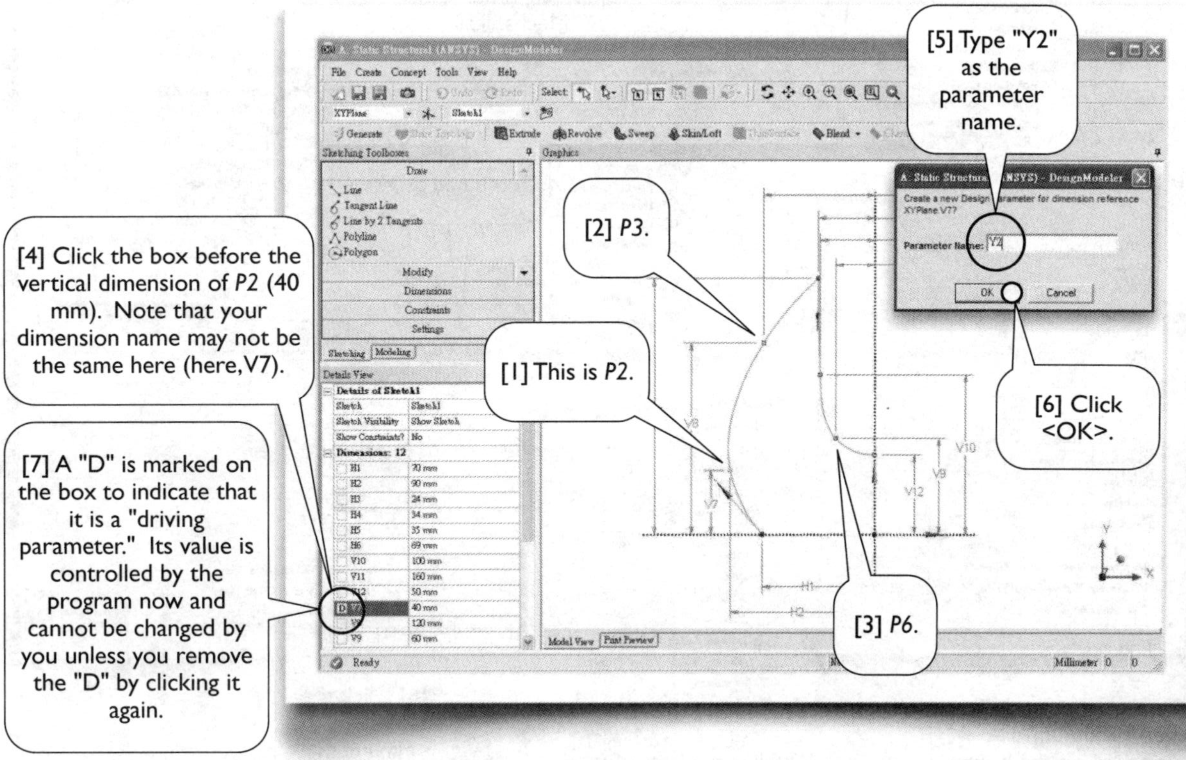

Repeat steps [4-6] for the vertical dimensions of *P3* and *P6* [8, 9]. Remember that your dimension names may not be the same as they appear here (here, they are V8 and V9 respectively).

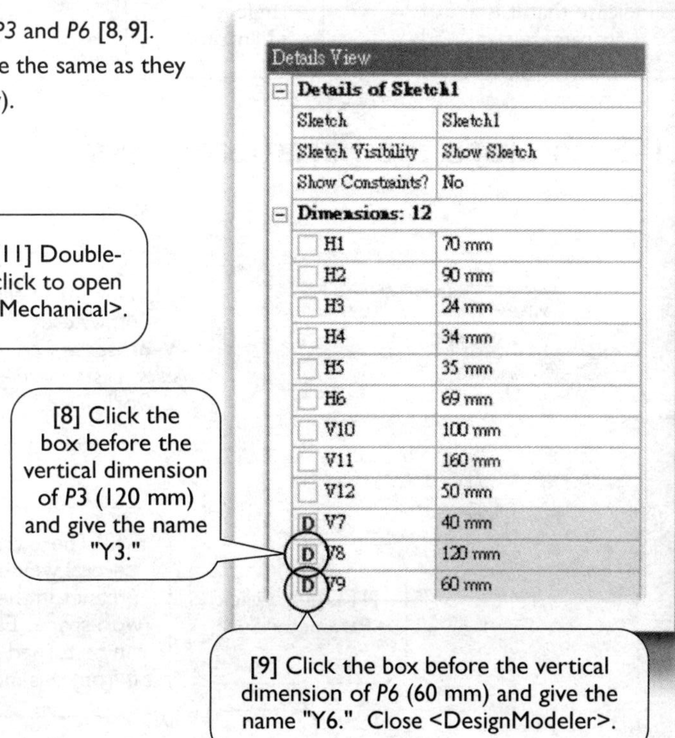

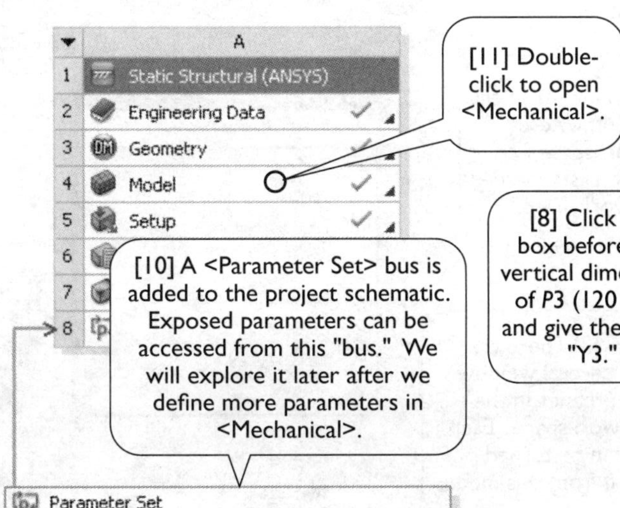

8.1-4 Define Parameters in <Mechanical>

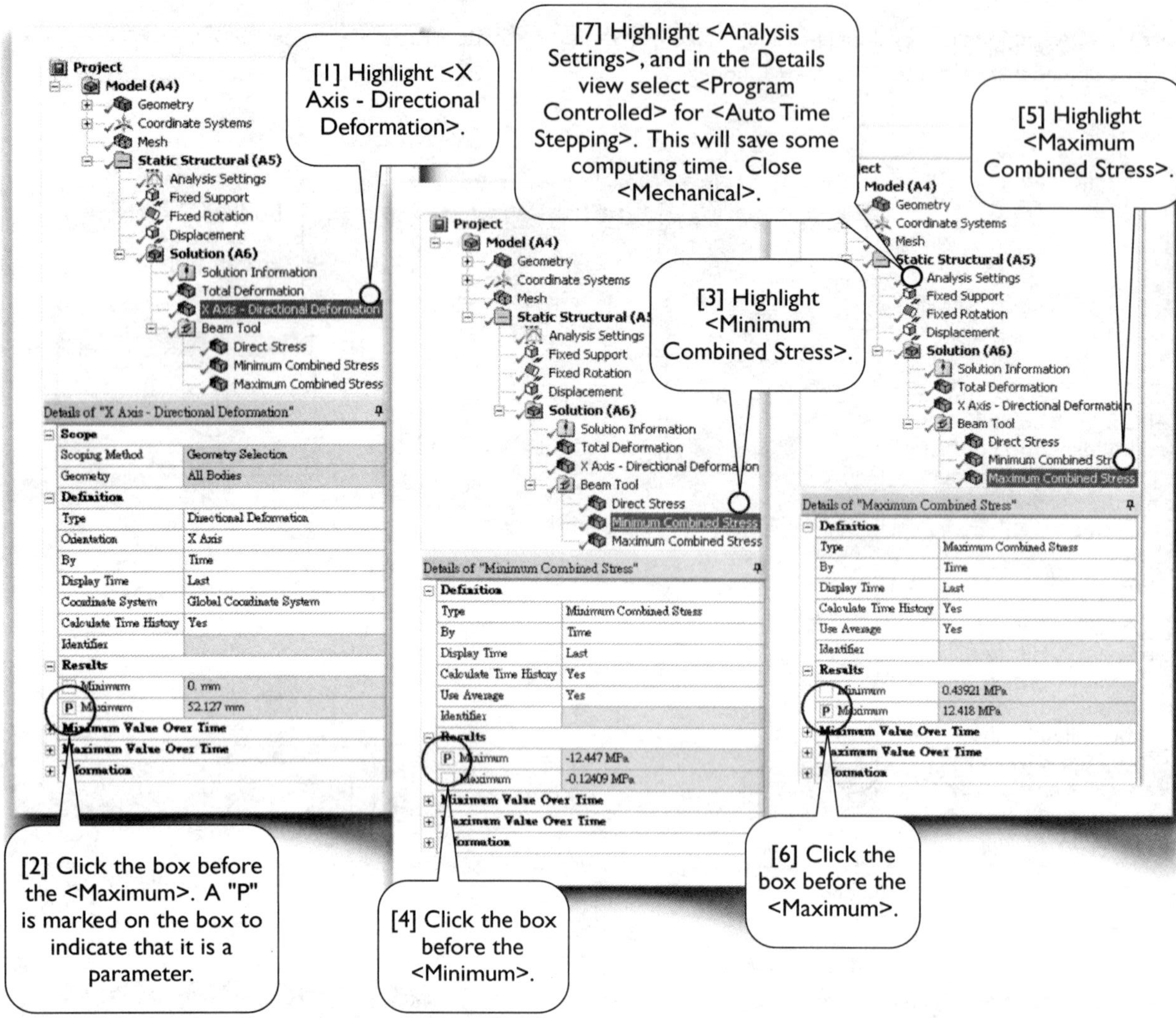

8.1-5 Explore the Parameter Sets

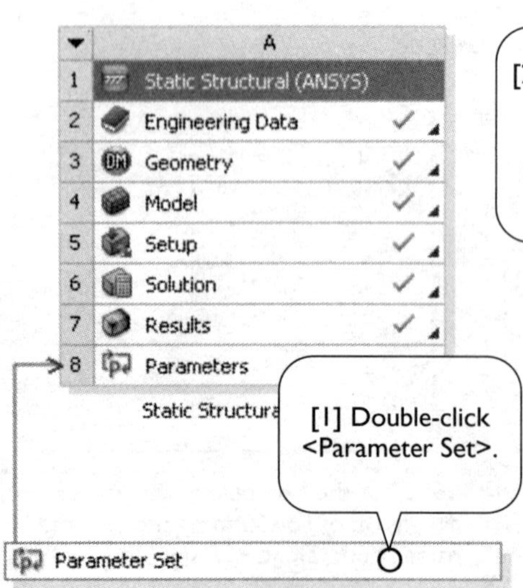

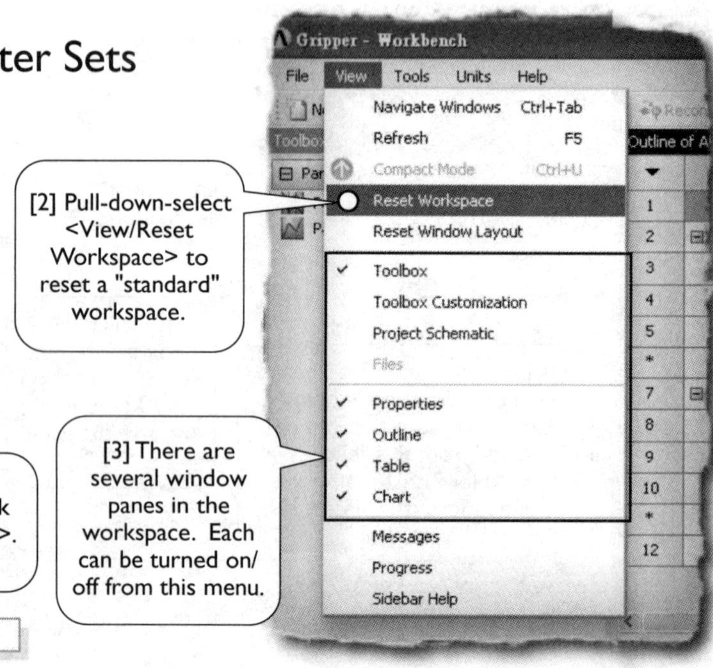

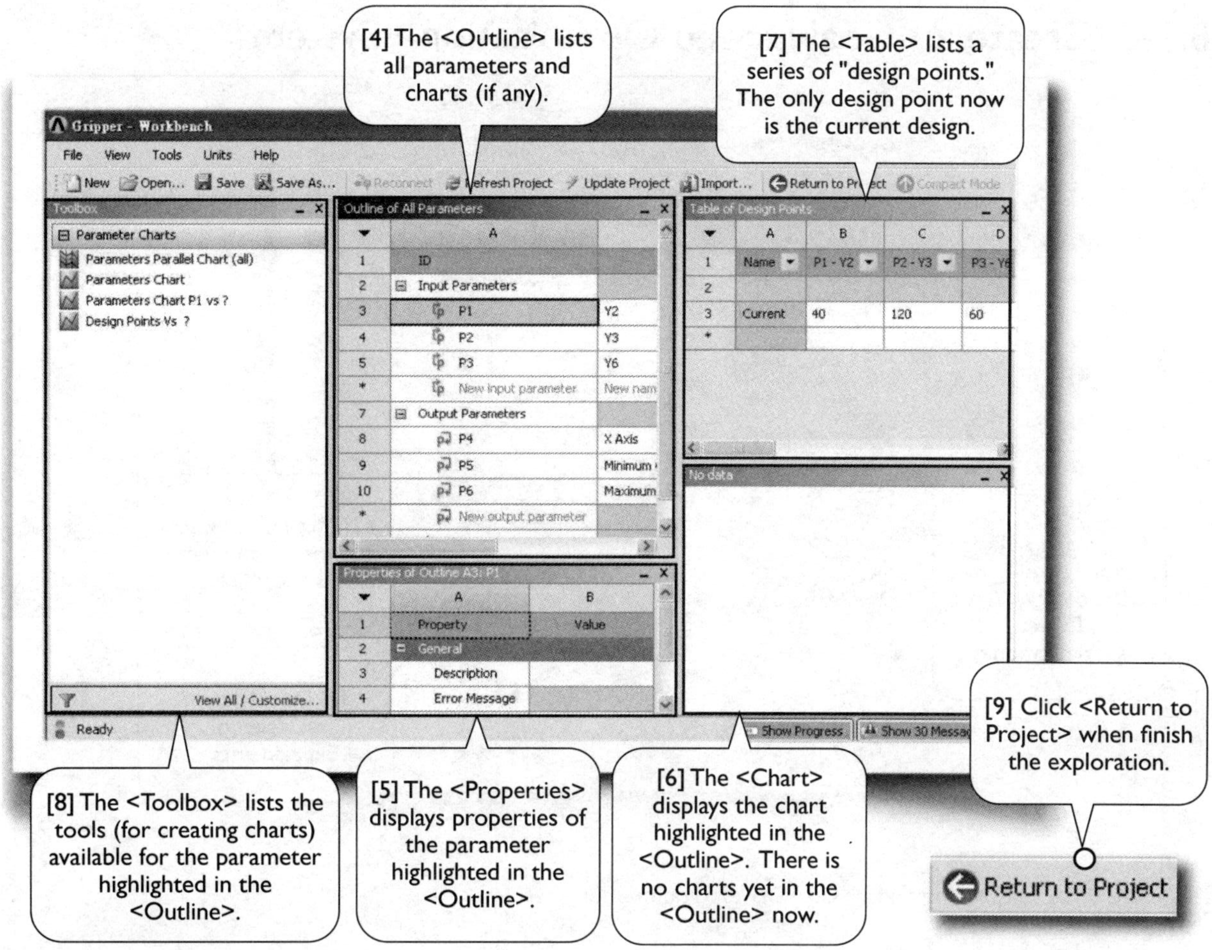

Input Parameters and Output Parameters

In optimization jargon, input parameters are also called *design variables*, and output parameters are also called *state variables*. Initial values of input parameters are set up by the user, and the Workbench subsequently change these values to improve the design. Values of output parameters are calculated from the simulation applications (e.g., <Mechanical>). In our case the input parameters are Y2, Y3, and Y6, and the output parameters are the maximum horizontal displacement, the minimum combined stress, and the maximum combined stress. Note that the input parameters are not necessarily defined in <DesignModeler>. For example, the loads defined in <Mechanical> could be defined as input parameters.

Design Space

The space spanned by the input parameters is called the *design space*. In our case, the space spanned by parameters Y2, Y3, and Y6 is the design space, which is a three-dimensional space. The optimization process can be thought of a process of searching a best point in the design space.

Design Point

Any point in the design space can be a *design point*. The <Table of Design Points> [5] lists a series of design points with which the simulations have been carried out. In our case, we have only one design point: Y2 = 40, Y3 = 120, Y6 = 60. This design point is now called *current design*.

Remark

The Workbench refers the parameters as P1, P2, P3 (non-italic), etc. [4]. In our case of flexible gripper, we use *P2*, *P3*, and *P6* (italic) for three control points of the shape. Be careful not to mix up these two sets of notations.

8.1-6 Create a <Goal Driven Optimization> System

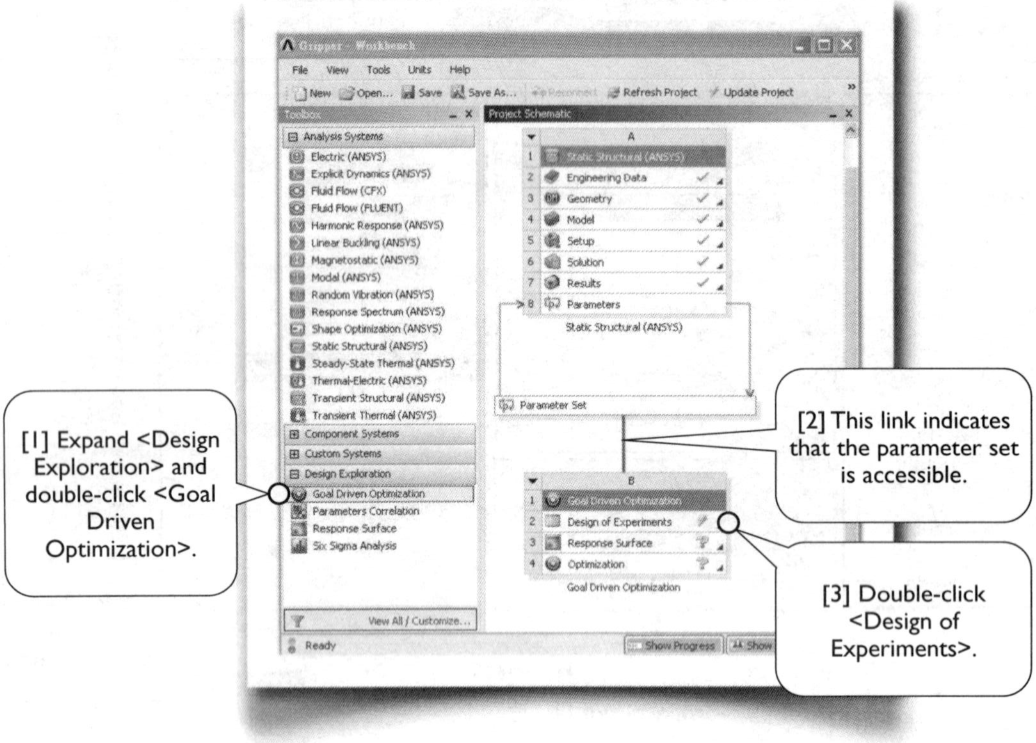

There are three cells, or steps, in a <Goal Driven Optimization> system.

Design of Experiments

In this step, simulations with several design points are performed. The design points are chosen according to a method of Design of Experiments (DOE). In our case, a total of 15 design points (including current design) will be chosen (8.1-7[11]). That implies a total of 15 times of simulation similar to Section 7.1 will be performed. The output parameters are recorded. The values of output parameters are also called the *responses*.

Response Surface

In this step, the design points and their response values are used to best-fit mathematical functions (typically second-order polynomials). The functions are called response surfaces. Each response value (output parameter) has a response surface, so three response surfaces are constructed in our case. The response surfaces are used to predict the output values for any point in the design space. Any point in a response surface is called a *response point*.

Optimization

In this step, the goal or constraint of each output parameter is specified. In our case, the goal is to maximize the horizontal displacement, subject to a constraint on the combined stress that its absolute value does not exceed 15 MPa. Knowing the goals and constraints of the output parameters, <DesignXplorer> searches through the response surfaces and suggests candidate designs for you. The <DesignXplorer> provides three algorithms for searching the response surfaces. The MOGA (multi-objective genetic algorithm) deals with both single- and multi-objective problems. The NLPQL (nonlinear programming by quadratic Lagrangian) deals with single-objective problems. Screening method divides the design space into grids and exhaustively searches the design space; the method can deal with problems involving discrete design variables.

8.1-7 Generate DOE Table and Results

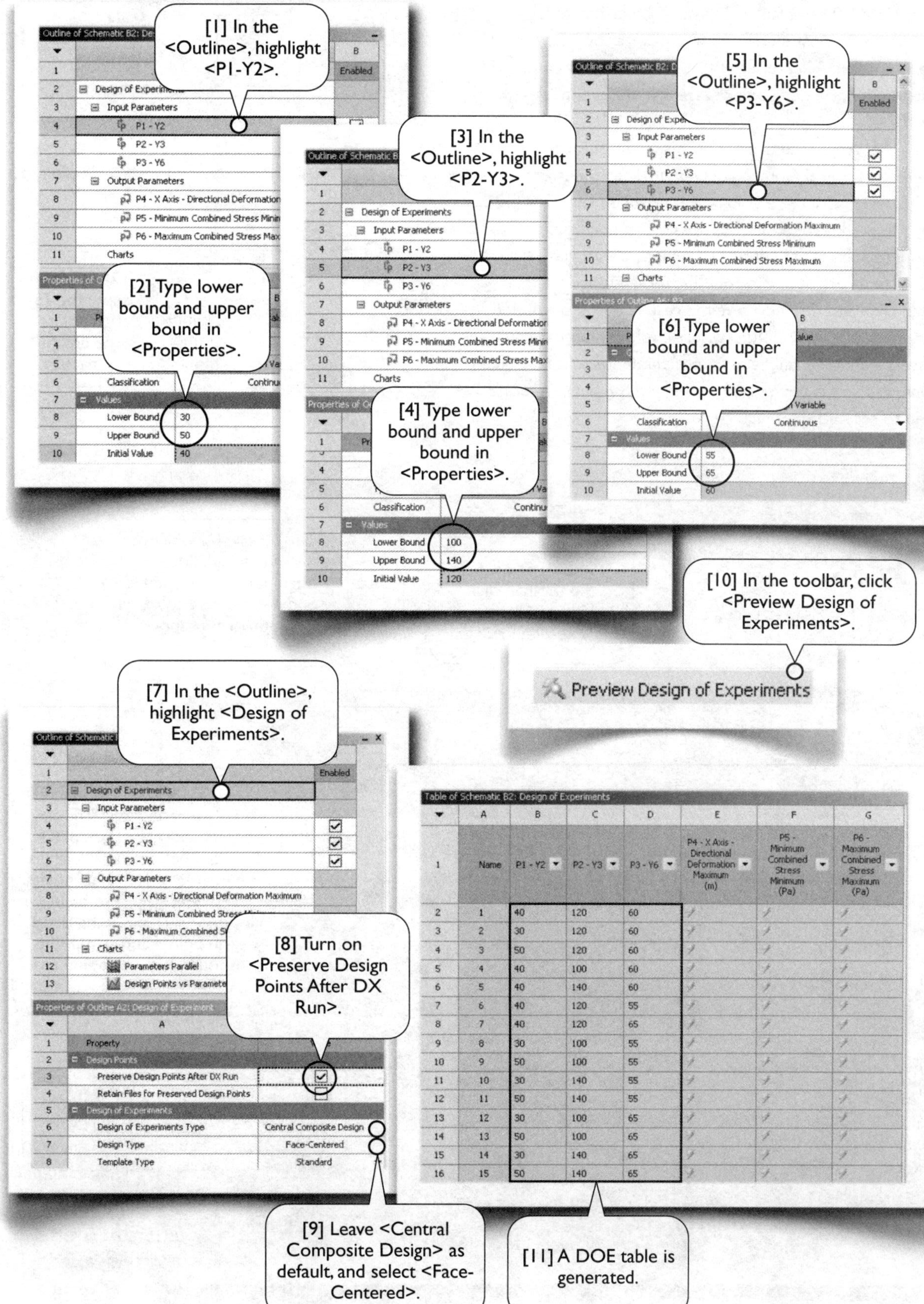

The DOE Table

With <Design of Experiments> highlighted [7], the <Properties> shows details of how the experimental array is generated. The default <Design of Experiments Type> is <Central Composite Design>. We change the <Design Type> to <Face-Centered> [9], just because it is easier to understand for a newcomer of Design of Experiments (DOE).

The experimental array [11] is a typical Face-Centered Central Composite Design. The 15 design points in the design space are graphically shown on the right [12]. With these design points, it is possible to construct response surfaces of full second order polynomials.

The effect of turning on <Preserve Design Points After DX Run> [8] is to save the results of the simulation of each design point. Otherwise, <DesignXplorer> would preserve only the values of output parameters. It may take much disk space, but, in case we need these data, we don't need to rerun the project.

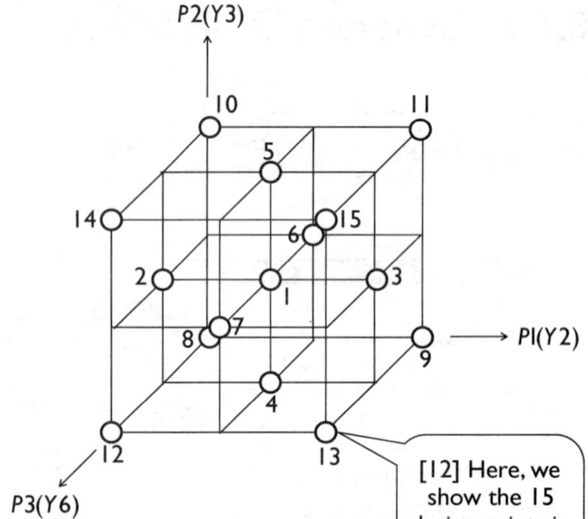

[12] Here, we show the 15 design points in the design space.

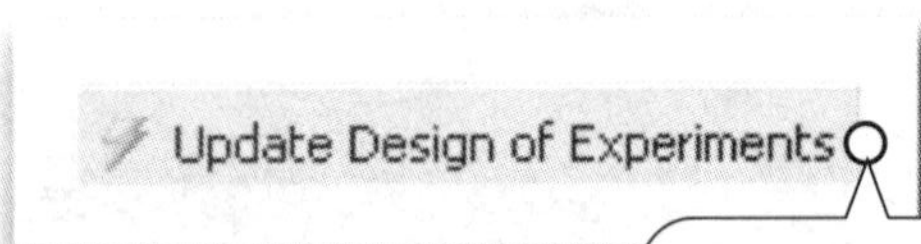

[13] Save project. In the toolbar, click <Update Design of Experiments>

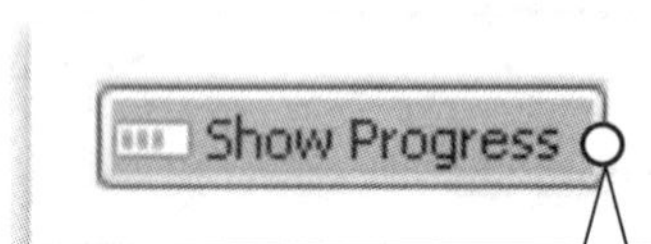

[14] It takes a while to finish the simulations of 15 design points. You can click <Show Progress> to watch the progress report.

Table of Schematic B2: Design of Experiments

	A	B	C	D	E	F	G
1	Name	P1 - Y2	P2 - Y3	P3 - Y6	P4 - X Axis - Directional Deformation Maximum (mm)	P5 - Minimum Combined Stress Minimum (MPa)	P6 - Maximum Co...
2	1	40	120	60	52.127	-12.447	12.
3	2	30	120	60	53.191	-12.747	12.
4	3	50	120	60	51.189	-12.19	12.
5	4	40	100	60	55.742	-13.914	13.
6	5	40	140	60	54.238	-11.536	11.
7	6	40	120	55	53.334	-11.571	
8	7	40	120	65	51.425	-12.729	12.709
9	8	30	100	55	58.107	-13.122	13.061
10	9	50	100	55	55.872	-12.54	12.483
11	10	30	140	55	57.436	-11.013	10.97
12	11	50	140	55	53.645	-10.632	10.591
13	12	30	100	65	56.156	-14.664	14.632
14	13	50	100	65	53.976	-13.934	13.907
15	14	30	140	65	55.414	-12.016	12
16	15	50	140	65	51.74	-11.556	11.543

[15] The results of 15 design points show the horizontal displacement can be as high as 58 mm among 15 design points. The next step is to build response surfaces using these design points and search the response surface to find an even higher value.

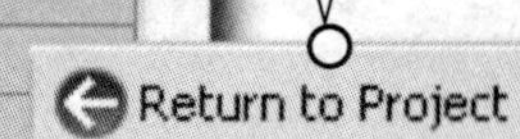

[16] Click <Return to Project>.

8.1-8 Build Response Surface

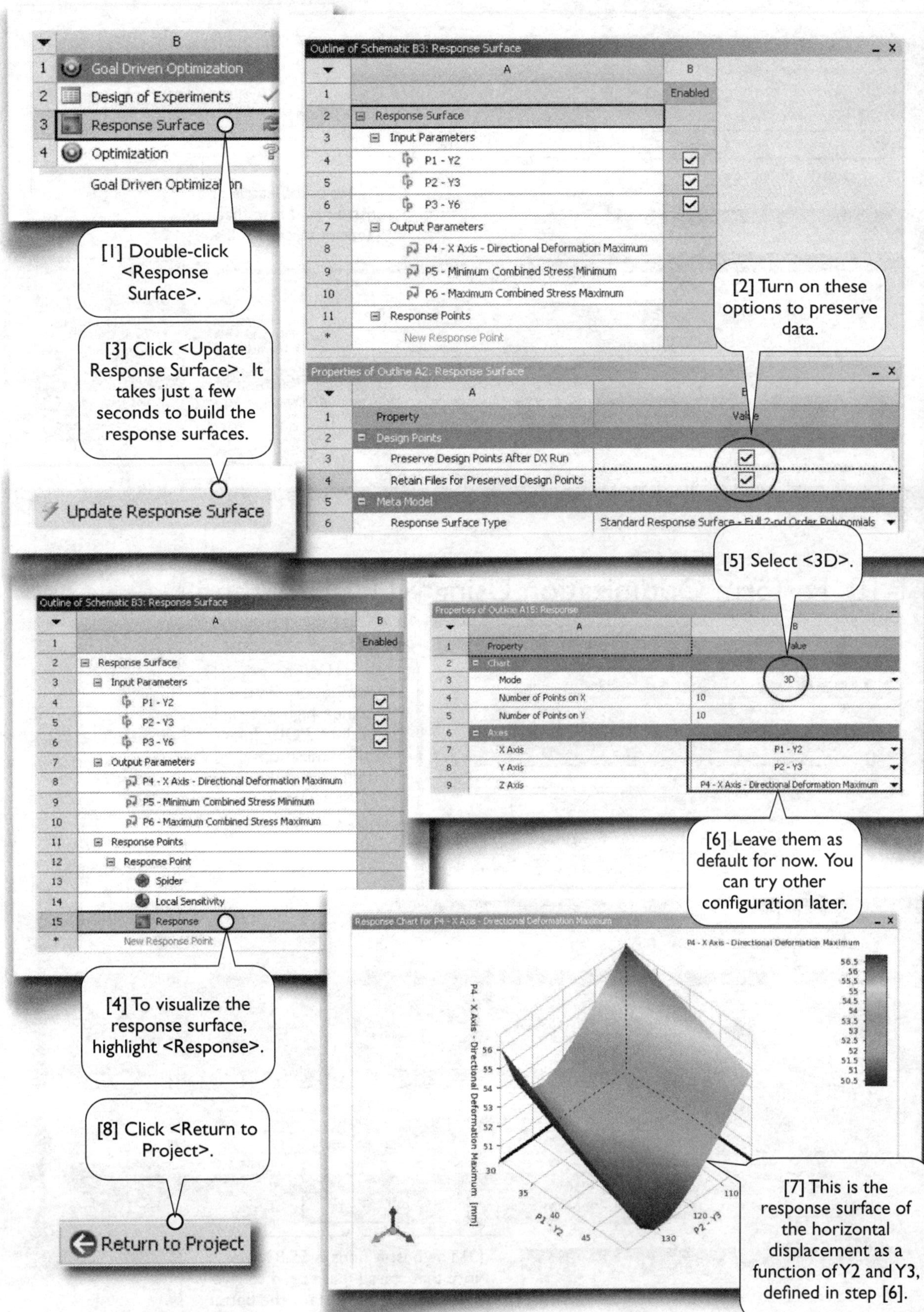

8.1-9 Set Up Objectives and Constraints

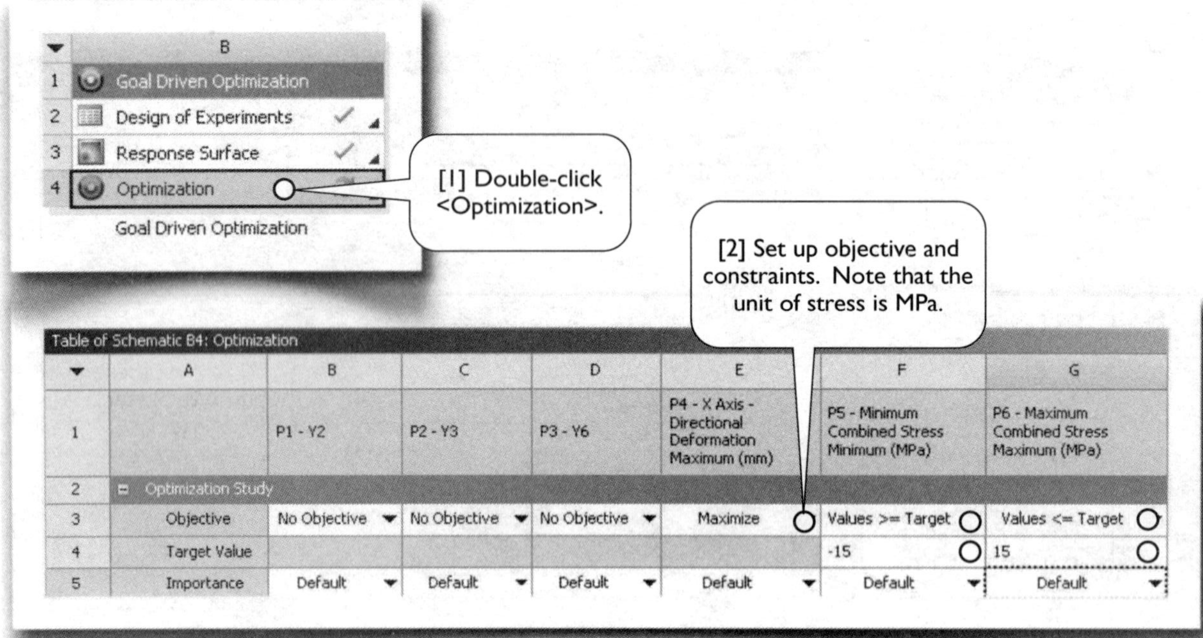

8.1-10 Perform Optimization Using NLPQL Method

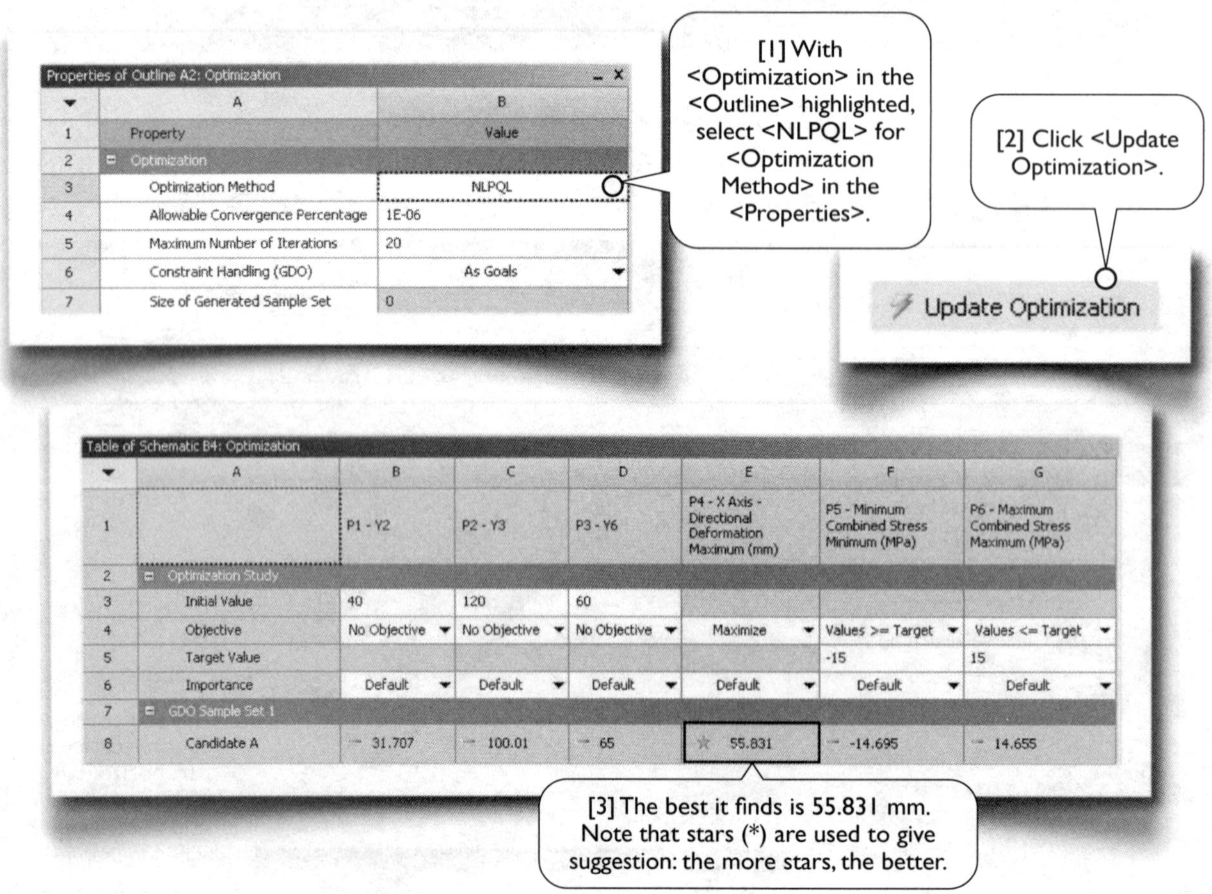

8.1-11 Perform Optimization Using MOGA Method

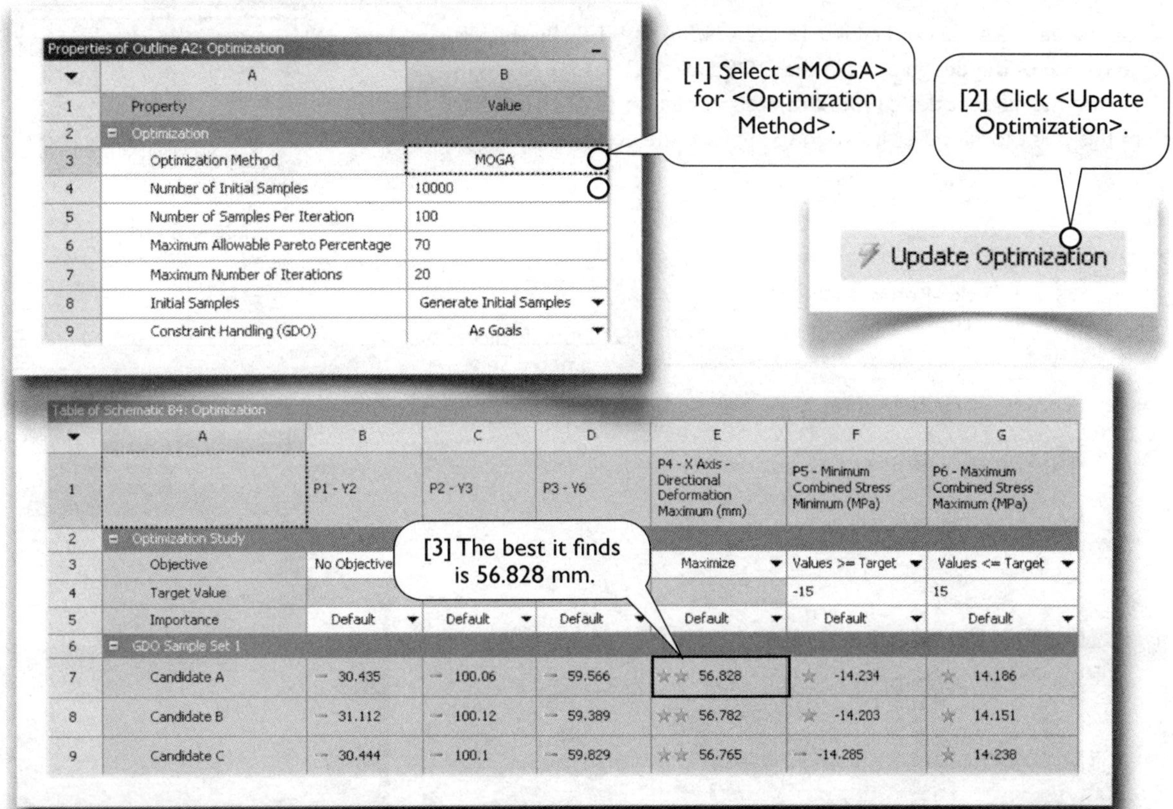

8.1-12 Perform Optimization Using Screening Method

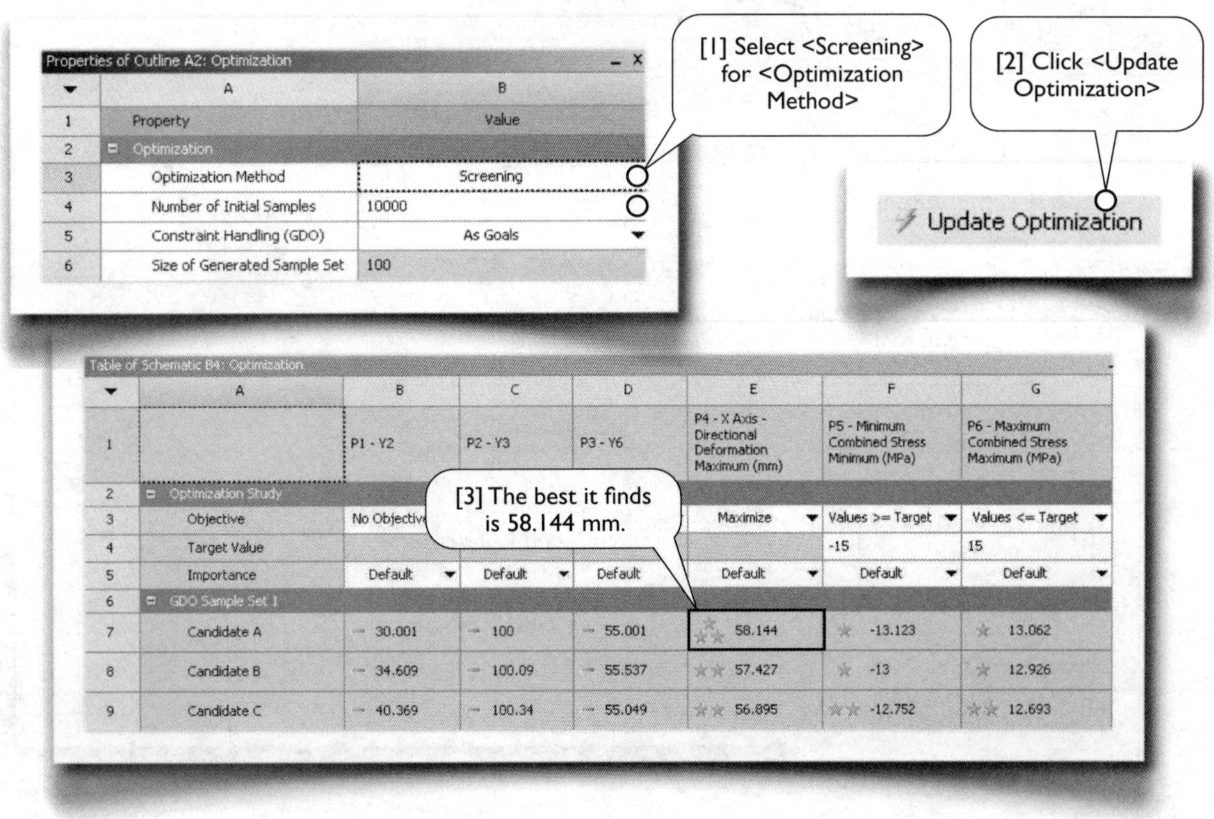

8.1-13 Update Current Design

So far, the best GA we can find is 1.16 (58.144/50) (8.1-12[3]), which is close to one of the design point in the DOE table (8.1-7[15]). We want to update the current design with this design point, so that we can start from this point for another iteration to improve the design.

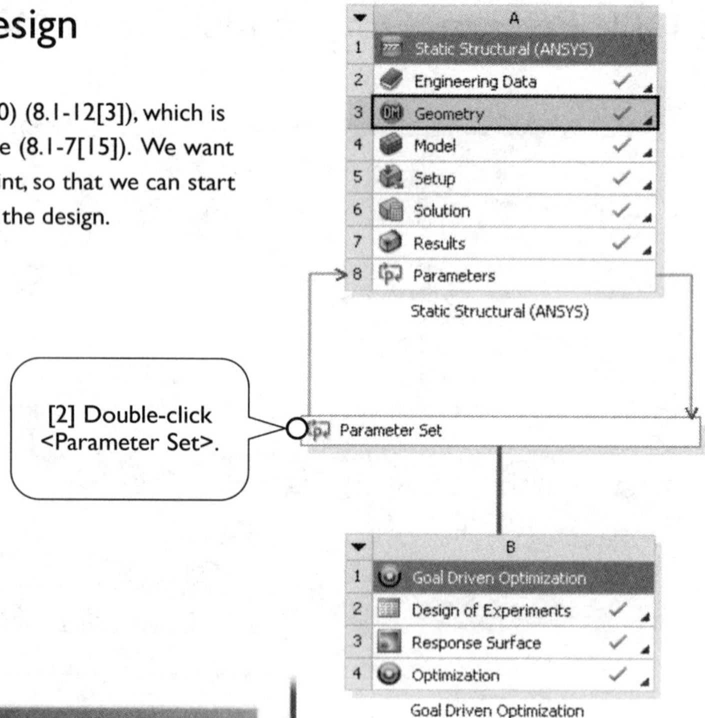

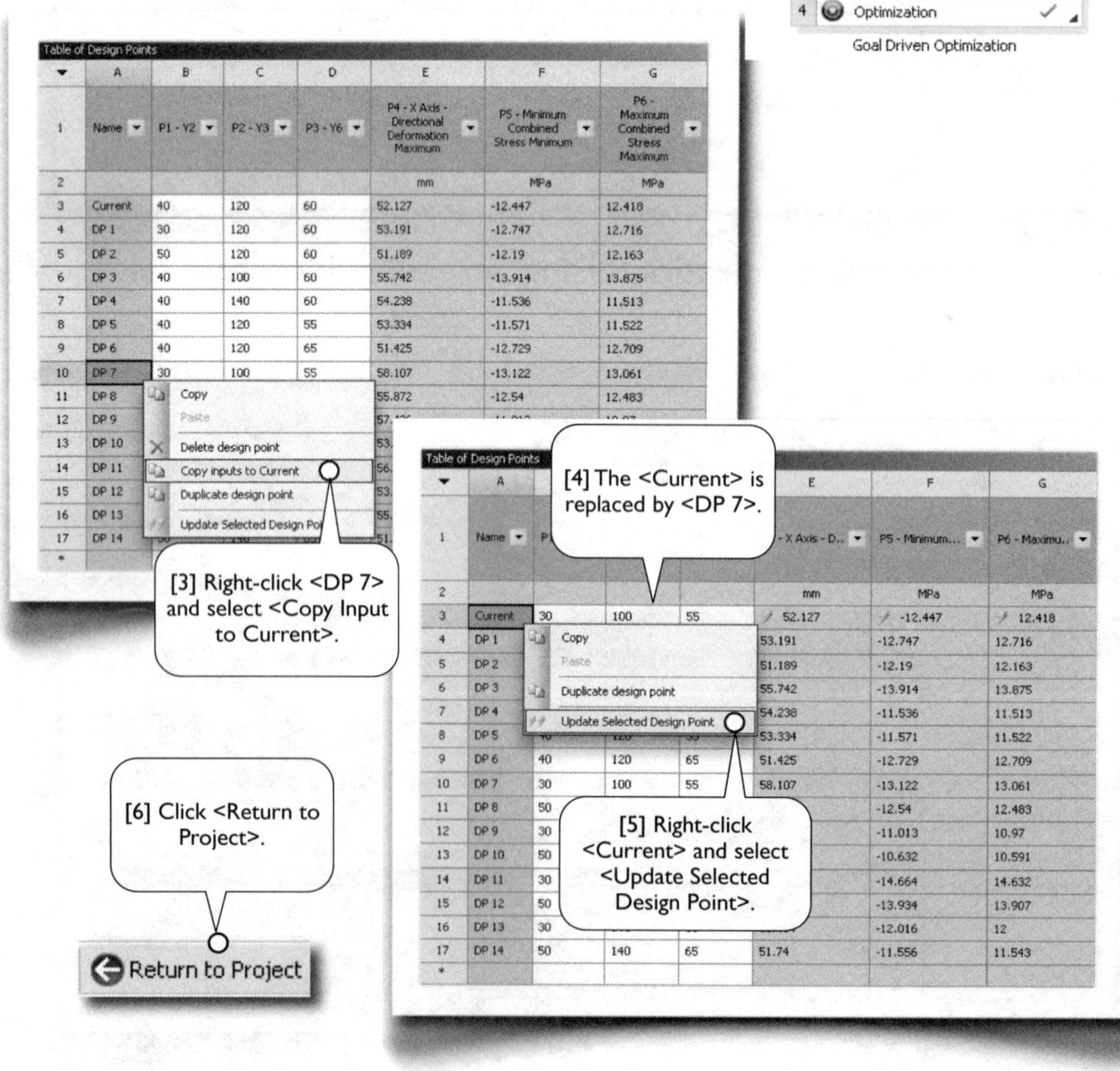

8.1-14 Check the Current Design

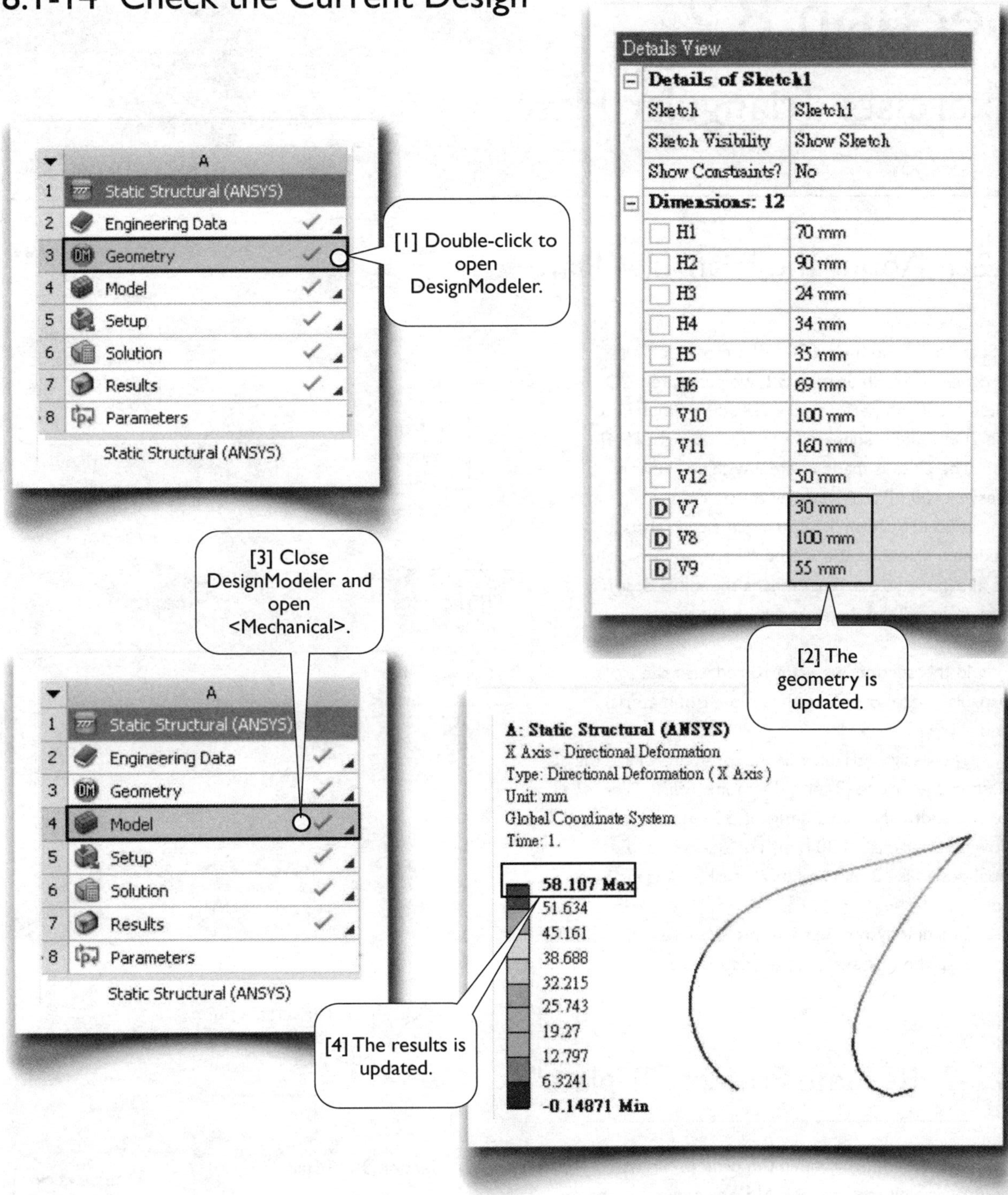

Wrap Up

Close <Mechanical>. Save the project and exit <Workbench>. As an exercise (8.3-2), you may perform another iteration of optimization using the updated design as "central design." Choose appropriate ranges of adjustment for the design variables.

Section 8.2

Exercise: Triangular Plate

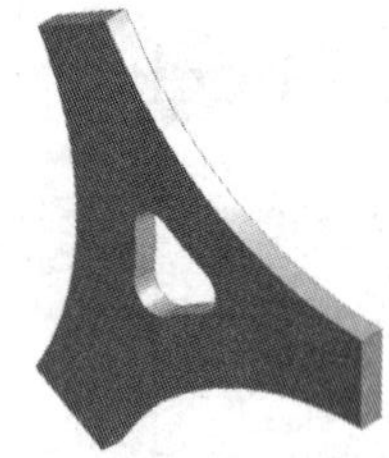

8.2-1 About the Triangular Plate

In Section 2.2, we built a 3D solid model for a triangular plate. In Section 3.1, we generate a 2D solid model and performed a 2D static simulation. The 2D model is repeated here on the right [1-4].

The plate is made of steel with an allowable stress of 100 MPa. According to the results of simulation in Section 3.1, the initial design gives a maximum stress of about 54.6 MPa, much less than the allowable stress. That means the initial design is over-designed: the material can be cut down somehow.

In this section, we want to redesign the triangular plate to reduce the amount of material used.

The design variables (input parameters) are the width of the bridge [3] and the radius of the fillet [4]. For the width, the initial design is 30 mm and its allowable range is 20-30 mm. For the radius, the initial design is 10 mm and its allowable range is 5-15 mm.

The unit system used in this exercise is mm-s-N (to set up the unit system, see Section 3.3-5).

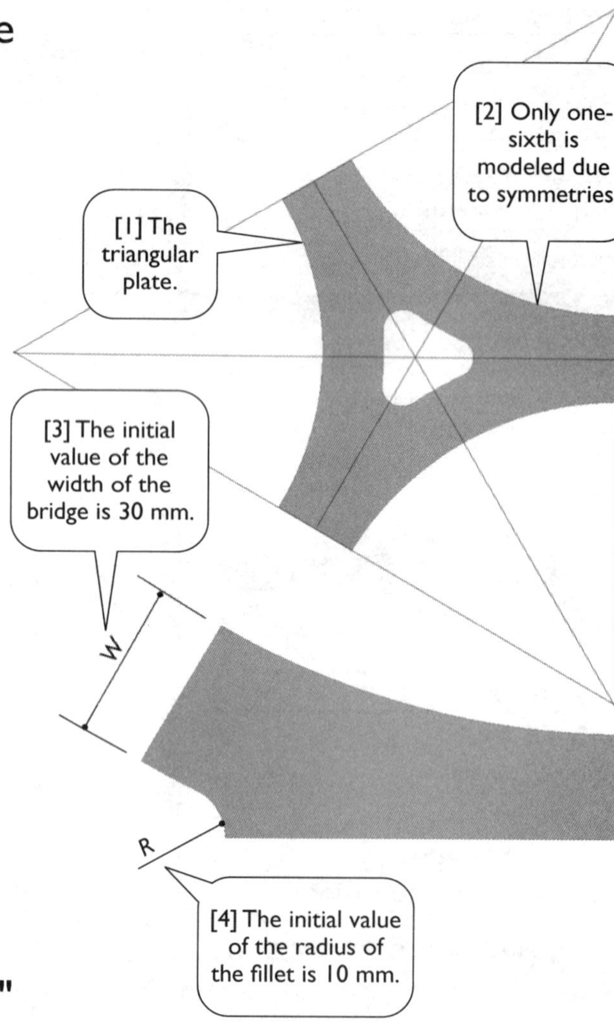

8.2-2 Resume Project "Triplate"

Launch <Workbench>, open the project "Triplate," which is saved in Section 3.1. Make sure the project unit is <kg-mm-s-N> or <tonne-mm-s-N>.

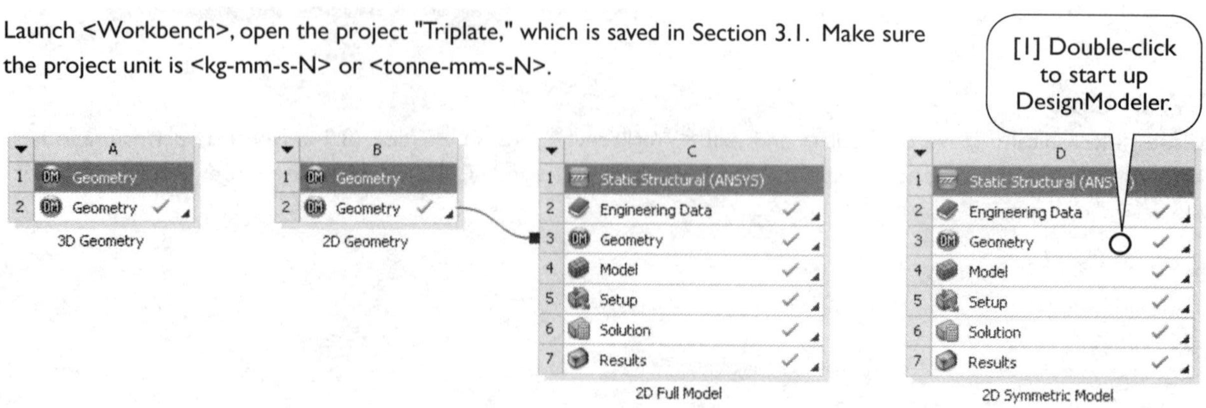

8.2-3 Define Input Parameters in DesignModeler

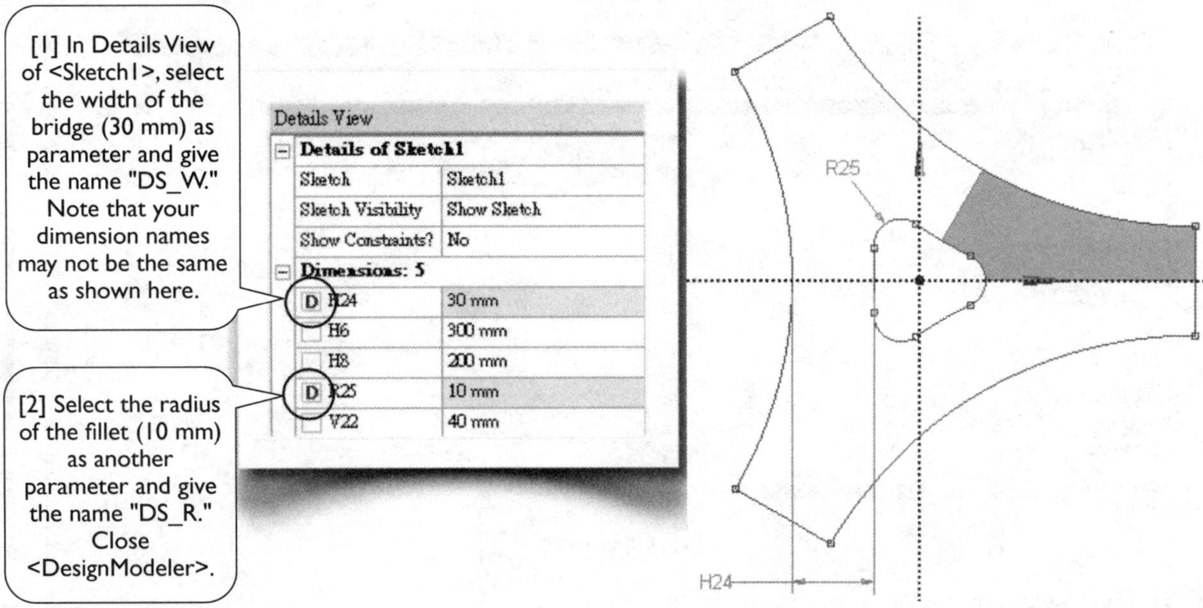

8.2-4 Define Output Parameters in <Mechanical>

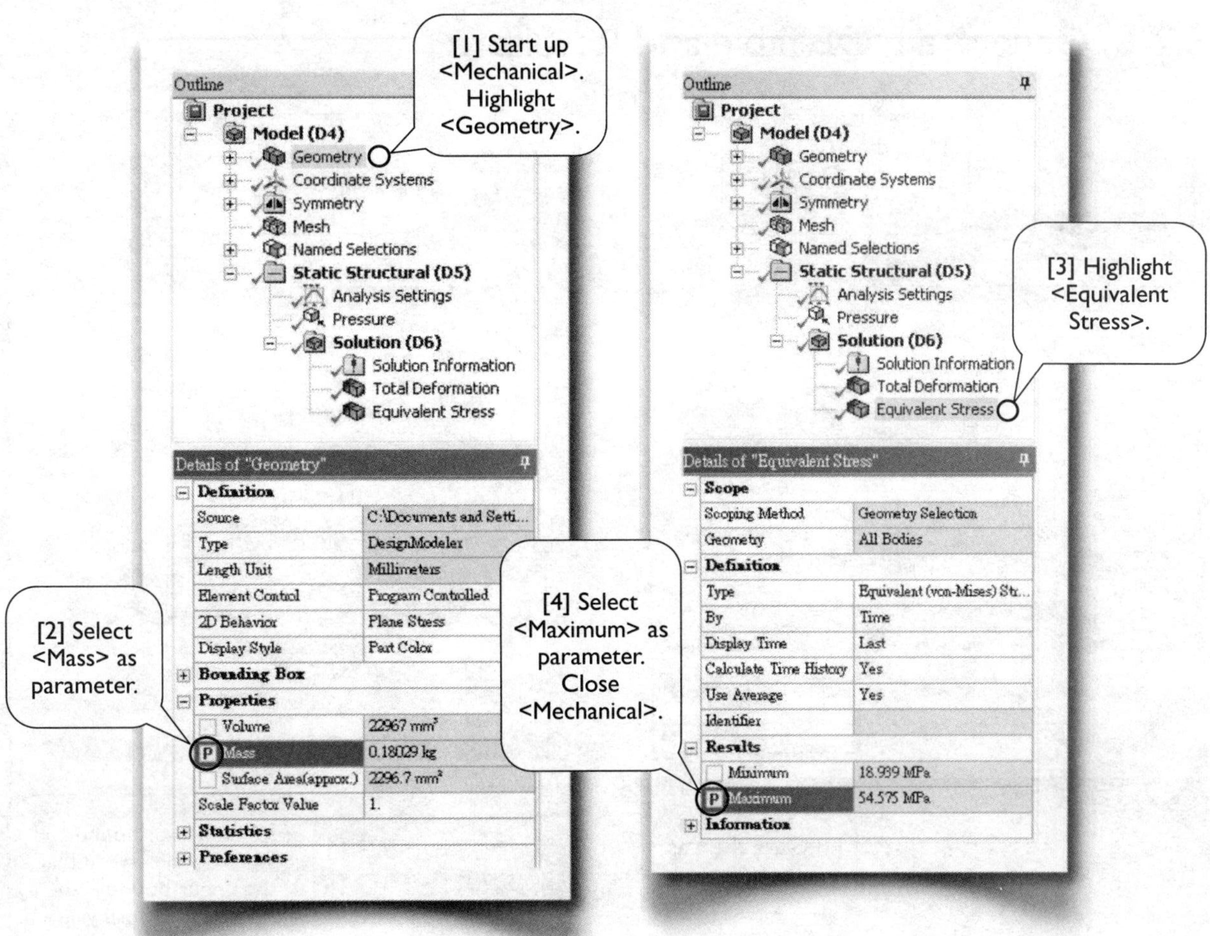

8.2-5 Create a <Goal Driven Optimization> System

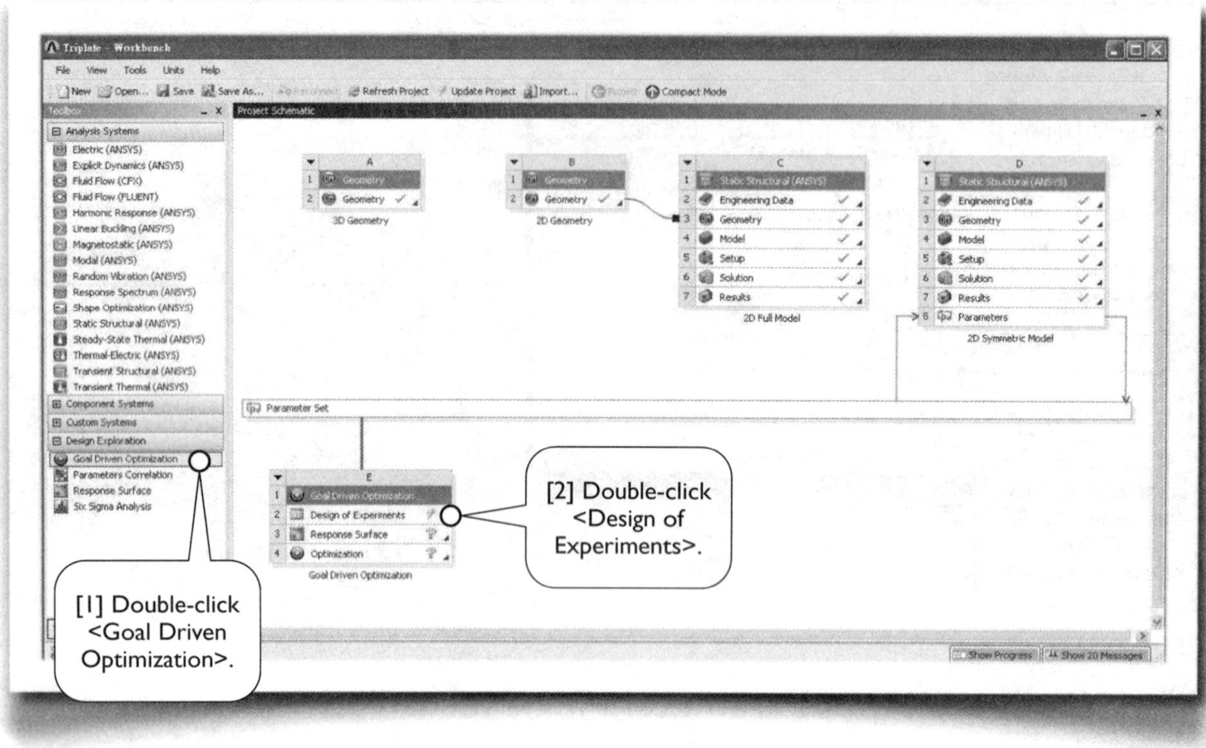

8.2-6 Generate DOE Table and Results

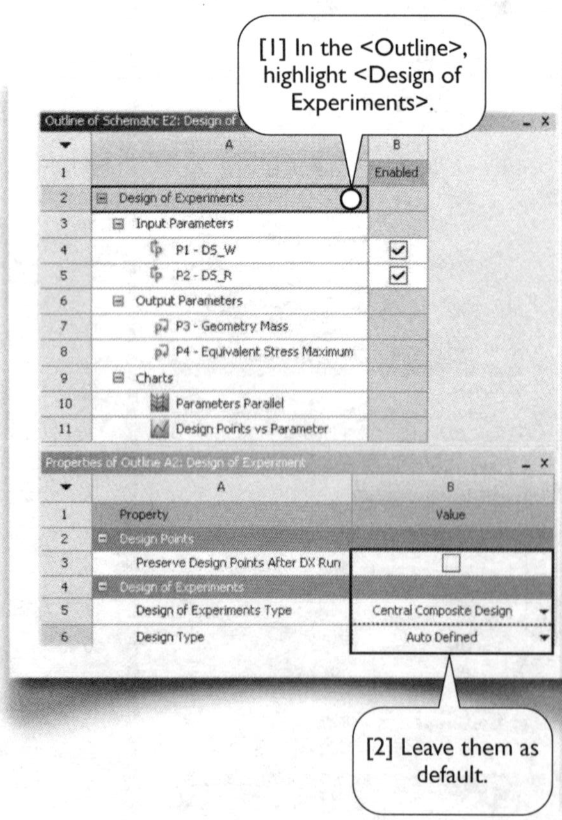

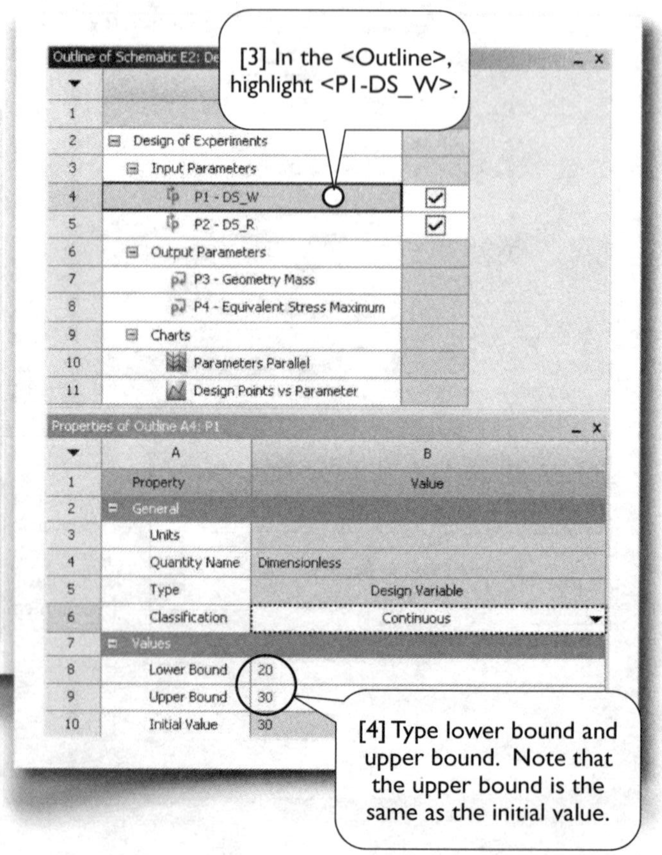

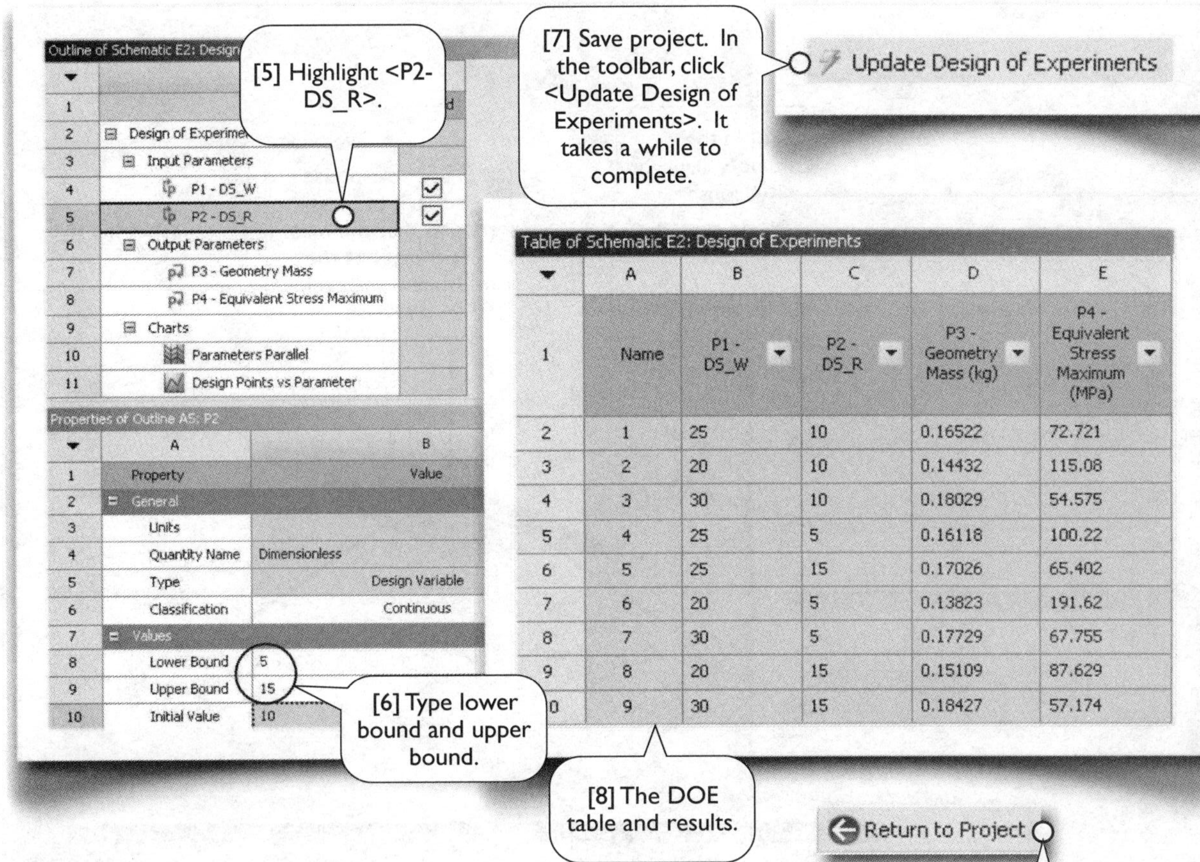

8.2-7 Build Response Surface

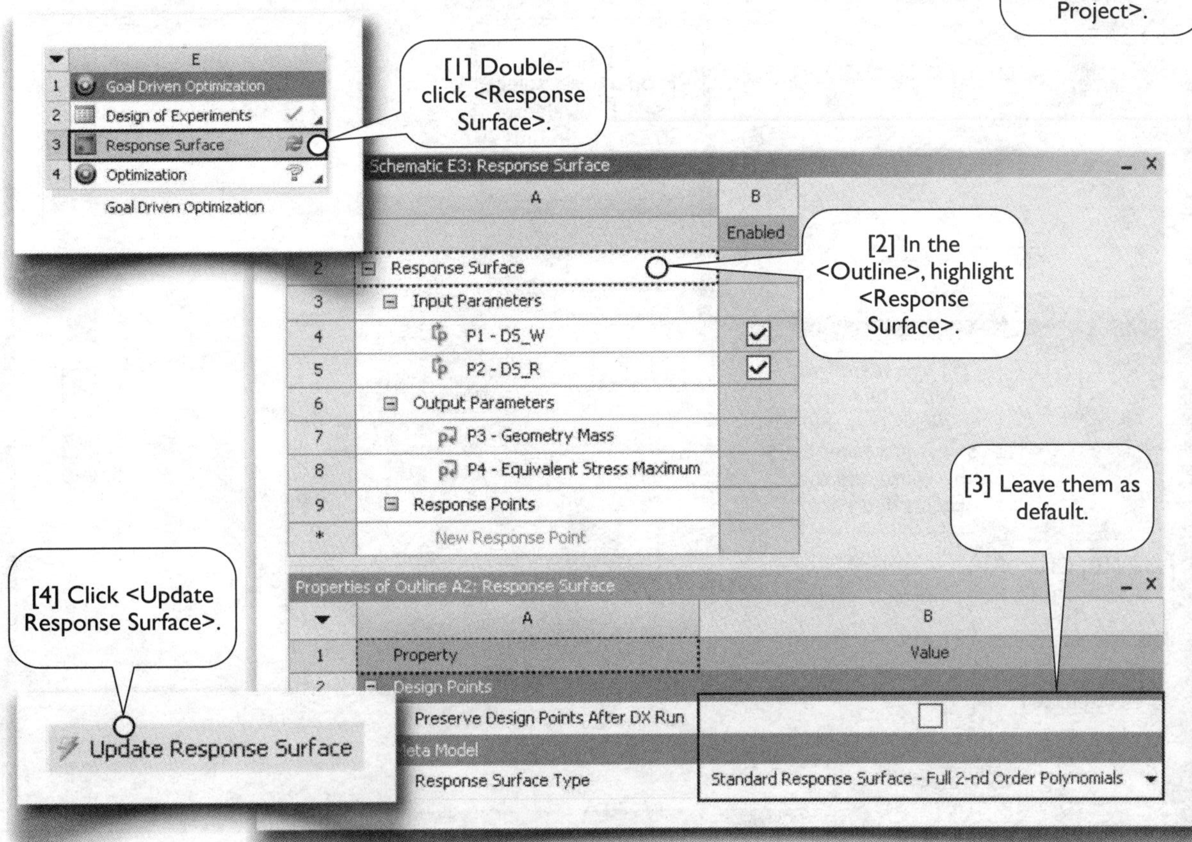

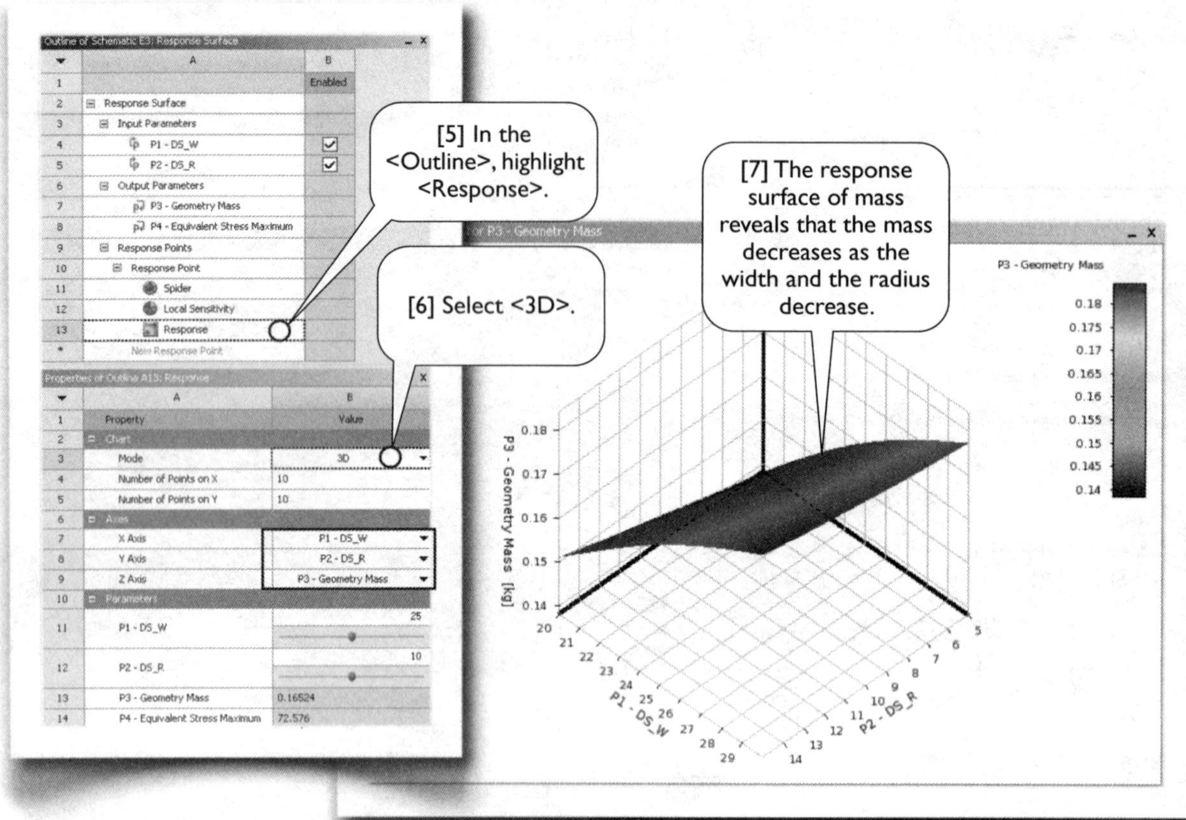
[5] In the <Outline>, highlight <Response>.
[6] Select <3D>.
[7] The response surface of mass reveals that the mass decreases as the width and the radius decrease.
Outline of Schematic E3: Response Surface
Response Surface
Input Parameters
P1 - DS_W
P2 - DS_R
Output Parameters
P3 - Geometry Mass
P4 - Equivalent Stress Maximum
Response Points
Response Point
Spider
Local Sensitivity
Response
New Response Point
Properties of Outline A13: Response
Property
Value
Chart
Mode
3D
Number of Points on X
10
Number of Points on Y
10
Axes
X Axis
P1 - DS_W
Y Axis
P2 - DS_R
Z Axis
P3 - Geometry Mass
Parameters
P1 - DS_W
25
P2 - DS_R
10
P3 - Geometry Mass
0.16524
P4 - Equivalent Stress Maximum
72.576
P3 - Geometry Mass [kg]
P1 - DS_W
P2 - DS_R
P3 - Geometry Mass

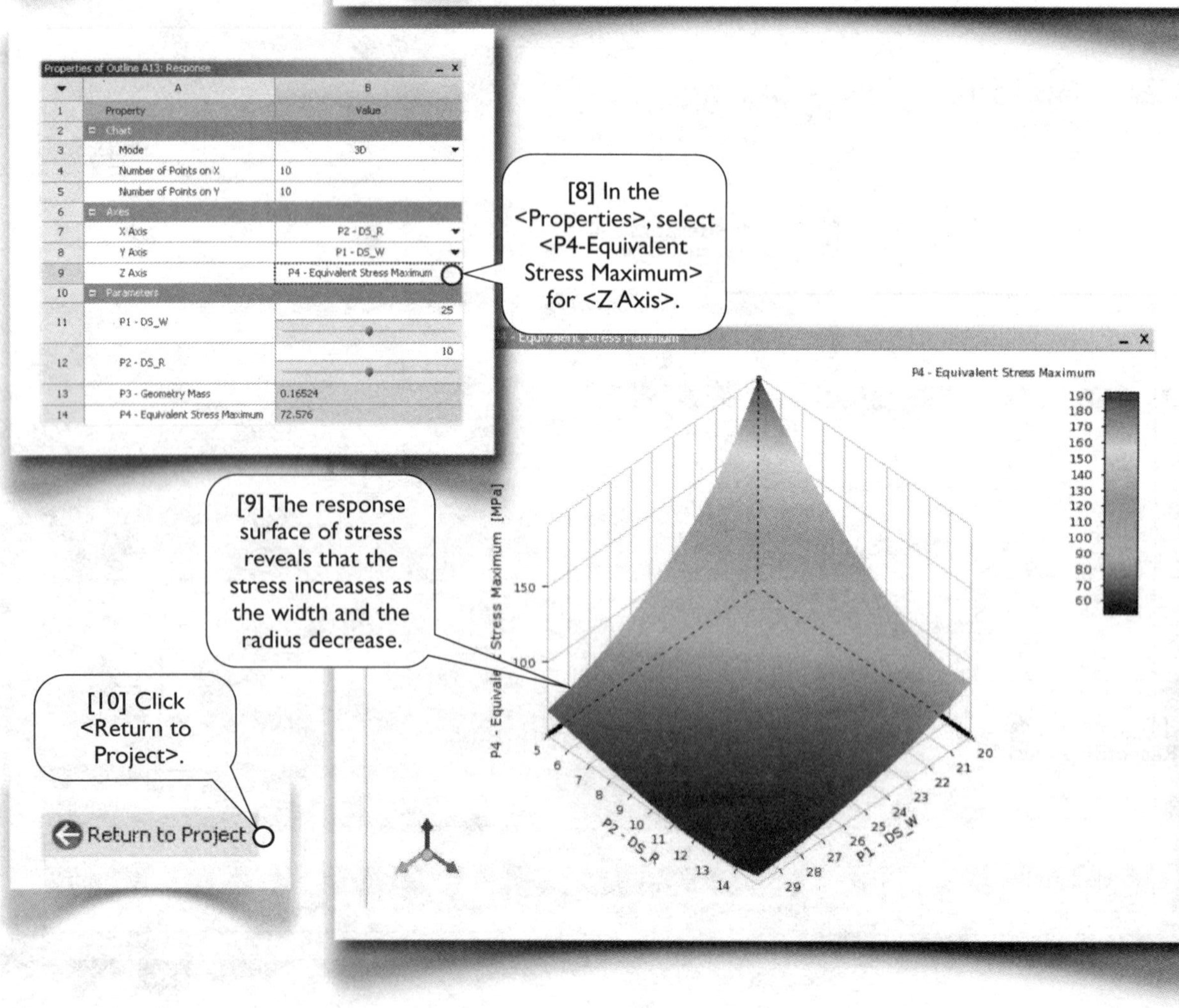
[8] In the <Properties>, select <P4-Equivalent Stress Maximum> for <Z Axis>.
[9] The response surface of stress reveals that the stress increases as the width and the radius decrease.
[10] Click <Return to Project>.
Return to Project
Properties of Outline A13: Response
Property
Value
Chart
Mode
3D
Number of Points on X
10
Number of Points on Y
10
Axes
X Axis
P2 - DS_R
Y Axis
P1 - DS_W
Z Axis
P4 - Equivalent Stress Maximum
Parameters
P1 - DS_W
25
P2 - DS_R
10
P3 - Geometry Mass
0.16524
P4 - Equivalent Stress Maximum
72.576
P4 - Equivalent Stress Maximum
P2 - DS_R
P1 - DS_W

8.2-8 Perform Optimization

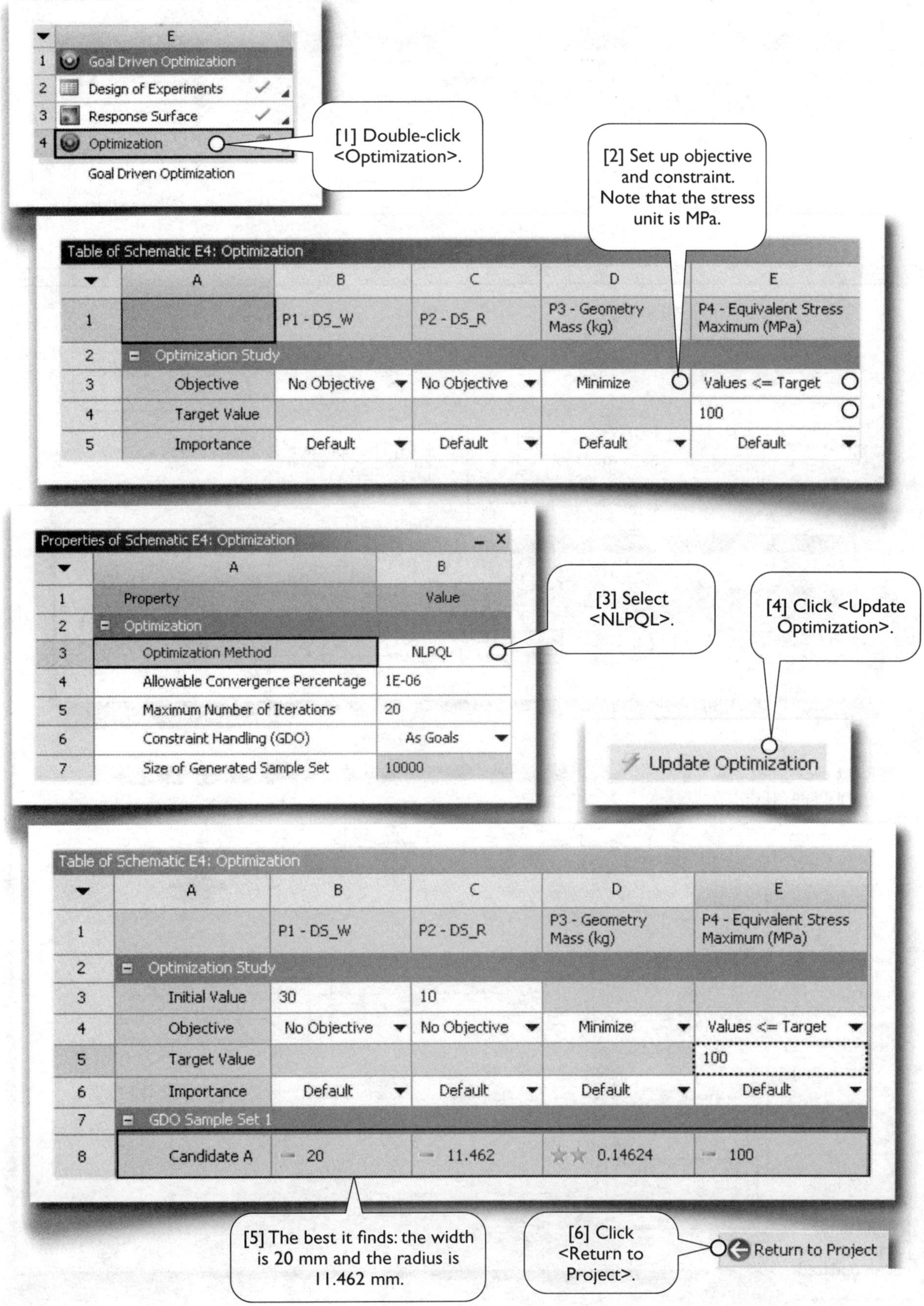

8.2-9 Update Current Design

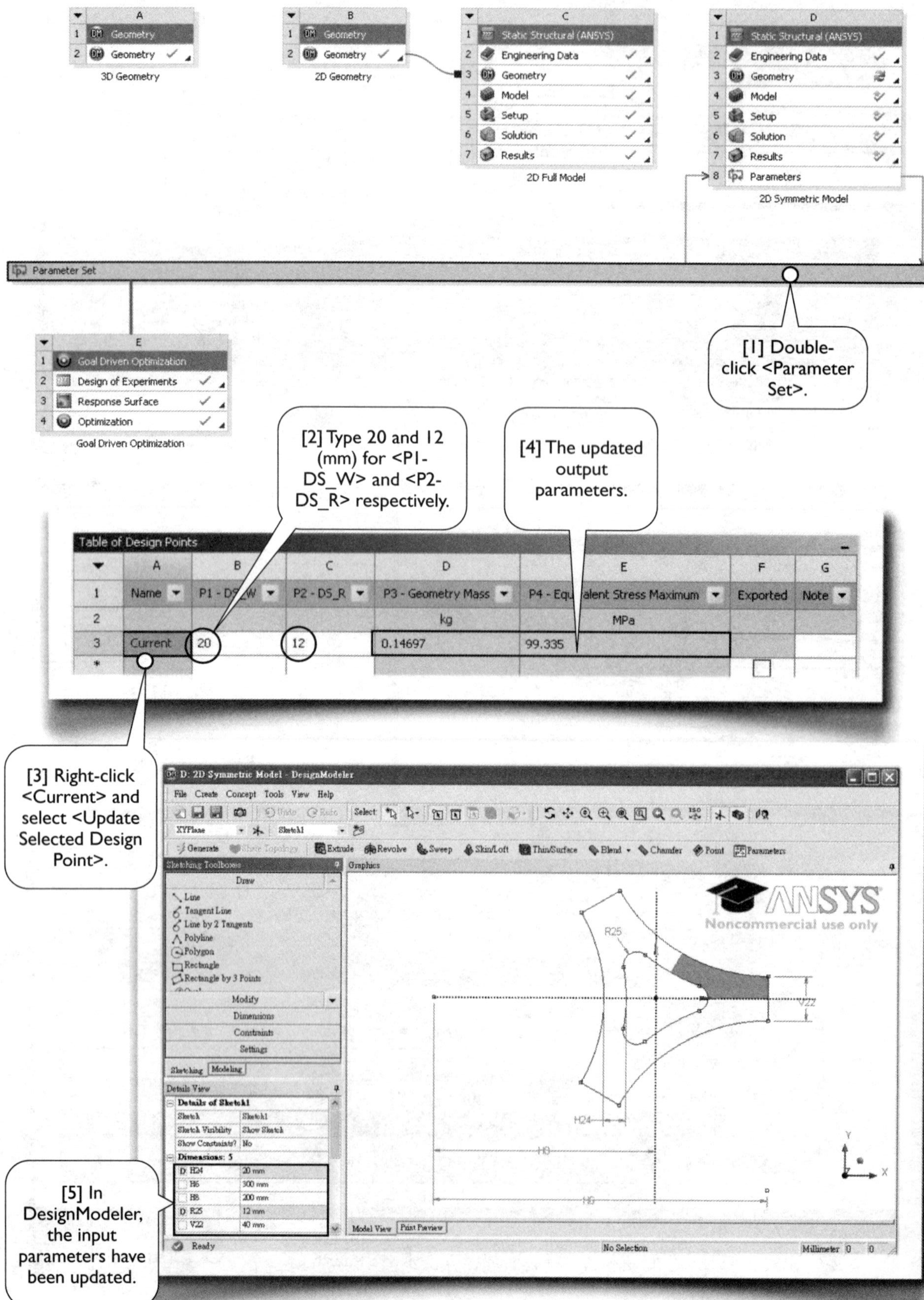

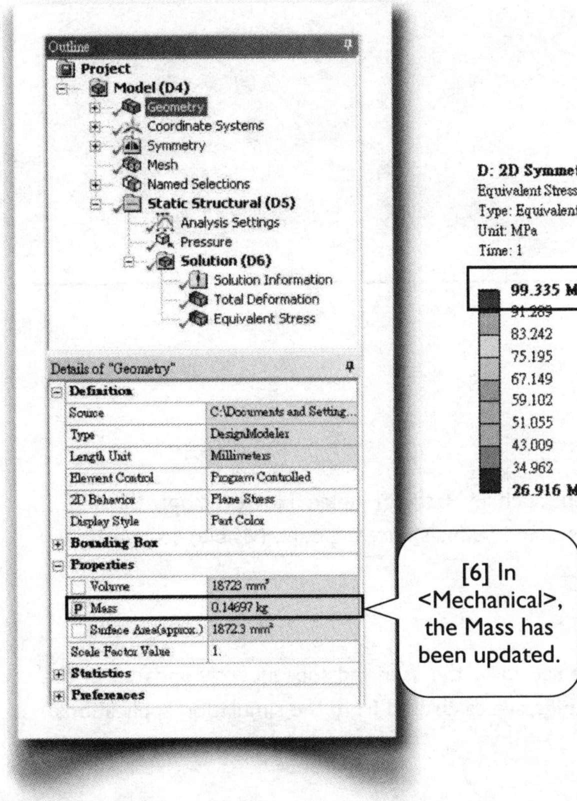

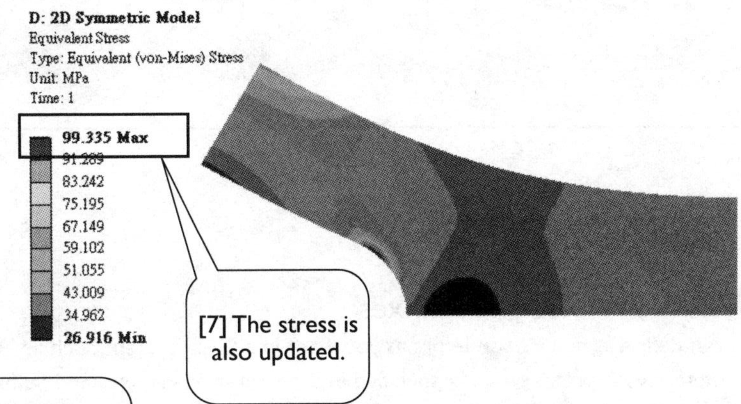

Wrap Up

Save the project, and exit the Workbench. As an exercise (8.3-2), you may perform another iteration of optimization using the updated design as "central design." Choose appropriate ranges of adjustment for the design variables.

Section 8.3

Problems

8.3-1 Key Concepts

Filtering Prefixes and Suffixes

You can define as many parameters as you want in a CAD system, such as DesignModeler. However, only those parameters with prefix or suffix specified in the <Filtering Prefixes and Suffixes> are exposed (visible) to other applications of the Workbench.

Input Parameters and Output Parameters

Initial values of input parameters, also called design variables, are set up by the user and subsequently updated by the Workbench. Values of output parameters, also called state variables, are calculated from the simulation applications.

Design Space

The space spanned by the input parameters, or design variables.

Design Points

In a broader sense, any point in the design space is called a design point. In the DesignXplorer, design points are those with which the simulations have been carried out.

Design of Experiments[1,2]

A method of determining design parameters by experiments. A series of experiments is carried out according to a system of experimental array. Results are analyzed and ways of adjusting the design parameters are drawn from the data analysis.

Response Surface

A mathematical function that describes the response of a system. A response surface is typically a second-order polynomial and built by best-fitting a set of experimental data. In the Workbench, the "experimental data" are produced by computer simulations.

Screening Method

A method of finding the optimum design. It divides the design space into grids and exhaustively searches the design space. The method can deals with problems involving discrete design variables.

NLPQL

Short for nonlinear programming by quadratic Lagrangian. A method of finding an optimal design. In each iteration, it approaches the problem using a quadratic polynomial and find the optimal design in the subproblem described by the quadratic polynomial. The process is repeated until the optimal design is found. The method deals with only single-objective problems.

MOGA

Short for multi-objective genetic algorithm. It deals with both single- and multi-objective problems.

8.3-2 Workbench Exercises

Another iteration for the gripper design

At the end of Section 8.1, the design has been updated to Y2 = 30 mm, Y3 = 100 mm, and Y6 = 55 mm. Starting with this design point, perform another iteration. Set up suitable upper and lower bounds by yourself.

Another iteration for the triangular plate design

At the end of Section 8.2, the design has been updated to DS_W = 20 mm and DS_R = 12 mm. Starting with this design point, perform another iteration. Set up suitable upper and lower bounds by yourself.

References

1. Box, G. E. P., Hunter, W. G., and Hunter, J. S., *Statistics for Experiments: An Introduction to Design, Data Analysis, and Model Building*, John Wiley & Sons, 1978.
2. Box, G. E. P., Hunter, J. S., and Hunter, W. G., *Statistics for Experiments: Design, Innovation, and Discovery*, John Wiley & Sons, 2005.

Chapter 9
Meshing

So far, we haven't emphasized much on meshing because, for linear static problems, we usually can solve them with global mesh controls (e.g., <Relevance Center>, <Relevance>, and <Element Size>) and obtain solutions which are acceptable both in computing time and accuracy. For the rest of the book, we will be dealing with dynamic or nonlinear problems. Solutions of dynamic and nonlinear problems are sensitive to meshing quality. With poor mesh quality, a simulation may end up with solutions of poor accuracy. Besides, since dynamic and nonlinear problems require much of computational resource, poor mesh quality may aggravate the situation and end up with an lengthy computing time. For nonlinear problems, it is possible to reduce much of runtime by improving the mesh quality so that they become easier to converge. On contrast, it is possible that a nonlinear problem fails to converge to a solution just because its mesh quality is not acceptable.

In short, mesh quality is not only a matter of good or bad (accuracy and runtime) for the solution but also a matter of life or death (success or failure) for the solution.

Purpose of the Chapter

This chapter introduces meshing methods provided by the Workbench and demonstrates how to use them using two hands-on examples. One of the mesh quality metrics, called *skewness*, is also introduced and used as a measure of mesh quality in this chapter.

About Each Section

Using the pneumatic finger example, Section 1 provides a step-by-step exercise to introduce some important concepts of meshing technology. Section 2 uses a more involved model, the cover of pressure cylinder, to demonstrate some complicated manipulations toward a better mesh quality. Section 3, a sequel of Section 3.5, studies the 3D finite element convergence behavior. We postpone the study of 3D element convergence because we need more meshing techniques to control the meshing density. The other reason is that the students should have enough curiosity about 3D elements convergence after so many exercises have been done in the previous chapters.

Section 9.1

Step-by-Step: Pneumatic Fingers

9.1-1 About the Pneumatic Fingers

The pneumatic finger was overviewed in Section 1.1. In this section, we will walk through the details, including geometric modeling and the simulation.

Besides the information in Section 1.1-1, detail dimensions are shown in the figure below [1-2]. Due to symmetry, we will model only half of the problem. The unit system used in this exercise is mm-s-N.

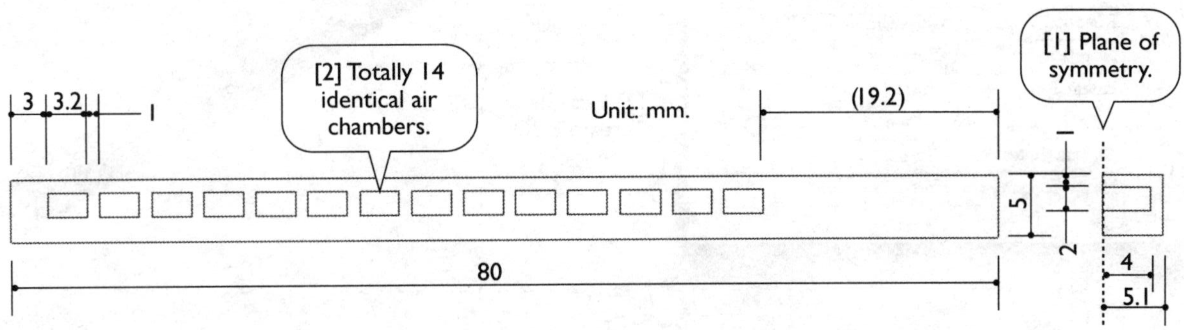

9.1-2 Start Up and Prepare Material Properties

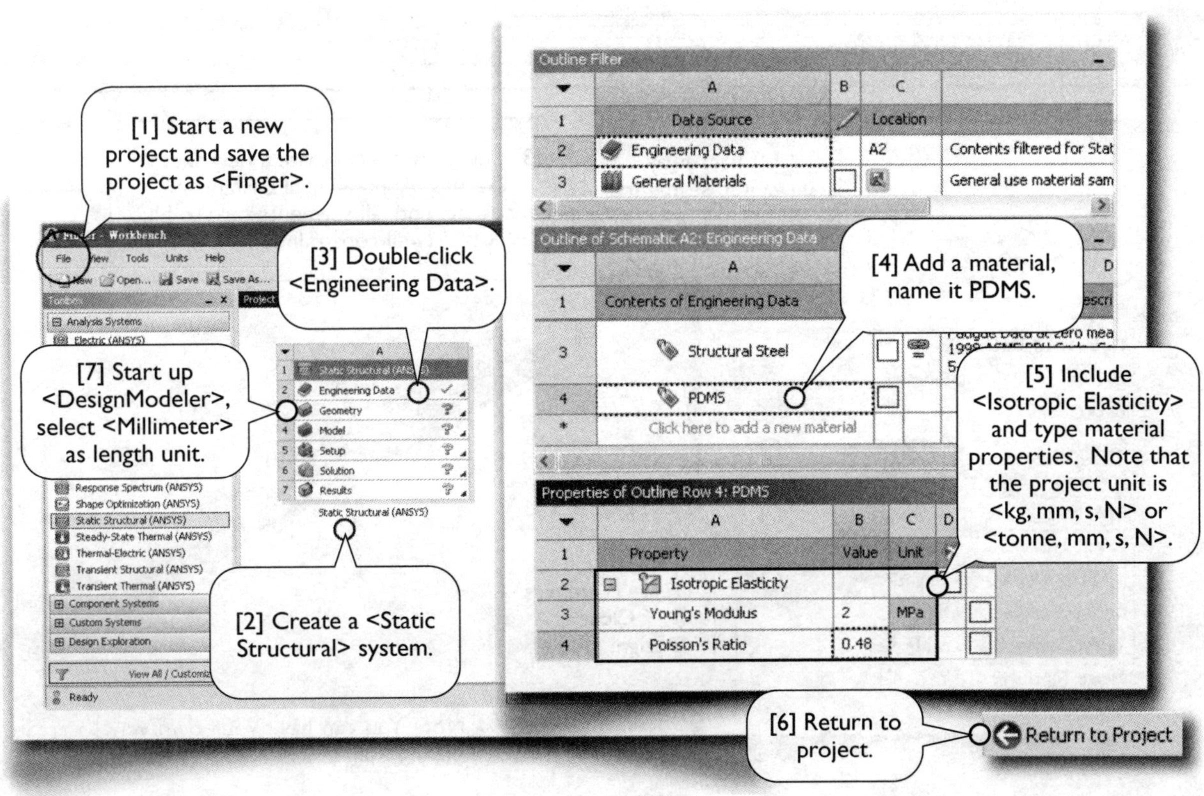

9.1-3 Create Geometry

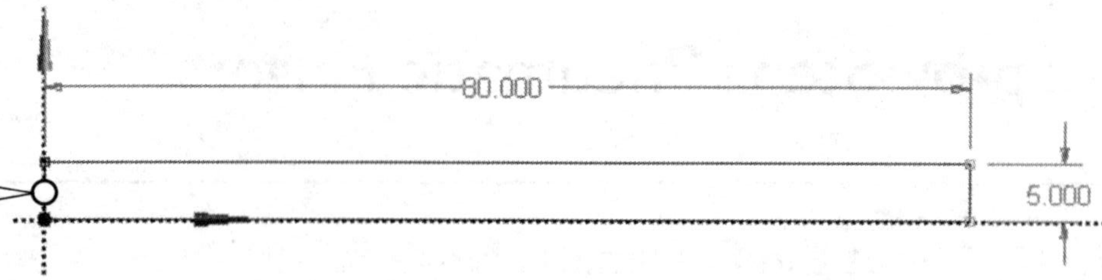

Details View	
Details of Extrude1	
Extrude	Extrude1
Base Object	Sketch1
Operation	Add Material
Direction Vector	None (Normal)
Direction	Reversed
Extent Type	Fixed
FD1, Depth (>0)	5.1 mm
As Thin/Surface?	No
Merge Topology?	Yes

[2] Extrude to create a 3D block.

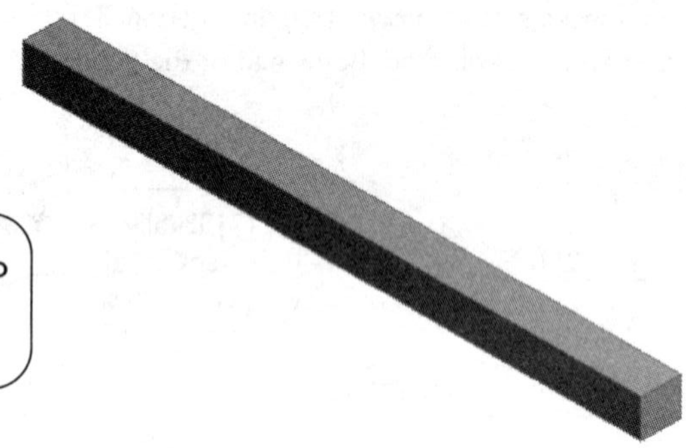

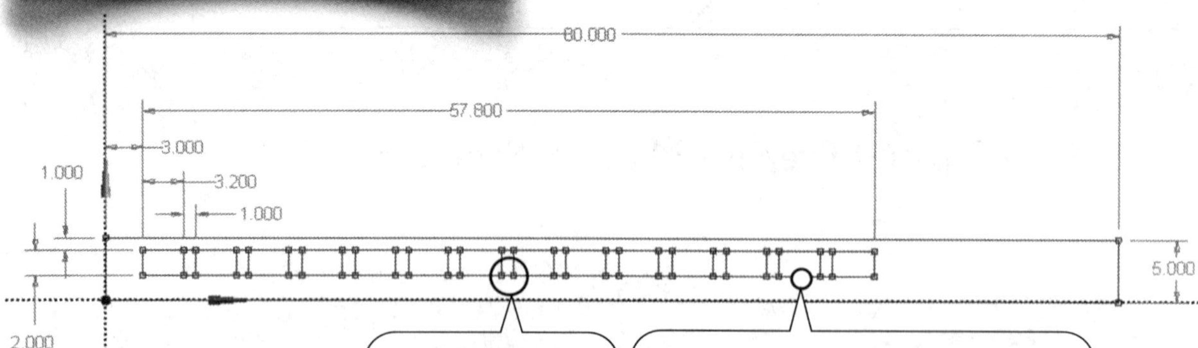

Details View	
Details of Extrude2	
Extrude	Extrude2
Base Object	Sketch2
Operation	Cut Material
Direction Vector	None (Normal)
Direction	Reversed
Extent Type	Fixed
FD1, Depth (>0)	4 mm
As Thin/Surface?	No
Target Bodies	All Bodies
Merge Topology?	Yes

[5] Extrude to create chambers. Close DesignModeler.

Note: You can have your own way to create the geometry.

9.1-4 Assign Material

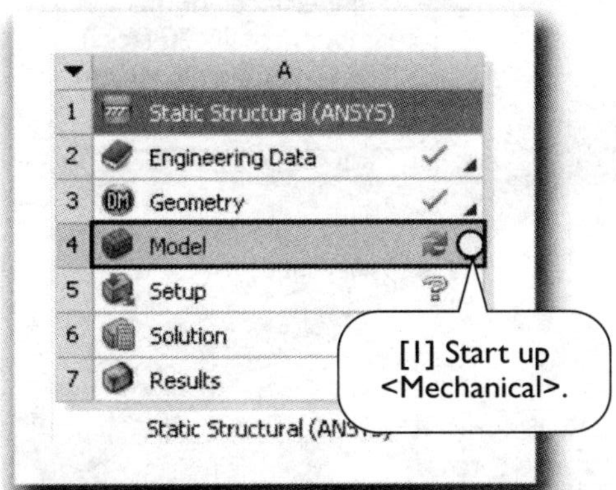

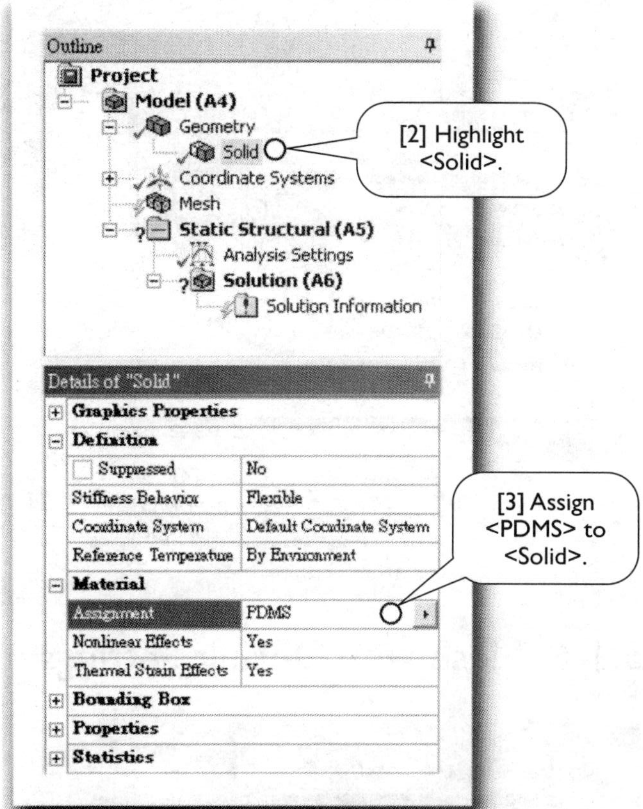

9.1-5 Set Up Environment Conditions

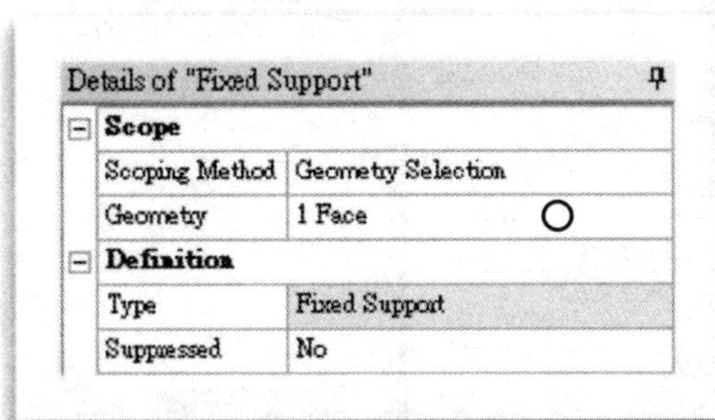

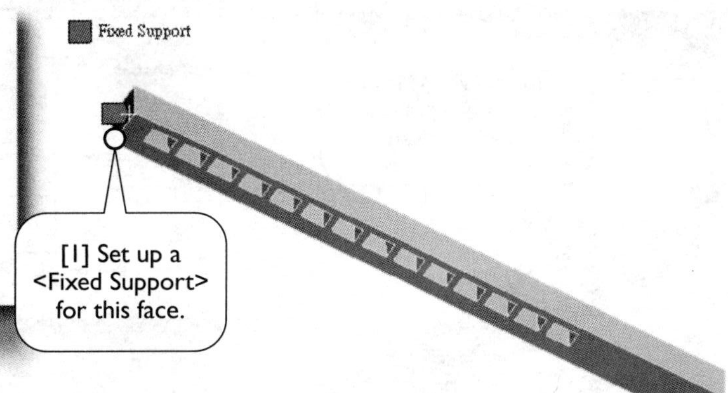

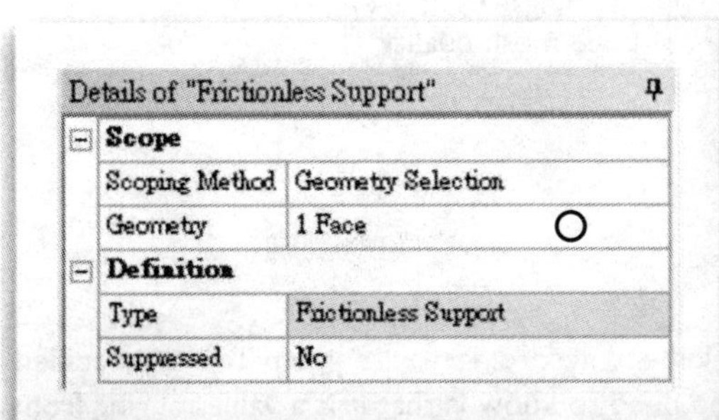

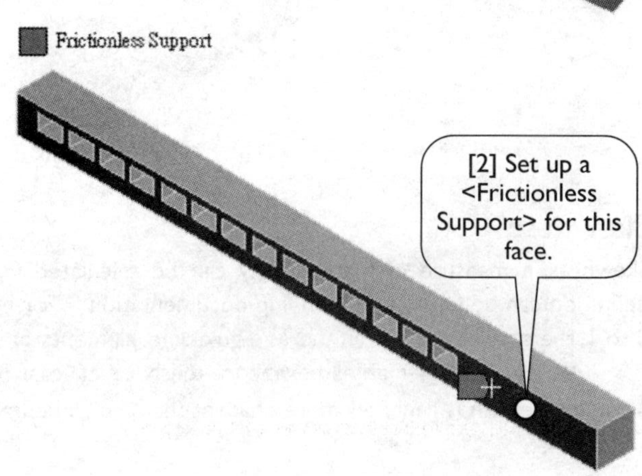

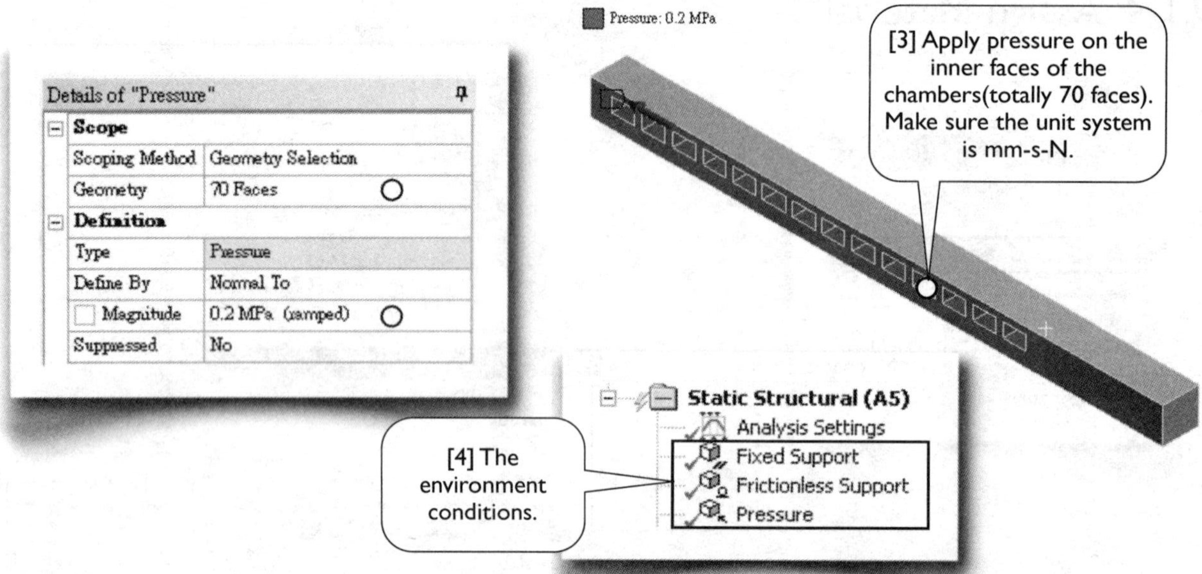

9.1-6 Mesh with Default Settings

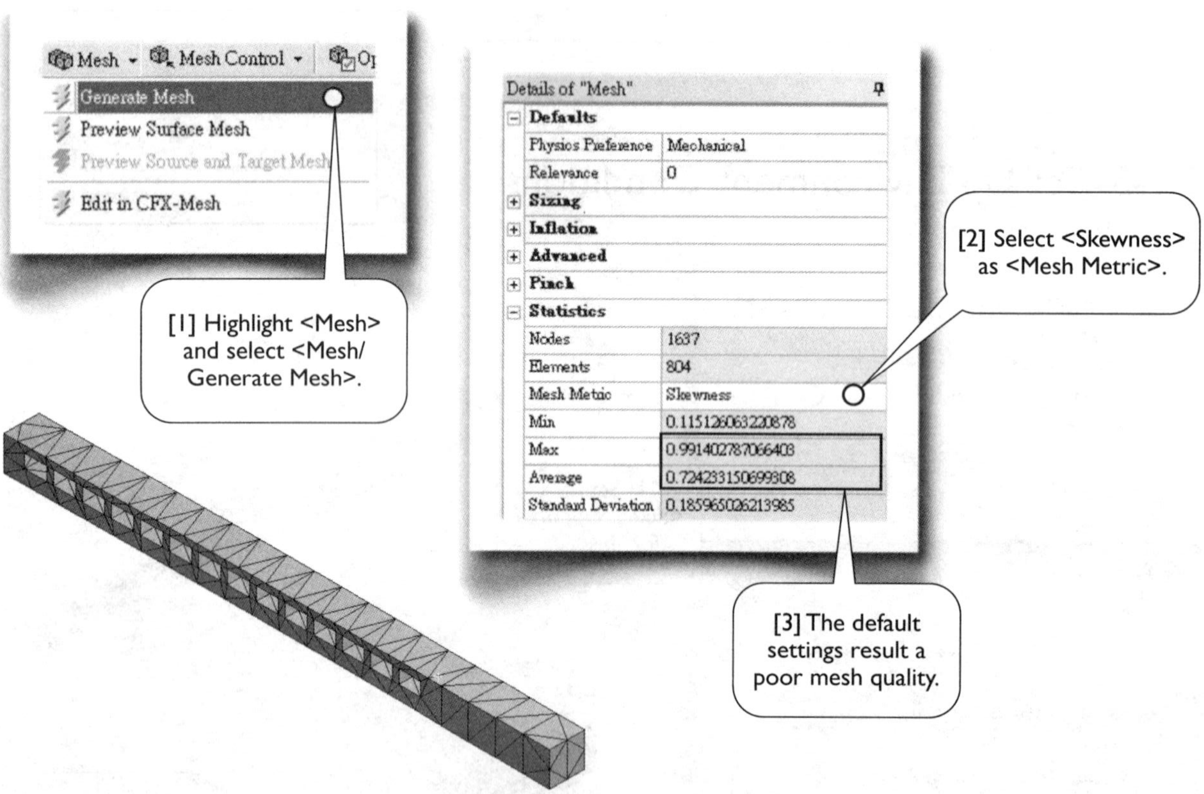

Skewness[1]

Skewness, a measure of mesh quality, can be calculated for each element according to its geometry. A detailed definition can be found in the on-line documentation[1]. For now, all you need to know is that it is a value ranging from 0 to 1, the smaller the better, and, as a guideline, elements of skewness of more than 0.95 are considered unacceptable.

We usually prefer an all-hexahedra mesh, or at least hexahedra-dominate mesh to a tetrahedral mesh, since a hexahedral mesh is generally more efficient than a tetrahedral mesh.

9.1-7 Improve Mesh Quality

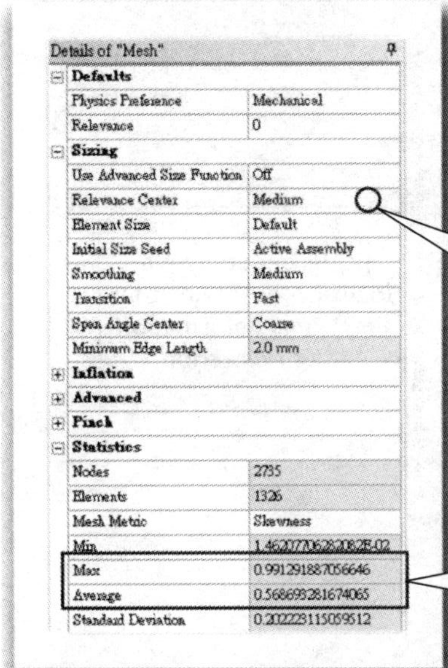

Details of "Mesh"	
Defaults	
Physics Preference	Mechanical
Relevance	0
Sizing	
Use Advanced Size Function	Off
Relevance Center	Medium
Element Size	Default
Initial Size Seed	Active Assembly
Smoothing	Medium
Transition	Fast
Span Angle Center	Coarse
Minimum Edge Length	2.0 mm
Inflation	
Advanced	
Pinch	
Statistics	
Nodes	2735
Elements	1326
Mesh Metric	Skewness
Min	1.46207706282082E-02
Max	0.991291887056646
Average	0.568693281674065
Standard Deviation	0.202223115059512

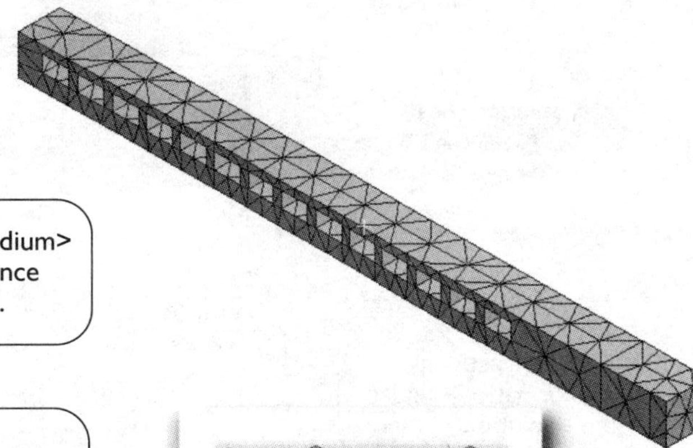

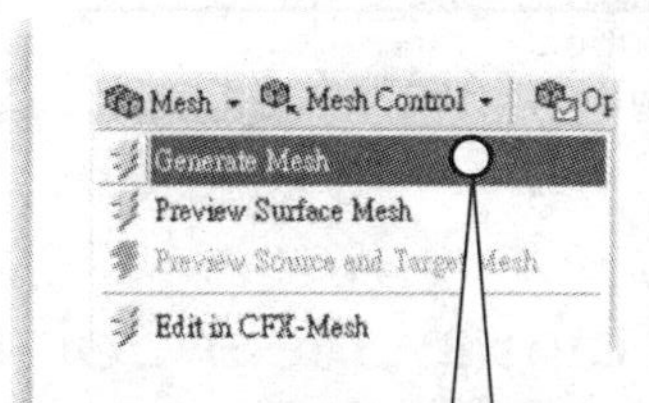

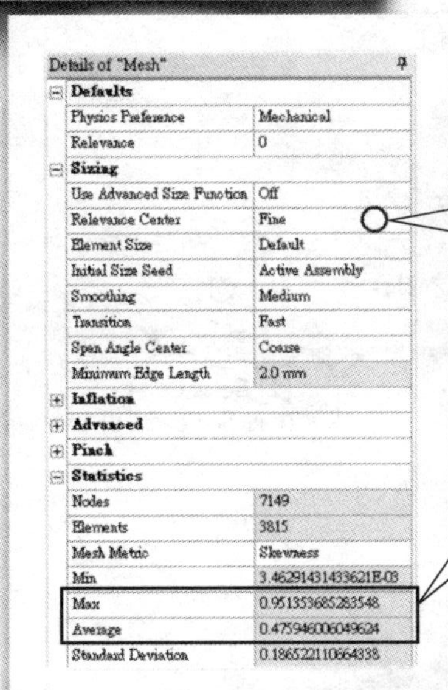

Details of "Mesh"	
Defaults	
Physics Preference	Mechanical
Relevance	0
Sizing	
Use Advanced Size Function	Off
Relevance Center	Fine
Element Size	Default
Initial Size Seed	Active Assembly
Smoothing	Medium
Transition	Fast
Span Angle Center	Coarse
Minimum Edge Length	2.0 mm
Inflation	
Advanced	
Pinch	
Statistics	
Nodes	7149
Elements	3815
Mesh Metric	Skewness
Min	3.46291431433621E-03
Max	0.951353685283548
Average	0.475946006049624
Standard Deviation	0.186522110664338

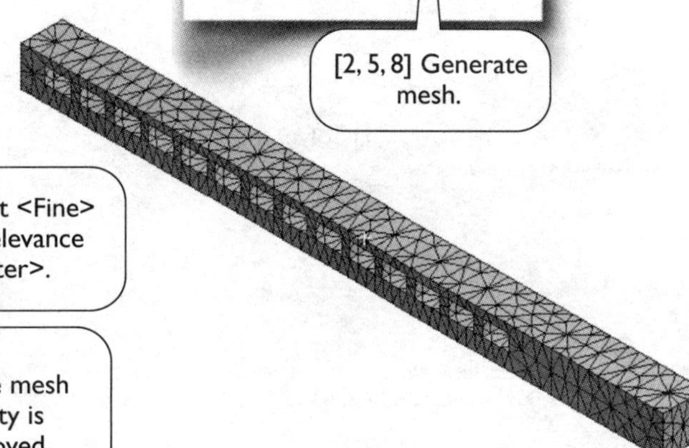

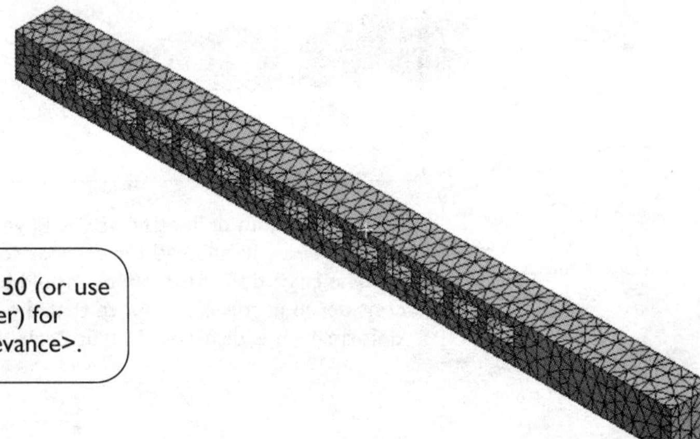

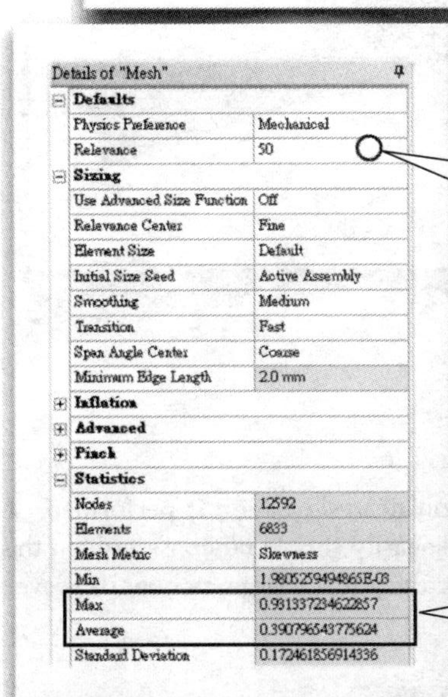

Details of "Mesh"	
Defaults	
Physics Preference	Mechanical
Relevance	50
Sizing	
Use Advanced Size Function	Off
Relevance Center	Fine
Element Size	Default
Initial Size Seed	Active Assembly
Smoothing	Medium
Transition	Fast
Span Angle Center	Coarse
Minimum Edge Length	2.0 mm
Inflation	
Advanced	
Pinch	
Statistics	
Nodes	12592
Elements	6833
Mesh Metric	Skewness
Min	1.98052594948651E-03
Max	0.981337234622857
Average	0.390796543775624
Standard Deviation	0.172461856914336

9.1-8 Set Up Solution Branch

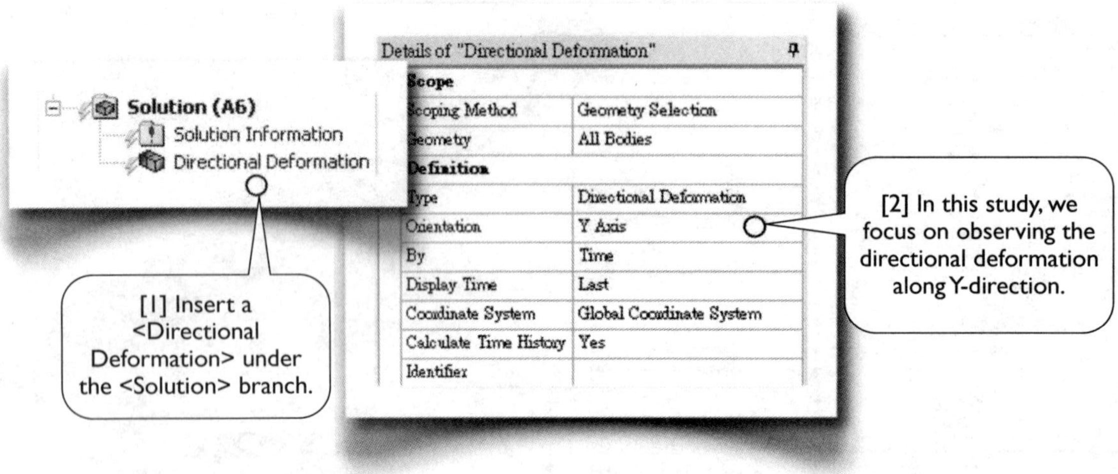

9.1-9 Obtain a Linear Solution

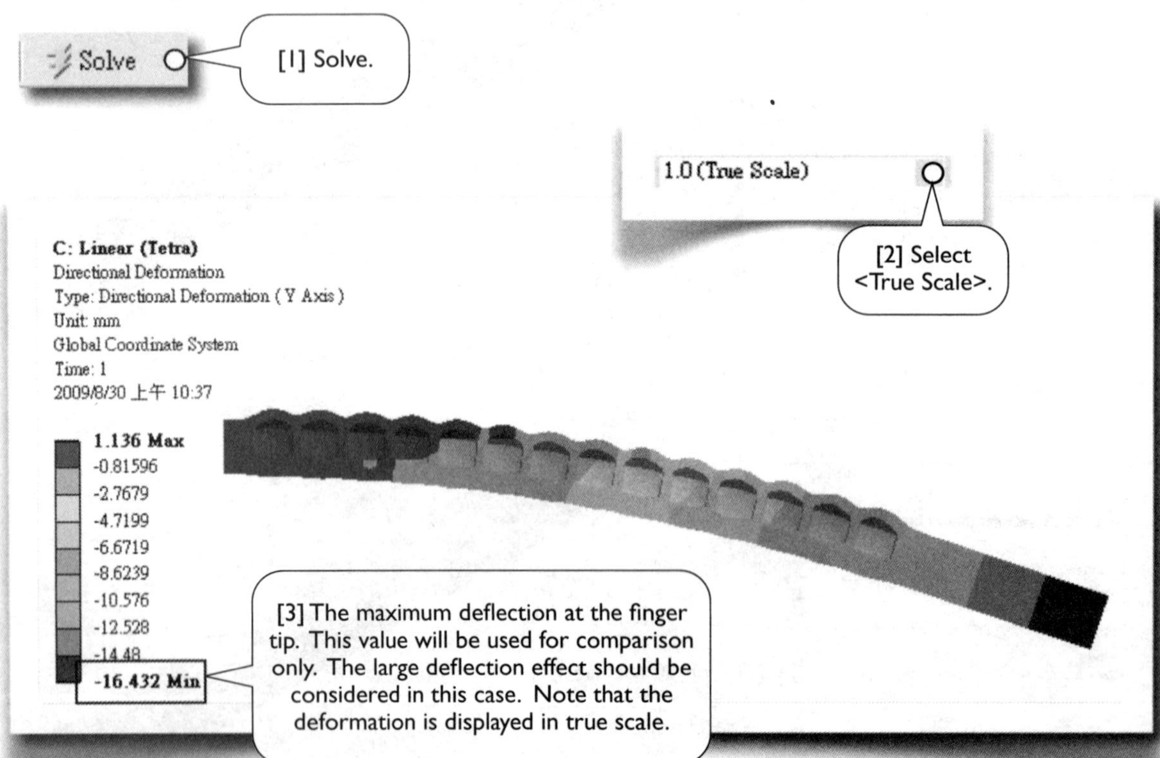

Obtain a Linear Solution before Nonlinear Simulation

It is a good practice to make sure a linear solution can be obtained before a nonlinear simulation is performed. A linear simulation needs much less computational time than a nonlinear one. Nonlinearity should be considered in this case, since the deflection is large. The linear solution, which may be out of accuracy for a large amount, however, provides an effective way of data checking.

9.1-10 Obtain a Nonlinear Solution

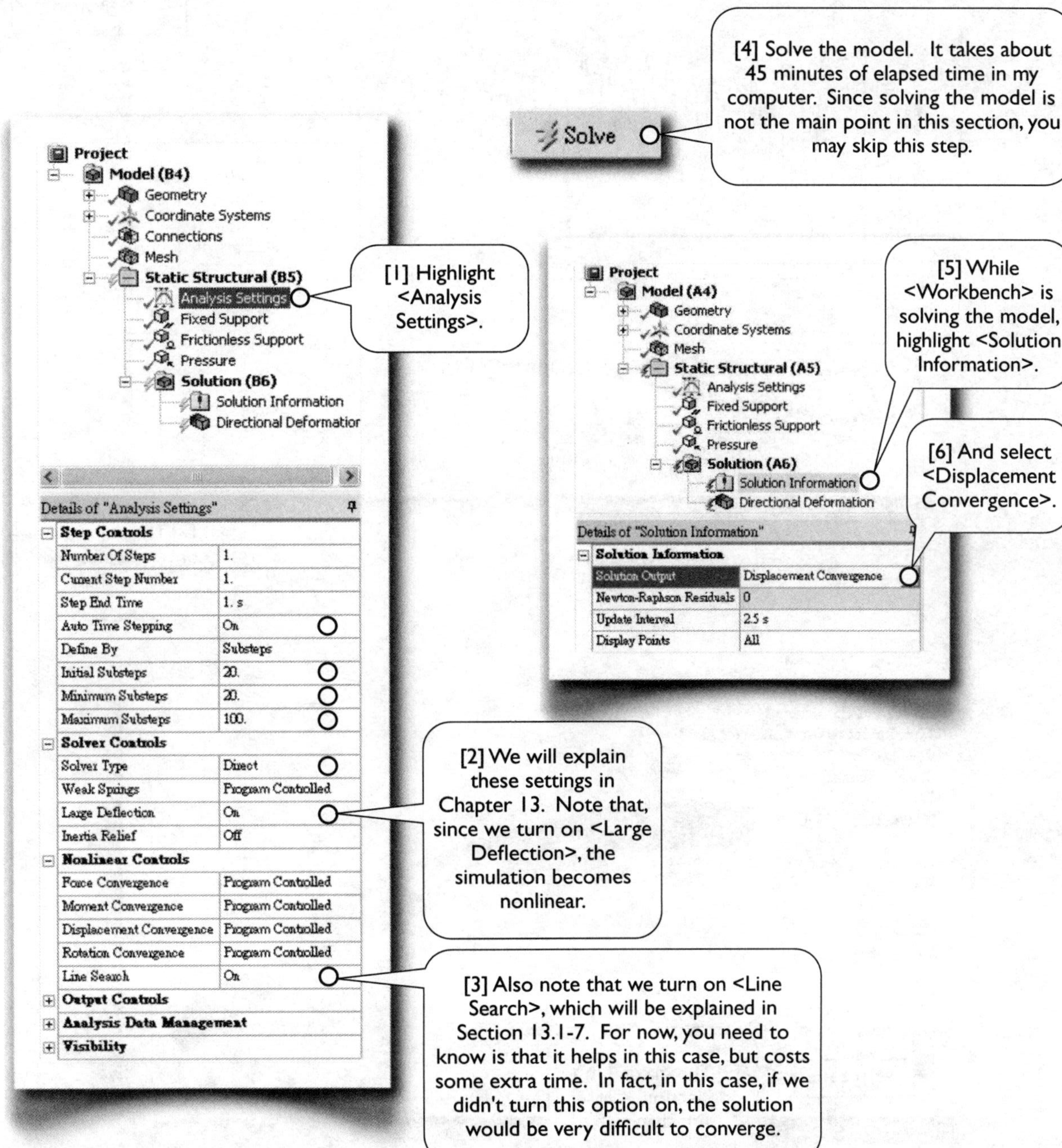

Displacement Convergence

Each substep of a nonlinear simulation involves an iterative process. Force and displacement are used as convergence criteria. Most of cases, you should look at force convergence behavior during the solution, because the convergence is usually governed by force criterion. However, for this particular case, the convergence is governed by displacement criterion. That is why we look at <Displacement Convergence> instead of <Force Convergence>. These terms will be defined in Section 13.1-5.

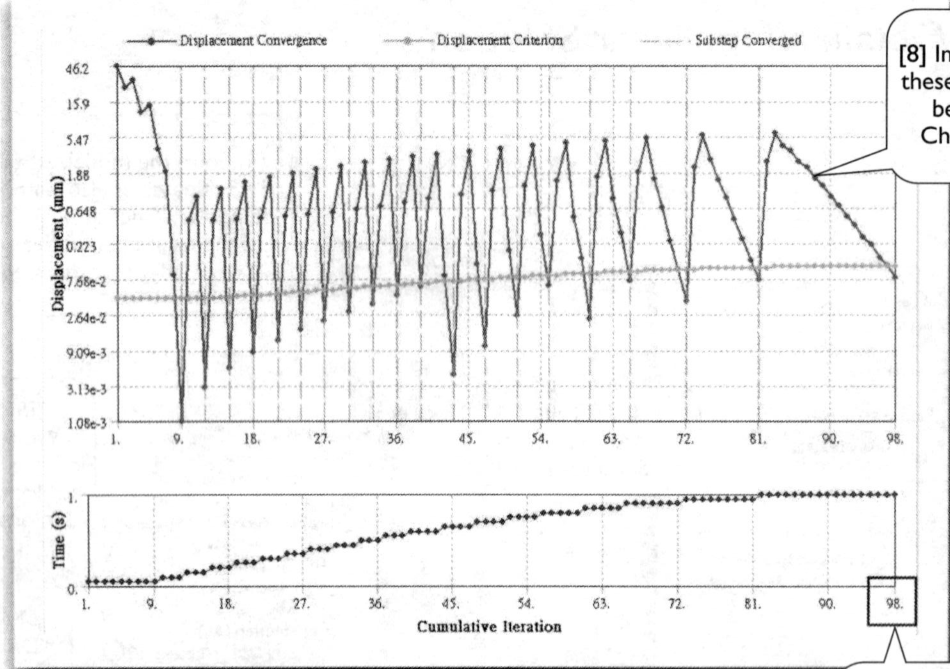

[8] Implication of these curves will be given in Chapters 13.

[7] The solution converges after 98 iterations.

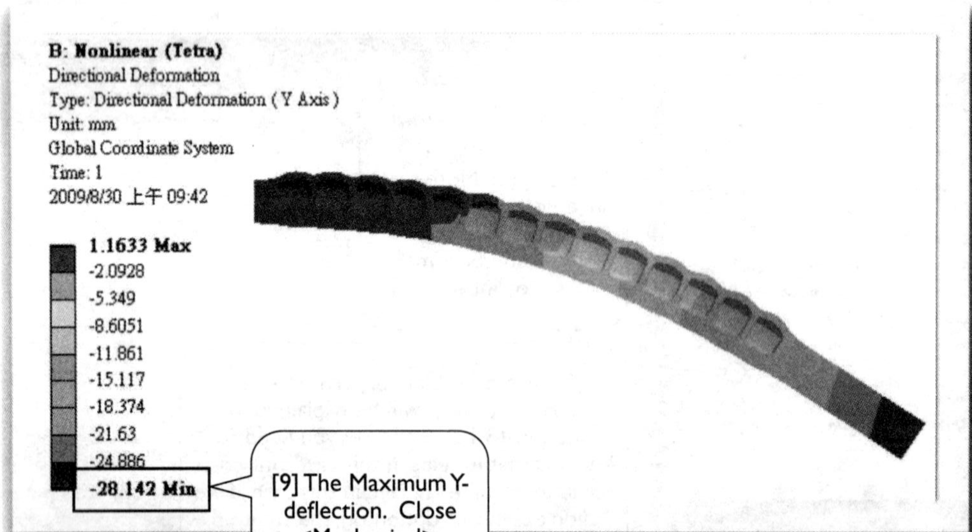

[9] The Maximum Y-deflection. Close <Mechanical>.

For this case, the nonlinear simulation proceeds quite smoothly without any problems, except it takes some computing time. But in general, nonlinear simulations are challenging and sometimes fail. A key issue is the meshing quality. The mesh metric (skewness) demonstrated in Sections 9.1-6 and 9.1-7 is a measure of mesh quality. It often can be improved by refining elements. It sometimes needs a large number of elements to achieve a mesh quality good enough to make the solution converge. The worse is that it sometimes never achieve an acceptable mesh quality by simply refining elements.

Another factor affecting convergence is the shapes of elements. In general, hexahedra are more efficient than tetrahedra. Let's try to mesh the model with hexahedra as many as possible and with the skewness as low as possible.

9.1-11 Mesh with <Hex Dominant> Method

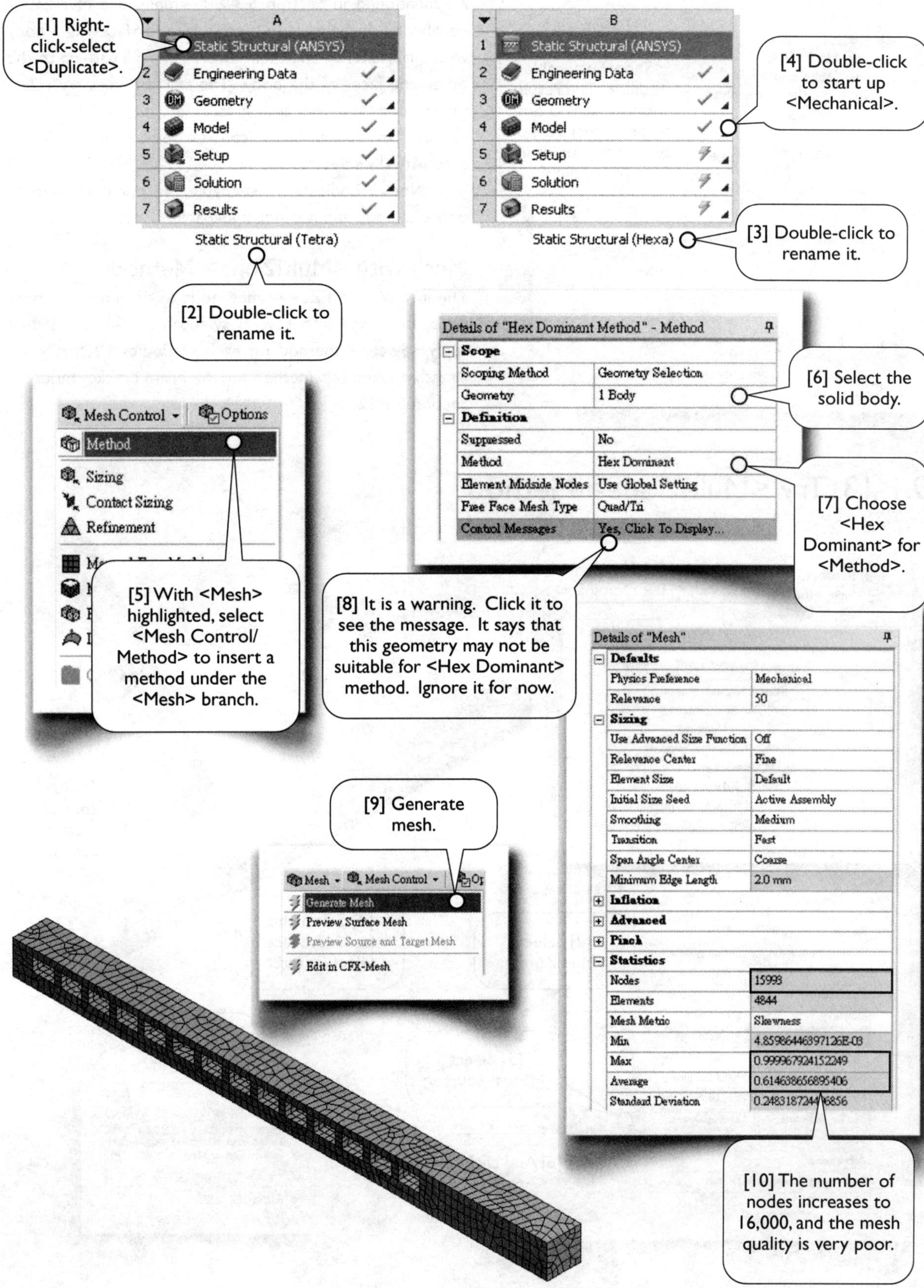

9.1-12 Try <Sweep> Method

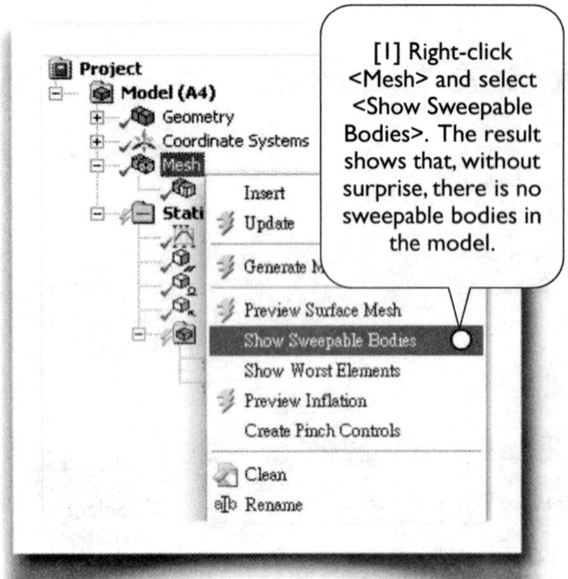

Mesh with <Sweep> Method

As mentioned in Section 5.3-2, a simple idea of creating hexahedral elements is to mesh a face (or faces) of a body with quadrilaterals and then "sweep" along a path up to the other end faces of the body. The starting faces are called *source faces* and the ending faces are *target faces*. The source or target faces can be either manually or automatically selected.

Not all bodies are sweepable. In our case, there is only one body, and it is not sweepable.

Mesh with <MultiZone> Method

The idea of <MultiZone> method is to decompose a non-sweepable body into several sweepable bodies, and then apply <Sweep> method on each of bodies. Actually, we already applied this method for the beam bracket model in Section 5.1-12.

9.1-13 Try <MultiZone> Method

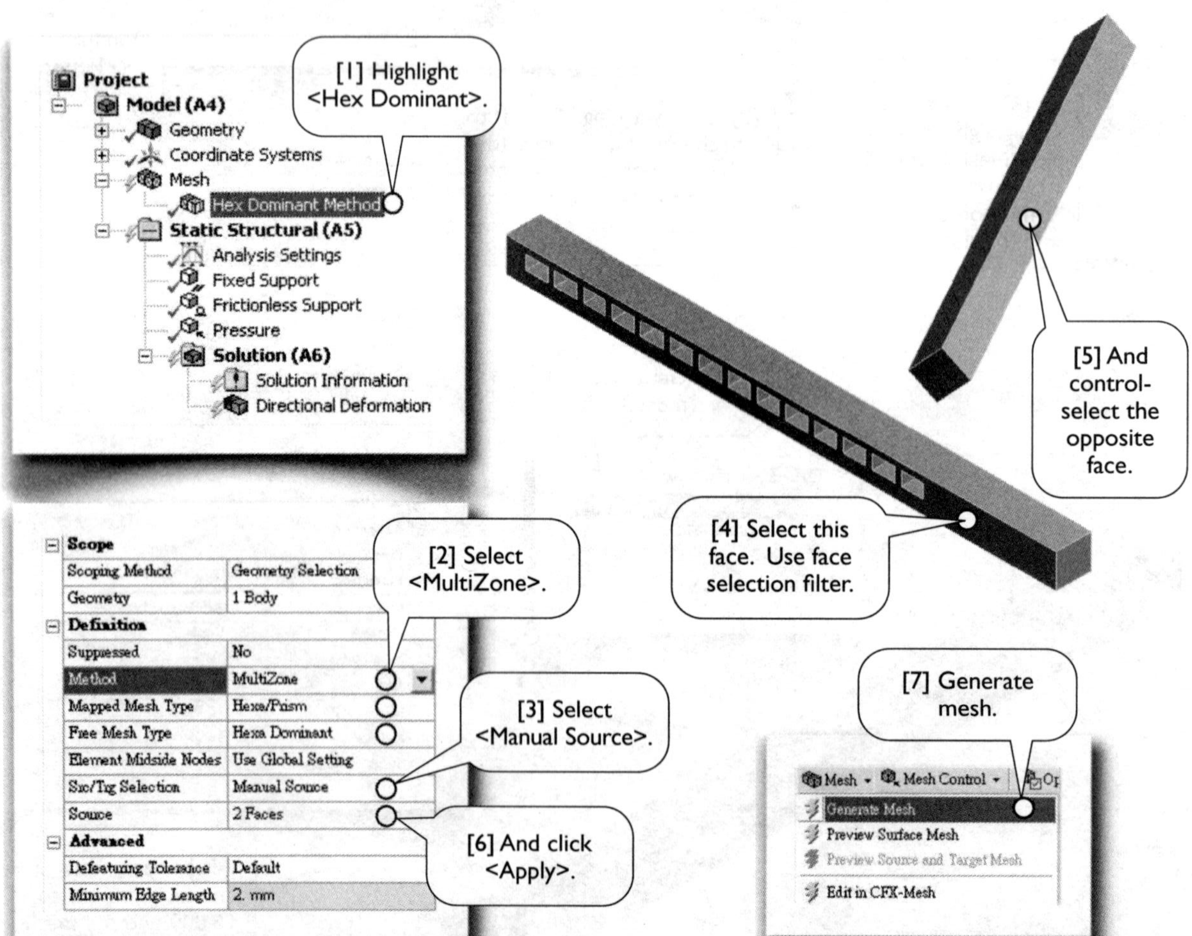

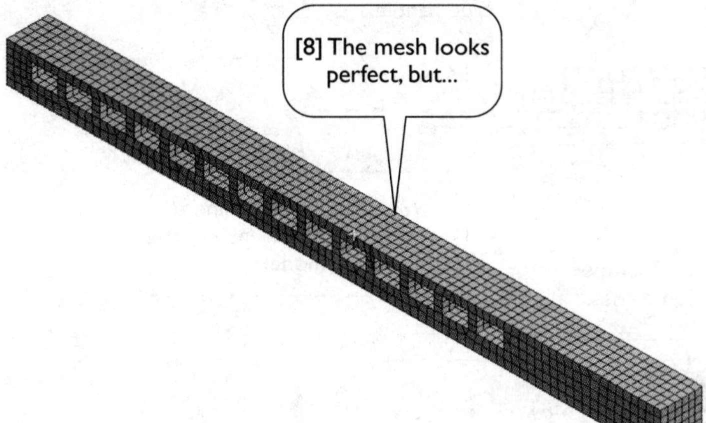

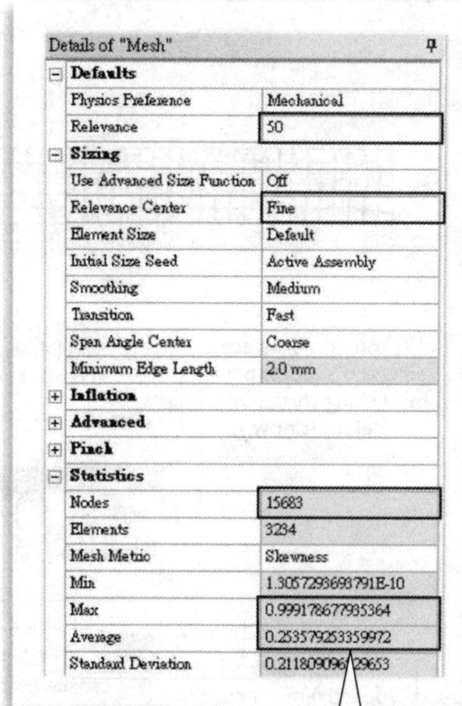

Defaults	
Physics Preference	Mechanical
Relevance	50
Sizing	
Use Advanced Size Function	Off
Relevance Center	Fine
Element Size	Default
Initial Size Seed	Active Assembly
Smoothing	Medium
Transition	Fast
Span Angle Center	Coarse
Minimum Edge Length	2.0 mm
Inflation	
Advanced	
Pinch	
Statistics	
Nodes	15683
Elements	3234
Mesh Metric	Skewness
Min	1.3057293693791E-10
Max	0.999178677935364
Average	0.253579253359972
Standard Deviation	0.211809096729653

9.1-14 Show Problematic Elements

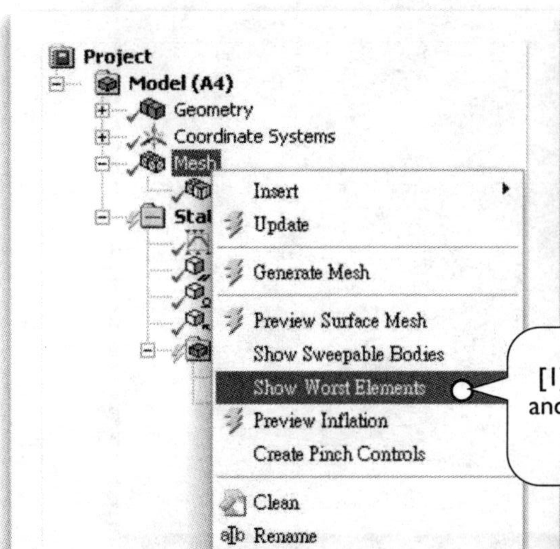

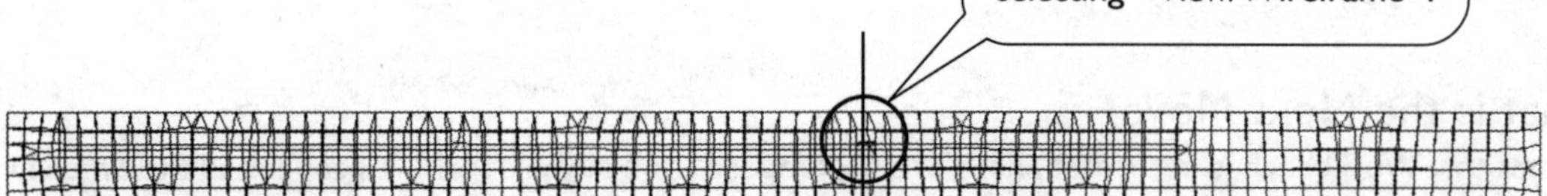

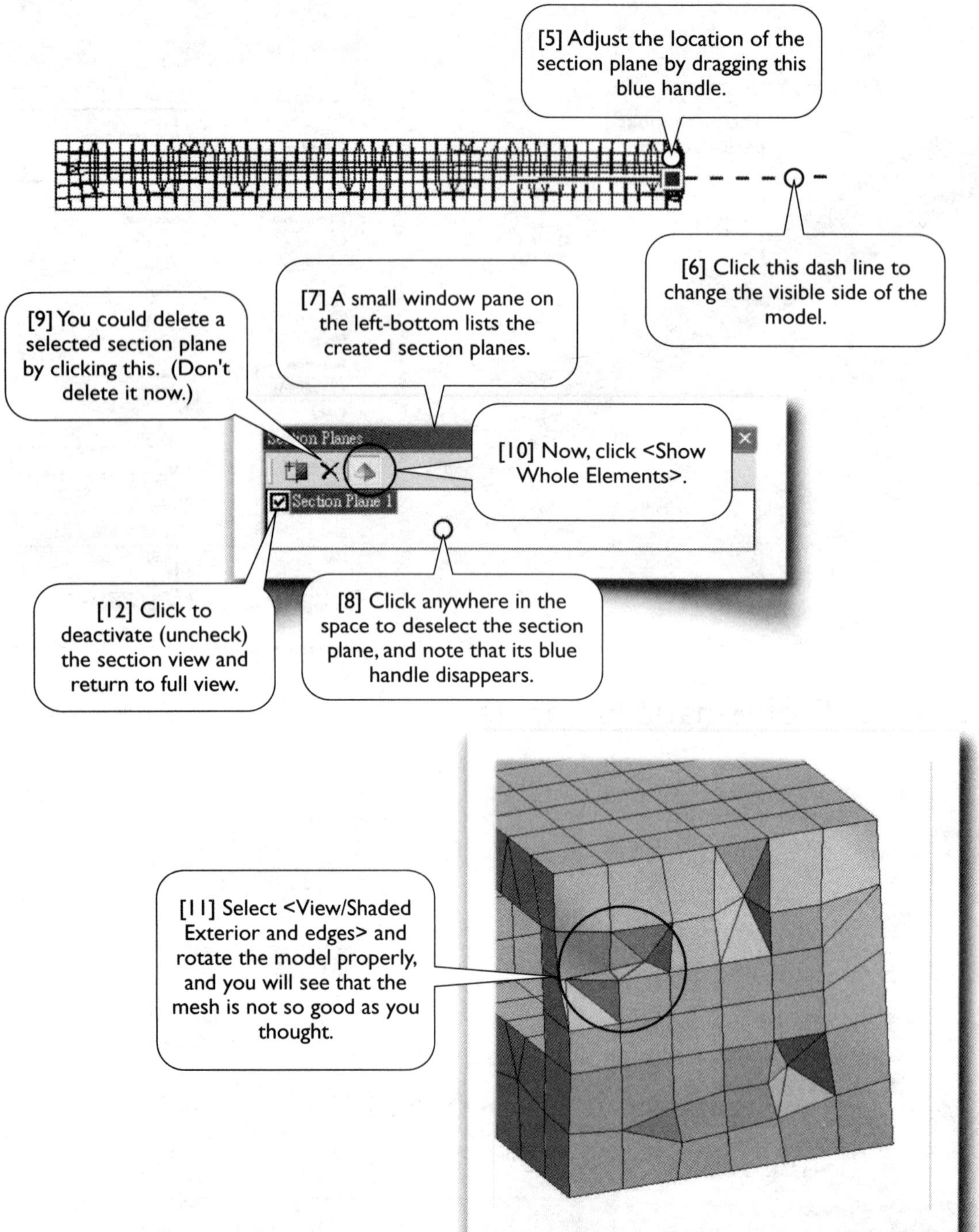

What is the Next Move?

It seems that Workbench is not smart enough to decompose the body properly. It happens all the time. In such cases, we may manually decompose the body. We now want to manually *slice* the body into two sweepable bodies. The two bodies will form a single part. When meshed, the bodies' boundaries will be compatible (i.e., they share the same nodes).

9.1-15 Slice the Body into Two Parts

[1] Close <Mechanical>. You don't have to close it, but I strongly suggest the beginners close it, because when you start it up again, it will automatically refresh the changes made in the DesignModeler.

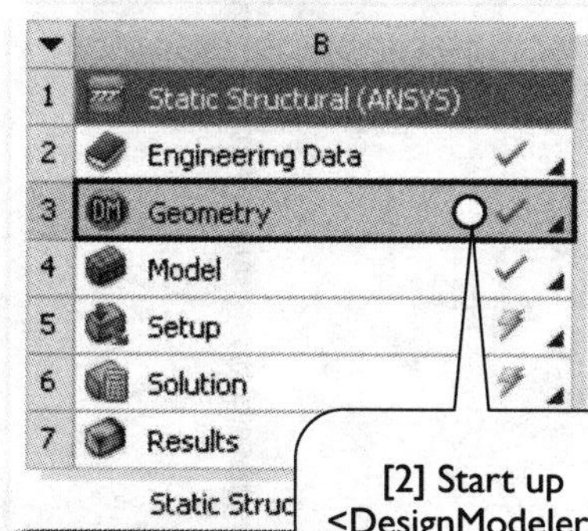

[2] Start up <DesignModeler>.

[3] Click <New Plane>. We want to use the new plane as slicing plane.

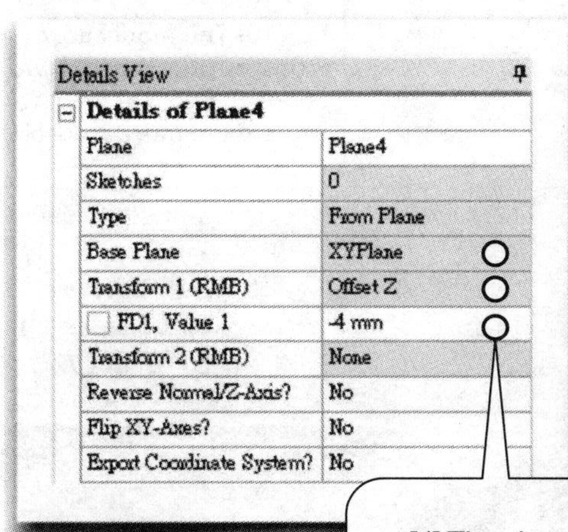
Details View

Details of Plane4	
Plane	Plane4
Sketches	0
Type	From Plane
Base Plane	XYPlane
Transform 1 (RMB)	Offset Z
FD1, Value 1	-4 mm
Transform 2 (RMB)	None
Reverse Normal/Z-Axis?	No
Flip XY-Axes?	No
Export Coordinate System?	No

[4] The plane is created by offsetting <XYPlane> -4 mm along local Z-direction. Click <Generate>.

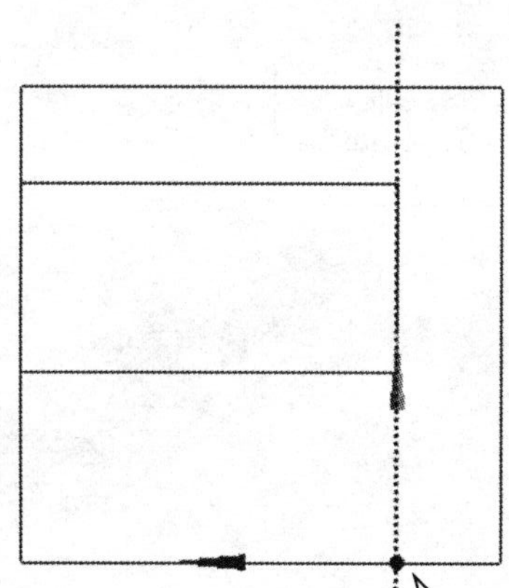

[5] The origin of the new plane.

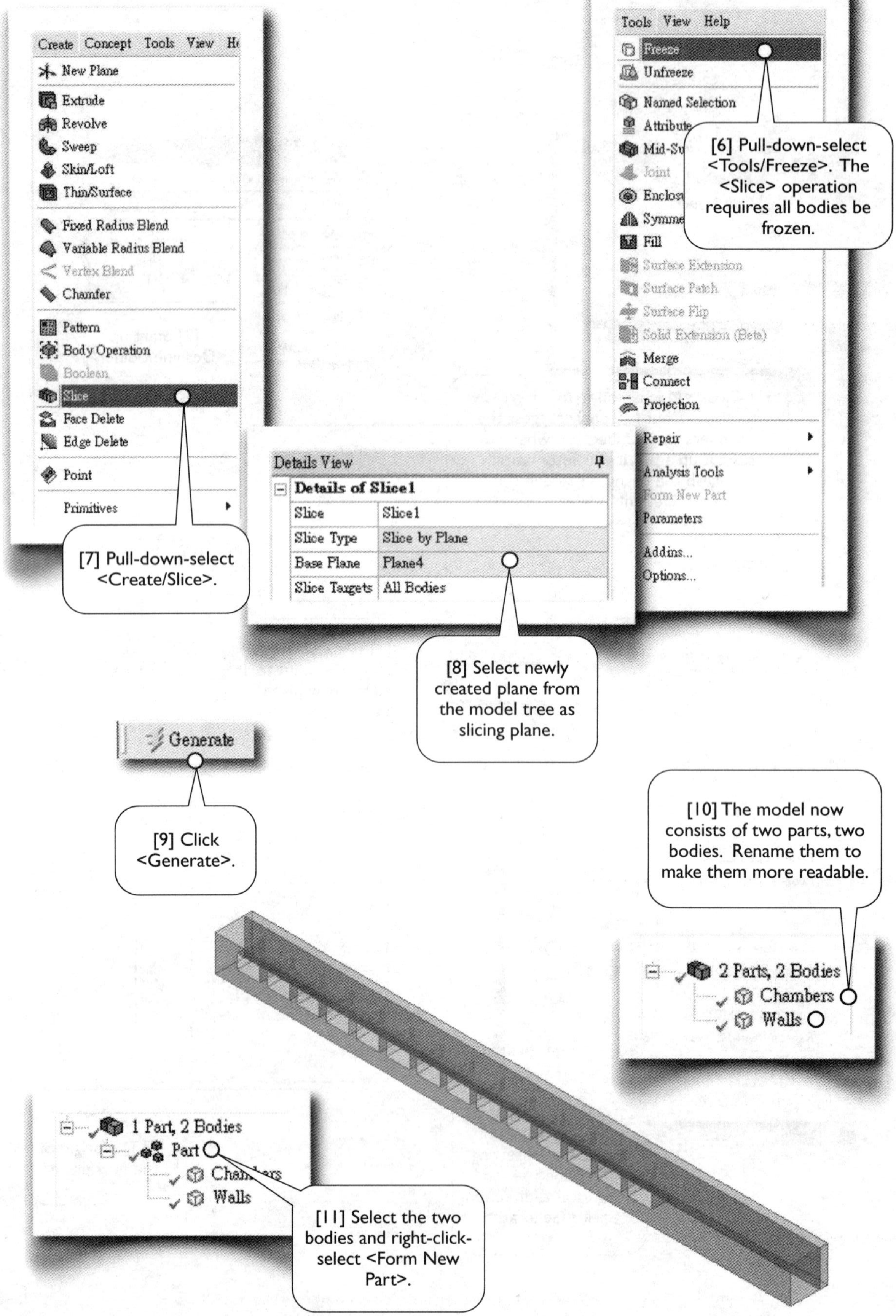
Create Concept Tools View He
New Plane
Extrude
Revolve
Sweep
Skin/Loft
Thin/Surface
Fixed Radius Blend
Variable Radius Blend
Vertex Blend
Chamfer
Pattern
Body Operation
Boolean
Slice
Face Delete
Edge Delete
Point
Primitives
[7] Pull-down-select <Create/Slice>.
Tools View Help
Freeze
Unfreeze
Named Selection
Attribute
Joint
Fill
Surface Extension
Surface Patch
Surface Flip
Solid Extension (Beta)
Merge
Connect
Projection
Repair
Analysis Tools
Form New Part
Parameters
Addins...
Options...
[6] Pull-down-select <Tools/Freeze>. The <Slice> operation requires all bodies be frozen.
Details View
Details of Slice1
Slice Slice1
Slice Type Slice by Plane
Base Plane Plane4
Slice Targets All Bodies
[8] Select newly created plane from the model tree as slicing plane.
Generate
[9] Click <Generate>.
[10] The model now consists of two parts, two bodies. Rename them to make them more readable.
2 Parts, 2 Bodies
Chambers
Walls
1 Part, 2 Bodies
Part
Walls
[11] Select the two bodies and right-click-select <Form New Part>.

9.1-16 Mesh with <Sweep> Method

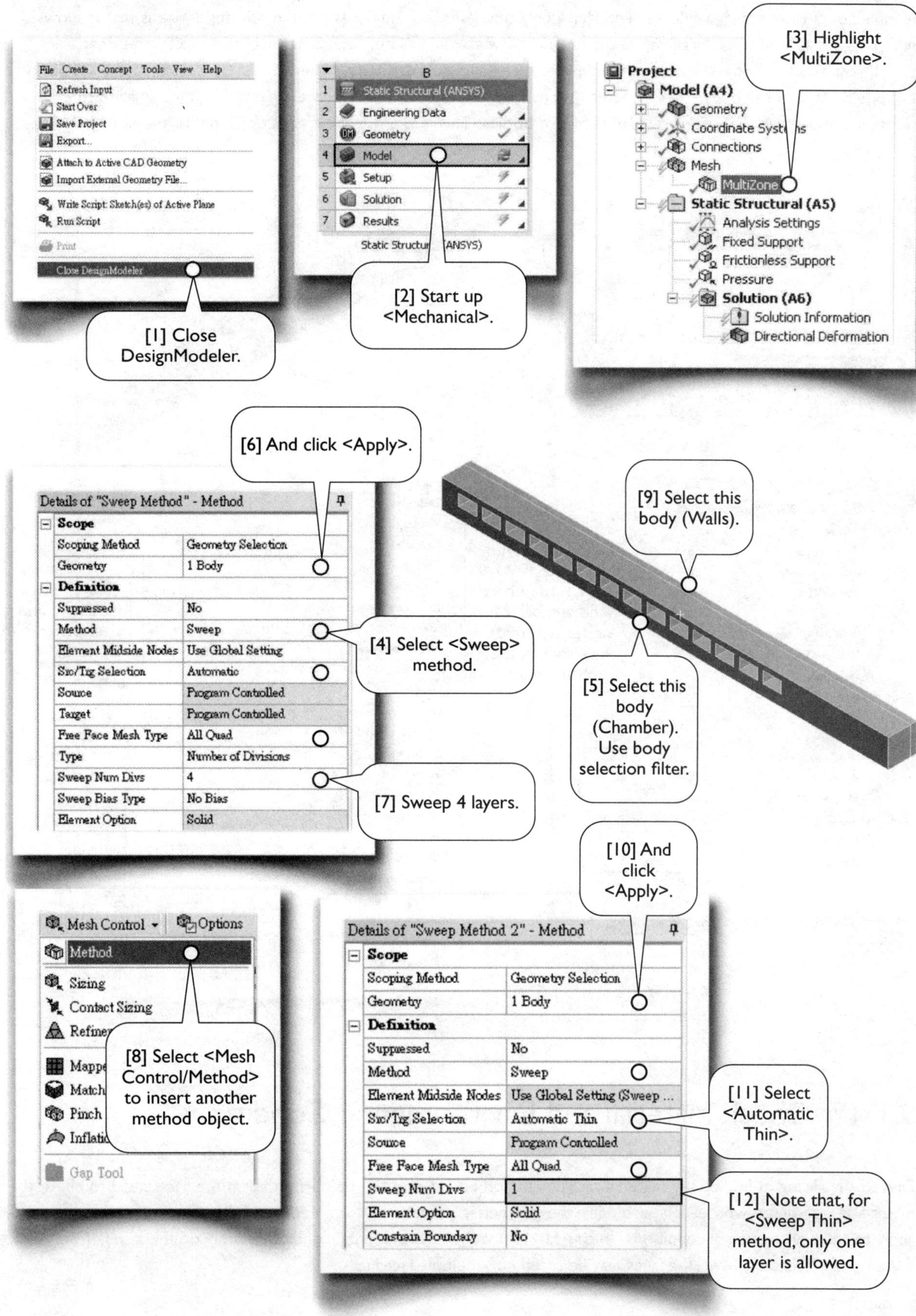

<Sweep Thin> Method

The <Sweep> method can be further classified into normal <Sweep> and <Sweep Thin>. The normal <Sweep> allows multiple layers of sweeping while <Sweep Thin> only one layer. The advantage of the <Sweep Thin> is that it allows multiple faces as source or target while the normal <Sweep> allows only one face for both source and target.

If you hide the body <Chambers> and make sure <View/Shaded Exterior and Edges> is selected, you will see that one surface of the body <Walls> actually consists of multiple faces. They are created by <Mechanical> to maintain compatibility between boundaries of two bodies. This is why we apply <Sweep Thin> on the body <Walls>.

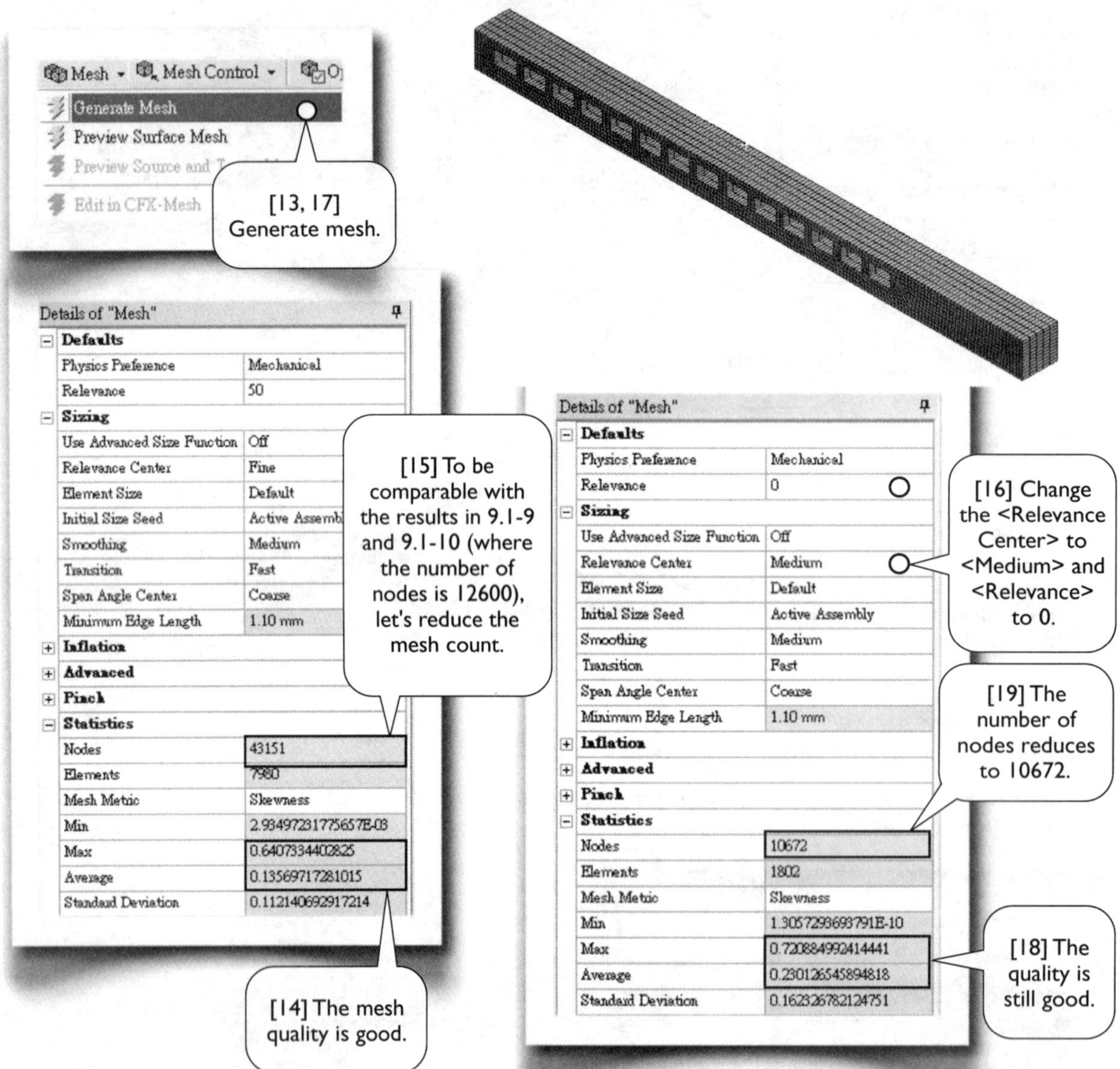

9.1-17 Check Material and Environmental Conditions

Due to the slicing of bodies, the material assignments on bodies may not be correct any more. You need to check the material assignments whenever you modify the geometric model in DesignModeler. The same considerations also apply to the environmental conditions. In this case, since the environmental conditions apply on the faces of the body, if the body is sliced into two, the faces may be sliced into multiple faces too.

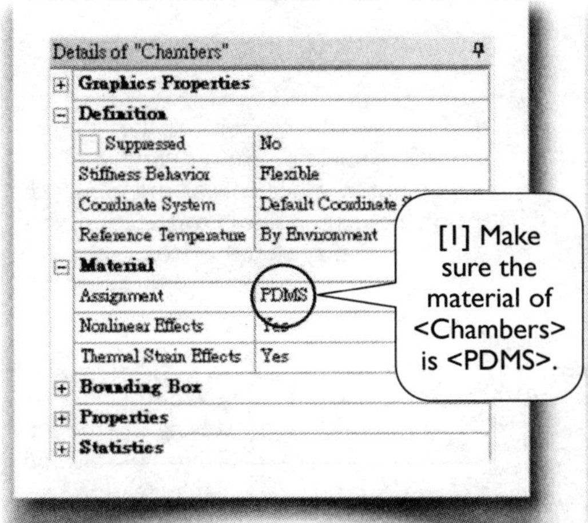

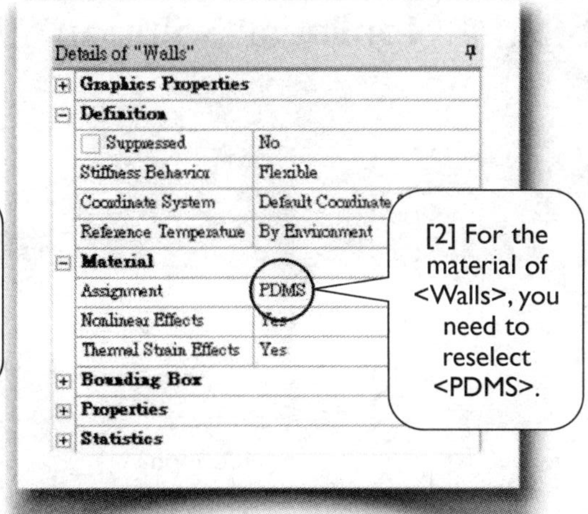

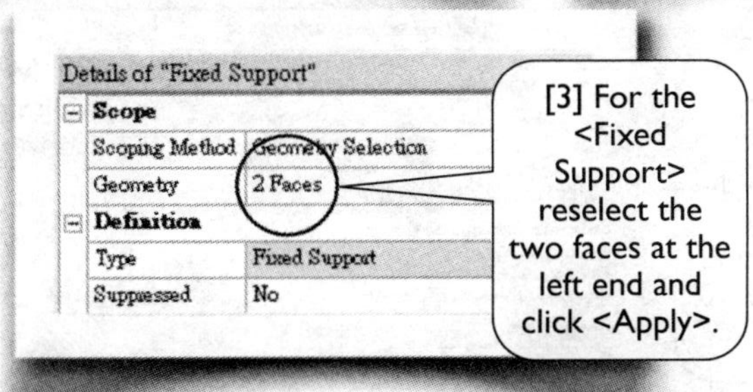

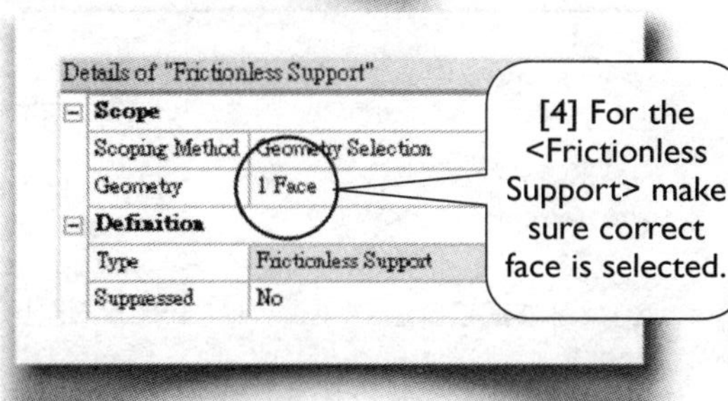

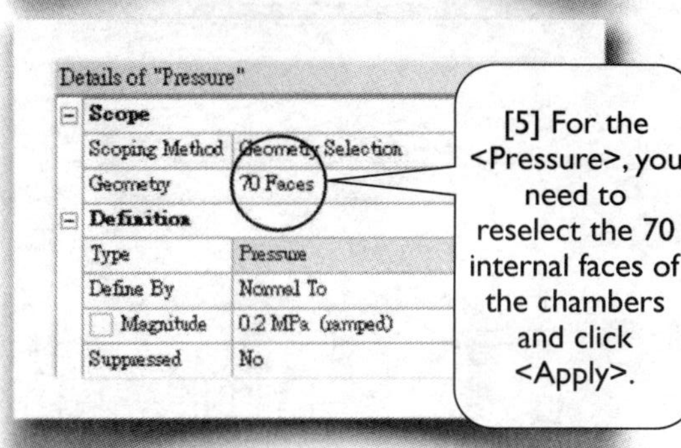

9.1-18 Obtain a Linear Solution

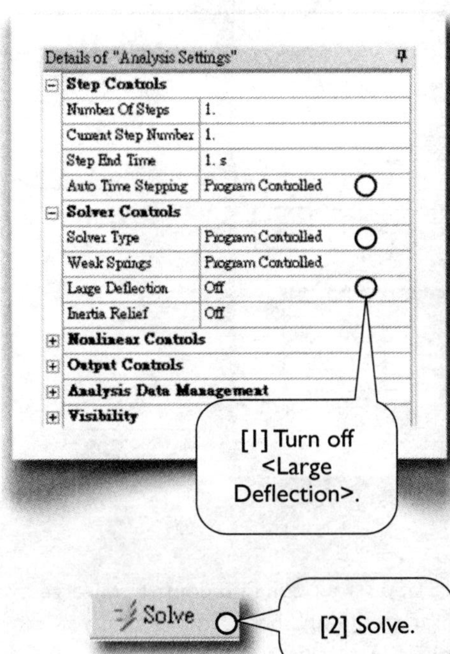

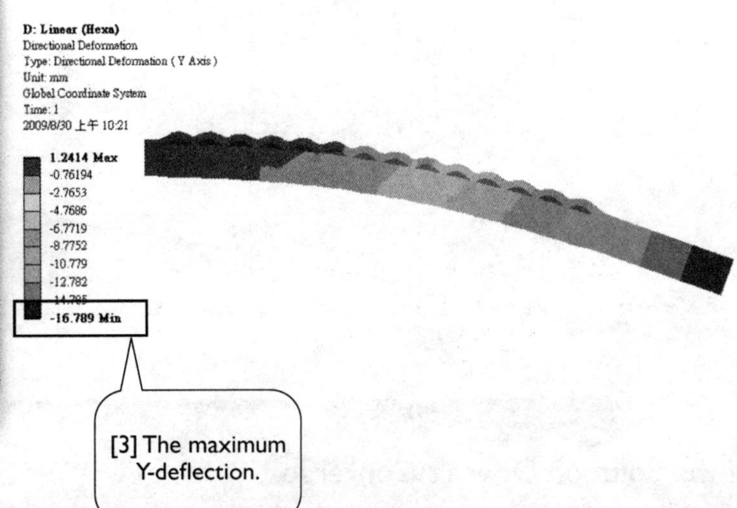

9.1-19 Obtain a Nonlinear Solution

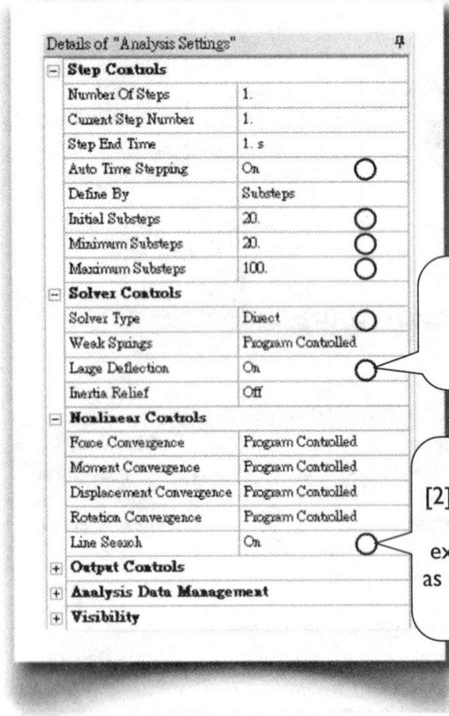

[1] Turn on <Large Deflection>.

[2] Make sure the settings are exactly the same as those in 9.1-10.

[3] Solve the model. It takes about 45 minutes of elapsed time in my computer. Since solving the model is not the main point in this section, you may skip this step.

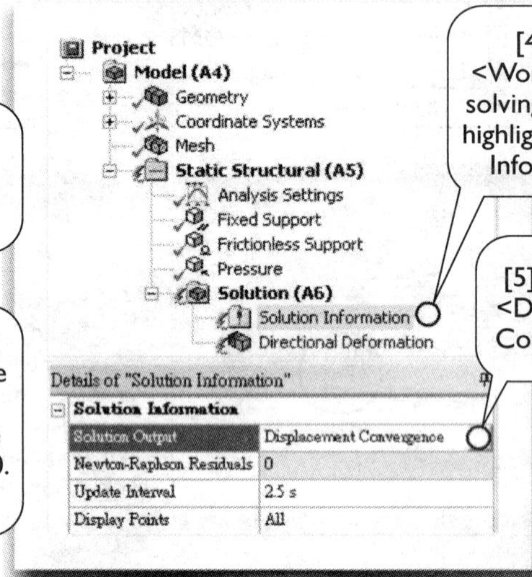

[4] While <Workbench> is solving the model, highlight <Solution Information>.

[5] And select <Displacement Convergence>.

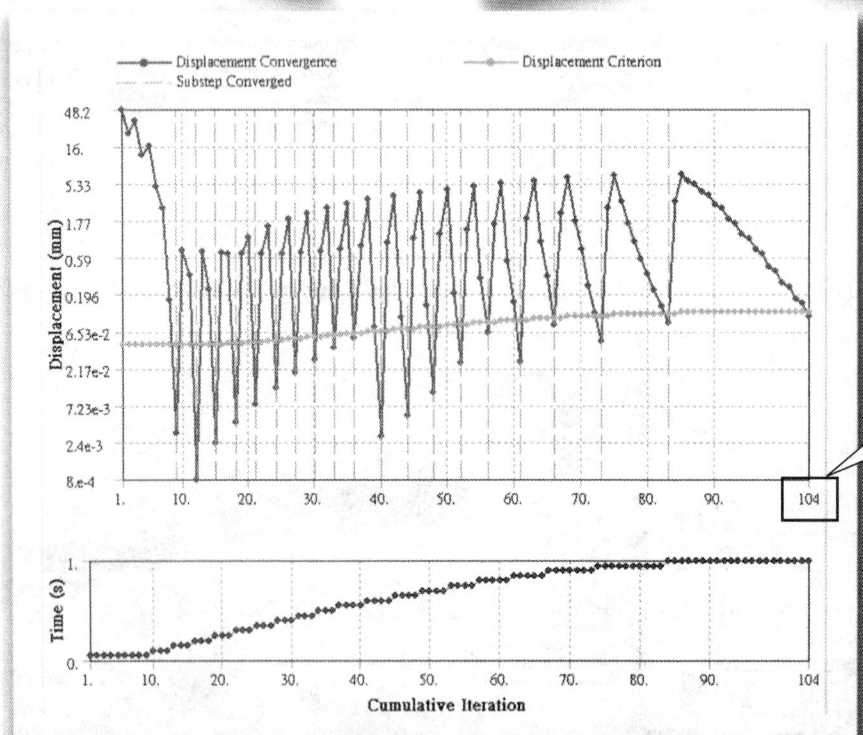

[6] The solution converges after 104 iterations.

If the Solution Doesn't Converge...

Nonlinear solution is sensitive to mesh. It is possible that, due to a mesh variation, your solution doesn't converge as shown here. Even that happens, the convergence curve should be very similar to the one here. In this case, you can increase the initial substeps (say, increase from 20 to 25), and rerun again. Increasing substeps (or equivalently, decreasing time step) usually helps convergence, but takes longer time.

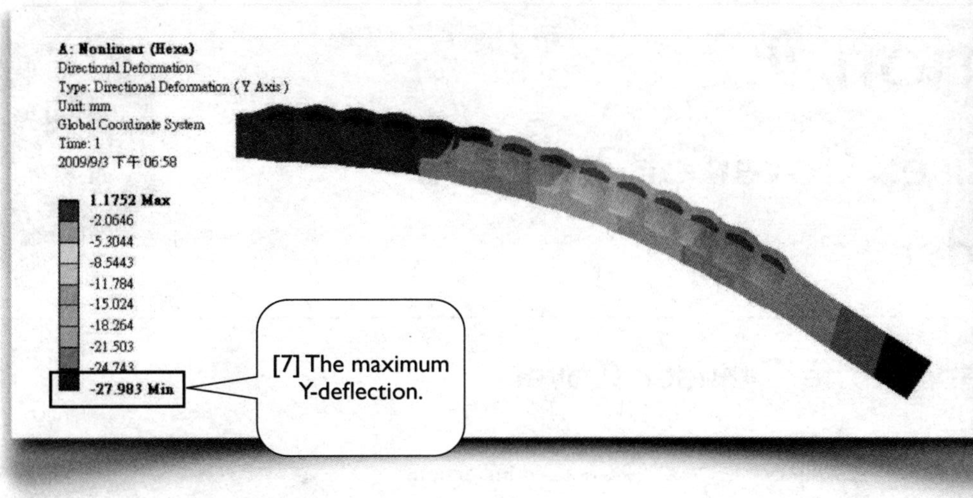

Wrap Up

Close everything and exit Workbench.

Remark

As mentioned in Section 1.1-8, when assuming a linear material, we are also assume the compressive behavior is the same as tensile behavior, but this is usually not true for an elastomer under such a large deformation. Hyperelasticity, a more accurate material model for elastomer under large deformation, will be introduced in Sections 14.1-7 to 14.1-9.

Reference

1. ANSYS Help System>Meshing>Global Mesh Control>Statistics Group>Mesh Metric>Skewness

Section 9.2

Exercise: Cover of Pressure Cylinder

9.2-1 About the Cylinder Cover

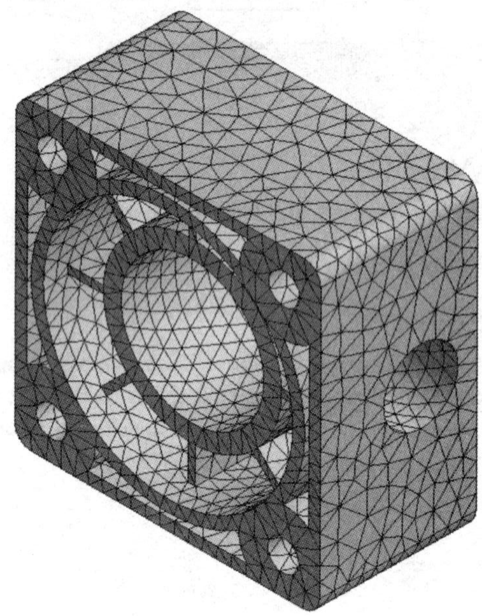

In this section we will use the cylinder cover introduced in Sections 4.2 and 5.2 to demonstrate some meshing techniques.

The geometry of the cover is quite complicated. It seems that the free mesh with tetrahedral elements is the only meshing method. There is nothing wrong with the tetrahedral mesh as long as the mesh quality is good enough. Examining the mesh generated in Section 5.2-5, we will see that the mesh quality is pretty bad (9.2-3[2]). The mesh quality needs to be improved. The simplest way is to globally adjust the relevance values. That sometimes works, although increasing the problem size, but not always work. For a linear static simulation, problem size seems no big deal. But for a nonlinear or dynamic simulation, the problem size should be kept minimum as possible, to maintain an acceptable computing time.

The purpose of this section is to demonstrate various meshing techniques, rather to find the best mesh for the cylinder cover.

9.2-2 Open the Project "Cover"

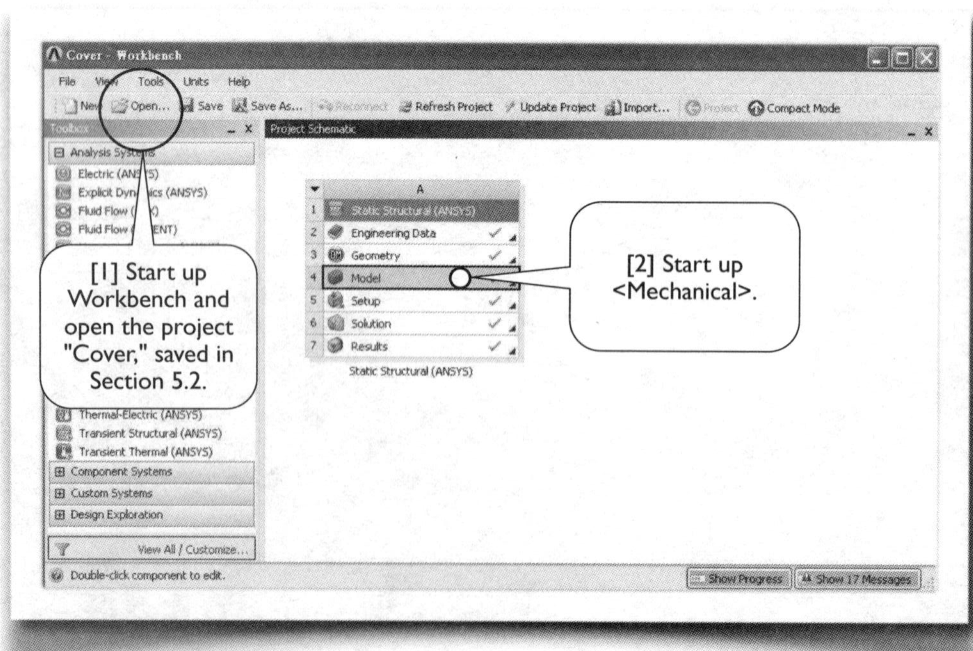

9.2-3 Increase Mesh Density Using Global Mesh Controls

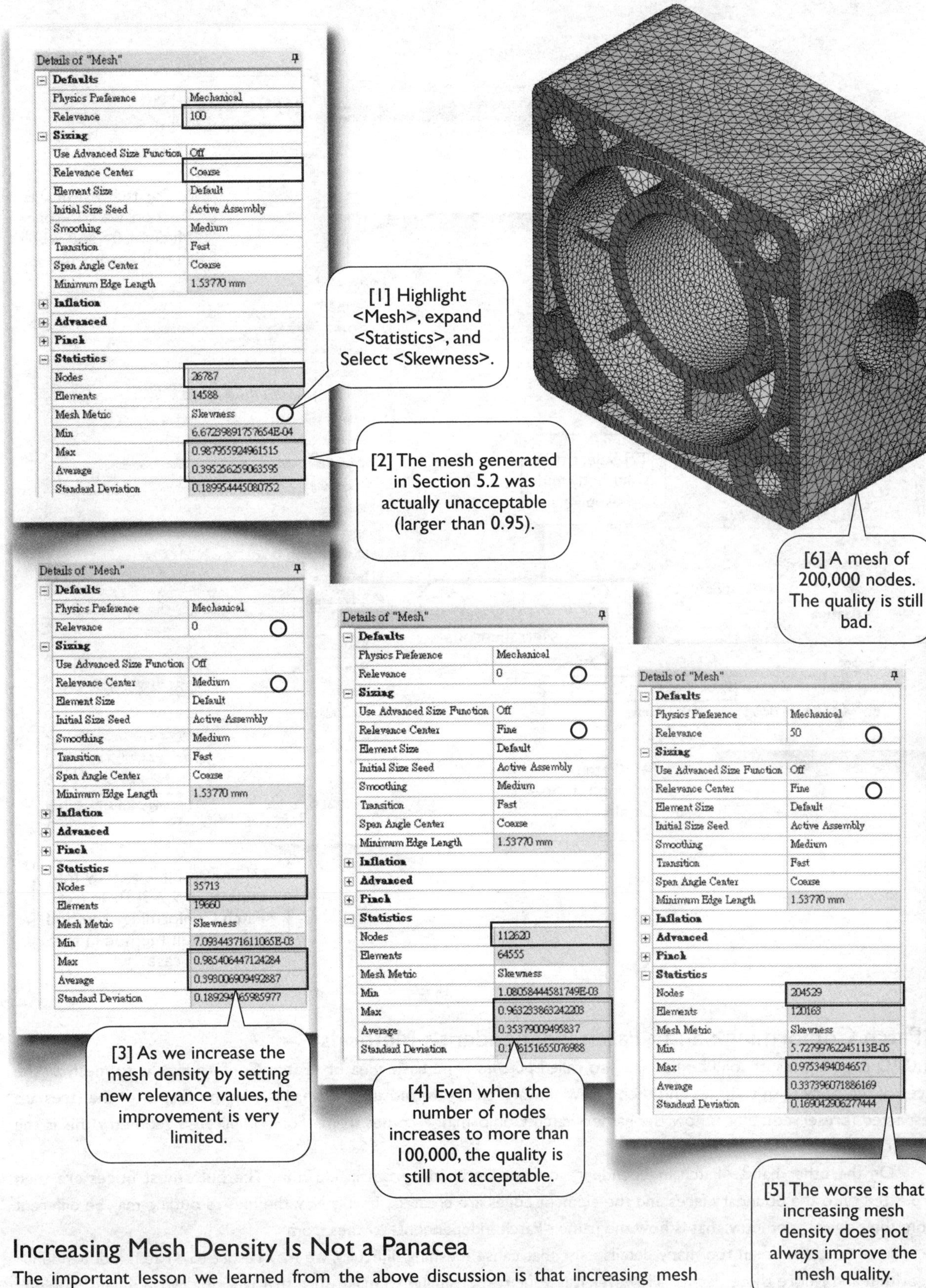

Increasing Mesh Density Is Not a Panacea

The important lesson we learned from the above discussion is that increasing mesh density is not a universal remedy. We need to learn other meshing techniques.

9.2-4 Mesh with <Patch Conforming> Method

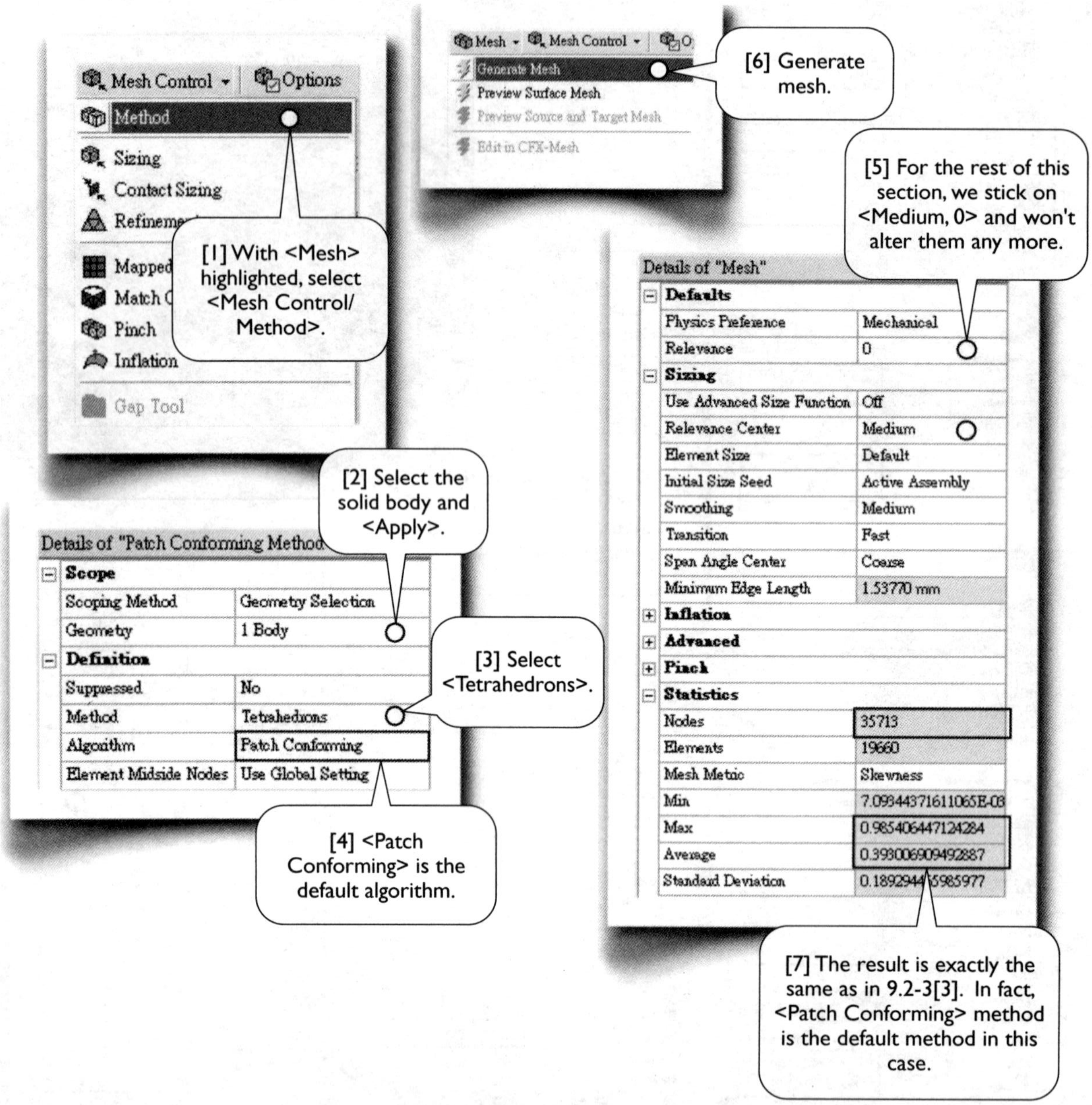

<Patch Conforming> and <Patch Independent> Methods

In CAD jargon, faces of solid bodies are also called *patches*. The basic idea of <Patch Conforming> is to mesh all the faces of the body with triangles and then "grow" inward to create tetrahedra. In this way, the shapes of the faces are respected (preserved); that is how the name <Patch Conforming> comes from. For complicated geometry, this is the default method.

On the other hand, <Patch Independent> creates tetrahedra from inside out. The outermost nodes are then projected onto the boundary faces and the element edges are created. In this way, the mesh's outline may be different from the original geometry; that is how the name <Patch Independent> comes from.

In some cases when too many details exist that cause meshing difficulty, we may resort to <Patch Independent> algorithm and ignore these details. However, it is your responsibility to make sure that ignoring those details wouldn't distort the geometry too much and raise an accuracy issue.

9.2-5 Mesh with <Patch Independent> Method

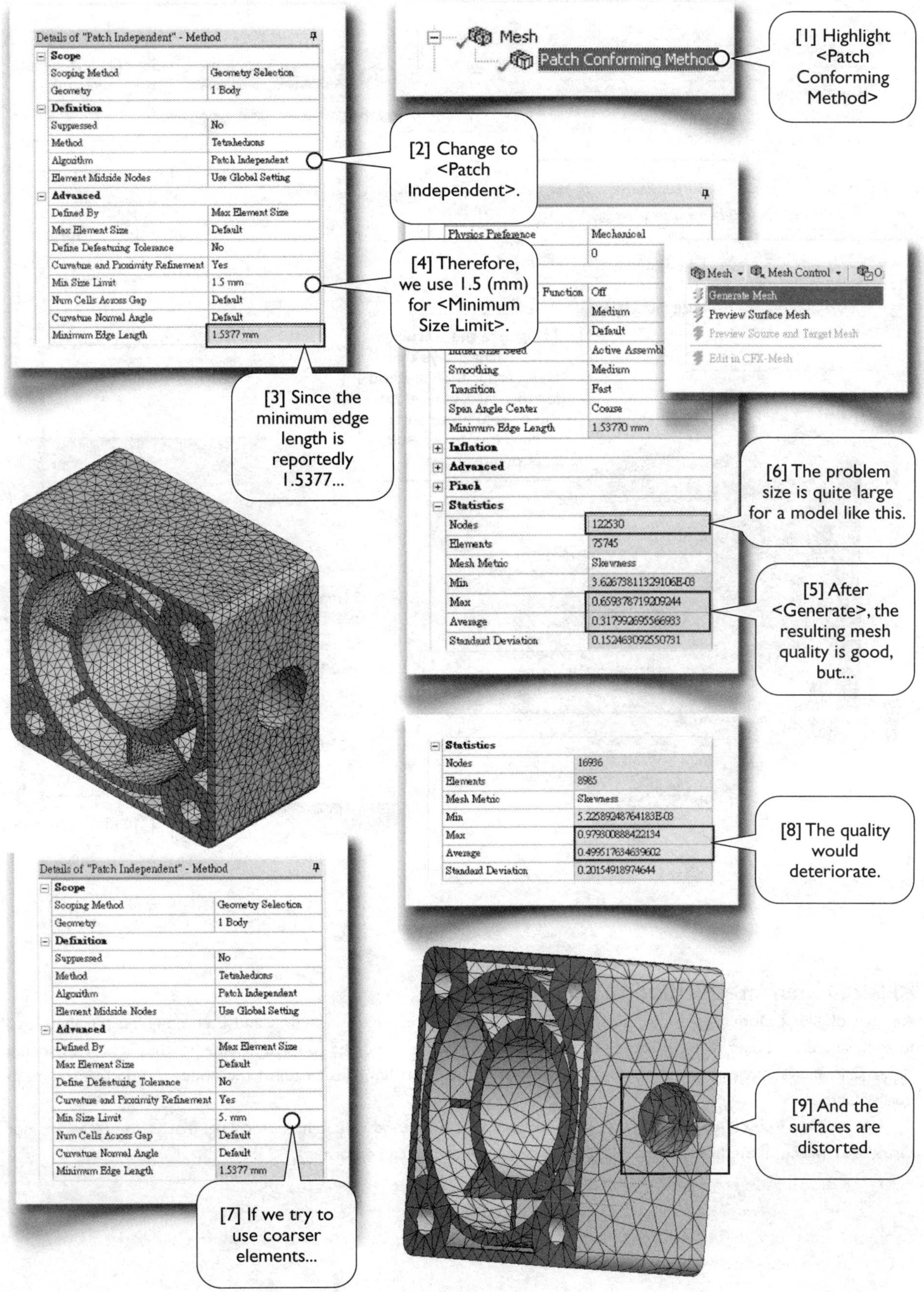

9.2-6 Mesh with <Hex Dominant> Method

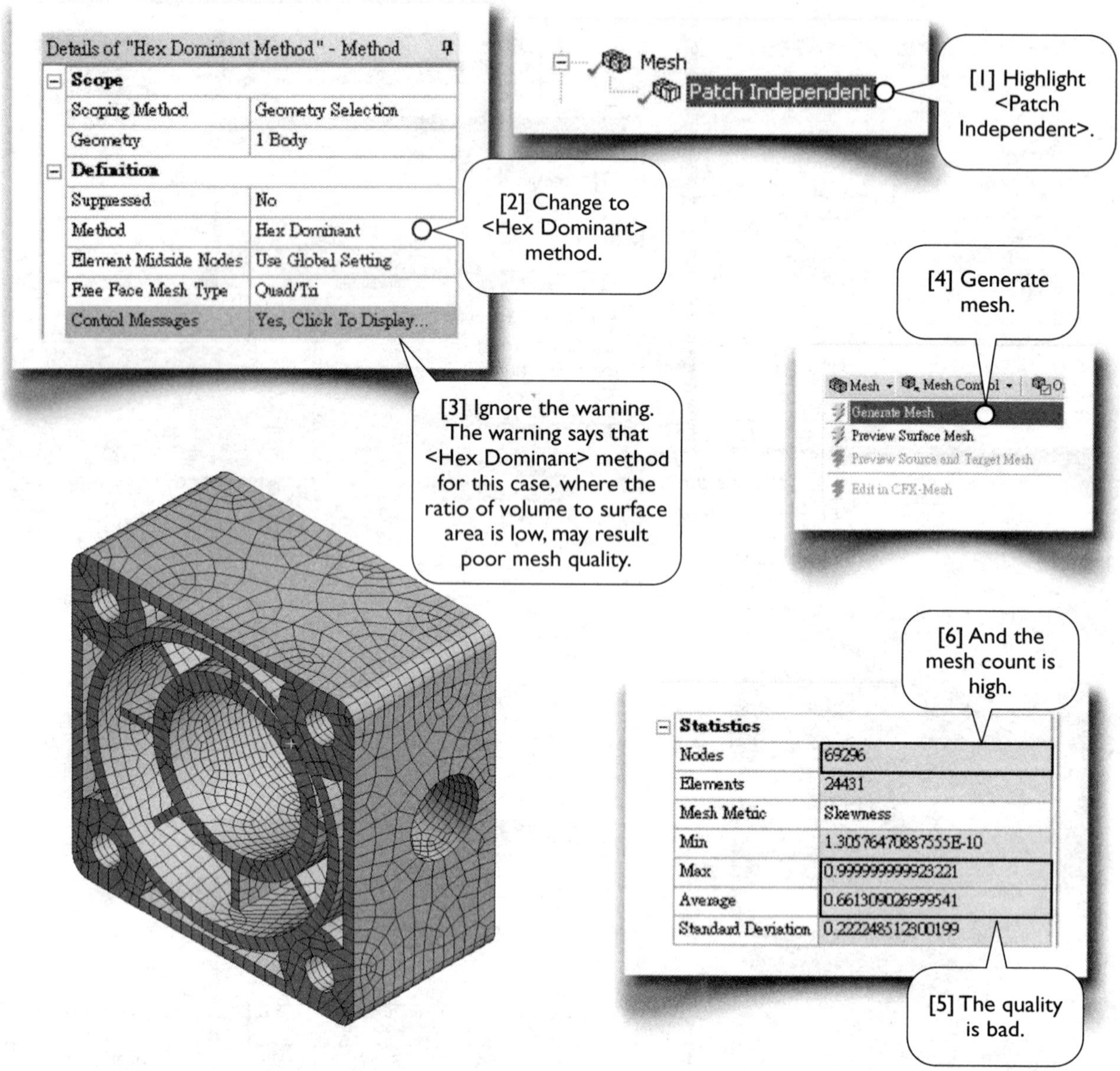

<Hex Dominant> Method

An idea of <Hex Dominant> is to mesh the body with <Patch Conforming> first and then combine tetrahedra to form hexahedra. It usually leaves some tetrahedra that cannot be combined to form hexahedra; that is how the name <Hex Dominant> comes from. After forming hexahedra, the algorithm tries to adjust the nodes to improve the mesh quality further.

Note that, <Hex Dominant> method, by its nature, is a method of patch conforming, that is, the faces are not distorted. In fact, all methods except <Patch Independent> are patch conforming.

9.2-7 Mesh with <MultiZone> Method

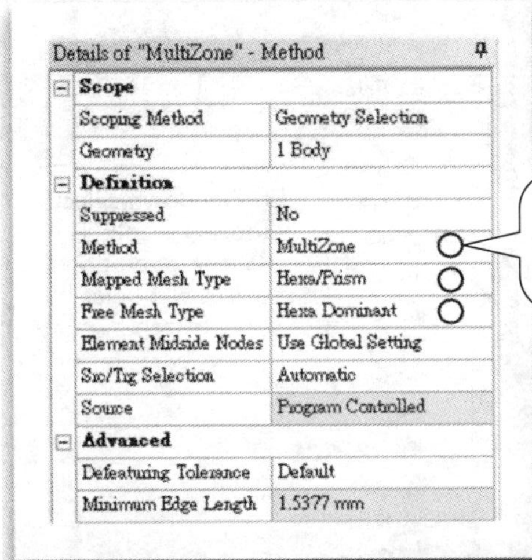

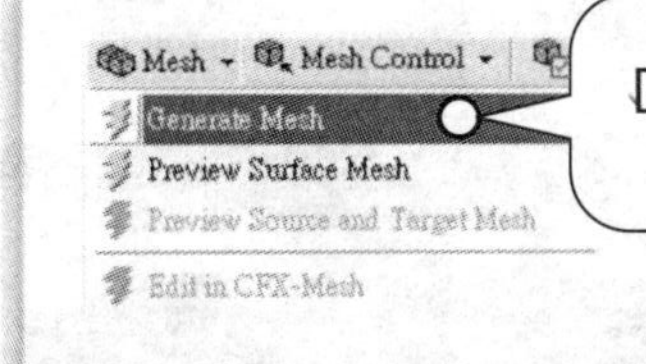

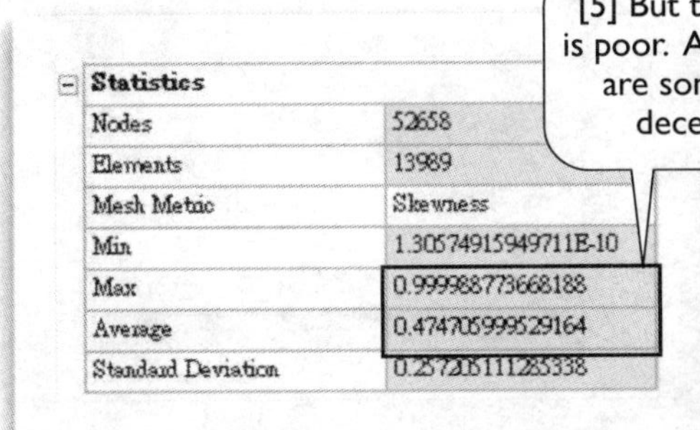

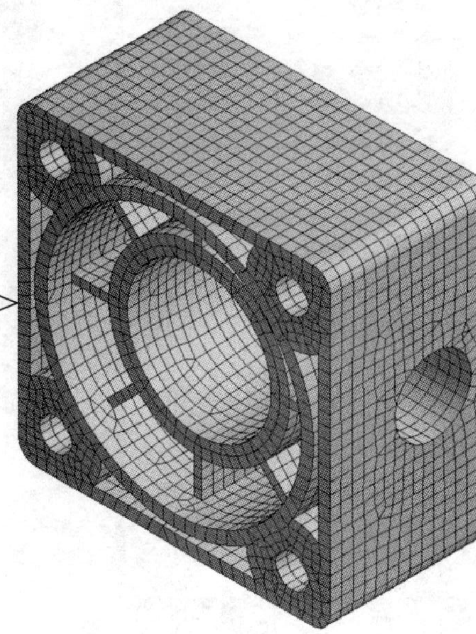

<MultiZone> Method

As mentioned, the idea of <MutiZone> method is to decompose a non-sweepable body into several sweepable bodies, and then apply <Sweep> method on each body. The selection of source faces can be automatic or manual. In this case, you could try to select source faces manually, but the result is the same.

<Workbench> is usually smart enough to decompose the body into sweepable bodies. But, since these bodies are integral part, the boundaries between the bodies must be conformal (the boundaries must have the same surface mesh), These constraints may complicate the meshing task.

To remove these constraints, we now manually slice the body into several parts and mesh each part independently.

9.2-8 Slice the Body into Parts

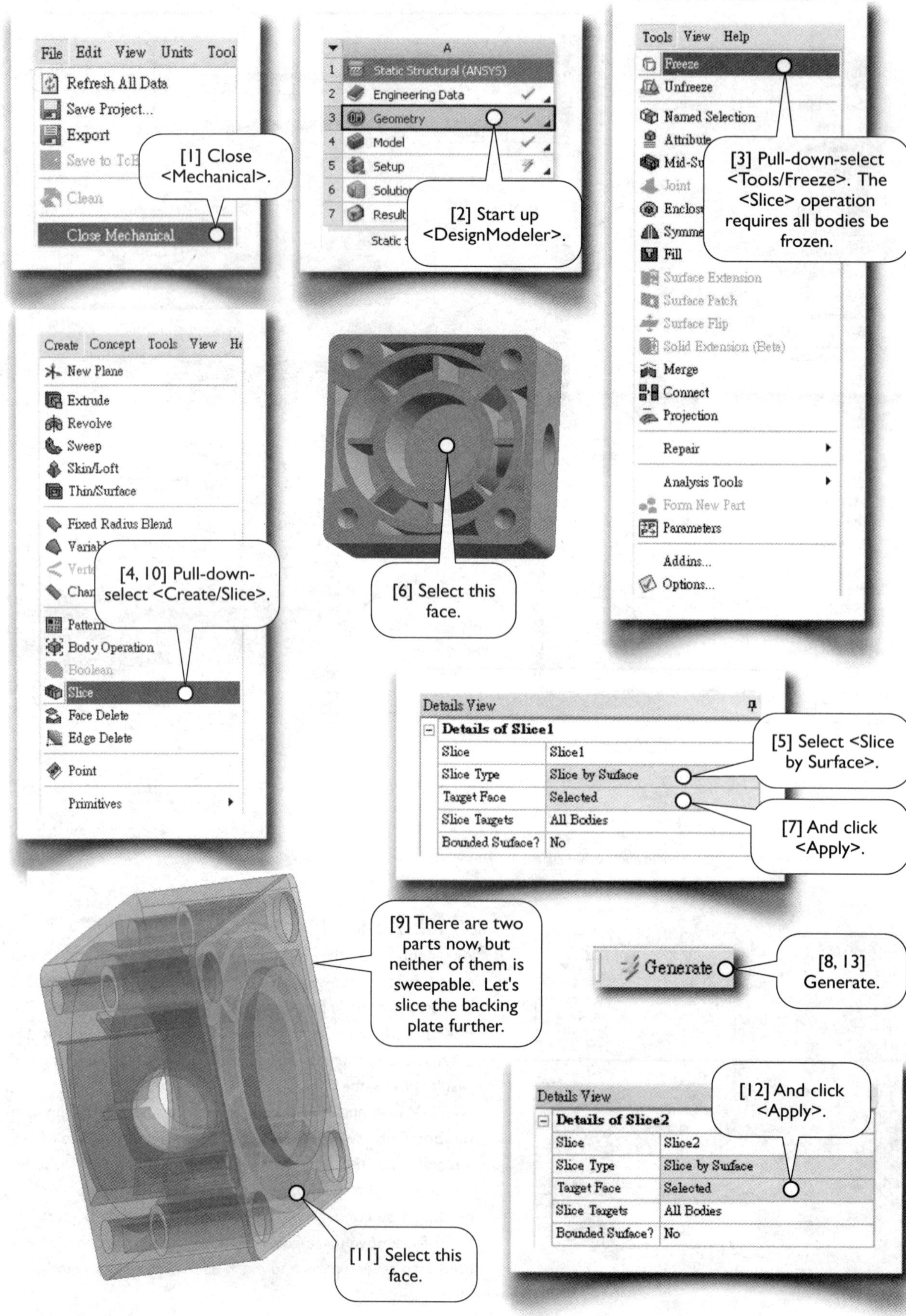

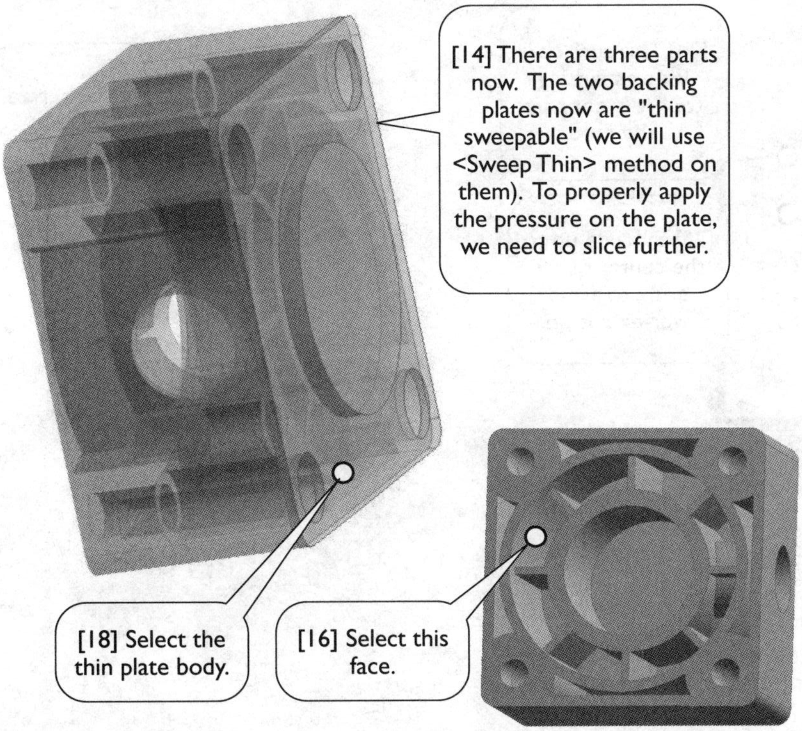

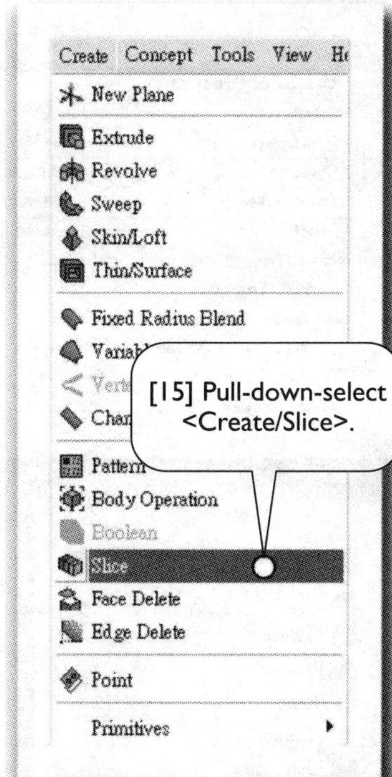

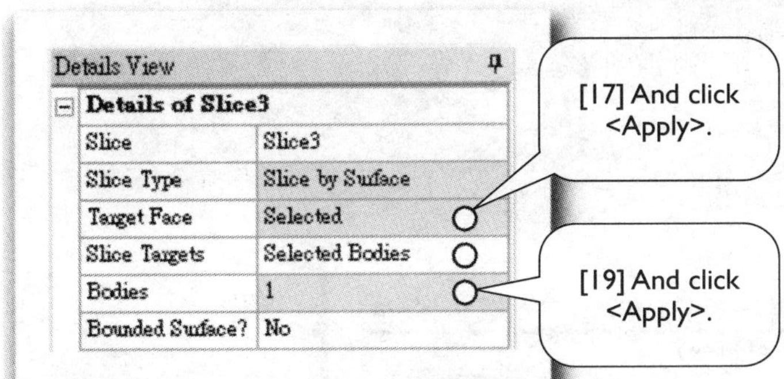

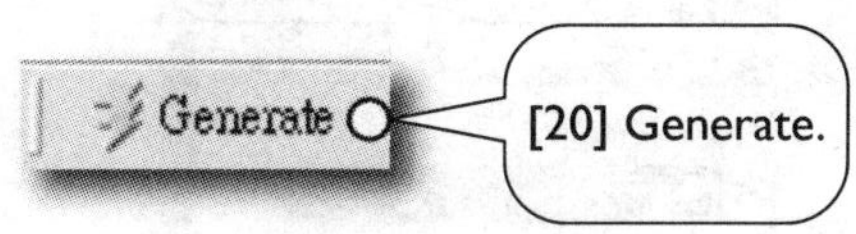

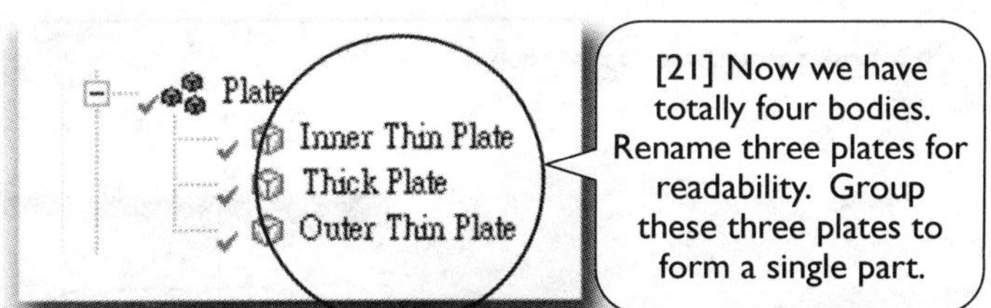

Next we want to slice the cylindrical inlet off from the body it belongs. To do that, we need to create a cylindrical surface first.

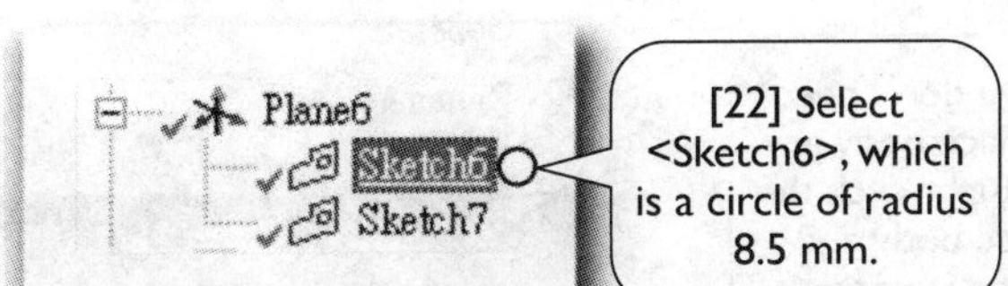

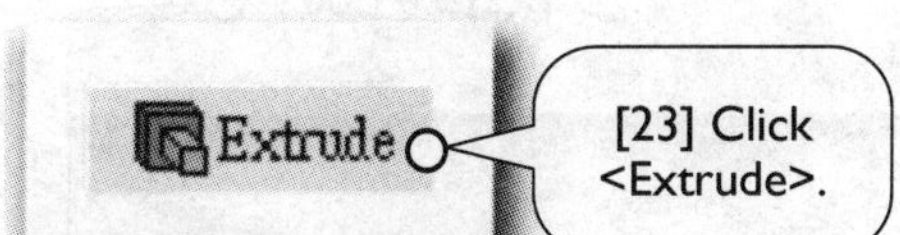

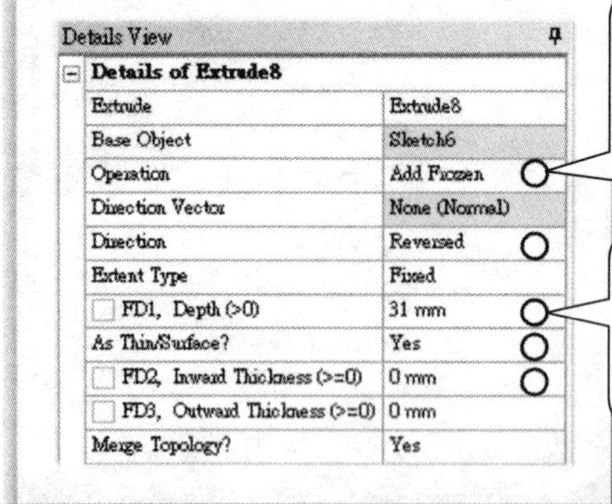

[24] This surface is used as cutting tool; it is not part of the model.

[25] Extrude up to the center of the body, to avoid over-extrusion.

[26] Generate.

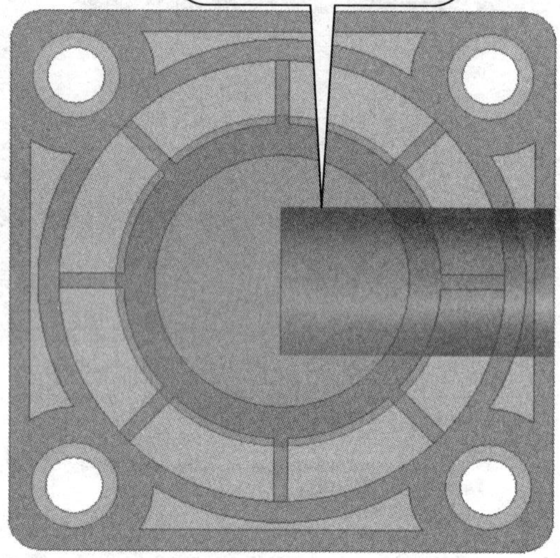

[27] A surface body is created. The surface will be used to slice off the cylindrical inlet.

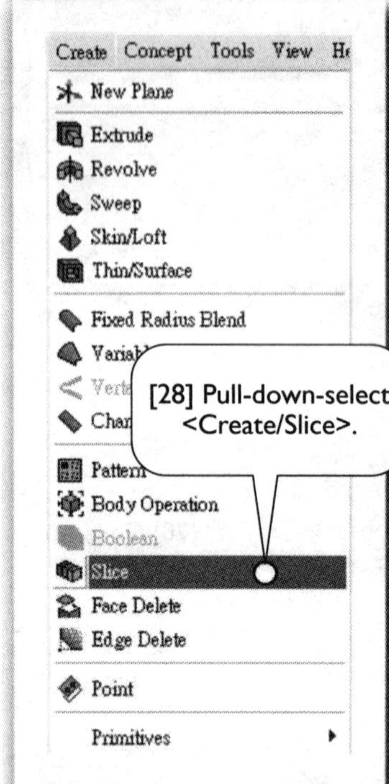

[28] Pull-down-select <Create/Slice>.

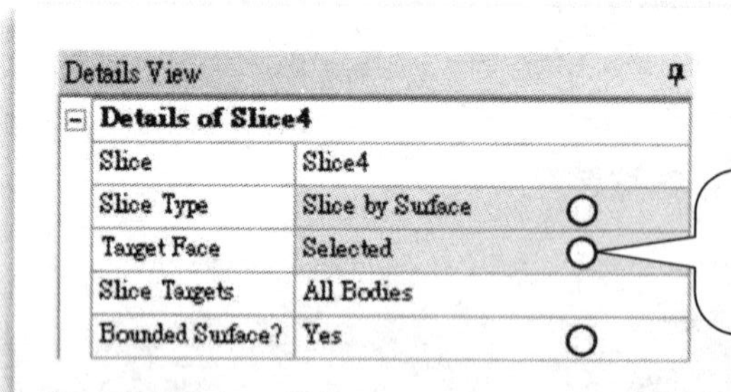

[29] Select newly created surface. Click <Generate>.

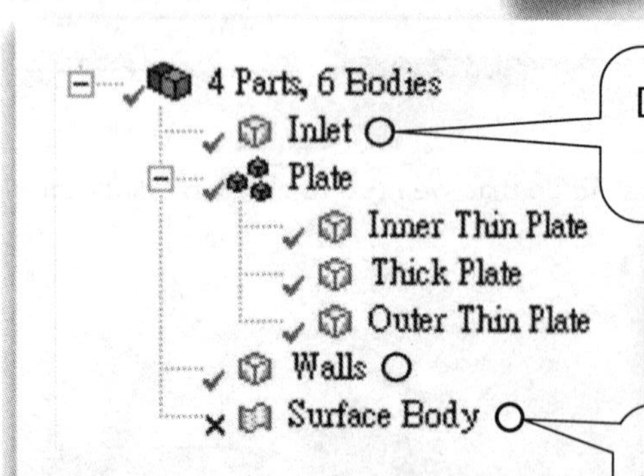

[30] Rename them for readability.

[31] We don't need the surface body any more. Right-click the surface body and select <Suppress Body>.

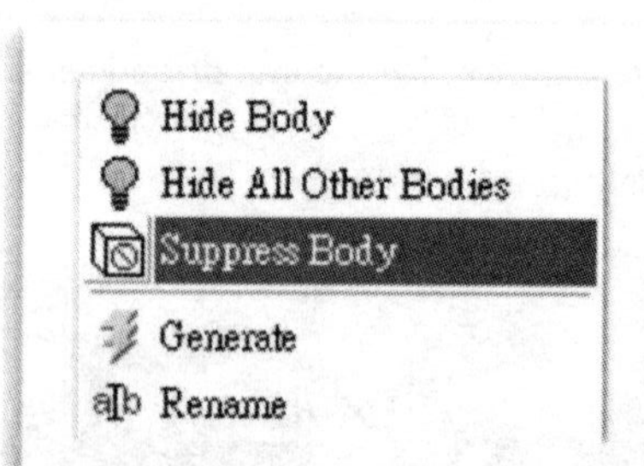

9.2-9 Return to <Mechanical>

Close <DesignModeler> and start up <Mechanical> again.

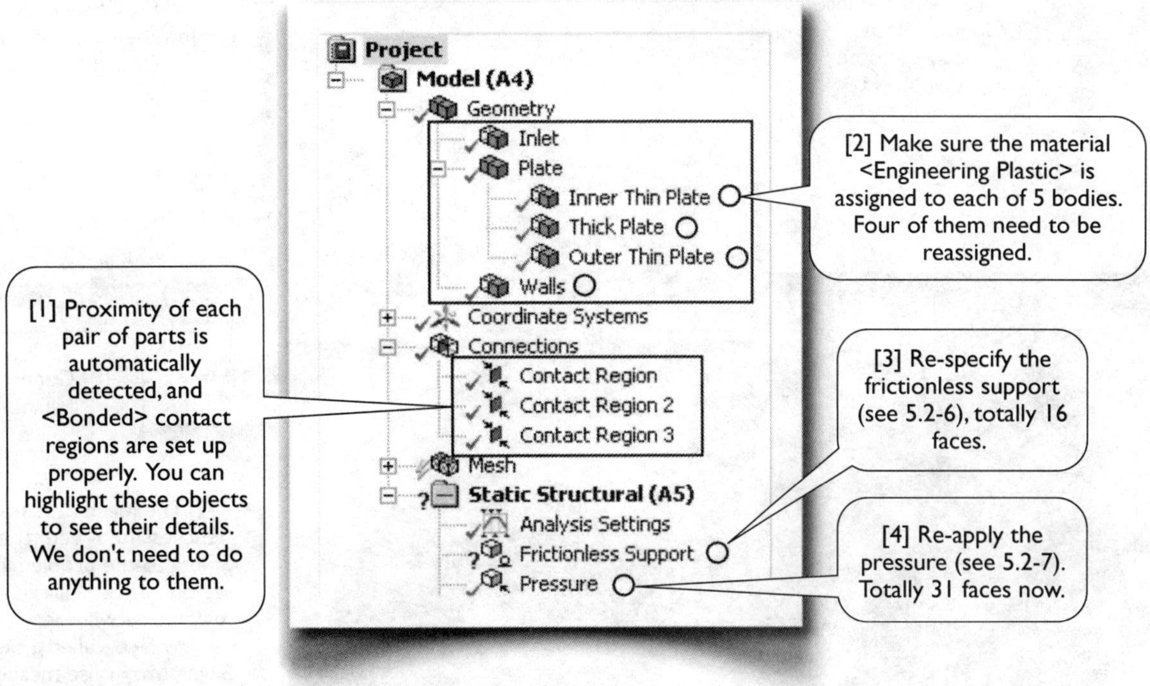

9.2-10 Specify Mesh Methods

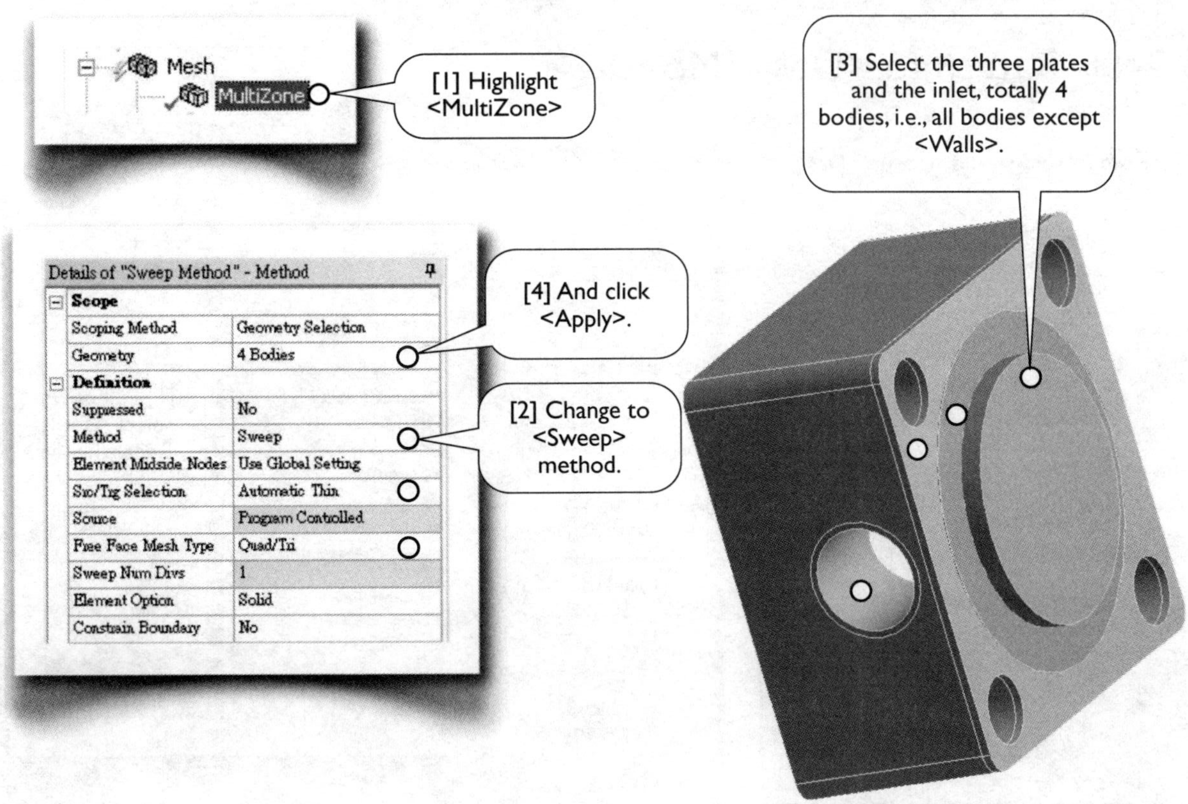

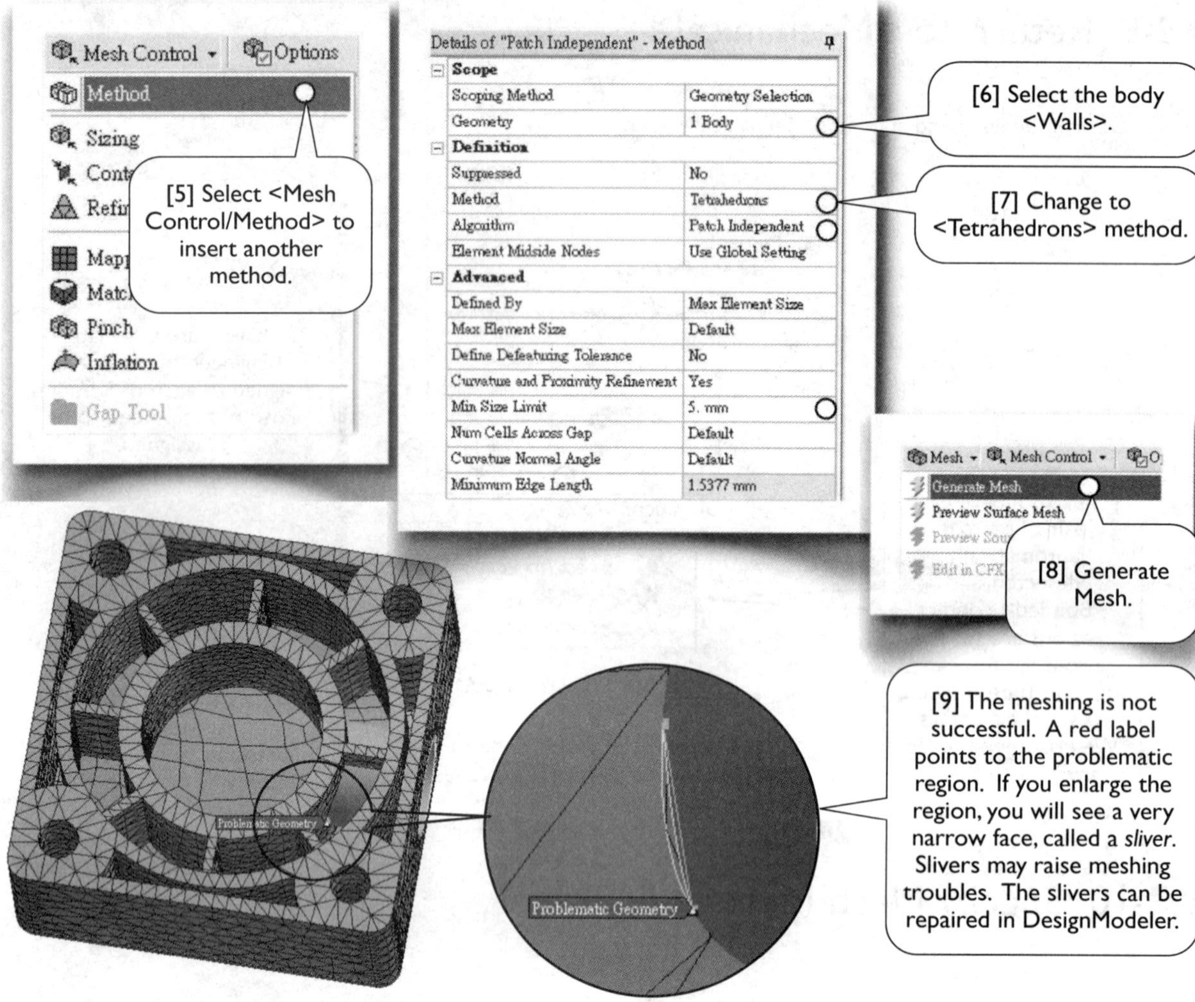

9.2-11 Return to <DesignModeler>

Close <Mechanical> and start up <DesignModeler> again.

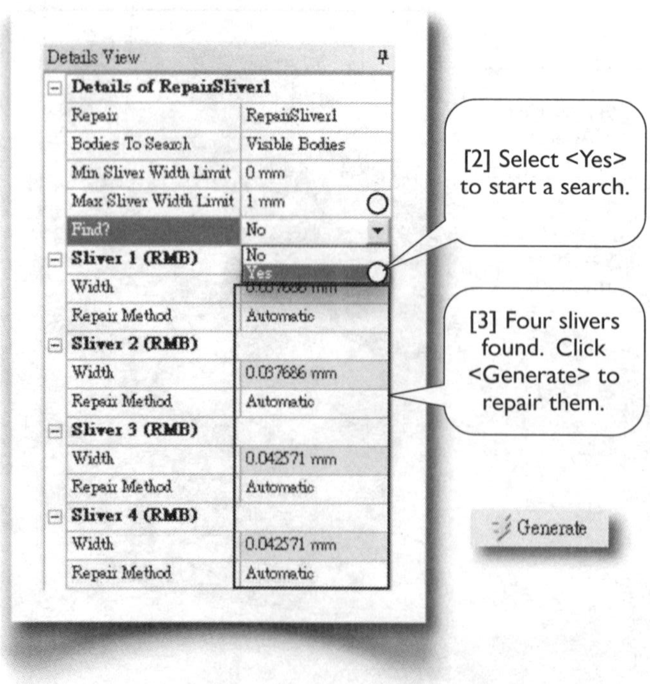

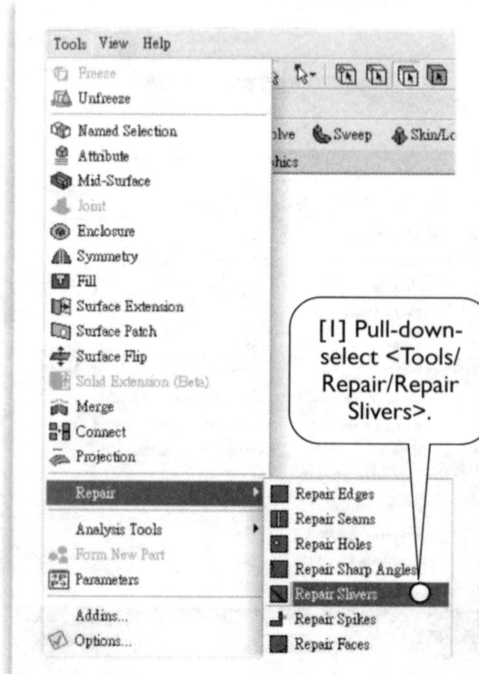

Short Edges, Cracking Seams, Small Holes, Sharp Angles, Narrow Slivers, Pointed Spikes, and Small Surfaces

These potential trouble makers can be repaired by DesignModeler automatically or semi-automatically. They most commonly occur when importing CAD files created by other software (than DesignModeler) to Workbench. That is one of the reasons that, when creating a geometry for Workbench simulations, you use DesignModeler whenever possible. In some cases, DesignModeler does generate these defects, but they are generally easy to repair.

9.2-12 Return to <Mechanical>

Close <DesignModeler> and start up <Mechanical> again.

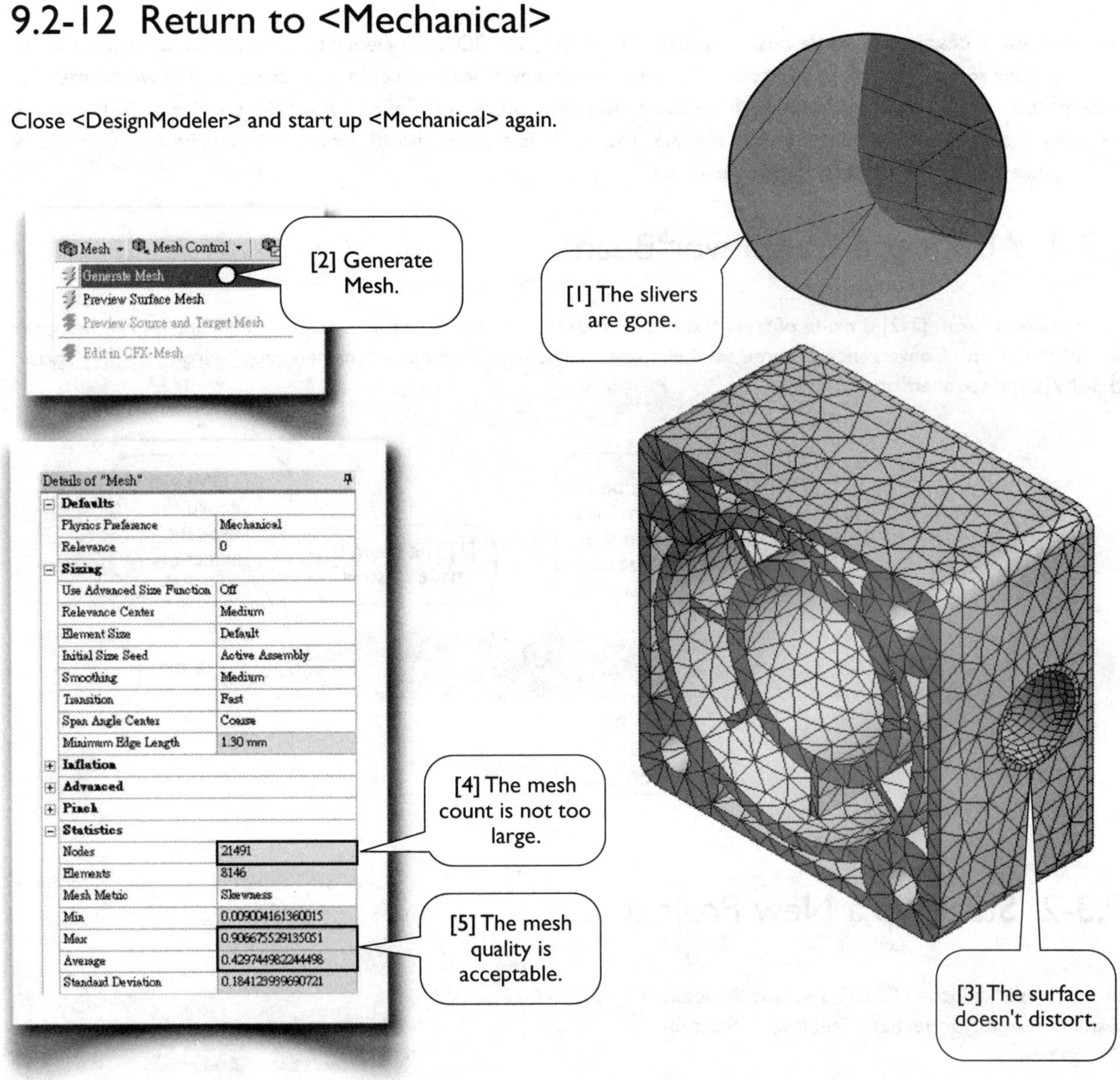

Wrap Up

Comparing with the initial mesh (9.2-3[2]), the mesh is improved in both the quality and the mesh count. However, that is a result of much effort. You may solve the model now. We won't discuss the solutions further.

Close <Mechanical> and exit <Workbench>.

Section 9.3

Exercise: 3D Solid Elements Convergence Study

This exercise is designed to serve dual purposes: (a) studying the 3D solid elements convergence behavior, and (b) demonstrating some of the mesh controls techniques. A cantilever beam of rectangular cross section will be used for these purposes. The conclusions drawn from the convergence study are useful to the CAE engineers. Although the concepts are already introduced in Section 3.5, the CAE engineers should have more insight about elements convergence behaviors after this hands-on exercise.

9.3-1 About the Cantilever Beam

The cantilever beam [1-2] is made of steel and of size 100x10x10 mm. A uniform load of 1 MPa applies on the upper face of the beam. Convergence of three solid element shapes will be compared, namely hexahedron (1.3-3[1]), prism (1.3-3[2]), and tetrahedron (1.3-3[4]).

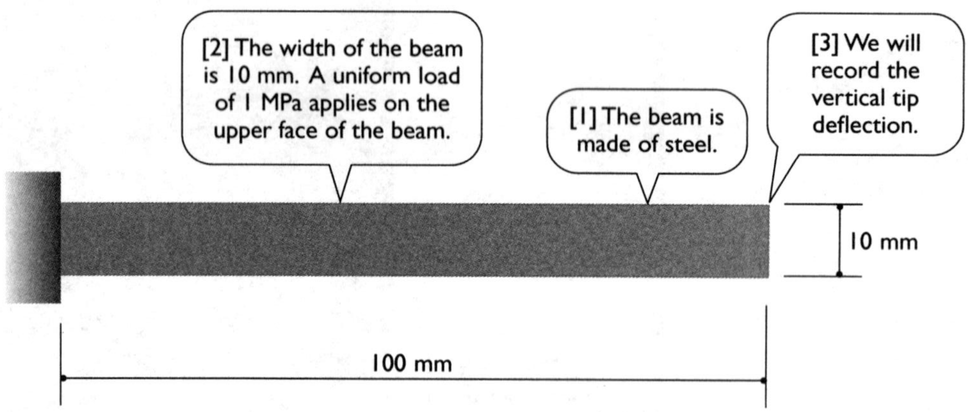

9.3-2 Start Up a New Project

Launch <Workbench>. Create a <Static Structural> system. Save the project as "Cantilever." Start up DesignModeler.

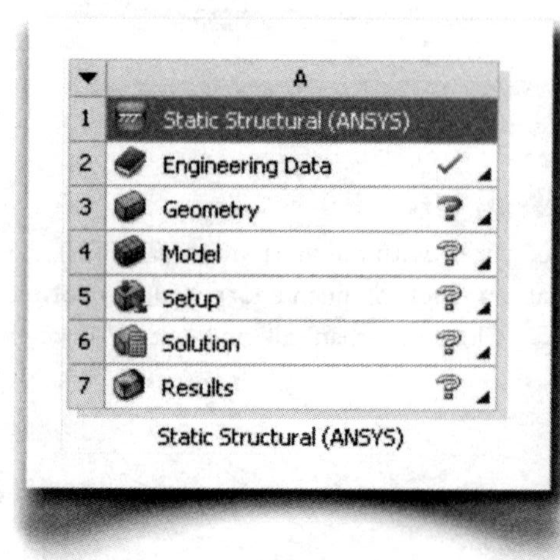

9.3-3 Create a 3D Model in DesignModeler

Create a sketch on XYPlane [1]. Extrude the sketch to create a 3D model [2]. Close DesignModeler.

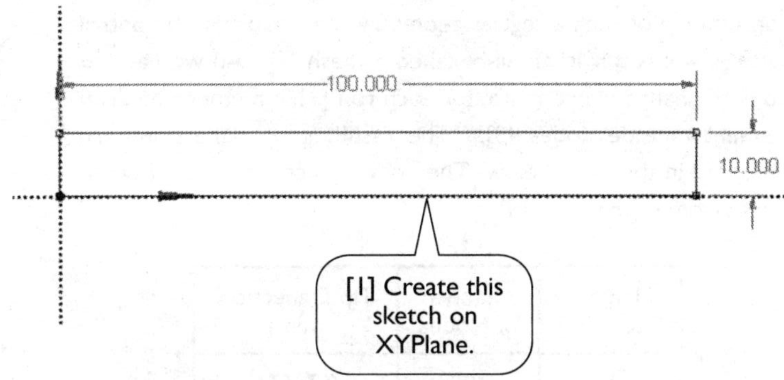

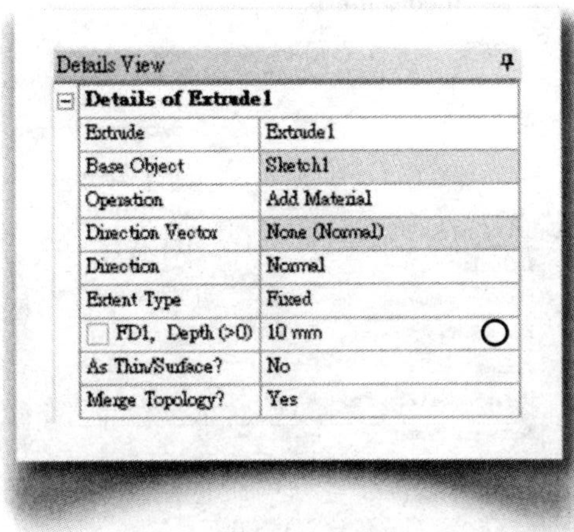

Details View	
Details of Extrude1	
Extrude	Extrude1
Base Object	Sketch1
Operation	Add Material
Direction Vector	None (Normal)
Direction	Normal
Extent Type	Fixed
FD1, Depth (>0)	10 mm
As Thin/Surface?	No
Merge Topology?	Yes

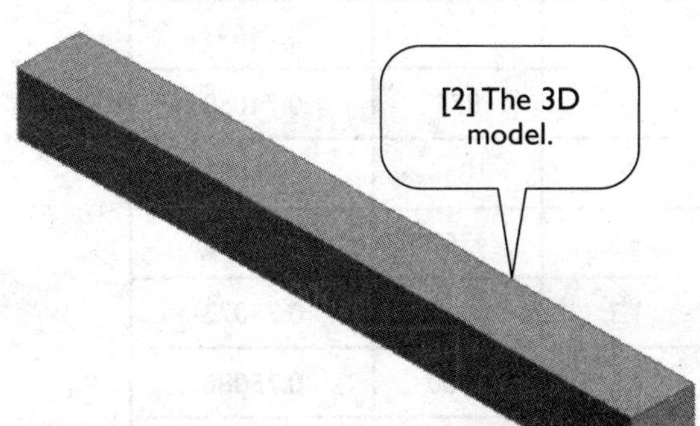

9.3-4 Set Up Support, Load, and Solution Objects

Specify <Fixed Support> on the left face [1]; apply a pressure of 1 MPa on the upper face [2]. Insert a <Directional Deformation> under the solution branch and set the orientation to <Y Axis> [3].

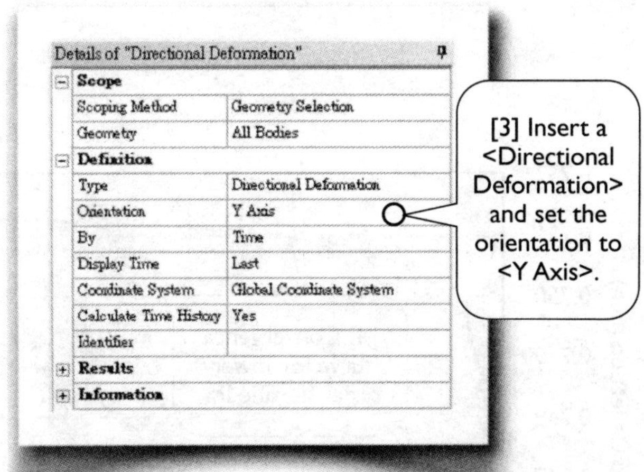

Details of "Directional Deformation"	
Scope	
Scoping Method	Geometry Selection
Geometry	All Bodies
Definition	
Type	Directional Deformation
Orientation	Y Axis
By	Time
Display Time	Last
Coordinate System	Global Coordinate System
Calculate Time History	Yes
Identifier	
Results	
Information	

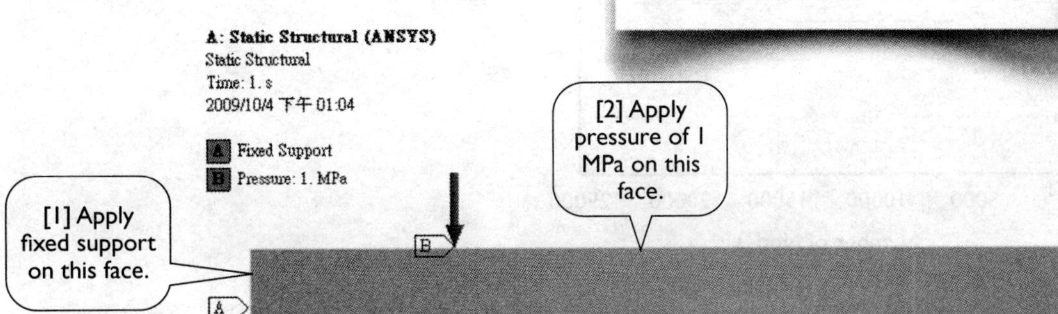

9.3-5 Lower-Order Hexahedra

For a model of such a regular geometry, the default mesh control settings will result in an all-hexahedra mesh [1]. All we have to do is to change element size for each run [2]; remember to drop element midside nodes [3]. The resulting tip deflections are recorded in the table below. The convergence curve is shown in the bottom of this page [4].

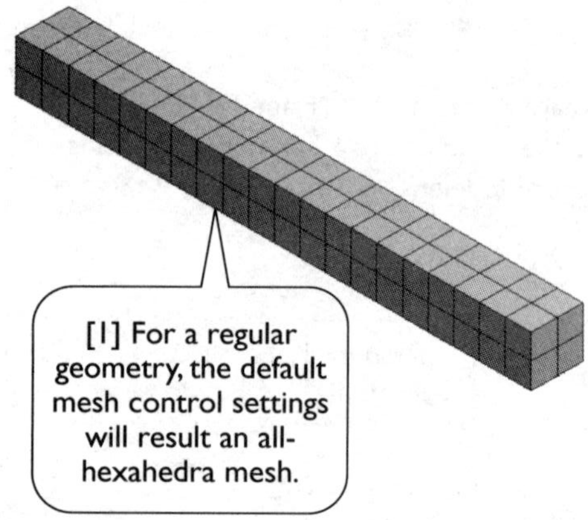

Element Size (mm)	Number of Nodes	Tip Deflection (mm)
5	189	0.74571
4	416	0.74693
3	875	0.74850
2	1836	0.74980
1.5	4352	0.75048
1.3	6318	0.75072
1.2	8500	0.75086
1	12221	0.75106
0.9	19097	0.75120
0.8	24696	0.75129

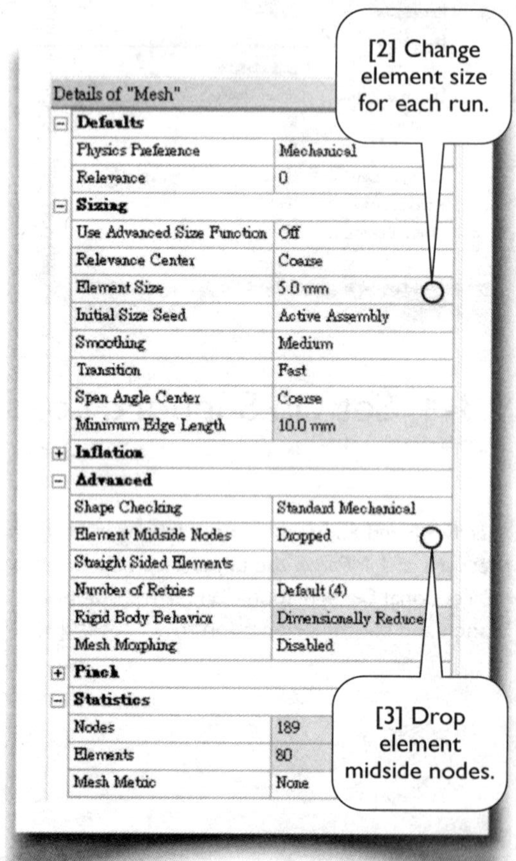

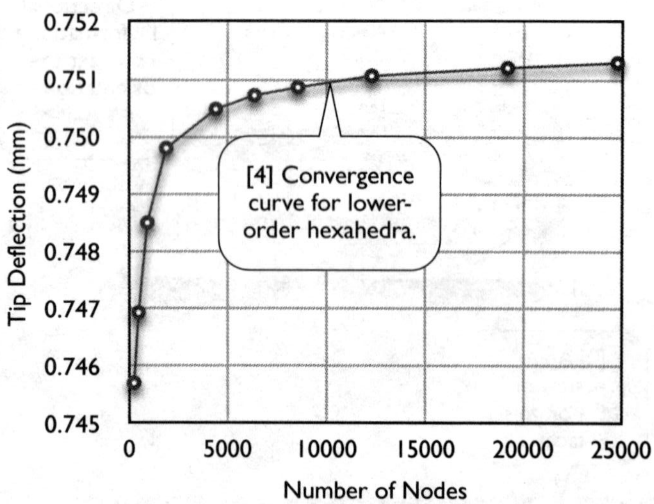

9.3-6 Lower-Order Tetrahedra

Highlight <Mesh> in the project tree and select <Mesh Control/Method> to insert a mesh control method. Select <Tetrahedrons> method [1]. Now, change element size for each run [2]. The resulting tip deflections are recorded in the table below. The convergence curve is shown in the bottom of this page [3].

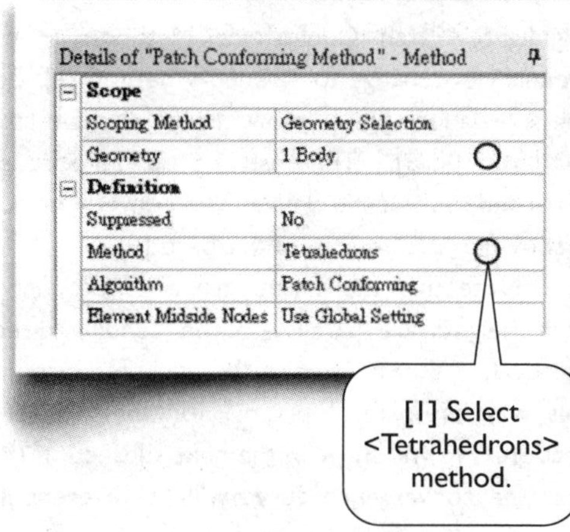

Element Size (mm)	Number of Nodes	Tip Deflection (mm)
5	104	0.31053
4	173	0.44116
2.5	310	0.50445
2	563	0.59422
1.5	808	0.61599
1.2	1340	0.63799
1	2010	0.65643
0.8	2869	0.67529
0.7	3960	0.68507
0.6	5271	0.69133
0.55	6314	0.69338
0.5	8112	0.70008

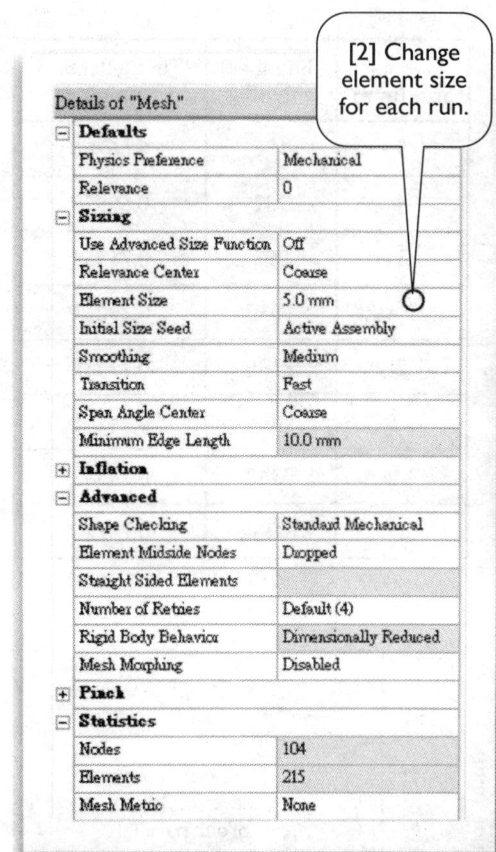

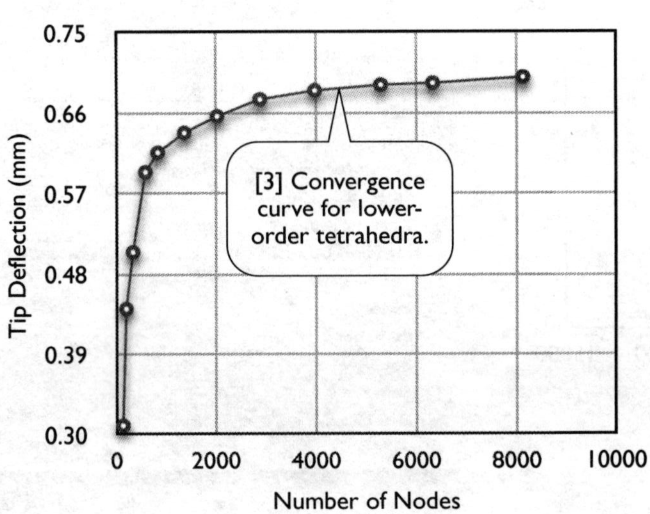

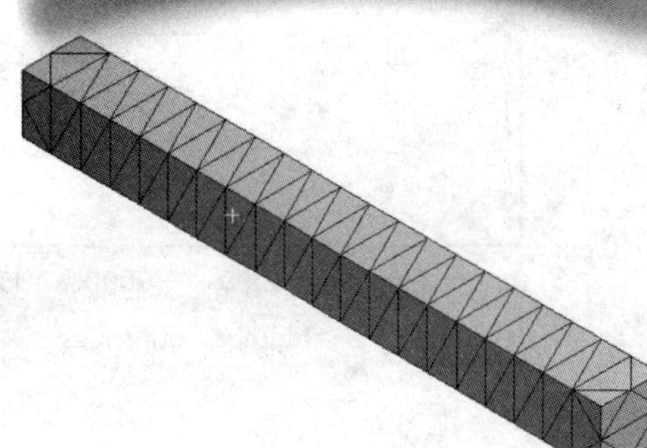

9.3-7 Lower-Order Prisms (Parallel to Bending Direction)

Highlight <Patch Conforming Method>. In the Details view, change to <Sweep> method [1]. Set up the source face [2, 3]. Now, change element size for each run [4, 5]. The resulting tip deflections are recorded in the table below. The convergence curve is shown in the bottom of this page [6].

Note that the prisms are oriented such that their heights are parallel to the bending direction (vertical). We will refer to the elements oriented in this way as "parallel prisms" for the rest of this section. We will show in the next subsection (9.3-8) that the convergence curve will be different if the prisms are oriented differently.

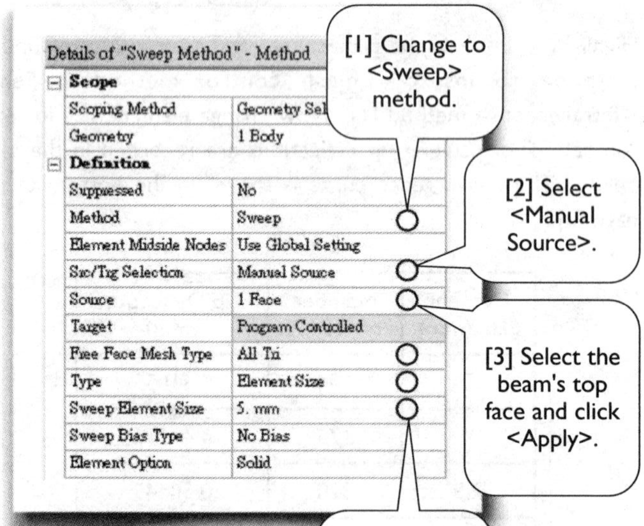

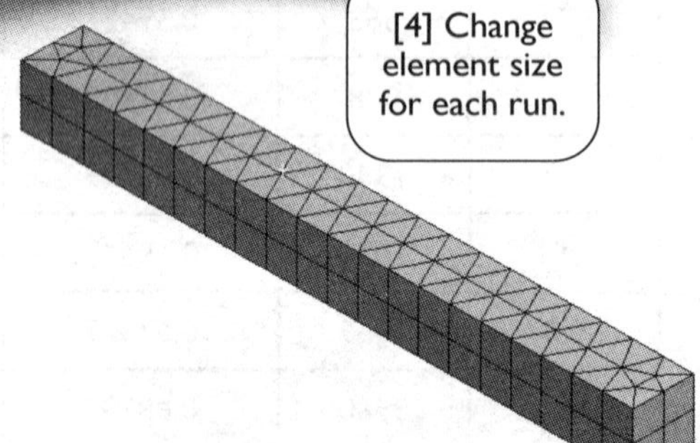

Element Size (mm)	Number of Nodes	Tip Deflection (mm)
5	198	0.66760
4	332	0.69979
3	895	0.71954
2.4	1350	0.73061
2	2136	0.73438
1.5	4896	0.74205
1.2	9340	0.74542
1	13332	0.74713

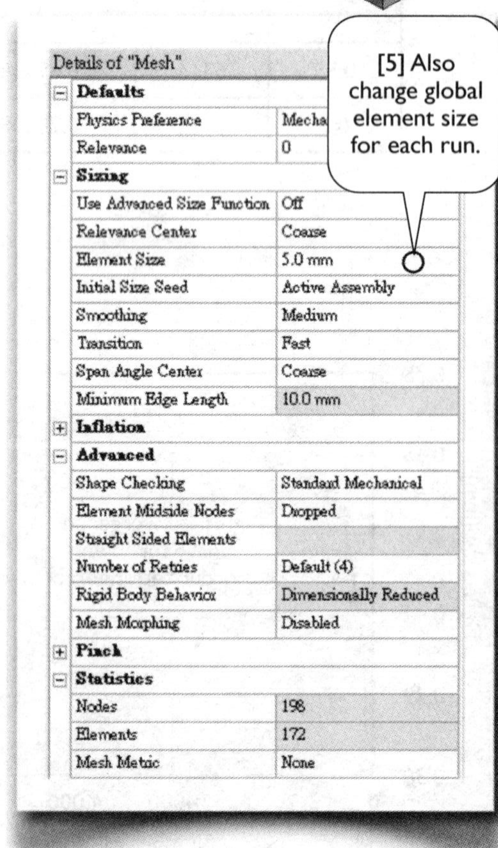

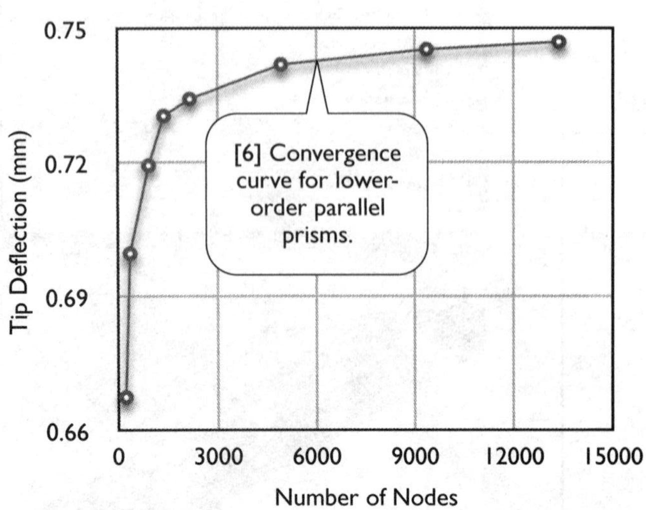

9.3-8 Lower-Order Prisms (Perpendicular to Bending Direction)

In the Details view of the <Sweep Method>, reselect the source face [1]. Now, change element size for each run [2, 3]. The resulting tip deflections are recorded in the table below. The convergence curve is shown in the bottom of this page [4].

Note that the prisms are oriented such that their heights are perpendicular to the bending direction (vertical). We will refer to the elements oriented in this way as "perpendicular prisms" for the rest of this section.

Element Size (mm)	Number of Nodes	Tip Deflection (mm)
5	198	0.50355
4	332	0.49298
3	895	0.66289
2.4	1350	0.66485
2	2136	0.70611
1.5	4896	0.72532
1.2	9340	0.73439
1	13332	0.73718

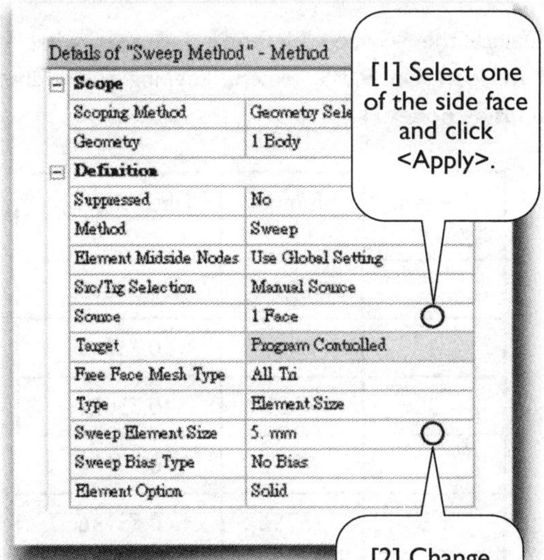

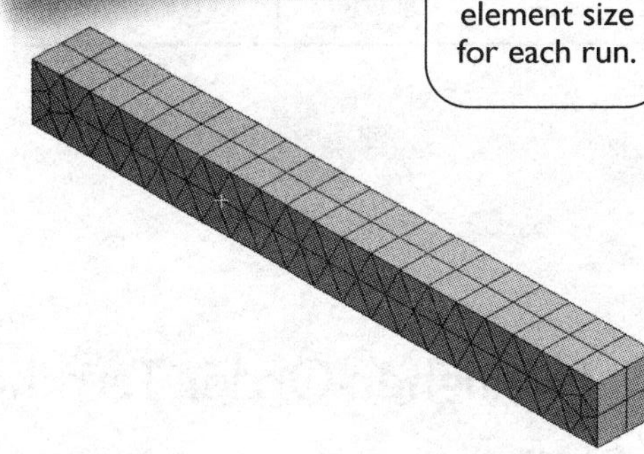

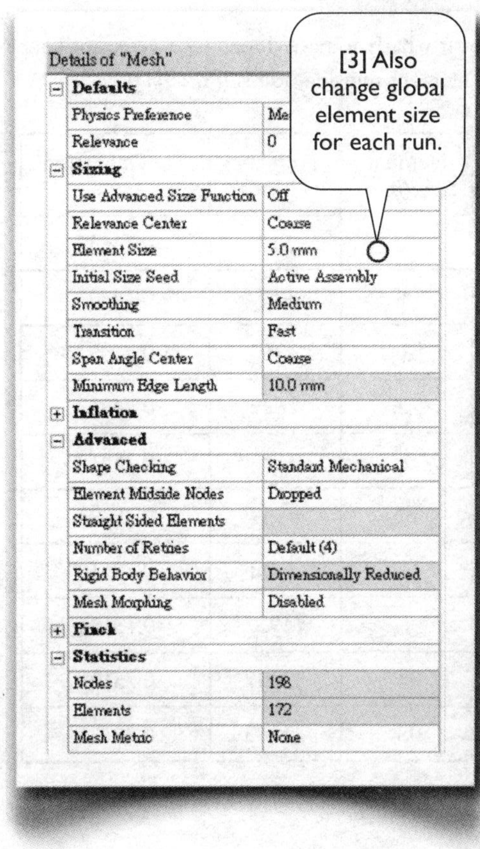

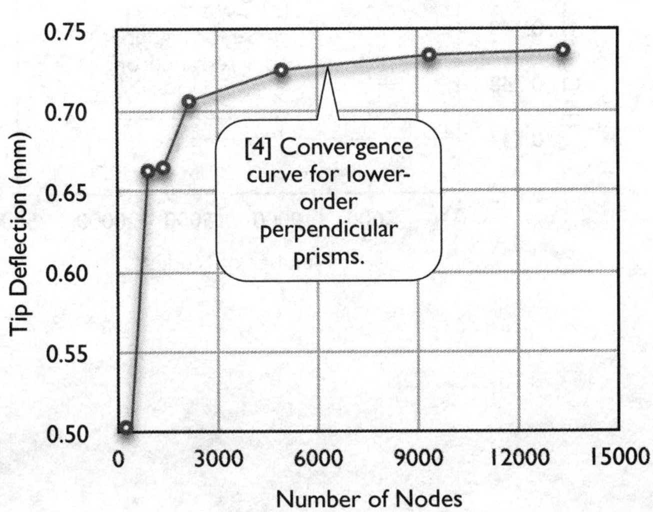

9.3-9 Higher-Order Hexahedra

Delete the <Sweep Method>. Repeat what you have done in 9.3-5, except keeping the element midside nodes [1].

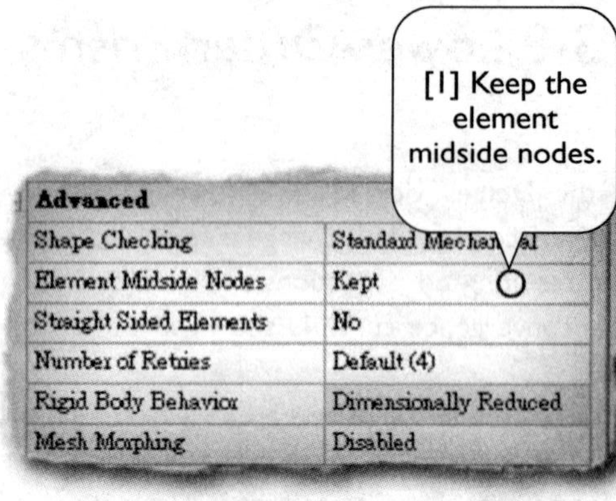

Element Size (mm)	Number of Nodes	Tip Deflection (mm)
5	621	0.74899
4	1440	0.75011
3	3125	0.75071
2	6696	0.75108
1.5	16256	0.75136
1.3	23787	0.75145

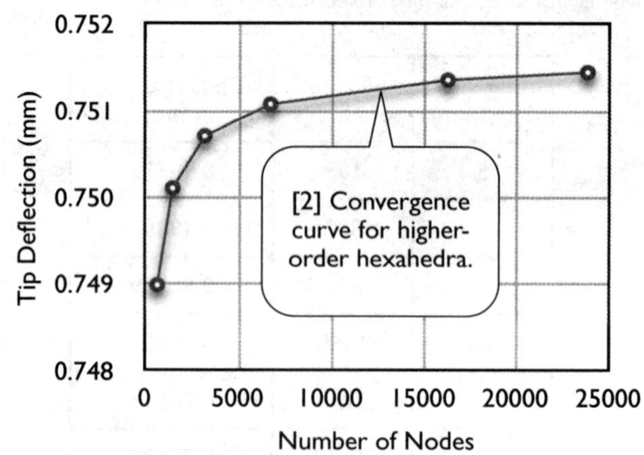

9.3-10 Higher-Order Tetrahedra

Repeat what you have done in 9.3-6, except keeping the element midside nodes ([9.3-9[1]).

Element Size (mm)	Number of Nodes	Tip Deflection (mm)
5	512	0.74637
4	857	0.74803
3	1360	0.74991
2.5	1639	0.74963
2	3135	0.75017
1.5	4549	0.75097
1.2	7808	0.75110
1	11952	0.75124
0.8	17237	0.75139
0.7	23963	0.75151

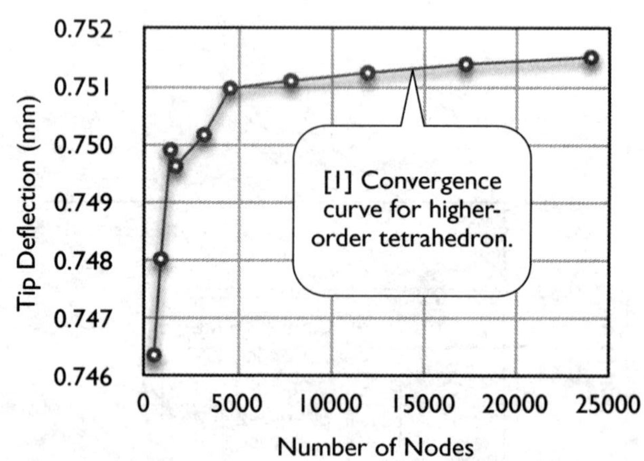

9.3-11 Higher-Order Parallel Prisms

Repeat what you have done in 9.3-7, except keeping the element midside nodes (9.3-9[1]).

Element Size (mm)	Number of Nodes	Tip Deflection (mm)
5	783	0.74964
4	1341	0.75042
3.3	2875	0.75084
3	3901	0.75089
2.4	5943	0.75115
2	9646	0.75120
1.8	12915	0.75134
1.6	19058	0.75143
1.4	27705	0.75151

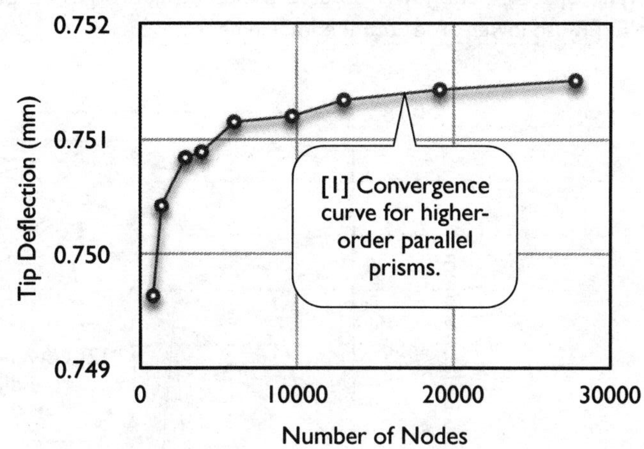

9.3-12 Higher-Order Perpendicular Prisms

Repeat what you have done in 9.3-8, except keeping the element midside nodes (9.3-9[1]).

Element Size (mm)	Number of Nodes	Tip Deflection (mm)
5	783	0.74953
4	1341	0.75013
3.3	2899	0.75080
3	3901	0.75089
2.4	5943	0.75115
2	9646	0.75126
1.8	12915	0.75138
1.6	19058	0.75147
1.4	27749	0.75154

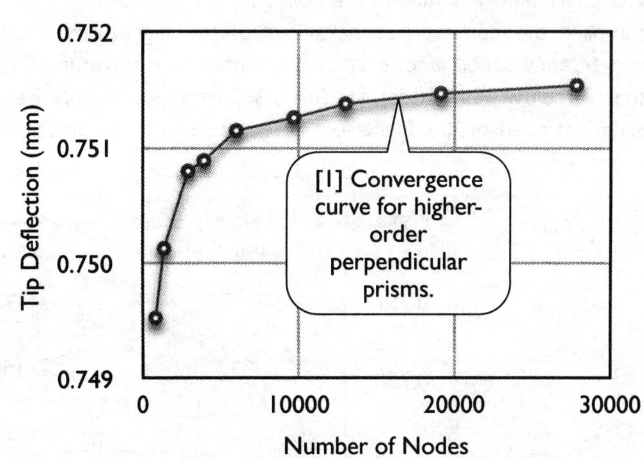

9.3-13 Comparison: Lower-Order Elements

The chart below is made by a collection of the convergence curves in Sections 9.3-5, 9.3-6, 9.3-7, and 9.3-8 to compare the convergence behaviors of the lower-order elements. The order of the convergence speed is, from fast to slow, hexahedron, parallel prism, perpendicular prism, tetrahedron. The differences between them are obvious and quite evenly spaced. The lower-order tetrahedron converges so poorly that it is not practically useful. As a guideline, NEVER use lower-order tetrahedral elements.

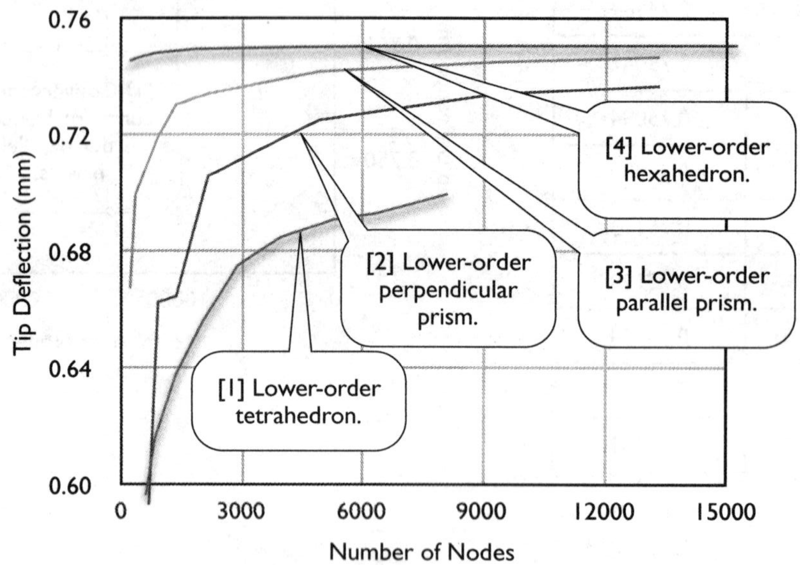

9.3-14 Comparison: Higher-Order Elements

The chart below is made by a collection of the convergence curves in Sections 9.3-9, 9.3-10, 9.3-11, and 9.3-12 to compare the convergence behaviors of the higher-order elements. Except the tetrahedron, the order of the convergence speed among other elements is not obvious. The tetrahedron performs poorly only when the mesh is coarse (below 5000 nodes, for this case), otherwise it may be as good as other elements. Contrasting to the lower-order tetrahedron, the higher-order tetrahedron is still practically useful as long as the mesh is fine enough.

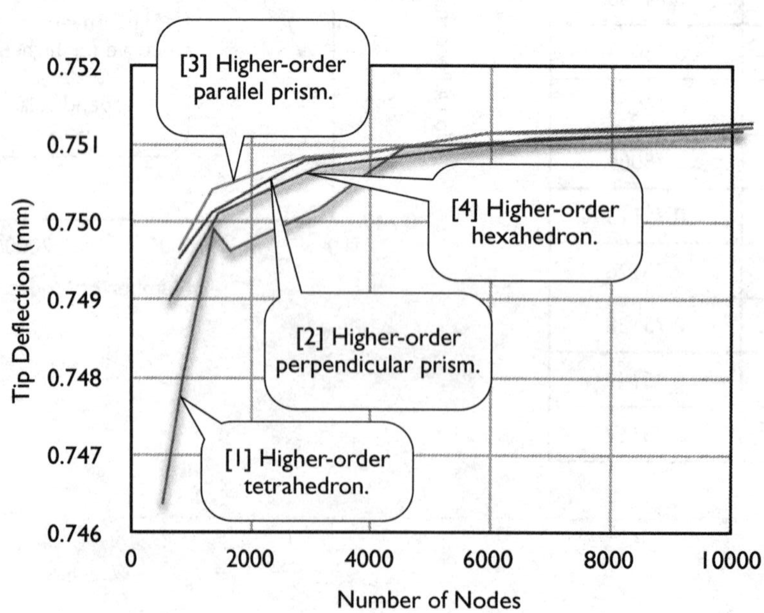

9.3-15 Comparison: Hexahedra

The chart below is made by a collection of the convergence curves in Sections 9.3-5 and 9.3-9 to compare the convergence behaviors of the lower- and higher-order hexahedra. It is obvious that higher-order element is better than the lower-order one.

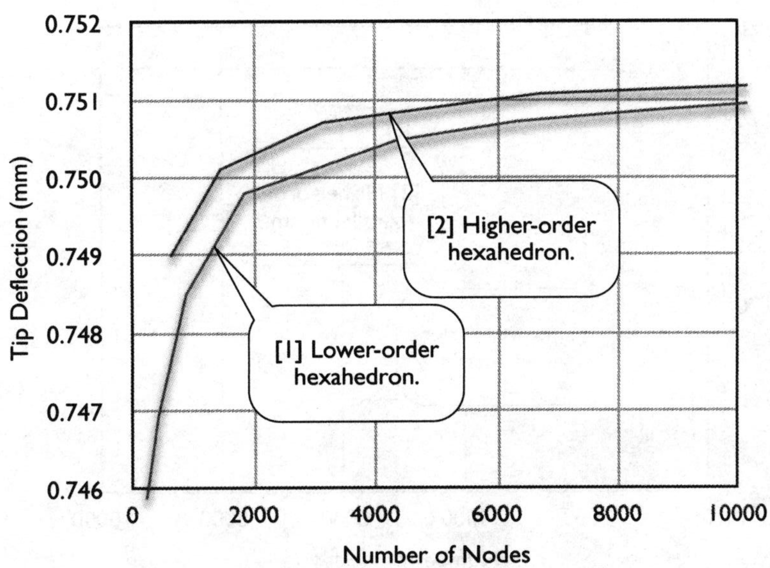

9.3-16 Comparison: Tetrahedra

The chart below is made by a collection of the convergence curves in Sections 9.3-6 and 9.3-10 to compare the convergence behaviors of the lower- and higher-order tetrahedra. It is obvious that higher-order element is much better than the lower-order one. Again, NEVER use lower-order tetrahedral elements.

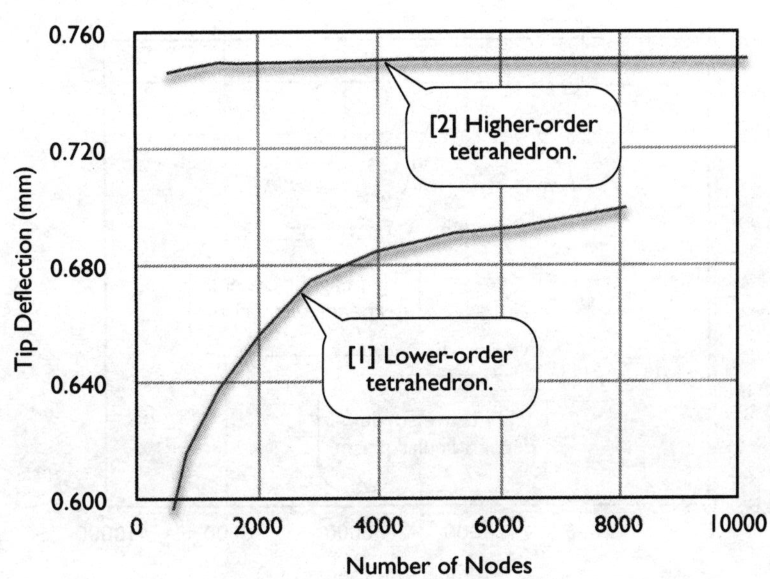

9.3-17 Comparison: Parallel Prisms

The chart below is made by a collection of the convergence curves in Sections 9.3-7 and 9.3-11 to compare the convergence behaviors of the lower- and higher-order parallel prisms. It is obvious that higher-order element is much better than the lower-order one. Generally, lower-order prismatic elements are not recommended, even if the sweeping direction is parallel to the bending direction.

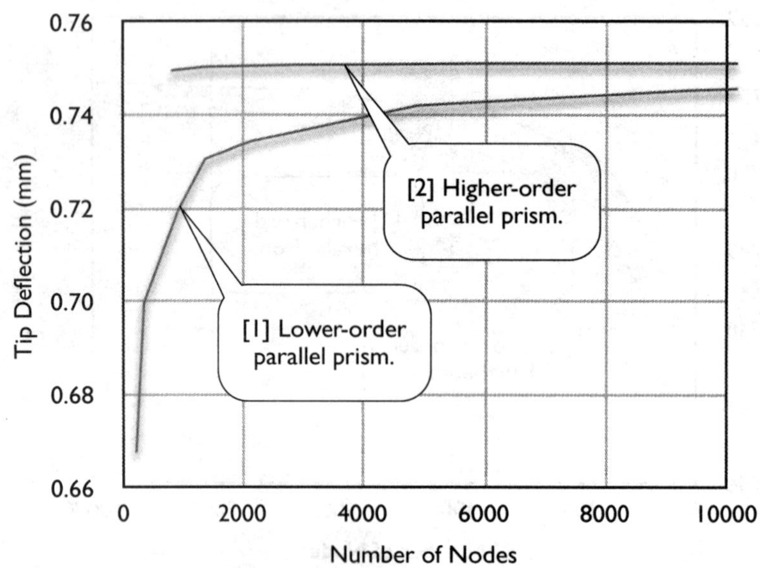

9.3-18 Comparison: Perpendicular Prisms

The chart below is made by a collection of the convergence curves in Sections 9.3-8 and 9.3-12 to compare the convergence behaviors of the lower- and higher-order perpendicular prisms. It is obvious that higher-order element is much better than the lower-order one. Again, lower-order prismatic elements are generally not recommended.

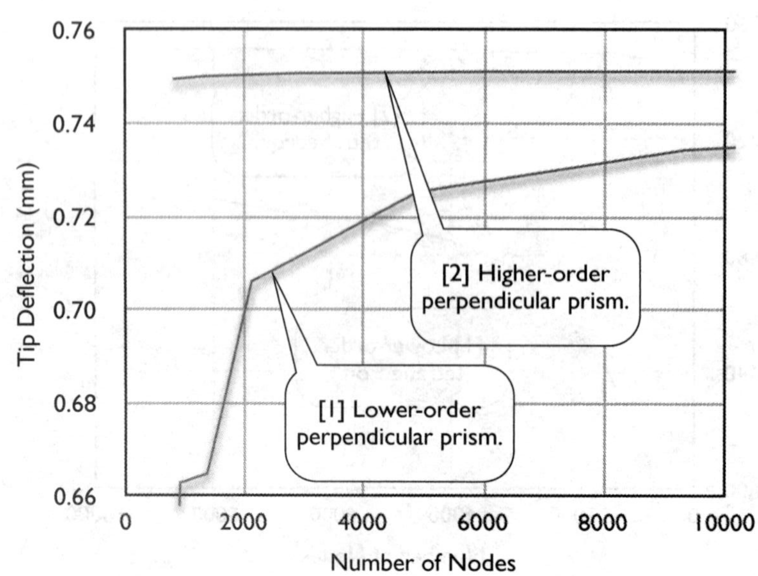

9.3-19 Summary and Guidelines

Combining the observations in Section 3.5 and this section, we may summarized the conclusions as follows: (a) Never use lower-order tetrahedra or triangles. (b) Higher-order tetrahedra or triangles can be as good as other elements as long as the mesh is fine enough. In cases of coarse mesh, however, they perform poorly and are not recommended. (c) Lower-order prisms are not recommended. (d) Lower-order hexahedra and quadrilaterals can be used, but they are not as efficient as their higher-order counterparts. (e) Higher-order hexahedra, prisms, and quadrilaterals are among the most efficient elements so far we have discussed. Mesh your models with these elements whenever possible. If that is not possible, than at least try to achieve a higher-order hexahedra-dominate or quadrilateral-dominate mesh.

Besides the above guidelines, mesh quality requirements, in terms of mesh metrics such as skewness, should also be met according to guidelines proposed in Section 9.1-6.

Remark

In Section 3.5 and this section, comparisons among elements are made under the same number of nodes. More reasonable comparisons should be made under the same CPU time. For a simulation task, the CPU time consists of three parts. First, the time required to establish Eq. 1.3-1(1). It involves numerical integrations element by element. This part of CPU time depends on the total number of elements as well as the number of integration points of each element. Second, the time required to solve the equation. This part of CPU time is determined solely by the number of degrees of freedom, which is in turn determined by the number of nodes and the dimensionality (2D or 3D). Third, the others (the overhead).

For small problems, the overall CPU time is dominated by the third part (the overhead). That is why we didn't use CPU time for comparison, since all cases are small when coarsely meshed. For large problems, the CPU time is essentially the sum of the first two parts.

Therefore, strictly speaking, our comparison was not perfectly reasonable. Nevertheless, the discussions and conclusions in this section pretty much reflect the reality. These guidelines should be useful.

Section 9.4

Problems

9.4-1 Key Concepts

Skewness

A measure of mesh quality, calculated for each element according to its geometry. Its value ranges from 0 to 1, the smaller the better. Elements of skewness of more than 0.95 are considered unacceptable.

Convergence Criteria

In nonlinear simulation, the loading are divided into substeps and applied substep by substep. By default, a substep is said to be complete when both displacement convergence criterion and force convergence criterion are met during the iterations.

Displacement Convergence Criterion

During the iterations of a substep of a nonlinear simulation, the displacement convergence criterion is met when the increment of displacement is less than a criterion, which is, by default, 0.5% of maximum displacement.

Force Convergence Criterion

During the iterations of a substep of a nonlinear simulation, the force convergence criterion is met when the unbalanced force is less than a criterion, which is, by default, 0.5% of applied force.

Sweep Thin Method

The <Sweep> mesh control method can be classified into normal <Sweep> and <Sweep Thin>. The normal <Sweep> allows multiple layers of sweeping, while <Sweep Thin> only one layer. The advantage of the <Sweep Thin> is that it allows multiple faces as source or target while the normal <Sweep> allows only one face for both source and target.

Patch Conforming Method

A mesh control method. It meshes all the faces of the body with triangles and then "grow" inward to create tetrahedra. In this way, the shapes of the faces are respected (preserved).

Patch Independent Method

A mesh control method. It creates tetrahedra from inside out. The outermost nodes are then projected onto the boundary faces and the element edges are created. In this way, the mesh's outline may be different from the original geometry.

Hex Dominant Method

A mesh control method. It meshes a body with Patch Conforming method first and then combine tetrahedra to form hexahedra. It usually leaves some tetrahedra that cannot be combined to form hexahedra.

Parallel Prisms

When a body is meshed with prismatic elements and the prisms are oriented such that their heights are parallel to the bending direction, the prismatic elements oriented in this way are referred as parallel prisms. (Note: this term is used in this book only.)

Perpendicular Prisms

When a body is meshed with prismatic elements and the prisms are oriented such that their heights are perpendicular to the bending direction, the prismatic elements oriented in this way are referred as parallel prisms. (Note: this term is used in this book only.)

9.4-2 Workbench Exercises

Convergence Study for the Higher-Order 2D Elements

In Section 9.3, we study the convergence of 3D elements, both higher-order and lower-order elements. In Section 3.5, we study the convergence of 2D elements, only for the lower-order elements. We haven't studied the higher-order 2D elements yet. Conduct a study of the higher-order 2D elements.

Chapter 10

Buckling and Stress Stiffening

As mentioned in the beginning of Section 1.4, functionality, safety, and reliability are the main purposes of structural simulations. Stresses usually relate to the safety and reliability. In the 3D truss example (Section 7.2), calculated stresses are well below the material's yield strength. Can we conclude that the design is safe? Not yet. For any structural members (particularly those slender or thin members) subject to compressive stresses, we need to check their stability before concluding their safety. This chapter mainly deals with *stability analysis*, or *buckling analysis*.

Buckling can be viewed as an ultimate case of a more general effect, called *stress stiffening*: a slender or thin structure member's bending stiffness increases with increasing axial tensile stress, and, on the other hand, the member's bending stiffness decreases with the increasing compressive stress. Buckling occurs when the compressive stress reaches a level such that the bending stiffness vanishes; the applying load is called a *buckling load* and the deformation is called a *buckling mode*. The purpose of buckling analyses is to find the buckling loads and the buckling modes.

Purpose of the Chapter

The main purpose of this chapter is to discuss linear buckling analysis. Since buckling can be viewed as an ultimate case of stress stiffening, the discussion will start with a thorough understanding of stress stiffening. As usual, the concepts are introduced using designed exercises.

About Each Section

Section 1 introduces the stress stiffening effects, using a simply supported beam as example. The results of these nonlinear analyses can be used to predict the buckling load using an extrapolation method; this procedure can be called a *nonlinear buckling analysis*. A linear buckling analysis is then carried out to find the buckling loads and buckling modes. Comparison between linear and nonlinear buckling analyses is made to show that linear buckling analysis tends to overestimate the buckling load.

Sections 2 performs a linear buckling analysis on the 3D truss structure introduced in Section 7.2. Section 3 carries out a linear buckling analysis on the beam bracket which has been discussed in Sections 4.1, 5.1, and 6.2.

Section 10.1

Step-by-Step: Stress Stiffening

This section introduces the *stress stiffening effect*, which is closely related to the buckling. Stress stiffening effect is often observed in slender or thin structures or structural members, such as cables, shells, columns, walls, towers, trusses, etc. In a slender structural member, such as a column, the bending stiffness can be affected by its axial stress. In a thin structure member, such as a wall, the bending stiffness are affected by its in-plane stress. More specifically, when subject to axial (or in-plane) tension, the bending stiffness will increase, while subject to axial (or in-plane) compression, the bending stiffness will decrease.

In this section, we will use a simply supported slender beam to demonstrate the stress stiffening effects.

10.1-1 About the Simply Supported Beam

Consider a simply supported beam shown below [1-3]. The beam is made of steel and has a uniform cross section of 10x10 mm [1]. A uniformly distributed load of 0.1 N/mm is applied downward on the beam's upper surface [2]. An axial force applies on the beam's end which is free to move horizontally.

The vertical load, which contributes to the bending, will be fixed in the following simulations, while the horizontal force P will be varied. The range of P will be from -500 N to 1000 N. Note the negative P produces a compressive axial stress while the positive P produces a tensile axial stress. We will focus on the beam's maximum vertical deflection, which occurs at the middle of the span.

Let δ_0 be the beam's maximum deflection when $P = 0$. Then, when the beam is subject to a positive P in the following simulations, we expect the deflection will be less than δ_0. We will conclude that the bending stiffness increases with the increasing tensile axial stress. On the other hand, when the beam is subject to a negative (compressive) P in the following simulations, we expect the deflection will be larger than δ_0. We will conclude that the bending stiffness decreases with the increasing compressive axial stress. This phenomenon is called the *stress stiifening*.

Since the bending stiffness decreases with the increasing compressive axial stress, you may easily raise a question: With how large the compressive force P, does the bending stiffness reduces to zero? A zero bending stiffness implies an unstable structure: a small vertical load would cause the beam to deflect indefinitely. This phenomenon is called the *buckling*.

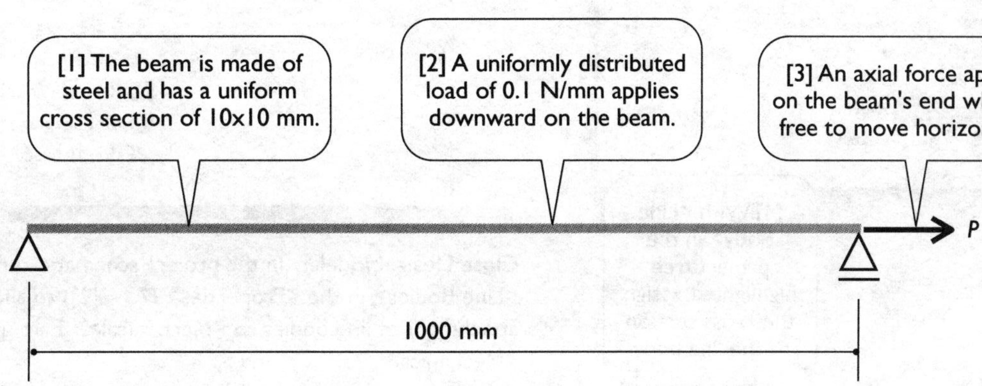

10.1-2 Start a New Project

Launch <Workbench>. Create a <Static Structural> system. Save the project as "SimpleBeam." Start up DesignModeler.

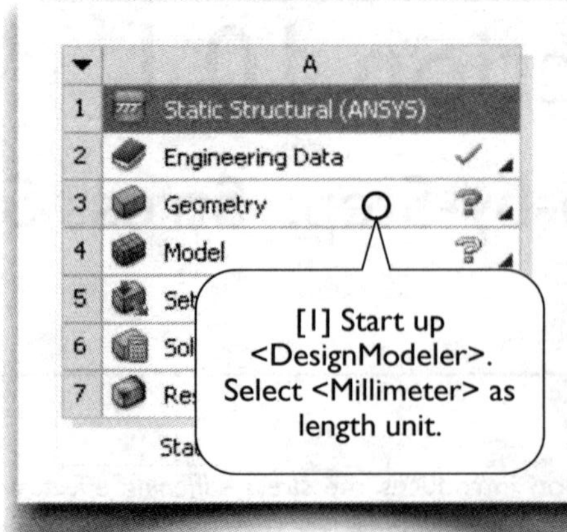

10.1-3 Create a Line Model in DesignModeler

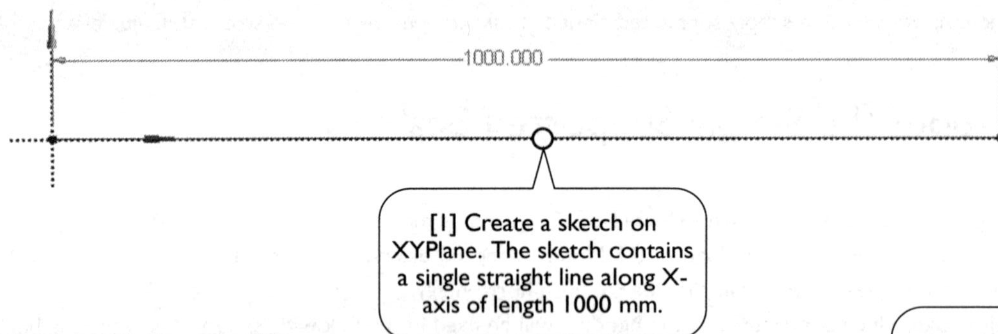

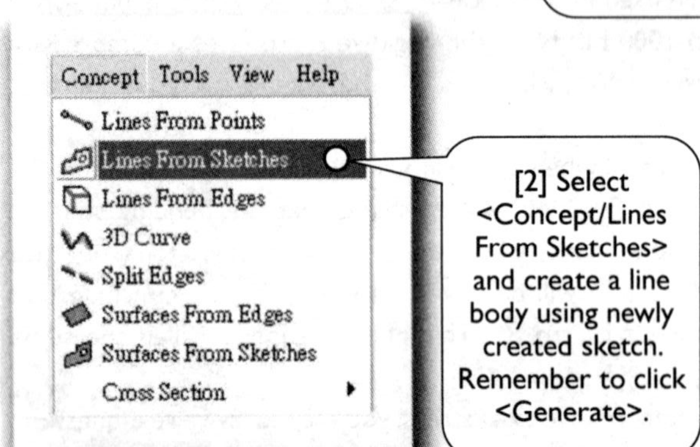

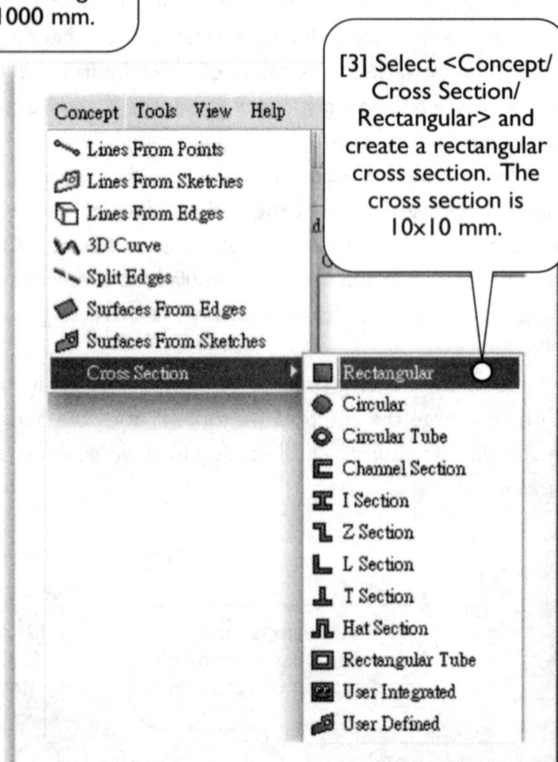

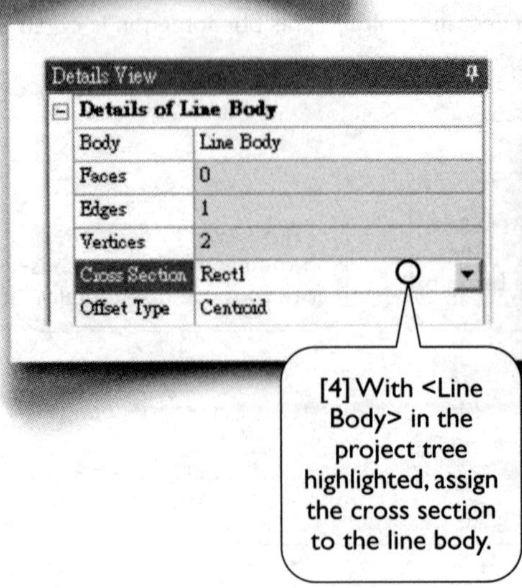

Close DesignModeler. In the project schematic, turn on the <Line Bodies> in the <Properties> (7.1-7[2]) to allow the attachment of line bodies to <Mechanical>. Start up <Mechanical>.

10.1-4 Set Up Supports

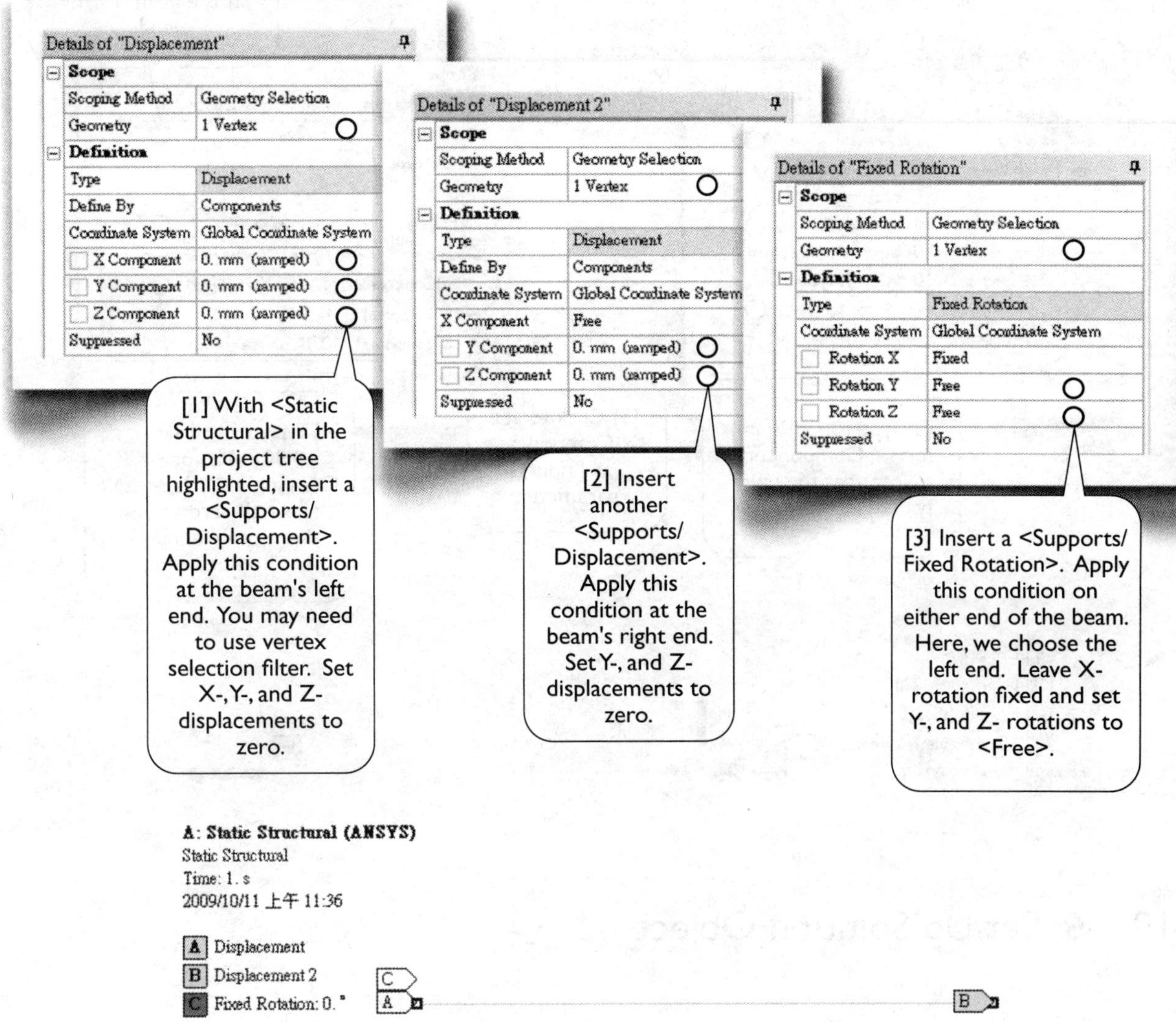

Provide Enough Supports to Avoid Rigid Body Modes

In Section 3.1-8, we mentioned that it is a good practice to provide enough supports. This becomes a necessity when working on dynamic simulations or buckling analysis, where the "rigid body modes" are not automatically eliminated.

In this case, the newcomers often fail to fix Z-displacements in steps [1, 2] and the X-rotation in step [3]. Fixing Z-displacements is to prevent the beam from translating in Z-direction, while fixing X-rotation is to prevent it from rotating in X-direction. Without these supports, the nonlinear simulation would run into convergence difficulties. In case of dynamic or buckling analyses, rigid body modes would present.

What's wrong with the presence of rigid body modes? The answer depends on the type of simulation. For <Static Structural> simulations, we already answer that question: the Workbench will add a weak spring to stop an uncontrolled large amount of rigid body motion (Section 3.1-8), and, instead, a small amount of rigid body motion will occur (Section 3.1-9).

For <Linear Buckling> and <Modal> simulations, rigid body modes are trivial but theoretically no harm. The buckling load corresponding to a rigid body mode is zero, and the natural frequency corresponding a rigid body mode is also zero. However, presence of rigid body modes may deteriorate the numerical accuracy.

For <Transient Structural> simulation, we usually don't need to artificially eliminate a rigid body if it exists by its natural. Let the rigid body modes be present, and the algorithm will take care them nicely. Sections 12.4, 15.1, and 15.2 provide good examples for these situations.

10.1-5 Set Up Loads

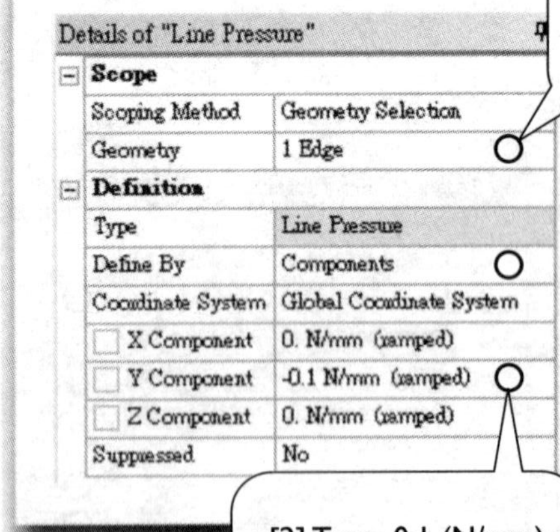

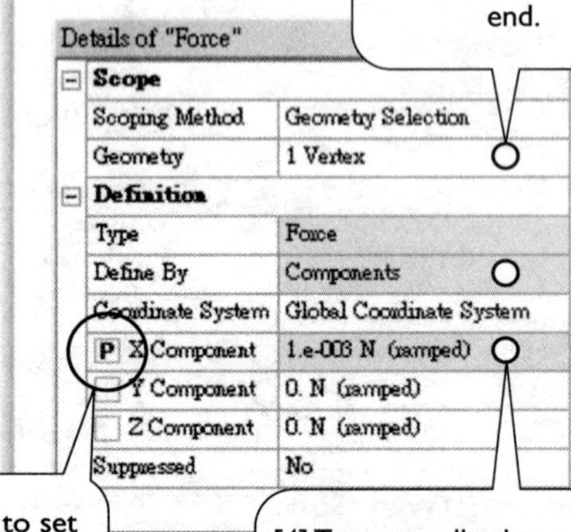

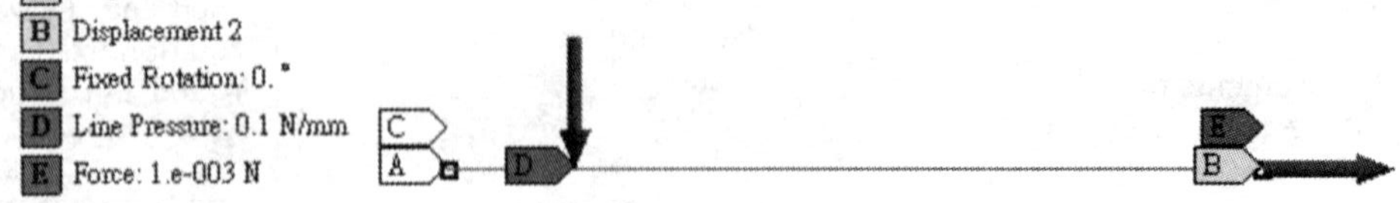

10.1-6 Set Up Solution Object

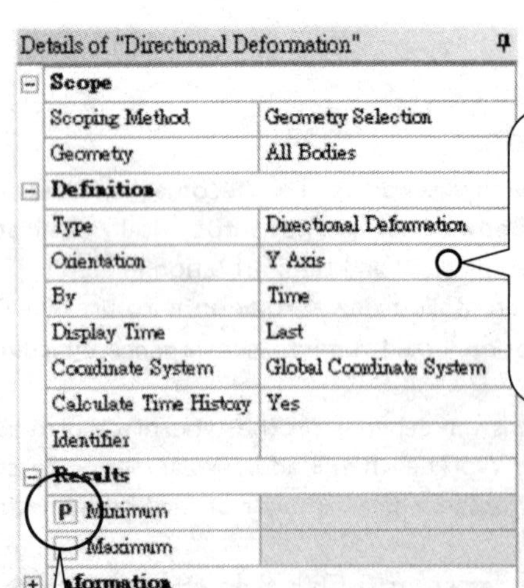

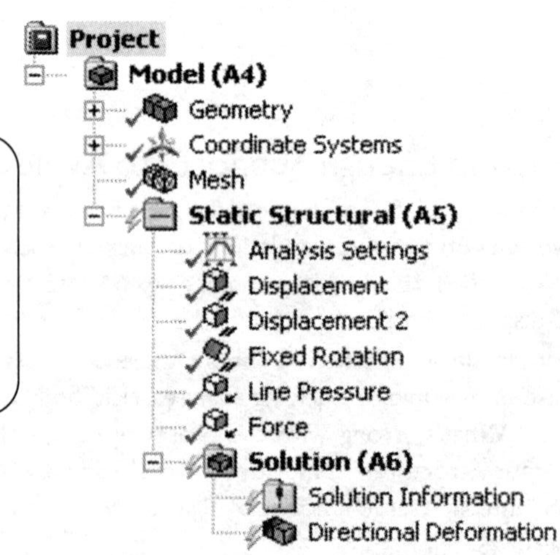

10.1-7 Set Up Mesh and Turn on Large Deflection Effect

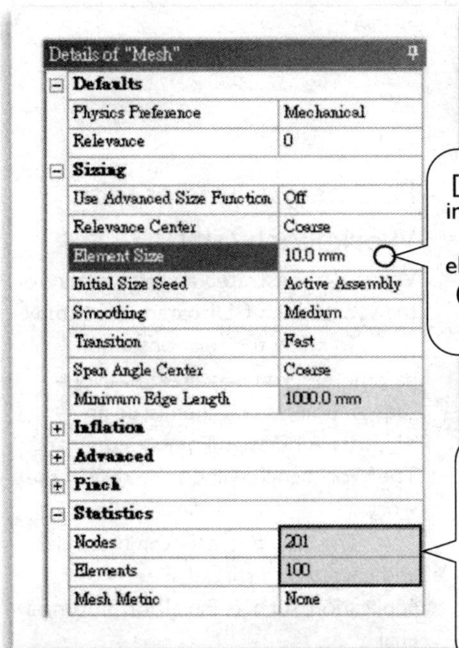

[1] With <Mesh> in the project tree highlighted, set element size to 10 (mm). Generate mesh.

[2] There are 100 beam elements for this model. We will use this element size for all the simulations in this section.

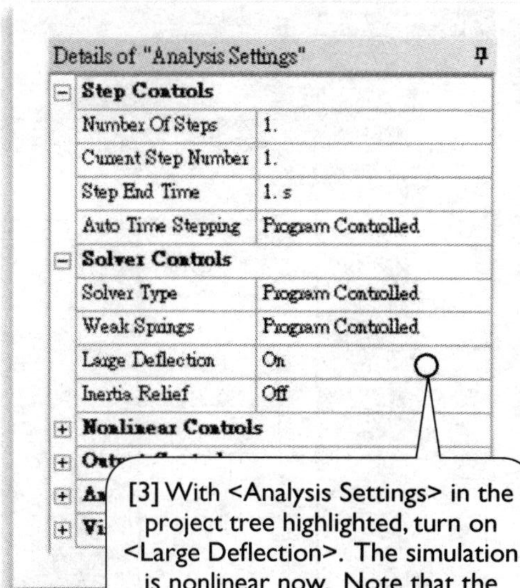

[3] With <Analysis Settings> in the project tree highlighted, turn on <Large Deflection>. The simulation is nonlinear now. Note that the stress stiffening effect is due to geometry interactions. Without turning on <Large Deflection>, the effect won't exist.

10.1-8 Create Design Points

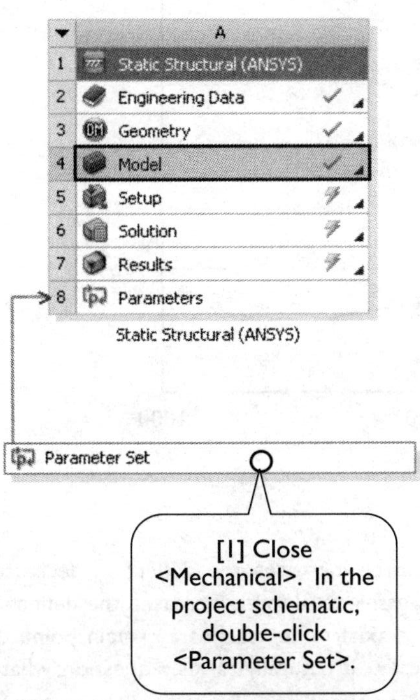

[1] Close <Mechanical>. In the project schematic, double-click <Parameter Set>.

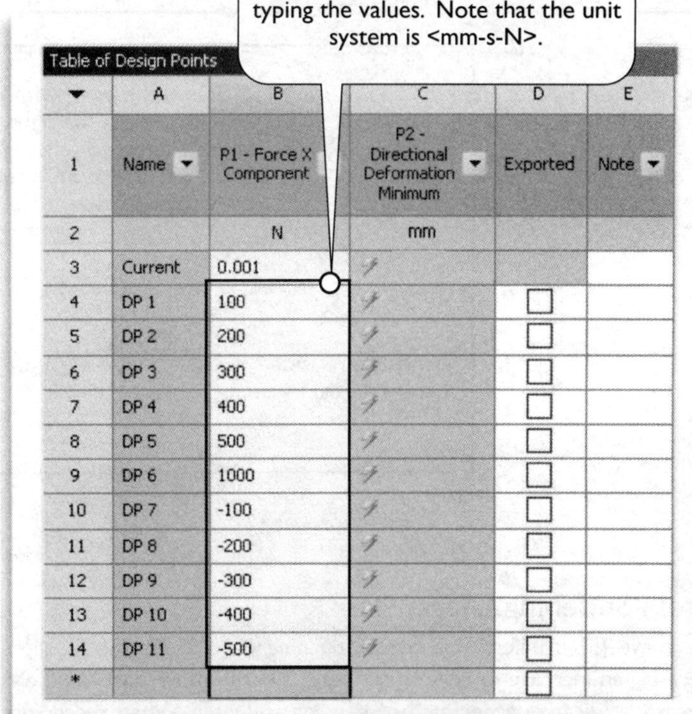

[2] In the <Table of Design Points>, add 11 design points by directly typing the values. Note that the unit system is <mm-s-N>.

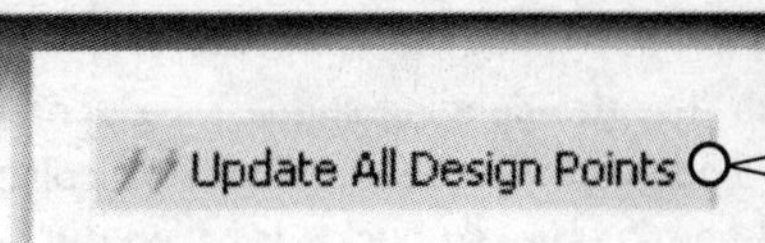

[3] Click <Update All Design Points>

10.1-9 The Results and Discussion

Table of Design Points

▼	A	B	C	D	E
1	Name	P1 - Force X Component	P2 - Directional Deformation Minimum	Exported	Note
2		N	mm		
3	Current	0.001	-5.7329		
4	DP 1	100	-5.411	☐	
5	DP 2	200	-5.1375	☐	
6	DP 3	300	-4.8913	☐	
7	DP 4	400	-4.6729	☐	
8	DP 5	500	-4.4771	☐	
9	DP 6	1000	-3.7287	☐	
10	DP 7	-100	-6.1153	☐	
11	DP 8	-200	-6.5849	☐	
12	DP 9	-300	-7.215	☐	
13	DP 10	-400	-7.8457	☐	
14	DP 11	-500	-9.2079	☐	
*				☐	

[1] The input forces are used as abscissa in the chart below.

[2] The output deflections are used as ordinate in the chart below.

Parameters Studies with Workbench GUI

We've demonstrated a useful feature of the Workbench GUI: parameters study.

To study the relations among parameters, you may create various "design points" and then issue an <Update All Design Points> command. The Workbench will do the rest of the work.

The resulting data can be copied and pasted to a spread sheet application, such as Excel, for plotting a chart.

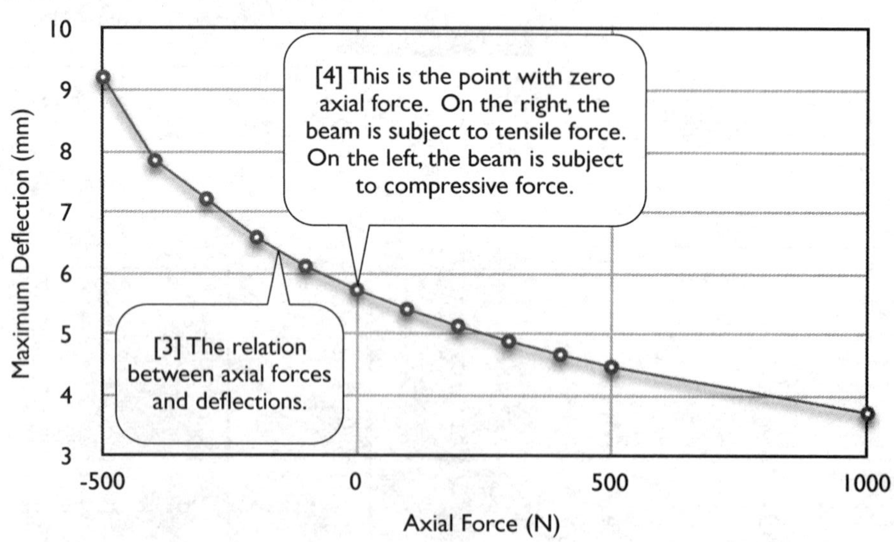

Stress Stiffening Effects

The curve [3] manifests the stress stiffening effects. As the tensile axial force increases, the deflection decreases, indicating an increase of bending stiffness. On the other hand, as the compressive axial force increases, the deflection increases, indicating a decrease of bending stiffness. When the compressive axial force reaches a certain point, the bending stiffness decreases so much that the deflection is enlarged dramatically. It naturally raises a question: what is the compressive force such that the bending stiffness reduces to zero? A zero bending stiffness implies an unstable structure: a small vertical load would cause the beam to collapse. This phenomenon is called the *buckling* and the compressive force causing the structure to buckle is called the *buckling load*, or *critical load* in some of other textbooks.

We could continue the above process and extend the curve [3] until a vertical asymptote can be drawn. The force value intercepted by the asymptote would be the buckling force. This approach is too tedious and is not practical. A more practical approach is to constantly increment the applied loads until the solution begins to diverge[1]. Either way, the deformation is so large that the convergence of the nonlinear solution is always an issue.

The workbench provide a linear buckling analysis capability to assess the buckling load. Comparing to nonlinear buckling analysis, it takes much less computing time, but usually takes more computing time than a static structural analysis.

The problem of the linear buckling analysis is that, it usually overestimates the buckling load. For example, from the curve [3], we may reasonably estimate the buckling load as no more than 600 N. The linear buckling theory, however, predicts the buckling load as

$$P_{buckling} = \frac{\pi^2 EI}{L^2} = \frac{\pi^2(200,000)(833.33)}{(1000)^2} = 1645 \text{ N}$$

The difference is huge. Note the above calculation doesn't include the distributed beam load (0.1 N/mm). Although tending to overestimate the buckling load and deviate from reality, the linear buckling analysis is still useful for two reasons: (a) It is computationally much cheaper than a nonlinear buckling analysis, and should be run as a first step to estimate the critical load. (b) It can be used to determine the possible buckling mode.

We will demonstrate the linear buckling analysis for this case in the rest of the section.

10.1-10 Set Up Project Schematic

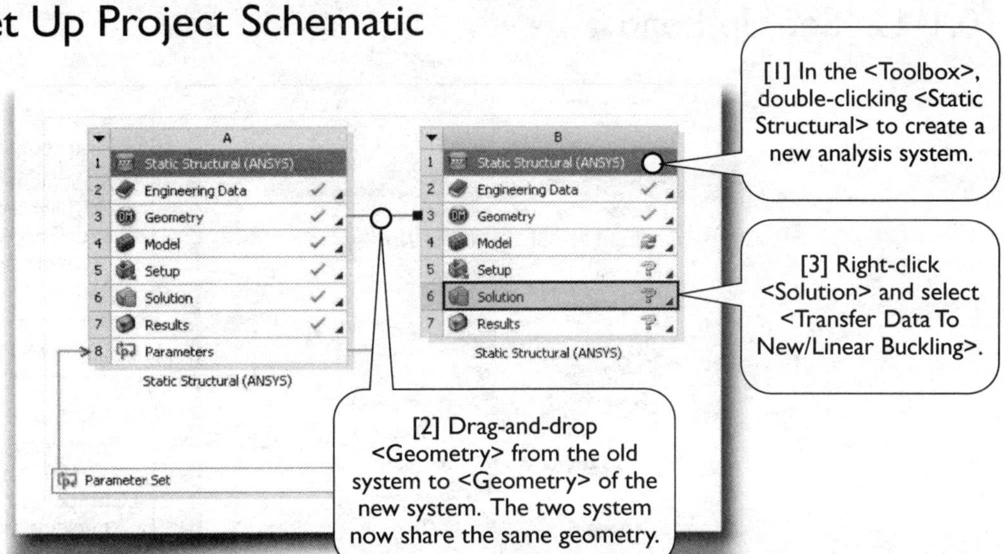

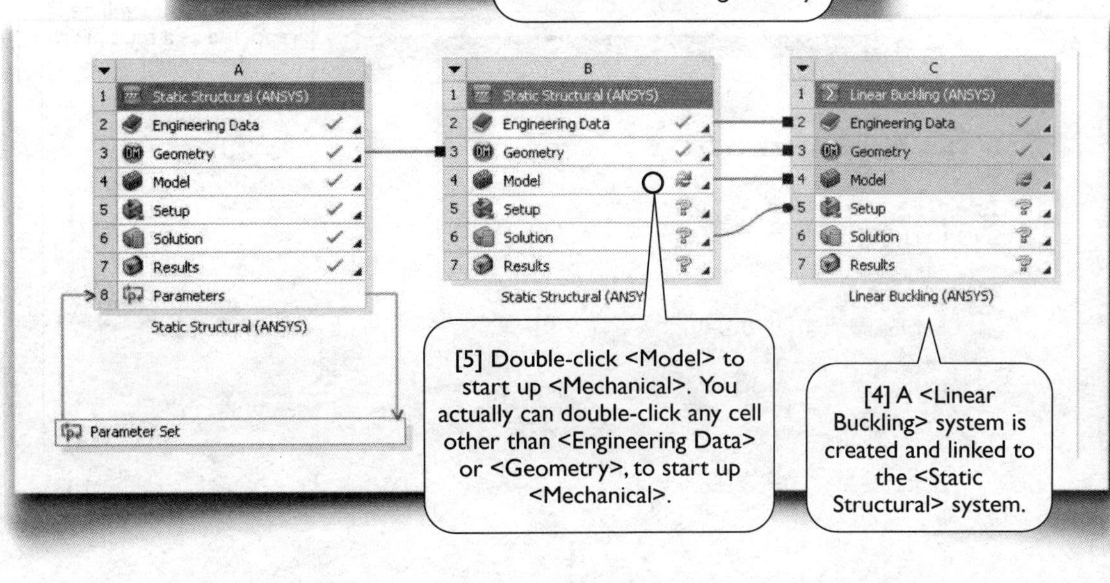

10.1-11 Set Up Supports

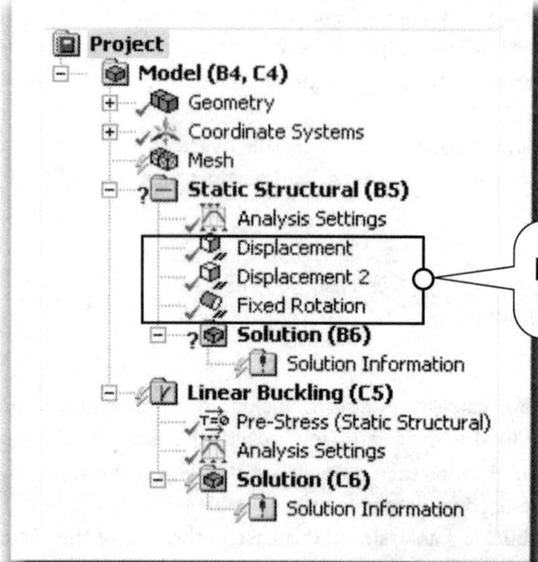

[1] Repeat the steps in Section 10.1-4.

10.1-12 Set Up Load

Details of "Force"

Scope	
Scoping Method	Geometry Selection
Geometry	1 Vertex
Definition	
Type	Force
Define By	Components
Coordinate System	Global Coordinate System
X Component	-100. N (ramped)
Y Component	0. N (ramped)
Z Component	0. N (ramped)
Suppressed	No

[1] With <Static Structural> still highlighted, insert a <Loads/Force>. Select the beam's right end.

[2] Type an arbitrary compressive value, say -100 (N), for <X Component>. After the buckling analysis, the critical load will be reported as a multiplier of the applied loads.

10.1-13 Set Up Mesh

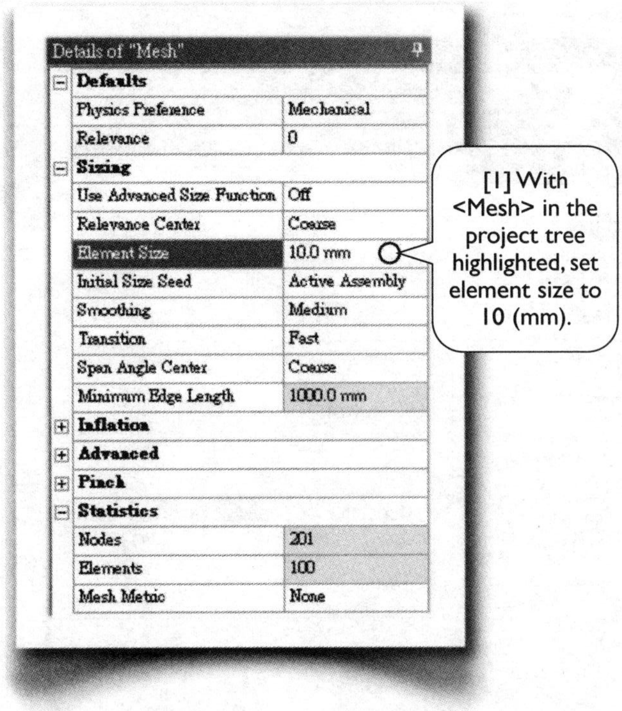

10.1-14 Specify Number of Buckling Modes and Solve

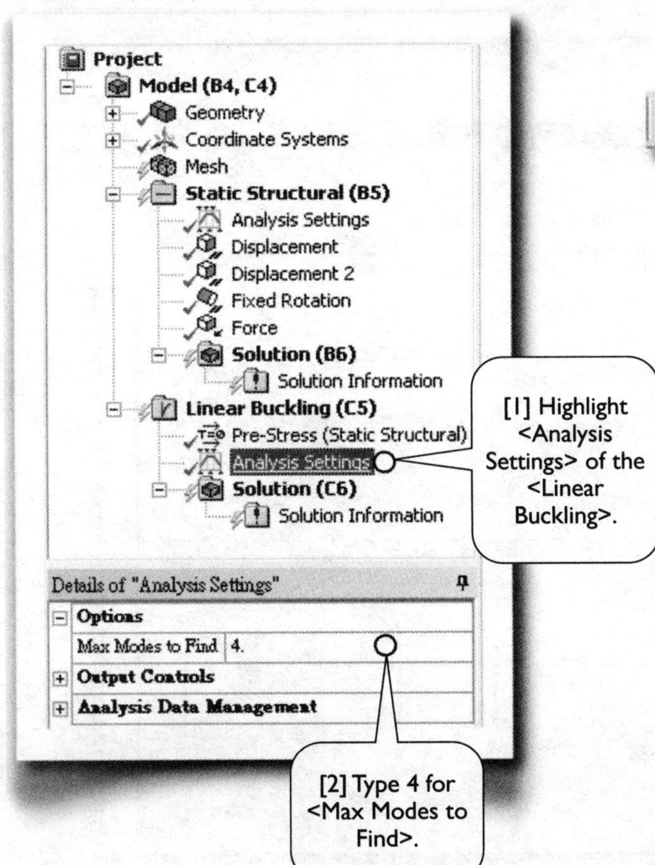

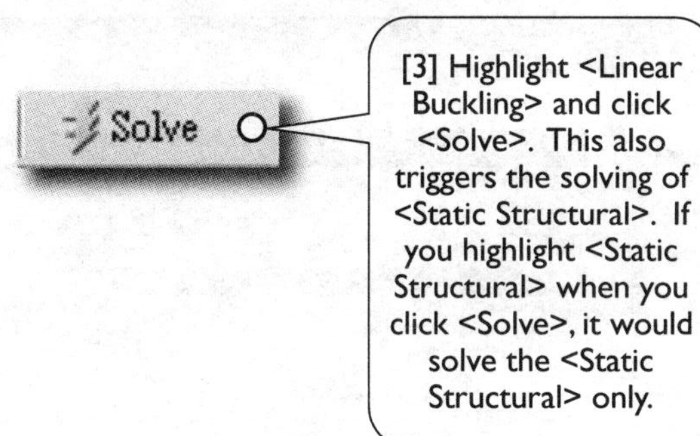

Number of Buckling Modes

In this case, the first buckling mode (mode with smallest critical load) is what we concern about. Other modes have little practical usage in this case.

Due to the same dimensions of the cross section in Y- and Z-direction, buckling modes should appear as pairs, that is, the first two modes are identical, the third and fourth modes are identical, and so on.

The reason we want to evaluate the third and the forth modes is to make sure they are far beyond our concern.

10.1-15 View the Results

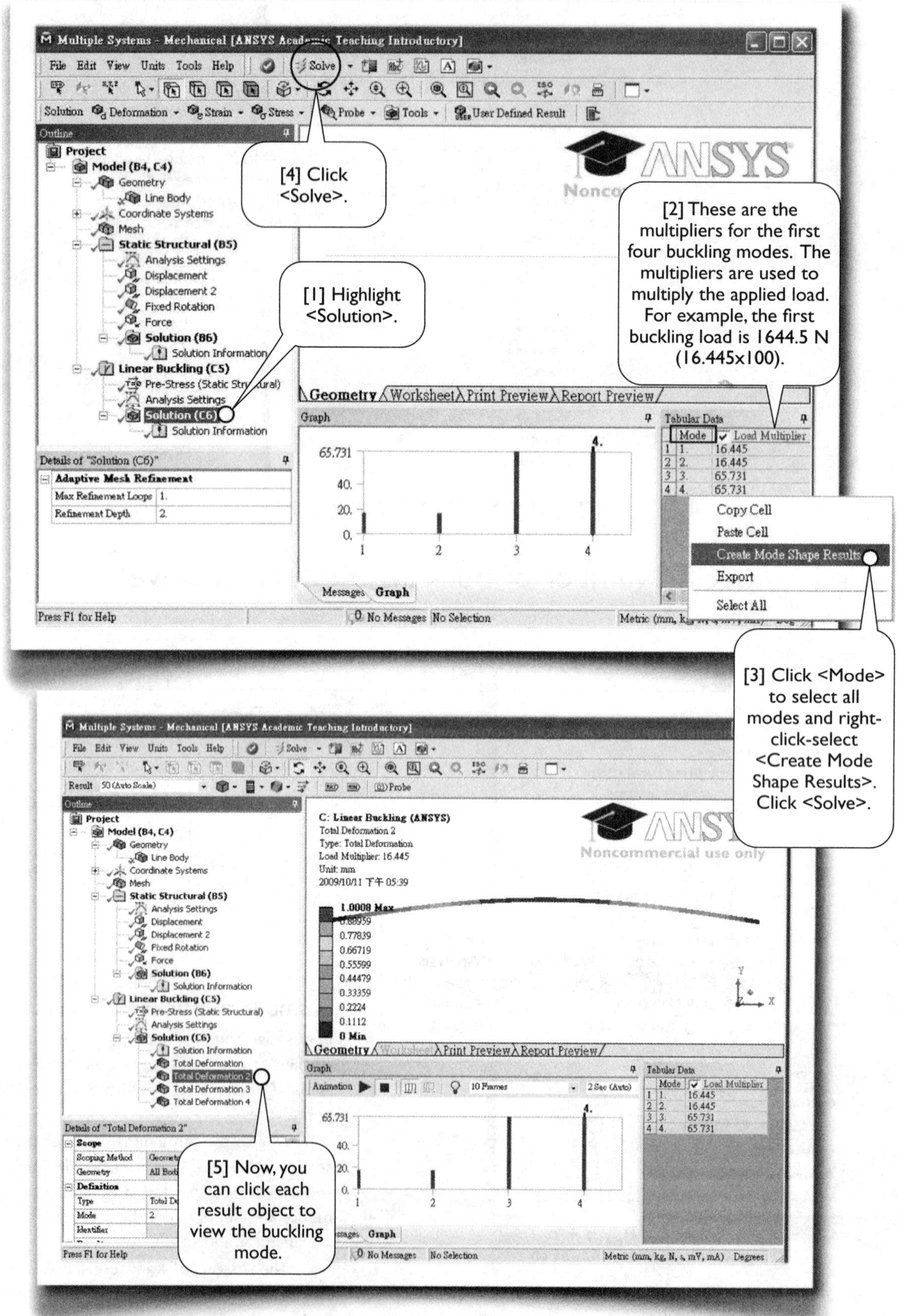

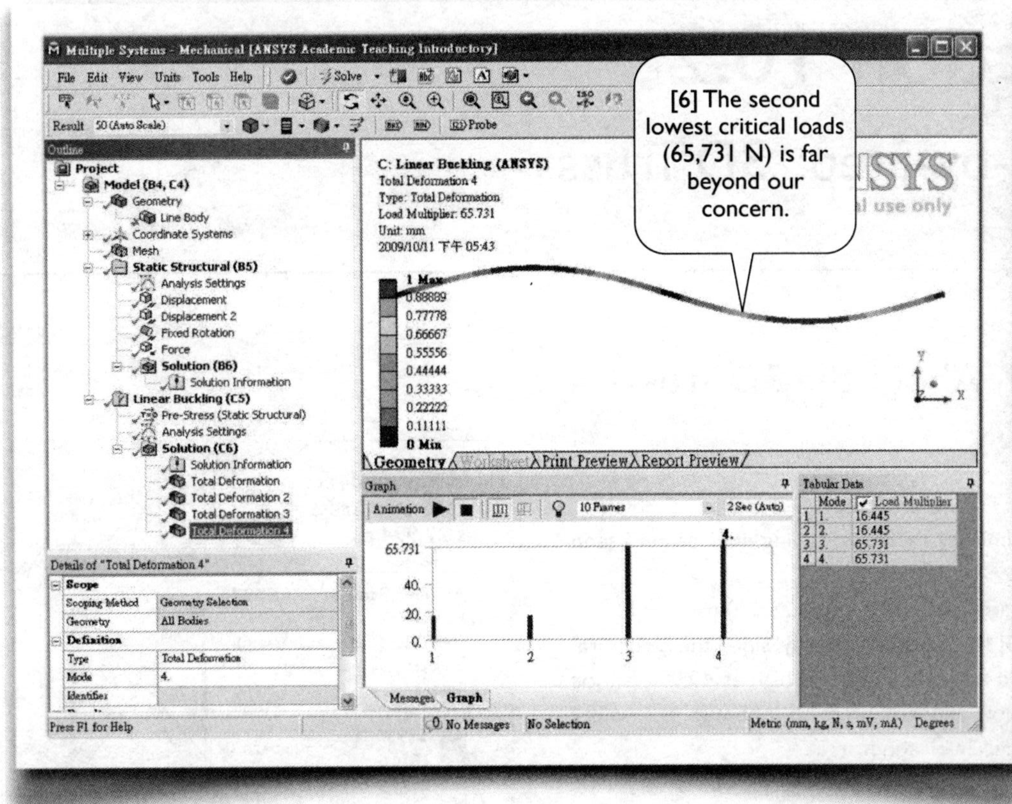

Buckling Mode Shapes

When displaying the buckling mode shapes, Workbench scales the values of deformation such that the maximum deformation is 1.0. The values of deformation have no physical significance. It is the mode shapes that concern us. Similarly, the stresses or strains have no physical meaning.

Wrap Up

Close <Mechanical>. Save the project and exit Workbench.

Reference

1. ANSYS Help System>Mechanical APDL>Structural Analysis Guide>7.3. Performing a Nonlinear Buckling Analysis.

Section 10.2

Step-by-Step: 3D Truss

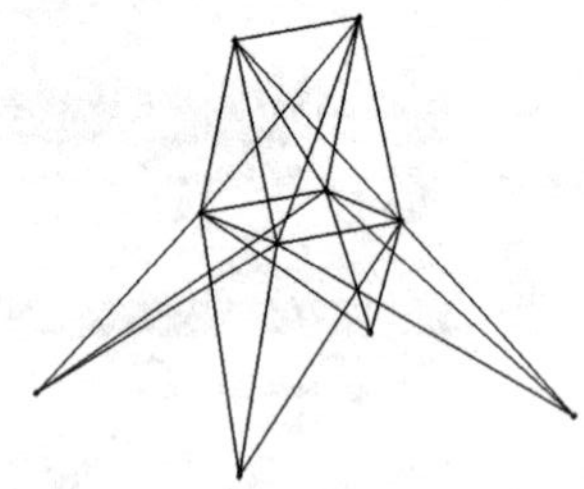

10.2-1 About the 3D Truss

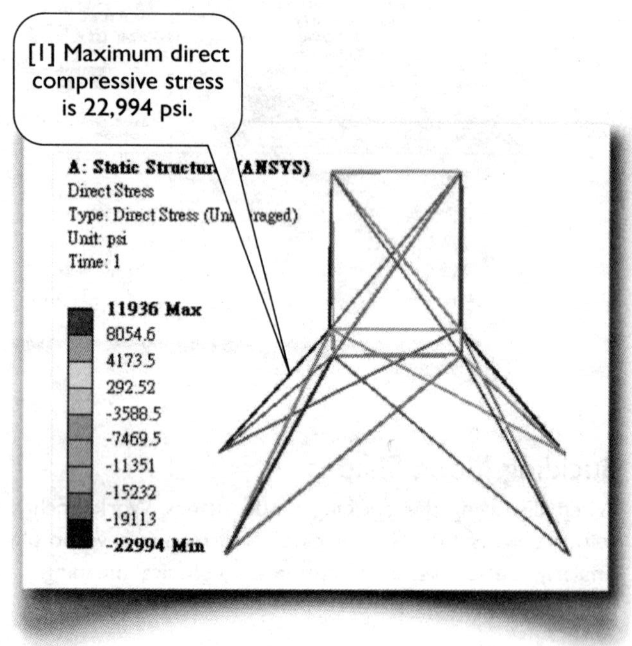

In Section 7.2, we analyzed a 3D truss and obtained some preliminary results, including displacement sand stresses.

The stresses range from -25,000 psi to +14,000 psi [7.2-15[4]). They seem okay, since the structural steel's yield strength can be as high as 40,000 psi for both tension and compression, although the safety factor is merely on the margin.

Stress is only one of the concerns regarding safety or reliability. Structural stability must be verified whenever compressive members are involved in the structure system.

Let's make some simple calculations to check whether structural stability should be an issue.

The maximum direct compressive stress occurs in a member which has a stress of 22,994 psi [1]. The member has a cross sectional area of 0.6875 in^2, therefore the direct compressive force is

$$P = 22{,}994 \times 0.6875 = 15808 \text{ lb}$$

The member has a length of 133.46 in and an area moment of inertia of 0.13852 in^4. Besides, the structural steel's Young's modulus is 29,000,000 psi. Its buckling load, according to linear buckling theory, is estimated to be

$$P_{buckling} = \frac{\pi^2 EI}{L^2} = \frac{\pi^2 (29{,}000{,}000)(0.13852)}{(133.46)^2} = 2226 \text{ lb} = 0.14P$$

In other word, only 14% of the design loads (7.2-1) would cause one of the structural member to buckle. It is now obvious that the structural stability might be an issue, at least in the members' level.

In this section, we want to perform a linear buckling analysis for the entire 3D truss structure, rather than a single member. We will come up with a much higher multiplier (higher than 14%). Two factors cause the deviation from the simple calculation. First, this truss is a statically indeterminate structure; buckling of one member does not necessarily cause a buckling of the entire structure. Second, the rigid joints provide additional rigidity to increase the buckling load.

The unit system used will be in-lb-s.

10.2-2 Resume the Project "Truss"

Launch <Workbench>. Open the project "Truss," saved in Section 7.2.

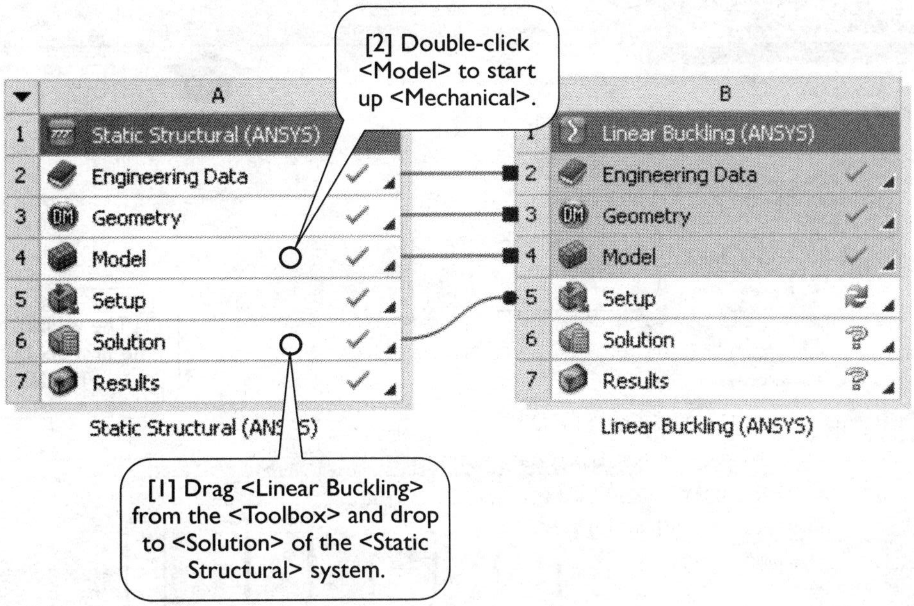

10.2-3 Perform Buckling Analysis

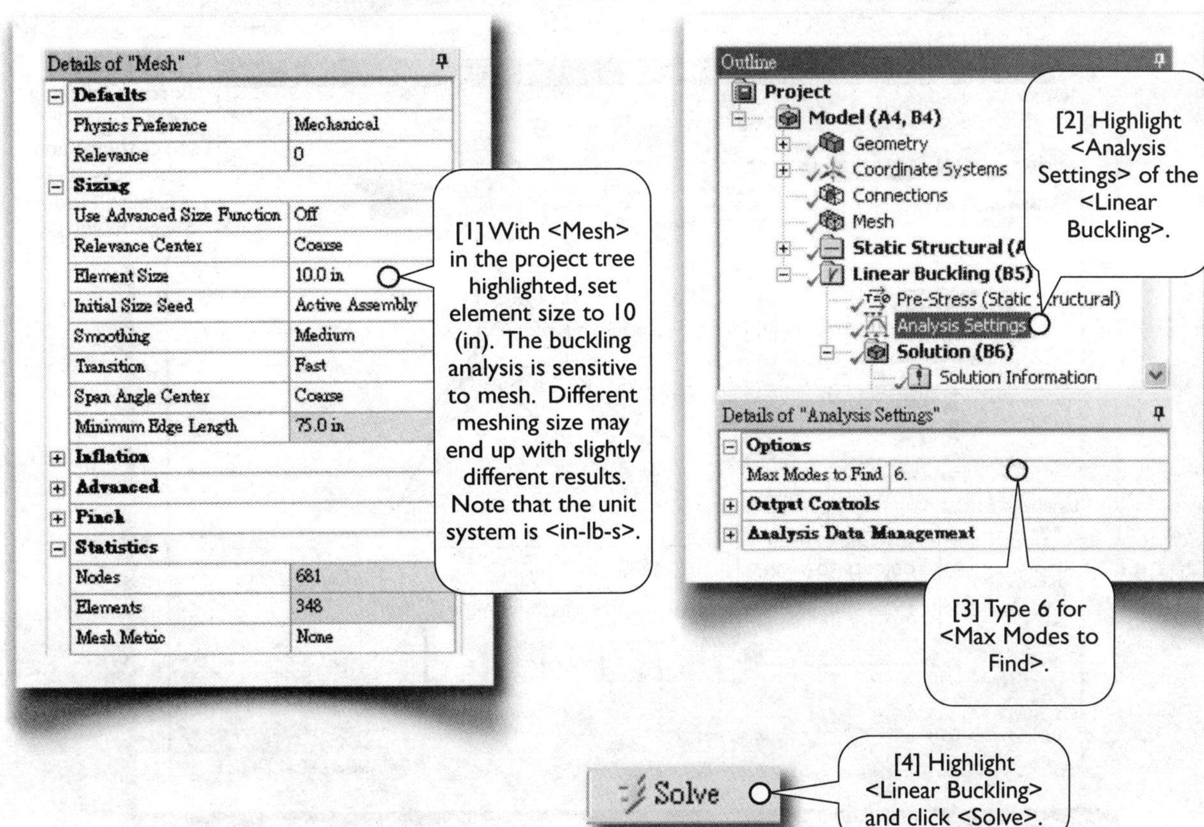

10.2-4 View the Results

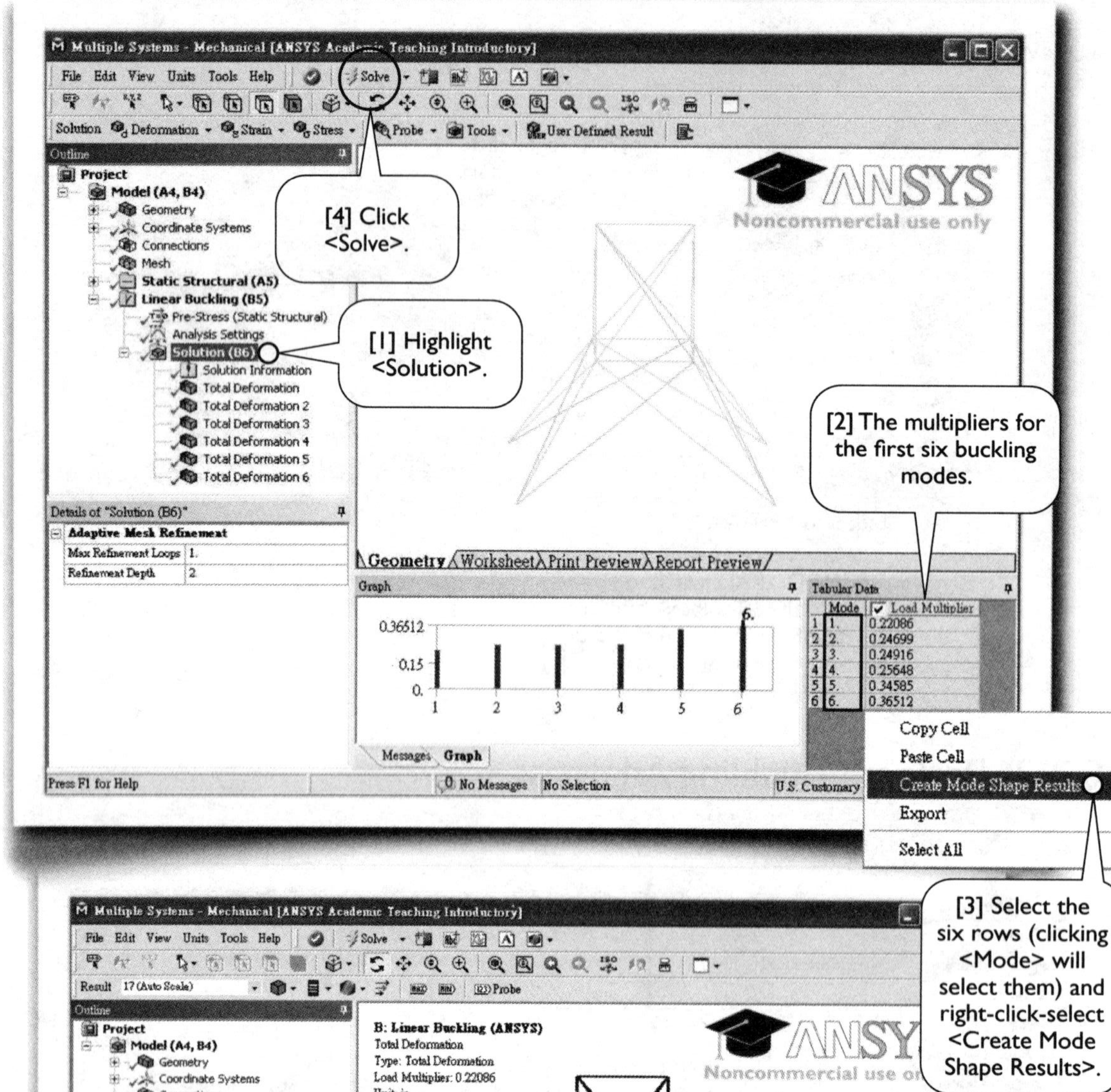

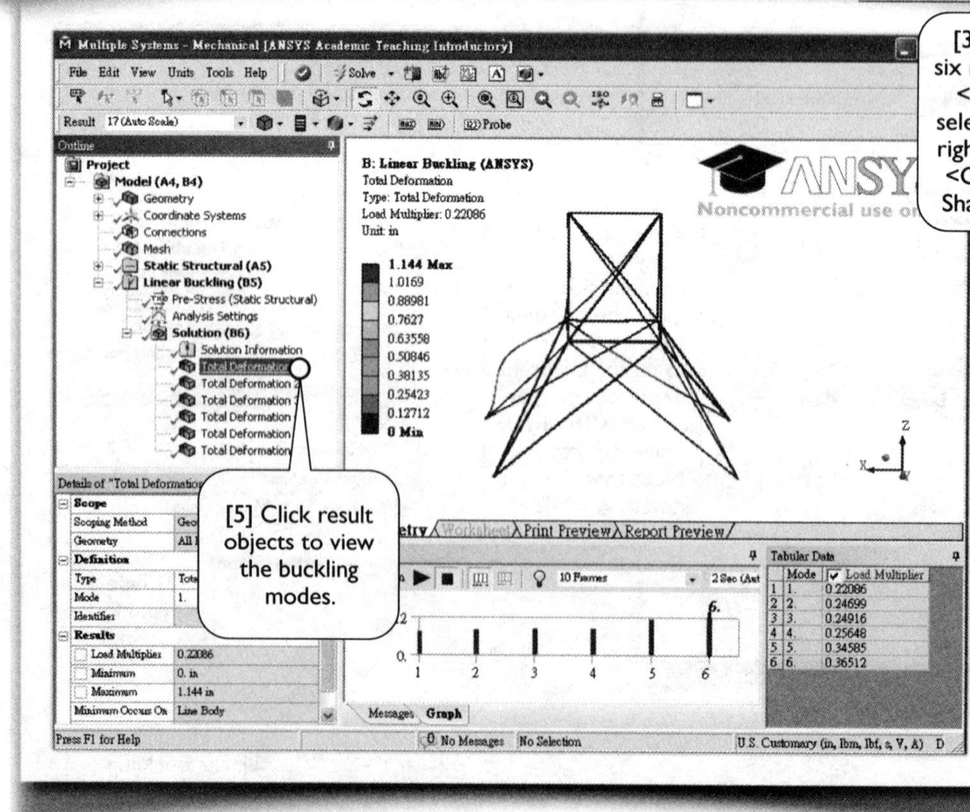

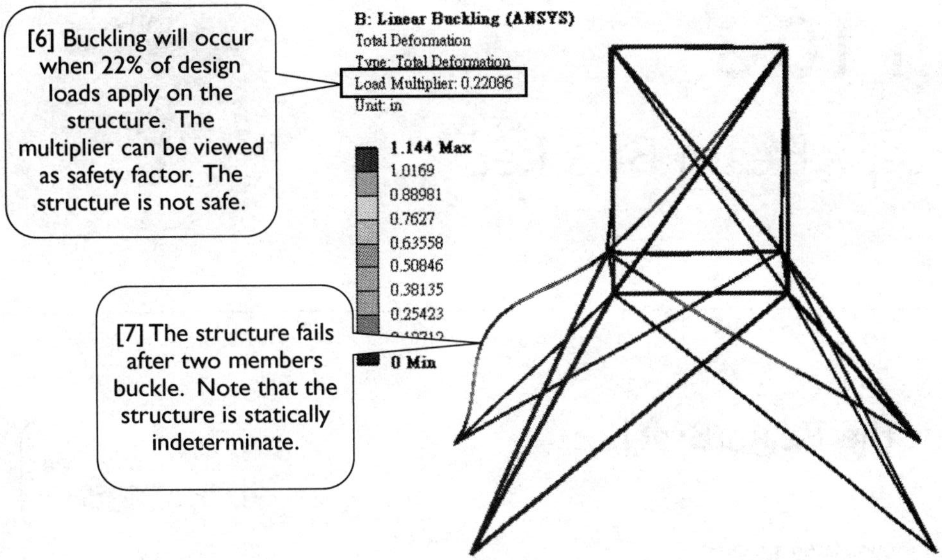

Wrap Up

Close <Mechanical>. Save the project and exit Workbench.

Section 10.3

Step-by-Step: Beam Bracket

10.3-1 About the Beam Bracket

In Sections 5.1 and 6.2, we simulated a beam bracket and obtained some preliminary results, including the deformation and the stress.

Under the design load, the maximum von Mises stress is 85 MPa [1], well below the yield strength, 250 MPa.

By examining minimum principle stress [2, 3], we see that the web is under compression. The maximum compressive stress is about 20-30 MPa. It is a good practice that an engineer always checks the structural stability whenever a mild compressive stress exists, until he has enough experience to judge that the checking is not needed.

In this section, we now want to make sure that, under the design load, the web does not buckle.

The unit system used in this section will be mm-s-N.

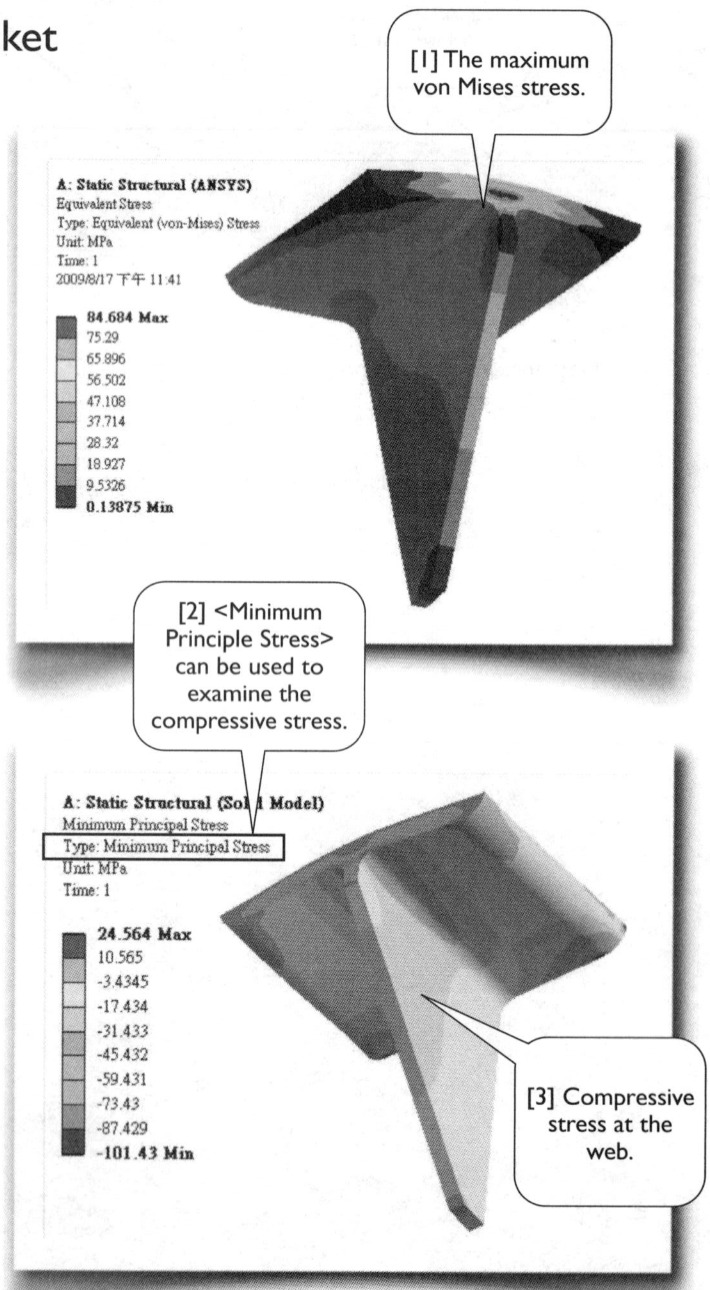

10.3-2 Resume the Project "Bracket"

Launch <Workbench>. Open the project "Bracket," saved in Section 6.2.

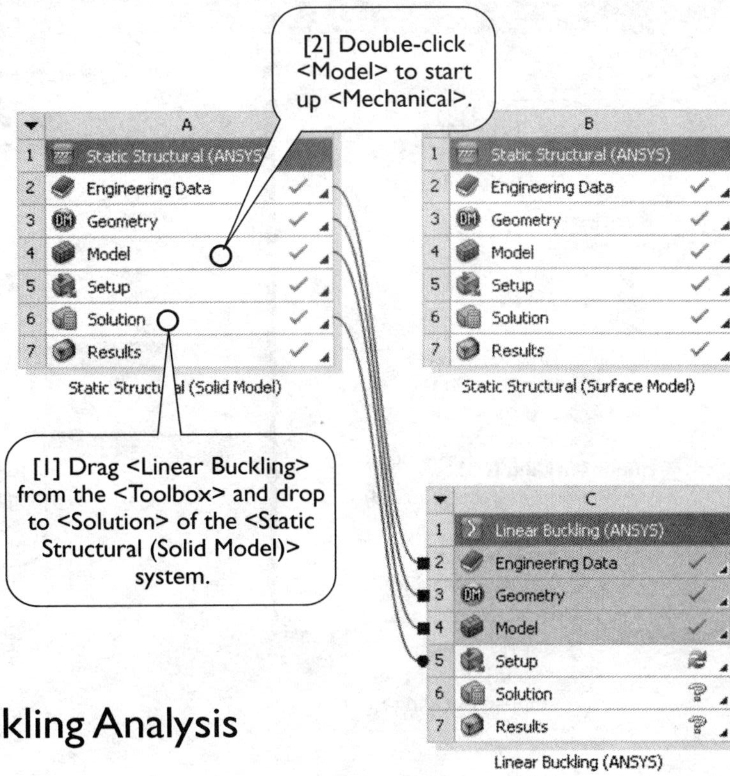

10.3-3 Perform Buckling Analysis

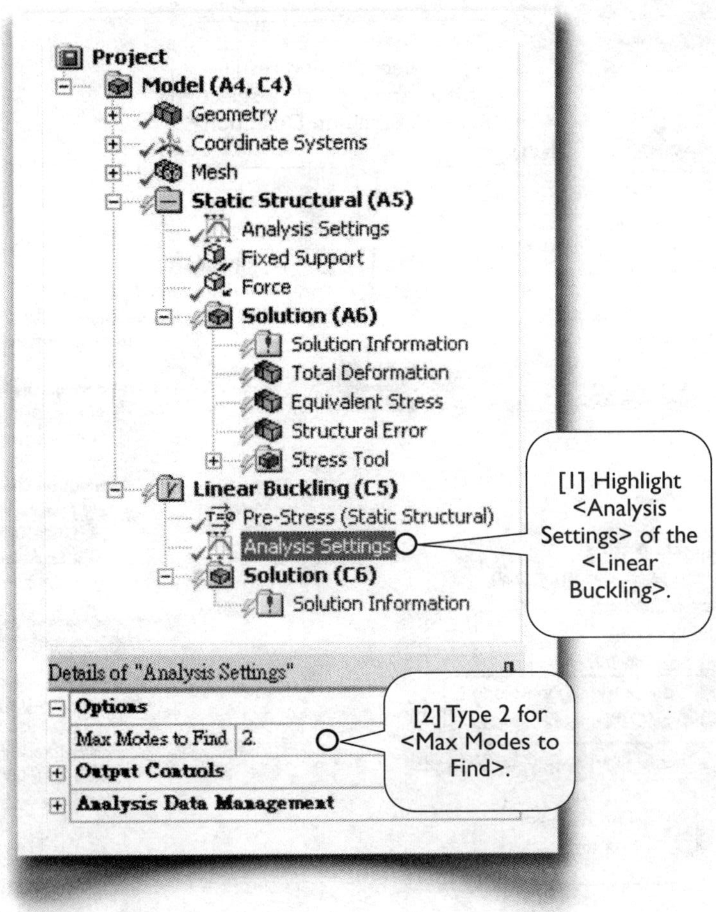

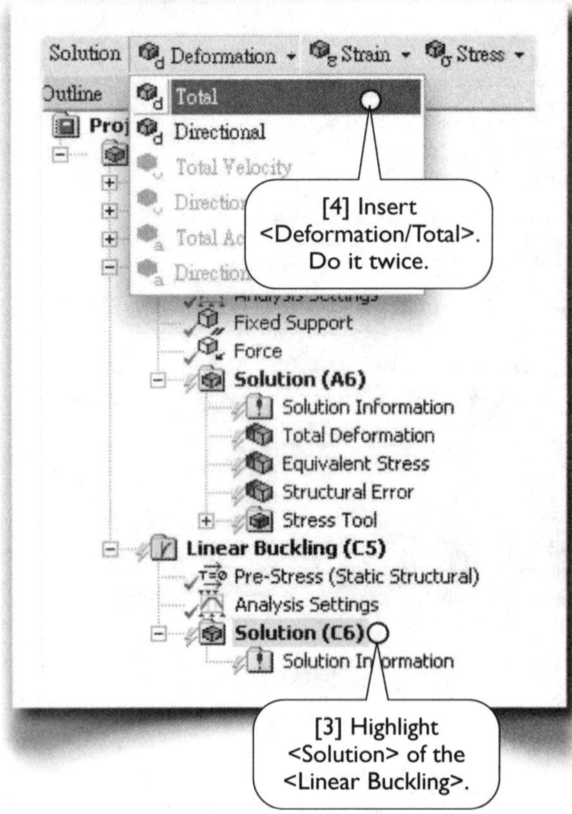
[4] Insert <Deformation/Total>. Do it twice.
[3] Highlight <Solution> of the <Linear Buckling>.

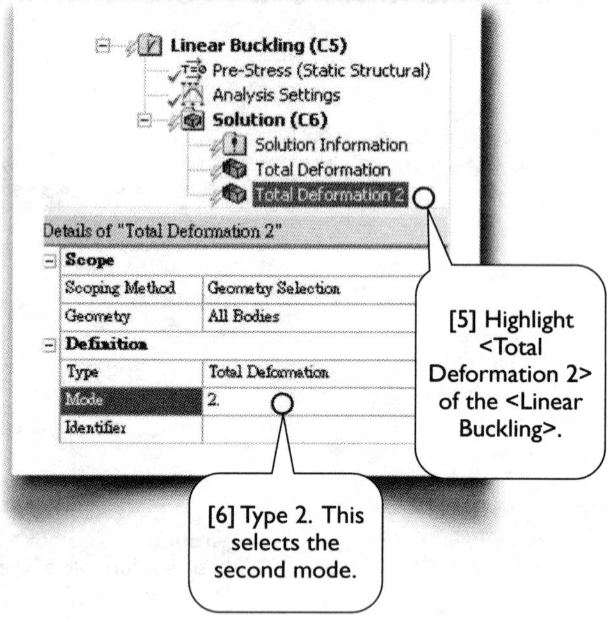
[5] Highlight <Total Deformation 2> of the <Linear Buckling>.
[6] Type 2. This selects the second mode.

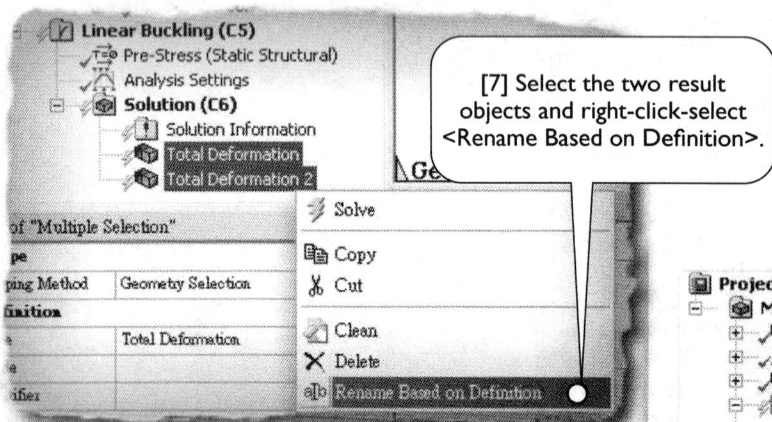
[7] Select the two result objects and right-click-select <Rename Based on Definition>.

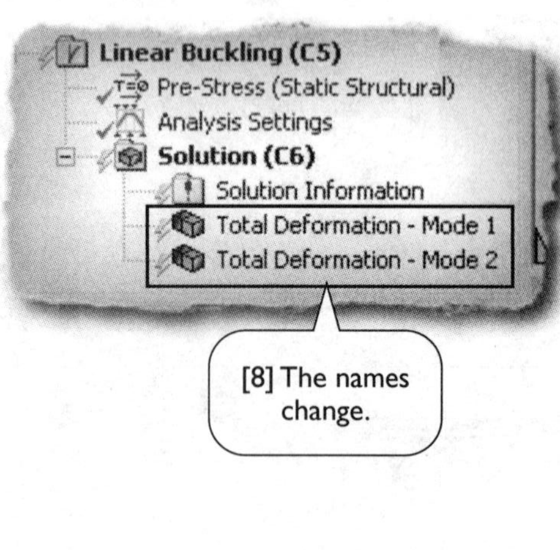
[8] The names change.

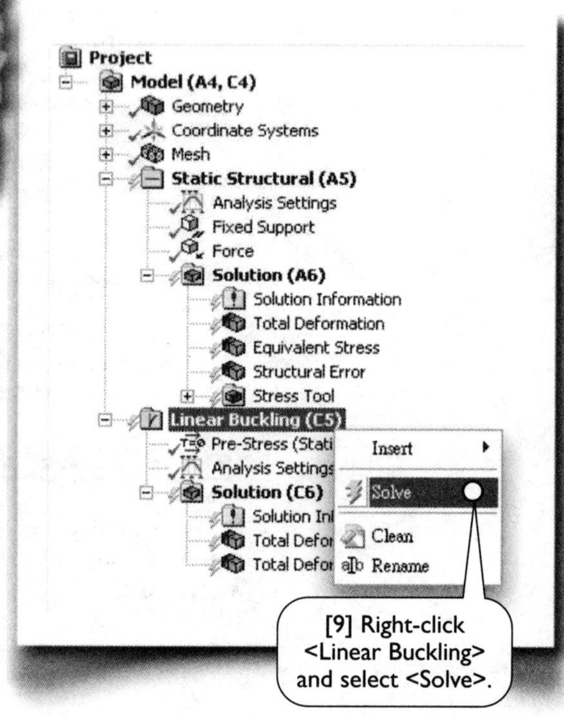
[9] Right-click <Linear Buckling> and select <Solve>.

10.3-4 View the Results

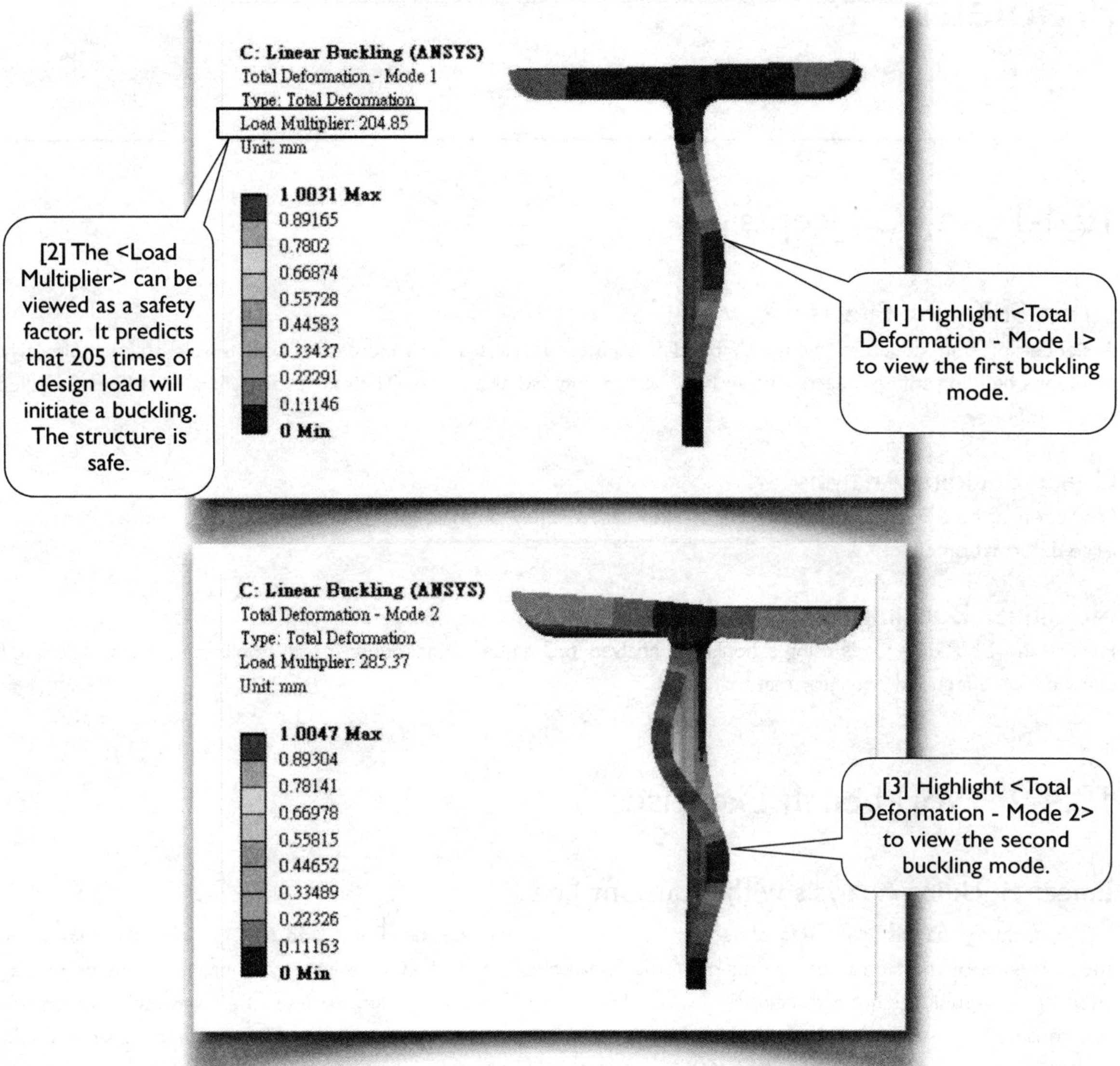

Wrap Up

Close <Mechanical>. Save the project and exit Workbench.

Section 10.4

Problems

10.4-1 Key Concepts

Stress Stiffening Effects

A slender or thin structural member's bending stiffness increases with increasing axial tensile stress. Similarly, the member's bending stiffness decreases with increasing compressive stress. The extra (or deficient) stiffness is called the stress stiffness.

Linear Buckling Analysis

Prediction of buckling loads and buckling modes based solely on initial stress stiffening effect. It doesn't account for large deformation effect.

Nonlinear Buckling Analysis

Prediction of buckling loads using a nonlinear analysis technique. It accounts for all nonlinear effects, including large deformation effect and nonlinear material effect.

10.4-2 Workbench Exercises

Linear Buckling Analysis with Constant Loads

In the buckling analysis at the end of Section 10.1, we didn't include the lateral load (0.1 N/mm). You may wonder if the existence of the lateral load would alter the linear buckling load. Our engineering intuition tells us that a little lateral load would significantly decrease the buckling load. In linear buckling analysis, the large deformation effect is not considered. As a result, the lateral load has limited influence on the buckling loads. In our case, since the lateral load is so small, the buckling load predicted by a linear buckling analysis will be essentially the same regardless of the presence of the lateral load. This exercise requires you to verify this point.

To do this, you are performing a linear buckling analysis with constant loads. Remember that a linear buckling analysis reports a multiplier. Buckling loads are ALL the applied loads multiply by the multiplier. If the model involves a constant load, then there is no sense to multiply that constant load unless the multiplier equals a unity. Iterating on buckling analysis and trying to obtain a multiplier of unity is exactly the approach you should use when performing a linear buckling analysis with constant loads.

Buckling Pressure of the Bellows Joints

The bellows joint, simulated in Section 6.1, is subject to external pressure when used in the deep ocean. If the external pressure is larger than the internal pressure, then its stability must be checked. This exercise asks you to predict the net pressure (difference between external and internal pressures) that causes the bellows joint to buckle. Study its buckling modes.

Buckling Torque of a Pipe

Applying a twist on a thin aluminum pipe will introduce tensile stress on part of the pipe and compressive stress on other part of the pipe. Excess compressive stress may cause the skin to buckle. Model an aluminum pipe of a diameter of 30 mm and a thickness of 0.2 mm, and predict the torque that causes the skin to buckle. Study the buckling modes.

Chapter 11

Modal Analysis

As mentioned in Section 1.1-10, when the material of a structure moves very fast, dynamic effects must be included in the simulation. Purpose of modal analyses is to investigate the dynamic characteristics of free vibrations, vibrations without external forces. The most important characteristics of free vibrations are the natural frequencies and their corresponding vibration mode shapes.

Purpose of the Chapter

Why do we need to know the natural frequencies and the mode shapes? First, these dynamic characteristics are rudimentary for more involved dynamic simulations, for examples, transient dynamic simulations or harmonic response analyses. Besides, modal analysis has many usages in its own right. This chapter provides several examples to demonstrate the usage of modal analyses.

About Each Section

Section 1 uses the gearbox, discussed in Section 6.3, as an example to illustrate a common consideration when designing a machine involving rotational parts: avoiding resonance. Section 2 uses the two-story building, discussed in Section 7.3, to demonstrate the use of modal analysis to find the weakest direction of a structure and improve the stiffness of that direction. Section 3 discusses a case in the popular TV series *Mythbusters*, in which they succeeded in shattering CDs with a high rotational speed. Some people may have a myth that the shattering is due to the excessive centrifugal stress (e.g., see Wikipedia>CD shattering). This section is designed to bust that myth, by proving that the shattering is due to vibrations rather than the centrifugal stress. Section 4 provides a discussion of the physics of music, which are closely related to modal analysis, using a guitar string as an example.

Section 11.1
Step-by-Step: Gearbox

11.1-1 About the Gearbox

In Section 6.3, we built a model for a gearbox and performed a static structural simulation using the model. Deformation and stresses were calculated, and they seem within safety margin under the static design loads. Dynamic behavior, however, should be investigated for a problem like this.

The gearbox is designed for a speed reducer. The maximum speed at input is 630 rpm (or 10.5 Hz). The gearbox must be stiff enough such that, during the operation, resonance does not occur. Resonance is harmful because it enlarges the deformation and the stresses. It also causes noises.

In this section, we want to perform a modal analysis to investigate the natural frequencies of the gearbox, to make sure these natural frequencies are much higher than the operational frequency (630 rpm).

The students may raise a question whether the design bearing loads (Section 6.3-7) should be applied or not, when evaluating the natural frequencies. Generally speaking, the answer is yes, since the prestress will modify the stiffness (called stress stiffening effect, see Section 10.1). In the old days, since these "prestressed modal analyses" were expensive to carry out, engineers tended to neglect the prestress effect when, according to their experiences, they knew that the prestress effect is negligible.

In this section, we will perform modal analysis twice, one with prestress, another without, to show that the effect of the prestress in this case is negligible. Note that, in other cases, the effect of prestress may be significant.

11.1-2 Resume the Project "GearBox"

Launch <Workbench>. Open the project "Gearbox," saved in Section 6.3.

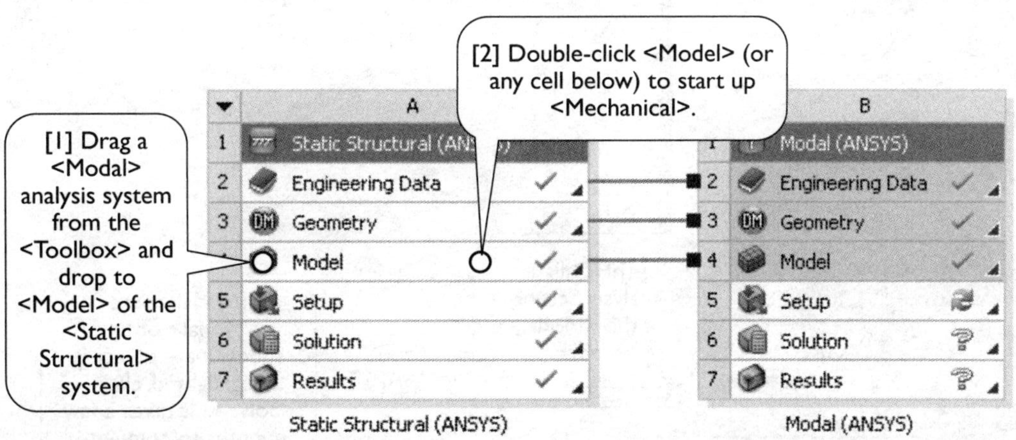

<Static Structural> Simulation is Not Always Needed for a Modal Analysis

We are now performing an "unprestressed modal analysis." When performing an unprestressed modal analysis, the <Static Structural> analysis is not needed. You could have dragged a <Modal> system to the <Geometry> of the <Static Structural> system, and then deleted the <Static Structural> system. We kept the <Static Structural> system just because we want to reuse the system (Section 11.1-5).

11.1-3 Perform Modal Analysis

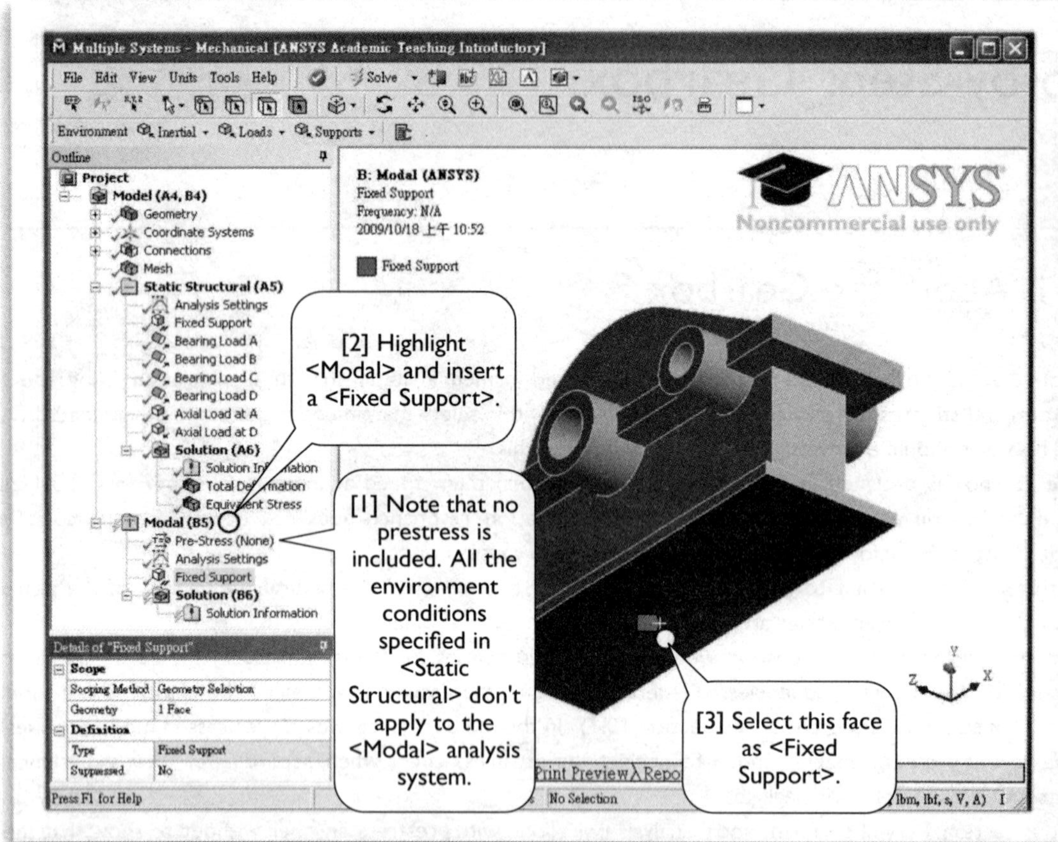

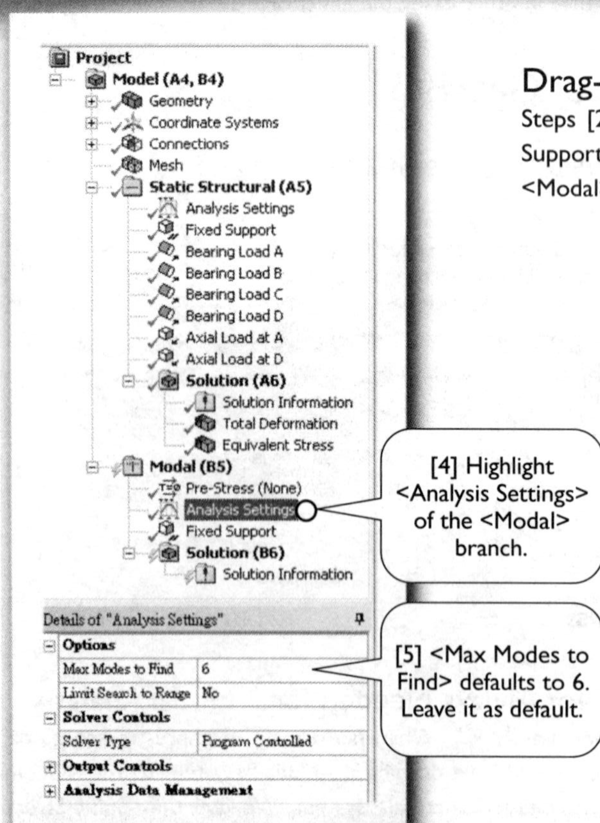

Drag-and-Drop a Tree Object

Steps [2, 3] can be replaced by dragging the <Fixed Support> of <Static Structural> and dropping to the <Modal> branch.

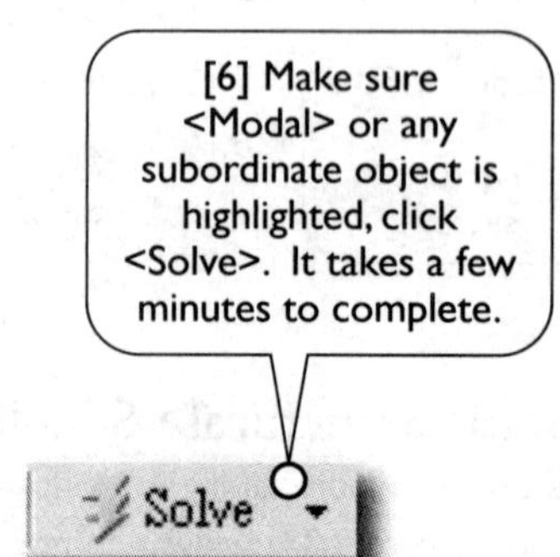

11.1-4 View the Results

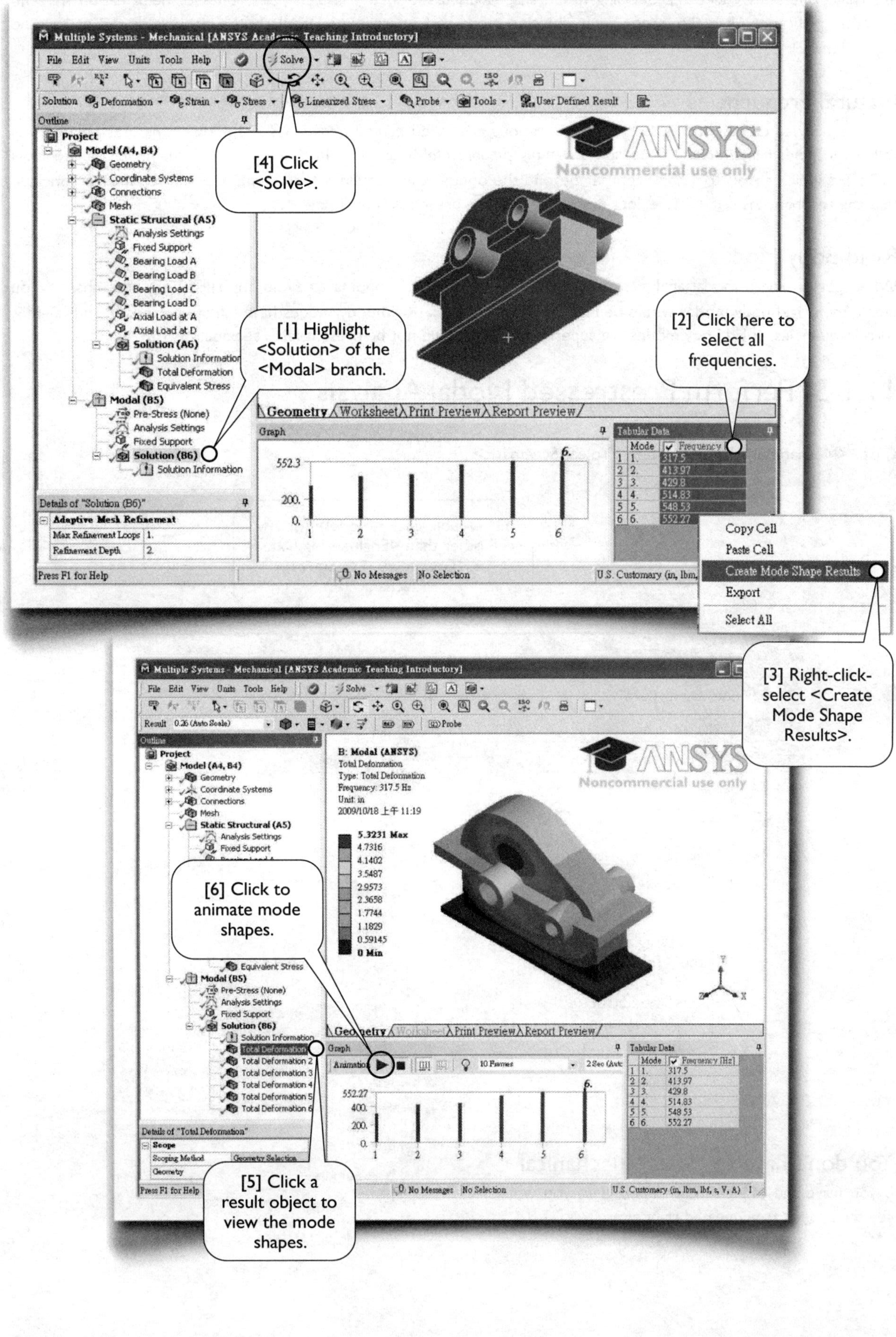

Free Vibration Mode Shapes

The vibrations obtained in the modal analysis are called *free vibrations* since the vibrations are not subject to any external excitations. Like the buckling mode shapes discussed in the last chapter, values of deformation have no physical significance. It is the "shape" of a vibration mode that interests us. Similarly, the stresses or strains have no physical meaning.

Natural Frequencies

The frequencies corresponding to the free vibrations are called *natural frequencies*. The lowest natural frequency is called the *fundamental natural frequency*, or simply *fundamental frequency*. In this case, the fundamental frequency is 317.5 Hz, which equals to 19,050 rpm, far beyond the operational frequency (630 rpm). Before we jump to conclude that the resonance is not an issue, let's make sure that the prestress is negligible.

Rigid Body Modes

When performing a modal analysis, you should provide enough supports to avoid any rigid body motions. If you didn't, then rigid body modes would be included in the results. Rigid body modes have infinite period, or, equivalently, zero frequencies. Rigid body modes are superfluous, and should not be present (also see Section 10.1-4).

11.1-5 Perform Prestressed Modal Analysis

Close <Mechanical>. Return to the <Project Schematic>.

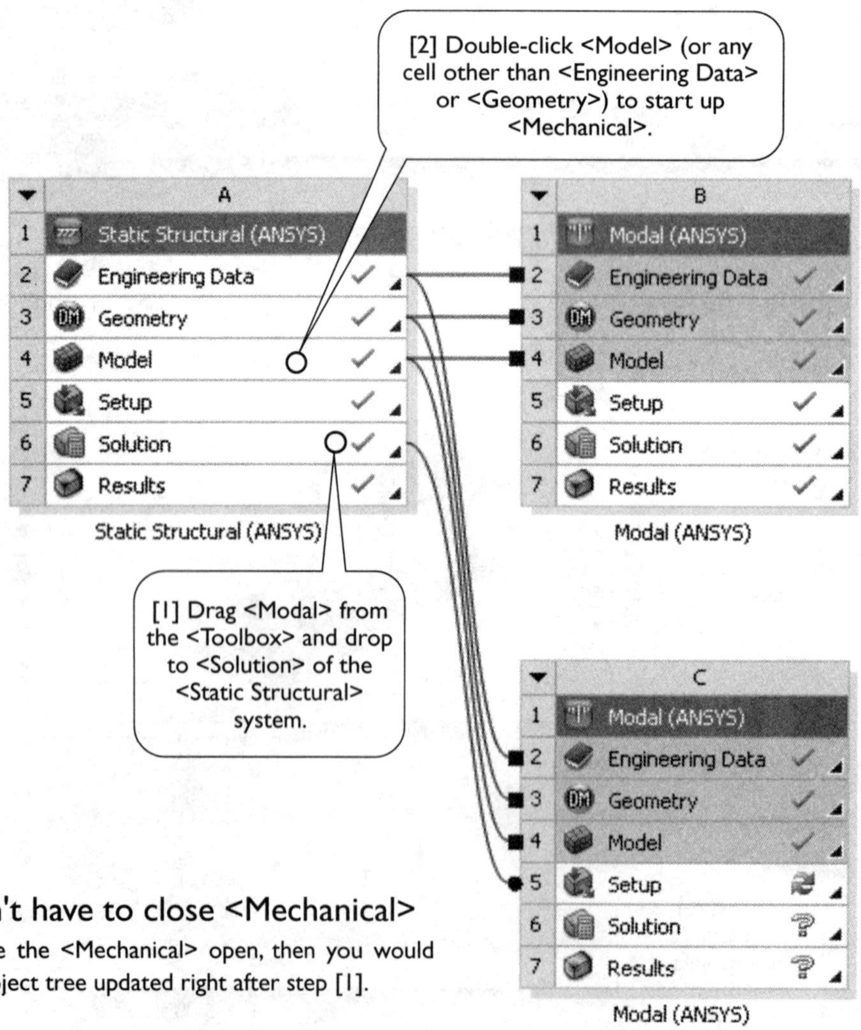

You don't have to close <Mechanical>

If you leave the <Mechanical> open, then you would see the project tree updated right after step [1].

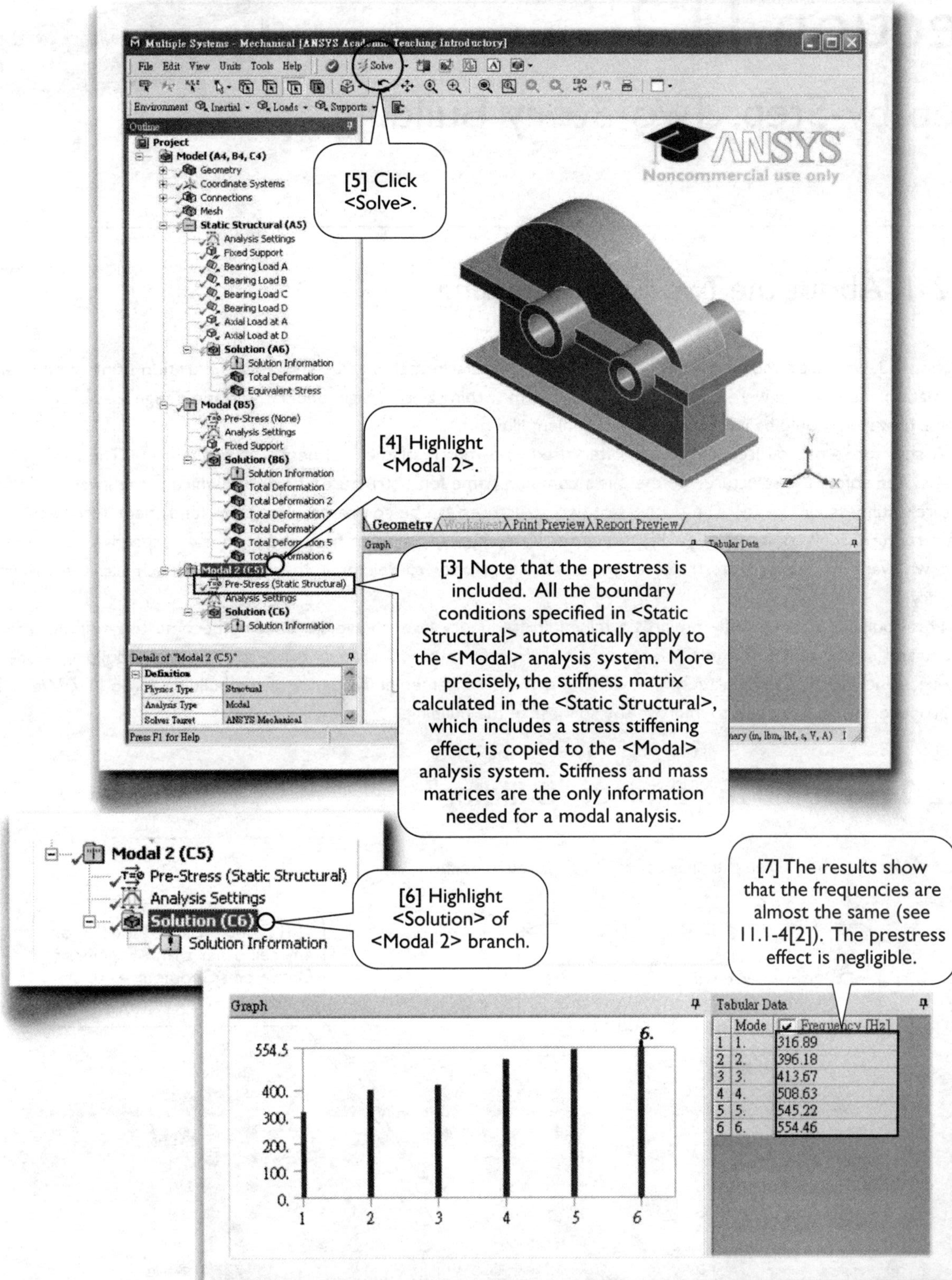

Wrap Up

Close <Mechanical>. Save the project and exit Workbench.

Section 11.2

Step-by-Step: Two-Story Building

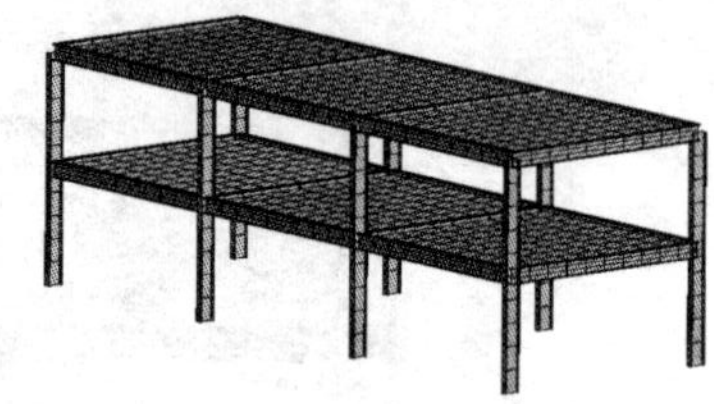

11.2-1 About the Two-Story Building

In Section 7.3, we built a model for a two-story building and performed a static structural simulation using the model. Deformation and stresses were calculated, and they seem within safety margin under the static design loads. Dynamic behavior, however, should be investigated for a problem like this.

A structure's natural frequencies are often used as a metric of the "softness" the structure. The lower the frequency, the softer the structure. Softness is a common name for a structure's flexibility, which is the inverse of the structure's stiffness, or rigidity. The softness of two structures can be compared using their fundamental frequencies. For a structure, softness in different directions can be compared using its frequencies in the respective directions. When we want to reinforce a structure, we may take priority to reinforce the direction which has the lowest frequency.

Local building codes usually requires a minimum frequency level to avoid a building become too soft, both for comfort and safety concerns. In this section, we will perform modal analysis using the two-story building model. Prestress is included in the simulation. We will find that the fundamental frequency of the building is too low. We will then propose a simple solution to improve the stiffness of the building.

11.2-2 Resume the Project "Building"

Launch <Workbench>. Open the project "Building," saved in Section 7.3.

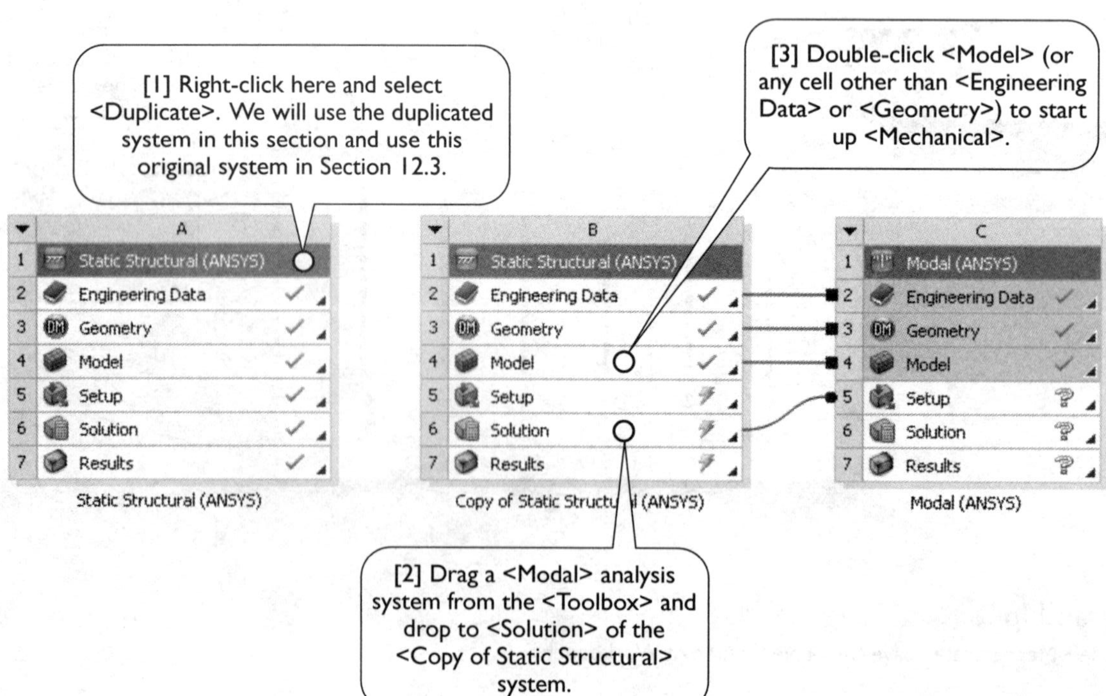

11.2-3 Perform Modal Analysis

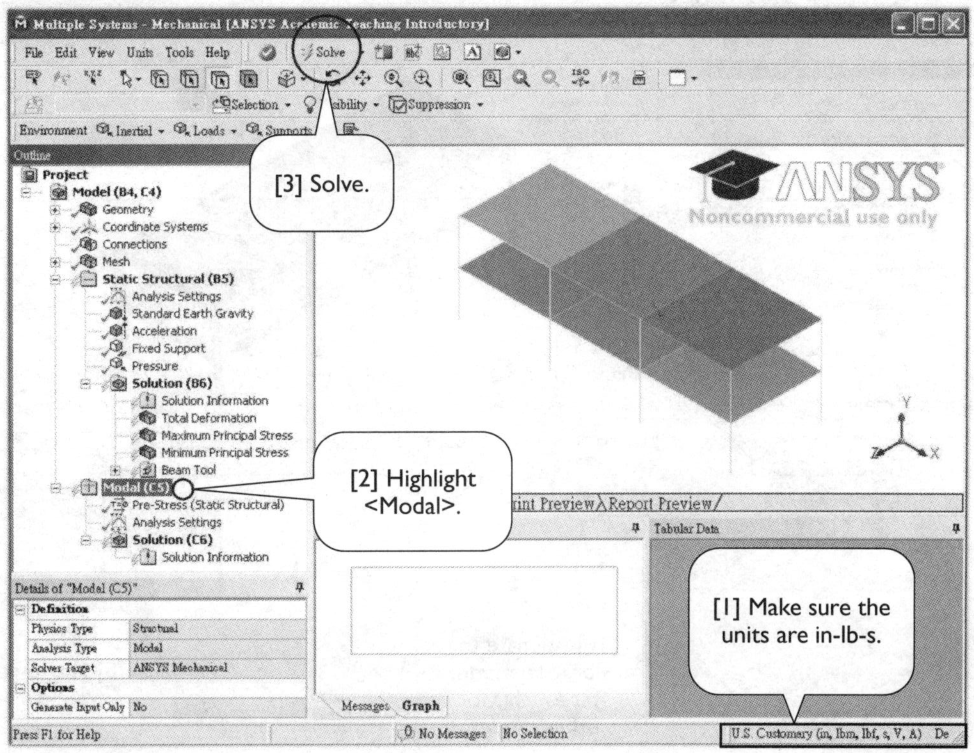

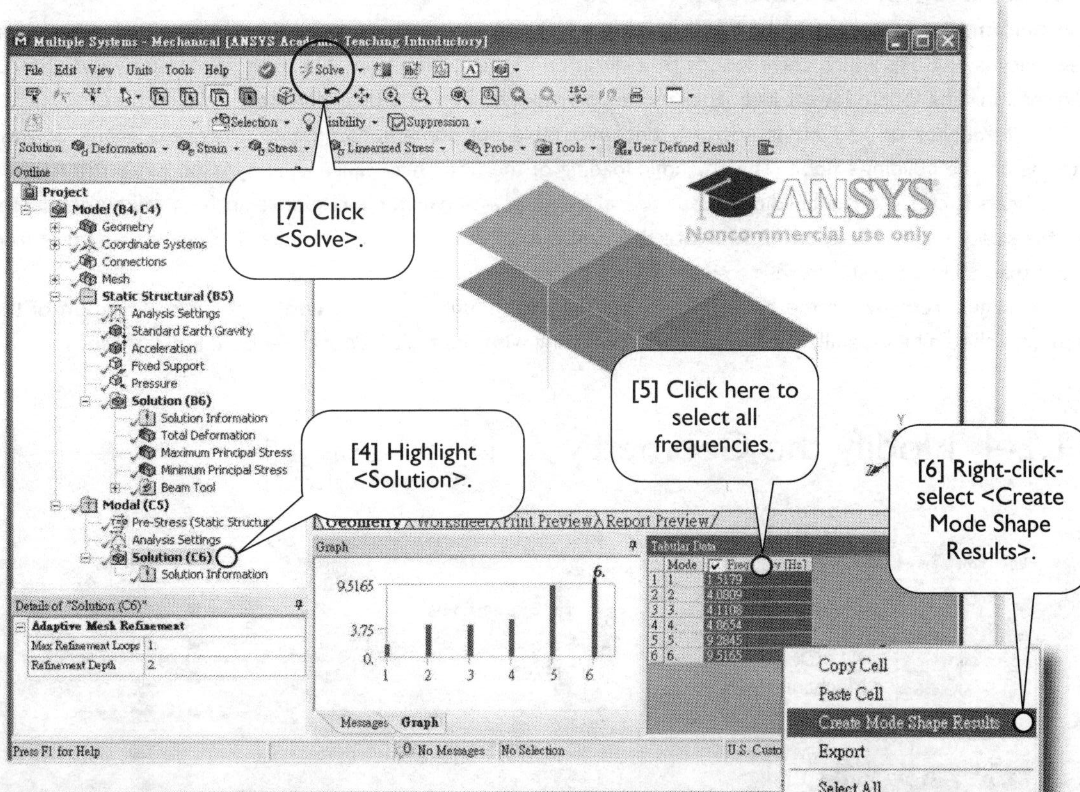

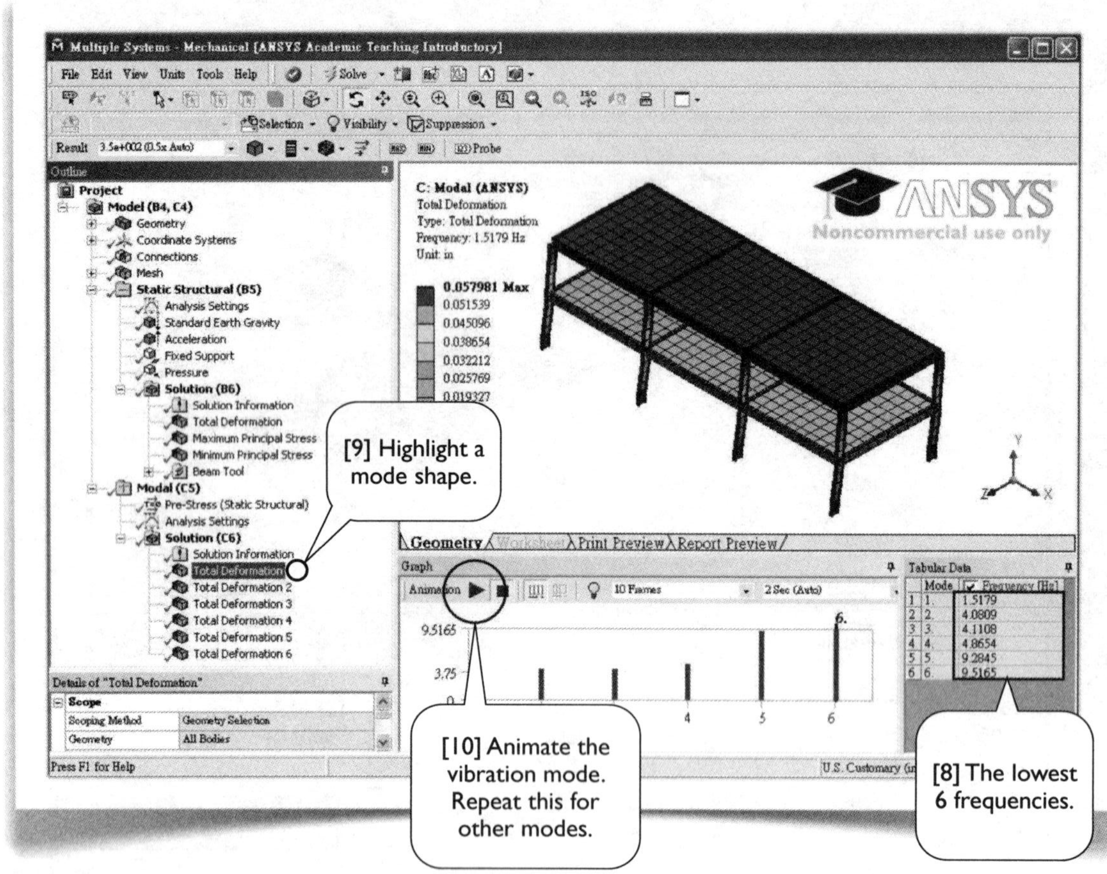

A Discussion of the Vibration Modes

The fundamental frequency is 1.52 Hz, which corresponds to a vibration in the X-direction. The second lowest frequency is 4.08 Hz, which corresponds to a vibration in the Z-direction. The third lowest frequency mode is also in X-direction. The fourth lowest frequency mode corresponds to a torsional vibration in Y-direction.

A frequency of 1.52 Hz is not only uncomfortable but sometimes unsafe. Imagine a group of young people dancing on the building's floor. The rhythmic loading of the floor may cause a safety issue, since the frequency of the music beats is close to the building's fundamental frequency. A harmonic response analysis will be conducted to clear up this safety issue in Section 12.3. Note that some local building codes require a structure's natural frequency be larger than 5 Hz if the structure is to be used as a dance floor in a venue.

A simple remedy for the building is to add diagonal members to the weak direction. Location of the diagonal members should be carefully chosen to avoid conflicting with the building's architectural functionalities.

11.2-4 Modify the Geometry

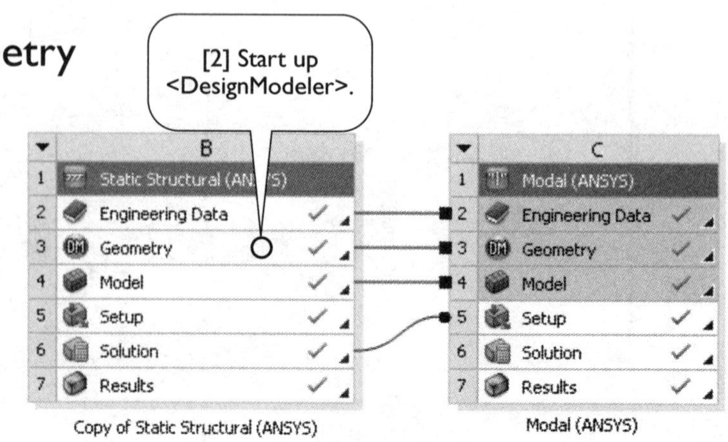

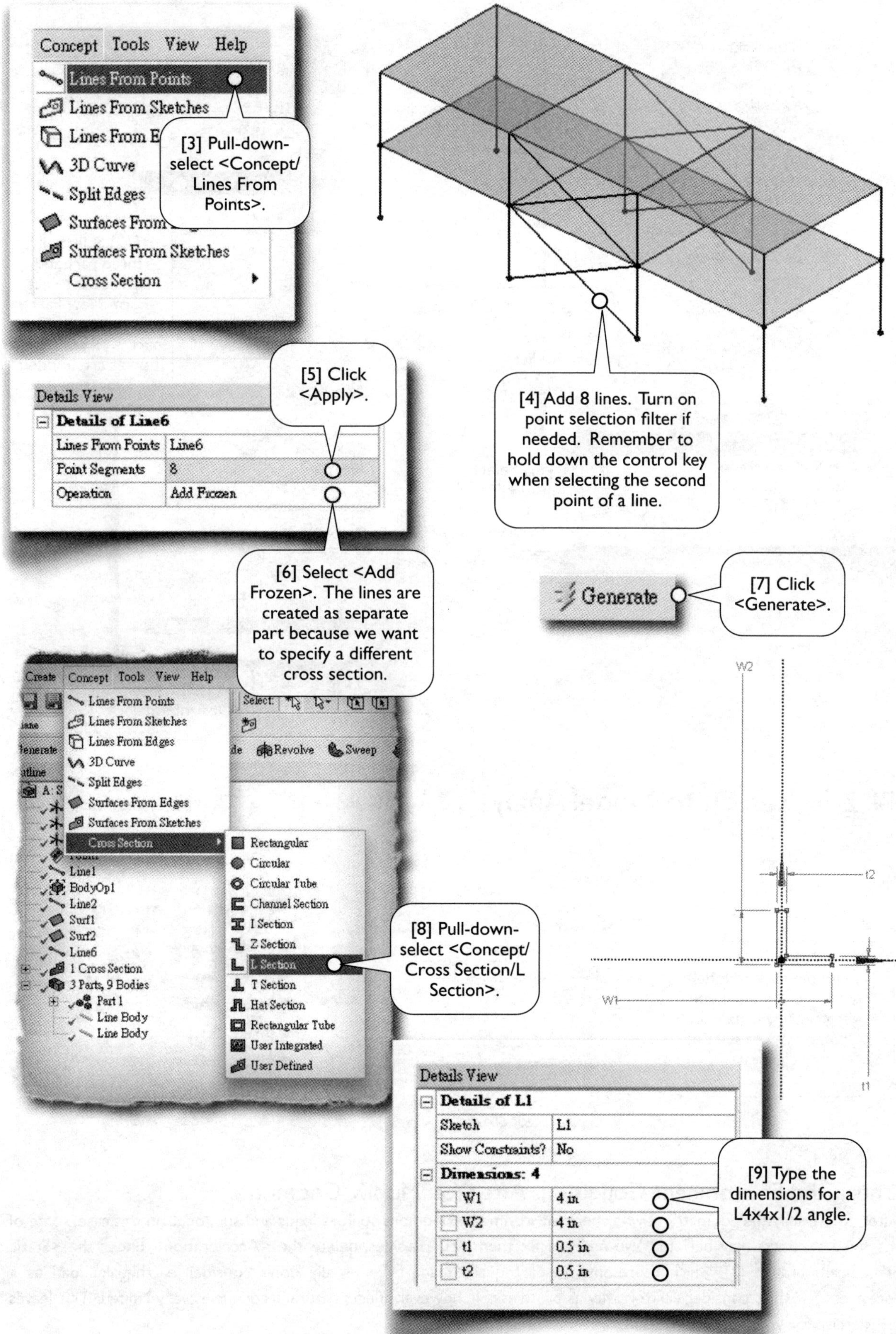
Concept Tools View Help
Lines From Points
Lines From Sketches
3D Curve
Split Edges
Surfaces From Sketches
Cross Section
[3] Pull-down-select <Concept/ Lines From Points>.
[4] Add 8 lines. Turn on point selection filter if needed. Remember to hold down the control key when selecting the second point of a line.
Details View
Details of Line6
Lines From Points Line6
Point Segments 8
Operation Add Frozen
[5] Click <Apply>.
[6] Select <Add Frozen>. The lines are created as separate part because we want to specify a different cross section.
Generate
[7] Click <Generate>.
Rectangular
Circular
Circular Tube
Channel Section
I Section
Z Section
L Section
T Section
Hat Section
Rectangular Tube
User Integrated
User Defined
[8] Pull-down-select <Concept/ Cross Section/L Section>.
W2
t2
W1
t1
Details of L1
Sketch L1
Show Constraints? No
Dimensions: 4
W1 4 in
W2 4 in
t1 0.5 in
t2 0.5 in
[9] Type the dimensions for a L4x4x1/2 angle.

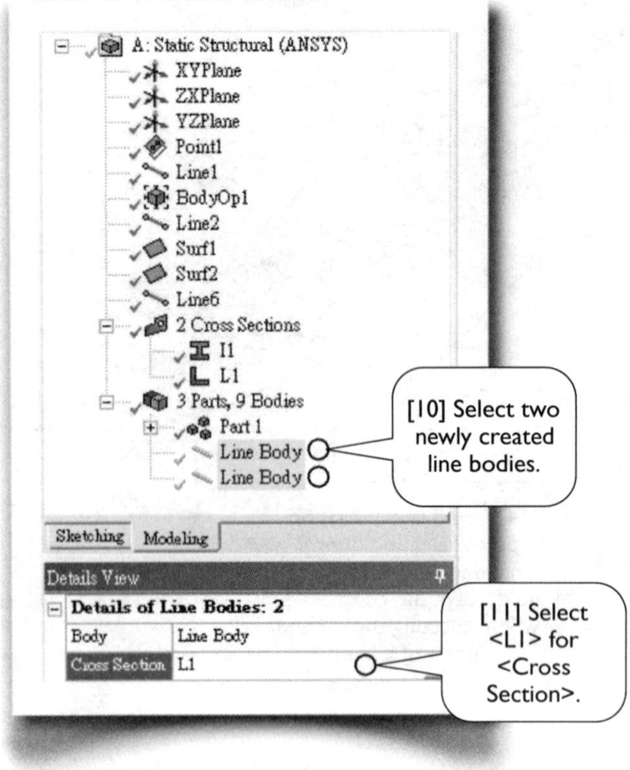

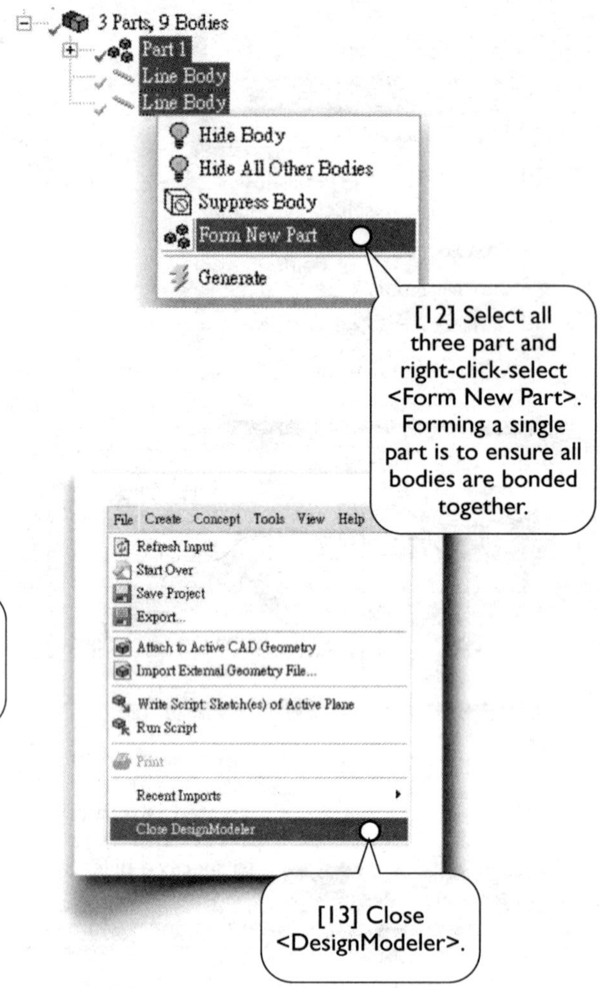

11.2-5 Return to Model Analysis

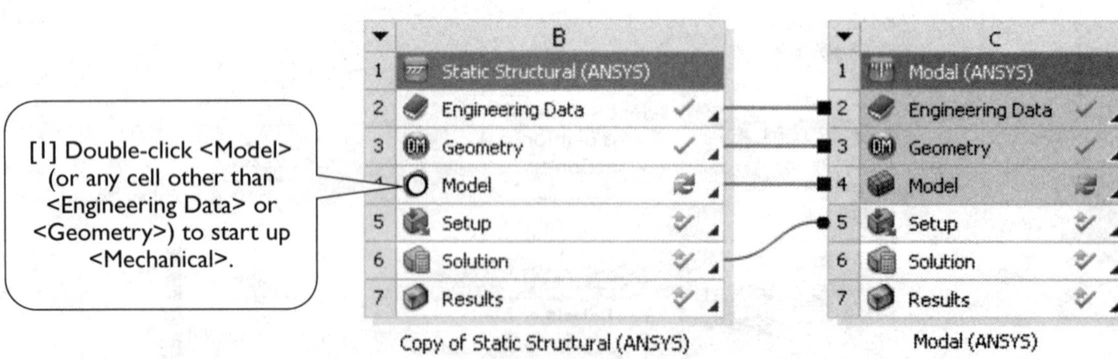

Check the Environment Conditions After You Modify Geometry

After you modify the geometry, always check environment conditions such as loads and supports. In this case, some of the fixed supports may be lost. We need to fix them [2]. Besides, delete the <Acceleration> under the <Static Structural> branch [3], which represents an earthquake load. We usually don't consider earthquake load as a "prestress." We do consider earth gravity as prestress. It, however, affects natural frequencies very limited. This leaves an exercise for you (Section 11.5-2).

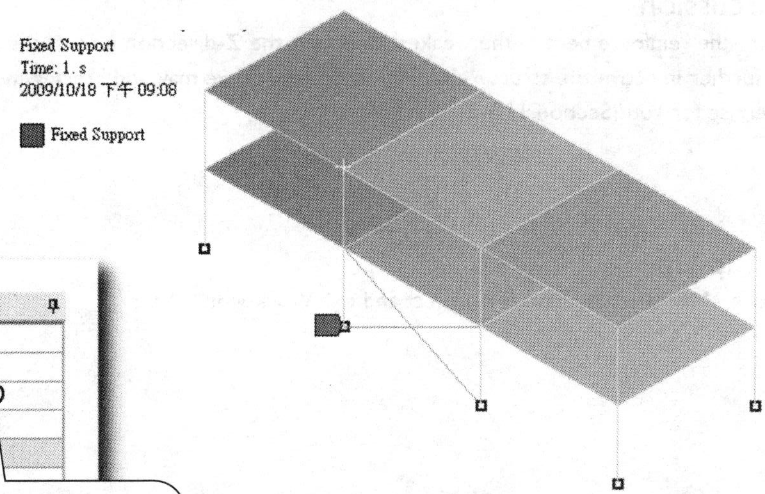

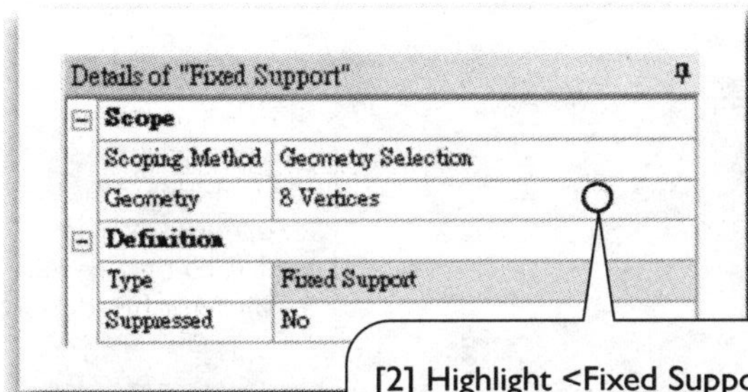

[2] Highlight <Fixed Support> in the <Static Structural> branch, select 8 vertices at the column bases, and click <Apply>. Turn on vertex selection filter if needed.

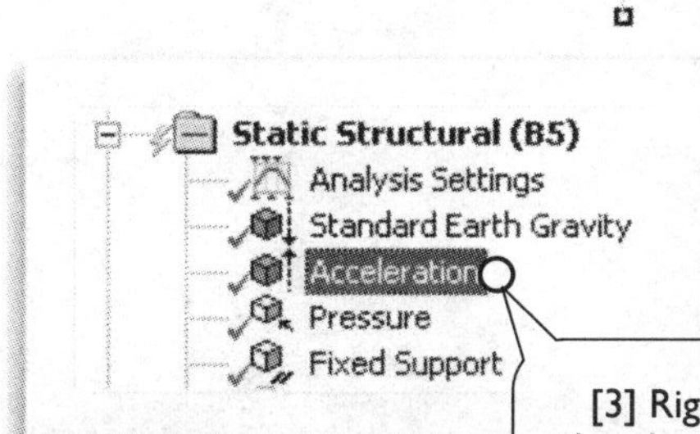

[3] Right-click <Acceleration> and select <Delete>.

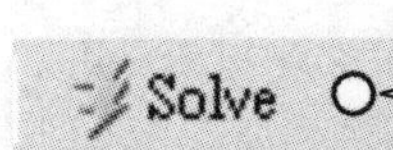

[4] Highlight <Modal> and click <Solve>.

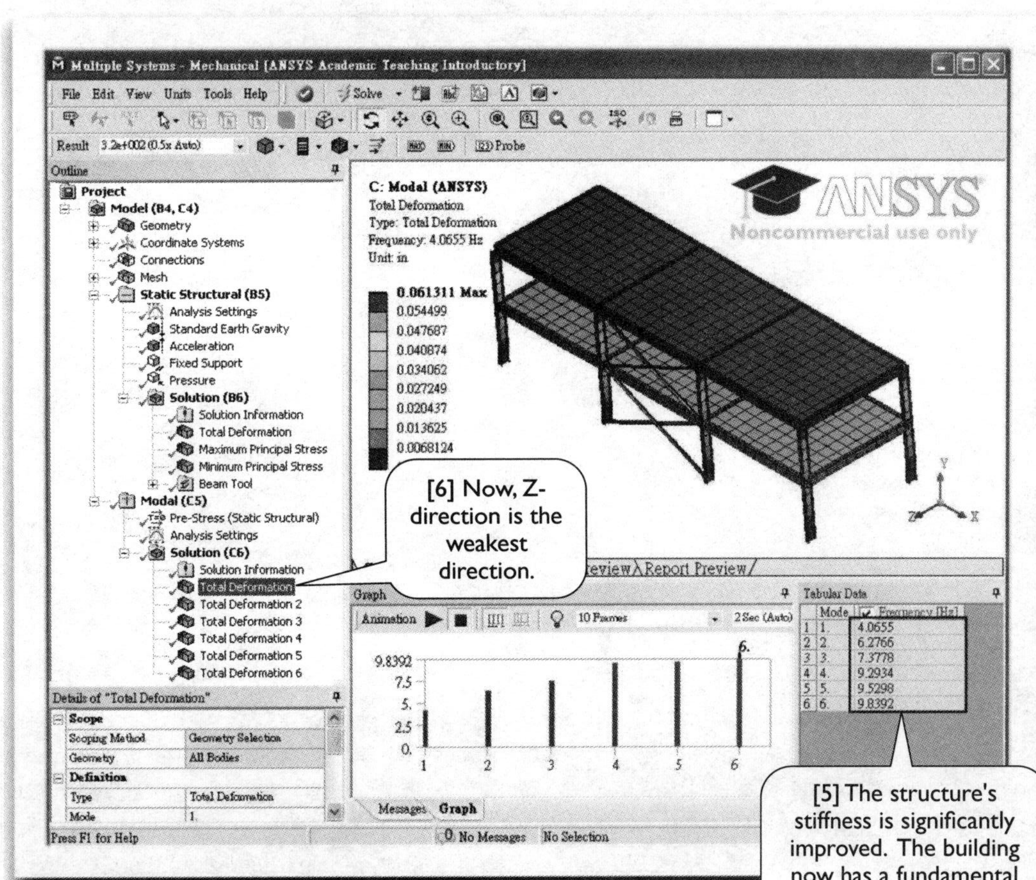

[6] Now, Z-direction is the weakest direction.

[5] The structure's stiffness is significantly improved. The building now has a fundamental frequency of 4.1 Hz.

Discussion

After the reinforcement in the weakest direction, the Z-direction now sticks out as the weakest direction. If we want to further improve the structure's stiffness, or rigidity, we may add bracing members in the Z-direction. This leaves an exercise for you (Section 11.5-2).

Wrap Up

Close <Mechanical>. Save the project and exit Workbench.

Section 11.3
Exercise: Compact Disk

11.3-1 About the Compact Disk

The CD is made of polycarbonate (PC) [1], with density 1200 kg/m^3, Young's modulus 2.2 GPa, Poisson ratio 0.37, and tensile strength 65 MPa. The sizes are 120 mm (outer diameter) by 15 mm (inner diameter) by 1.2 mm (thickness). For a 52x CD drive, the maximum rotational speed can reach 27,500 rpm (458 Hz) when reading the inner tracks, and the minimum speed is 11,000 rpm (183 Hz) when reading the outer tracks.

The television series *MythBusters* conducted experiments[1] in which they succeeded in shattering CDs at speeds of 23,000 rpm. In this section, we want to find out the maximum stress in the CD due to the centrifugal force when rotating in 27,500 rpm, to justify if the shattering is indeed due to the high stress.

Second, we want to find the natural frequencies of the CD to investigate the possibility of resonant vibrations. We will conclude that the CD shattering may be due to sustaining vibrations rather than centrifugal stress. Also, we want to demonstrate that the natural frequencies increase with increasing rotational speed.

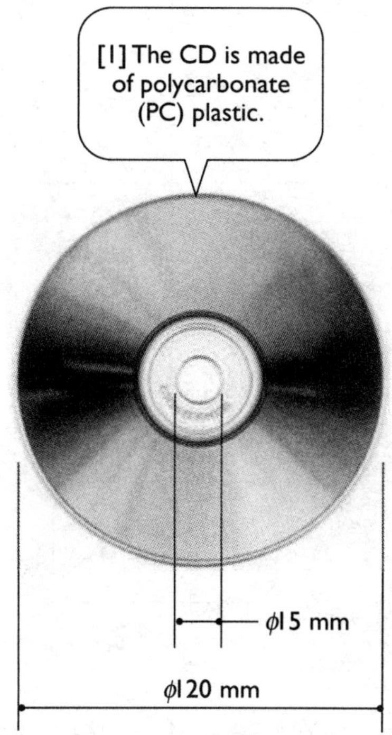

11.3-2 Start Up a new Project

Launch <Workbench>. Create a <Static Structural> analysis system [1]. Save the project as "CD." Double-click <Engineering Data> and create a new material with the name "PC" [2]. Input the material properties, including density (1200 kg/m3), Young's modulus (2.2 GPa), and Poisson's ratio (0.37) [3]. Start up DesignModeler, select <Millimeter> as length unit [4].

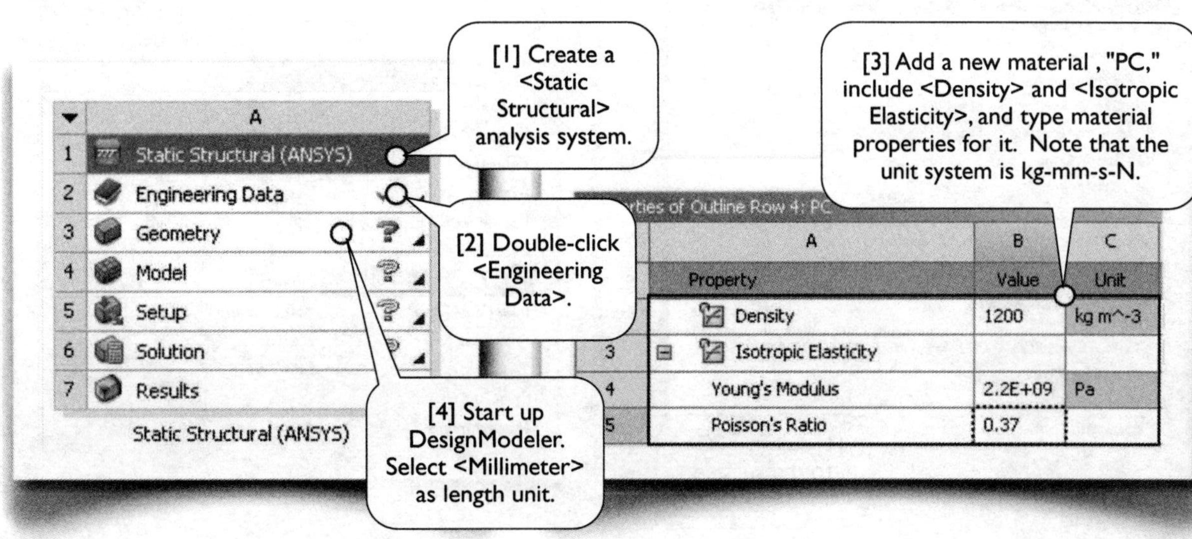

11.3-3 Create Geometry in DesignModeler

Draw a sketch on the XYPlane as shown [1]. Pull-down-select <Concept/Surfaces From Sketches> to create a surface body [2]. Close DesignModeler.

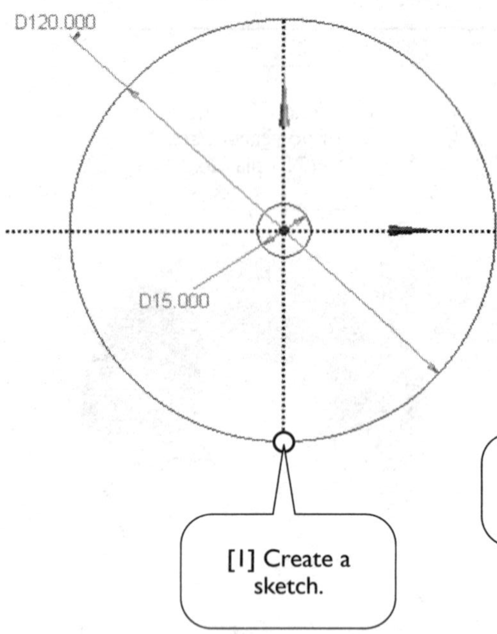

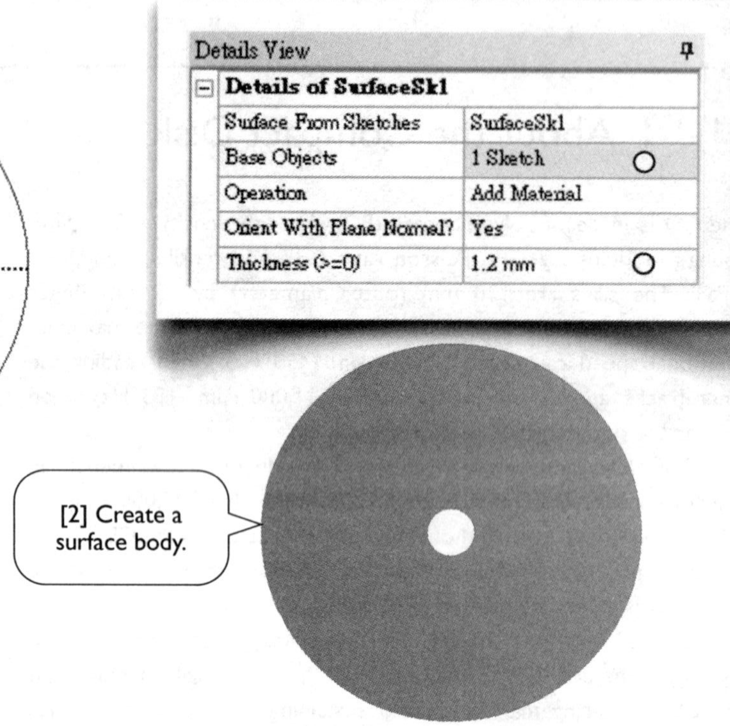

11.3-4 Assess Centrifugal Stress

Start up <Mechanical>. Make sure the unit system is mm-s-N. Assign the material <PC> to the surface body [1]. Specify 2.0 (mm) for the global element size [2]. Select inner rim of the CD and insert a <Fixed Support> [3]. Insert a <Rotational Velocity> load and type 27500 (RPM) for <Z Component> [4, 5]. Insert a <Maximum Principle Stress> [6]. Solve the model [7].

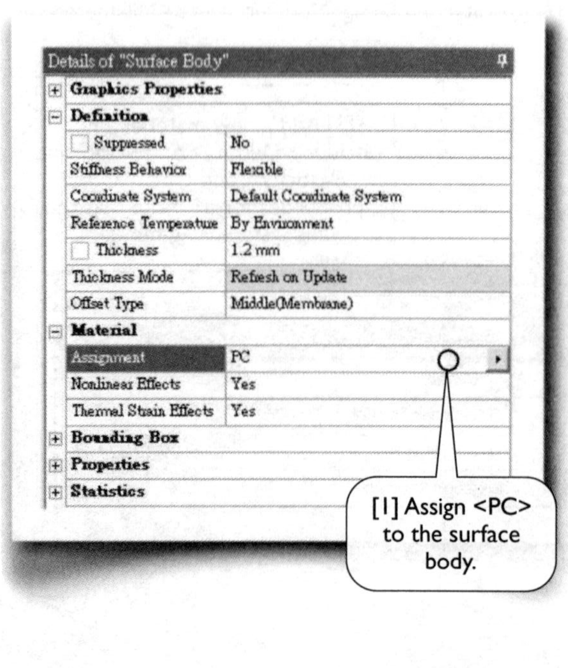

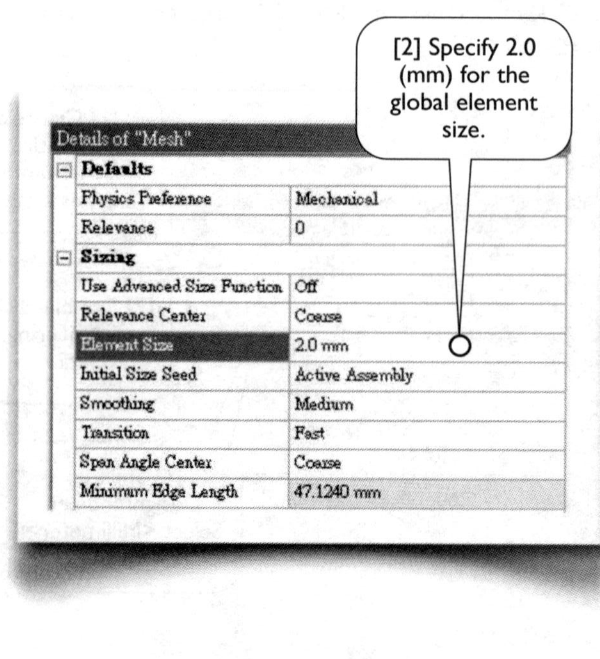

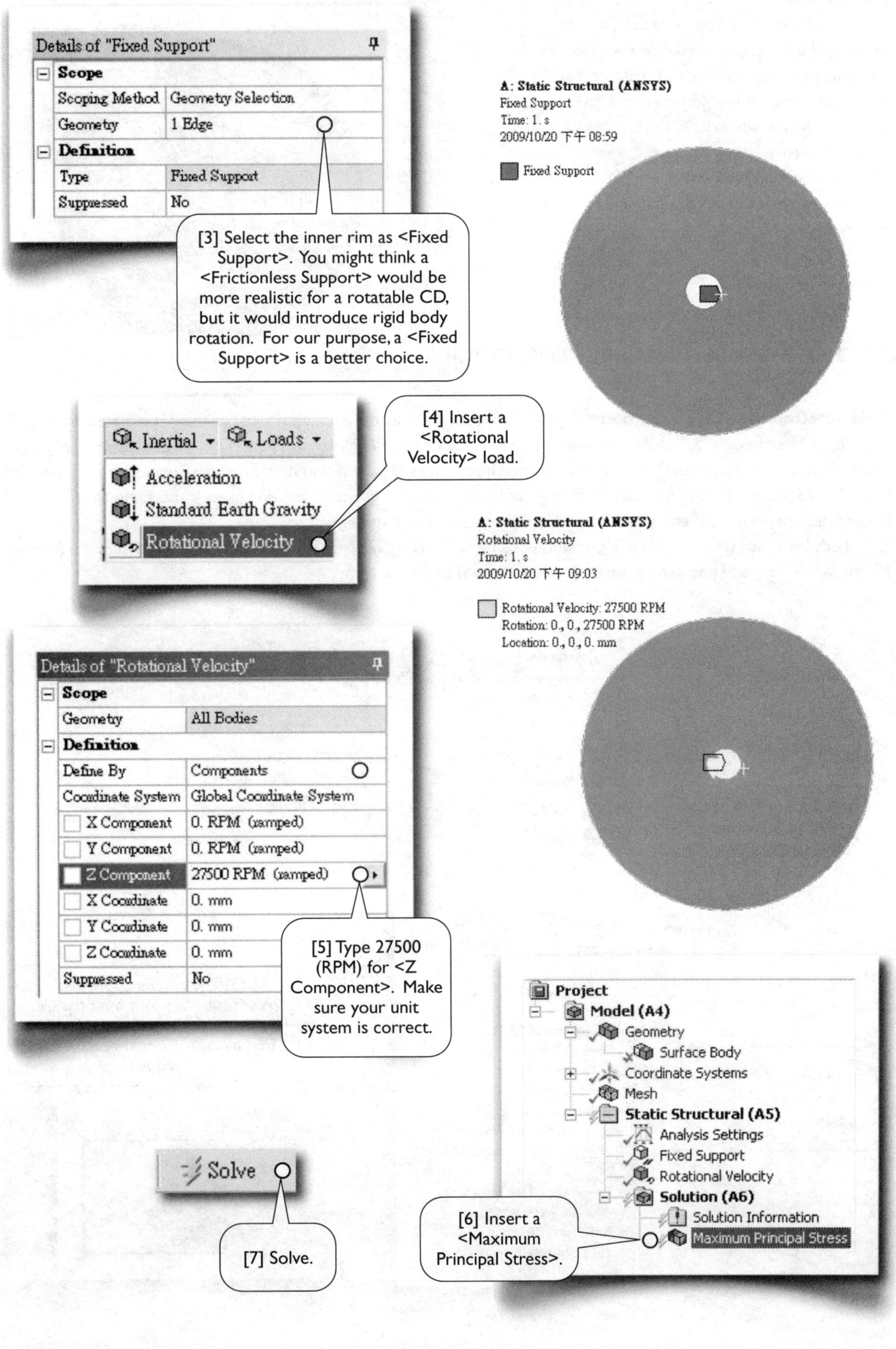
Details of "Fixed Support"
Scope
Scoping Method | Geometry Selection
Geometry | 1 Edge
Definition
Type | Fixed Support
Suppressed | No
[3] Select the inner rim as <Fixed Support>. You might think a <Frictionless Support> would be more realistic for a rotatable CD, but it would introduce rigid body rotation. For our purpose, a <Fixed Support> is a better choice.
A: Static Structural (ANSYS)
Fixed Support
Time: 1. s
2009/10/20 下午 08:59
Fixed Support
Inertial
Loads
Acceleration
Standard Earth Gravity
Rotational Velocity
[4] Insert a <Rotational Velocity> load.
A: Static Structural (ANSYS)
Rotational Velocity
Time: 1. s
2009/10/20 下午 09:03
Rotational Velocity: 27500 RPM
Rotation: 0., 0., 27500 RPM
Location: 0., 0., 0. mm
Details of "Rotational Velocity"
Scope
Geometry | All Bodies
Definition
Define By | Components
Coordinate System | Global Coordinate System
X Component | 0. RPM (ramped)
Y Component | 0. RPM (ramped)
Z Component | 27500 RPM (ramped)
X Coordinate | 0. mm
Y Coordinate | 0. mm
Z Coordinate | 0. mm
Suppressed | No
[5] Type 27500 (RPM) for <Z Component>. Make sure your unit system is correct.
Project
Model (A4)
Geometry
Surface Body
Coordinate Systems
Mesh
Static Structural (A5)
Analysis Settings
Fixed Support
Rotational Velocity
Solution (A6)
Solution Information
Maximum Principal Stress
[6] Insert a <Maximum Principal Stress>.
Solve
[7] Solve.

The maximum stress is 20.8 MPa [8], which occurs at the inner rim as expected and is far less than the material's tensile strength (65 MPa). It is unlikely that the CD shatters due to the deficiency of tensile strength, unless some defects already exist in the CD before the experiments.

As next step, let's assess the CD's natural frequencies under the spinning prestress.

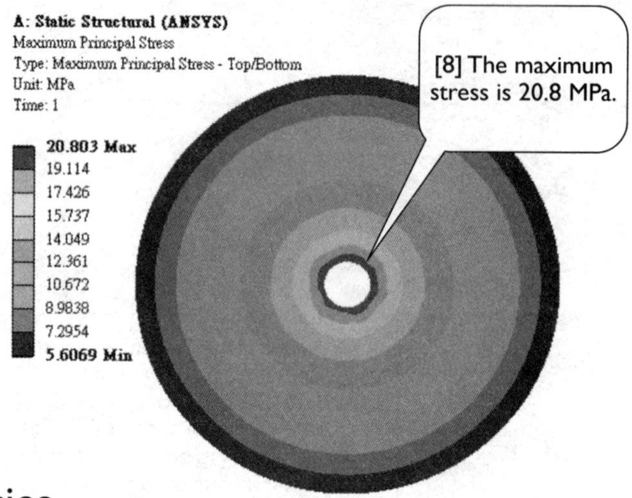

11.3-5 Assess Natural Frequencies

Close <Mechanical>. Drag-and-drop a <Modal> analysis system to the <Solution> cell of the <Static Structural> [1]. Start up <Mechanical> by double-clicking any cells other than <Engineering Data> or <Geometry>. Highlight <Model> and solve the model [2]. The lowest three frequencies [3] are within or close to the operational frequencies (11,000-2,7500 rpm, or 183-458 Hz). Although the operational frequencies are not exactly the same as the natural frequencies, they are close enough to excite the CD and may cause damage.

Let's look into this issue of resonant vibrations more thoroughly. We'll assess the prestressed natural frequencies for the whole range of possible operational speeds, from 0 to 30,000 rpm.

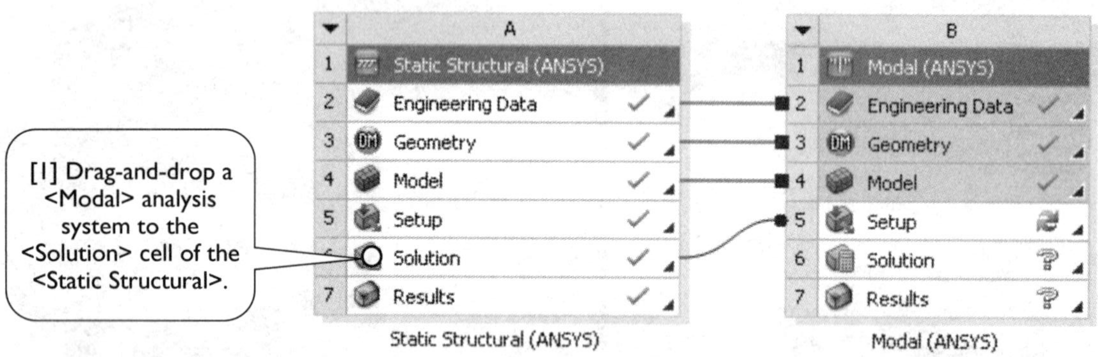

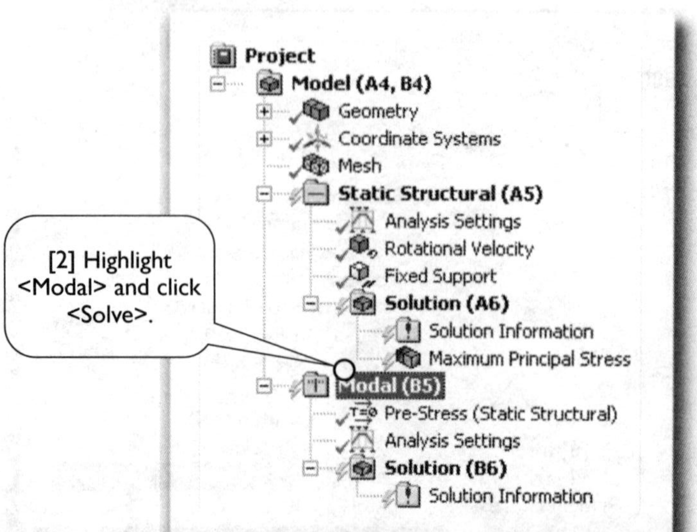

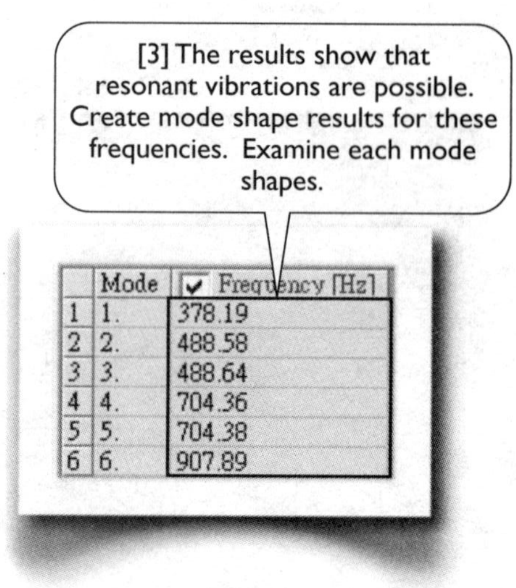

	Mode	Frequency [Hz]
1	1.	378.19
2	2.	488.58
3	3.	488.64
4	4.	704.36
5	5.	704.38
6	6.	907.89

11.3-6 Assess Natural Frequencies Under the Range of Rotational Speeds

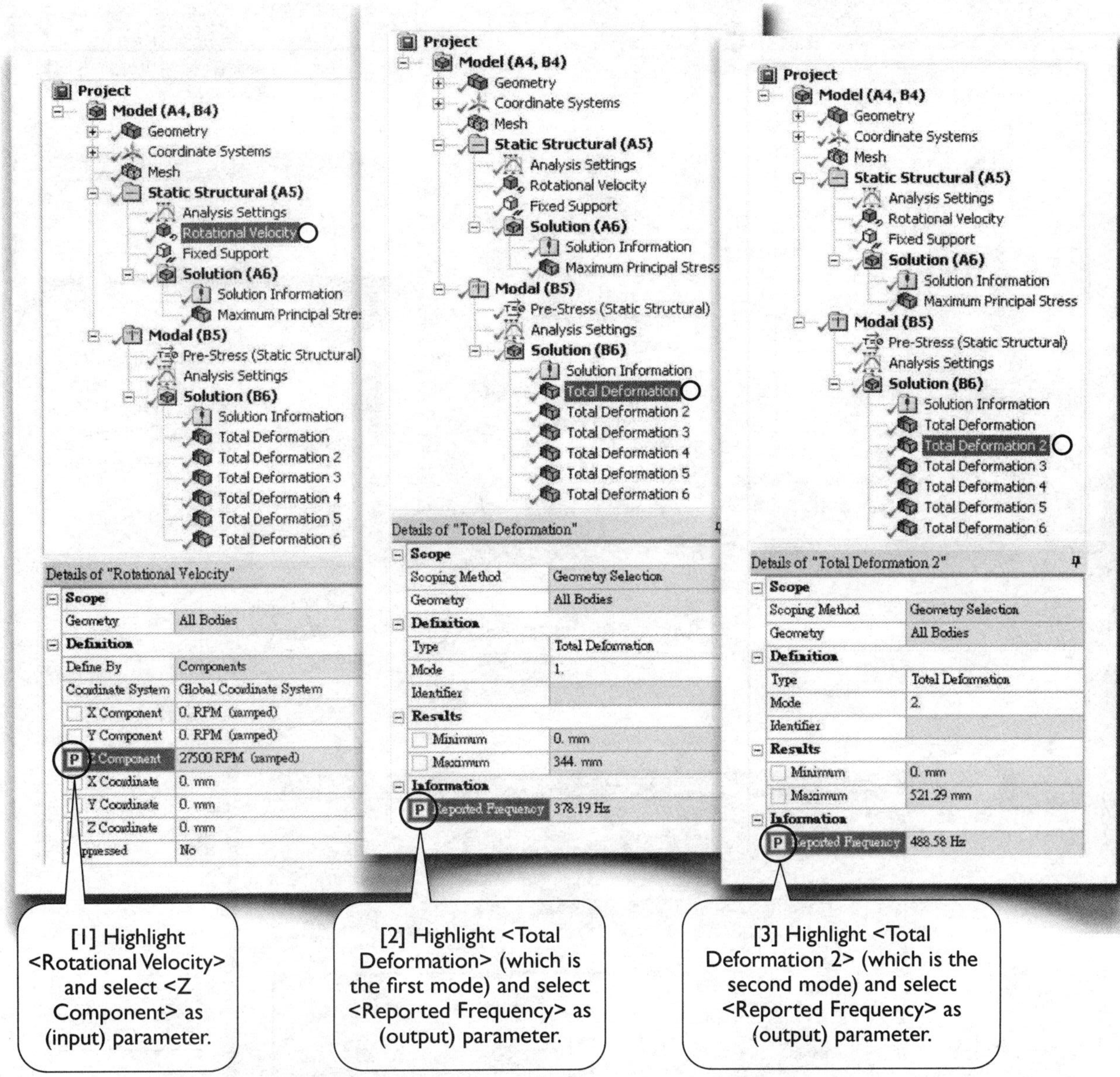

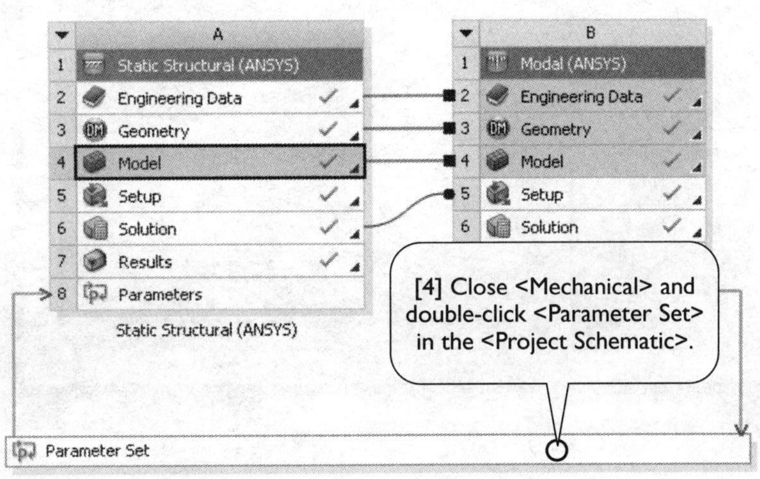

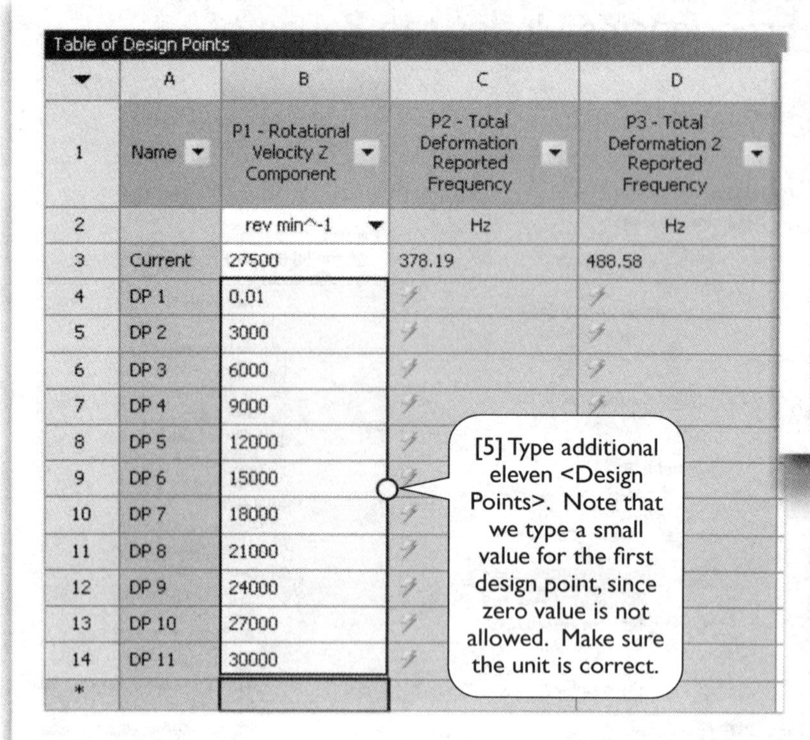

Table of Design Points

	A	B	C	D
1	Name	P1 - Rotational Velocity Z Component	P2 - Total Deformation Reported Frequency	P3 - Total Deformation 2 Reported Frequency
2		rev min^-1	Hz	Hz
3	Current	27500	378.19	488.58
4	DP 1	0.01		
5	DP 2	3000		
6	DP 3	6000		
7	DP 4	9000		
8	DP 5	12000		
9	DP 6	15000		
10	DP 7	18000		
11	DP 8	21000		
12	DP 9	24000		
13	DP 10	27000		
14	DP 11	30000		
*				

[5] Type additional eleven <Design Points>. Note that we type a small value for the first design point, since zero value is not allowed. Make sure the unit is correct.

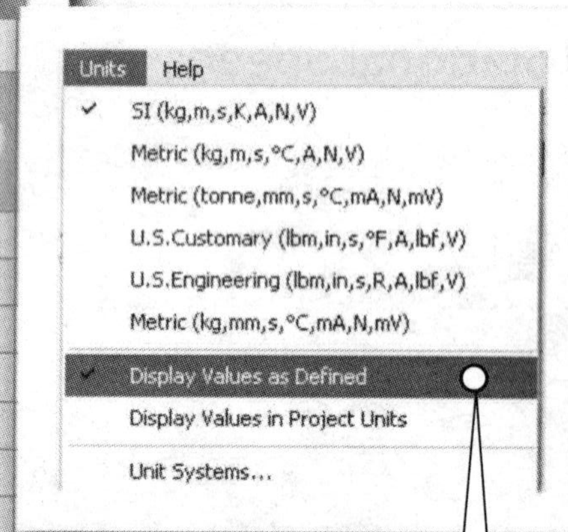

[6] If the unit of rotational velocity is not <rpm>, turn on <Units/Display Values as Defined>.

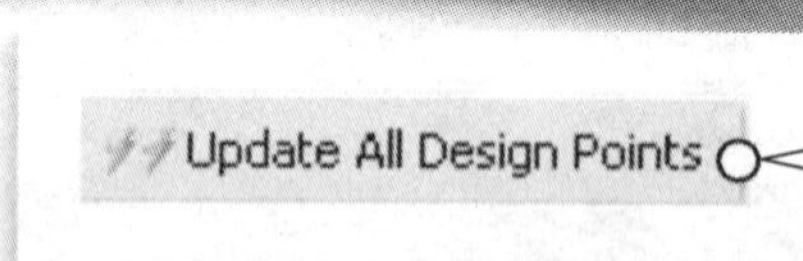

[7] Click <Update All Design Points>.

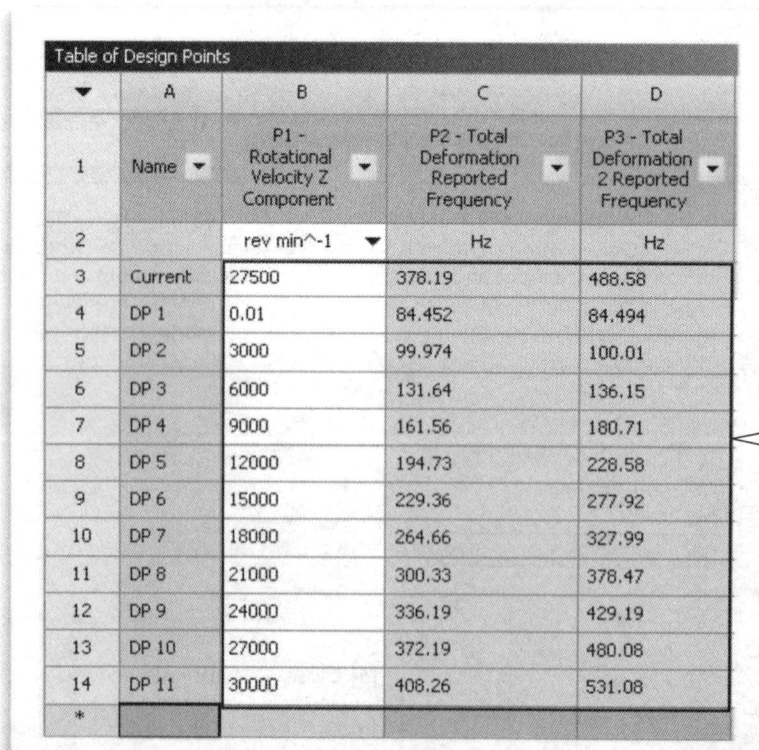

Table of Design Points

	A	B	C	D
1	Name	P1 - Rotational Velocity Z Component	P2 - Total Deformation Reported Frequency	P3 - Total Deformation 2 Reported Frequency
2		rev min^-1	Hz	Hz
3	Current	27500	378.19	488.58
4	DP 1	0.01	84.452	84.494
5	DP 2	3000	99.974	100.01
6	DP 3	6000	131.64	136.15
7	DP 4	9000	161.56	180.71
8	DP 5	12000	194.73	228.58
9	DP 6	15000	229.36	277.92
10	DP 7	18000	264.66	327.99
11	DP 8	21000	300.33	378.47
12	DP 9	24000	336.19	429.19
13	DP 10	27000	372.19	480.08
14	DP 11	30000	408.26	531.08
*				

[8] We will use these data to plot a chart.

The data [8] are plotted in a chart as shown [9-11]. Although all natural frequencies are not exactly on the "line of resonance" [11], they are close enough to be excited and in turn cause damage. Note that the resonant excitation may initiate when the rotational speed is 11,000 rpm, which is close to the speed of popular 20x and 24x CD drivers.

According to these studies, we may conclude that the CD shattering in the experiments conducted by TV series *Mythbusters* is probably due to resonant vibration effects, rather than the centrifugal stress.

In the real-world, the mechanisms of the CD drives usually provide supports for the CDs, to reduce the vibrations as well as the radial deformations, therefore, the vibrations may not be an issue.

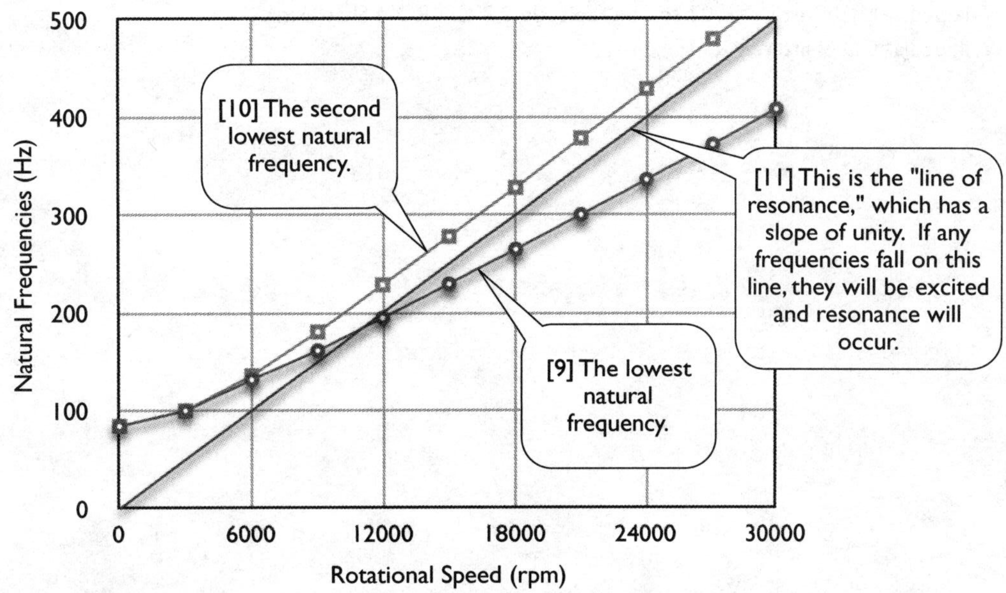

11.3-7 How about Double the Thickness?

A simple remedy for the vibrations issue is to increase the thickness of the CD. After doubling the thickness (changing the thickness from 1.2 mm to 2.4 mm), and rerunning the simulations (see an exercise in Section 11.4-2), the resulting curves [12-14] show that the vibrations should be alleviated significantly, at least for the rotational speeds up to 20,000 rpm.

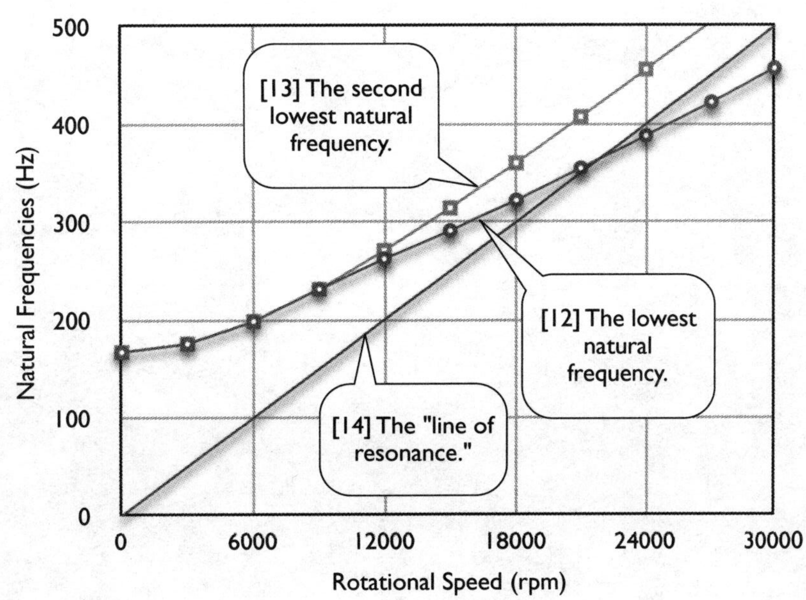

Wrap Up

Save the project and exit Workbench.

Reference

1. Wikipedia>MythBusters>2003 season>Episode 2.3 CD-ROM Shattering.
2. Wikipedia>CD Shattering

Section 11.4

Exercise: Guitar String

Meanings of sound quality may be different from the points of view between engineers and musicians. This section tries to build a bridge for the engineers to the territory of music. When designing or improving a musical instrument, an engineer must know the physics of music. On the other hand, to fully appreciate the theory of music, a musician needs to know the physics behind the music.

We will use a guitar string to demonstrate some of the physics of music in this section and Section 12.5. For those students who are not interested in music theory at all, you can read only the first two subsections (11.4-1 and 11.4-2) and skip the rest of this section. On the other hand, if you want to introduce this article to a friend who does not have enough background in modal analyses, he can skip the first two subsections and jump to 11.4-3 directly.

11.4-1 About the Guitar String

The guitar string in our case is made of steel, which has a mass density of 7850 kg/m^3, a Young's modulus of 200 GPa, and a Poisson's ratio of 0.3. It has a circular cross section of diameter 0.28 mm and a length of 1.0 m. The string is stretched with a tension T, and is in tune with a standard A note (*la*), which has been defined to be exactly 440 Hz in the modern music. In the next subsection (11.4-2), we will perform a modal analysis to find the required tension T.

Before the simulation, let's make some simple calculation. According to the basic physics, the wave traveling on a string has a speed of

$$v = \sqrt{\frac{T}{\mu}}$$

Where μ is the linear density (kg/m) of the string. The standing wave corresponding to the lowest frequency is called the *first harmonic mode*, which has a wavelength of twice the string length ($2L$). According to the relation between the velocity, the frequency, and the wavelength

$$f = \frac{v}{\lambda} = \frac{v}{2L}$$

we can estimate the required tension

$$T = \mu(2fL)^2 = 7850 \times \frac{\pi(0.00028)^2}{4}(2 \times 440 \times 1.0)^2 = 374.32 \text{ N}$$

11.4-2 Perform Modal Analysis

Launch the Workbench. Create a <Static Structural> System. Save the project as "String." Drag-and-drop a <Modal> analysis system to the <Solution> cell of the <Static Structural> system. In the <Engineering Data>, make sure the material properties for the <Structural Steel> are consistent with those of the guitar string.

Enter the DesignModeler (using <Millimeter> as length unit), create a sketch and use the sketch to create a line body of 1.0 m. Create a circular cross section of radius 0.14 mm, and associate the line body with the cross section.

Before starting up <Mechanical>, don't forget to turn on <Line Bodies> in the <Properties> (7.1-7[2]). In the <Mechanical>, specify environment conditions under the <Static Structural> [1]: a <Fixed Support> [2], a <Displacement> [3], a <Fixed Rotation> [4], and a <Force> [5]. Note that we suppressed all rigid body modes.

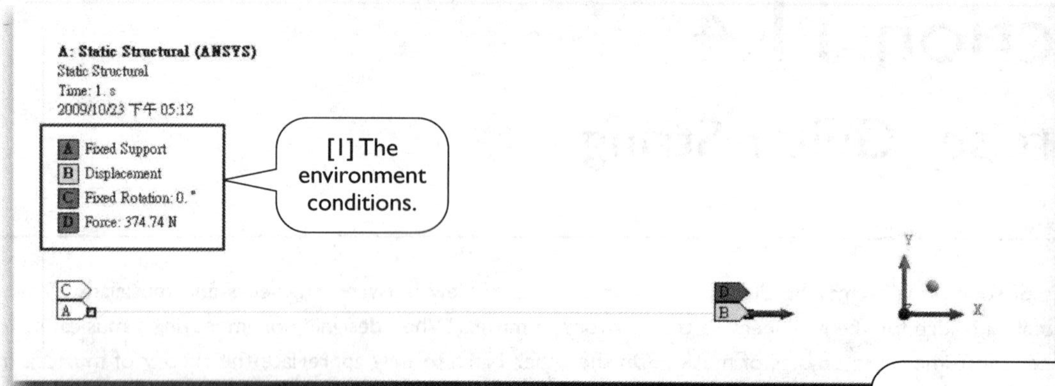

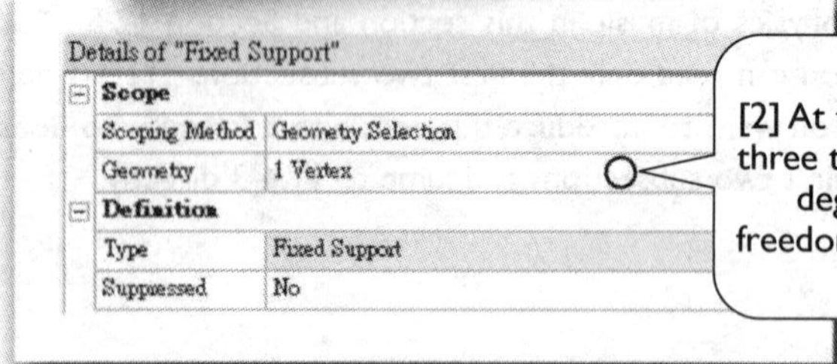

Details of "Fixed Support"

Scope	
Scoping Method	Geometry Selection
Geometry	1 Vertex
Definition	
Type	Fixed Support
Suppressed	No

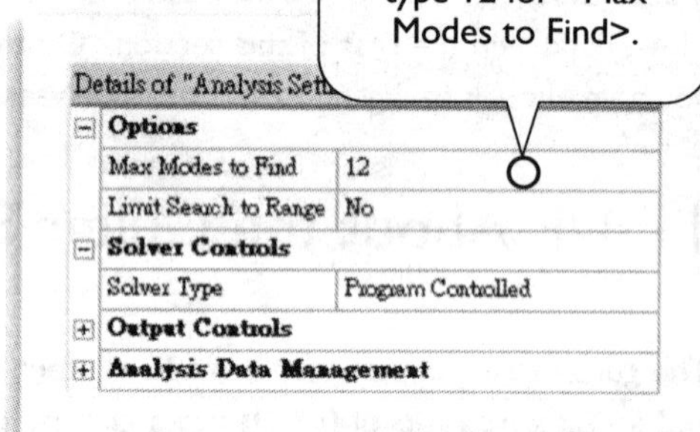

Details of "Analysis Sett

Options	
Max Modes to Find	12
Limit Search to Range	No
Solver Controls	
Solver Type	Program Controlled
Output Controls	
Analysis Data Management	

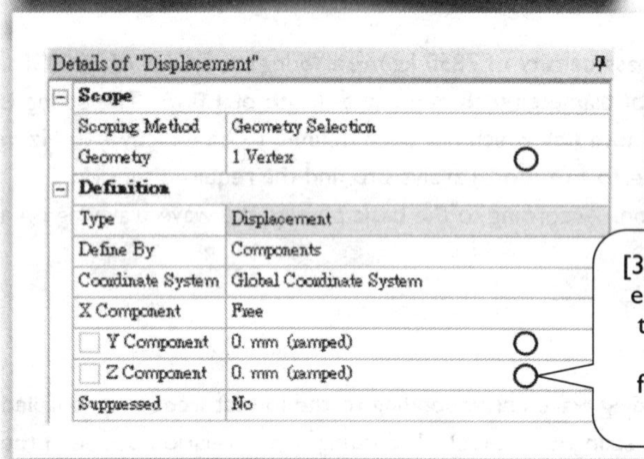

Details of "Displacement"

Scope	
Scoping Method	Geometry Selection
Geometry	1 Vertex
Definition	
Type	Displacement
Define By	Components
Coordinate System	Global Coordinate System
X Component	Free
Y Component	0. mm (ramped)
Z Component	0. mm (ramped)
Suppressed	No

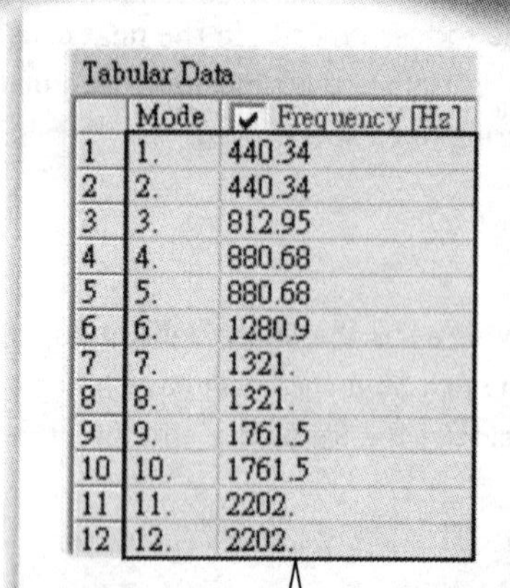

Tabular Data

	Mode	Frequency [Hz]
1	1.	440.34
2	2.	440.34
3	3.	812.95
4	4.	880.68
5	5.	880.68
6	6.	1280.9
7	7.	1321.
8	8.	1321.
9	9.	1761.5
10	10.	1761.5
11	11.	2202.
12	12.	2202.

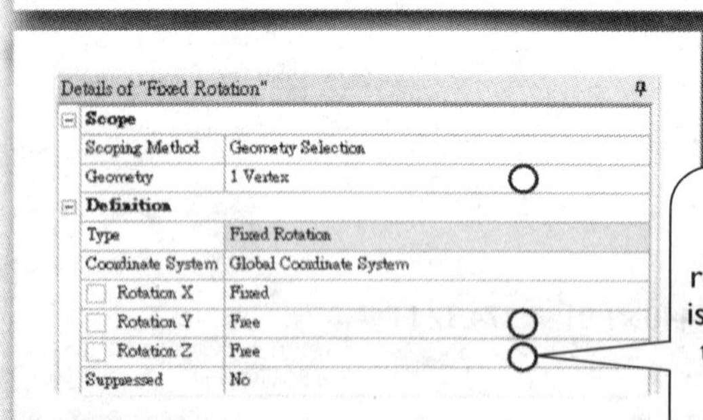

Details of "Fixed Rotation"

Scope	
Scoping Method	Geometry Selection
Geometry	1 Vertex
Definition	
Type	Fixed Rotation
Coordinate System	Global Coordinate System
Rotation X	Fixed
Rotation Y	Free
Rotation Z	Free
Suppressed	No

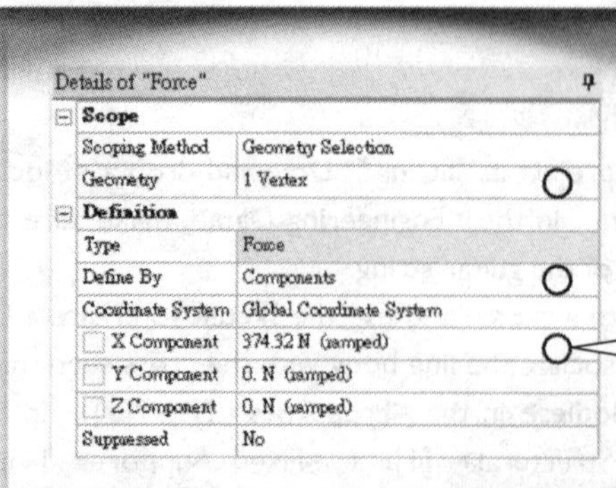

Details of "Force"

Scope	
Scoping Method	Geometry Selection
Geometry	1 Vertex
Definition	
Type	Force
Define By	Components
Coordinate System	Global Coordinate System
X Component	374.32 N (ramped)
Y Component	0. N (ramped)
Z Component	0. N (ramped)
Suppressed	No

The results of the modal analysis [7] show that the lowest frequency is not exactly 440 Hz. It slightly deviates from what we've calculated. The main reason is that when applying the tension, the length of the string increases (for about 30 mm). Another reason is due to the use of beam model, which is slightly different from the pure tension-only model used in our hand-calculation.

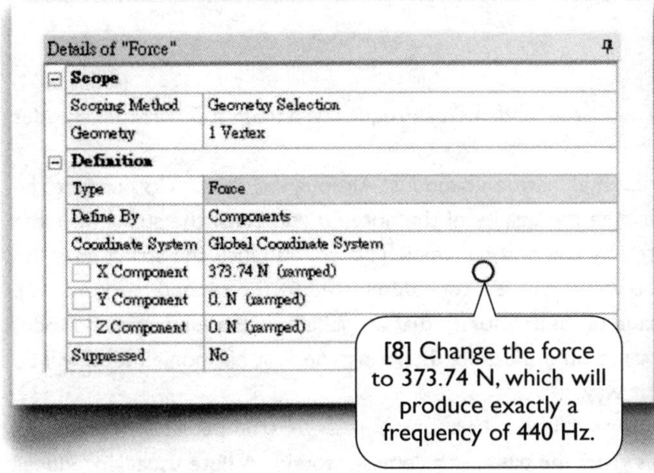

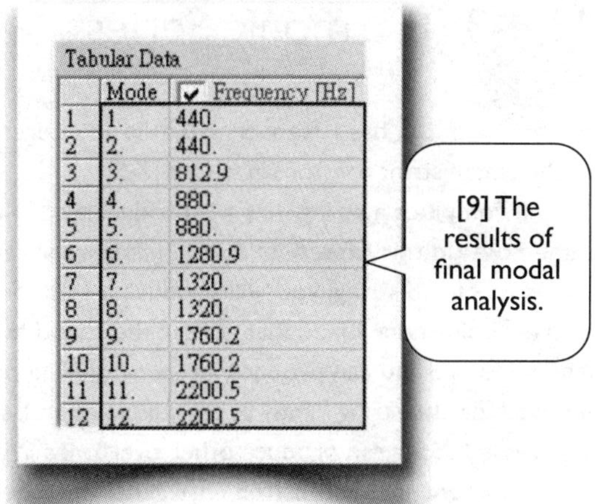

After several trial-and-errors, we will come up with a tension of 373.74 N that produces exactly a fundamental frequency of 440 Hz [8, 9].

As expected, the spectrum of frequencies [9] includes 440 Hz, 880 Hz, 1320 Hz, 1760 Hz, etc., with negligible numerical errors. Some modes need to be further explained.

The third mode (812.9 Hz) is a rotation mode in X-direction [10, 11]. There is no way to visualize it from the animation. In the real-world, it exists, but its magnitude usually very small, and our ears hardly sense it since the air pressure is hard to be excited in this way.

The sixth mode (1280.9 Hz) is a stretching mode in X-direction [12]. We can visualize it from the animation. In the real-world, it exists too, but again, we hardly sense it since the air pressure is hard to be excited in this way.

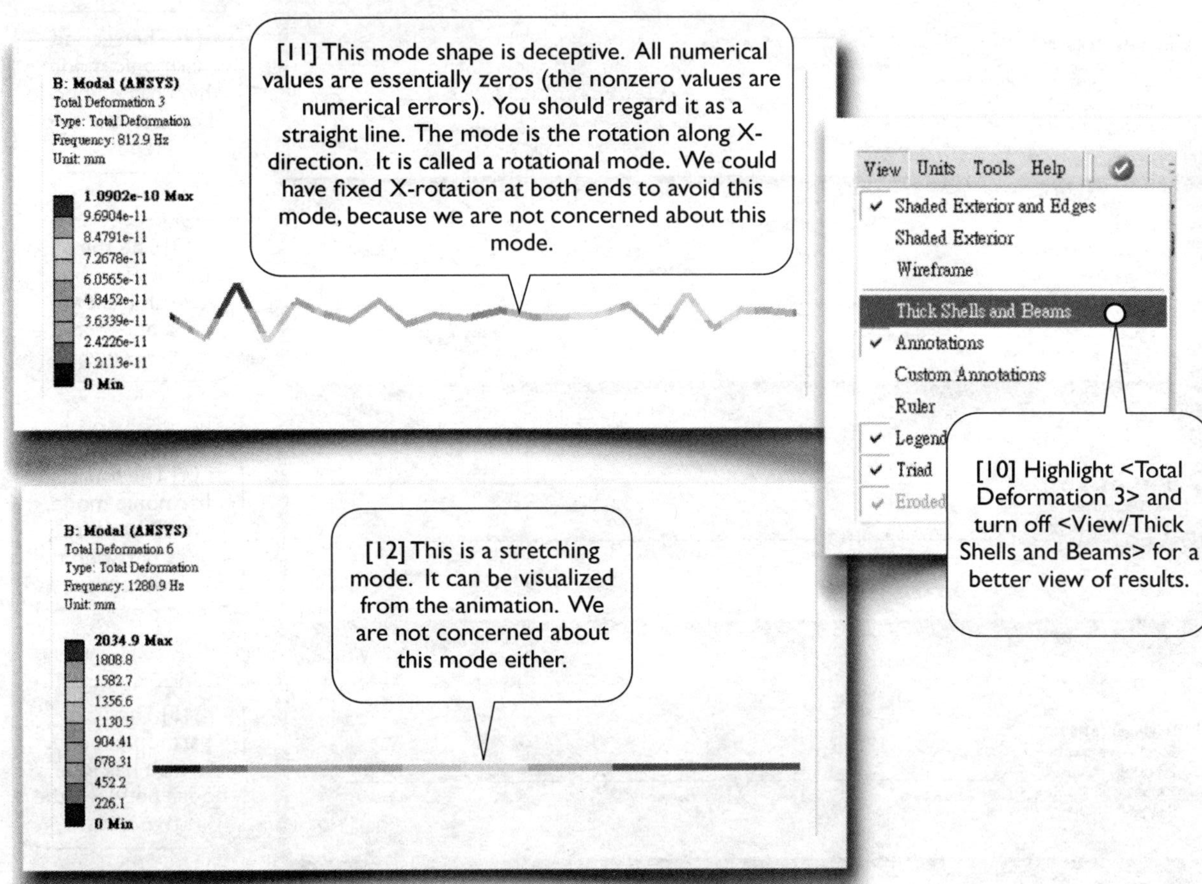

11.4-3 Harmonic Series

A *harmonic mode* has a frequency that is an integer multiple of the fundamental frequency. The first 5 harmonic modes of the guitar string are shown below [1-5].

If you pluck a string, you will produce a tone made up of all harmonic modes. Although all the plucks produce the same note (in this case, note *A*), the *harmonic mixes* determine the quality of the note. If you pluck the string near the midpoint of the string, you will produce a tone dominated by the first harmonic [1]. If you pluck the string near the quarter point (in a guitar, that is near the sound hole), you will produce a tone dominated by the second harmonic [2]. And so forth. You can produce an "overtone" (a tone made up of harmonics that are all above the fundamental mode) by touching the string lightly at the midpoint and, at the same time, plucking the string; the first harmonic mode will be suppressed. Your can produce other overtones in a similar way.

Different musical instruments generate tones that have different harmonic mixes. A trumpet usually produces much of higher harmonics in its frequency spectrum. This gives the trumpet a "brassy" sound. A flute usually produces a tone dominated by the first harmonic with almost no higher harmonics. This gives the flute a unique "pure" sound.

Knowing these physics, an engineer should be able to produce the sound of any musical instruments using a frequency-generating device, including human voices.

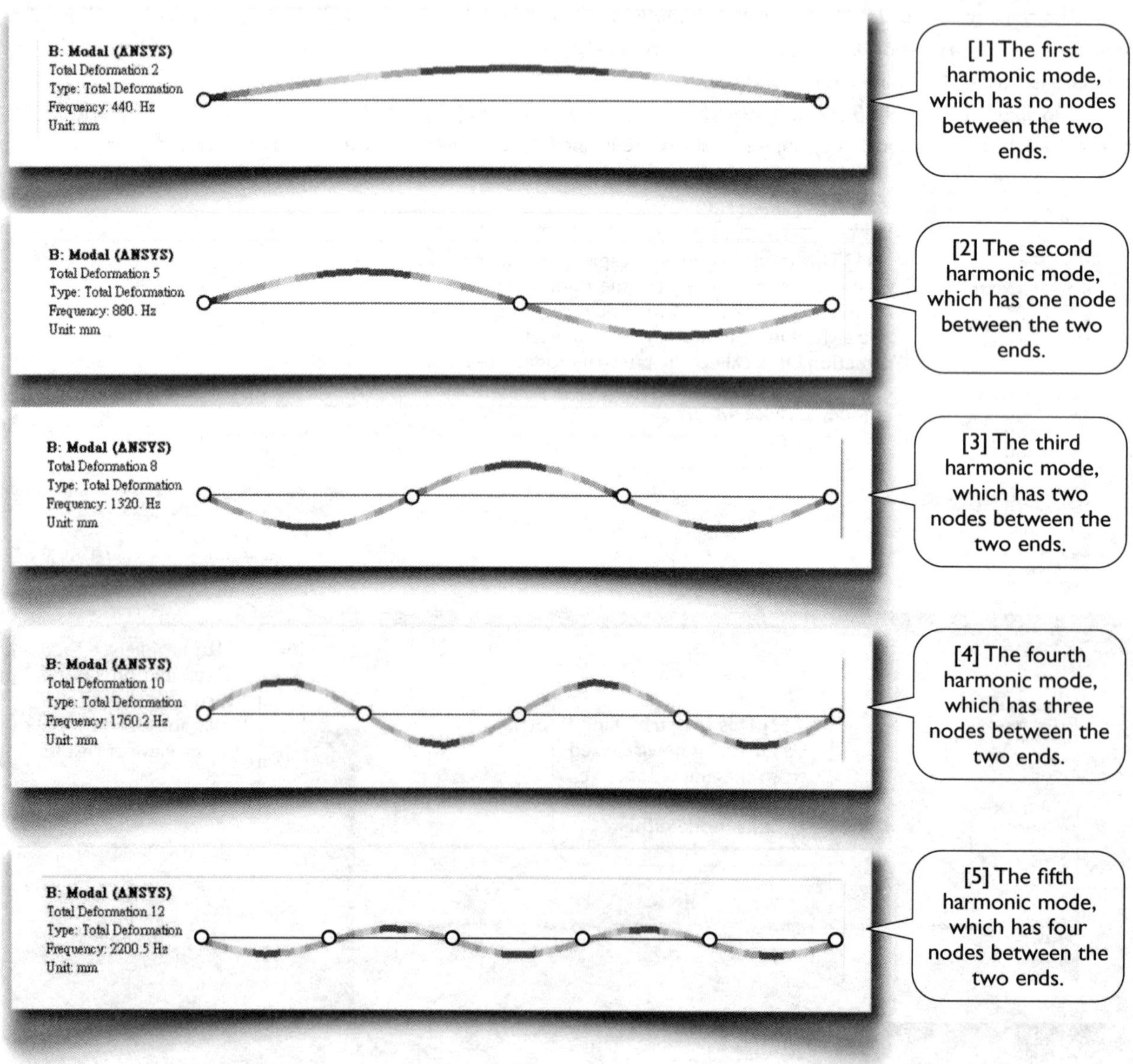

11.4-4 Just Tuning System[1]

Why do some notes sound pleasing to our ears when played together, while others do not? We know from the experience that when two notes have a simple frequency ratio, they sound harmonious with each other. The simpler the ratio, the more harmonious it sounds. The details will be explained in Section 11.4-6. For now, we simply believe it.

In Western music, an 8-tone musical scale has traditionally been used. When learning to sing, we identify the eight tones in the scale by the syllables *do, re, mi, fa, sol, la, ti, do*. For a *C*-major scale in a piano, there are 8 white keys from a *C* to the higher pitch of *C* [1]. The two *C*'s has a frequency ratio of 2:1, and are said to be an *octave* apart. If we play two notes an octave apart, they sound very similar. In fact, we often have difficulty telling the difference between two notes having an octave apart. This is because that, except the fundamental harmonic of the lower note, two notes have most of the same higher harmonics.

For the following discussion, let's arbitrarily assume the frequency of the lower pitch *C* as 1. (In a modern piano, the middle *C* has a frequency of 261.63 Hz; see the table in Section 11.4-5.) Then the frequency of the higher pitch *C* is 2. Before being replaced by the "equal temperament" (Section 11.4-5) in the early 20th century, the "just tuning" systems prevail in the music world. In a just tuning music system, the frequencies of the notes between the 2 *C*'s are chosen according to the "simple ratio" rule, in order to be harmonious to each other. The result is as shown [2]. Note that we didn't show the frequency ratios for the black keys (the semitones) to simplify our discussion.

Now, you can appreciate that if we play the notes *do* and *sol* together, the sound is pleasing to our ears, since they have the simplest frequency ratio between 1 and 2. You also can appreciate that the major cord *C* consists of the notes *do, me, sol, do*, the simplest frequency ratios (but not too "close," to avoid *beats*; see Section 11.4-6) between 1 and 2.

The problem of the just tuning system is that it is almost impossible to play in another key. For example, when we play in *D* key, then the frequency ratio between *D* and its *fifth* (*A*) is no longer 3/2. Instead, the frequency ratio is an awkward 40/27; the two notes are not harmonious enough any more.

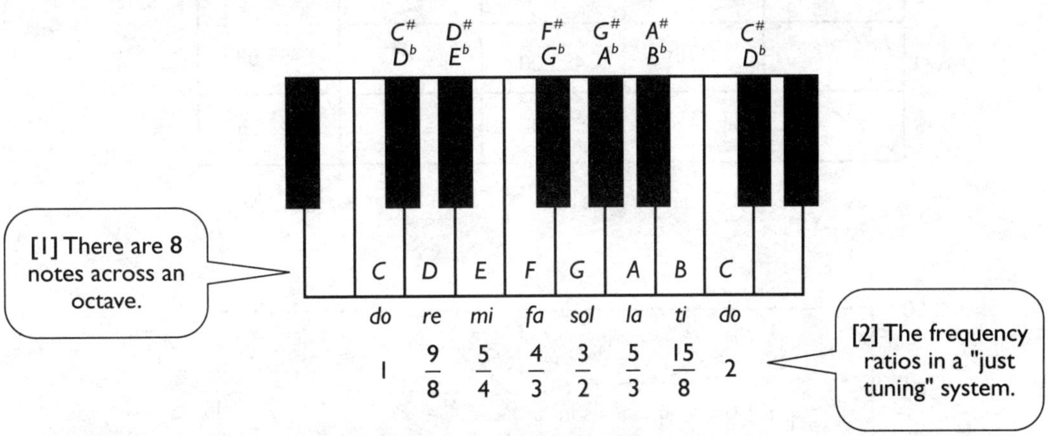

11.4-5 Twelve-Tone Equally Tempered Tuning System[2]

Modern Western music is dominated by a 12-*tone equally tempered tuning system*, or simply *equal temperament*. The idea is to compromise on the frequency ratios between the notes, so that they can be played in different keys. In this system, an octave is equally divided into 12 tones (including semitones) in logarithmic scale. In other words, the adjacent tones has a frequency ratio of $2^{1/12}$, or 1.05946. For example, the frequency ratio between the $C^\#$ and the *C* is $2^{1/12}$; the frequency ratio between the *A* and the lower *C* is $2^{5/12}$. According to this idea, frequencies of the notes can be calculated and listed in the table below. For comparison, we also list the frequencies of the notes in the just tuning system. The data in the table are plotted into a chart as shown [1, 2]. The compromised frequencies are close enough to the just tuning system that most of musicians are satisfied with this system for centreis.

Note	Just Tuning		Equal Temperament	
	Frequency Ratio	Frequency	Frequency Ratio	Frequency
C	1	264.00	1	261.63
$C^{\#}$ (D^{b})			$2^{1/12}$	277.18
D	9/8	297.00	$2^{2/12}$	293.66
$D^{\#}$ (E^{b})			$2^{3/12}$	311.13
E	5/4	330.00	$2^{4/12}$	329.63
F	4/3	352.00	$2^{5/12}$	349.23
$F^{\#}$ (G^{b})			$2^{6/12}$	369.99
G	3/2	396.00	$2^{7/12}$	392.00
$G^{\#}$ (A^{b})			$2^{8/12}$	415.30
A	5/3	440.00	$2^{9/12}$	440.00
$A^{\#}$ (B^{b})			$2^{10/12}$	466.16
B	15/8	495.00	$2^{11/12}$	493.88
C	2	528.00	2	523.25

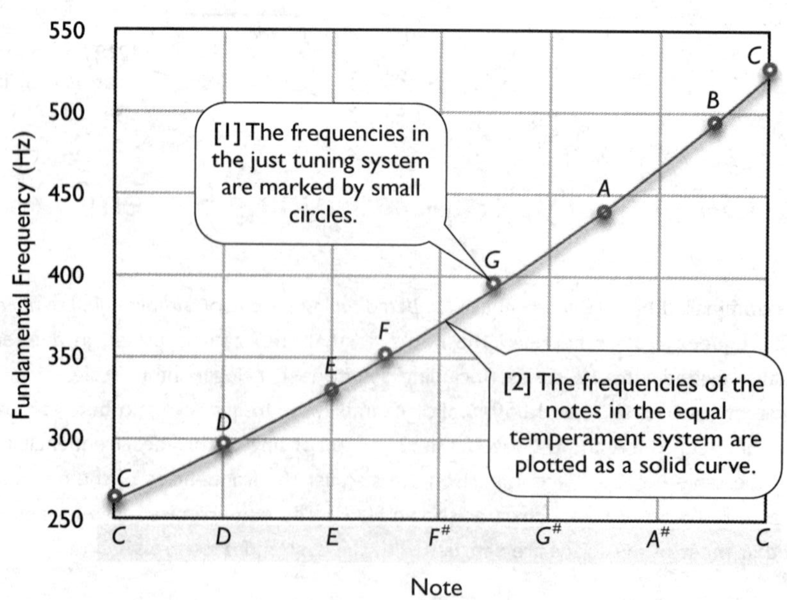

11.4-6 Beat Frequency[3, 4]

Return to the question in the beginning of Section 11.4-4: Why do some notes sound pleasing to our ears when played together, while others do not? Why does a simple frequency ratio imply a harmonious sound? To explain this, another physical phenomenon called *beats* is at work.

When two waves of different frequencies are combined, they interfere with each other. When they are in phase, the combined wave has a large amplitude. When they are out of phase, the amplitude becomes smaller. This fluctuation in amplitude of the combined wave is called *beats*, and the frequency is called the *beat frequency*.

The beat frequency is equal to the frequency difference of the two waves. If the two notes are very close in frequency, the beat frequency is slow enough to be heard as a variation in amplitude, that is, you can hear the sound getting louder and softer in a repetitive pattern. This effect can be useful in tuning a musical instrument, since the beats disappear when two frequencies are in tune.

What happens when we play *C* and *D* together? The beat frequency is 32.03 Hz (293.66 - 261.63; see the table in 11.4-5), which is large enough that we hear a harsh buzz, which is unpleasant for our ears. In music, however, a dissonant sound is sometimes used to produce desired effects, for example, a sad mood.

What happens when we play *C* and *G* together? The beat frequency is 130.37 Hz (392.00 - 261.63; see the table in 11.4-5), which is very close to one half of the middle *C* (261.63 Hz). In other words, the beat frequency is an octave below middle *C*. Therefore, it fits nicely within a chord containing *C* and *G*. Thus, beats can explain the harmony when we play major chords.

Wrap Up

Save the project and exit Workbench.

References

1. Wikipedia>Just Intonation.
2. Wikipedia>Equal Temperament.
3. Wikipedia>Beat.
4. Griffith, W.T., The Physics of Everyday Phenomena, Fourth Edition, McGraw-Hill, 2004.

Section 11.5
Problems

11.5-1 Key Concepts

Structural Dynamic Analysis
Technique used to determine the dynamic behavior of a structure.

Dynamic Behavior
Structural dynamic behavior includes vibration characteristics, effect of harmonic loads, and effect of general time-varying loads.

Modal Analysis
A dynamic analysis to investigate the vibration characteristics, specifically the frequencies and shapes, of a structure without any time-varying loads. The frequencies are called natural frequencies.

Transient Structural Analysis
A dynamic analysis to investigate the response of a structure under general time-varying loads.

Free Vibration
The vibration of a structural without any external forces.

Natural Frequencies
The frequencies corresponding to the free vibrations are called natural frequencies.

Fundamental Natural Frequency
The lowest frequency of free vibration.

Rigid Body Modes
Rigid body modes have infinite period, or, equivalently, zero frequencies. In general, rigid body modes should not be present.

Harmonic Mode
A harmonic mode has a frequency that is an integer multiple of the fundamental frequency.

11.5-2 Workbench Exercises

Gravity Are Negligible When Evaluating Frequencies of the Two-Story Building

In Section 11.2-5, we mentioned that the earth gravity affects natural frequencies of the two-story building very limited. Verify this.

Improving the Stiffness of the Two-Story Building

In the end of Section 11.2, we mentioned that if we want to further improve the structure's solidity, we may add bracing members in the Z-direction. Implement this idea.

Double the CD Thickness

Perform simulations and generate a chart like the one in Section 11.3-7.

Model Airplane Wing

The wing of a model airplane is detailed in the ANSYS Help System[1]. Carry out the modal analysis for the airplane wing. How do you stiffen the wing further without increasing the weight?

Reference

1. ANSYS Help System>Mechanical APDL>Tutorials>9. Modal Tutorial.

Chapter 12
Structural Dynamics

In the real world, all loads are time-varying, so do the structural responses. For example, after you hang a weight on a spring and release it, the weight moves up and down for a while and finally stops. To know the whole process, you need to perform a *dynamic simulation*. If you are concerning only the final state, called the *steady state*, of the response, a static analysis is adequate, since the dynamic effect (Section 1.1-10) vanishes then. The response before the steady state is called a *transient state*. To know the transient state, a transient dynamic simulation is needed. Another situation that a dynamic simulation can be replaced by a series of static simulations is that if the loads are applied so slowly, that the structure displaces very slow so that the dynamic effect is negligible. The series of static simulations is called a *quasistatic simulation*.

Other than these two kinds of cases (in cases of finding a steady state solution or in cases that the structure displaces slowly), dynamic effect must be taken into account; dynamic simulations are needed.

Purpose of the Chapter

The purpose of this chapter is to provide background knowledge as well as practical examples for the students to master the techniques for dynamics simulations. It is a sequel of the last chapter, modal analysis. Except Section 12.3, which is performed with <Harmonic Response> analysis system, all the other exercises are performed with <Transient Structural> analysis system, which uses an implicit integration method to calculate the response. The <Explicit Dynamics> analysis system, on the other hand, uses an explicit integration method. The explicit dynamics will be introduced in Chapter 15, which concludes our discussion of structural dynamics.

About Each Section

Section 1 intends to equip the students with background knowledge of structural dynamics. Again, it is the concepts, rather than the mathematics details, that we want to emphasize. We will use a single-degree-of-freedom system to illustrate these ideas. Section 2 provides a practical example to demonstrate the application of dynamic loads and other considerations such as integration time steps and damping.

Section 3, using the two-story building as example, demonstrates the procedure of harmonic response analysis. Section 4 performs an impact simulation. One of its purpose is to demonstrate how to specify a simple initial condition, namely uniform velocity. Another purpose is to show the limitation of implicit integration method and the necessity of explicit dynamics for high-speed impact simulations.

Section 5 is a sequel of Section 11.4. As mentioned, in the beginning of Section 11.4-3, if you pluck a string, you will produce a tone made up of all harmonic modes. We will apply plucks at different location of the string to observe the responses. The other purpose of Section 5 is to demonstrate how to specify a general initial condition. Some initial conditions are so complicated that they need a static simulation themselves. In this section, we will use the results of a static simulation as an initial condition of a transient simulation.

Section 12.1

Basics of Structural Dynamics

The purpose of this section is to provide basics of structural dynamics, which is crucial for understanding the procedure demonstrated in this chapter. We will emphasize on concepts and terminologies, which will be used throughout in this chapter and the rest of the book. We will use a single-degree-of-freedom lumped mass model for explaining some basic behavior of dynamic response. The results will be conceptually extend to the general multiple-degrees-of-freedom cases (not limiting to lumped mass models).

12.1-1 Lumped Mass Model

In the old days, when computation was expensive or not fast enough, many dynamics problems were modeled as lumped mass systems. As an example, to find the lateral displacements (in X-direction or Z-direction), the two-story building (Sections 7.3, 11.2) is modeled as a two-degrees-of-freedom system as shown [1-7].

The parameters (m_1, m_2, k_1, k_2, c_1, c_2) should be carefully evaluated to reflect the real situation. The masses m_1 and m_2 [2, 3] may include the respective floor mass, the mass of the live load on the floor, the mass of the upper half of the lower floor columns, and the mass of the lower half of the upper floor columns. The spring constants k_1 and k_2 [4, 5] are calculated according to the bending stiffnesses of the columns and beams at the respective floor. The damping coefficients c_1 and c_2 [6, 7] represent all energy dissipating mechanisms of the respective floor.

The energy dissipating mechanisms include frictions between the building and the surrounding air, material's internal frictions, and the frictions in the joints connecting structural members. Evaluating damping is one of the most challenging tasks of engineering practice. Fortunately, damping in most structures are very small. Consequently, it may not be crucial in many cases, and we may choose a reasonable value according to engineering experiences. In other cases, conducting experiments to find out the damping values may be needed. Section 12.1-3 will provide concepts that are needed when dealing with damping.

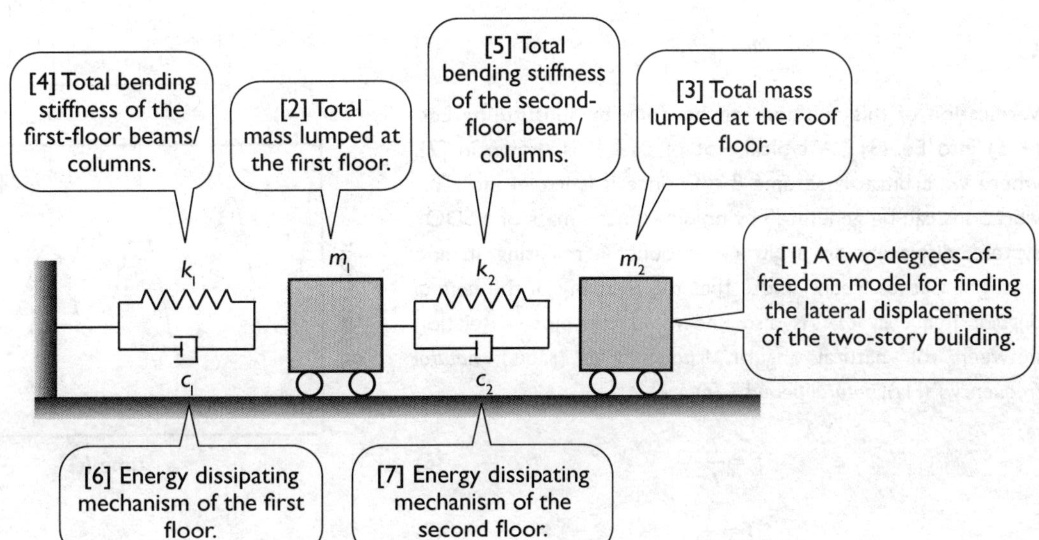

12.1-2 Single Degree of Freedom

Consider a single-degree-of-freedom (SDOF) model as shown [1]. Apply Newton's law of motion on the block of mass m,

$$\sum F = ma$$
$$p - kx - c\dot{x} = m\ddot{x}$$

or

$$m\ddot{x} + c\dot{x} + kx = p \qquad (1)$$

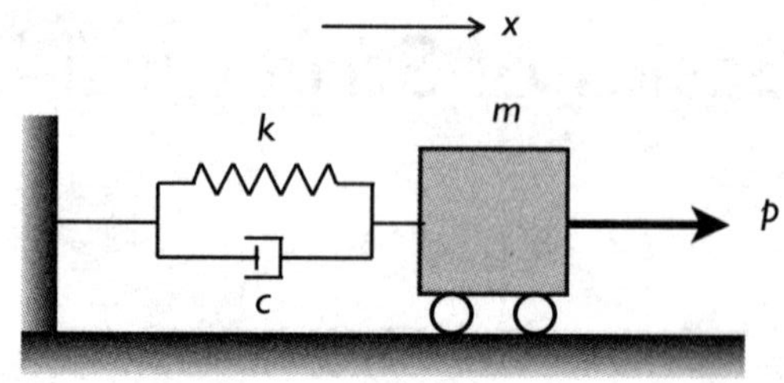

[1] A single-degree-of-freedom model.

Eq. (1) is the governing equation of the SDOF model [1]. Note that we assume that the spring force is linearly proportional to the displacement, and the damping force is linearly proportional to the velocity. This kind of damping is called a *viscous damping*. We will discuss this assumption of damping in Section 12.1-3.

If the external force vanishes, the equation becomes

$$m\ddot{x} + c\dot{x} + kx = 0 \qquad (2)$$

Eq. (2) represents a SDOF system under *free vibrations*.

If the damping is negligible, then the equation becomes

$$m\ddot{x} + kx = 0 \qquad (3)$$

Eq. (3) represents a SDOF system under *undamped free vibration*.

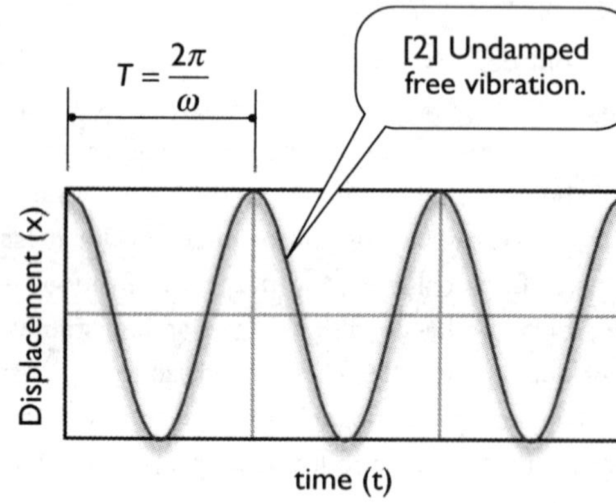

[2] Undamped free vibration.

Undamped Free Vibration

The general solution of Eq. (3) is

$$x = A\sin(\omega t + B) \qquad (4)$$

where A and B are arbitrary real numbers and

$$\omega = \sqrt{\frac{k}{m}} \qquad (5)$$

Verification of this solution can be done by substituting Eqs. (4, 5) into Eq. (3). A typical plot of Eq. (4) is shown in [2], where we arbitrarily assume B = 0, since it is irrelevant. This vibrations can be generated by holding up the mass of a SDOF system, displacing an arbitrary amount A, releasing it, and letting it vibrate freely. Note that the meaning of the *natural angular frequency* ω is also shown in the plot. Relation between the natural angular frequency ω (rad/s), *natural frequency* f (Hz), *natural period* T (s) are

$$f = \frac{\omega}{2\pi} \qquad (6)$$

$$T = \frac{1}{f} \qquad (7)$$

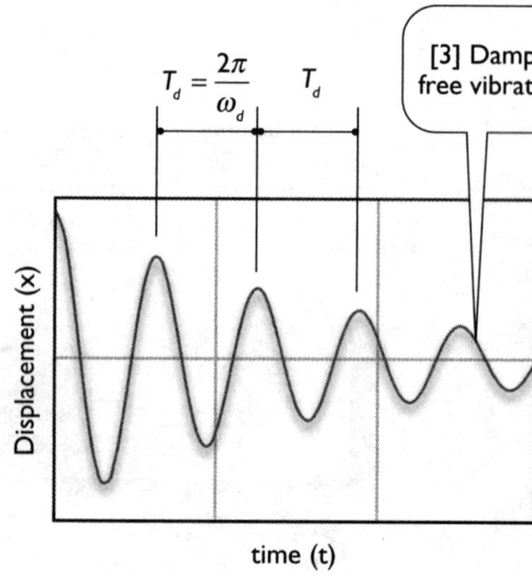

[3] Damped free vibration.

Damped Free Vibration

Assuming the damping c is smaller than the critical damping (to be defined), then the general solution of Eq. (2) is

$$x = Ae^{-\xi\omega t}\sin\left(\omega_d t + B\right) \tag{8}$$

where A and B are arbitrary real numbers and

$$\omega_d = \omega\sqrt{1-\xi^2} \tag{9}$$

$$\xi = \frac{c}{c_c} \tag{10}$$

$$c_c = 2m\omega \tag{11}$$

Verification of this solution can be done by substituting Eqs. (8-11) into Eq. (2). A typical plot of Eq. (8) is shown in [3]. Again, this vibrations can be generated by holding up the mass of a SDOF system, displacing an arbitrary amount A, releasing it, and letting it vibrate freely.

The quantity c_c, defined in (11), is called the *critical damping coefficient.* It can be shown that if the damping c is larger than or equal to c_c, than the Eq. (8) is no longer valid. Actually, the motion is no longer oscillatory, and the system is called *over-damped* (if $c > c_c$) or *critically damped* (if $c = c_c$). For most of structures, we may reasonably assume that the system is under-damped ($c < c_c$), and the Eq. (8) is always valid.

The quantity ξ, defined in Eq. (10), is called the *damping ratio.* Values of damping ratio for typical structures range from about 0.02 (for piping systems) to about 0.07 (for bolted structures and reinforced concrete)[1].

The quantity ω_d, defined in Eq. (9), is called *damped natural angular frequency.* Note that, for a small damping ratio, ω_d and ω is practically no difference. For example, with $\xi = 0.07$, $\omega_d = 0.9975\omega$.

Measuring Damping Coefficient

Given the mass m and the spring constant k of a SDOF system, and if we can obtain a damped free vibration curve [3], then we can calculate the damping coefficient from these information. From Eq. (8), the peak displacement is

$$x_{peak} = Ae^{-\xi\omega t}$$

Recognizing the time between two peaks is $T = 2\pi/\omega_d \approx 2\pi/\omega$, we can write down the *displacement ratio R* between two consecutive peaks

$$R = \frac{x_{peak2}}{x_{peak1}} = \frac{Ae^{-\xi\omega(t+\frac{2\pi}{\omega})}}{Ae^{-\xi\omega t}} = e^{-2\pi\xi} \tag{12}$$

For example, with $\xi = 0.07$, the displacement ratio between two consecutive peaks is $R = 0.64$. In practice, the displacement ratio can be calculated by averaging the displacement ratios of *several* cycles of vibration. The damping ratio ξ then can be calculated from Eq. (12)

$$\xi = \frac{-\ln R}{2\pi} \tag{13}$$

The damping coefficient can be calculated using Eqs. (10) and (11),

$$c = \frac{-\ln R}{\pi} m\omega \tag{14}$$

Viscous damping coefficient c is not an intrinsic property of material

Imaging that the SDOF system [1] is entirely made up of a material and you want to characterize the damping property for the material. You make a piece of specimen, generate a free vibration curve [3], and calculate the damping coefficient according to Eq. (14). It seems easy. The problem is that, in this way, the damping depends on the geometry of the specimen, since the geometry determine the natural frequency ω . In other words, different geometries end up with different damping coefficients.

12.1-3 Damping

Damping Mechanisms

As mentioned, damping is the collection of all energy dissipating mechanisms in a structure. In a structural system, all energy dissipating mechanisms boil down to one word: friction. In a structure system, three categories of frictions can be identified: (a) friction between the structure and its surrounding fluid, called *viscous damping*; (b) internal friction in the material, called *material damping, solid damping,* or *elastic hysteresis*; and (c) friction in the connection between structural members, called *dry friction* or *Coulomb friction*. When the structure is surrounded by the air, the viscous damping is usually very small, and the major sources of damping are elastic hysteresis and Coulomb friction.

Viscous Damping

Viscous damping is the friction between a structure and its surrounding fluid. Viscous damping force can reasonably assume to be proportional to the velocity of the structural displacement

$$F_D = c\dot{x} \tag{1}$$

The viscous damping coefficient c can be input directly as an element parameter, such as a spring element [1]. In some analysis systems, the viscous damping can be specified using a global damping ratio ξ [2]. The damping coefficient c is then calculated according to Eqs. 12.1-2(10)-(11),

$$c = 2m\xi\omega = 2\xi\sqrt{mk} \tag{2}$$

Note that Eq. (2) involves a frequency; the damping c is frequency dependent. In some analysis systems, such as <Harmonic Response> analysis (Section 12.3), which calculates the response under various frequencies, the frequencies are well understood, so that Eq. (2) can be applied. For other analysis systems, such as <Transient Structural> analysis (Section 12.2), there is no way to apply Eq. (2) since frequencies are not known beforehand. Therefore, for a <Transient Structural> analysis, input of a constant damping ratio [2] is not allowed, that is, viscous damping is not considered as a global parameter. To introduce viscous damping to a structure for transient analyses, you may add individual elements involving viscous damping, such as spring elements [1].

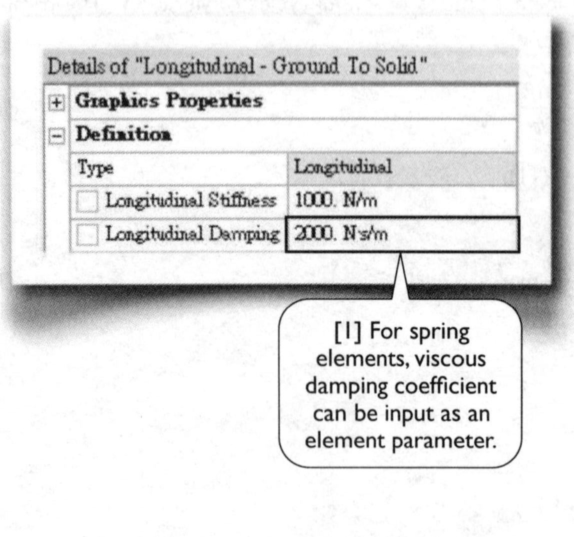

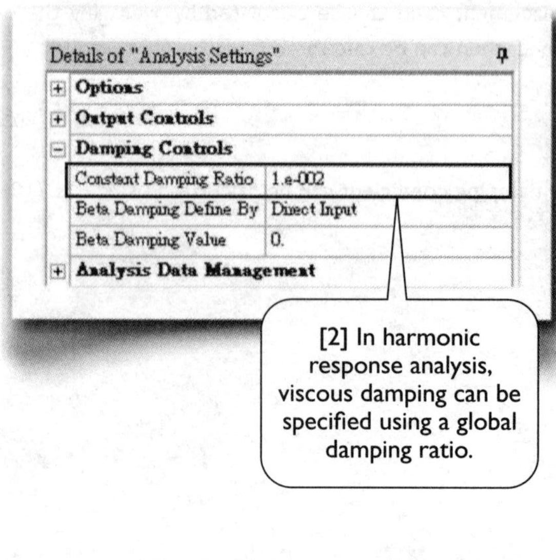

Material Damping

Material damping is the internal friction in the material. Other names of material damping include *solid damping* and *elastic hysteresis*. It is one of the major sources of damping.

To understand the material damping, consider a typical stress-strain relation in a uniaxial material test [3-5]. Unlike the tests shown in 1.4-1[1-5], here we repeatedly increase the stress [1] and then release the stress [2]. If the plastic deformation (permanent deformation) is not present, the strain will return to the original state when releasing the stress, and the curve of releasing stress is likely to be a straight line. A material in which the strain state returns to the original state when the stress is released is called an *elastic material.*

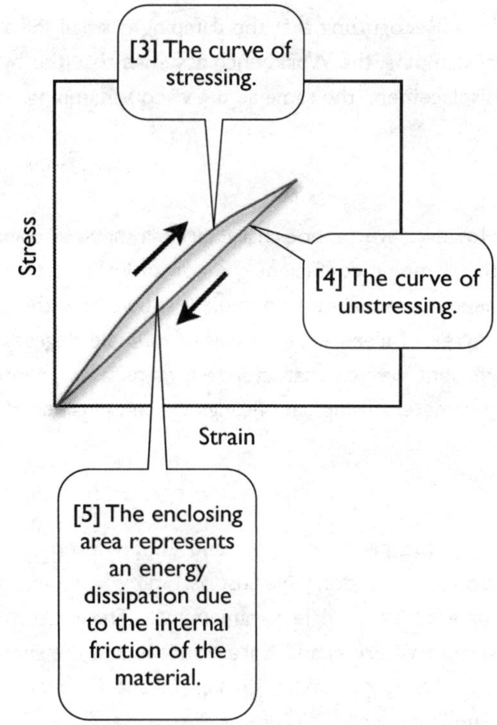

The area enclosed by the curves [5] represents the energy dissipation due to the internal friction of the material. Note that this area is typically very small; the plot [3-5] is exaggerated for instructional purpose. In linear elasticity, we assume that both curves [3, 4] are linear, and the energy loss is considered only when cyclic deformation (such as vibrations) is involved.

The plot [3-5] is similar to the *B-H* curve of a magnetic material [6], where *B* is the *magnetic flux density* and *H* is the *magnetic filed intensity*. A magnetic field *H* is applied on a magnetic material to create a *B* field within the material (i.e., the material is magnetized). The area enclosed by the *B-H* curve represents an energy dissipation, and is called the *magnetic hysteresis*. Because of the similarity, the energy dissipation in a stress-strain curve is called the *elastic hysteresis*.

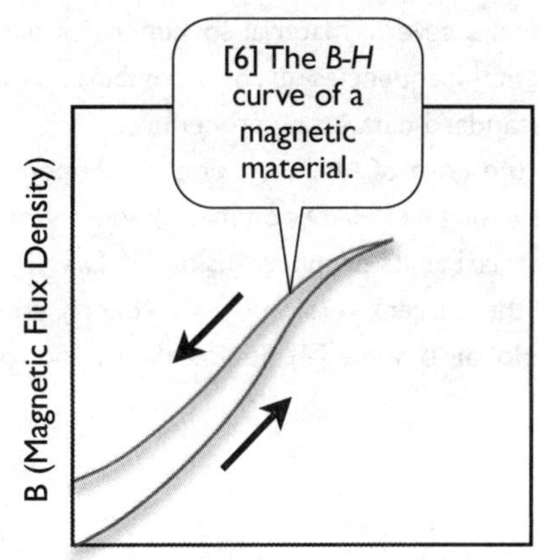

Hysteresis damping is difficult to be included in a mathematical model, such as Eq. 12.1-2(1). As far as a simulation is concerned, hysteresis damping force can be more reasonably assume to be proportional to the structural displacement rather than the velocity. Thus, we might assume the hysteris damping force is proportional to the displacement and its direction is opposite to the velocity,

$$F_D = hxi \qquad (3)$$

Where h is a proportional constant and $i = \sqrt{-1}$ is the imaginary unit. The inclusion of the imaginary unit is an additional assumption that the velocity is 90 degrees out of phase with the displacement; that is true for harmonic vibrations. Including the hysteris damping, Eq. (3), into Eq. 12.1-2(1), the governing equation becomes

$$m\ddot{x} + c\dot{x} + (k + hi)x = p \qquad (4)$$

The Eq. (4) needs a more sophisticated algorithm and the Workbench doesn't use Eq. (4); it uses Eq. 12.1-2(1).

Recognizing that the damping is small for a structure and the global behavior is similar regardless of the sources of damping, the Workbench assumes that the hysteris damping force is proportional to the velocity of the structural displacement, the same as the viscous damping,

$$F_D = c\dot{x} \tag{5}$$

However, we cannot characterize a material using a damping coefficient c. As mentioned in the end of Section 12.1-2, the damping coefficient c is not an intrinsic property of a material. To filter out other factors, such as geometry, we need more elaboration. Eq. (2) shows how the coefficient c relates to the mass m and stiffness k for the case of single degree of freedom; for cases of multiple degrees of freedom, the relation is not so simple. In engineering practice, an efficient way to characterize a material is proposing a mathematics form with parameters and then determining the parameters using data fitting. We assume that the coefficient c is a linear combination of the mass m and the stiffness k, that is,

$$c = \alpha m + \beta k \tag{6}$$

Now, the parameters α and β are used to characterize the damping property of a material. The students may wonder why don't we just assume $c = \gamma\sqrt{mk}$, which would be closer to the form of Eq. (2), and characterize the material by a single parameter γ. The reason is that, in general, we are dealing with multiple degrees of freedom system, where m and k are matrices, and the simple relation of Eq. (2) doesn't exist.

Using $c = 2m\xi\omega$ in Eq. (2) and $k = m\omega^2$ in Eq. 12.1-2(5), Eq. (6) can be rewritten in terms of frequency and damping ratio,

$$2\xi\omega = \alpha + \beta\omega^2 \tag{7}$$

If we can make a single material specimen and measure the damping ratios ξ_i under different excitation frequencies ω_i, or make several material specimens of different sizes, and measure the damping ratios ξ_i under their respective fundamental frequencies ω_i, or a combination of the above ideas, then we can evaluate the material parameters α and β by a standard data fitting procedure.

In the core of ANSYS, it does implement the idea of Eq. (6). Using the APDL commands[2], you can input a global α value (using ALPHAD command) and a global β value (using BETAD command). You also can input β value for each material as its property (using MP, DAMP).

In the current version of Workbench, you cannot input a global α value (it assumes $\alpha = 0$), but it allows you to input a global β value [7]. It also allows you to input a β value for each material as a material property [8, 9].

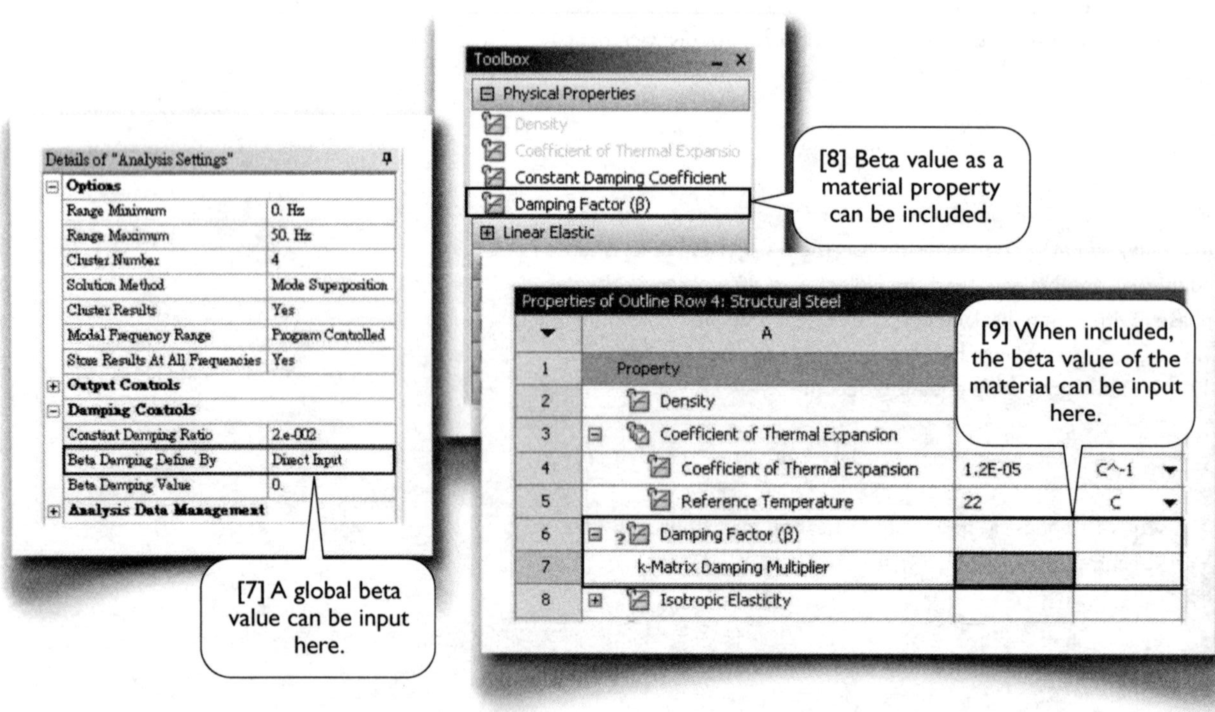

Since the Workbench assumes $\alpha = 0$, Eq. (7) becomes

$$\beta = \frac{2\xi}{\omega} \tag{8}$$

Eq. (8) is a simple relation between the β value and the damping ratio ξ. It can be used to estimate one value when knowing the other one, if the frequency is also known.

Although the damping ratio is meant to be used for the viscous damping [2] rather than the material damping, in practice, the engineers often use a damping ratio to simplify the overall damping effect, when the damping is not critical to the response. As mentioned in Section 12.1-2, values of damping ratio for typical structures range from 0.02 to 0.07.

Coulomb Friction

Another major source of damping is the friction in the connection between structural members. It is called the *dry friction* or *Coulomb friction*. In the Workbench, it is implemented as *frictional contacts*. To include the Coulomb friction, you have to specify frictional contacts between parts, which will be discussed in Chapter 13.

12.1-4 Analysis Systems

Generally, we are dealing with multiple-degrees-of-freedom systems. The foregoing concepts may be generalized to include general cases. Specifically, Eq. 12.1-2(1) can be generalized for general cases,

$$[M]\{\ddot{D}\}+[C]\{\dot{D}\}+[K]\{D\}=\{F\} \tag{1}$$

Where $\{D\}$ is the nodal displacements vector, $\{F\}$ is the nodal external forces vector, $[M]$ is called the *mass matrix*, $[C]$ is called the *damping matrix*, and $[K]$ is the stiffness matrix. Eq. (1) also can be viewed as a generalization of Eq. 1.3-1(1).

Eq. (1) represents the governing equation of a transient structural simulation. It can be viewed as a force equilibrium relation. On the right hand side of the equation is the external force $\{F\}$. The first item on the left hand side, $[M]\{\ddot{D}\}$, is termed the *inertia force*; the second item, $[C]\{\dot{D}\}$, is called the *damping force*, and the third item, $[K]\{D\}$, is called the *elastic force*. Combination of the inertia force, damping force, and the elastic force balances with the external force.

Let's look at some specialized cases of Eq. (1) [1].

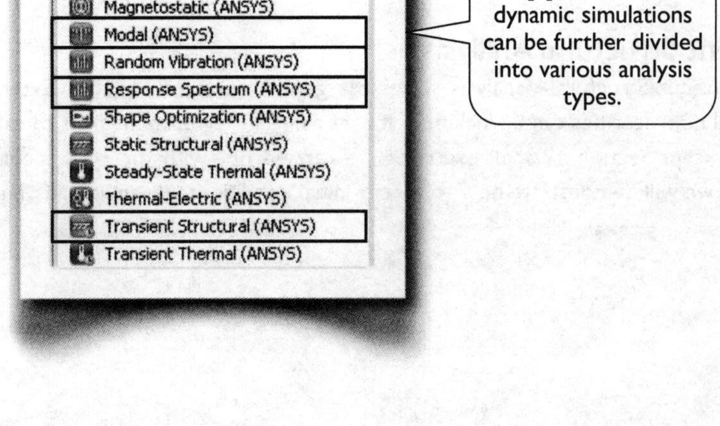

Modal Analysis

Imagine that you displace a structure a certain amount and then release. There is no external force involved; it is called a free vibration. Eq. (1), since there is no external forces, becomes

$$[M]\{\ddot{D}\}+[C]\{\dot{D}\}+[K]\{D\}=0 \qquad (2)$$

Solution of Eq. (2) is not unique. For a problems of n degrees of freedom, it has at most n solutions, denoted by $\{D_i\}, i=1,2,...,n$. These solutions are called *mode shapes* of the structure. Each mode shape $\{D_i\}$ can be resonantly excited by an external excitation of frequency ω_i, called the natural frequency of the mode. The lowest frequency is called the *fundamental natural frequency*, or simply *fundamental frequency*. Finding all or some of the mode shapes and their corresponding natural frequencies is called a *modal analysis*.

In a modal analysis, since we are usually interested only in the natural frequencies and the relative shapes of the vibration modes (the absolute values of deformation depend on the energy that excites the structure), the damping effect can be neglected (see Eq. 12.1-2(9)) to simplify the calculation; Eq. (2) becomes

$$[M]\{\ddot{D}\}+[K]\{D\}=0 \qquad (3)$$

It is Eq. (3) that the Workbench solves in a <Modal> analysis system. Note that modal analysis is a linear analysis; all nonlinearities are ignored.

Harmonic Response Analysis

Imagine that a rotatory machine is installed on the floor of the two-story building (Sections 7.3, 11.2). Assume the operational speed of the machine is 3000 rpm. Due to an inevitable eccentricity of the rotation, the machine may generate an up-and-down harmonic force on the floor. When started up, the machine's speed increases from zero up to 3000 rpm. Any natural frequencies of the building ranging from zero to 3000 rpm may be excited by the harmonic force. Vibrations of the building or its structural components are unavoidable; the question is how large amplitude of the vibrations will happen. Do the vibrations cause any safety concern or psychological annoyance? A <Harmonic Response> analysis can be carried out to answer that question.

The <Harmonic Response> analysis solves a special form of Eq. (1), in which the external force on *i*th degree of freedom is of the form

$$F_i = A_i \sin(\Omega t+\phi_i) \qquad (4)$$

where A_i is the amplitude of the force, ϕ_i is the phase angle of the force, and Ω is the angular frequency of the external force. Due to the special form of the external forces, the calculation is much more efficient than a general transient response analysis. The steady-state solution of the equation will be of the form

$$D_i = B_i \sin(\Omega t+\varphi_i) \qquad (5)$$

The goal of the harmonic response analysis to find the magnitude B_i and the phase angle φ_i of the response for each degree of freedom. Note that harmonic response analysis is a linear analysis; all nonlinearities are ignored.

In Section 12.3, we will use the two-story building to demonstrate the procedure of the harmonic response analysis.

Transient Structural Analysis

The <Transient Structural> analysis solves the general form of Eq. (1). External force $\{F\}$ can be time-dependent forces. All nonlinearities can be included. It uses a *direct integration methods* to calculated the dynamic response. In this chapter, except Section 12.3, all exercises are carried out with the <Transient Structural> system. Through these exercises, we will demonstrate how to specify initial conditions, dynamic loads, and set up the <Analysis Settings>.

Explicit Dynamics

Similar to the <Transient Structural>, the <Explicit Dynamics> also solves the general form of Eq. (1). External force $\{F\}$ can be time-dependent forces. All nonlinearities can be included. It also uses a direct integration methods to calculated the dynamic response. The difference is described as follows.

The direct integration method used in the <Transient Structural> analysis is called an *implicit integration method*. The implicit method works fine for most of applications except for high-speed impact simulations.

In high-speed impact simulations, the duration of impact time is so short that the integration time needs to be extremely small (e.g., micro to nano seconds) to catch the details behavior. The total number of time steps becomes huge that the computational time is unbearable. That calls for an *explicit integration method*, implemented in the <Explicit Dynamics> analysis system.

For most of transient dynamic simulations, the explicit method is not popular for one reasons: it requires very small integration time steps to achieve an accurate solution. A small integration time is exactly what a high-speed impact simulation needs, therefore it is not a disadvantage any more. The advantage, on the other hand, is that the calculation is very efficient in each time step. Overall, the high-speed impact simulations are possible only with the explicit integration method.

There are cases, other than high-speed impact simulations, that are benefited by using the explicit method. Highly nonlinear simulations usually require very small time steps to overcome the convergence difficulties. In such cases, explicit method is often used.

In this chapter, we will restrict the discussion in implicit dynamics only (i.e., using <Transient Structural> analysis system). The applications of <Explicit Dynamics> will be postponed until Chapter 15. The reason is that, since explicit dynamics usually involves nonlinearities, we need more background on nonlinear simulations, which will be covered in Chapters 13 and 14.

For the beginners, the origination of the names "implicit" or "explicit" may not be very important. You may regard them as code names. For those students with strong curiosity, you will learn it in Section 15.1.

Response Spectrum Analysis

We often design an engineering object such that it can withstand oscillatory or repeated loadings. For example, a building must withstand the strikes of earthquakes. When designing a building, we may use a well-recorded earthquake as a "design earthquake." The history of the earthquake (typically a history of acceleration versus time) can be input as loads and a transient structural simulation is then carried out. After the simulation, the maximum stress (or any other responses) at each location of the structure is collected. The members of the structure is designed according to these maximum values of responses. If the maximum response is the sole purpose of the simulation, a much inexpensive way of simulation is available, response spectrum analysis.

A time history of earthquake can be transformed to a response spectrum, a maximum response versus frequency (or period) plot. The response spectrum is then input to a <Response Spectrum> analysis system. The output is the maximum response (e.g., maximum stress) at each location of the structure.

Random Vibration Analysis

There exists a design philosophy that speaks in a language of probability. The probabilistic loads are described by a spectrum representing probability distribution of excitation at varying frequencies in known directions. The technique is used to design structures withstanding random loadings, for example, a space vehicle subject to random strikes of meteorites or asteroids.

References

1. Cook, R.D., Milkus, D. S., Plesha, M. E., and Witt, R. J., *Concepts and Applications of Finite Element Analysis, Fourth Edition*, John Wiley & Sons, Inc., 2002; Section 11.5 Damping.
2. ANSYS Help System>Mechanical APDL>Theory Reference>15.3. Damping Matrices.

Section 12.2

Step-by-Step: Lifting Fork

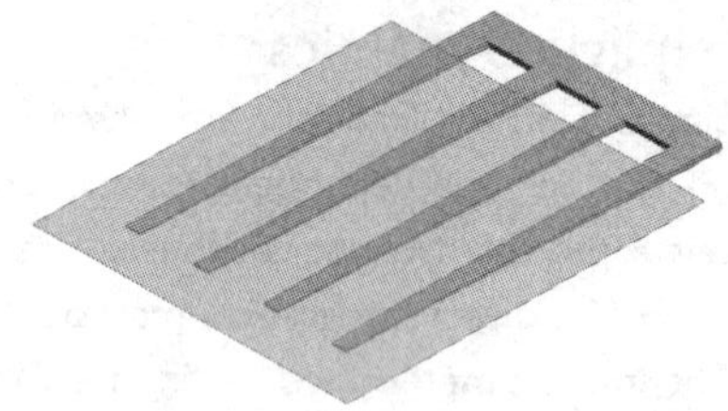

12.2-1 About the Lifting Fork

In Section 4.3, we built a model for a lifting fork and glass. The lifting fork [1] is used in an LCD factory to handle the glass panel [2]. The fork is modeled as solid body and the glass as surface body. The glass panel is so unprecedentedly large that the engineers concern about its vertical deflections during the dynamic handling.

The fork is made of steel with a density of 7850 kg/m^3, Young's modulus of 200 GPa, and Poisson's ratio of 0.3. The glass has a density of 2370 kg/m^3, Young's modulus of 70 GPa, and Poisson's ratio of 0.22.

In this section we will perform a static structural simulation first, to evaluate the vertical deflection of the glass panel under the gravitational force. This is a critical when determining the clearance of the processing machine [3]. During the dynamic handling, the fork accelerates upward to 6 m/s in 0.3 second and then decelerates to stop in another 0.3 second, causing the glass panel vibrate [4]. We want to know the time duration when the vibration is settled to a certain amount so that the glass can be pushed into the processing machine [3]. We also want to know the maximum stress during the handling. Before the simulation of the dynamic handling, we will perform a modal analysis to obtain the vibration frequency of the system. This frequency will help us estimate the initial integration time step.

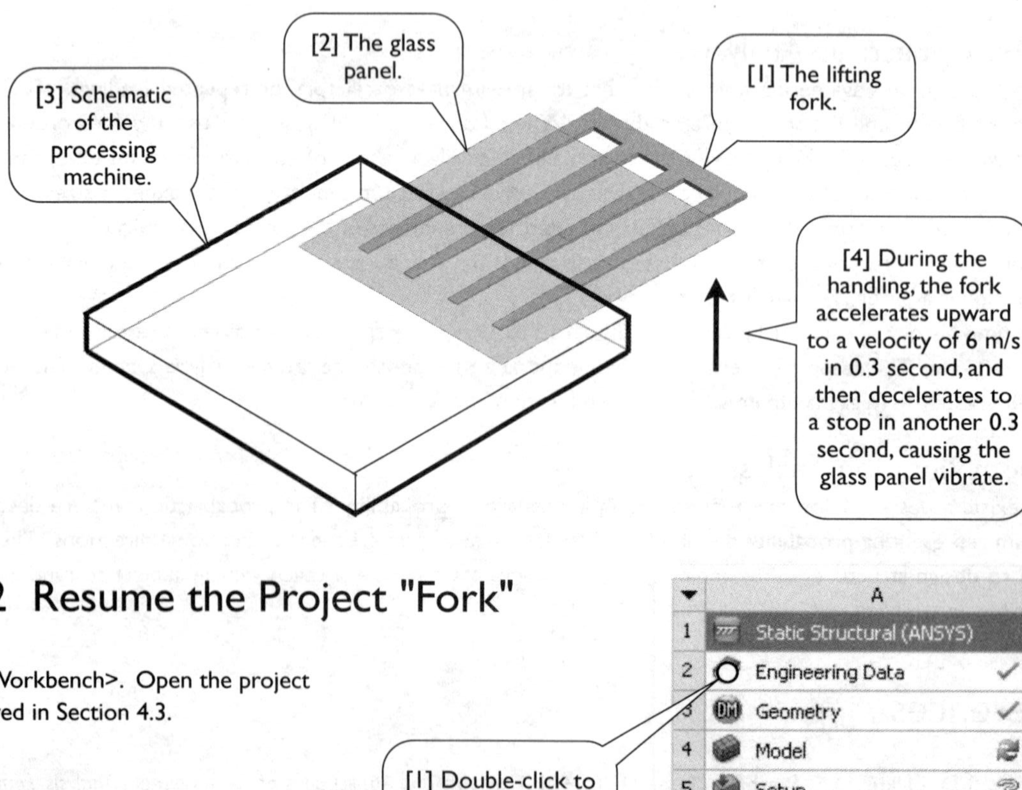

12.2-2 Resume the Project "Fork"

Launch <Workbench>. Open the project "Fork," saved in Section 4.3.

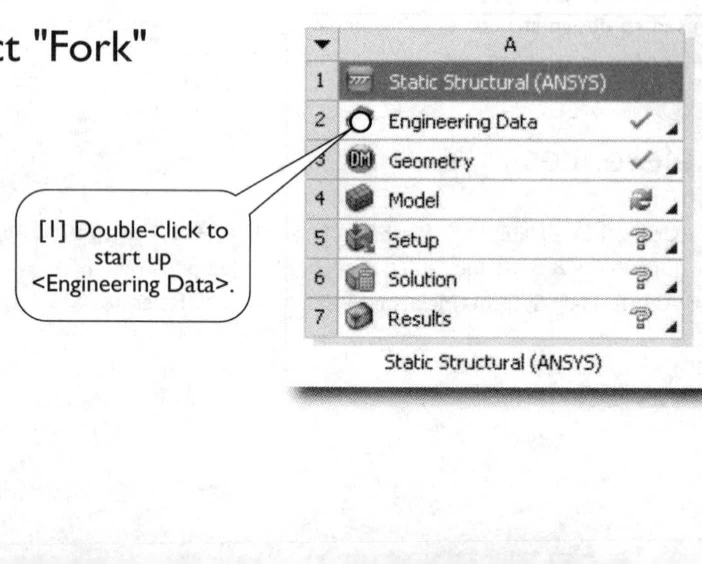

12.2-3 Set Up the Model

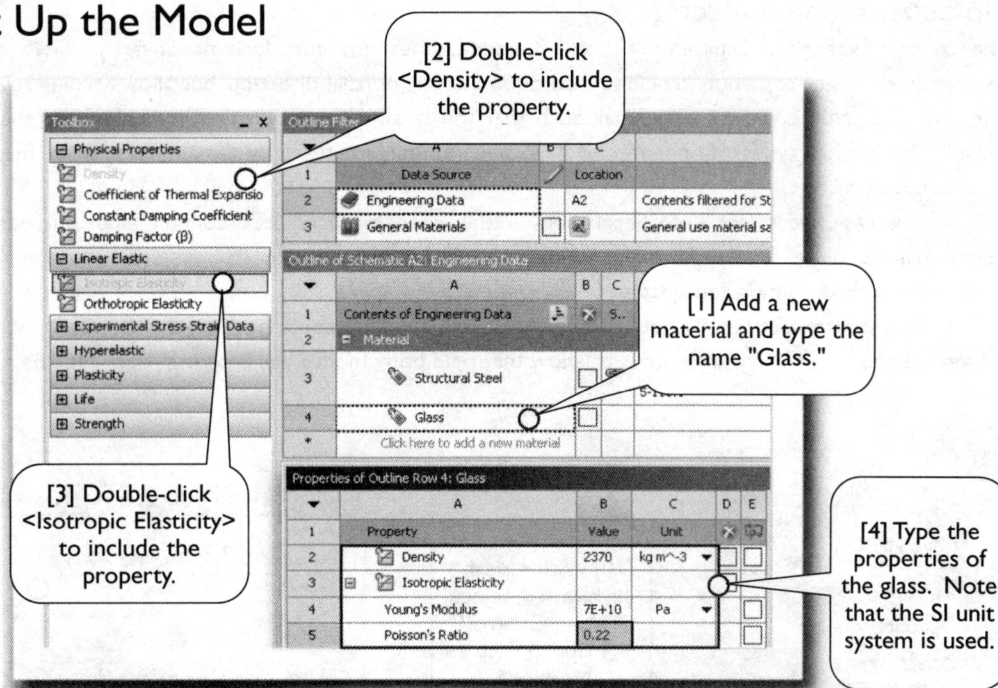

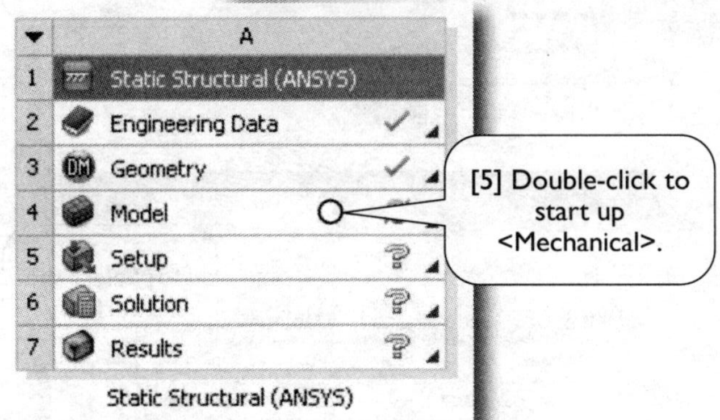

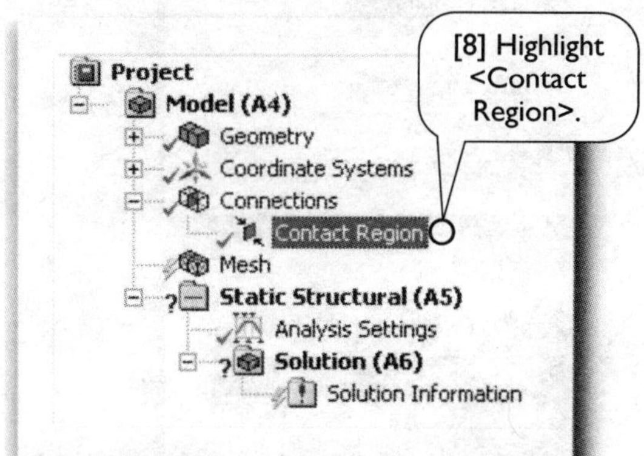

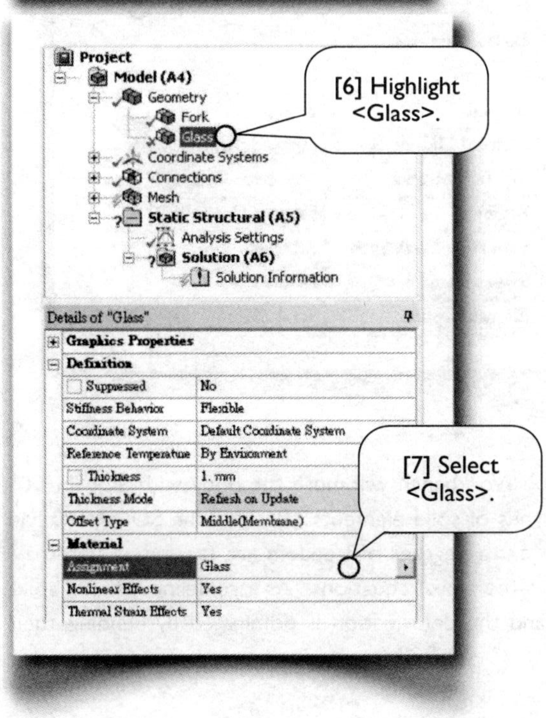

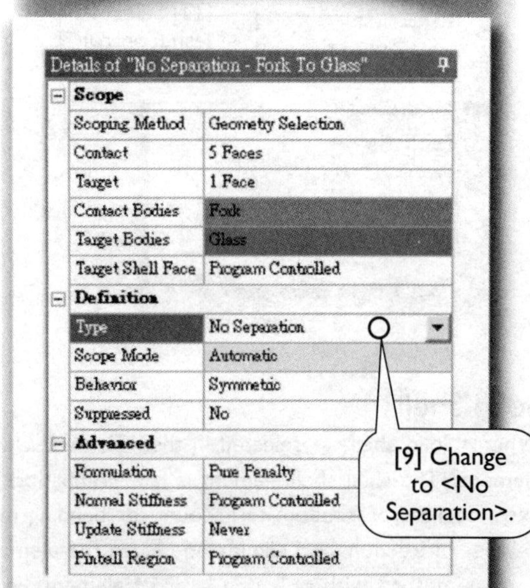

No Separation Contact

The contact type <No Separation>, like <Bonded>, does not introduce nonlinearity. Two surfaces with <No Separation> contact condition prohibits separation in their normal direction, but allows sliding relative to each other. The sliding is assumed to be very small such that the small-deformation theory applies and the simulation remain linear. The contact types <Bonded> and <No Separation> are the only two contact types that do not introduce contact nonlinearity.

In this case, we select <No Separation> rather than more realistic contact types such as <Frictionless> or <Frictional>, because small-deformation theory should be adequate for this case and we don't want to introduce nonlinearity into the simulation system.

In fact, the contact type is not crucial in this example. You could have select <Bonded> type in step [9]. One reason we assume <No Separation> is to show that rigid body modes will appear in the <Modal> analysis (12.2-5[4]).

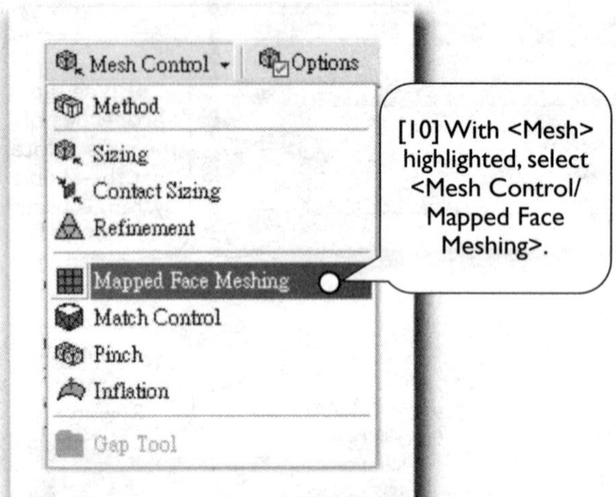

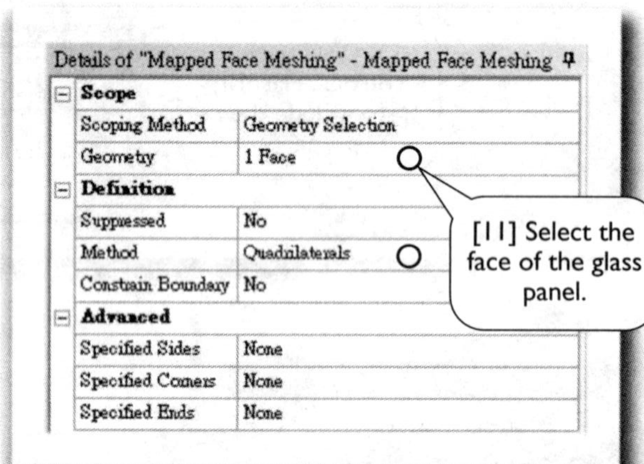

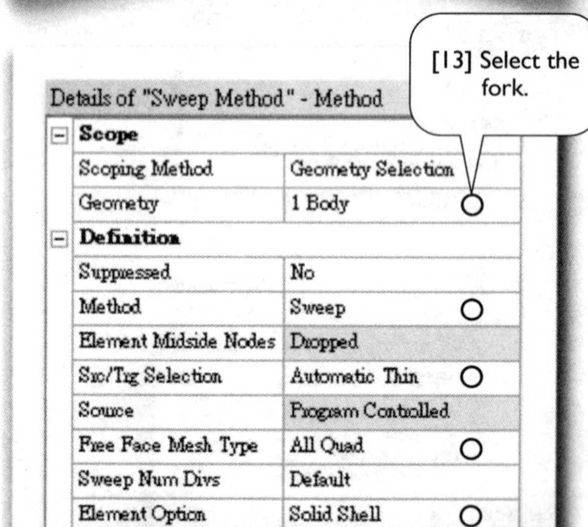

Solid Shell

When <Solid Shell> is selected in the <Element Option> [13], the Workbench will mesh the body with SOLSH190[1] element. The solid shell element is fully compatible with other types of solid elements. Besides, the SOLSH190 has extra degrees of freedom to account for bending modes. These extra degrees of freedom are treated as "internal" degrees of freedom and eliminated before the element is added to the global equations. As a guideline, when a solid body is meshed with only one layer of elements in a direction and the deformation is dominated by bending, then <Solid Shell> is an appropriate choice.

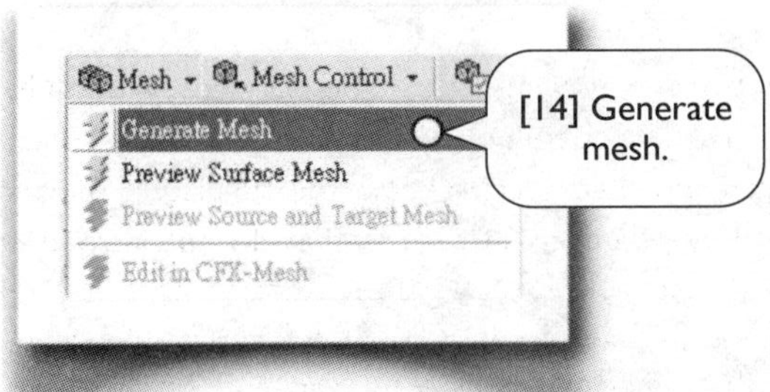

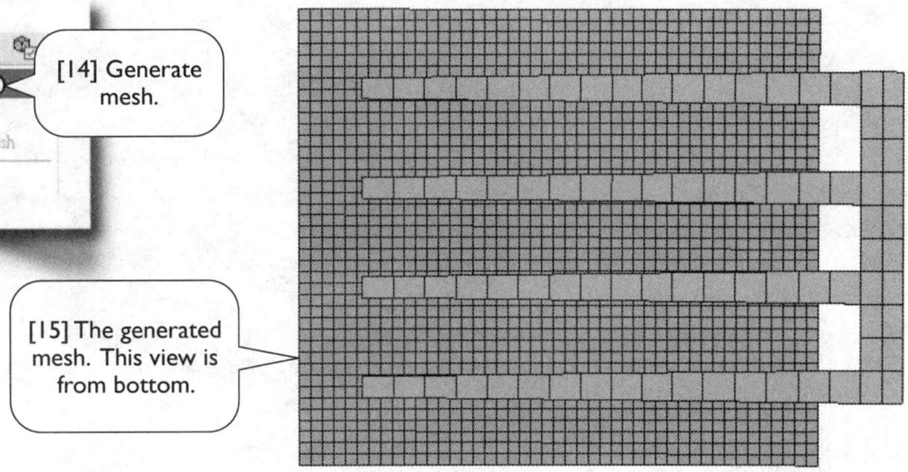

12.2-4 Evaluate Deflection Under Gravity

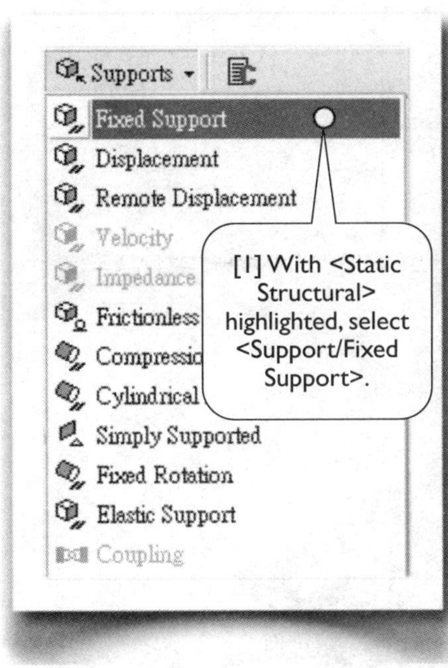

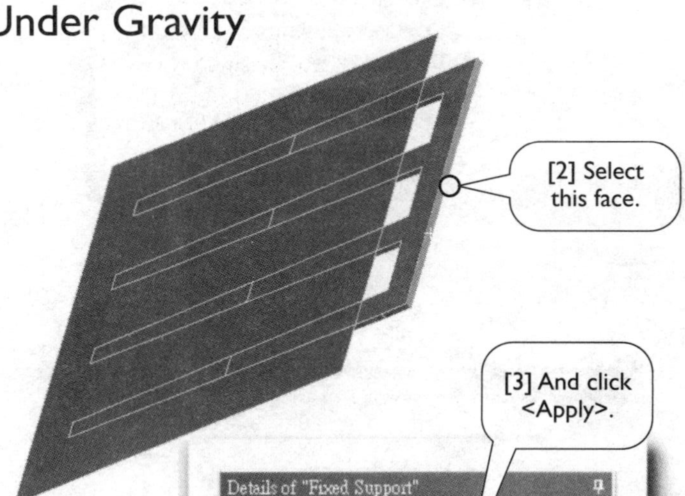

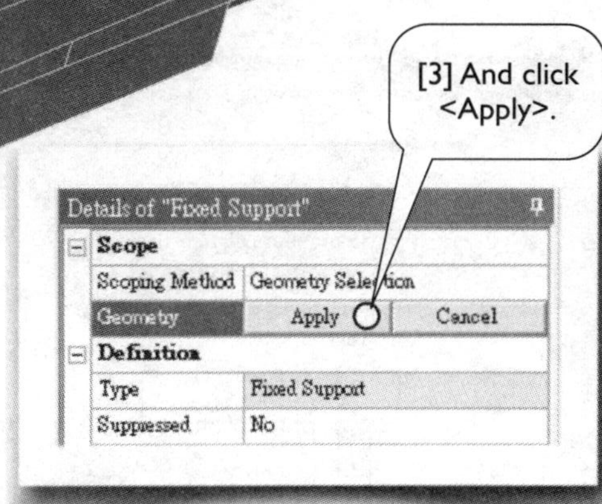

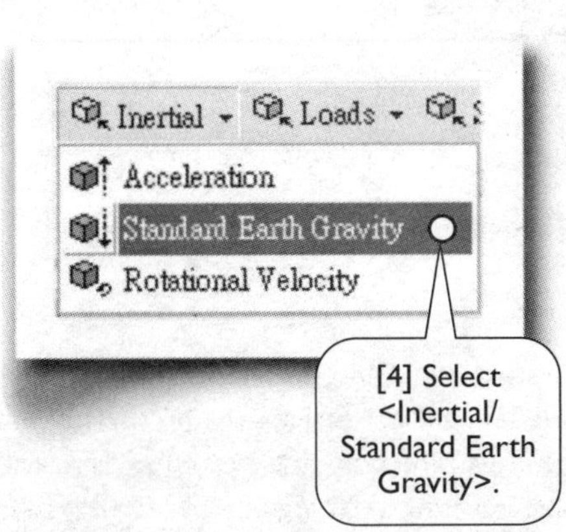

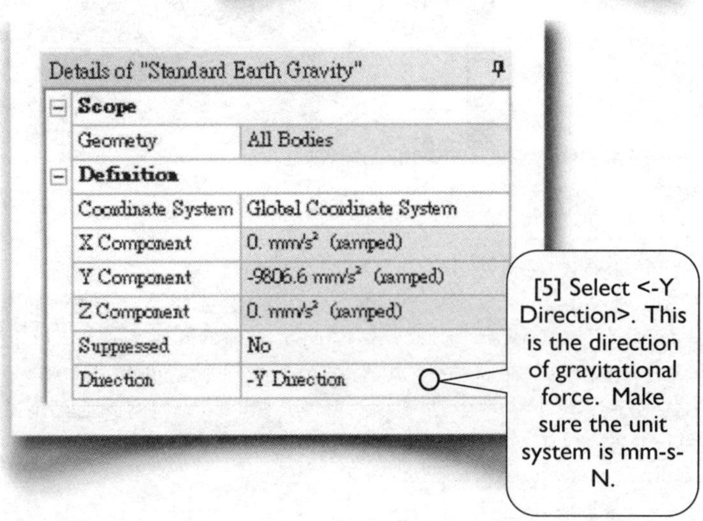

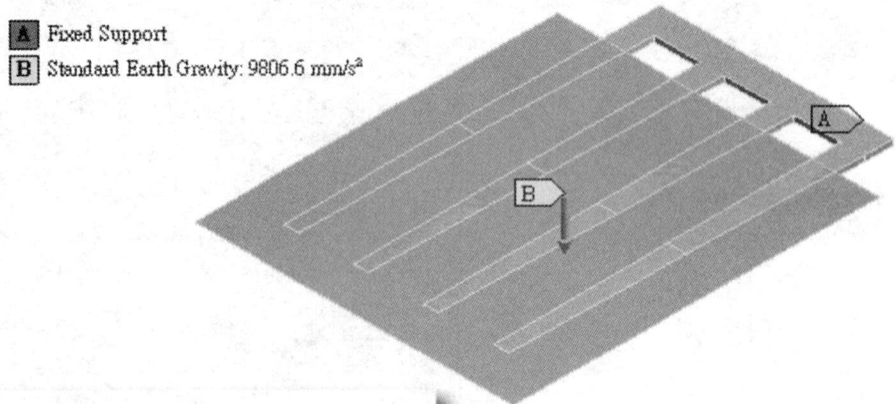

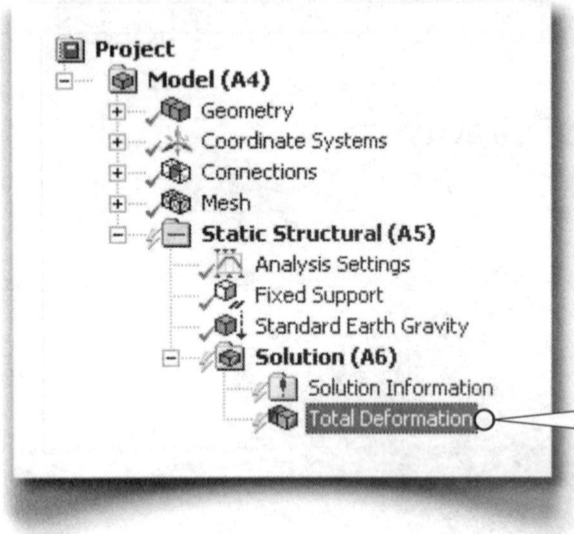

[6] Insert a <Total Deformation> under the <Solution> and solve the model.

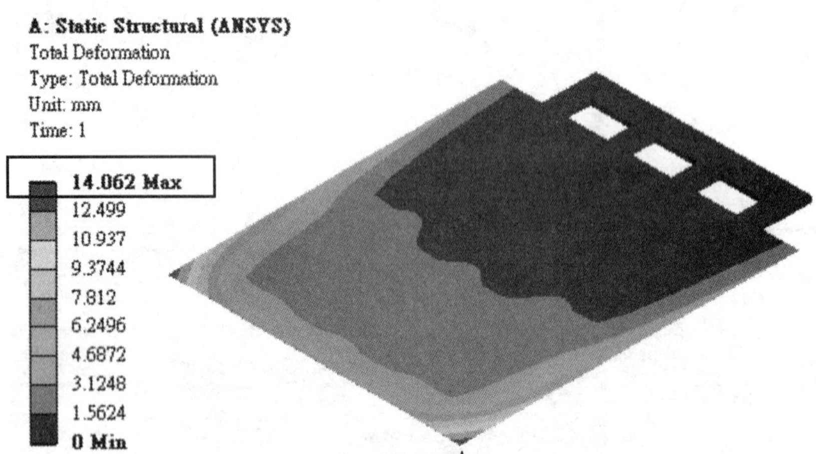

[7] The maximum deflection is 14 mm.

12.2-5 Evaluate Natural Frequencies

[1] Leave the <Mechanical> open. Drag-and-drop a <Modal> system to <Model>. Note that we neglect the effect of prestress, since the prestress has little effect in this case.

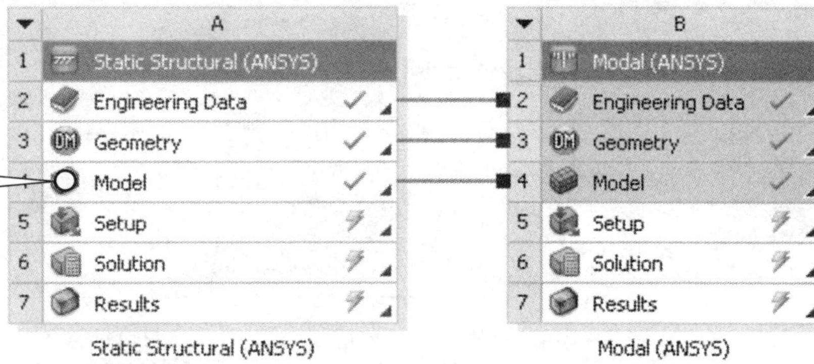

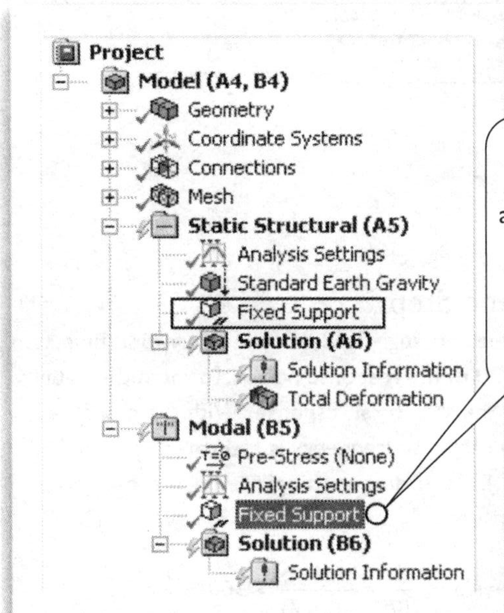

[2] Note that the project tree is automatically updated. Drag-and-drop the <Fixed Support> from <Static Structural> to <Modal>.

[3] Solve.

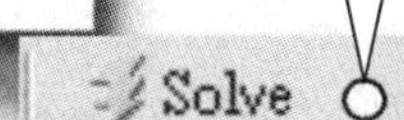

[4] Rigid body modes.

Tabular Data

	Mode	Frequency [Hz]
1	1.	0.
2	2.	0.
3	3.	0.
4	4.	6.6821
5	5.	6.6822
6	6.	9.4258

[5] The lowest nonzero frequency is the fundamental frequency.

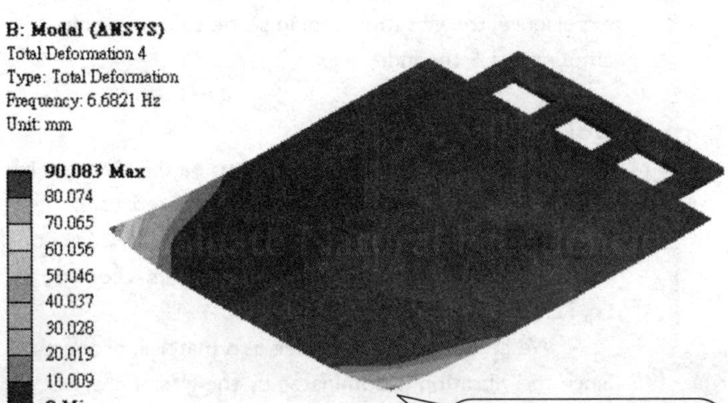

[6] The mode shape corresponding to the fundamental frequency.

Exploring Free Vibration Modes

Since the <No Separation> contact allows sliding between the surfaces of the glass panel and the fork, there are 3 rigid body modes: X-translation, Z-translation, and Y-rotation of the glass [4]. The rigid body motions have infinite large value of period, or zero values of frequency, since they are not oscillatory motions.

The lowest nonzero frequency mode [5, 6] is what we concern, since the vibrations will be dominated by the fundamental mode (12.2-1[4]). The frequency of vibrations is estimated to be 6.7 Hz.

12.2-6 Perform Transient Structural Simulation

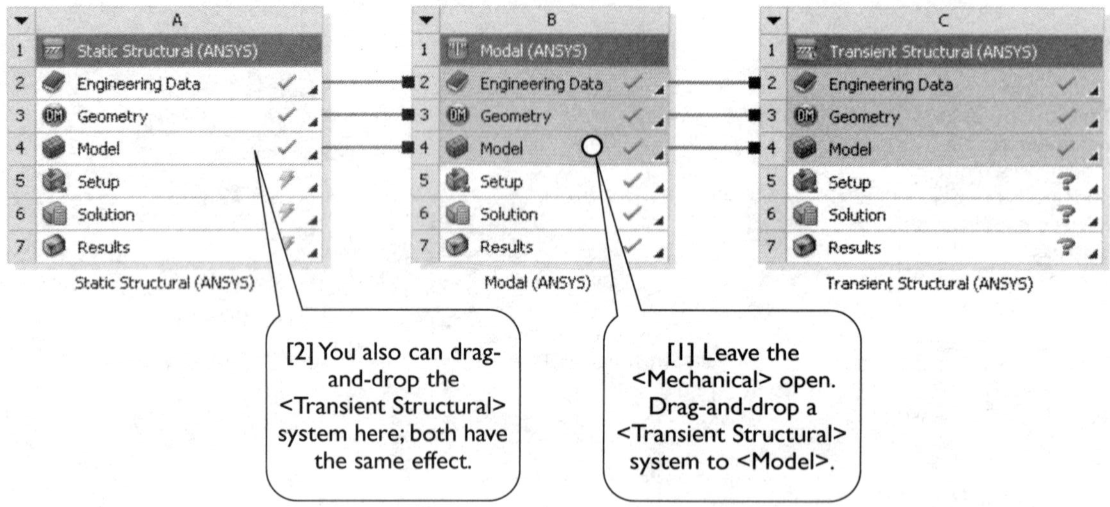

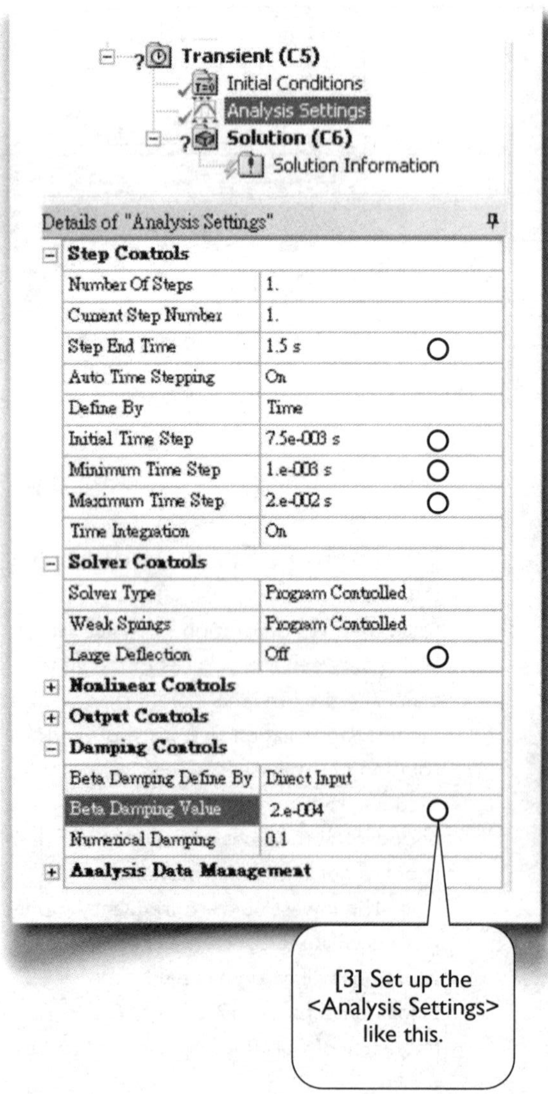

Initial Time Step

As a guideline, it is suggested that the integration time step be about 1/20 of the response period, to catch the detail behavior of the structural response. With the modal analysis, the response frequency is estimated to be 6.7 Hz (12.2-5[5, 6]). According to this guideline, the integration time step is about

$$ITS = \frac{1}{20f} = \frac{1}{20(6.7)} = 0.0075 \text{ sec.}$$

Step End Time

This is the total simulation time. According to the experience, the vibration should settle to a negligible amount in 1.5 second.

Beta Damping Value

The beta damping value is reported to be 0.0002 from lab experiments. The experiments are conducted, using specimens of the glass, as described in the end of Section 12.1-3. The beta damping value is calculated according to Eq. 12.1-3(8).

We could specify this value as a material property. Since the vibration is dominated by the glass, here, we choose to input the beta value as a global damping value, that is, neglecting the difference caused by the steel material.

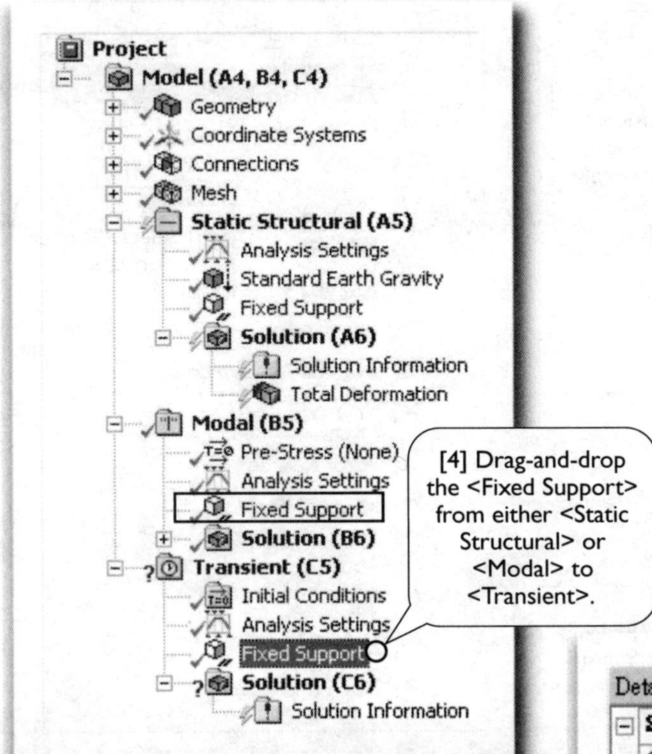

Why Fixed Support?

During the handling process, the fork is not fixed. It can freely move in the vertical direction. We could have set up a <Frictionless> support for the same face and allowed the fork to move vertically. Obtaining absolute values of vertical displacement, however, is not what we concern. Our goal is to investigate the vibration behavior. If we let the fork move with such a large displacement, the small displacement of vibrations would be numerically overwhelmed, so that you would not see the vibrations at all.

By setting up <Fixed Support> at the face of the fork, and applying inertia force downward (since the fork accelerates upward), we will have the same effect and avoid the numerical problems.

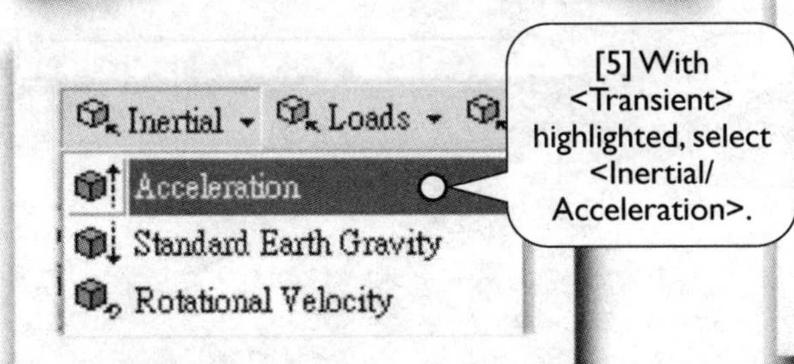

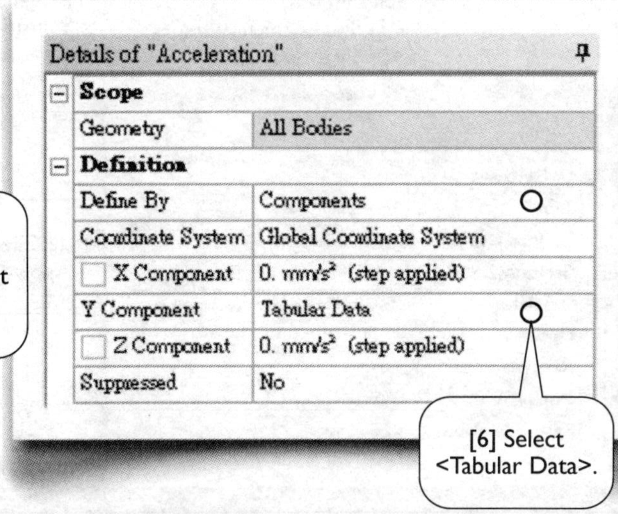

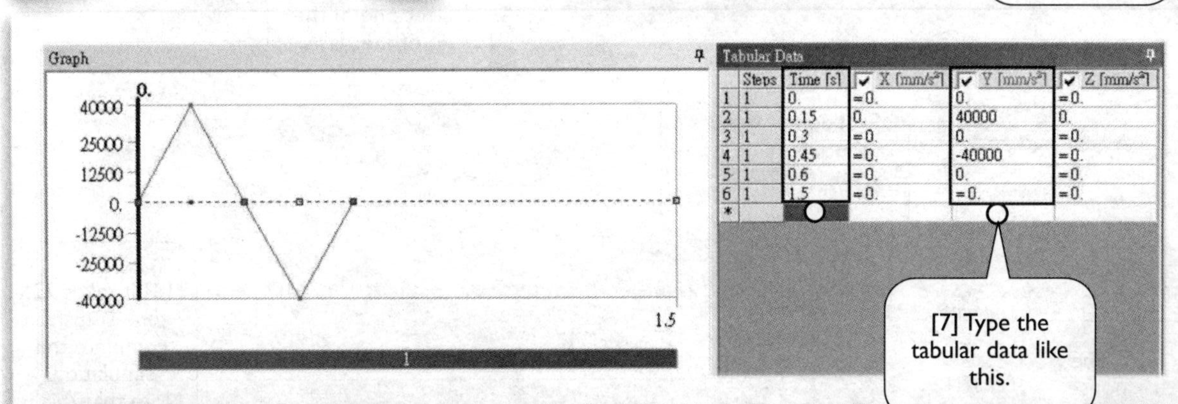

	Steps	Time [s]	X [mm/s²]	Y [mm/s²]	Z [mm/s²]
1	1	0.	=0.	0.	=0.
2	1	0.15	0.	40000	0.
3	1	0.3	=0.	0.	=0.
4	1	0.45	=0.	-40000	=0.
5	1	0.6	=0.	0.	=0.
6	1	1.5	=0.	=0.	=0.
*					

How does the tabular data come from?

During the handling, the fork accelerates upward until a speed of 6 m/s in 0.3 second and then decelerates until a full stop in another 0.3 second. The average acceleration is thus 20 m/s^2, but it is not a constant acceleration. The control system controls the acceleration such that it increases linearly to 40 m/s^2 and than decreases to zero linearly. That way, the impact will be minimized and thus the amplitude of vibrations will be minimized too. The same idea applies during the deceleration.

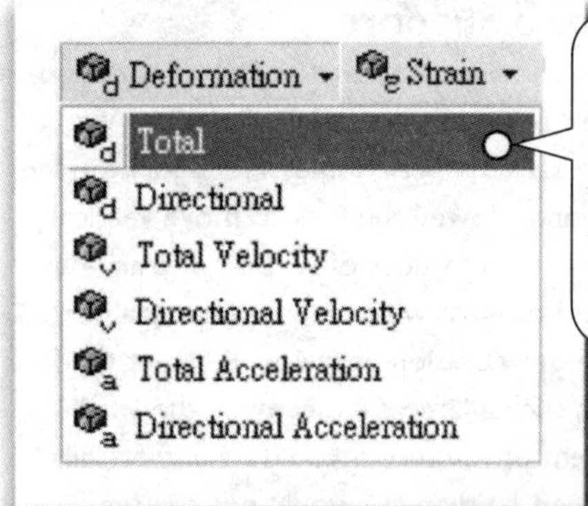

[8] With <Solution> of the <Transient> highlighted, select <Deformation/Total>.

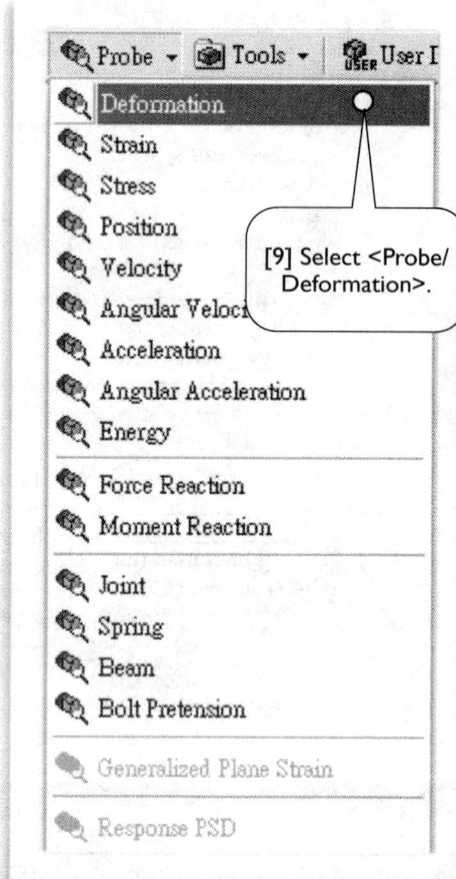

[9] Select <Probe/ Deformation>.

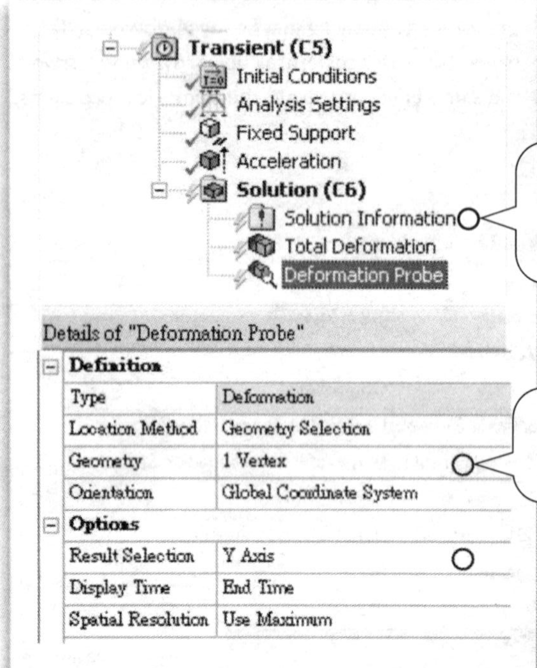

[12] Highlight <Solution Information>.

[11] Click <Apply>.

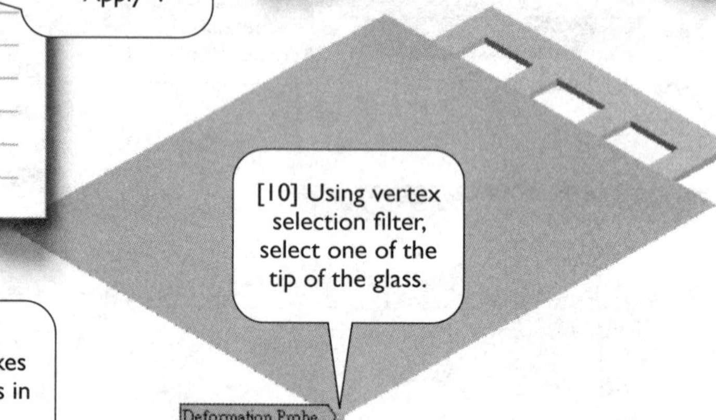

[10] Using vertex selection filter, select one of the tip of the glass.

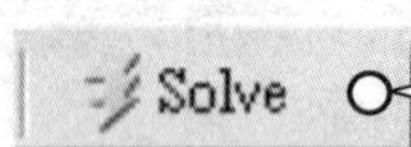

[13] Solve. It takes about 25 minutes in my computer.

```
  FORCE CONVERGENCE VALUE  =  21.50       CRITERION=  3.183
  MOMENT CONVERGENCE VALUE = 0.8528E-03  CRITERION=  115.9
* LOAD STEP     1   SUBSTEP   224  COMPLETED.    CUM ITER =     224
* TIME =   1.49742          TIME INC =  0.669661E-02  NEW TRIANG MATRIX
* RESPONSE FREQ =  10.46       PERIOD=  0.9556E-01  PTS/CYC =  14.
* AUTO TIME STEP:  NEXT TIME INC = 0.25762E-02  DECREASED (FACTOR = 0.3847)

  FORCE CONVERGENCE VALUE  =  36.24       CRITERION=  2.893
  MOMENT CONVERGENCE VALUE = 0.3740E-02  CRITERION=  105.3
*** LOAD STEP     1   SUBSTEP   225  COMPLETED.    CUM ITER =     225
*** TIME =   1.50000          TIME INC =  0.257621E-02  NEW TRIANG MATRIX
*** RESPONSE FREQ =  10.26       PERIOD=  0.9746E-01  PTS/CYC =  38.
```

[15] The response frequency is 10-11 Hz.

[14] It takes 225 time steps to complete the simulation. Note that this is a linear simulation. There is no nonlinearity involved. Each time step needs only one iteration.

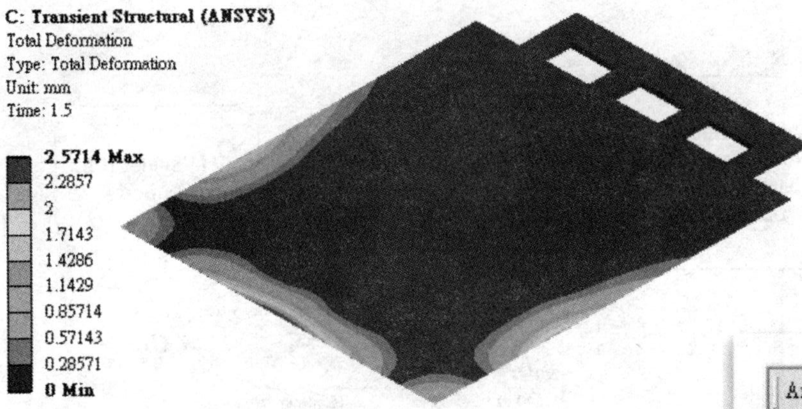

[16] Highlight <Total Deformation> to animate the dynamic response.

[17] Remember to select <Result Sets>.

[18] Highlight <Deformation Probe> to study the displacement of the tip.

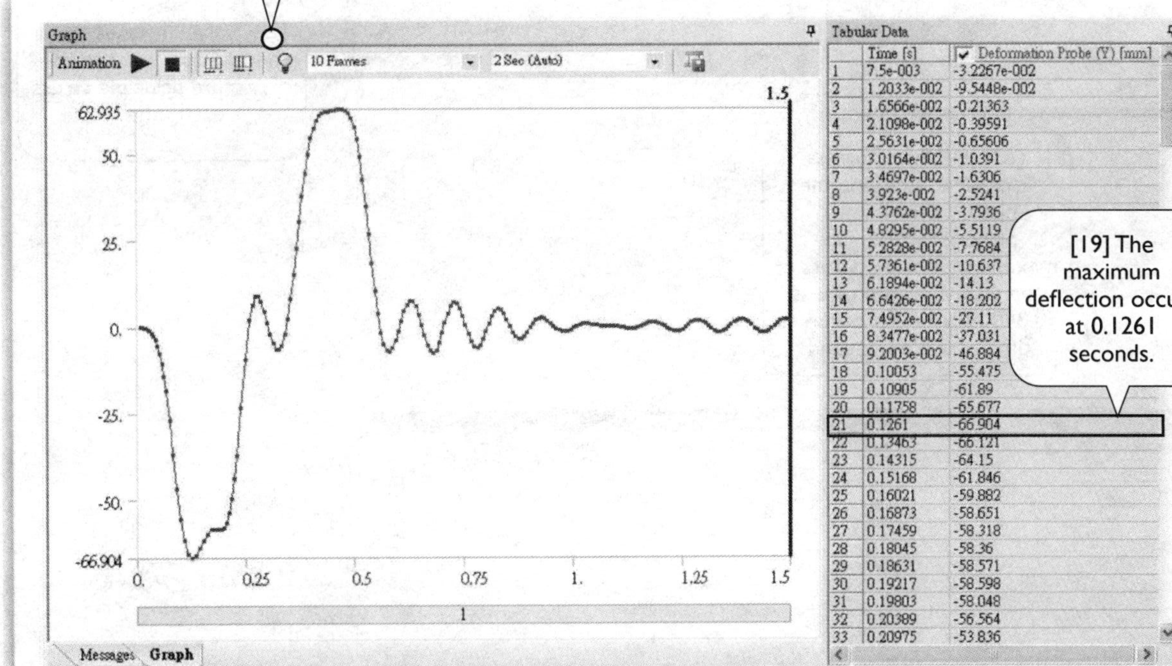

[19] The maximum deflection occurs at 0.1261 seconds.

Observation

The maximum deflection is 67 mm (downward), which occurs at 0.1261 seconds. The vibrations damps out very fast. The vibration reduces to a negligible amount at about 1.0 second. The response frequency is about 10-11 Hz [15], which deviates from our estimation (6.7 Hz) a substantial amount, but it doesn't matter since the estimated frequency is used for calculating the initial time step only. The Workbench automatically adjusts the time step according to the response frequency.

Next, we want to investigate the maximum stress and its location.

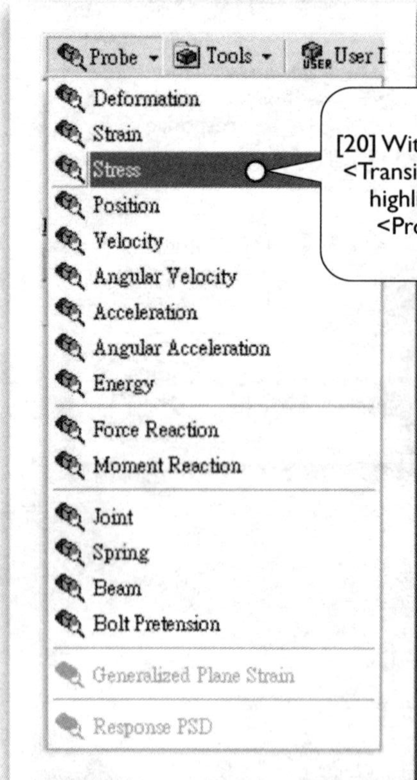

[20] With <Solution> of <Transient Structural> highlighted, select <Probe/Stress>.

[21] Select the glass body.

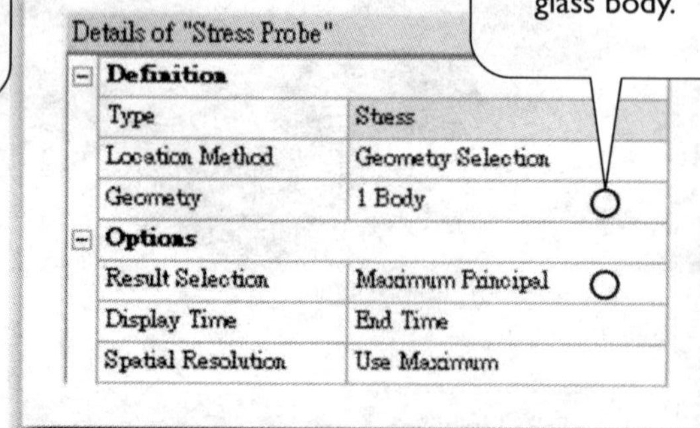

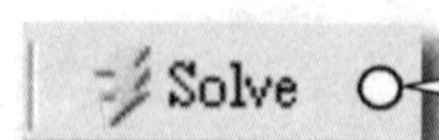

[22] Solve. It takes a few minutes to evaluate the maximum principle stress at each time step.

[23] Highlight <Stress Probe> to examine the history of maximum principal stress. The maximum principle stress of the glass over the time is 40.849 MPa, which occurs at time of 0.1261 second.

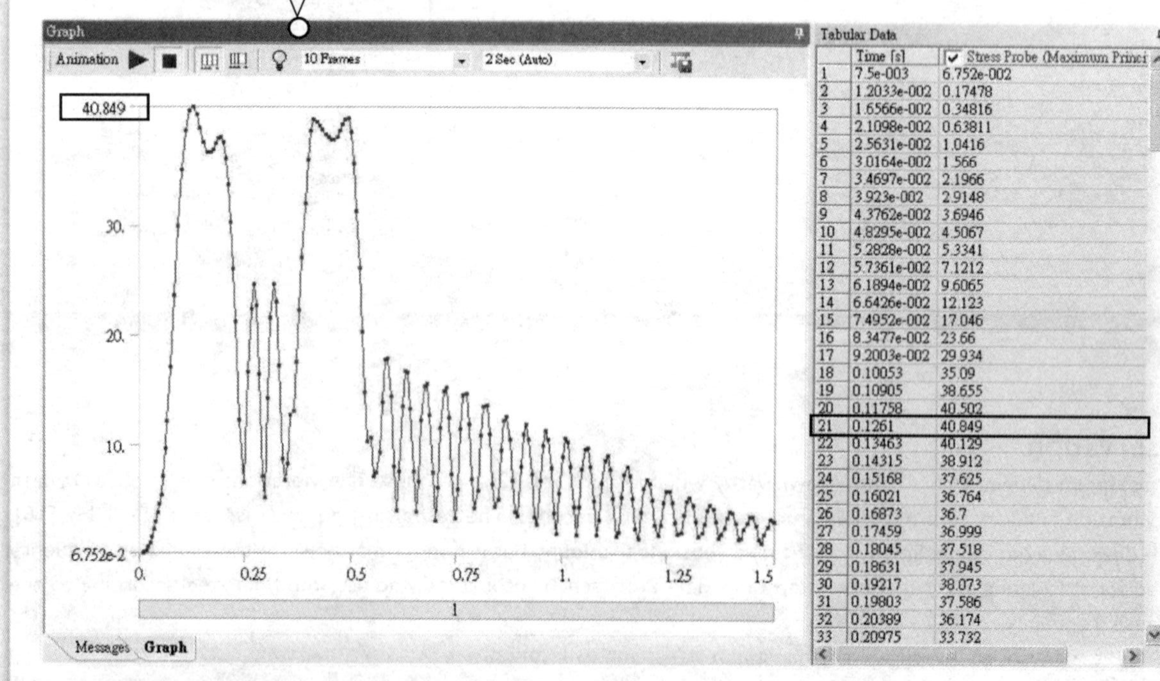

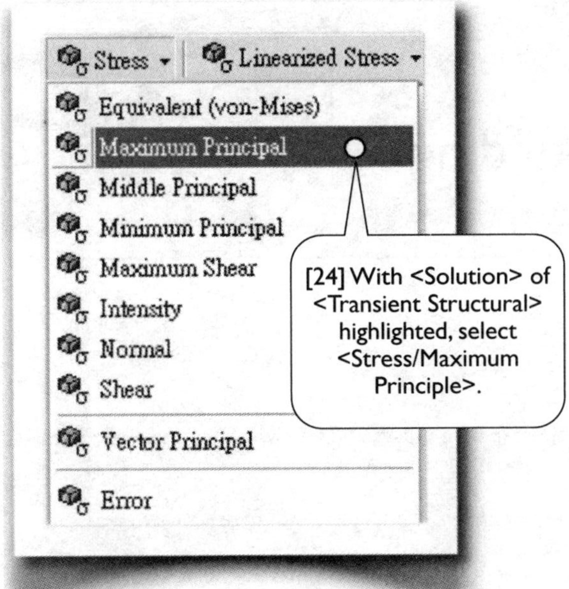

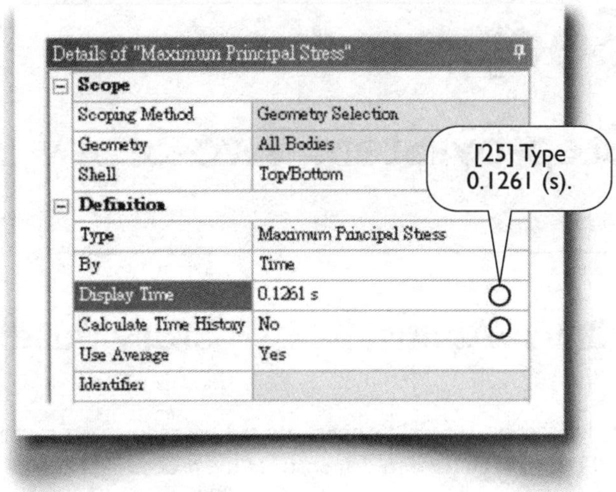

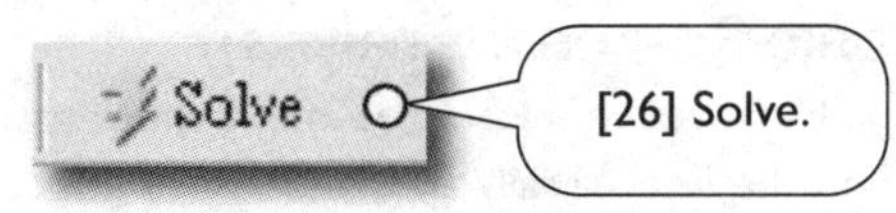

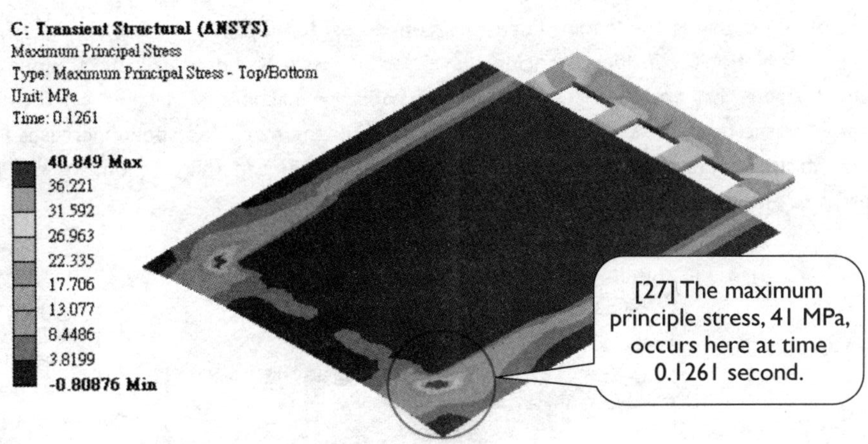

Wrap Up

Close <Mechanical>. Save the project and exit Workbench.

Reference

1. ANSYS Help System>Mechanical APDL>Element Reference>SOLSH190.

Section 12.3

Step-by-Step: Two-Story Building

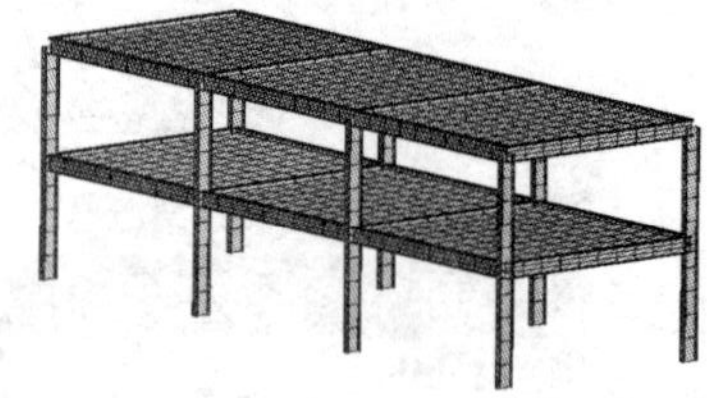

12.3-1 About the Two-Story Building

In this section, we will demonstrate the procedure of a harmonic response analysis. The two-story building (Sections 7.3, 11.2) will be used to demonstrate the procedures.

Harmonic Response Analysis

At the end of Section 11.2-3, we mentioned that the rhythmic loading on the floor may cause a safety issue. Is "dancing on the floor" really an issue? Since the building is designed to withstand a live load of 50 psf (lb/ft^2), we will assume that a group of young people of 50 psf is dancing on a side-span floor deck [1] to simulate an asymmetric loading that will cause the building side sway. The dancing is so hard that the young people generate a vertical harmonic force of 10 psf, that is, the loading fluctuates from 40 psf to 60 psf.

Engineers usually don't consider "dancing" as a serious issue. Let's look at a more realistic engineering consideration. Imagine that an electric motor or any rotatory machine is installed on the floor deck [1]. The operational speed of the machine is 3000 rpm. When started up, the machine's speed increases from zero up to 3000 rpm. Are the vibrations caused by the rotatory machine an issue? In this section, we will perform a harmonic response analysis to answer the above questions.

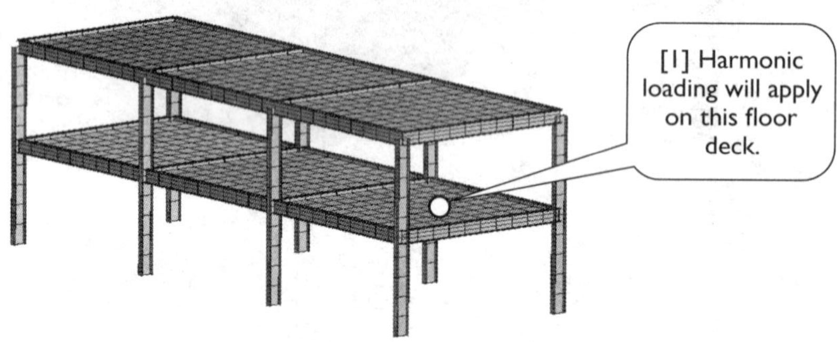

12.3-2 Perform an Unprestressed Modal Analysis

Launch <Workbench>. Open the project "Building," saved in Section 11.2.

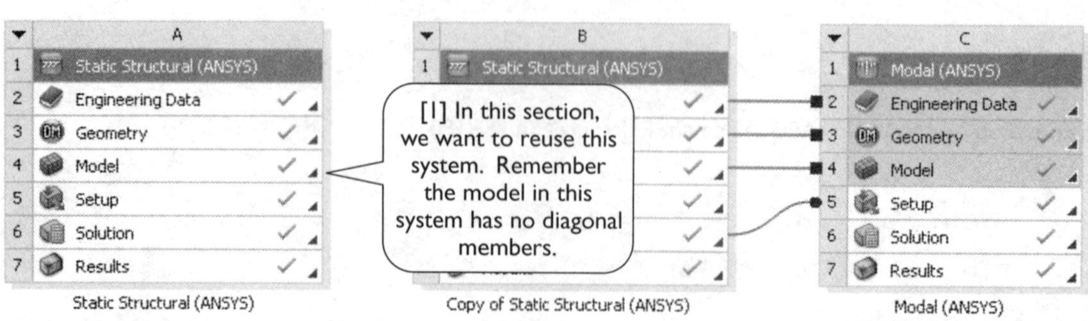

[2] Drag-and-drop a <Modal> analysis system to <Model>. Don't drop to <Solution>.

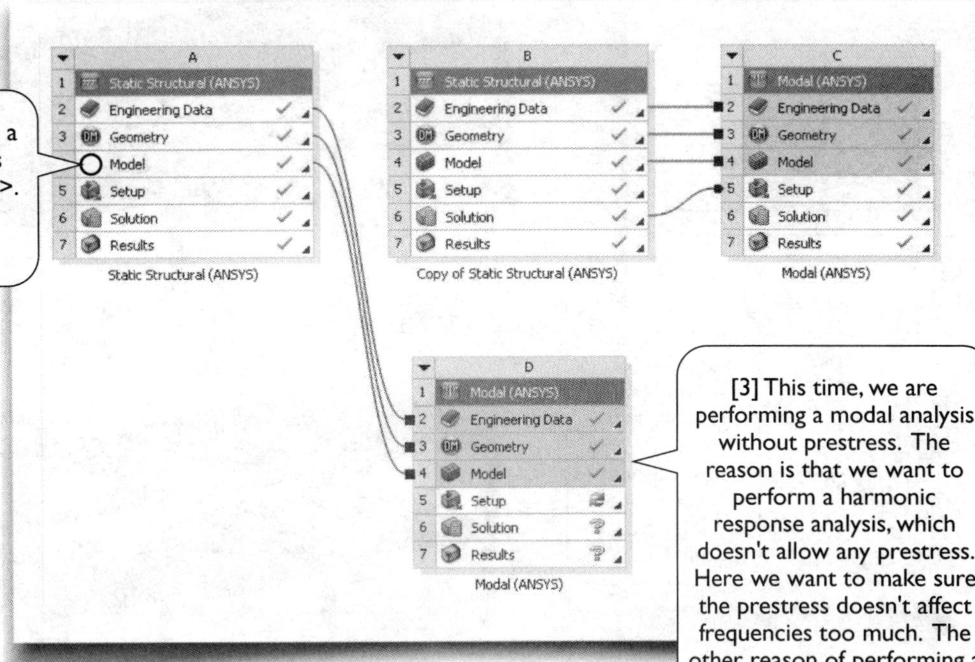

[3] This time, we are performing a modal analysis without prestress. The reason is that we want to perform a harmonic response analysis, which doesn't allow any prestress. Here we want to make sure the prestress doesn't affect frequencies too much. The other reason of performing a modal analysis is to investigate more vibration modes. Click any clickable cell in this system to start up <Mechanical>.

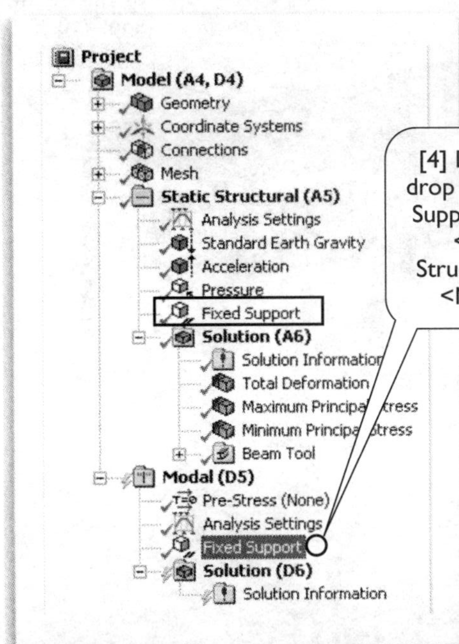

[4] Drag-and-drop the <Fixed Support> from <Static Structural> to <Modal>.

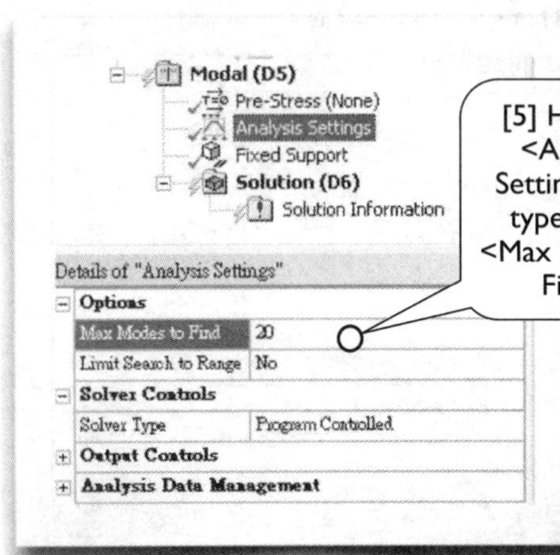

[5] Highlight <Analysis Settings> and type 20 for <Max Modes to Find>.

[6] Solve. It takes about one minute.

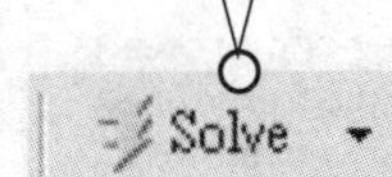

	Mode	Frequency [Hz]
1	1.	1.5537
2	2.	4.0917
3	3.	4.1814
4	4.	4.877
5	5.	9.2886
6	6.	9.5179
7	7.	9.8231
8	8.	10.232
9	9.	10.615
10	10.	11.359
11	11.	13.636
12	12.	16.31
13	13.	17.37
14	14.	18.041
15	15.	19.032
16	16.	19.83
17	17.	20.538
18	18.	20.81
19	19.	21.318
20	20.	22.773

[7] Explore all of vibration modes, particularly the first, sixth, and eighth modes. These modes are important in our study.

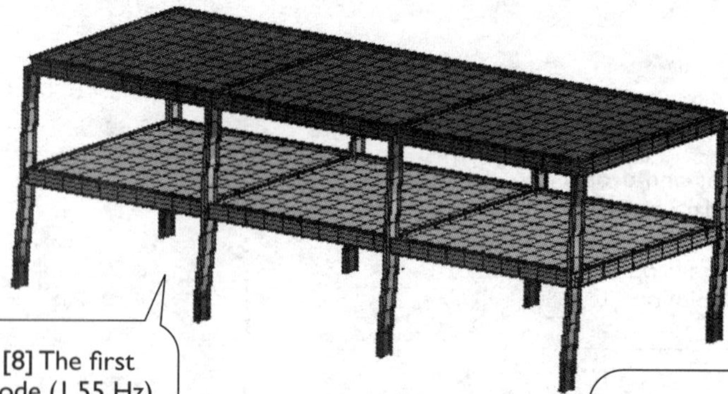

[8] The first mode (1.55 Hz).

[9] The sixth mode (9.52 Hz).

[10] The eighth mode (10.23 Hz)

Remember that we are studying the effect of dancing and the rotatory machine on a side-span floor deck. The dancing frequency is close to the fundamental mode (1.55 Hz), that's why we pay attention on this mode. For the rotatory machine, we are concerning the floor vibrations. That's why we pay attention on the sixth and eighth modes.

12.3-3 Perform Harmonic Response Analysis

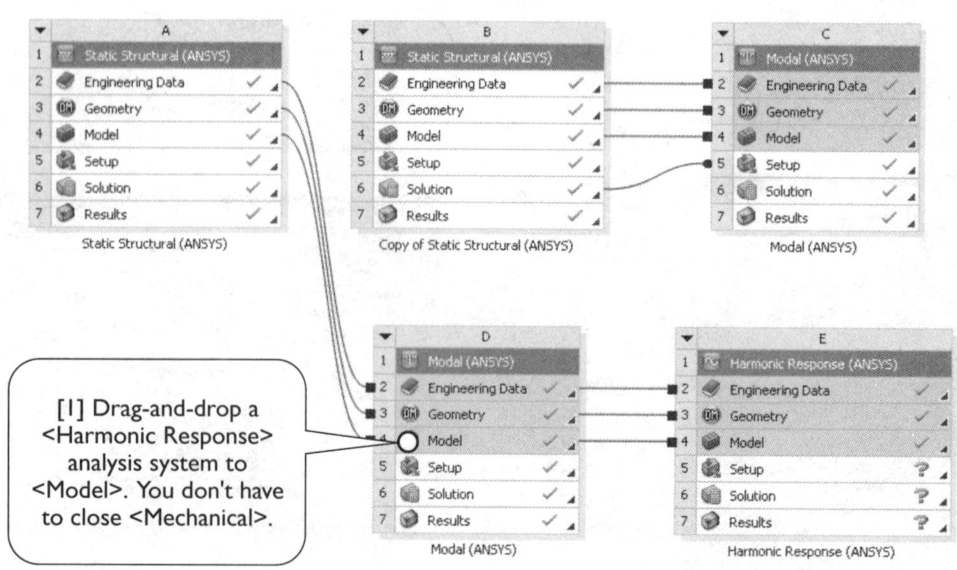

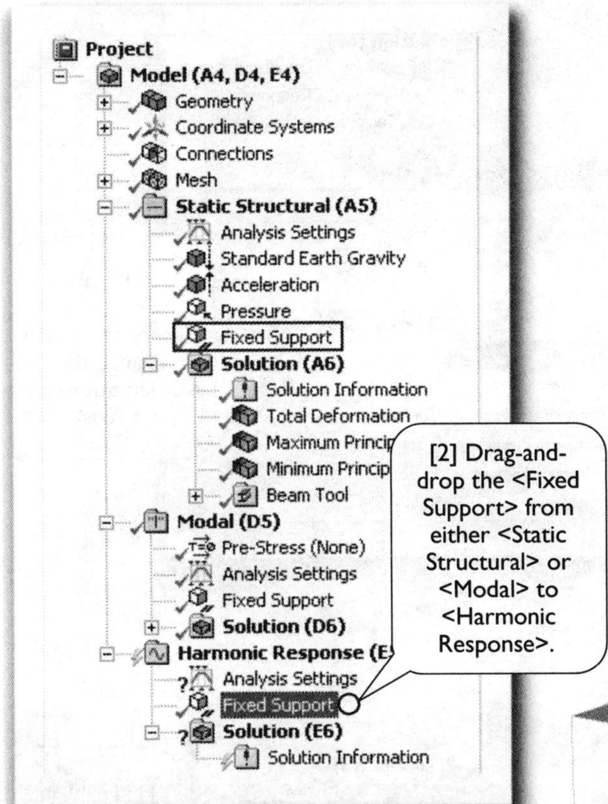
Project
Model (A4, D4, E4)
Geometry
Coordinate Systems
Connections
Mesh
Static Structural (A5)
Analysis Settings
Standard Earth Gravity
Acceleration
Pressure
Fixed Support
Solution (A6)
Solution Information
Total Deformation
Maximum Princip
Minimum Princip
Beam Tool
Modal (D5)
Pre-Stress (None)
Analysis Settings
Fixed Support
Solution (D6)
Harmonic Response (E
Analysis Settings
Fixed Support
Solution (E6)
Solution Information
[2] Drag-and-drop the <Fixed Support> from either <Static Structural> or <Modal> to <Harmonic Response>.

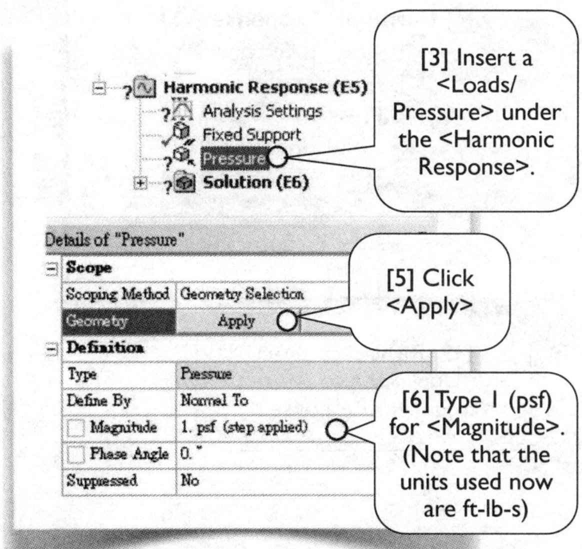
Harmonic Response (E5)
Analysis Settings
Fixed Support
Pressure
Solution (E6)
[3] Insert a <Loads/ Pressure> under the <Harmonic Response>.
Details of "Pressure"
Scope
Scoping Method
Geometry Selection
Geometry
Apply
[5] Click <Apply>
Definition
Type
Pressure
Define By
Normal To
Magnitude
1. psf (step applied)
Phase Angle
0. °
Suppressed
No
[6] Type 1 (psf) for <Magnitude>. (Note that the units used now are ft-lb-s)

[4, 9] Select this face.

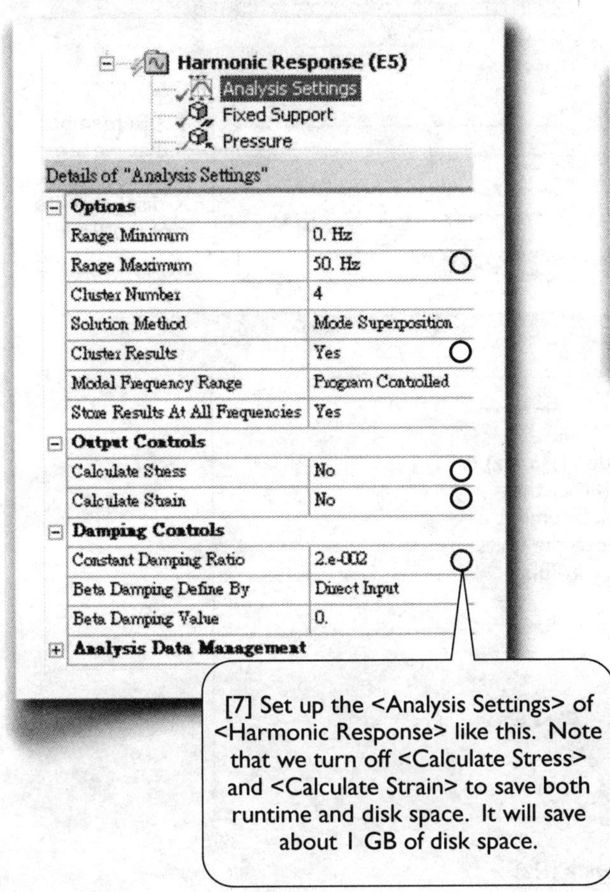
Harmonic Response (E5)
Analysis Settings
Fixed Support
Pressure
Details of "Analysis Settings"
Options
Range Minimum
0. Hz
Range Maximum
50. Hz
Cluster Number
4
Solution Method
Mode Superposition
Cluster Results
Yes
Modal Frequency Range
Program Controlled
Store Results At All Frequencies
Yes
Output Controls
Calculate Stress
No
Calculate Strain
No
Damping Controls
Constant Damping Ratio
2.e-002
Beta Damping Define By
Direct Input
Beta Damping Value
0.
Analysis Data Management
[7] Set up the <Analysis Settings> of <Harmonic Response> like this. Note that we turn off <Calculate Stress> and <Calculate Strain> to save both runtime and disk space. It will save about 1 GB of disk space.

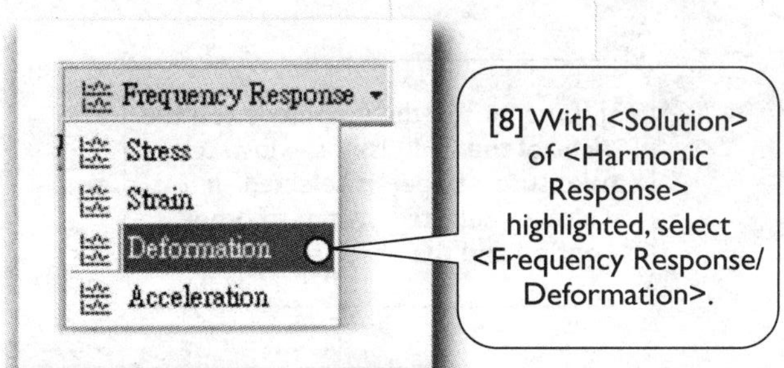
Frequency Response
Stress
Strain
Deformation
Acceleration
[8] With <Solution> of <Harmonic Response> highlighted, select <Frequency Response/ Deformation>.

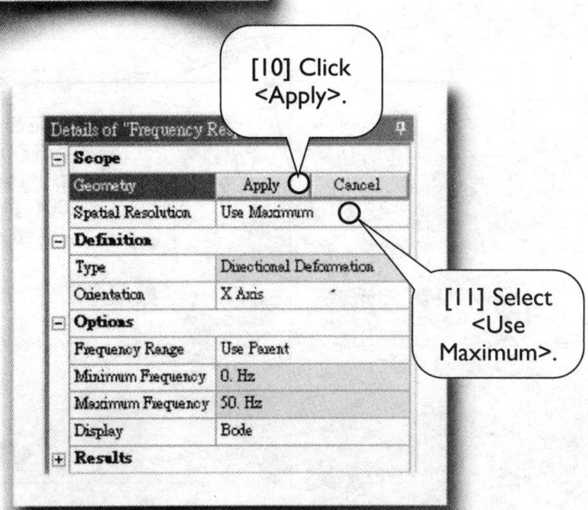
[10] Click <Apply>.
Details of "Frequency Re
Scope
Geometry
Apply
Cancel
Spatial Resolution
Use Maximum
Definition
Type
Directional Deformation
Orientation
X Axis
Options
Frequency Range
Use Parent
Minimum Frequency
0. Hz
Maximum Frequency
50. Hz
Display
Bode
Results
[11] Select <Use Maximum>.

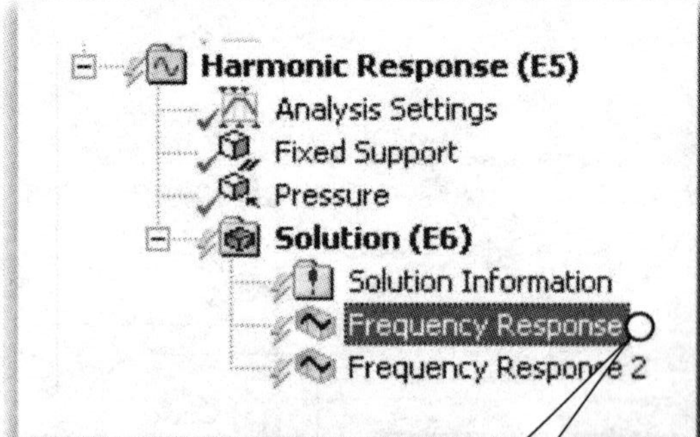

[12] Right-click-select <Duplicate> to create <Frequency Response 2>.

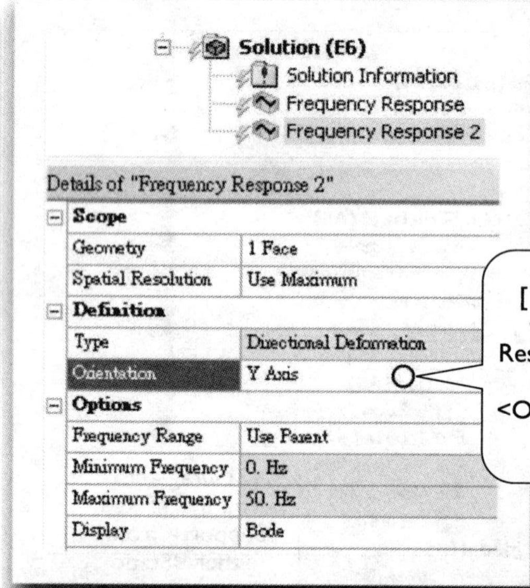

[13] Highlight <Frequency Response 2>, and change the <Orientation> to <Y Axis>.

[14] Solve. It takes about 1 minute.

12.3-4 Effect of Dancing

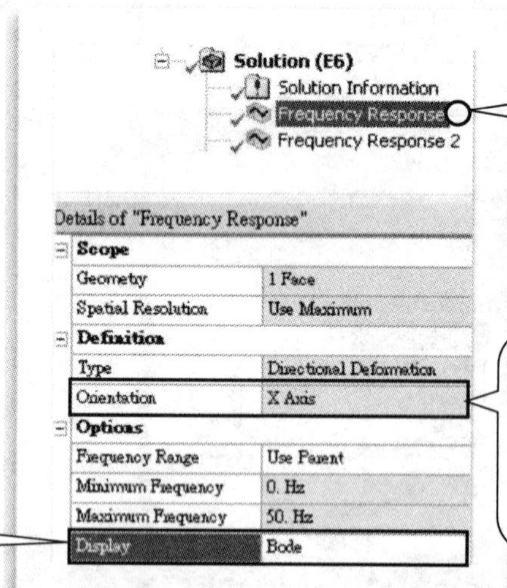

[1] Highlight <Frequency Response>.

[2] Remember that we are investigating the X-displacement of the floor.

[3] If the plot of the Amplitude (on the right of the GUI) is not in log scale, make sure <Bode> is selected. If it is already selected, switch to other option and then back to <Bode>.

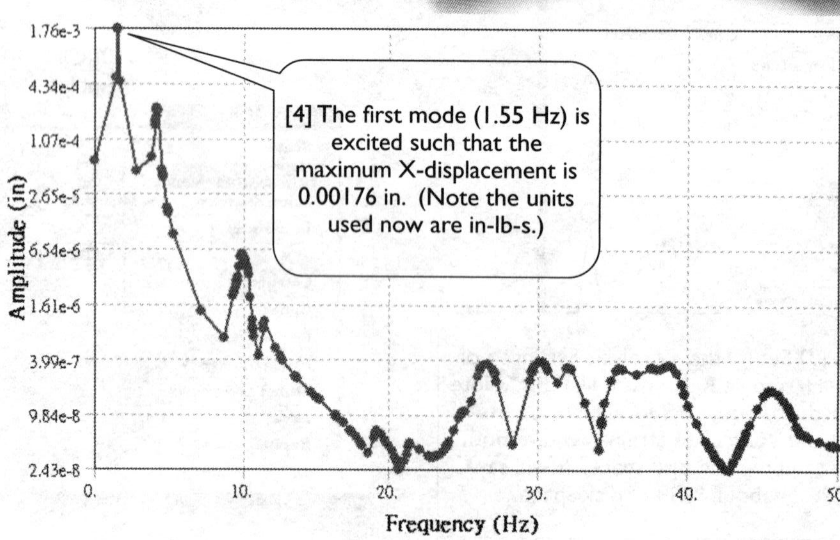

[4] The first mode (1.55 Hz) is excited such that the maximum X-displacement is 0.00176 in. (Note the units used now are in-lb-s.)

Interpretation of Harmonic Response Plot

The harmonic response plot [4] is an amplitude versus frequency plot. Because we are investigating the effect of the dancing, we should look at the frequencies that don't exceed 3 or 4 Hz (people don't dance faster than that). At dancing frequency of 1.55 Hz, the structure is excited such that the maximum X-displacement is 0.00176 in. Remember that in 12.3-1, we estimate the dancing loading is about 10 psf harmonically. In 12.3-3[6], we input a unit of harmonic load (1 psf), therefore the estimated response should be 10 times of 0.00176 in, that is 0.0176 in. (0.45 mm). This value is too small to be worried about.

We conclude that dancing is not an issue for this building.

12.3-5 Effect of Rotatory Machine

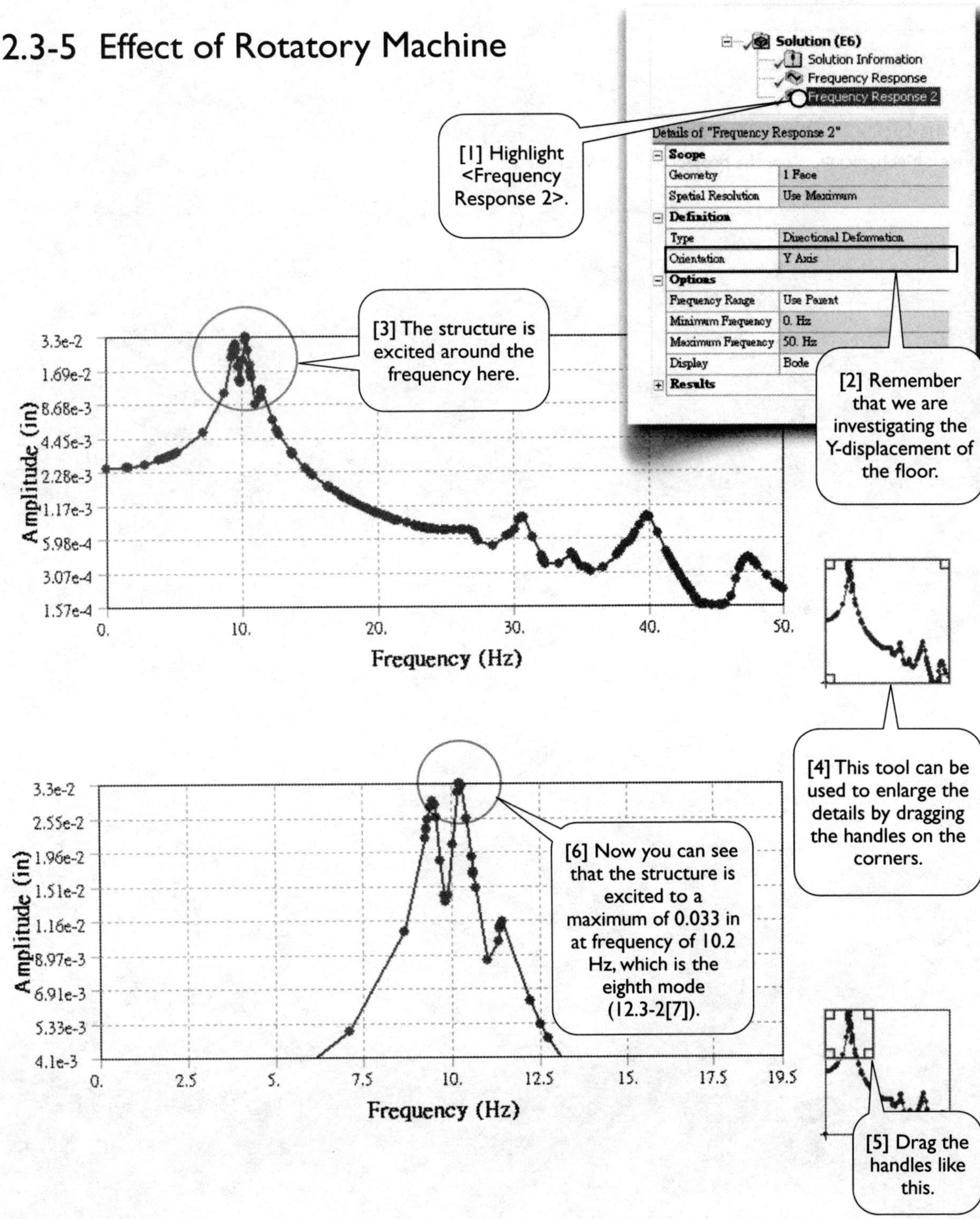

Interpretation of Harmonic Response Plot

Now we are investigating the effect of the rotatory machine from 0 to 3000 rpm (50 Hz). We estimate that the amplitude of the harmonic load should be no more than 0.1 psf distributing on the floor (that totals to 40 lb). In 12.3-3[6], we input a unit of harmonic load (1 psf), therefore the estimated response should be 0.1 times of the response shown in [3] or [6].

Although high frequencies do excite the floor, but the values are very small. At frequency of 10.2 Hz, the excitation reaches a maximum of 0.0033 in (0.1 times 0.033 in), that is even smaller than the dancing effect. The value is too small to cause an issue.

We conclude that the rotatory machine is safe for this building.

Wrap Up

Close <Mechanical>. Save the project and exit Workbench.

Section 12.4

Exercise: Disk and Block

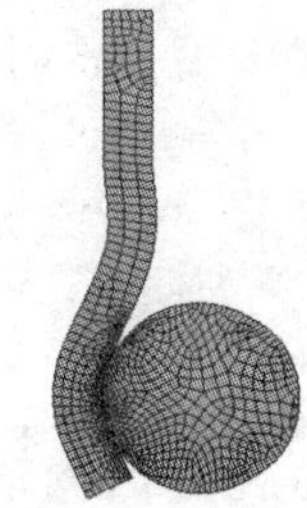

This exercise serves two purposes: (1) to demonstrate how to apply a simple initial condition, namely uniform velocity, on a body, and (2) to show the limitation of the <Transient Structural> analysis system for impact simulations, and to build the learning motivation for the <Explicit Dynamics> (Section 12.1-4 and Chapter 15).

12.4-1 About the Disk and Block

Consider a disk of radius of 40 mm and a block of 200x20 mm, both have a thickness of 10 mm, on a non-frictional horizontal surface. Both are made of a very soft polymer of Young's modulus of 10 kPa, Poisson's ratio of 0.4, and mass density of 1000 kg/m^3.

Right before the impact, the disk moves toward the block with a velocity of 0.5 m/s, and the positions of the disk and the block are as shown [1, 2].

We purposely use an unrealistically soft material (Young's modulus of 10 kPa) and consider a very slow-speed impact (velocity of 0.5 m/s) to relieve the numerical difficulty. Increasing either of them will make the impact duration shorter, and call for a shorter integration time step. This will leave an exercise for you at the end of this chapter.

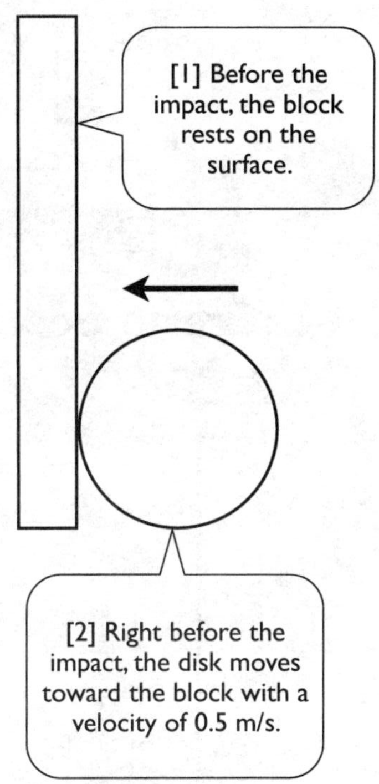

12.4-2 Start Up

Launch <Workbench>. Create a <Transient Structural> analysis system [1] by double-click it in the <Toolbox>. Save the project as "Disk."

Double-click <Engineering Data> to prepare material data [2]. Create a new material and name it "Polymer" [3] and input the material properties as shown [4].

Return to the <Project Schematic> and Double-click <Geometry> to start up DesignModeler. Choose <Millimeter> as unit.

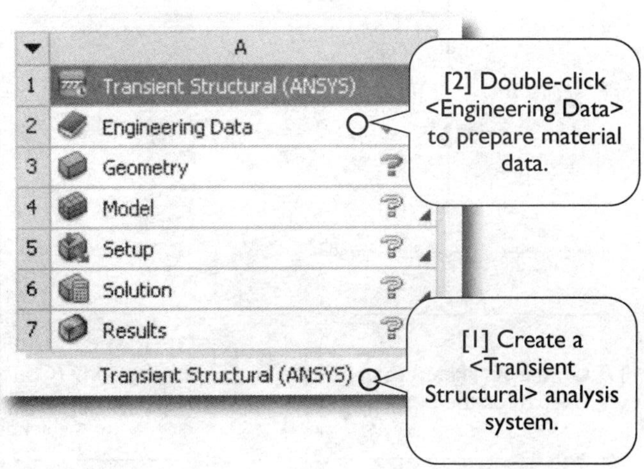

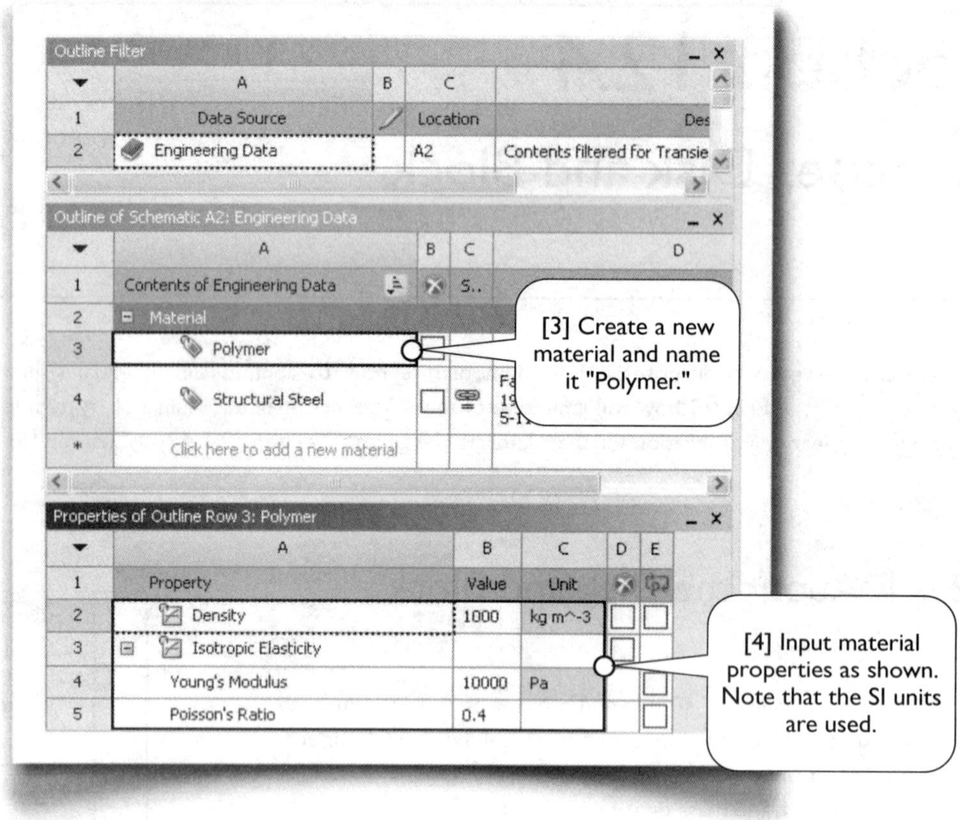

12.4-3 Create Geometry in DesignModeler

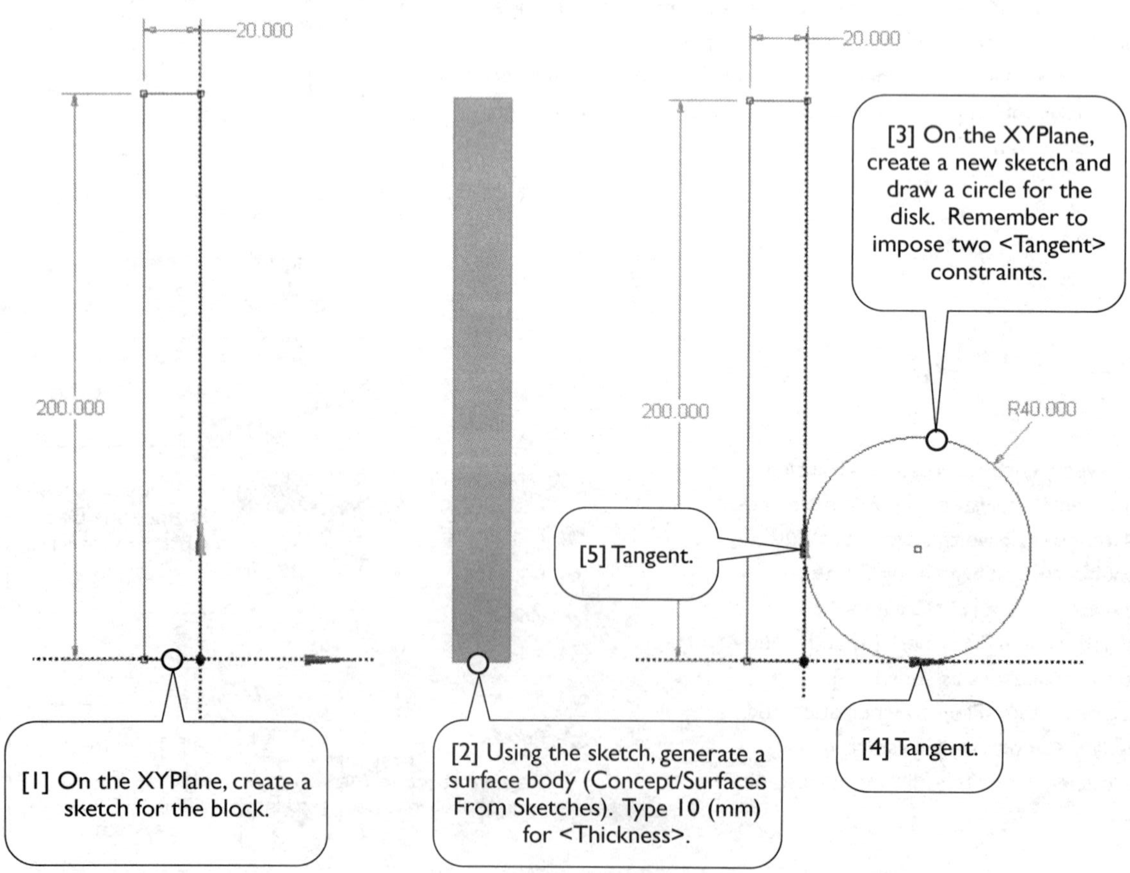

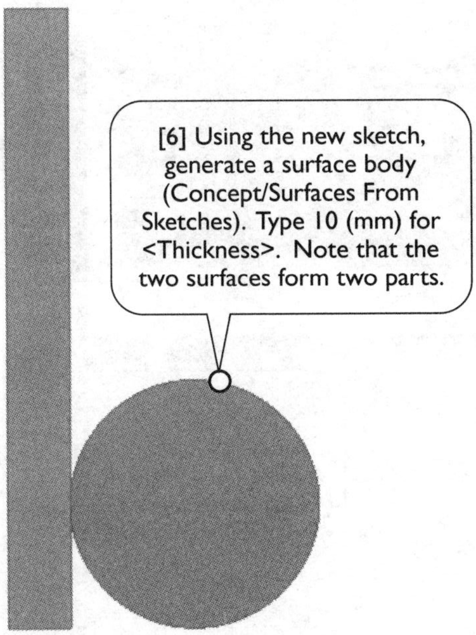

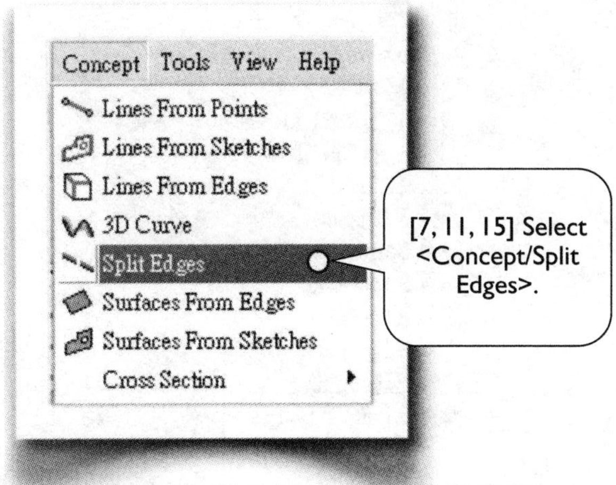

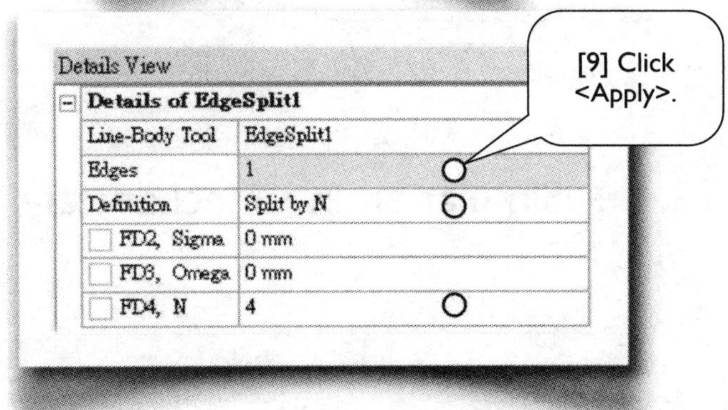

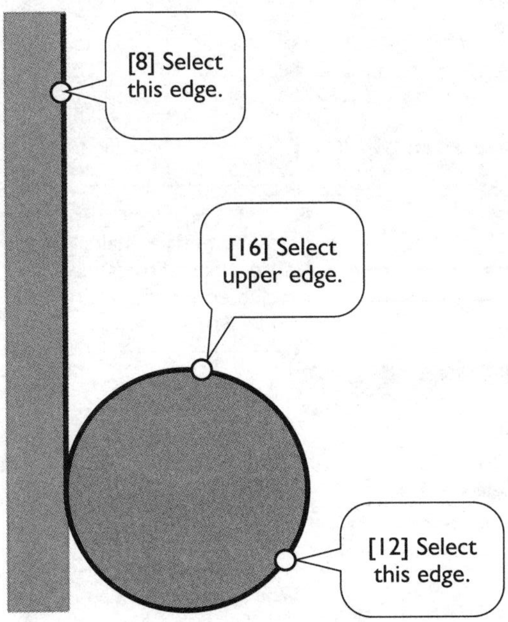

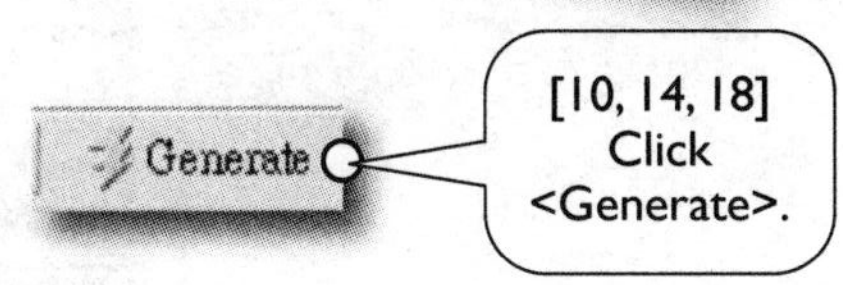

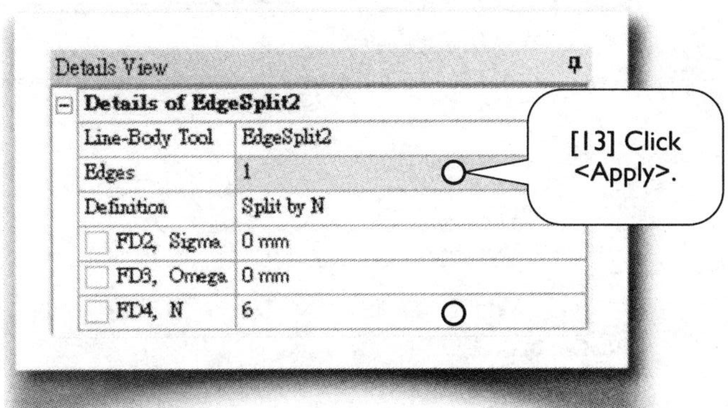

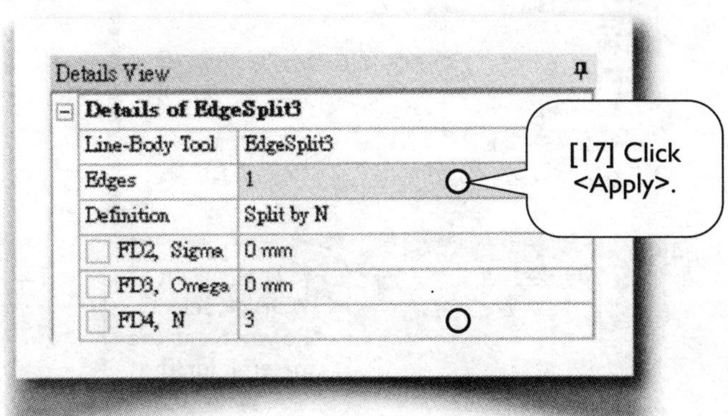

Why Split Edges?

The purpose of splitting the edges into segments is that, when meshed, each segment can have its own mesh density. Specifically, we need finer mesh around the contact region.

A Bug?

When I try to split the circular edge into 6 edges [11-14], oddly enough, it splits only the lower part of the circular edge. Therefore, I have to split the upper circular edge further into three edges [15-18]. Fortunately, we should be able to live with this kind of small problems.

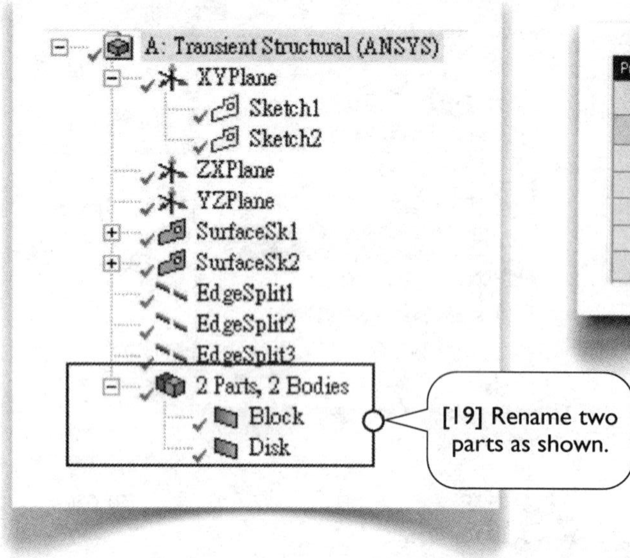

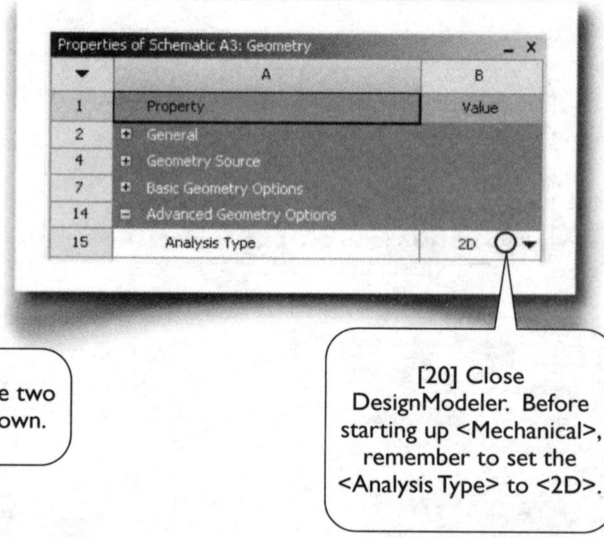

12.4-4 Simulation in <Mechanical>

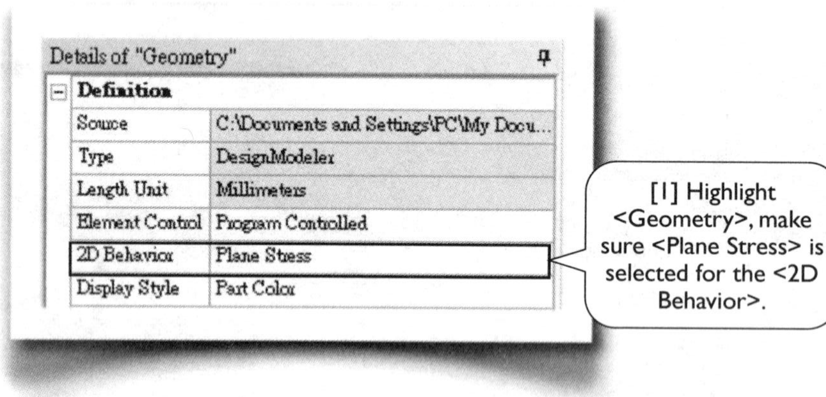

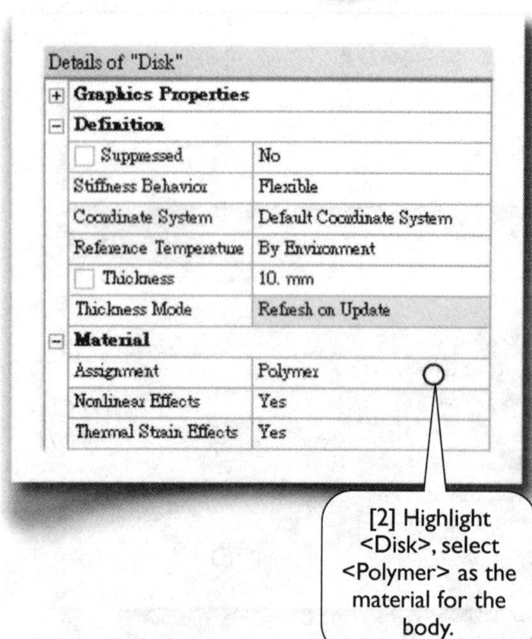

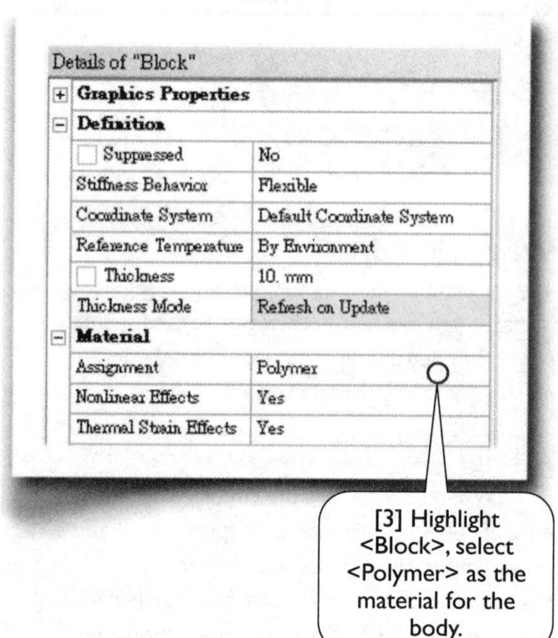

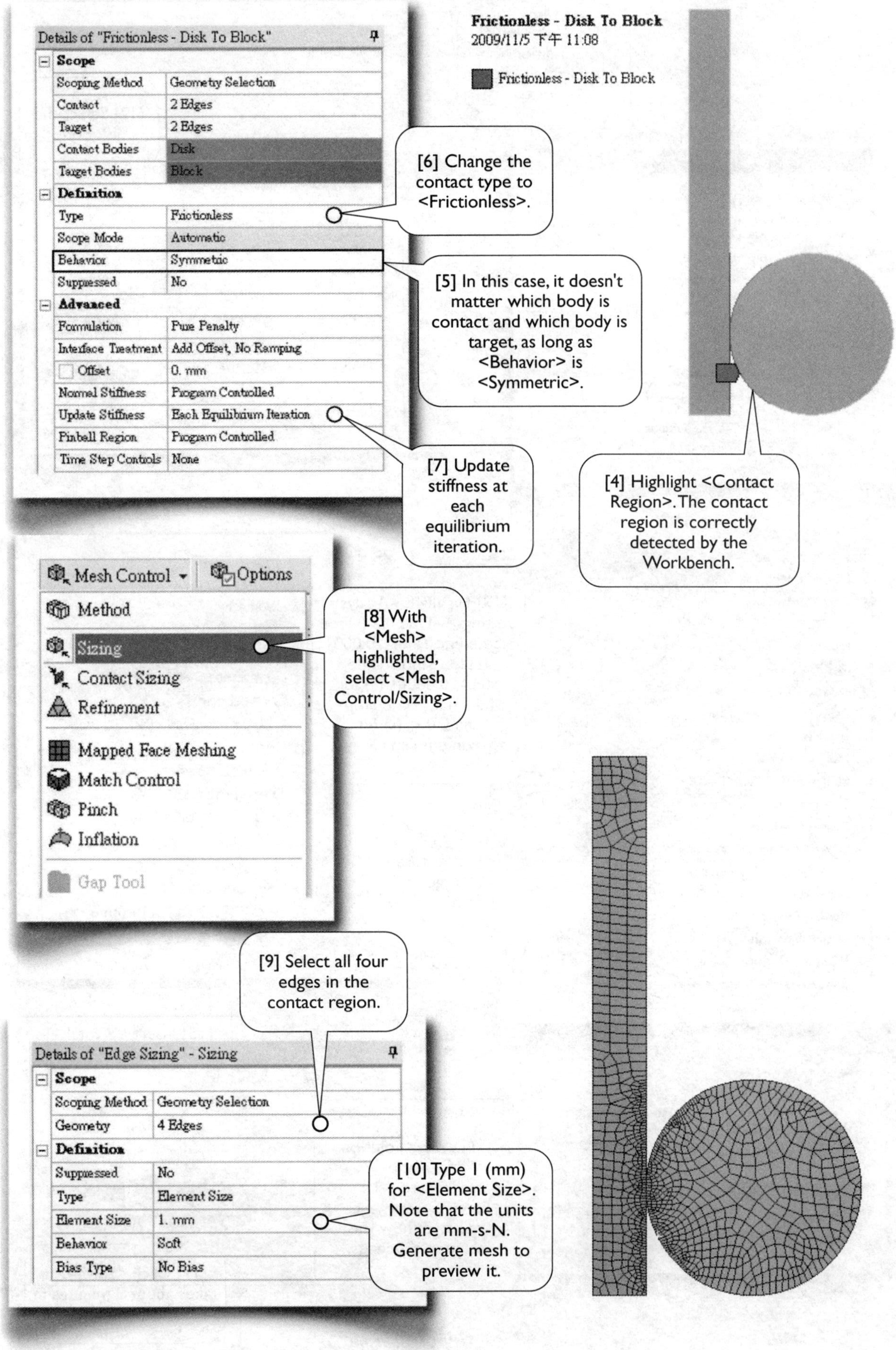
Details of "Frictionless - Disk To Block"
Scope
Scoping Method Geometry Selection
Contact 2 Edges
Target 2 Edges
Contact Bodies Disk
Target Bodies Block
Definition
Type Frictionless
Scope Mode Automatic
Behavior Symmetric
Suppressed No
Advanced
Formulation Pure Penalty
Interface Treatment Add Offset, No Ramping
Offset 0. mm
Normal Stiffness Program Controlled
Update Stiffness Each Equilibrium Iteration
Pinball Region Program Controlled
Time Step Controls None
Frictionless - Disk To Block
2009/11/5 下午 11:08
Frictionless - Disk To Block
[6] Change the contact type to <Frictionless>.
[5] In this case, it doesn't matter which body is contact and which body is target, as long as <Behavior> is <Symmetric>.
[7] Update stiffness at each equilibrium iteration.
[4] Highlight <Contact Region>. The contact region is correctly detected by the Workbench.
Mesh Control
Options
Method
Sizing
Contact Sizing
Refinement
Mapped Face Meshing
Match Control
Pinch
Inflation
Gap Tool
[8] With <Mesh> highlighted, select <Mesh Control/Sizing>.
[9] Select all four edges in the contact region.
Details of "Edge Sizing" - Sizing
Scope
Scoping Method Geometry Selection
Geometry 4 Edges
Definition
Suppressed No
Type Element Size
Element Size 1. mm
Behavior Soft
Bias Type No Bias
[10] Type 1 (mm) for <Element Size>. Note that the units are mm-s-N. Generate mesh to preview it.

[11] With <Initial Condition> highlighted, click <Velocity>.

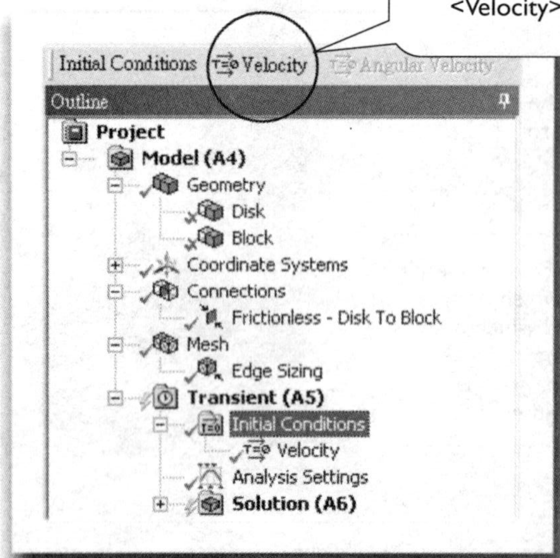

[12] Select the disk body.

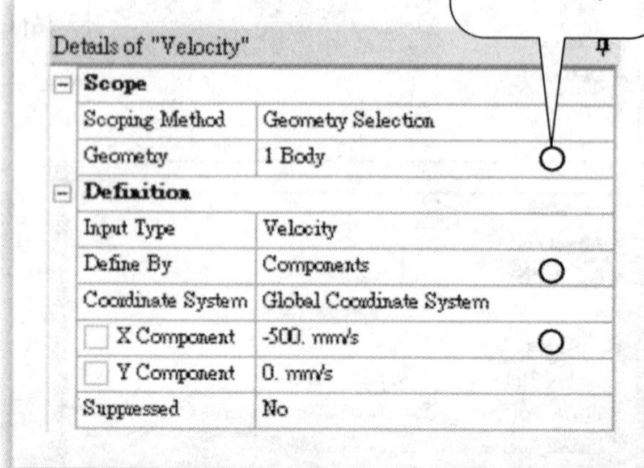

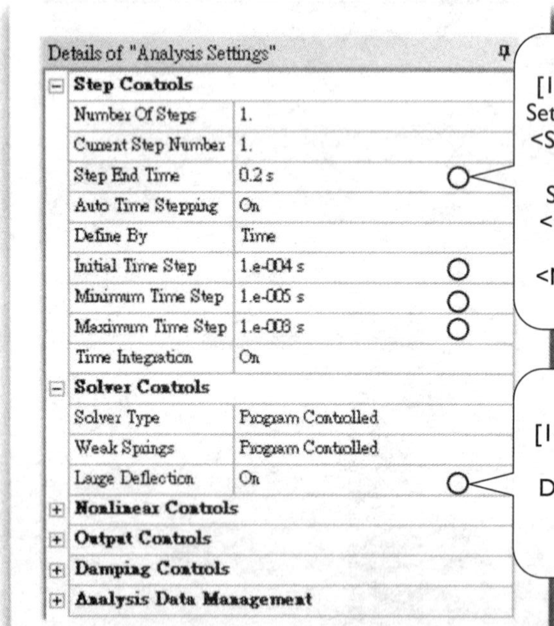

[13] Highlight <Analysis Settings>. Type 0.2 (s) for <Setp End Time>, 0.0001 (s) for <Intial Time Step>, 0.00001 (s) for <Minimum Time Step>, and 0.001 (s) for <Maximum Time Step>.

[14] Make sure <Large Deflection> is turned on.

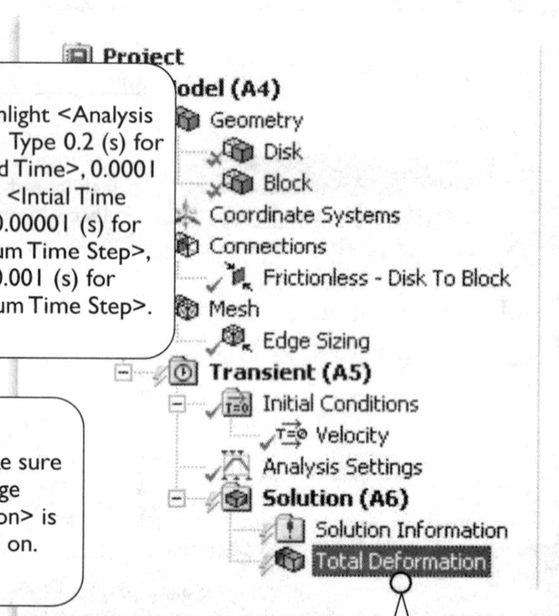

[15] Insert a <Total Deformation>.

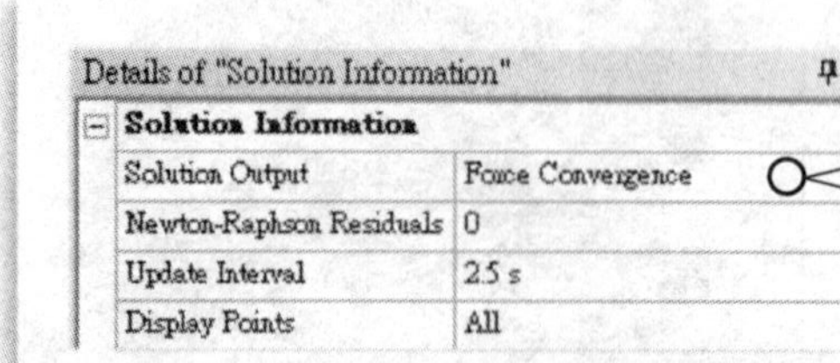

[16] With <Solution Information> highlighted, select <Force Convergence>, to watch how the solution proceeds.

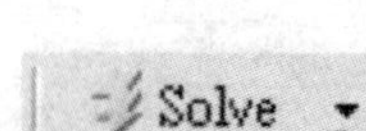

[17] Click <Solve>. It takes about 7 minutes in my computer.

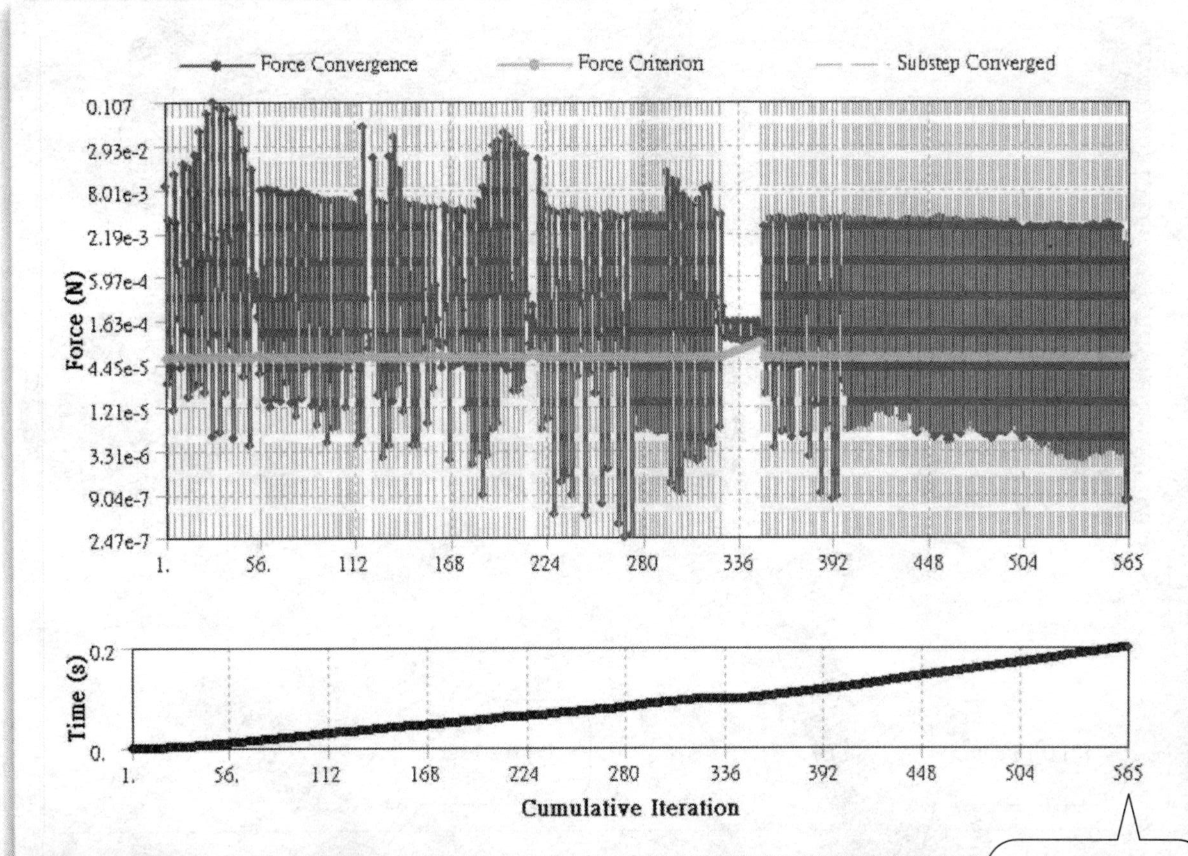

[18] It takes 565 iterations to complete the simulations.

12.4-5 Animate the Impact

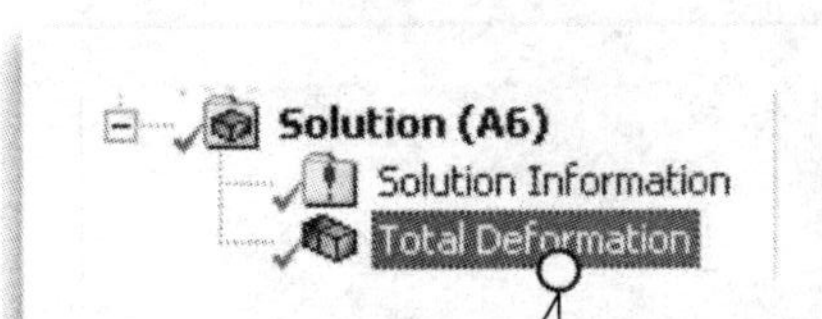

[1] Highlight <Total Deformation>.

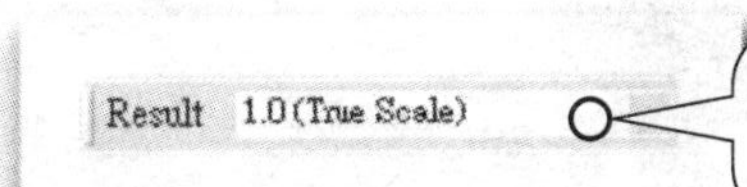

[2] Select <True Scale>.

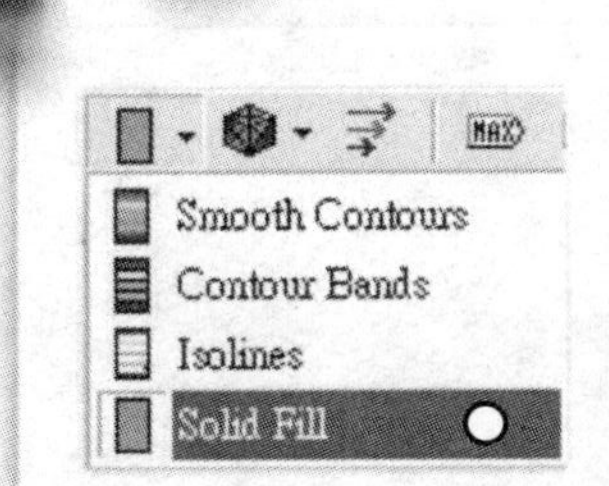

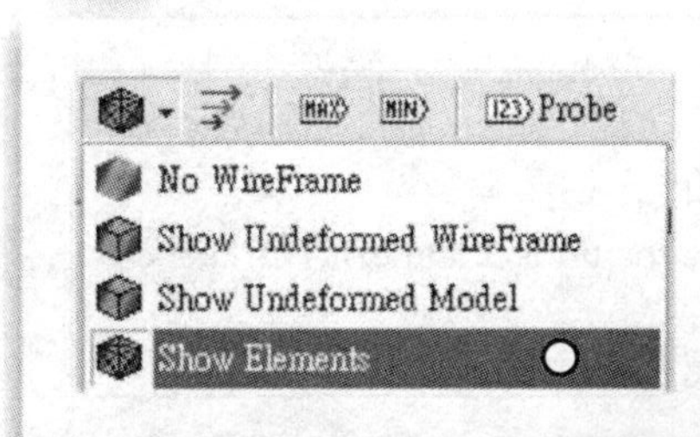

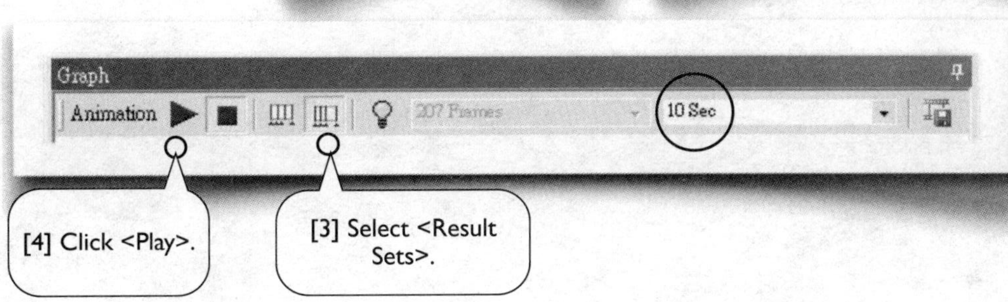

[4] Click <Play>.

[3] Select <Result Sets>.

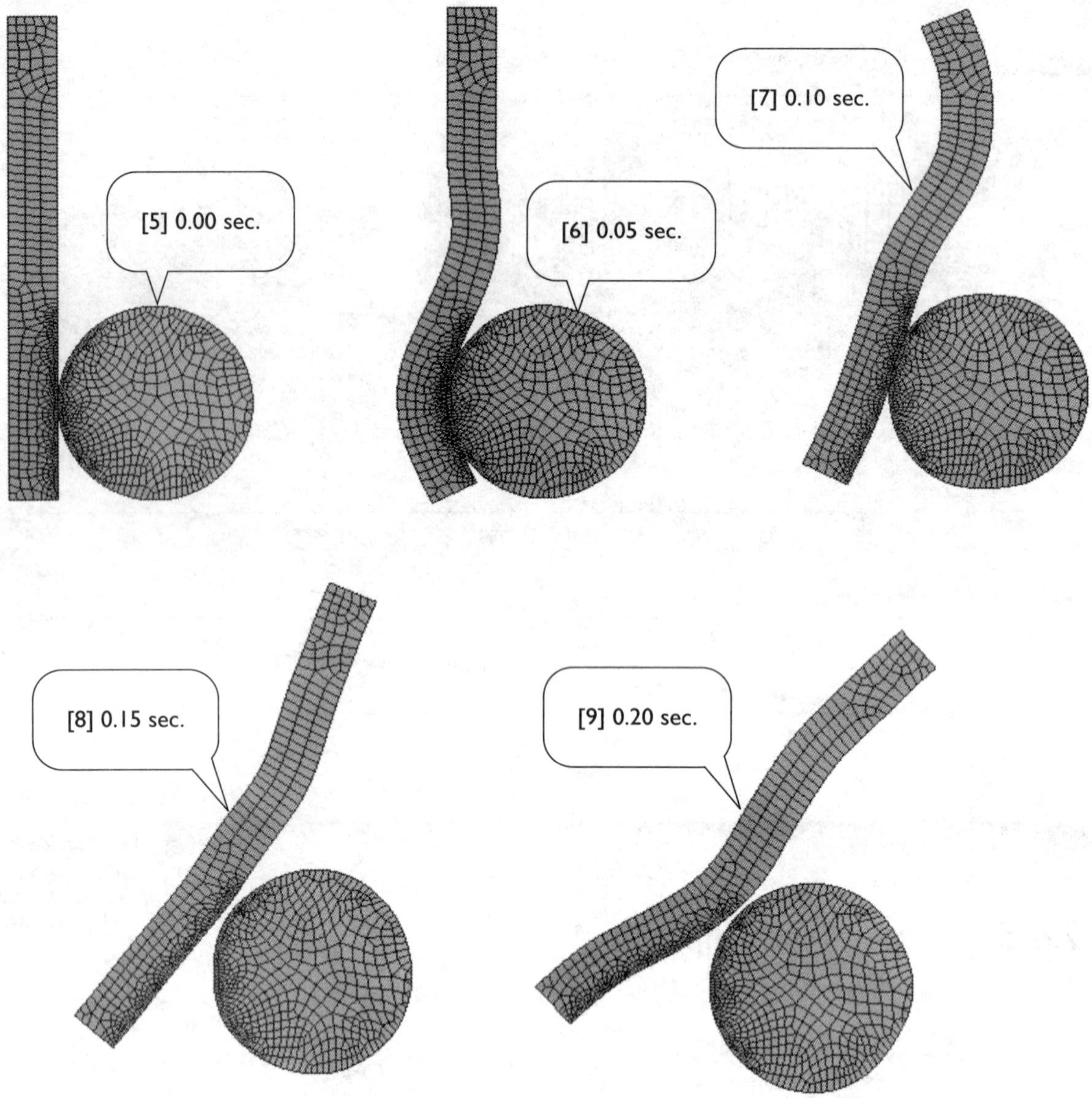

Wrap Up

Save the project and exit Workbench.

Section 12.5

Exercise: Guitar String

The exercise serves two purposes: (1) to demonstrate how to use the results of a static simulation as an initial condition of a transient dynamic simulation, and (2) to show the transient behavior of a guitar string, as a sequel of Section 11.4.

12.5-1 About the Guitar String

As mentioned, in Section 11.4-3, if you pluck a string, you will produce a tone made up of all harmonic modes. It is the harmonic mixes that differentiates the sound of one music instrument from others. A good guitar player knows very well that he/she can control the quality of sound by plucking the string at different locations. We will explore this phenomenon in this section, using the guitar string introduced in Section 11.4.

The string is plucked at the middle, quarter, and eighth points respectively, and its transient responses are observed. To be more precisely, the string is applied a vertical displacement of 10 mm at the respective locations, and then instantaneously released to produce vibrations. The vibrations will eventually reach a steady state, that is, free vibrations, after a certain duration of time. It, however, is the transient vibrations that impress our ears most.

12.5-2 Using Results of Static Analysis as Initial Condition

Applying the vertical displacement requires a <Static Structural> analysis, while releasing the string to produce vibrations requires a <Transient Structural> analysis using the results of the static analysis as the initial condition. In a <Transient Structural>, it is possible to specify the first step as a static simulation. The results automatically become an initial condition of the next step of transient simulation. This two-step method has become a standard procedure, when the simulation requires a static simulation as an initial condition.

Before we explain further about the two-step method, let's clear up a concept. In transient dynamic simulation, each time step needs an initial condition to carry on. The results of the last time step become the initial condition of the next time step. The initial condition, to be more precise, is the position and velocity of each node.

A key of the two-step method is that, in a <Transient Structural> simulation, the Workbench allows you to turn off/on the <Time Integration> [1]. Turning <Time integration> off means turning the dynamic effects (Section 1.1-10) off, and Eq. 12.1-4(1) reduces to Eq. 1.3-1(1), that is, a static simulation. You can turn on/off the <Time Integration> for each step (load step).

Make sure you don't confuse with steps, substeps, and equilibrium iterations. Multiple steps (or load steps) are created when you need to specify different <Analysis Settings> for each step. Each step is further divided into substeps (or time steps) for two reasons: (a) in a transient dynamic simulation, each substep is a time integration step, and (b) in a nonlinear simulation, a substep must be small enough to guarantee convergence within that substep. For nonlinear simulations (either dynamic or static), each substep may need multiple equilibrium iterations to achieve convergence.

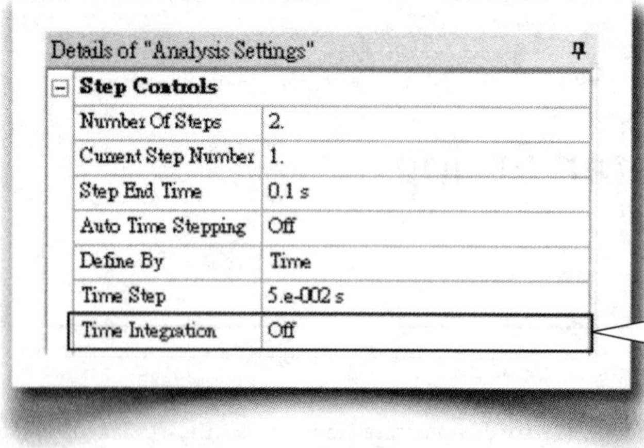

[1] In a <Transient Structural> simulation, if the <Time Integration> is turned off, i.e., dynamic effects are turned off, the simulation reduces to a static one.

12.5-3 Resume the Project "String"

Launch <Workbench>. Open the project "String," saved in Section 11.4.

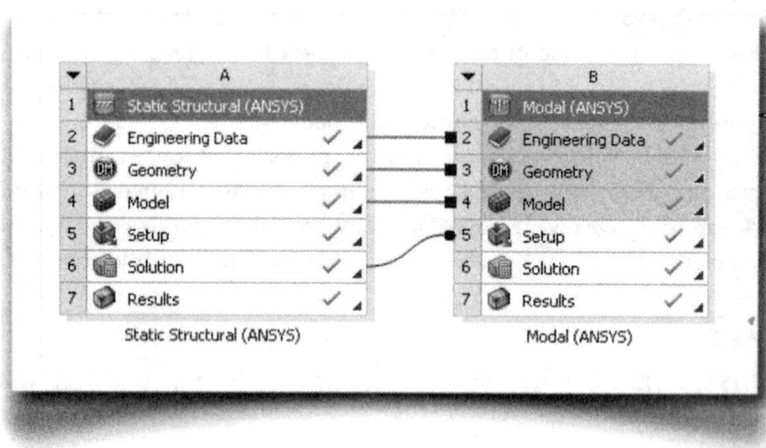

[1] This is the project schematic at the end of Section 11.4.

[3] Double-click <Geometry> to start up <DesignModeler>.

[2] Drag-and-drop a <Transient Structural> analysis system to <Model> of the <Modal> analysis system. You also can drop to the <Static Structural>; although the schematic is different, the effect is exactly the same.

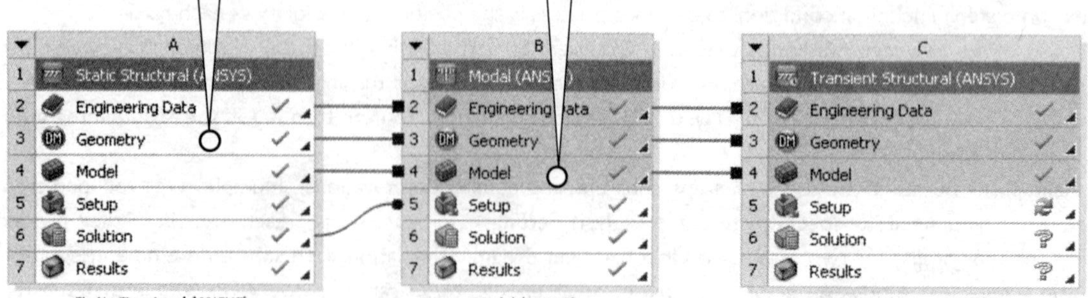

12.5-4 Modify the Geometry in DesignModeler

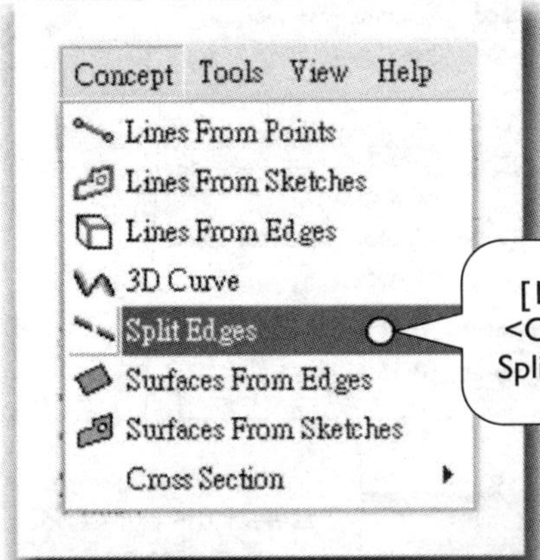

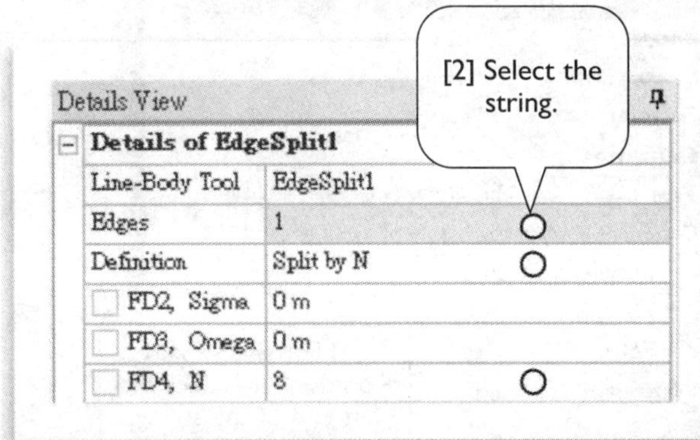

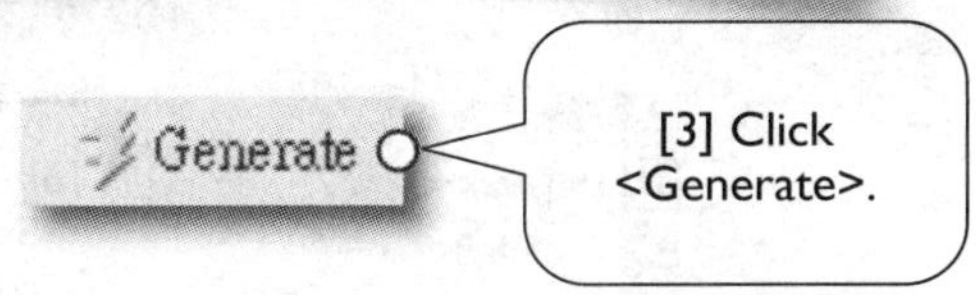

Close DesignModeler. On the <Project Schematic>, double-click any cells other than <Geometry> or <Engineering Data> to start up <Mechanical>.

12.5-5 Correct the Environment Conditions

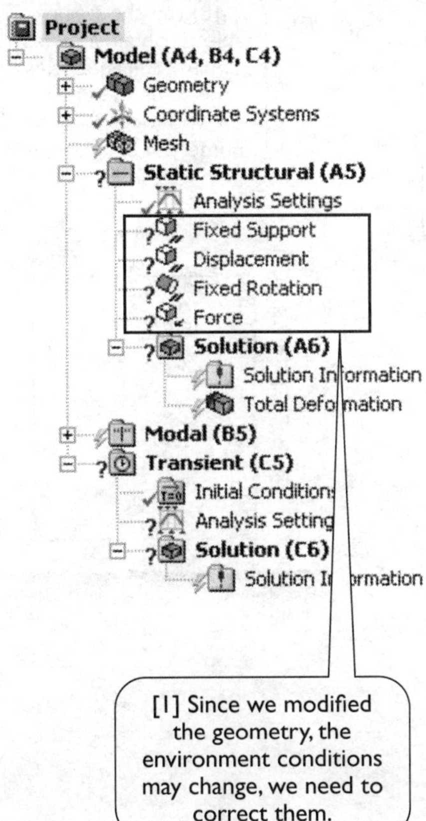

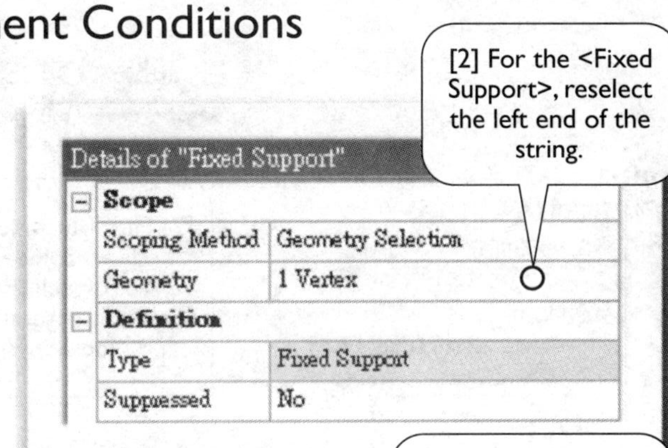

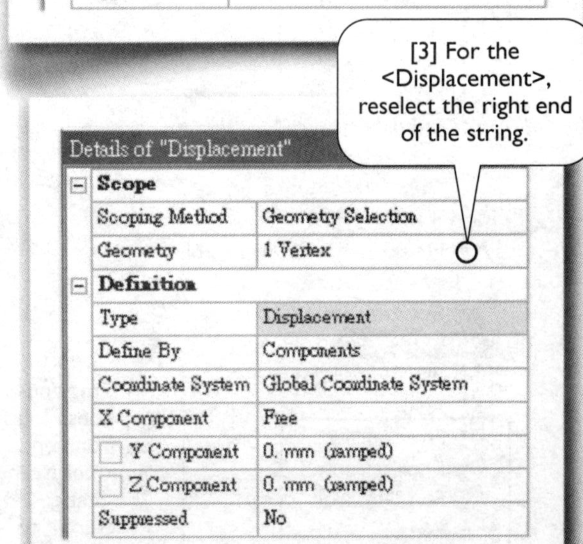

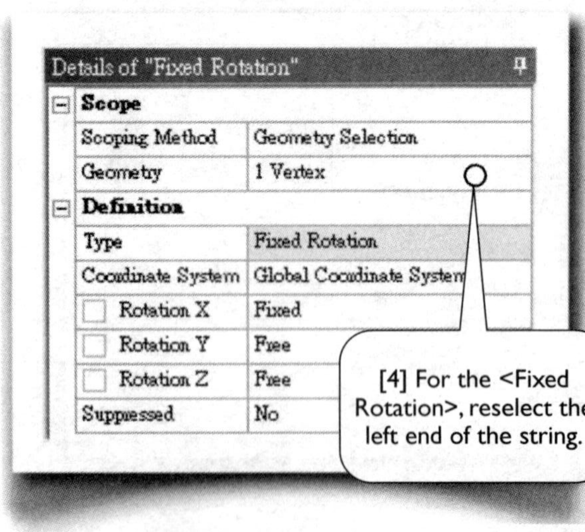

[4] For the <Fixed Rotation>, reselect the left end of the string.

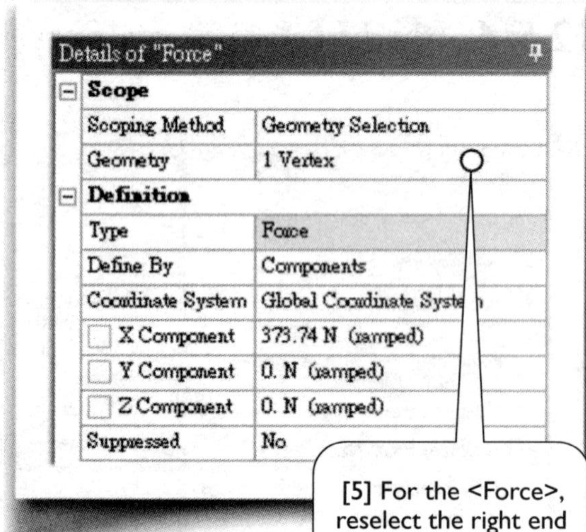

[5] For the <Force>, reselect the right end of the string.

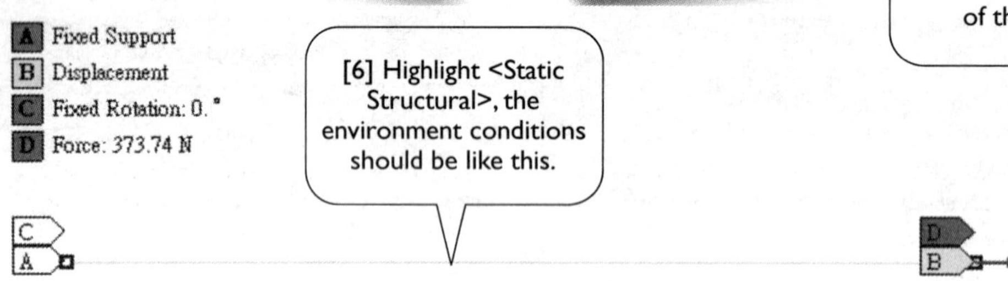

[6] Highlight <Static Structural>, the environment conditions should be like this.

[7] Highlight <Modal> and click <Solve>. The Workbench is solving <Static Structural> and the <Modal> systems.

[8] You should be able to obtain a series of natural frequencies the same as before, with negligible numerical differences.

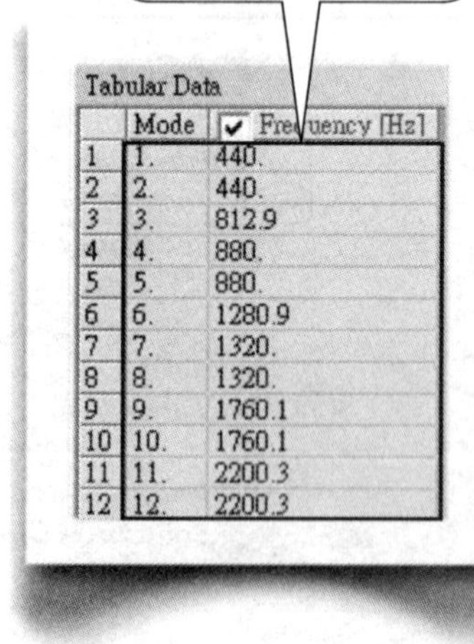

Tabular Data

	Mode	Frequency [Hz]
1	1.	440.
2	2.	440.
3	3.	812.9
4	4.	880.
5	5.	880.
6	6.	1280.9
7	7.	1320.
8	8.	1320.
9	9.	1760.1
10	10.	1760.1
11	11.	2200.3
12	12.	2200.3

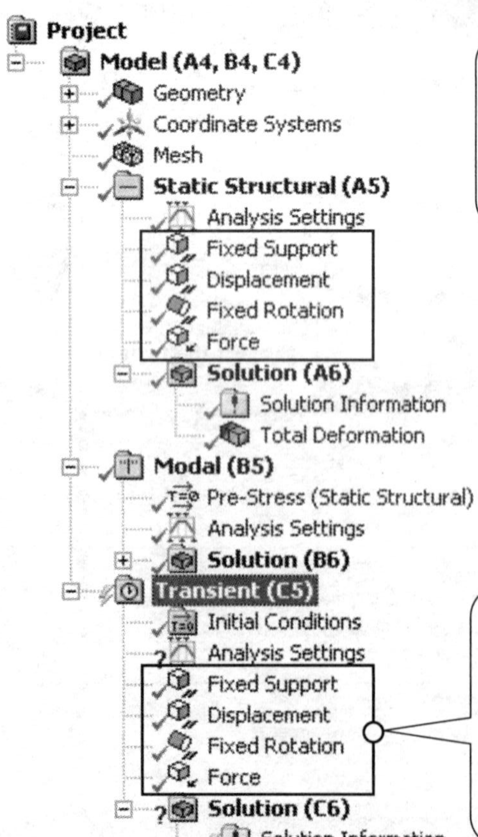

[9] Drag-and-drop these four environment conditions from <Static Structural> to <Transient>.

12.5-6 Set Up <Analysis Settings>

Highlight <Analysis Settings> of the <Transient>.

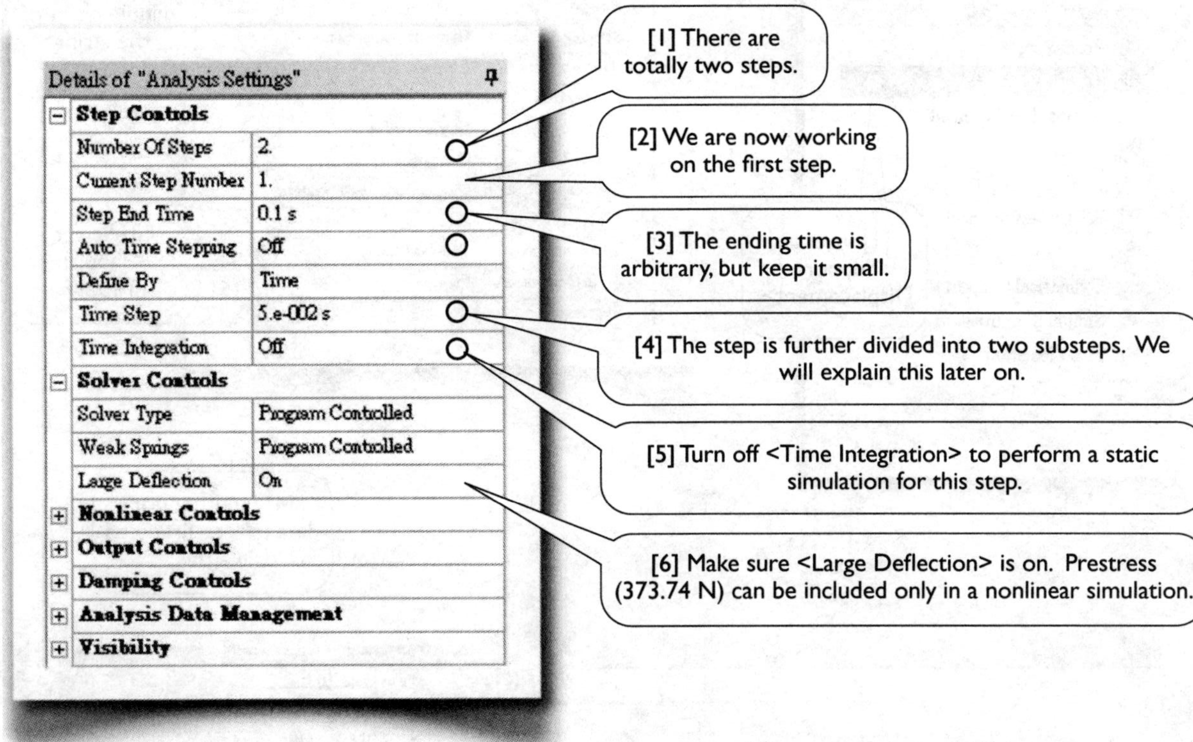

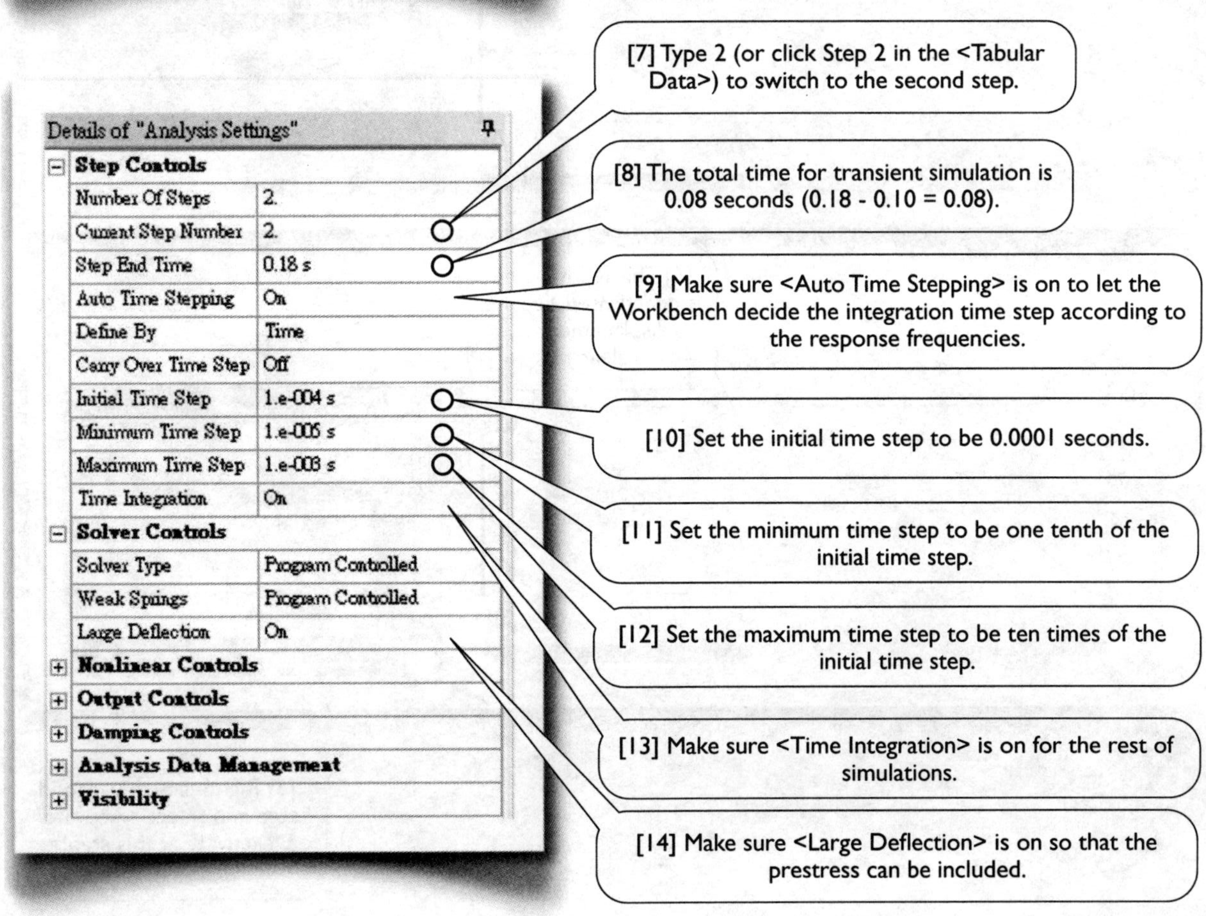

12.5-7 Set Up the Initial Displacement

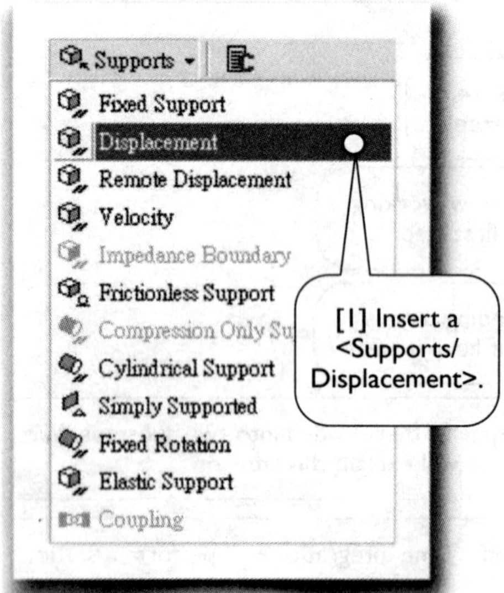

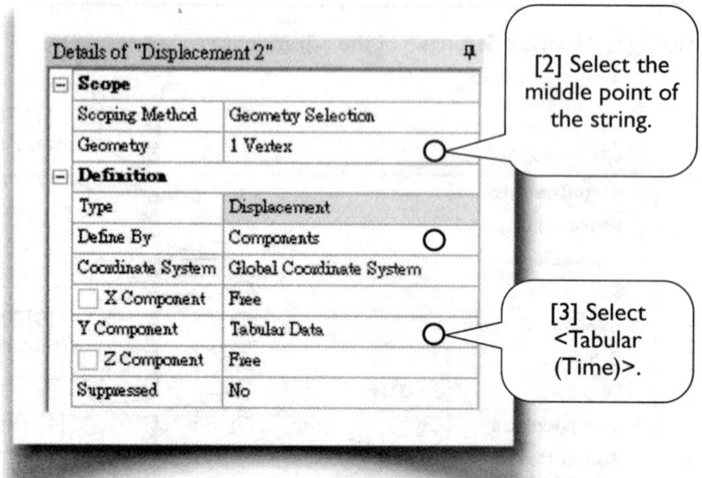

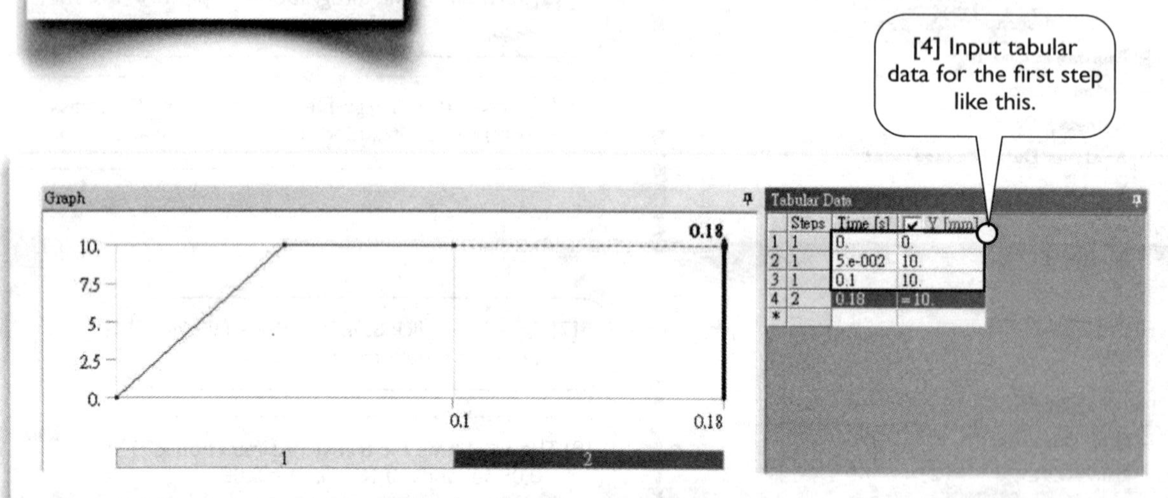

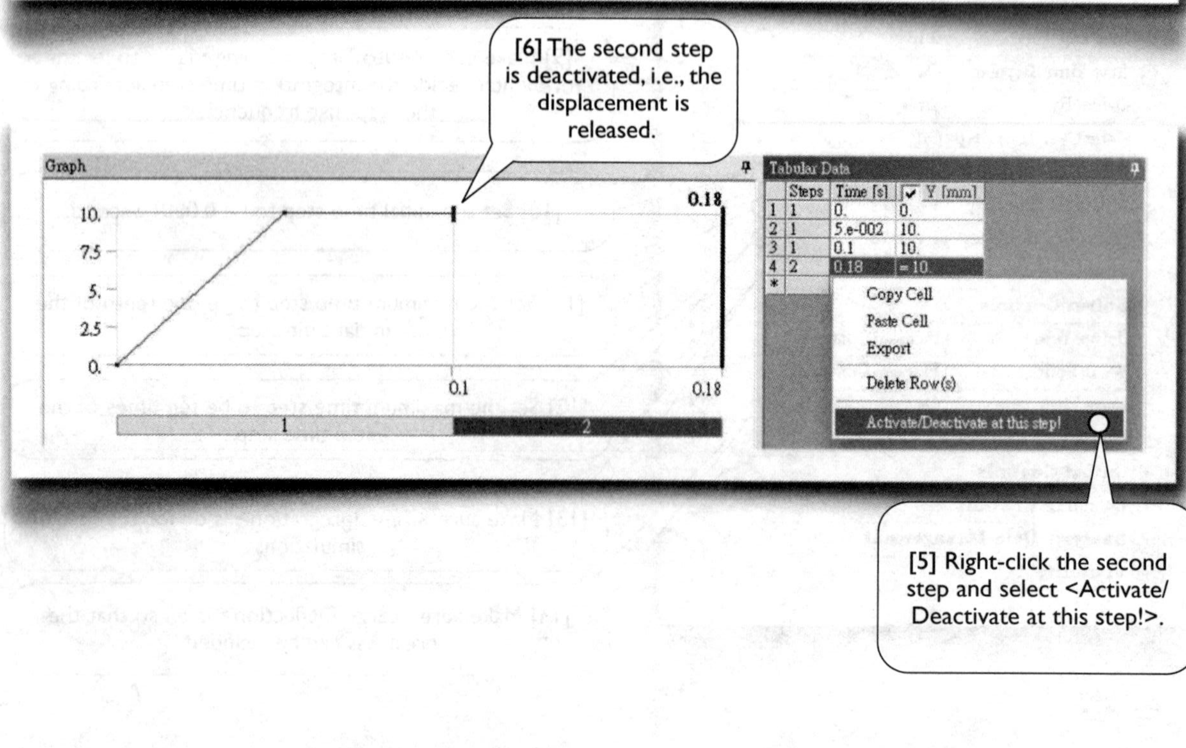

12.5-8 Insert Result Objects and Solve the Model

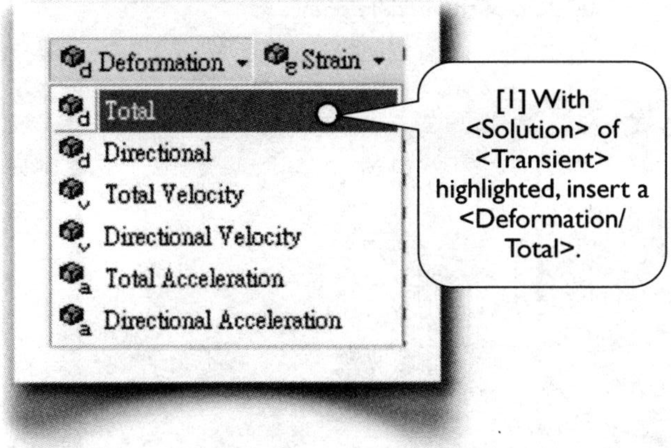

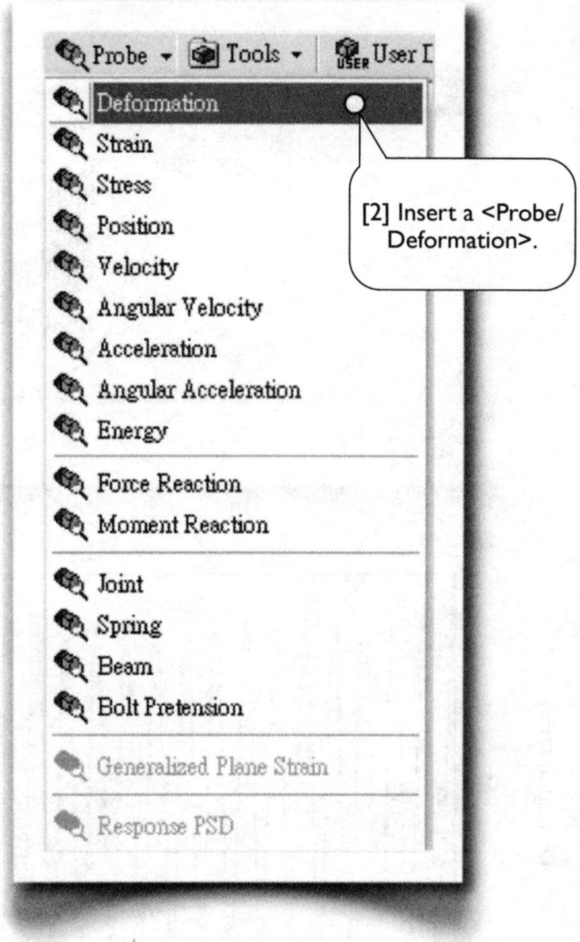

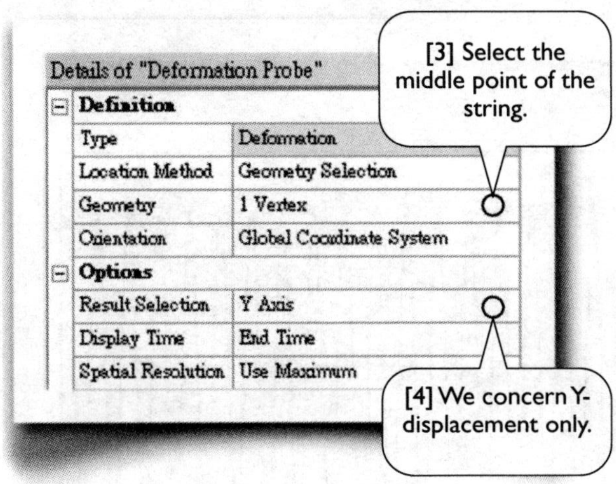

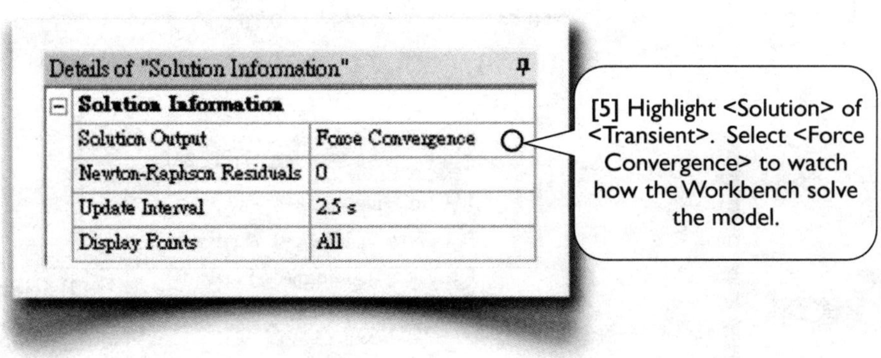

12.5-9 View the Results

[1] Highlight <Deformation Probe>, it shows a deflection versus time of the middle point.

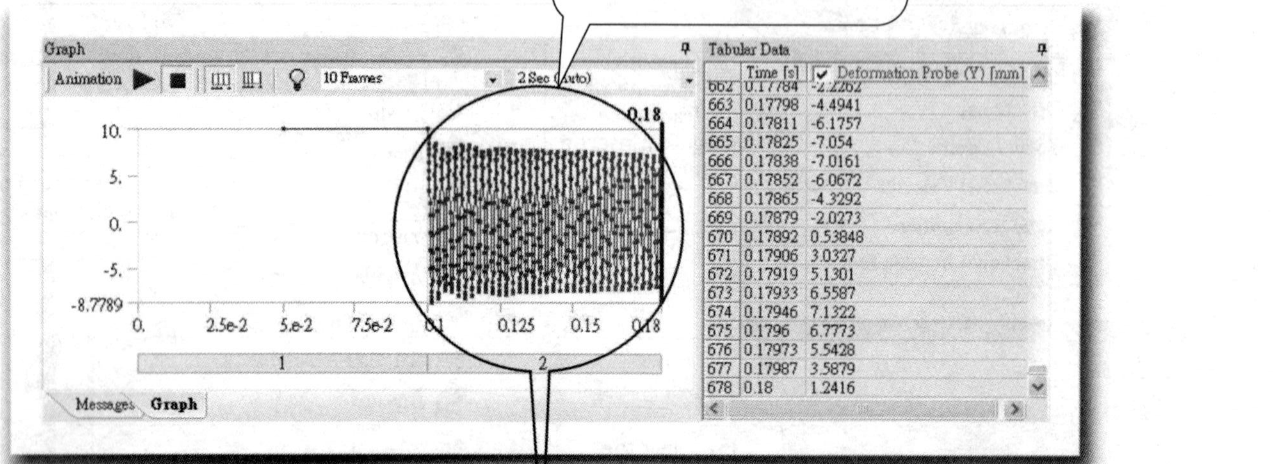

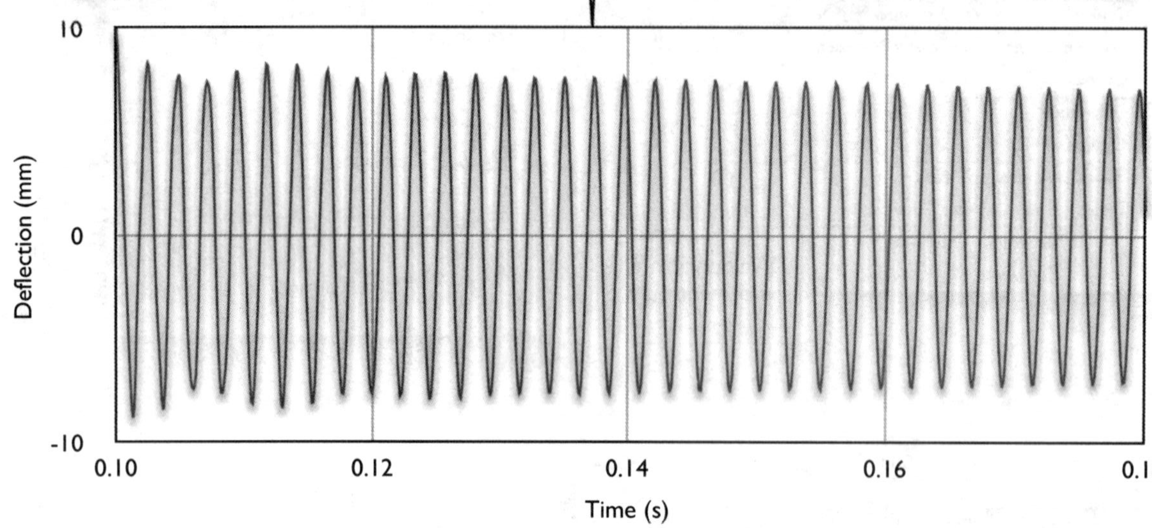

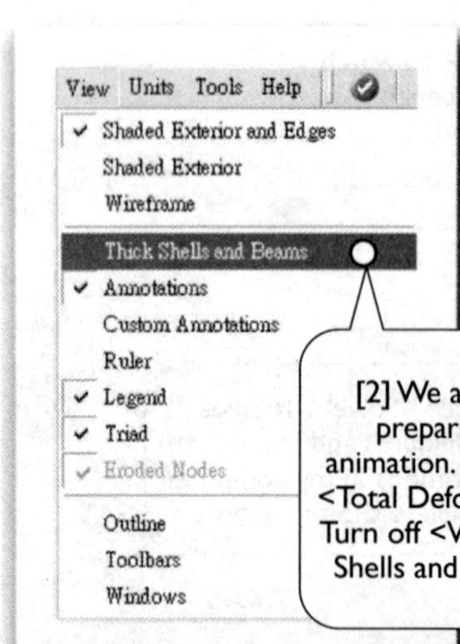

[2] We are now preparing an animation. Highlight <Total Deformation>. Turn off <View/Thick Shells and Beams>.

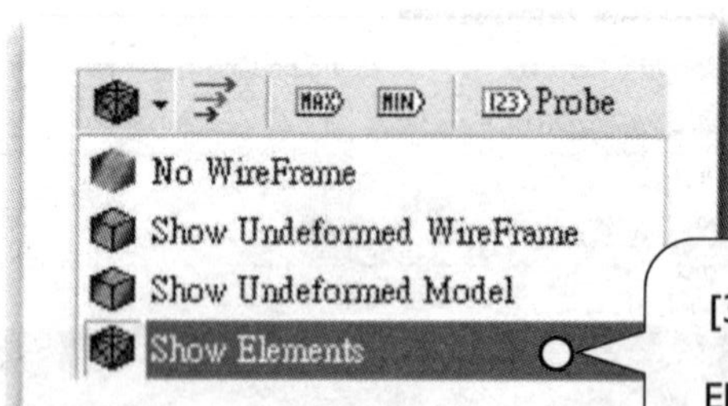

[3] Select <Show Element>.

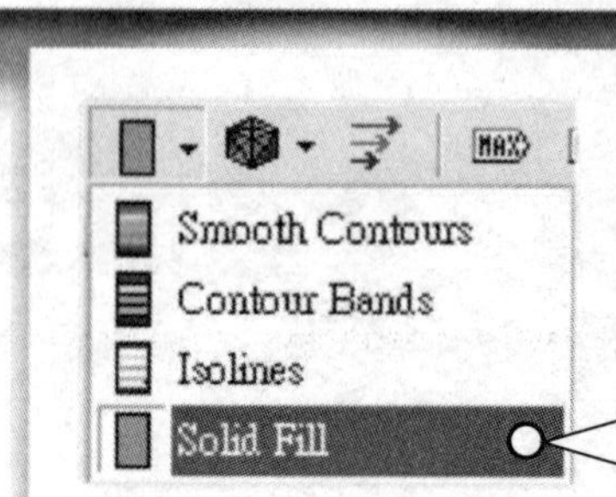

[4] Select <Solid Fill>.

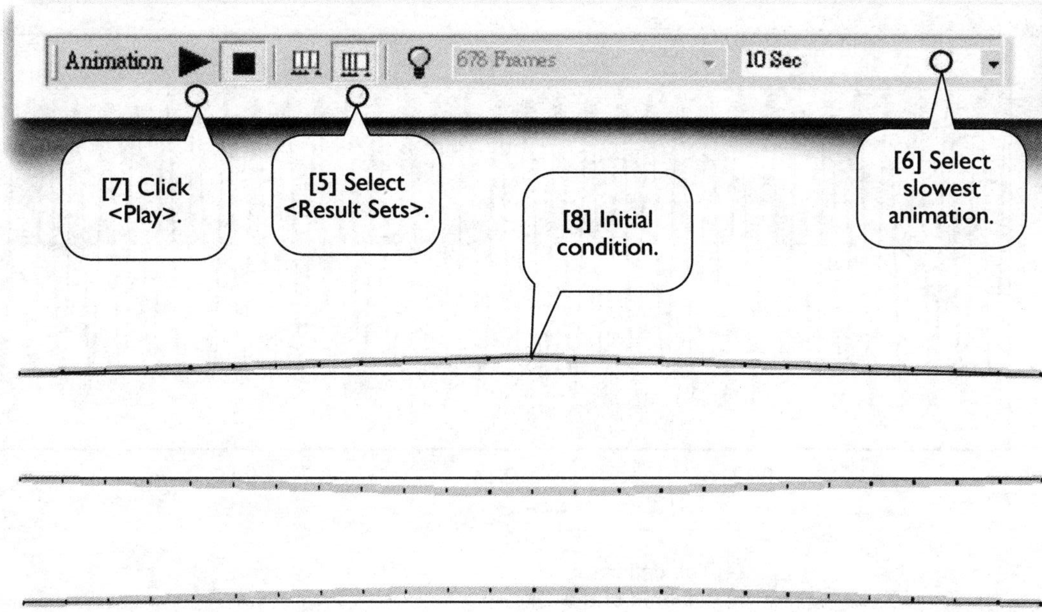

12.5-10 Pluck at Quarter Point

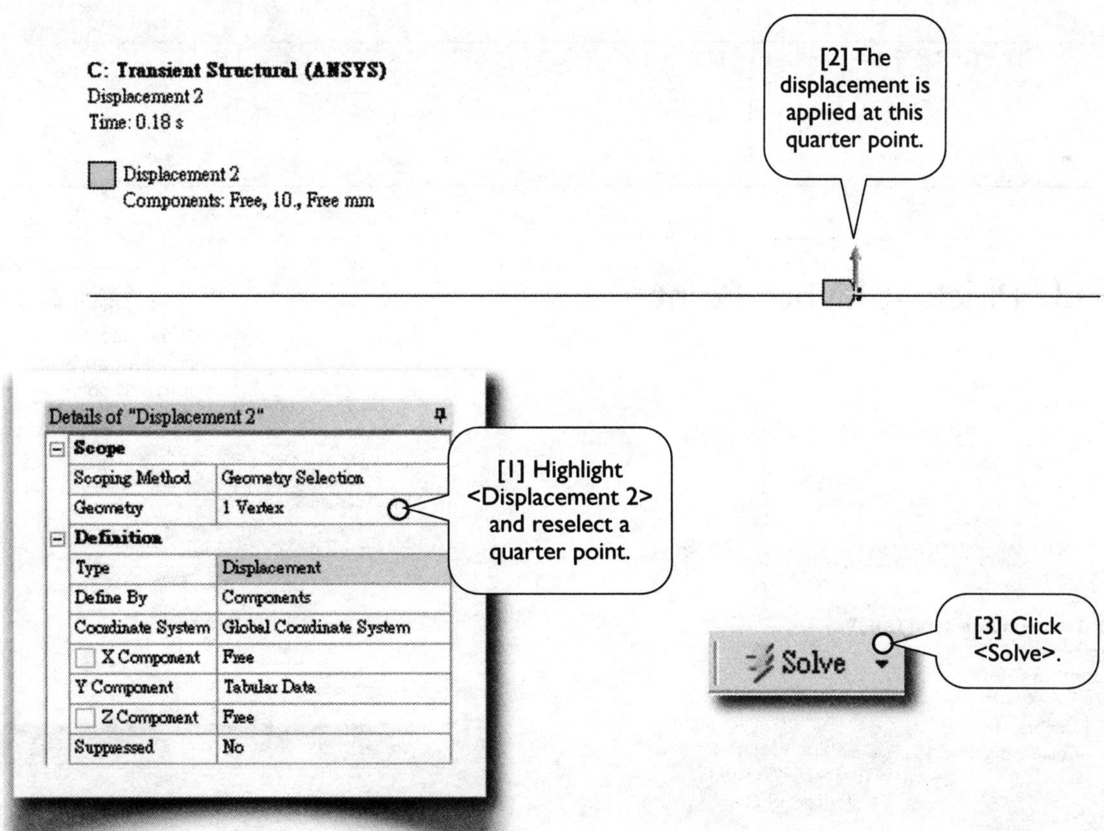

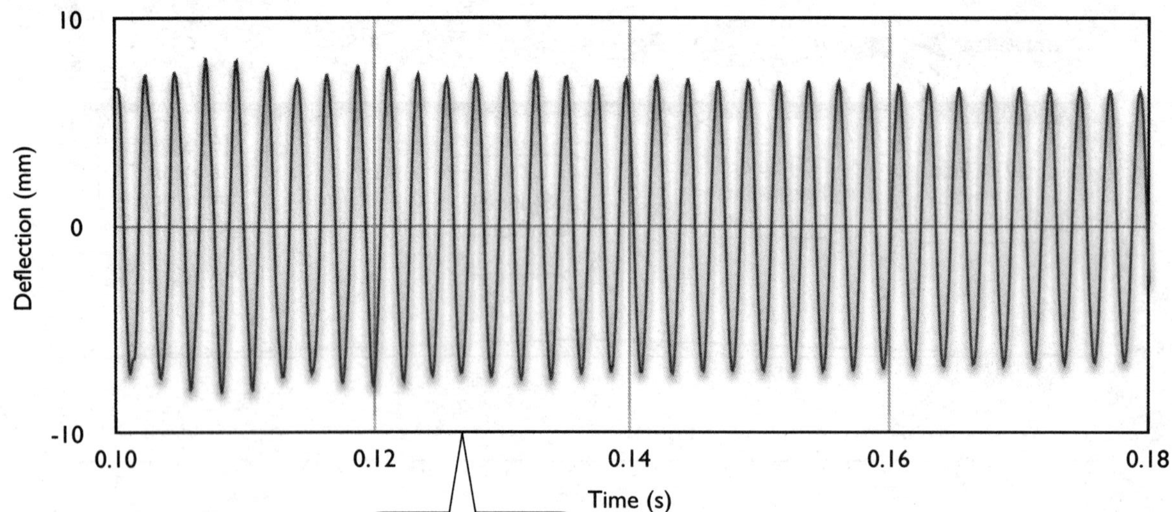

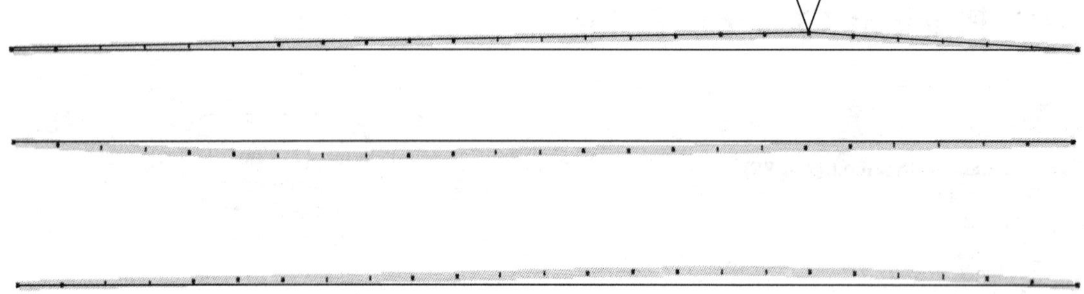

12.5-11 Pluck at Eighth Point

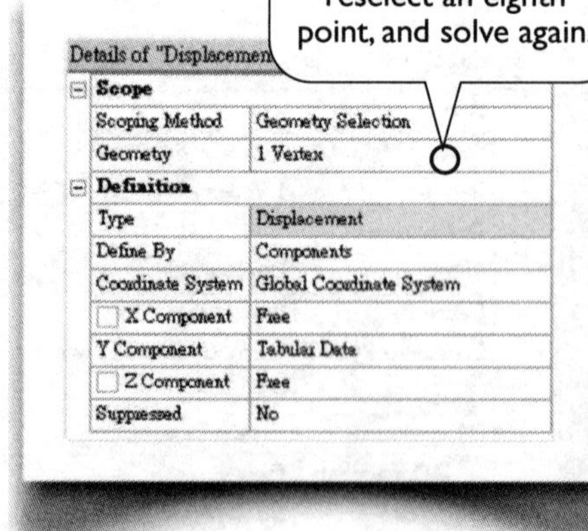

Details of "Displacemen

Scope	
Scoping Method	Geometry Selection
Geometry	1 Vertex
Definition	
Type	Displacement
Define By	Components
Coordinate System	Global Coordinate System
X Component	Free
Y Component	Tabular Data
Z Component	Free
Suppressed	No

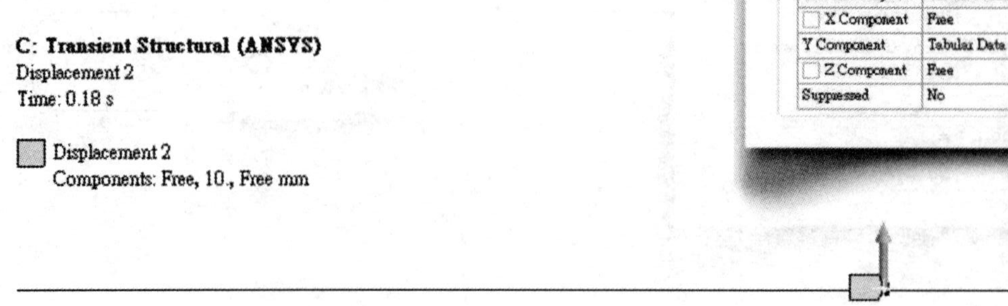

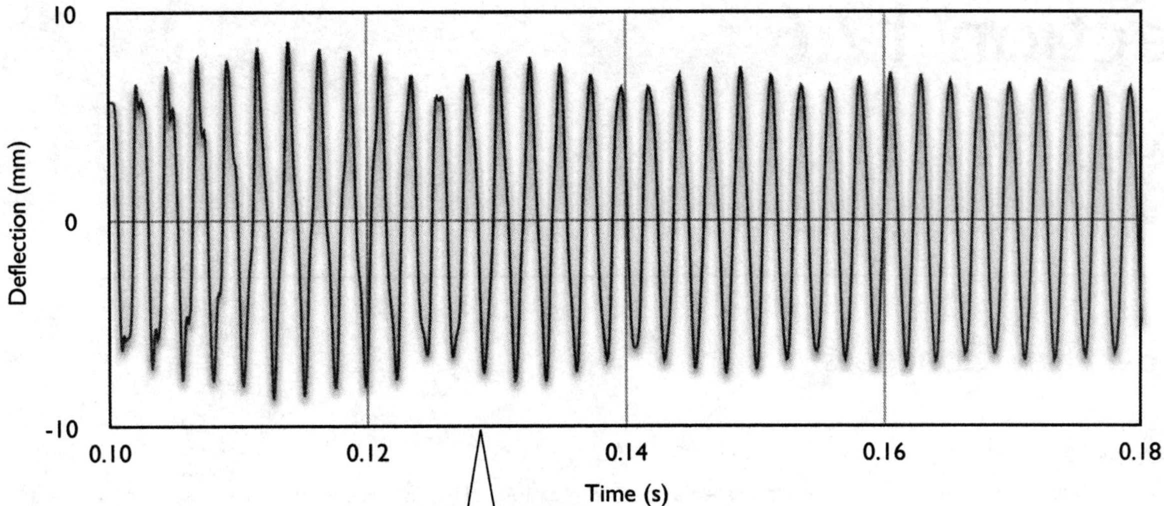

[2] The deflection versus time of the middle point.

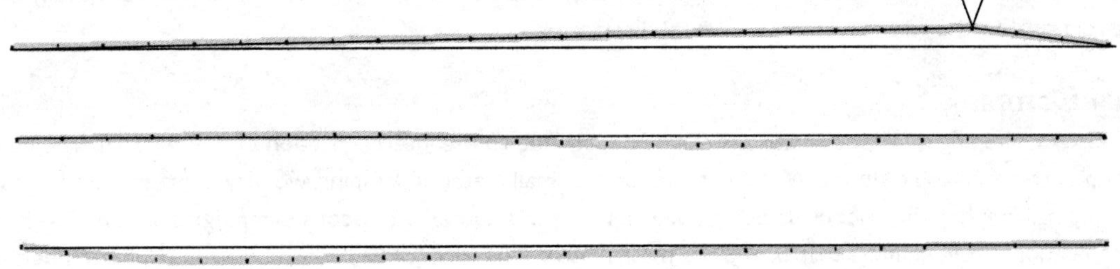

[3] Initial condition.

Wrap Up

Save the project and exit Workbench.

Section 12.6

Problems

12.6-1 Key Concepts

Lumped Mass Model

Analysis models that assume the mass concentrated at certain locations. The discrete masses are typically connected by springs and dampers. The models are often used to study dynamic systems.

Critical Damping

When the damping of a dynamic system is smaller than a critical value, its free vibration is oscillatory. On the other hand, if the damping is larger than the critical value, the motion is not oscillatory.

Viscous Damping

The damping due to the friction between the structure and its surrounding fluid. The damping force typically assumes to be proportional to the velocity of the structural displacement.

Material Damping

Also called solid damping or elastic hysteresis. The damping due to the internal friction in the material. The behavior is still an open research topic. In the Workbench, assuming small material damping, we may express it by an equivalent viscous damping. Further, the viscous damping coefficient (of this equivalent viscous damping) is assumed to be a linear combination of the stiffness matrix and the mass matrix. The form of linear combination (alpha and beta) is then determined by lab experiments and data fittings.

Coulomb Damping

Also called Coulomb friction or dry friction. The damping due to the friction in the connection between structural members. In the Workbench, it can be modeled using frictional contact.

Harmonic Response Analysis

A dynamic analysis to investigate the maximum response of a structure under steady harmonic (sinusoidal) loads.

Response Spectrum Analysis

A dynamic analysis to evaluate the maximum response of a structure under loading conditions described by a spectrum representing the maximum response at varying frequencies in known directions to a specific time history. The technique is often used to design structures withstanding multiple short-duration loadings, such as earthquakes.

Random Vibration Analysis

A dynamic analysis to evaluate the probabilistic response of a structure under probabilistic loads described by a spectrum representing probability distribution of excitation at varying frequencies in known directions. The technique is used to design structures withstanding random loadings.

Explicit Dynamics
A technique for transient dynamic analysis. Explicit integration method is used, which requires a very small integration time step to achieve solution accuracy. For a single time step, it is much more efficient than an implicit method, which is used in the <Transient Structural> analysis system. These features make it very efficient for a high-speed impact simulation, or highly nonlinear simulations.

Steps, Substeps, and Equilibrium Iterations
We may divide the whole loading history into steps, to specify different <Analysis Settings> for each step. Each step can be further divided into substeps. For transient dynamic simulation, each substep is an integration time step. For nonlinear simulation, dividing into substeps is to expedite convergence. In nonlinear simulations, each substep may need several equilibrium iterations to find its solution.

No Separation Contact
Two surfaces with <No Separation> contact condition prohibits separation in their normal direction, but allows small sliding relative to each other. Both <Bonded> and <No Separation> contact types do not introduce contact nonlinearity.

Solid Shell Element
A solid element that includes additional deformation modes to improve the bending accuracy; useful when meshing thin solid bodies.

12.6-2 Workbench Exercises

High-Speed Impact Simulation
The impact simulation in the Section 12.4 is actually not useful, since the material (of Young's Modulus 10 kPa) is not realistic and the impact speed (0.5 m/s) is slow. Try more realistic simulations by yourself using the same geometric model. Gradually increase the Young's modulus and the impact speed. Each time you may need to decrease the integration time step. This exercise is to experience the limitation of the implicit method, which is used in the <Transient Structural> analysis system. High-speed impact simulations are more suitable by using <Explicit Dynamics> analysis system (Chapter 15).

Chapter 13

Nonlinear Simulations

When the relation between the response and the load of a structure is linear, the structure is called a *linear structure*, and the simulation is called a *linear simulation*. Otherwise, the structure is called a *nonlinear structure* and the simulation is called a *nonlinear simulation*. In the real world, all structures are nonlinear in some degree. In many cases, when nonlinearities are negligible, we may predict their behavior using linear simulations, and the results are often accurate enough. For other cases, when nonlinearities are not negligible, nonlinear simulations are needed.

Structural nonlinearities come from three sources: large deformation, change of connectivity, and nonlinear stress-strain relations. Nonlinearity due to large deformation is called *geometry nonlinearity*. Nonlinearity due to the change of connectivity is called *topology nonlinearity*, which includes failure of structural members or materials, and change of contact status. In this chapter, we discuss the change of contact status only. This kind of nonlinearity can also be termed *contact nonlinearity*. Nonlinearity due to the nonlinear stress-strain relations is called *material nonlinearity* and will be covered in Chapter 14.

In general, nonlinear simulations are much more challenging than linear simulations. They not only take much of computing time, but sometime fail to converge to a solution. These solution behaviors highly depend on the settings of solution parameters. A thorough comprehension of these solution parameters becomes critical when you want to adjust these parameters to reduce the computing time, or try to succeed in finding a solution.

Purpose of the Chapter

This chapter deals with nonlinear solution algorithms and focuses on geometry nonlinearity and contact nonlinearity. Material nonlinearity will be covered in Chapter 14. This chapter provides some basics of nonlinear simulations process, so that you can understand and harness the solution parameters.

About Each Section

Section 1 introduces the basics of nonlinear simulations, including the Newton-Raphson method, the solution method used in the Workbench. Concepts of convergence follow the introduction. Section 2 provides a step-by-step example of geometric nonlinearity. Sections 3 provides a step-by-step example of contact nonlinearity. Section 4 provides an additional exercise of contact nonlinearity.

Section 13.1

Basics of Nonlinear Simulations

PART A. NONLINEARITY IN GENERAL

13.1-1 What Are Nonlinear Simulations

In a linear simulation, the response is linearly proportional to the load. To be more specific, let's use Eq. 1.3-1(1) for the upcoming discussion

$$[K]\{D\}=\{F\} \qquad \text{Copy of 1.3-1(1)}$$

The nodal force $\{F\}$ is the synthesis of all loads; the nodal displacement $\{D\}$ represents the responses (stress and strain can be computed from the displacement); the stiffness matrix $[K]$ is the proportionality coefficient between the force and the displacement. Eq. 1.3-1(1) can be conceptually plotted as shown below [1]. Note that both the abscissa (displacement) and the ordinate (force) are multi-dimensional (i.e., vectors), and $[K]$ is the "slope" of the conceptual "straight line."

Performing a linear simulation means to solve Eq. 1.3-1(1), once and for all. For linear transient dynamic simulations, Eq. 12.1-4(1) is solved instead; it involves the integration over the time domain. In each integration time step, the equation is solved only once.

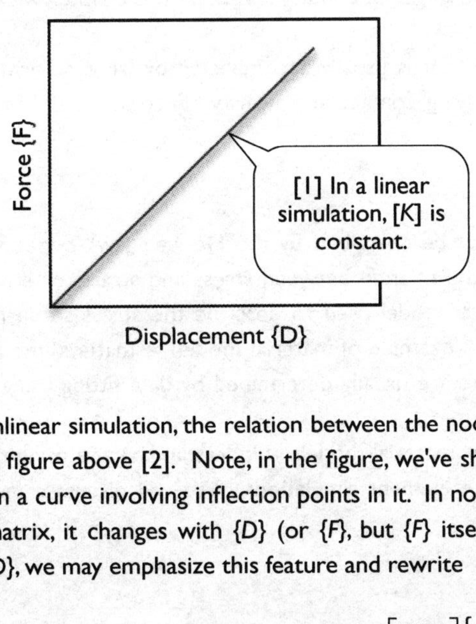

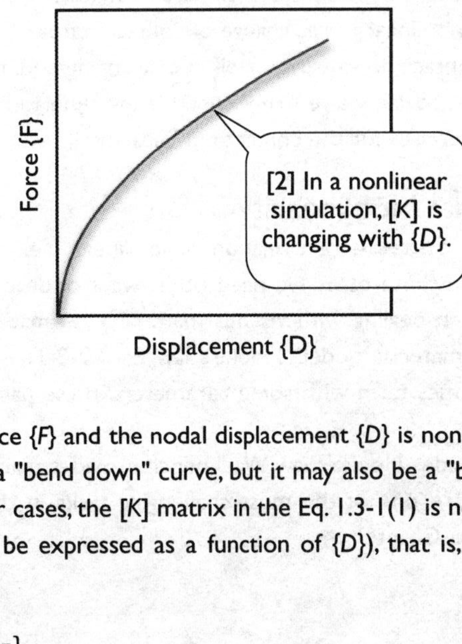

In a nonlinear simulation, the relation between the nodal force $\{F\}$ and the nodal displacement $\{D\}$ is nonlinear, as shown in the figure above [2]. Note, in the figure, we've shown a "bend down" curve, but it may also be a "bend up" curve, or even a curve involving inflection points in it. In nonlinear cases, the $[K]$ matrix in the Eq. 1.3-1(1) is no longer a constant matrix, it changes with $\{D\}$ (or $\{F\}$, but $\{F\}$ itself can be expressed as a function of $\{D\}$), that is, $[K]$ is a function of $\{D\}$, we may emphasize this feature and rewrite

$$[K(D)]\{D\}=\{F\} \qquad (1)$$

Challenges of nonlinear simulations come from the difficulties of solving Eq. (1).

13.1-2 Causes of Structural Nonlinearities

As mentioned in the opening of this chapter, sources of structural nonlinearities can be classified into three categories: geometry nonlinearity, topology nonlinearity, and material nonlinearity. Note that a problem may mix up two or more categories of nonlinearities.

A linear simulation implies none of the nonlinearities are present; it in turn implies: (a) the deformation is very small, (b) there is no topological changes, and (c) the stress-strain relation is linear, i.e., described by Hooke's law. It also implies that the principle of superposition is applicable, and, so that the solution is independent of loading history. On the other hand, for nonlinear problems, the principle of superposition is not applicable and the solution may depend on loading history.

Geometry Nonlinearity

Geometry nonlinearity is due to the large deformation of the structure. The stiffness matrix $[K]$ is composed by element stiffness matrices, and each element stiffness depends on the element's material properties and geometry. When the deformation of the structure is so large that the stiffness matrix $[K]$ is changed substantially, geometry nonlinearity must be considered. To include the geometry nonlinearity, simply turn on <Large Deflection> in the <Analysis Settings> [1]. Among the three sources of nonlinearities, geometry nonlinearity causes fewest troubles in convergence; reducing the time step is usually enough to improve the convergence. Some exceptions (e.g., the pneumatic finger of Section 9.1) need special treatments. In this textbook, so far, we've experienced many simulations involving geometry nonlinearity. Section 13.2 provides one more step-by-step exercise for the geometry nonlinearity.

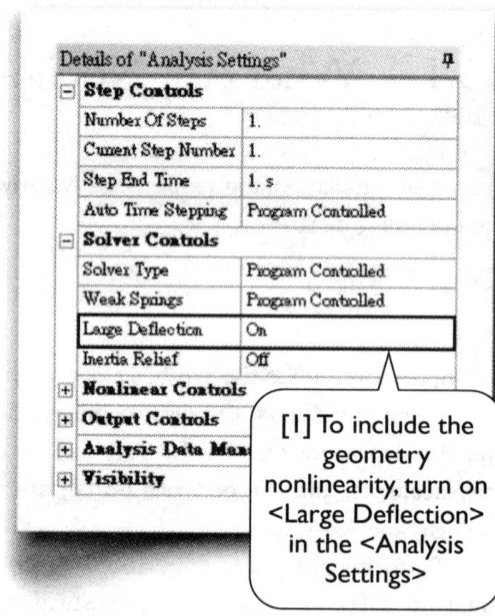

Topology Nonlinearity

When the topology (or connectivity) of a structure changes, its stiffness matrix will also change. Topology changes include failure of structural members or materials, and the changes of contact status. In this chapter, we only deal with contact nonlinearity, i.e., change of contact status.

Contact nonlinearity itself is challenging and, moreover, it is usually accompanied by large deformation. In this textbook, so far, we've experienced many simulations involving contact nonlinearity. Sections 13.3 and 13.4 are two more exercises for the contact nonlinearity.

Material Nonlinearity

When the stress-strain relation is not linear (i.e., it cannot be described by the Hooke's law), material nonlinearity raises. In these cases, we need other ways of describing the relation between stress and strain (or stress and strain rate, when dealing with viscous materials). A mathematical model used to describe the stress-strain relationship is called a material model. Hooke's law, Eq. 1.2-8(1), is a good example of material model. A material model is usually a mathematics form with some parameters; these parameters are usually determined by data fitting using material test data.

Besides Hooke's law, Workbench provides many other material models. Understanding and using these material models are one of the most challenging tasks in the finite element simulations. We will discuss a few of material models in Chapter 14.

13.1-3 Load Steps, Substeps, and Equilibrium Iterations

Steps (Load Steps)

To fully control the <Analysis Settings>, the user can divide the entire loading history into one or more *load steps*, or simply *steps*. The number of steps can be specified in the Details view of <Analysis Settings> [1]. Each step can have its own analysis settings [2]. To switch between steps, you can directly type a step number in the Details view [3], click a step number on the <Graph> [4], or click a step number on the <Tabular Data> [5].

Time Steps (Substeps)

Each load step is further divided into *substeps*, or *time steps*. In dynamic simulations, time step is used for integration over the time domain (Chapter 12); main consideration of the time step size is to capture the response characteristics. In static simulation, a load step can be divided into substeps to achieve or enhance convergence. Smaller time step size usually converges easier, but, of course, needs more number of time steps to complete a load step.

Iterations (Equilibrium Iterations)

For nonlinear problems, each time step itself needs several iterations to solve Eq. 13.1-1(1). Each iteration involves the solving of a subproblem, Eq. 1.3-1(1), the linearized equilibrium equation. Solving of Eq. 1.3-1(1) is called an *equilibrium iterations*, or simply *iteration*. We will present details about the process of equilibrium iterations, known as the Newton-Rapshon method, in the next subsection.

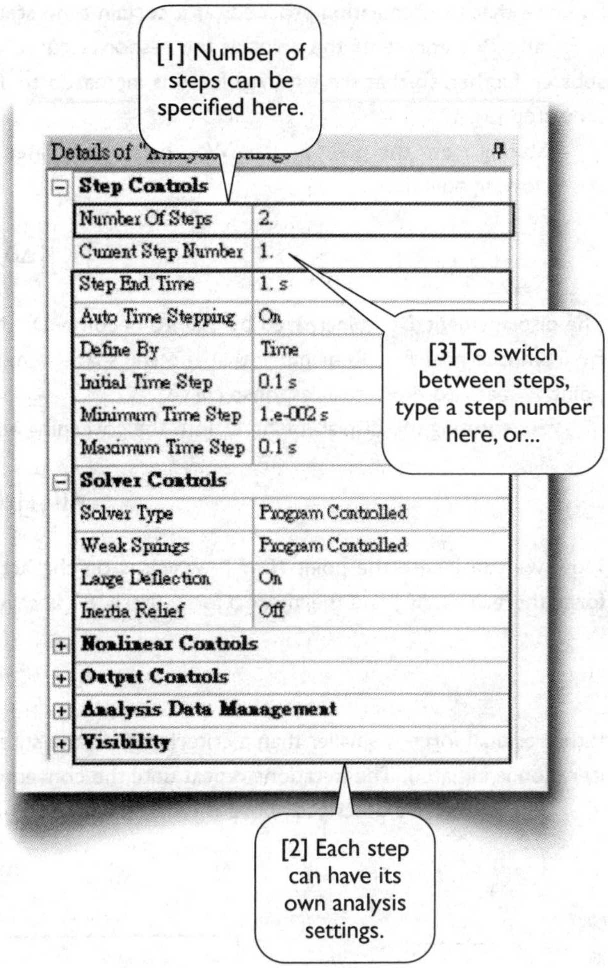

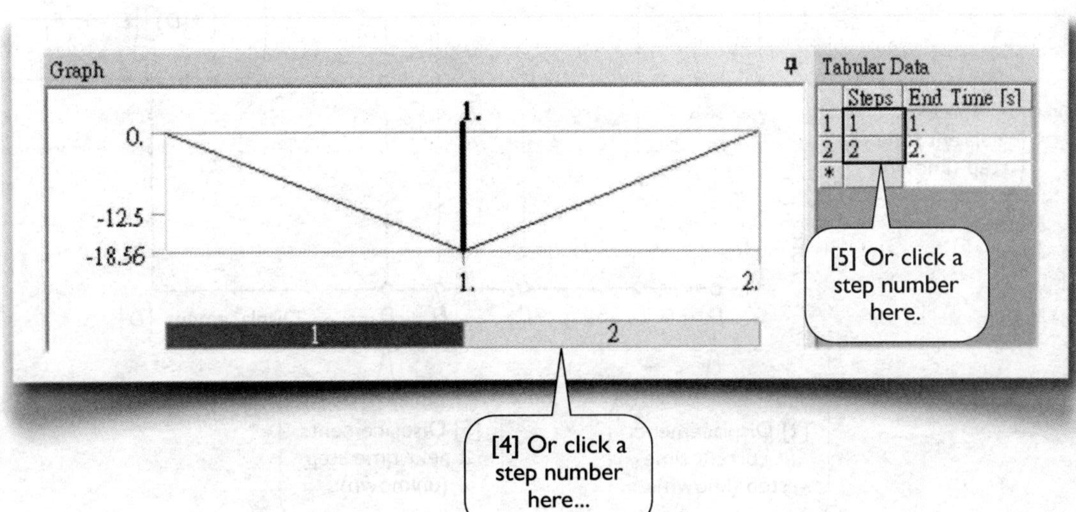

13.1-4 Newton-Raphson Method

Suppose that the simulation proceeds at a certain time step [1-3], at which the displacement is D_0, the external force is F_0, and P_0 represents the point at the response curve described by Eq. 13.1(1). Now, the time is increased one substep further, so that the external force is increased to $F_0 + \Delta F$ [4], and we want to find the displacement at next time step [5].

Staring from the point P_0, the Workbench calculates the *tangent stiffness* [K], the linearized stiffness, and solves the following equation

$$[K]\{\Delta D\} = \{\Delta F\} \quad (1)$$

The displacement D_0 is increased by ΔD to become D_1. Now, in the *D-F* space, we are at $(D_1, F_0 + \Delta F)$, the point P_1', far from our goal P_4. Remember that the *D-F* space is multi-dimensional space. To proceed, we need to "drive" the point P_1' back to the actual response curve.

Substituting the displacement D_1 into the governing equation, Eq. 13.1-1(1), we can calculate the *internal force* F_1,

$$[K(D_1)]\{D_1\} = \{F_1\}$$

Now we can locate the point (D_1, F_1), which is on the actual response curve. The difference between the external force (here, $F_0 + \Delta F$) and the internal force (here, F_1) is called the *residual force* of that equilibrium iteration,

$$F_1^R = (F_0 + \Delta F) - F_1$$

If the residual force is smaller than a criterion, then the substep is said to be converged, otherwise, another equilibrium iteration is initiated. The iterations repeat until the convergence criterion satisfies.

The procedure described above is called the Newton-Raphson Method.

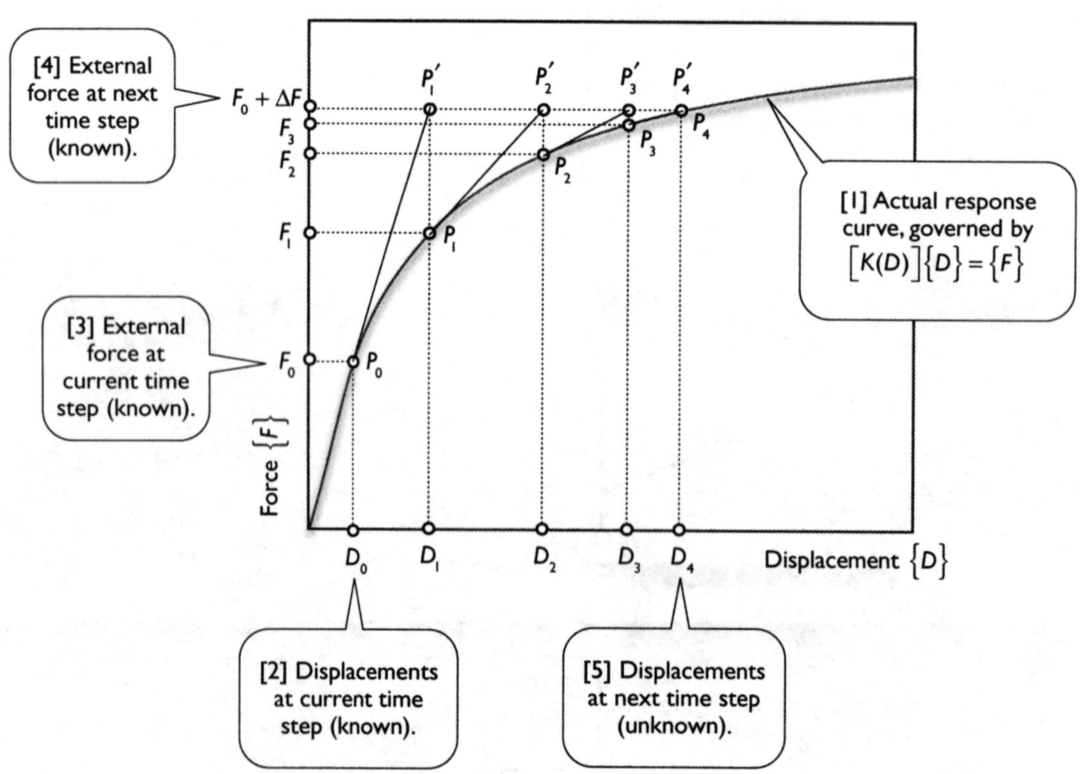

13.1-5 Force Convergence and Displacement Convergence

In the last subsection, we stated that when the residual force F^R is smaller than a criterion, then the substep is said to be converged. This statement is not strictly correct. There are at most four convergence criteria that can be activated under your control, namely, force convergence [1], displacement convergence [2], moment convergence [3], and rotation convergence [4]. The moment convergence and rotation convergence can be activated only when shell elements or beam elements are used in the model. These convergence monitoring methods are all default to <Program Controlled>, that is, the Workbench automatically turns on any of them when it is appropriate. You may manually turn off or turn on any of them.

When you turn on any of them, you may specify a <Value>, a <Tolerance>, and a <Minimum Reference>. The criterion is then

$$\text{Criterion} = \text{maximum}(\text{Tolerance} \times \text{Value},\ \text{Minimum Reference})$$

The force (or moment) convergence satisfies when

$$\left\| F^R \right\| < \text{Criterion} \qquad (1)$$

The displacement (or rotation) convergence satisfies when

$$\left\| \Delta D \right\| < \text{Criterion} \qquad (2)$$

Where $\|\cdot\|$ denotes the norm of the underlying vector, and is called a *convergence value*. The <Value> defaults to <ANSYS Calculated>, which usually means the current maximum value. For example, in the example of Section 13.1-4, the current maximum force value is $\|F_0\|$, and the current maximum displacement value is $\|D_0\|$. The <Tolerance> defaults to 0.5%. Note that setting up a <Minimum Reference> is to avoid a never-convergent situation when <Value> is near zero.

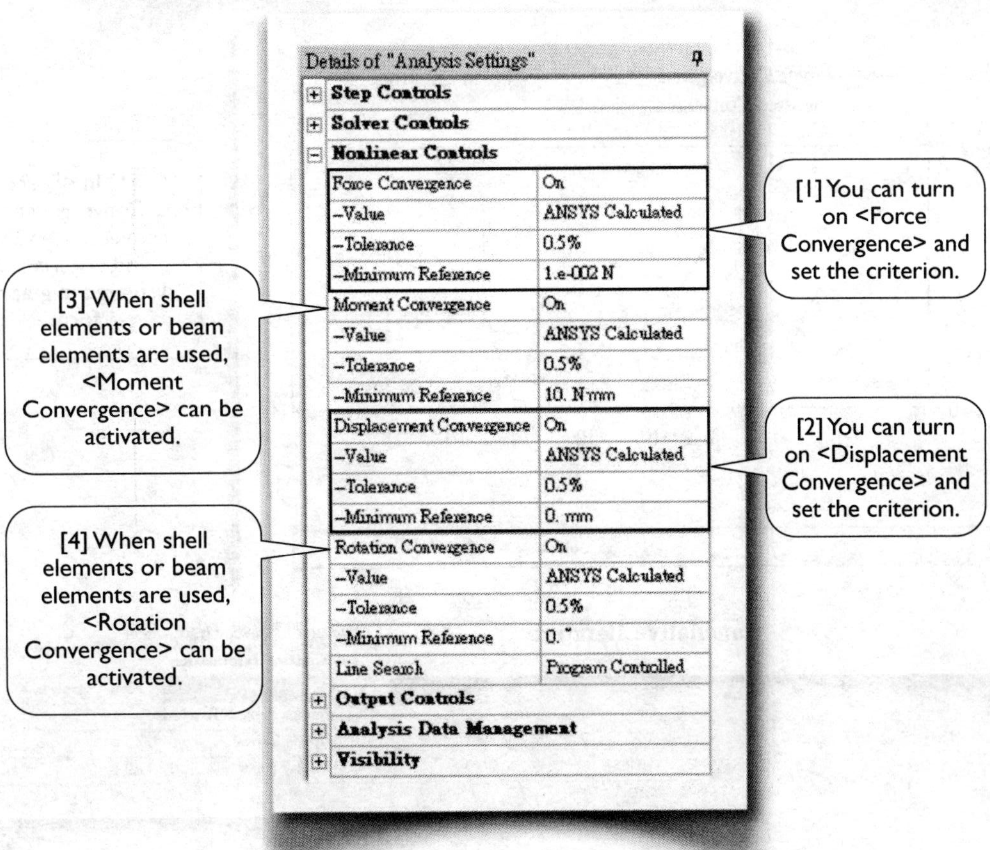

13.1-6 Solution Information

A text form of convergence values and criteria for each iteration is available in the <Solution Information> [1]. A graphics form of this information is also available [2]. A key to tackle nonlinear problems is the ability to interpret and draw conclusions from these data.

Details of "Solution Information"	
Solution Information	
Solution Output	Solver Output
Newton-Raphson Residuals	0
Update Interval	2.5 s
Display Points	All

[1] In <Solver Output>, convergence values and criteria are listed in text form.

```
   FORCE CONVERGENCE VALUE   = 0.9949E-01  CRITERION= 0.2227E-01
  EQUIL ITER   1 COMPLETED.  NEW TRIANG MATRIX.  MAX DOF INC=  0.9229E-02
   LINE SEARCH PARAMETER =   1.000       SCALED MAX DOF INC =  0.9229E-02
   FORCE CONVERGENCE VALUE   = 0.6719E-02  CRITERION= 0.2173E-01 <<< CONVERGED
  >>> SOLUTION CONVERGED AFTER EQUILIBRIUM ITERATION   1
*** LOAD STEP     1   SUBSTEP     9  COMPLETED.    CUM ITER =     20
*** TIME =   0.900000         TIME INC =  0.100000

   FORCE CONVERGENCE VALUE   = 0.9542E-01  CRITERION= 0.2455E-01
  EQUIL ITER   1 COMPLETED.  NEW TRIANG MATRIX.  MAX DOF INC=  0.9888E-02
   LINE SEARCH PARAMETER =   1.000       SCALED MAX DOF INC =  0.9888E-02
   FORCE CONVERGENCE VALUE   = 0.4753E-02  CRITERION= 0.2415E-01 <<< CONVERGED
  >>> SOLUTION CONVERGED AFTER EQUILIBRIUM ITERATION   1
*** LOAD STEP     1   SUBSTEP    10  COMPLETED.    CUM ITER =     21
*** TIME =   1.00000          TIME INC =  0.100000
```

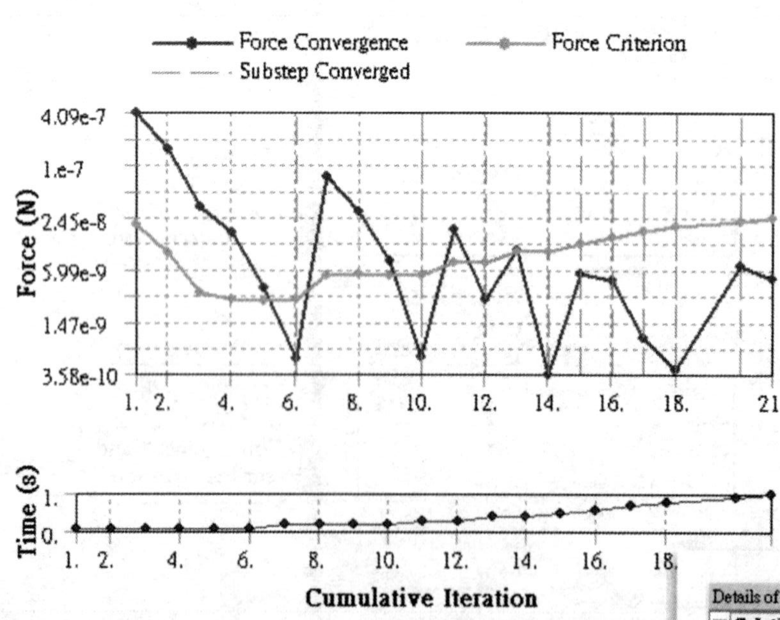

[1] In <Force Convergence>, convergence values and criteria are displayed in graphics form.

Details of "Solution Information"	
Solution Information	
Solution Output	Force Convergence
Newton-Raphson Residuals	0
Update Interval	2.5 s
Display Points	All

13.1-7 Line Search

In the example of 13.1-4[1-5], each equilibrium iteration (Eq. 13.1-4(1)) calculates a displacement ΔD, that is smaller than the goal, therefore several iterations is needed to reach the goal. That is true in many cases when the *F-D* curves are monotonically "concave down."

In some cases when *F-D* curves are highly nonlinear or "concave up," (e.g., the pneumatic finger, see 1.1-8[4] and 9.1-10[3]) the calculated displacement ΔD in a single iteration may overshoot the goal [1]. In such cases, a numerical technique called *line search* can be activated to "scale down" the incremental displacement [2]. Line searching is useful, but takes extra computing time.

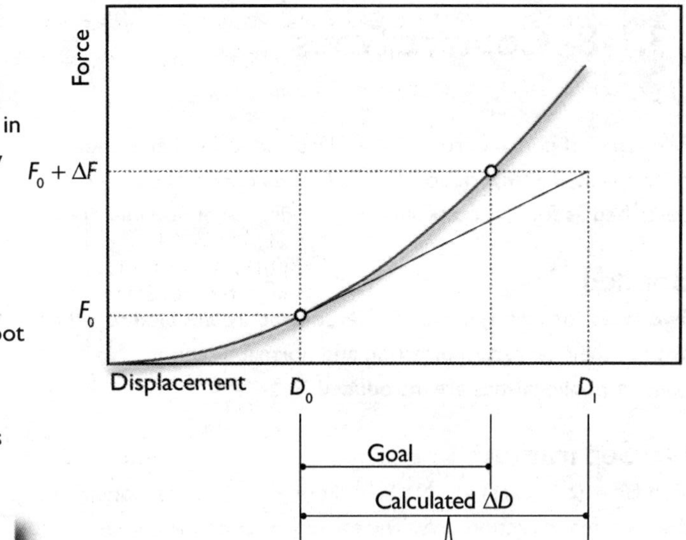

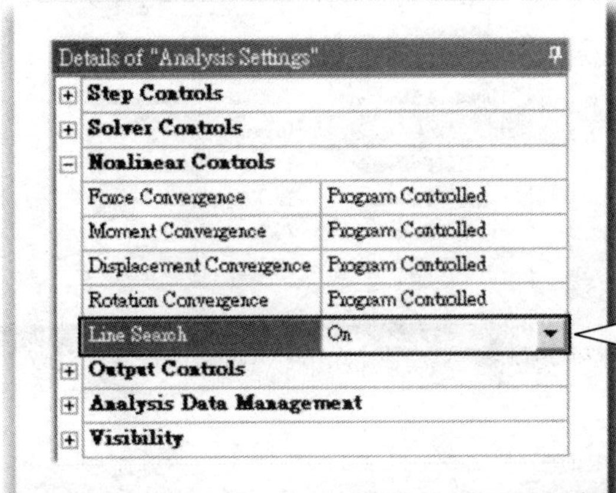

[3] Line search parameter scales down the incremental displacement.

```
 FORCE CONVERGENCE VALUE  =  327.2      CRITERION= 0.2962
EQUIL ITER   1 COMPLETED.  NEW TRIANG MATRIX.  MAX DOF INC= -0.1956
 LINE SEARCH PARAMETER =  0.5779      SCALED MAX DOF INC = -0.1131
 FORCE CONVERGENCE VALUE  =  179.4      CRITERION= 0.2133
EQUIL ITER   2 COMPLETED.  NEW TRIANG MATRIX.  MAX DOF INC=  0.1267E-01
 LINE SEARCH PARAMETER =  1.000       SCALED MAX DOF INC =  0.1267E-01
 FORCE CONVERGENCE VALUE  =  34.92      CRITERION= 0.2253
EQUIL ITER   3 COMPLETED.  NEW TRIANG MATRIX.  MAX DOF INC=  0.1004
 LINE SEARCH PARAMETER =  0.6958      SCALED MAX DOF INC =  0.6985E-01
 FORCE CONVERGENCE VALUE  =  30.58      CRITERION= 0.2916
EQUIL ITER   4 COMPLETED.  NEW TRIANG MATRIX.  MAX DOF INC=  0.1047E-01
 LINE SEARCH PARAMETER =  1.000       SCALED MAX DOF INC =  0.1047E-01
 FORCE CONVERGENCE VALUE  =  5.867      CRITERION= 0.3076
EQUIL ITER   5 COMPLETED.  NEW TRIANG MATRIX.  MAX DOF INC=  0.1734E-01
 LINE SEARCH PARAMETER =  0.8577      SCALED MAX DOF INC =  0.1487E-01
 FORCE CONVERGENCE VALUE  =  2.724      CRITERION= 0.3313
EQUIL ITER   6 COMPLETED.  NEW TRIANG MATRIX.  MAX DOF INC=  0.3472E-03
 LINE SEARCH PARAMETER =  1.000       SCALED MAX DOF INC =  0.3472E-03
 FORCE CONVERGENCE VALUE  = 0.2257      CRITERION= 0.3382     <<< CONVERGED
 >>> SOLUTION CONVERGED AFTER EQUILIBRIUM ITERATION   6
*** LOAD STEP     2   SUBSTEP  114  COMPLETED.    CUM ITER =   1889
*** TIME =   1.89395          TIME INC =  0.288325E-01
*** AUTO TIME STEP:  NEXT TIME INC = 0.43249E-01  INCREASED (FACTOR = 1.5000)
```

PART B. CONTACT NONLINEARITY

13.1-8 Contact Types

Five types of contact are available [1]: Bonded, No Separation, Frictionless, Rough, Frictional. These types of contact are described as follows according to their degree of nonlinearity.

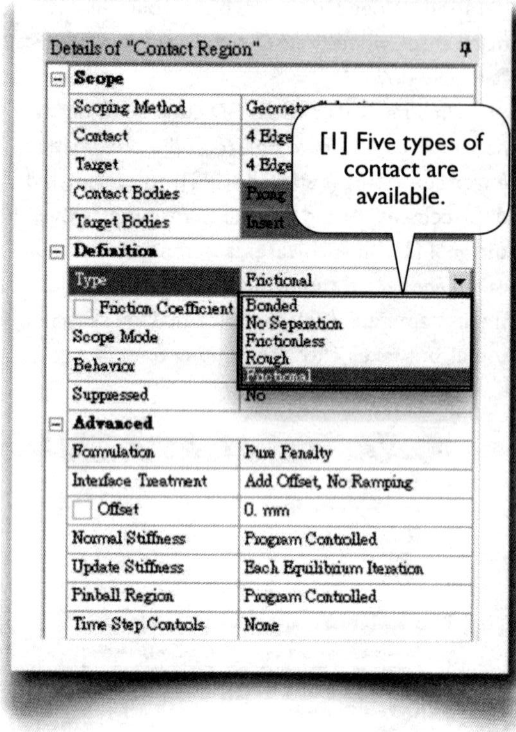

Bonded

Two faces (or edges) in <Bonded> contact are coupled together both in their tangential direction and normal direction. No contact nonlinearities are introduced.

No Separation

Two faces (or edges) in <No Separation> contact are coupled in their normal direction only. The tangential direction allows a small sliding on each other. No contact nonlinearities are introduced since small displacement theory is assumed for the sliding.

Frictionless

Two faces (or edges) in <Frictionless> contact are free to separate in normal direction and sliding in tangential direction without any friction force between them. This contact type does introduce contact nonlinearities. No small displacement theory is assumed.

Rough

Two faces (or edges) in <Rough> contact are free to separate in their normal direction. In their tangential direction, however, it is assumed that the friction is so large that no sliding occurs between two points. In other word, two faces are coupled in their tangential direction. This contact type also introduce contact nonlinearities. No small displacement theory is assumed.

Frictional

Two faces (or edges) in <Frictional> contact are free to separate in their normal direction. In their tangential direction, sliding occurs only when the shear stress exceeds the value multiplying the normal stress by a friction coefficient, which is input as a contact property. This contact type also introduce contact nonlinearities. No small displacement theory is assumed.

Linear versus Nonlinear Contacts

The contact types <Bonded> and <No Separation> are called linear contacts. The contact types <Frictionless>, <Rough>, and <Frictional> are called nonlinear contacts.

13.1-9 Contact versus Target

To specify a contact region, you have to select a set of <Contact> faces (or edges), and select a set of <Target> faces (or edges) [1]. During the solution, Workbench will check the contact status for each point (typically a node or an integration point) on the <Contact> faces against the <Target> faces.

If the <Behavior> is set to <Symmetric>, the roles of <Contact> and <Target> will be symmetric [2], i.e., Workbench checks each point on the <Contact> against the <Target>, as well as each point on the <Target> against the <Contact>. If the <Behavior> is set to <Asymmetric>, the checking is only one-sided.

Consider a point, on a <Contact> face, which is approaching a <Target> face. The point is called a *contacting point.* The Workbench keep tracing the contacting point so that it won't penetrate into the target face. When the point is in contact with the surface, the Workbench calculates the contact force between the point and the face.

In some cases, when <Symmetric> behavior is not available, or when you want to set to <Asymmetric>, to save the run time, selection of <Contact> and <Target> becomes important. In general, we select faces with following characteristics as <Target>: the faces belong to a body with fixed supports, the faces belong to a body with more rigid material (higher Young's modulus), the faces with less curvature, etc.

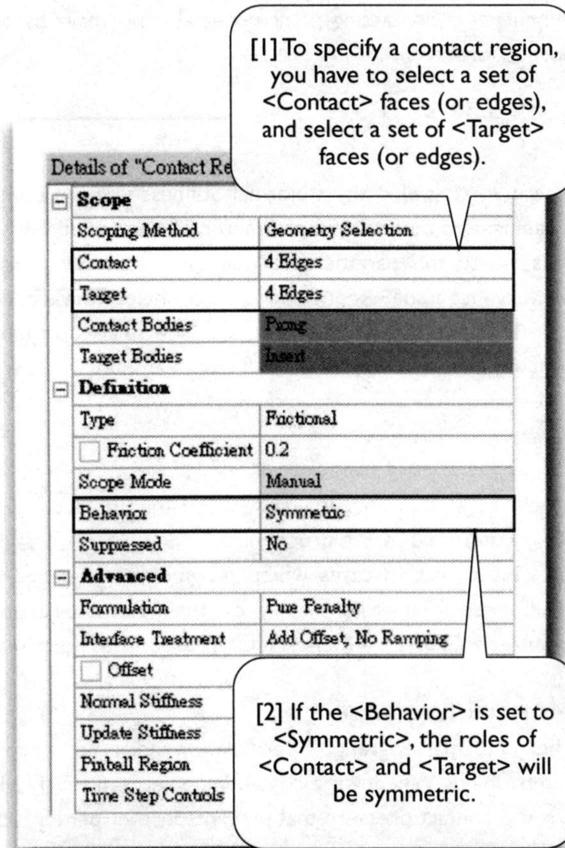

13.1-10 Contact Formulations

Workbench offers several <Formulations> [1] to enforce contact compatibility at the contact interface, i.e., preventing penetration of the contacting point into the target faces. These formulations are: <Pure Penalty>, <Augmented Lagrange>, <MPC>, <Normal Lagrange>.

MPC

For linear contact types (<Bonded> and <No Separation>), a multi-point constraint (MPC) formulation is available. MPC internally adds constraint equations to couple the displacements between contacting faces. Although you can use other formulations for <Bonded> and <No Separation> contact types, <MPC> is recommended for these linear contact types, since it is a direct, efficient formulation.

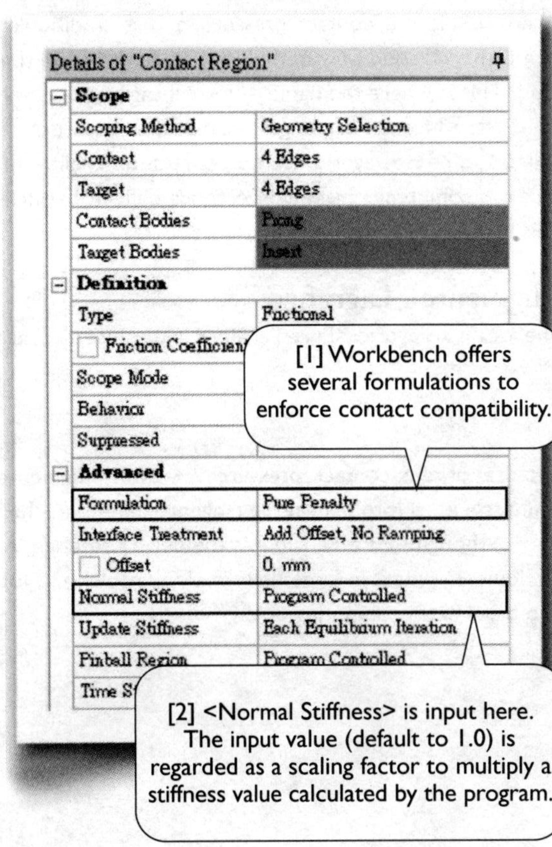

Pure Penalty

Whenever a contacting point penetrates normally by an amount x_n into a target face, it will be pushed back by a normal force F_n,

$$F_n = k_n x_n \tag{1}$$

where k_n is called the <Normal Stiffness> of the contact region [2]. The <Normal Stiffness> has no real physical meaning; it is a numerical parameter of the penalty algorithm. In many cases, solution convergence behavior may be sensitive to this parameter. A larger k_n usually gives a more accurate solution (less penetration), but may raise convergence issue. Reducing k_n usually helps convergence, but results an increasing penetration.

If the sliding in tangential direction is also prohibited, a similar treatment can be implemented. Whenever a contacting point slides tangentially by an amount x_t, it will be pushed back by a tangential force F_t,

$$F_t = k_t x_t \tag{2}$$

where k_t is the tangential stiffness of the contact region. Unlike the <Normal Stiffness>, the tangential stiffness is alway controlled by the program.

Note that, in cases when <Augmented Lagrange> or <Normal Lagrange> (to be discussed) formulations are used, these formulations apply on the normal direction only. The tangential direction still uses <Pure Penalty> formulation, Eq. (2). When <MPC> is used, both normal and tangential directions use <MPC> formulation.

Normal Lagrange

The <Normal Lagrange> formulation adds an extra degree of freedom, namely, contact pressure, to satisfy compatibility. Whenever a contacting point is in touch with the target face, the contact pressure is explicitly calculated. It is the contact pressure that prevents further penetration,

$$F_n = \lambda \tag{3}$$

where λ is the contact pressure, and is traditionally called a *Lagrange multipler*. Note that, as mentioned, this formulation is used only in the normal direction. In the tangential direction, the <Pure Penalty> formulation, Eq. (2), is used. This is where the name <Normal Lagrange> comes from.

The <Normal Lagrange> formulation does not require a normal stiffness, and theoretically, it can enforce zero penetration. However, since no penetration is allowed, the contact status is either open or closed (a step function). This can sometimes make convergence difficult because contact points may oscillate between open and closed status. This is called *chattering*.

Augmented Lagrange

The idea is to hybrid <Pure Penalty> with <Normal Lagrange>, i.e., the push-back normal force is

$$F_n = k_n x_n + \lambda \tag{4}$$

Because of the contact pressure λ, the <Augmented Lagrange> formulation is less sensitive to the <Normal Stiffness> k_n. Note that, in the tangential direction, the <Pure Penalty> formulation, Eq. (2), is used.

Although <Pure Penalty> is the default setting, <Augmented Lagrange> is recommended for general frictional or frictionless contact in large deformation problems. Note that, since Lagrange method add extra degree of freedom, it also takes extra computing time.

13.1-11 Other Advanced Contact Settings

Pinball Region

The pinball is a sphere region, its radius can be defined in <Pinball Region>. Consider again that a contacting point approaches a target face. Using the contacting point as the center of a pinball, for the nodes on the target face that are within the pinball region, they are considered to be in "near" contact and will be monitored. Nodes outside of the pinball region will not be monitored.

If the <Bonded> type is specified, surfaces that have gap smaller than the pinball radius is treated as bonded.

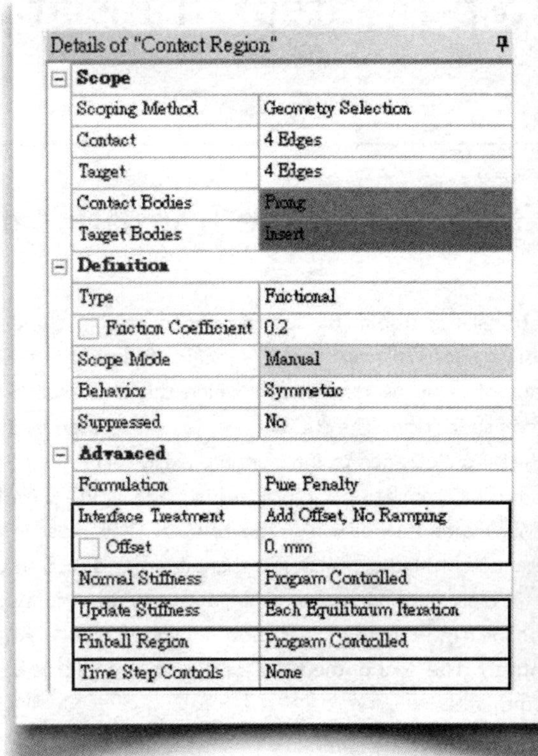

Details of "Contact Region"	
Scope	
Scoping Method	Geometry Selection
Contact	4 Edges
Target	4 Edges
Contact Bodies	Prong
Target Bodies	Insert
Definition	
Type	Frictional
Friction Coefficient	0.2
Scope Mode	Manual
Behavior	Symmetric
Suppressed	No
Advanced	
Formulation	Pure Penalty
Interface Treatment	Add Offset, No Ramping
Offset	0. mm
Normal Stiffness	Program Controlled
Update Stiffness	Each Equilibrium Iteration
Pinball Region	Program Controlled
Time Step Controls	None

Interface Treatment

For <Bonded> contact type, a large enough pinball radius may allow any gap between contacting faces to be ignore. For <Frictional> or <Frictionless> contact types, an initial gap is not automatically ignored, no matter how large the pinball is used, since the gap may represents the geometry.

If an initial gap is present [1] and a force is applied, one part may "fly away" relative to another part [2] if the initial contact is not established right at the end of the time step.

To alleviate situations where a gap (clearance) is modeled but needs to be ignored to establish initial contact for <Frictional> or <Frictionless> contact types, the <Interface Treatment> can internally offset the contact surfaces by a specified amount. Note that this treatment is intended for small gaps. Don't apply it in a large gap.

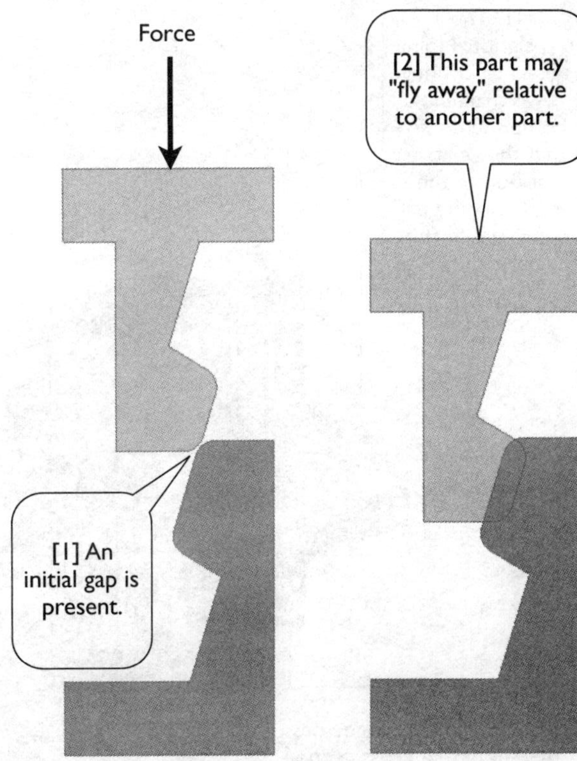

Time Step Controls

<Time Step Controls> tries to enhance convergence by allowing adjustments of time step size based on changes in contact behavior.

By default, contact behavior does not affect auto time stepping, since adjustment of time step based on contact behavior may increase computing time too much.

When turning on <Time Step Controls>, Workbench will adjust the time step size based on contact behavior.

Update Stiffness

By default, structural stiffness is not updated upon the change of contact behavior, to save the computing time. Turning on <Update Stiffness> enhance convergence, with the cost of computing time.

Section 13.2

Step-by-Step: Translational Joint

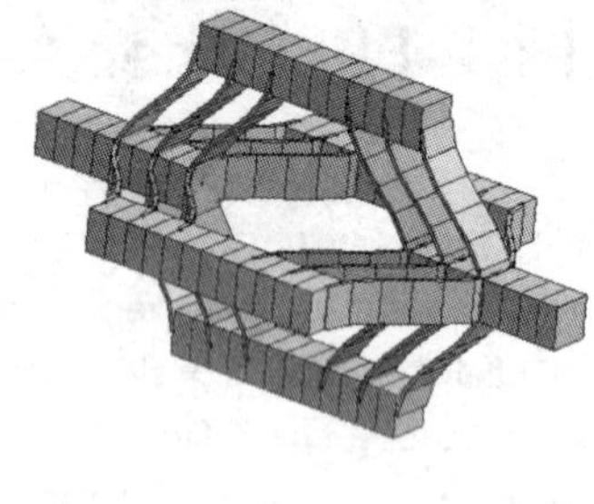

13.2-1 About the Translational Joint

A translational joint is used to connect two machine components, so that the relative motion of two components is restricted to translate in a specific direction. Conventionally, translational joints are designed as mechanisms, composed by parts, between which the clearance or interference are inevitable; they either decrease precision or increase friction. The translational joint discussed in this section is not a mechanism; it is a unitary flexible structure, in which no clearance or interference exist.

The translational joint [1-4] is made of POM (polyoxymethylene, a plastic polymer), which has a Young's modulus of 2 GPa and a Poisson's ratio of 0.35. The most important design consideration is that the rigidity of translational direction should be much less than all other directions, so that the motion can be restricted in that direction only.

Here, we want to explore the geometric nonlinearity of the structure: how the applied force increases nonlinearly with the translational displacement. For this purpose, we will model the structure using line bodies entirely. The goal of the simulation is to plot a force-versus-displacement chart. The unit system used in the simulation is mm-s-N.

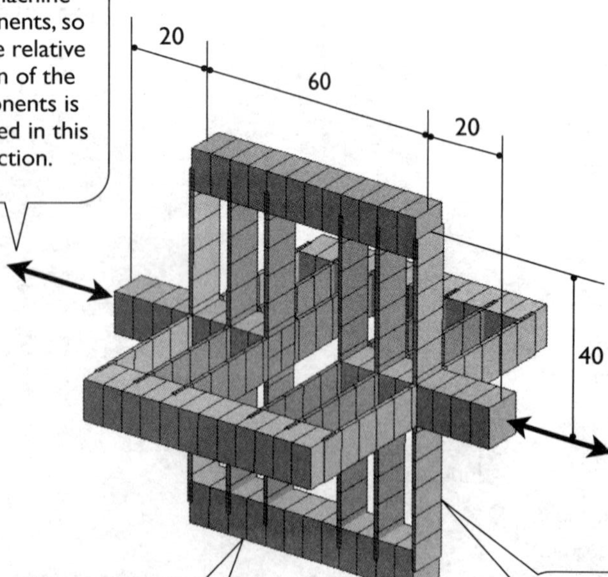

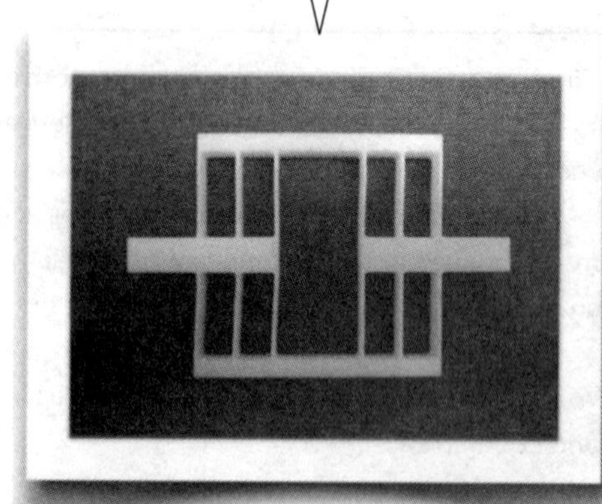

13.2-2 Start Up

Launch <Workbench>. Create a <Static Structural> analysis system. Save the project as "Transjoint."

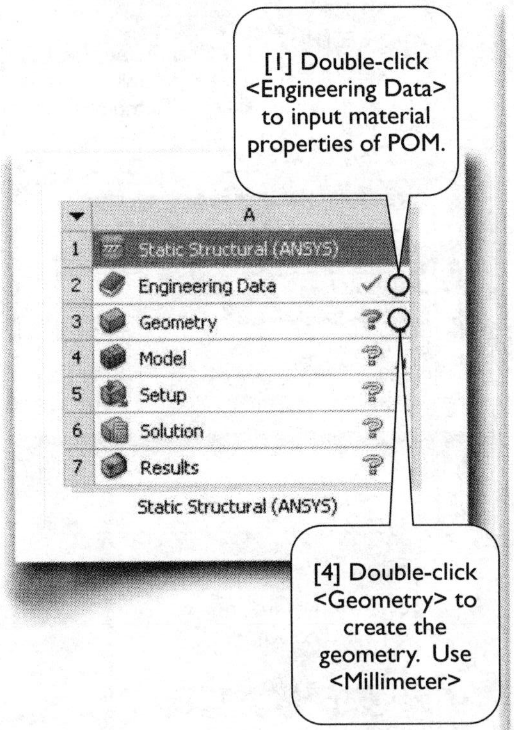

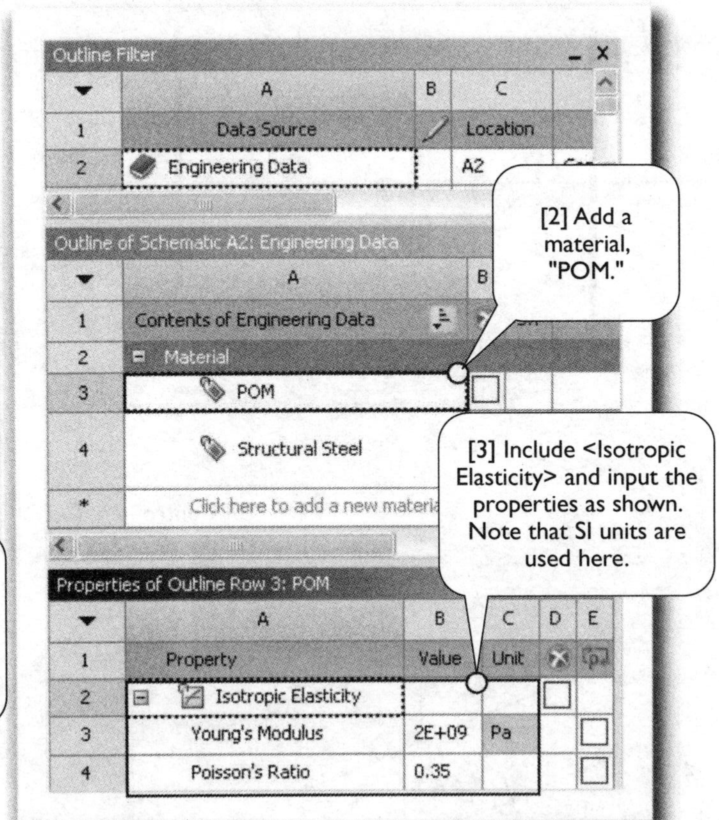

13.2-3 Create Geometry in DesignModeler

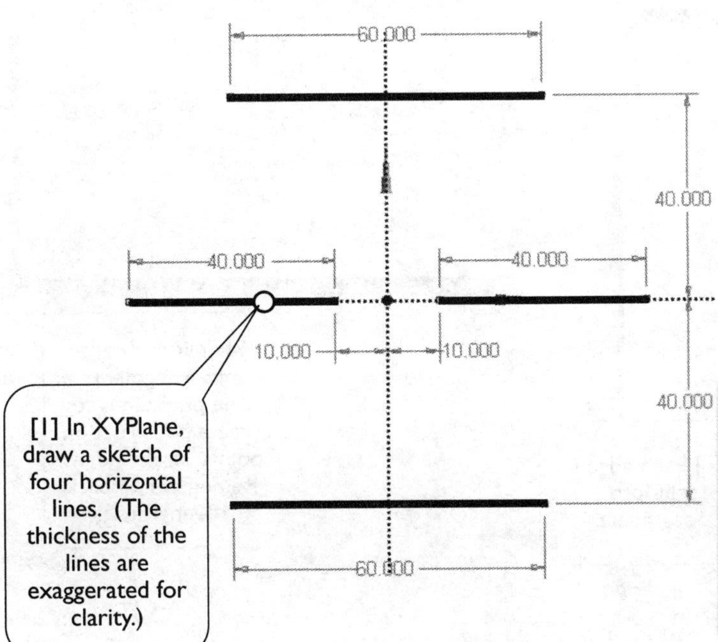

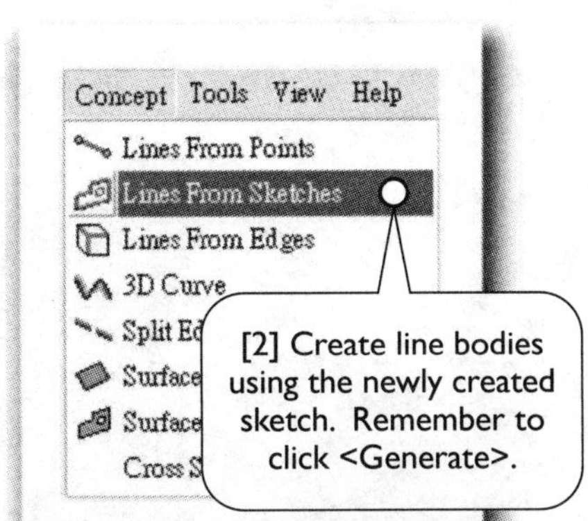

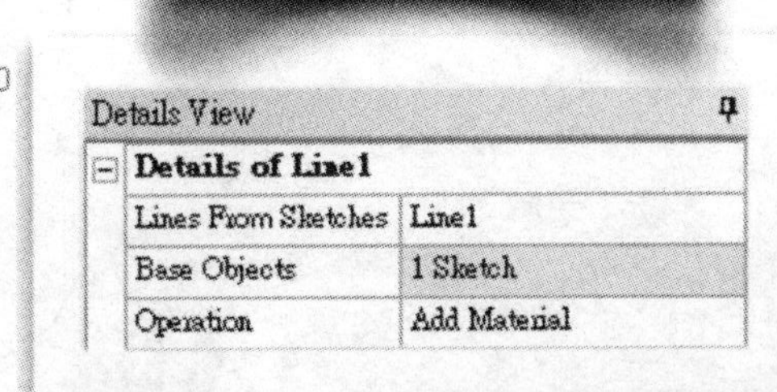

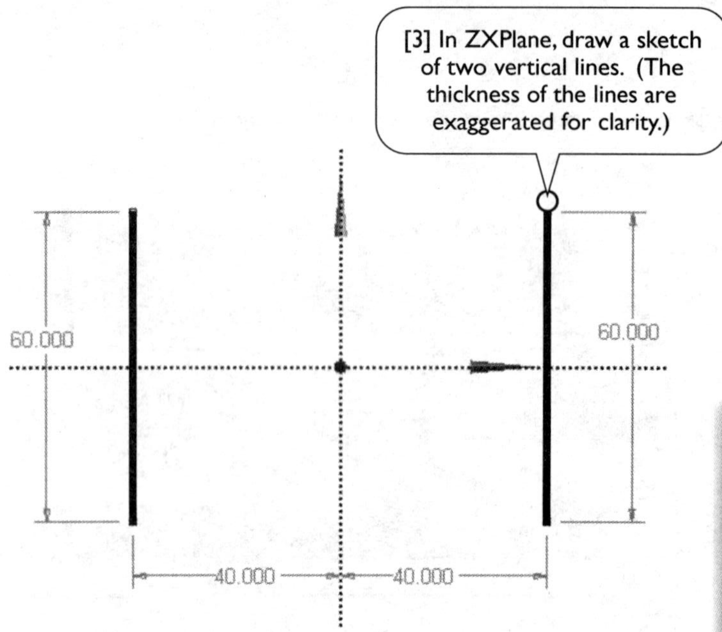
[3] In ZXPlane, draw a sketch of two vertical lines. (The thickness of the lines are exaggerated for clarity.)
60.000
60.000
40.000
40.000

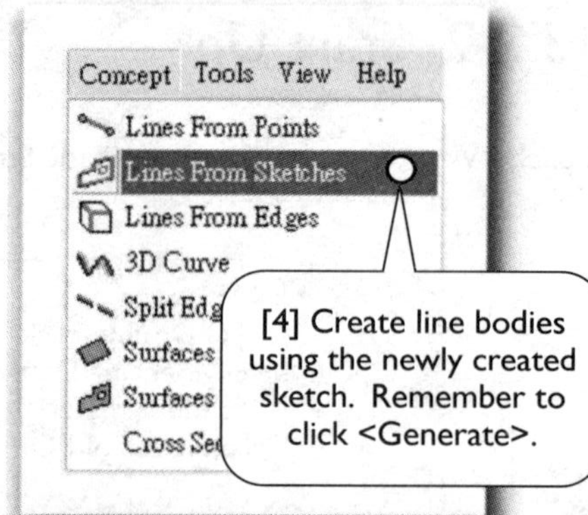
Concept Tools View Help
Lines From Points
Lines From Sketches
Lines From Edges
3D Curve
Split Edg
Surfaces
Surfaces
Cross Se
[4] Create line bodies using the newly created sketch. Remember to click <Generate>.

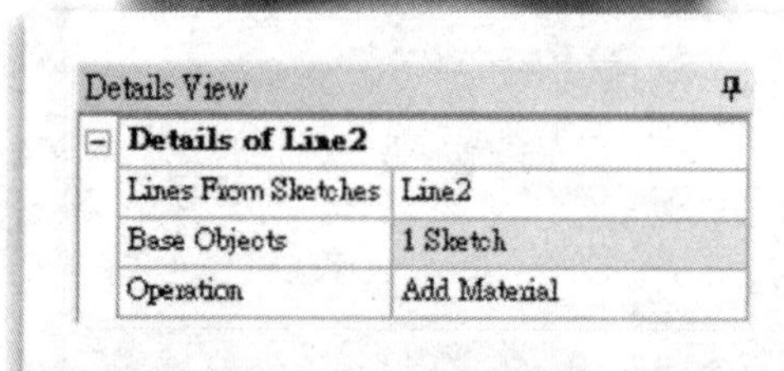
Details View
Details of Line2
Lines From Sketches
Line2
Base Objects
1 Sketch
Operation
Add Material

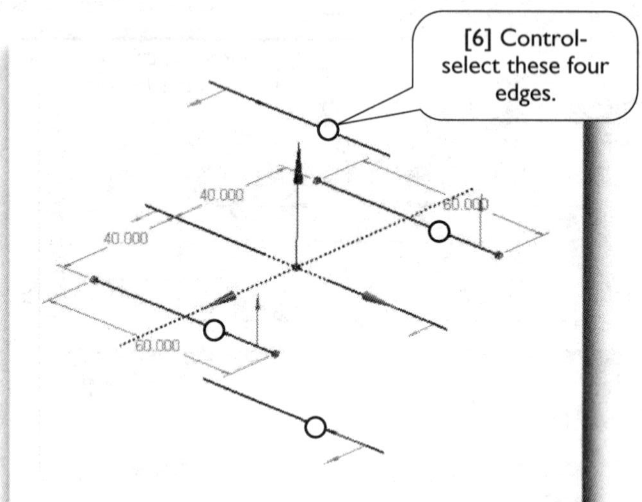
[6] Control-select these four edges.
40.000
40.000
60.000
60.000

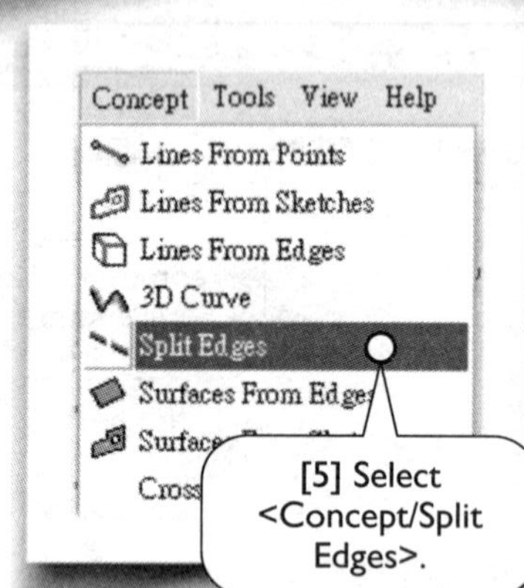
Concept Tools View Help
Lines From Points
Lines From Sketches
Lines From Edges
3D Curve
Split Edges
Surfaces From Edges
[5] Select <Concept/Split Edges>.

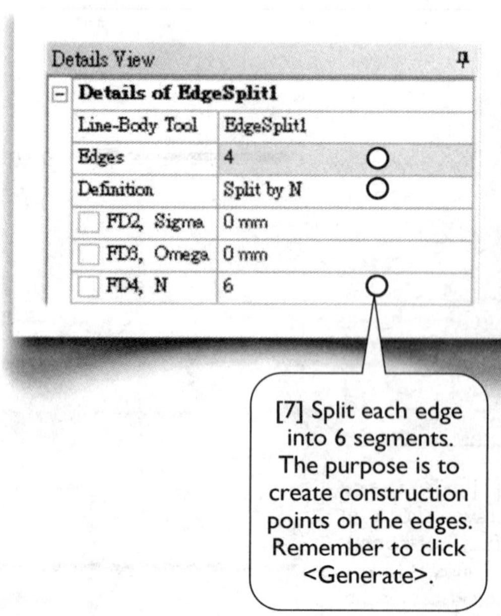
Details View
Details of EdgeSplit1
Line-Body Tool
EdgeSplit1
Edges
4
Definition
Split by N
FD2, Sigma
0 mm
FD3, Omega
0 mm
FD4, N
6
[7] Split each edge into 6 segments. The purpose is to create construction points on the edges. Remember to click <Generate>.

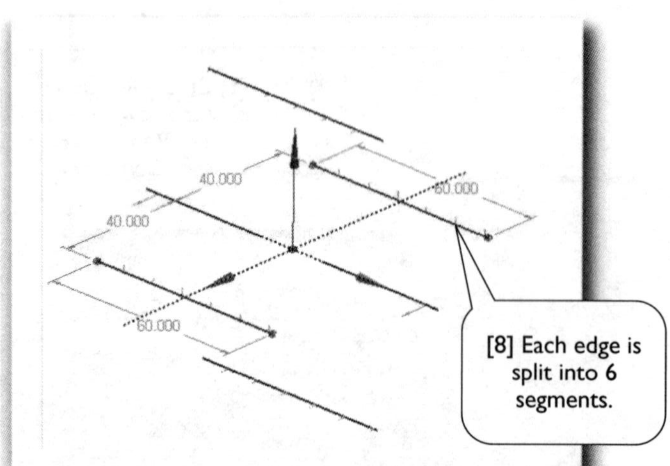
40.000
40.000
60.000
60.000
[8] Each edge is split into 6 segments.

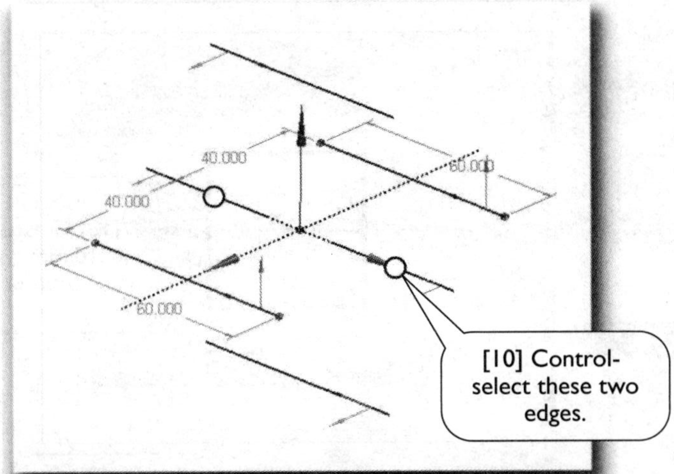
40.000
40.000
60.000
60.000
[10] Control-select these two edges.

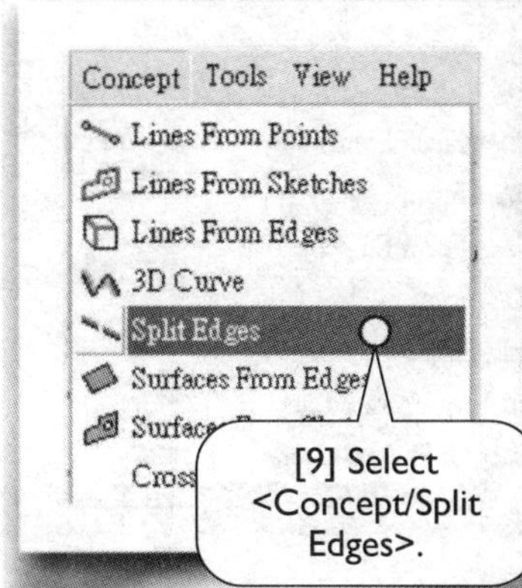
Concept Tools View Help
Lines From Points
Lines From Sketches
Lines From Edges
3D Curve
Split Edges
Surfaces From Edges
Cross
[9] Select <Concept/Split Edges>.

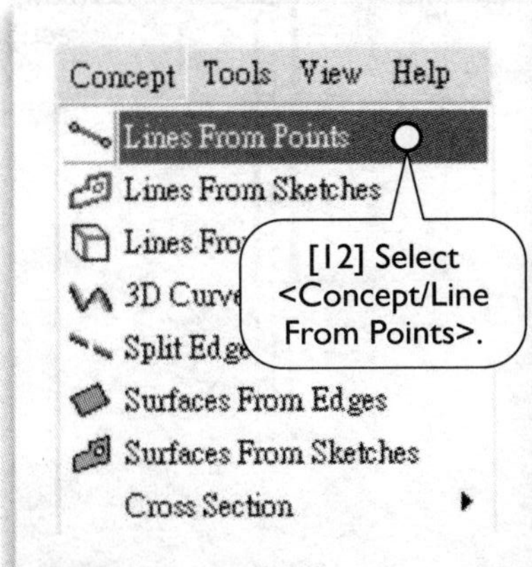
Concept Tools View Help
Lines From Points
Lines From Sketches
3D Curve
Surfaces From Edges
Surfaces From Sketches
Cross Section
[12] Select <Concept/Line From Points>.

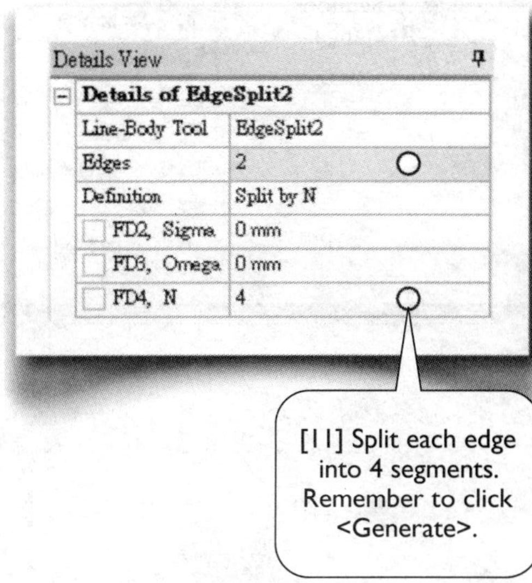
Details View
Details of EdgeSplit2
Line-Body Tool EdgeSplit2
Edges 2
Definition Split by N
FD2, Sigma 0 mm
FD3, Omega 0 mm
FD4, N 4
[11] Split each edge into 4 segments. Remember to click <Generate>.

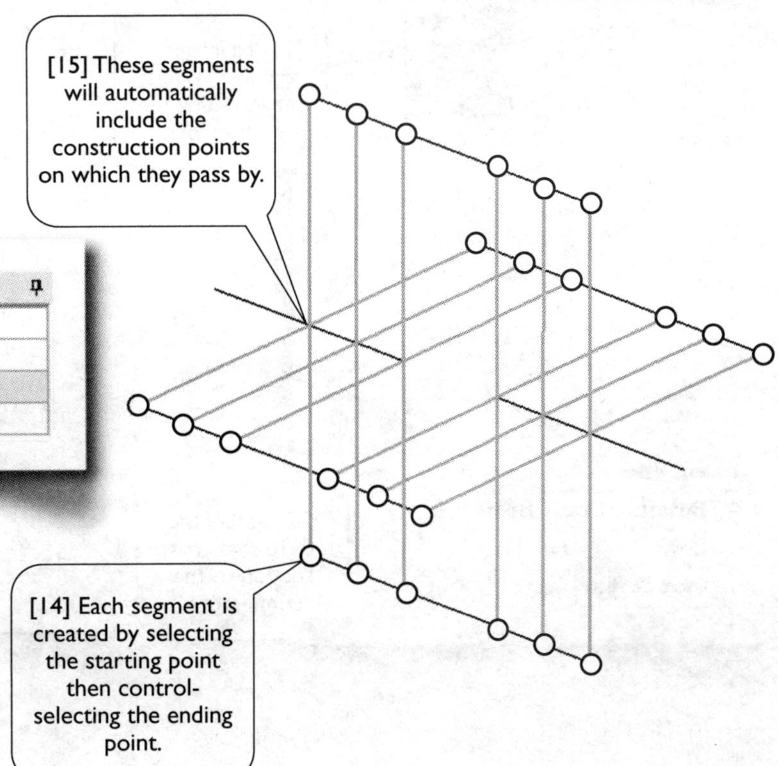
[15] These segments will automatically include the construction points on which they pass by.
[14] Each segment is created by selecting the starting point then control-selecting the ending point.

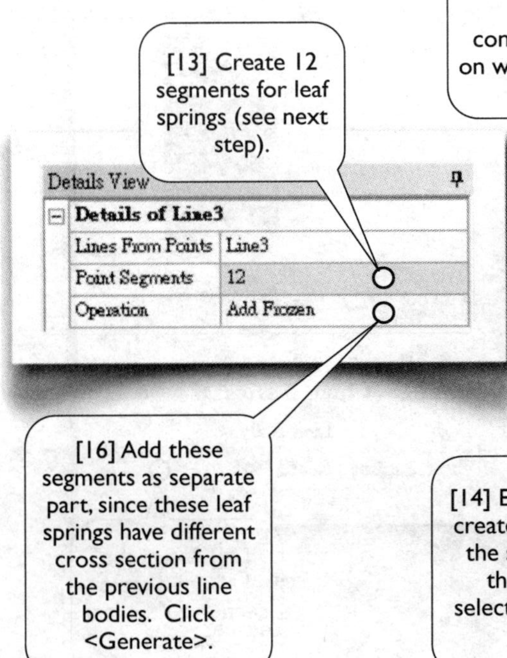
Details View
Details of Line3
Lines From Points Line3
Point Segments 12
Operation Add Frozen
[13] Create 12 segments for leaf springs (see next step).
[16] Add these segments as separate part, since these leaf springs have different cross section from the previous line bodies. Click <Generate>.

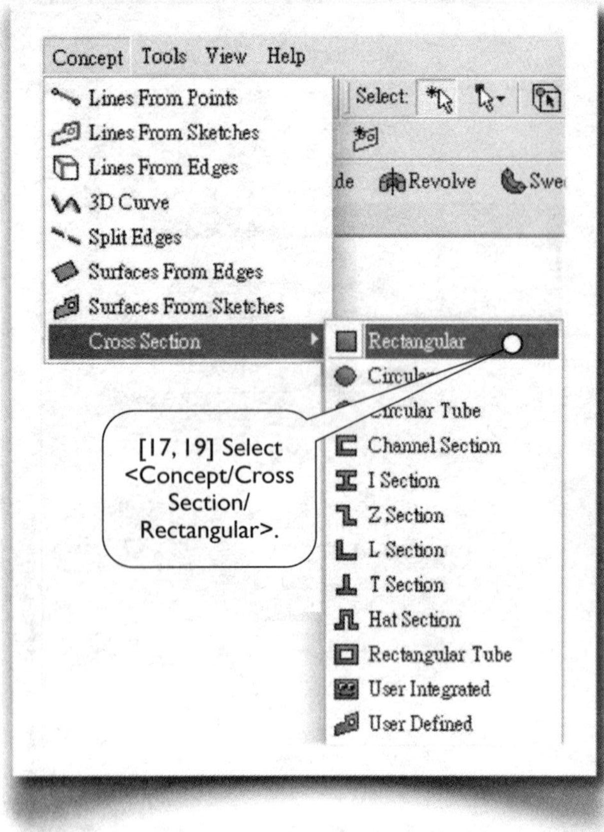
Concept Tools View Help
Lines From Points
Lines From Sketches
Lines From Edges
3D Curve
Split Edges
Surfaces From Edges
Surfaces From Sketches
Cross Section
Select:
Revolve
Rectangular
Channel Section
I Section
Z Section
L Section
T Section
Hat Section
Rectangular Tube
User Integrated
User Defined
[17, 19] Select <Concept/Cross Section/ Rectangular>.

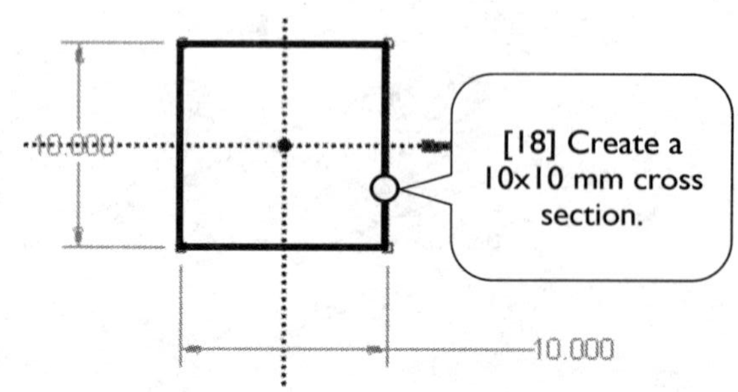
10.000
[18] Create a 10x10 mm cross section.

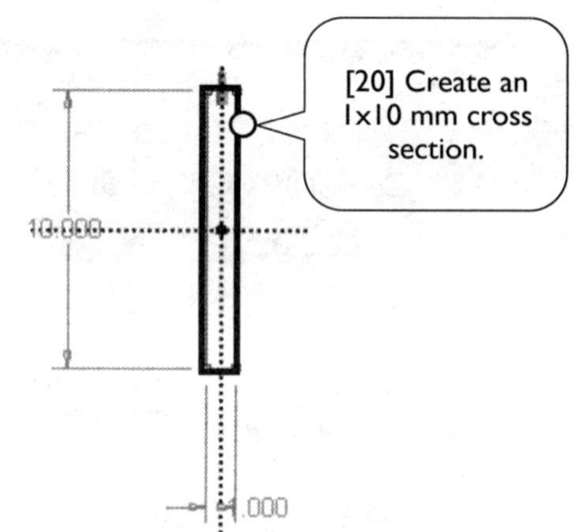
[20] Create an 1x10 mm cross section.

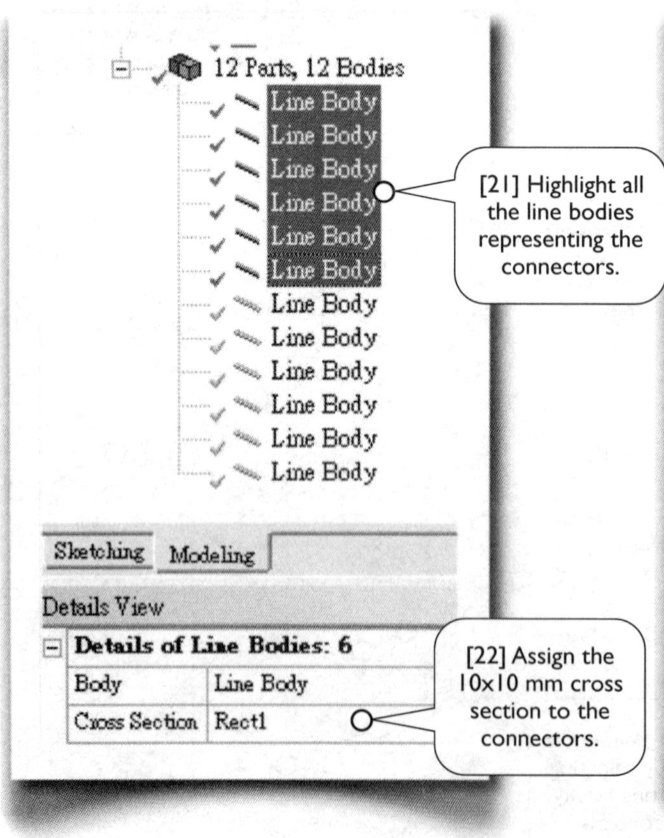
12 Parts, 12 Bodies
Line Body
Sketching
Modeling
Details View
Details of Line Bodies: 6
Body
Line Body
Cross Section
Rect1
[21] Highlight all the line bodies representing the connectors.
[22] Assign the 10x10 mm cross section to the connectors.

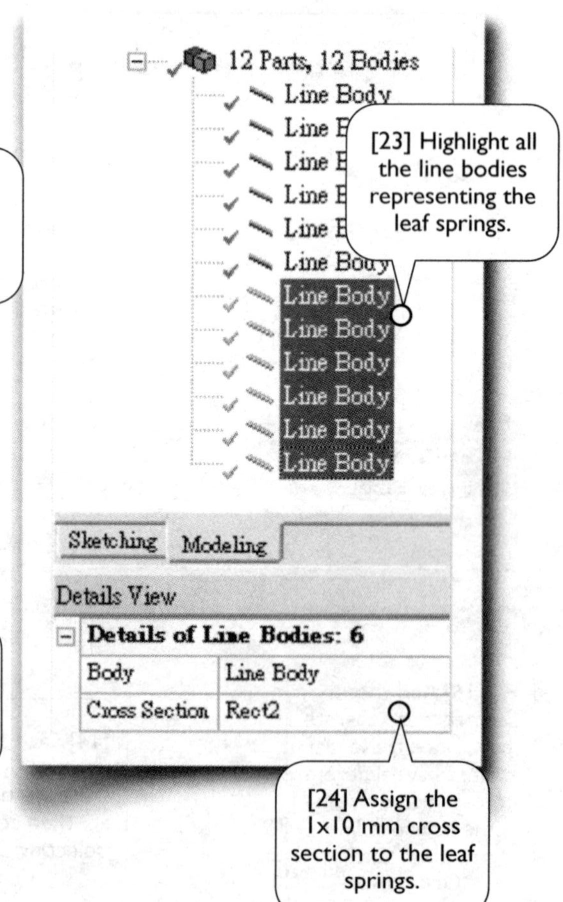
12 Parts, 12 Bodies
Line Body
Sketching
Modeling
Details View
Details of Line Bodies: 6
Body
Line Body
Cross Section
Rect2
[23] Highlight all the line bodies representing the leaf springs.
[24] Assign the 1x10 mm cross section to the leaf springs.

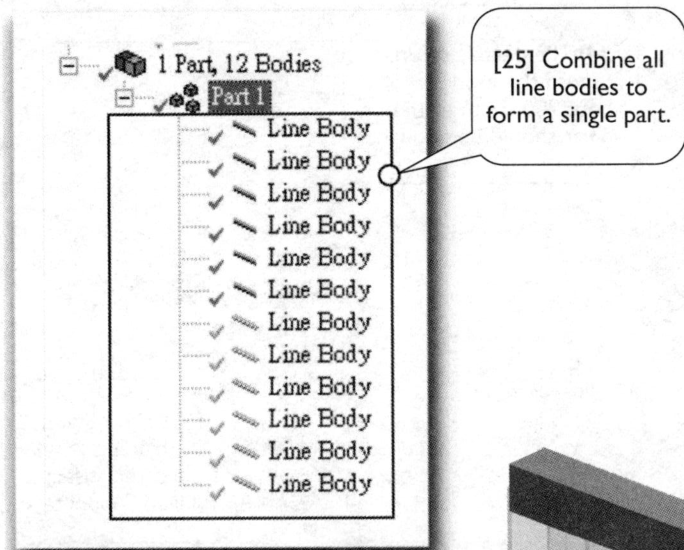

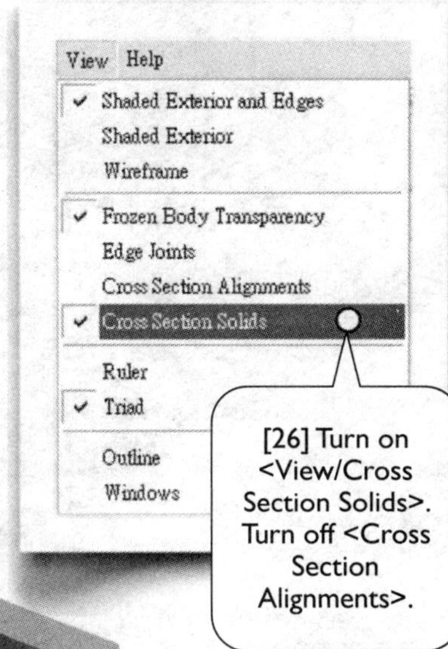

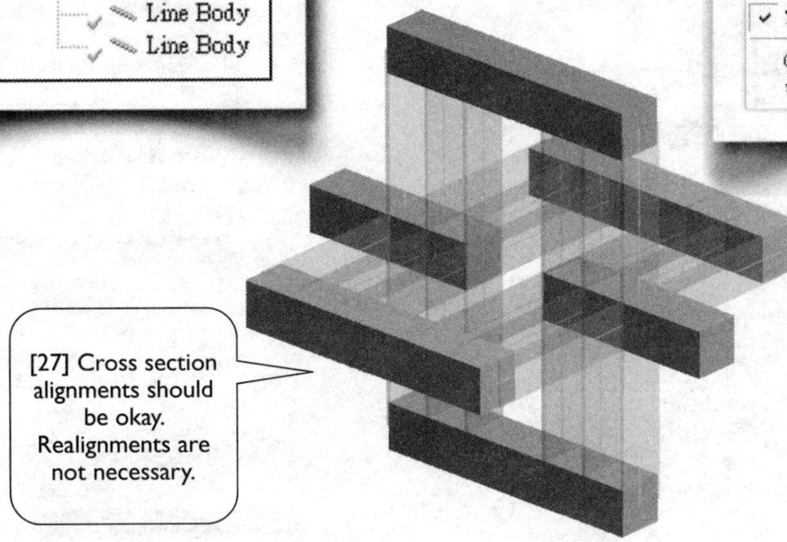

13.2-4 Linear Simulation

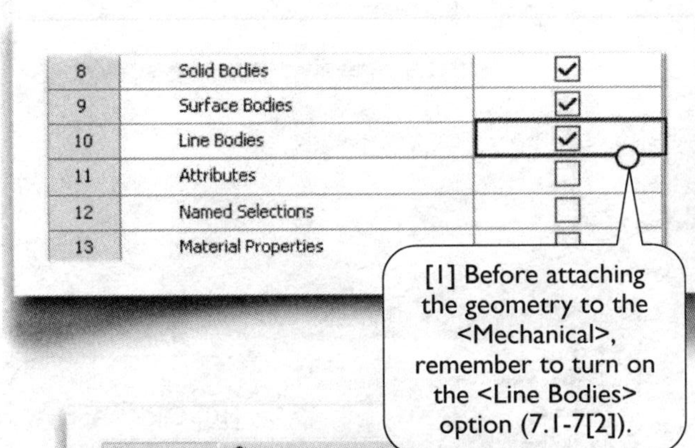

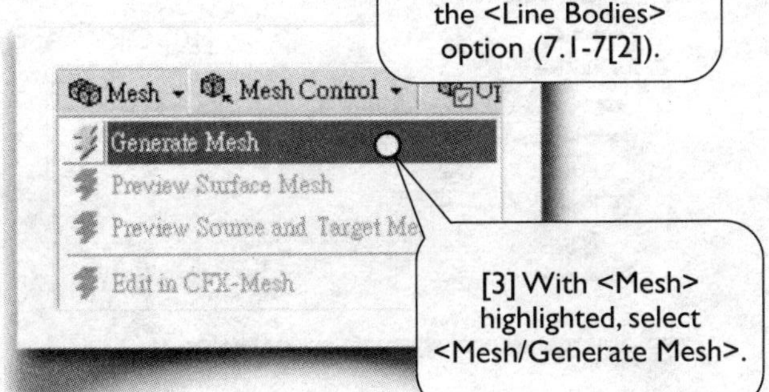

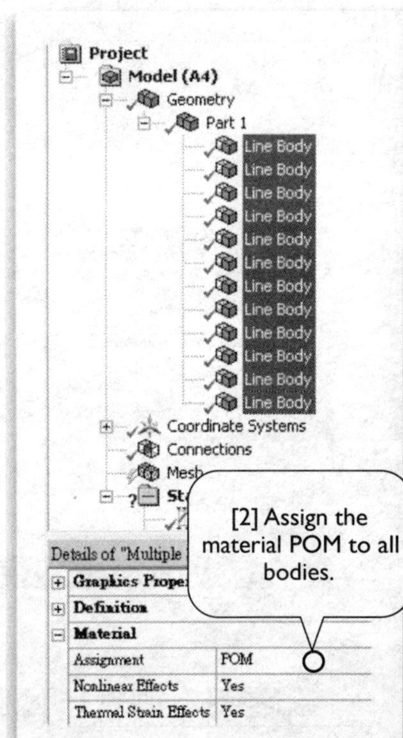

[4] The default settings mesh the model with about 200 beam elements. That should be enough.

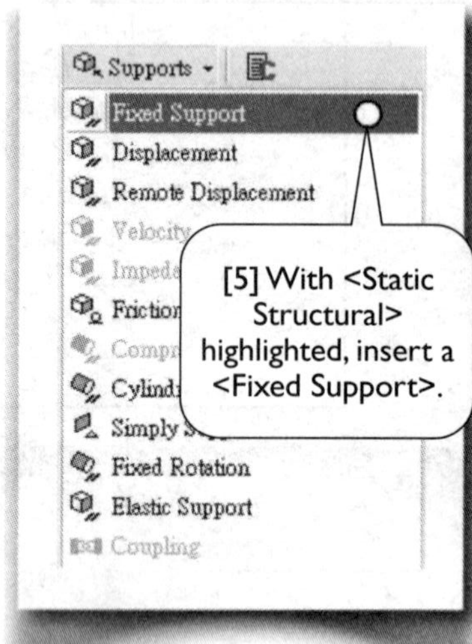
Supports
Fixed Support
Displacement
Remote Displacement
Velocity
Frictio
Cylind
Simply S
Fixed Rotation
Elastic Support
Coupling
[5] With <Static Structural> highlighted, insert a <Fixed Support>.

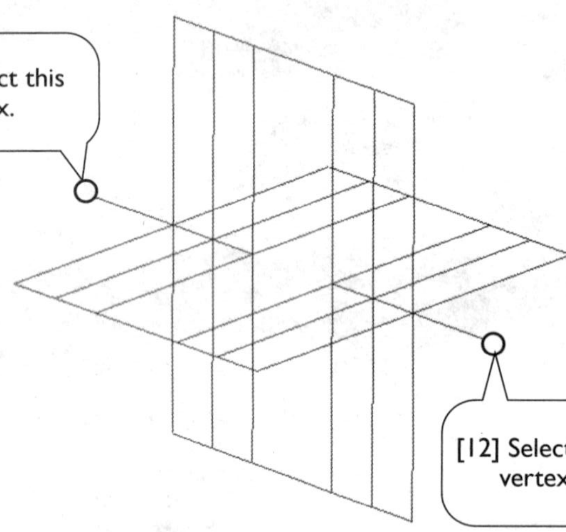
[6, 9] Select this vertex.
[12] Select this vertex.

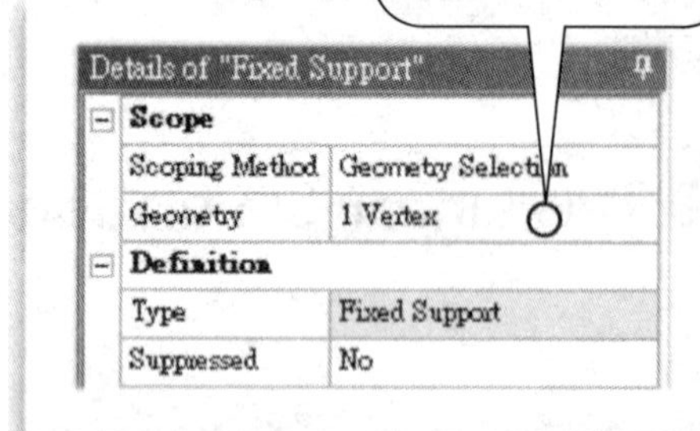
[7] Click <Apply>.
Details of "Fixed Support"
Scope
Scoping Method
Geometry Selection
Geometry
1 Vertex
Definition
Type
Fixed Support
Suppressed
No

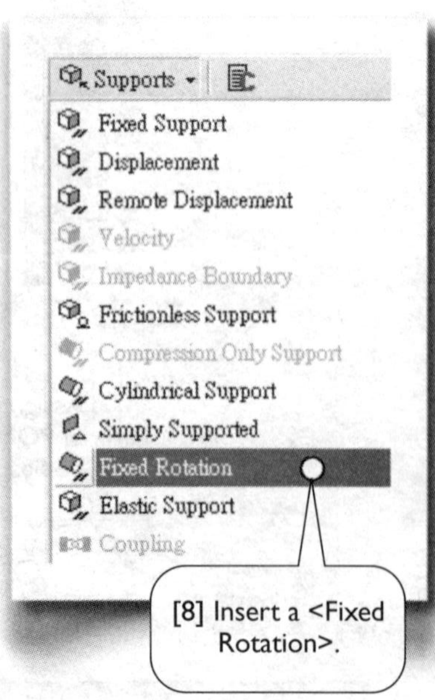
Supports
Fixed Support
Displacement
Remote Displacement
Velocity
Impedance Boundary
Frictionless Support
Compression Only Support
Cylindrical Support
Simply Supported
Fixed Rotation
Elastic Support
Coupling
[8] Insert a <Fixed Rotation>.

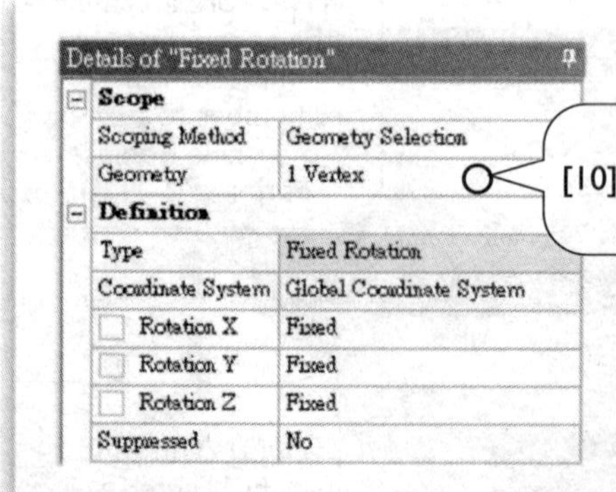
Details of "Fixed Rotation"
Scope
Scoping Method
Geometry Selection
Geometry
1 Vertex
Definition
Type
Fixed Rotation
Coordinate System
Global Coordinate System
Rotation X
Fixed
Rotation Y
Fixed
Rotation Z
Fixed
Suppressed
No
[10] Click <Apply>.

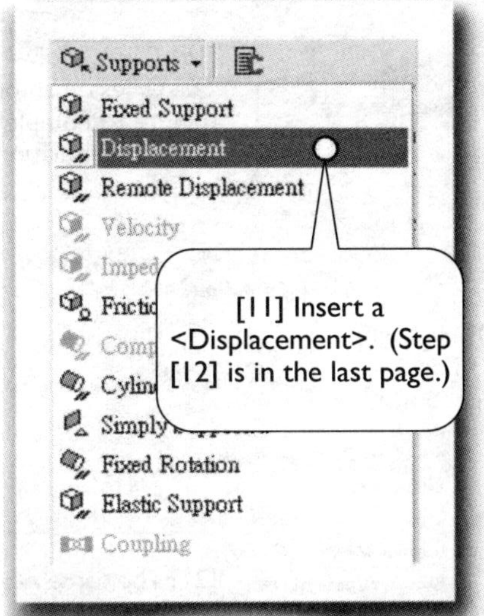

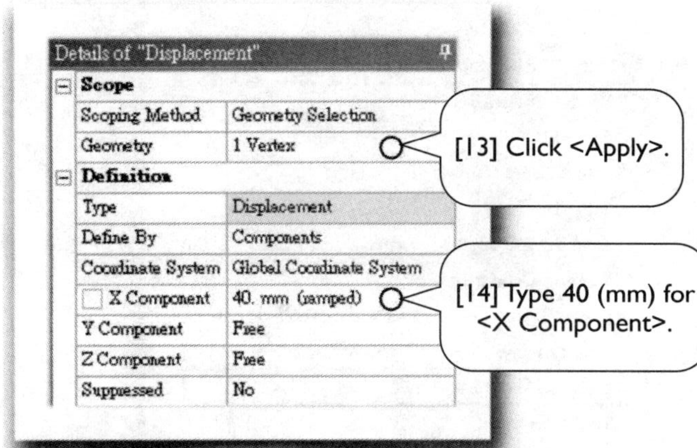

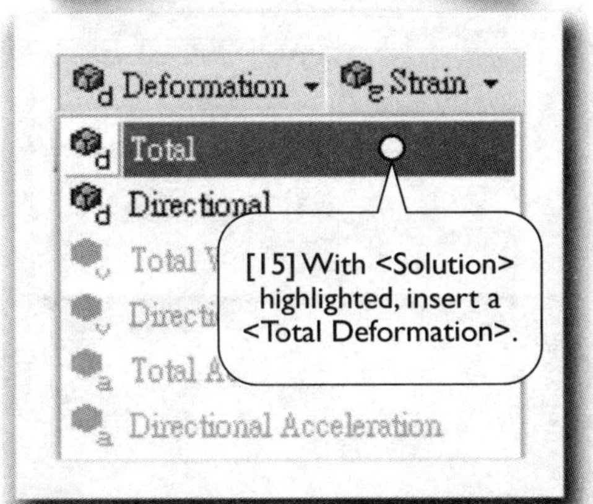

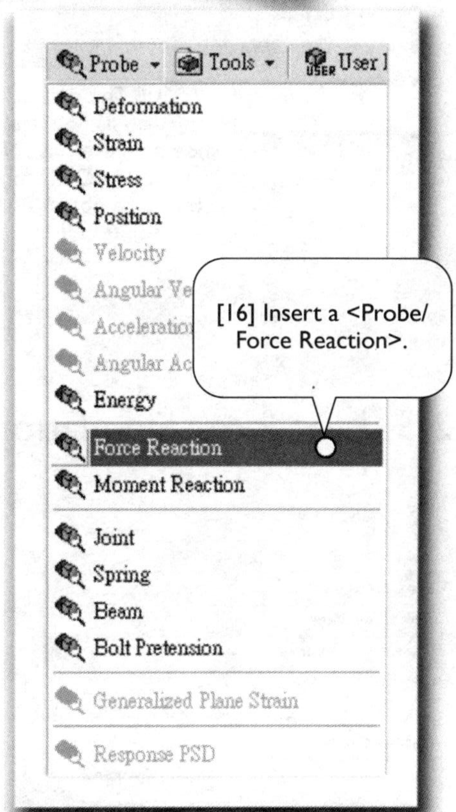

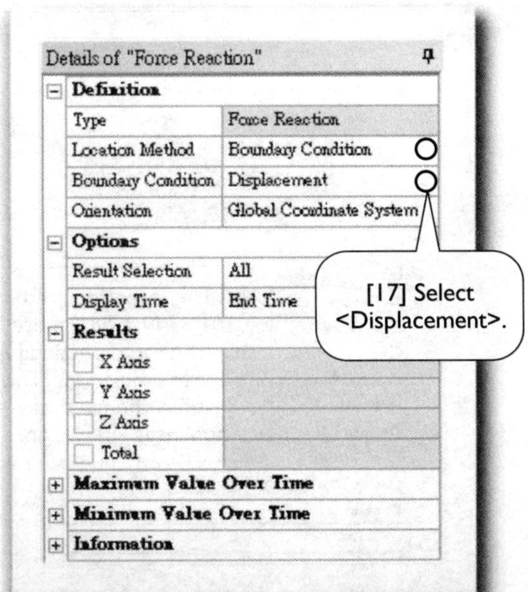

Force Reaction

Forces are needed to maintain a displacement condition. For example, if a point of a structure is to be held still (i.e., a fixed support), forces are needed to maintain the zero-displacement condition. The forces are called *reaction forces*.

This concept can be generalized to a nonzero displacement condition. In our case, we want to maintain a displacement of 40 mm in X-direction, the force required is called the reaction force of that displacement.

The purpose of <Force Reaction> object is to evaluate the force required for the 40 mm displacement.

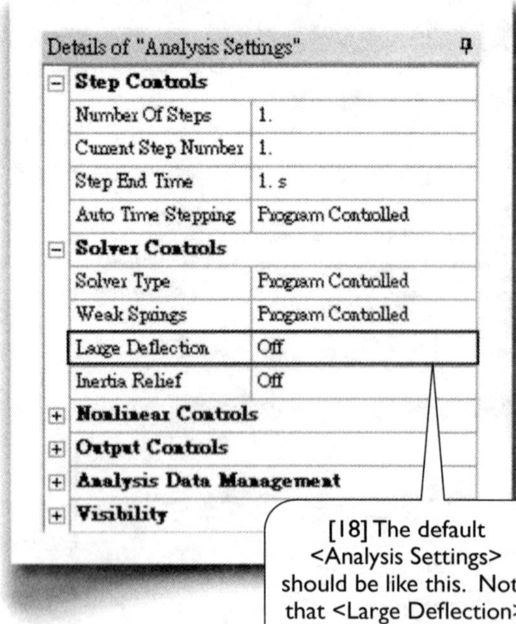

[18] The default <Analysis Settings> should be like this. Note that <Large Deflection> is off. Let's obtain a linear solution first.

[19] Click <Solve>. It takes less than one minute to complete a linear simulation.

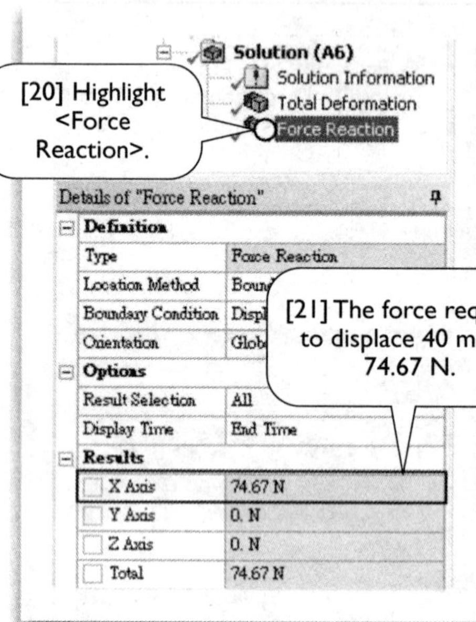

[20] Highlight <Force Reaction>.

[21] The force required to displace 40 mm is 74.67 N.

13.2-5 Nonlinear Simulation

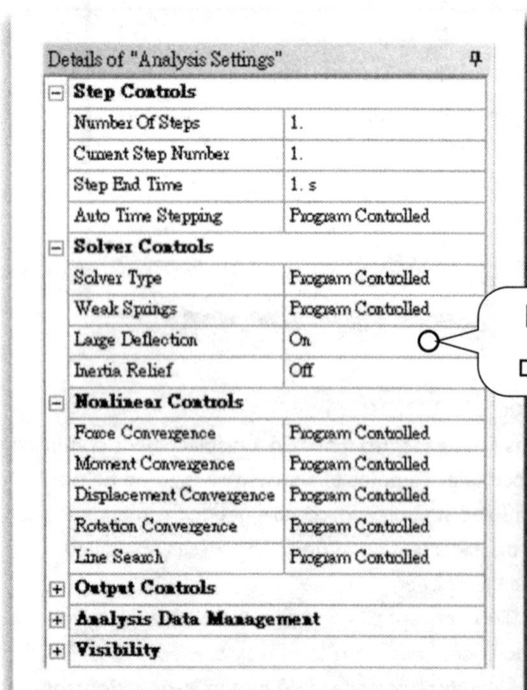

[1] Turn on <Large Deflection>.

[2] Click <Solve>. It takes less than one minute.

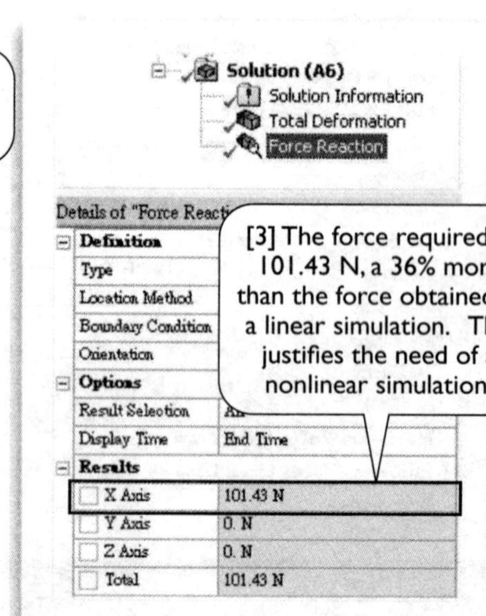

[3] The force required is 101.43 N, a 36% more than the force obtained in a linear simulation. This justifies the need of a nonlinear simulation.

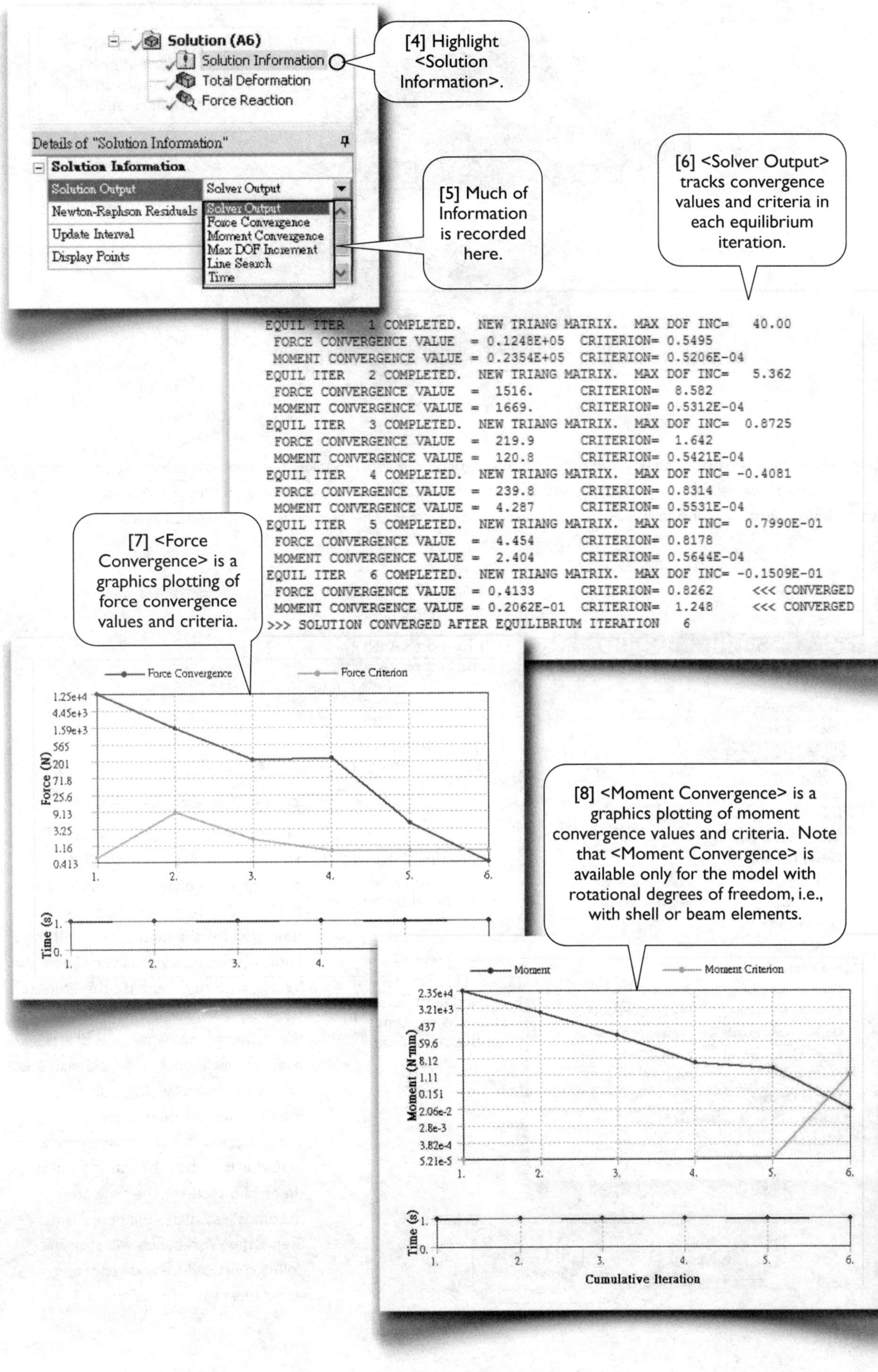
Solution (A6)
Solution Information
Total Deformation
Force Reaction
[4] Highlight <Solution Information>.
Details of "Solution Information"
Solution Information
Solution Output
Solver Output
Newton-Raphson Residuals
Update Interval
Display Points
Solver Output
Force Convergence
Moment Convergence
Max DOF Increment
Line Search
Time
[5] Much of Information is recorded here.
[6] <Solver Output> tracks convergence values and criteria in each equilibrium iteration.
EQUIL ITER 1 COMPLETED. NEW TRIANG MATRIX. MAX DOF INC= 40.00
FORCE CONVERGENCE VALUE = 0.1248E+05 CRITERION= 0.5495
MOMENT CONVERGENCE VALUE = 0.2354E+05 CRITERION= 0.5206E-04
EQUIL ITER 2 COMPLETED. NEW TRIANG MATRIX. MAX DOF INC= 5.362
FORCE CONVERGENCE VALUE = 1516. CRITERION= 8.582
MOMENT CONVERGENCE VALUE = 1669. CRITERION= 0.5312E-04
EQUIL ITER 3 COMPLETED. NEW TRIANG MATRIX. MAX DOF INC= 0.8725
FORCE CONVERGENCE VALUE = 219.9 CRITERION= 1.642
MOMENT CONVERGENCE VALUE = 120.8 CRITERION= 0.5421E-04
EQUIL ITER 4 COMPLETED. NEW TRIANG MATRIX. MAX DOF INC= -0.4081
FORCE CONVERGENCE VALUE = 239.8 CRITERION= 0.8314
MOMENT CONVERGENCE VALUE = 4.287 CRITERION= 0.5531E-04
EQUIL ITER 5 COMPLETED. NEW TRIANG MATRIX. MAX DOF INC= 0.7990E-01
FORCE CONVERGENCE VALUE = 4.454 CRITERION= 0.8178
MOMENT CONVERGENCE VALUE = 2.404 CRITERION= 0.5644E-04
EQUIL ITER 6 COMPLETED. NEW TRIANG MATRIX. MAX DOF INC= -0.1509E-01
FORCE CONVERGENCE VALUE = 0.4133 CRITERION= 0.8262 <<< CONVERGED
MOMENT CONVERGENCE VALUE = 0.2062E-01 CRITERION= 1.248 <<< CONVERGED
>>> SOLUTION CONVERGED AFTER EQUILIBRIUM ITERATION 6
[7] <Force Convergence> is a graphics plotting of force convergence values and criteria.
Force Convergence
Force Criterion
Force (N)
1.25e+4
4.45e+3
1.59e+3
565
201
71.8
25.6
9.13
3.25
1.16
0.413
Time (s)
[8] <Moment Convergence> is a graphics plotting of moment convergence values and criteria. Note that <Moment Convergence> is available only for the model with rotational degrees of freedom, i.e., with shell or beam elements.
Moment
Moment Criterion
Moment (N·mm)
2.35e+4
3.21e+3
437
59.6
8.12
1.11
0.151
2.06e-2
2.8e-3
3.82e-4
5.21e-5
Time (s)
Cumulative Iteration

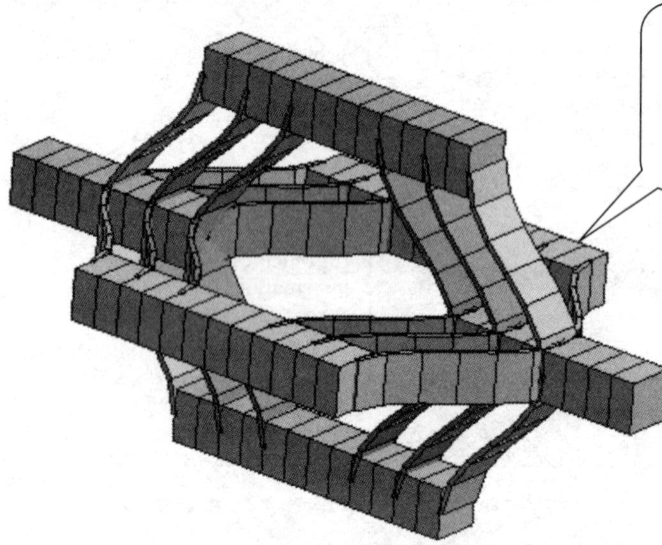

[9] Highlight <Total Deformation> to examine the deformation.

The Workbench solves this case easily in only one substep, and the substep takes 6 equilibrium iterations to converge.

To plot a force-versus-displacement chart, let's specify a small initial substep value, but let the Workbench automatically adjust the substep values for the subsequent substeps. This feature is called <Auto Time Stepping>.

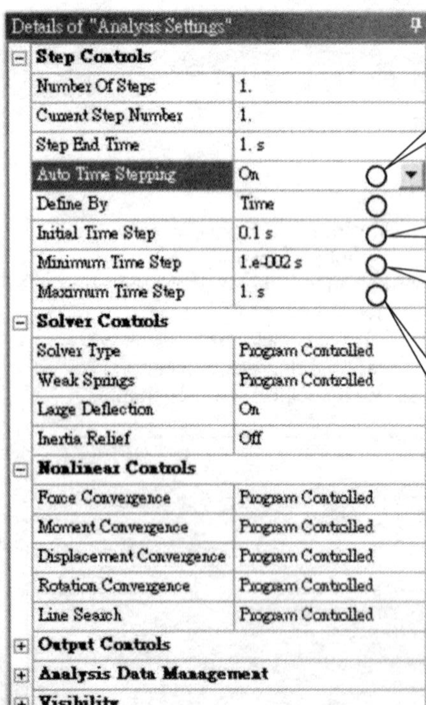

[10] Turn on <Auto Time Stepping>.

[11] Type 0.1 (sec) for <Initial Time Step>.

[12] Set <Minimum Time Step> to one-tenth of the initial time step.

[13] Set <Maximum Time Step> to ten times of the initial time step.

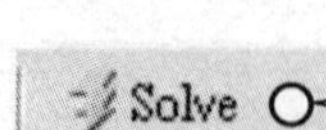

[14] Click <Solve>.

Auto Time Stepping

The Workbench uses the <Initial Time Step> for the first substep. If the convergence behavior is merely okay, the Workbench continues to use that time step for the next substep. If the convergence behavior is very good, the Workbench may increase the time step (typically 50%) for the next substep. If the convergence behavior is pretty bad, the workbench may decrease the time step (typically 50%; called *bisection*) for the next substep.

In cases that the convergence behavior is so bad that, after several times of bisections, the time step becomes less than <Minimum Time Step>, the Workbench will stop the solution procedure and report an error message for you.

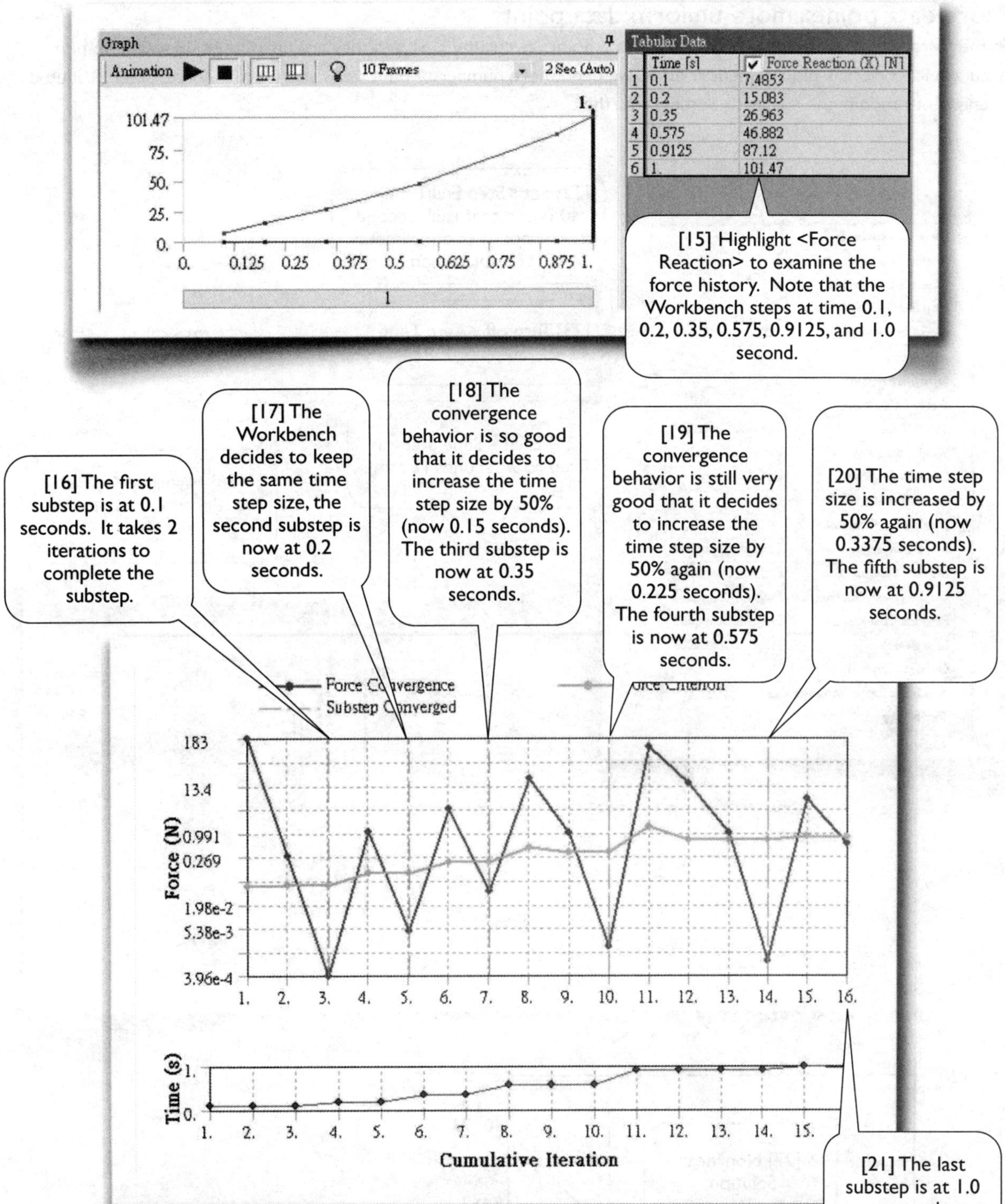

Time is used as a counter in static simulations

In a static simulation, in which time has no real meaning, the Workbench uses time as a counter. By default, it set 1.0 second for each step. You, of course, can change that value as you wish. In our case, since the total displacement is 40 mm, we may set the <Step End Time> to 40 seconds, so that each second corresponds to a millimeter of displacement.

More data points; more uniform data points

In the foregoing simulation, there are only 6 data points calculated [15], and they are distributed unevenly. To plot an accurate force-versus-displacement relation, we need more number of time steps and they had better be distributed evenly. Let's modify the <Analysis Settings> further.

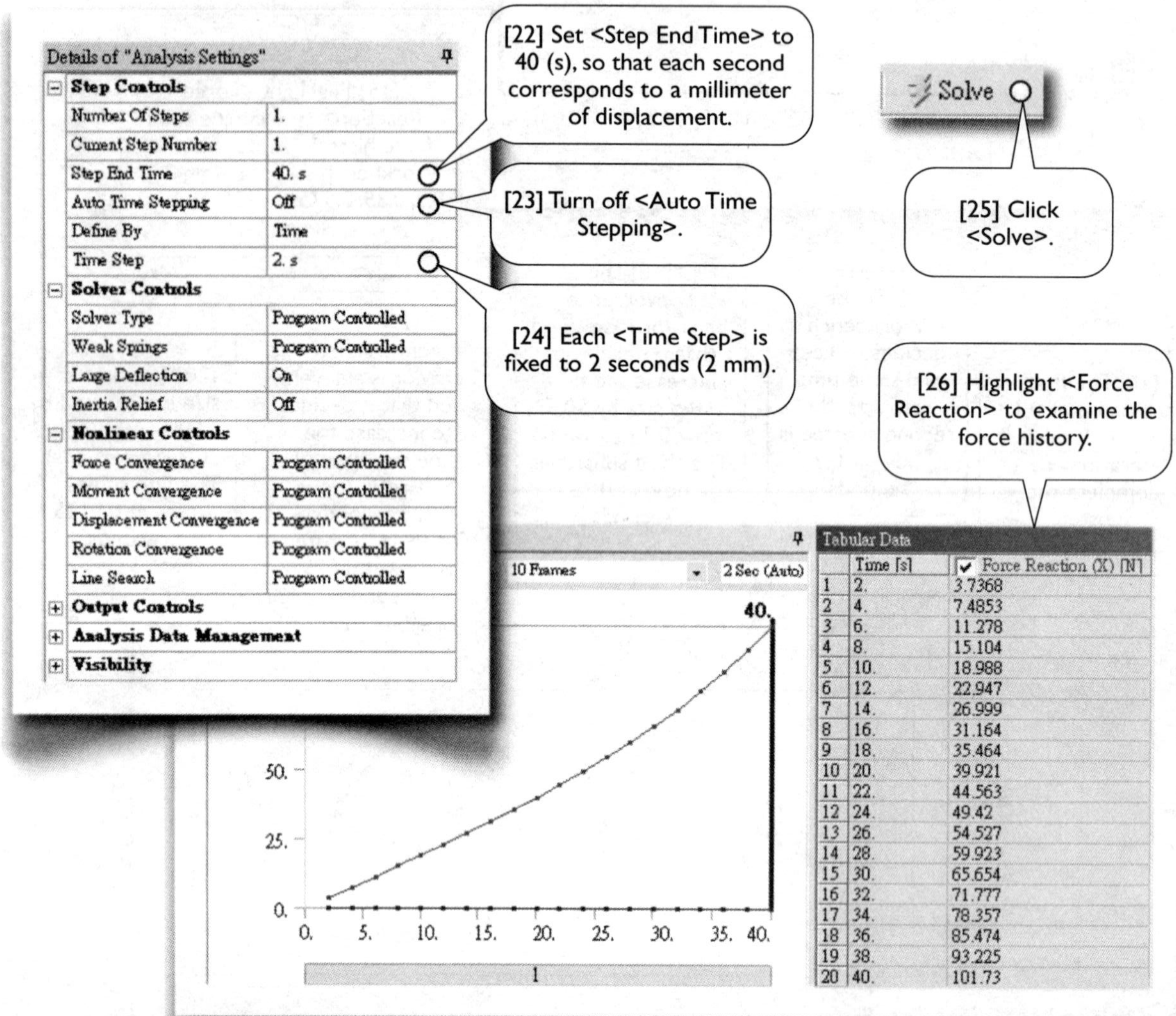

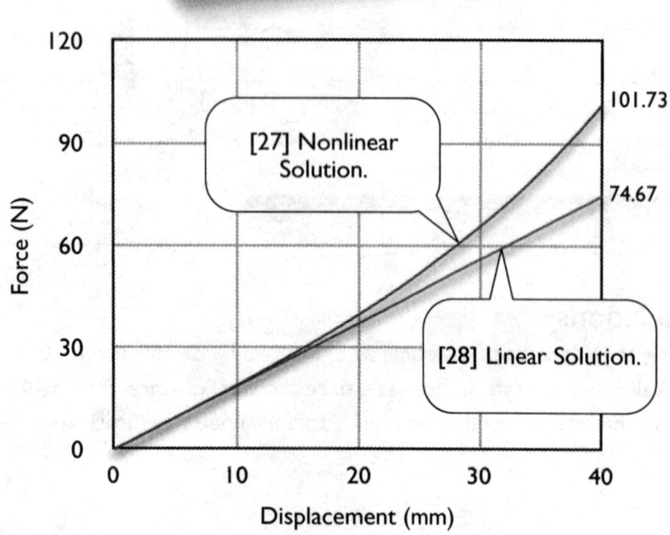

Wrap Up

Save the project and exit Workbench.

Section 13.3

Step-by-Step: Microgripper

13.3-1 About the Microgripper

In Section 2.6, we introduced the microgripper and created a solid model for it. As mentioned in that section, the microgripper is made of PDMS and actuated by a SMA (shape memory alloy) actuator; it is tested by gripping a glass bead in a lab. In this section, we want to assess the gripping forces on the glass bead under an actuation force of 40 μN exerted by the SMA device. More specifically, we will plot a gripping force-versus-actuation-force chart. Since the glass bead is much more rigid than the PDMS material, we will model the glass bead as a rigid body. This will ease some of the convergence difficulty. By taking advantage of symmetries, we will model only one quarter of the microgripper.

13.3-2 Resume the Project "Microgripper"

Launch <Workbench>. Open the project "Microgripper," saved in Section 2.6.

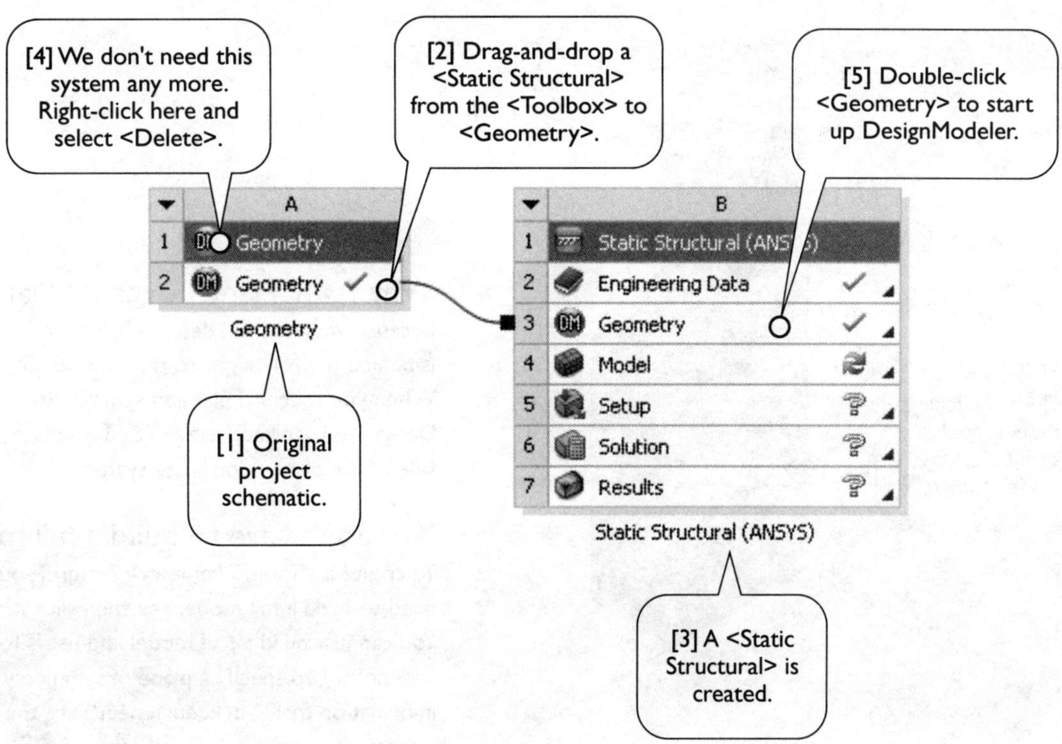

13.3-3 Modify the Geometry in DesignModeler

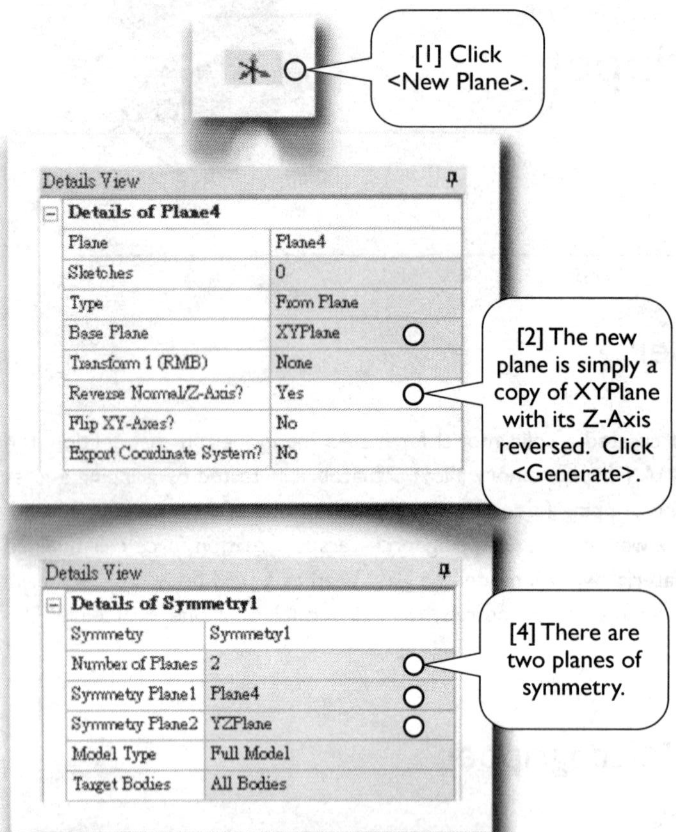

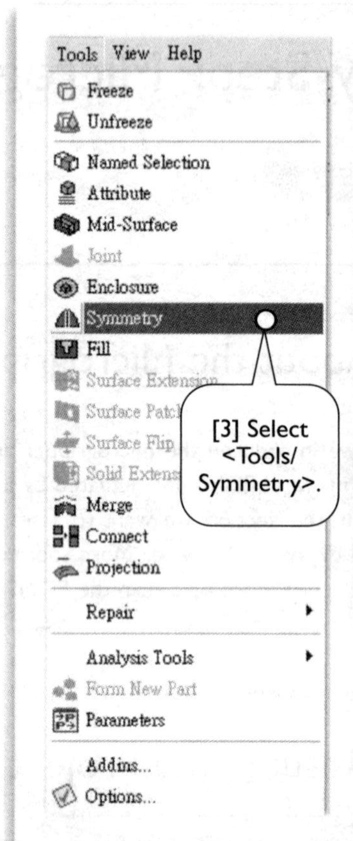

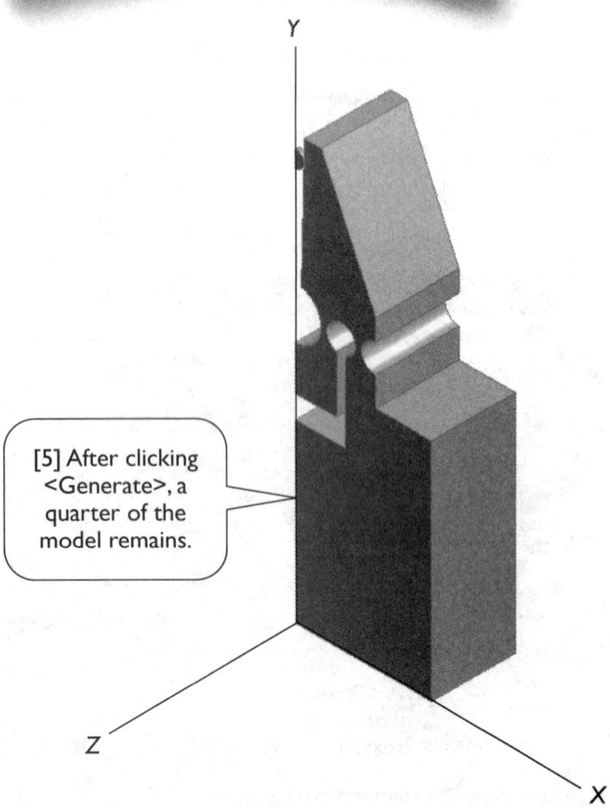

Why favor Plane4 over XYPlane?

Because we want to keep the half of the model that is behind the XY plane, so that it is visually better. When you specify a plane of symmetry, DesignModeler keep the portion that is in the +Z side of the plane coordinate system.

You don't have to build a full model

To create a <Tools/Symmetry> feature, you don't need to build a full model and then slice it to a half. You can just build a half model and use <Tools/ Symmetry> to specify a plane of symmetry. The information that Workbench needs are the planes of symmetry, not the other half of the model.

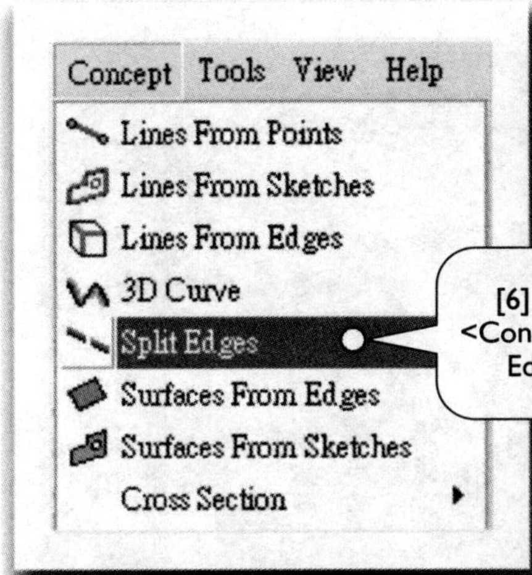
Concept Tools View Help
Lines From Points
Lines From Sketches
Lines From Edges
3D Curve
Split Edges
Surfaces From Edges
Surfaces From Sketches
Cross Section
[6] Select <Concept/Split Edges>.

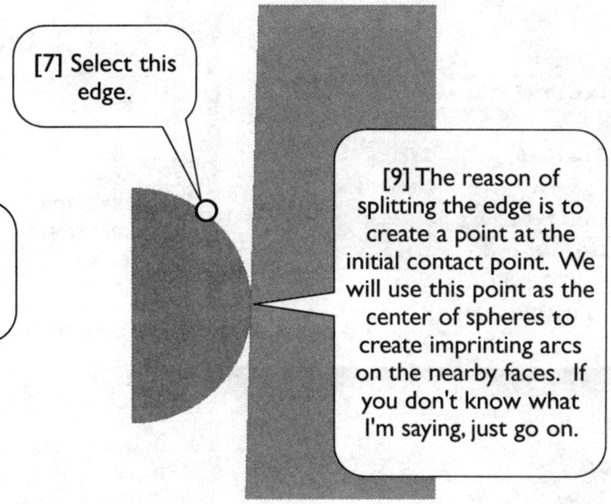
[7] Select this edge.
[9] The reason of splitting the edge is to create a point at the initial contact point. We will use this point as the center of spheres to create imprinting arcs on the nearby faces. If you don't know what I'm saying, just go on.

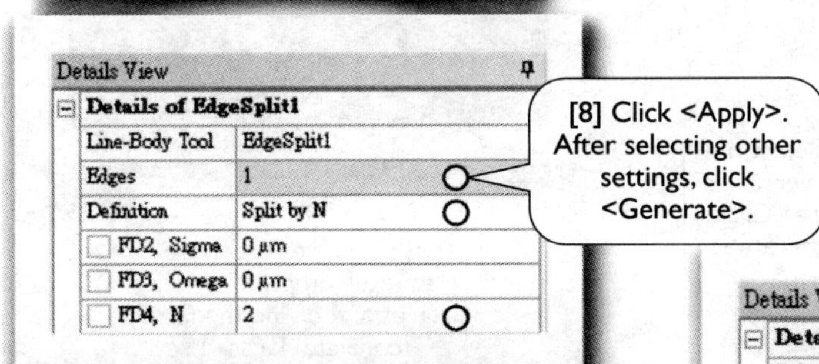
Details View
Details of EdgeSplit1
Line-Body Tool EdgeSplit1
Edges 1
Definition Split by N
FD2, Sigma 0 µm
FD3, Omega 0 µm
FD4, N 2
[8] Click <Apply>. After selecting other settings, click <Generate>.

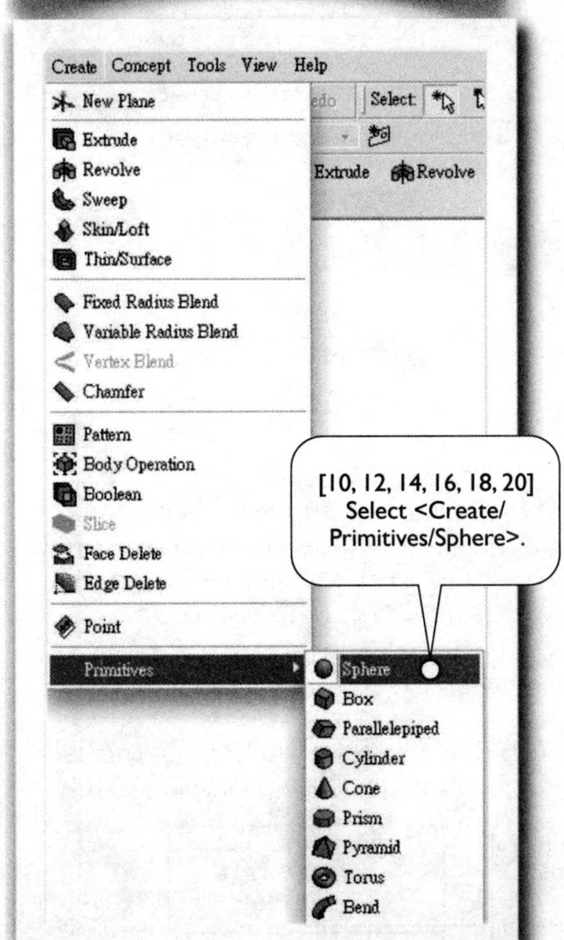
Create Concept Tools View Help
New Plane
Extrude
Revolve
Sweep
Skin/Loft
Thin/Surface
Fixed Radius Blend
Variable Radius Blend
Vertex Blend
Chamfer
Pattern
Body Operation
Boolean
Slice
Face Delete
Edge Delete
Point
Primitives
Sphere
Box
Parallelepiped
Cylinder
Cone
Prism
Pyramid
Torus
Bend
[10, 12, 14, 16, 18, 20] Select <Create/ Primitives/Sphere>.

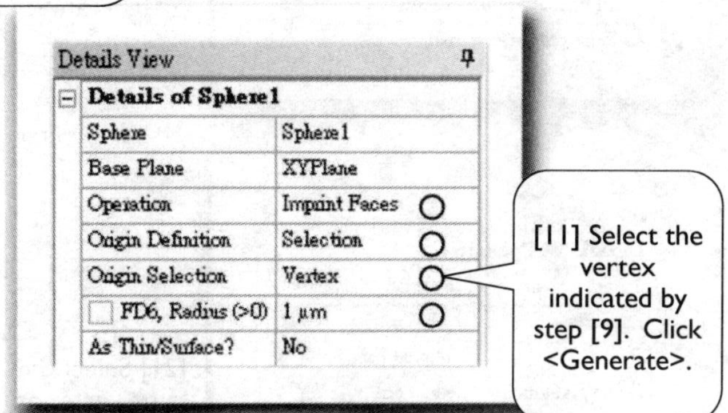
Details View
Details of Sphere1
Sphere Sphere1
Base Plane XYPlane
Operation Imprint Faces
Origin Definition Selection
Origin Selection Vertex
FD6, Radius (>0) 1 µm
As Thin/Surface? No
[11] Select the vertex indicated by step [9]. Click <Generate>.

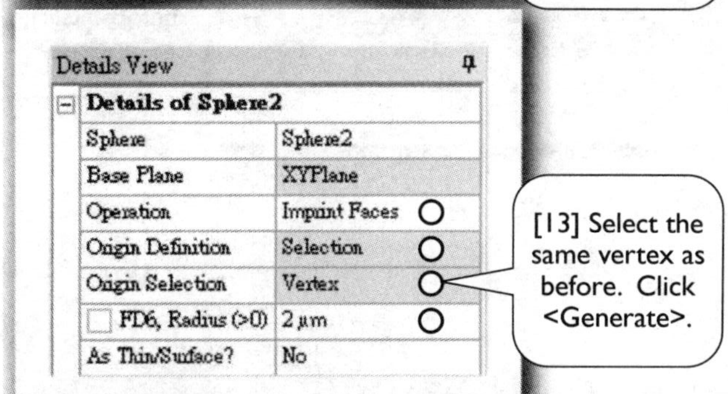
Details View
Details of Sphere2
Sphere Sphere2
Base Plane XYPlane
Operation Imprint Faces
Origin Definition Selection
Origin Selection Vertex
FD6, Radius (>0) 2 µm
As Thin/Surface? No
[13] Select the same vertex as before. Click <Generate>.

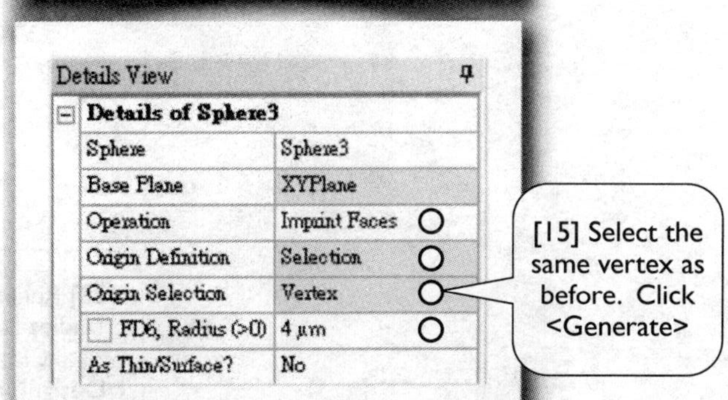
Details View
Details of Sphere3
Sphere Sphere3
Base Plane XYPlane
Operation Imprint Faces
Origin Definition Selection
Origin Selection Vertex
FD6, Radius (>0) 4 µm
As Thin/Surface? No
[15] Select the same vertex as before. Click <Generate>

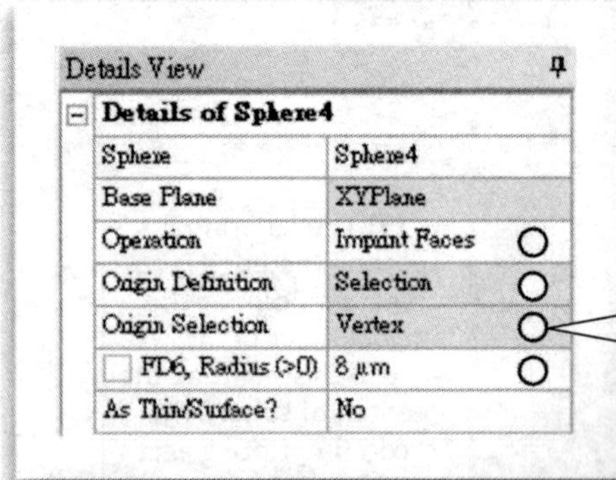

[17] Select the same vertex as before. Click <Generate>.

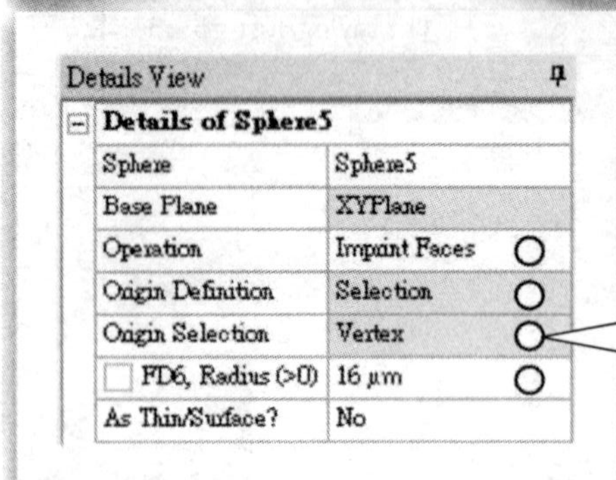

[19] Select the same vertex as before. Click <Generate>.

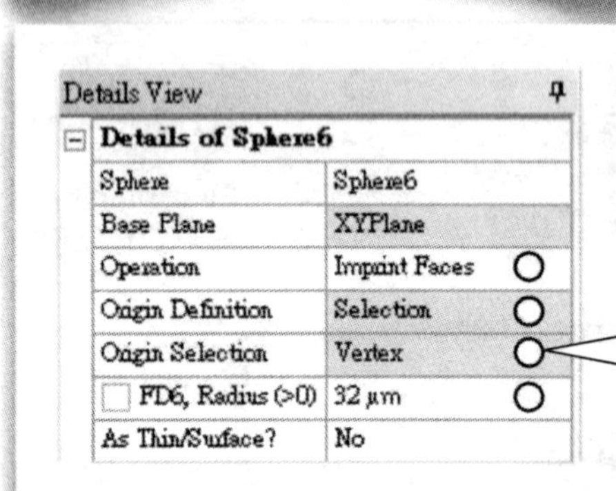

[21] Select the same vertex as before. Click <Generate>.

[22] Note that these spheres "imprint" on the faces and divide the faces to several faces. The spheres don't "slice" into the solid bodies. The reason we create these faces is to better control the meshing density.

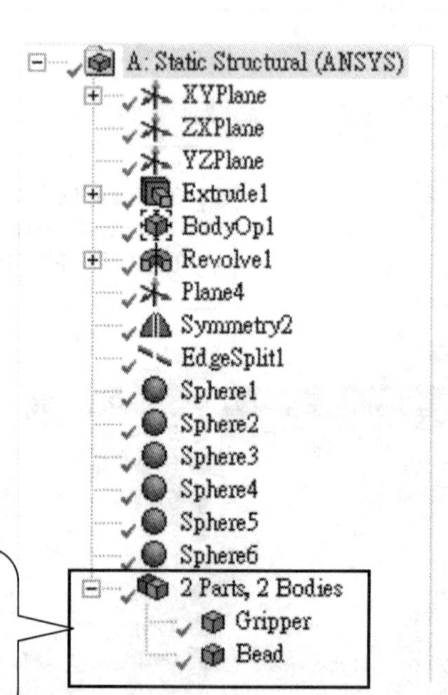

[23] Rename two bodies like this. Close DesignModeler.

13.3-4 Set Up Material in <Engineering Data>

Model the Bead as Rigid Body

The Young's modulus of glass (70 GPa) is 35,000 times of that of the PDMS (2 MPa). Whenever two bodies are so different in rigidity, you should model the more rigid one as rigid body whenever possible. This not only reduces the problem size (rigid bodies won't deform, they don't need to be meshed), but also eases the numerical difficulty.

Rigid bodies won't deform, therefore its Young's modulus and Poisson's ratio are not relevant. For a static simulation, we can assign any material to a rigid body. (For dynamic simulation, the mass density should be specified.) We will leave <Structural Steel> for the glass bead.

Start up <Mechanical> now.

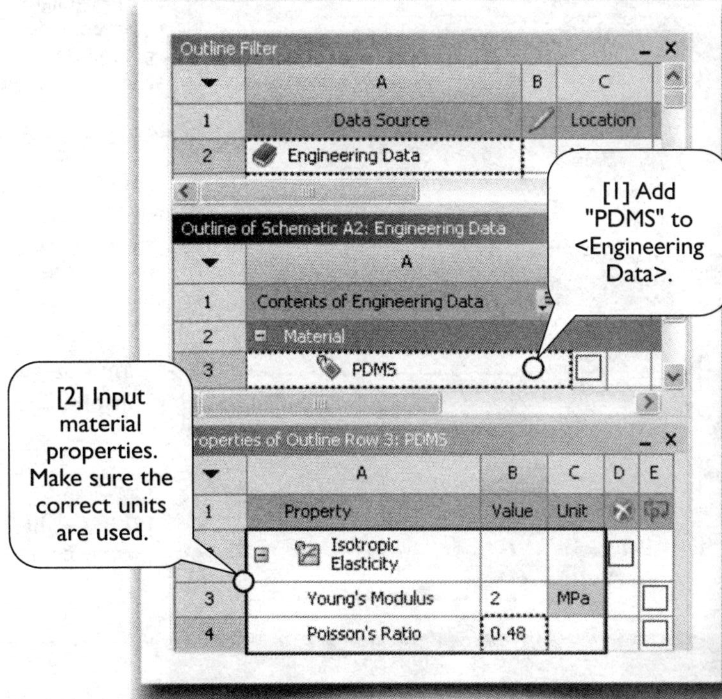

13.3-5 Set Up Model

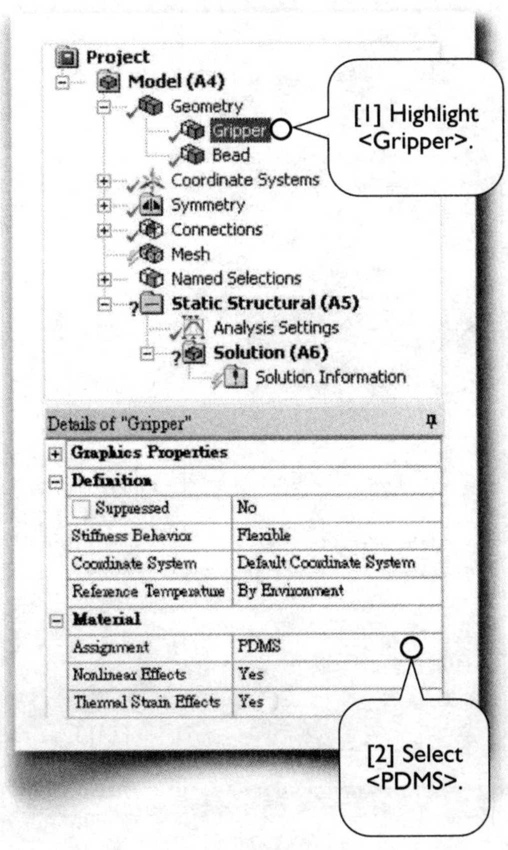

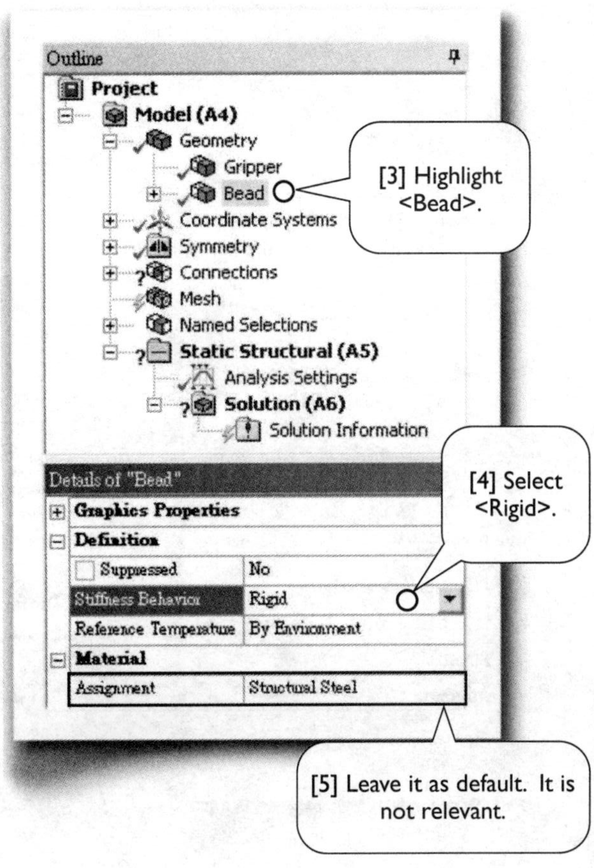

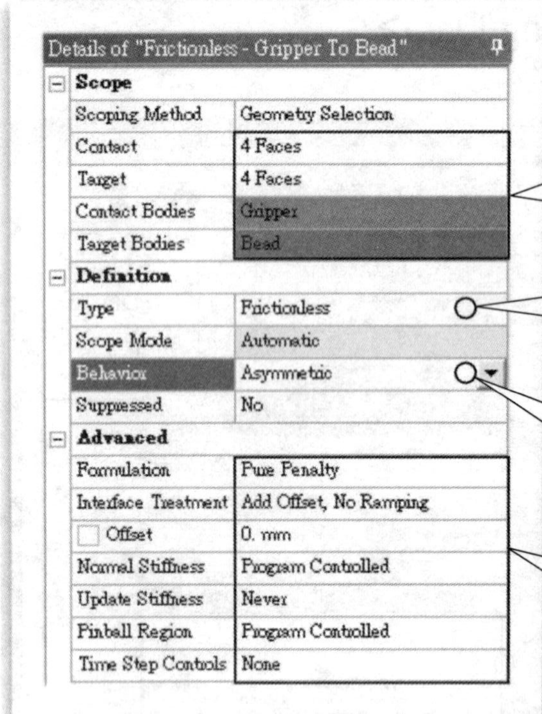

[6] Highlight <Contact Region>. Workbench correctly detect a contact region. You should examine these contact/target faces. Note that whenever a rigid body is involved, it is chosen as <Target Bodies>.

[7] Select <Frictionless>. Although there does exist friction between the PDMS and the glass, for our purpose of assessing gripping force, we may neglect the friction force to ease computation.

[8] Select <Asymmetric>. When a rigid is involved, you must choose <Asymmetric>.

[9] Leave these options as default for now. We may come back to modify them later on.

[10] Click <-X> to rotate the model.

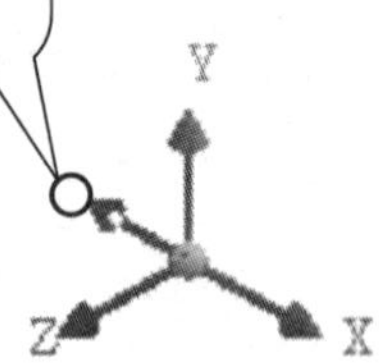

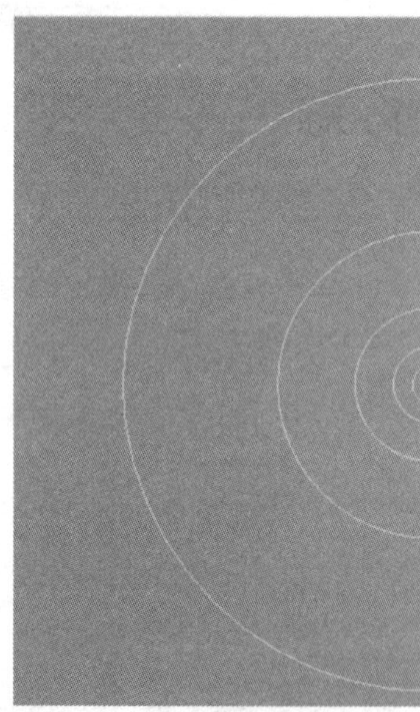

[11] Right-click <Bead> in the project tree and select <Hide Body>. Enlarge the contact region in the <Gripper>.

[12, 15, 17, 19, 21, 23] With <Mesh> highlighted, insert a <Sizing>.

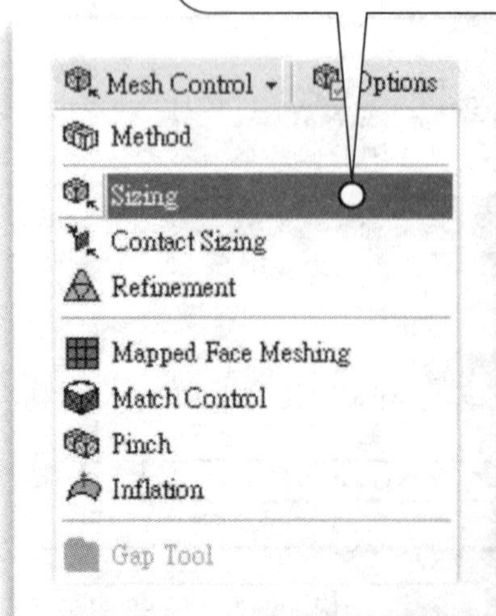

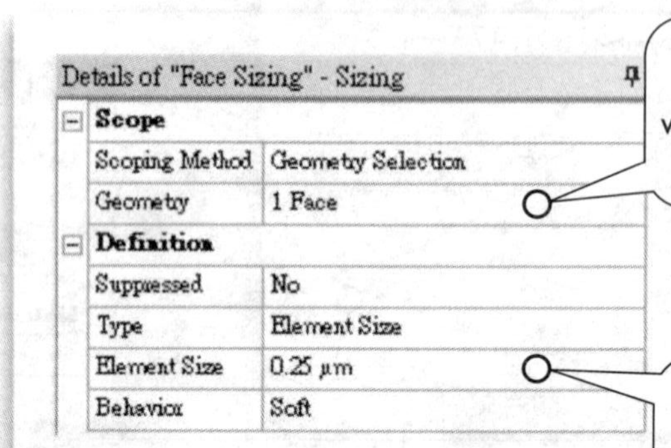

[13] Select the inner circular face, which has a radius of 1 μm .

[14] Type the element size. Note that the unit is micron.

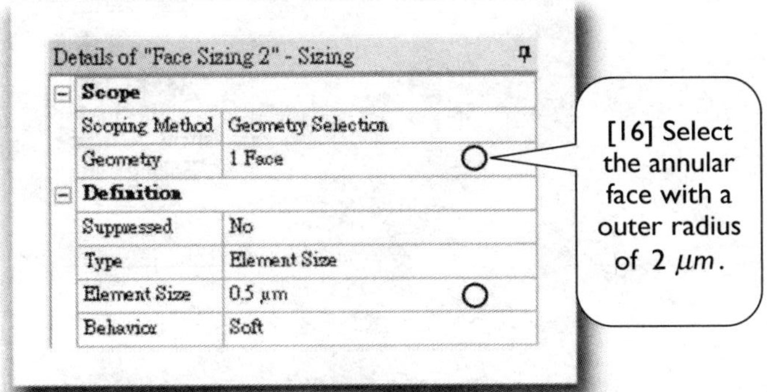
Details of "Face Sizing 2" - Sizing
Scope
Scoping Method | Geometry Selection
Geometry | 1 Face
Definition
Suppressed | No
Type | Element Size
Element Size | 0.5 µm
Behavior | Soft
[16] Select the annular face with a outer radius of 2 µm.

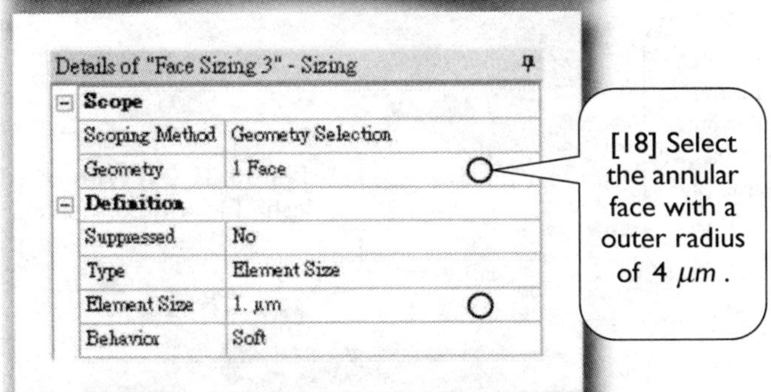
Details of "Face Sizing 3" - Sizing
Scope
Scoping Method | Geometry Selection
Geometry | 1 Face
Definition
Suppressed | No
Type | Element Size
Element Size | 1. µm
Behavior | Soft
[18] Select the annular face with a outer radius of 4 µm.

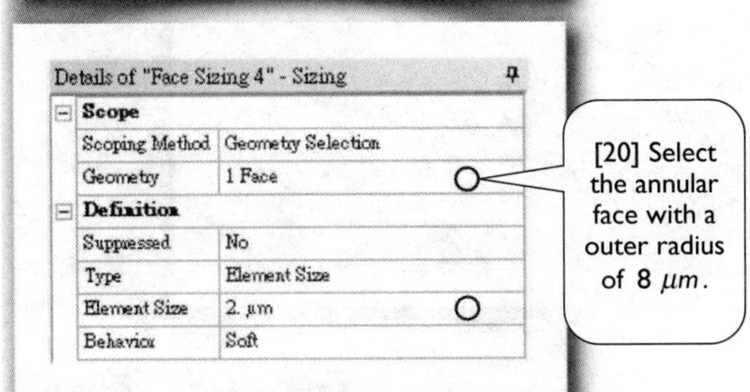
Details of "Face Sizing 4" - Sizing
Scope
Scoping Method | Geometry Selection
Geometry | 1 Face
Definition
Suppressed | No
Type | Element Size
Element Size | 2. µm
Behavior | Soft
[20] Select the annular face with a outer radius of 8 µm.

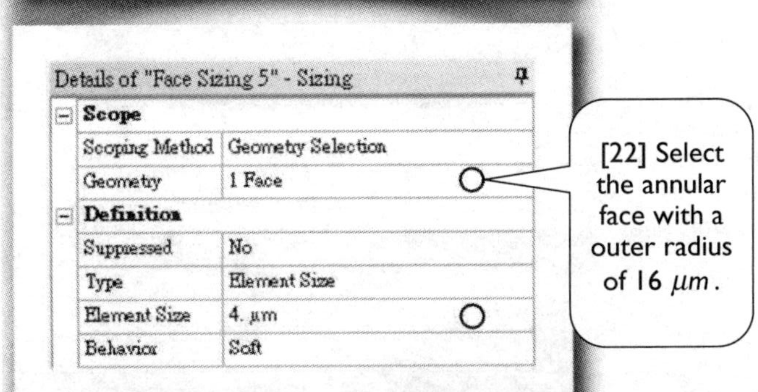
Details of "Face Sizing 5" - Sizing
Scope
Scoping Method | Geometry Selection
Geometry | 1 Face
Definition
Suppressed | No
Type | Element Size
Element Size | 4. µm
Behavior | Soft
[22] Select the annular face with a outer radius of 16 µm.

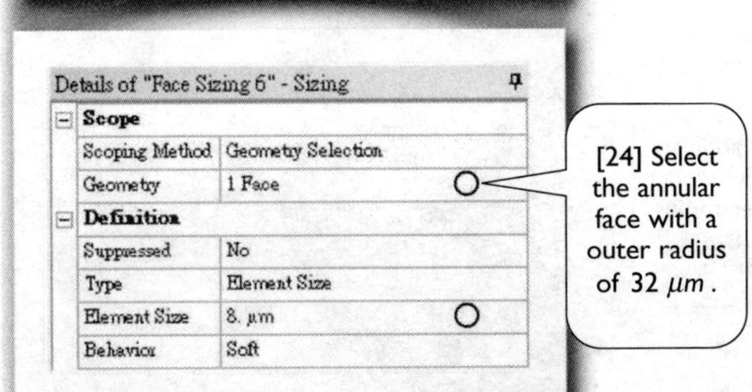
Details of "Face Sizing 6" - Sizing
Scope
Scoping Method | Geometry Selection
Geometry | 1 Face
Definition
Suppressed | No
Type | Element Size
Element Size | 8. µm
Behavior | Soft
[24] Select the annular face with a outer radius of 32 µm.

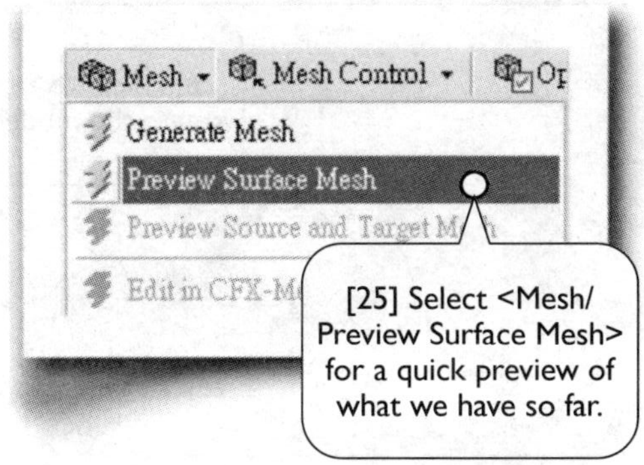
Mesh
Mesh Control
Generate Mesh
Preview Surface Mesh
Preview Source and Target Mesh
[25] Select <Mesh/ Preview Surface Mesh> for a quick preview of what we have so far.

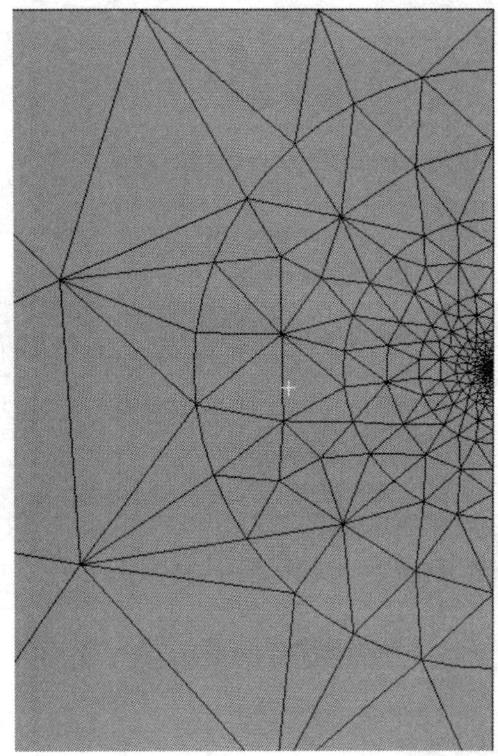

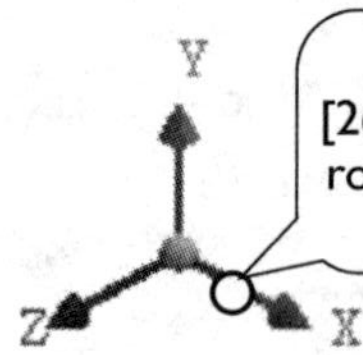

[26] Click <X> to rotate the model.

[27] Hide <Gripper> and show <Bead>. Enlarge the <Bead>.

[28, 30, 32, 34] With <Mesh> highlighted, insert a <Sizing>.

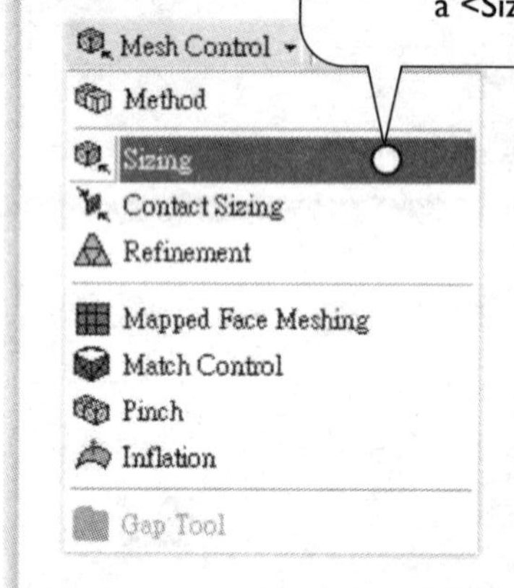

Details of "Face Sizing 7" - Sizing

Scope	
Scoping Method	Geometry Selection
Geometry	1 Face
Definition	
Suppressed	No
Type	Element Size
Element Size	0.25 μm
Behavior	Soft

[29] Select the inner circular face, which has a radius of 1 μm .

Details of "Face Sizing 8" - Sizing

Scope	
Scoping Method	Geometry Selection
Geometry	1 Face
Definition	
Suppressed	No
Type	Element Size
Element Size	0.5 μm
Behavior	Soft

[31] Select the annular face with a outer radius of 2 μm.

Details of "Face Sizing 9" - Sizing

Scope	
Scoping Method	Geometry Selection
Geometry	1 Face
Definition	
Suppressed	No
Type	Element Size
Element Size	1. μm
Behavior	Soft

[33] Select the annular face with a outer radius of 4 μm .

Details of "Face Sizing 10" - Sizing

Scope	
Scoping Method	Geometry Selection
Geometry	1 Face
Definition	
Suppressed	No
Type	Element Size
Element Size	2. μm
Behavior	Soft

[35] Select the annular face with a outer radius of 8 μm.

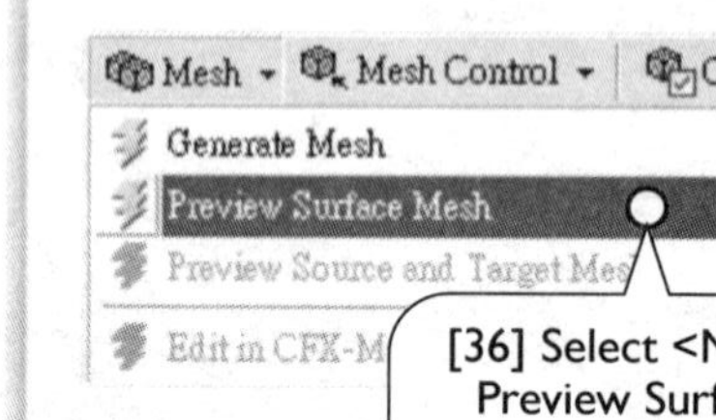

[36] Select <Mesh/ Preview Surface Mesh> for a quick preview.

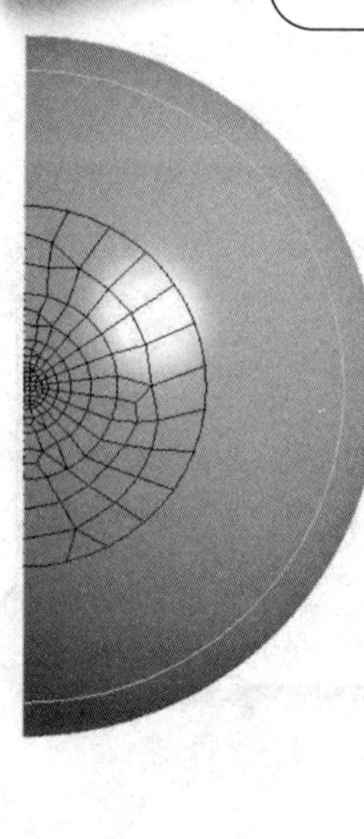

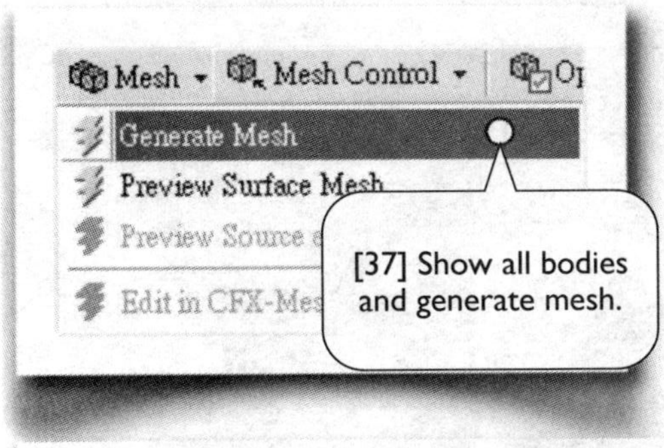

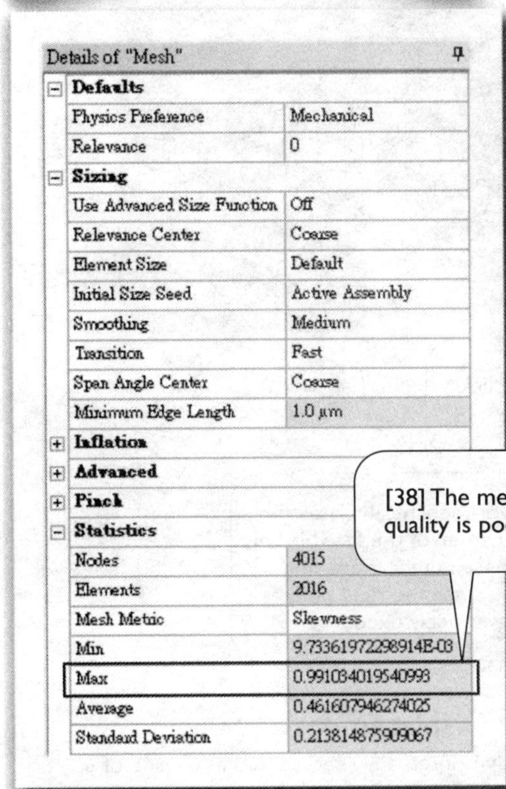

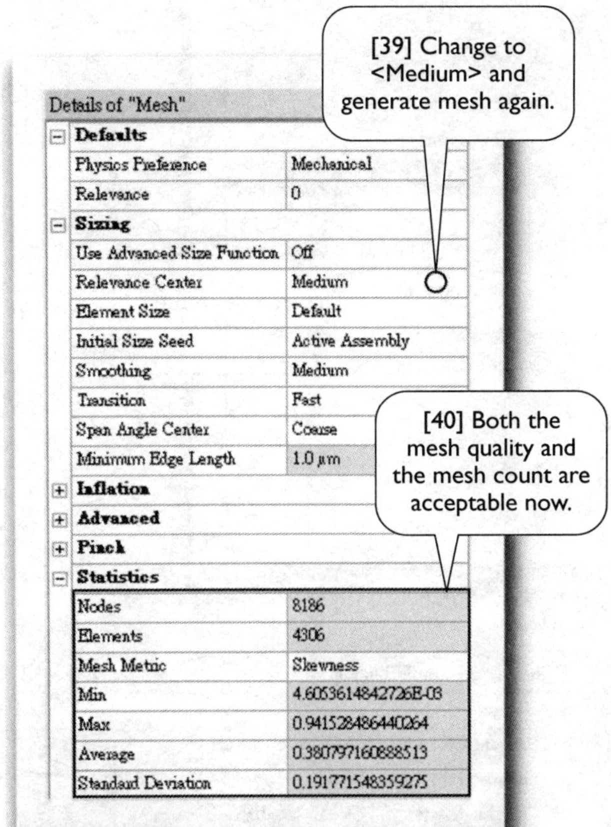

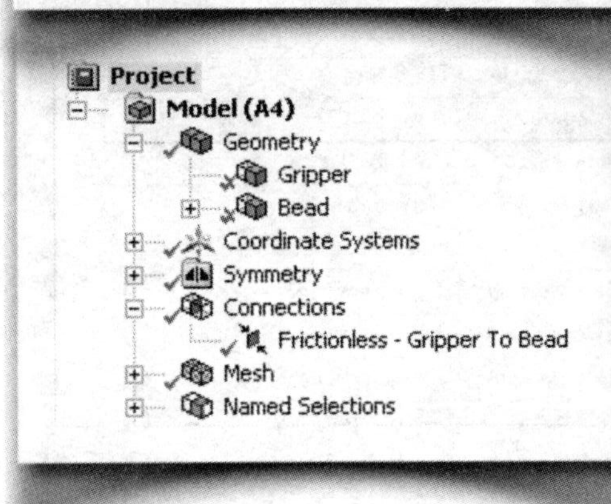

13.3-6 Set Up Environment Conditions

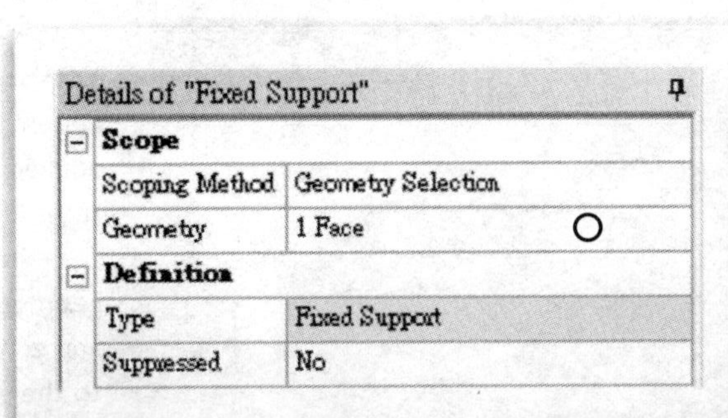

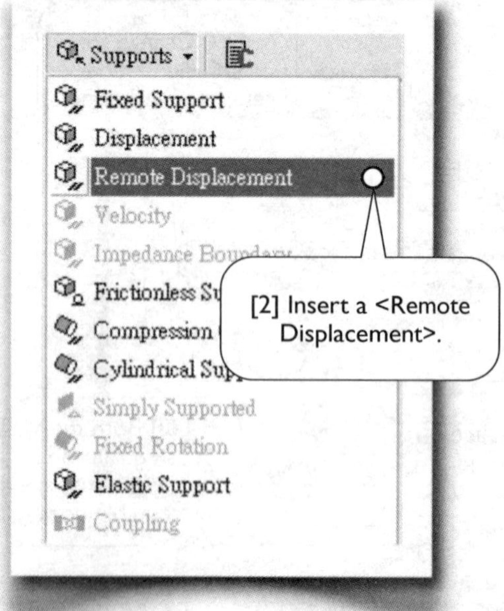

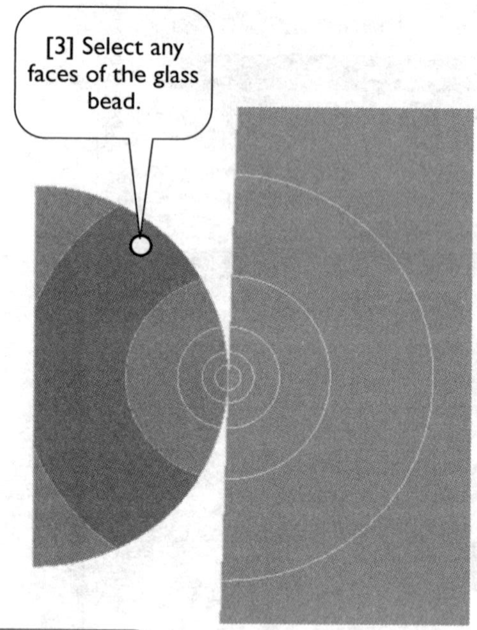

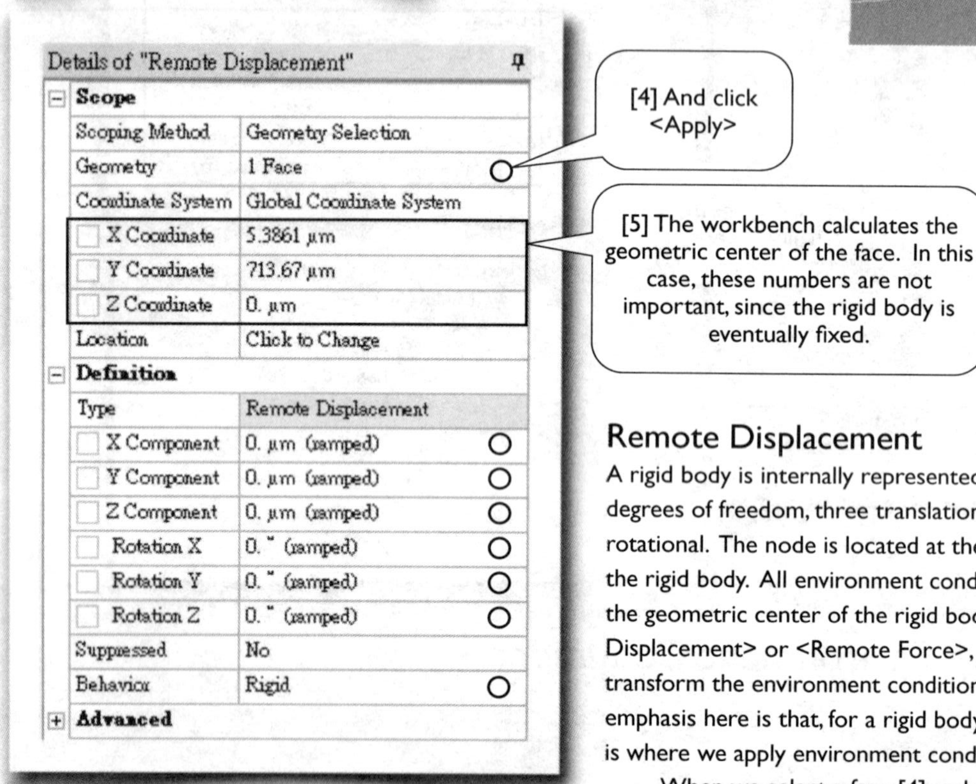

Remote Displacement

A rigid body is internally represented as a node of 6 degrees of freedom, three translational and three rotational. The node is located at the geometric center of the rigid body. All environment conditions are applied at the geometric center of the rigid body. With <Remote Displacement> or <Remote Force>, the Workbench will transform the environment conditions to the node. The emphasis here is that, for a rigid body, its geometry center is where we apply environment conditions.

When we select a face [4] and apply a <Remote Displacement>, the Workbench will calculate the geometry center for that face, and the specified displacement is applied at that location. That displacement is then transformed to the geometry center of the rigid body.

In our case, we arbitrarily select a face [3]. The geometric center of that face will have zero displacements and zero rotations. These conditions will be transformed to the geometry center of the rigid body. The bottom line is that the rigid body is entirely fixed, both translationally and rotationally. That's what we want for this rigid body.

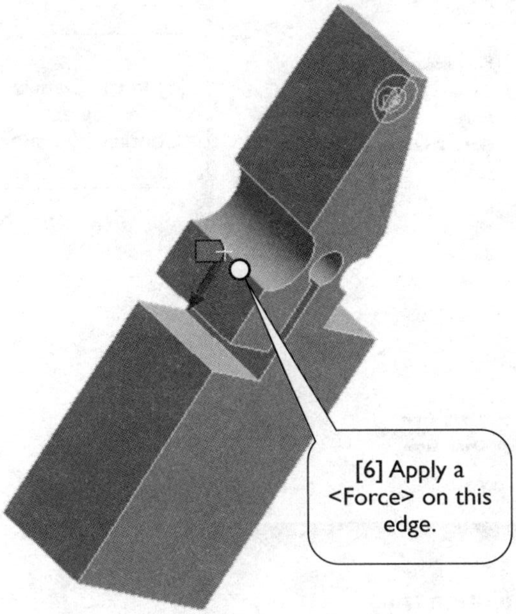

[6] Apply a <Force> on this edge.

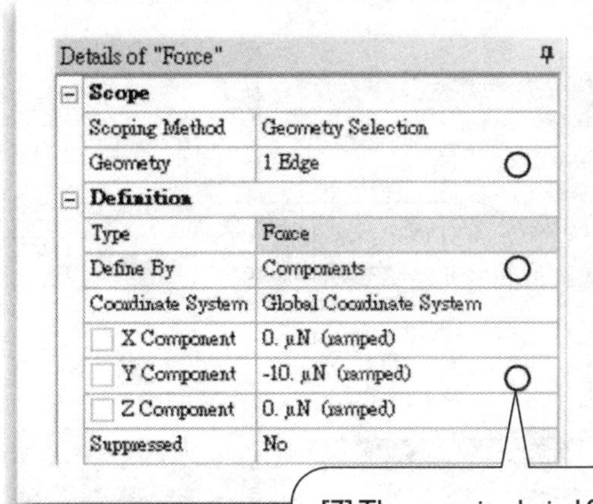

[7] The magnitude is 10 μN downward. Note that, since the simulation model is only a quarter of the real model, only a quarter of the total load is applied.

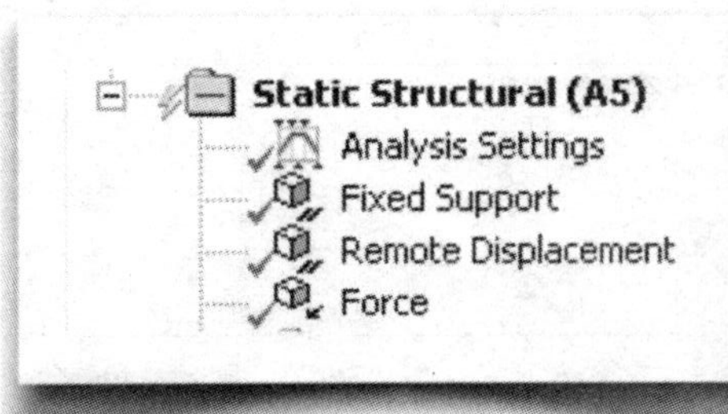

13.3-7 Set Up Result Objects

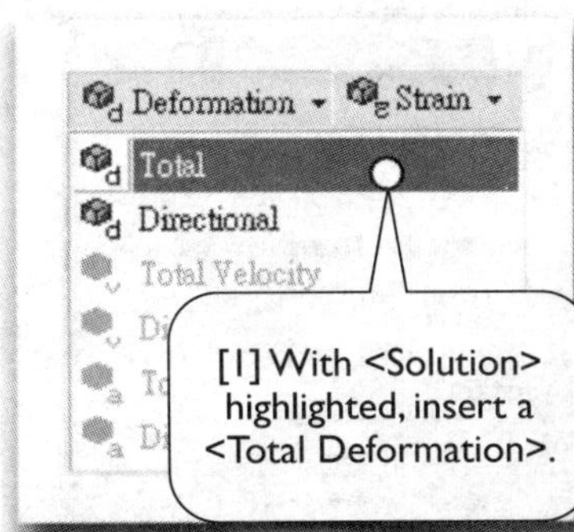

[1] With <Solution> highlighted, insert a <Total Deformation>.

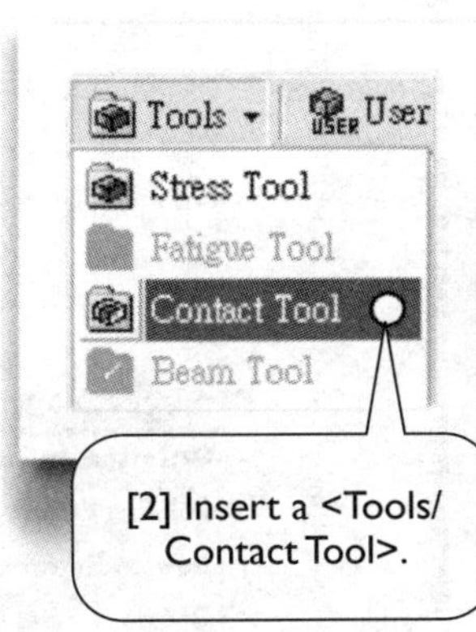

[2] Insert a <Tools/ Contact Tool>.

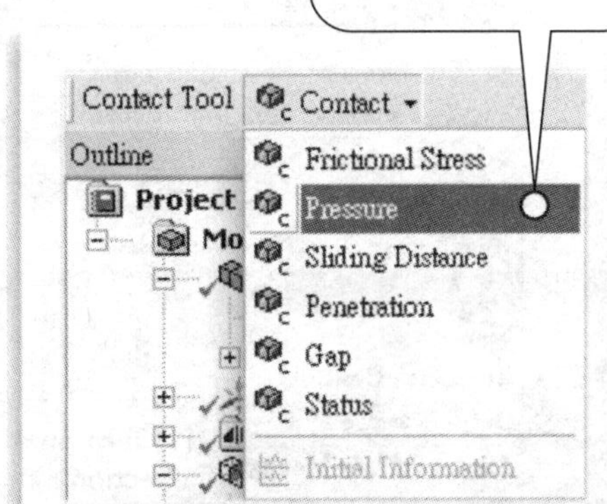

[4] With <Contact Tool> still highlighted, insert a <Contact/Pressure>.

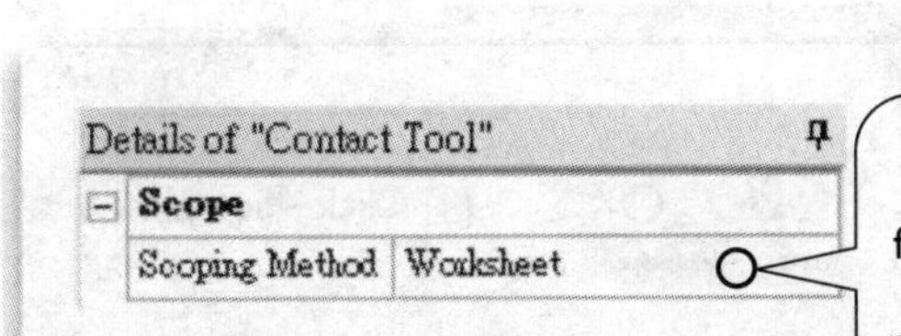

[3] Make sure that <Worksheet> is selected for <Scoping Method> and leave the settings in the <Worksheet> (right side of the GUI) as default.

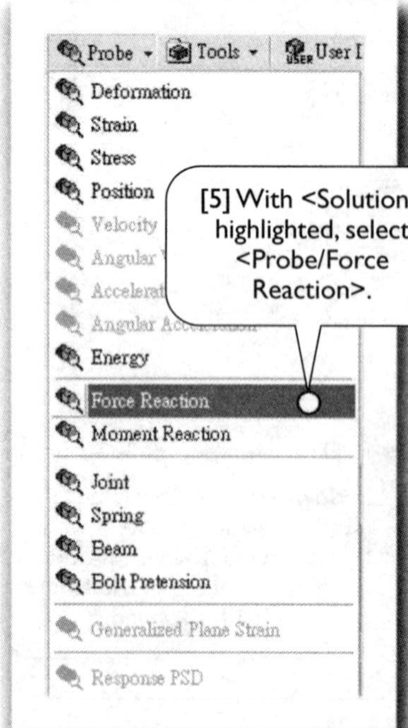

[5] With <Solution> highlighted, select <Probe/Force Reaction>.

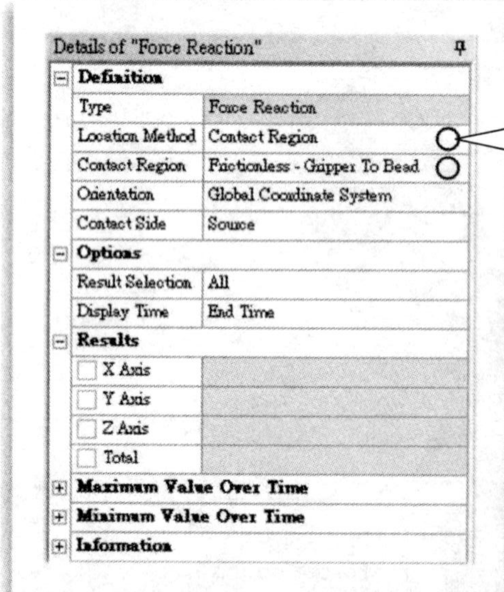

[6] In the Details view, select <Contact Region>.

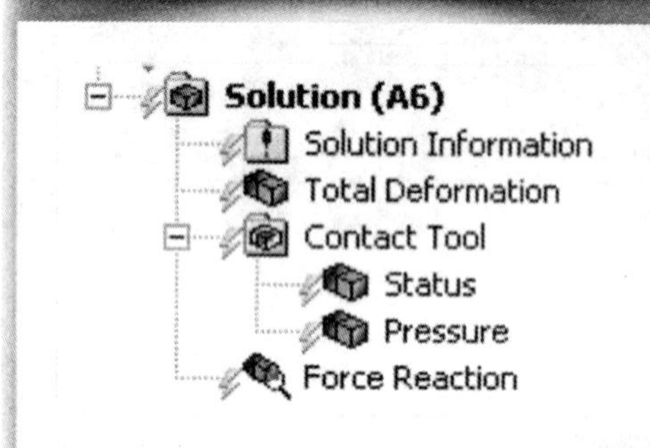

13.3-8 Solve the Model and View the Results

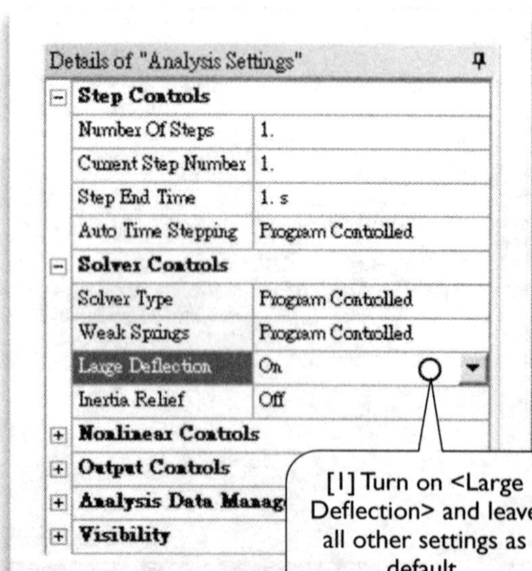

[1] Turn on <Large Deflection> and leave all other settings as default.

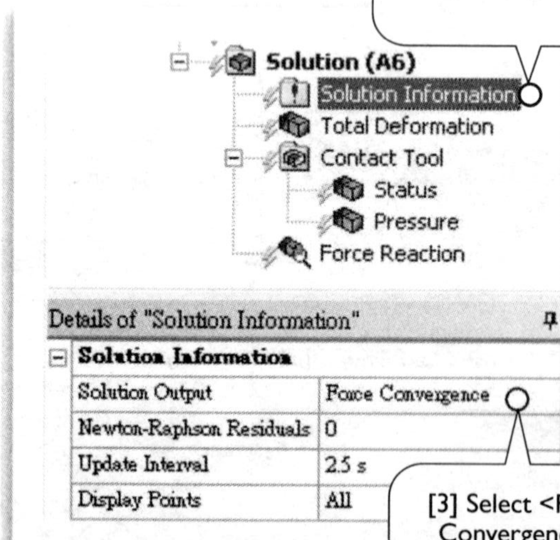

[2] Highlight <Solution Information>.

[3] Select <Force Convergence>.

[4] Click <Solve>.

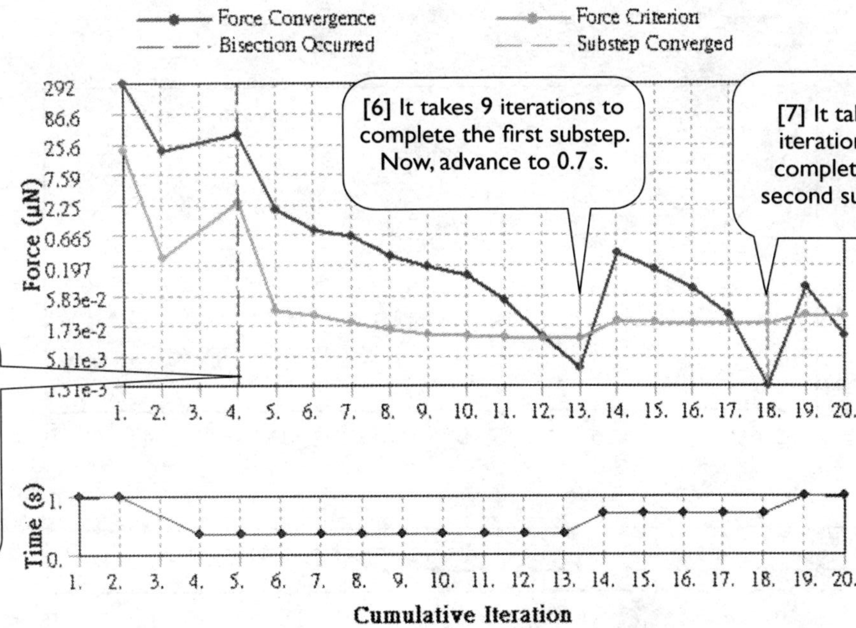

Interpretation of the Convergence Curve

There are two problems. First, bisections should avoid if possible, since they are wasting time. Second, It takes 9 iterations to complete the first substep; that may be too many and should be reduced if possible.

Tabular Data

	Time [s]	Force Reaction (X) [μN]
1	0.35	0.8631
2	0.7	1.7322
3	1.	2.4885

[8] Highlight <Force Reaction>, it records the gripping force at each time step.

Details of "Analysis Settings"

Step Controls	
Number Of Steps	1.
Current Step Number	1.
Step End Time	1. s
Auto Time Stepping	On
Define By	Time
Initial Time Step	0.3 s
Minimum Time Step	3.e-002 s
Maximum Time Step	0.5 s
Solver Controls	
Solver Type	Program Controlled
Weak Springs	Program Controlled
Large Deflection	On
Inertia Relief	Off

[9] Set up an appropriate initial time step to avoid bisection.

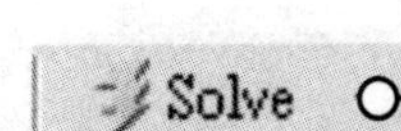

[10] Click <Solve>.

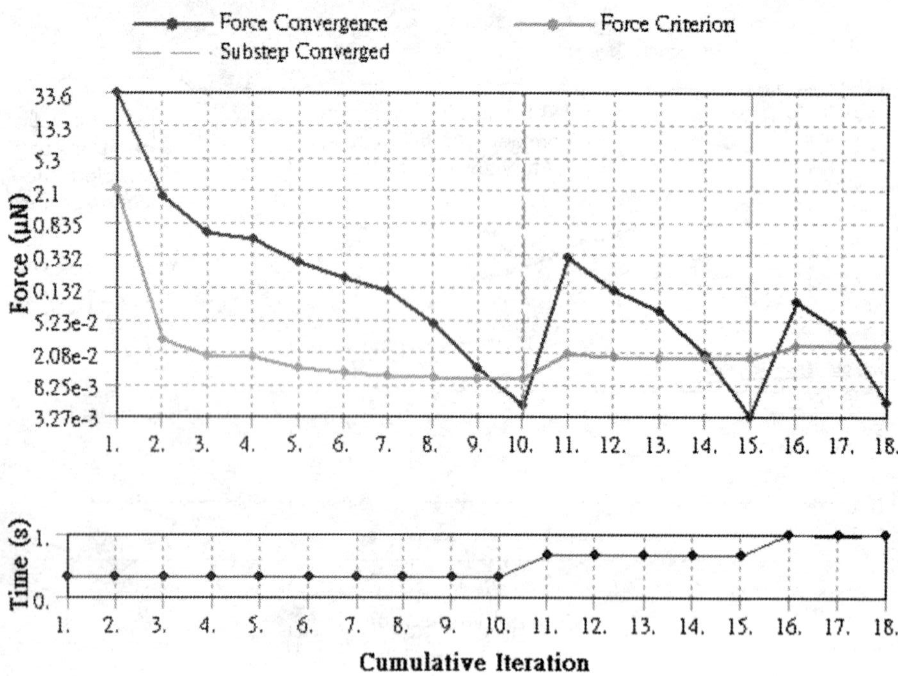

[11] Now, the bisection doesn't occur and the total number of iteration reduces to 18.

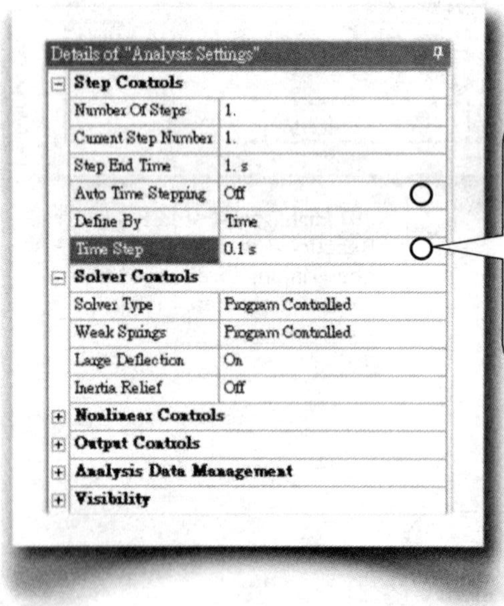

[12] If we want to plot the gripping-force-versus-actuation-force more accurately, a smaller time step may be necessary. Solve again.

[13] Small time step usually requires less iterations for each substep. The total iterations, however, is increased.

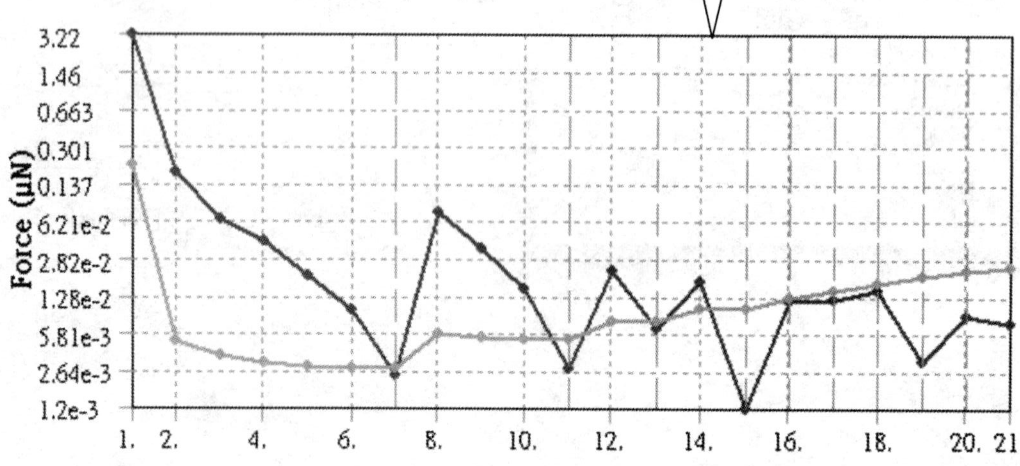

Tabular Data

	Time [s]	Force Reaction (X) [uN]
1	0.1	0.24399
2	0.2	0.49123
3	0.3	0.74033
4	0.4	0.9884
5	0.5	1.2352
6	0.6	1.4854
7	0.7	1.7337
8	0.8	1.9799
9	0.9	2.2293
10	1.	2.4768

[14] Highlight <Force Reaction> to view the gripping forces.

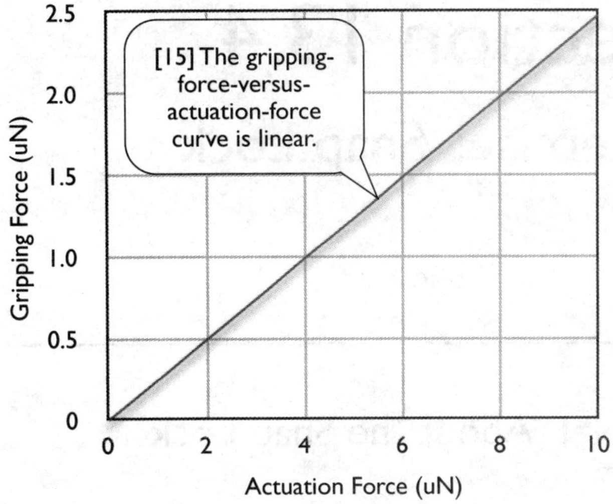

[15] The gripping-force-versus-actuation-force curve is linear.

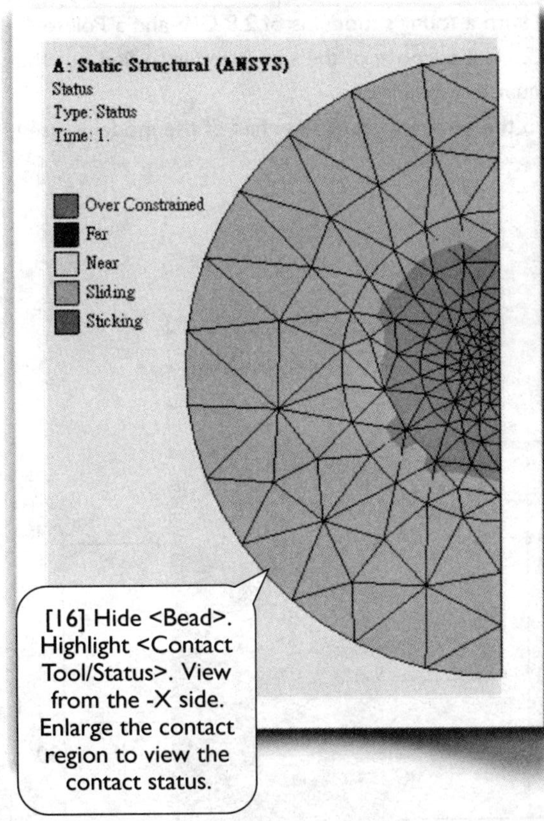

[16] Hide <Bead>. Highlight <Contact Tool/Status>. View from the -X side. Enlarge the contact region to view the contact status.

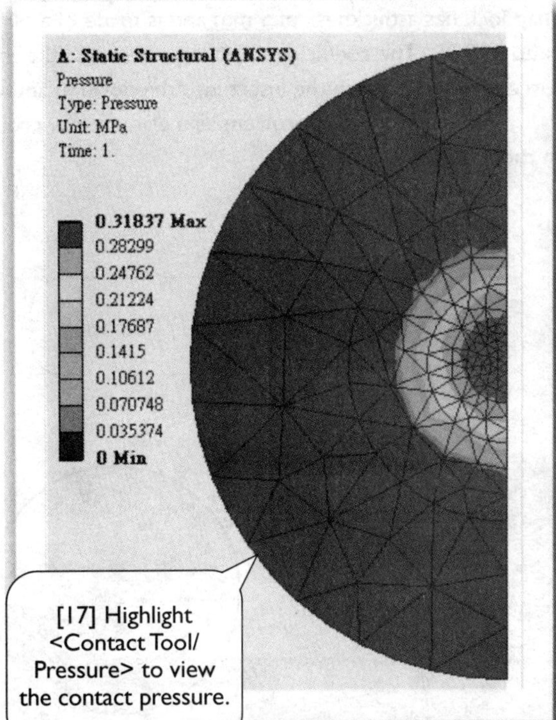

[17] Highlight <Contact Tool/Pressure> to view the contact pressure.

Wrap Up

Animate the deformation. Save the project and exit Workbench.

Section 13.4
Exercise: Snap Lock

13.4-1 About the Snap Lock

The snap lock consists of two parts: the insert [1] and the prongs [2]; it is fastened when pushed into position [3]. The snap lock has a thickness of 5 mm and is made of a plastic material with a Young's modulus of 2.8 GPa and a Poisson's ratio of 0.35. The coefficient of friction between the materials is 0.2. The purpose of the simulation is to find out the force required to push the insert into the position and the force required to pull it out.

We will model the problem as a plane stress problem. Due to the symmetry, only one half of the model is used in the simulation.

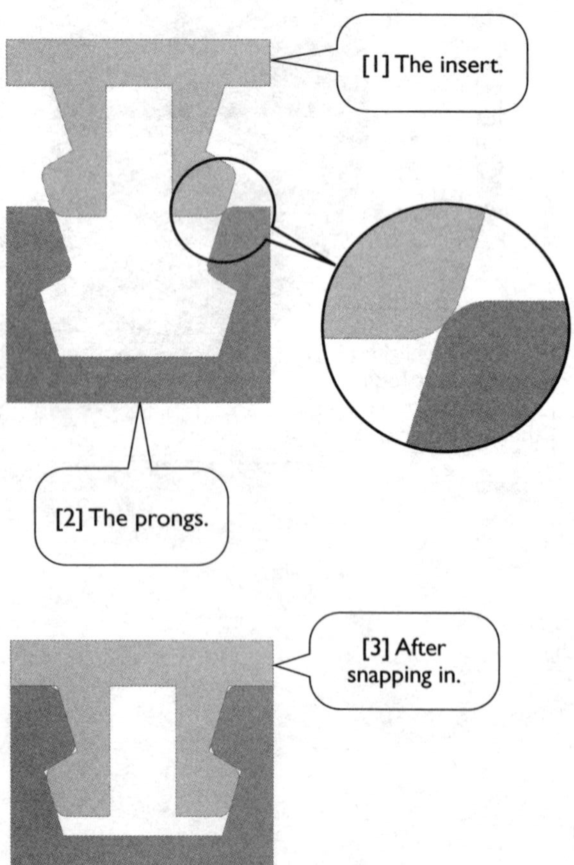

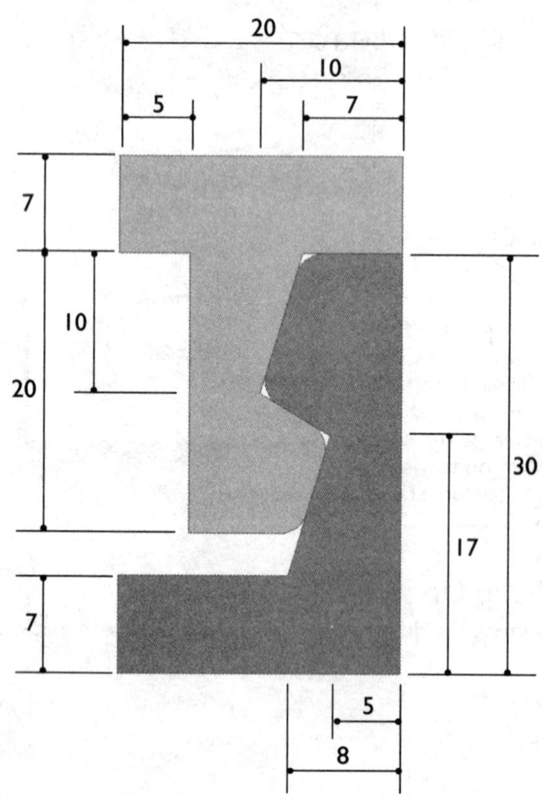

Unit: mm.

All fillets has radius of 2 mm.

13.4-2 Start Up

Launch <Workbench>. Create a <Static Structural> analysis system. Save the project as "Snap."

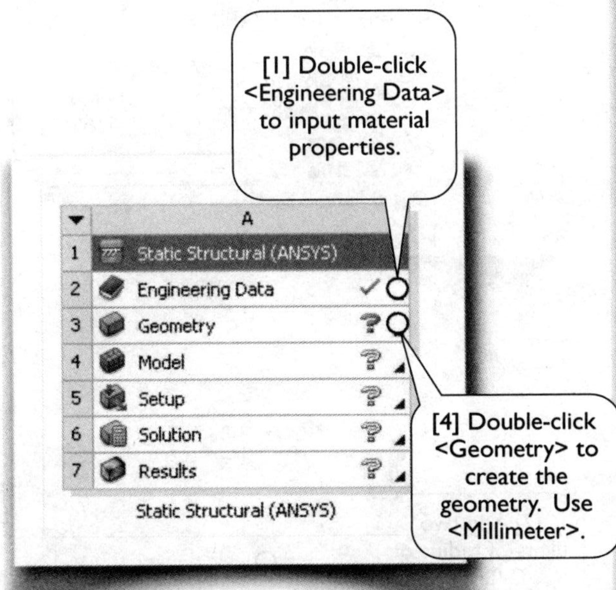

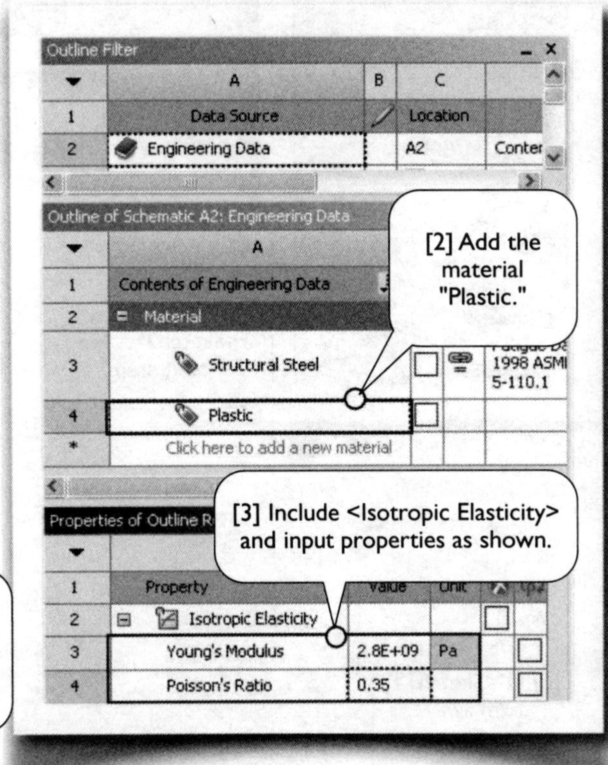

13.4-3 Create Geometry in DesignModeler

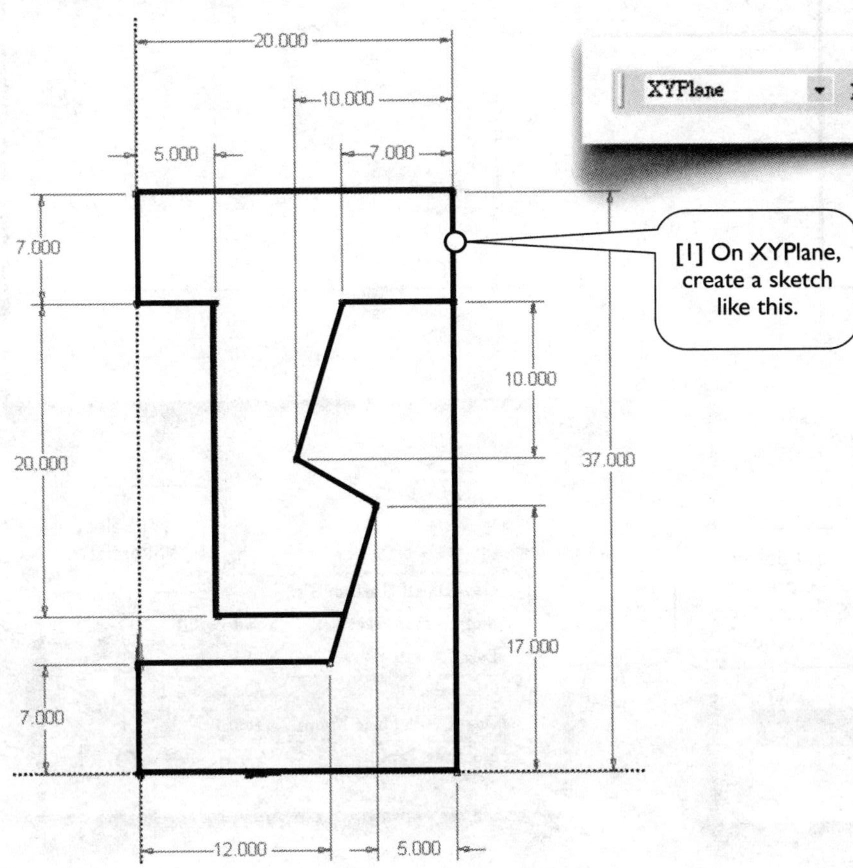

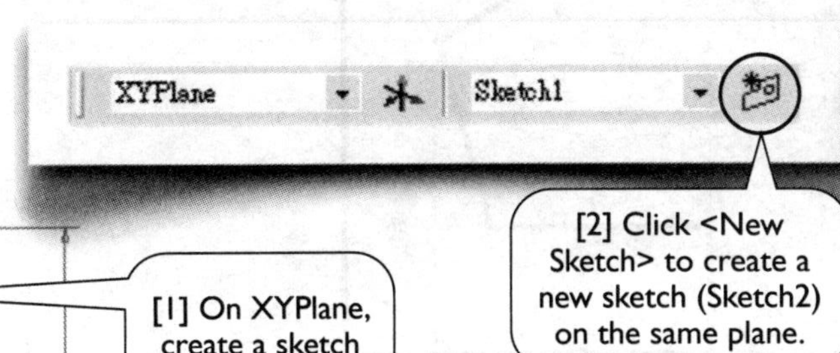

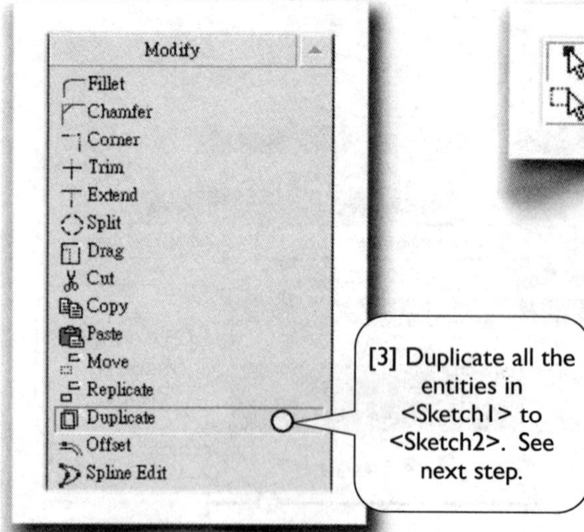
Modify
Fillet
Chamfer
Corner
Trim
Extend
Split
Drag
Cut
Copy
Paste
Move
Replicate
Duplicate
Offset
Spline Edit
[3] Duplicate all the entities in <Sketch1> to <Sketch2>. See next step.

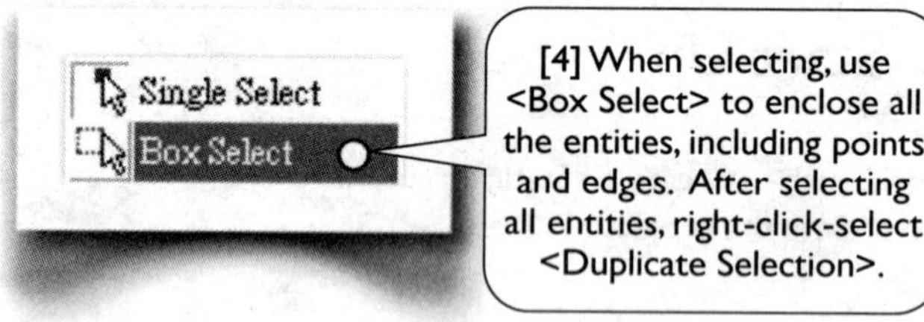
Single Select
Box Select
[4] When selecting, use <Box Select> to enclose all the entities, including points and edges. After selecting all entities, right-click-select <Duplicate Selection>.

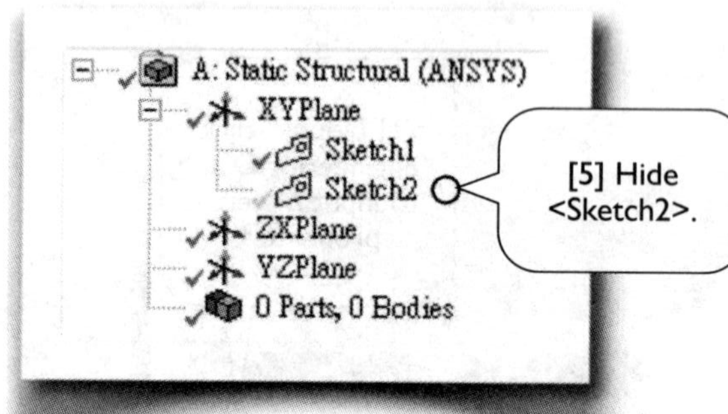
A: Static Structural (ANSYS)
XYPlane
Sketch1
Sketch2
ZXPlane
YZPlane
0 Parts, 0 Bodies
[5] Hide <Sketch2>.

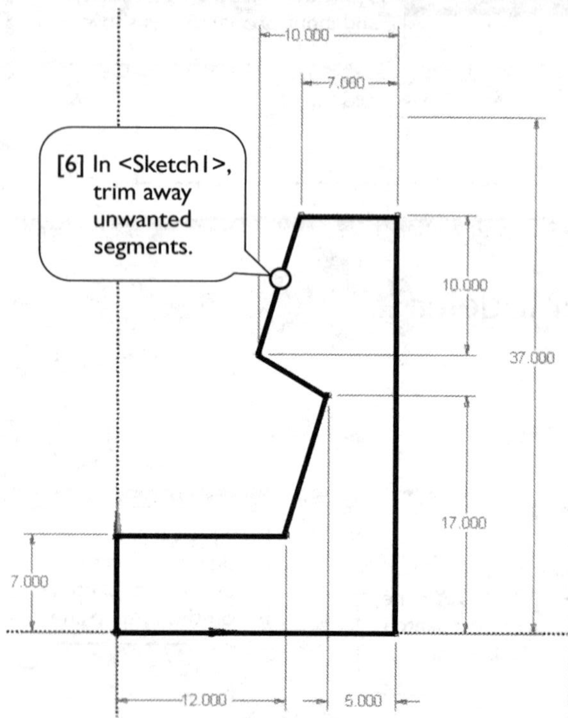
10.000
7.000
[6] In <Sketch1>, trim away unwanted segments.
10.000
37.000
17.000
7.000
12.000
5.000

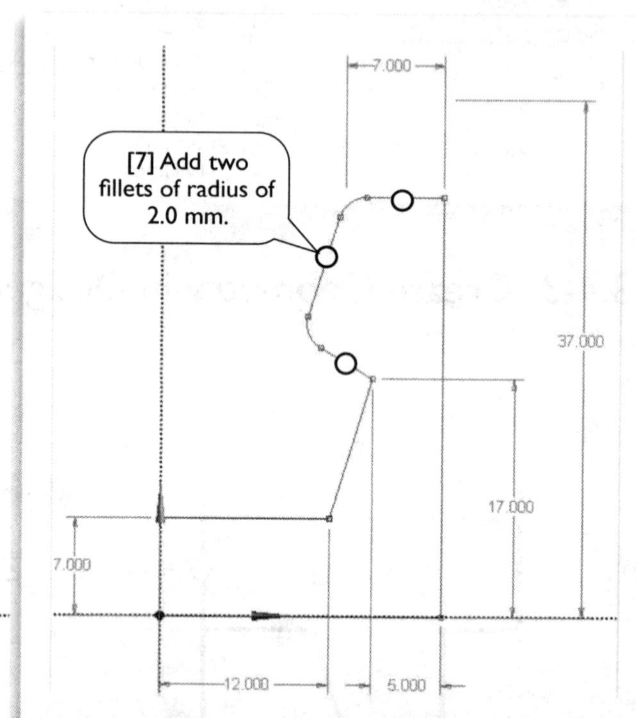
7.000
[7] Add two fillets of radius of 2.0 mm.
37.000
17.000
7.000
12.000
5.000

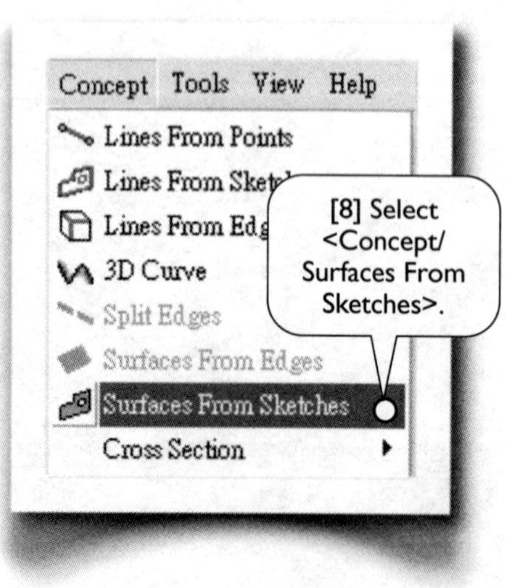
Concept
Tools
View
Help
Lines From Points
Lines From Sketc
Lines From Edg
3D Curve
Split Edges
Surfaces From Edges
Surfaces From Sketches
Cross Section
[8] Select <Concept/ Surfaces From Sketches>.

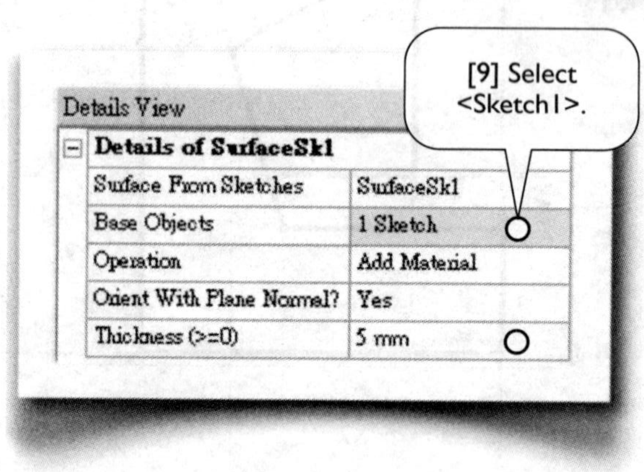
Details View
Details of SurfaceSk1
Surface From Sketches
SurfaceSk1
Base Objects
1 Sketch
Operation
Add Material
Orient With Plane Normal?
Yes
Thickness (>=0)
5 mm
[9] Select <Sketch1>.

[10] After
<Generate>, the
prong is
complete.

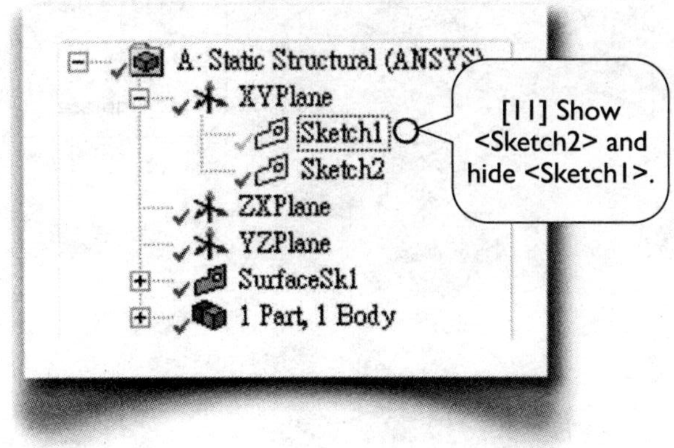
A: Static Structural (ANSYS)
XYPlane
Sketch1
Sketch2
ZXPlane
YZPlane
SurfaceSk1
1 Part, 1 Body
[11] Show
<Sketch2> and
hide <Sketch1>.

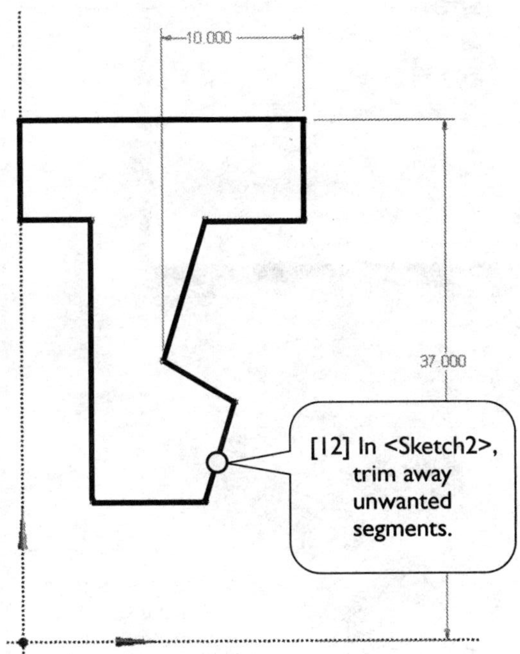
10.000
37.000
[12] In <Sketch2>,
trim away
unwanted
segments.

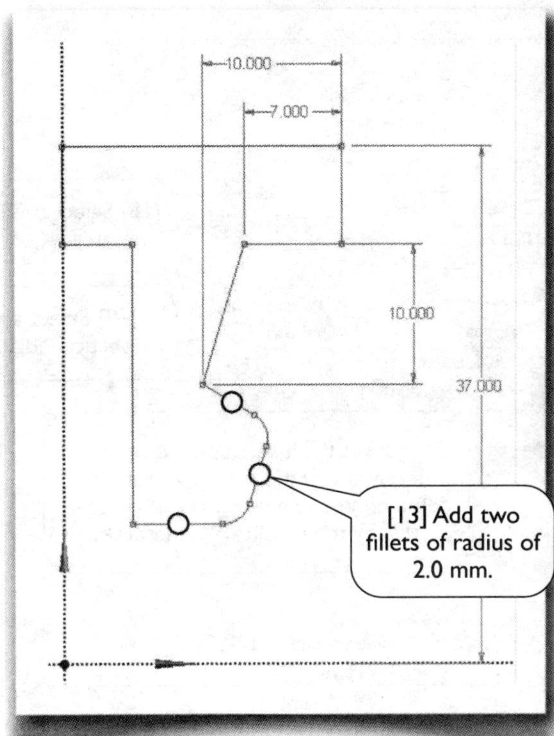
10.000
7.000
10.000
37.000
[13] Add two
fillets of radius of
2.0 mm.

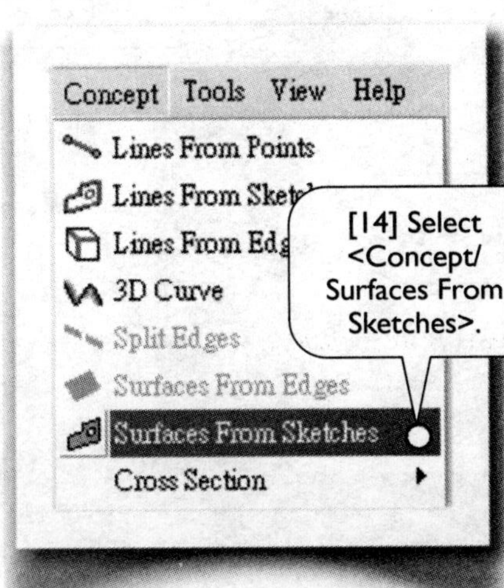
Concept Tools View Help
Lines From Points
Lines From Sket
Lines From Edg
3D Curve
Split Edges
Surfaces From Edges
Surfaces From Sketches
Cross Section
[14] Select
<Concept/
Surfaces From
Sketches>.

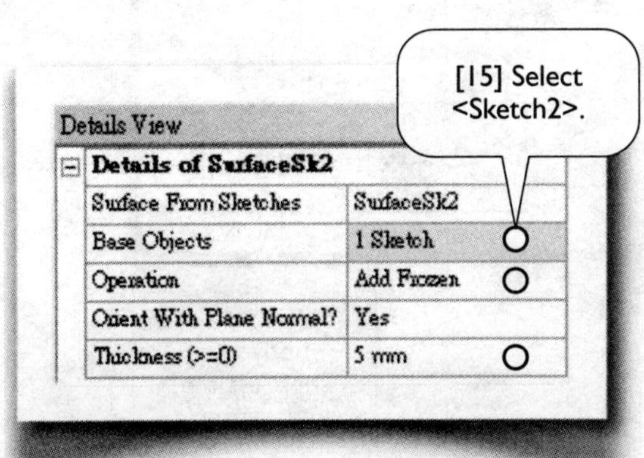
Details View
Details of SurfaceSk2
Surface From Sketches SurfaceSk2
Base Objects 1 Sketch
Operation Add Frozen
Orient With Plane Normal? Yes
Thickness (>=0) 5 mm
[15] Select
<Sketch2>.

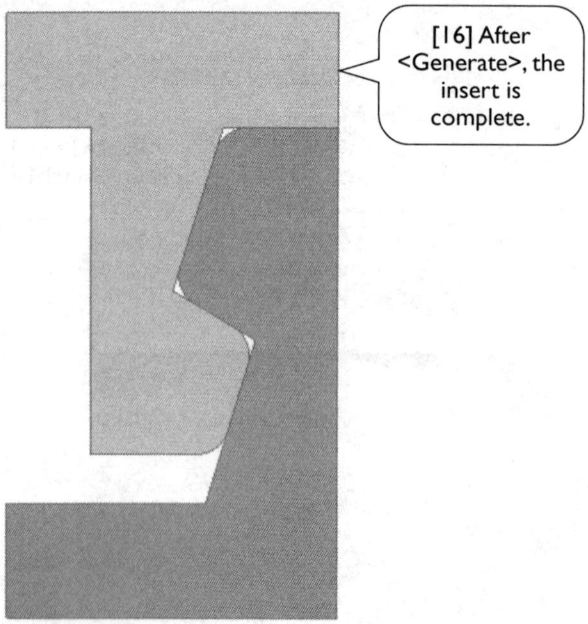
[16] After <Generate>, the insert is complete.

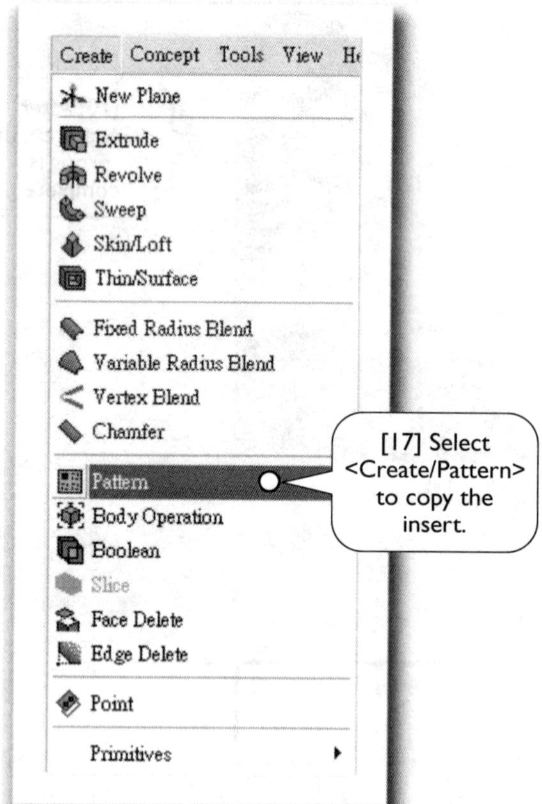
Create Concept Tools View H
New Plane
Extrude
Revolve
Sweep
Skin/Loft
Thin/Surface
Fixed Radius Blend
Variable Radius Blend
Vertex Blend
Chamfer
Pattern
Body Operation
Boolean
Slice
Face Delete
Edge Delete
Point
Primitives
[17] Select <Create/Pattern> to copy the insert.

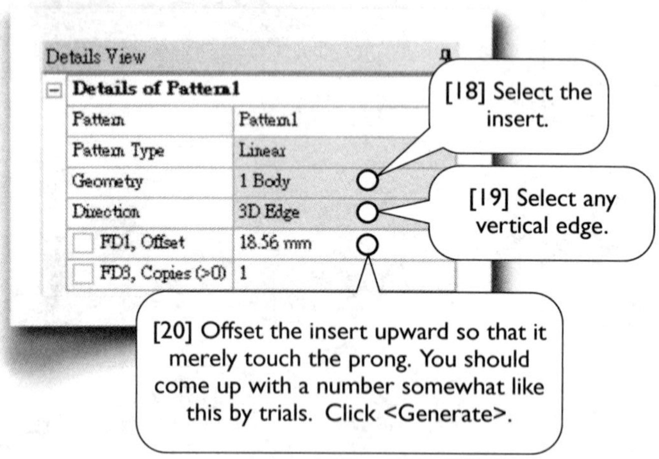
Details View
Details of Pattern1
Pattern | Pattern1
Pattern Type | Linear
Geometry | 1 Body
Direction | 3D Edge
FD1, Offset | 18.56 mm
FD3, Copies (>0) | 1
[18] Select the insert.
[19] Select any vertical edge.
[20] Offset the insert upward so that it merely touch the prong. You should come up with a number somewhat like this by trials. Click <Generate>.

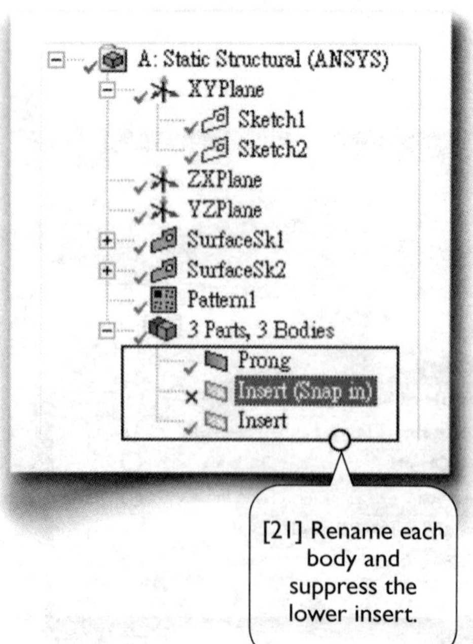
A: Static Structural (ANSYS)
XYPlane
Sketch1
Sketch2
ZXPlane
YZPlane
SurfaceSk1
SurfaceSk2
Pattern1
3 Parts, 3 Bodies
Prong
Insert (Snap in)
Insert
[21] Rename each body and suppress the lower insert.

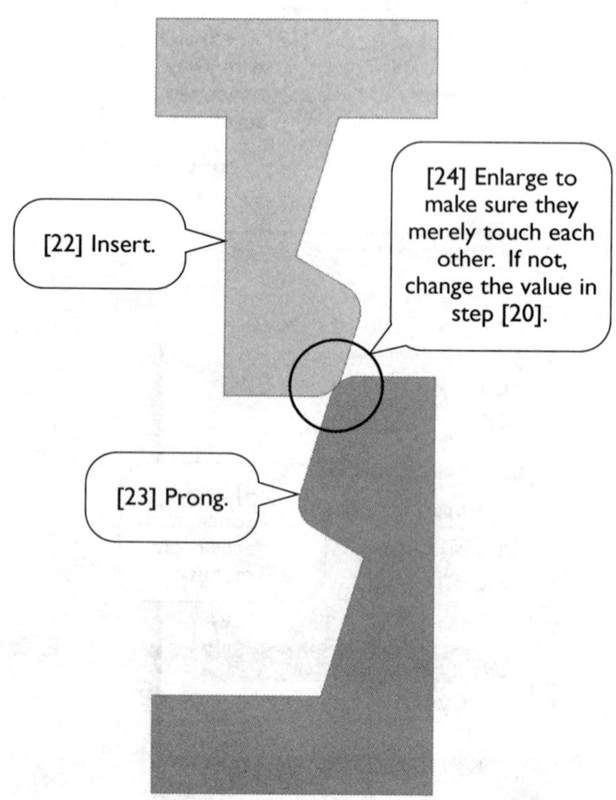
[22] Insert.
[24] Enlarge to make sure they merely touch each other. If not, change the value in step [20].
[23] Prong.

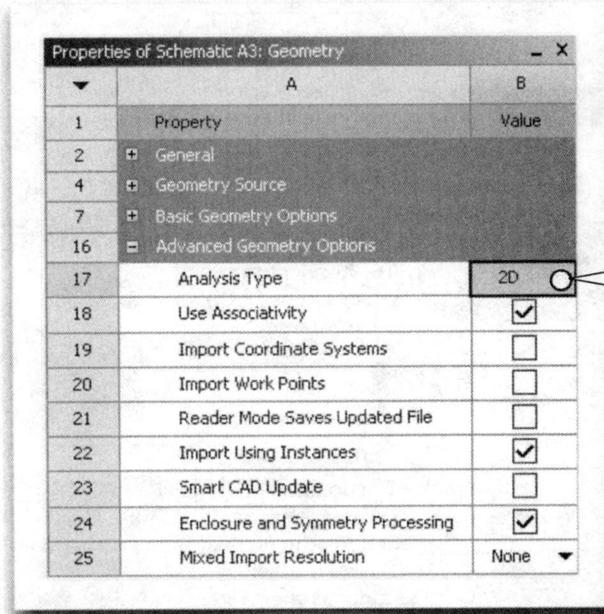

[25] Before attaching the geometry to <Mechanical>, remember to select <2D> option (3.1-4[7]).

13.4-4 Set Up Model

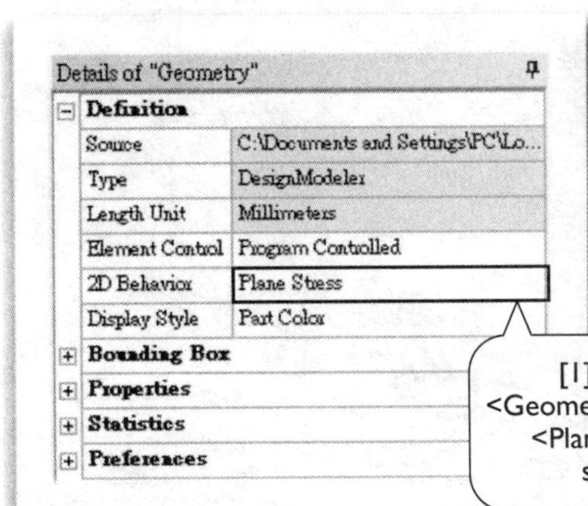

[1] Highlight <Geometry>, make sure <Plane Stress> is selected.

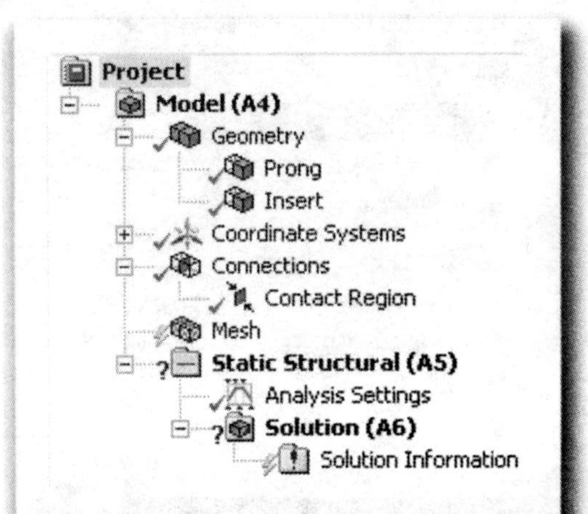

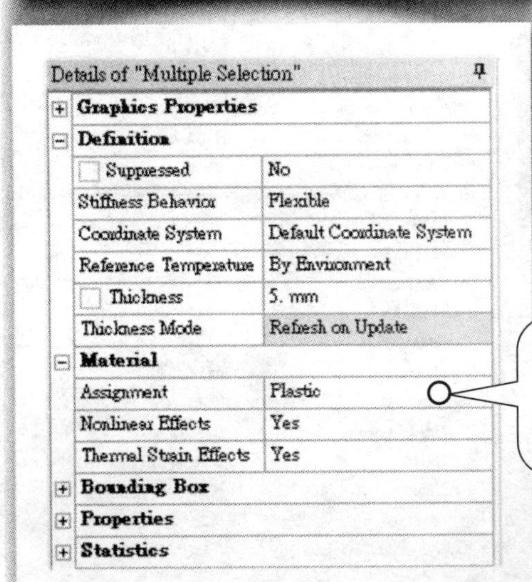

[2] Highlight <Prong> and <Insert>, assign <Plastic> to two bodies.

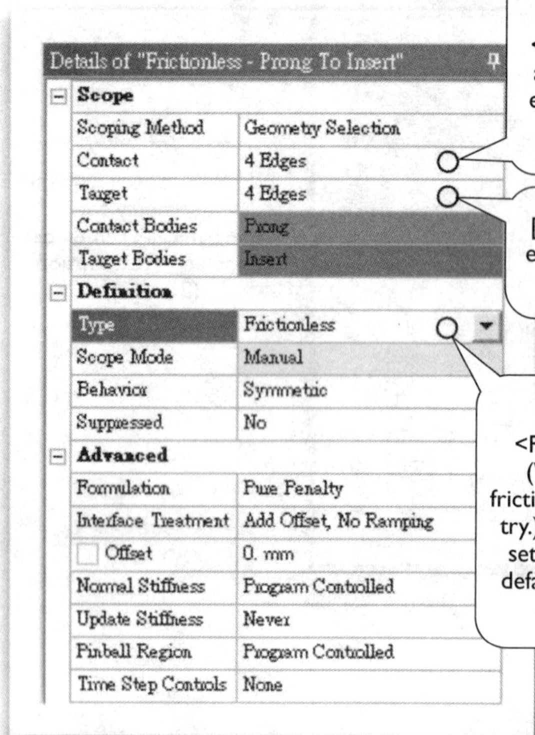

[3] Highlight <Contact Region> and reselect the 4 edges (steps [4, 5]) as <Contact>.

[6] Reselect the 4 edges (steps [7, 8]) as <Target>.

[9] Select <Frictionless>. (We neglect friction for the first try.) Leave other settings as their default values for now.

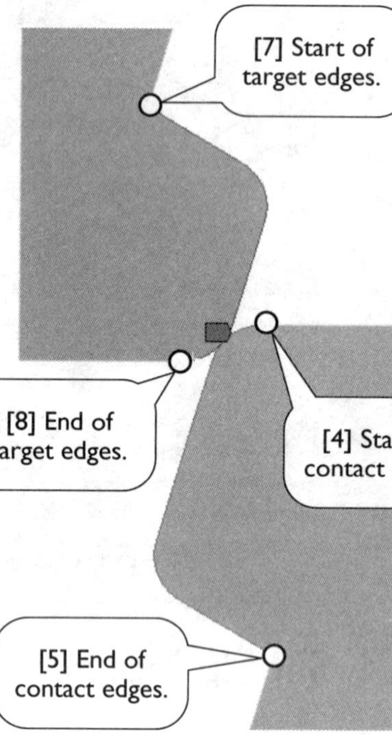

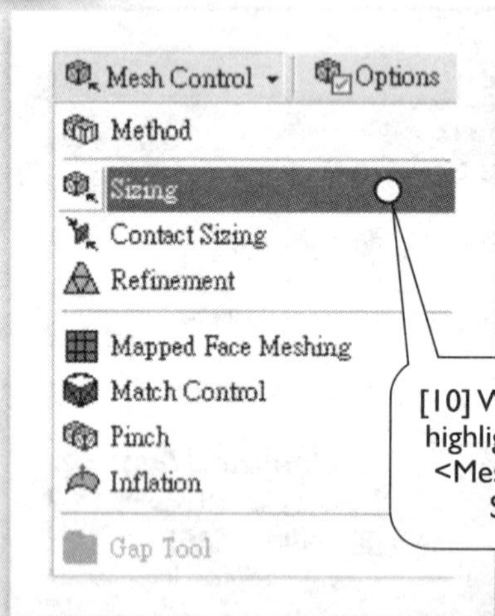

[10] With <Mesh> highlighted, select <Mesh Control/ Sizing>.

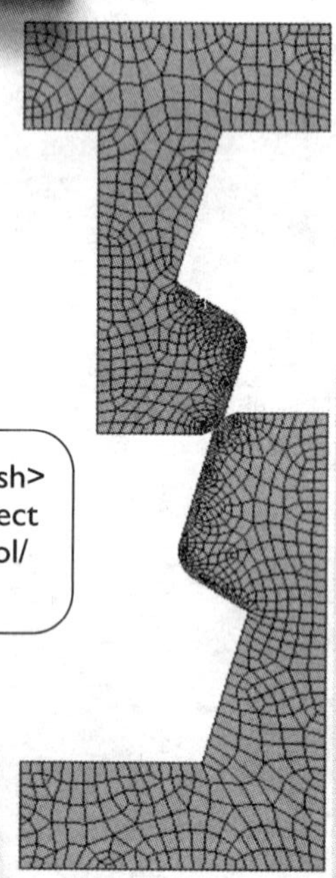

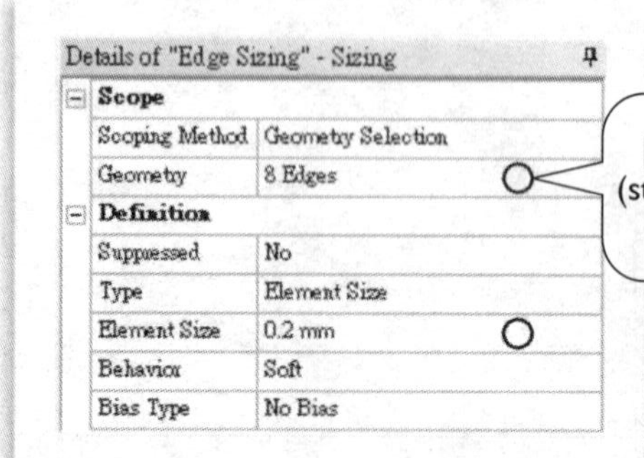

[11] Select all edges (steps [4, 5, 7, 8]) of the contact region.

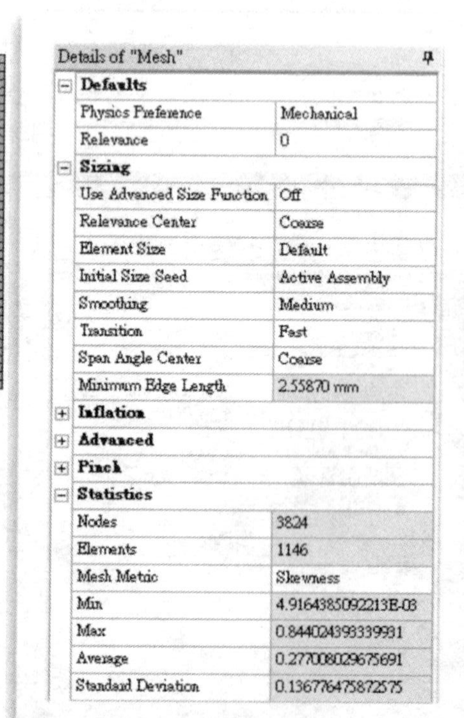

13.4-5 Set Up Analysis Settings

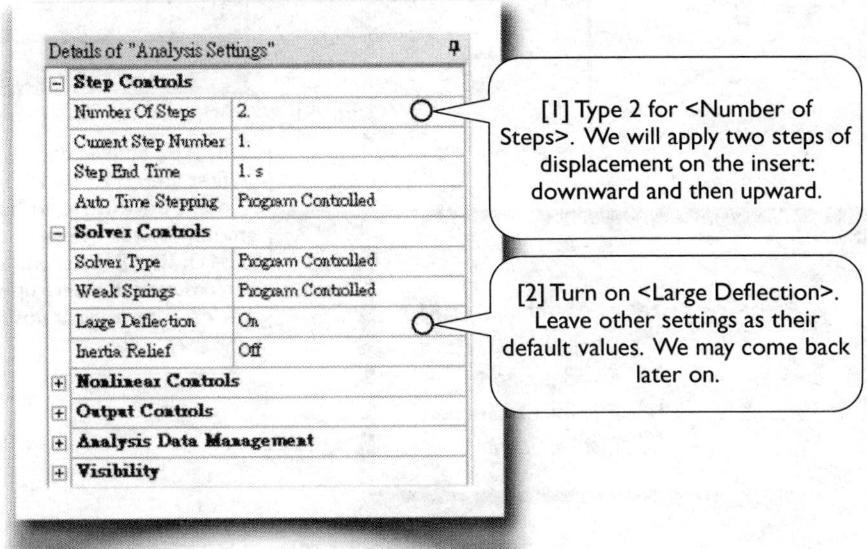

13.4-6 Set Up Environment Conditions

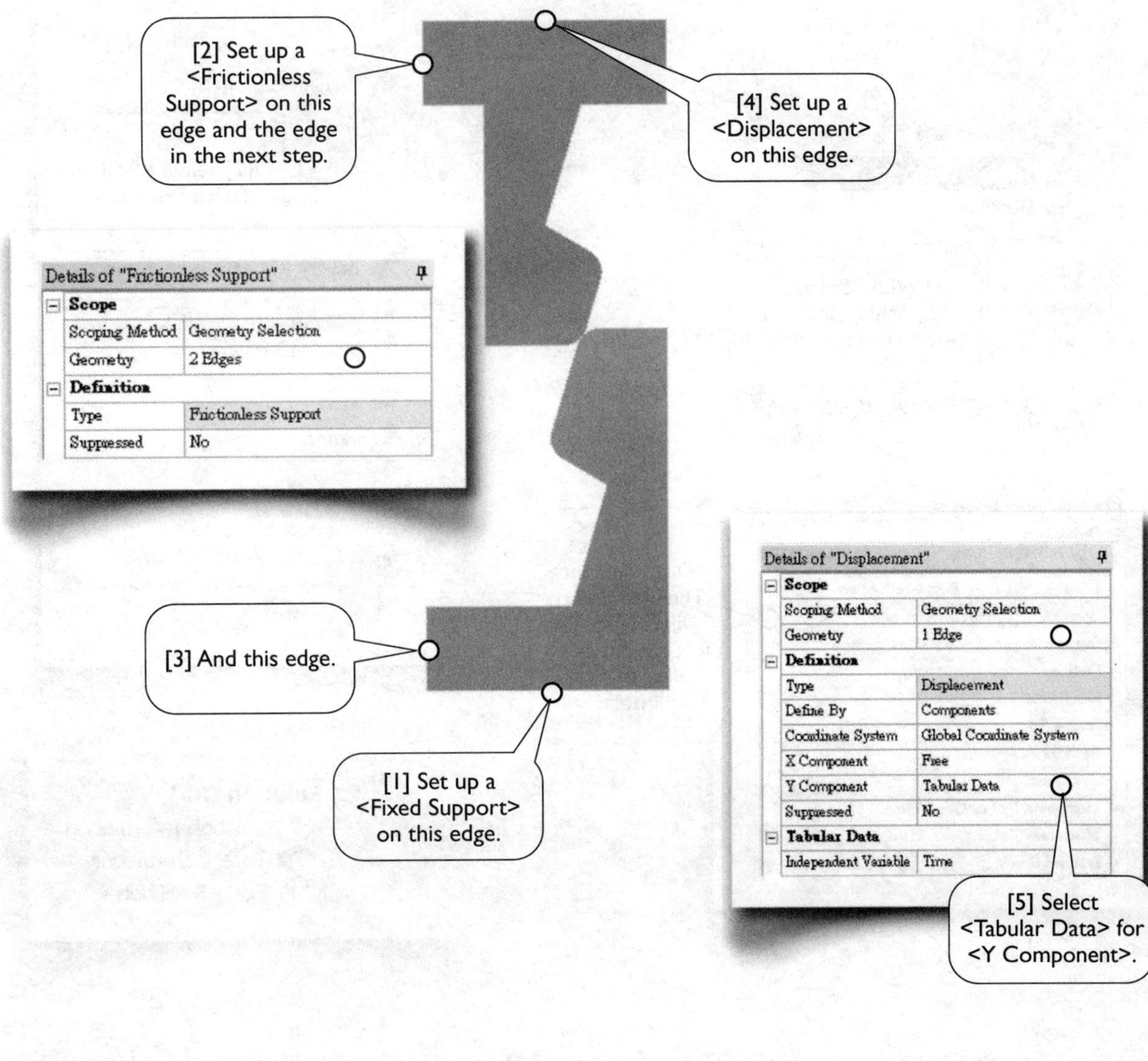

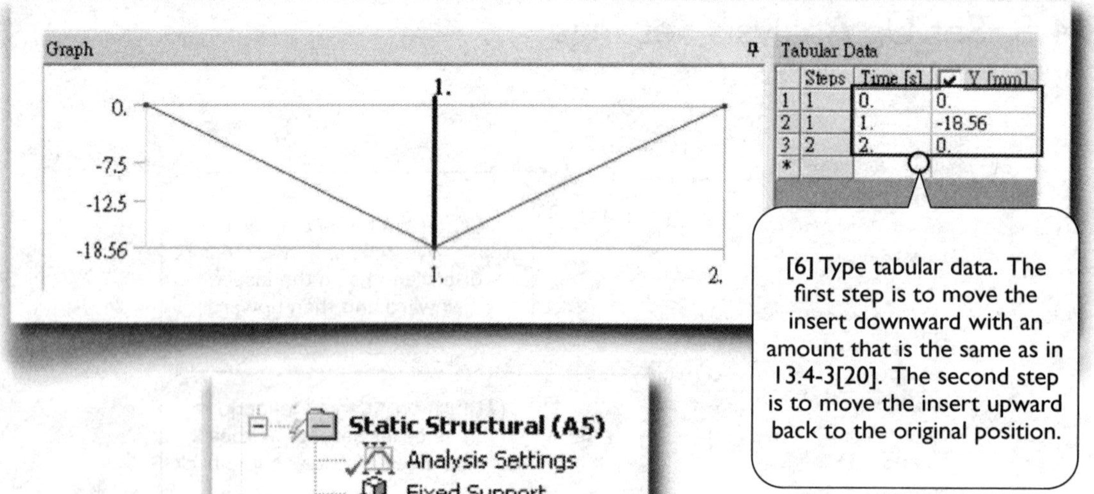

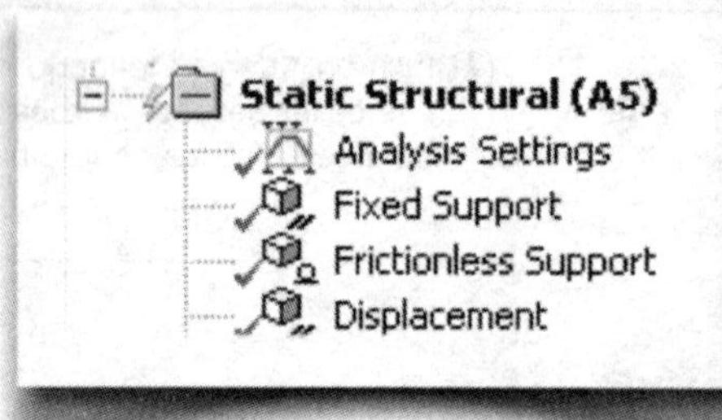

13.4-7 Set Up Result Objects

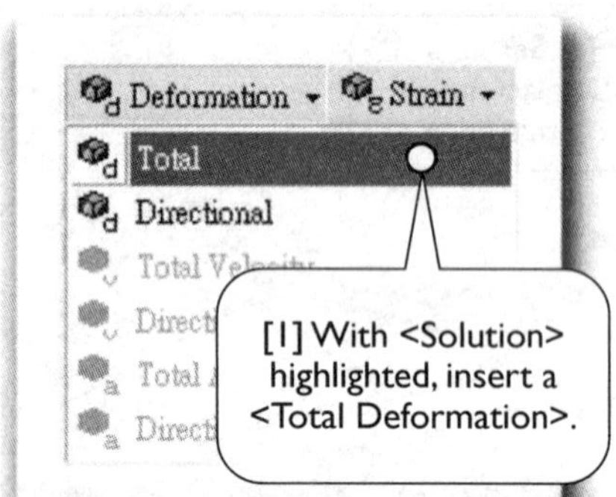

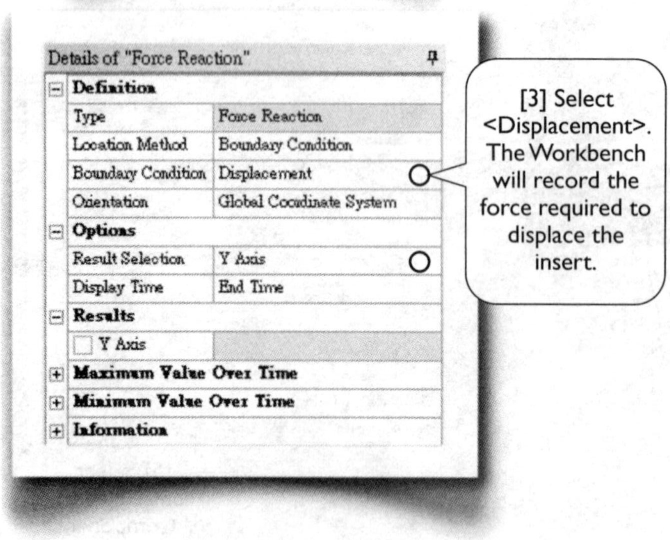

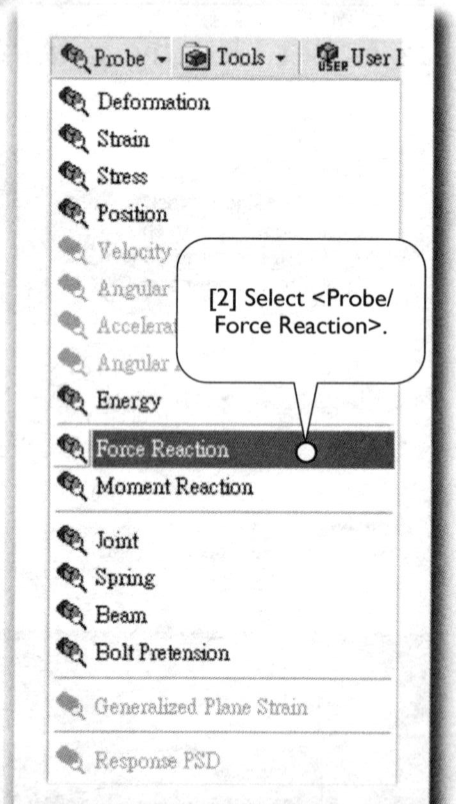

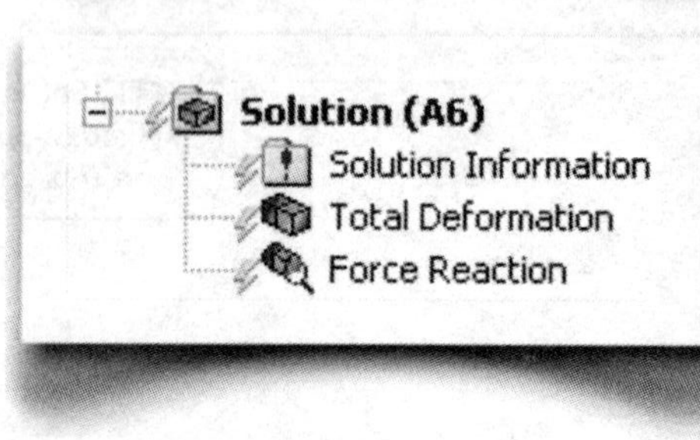

13.4-8 Solve the Model and View the Results

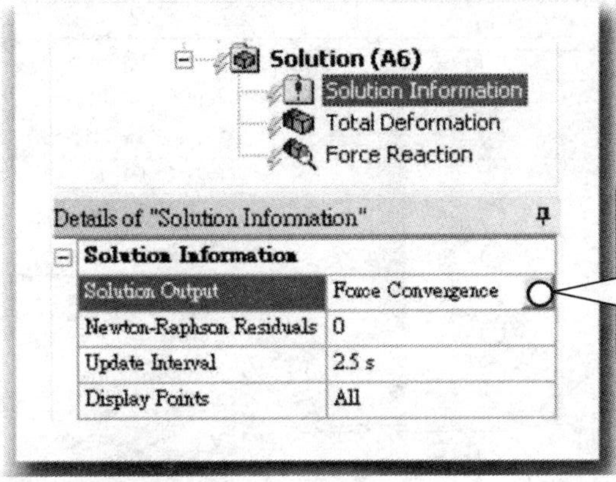

[1] Highlight <Solution Information>, select <Force Convergence>, and click <Solve>.

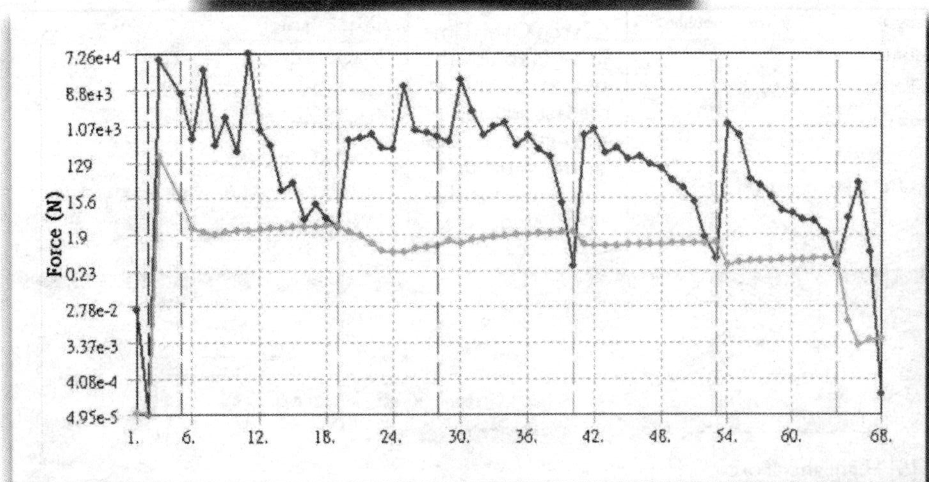

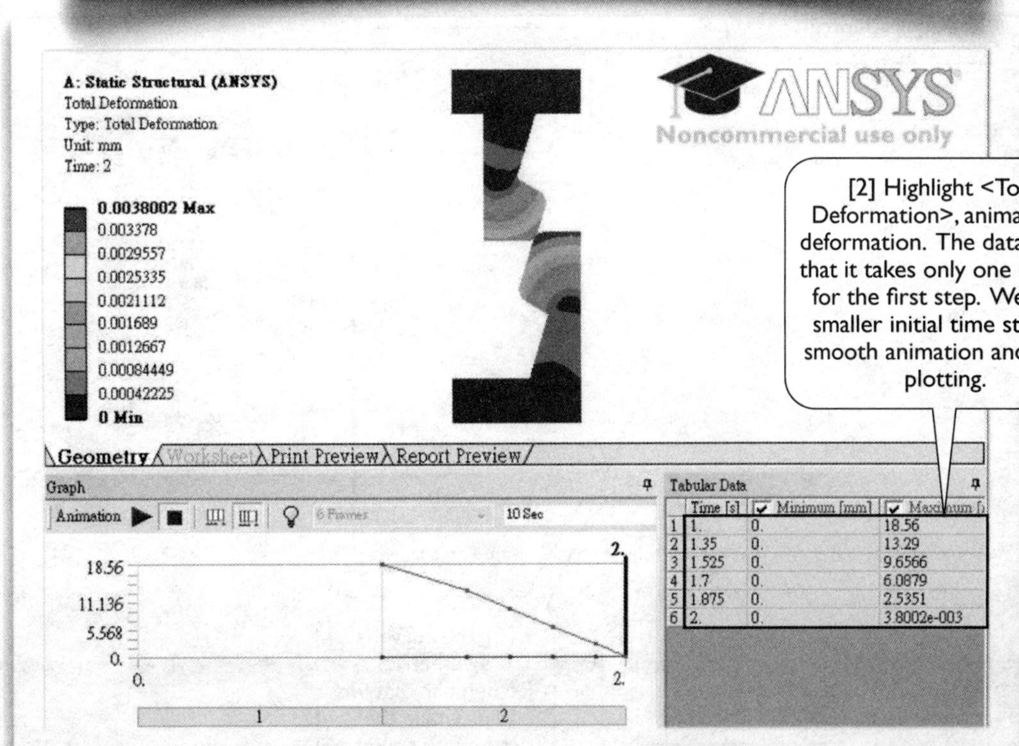

[2] Highlight <Total Deformation>, animate the deformation. The data shows that it takes only one substep for the first step. We need smaller initial time step for smooth animation and curve plotting.

[1] Set up <Analysis Settings> for the first step.

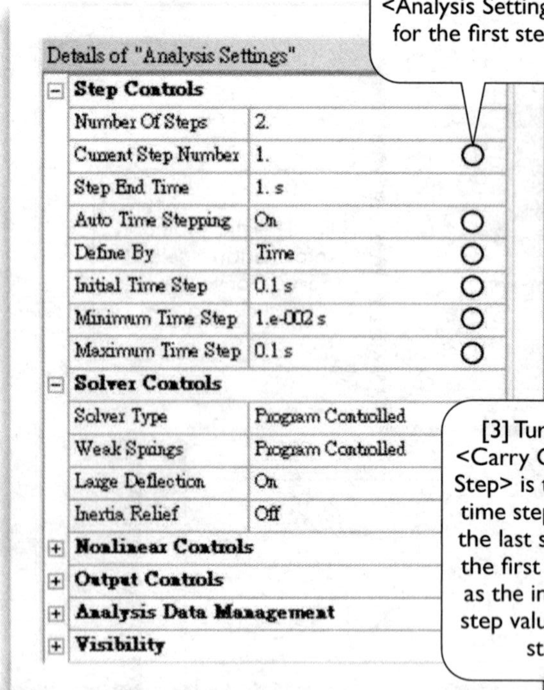

[2] Set up <Analysis Settings> for the second step.

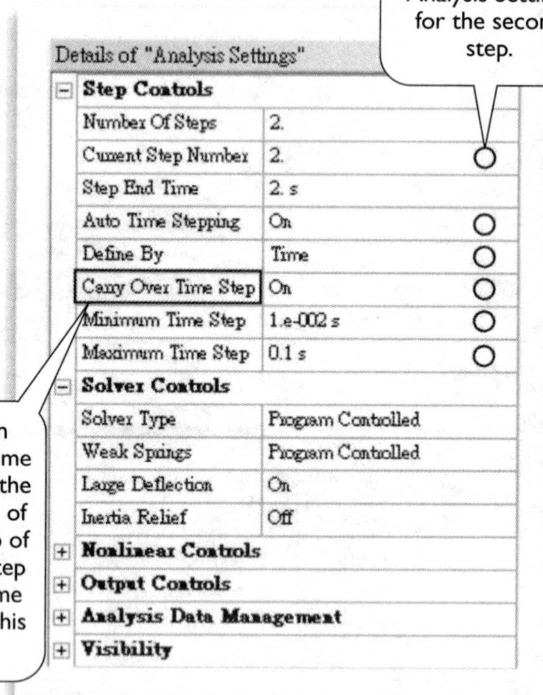

[3] Turning on <Carry Over Time Step> is to use the time step value of the last substep of the first load step as the initial time step value for this step.

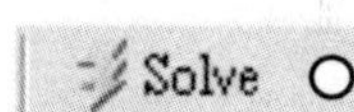

[4] Solve.

[5] Highlight <Force Reaction> to view the required forces.

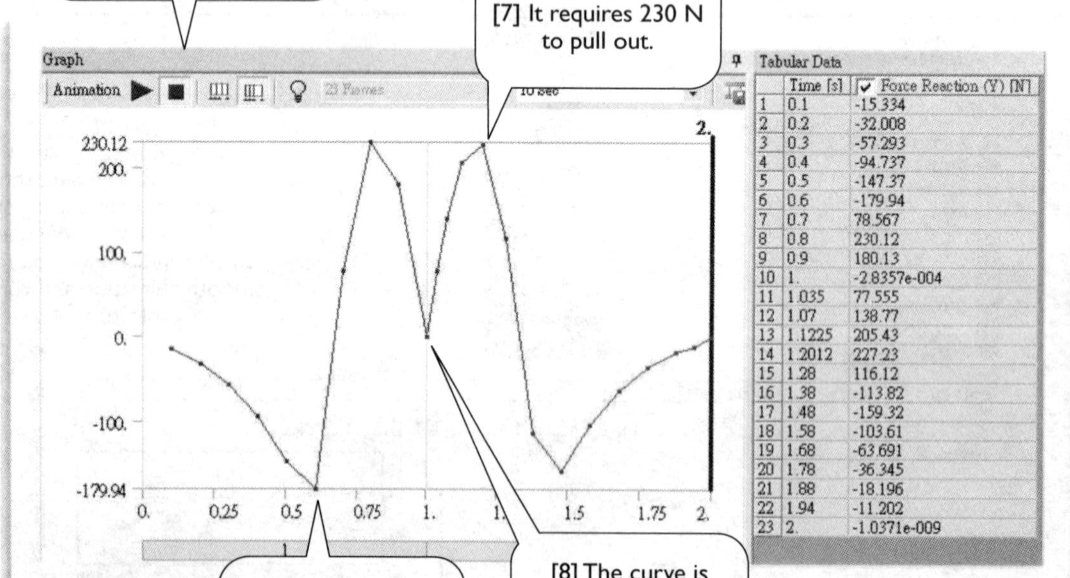

[7] It requires 230 N to pull out.

[6] It requires 180 N to snap in.

[8] The curve is symmetric. Remember that we didn't take the friction into account.

Details of "Frictional - Prong To Insert"

Scope	
Scoping Method	Geometry Selection
Contact	4 Edges
Target	4 Edges
Contact Bodies	Prong
Target Bodies	Insert
Definition	
Type	Frictional
Friction Coefficient	0.2
Scope Mode	Manual
Behavior	Symmetric
Suppressed	No
Advanced	
Formulation	Pure Penalty
Interface Treatment	Add Offset, No Ramping
Offset	0. mm
Normal Stiffness	Program Controlled
Update Stiffness	Never
Pinball Region	Program Controlled
Time Step Controls	None

[9] Highlight <Frictionless - Prong To Insert>, change the <Type> to <Frictional>, and type 0.2 for <Friction Coefficient>

[10] Solve again. It fails after a few iterations, because of too many bisections.

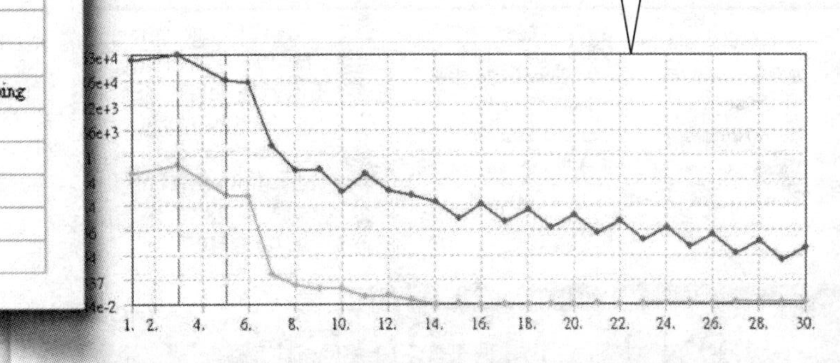

Details of "Analysis Settings"

Step Controls	
Number Of Steps	2.
Current Step Number	1.
Step End Time	1. s
Auto Time Stepping	On
Define By	Time
Initial Time Step	2.e-002 s
Minimum Time Step	2.e-003 s
Maximum Time Step	0.1 s
Solver Controls	
Solver Type	Program Controlled
Weak Springs	Program Controlled
Large Deflection	On
Inertia Relief	Off

[11] Reduce the initial time step to 0.02 s.

Details of "Analysis Settings"

Step Controls	
Number Of Steps	2.
Current Step Number	2.
Step End Time	2. s
Auto Time Stepping	On
Define By	Time
Carry Over Time Step	On
Minimum Time Step	2.e-003 s
Maximum Time Step	0.1 s
Solver Controls	
Solver Type	Program Controlled
Weak Springs	Program Controlled
Large Deflection	On
Inertia Relief	Off

[12] Solve again. It again fails after a few iterations.

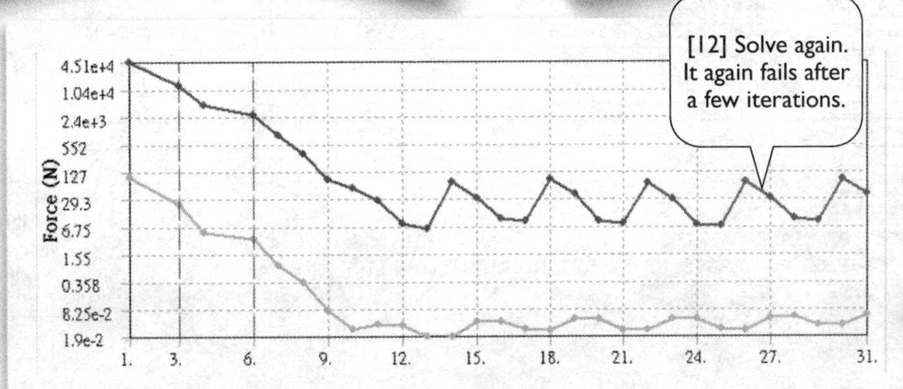

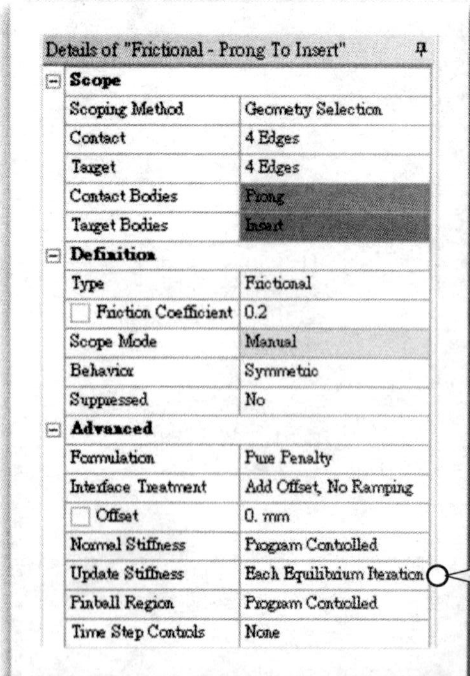

[13] Highlight <Frictional - Prong To Insert>, select <Each Equilibrium Iteration> for <Update Stiffness>. This usually helps convergence.

[14] Solve again. It takes a while (about 25 minutes in my computer) to complete the solution.

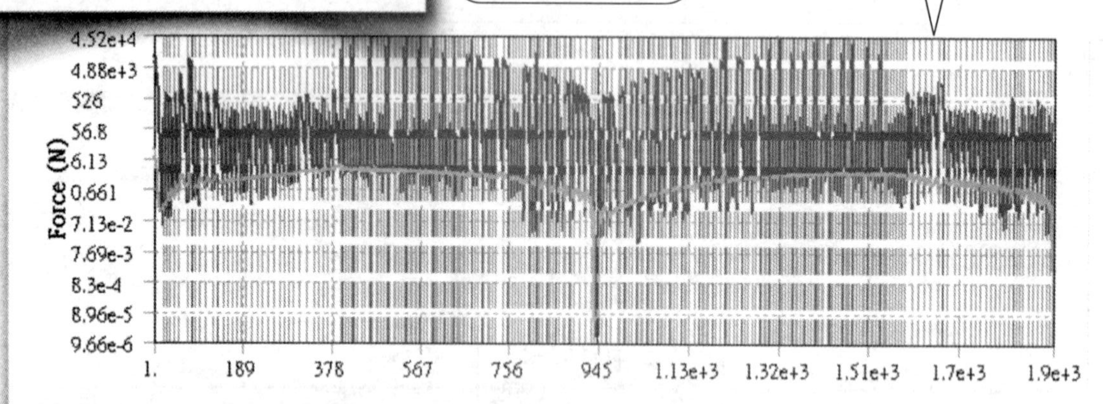


```
 FORCE CONVERGENCE VALUE  =  327.2      CRITERION= 0.2962
EQUIL ITER   1 COMPLETED.  NEW TRIANG MATRIX.  MAX DOF INC= -0.1956
 LINE SEARCH PARAMETER =  0.5779     SCALED MAX DOF INC = -0.1131
 FORCE CONVERGENCE VALUE  =  179.4      CRITERION= 0.2133
EQUIL ITER   2 COMPLETED.  NEW TRIANG MATRIX.  MAX DOF INC=  0.1267E-01
 LINE SEARCH PARAMETER =   1.000     SCALED MAX DOF INC =  0.1267E-01
 FORCE CONVERGENCE VALUE  =  34.92      CRITERION= 0.2253
EQUIL ITER   3 COMPLETED.  NEW TRIANG MATRIX.  MAX DOF INC=  0.1004
 LINE SEARCH PARAMETER =  0.6958     SCALED MAX DOF INC =  0.6985E-01
 FORCE CONVERGENCE VALUE  =  30.58      CRITERION= 0.2916
EQUIL ITER   4 COMPLETED.  NEW TRIANG MATRIX.  MAX DOF INC=  0.1047E-01
 LINE SEARCH PARAMETER =   1.000     SCALED MAX DOF INC =  0.1047E-01
 FORCE CONVERGENCE VALUE  =  5.867      CRITERION= 0.3076
EQUIL ITER   5 COMPLETED.  NEW TRIANG MATRIX.  MAX DOF INC=  0.1734E-01
 LINE SEARCH PARAMETER =  0.8577     SCALED MAX DOF INC =  0.1487E-01
 FORCE CONVERGENCE VALUE  =  2.724      CRITERION= 0.3313
EQUIL ITER   6 COMPLETED.  NEW TRIANG MATRIX.  MAX DOF INC=  0.3472E-0
 LINE SEARCH PARAMETER =   1.000     SCALED MAX DOF INC =  0.3472E-03
 FORCE CONVERGENCE VALUE  = 0.2257      CRITERION= 0.3382      <<< CON
>>> SOLUTION CONVERGED AFTER EQUILIBRIUM ITERATION   6
*** LOAD STEP     2 . SUBSTEP   114  COMPLETED.    CUM ITER =   1889
*** TIME =   1.89395          TIME INC =  0.288325E-01
*** AUTO TIME STEP:  NEXT TIME INC = 0.43249E-01  INCREASED (FACTOR = 1.5000)
```

[15] Many of line search take place.

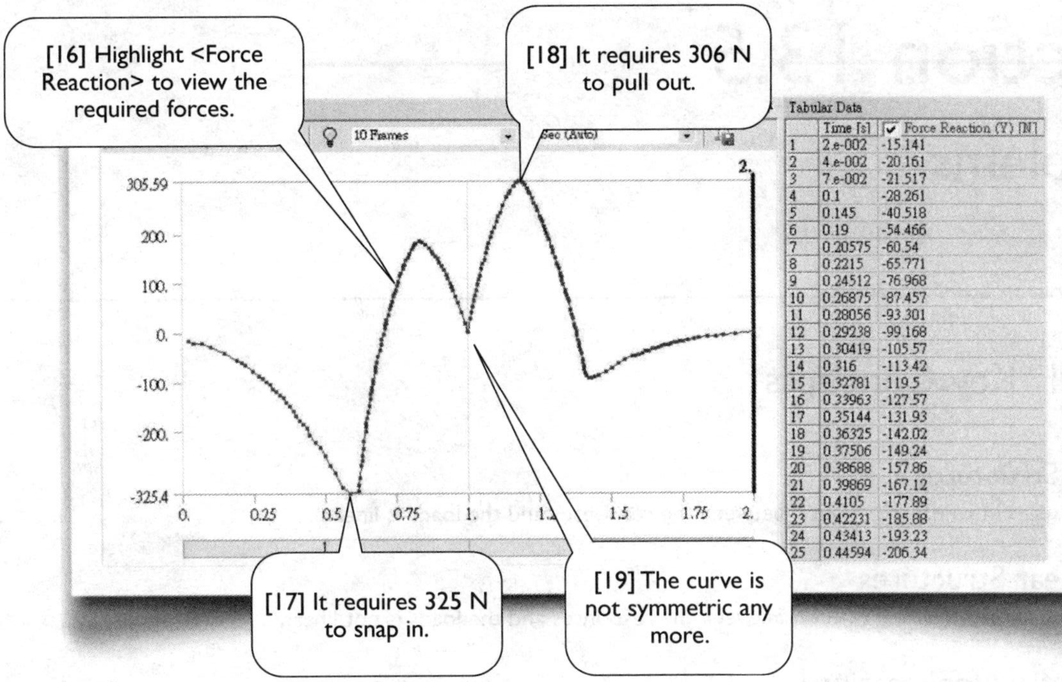

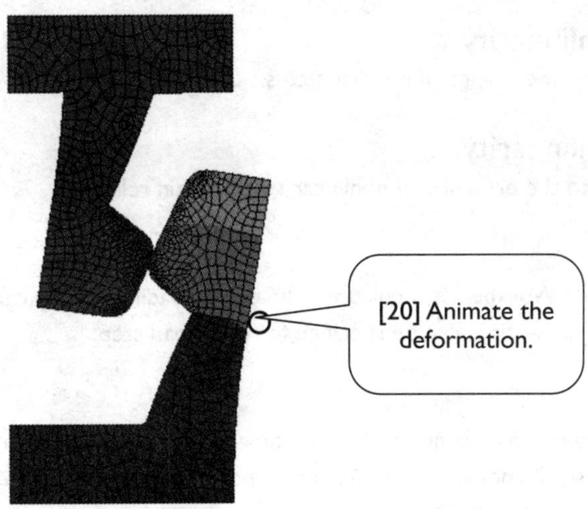

Wrap Up

Save the project and exit Workbench.

Section 13.5

Problems

13.5-1 Key Concepts

Linear Structures
The structures in which the relation between the responses and the loads is linear.

Nonlinear Structures
The structures in which the relation between the responses and the loads is not linear.

Geometry Nonlinearity
Nonlinearity due to large deformation.

Contact Nonlinearity
Nonlinearity due to the change of contact status.

Material Nonlinearity
Nonlinearity due to the presence of nonlinear stress-strain relation.

Load Steps
Also called steps. In Workbench simulations, the entire loading history can be divided into one or more load steps, so that different analysis settings can be specified for each load step.

Substeps
Also called time steps. In dynamic simulations, time step size is used for integration over the time domain; the time step size must be small enough to capture the response characteristics. In static simulation, a load step can be divided into substeps small enough to achieve or enhance convergence.

Equilibrium Iterations
Also called iterations. For nonlinear problems, each time step needs several iterations to complete. For linear problems, each time step requires exactly one equilibrium iteration.

Newton-Raphson Method
The method used by Workbench to solve a substep in a nonlinear simulation. External force of that substep is applied. Equilibrium equation is solved for the displacement using the tangent stiffness. Internal force is calculated using updated displacement and stiffness. This completes an iteration. The process iterates until all the active convergence criteria are satisfied.

Residual Force
During the Newton-Raphson equilibrium iterations, the difference between external force and the calculated internal force is call a residual force.

Force Convergence

A substep is said to satisfy the force convergence when the norm of the residual force is less than a criterion.

Displacement Convergence

A substep is said to satisfy the displacement convergence when the norm of the difference of displacements between two iteration is less than a criterion.

Moment Convergence

When shell or beam elements are used in a model, moment convergence can be activated. A substep is said to satisfy the moment convergence when the norm of the residual moment is less than a criterion.

Rotation Convergence

When shell or beam elements are used in a model, rotation convergence can be activated. A substep is said to satisfy the rotation convergence when the norm of the difference of rotations between two iteration is less than a criterion.

Line Search

In some cases when a force-displacement relation is highly nonlinear or "concave up," during the Newton-Rapshon iterations of a substep, the calculated displacement in a single iteration may overshoot the goal. In such cases, a numerical technique called line search can be activated to "scale down" the incremental displacement. Line search often helps convergence, but takes extra computing time.

13.5-2 Workbench Exercises

Contact Stiffness Study

In Section 13.1-10, when introducing <Pure Penalty> formulation, we mentioned that, in many cases, solution convergence behavior may be sensitive to the <Normal Stiffness>. VM63[1] of the <Verification Manual for the Mechanical APDL Application> is a good exercise to study this behavior. First, complete a simulation using all the parameters given in the verification manual, and verify the solution with the verification manual. Next, increase the Young's modulus from the original value (1 GPa) to 200 GPa (which is the Young's modulus of steel). This should creates a convergence difficulty. When you run into a convergence difficulty, try to ease the difficulty by decreasing the <Normal Stiffness>. This will introduces more penetration into the solution. Tabulate data (or draw curve) to show how <Normal Stiffness> affects penetration and other results.

Reference

1. ANSYS Help System>Mechanical APDL>Verification Manual for the Mechanical APDL Application>I. Verification Test Case Descriptions>VM63

Chapter 14
Nonlinear Materials

When the stress-strain relation of a material is linear, it is called a *linear material*. On the other hand, if the stress-strain relation is not linear, it is called a *nonlinear material*. Stress-strain relation of a linear material can be expressed by Hooke's law, Eq. 1.2-8(1) (or 1.2-8(3)), in which two independent material parameters are used to completely defined the stress-strain relation. Note that Eq. 1.2-8(1) assumes an isotropic material properties, that is, the Young's modulus and the Poisson's ratio are independent of directions. So far, in our foregoing simulations, we assumed the materials are linear.

In reality, most of materials exhibit more or less nonlinearity. In many cases, the nonlinearities are negligible, and we use Hooke's law to describe the stress-strain relation. In some other cases, when the material nonlinearities are not negligible, *nonlinear material models* must be used to define stress-strain relations. A material model is usually a mathematics form with some parameters, called *material parameters*. To fully define a material, you select a material model and provide the material parameters. The material parameters are usually obtained by data-fitting the results of a series of material testings.

Purpose of the Chapter
The Workbench provides a variety of nonlinear material models. In this chapter, we will introduced two categories of nonlinear material models: *plasticity* and *hyperelasticity*. Background knowledge will be introduced first, and two step-by-step exercises will follow to demonstrate their applications.

About Each Section
Section 1 gives basics of plasticity and hyperelasticity. Section 2 provides a step-by-step example to demonstrate the use of a plastic material model. Section 3 uses another step-by-step example demonstrate the application of a hyperelastic material model.

Section 14.1

Basics of Nonlinear Materials

PART A. INTRODUCTION

14.1-1 Linear versus Nonlinear Materials

When the stress-stain relation of a material is linear, it is called a *linear material* [1], otherwise the material is called a *nonlinear material.* For a linear material, the stress-strain relation is expressed by Hooke's law, Eq. 1.2-8(1), in which two independent material parameters are needed to completely define the material. Note that Eq. 1.2-8(1) assumes an isotropic material properties, that is, the Young's modulus and the Poisson's ratio are independent of directions. Generalization of Eq. 1.2-8(1) to include orthotropic elasticity is available in the Workbench [2].

Besides a linear relation, the Hooke's law also implies that the stress-strain relation is (a) elastic, (b) time-independent, and (c) rate-independent. Materials that violate any of these behaviors cannot be described by the Hooke's law, and are categorized as nonlinear materials, even though the stress-strain relation is linear for both stressing and unstressing [3].

The Workbench provides non-elastic material model, called plastic material models. Current version of Workbench does not provide time-dependent models (also called creep models) or rate-dependent models. It is available only through the use of APDL.

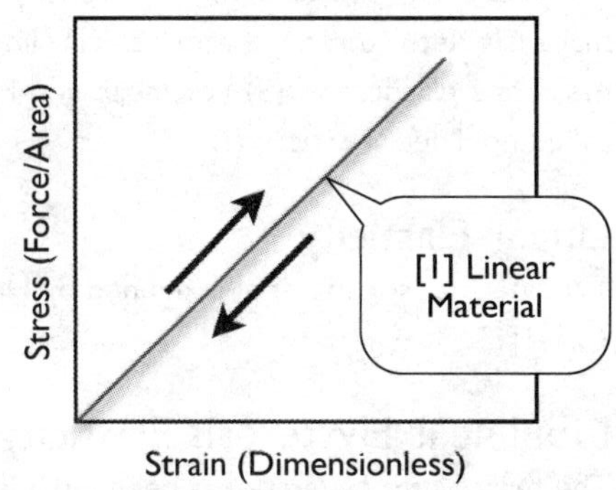

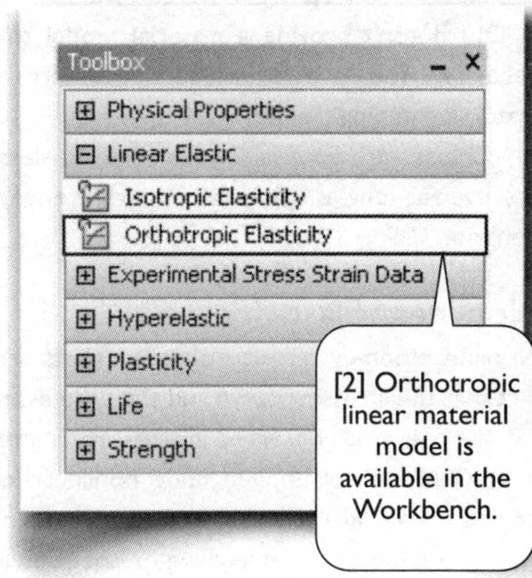

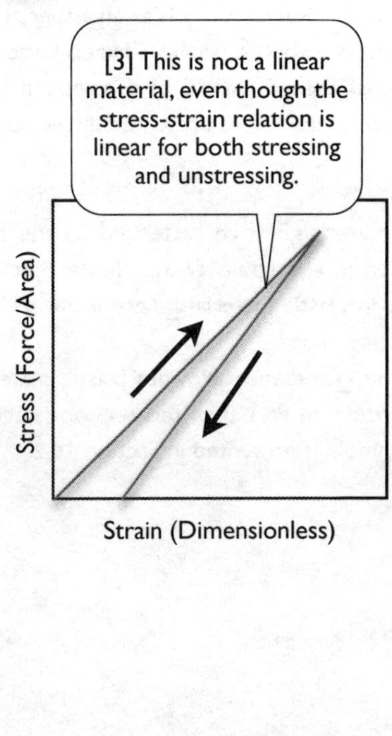

Time-Dependent Stress-Strain Relations

When you apply a stress on a steel, the strain occurs instantaneously and remains the same forever. This statement is not strictly true. A more rigorous statement should be like this, "The strain occurs ALMOST instantaneously and ALMOST remains the same forever."

Consider a big water tank made of plastic material. Starting from the moment right after you fill up the water, the plastic tank begins to deform: the diameter expands slowly. It may takes months until the deformation stops. This teaches us a lesson that the deformation may take time. This time-dependent stress-strain behavior is called creeping, or viscosity.

For the steel under room temperature, the creeping behavior is practically negligible. In engineering practice, we often neglect creeping for solid materials under a fairly lower temperature, for example, below half of the melting point.

We will not discuss time-dependent behavior for the rest of this chapter.

14.1-2 Elastic versus Plastic Materials

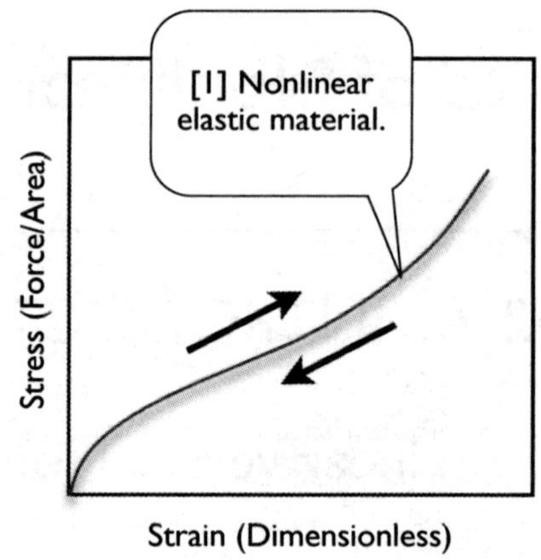

In 14.1-1[3], the strain is not totally recovered after complete release of the stress. This behavior is called plasticity, and the residual strain is called a plastic strain. If the strain is totally recoverable, that is, there is no residual strain after complete release of stress, the behavior is called elasticity, and the material is said to be elastic.

Following this definition of elasticity, we may classify the elastic materials into three categories: (1) linear elastic, (2) nonlinear hysteresis elastic, and (3) nonlinear non-hysteresis elastic, or simply called nonlinear elastic.

Linear Elasticity

The linear elastic material is defined by Hooke's law and depicted in 14.1-1[1].

Nonlinear Hysteresis Elasticity

The term *elastic hysteresis* has been introduced in Section 12.1-3, and depicted in 12.1-3[3-5]. The current version of ANSYS (including APDL) doesn't provide a material model to include the hysteresis behavior. You have to include the hysteresis behavior in terms of material damping (Section 12.1-3).

Most of materials have more-or-less hysteresis behavior, however, as long as it is small enough, we may neglect the hysteresis behavior.

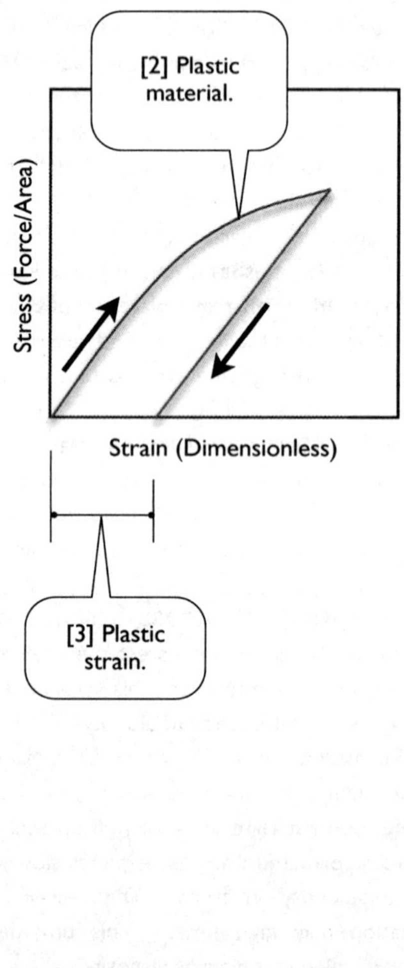

Nonlinear Elasticity

Nonlinear non-hysteresis elastic materials are characterized by the fact that the stressing curve and the unstressing curve are coincident [1]: the energy is conserved in stressing-unstressing cycles.

Challenge of implementing nonlinear elastic material models comes from that the strain may be as large as 100% or even 200%, such as rubber under stretching or compression. This kind of super-large deformation elasticity is given a special name: *hyperelasticity*.

The Workbench provides hyperelastic material models and we will discuss them in Part C of this section (starting from 14.1-7). A step-by-step example is presented in Section 14.3.

Plasticity

Plastic materials are characterized by the presence of the residual strain, or plastic strain [2-3]. Note that the hysteresis is always present in plastic materials: there is always energy loss in stressing-unstressing cycles.

The Workbench provides plastic material models and we will discuss them in Part B of this section (starting 14.1-3). A step-by-step example is presented in Section 14.2.

PART B. PLASTICITY

14.1-3 Idealized Stress-Strain Curve for Plasticity

Plasticity behavior typically occurs in ductile metals subject to large deformation. Plastic strain results from slip between planes of atoms due to shear stresses. This dislocation deformation is a rearrangement of atoms in the crystal structure.

In the Workbench, a typical stress-strain relation, such as 14.1-2[2], is idealized to the one as shown [1-4]. The stress-strain curve is composed of several straight segments. The slope of the first segment is the Young's modulus [3]. When the stress is released, the strain decreases with a slope equal to the Young's modulus [4]. This implies that if the stress/strain state is on the first segment, the behavior is elastic: no plastic strain remains after releasing the stress. The point at the end of the first segment is called *elastic limit*, or *initial yield point*. All points higher than the initial yield point are called *subsequent yield points*, since they all represent yielding state.

A stress-strain relation such as [1-4] is not sufficient to fully define a plasticity behavior. There are other questions that must be answered: (a) What is the yield criterion? (b) What is the hardening rule?

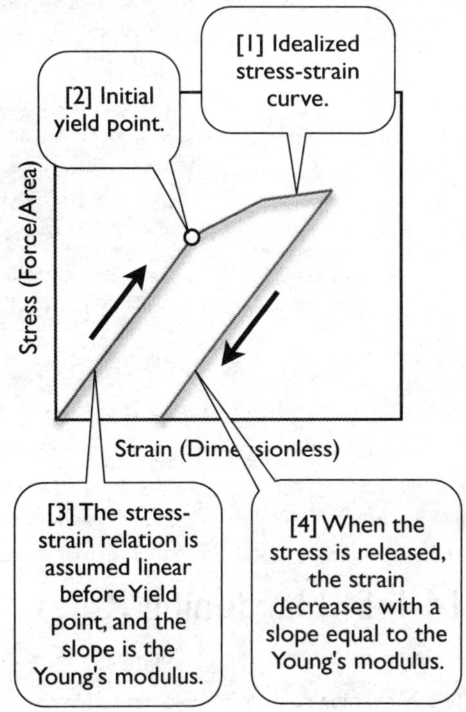

14.1-4 Yield Criteria

A stress-strain curve such as 14.1-3[1-4] is usually obtained by a uniaxial tensile test. It provides an initial yield strength σ_y of uniaxial tensile test. In three-dimensional cases, the stress state is multiaxial. According to what criteria can we say that a stress state reaches a yield state? The Workbench uses von Mises criterion (Section 1.4-5) as the yield criterion, that is, a stress state reaches yield state when the von Mises stress σ_e is equal to the *current uniaxial yield strength* σ_y', or

$$\sqrt{\frac{1}{2}\left[(\sigma_1-\sigma_2)^2+(\sigma_2-\sigma_3)^2+(\sigma_3-\sigma_1)^2\right]}=\sigma_y' \tag{1}$$

The yielding initially occurs when $\sigma_y' = \sigma_y$, and the "current" uniaxial yield strength σ_y' may change subsequently. As mentioned at the end of Section 1.4-5, when plotted in the $\sigma_1 - \sigma_2 - \sigma_3$ space, Eq. (1) is a cylindrical surface aligned with the axis $\sigma_1 = \sigma_2 = \sigma_3$ and with a radius of $\sqrt{2}\sigma_y'$. It is called a *von Mises yield surface* [1]. If the stress state is inside the cylinder, no yielding occurs. If the stress state is on the surface, yielding occurs. No stress state can exist outside the yield surface. If the stress state is on the surface and the stress state continue to "push" the yield surface outward, the size (radius) or the location of the yield surface will change. The rule that describes how the yield surface changes its size or location is called a *hardening rule*.

The concept of yield surface is worth emphasis again. In a uniaxial test, we are talking about "yield points" in stress axis. In a biaxial case, the yielding state form a "yield line," while in a 3D cases, the yielding state is a "yield surface."

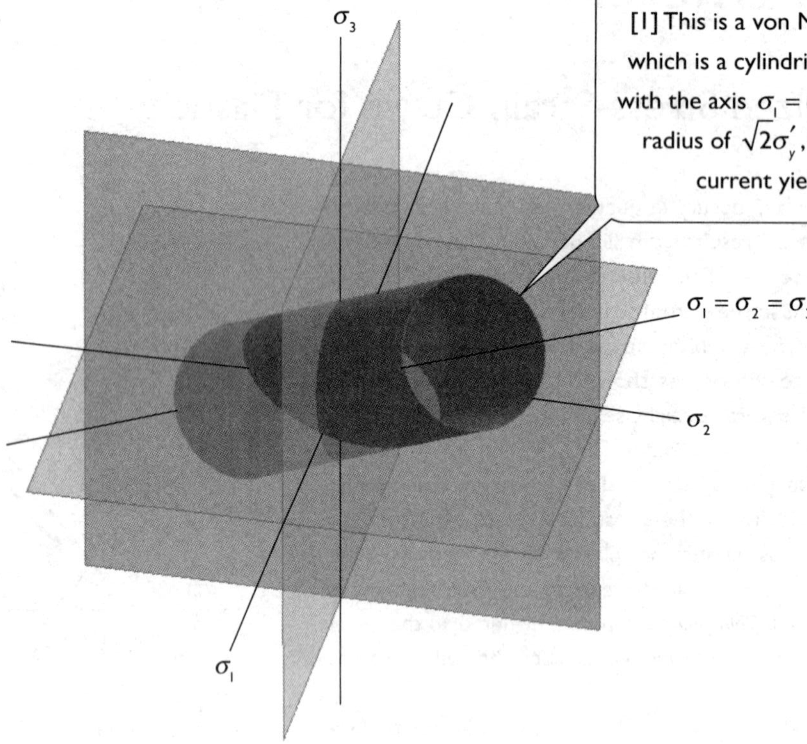

[1] This is a von Mises yield surface, which is a cylindrical surface aligned with the axis $\sigma_1 = \sigma_2 = \sigma_3$ and with a radius of $\sqrt{2}\sigma_y'$, where σ_y' is the current yield strength.

14.1-5 Hardening Rules

Two hardening rules are implemented in the Workbench: (a) kinematic hardening, and (b) isotropic hardening. It should be noted that, in metal plasticity, hardening behavior is often a mix-up of kinematic and isotropic. Since the Workbench implements only two extremities, you have to choose either one that is suitable to describe your application.

Kinematic Hardening

The kinematic hardening assumes that, when a stress state continues to "push" a yield surface outward, the yield surface will change its location, according to the "push direction," but preserve the size of the yield surface. In a uniaxial test, It is equivalent to say that the difference between the tensile yield strength and the compressive yield strength remains a constant of $2\sigma_y$ [1].

Kinematic hardening is generally used for small strain, cyclic loading applications.

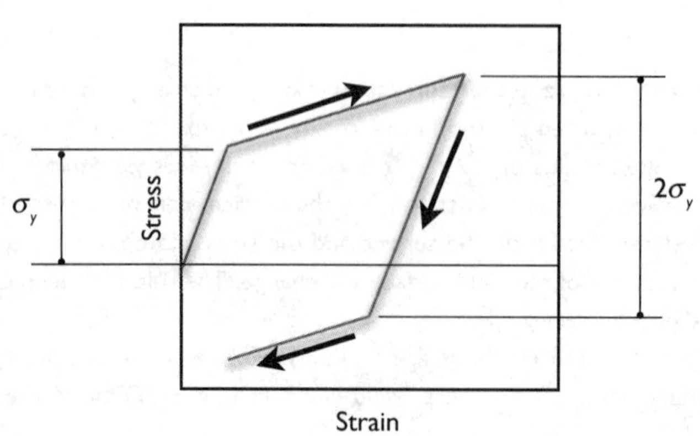

[1] The kinematic hardening assumes that the difference between tensile yield strength and the compressive yield strength remains a constant of $2\sigma_y$.

Isotropic Hardening

The isotropic hardening assumes that, when a stress state continues to "push" a yield surface, the yield surface will expand its size, but preserve the axis of the yield surface. It is equivalent to say that, in a uniaxial test, the tensile yield strength and the compressive yield strength remain equal in magnitude [2].

Isotropic hardening is often used for large strain simulations. It is usually not applicable for cyclic loading applications.

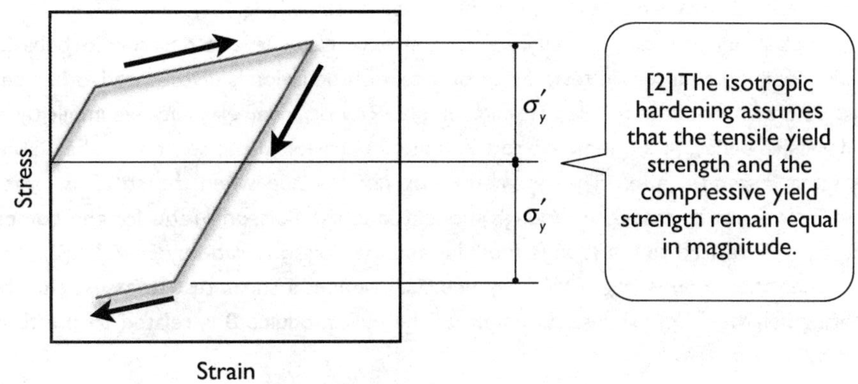

14.1-6 Plasticity Models in Workbench

The Workbench provides four plasticity models [1]. Besides choosing from either of hardening rules, you can choose from either type of stress-strain curves: bilinear or multilinear.

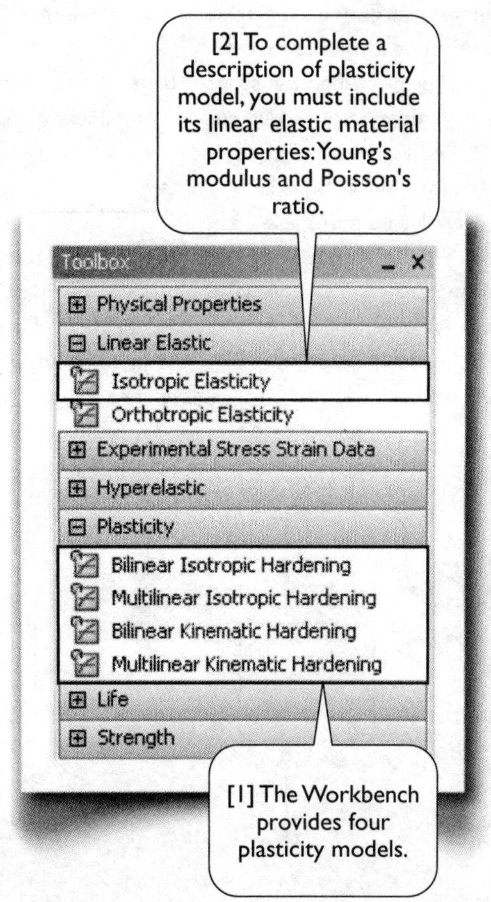

Linear Elastic Material Properties Must be Supplied

To describe a material model for plasticity, you must include a set of linear elastic material properties (Young's modulus and Poisson's ratio). The Young's modulus is used for the slope of the first segment of the stress-strain curve, in which the material behaves as linear elasticity.

Bilinear Stress-Strain Curve

Examples of bilinear models are shown in 14.1-5[1-2]; the stress-strain curve is composed by two straight segments. Besides the Young's modulus and Poisson's ratio, you need to supply an *initial yield stress* and a *tangent modulus* (the slope for the second segment).

Multilinear Stress-Strain Curve

An example of multilinear models is shown in 14.1-3[1-4]; the stress-strain curve is composed by several straight segments. Besides the Young's modulus and Poisson's ratio, you need to supply a tabular form of data describing the *subsequent yield stresses* and the corresponding *plastic strains*. A hands-on example will be shown in Section 14.2.

PART C. HYPERELASTICITY

14.1-7 Test Data Needed for Hyperelasticity

As mentioned in Section 14.1-2, challenge of implementing nonlinear elastic models comes from that the strain may be as large as 100% or even 200%, such as rubber under stretching.

In plasticity or linear elasticity, we use a stress-strain curve to describe its behavior, and the stress-strain curve is usually obtained by a tensile test. Since only tension behavior is investigated, other behaviors (compression, shearing) must be drawn from the tensile test data. In plasticity or linear elasticity, we implicitly made some assumptions: (a) The compressive behavior is symmetric to the tension behavior in the sense that they have the same Young's modulus, and the same Poisson's ratio. The symmetry may not be true when the strain is large. We may need to conduct a compressive test to assess the Young's modulus and the Poisson's ratio for the compressive behavior. (b) The shear modulus G is related to the Young's modulus and the Poisson's ratio by Eq. 1.2-8(2). Again, this assumption may not be true when the strain is large. We may need to conduct a shear test to assess the shear modulus for describing the shearing behavior. (c) We also assume that the bulk modulus B is related to the Young's modulus and the Poisson's ratio by

$$B = \frac{E}{3(1-2\nu)} \qquad (1)$$

Again, this assumption may not be true when the strain is large. We may need to conduct a volumetric test to assess the bulk modulus for describing the volumetric behavior. Note that, in many cases, the bulk modulus is almost infinitely large (i.e., the material is incompressible). For these cases, we usually assume incompressibility without conducting a volumetric test.

Further, when the strain is large, all the moduli (tensile, compressive, shear, and bulk) are no longer constant; they change along stress-strain curves. Nonlinear elasticity with large strain is also called *hyperelasticity*.

As a summary, to describe hyperelasticity behavior, we need following test data: (a) a set of uniaxial tensile test data, (b) a set of uniaxial compressive test data, (c) a set of shear test data, and (d) a set of volumetric test data if the material is compressible.

Note that it is possible that a set of test data is obtained by superposing two sets of other test data. For example, the set of uniaxial compressive test data can be obtained by adding a set of hydrostatic compressive test data to a set of equibiaxial tensile test data [1-3]. Reasons of doing this are as follows. (a) Biaxial tesile test may be easier to conduct than compressive test in some testing devices; (b) For incompressible materials, hydrostatic compressive test data are trivial: all strains have zero values.

An example of test data for hyperelasticity is shown below [4-6], which will be used in of Section 14.3.

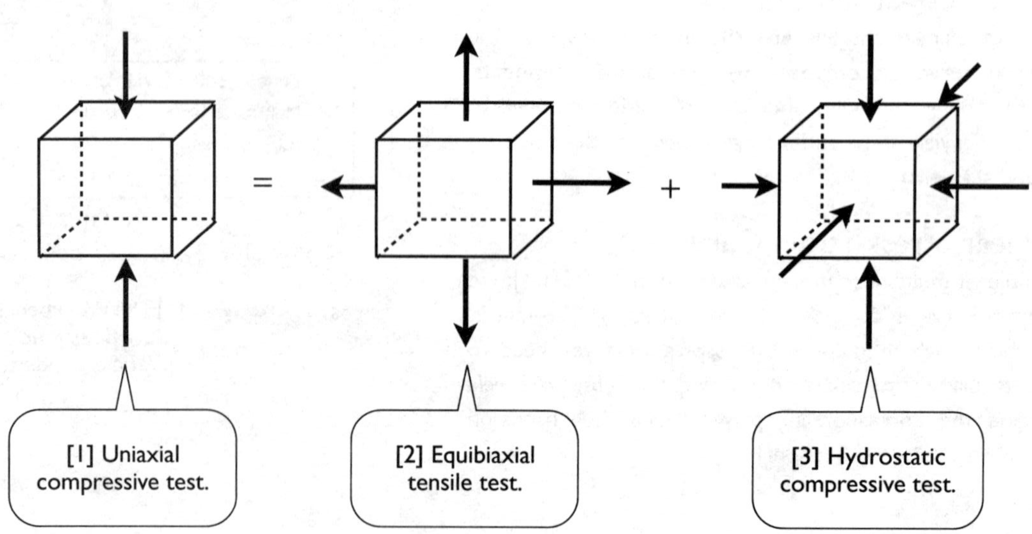

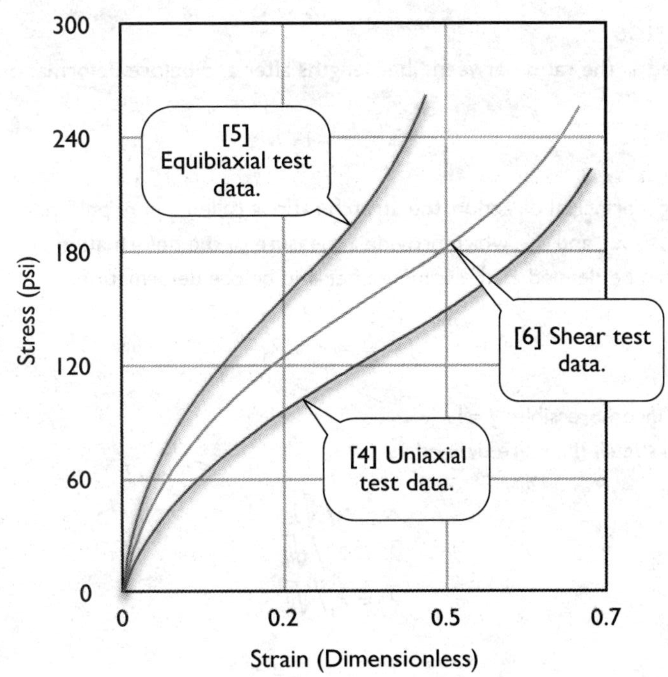

14.1-8 Strain Energy Function

Raw test data such as 14.1-7[4-6] are not convenient for internal calculations in the Workbench. It is usually preferable to use mathematical forms to describe material behavior (such as Eq. 1.2-8(1)). The idea is to propose mathematical forms with parameters, and determine the parameters that best-fit the test data.

Since there are three sets of test data, a rudimentary idea is to propose a mathematical form for each set of data. This idea is not workable since, as discussed in Section 1.2, components of a stress state or a strain state are not arbitrary values; they must satisfy some relations, such as Eq. 1.2-6(2). For example, given a strain state, it is possible to look up the mathematical forms and obtain components of a "stress state," which is, however, not necessarily satisfy the equilibrium relation (Eqs. 1.2-6(2) or 1.2-6(3)); the components may not be a "legal" stress state.

We need better ideas.

As mentioned in Section 14.1-2, hyperelasticity is characterized by the fact that the stressing curve and the unstressing curve are coincident (14.1-2[1]): during the stressing and unstressing, the energy is conserved, or, equivalently, the stressing and unstressing are path independent. The stress state depends only on the strain state, and vice versa. They are independent of the stressing/unstressing history. This implies that there exists a potential energy function that depends on the state of the stress or strain. It reminds us the strain energy density function W, which does depend only on the state of stress or strain. We may propose a mathematical form for the strain energy

$$W = W(\varepsilon_{ij}) \tag{1}$$

And the stress can be calculated from the strain energy using

$$\sigma_{ij} = \frac{\partial W}{\partial \varepsilon_{ij}} \tag{2}$$

The strain state ε_{ij} consists of 6 strain components (Eq. 1.2-4(4)). To further simply the strain energy function and develop a coordinate-independent expression, we may replace the 6 strain components (which are coordinate-dependent) with 3 strain invariants (which are coordinate-independent). To go further, we need more background. Let's refresh some terms in solid mechanics.

Principal Stretch Ratios

The *stretch ratio* λ is defined as the ratio between fiber lengths after and before deformation,

$$\lambda = \frac{L}{L_0} = 1 + \varepsilon \tag{3}$$

When the direction is along a principal direction, the stretch ratio is called a *principal stretch ratio*. There are 3 principal stretch ratios, denoting by λ_1, λ_2, and λ_3, which provide a measure of the deformation.

The *volumetric ratio* J can be defined as the volume after and before deformation,

$$J = \frac{V}{V_0} = \lambda_1 \lambda_2 \lambda_3 \tag{4}$$

Note that, if the material is incompressible, $J = 1$.

The *deviatoric principal stretch ratios* are defined as

$$\begin{aligned} \bar{\lambda}_1 &= \lambda_1 / \sqrt[3]{J} \\ \bar{\lambda}_2 &= \lambda_2 / \sqrt[3]{J} \\ \bar{\lambda}_3 &= \lambda_3 / \sqrt[3]{J} \end{aligned} \tag{5}$$

Strain Invariants

The 3 strain invariants, I_1, I_2, and I_3, are the characteristic values (eigenvalues) of the strain state; it can be proved that

$$\begin{aligned} I_1 &= \lambda_1^2 + \lambda_2^2 + \lambda_3^2 \\ I_2 &= \lambda_1^2\lambda_2^2 + \lambda_2^2\lambda_3^2 + \lambda_3^2\lambda_1^2 \\ I_3 &= \lambda_1^2\lambda_2^2\lambda_3^2 \end{aligned} \tag{6}$$

The *deviatoric strain invariants* are defined as

$$\begin{aligned} \bar{I}_1 &= \lambda_1 / \sqrt[3]{J^2} \\ \bar{I}_2 &= \lambda_2 / \sqrt[3]{J^2} \\ \bar{I}_3 &= \lambda_3 / \sqrt[3]{J^2} \end{aligned} \tag{7}$$

Strain Energy Functions

We can replace the 6 strain components in Eq. (1) with either strain invariants or principle stretch ratios,

$$W = W(I_1, I_2, I_3)$$

or

$$W = W(\lambda_1, \lambda_2, \lambda_3)$$

Or, we can split the strain energy into deviatoric part and volumetric part, and write

$$W = W_d(\bar{I}_1, \bar{I}_2) + W_b(J) \tag{8}$$

or

$$W = W_d(\bar{\lambda}_1, \bar{\lambda}_2, \bar{\lambda}_3) + W_b(J) \tag{9}$$

Note that $I_3 = J^2$, so $\bar{I}_3$ is not used in the definition of W.

14.1-9 Hyperelasticity Models in Workbench

The Workbench provides many hyperelasticity models [1]; they are based on either Eq. (8) or Eq. (9).

Polynomial Form

The polynomial form is based on Eq. (8),

$$W = \sum_{i+j=1}^{N} c_{ij}(\bar{I}_1 - 3)^i(\bar{I}_2 - 3)^j + \sum_{k=1}^{N} \frac{1}{d_k}(J-1)^{2k} \quad (10)$$

For example, the <Polynomial 1st Order> ($N = 1$) is

$$W = c_{10}(\bar{I}_1 - 3) + c_{01}(\bar{I}_2 - 3)^1 + \frac{1}{d_1}(J-1)^2 \quad (11)$$

It has three parameters, c_{10}, c_{01}, and d_1. Note that, for incompressible materials, $J = 1$, $d_1 = 0$, and the last term is dropped.

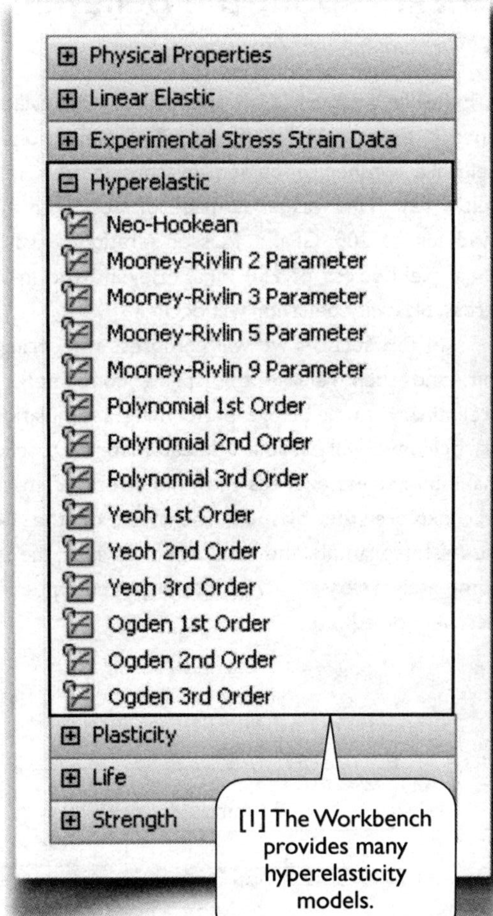

[1] The Workbench provides many hyperelasticity models.

Ogden Form

The Ogden form is based on Eq. (9),

$$W = \sum_{i=1}^{N} \frac{\mu_i}{\alpha_i}(\bar{\lambda}_1^{\alpha_i} + \bar{\lambda}_2^{\alpha_i} + \bar{\lambda}_3^{\alpha_i} - 3) + \sum_{i=1}^{N} \frac{1}{d_i}(J-1)^{2i} \quad (12)$$

For example, the <Ogden 1st Order> ($N = 1$) is

$$W = \frac{\mu_1}{\alpha_1}(\bar{\lambda}_1^{\alpha_1} + \bar{\lambda}_2^{\alpha_1} + \bar{\lambda}_3^{\alpha_1} - 3) + \frac{1}{d_1}(J-1)^2 \quad (13)$$

It has three parameters, μ_1, α_1, and d_1.

Mooney-Rivlin, Yeoh, and Neo-Hookean

These are reduced forms of the generalized polynomial.

Which Form to Use?

The choice depends on type of material, maximum strain, and the test data available. In general, the best form of strain energy density function is the one that produces the closest curve fit of the test data.

Section 14.3 provides an example to demonstrate some details.

Section 14.2

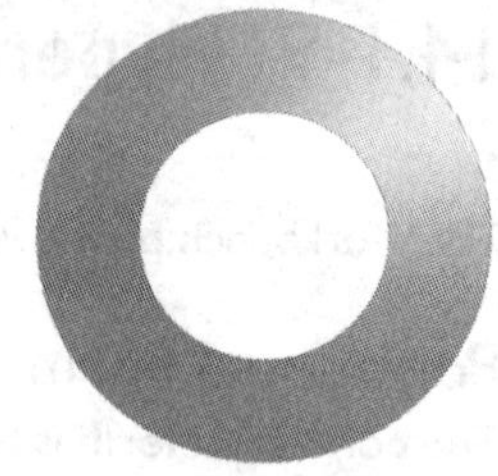

Step-by-Step: Belleville Washer

14.2-1 About the Belleville Washer

A Belleville washer[1] [1] is also called a Belleville spring, since it behaves like a spring. The dimensions of the Belleville washer discussed in this section is shown below [2]. The washer is made of steel with a Young's modulus of 200 GPa, a Poisson's ratio of 0.3, and an initial yield stress of 250 MPa. Beyond the initial yield stress, plasticity behavior will occur [3].

In this section, we will compress the spring by 1.0 mm and then release the spring completely. As a preliminary study, before performing a simulation using plasticity, we will assume a linear material to see if the maximum stress exceeds the yield stress. If so, then we will explore the plasticity behavior of the Belleville spring, for example, the residual stress after the spring is completely released. A force-displacement curve will also be plotted.

[1] The Belleville washer[1].

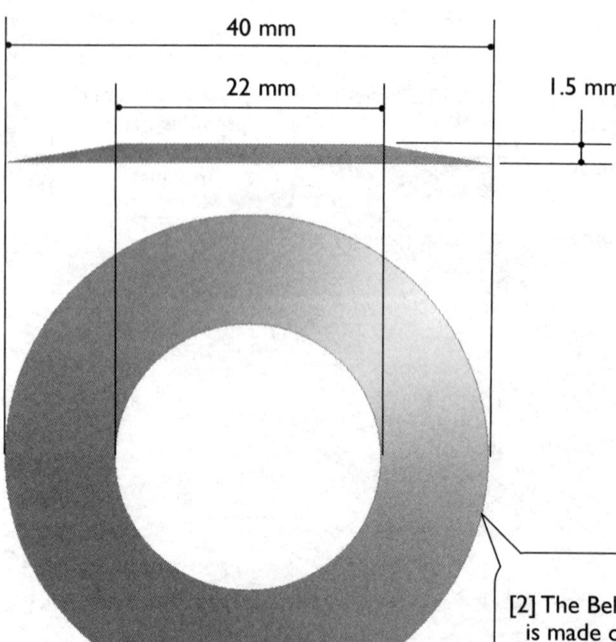

[2] The Belleville washer is made of steel, with thickness of 1.0 mm.

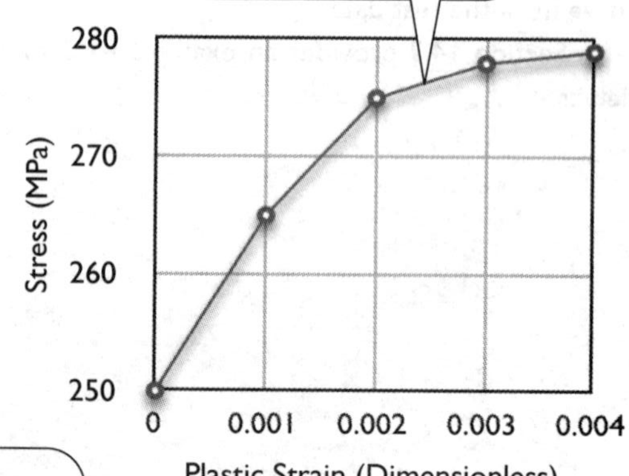

[3] Plasticity behavior of the steel in this case.

14.2-2 Start Up

Launch <Workbench>. Create a <Static Structural> analysis system. Save the project as "Belleville."

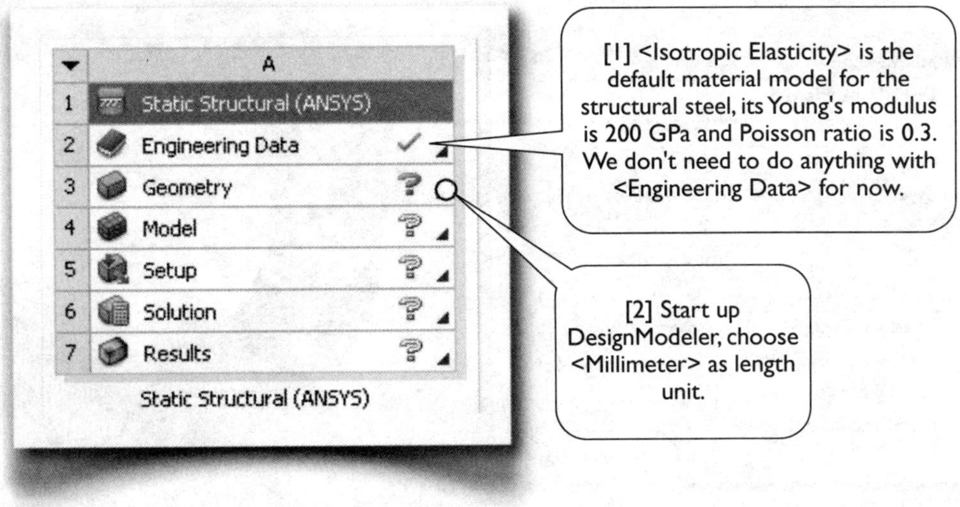

14.2-3 Create Geometry

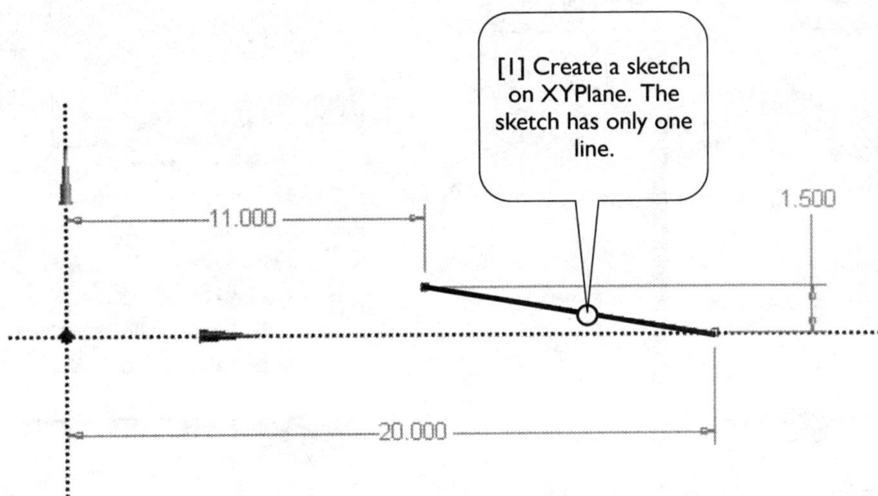

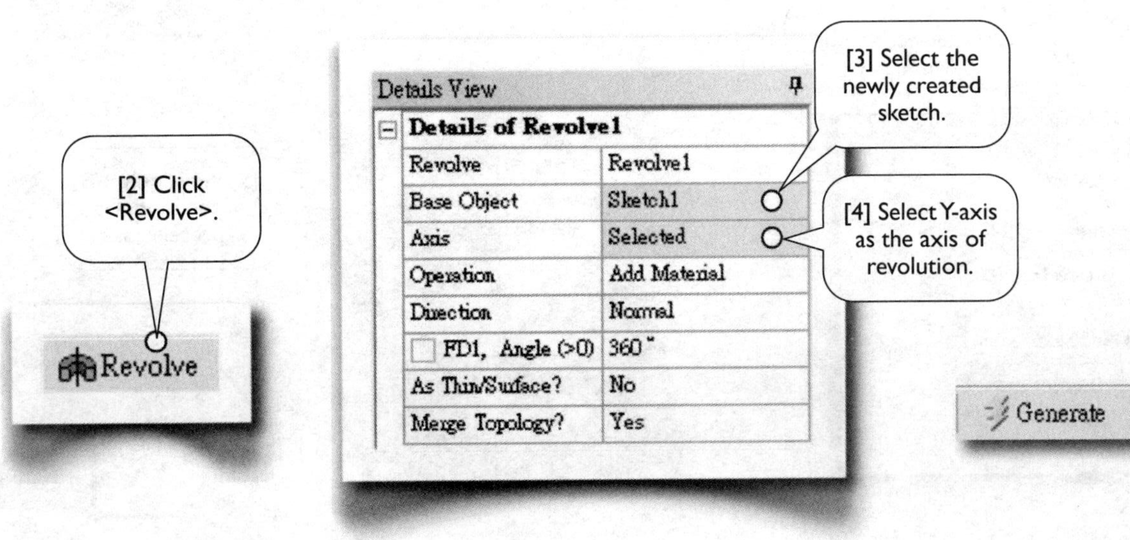

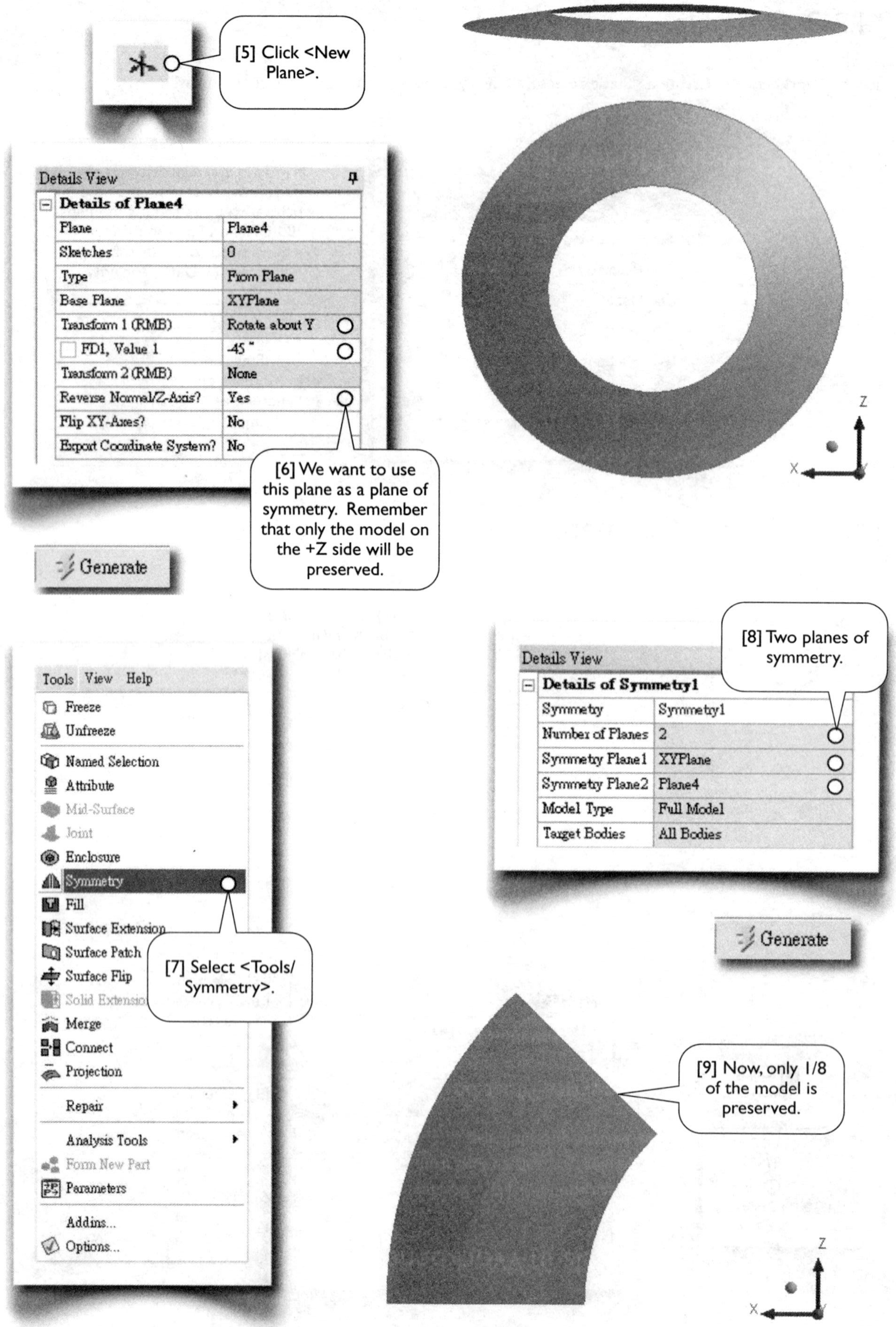
[5] Click <New Plane>.
Details View
Details of Plane4
Plane | Plane4
Sketches | 0
Type | From Plane
Base Plane | XYPlane
Transform 1 (RMB) | Rotate about Y
FD1, Value 1 | -45 °
Transform 2 (RMB) | None
Reverse Normal/Z-Axis? | Yes
Flip XY-Axes? | No
Export Coordinate System? | No
[6] We want to use this plane as a plane of symmetry. Remember that only the model on the +Z side will be preserved.
Generate
Z
X
Tools View Help
Freeze
Unfreeze
Named Selection
Attribute
Mid-Surface
Joint
Enclosure
Symmetry
Fill
Surface Extension
Surface Patch
Surface Flip
Solid Extensio
Merge
Connect
Projection
Repair
Analysis Tools
Form New Part
Parameters
Addins...
Options...
[7] Select <Tools/ Symmetry>.
Details View
Details of Symmetry1
Symmetry | Symmetry1
Number of Planes | 2
Symmetry Plane1 | XYPlane
Symmetry Plane2 | Plane4
Model Type | Full Model
Target Bodies | All Bodies
[8] Two planes of symmetry.
Generate
[9] Now, only 1/8 of the model is preserved.
Z
X

In this case, any plane derived from rotating XYPlane about Y-axis will be a plane of symmetry. In other words, there are infinitely many planes of symmetry for this case. In fact, an axisymmetric geometry has infinitely number of planes of symmetry. We can choose any two of them. In this case, we decide to use 1/8 of the model. In practice, a 45° sector of the model is a good choice. The other possibility is to model it as an axisymmetric problem using 2D option. This leaves an exercise for you (Section 14.4-2).

14.2-4 Set Up for Simulation with Linear Material

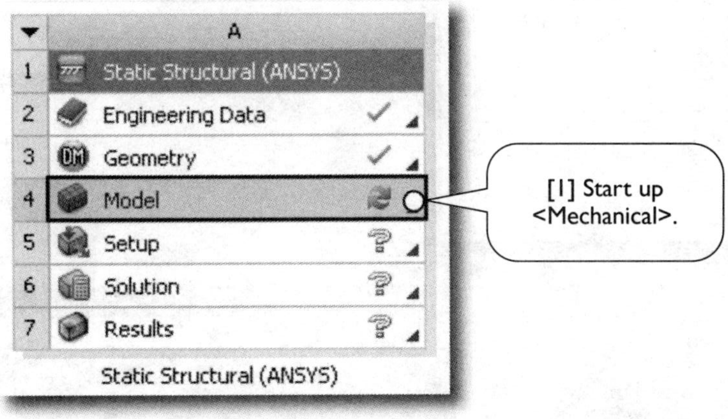

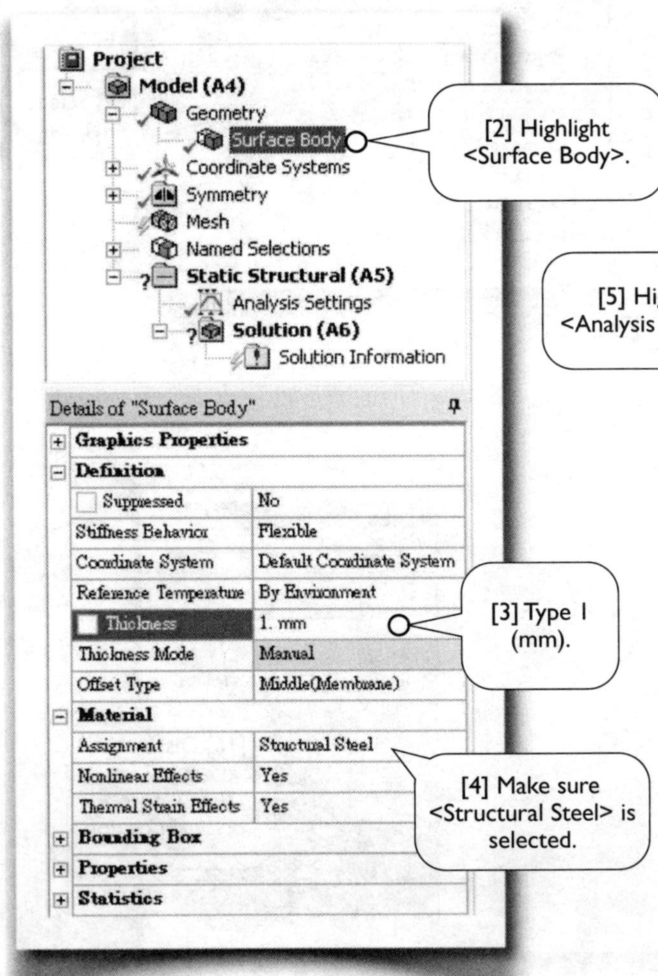

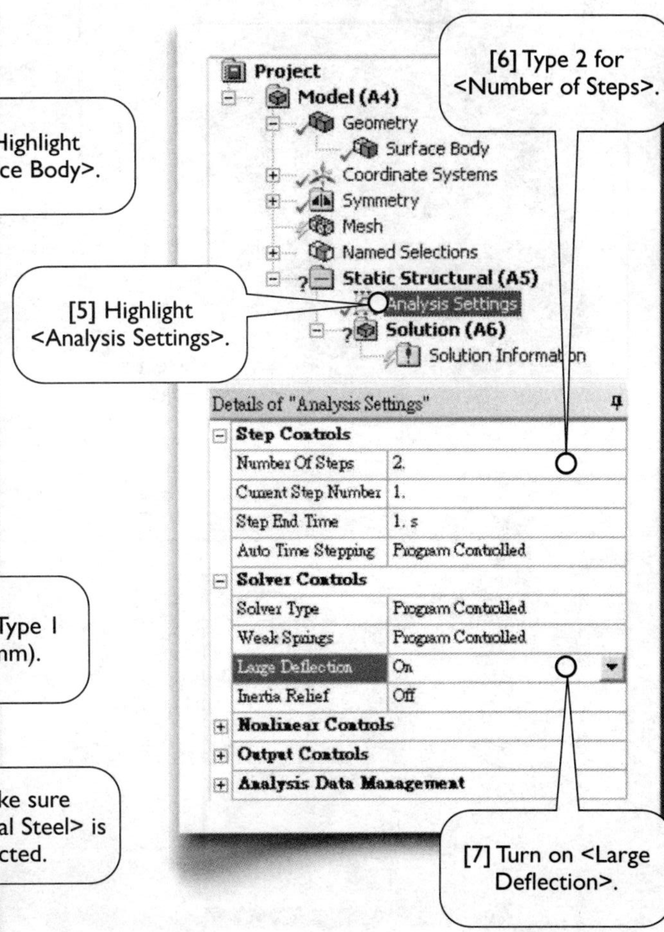

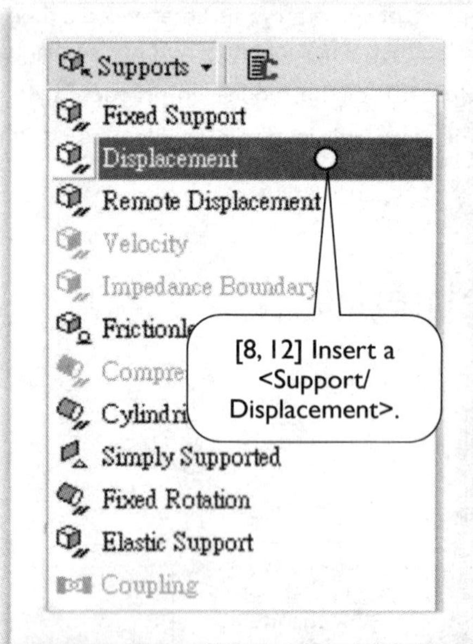
Supports
Fixed Support
Displacement
Remote Displacement
Velocity
Impedance Boundary
Simply Supported
Fixed Rotation
Elastic Support
Coupling
[8, 12] Insert a <Support/ Displacement>.

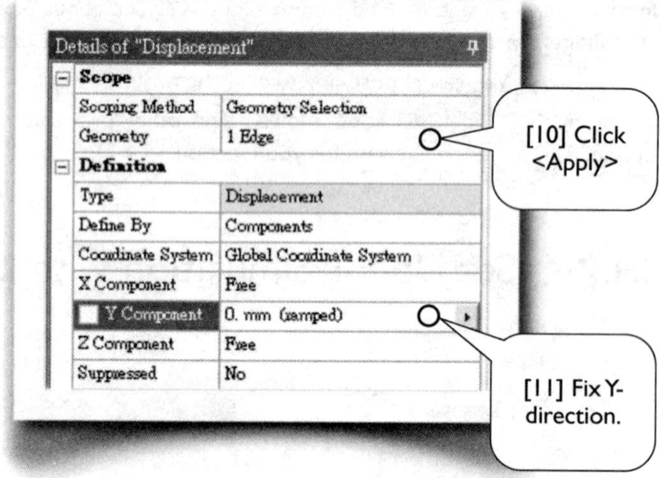
Details of "Displacement"
Scope
Scoping Method | Geometry Selection
Geometry | 1 Edge
Definition
Type | Displacement
Define By | Components
Coordinate System | Global Coordinate System
X Component | Free
Y Component | 0. mm (ramped)
Z Component | Free
Suppressed | No
[10] Click <Apply>
[11] Fix Y-direction.

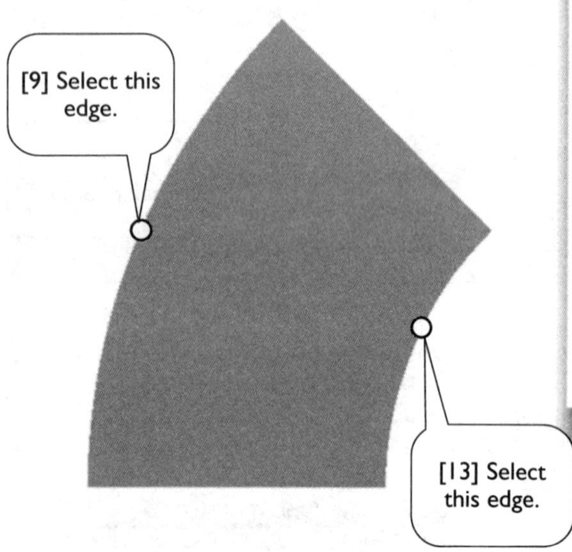
[9] Select this edge.
[13] Select this edge.

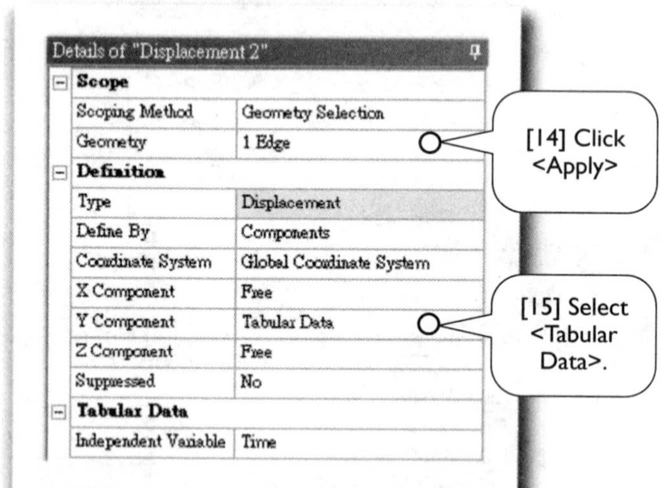
Details of "Displacement 2"
Scope
Scoping Method | Geometry Selection
Geometry | 1 Edge
Definition
Type | Displacement
Define By | Components
Coordinate System | Global Coordinate System
X Component | Free
Y Component | Tabular Data
Z Component | Free
Suppressed | No
Tabular Data
Independent Variable | Time
[14] Click <Apply>
[15] Select <Tabular Data>.

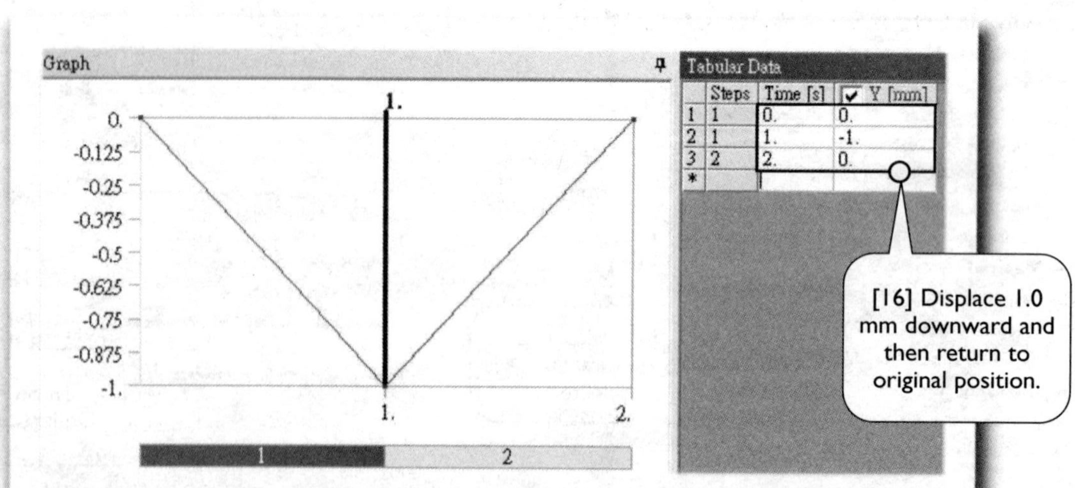
Graph
0.
-0.125
-0.25
-0.375
-0.5
-0.625
-0.75
-0.875
-1.
1.
2.
Tabular Data
Steps | Time [s] | Y [mm]
1 | 1 | 0. | 0.
2 | 1 | 1. | -1.
3 | 2 | 2. | 0.
[16] Displace 1.0 mm downward and then return to original position.

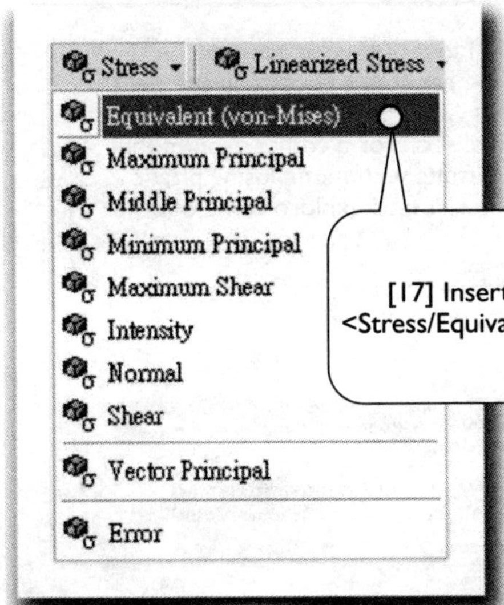

[17] Insert a <Stress/Equivalent>.

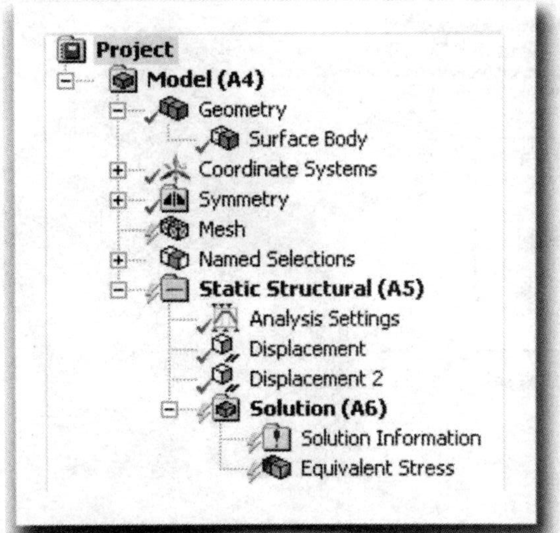

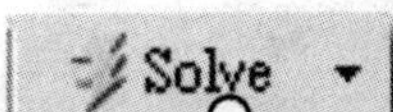

[18] Solve. The Workbench completes the solution in two substeps.

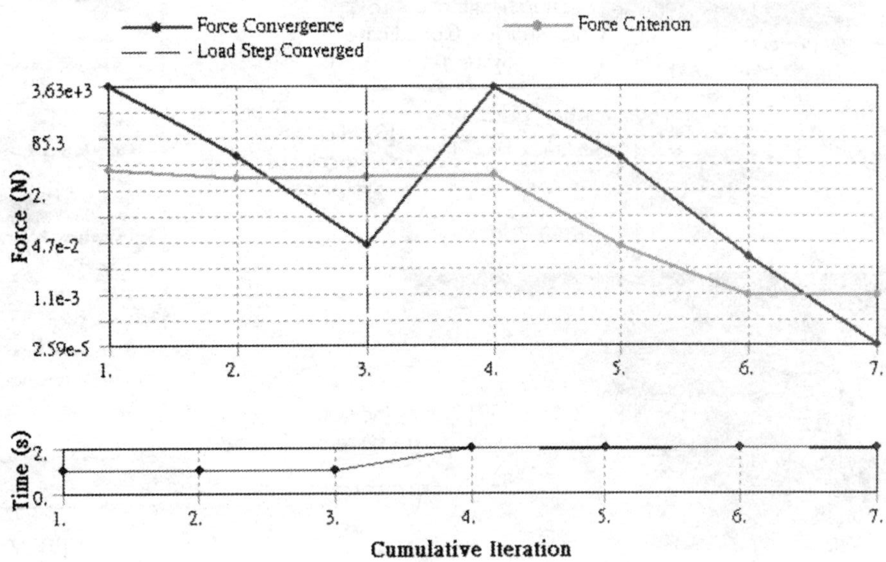

14.2-5 Results of the Linear Material Simulation

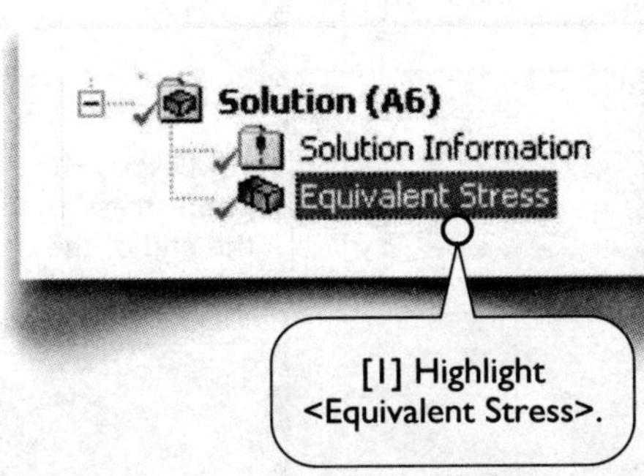

[1] Highlight <Equivalent Stress>.

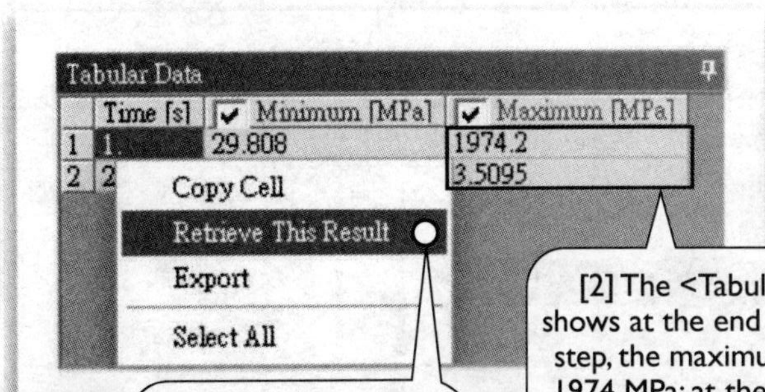

[3] Right-click the first load step and select <Retrieve This Result>.

[2] The <Tabular Data> shows at the end of first load step, the maximum stress is 1974 MPa; at the end of the second load step, the maximum stress is essentially zero. (It must be so for an elastic material.)

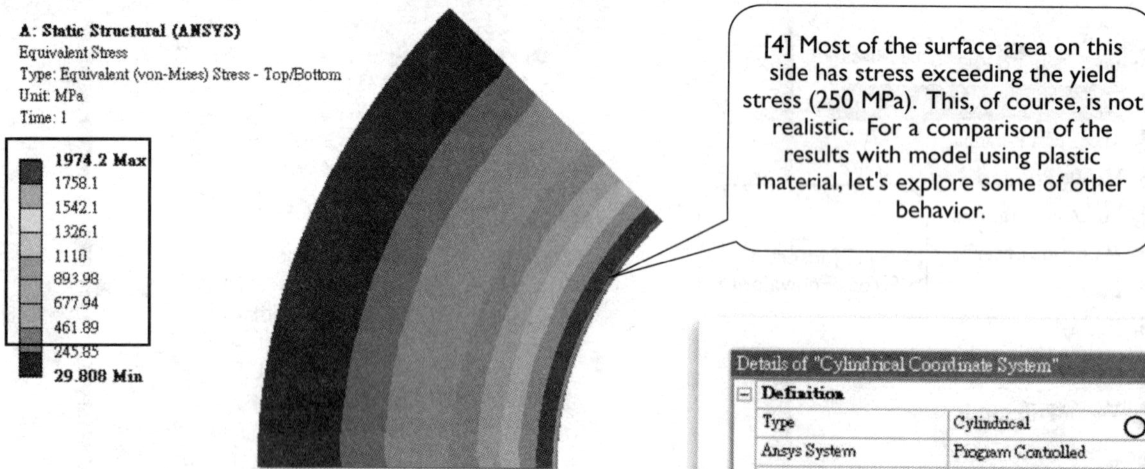
A: Static Structural (ANSYS)
Equivalent Stress
Type: Equivalent (von-Mises) Stress - Top/Bottom
Unit: MPa
Time: 1
1974.2 Max
1758.1
1542.1
1326.1
1110
893.98
677.94
461.89
245.85
29.808 Min
[4] Most of the surface area on this side has stress exceeding the yield stress (250 MPa). This, of course, is not realistic. For a comparison of the results with model using plastic material, let's explore some of other behavior.

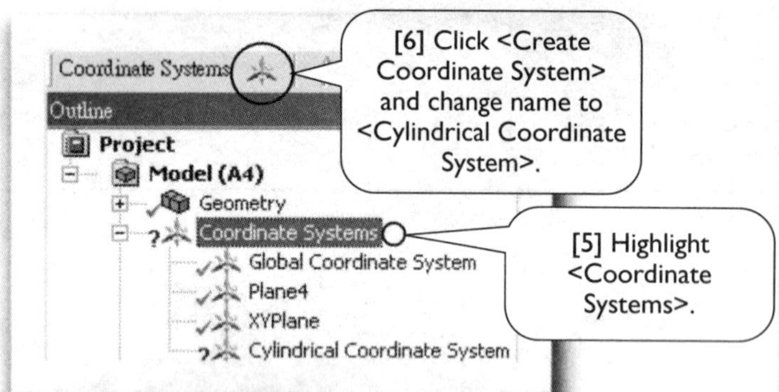
Coordinate Systems
Outline
Project
Model (A4)
Geometry
Coordinate Systems
Global Coordinate System
Plane4
XYPlane
Cylindrical Coordinate System
[6] Click <Create Coordinate System> and change name to <Cylindrical Coordinate System>.
[5] Highlight <Coordinate Systems>.

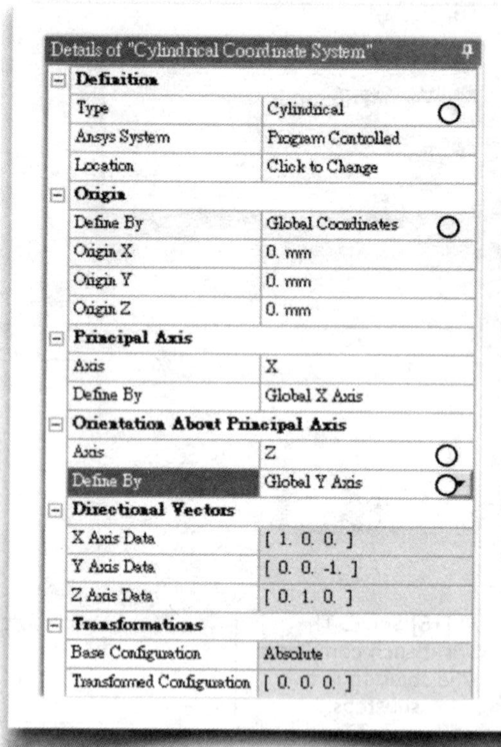
Details of "Cylindrical Coordinate System"
Definition
Type | Cylindrical
Ansys System | Program Controlled
Location | Click to Change
Origin
Define By | Global Coordinates
Origin X | 0. mm
Origin Y | 0. mm
Origin Z | 0. mm
Principal Axis
Axis | X
Define By | Global X Axis
Orientation About Principal Axis
Axis | Z
Define By | Global Y Axis
Directional Vectors
X Axis Data | [1. 0. 0.]
Y Axis Data | [0. 0. -1.]
Z Axis Data | [0. 1. 0.]
Transformations
Base Configuration | Absolute
Transformed Configuration | [0. 0. 0.]

[7] The cylindrical coordinate system.
X
Z
Y

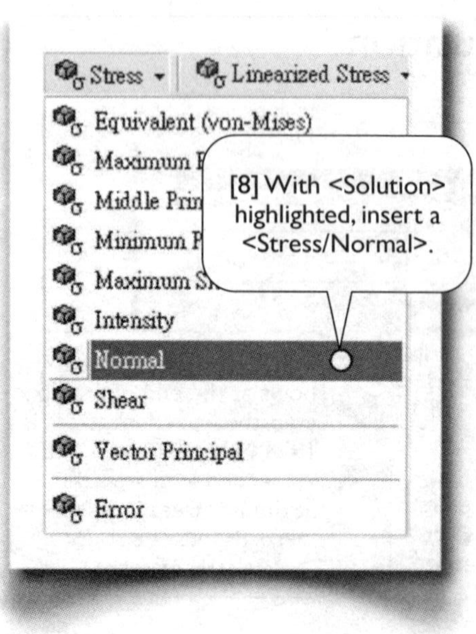
Stress
Linearized Stress
Equivalent (von-Mises)
Maximum P
Middle Prin
Minimum P
Maximum Sh
Intensity
Normal
Shear
Vector Principal
Error
[8] With <Solution> highlighted, insert a <Stress/Normal>.

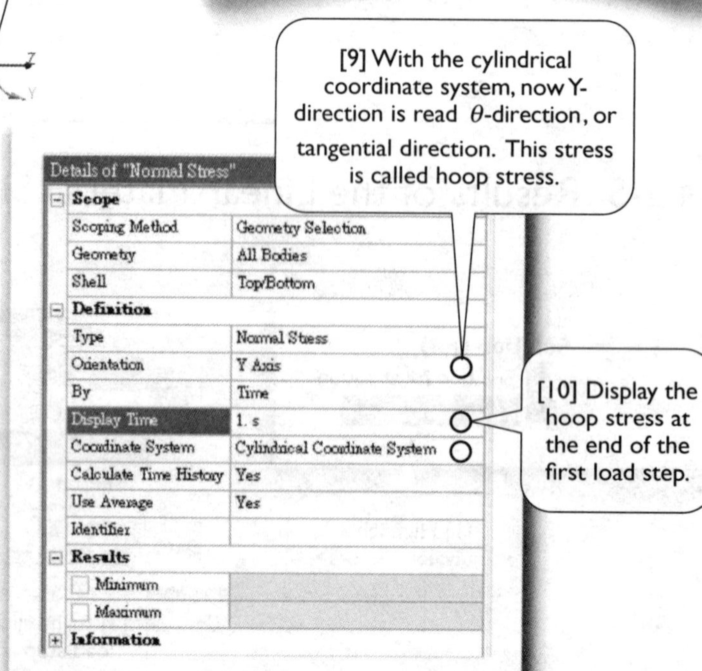
[9] With the cylindrical coordinate system, now Y-direction is read θ-direction, or tangential direction. This stress is called hoop stress.
Details of "Normal Stress"
Scope
Scoping Method | Geometry Selection
Geometry | All Bodies
Shell | Top/Bottom
Definition
Type | Normal Stress
Orientation | Y Axis
By | Time
Display Time | 1. s
Coordinate System | Cylindrical Coordinate System
Calculate Time History | Yes
Use Average | Yes
Identifier
Results
Minimum
Maximum
Information
[10] Display the hoop stress at the end of the first load step.

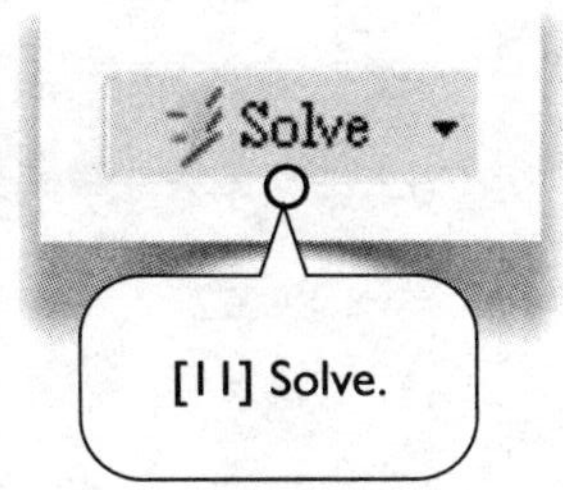
Solve
[11] Solve.

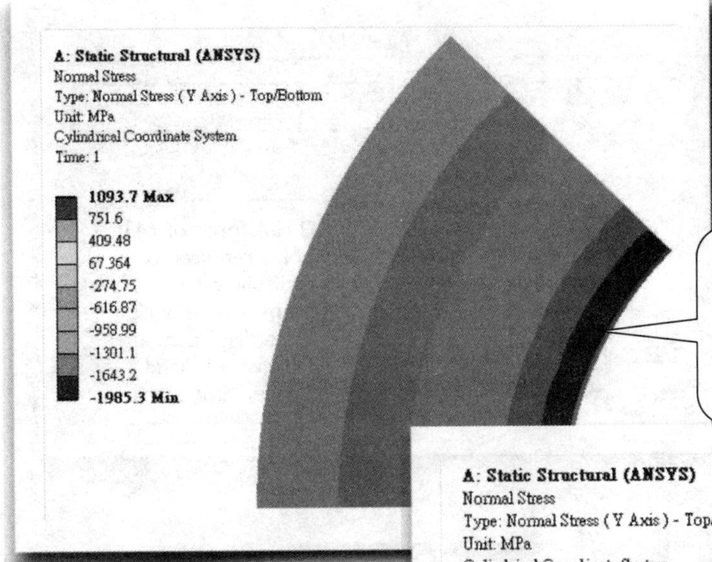
A: Static Structural (ANSYS)
Normal Stress
Type: Normal Stress (Y Axis) - Top/Bottom
Unit: MPa
Cylindrical Coordinate System
Time: 1
1093.7 Max
751.6
409.48
67.364
-274.75
-616.87
-958.99
-1301.1
-1643.2
-1985.3 Min
[12] Compressive hoop (tangential) stress dominates the top surface

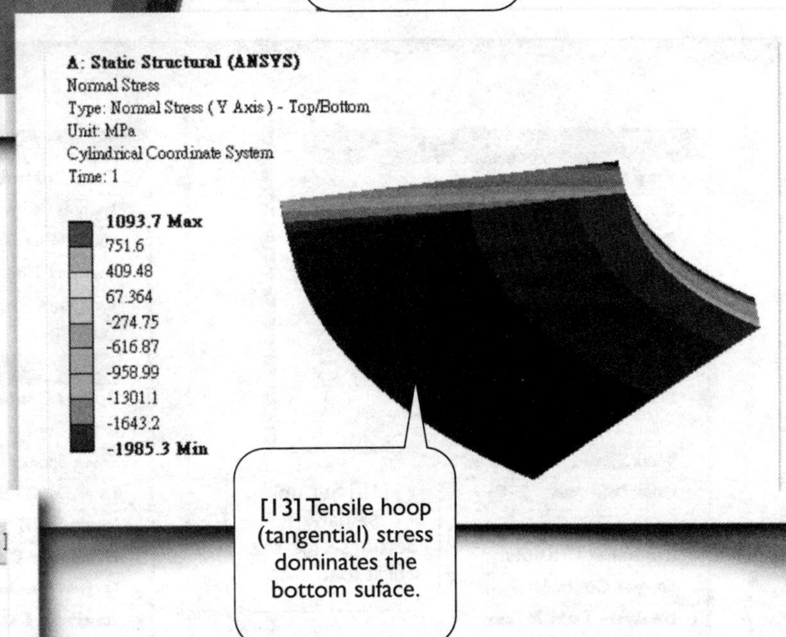
A: Static Structural (ANSYS)
Normal Stress
Type: Normal Stress (Y Axis) - Top/Bottom
Unit: MPa
Cylindrical Coordinate System
Time: 1
1093.7 Max
751.6
409.48
67.364
-274.75
-616.87
-958.99
-1301.1
-1643.2
-1985.3 Min
[13] Tensile hoop (tangential) stress dominates the bottom suface.

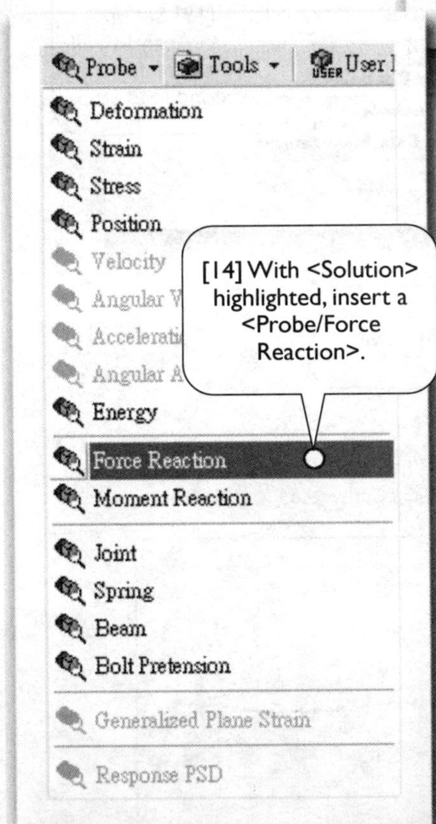
Probe
Tools
Deformation
Strain
Stress
Position
Velocity
Energy
Force Reaction
Moment Reaction
Joint
Spring
Beam
Bolt Pretension
Generalized Plane Strain
Response PSD
[14] With <Solution> highlighted, insert a <Probe/Force Reaction>.

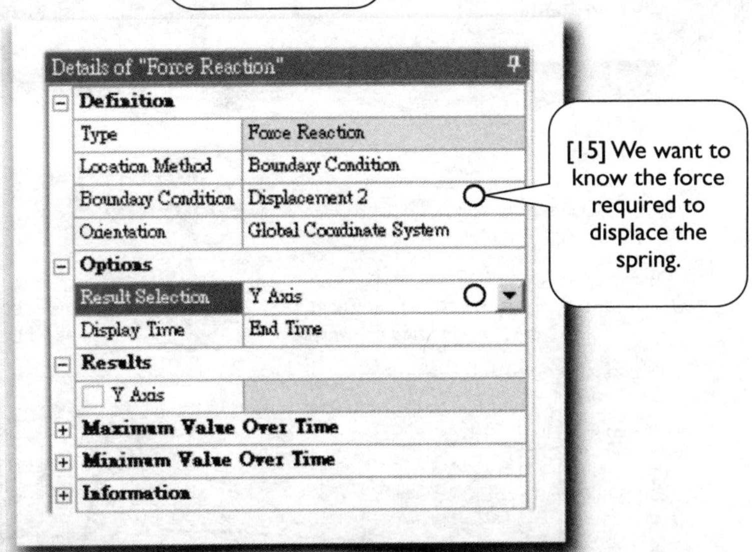
Details of "Force Reaction"
Definition
Type
Force Reaction
Location Method
Boundary Condition
Boundary Condition
Displacement 2
Orientation
Global Coordinate System
Options
Result Selection
Y Axis
Display Time
End Time
Results
Y Axis
Maximum Value Over Time
Minimum Value Over Time
Information
[15] We want to know the force required to displace the spring.

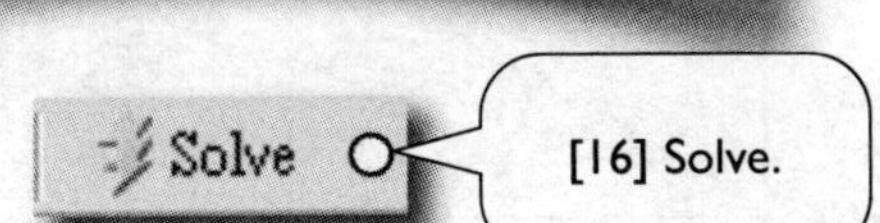
Solve
[16] Solve.

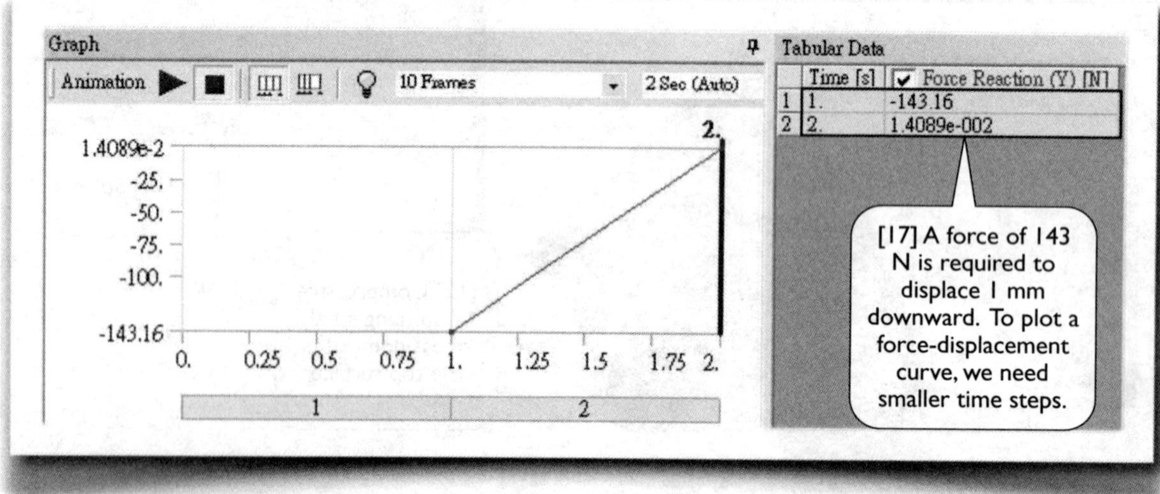
Graph
Animation
10 Frames
2 Sec (Auto)
1.4089e-2
-25.
-50.
-75.
-100.
-143.16
0.
0.25
0.5
0.75
1.
1.25
1.5
1.75
2.
Tabular Data
Time [s]
Force Reaction (Y) [N]
1 1. -143.16
2 2. 1.4089e-002
[17] A force of 143 N is required to displace 1 mm downward. To plot a force-displacement curve, we need smaller time steps.

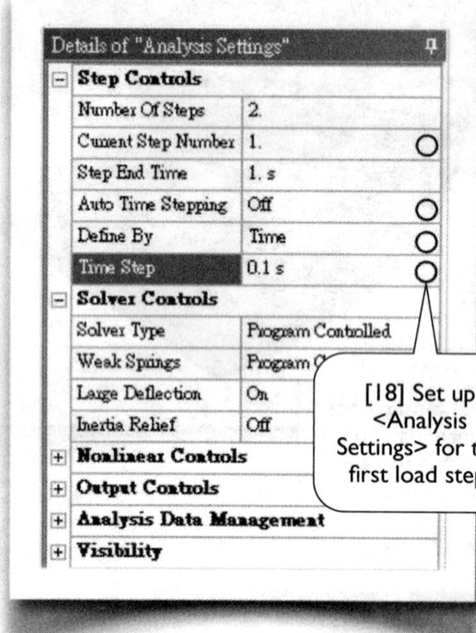
Details of "Analysis Settings"
Step Controls
Number Of Steps 2.
Current Step Number 1.
Step End Time 1. s
Auto Time Stepping Off
Define By Time
Time Step 0.1 s
Solver Controls
Solver Type Program Controlled
Weak Springs
Large Deflection On
Inertia Relief Off
Nonlinear Controls
Output Controls
Analysis Data Management
Visibility
[18] Set up <Analysis Settings> for the first load step.

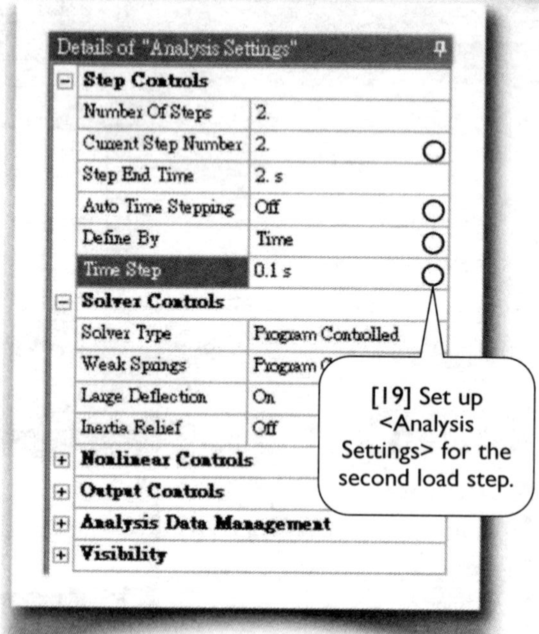
Details of "Analysis Settings"
Step Controls
Number Of Steps 2.
Current Step Number 2.
Step End Time 2. s
Auto Time Stepping Off
Define By Time
Time Step 0.1 s
Solver Controls
Solver Type Program Controlled
Weak Springs
Large Deflection On
Inertia Relief Off
Nonlinear Controls
Output Controls
Analysis Data Management
Visibility
[19] Set up <Analysis Settings> for the second load step.

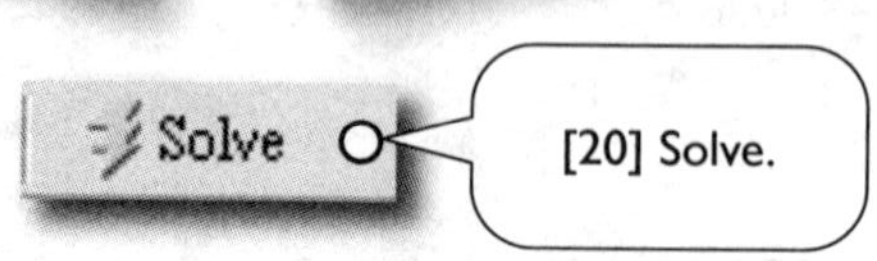
Solve
[20] Solve.

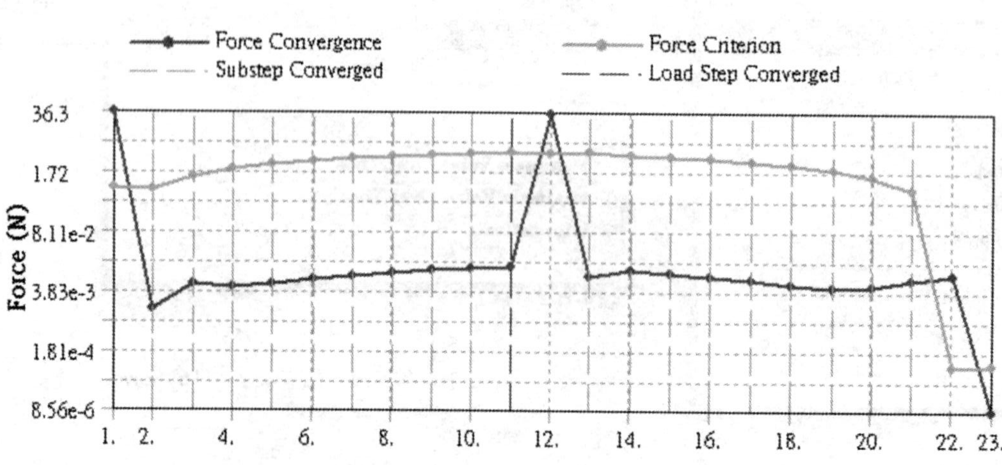
Force Convergence
Substep Converged
Force Criterion
Load Step Converged
Force (N)
36.3
1.72
8.11e-2
3.83e-3
1.81e-4
8.56e-6
1.
2.
4.
6.
8.
10.
12.
14.
16.
18.
20.
22.
23.

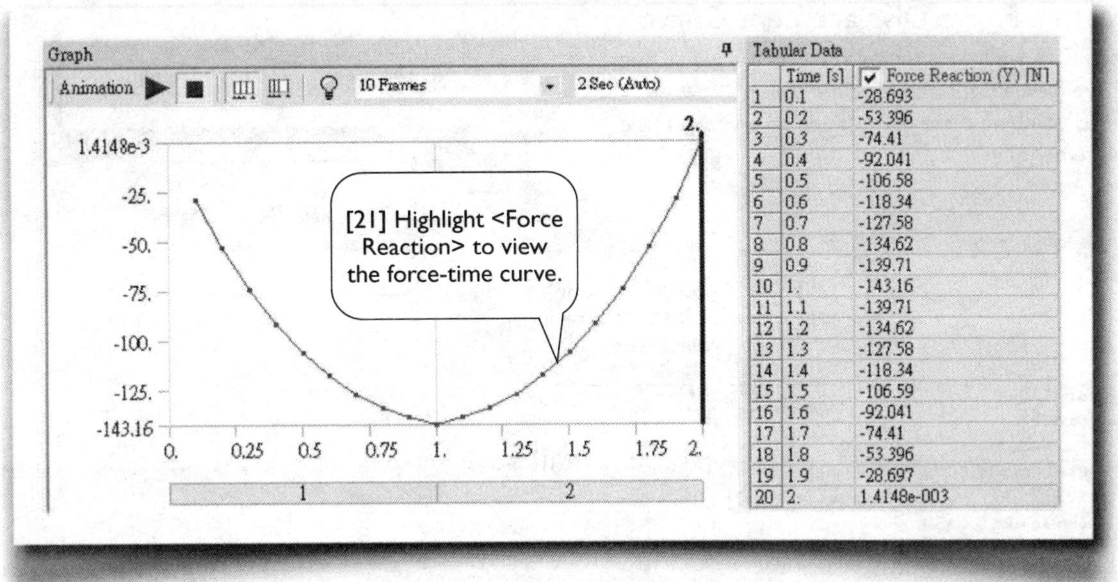

	Time [s]	Force Reaction (Y) [N]
1	0.1	-28.693
2	0.2	-53.396
3	0.3	-74.41
4	0.4	-92.041
5	0.5	-106.58
6	0.6	-118.34
7	0.7	-127.58
8	0.8	-134.62
9	0.9	-139.71
10	1.	-143.16
11	1.1	-139.71
12	1.2	-134.62
13	1.3	-127.58
14	1.4	-118.34
15	1.5	-106.59
16	1.6	-92.041
17	1.7	-74.41
18	1.8	-53.396
19	1.9	-28.697
20	2.	1.4148e-003

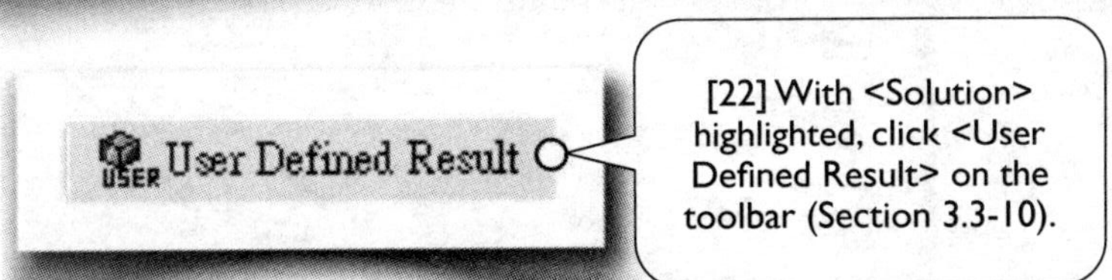

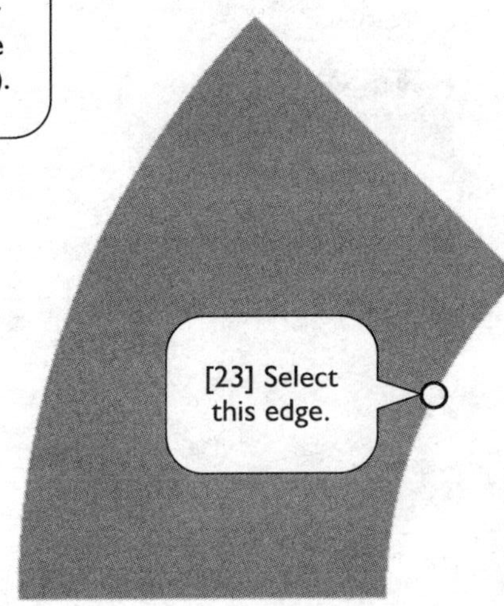

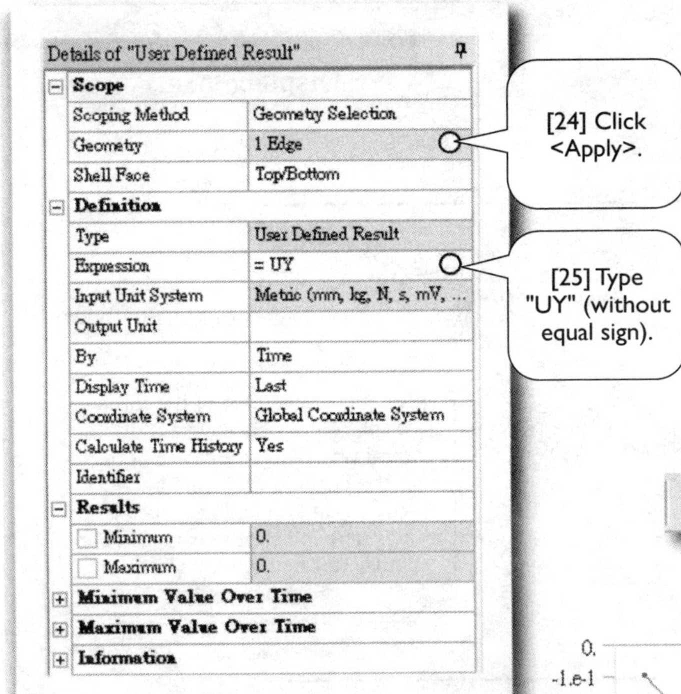

Details of "User Defined Result"

Scope	
Scoping Method	Geometry Selection
Geometry	1 Edge
Shell Face	Top/Bottom
Definition	
Type	User Defined Result
Expression	= UY
Input Unit System	Metric (mm, kg, N, s, mV, ...
Output Unit	
By	Time
Display Time	Last
Coordinate System	Global Coordinate System
Calculate Time History	Yes
Identifier	
Results	
Minimum	0.
Maximum	0.
Minimum Value Over Time	
Maximum Value Over Time	
Information	

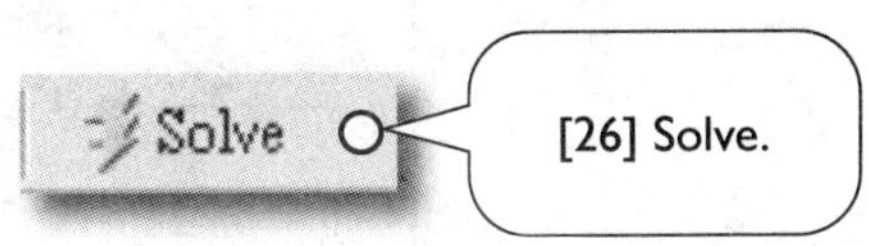

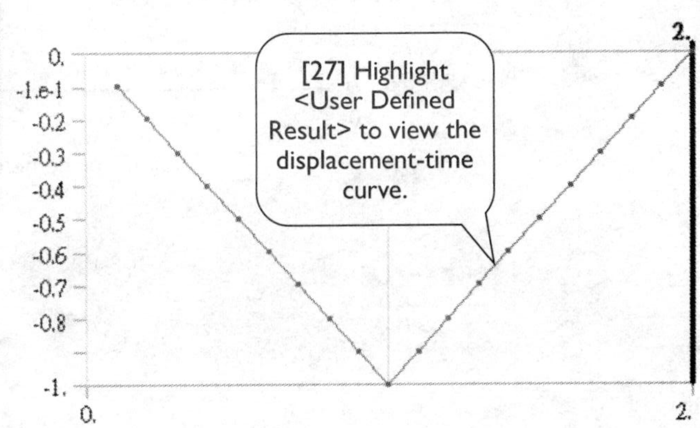

Create a Force-Displacement Curve

In step [21], we have a force-time curve while in step [27], we have a displacement-time curve. Now, we want to combine these information to create a force-displacement curve.

[28] Click <New Chart and Table> on the toolbar.

[29] Select <Force Reaction> and <User Defined Result> in the project tree.

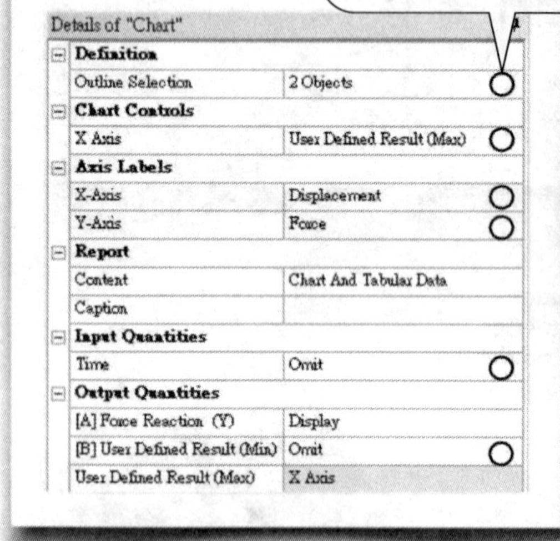

Details of "Chart"

Definition	
Outline Selection	2 Objects
Chart Controls	
X Axis	User Defined Result (Max)
Axis Labels	
X-Axis	Displacement
Y-Axis	Force
Report	
Content	Chart And Tabular Data
Caption	
Input Quantities	
Time	Omit
Output Quantities	
[A] Force Reaction (Y)	Display
[B] User Defined Result (Min)	Omit
User Defined Result (Max)	X Axis

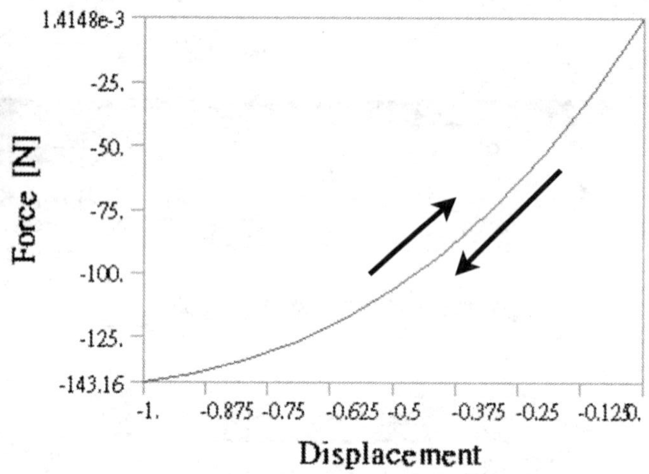

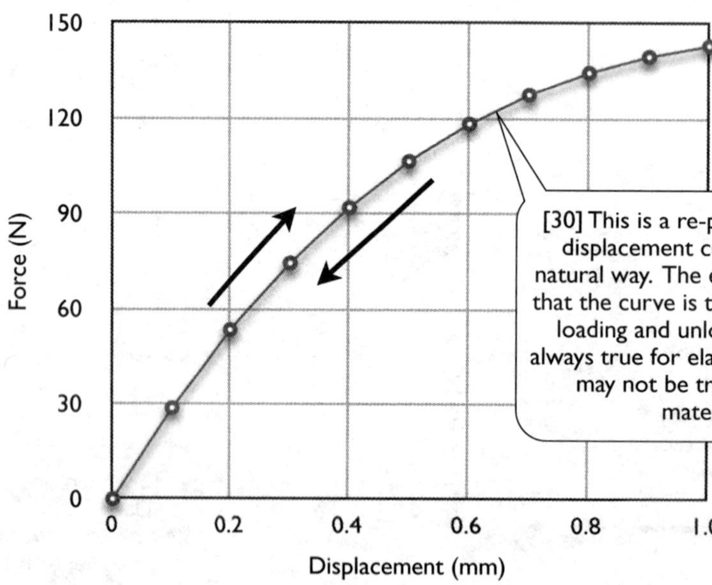

[30] This is a re-plot of the force-displacement curve in a more natural way. The emphasize here is that the curve is the same between loading and unloading, which is always true for elastic materials, but may not be true for plastic materials.

14.2-6 Set Up for Simulation with Plastic Material Model

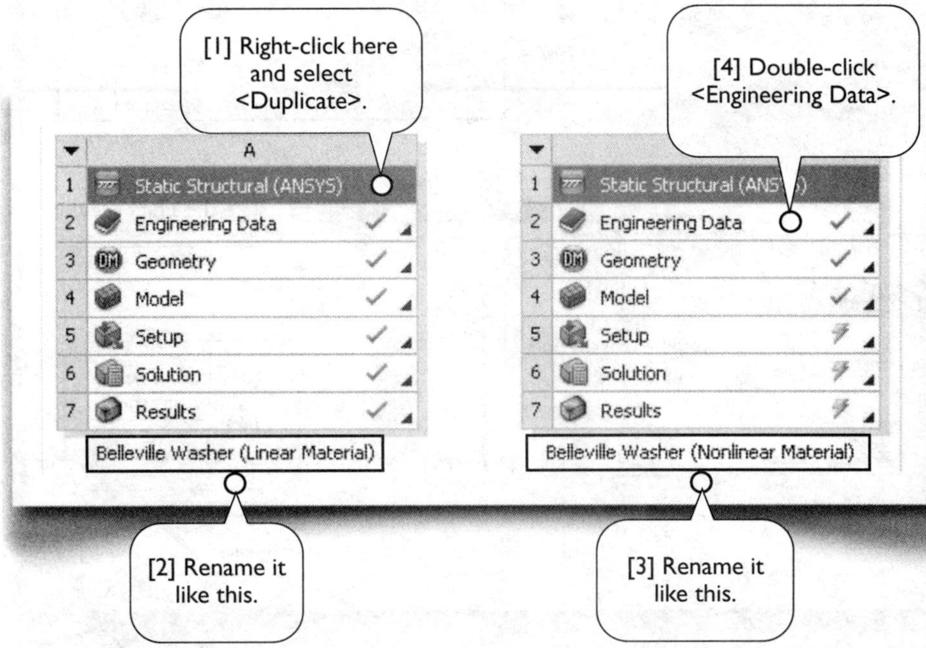

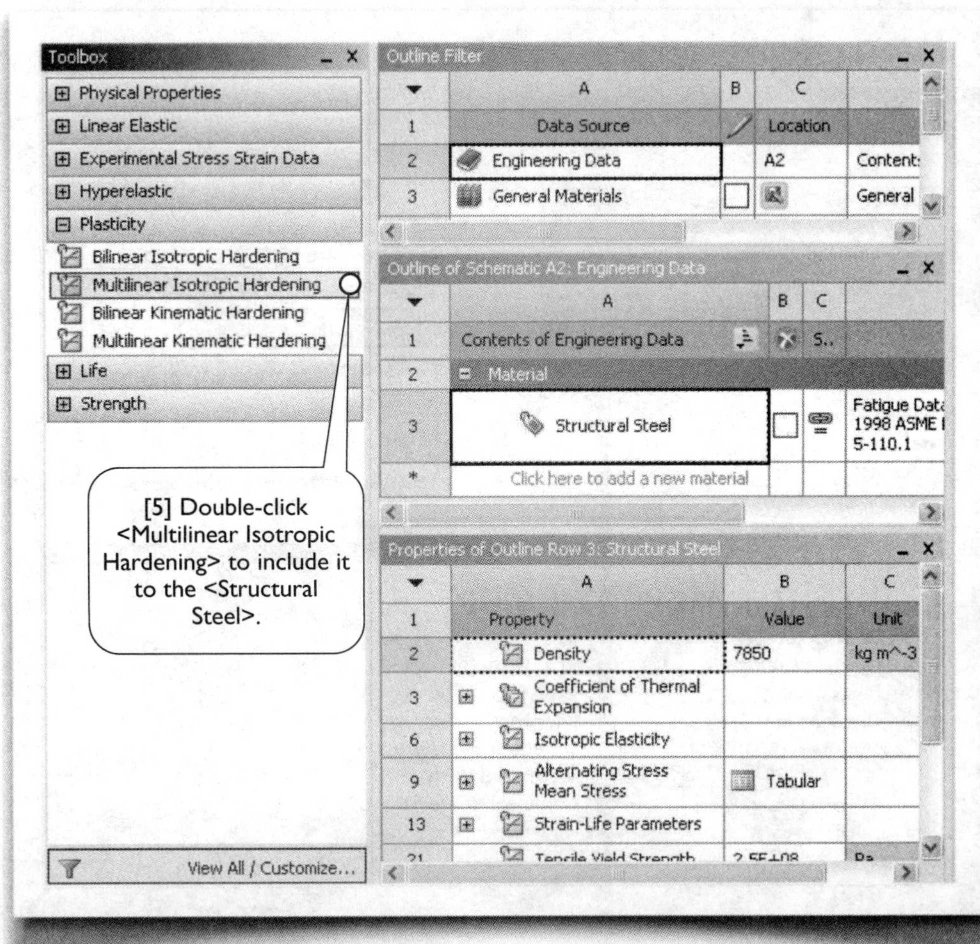

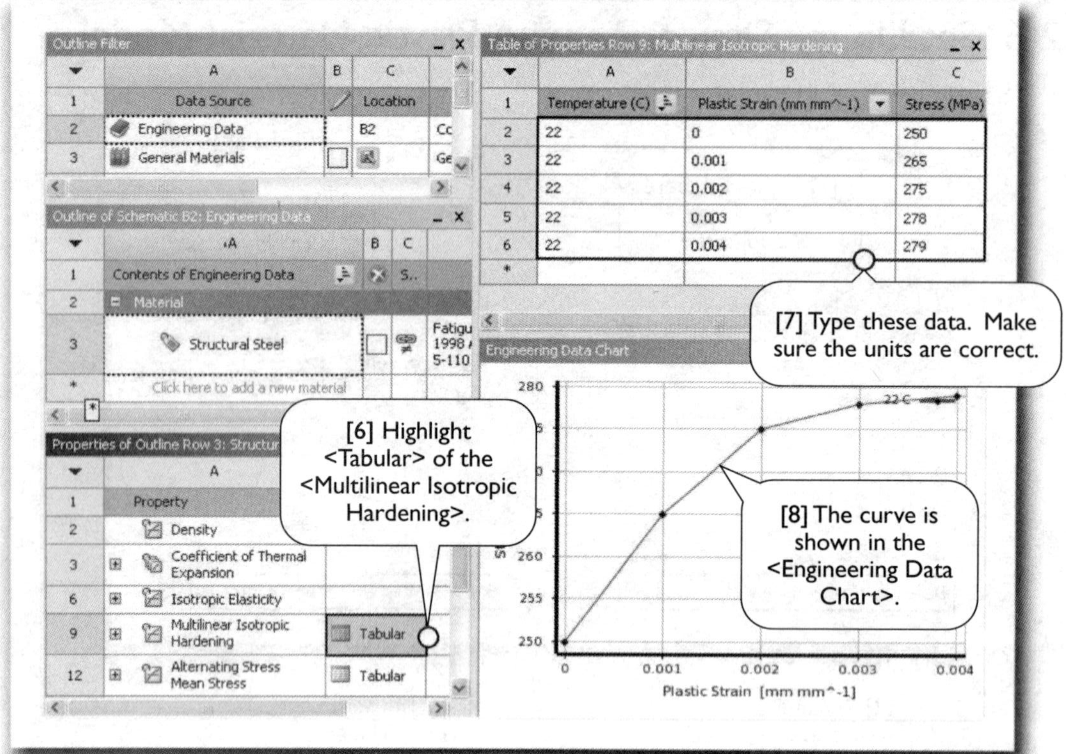
[6] Highlight <Tabular> of the <Multilinear Isotropic Hardening>.
[7] Type these data. Make sure the units are correct.
[8] The curve is shown in the <Engineering Data Chart>.

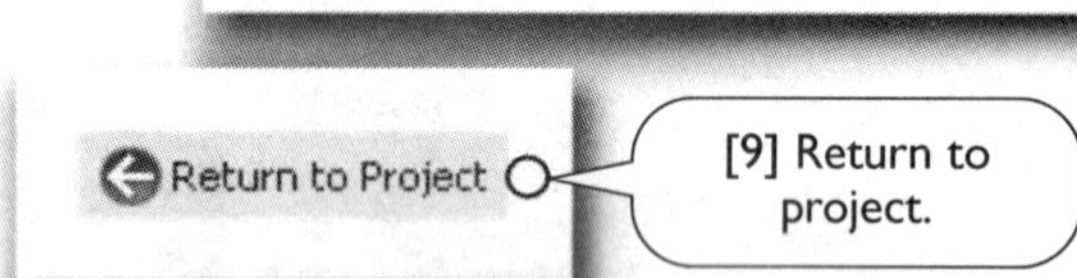
[9] Return to project.

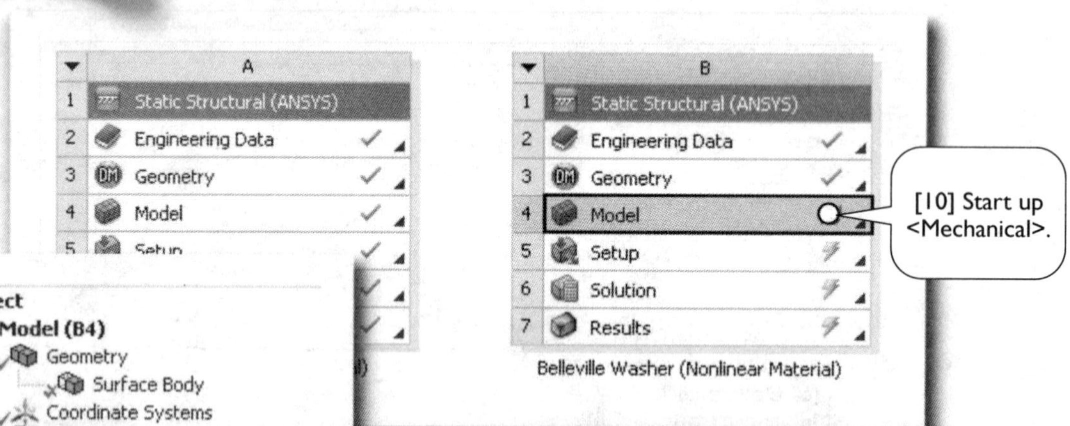
[10] Start up <Mechanical>.

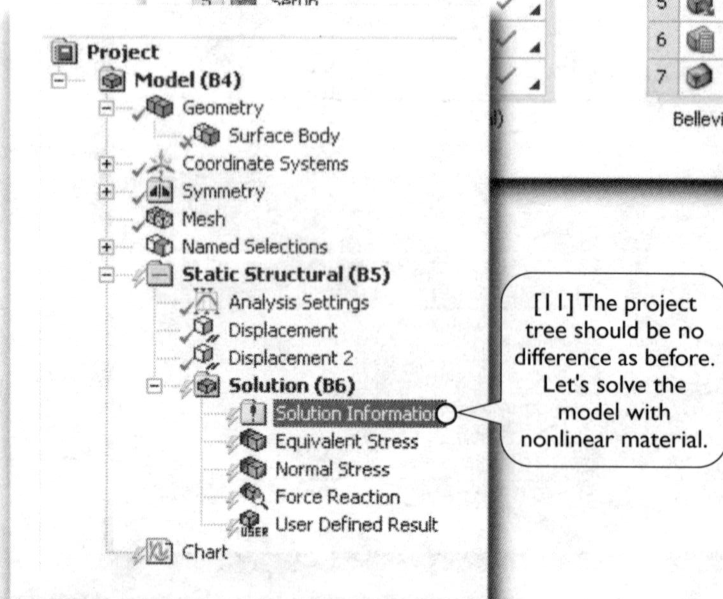
[11] The project tree should be no difference as before. Let's solve the model with nonlinear material.

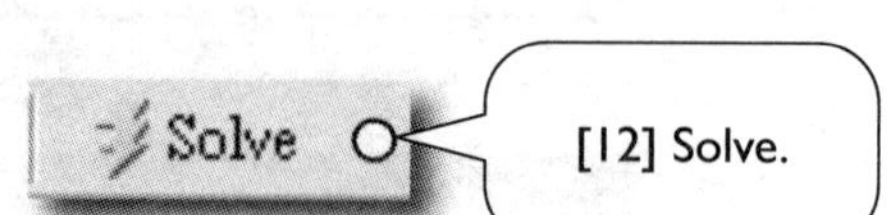
[12] Solve.

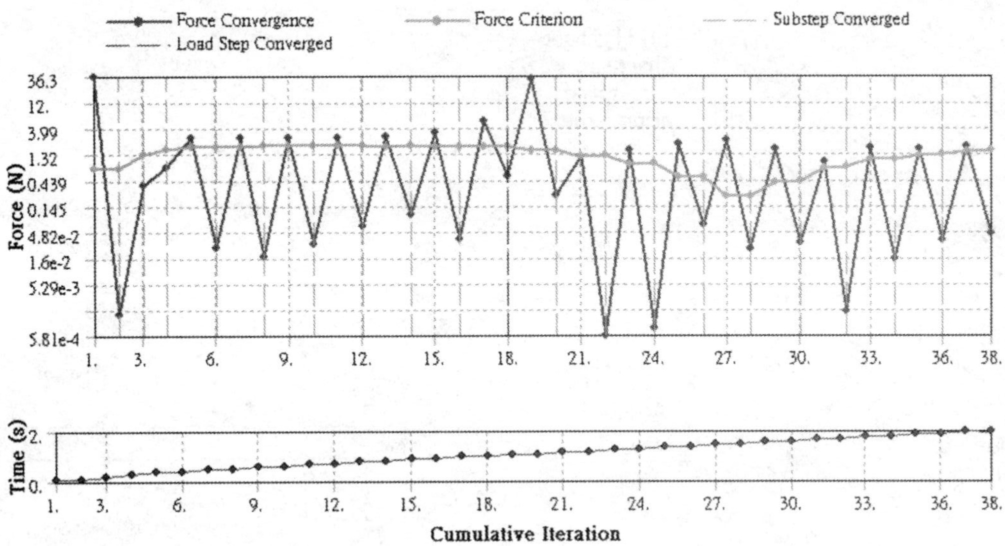

14.2-7 Results of the Nonlinear Material Simulation

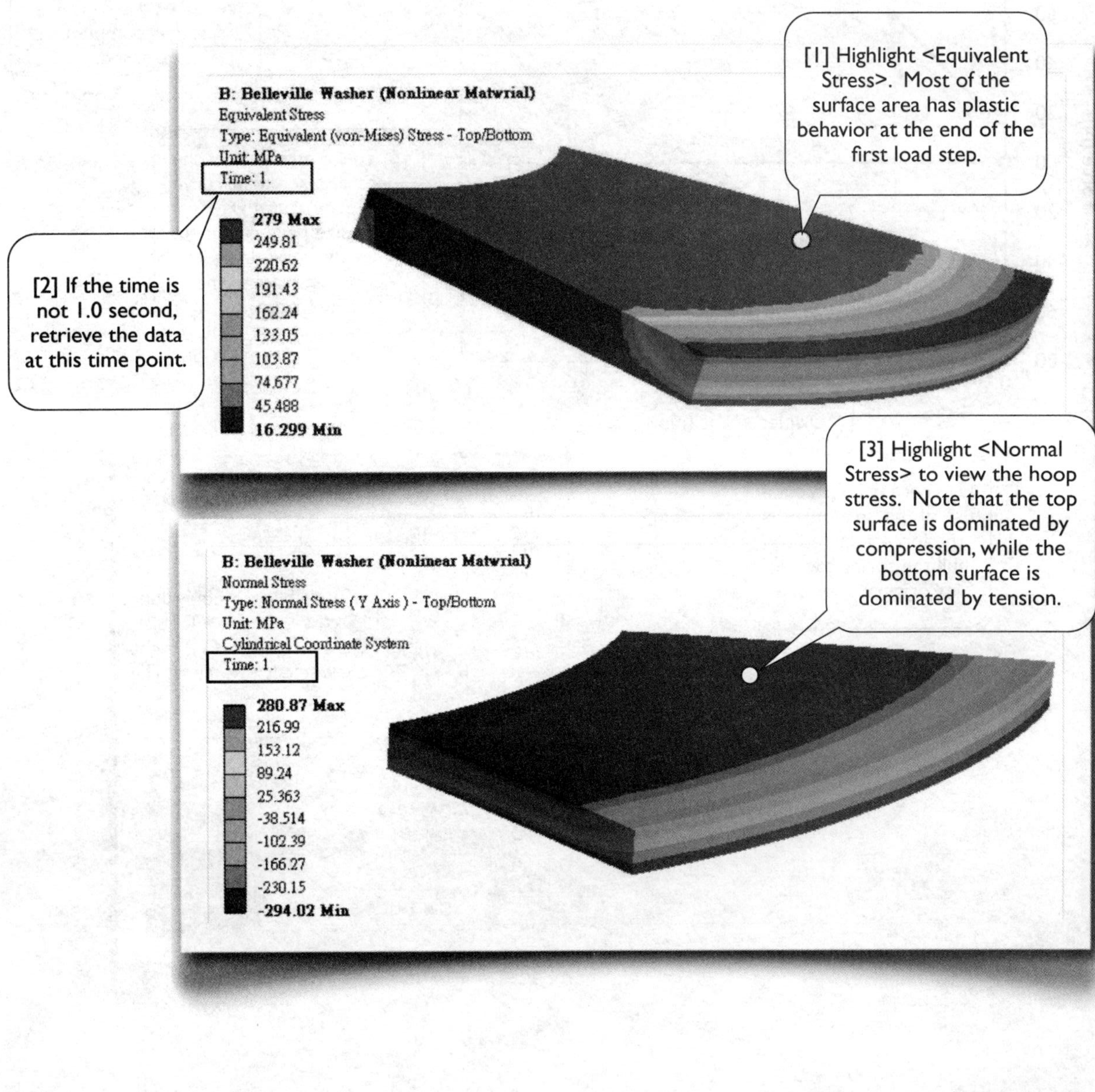

[4] Highlight <Chart> to view the force-displacement curve.

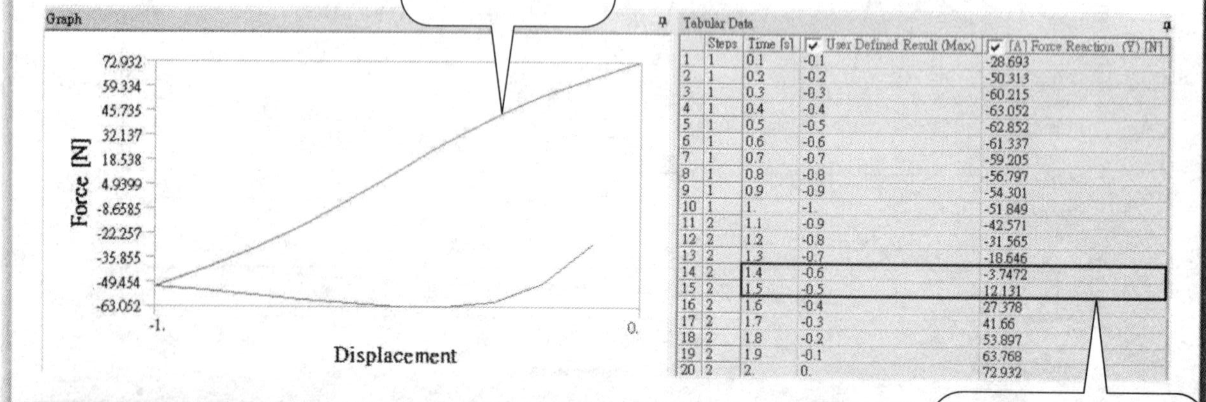

	Steps	Time [s]	User Defined Result (Max)	[A] Force Reaction (Y) [N]
1	1	0.1	-0.1	-28.693
2	1	0.2	-0.2	-50.313
3	1	0.3	-0.3	-60.215
4	1	0.4	-0.4	-63.052
5	1	0.5	-0.5	-62.852
6	1	0.6	-0.6	-61.337
7	1	0.7	-0.7	-59.205
8	1	0.8	-0.8	-56.797
9	1	0.9	-0.9	-54.301
10	1	1.	-1.	-51.849
11	2	1.1	-0.9	-42.571
12	2	1.2	-0.8	-31.565
13	2	1.3	-0.7	-18.646
14	2	1.4	-0.6	-3.7472
15	2	1.5	-0.5	12.131
16	2	1.6	-0.4	27.378
17	2	1.7	-0.3	41.66
18	2	1.8	-0.2	53.897
19	2	1.9	-0.1	63.768
20	2	2.	0.	72.932

[5] The data show that, at time of 1.4 second, or displacement of 0.6 mm, the reaction force is zero, i.e., the Belleville spring is completely released.

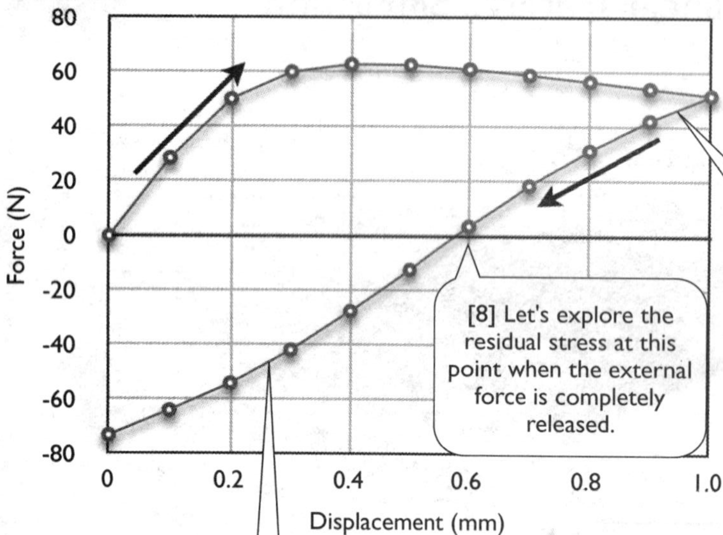

[6] This is a re-plot of the force-displacement curve in a more natural way. The emphasize here is that the curve is quite different between loading and unloading.

[8] Let's explore the residual stress at this point when the external force is completely released.

[7] There is no practice use of this section. It is the force required to pull the spring back to its original position.

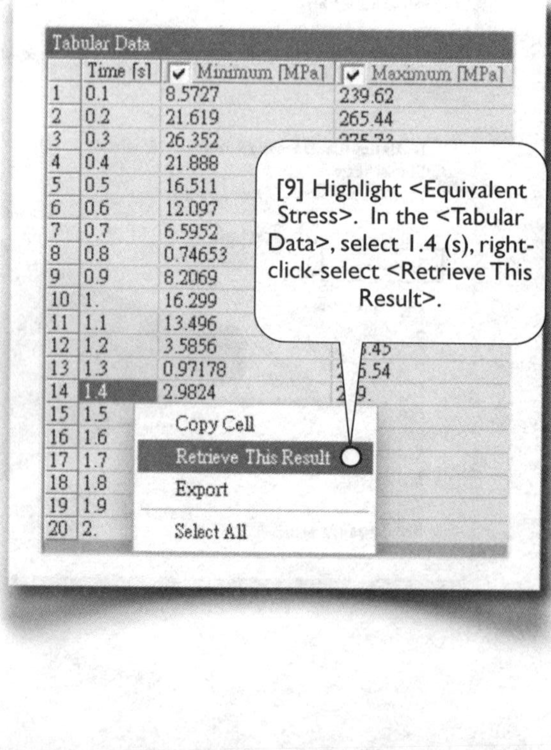

	Time [s]	Minimum [MPa]	Maximum [MPa]
1	0.1	8.5727	239.62
2	0.2	21.619	265.44
3	0.3	26.352	
4	0.4	21.888	
5	0.5	16.511	
6	0.6	12.097	
7	0.7	6.5952	
8	0.8	0.74653	
9	0.9	8.2069	
10	1.	16.299	
11	1.1	13.496	
12	1.2	3.5856	
13	1.3	0.97178	
14	1.4	2.9824	
15	1.5		
16	1.6		
17	1.7		
18	1.8		
19	1.9		
20	2.		

[9] Highlight <Equivalent Stress>. In the <Tabular Data>, select 1.4 (s), right-click-select <Retrieve This Result>.

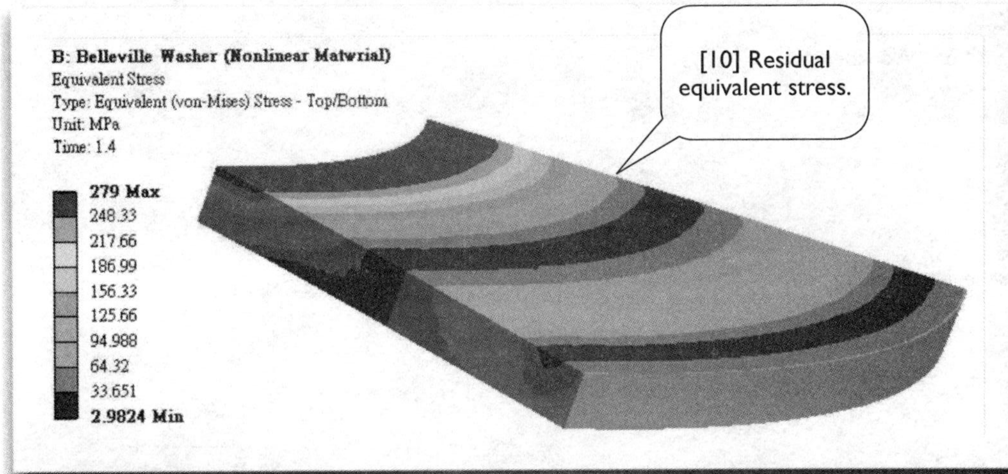
B: Belleville Washer (Nonlinear Matwrial)
Equivalent Stress
Type: Equivalent (von-Mises) Stress - Top/Bottom
Unit: MPa
Time: 1.4
279 Max
248.33
217.66
186.99
156.33
125.66
94.988
64.32
33.651
2.9824 Min
[10] Residual equivalent stress.

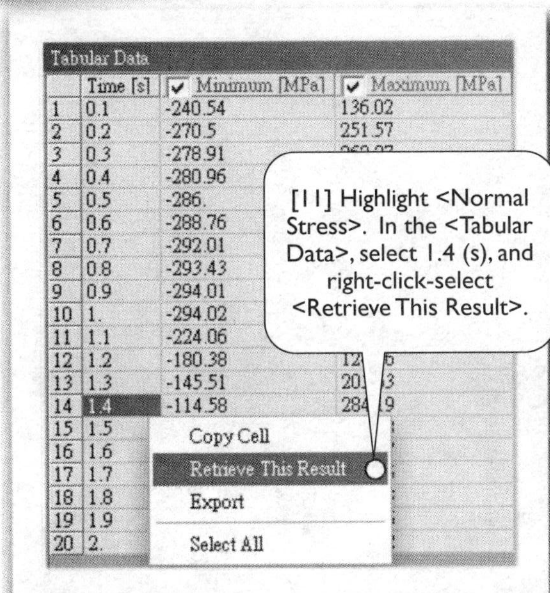
Tabular Data
Time [s]
Minimum [MPa]
Maximum [MPa]
1 0.1 -240.54 136.02
2 0.2 -270.5 251.57
3 0.3 -278.91
4 0.4 -280.96
5 0.5 -286.
6 0.6 -288.76
7 0.7 -292.01
8 0.8 -293.43
9 0.9 -294.01
10 1. -294.02
11 1.1 -224.06
12 1.2 -180.38
13 1.3 -145.51
14 1.4 -114.58
15 1.5
16 1.6
17 1.7
18 1.8
19 1.9
20 2.
Copy Cell
Retrieve This Result
Export
Select All
[11] Highlight <Normal Stress>. In the <Tabular Data>, select 1.4 (s), and right-click-select <Retrieve This Result>.

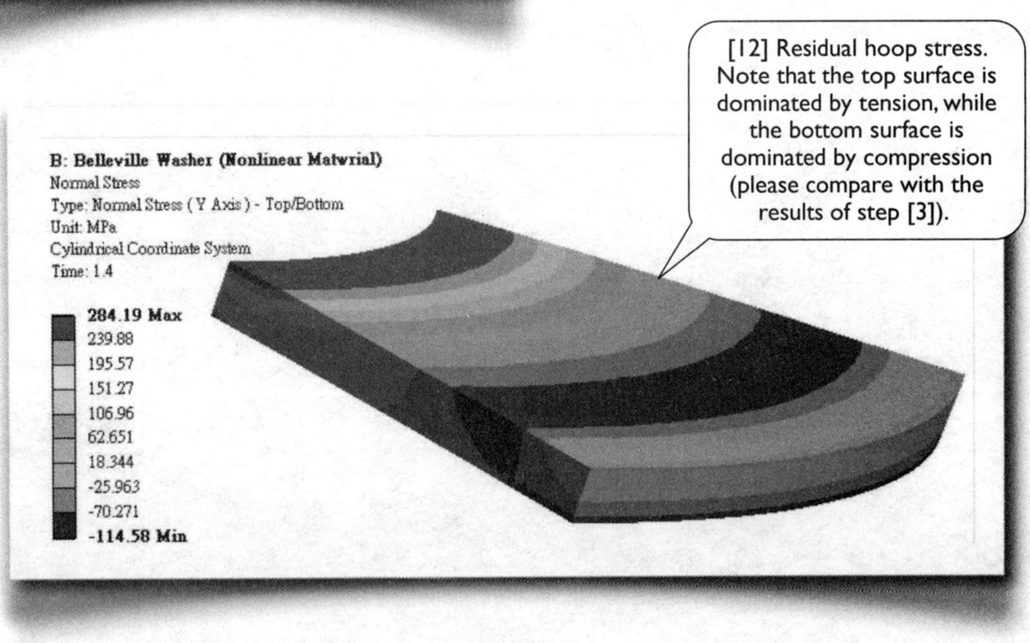
B: Belleville Washer (Nonlinear Matwrial)
Normal Stress
Type: Normal Stress (Y Axis) - Top/Bottom
Unit: MPa
Cylindrical Coordinate System
Time: 1.4
284.19 Max
239.88
195.57
151.27
106.96
62.651
18.344
-25.963
-70.271
-114.58 Min
[12] Residual hoop stress. Note that the top surface is dominated by tension, while the bottom surface is dominated by compression (please compare with the results of step [3]).

Wrap Up

Save the project and exit Workbench.

Reference

1. Wikipedia>Belleville Washer.

Section 14.3

Step-by-Step: Planar Seal

14.3-1 About the Planar Seal

The seal [1-4] is used in the door of a refrigerator. The seal is a long strip, and we will model it as a plane strain problem. The seal is made of a rubber. A series of material tests with the rubber have been conducted, including a uniaxial tensile test, a biaxial tensile test, and a shear test [5-7].

The strain range of the original test data covers much more extent than the data shown here [5-7]. However, a preliminary study of the problem shows that the maximum strain does not exceed 0.3. Therefore, we decided to used the portion of data up to a strain of 0.3. The data fitting will be better if we use only the relevant data. A series of trials of data fitting shows that, for these material testing data, the two-parameters Mooney-Rivlin hyperelastic model fits the data better than other models. We decide to use two-parameter Mooney-Rivlin model.

The unit system used in this section is in-lb-s.

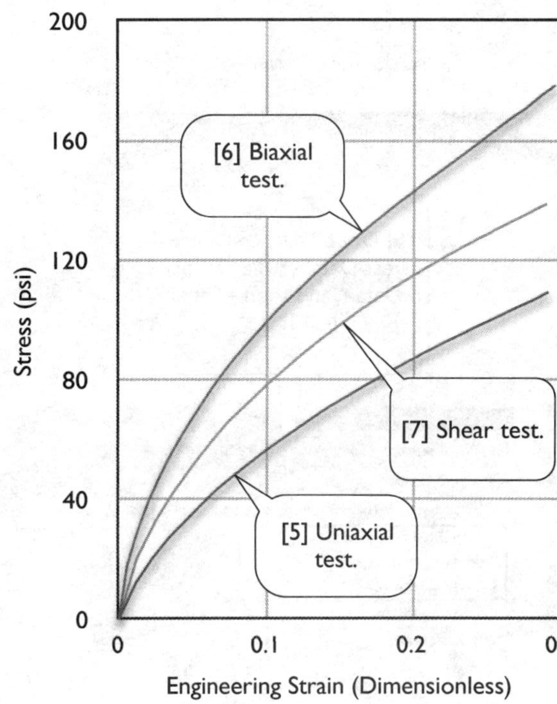

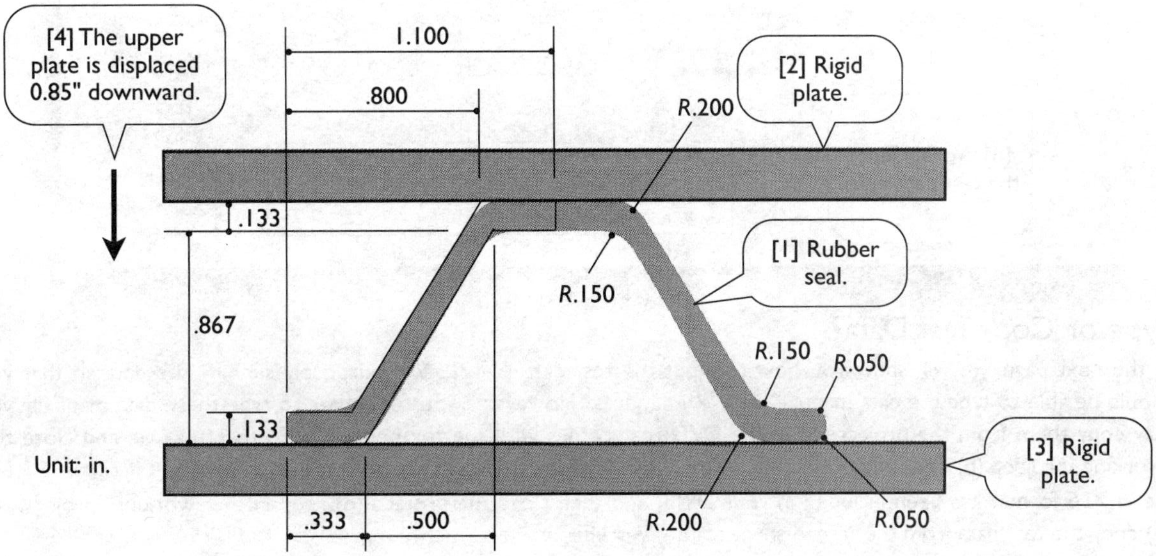

14.3-2 Prepare Material Properties for the Rubber

Launch <Workbench>. Create a <Static Structural> analysis system. Save the project as "Seal."

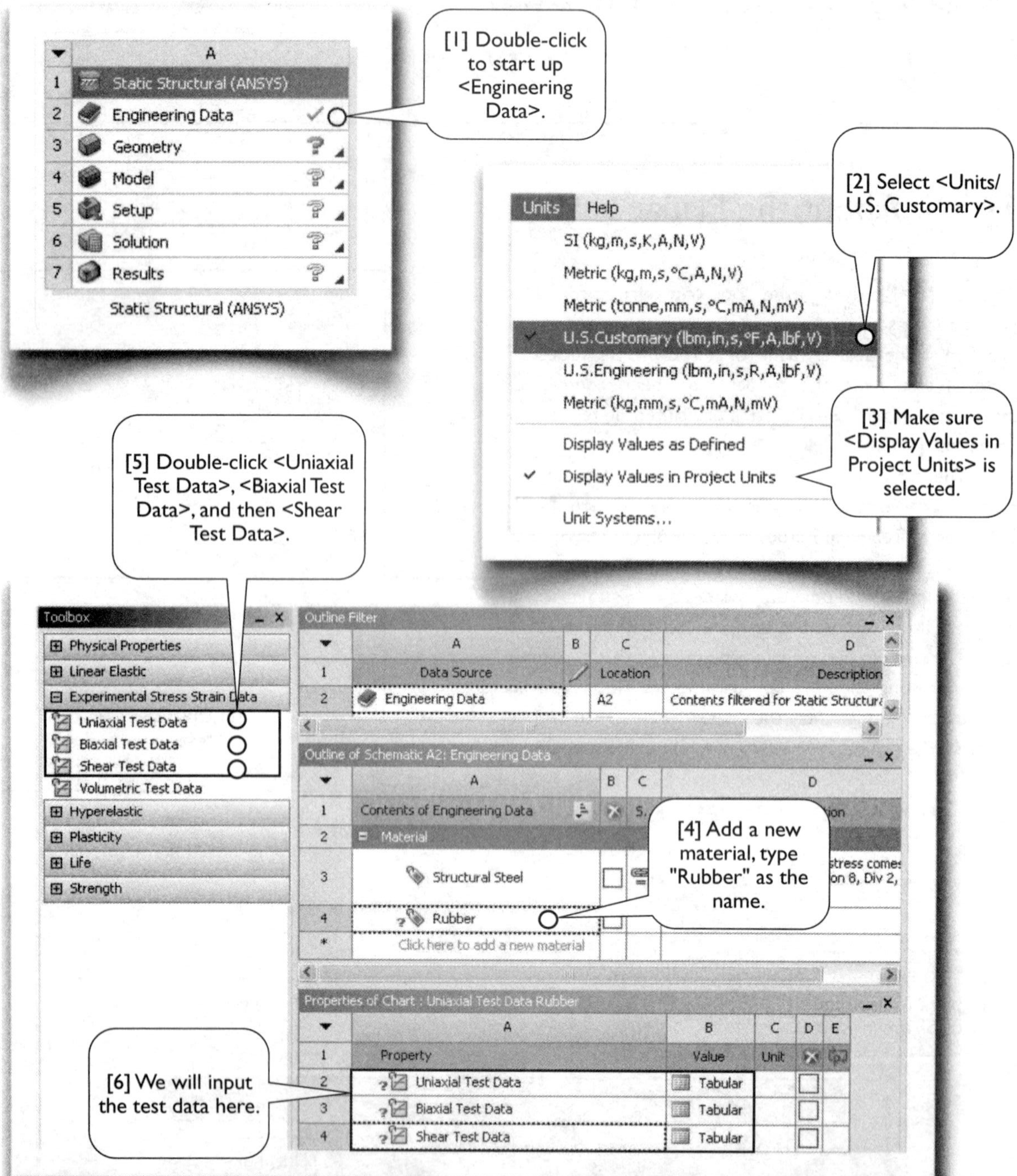

Type or Copy Test Data?

In the next page, we will show you how to input the test data [7-12]. We purposely simplify the data so that you should be able to type the data manually in a few minutes. However, if you really hate to type these data manually, you may copy them from the project file in the DVD that comes with the textbook. To do that, (a) save and close this "working" project, (b) open the project file in the DVD, (c) copy the test data to a spread sheet (e.g., Microsoft Excel; a file in XLS format has been included in your DVD) and then close the project, (d) reopen the "working" project, and (e) copy the test data from the spread sheet to the "working" project.

Properties of Outline Row 3: Rubber

	A	B	C	D	E
1	Property	Value	Unit		
2	Uniaxial Test Data	Tabular			
5	Biaxial Test Data	Tabular			
8	Shear Test Data	Tabular			
9	Scale	1			
10	Offset	0	psi		

[7] Highlight <Tabular> of the <Uniaxial Test Data>

[9] Highlight <Tabular> of the <Biaxial Test Data>

[11] Highlight <Tabular> of the <Shear Test Data>

[8] Type the data as shown. If <Table of Properties> doesn't show up, turn on <View/ Table>.

Table of Properties Row 2: Uniaxial Test Data

	A	B
1	Strain (in in^-1)	Stress (psi)
2	0	0
3	0.0116	12.34
4	0.0227	20.35
5	0.0339	27.28
6	0.0451	33.06
7	0.0557	38.29
8	0.0664	43.45
9	0.0773	47.86
10	0.088	52.12
11	0.0989	56.3
12	0.1095	60.06
13	0.1203	63.74
14	0.131	67.28
15	0.1415	70.67
16	0.1524	73.77
17	0.1628	76.84
18	0.1737	79.87
19	0.184	82.8
20	0.1947	85.61
21	0.2051	88.5
22	0.2154	91.13
23	0.2259	93.77
24	0.2366	96.37
25	0.2475	99.07
26	0.2584	101.6
27	0.2687	104.09
28	0.2797	106.58
29	0.2903	109.29
*		

[10] Type the data as shown.

Table of Properties Row 5: Biaxial Test Data

	A	B
1	Strain (in in^-1)	Stress (psi)
2	0	0
3	0.0056	17.94
4	0.0124	29.12
5	0.0192	38.22
6	0.0264	46.45
7	0.0337	53.81
8	0.041	60.37
9	0.0481	66.18
10	0.0555	71.76
11	0.0628	77.06
12	0.0702	81.97
13	0.0775	86.67
14	0.0851	91.21
15	0.0924	95.29
16	0.1	99.56
17	0.1078	103.8
18	0.1154	107.33
19	0.1231	110.94
20	0.1312	114.72
21	0.1394	118.19
22	0.1475	121.68
23	0.1558	125.28
24	0.1642	128.86
25	0.1726	132.26
26	0.1813	135.78
27	0.19	139.2
28	0.1992	142.49
29	0.2083	146.07
30	0.2174	149.37
31	0.2266	152.75
32	0.2361	156.28
33	0.2458	160.03
34	0.2551	163.66
35	0.2649	167.41
36	0.2748	170.67
37	0.2847	174.77
38	0.2948	178.44
*		

[12] Type the data as shown.

Table of Properties Row 8: Shear Test Data

	A	B
1	Strain (in in^-1)	Stress (psi)
2	0	0
3	0.012	20.22
4	0.0252	33.06
5	0.0376	43.07
6	0.0499	51.64
7	0.0624	59.27
8	0.0744	66.15
9	0.0874	72.3
10	0.0999	78.36
11	0.1124	83.77
12	0.1243	88.93
13	0.1371	93.76
14	0.1498	98.36
15	0.1619	102.75
16	0.1744	106.86
17	0.187	110.9
18	0.1998	114.76
19	0.2126	118.48
20	0.2252	122.09
21	0.238	125.61
22	0.2511	129.05
23	0.2633	132.32
24	0.2763	135.64
25	0.2892	138.91
*		

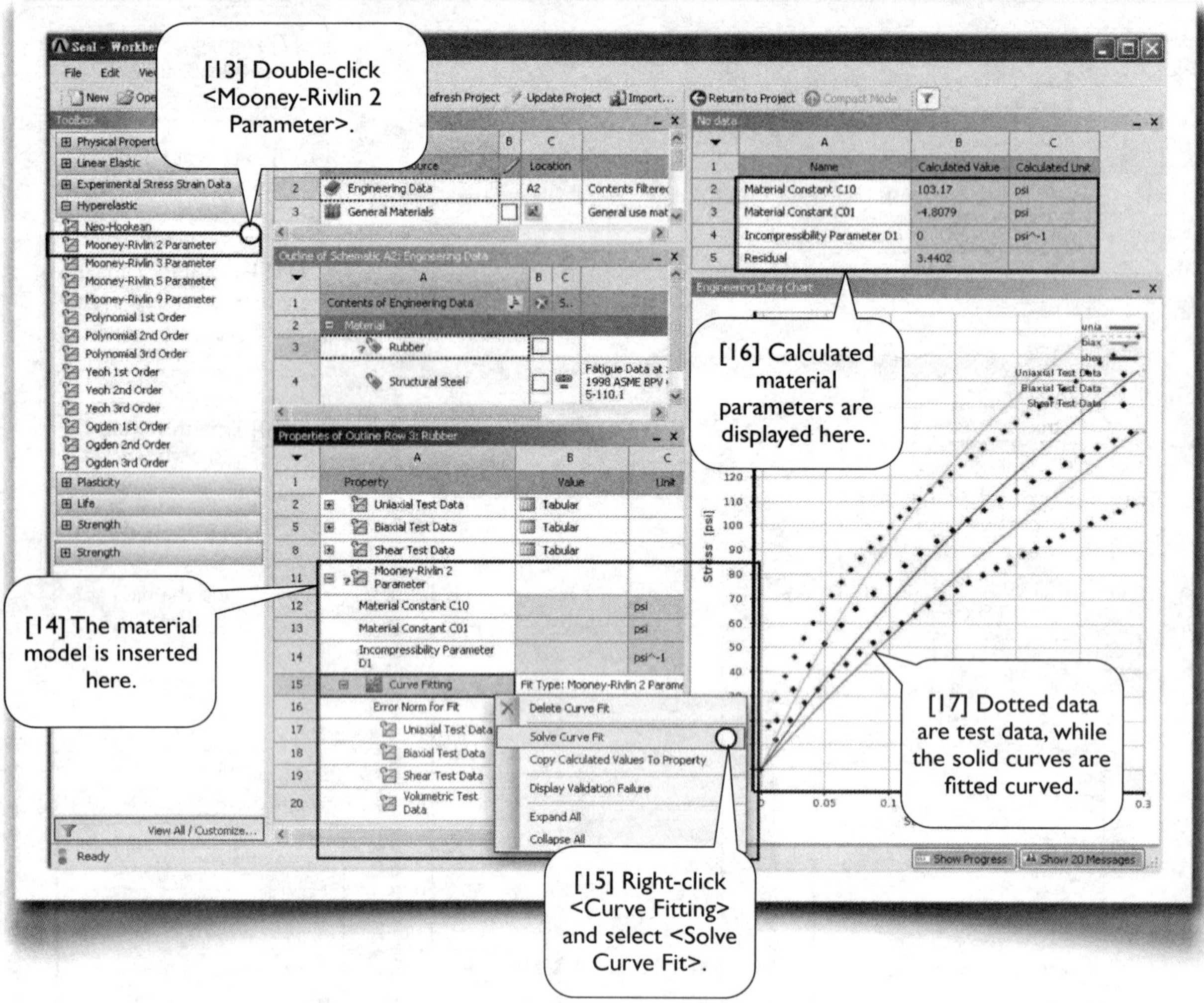
[13] Double-click <Mooney-Rivlin 2 Parameter>.
[14] The material model is inserted here.
[15] Right-click <Curve Fitting> and select <Solve Curve Fit>.
[16] Calculated material parameters are displayed here.
[17] Dotted data are test data, while the solid curves are fitted curved.
Material Constant C10
103.17
psi
Material Constant C01
-4.8079
psi
Incompressibility Parameter D1
0
psi^-1
Residual
3.4402

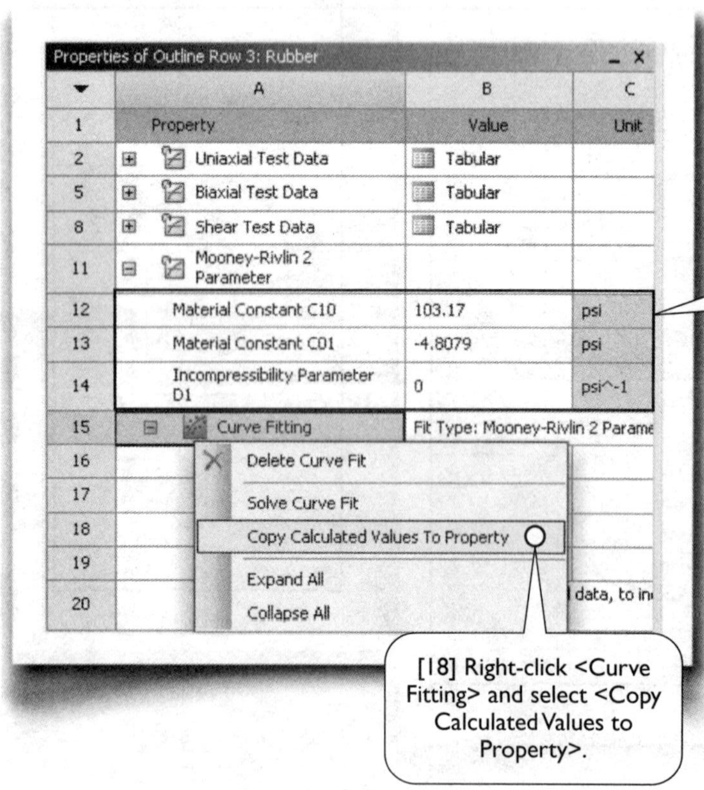
Properties of Outline Row 3: Rubber
Property
Value
Unit
Uniaxial Test Data
Biaxial Test Data
Shear Test Data
Tabular
Mooney-Rivlin 2 Parameter
Material Constant C10
103.17
psi
Material Constant C01
-4.8079
psi
Incompressibility Parameter D1
0
psi^-1
Curve Fitting
Fit Type: Mooney-Rivlin 2 Parame
Delete Curve Fit
Solve Curve Fit
Copy Calculated Values To Property
Expand All
Collapse All
[18] Right-click <Curve Fitting> and select <Copy Calculated Values to Property>.
[19] Now, the material parameters are formally input here.

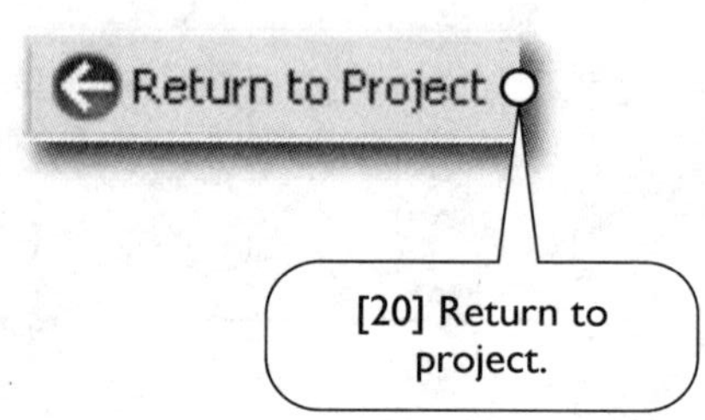
Return to Project
[20] Return to project.

14.3-3 Create 2D Geometry

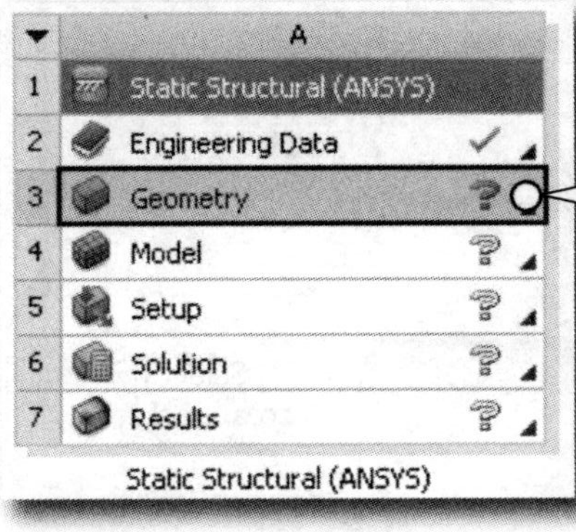

[1] Start up DesignModeler. Select <Inch> as length unit.

[2] Create a sketch on XYPlane.

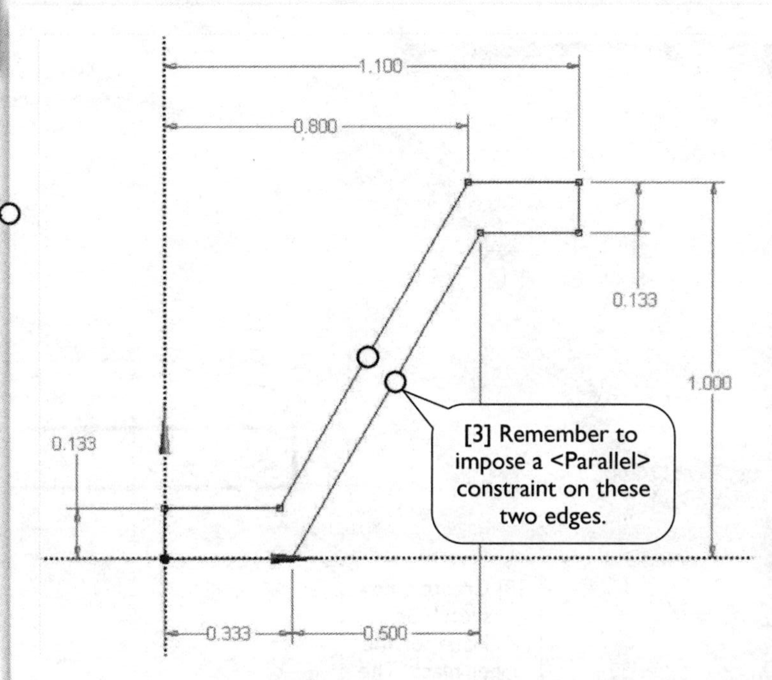

[3] Remember to impose a <Parallel> constraint on these two edges.

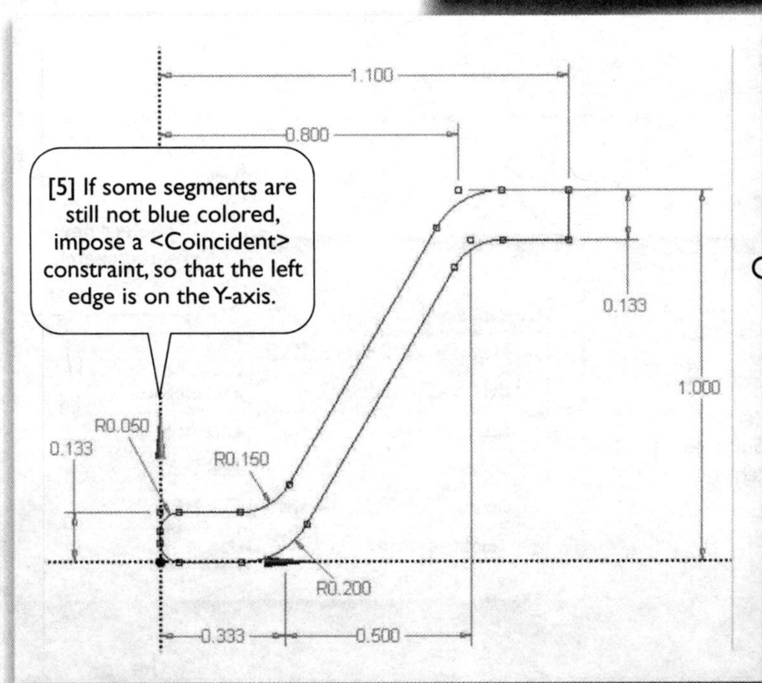

[5] If some segments are still not blue colored, impose a <Coincident> constraint, so that the left edge is on the Y-axis.

[4] Add fillets and specify their radii. (For the radii of the fillets, please refer to Section 14.3.1.)

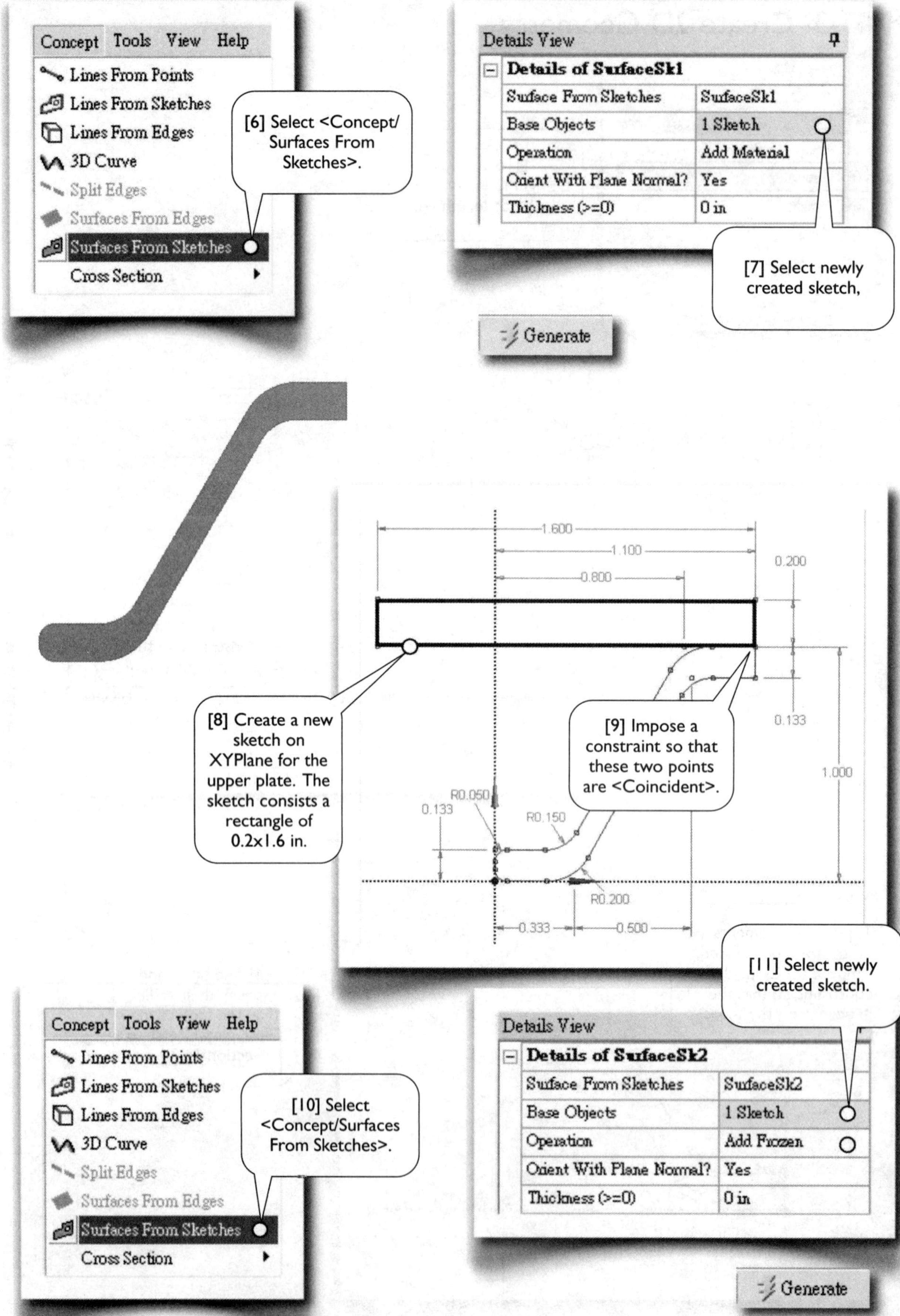
Concept Tools View Help
Lines From Points
Lines From Sketches
Lines From Edges
3D Curve
Split Edges
Surfaces From Edges
Surfaces From Sketches
Cross Section
[6] Select <Concept/ Surfaces From Sketches>.
Details View
Details of SurfaceSk1
Surface From Sketches SurfaceSk1
Base Objects 1 Sketch
Operation Add Material
Orient With Plane Normal? Yes
Thickness (>=0) 0 in
[7] Select newly created sketch,
Generate
1.600
1.100
0.800
0.200
0.133
1.000
R0.050
0.133
R0.150
R0.200
0.333
0.500
[8] Create a new sketch on XYPlane for the upper plate. The sketch consists a rectangle of 0.2x1.6 in.
[9] Impose a constraint so that these two points are <Coincident>.
Concept Tools View Help
Lines From Points
Lines From Sketches
Lines From Edges
3D Curve
Split Edges
Surfaces From Edges
Surfaces From Sketches
Cross Section
[10] Select <Concept/Surfaces From Sketches>.
[11] Select newly created sketch.
Details View
Details of SurfaceSk2
Surface From Sketches SurfaceSk2
Base Objects 1 Sketch
Operation Add Frozen
Orient With Plane Normal? Yes
Thickness (>=0) 0 in
Generate

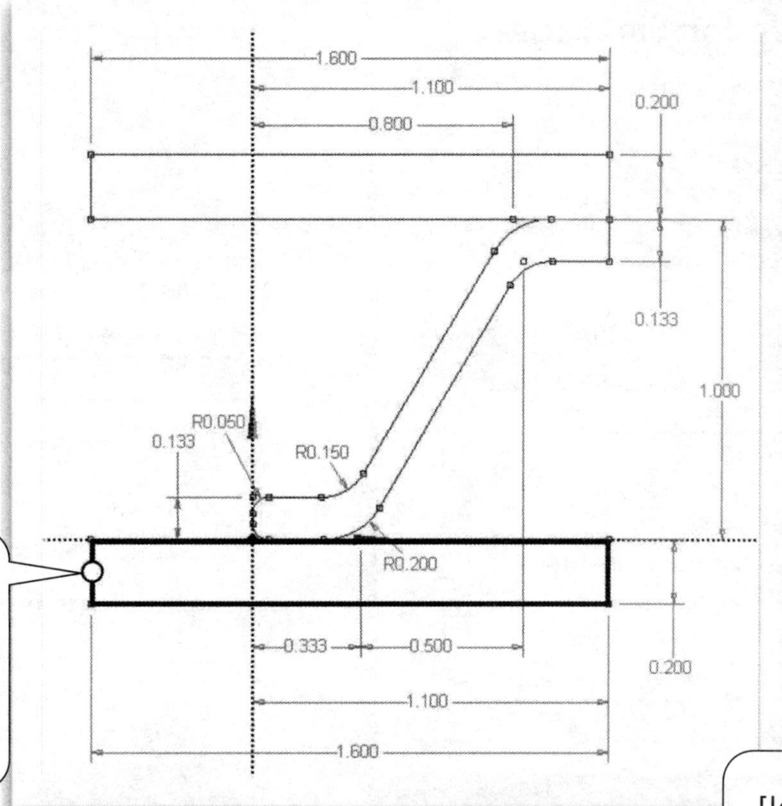

[12] Create a new sketch on XYPlane for the lower plate. The sketch consists a rectangle of the same size of the upper plate.

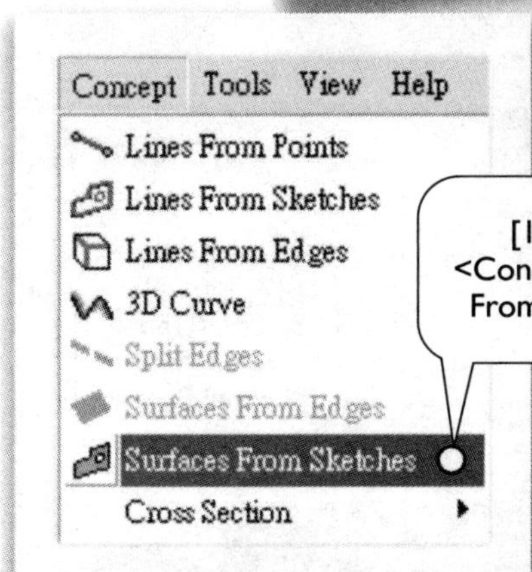

[13] Select <Concept/Surfaces From Sketches>.

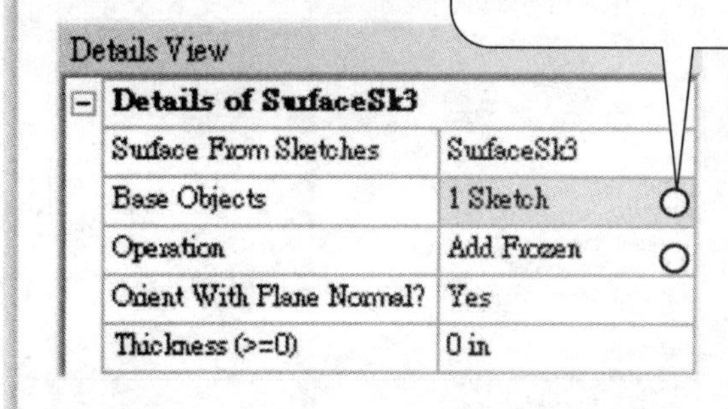

[14] Select newly created sketch.

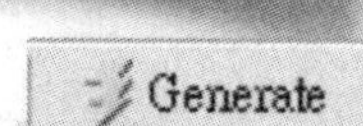

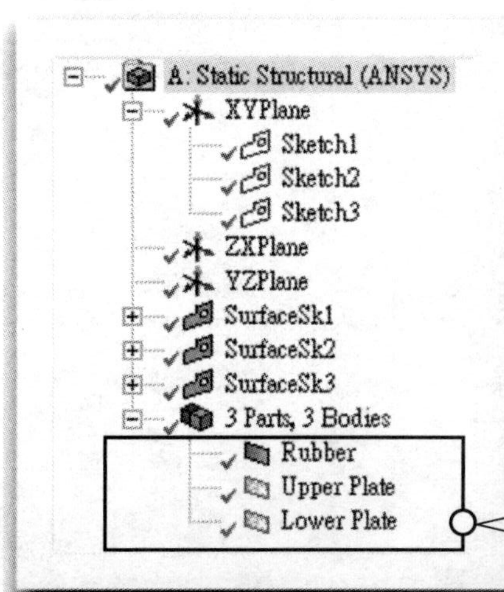

[15] Rename three parts.

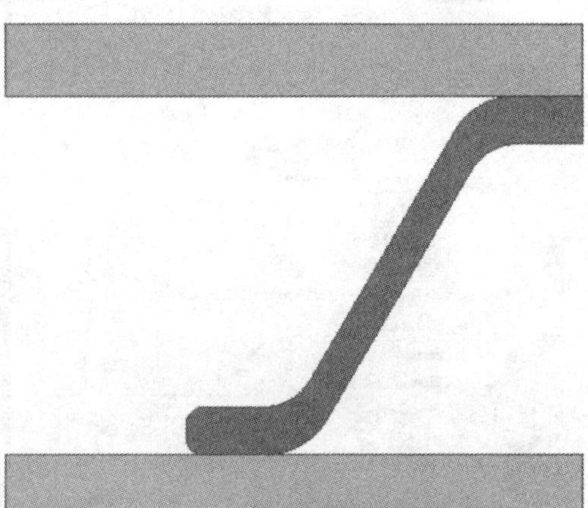

14.3-4 Set Up for Simulation

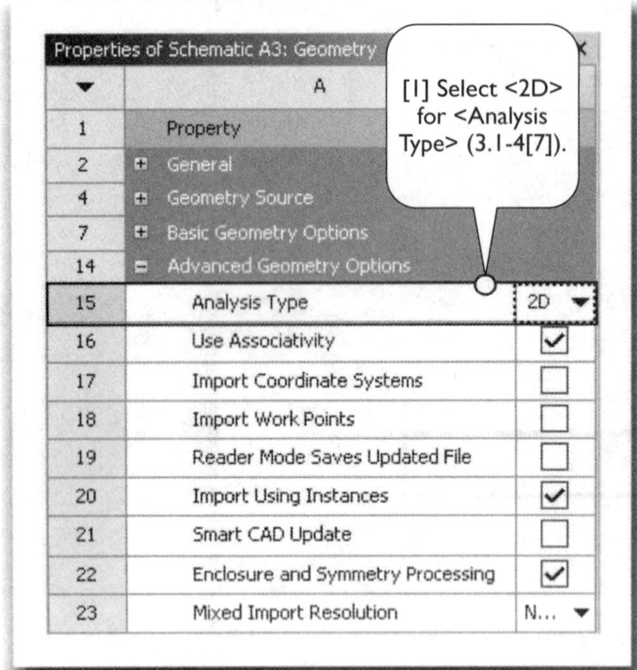

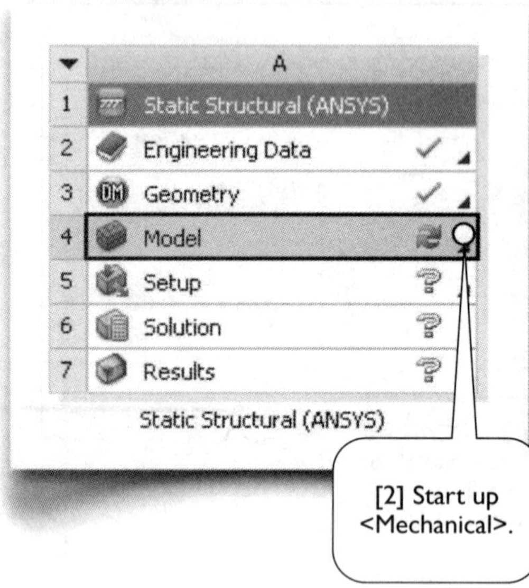

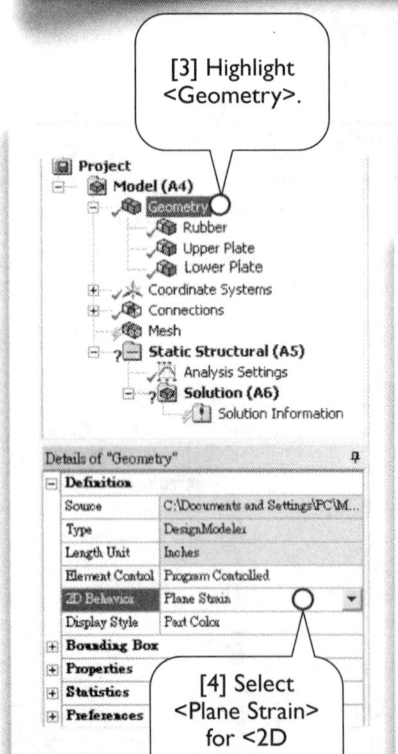

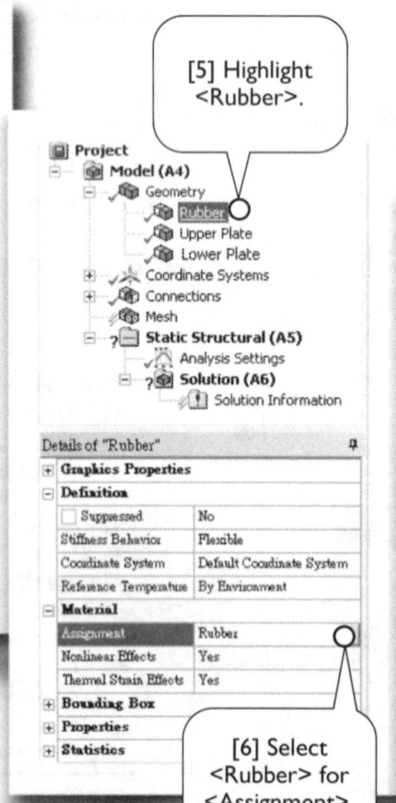

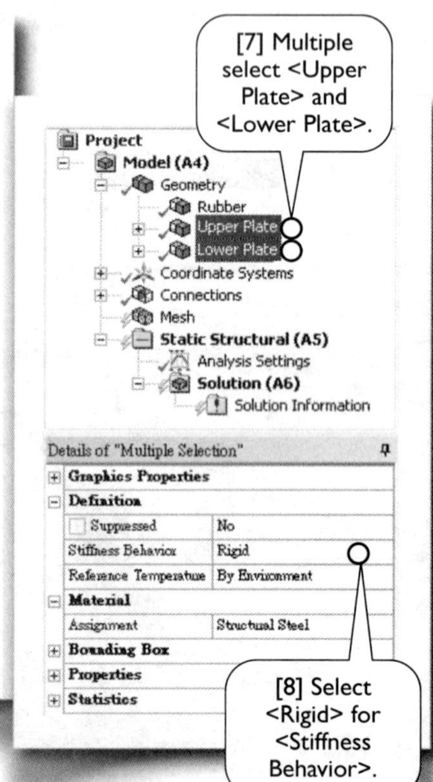

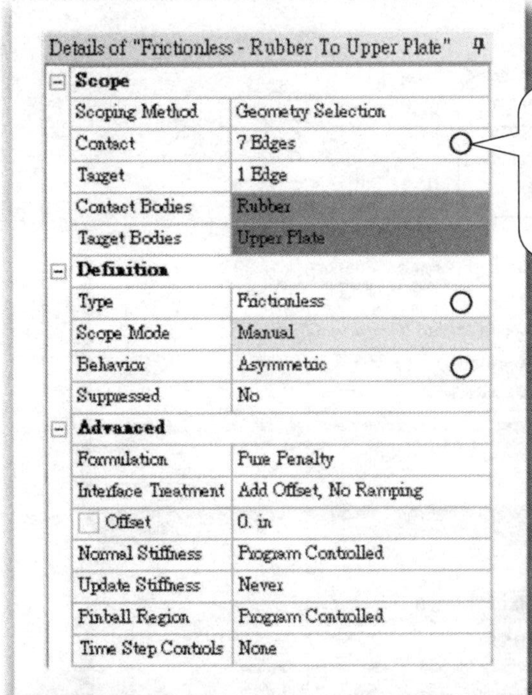

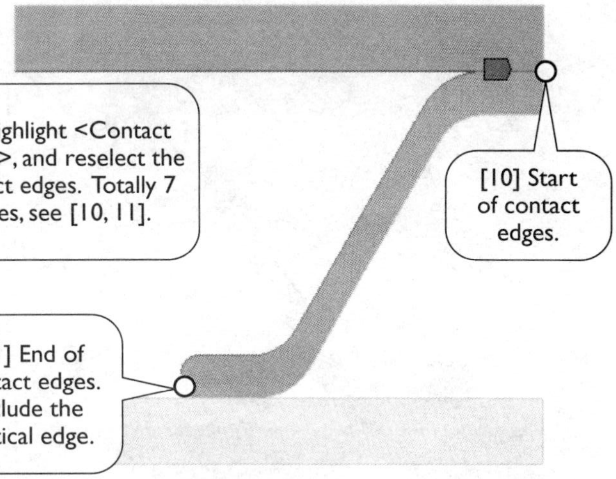

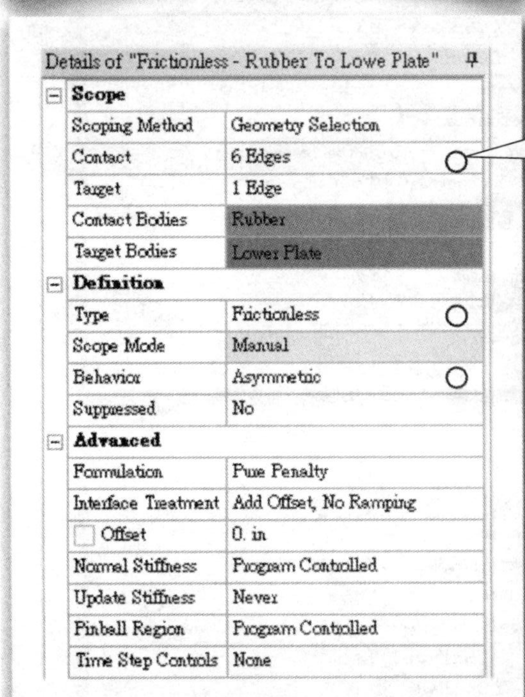

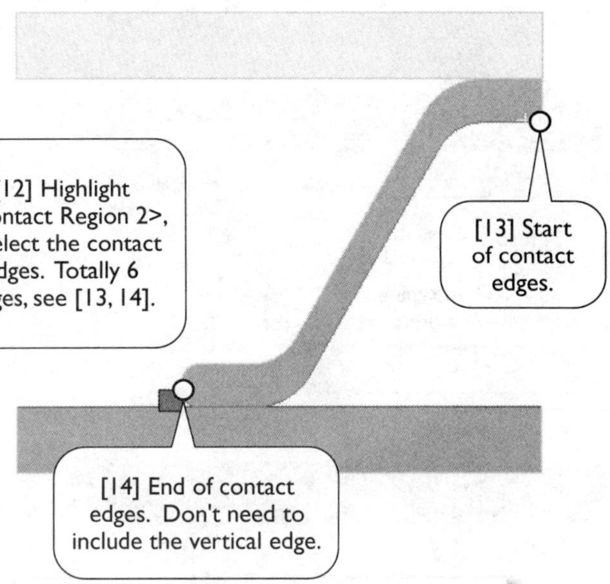

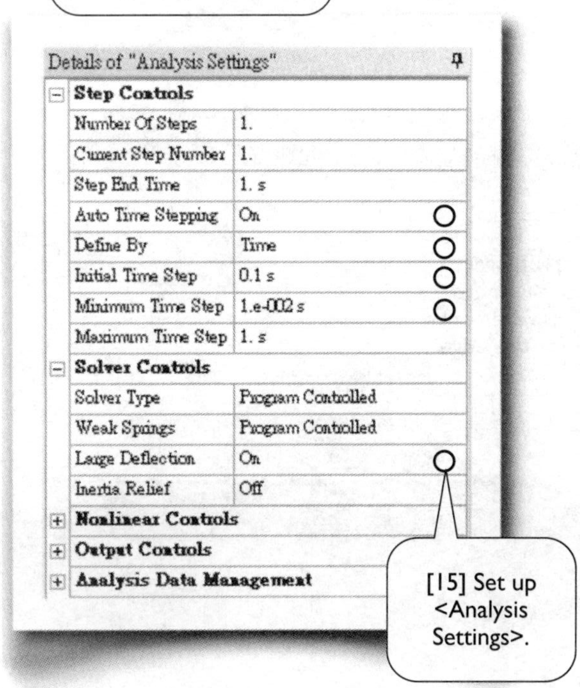

Asymmetric Behavior

When a rigid is involved, <Asymmetric> is the only choice for <Behavior> (also see 13.3-5[8]).

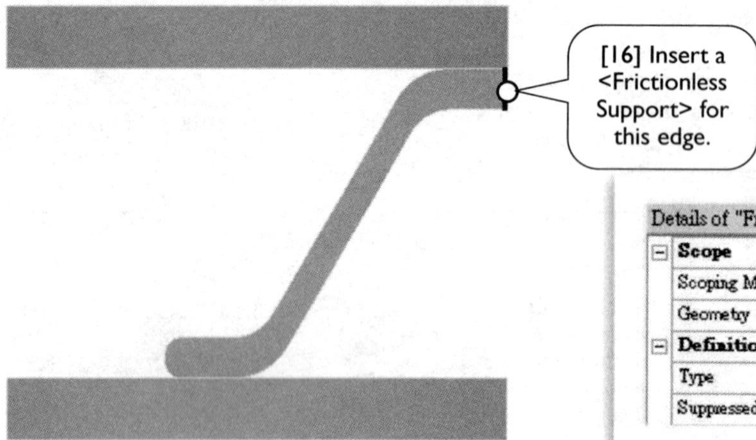

Details of "Frictionless Support"

Scope		
Scoping Method	Geometry Selection	
Geometry	1 Edge	○
Definition		
Type	Frictionless Support	
Suppressed	No	

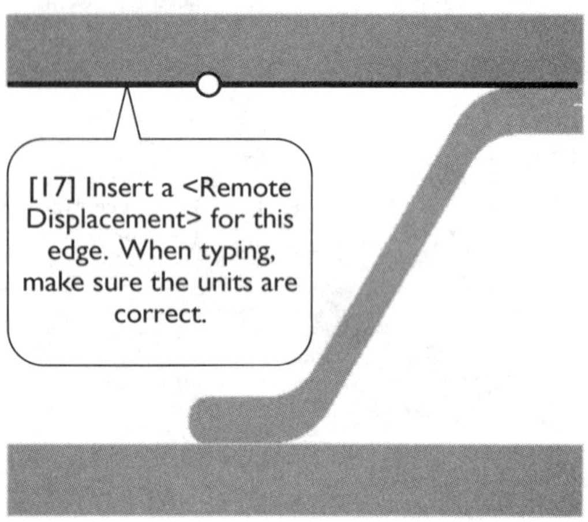

Details of "Remote Displacement"

Scope		
Scoping Method	Geometry Selection	
Geometry	1 Edge	○
Coordinate System	Global Coordinate System	
X Coordinate	0.3 in	
Y Coordinate	1. in	
Location	Click to Change	
Definition		
Type	Remote Displacement	
X Component	0. in (ramped)	○
Y Component	-0.85 in (ramped)	○
Rotation Z	0. ° (ramped)	○
Suppressed	No	
Behavior	Rigid	○
Advanced		

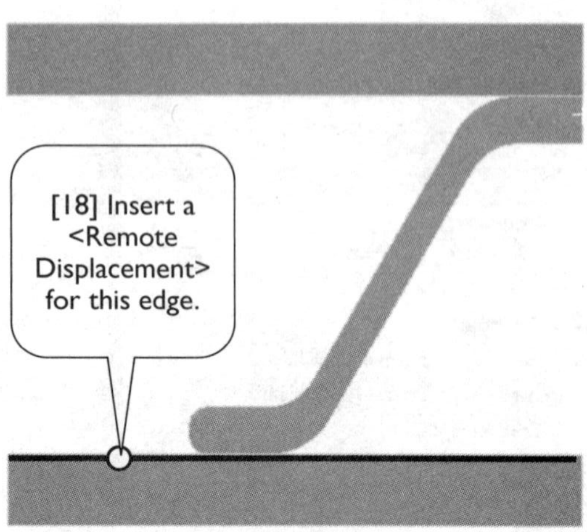

Details of "Remote Displacement 2"

Scope		
Scoping Method	Geometry Selection	
Geometry	1 Edge	○
Coordinate System	Global Coordinate System	
X Coordinate	0.3 in	
Y Coordinate	0. in	
Location	Click to Change	
Definition		
Type	Remote Displacement	
X Component	0. in (ramped)	○
Y Component	0. in (ramped)	○
Rotation Z	0. ° (ramped)	○
Suppressed	No	
Behavior	Rigid	○
Advanced		

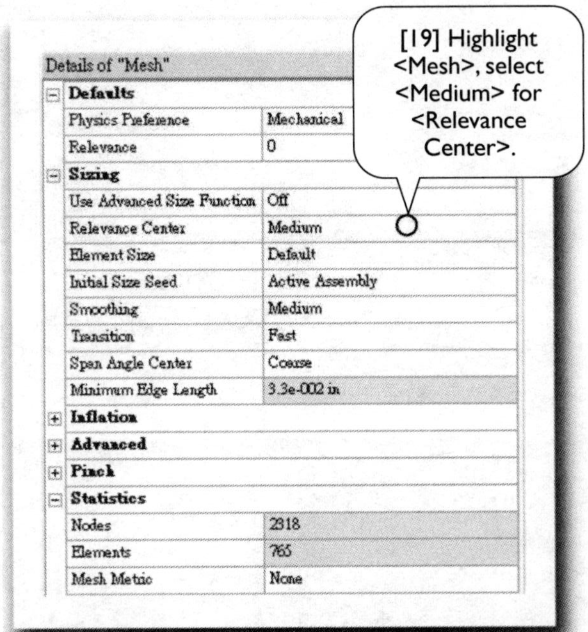
Details of "Mesh"
Defaults
Physics Preference | Mechanical
Relevance | 0
Sizing
Use Advanced Size Function | Off
Relevance Center | Medium
Element Size | Default
Initial Size Seed | Active Assembly
Smoothing | Medium
Transition | Fast
Span Angle Center | Coarse
Minimum Edge Length | 3.3e-002 in
Inflation
Advanced
Pinch
Statistics
Nodes | 2318
Elements | 765
Mesh Metric | None
[19] Highlight <Mesh>, select <Medium> for <Relevance Center>.

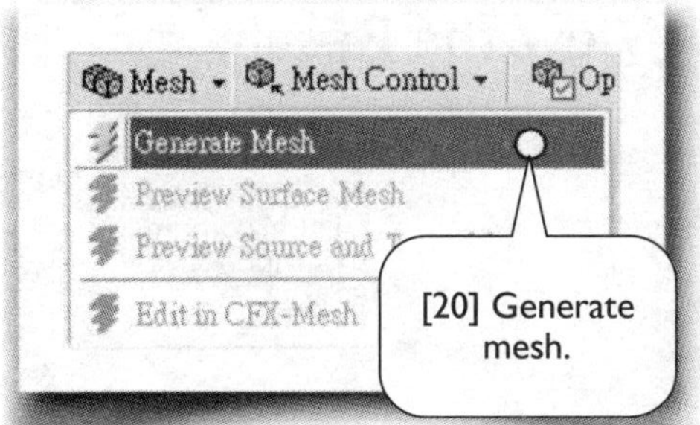
Mesh
Mesh Control
Generate Mesh
Preview Surface Mesh
Edit in CFX-Mesh
[20] Generate mesh.

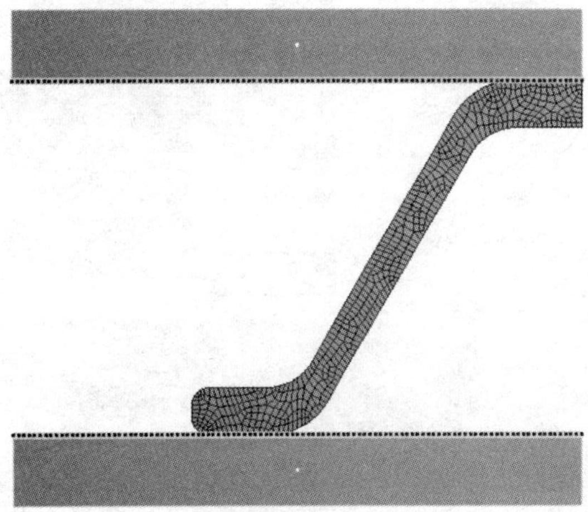

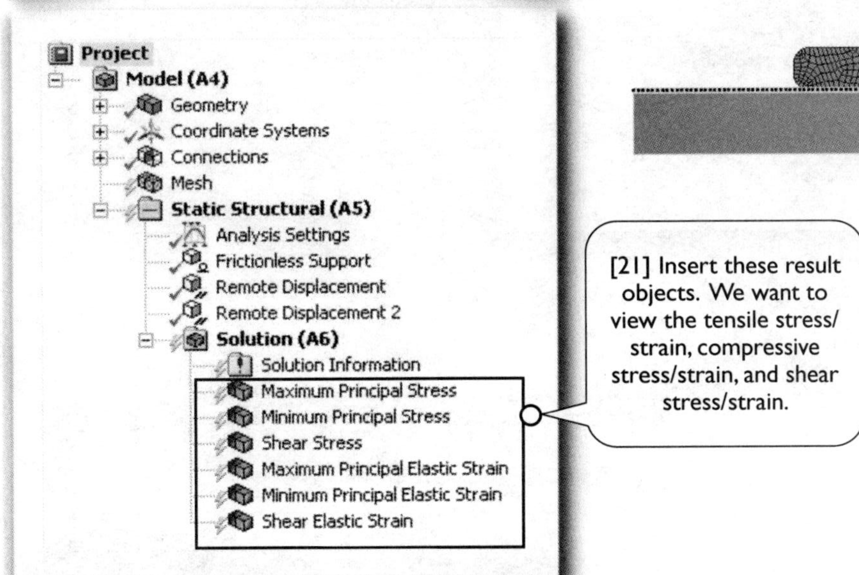
Project
Model (A4)
Geometry
Coordinate Systems
Connections
Mesh
Static Structural (A5)
Analysis Settings
Frictionless Support
Remote Displacement
Remote Displacement 2
Solution (A6)
Solution Information
Maximum Principal Stress
Minimum Principal Stress
Shear Stress
Maximum Principal Elastic Strain
Minimum Principal Elastic Strain
Shear Elastic Strain
[21] Insert these result objects. We want to view the tensile stress/strain, compressive stress/strain, and shear stress/strain.

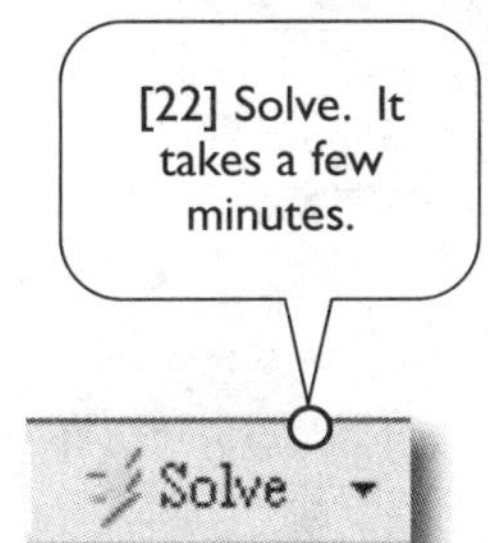
[22] Solve. It takes a few minutes.
Solve

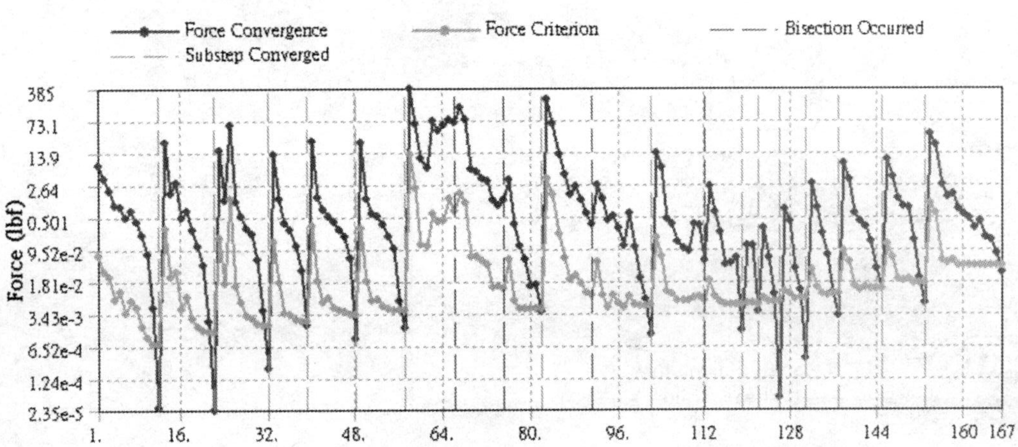
Force Convergence
Force Criterion
Bisection Occurred
Substep Converged
Force (lbf)
385
73.1
13.9
2.64
0.501
9.52e-2
1.81e-2
3.43e-3
6.52e-4
1.24e-4
2.35e-5
1.
16.
32.
48.
64.
80.
96.
112
128
144
160
167

14.3-5 View the Results

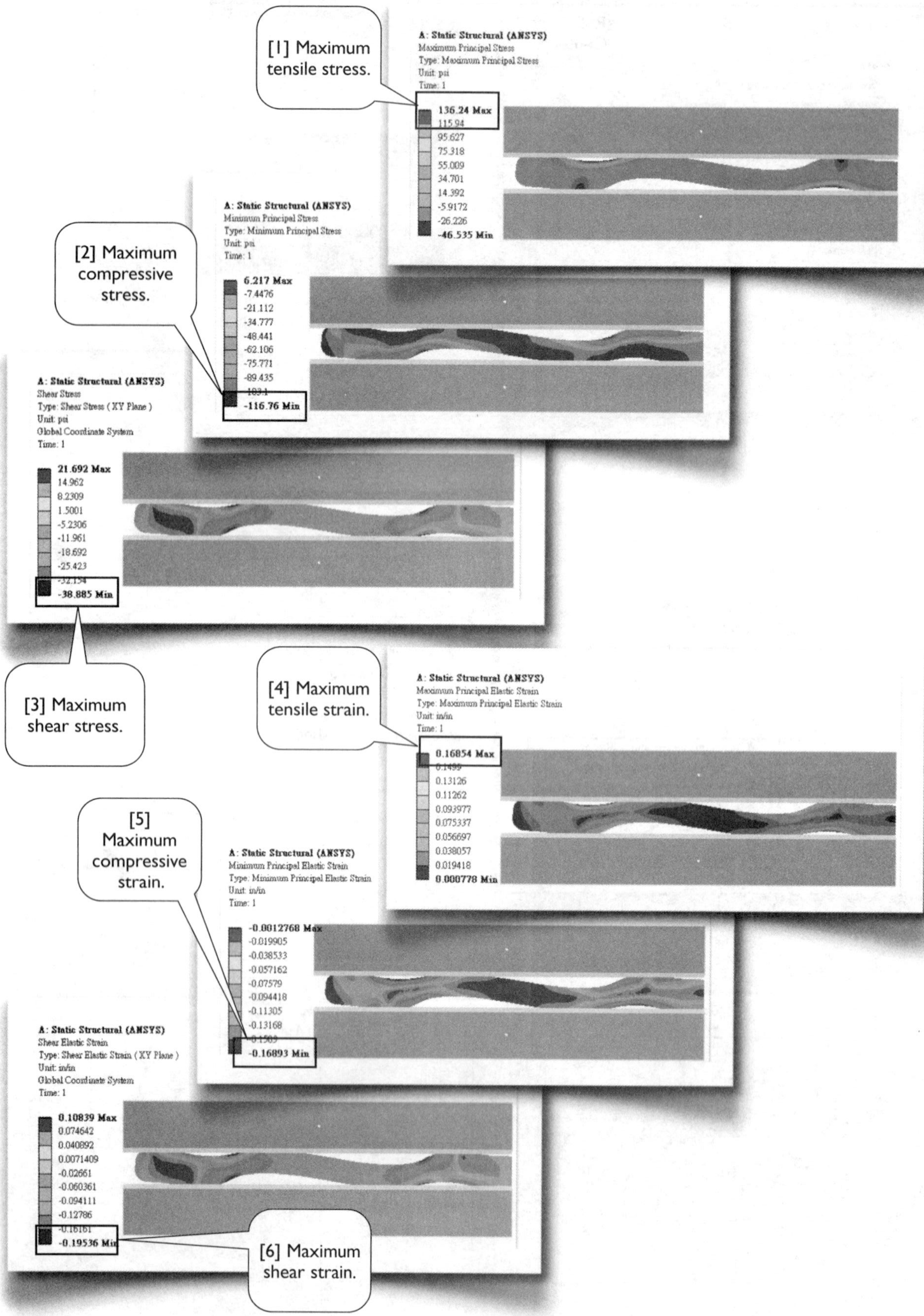

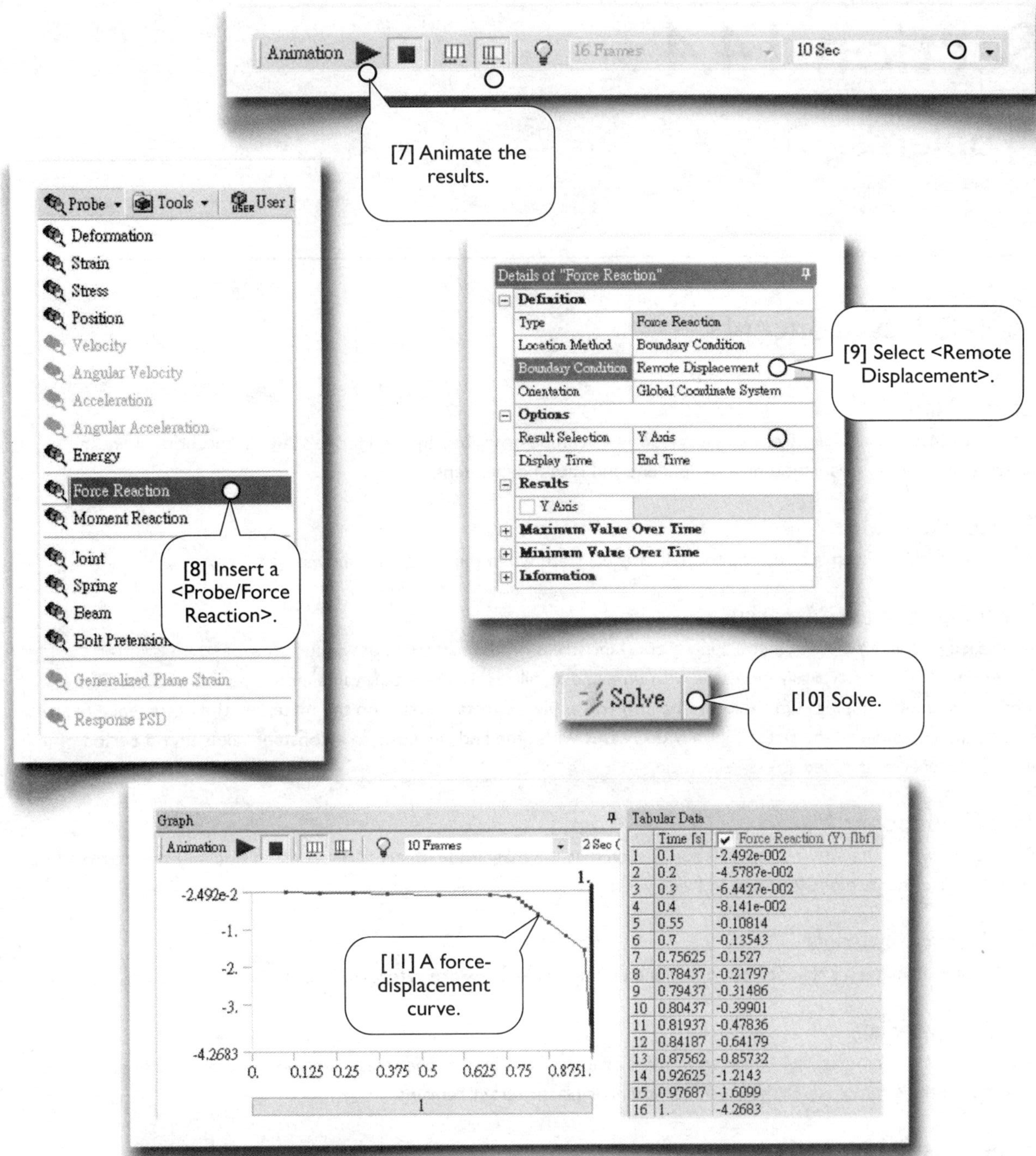

Wrap Up

Save the project and exit Workbench.

Reference

1. Wikipedia>Belleville Washer.

Section 14.4
Problems

14.4-1 Key Concepts

Linear Materials
A material that has a linear stress-strain relation and can be described by the Hooke's law. In this book, a linear material also implies elasticity, time-independent, and rate-independent.

Elastic Material
Materials of which the strain returns to their original state when the stress is removed.

Time-Dependent Materials
Also called viscous materials. If you apply a constant stress on the materials, the occurrence of strain is time-dependent. The strain typically increases with time and stabilizes to a constant value after a period of time. This behavior is called creeping. On the other hand, If you apply a constant strain on the materials, the occurrence of stress is also time-dependent. The stress typically decreases with time and stabilizes to a constant value after a period of time. This behavior is called stress-relaxation.

Rate-Dependent Materials
Materials of which the stress-strain relation is such that the magnitude of stress depends on not only the magnitude of strain but also the rate of the strain, and vice versa.

Nonlinear Materials
In this book, all materials that are not described by the Hooke's law are categorized as nonlinear materials.

Plastic Materials
Materials that exhibit plasticity behavior, which is characterized by that the strain does not return to its original state after the stress is removed. Rather, residual strain, or plastic strain, remains.

Hyperelastic Materials
Material that remain elastic under a very large strain.

Initial Yield Point
In plasticity, yield point may change. Stress at the elastic limit is called the initial yield point.

Yield Surface
In a uniaxial test, yielding occurs at certain stress values; they are called yield points. In 3D cases, yielding occurs at certain stress states; these stress states form a "surface" (or hyper-surface) in the multiaxial stress space. The surface is called a yield surface. During stressing, the yield surface may change in size as well as location.

Von Mises Yield Surface

Different yield criterion results in different yield surface. If von Mises yield criterion is used, the yield surface is a cylindrical surface in the $\sigma_1 - \sigma_2 - \sigma_3$ space.

Initial Yield Surface

In plasticity, yield surface may change in size as well as location during stressing. The original yield surface before any yielding occurs (i.e., the behavior is still elastic) is called the initial yield surface.

Subsequent Yield Surface

In plasticity, during stressing, yield surface may change in size as well as location. All possible yield surfaces except the initial yield surface is called the subsequent yield surface.

Hardening Rules

Rules that describe how yield surface changes its size and location.

Kinematic Hardening

Kinematic hardening assumes that the yield surface changes only the location but not the size.

Isometric Hardening

Isometric hardening assumes that the yield surface changes only the size but not the location.

14.4-2 Workbench Exercises

Model the Belleville Washer as a 2D Problem

In Section 14.2, we modeled the Belleville washer as a surface body and meshed it with shell elements. It is possible to model it as a 2D problem and mesh it with 2D axisymmetric solid elements. Do it and draw the pros and cons for both modeling methods.

Pneumatic Finger

Replace the material of the pneumatic finger, simulated in Section 9.1, with the rubber used in the Section 14.3. Redo the simulation for the pneumatic finger.

Chapter 15

Explicit Dynamics

Many transient dynamic simulations require extremely small integration time steps, for examples, high-speed impact, drop test, or highly nonlinear problems. In such cases, the time steps may be as small as several nanoseconds, and the use of <Transient Structural> analysis system becomes impractical, since the run time would be too enormous to be accepted. The integration method used in the <Transient Structural> analysis system is called an *implicit method*.

The <Explicit Dynamics> analysis system also deals with transient structural dynamics. It uses an *explicit integration method*. The explicit method is very efficient for each time step. It thus allows a huge number of time steps to be calculated within an acceptable time. The disadvantage of the explicit method is that the integration time steps must be very small (typically microseconds to nanoseconds) to achieve a stable solution. If the dynamic behavior must be observed within a long duration (say, several seconds), then millions or billions of time step is required to complete the simulation. The runtime becomes impractical, unless supercomputing facilities are used.

Purpose of the Chapter

This chapter provides the basics of explicit dynamics so that the students have enough background knowledge to perform some simple <Explicit Dynamics> simulations. A high-speed impact simulation and a drop test simulation are designed as step-by-step exercises to demonstrate the applications of the <Explicit Dynamics> analysis system.

About Each Section

Section 1 provides the basics of explicit dynamics. Section 2 presents a high-speed impact example and section 3 presents a drop test simulation. Both examples are simple yet instructional. We will use default settings as much as possible, so that the students can learn the built-in capability of the <Explicit Dynamics> analysis system.

Section 15.1
Basics of Explicit Dynamics

15.1-1 Implicit Integration Methods

Consider solving Eq. 12.1-4(1) again,

$$[M]\{\ddot{D}\}+[C]\{\dot{D}\}+[K]\{D\}=\{F\} \qquad \text{Copy of 12.1-4(1)}$$

Consider a typical time step $\Delta t = t_{n+1} - t_n$. Let D_n, $\dot{D}_n$, and $\ddot{D}_n$ be the displacement, velocity, and acceleration at t_n, and D_{n+1}, $\dot{D}_{n+1}$, and $\ddot{D}_{n+1}$ be those at t_{n+1}. Consider a special case that the acceleration is linear over the time step (i.e., $\ddddot{D}_n = \ddddot{D}_{n+1} = 0$), then, by Taylor series expansions at t_n,

$$\dot{D}_{n+1} = \dot{D}_n + \Delta t \ddot{D}_n + \frac{\Delta t^2}{2} \dddot{D}_n \tag{1}$$

$$D_{n+1} = D_n + \Delta t \dot{D}_n + \frac{\Delta t^2}{2} \ddot{D}_n + \frac{\Delta t^3}{6} \dddot{D}_n \tag{2}$$

The quantity $\dddot{D}_n$ can be approached by

$$\dddot{D}_n = \frac{\ddot{D}_{n+1} - \ddot{D}_n}{\Delta t} \tag{3}$$

Substitution of Eq. (3) into Eqs. (1) and (2) respectively yields

$$\dot{D}_{n+1} = \dot{D}_n + \frac{\Delta t}{2}\left(\ddot{D}_{n+1} + \ddot{D}_n\right) \tag{4}$$

$$D_{n+1} = D_n + \Delta t \dot{D}_n + \Delta t^2 \left(\frac{1}{6}\ddot{D}_{n+1} + \frac{1}{3}\ddot{D}_n\right) \tag{5}$$

Eqs. (4) and (5) can be regarded as a special case of the Newmark method,

$$\dot{D}_{n+1} = \dot{D}_n + \Delta t\left[\gamma \ddot{D}_{n+1} + (1-\gamma)\ddot{D}_n\right] \tag{6}$$

$$D_{n+1} = D_n + \Delta t \dot{D}_n + \frac{1}{2}\Delta t^2\left[2\beta \ddot{D}_{n+1} + (1-2\beta)\ddot{D}_n\right] \tag{7}$$

If you substitute $\gamma = 1/2$ and $\beta = 1/6$ into Eqs. (6) and (7) respectively, you will obtain Eqs. (4) and (5).

Eqs. (6) and (7) are used in <Transient Structural> analysis system. The parameters γ and β are chosen to control characteristics of the algorithm such as accuracy, numerical stability, etc. It is called an *implicit method* because the calculation of $\dot{D}_{n+1}$ and D_{n+1} requires knowledge of $\ddot{D}_{n+1}$. That is, the response at the current time step depends on not only the historical information but also the current information; iterations are needed to solve Eqs. (6) and (7).

Calculation of the response at time t_{n+1} is conceptually depicted in [1-6]. In the beginning [1], the displacement D_n, velocity $\dot{D}_n$, and acceleration $\ddot{D}_n$ of the last step are already known (For $n = 0$, we may assume $\ddot{D}_0 = 0$). Since $\ddot{D}_{n+1}$ is needed in Eqs. (6) and (7), we use $\ddot{D}_n$ as an initial gauss of $\ddot{D}_{n+1}$. Knowing D_n, $\dot{D}_n$, and $\ddot{D}_{n+1}$, the quantities $\dot{D}_{n+1}$ and D_{n+1} can be calculated according to Eqs. (6) and (7) [2]. The next step [3] is to substitute $\ddot{D}_{n+1}$, $\dot{D}_{n+1}$, and D_{n+1} into Eq. 12.1-4(1). If Eq. 12.1-4(1) is satisfied, then the calculation of the response at time t_{n+1} is complete [5], otherwise, $\ddot{D}_{n+1}$ is updated and another iteration is initiated [6]. Update of $\ddot{D}_{n+1}$ [6] is similar to the Newton-Raphson method described in Section 13.1-4.

With implicit methods, a typical integration time step is about 0.0001 to 0.01 seconds; a typical simulation time is about 0.1 to 10 seconds, which involves hundreds or thousands of integration time steps.

Implicit methods can be used for most of transient structural simulations. However, for highly nonlinear problems, it often fails due to convergence issues; for high-speed impact problems, the integration time is so small that the computing time becomes intolerable. In such cases, explicit methods are more applicable.

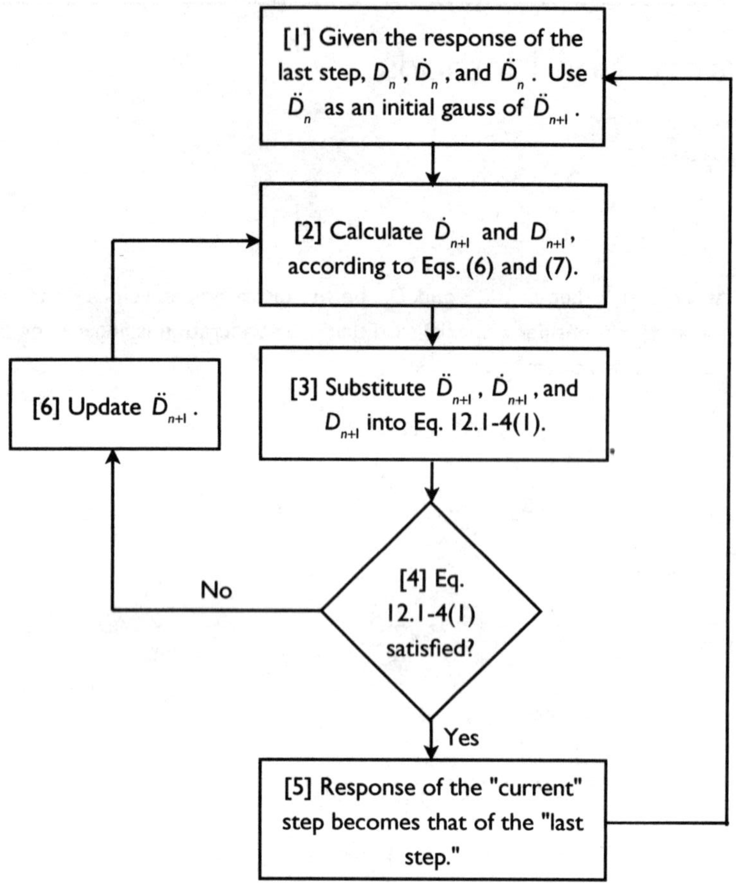

15.1-2 Explicit Integration Methods

The explicit method used in <Explicit Dynamics> analysis system is based on half-step central differences

$$\ddot{D}_n = \frac{\dot{D}_{n+\frac{1}{2}} - \dot{D}_{n-\frac{1}{2}}}{\Delta t}, \text{ or } \dot{D}_{n+\frac{1}{2}} = \dot{D}_{n-\frac{1}{2}} + \ddot{D}_n \Delta t \qquad (1)$$

$$\dot{D}_{n+\frac{1}{2}} = \frac{D_{n+1} - D_n}{\Delta t}, \text{ or } D_{n+1} = D_n + \dot{D}_{n+\frac{1}{2}} \Delta t \qquad (2)$$

Eqs. (1) and (2) are called *explicit methods* because the calculation of $\dot{D}_{n+\frac{1}{2}}$ and D_{n+1} requires knowledge of historical information only. That is, the response at the current time can be calculated explicitly; no iterations within a time step is needed. Therefore, it is very efficient to complete a time step, also called a *cycle*. One of the distinct characteristics of the explicit method is that its integration time step needs to be very small in order to achieve an accurate solution.

The procedure used in the <Explicit Dynamics> analysis system is illustrated in [1-9]. In the beginning of a cycle [2], the displacement D_n and velocity $\dot{D}_n$ of the last cycle are already known. With these information, we can calculate the strain and strain rate for each element [3], using the relations such as Eqs. 1.3-2(2) and 1.2-7(1). The volume change for each element is then calculated, according to the equations of state, and the mass density is updated [4]. The volumetric information is needed for the calculation of stresses. With these information, the element stresses can be calculated [5] according to a constitutive model, relation between stresses and strains/strain rates, such as Eq. 1.2-8(1). The stresses are integrated over the elements, and the external loads are added to form the nodal forces F_n [6]. The nodal accelerations are then calculated [7] according to

$$\ddot{D}_n = \frac{F_n}{m} + \frac{b}{\rho} \tag{3}$$

where b is the body force (see Eq. 1.2-6(2)), m is the nodal mass, and ρ is the mass density. The nodal velocities at $t_{n+\frac{1}{2}}$ are calculated [8] according to Eq. (1) and the nodal displacements at t_{n+1} are calculated [9] according to Eq. (2).

With explicit methods, a typical integration time step is about 1 nanosecond to 1 microsecond; a typical simulation time is about 1 millisecond to 1 second, which involves thousands or millions of cycles.

Explicit methods is useful for high-speed impact problems and highly nonlinear problems. For low-speed problems, using explicit methods becomes impractical due to an enormous computing time, since it requires very small integration time steps.

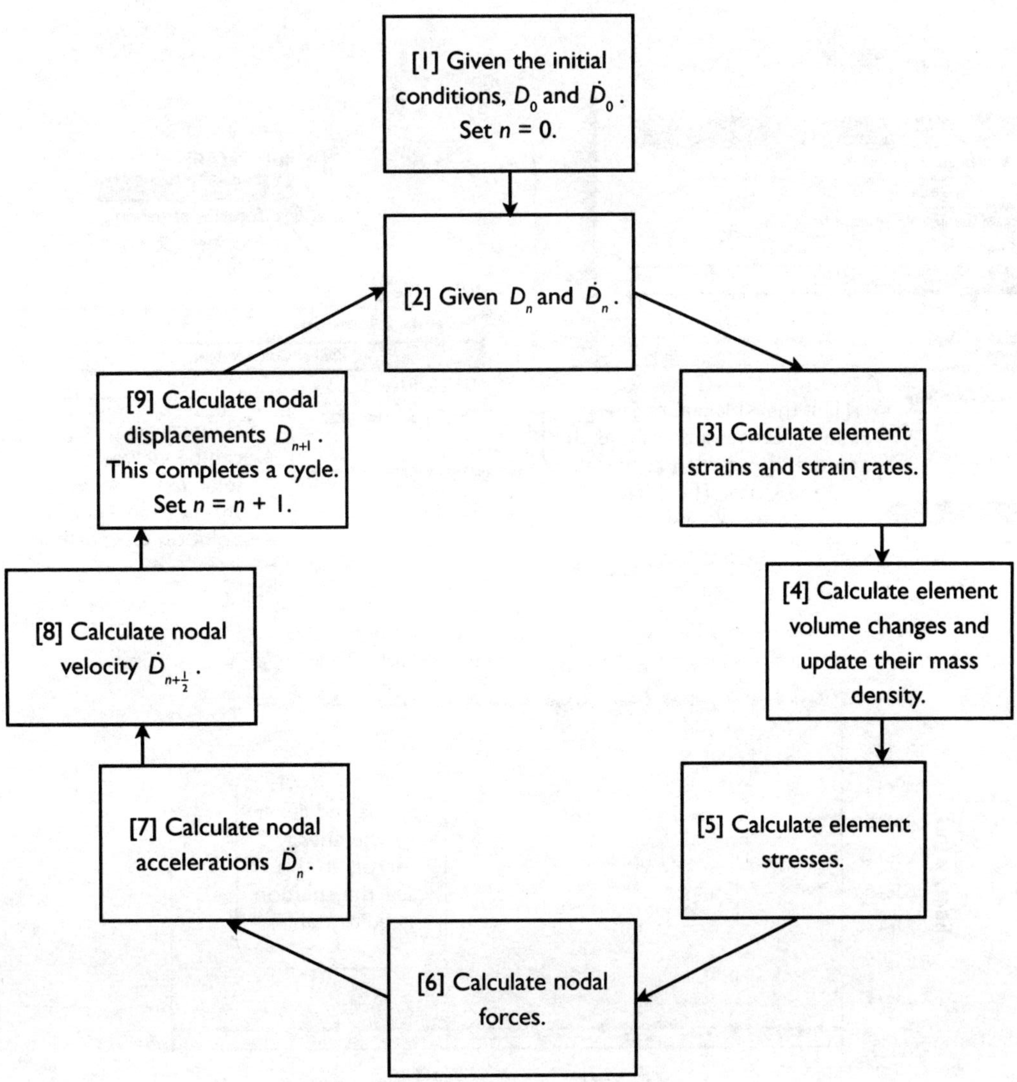

15.1-3 Solution Accuracy

In <Transient Structural>, in which an implicit method is used, convergence criteria are used to control the solution accuracy, similar to the Newton-Raphson method described in Section 13.1-4. In <Explicit Dynamics>, since no iterations are involved, solution accuracy is not controlled with convergence criteria. Instead, it uses the *principle of conservation of energy* to monitor the solution accuracy. It calculates overall energy at each cycle. If the energy error, which will be defined in the next paragraph, reaches a threshold, the solution is regarded as unstable and stops [1]. The default threshold is 10%. Energy statistics can be viewed by selecting <Energy Conservation> in the <Solution Output> [2, 3].

At any time, *Current energy* of the system can be calculated, including its kinetic energy and strain energy. Current energy at any time can be taken as *reference energy*, default to the energy at start cycle. One form of the principle of conservation of energy is called the *principle of work and energy*, which states that

$$(\text{Reference Energy}) + (\text{Work Done})_{\text{Reference}\rightarrow\text{Current}} = (\text{Current Energy}) \tag{1}$$

The *Energy error* is defined by

$$\text{Energy Error} = \frac{\left|(\text{Current Energy})-(\text{Reference Energy}) - (\text{Work Done})_{\text{Reference}\rightarrow\text{Current}}\right|}{\max\left(\left|\text{Current Energy}\right|, \left|\text{Reference Energy}\right|, \left|\text{Kinetic Energy}\right|\right)} \tag{2}$$

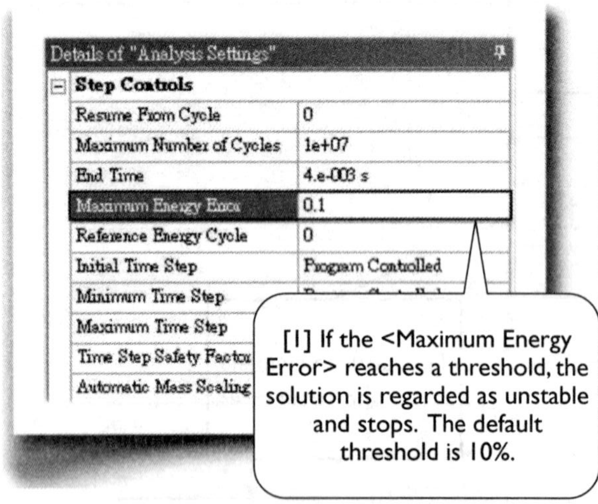

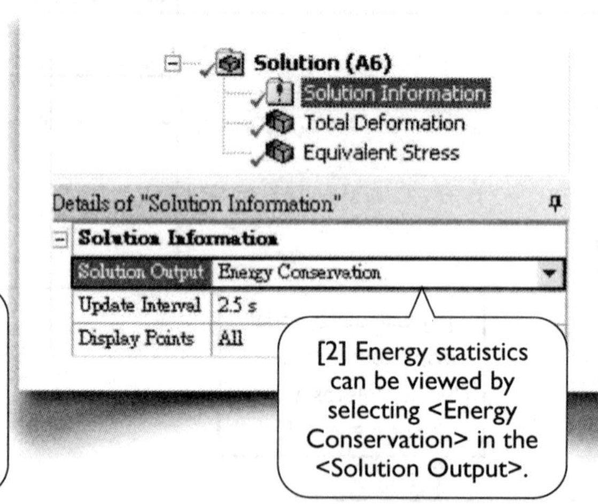

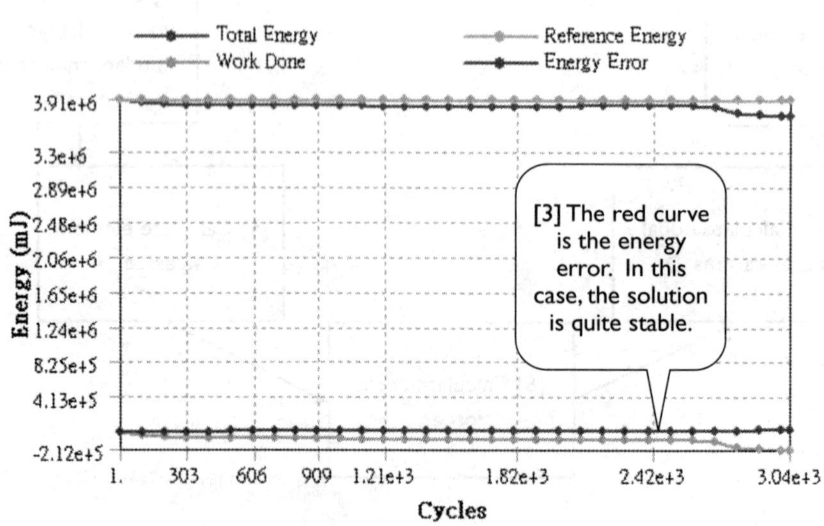

15.1-4 Integration Time Step

With explicit methods, the integration time step needs to be small enough to ensure stability and accuracy of the solution. How small should the time step be? The German mathematicians, Courant, Friedrichs, and Lewy[1, 2], suggested that, in a single time step, a wave should not travel further than the smallest element size, i.e.,

$$\Delta t \le \frac{h}{c} \qquad (1)$$

where h is the smallest element size, c is the wave speed in the element. Eq. (1) is called the *CFL condition*. In <Explicit Dynamics> a safety factor f is used to further ensure the solution stability [1, 2], i.e.,

$$\Delta t \le f\frac{h}{c} \qquad (2)$$

Because of the CFL condition, when generating meshes for <Explicit Dynamics>, make sure that one or two very small elements do not control the time step. In general, a uniform mesh size is desirable for <Explicit Dynamics> simulations.

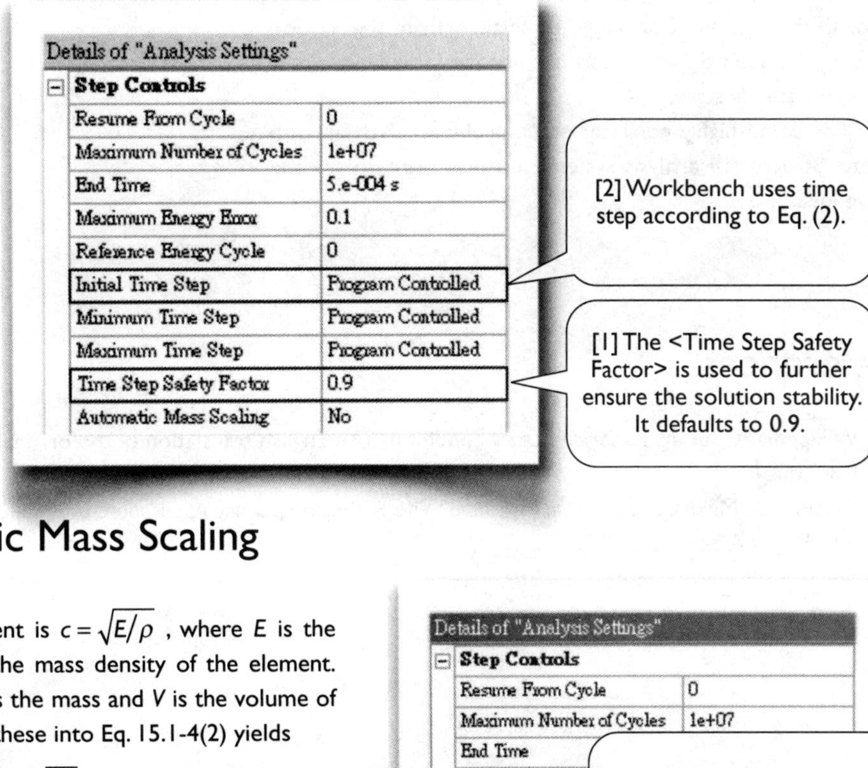

15.1-5 Automatic Mass Scaling

The wave speed in an element is $c=\sqrt{E/\rho}$, where E is the Young's modulus and ρ is the mass density of the element. Further, $\rho = m/V$, where m is the mass and V is the volume of the element. Substitution of these into Eq. 15.1-4(2) yields

$$\Delta t \le fh\sqrt{\frac{m}{VE}} \qquad (1)$$

The idea of mass scaling is to artificially increase the mass of small elements, so that the stability time step can be increased. Mass scaling is applied only to those elements which have a calculated stability time step less than a specified value, default to 1e-20 s [1], which is to ensure that no mass scaling takes place. If a mesh contains very few small elements, this idea can be useful. Mass scaling changes the inertial properties of the model. Be careful to ensure that the model remains valid for the physical problem.

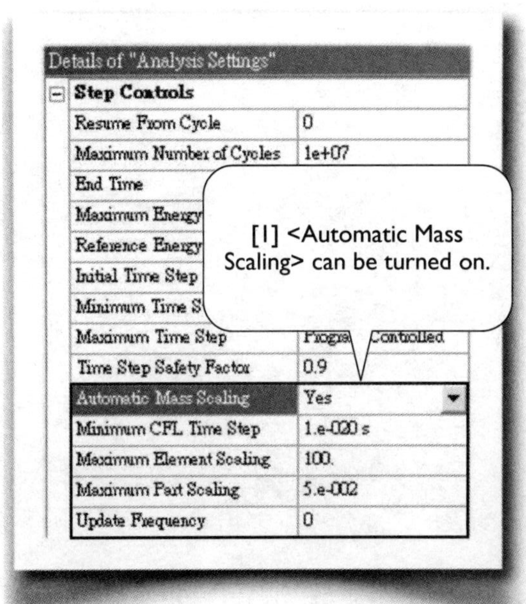

15.1-6 Static Damping

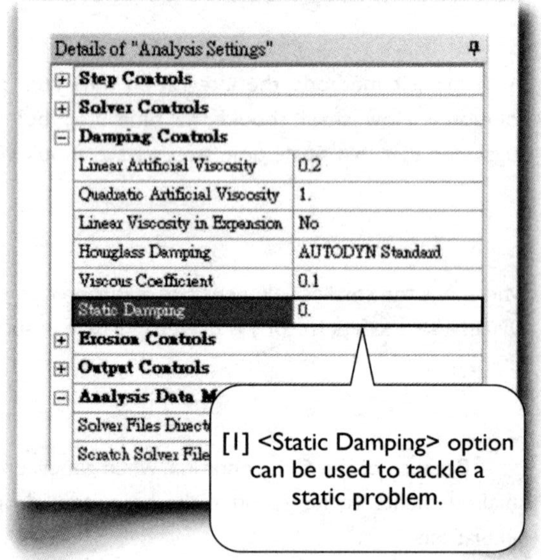

The <Explicit Dynamics> is primarily designed for solving transient dynamic problems. Using the <Static Damping> option, a steady-state solution can also be obtained. The idea is to introduce a damping force, to critically damp the lowest mode of oscillation.

Value of <Static Damping> for critical damping of the lowest mode of vibration is

$$\frac{2f\Delta t}{1+2\pi f\Delta t} \qquad (1)$$

where f is the lowest frequency of the system.

Input a critical damping is to minimize the simulation run time. If the <Static Damping> is large than the critical damping, the solution would take unnecessarily longer time (than critical damping) to reach a steady state. On the other hand, if the <Static Damping> is smaller than the critical damping, the solution would oscillate unnecessarily many times to reach a steady state.

For some highly-nonlinear static problems that fail with <Static Structural> analysis system, you may want to try the above idea.

References

1. Wikipedia>Courant-Friedrichs-Lewy condition. (An English translation of the original paper can be downloaded from this link.)
2. Cook, R.D., Milkus, D. S., Plesha, M. E., and Witt, R. J., *Concepts and Applications of Finite Element Analysis, Fourth Edition,* John Wiley & Sons, Inc., 2002.

Section 15.2

Step-by-Step: High-Speed Impact

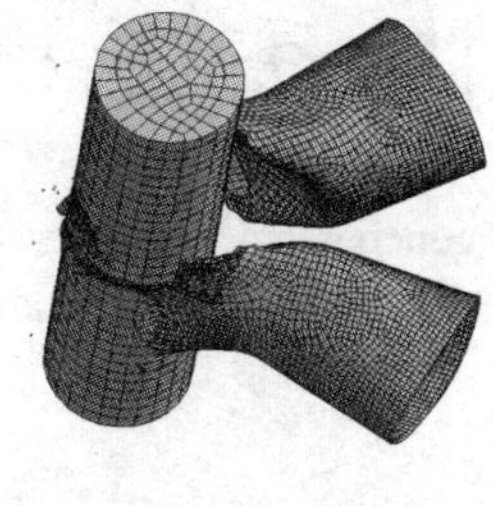

15.2-1 About the High-Speed Impact Simulation

Imagine, during an explosion, an aluminum pipe that was blasted away under the explosive pressure. The pipe hit a steel solid column, deformed, and finally torn to fragments due to excessive strain [1-6]. In this section, we will demonstrate the simulation of this scenario. We will use the default settings as much as possible to demonstrate that a complicated simulation like this can be done in <Explicit Dynamic> analysis system with just a few input data.

Both the aluminum pipe and the steel solid column have a diameter of 50 mm and a length of 200 mm. The steel column is modeled as a rigid body and fixed in the space. The aluminum pipe has a thickness of 1 mm and, when hitting the pipe, has a speed of 300 m/s (about the speed of sound). The aluminum is modeled as a bilinear isotropic plasticity material (Section 14.1) using the material parameters stored in the <Engineering Data> with a modification that the tangent modulus is set to zero, i.e., the aluminum is modeled as a perfectly elastic-plastic material. To simulate the fragmentation, it is assumed that the aluminum will be torn apart (failed) when the plastic strain is larger than 75%.

The millimeter will be used to create the geometry and the MKS or SI unit systems will be used in the simulation.

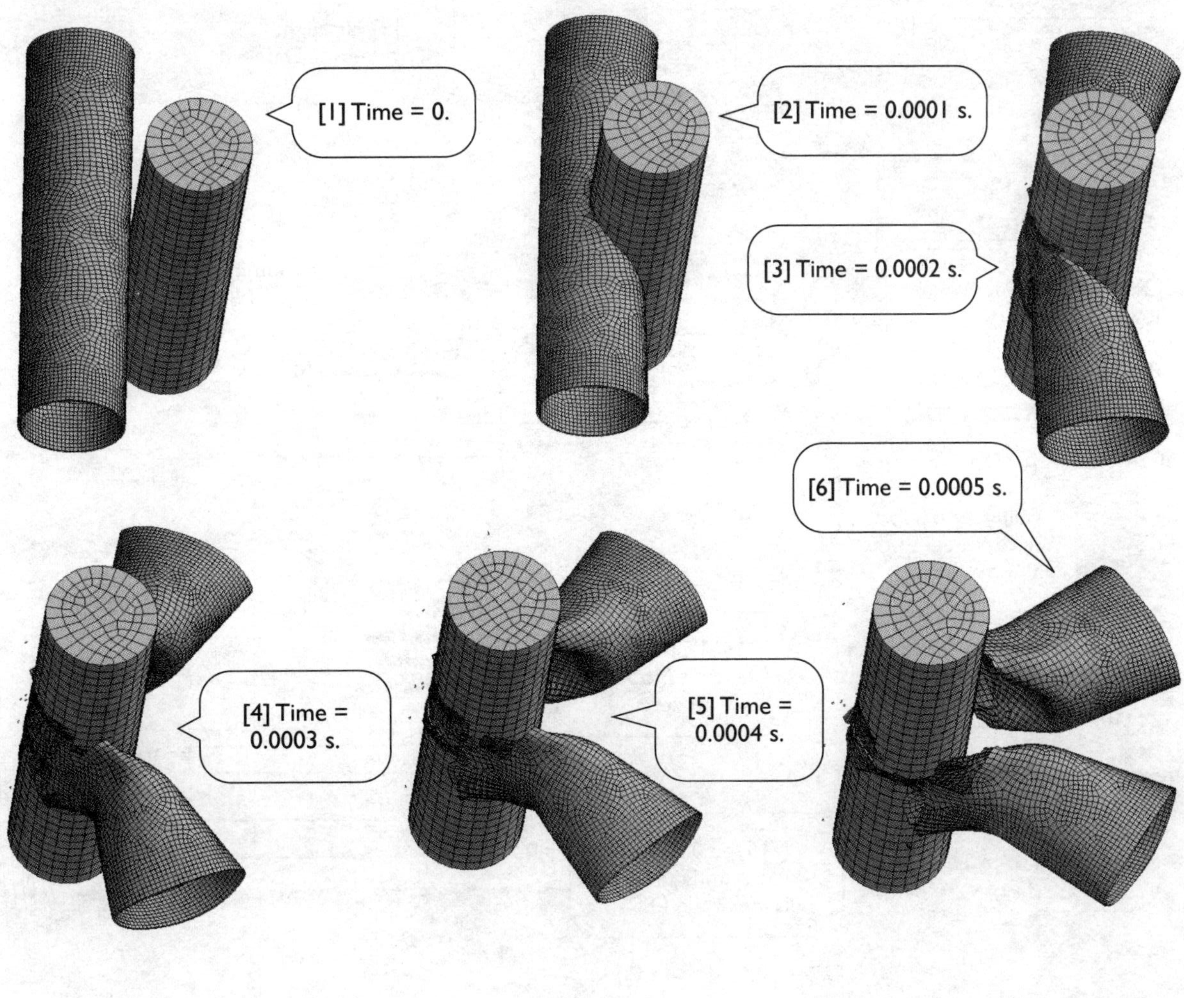

15.2-2 Start Up

Launch <Workbench>. Create an <Explicit Dynamics (ANSYS)> analysis system by double-clicking it in the <Toolbox>. Save the project as "Impact."

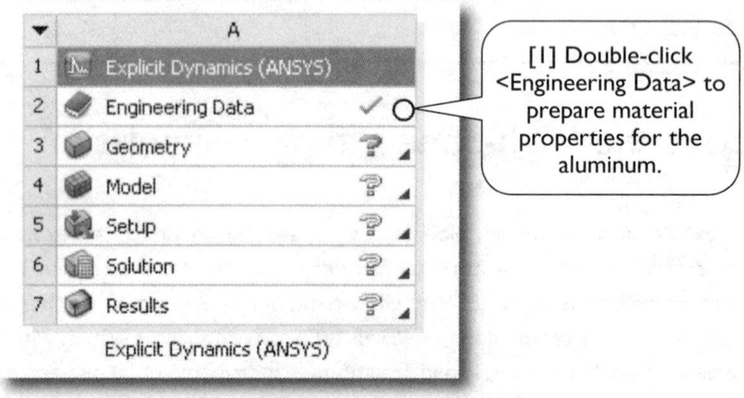

15.2-3 Prepare Material Properties for Aluminum

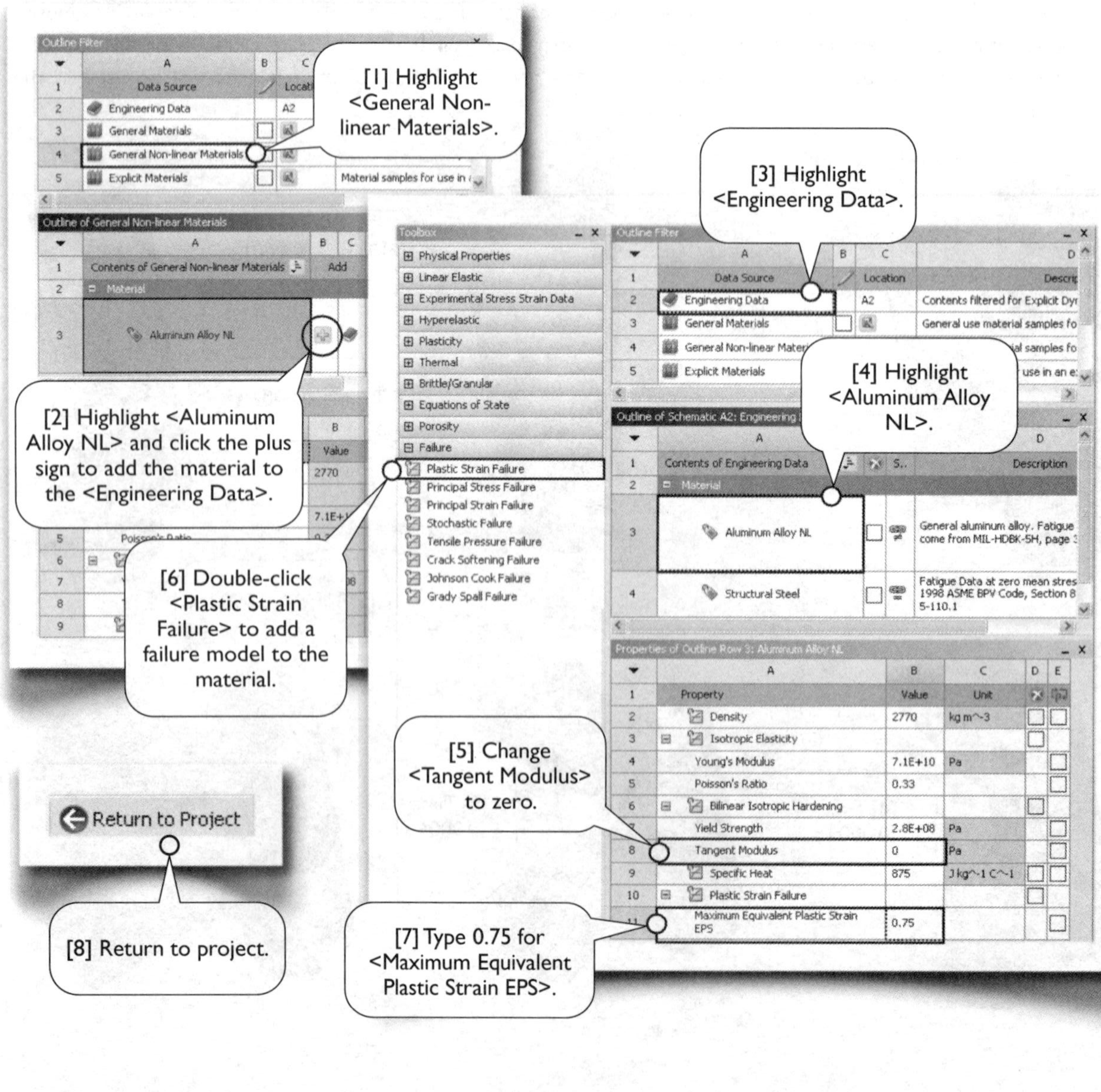

15.2-4 Create Geometry

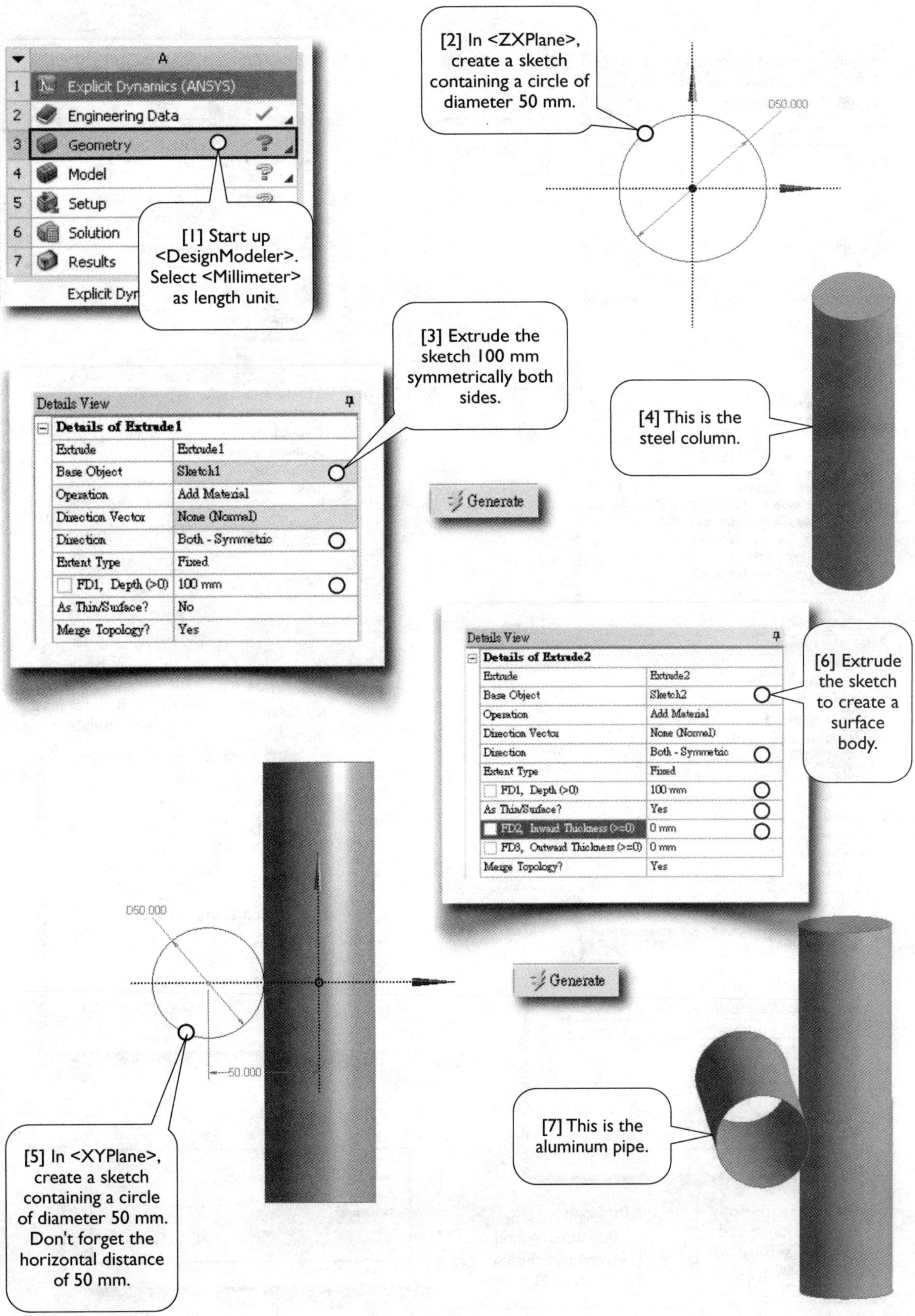

15.2-5 Set Up for Simulation

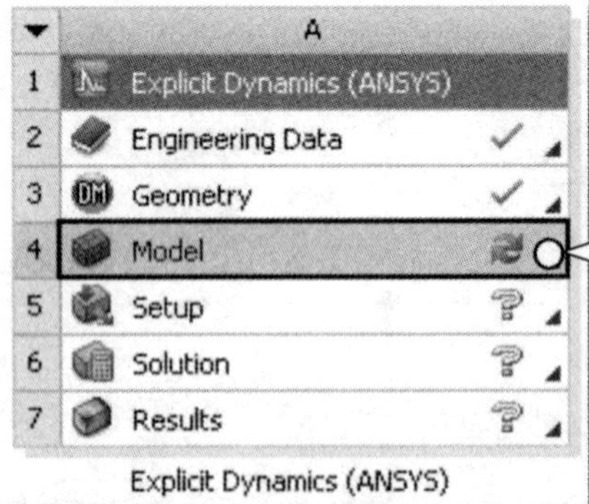

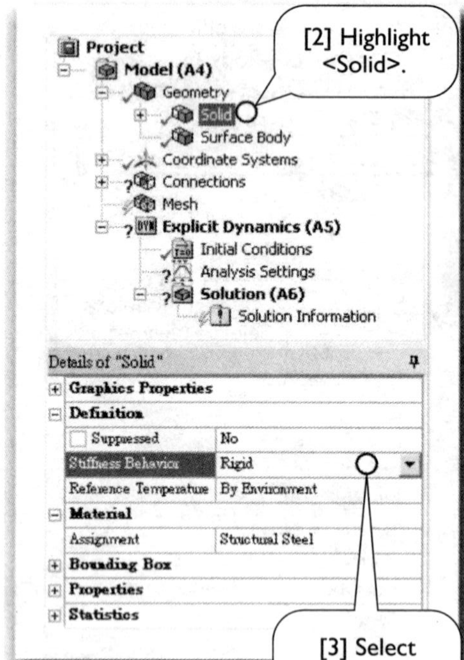

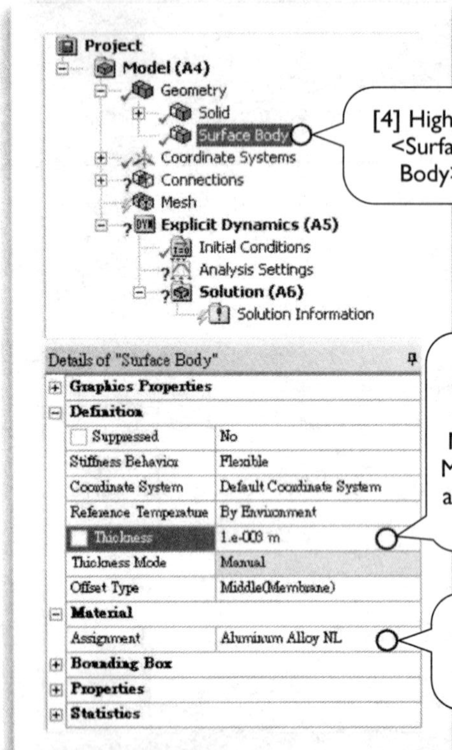

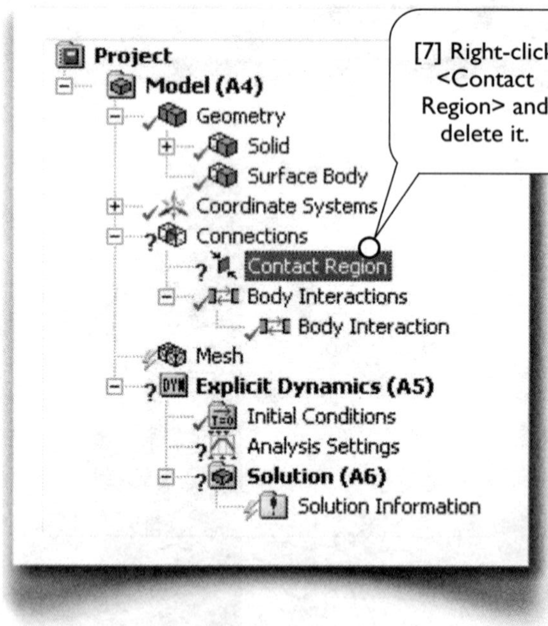

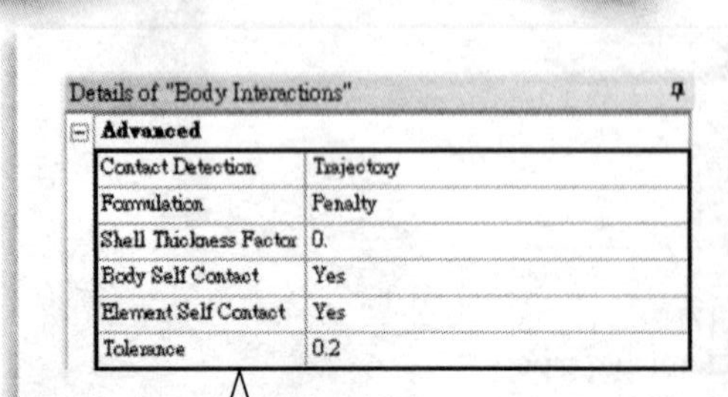

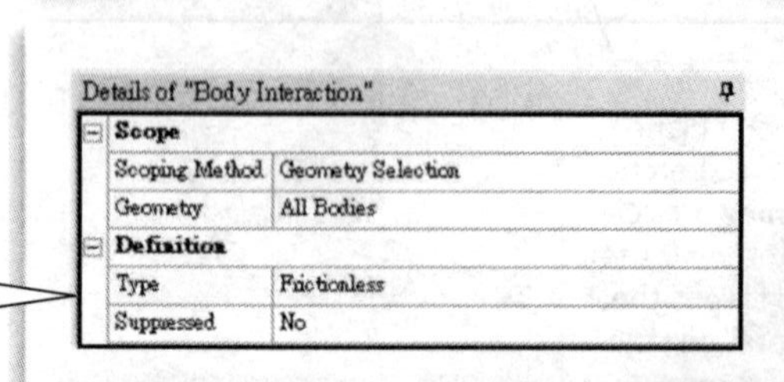

Contact Regions and Body Interactions

<Body Interactions> is to specify contacts between bodies while <Contact Regions> is to specify contact between surfaces. You can choose either way to specify the contact relations. <Body Interactions> is simpler but <Contact Regions> may be more efficient. A default <Frictionless> interaction is scoped to all bodies.

A feature of <Body Interactions> is that two bodies can be specified as both <Bonded> and <Frictionless> (or <Frictional>). In that case, two bodies are bonded initially. After the bond breaks during the simulation, the frictionless (or frictional) contact will take place.

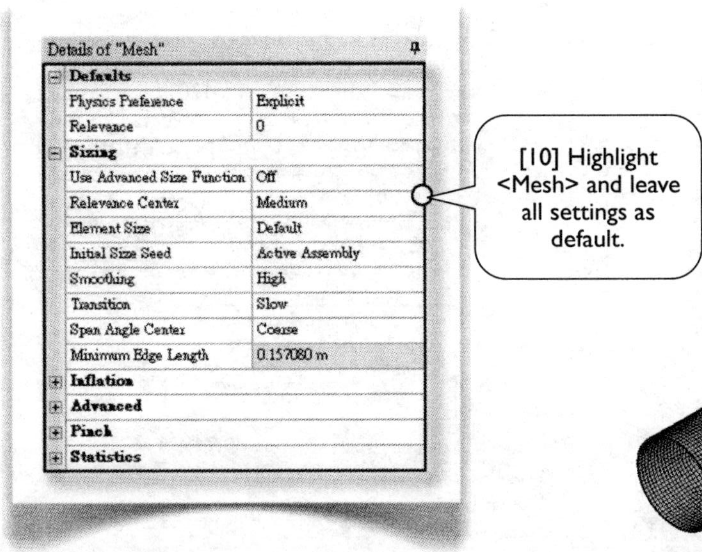

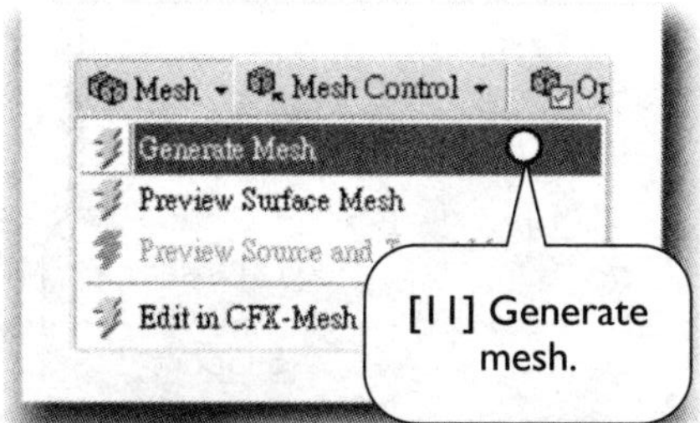

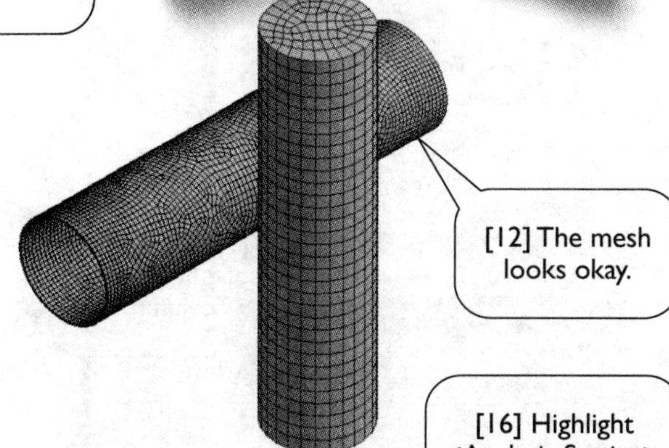

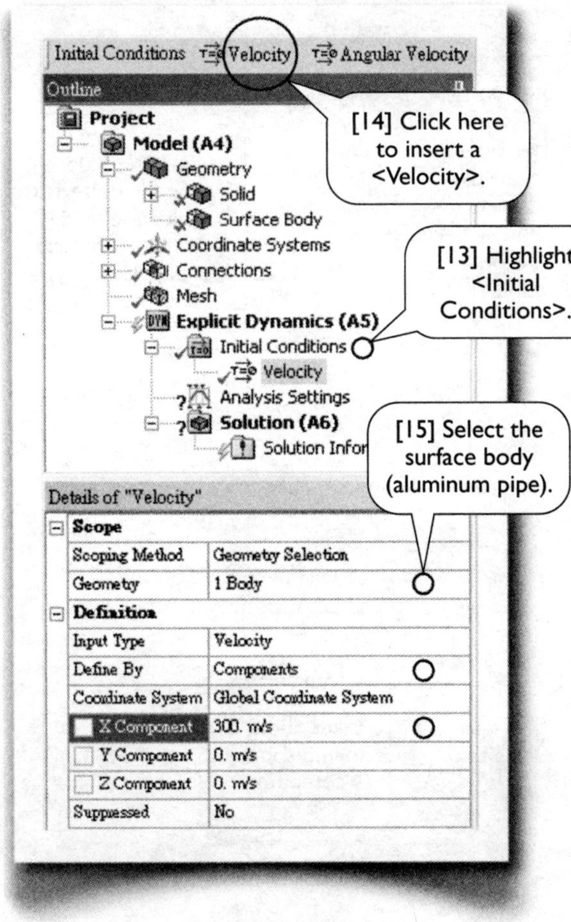

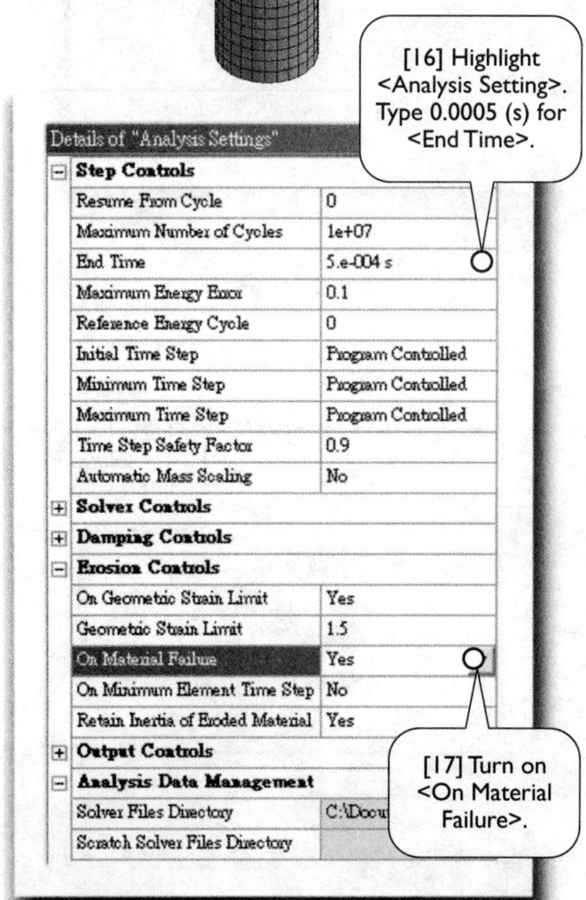

Erosion Controls

<Erosion Controls> in the <Analysis Settings> determine the conditions that an element will be removed. The default condition is that an element is removed when its geometric strain (effective strain, Eq. 1.4-5(16)) exceeds a limit of 150%. This value is large enough to assure that no elements are removed by default.

In this case, we add another failure condition: an element is removed when its plastic strain exceeds 75% ([17] and 15.2-3[7]).

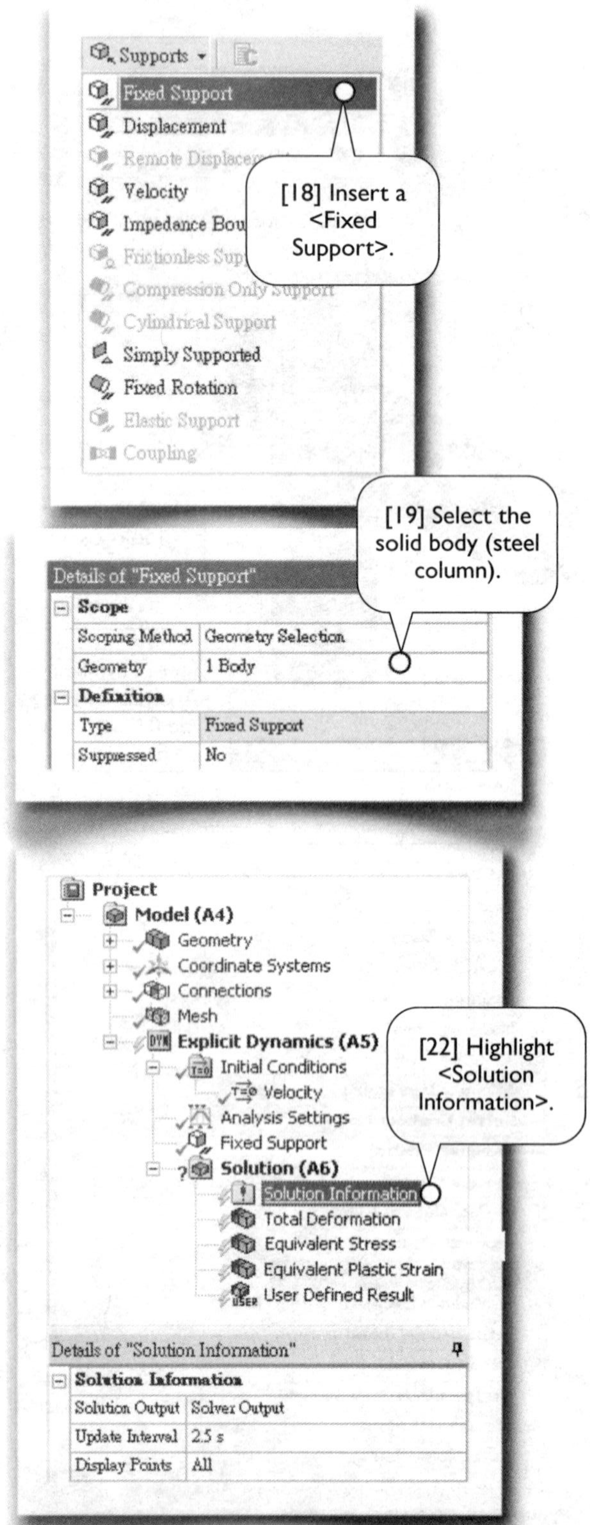

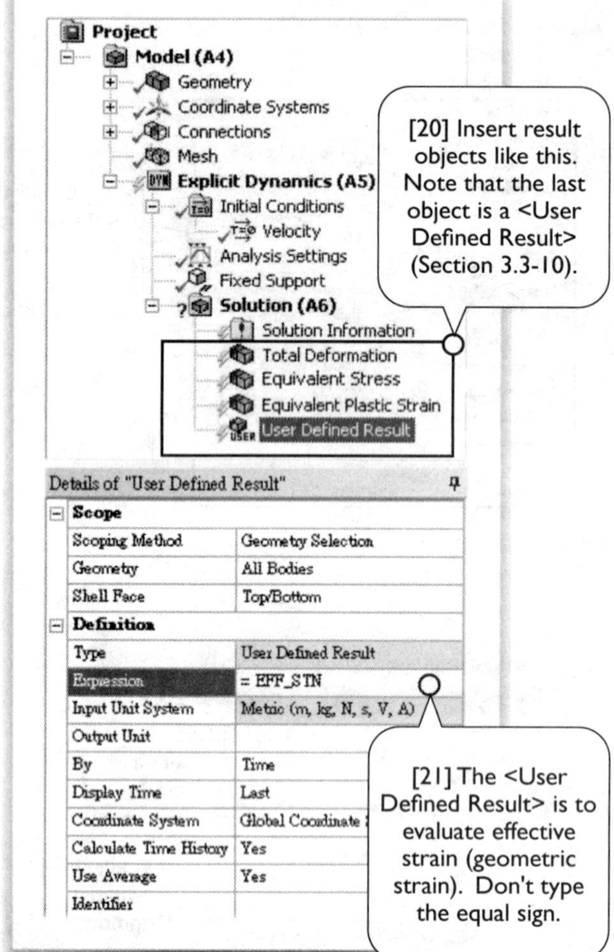

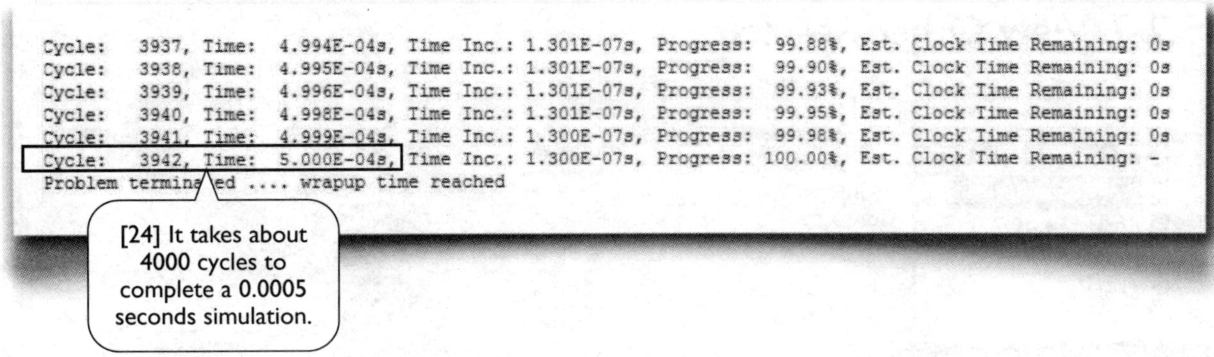

```
Cycle:   3937, Time:  4.994E-04s, Time Inc.: 1.301E-07s, Progress:  99.88%, Est. Clock Time Remaining: 0s
Cycle:   3938, Time:  4.995E-04s, Time Inc.: 1.301E-07s, Progress:  99.90%, Est. Clock Time Remaining: 0s
Cycle:   3939, Time:  4.996E-04s, Time Inc.: 1.301E-07s, Progress:  99.93%, Est. Clock Time Remaining: 0s
Cycle:   3940, Time:  4.998E-04s, Time Inc.: 1.301E-07s, Progress:  99.95%, Est. Clock Time Remaining: 0s
Cycle:   3941, Time:  4.999E-04s, Time Inc.: 1.300E-07s, Progress:  99.98%, Est. Clock Time Remaining: 0s
Cycle:   3942, Time:  5.000E-04s, Time Inc.: 1.300E-07s, Progress: 100.00%, Est. Clock Time Remaining: -
Problem terminated .... wrapup time reached
```


15.2-6 Animate the Deformation

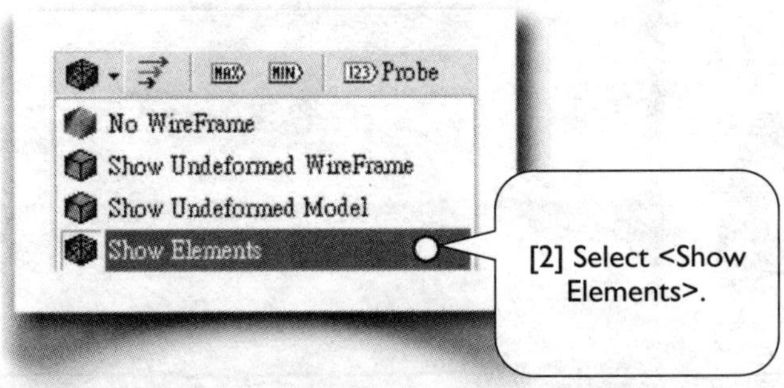

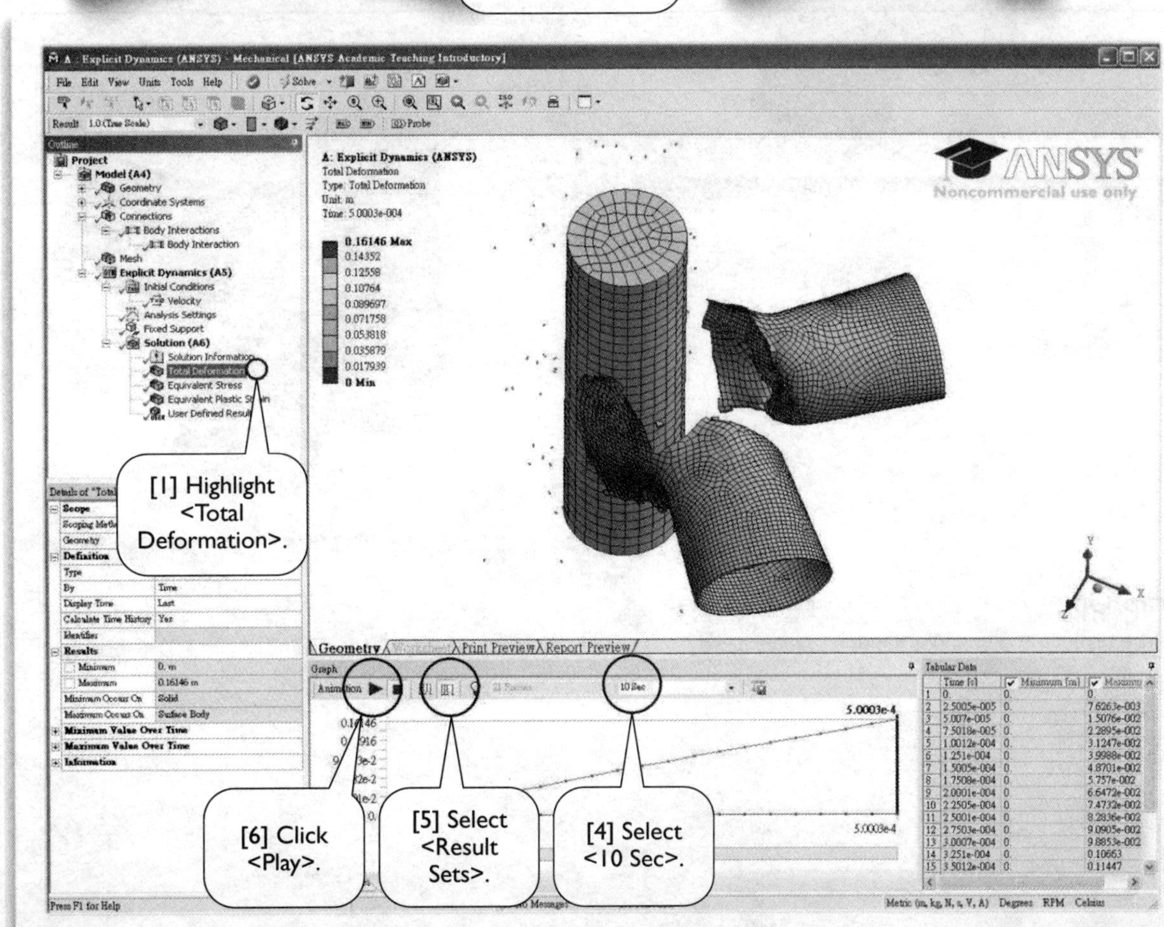

15.2-7 View Other Results

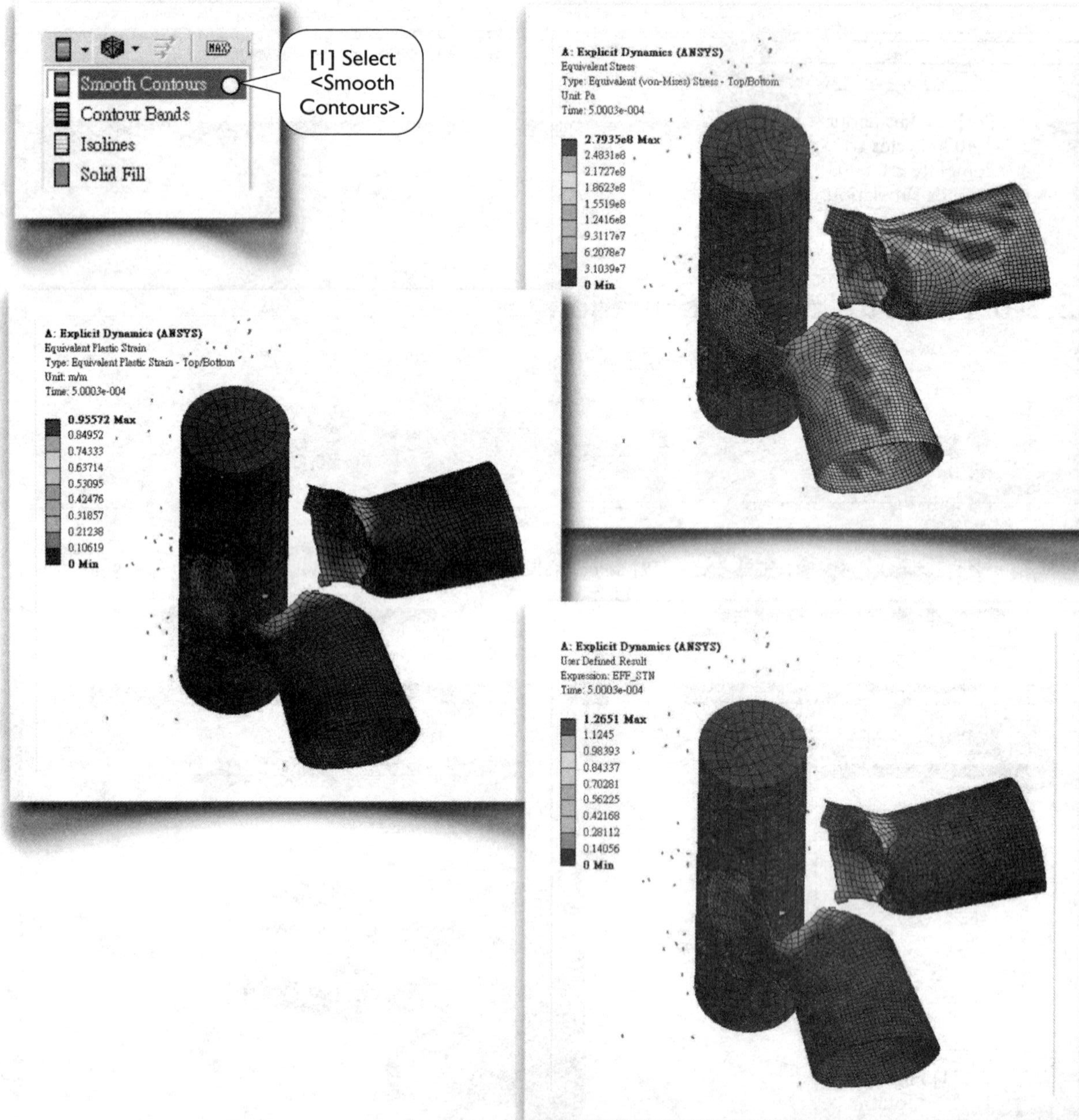

Wrap Up

Save the project and exit Workbench.

Section 15.3
Step-by-Step: Drop Test

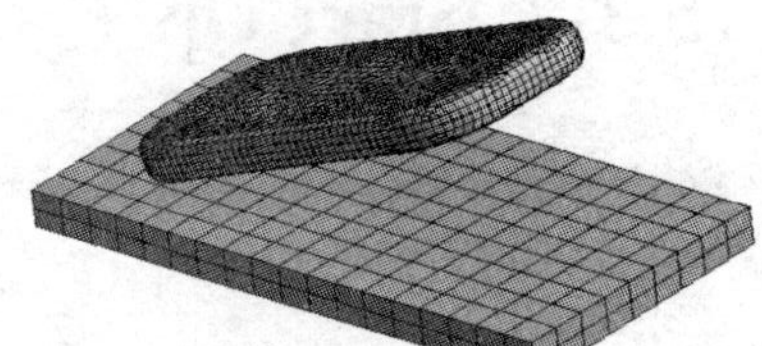

15.3-1 About the Drop Test Simulation

Drop test simulation is a special case of impact simulation, in which one of the impacting objects is a stationary floor, typically made of concrete, steel, or stone. In this section, we will simulate a scenario that a mobile phone falls off from your pocket and drops on a concrete floor. This kind of simulations typically take hours of computing time. From the experience of Section 15.2, a typical integration time step in <Explicit Dynamics> is 10^{-7} to 10^{-8} seconds. It would take about 100,000 to 1000,000 cycles to complete a 0.01 seconds of drop test. In this section, we will simplify the model to shorten the run time. A more realistic model will be suggested and leave for the students as an exercise (Section 15.4-2).

The phone body is a shell of thickness 0.5 mm and made of an aluminum alloy [1]. The concrete floor is modeled as an 160x40x10 (mm) block [2]. When the phone hits the floor, its velocity is 5 m/s, which is equivalent to a free fall from a height of 1.25 m. We will assume that the phone body forms an angle of 20° with the horizon when it hits the floor.

We will use the kg-mm-s-N unit system in both <DesignModeler> and <Mechanical>.

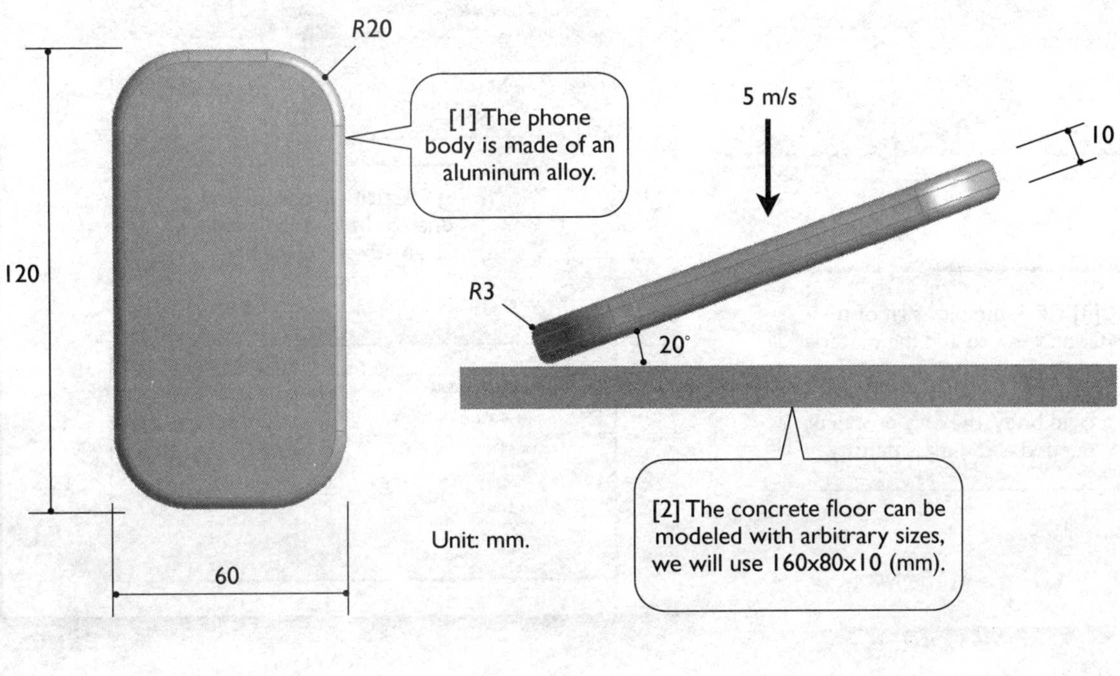

15.3-2 Start Up

Launch <Workbench>. Create a <Explicit Dynamic (ANSYS)> analysis system by double-clicking it in the <Toolbox>. Save the project as "Drop."

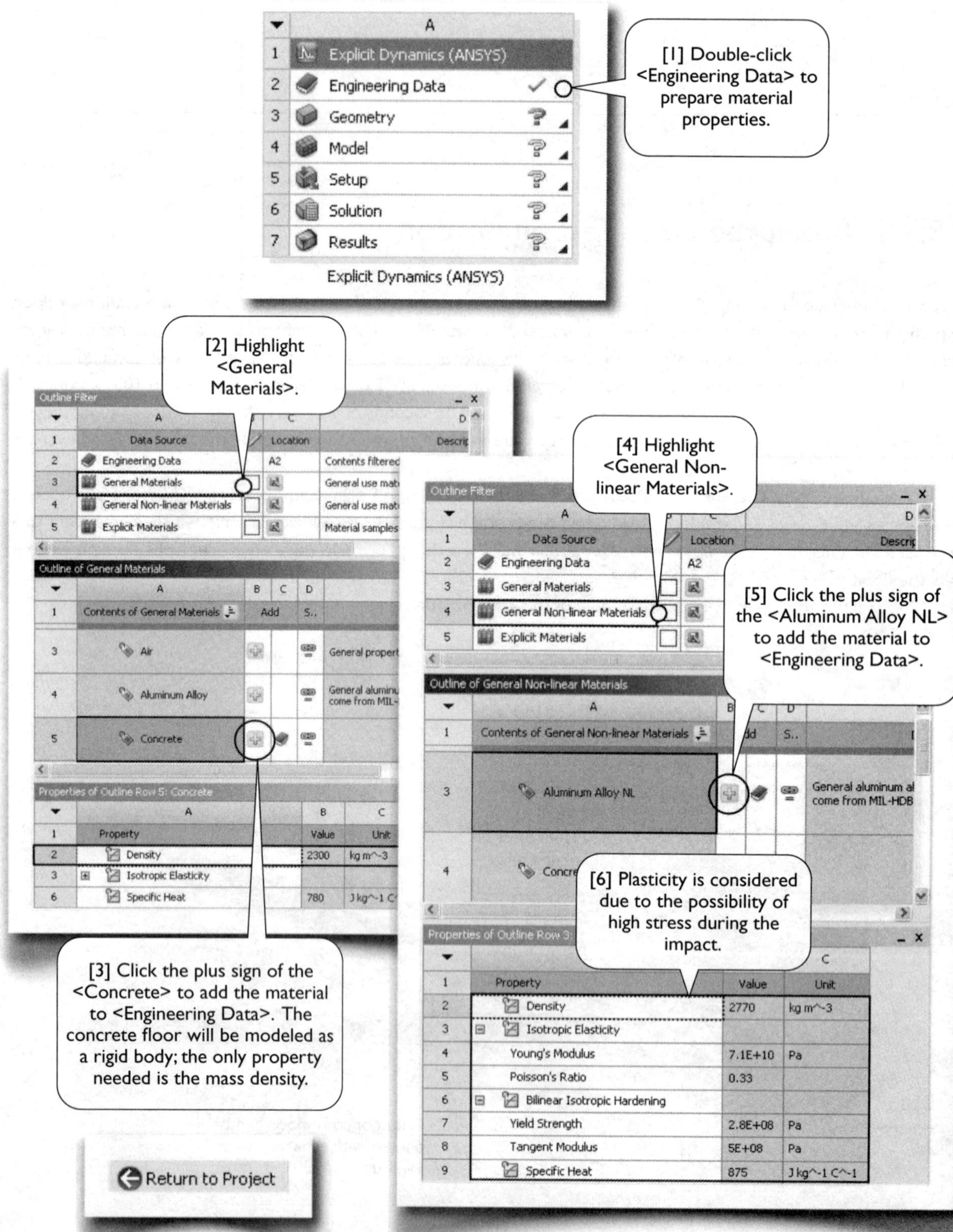

15.3-3 Create Geometry

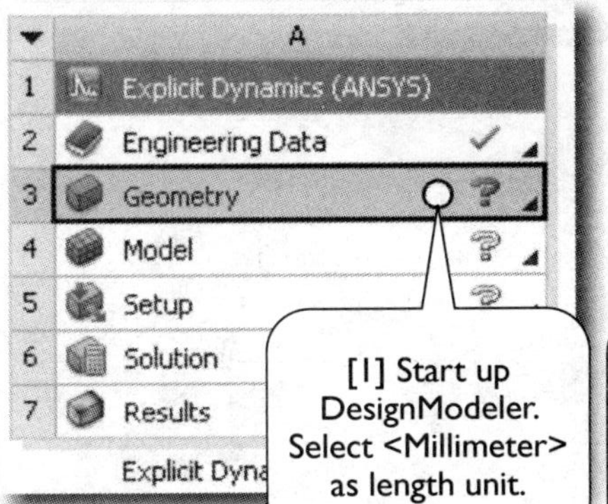

[1] Start up DesignModeler. Select <Millimeter> as length unit.

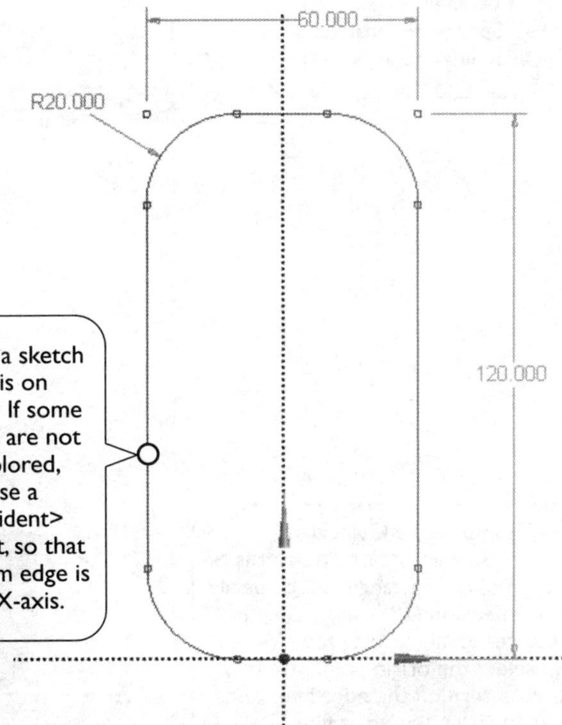

[2] Draw a sketch like this on XYPlane. If some segments are not blue colored, impose a <Coincident> constraint, so that the bottom edge is on the X-axis.

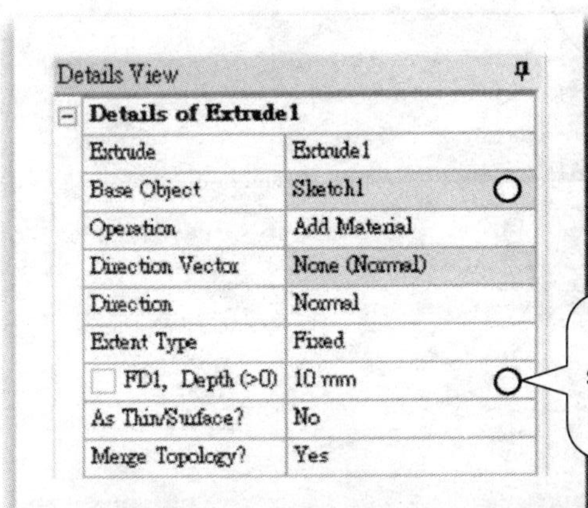

[3] Extrude the sketch to create a phone body.

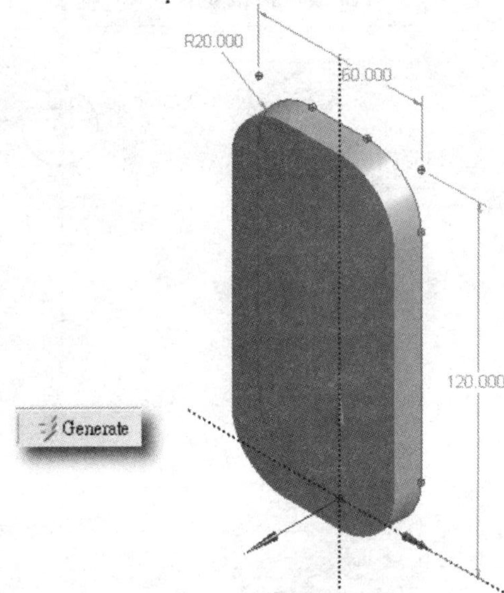

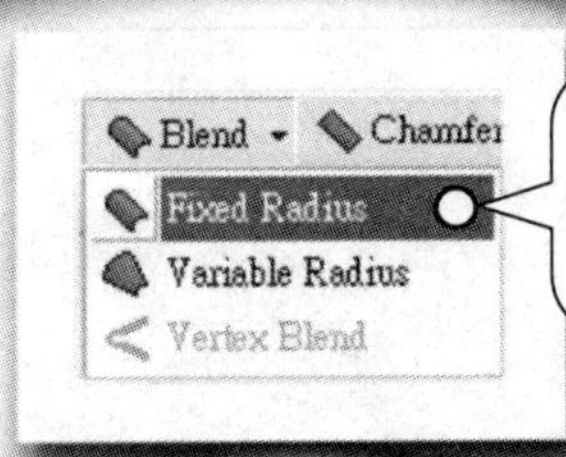

[4] Select <Blend/ Fixed Radius>.

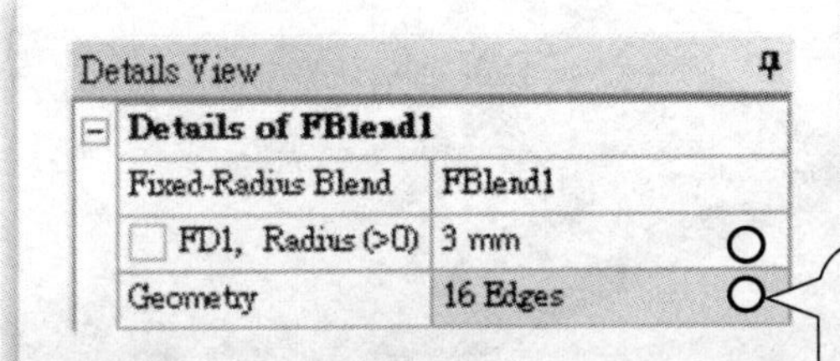

[5] Select all the sharp edges. You may use <Extend to Limits> (4.4-4[3]) to help the selection.

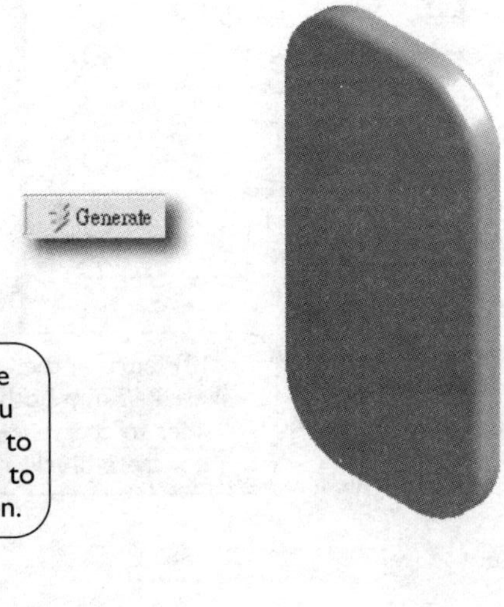

[6] In YZPlane, draw a rectangle using <Rectangle by 3 Points> tool. Specify dimensions, including the angle.

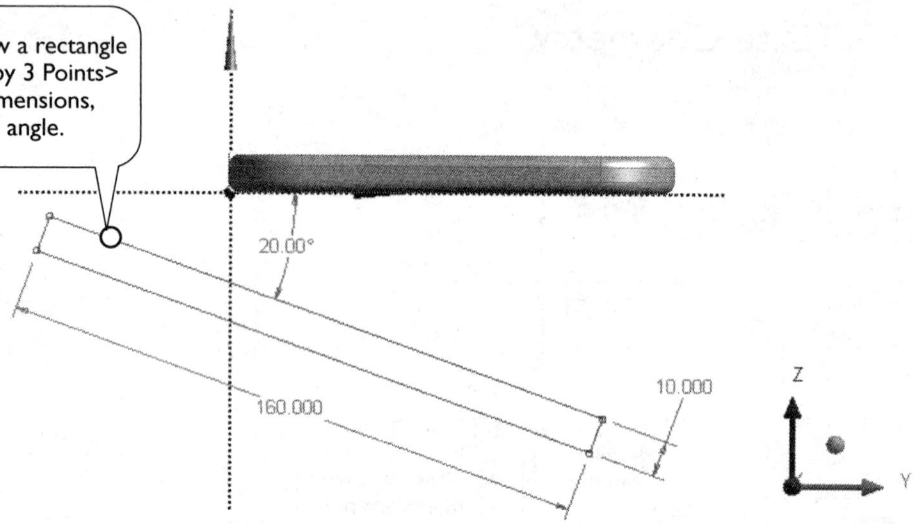

[7] Impose a <Coincident> constraint so that the origin point is on the edge of the rectangle. Also specify the dimension (20) using <Length/Distance> dimensioning tool. When you select the origin point, you may need to turn off the edge filter and turn on the point filter.

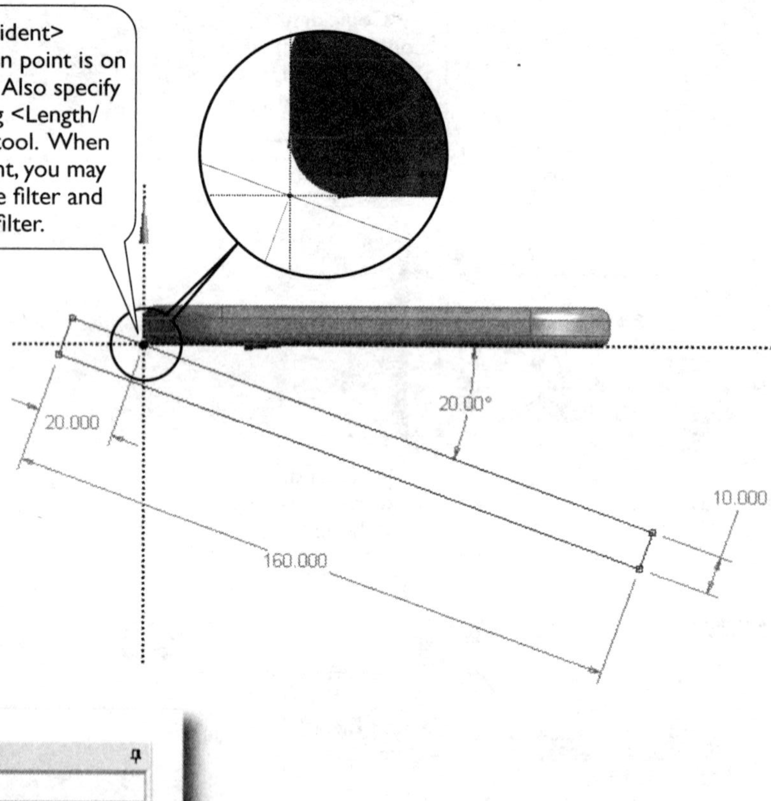

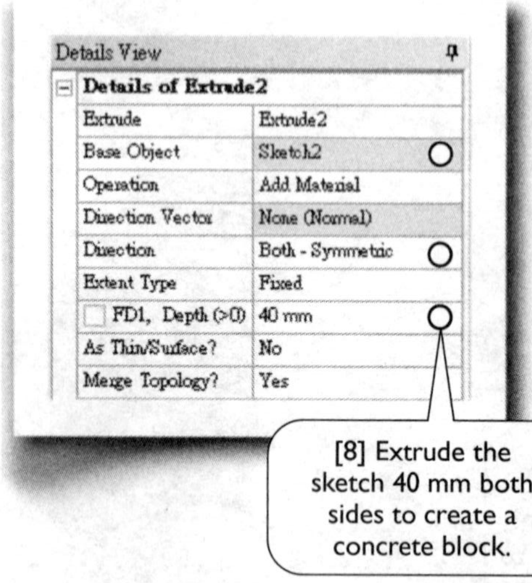

Details View	
Details of Extrude2	
Extrude	Extrude2
Base Object	Sketch2
Operation	Add Material
Direction Vector	None (Normal)
Direction	Both - Symmetric
Extent Type	Fixed
FD1, Depth (>0)	40 mm
As Thin/Surface?	No
Merge Topology?	Yes

[8] Extrude the sketch 40 mm both sides to create a concrete block.

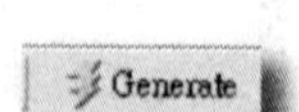

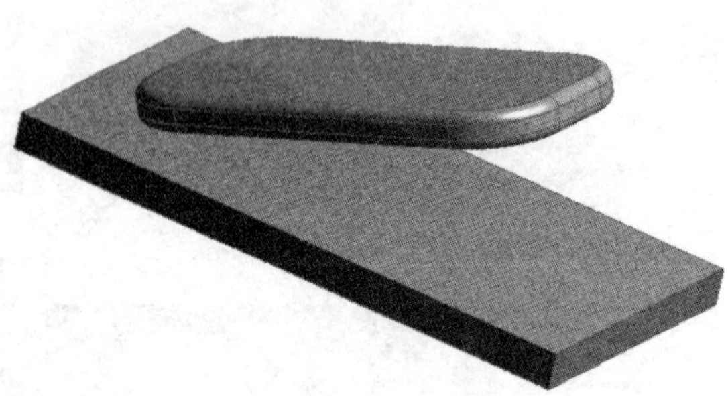

Thin/Surface
[9] Click <Thin/ Surface>.

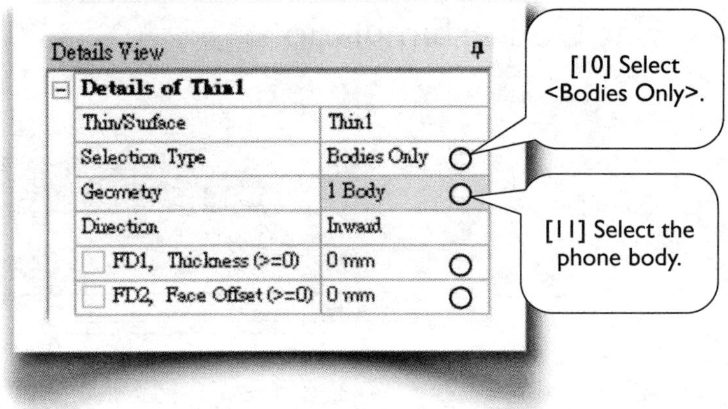
Details View
Details of Thin1
Thin/Surface
Thin1
Selection Type
Bodies Only
Geometry
1 Body
Direction
Inward
FD1, Thickness (>=0)
0 mm
FD2, Face Offset (>=0)
0 mm
[10] Select <Bodies Only>.
[11] Select the phone body.

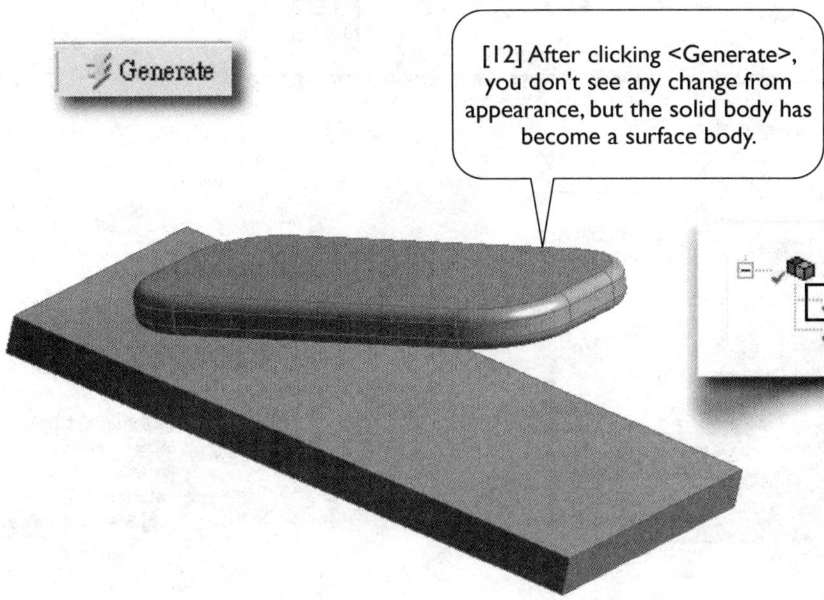
Generate
[12] After clicking <Generate>, you don't see any change from appearance, but the solid body has become a surface body.

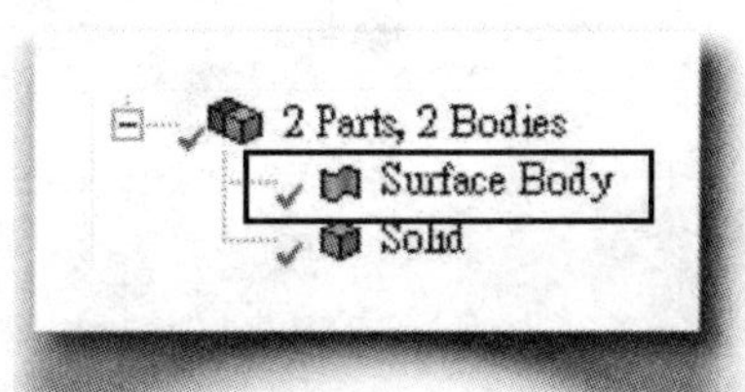
2 Parts, 2 Bodies
Surface Body
Solid

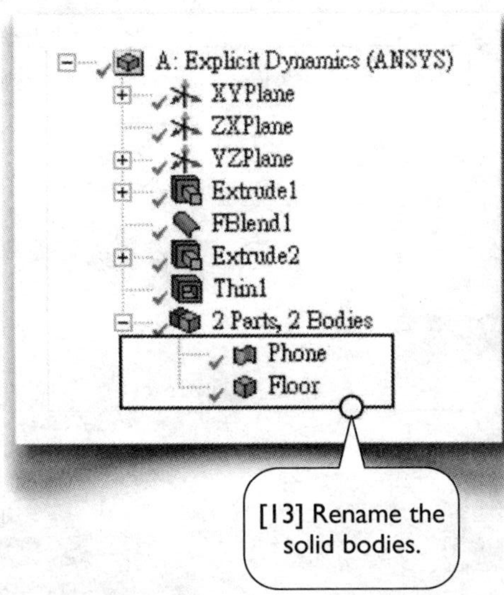
A: Explicit Dynamics (ANSYS)
XYPlane
ZXPlane
YZPlane
Extrude1
FBlend1
Extrude2
Thin1
2 Parts, 2 Bodies
Phone
Floor
[13] Rename the solid bodies.

15.3-4 Set Up for Simulation

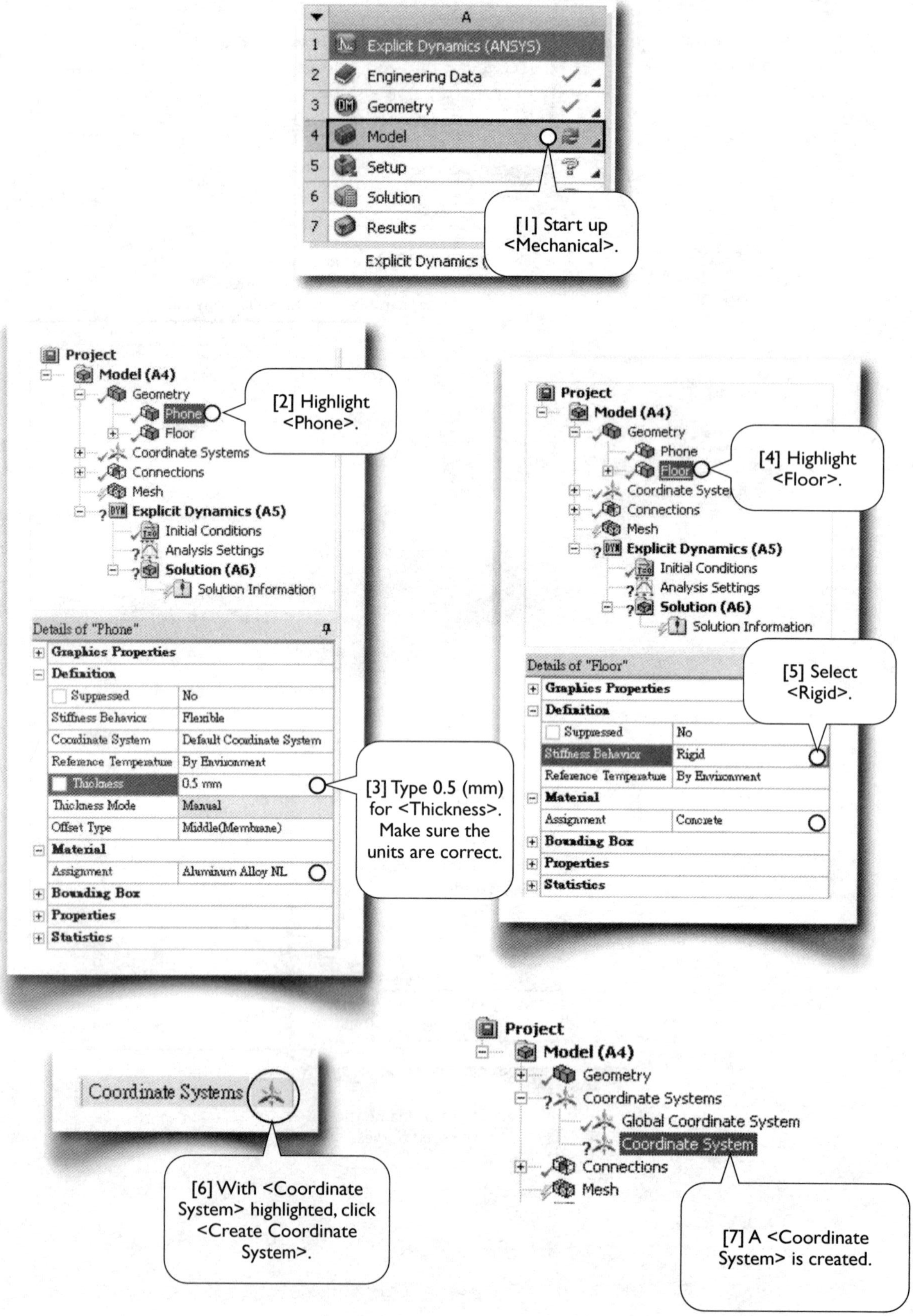

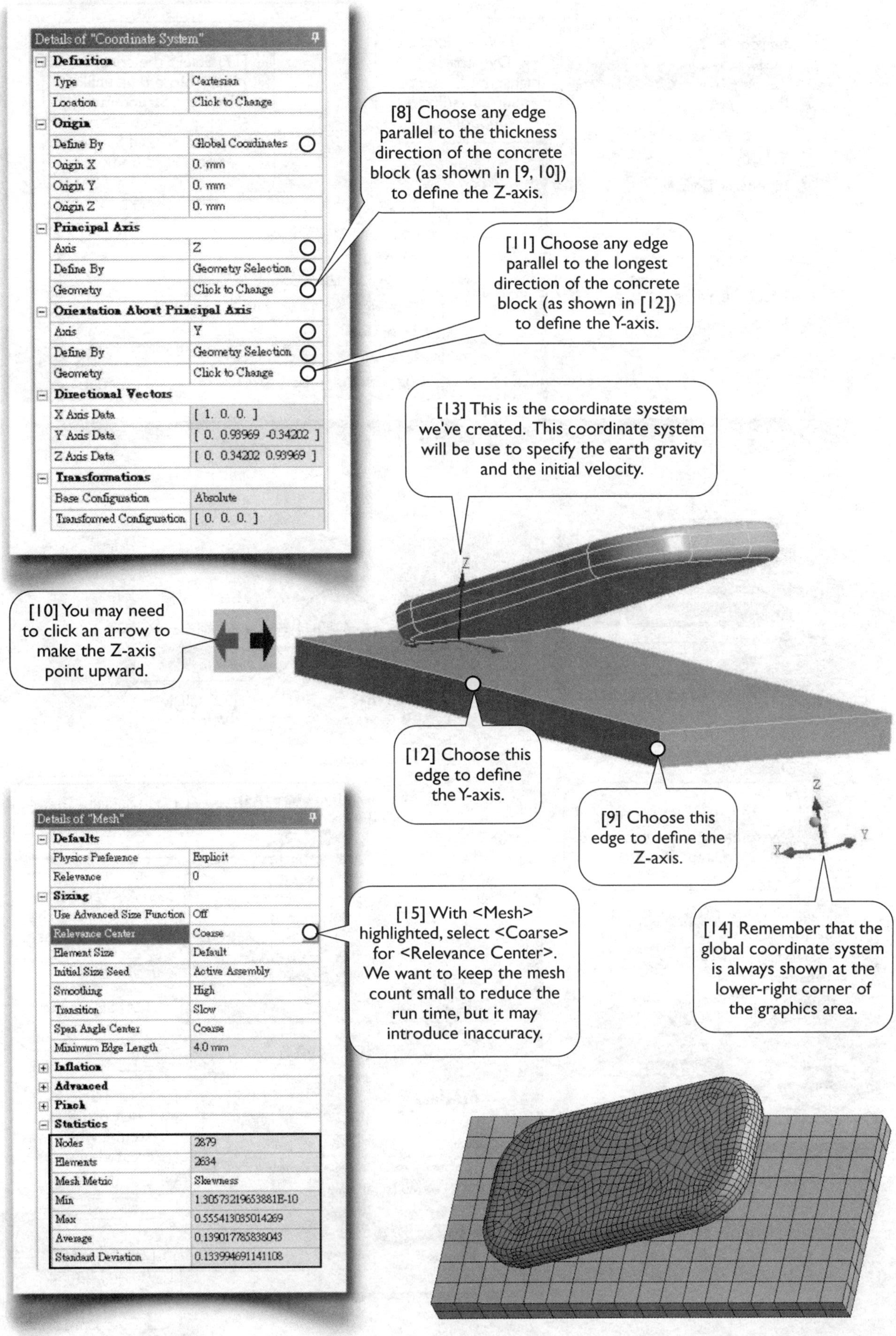
Details of "Coordinate System"
Definition
Type Cartesian
Location Click to Change
Origin
Define By Global Coordinates
Origin X 0. mm
Origin Y 0. mm
Origin Z 0. mm
Principal Axis
Axis Z
Define By Geometry Selection
Geometry Click to Change
Orientation About Principal Axis
Axis Y
Define By Geometry Selection
Geometry Click to Change
Directional Vectors
X Axis Data [1. 0. 0.]
Y Axis Data [0. 0.93969 -0.34202]
Z Axis Data [0. 0.34202 0.93969]
Transformations
Base Configuration Absolute
Transformed Configuration [0. 0. 0.]
[8] Choose any edge parallel to the thickness direction of the concrete block (as shown in [9, 10]) to define the Z-axis.
[11] Choose any edge parallel to the longest direction of the concrete block (as shown in [12]) to define the Y-axis.
[13] This is the coordinate system we've created. This coordinate system will be use to specify the earth gravity and the initial velocity.
Z
[10] You may need to click an arrow to make the Z-axis point upward.
[12] Choose this edge to define the Y-axis.
[9] Choose this edge to define the Z-axis.
Z
X
Y
Details of "Mesh"
Defaults
Physics Preference Explicit
Relevance 0
Sizing
Use Advanced Size Function Off
Relevance Center Coarse
Element Size Default
Initial Size Seed Active Assembly
Smoothing High
Transition Slow
Span Angle Center Coarse
Minimum Edge Length 4.0 mm
Inflation
Advanced
Pinch
Statistics
Nodes 2879
Elements 2634
Mesh Metric Skewness
Min 1.30573219653881E-10
Max 0.555413035014269
Average 0.139017785838043
Standard Deviation 0.133994691141108
[15] With <Mesh> highlighted, select <Coarse> for <Relevance Center>. We want to keep the mesh count small to reduce the run time, but it may introduce inaccuracy.
[14] Remember that the global coordinate system is always shown at the lower-right corner of the graphics area.

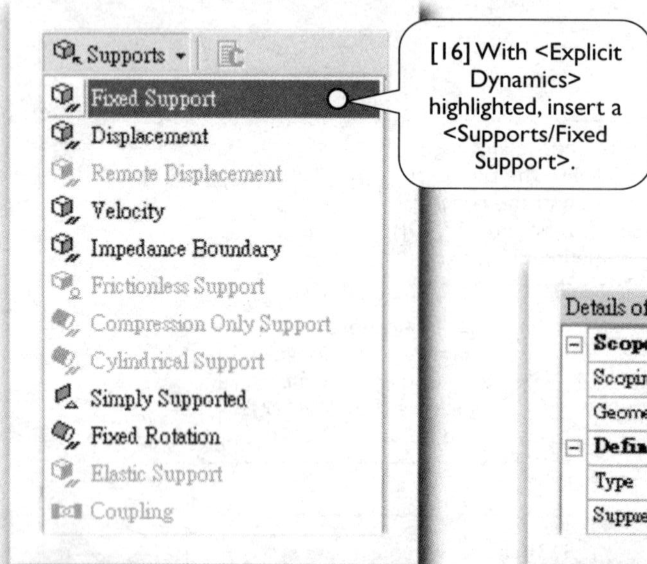
Supports
Fixed Support
Displacement
Remote Displacement
Velocity
Impedance Boundary
Frictionless Support
Compression Only Support
Cylindrical Support
Simply Supported
Fixed Rotation
Elastic Support
Coupling
[16] With <Explicit Dynamics> highlighted, insert a <Supports/Fixed Support>.

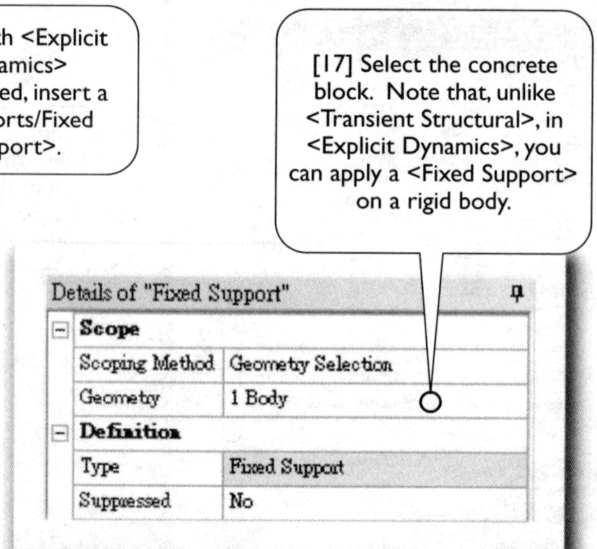
[17] Select the concrete block. Note that, unlike <Transient Structural>, in <Explicit Dynamics>, you can apply a <Fixed Support> on a rigid body.
Details of "Fixed Support"
Scope
Scoping Method Geometry Selection
Geometry 1 Body
Definition
Type Fixed Support
Suppressed No

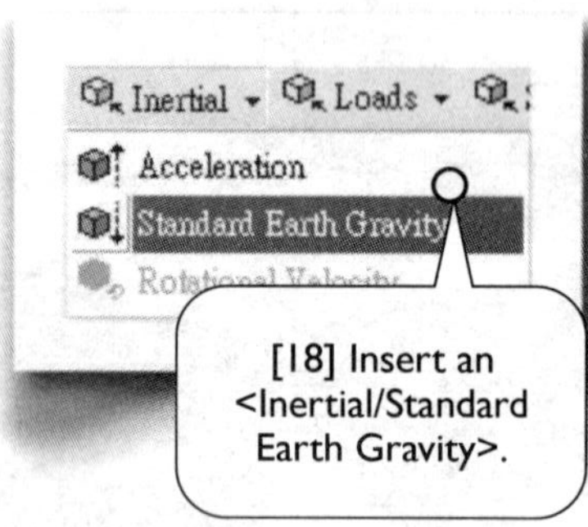
Inertial
Loads
Acceleration
Standard Earth Gravity
[18] Insert an <Inertial/Standard Earth Gravity>.

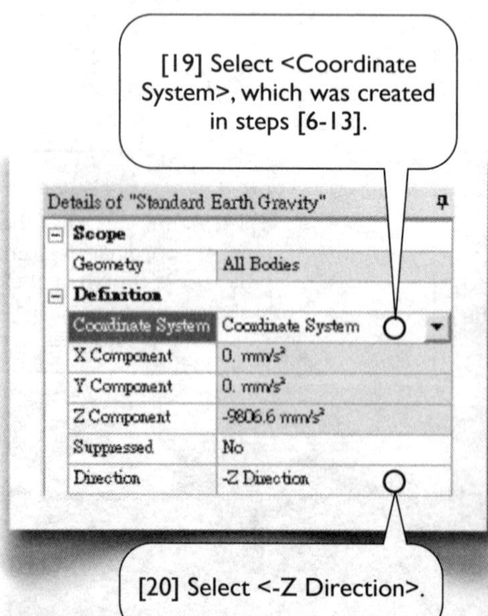
[19] Select <Coordinate System>, which was created in steps [6-13].
Details of "Standard Earth Gravity"
Scope
Geometry All Bodies
Definition
Coordinate System Coordinate System
X Component 0. mm/s²
Y Component 0. mm/s²
Z Component -9806.6 mm/s²
Suppressed No
Direction -Z Direction
[20] Select <-Z Direction>.

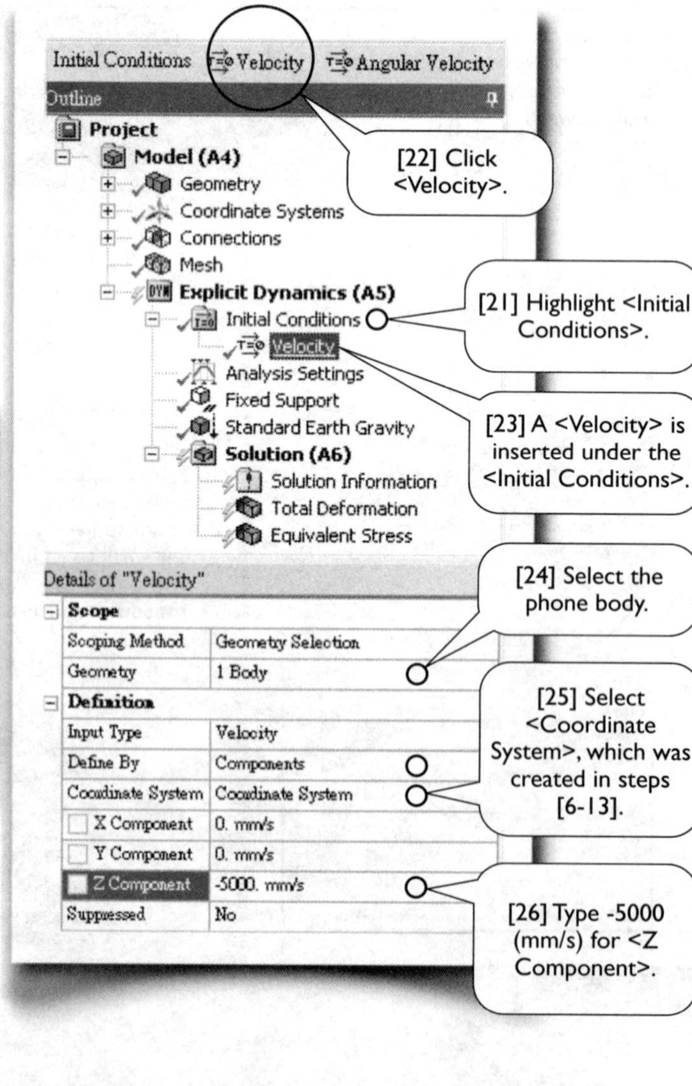
Initial Conditions
Velocity
Angular Velocity
Outline
Project
Model (A4)
Geometry
Coordinate Systems
Connections
Mesh
Explicit Dynamics (A5)
Initial Conditions
Velocity
Analysis Settings
Fixed Support
Standard Earth Gravity
Solution (A6)
Solution Information
Total Deformation
Equivalent Stress
[22] Click <Velocity>.
[21] Highlight <Initial Conditions>.
[23] A <Velocity> is inserted under the <Initial Conditions>.
Details of "Velocity"
Scope
Scoping Method Geometry Selection
Geometry 1 Body
Definition
Input Type Velocity
Define By Components
Coordinate System Coordinate System
X Component 0. mm/s
Y Component 0. mm/s
Z Component -5000. mm/s
Suppressed No
[24] Select the phone body.
[25] Select <Coordinate System>, which was created in steps [6-13].
[26] Type -5000 (mm/s) for <Z Component>.

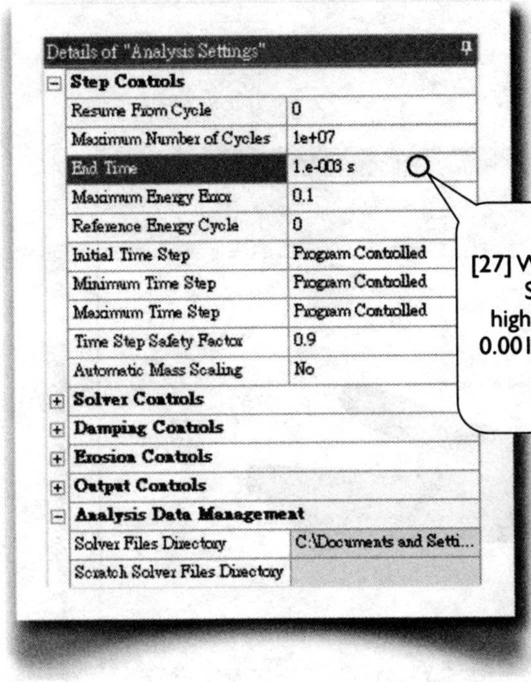

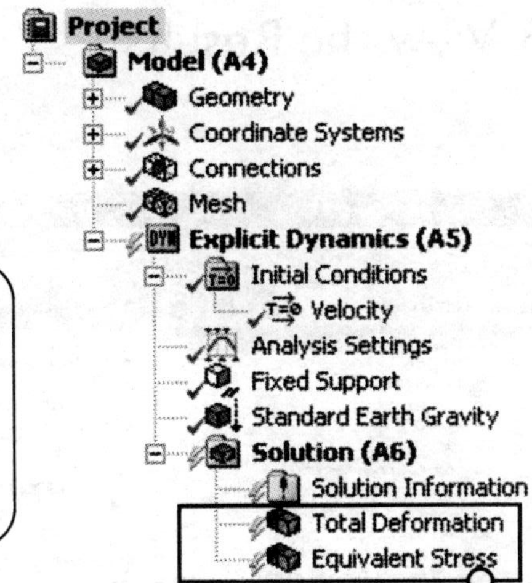

Perform Simulation Incrementally

As mentioned, a drop test simulation typically takes hours of computing time. If you had made a mistake, it might waste much of time. As a good practice, always perform the simulation incrementally. In this case, we perform a 0.001 seconds of simulation first to see if anything goes wrong. If everything is okay, then we can continue the simulation starting from the last cycle. This feature is called the "restart" of the simulation.

```
Cycle:  12127, Time:  9.994E-04s, Time Inc.: 8.241E-08s, Progress:  99.94%, Est. Clock Time Remaining: 0s
Cycle:  12128, Time:  9.995E-04s, Time Inc.: 8.241E-08s, Progress:  99.95%, Est. Clock Time Remaining: 0s
Cycle:  12129, Time:  9.995E-04s, Time Inc.: 8.241E-08s, Progress:  99.95%, Est. Clock Time Remaining: 0s
Cycle:  12130, Time:  9.996E-04s, Time Inc.: 8.241E-08s, Progress:  99.96%, Est. Clock Time Remaining: 0s
Cycle:  12131, Time:  9.997E-04s, Time Inc.: 8.241E-08s, Progress:  99.97%, Est. Clock Time Remaining: 0s
Cycle:  12132, Time:  9.998E-04s, Time Inc.: 8.241E-08s, Progress:  99.98%, Est. Clock Time Remaining: 0s
Cycle:  12133, Time:  9.999E-04s, Time Inc.: 8.241E-08s, Progress:  99.99%, Est. Clock Time Remaining: 0s
Cycle:  12134, Time:  1.000E-03s, Time Inc.: 8.241E-08s, Progress: 100.00%, Est. Clock Time Remaining: 0s
Cycle:  12135, Time:  1.000E-03s, Time Inc.: 8.241E-08s, Progress: 100.00%, Est. Clock Time Remaining: -
Problem terminated .... wrapup time reached
```

[30] Each cycle takes about 82 nanoseconds.

Increasing Integration Time Step

In this case, the integration time step is 82 nanoseconds. This number, proportional to the size of the smallest element, controls the overall run time. In <Explicit Dynamics>, a mesh of uniform element size is the most efficient mesh. It is possible to improve the mesh by adding sophisticated mesh controls. This leaves an exercise for the students (Section 15.4-2).

15.3-5 View the Results

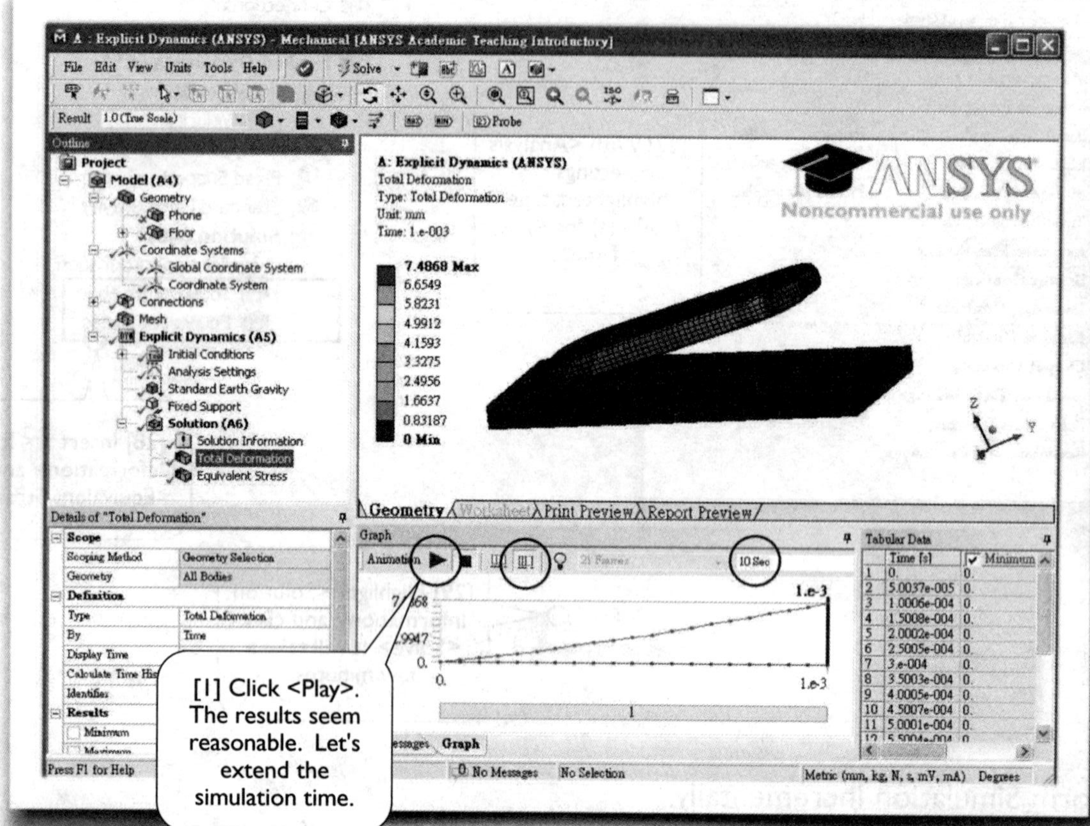

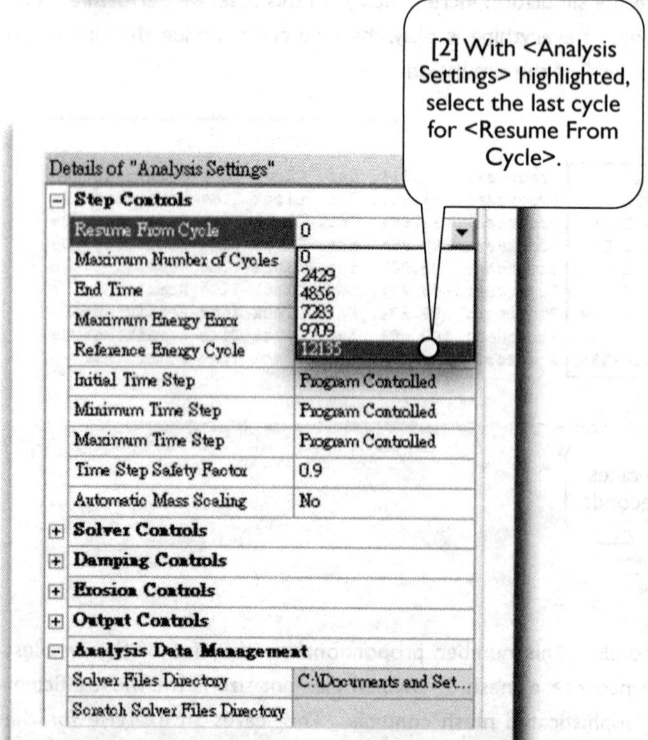

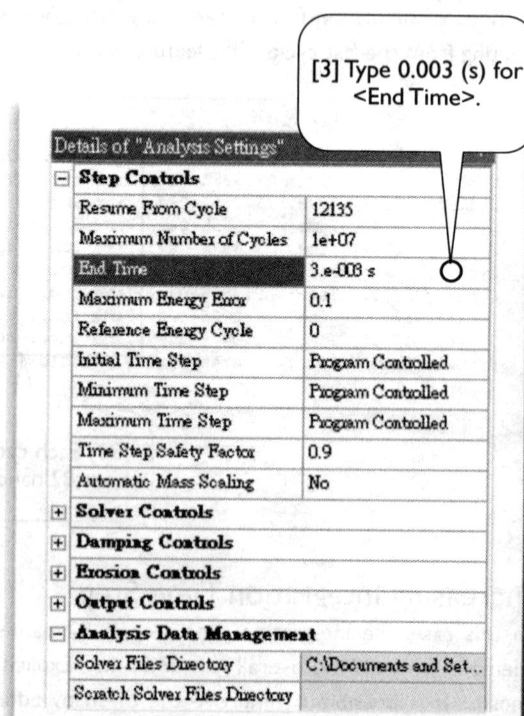

[4] Click <Solve>. It will take twice the time as before.

```
Cycle:  36398, Time:  3.000E-03s, Time Inc.: 8.241E-08s, Progress:  99.98%, Est. Clock Time Remaining: 0s
Cycle:  36399, Time:  3.000E-03s, Time Inc.: 8.241E-08s, Progress:  99.99%, Est. Clock Time Remaining: 0s
Cycle:  36400, Time:  3.000E-03s, Time Inc.: 8.241E-08s, Progress:  99.99%, Est. Clock Time Remaining: 0s
Cycle:  36401, Time:  3.000E-03s, Time Inc.: 8.241E-08s, Progress:  99.99%, Est. Clock Time Remaining: 0s
Cycle:  36402, Time:  3.000E-03s, Time Inc.: 8.241E-08s, Progress:  99.99%, Est. Clock Time Remaining: 0s
Cycle:  36403, Time:  3.000E-03s, Time Inc.: 8.241E-08s, Progress: 100.00%, Est. Clock Time Remaining: 0s
Cycle:  36404, Time:  3.000E-03s, Time Inc.: 8.241E-08s, Progress: 100.00%, Est. Clock Time Remaining: -
Problem terminated .... wrapup time reached
```

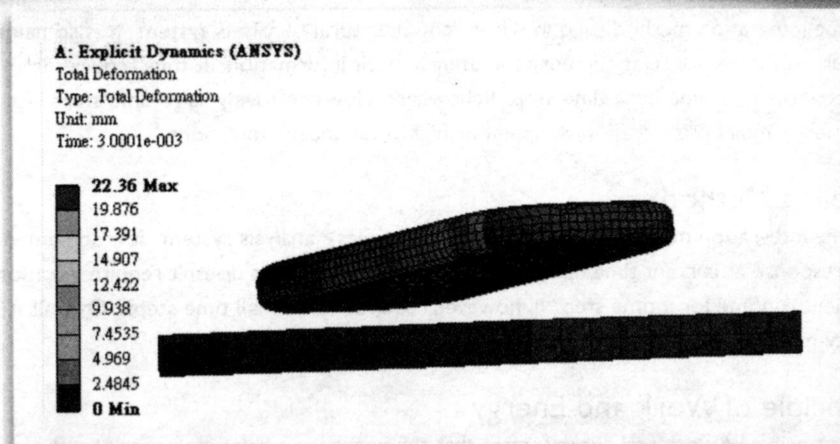

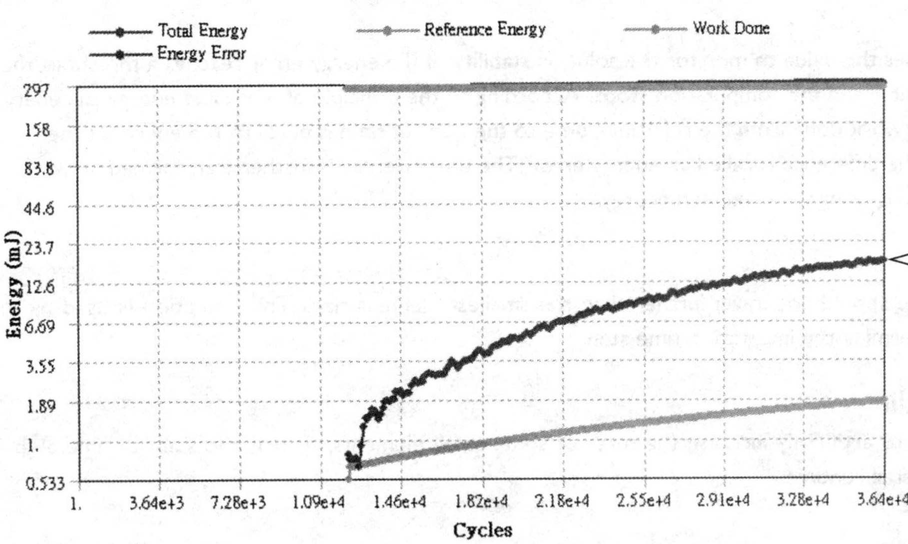

[5] Highlight <Solution Information> and select <Energy Conservation> in the Details view. The energy error starts to accumulate. This is due to the inadequacy of mesh density (see 15.3-4[15]).

Wrap Up

Animate the results. Save the project and exit Workbench.

Section 15.4

Problems

15.4-1 Key Concepts

Implicit Method

A time integration method used in <Transient Structural> analysis system. It is so named because the method calculates the response at current time using implicit information. It thus requires iterations for a time step, implying an expensive runtime for a time step. It, however, allows relatively large time steps. Overall, it is suitable for most of transient simulations except high-speed or highly-nonlinear simulations.

Explicit Method

A time integration method used in <Explicit Dynamics> analysis system. It is so named because the method calculates the response at current time using explicit information. It thus doesn't require iterations for a time step, implying an efficient runtime for a time step. It, however, requires very small time steps. Overall, it is suitable for high-speed or highly-nonlinear simulations.

Principle of Work and Energy

The principle of work and energy states that the energy at a reference time plus the work done from the reference time to a specific time is equal to the energy at that specific time.

Energy Error

The <Explicit Dynamics> uses this value to monitor the solution stability. If the energy error reaches a threshold, the solution is regarded as unstable and the computation stops. According to the principle of work and energy, the energy at a reference time plus the work done from the reference time to the current time is equal to the energy at the current time. If not equal, the difference is called an energy error. The energy error is further transformed into a dimensionless value by dividing using the maximum energy.

CFL Condition

In a single time step, a wave should not travel further than the smallest element size. This condition is used by the <Explicit Dynamics> to determine the integration time step.

Automatic Mass Scaling

The idea of mass scaling is to artificially increase the mass of some small elements, so that the stability time step is increased, to reduce the overall runtime.

Static Damping

The <Explicit Dynamics> is primarily for solving transient dynamic problems. However, a steady-state solution may also be obtained by introducing a damping force to critically damp the lowest mode of oscillation.

15.4-2 Workbench Exercises

Performing a More Realistic Drop Test

As mentioned at the end of Section 15.3-4, It is possible to improve the mesh by adding sophisticated mesh controls, so that the stability time step is increased and the overall runtime is decreased. Another problem of this simulation is that, because of the coarse mesh, the error would reach the threshold if we extend the simulation time further. Try to redo the drop test using a finer mesh.

Also mentioned in Section 15.3-1, to reduce the runtime, the model is over-simplified. In reality, the housing of a mobile phone may include a battery compartment. Include a slide-in battery in the model, perform a drop test to see if the battery will fall off during the impact with the floor.

Index

Note: ANSYS Workbench keywords are capitalized.